Dictionary

GERMAN–ENGLISH
ENGLISH–GERMAN

DEUTSCH–ENGLISCH
ENGLISCH–DEUTSCH

Gunhild Prowe
Jill Schneider

OXFORD
UNIVERSITY PRESS

OXFORD
UNIVERSITY PRESS

Great Clarendon Street, Oxford OX2 6DP

Oxford University Press is a department of the University of Oxford.
It furthers the University's objective of excellence in research, scholarship,
and education by publishing worldwide in

Oxford New York

Athens Auckland Bangkok Bogotá Buenos Aires Calcutta
Cape Town Chennai Dar es Salaam Delhi Florence Hong Kong Istanbul
Karachi Kuala Lumpur Madrid Melbourne Mexico City Mumbai
Nairobi Paris São Paulo Singapore Taipei Tokyo Toronto Warsaw

with associated companies in Berlin Ibadan

Oxford is a registered trade mark of Oxford University Press
in the UK and in certain other countries

© *Oxford University Press 1997, 2000*

First published 1997
First published as Oxford Take off in German Dictionary 2000

British Library Cataloguing in Publication Data

Data available

Library of Congress Cataloging in Publication Data

Data available

ISBN 0–19–860332–0

10 9 8 7 6 5 4 3 2 1

Typeset in Monotype Nimrod and Arial by
Latimer Trend & Company Ltd.
Printed in Great Britain
by Mackays of Chatham plc
Chatham, Kent

Contents

Preface

Oxford Take off in German Dictionary incorporates the changes to the spelling of German ratified by the governments of Germany, Austria, and Switzerland in July 1996.

It provides a handy and comprehensive reference work for tourists and business people, and covers the needs of the student for GCSE.

G. P. & J. S.

Introduction

The text of this new edition reflects recent changes to the spelling of German ratified in July 1996. The symbol ⓃᴇⱲ has been introduced to refer from the old spelling to the new, preferred one:

A̲s *nt* -ses,-se ⓃᴇⱲ**Ass**

Diät *f* -,-en (*Med*) diet; **D~ leben** be on a diet. **d~** *adv* **d~ leben** ⓃᴇⱲ **D~ leben**, *s.* **Diät**.

a̲bsein† *vi sep* (*sein*) ⓃᴇⱲ **ab sein**, *s.* **ab**

schne̲uzen (sich) *vr* ⓃᴇⱲ **schnäuzen (sich)**

Ro̲lladen *m* ⓃᴇⱲ**Rollladen**

When the two forms follow each other alphabetically or are used in phrases, the old form is shown in brackets after the new, preferred one:

A̲bfluss (A̲bfluß) *m* drainage; (*Öffnung*) drain. **A~rohr** *nt* drain-pipe

arm *a* (**ärmer, ärmst**) poor; **Arm und Reich (arm und reich)** rich and poor

Where both the old and new forms are valid, an equals sign = is used to refer to the preferred form:

a̲ufwändig *a* = **aufwendig**

Tu̲nfisch *m* = **Thunfisch**

Ra̲nd *m* . . . **zu R~e kommen mit** = **zurande kommen mit**, *s.* **zurande**

Sta̲nd *m* . . . **in S~ halten/setzen** = **instand halten/setzen**, *s.* **instand**

When such forms follow each other alphabetically, they are given with commas, with the preferred form in first place:

Pa̲nther, Pa̲nter *m* -s, - panther

In phrases, *od* (oder) is used:

. . . **d~e(r,s)** *poss pron* yours; **die D~en** *od* **d~en** *pl* your family *sg*.

. . . **s~e(r,s)** *poss pron* his . . . **das S~e** *od* **seine tun** do one's share

On the English–German side, only the preferred German
form is given.

- A swung dash ~ represents the headword or that part of
  the headword preceding a vertical bar |. The initial
  letter of a German headword is given to show whether
  or not it is a capital.
- The vertical bar | follows the part of the headword
  which is not repeated in compounds or derivatives.
- Square brackets [ ] are used for optional material.
- Angled brackets < > are used after a verb translation to
  indicate the object; before a verb translation to indicate
  the subject; before an adjective to indicate a typical
  noun which it qualifies.
- Round brackets ( ) are used for field or style labels (see
  list on page vii) and for explanatory matter.
- A box □ indicates a new part of speech within an entry.
- *od* (oder) and *or* denote that words or portions of a
  phrase are synonymous. An oblique stroke / is used
  where there is a difference in usage or meaning.
- ≈ is used where no exact equivalent exists in the other
  language.
- A dagger † indicates that a German verb is irregular
  and that the parts can be found in the verb table on page
  503. Compound verbs are not listed there as they follow
  the pattern of the basic verb.
- The stressed vowel is marked in a German headword by
  _ (long) or . (short). A phonetic transcription is only
  given for words which do not follow the normal rules of
  pronunciation. These rules can be found on page 501.
- Phonetics are given for all English headwords and for
  derivatives where there is a change of pronunciation or
  stress. In blocks of compounds, if no stress is shown, it
  falls on the first element.
- A change in pronunciation or stress shown within a
  block of compounds applies only to that particular word

(subsequent entries revert to the pronunciation and stress of the headword).

- German headword nouns are followed by the gender and, with the exception of compound nouns, by the genitive and plural. These are only given at compound nouns if they present some difficulty. Otherwise the user should refer to the final element.

- Nouns that decline like adjectives are entered as follows: **-e(r)** *m/f*, **-e(s)** *nt*.

- Adjectives which have no undeclined form are entered in the feminine form with the masculine and neuter in brackets **-e(r,s)**.

- The reflexive pronoun **sich** is accusative unless marked (*dat*).

Proprietary terms

This dictionary includes some words which are, or are asserted to be, proprietary names or trademarks. Their inclusion does not imply that they have acquired for legal purposes a non-proprietary or general significance, nor is any other judgement implied concerning their legal status. In cases where the editor has some evidence that a word is used as a proprietary name or trademark this is indicated by the letter (P), but no judgement concerning the legal status of such words is made or implied thereby.

Abbreviations / Abkürzungen

adjective	a	Adjektiv
abbreviation	abbr	Abkürzung
accusative	acc	Akkusativ
Administration	Admin	Administration
adverb	adv	Adverb
American	Amer	amerikanisch
Anatomy	Anat	Anatomie
Archaeology	Archaeol	Archäologie
Architecture	Archit	Architektur
Astronomy	Astr	Astronomie
attributive	attrib	attributiv
Austrian	Aust	österreichisch
Motor vehicles	Auto	Automobil
Aviation	Aviat	Luftfahrt
Biology	Biol	Biologie
Botany	Bot	Botanik
Chemistry	Chem	Chemie
collective	coll	Kollektivum
Commerce	Comm	Handel
conjunction	conj	Konjunktion
Cookery	Culin	Kochkunst
dative	dat	Dativ
definite article	def art	bestimmter Artikel
demonstrative	dem	Demonstrativ-
dialect	dial	Dialekt
Electricity	Electr	Elektrizität
something	etw	etwas
feminine	f	Femininum
familiar	fam	familiär
figurative	fig	figurativ
genitive	gen	Genitiv
Geography	Geog	Geographie
Geology	Geol	Geologie
Geometry	Geom	Geometrie
Grammar	Gram	Grammatik
Horticulture	Hort	Gartenbau

impersonal	impers	unpersönlich
indefinite article	indef art	unbestimmter Artikel
indefinite pronoun	indef pron	unbestimmtes Pronomen
infinitive	inf	Infinitiv
inseparable	insep	untrennbar
interjection	int	Interjektion
invariable	inv	unveränderlich
irregular	irreg	unregelmäßig
someone	jd	jemand
someone	jdm	jemandem
someone	jdn	jemanden
someone's	jds	jemandes
Journalism	Journ	Journalismus
Law	Jur	Jura
Language	Lang	Sprache
literary	liter	dichterisch
masculine	m	Maskulinum
Mathematics	Math	Mathematik
Medicine	Med	Medizin
Meteorology	Meteorol	Meteorologie
Military	Mil	Militär
Mineralogy	Miner	Mineralogie
Music	Mus	Musik
noun	n	Substantiv
Nautical	Naut	nautisch
North German	N Ger	Norddeutsch
nominative	nom	Nominativ
neuter	nt	Neutrum
or	od	oder
Proprietary term	P	Warenzeichen
pejorative	pej	abwertend
Photography	Phot	Fotografie
Physics	Phys	Physik
plural	pl	Plural
Politics	Pol	Politik
possessive	poss	Possessiv-

past participle	pp	zweites Partizip
predicative	pred	prädikativ
prefix	pref	Präfix
preposition	prep	Präposition
present	pres	Präsens
present participle	pres p	erstes Partizip
pronoun	pron	Pronomen
Psychology	Psych	Psychologie
past tense	pt	Präteritum
Railway	Rail	Eisenbahn
reflexive	refl	reflexiv
regular	reg	regelmäßig
relative	rel	Relativ-
Religion	Relig	Religion
see	s.	siehe
School	Sch	Schule
separable	sep	trennbar
singular	sg	Singular
South German	S Ger	Süddeutsch
slang	sl	salopp
someone	s.o.	jemand
something	sth	etwas
Technical	Techn	Technik
Telephone	Teleph	Telefon
Textiles	Tex	Textilien
Theatre	Theat	Theater
Television	TV	Fernsehen
Typography	Typ	Typographie
University	Univ	Universität
auxiliary verb	v aux	Hilfsverb
intransitive verb	vi	intransitives Verb
reflexive verb	vr	reflexives Verb
transitive verb	vt	transitives Verb
vulgar	vulg	vulgär
Zoology	Zool	Zoologie

Pronunciation of the alphabet
Aussprache des Alphabets

English/Englisch		*German/Deutsch*
eɪ	a	aː
biː	b	beː
siː	c	tseː
diː	d	deː
iː	e	eː
ef	f	ɛf
dʒiː	g	geː
eɪtʃ	h	haː
aɪ	i	iː
dʒeɪ	j	jɔt
keɪ	k	kaː
el	l	ɛl
em	m	ɛm
en	n	ɛn
əʊ	o	oː
piː	p	peː
kjuː	q	kuː
ɑː(r)	r	ɛr
es	s	ɛs
tiː	t	teː
juː	u	uː
viː	v	faʊ
ˈdʌbljuː	w	veː
eks	x	ɪks
waɪ	y	ˈʏpsilɔn
zed	z	tsɛt
eɪ umlaut	ä	ɛː
əʊ umlaut	ö	ø
juː umlaut	ü	yː
esˈzed	ß	ɛsˈtsɛt

A

Aal *m* -[e]s,-e eel. **a~en (sich)** *vr* laze; *(ausgestreckt)* stretch out

Aas *nt* -es carrion; *(sl)* swine

ab *prep* (+ *dat*) from; **ab Montag** from Monday □ *adv* off; *(weg)* away; *(auf Fahrplan)* departs; **ab sein** *(fam)* have come off; *(erschöpft)* be worn out; **von jetzt ab** from now on; **ab und zu** now and then; **auf und ab** up and down

abändern *vt sep* alter; *(abwandeln)* modify

abarbeiten *vt sep* work off; **sich a~** slave away

Abart *f* variety. **a~ig** *a* abnormal

Abbau *m* dismantling; *(Kohlen-)* mining; *(fig)* reduction. **a~en** *vt sep* dismantle; mine *(Kohle)*; *(fig)* reduce, cut

abbeißen† *vt sep* bite off

abbeizen *vt sep* strip

abberufen† *vt sep* recall

abbestellen *vt sep* cancel; **jdn a~** put s.o. off

abbiegen† *vi sep (sein)* turn off; **[nach] links a~** turn left

Abbild *nt* image. **a~en** *vt sep* depict, portray. **A~ung** *f* -,-en illustration

Abbitte *f* **A~ leisten** apologize

abblättern *vi sep (sein)* flake off

abblend|en *vt/i sep (haben)* **[die Scheinwerfer] a~en** dip one's headlights. **A~licht** *nt* dipped headlights *pl*

abbrechen† *v sep* □ *vt* break off; *(abreißen)* demolish □ *vi (sein/haben)* break off

abbrennen† *v sep* □ *vt* burn off; *(niederbrennen)* burn down; let off *(Feuerwerkskörper)* □ *vi (sein)* burn down

abbringen† *vt sep* dissuade **(von** from)

Abbruch *m* demolition; *(Beenden)* breaking off; **etw** *(dat)* **keinen A~ tun** do no harm to sth

abbuchen *vt sep* debit

abbürsten *vt sep* brush down; *(entfernen)* brush off

abdank|en *vi sep (haben)* resign; *(Herrscher:)* abdicate. **A~ung** *f* -,-en resignation; abdication

abdecken *vt sep* uncover; *(abnehmen)* take off; *(zudecken)* cover; **den Tisch a~** clear the table

abdichten *vt sep* seal

abdrehen *vt sep* turn off

Abdruck *m* (*pl* -e) impression; *(Finger-)* print; *(Nachdruck)* reprint. **a~en** *vt sep* print

abdrücken *vt/i sep (haben)* fire; **sich a~** leave an impression

Abend *m* -s,-e evening; **am A~** in the evening; **heute A~** this evening, tonight; **gestern A~** yesterday evening, last night. **a~** *adv* **heute/gestern a~** ⓃⒺⓌ **heute/gestern A~**, s. **Abend. A~brot** *nt* supper. **A~essen** *nt* dinner; *(einfacher)* supper. **A~kurs[us]** *m* evening class. **A~mahl** *nt (Relig)* [Holy] Communion. **a~s** *adv* in the evening

Abenteuer *nt* -s,- adventure; *(Liebes-)* affair. **a~lich** *a* fantastic; *(gefährlich)* hazardous

Abenteurer *m* -s,- adventurer

aber *conj* but; **oder** or else □ *adv (wirklich)* really; **a~ ja!** but of course! **Tausende und a~ Tausende** thousands upon thousands

Aber|glaube *m* superstition. **a~gläubisch** *a* superstitious

aber|mals *adv* once again. **A~tausende**, **a~tausende** *pl* thousands upon thousands

abfahr|en† *v sep* □ *vi (sein)* leave; *(Auto:)* drive off □ *vt* take away; *(entlangfahren)* drive along; use *(Fahrkarte)*; **abgefahrene Reifen** worn tyres. **A~t** *f* departure; *(Talfahrt)* descent; *(Piste)* run; *(Ausfahrt)* exit

Abfall *m* refuse, rubbish, *(Amer)* garbage; *(auf der Straße)* litter; *(Industrie-)* waste. **A~eimer** *m* rubbish-bin; litter-bin

abfallen† *vi sep (sein)* drop, fall; *(übrig bleiben)* be left **(für** for); *(sich neigen)* slope away; *(fig)* compare badly **(gegen** with); **vom Glauben a~** renounce one's faith. **a~d** *a* sloping

Abfallhaufen *m* rubbish-dump

abfällig *a* disparaging, *adv* -ly

abfangen† *vt sep* intercept; *(beherrschen)* bring under control

abfärben *vi sep (haben) (Farbe:)* run; *(Stoff:)* not be colour-fast; **a~ auf** (+ *acc*) *(fig)* rub off on

abfassen *vt sep* draft

abfertigen *vt sep* attend to; *(zollamtlich)* clear; **jdn kurz a~** *(fam)* give s.o. short shrift

abfeuern *vt sep* fire

abfind|en† *vt sep* pay off; (*entschädigen*) compensate; **sich a~en mit** come to terms with. **A~ung** *f* -,-**en** compensation

abflauen *vi sep* (*sein*) decrease

abfliegen† *vi sep* (*sein*) fly off; (*Aviat*) take off

abfließen† *vi sep* (*sein*) drain *or* run away

Abflug *m* (*Aviat*) departure

Abfluss (**Abfluß**) *m* drainage; (*Öffnung*) drain. **A~rohr** *nt* drain-pipe

abfragen *vt sep* jdn *od* jdm Vokabeln a~ test s.o. on vocabulary

Abfuhr *f* - removal; (*fig*) rebuff

abführ|en *vt sep* take *or* lead away. **a~end** *a* laxative. **A~mittel** *nt* laxative

abfüllen *vt sep* **auf** *od* **in Flaschen a~** bottle

Abgabe *f* handing in; (*Verkauf*) sale; (*Fußball*) pass; (*Steuer*) tax

Abgang *m* departure; (*Theat*) exit; (*Schul-*) leaving

Abgase *ntpl* exhaust fumes

abgeben† *vt sep* hand in; (*abliefern*) deliver; (*verkaufen*) sell; (*zur Aufbewahrung*) leave; (*Fußball*) pass; (*ausströmen*) give off; (*abfeuern*) fire; (*verlauten lassen*) give; cast (*Stimme*); **jdm etw a~** give s.o. a share of sth; **sich a~ mit** occupy oneself with

abgedroschen *a* hackneyed

abgehen† *v sep* □ *vi* (*sein*) leave; (*Theat*) exit; (*sich lösen*) come off; (*abgezogen werden*) be deducted; (*abbiegen*) turn off; (*verlaufen*) go off; **ihr geht jeglicher Humor ab** she totally lacks a sense of humour □ *vt* walk along

abgehetzt *a* harassed. **abgelegen** *a* remote. **abgeneigt** *a* etw (*dat*) **nicht abgeneigt sein** not be averse to sth. **abgenutzt** *a* worn. **Abgeordnete(r)** *m/f* deputy; (*Pol*) Member of Parliament. **abgepackt** *a* pre-packed. **abgerissen** *a* ragged

abgeschieden *a* secluded. **A~heit** *f* - seclusion

abgeschlossen *a* (*fig*) complete; (*Wohnung*) self-contained. **abgeschmackt** *a* (*fig*) tasteless. **abgesehen** *prep* apart (from **von**). **abgespannt** *a* exhausted. **abgestanden** *a* stale. **abgestorben** *a* dead; (*Glied*) numb. **abgetragen** *a* worn. **abgewetzt** *a* threadbare

abgewinnen† *vt sep* win (**jdm** from s.o.); **etw** *a* (*dat*) **Geschmack a~** get a taste for sth

abgewöhnen *vt sep* **jdm/sich das Rauchen a~** cure s.o. of/ give up smoking

abgezehrt *a* emaciated

abgießen† *vt sep* pour off; drain (*Gemüse*)

abgleiten† *vi sep* (*sein*) slip

Abgott *m* idol

abgöttisch *adv* **a~ lieben** idolize

abgrenz|en *vt sep* divide off; (*fig*) define. **A~ung** *f* - demarcation

Abgrund *m* abyss; (*fig*) depths *pl*

abgucken *vt sep* (*fam*) copy

Abguss (**Abguß**) *m* cast

abhacken *vt sep* chop off

abhaken *vt sep* tick off

abhalten† *vt sep* keep off; (*hindern*) keep, prevent (**von** from); (*veranstalten*) hold

abhanden *adv* **a~ kommen** get lost

Abhandlung *f* treatise

Abhang *m* slope

abhängen[1] *vt sep* (*reg*) take down; (*abkuppeln*) uncouple

abhäng|en[2]† *vi sep* (*haben*) depend (**von** on). **a~ig** *a* dependent (**von** on). **A~igkeit** *f* - dependence

abhärten *vt sep* toughen up

abhauen† *v sep* □ *vt* chop off □ *vi* (*sein*) (*fam*) clear off

abheben† *v sep* □ *vt* take off; (*vom Konto*) withdraw; **sich a~** stand out (**gegen** against) □ *vi* (*haben*) (*Cards*) cut [the cards]; (*Aviat*) take off; (*Rakete:*) lift off

abheften *vt sep* file

abhelfen† *vt sep* (+ *dat*) remedy

Abhilfe *f* remedy; **A~ schaffen** take [remedial] action

abholen *vt sep* collect; call for (*Person*); **jdn am Bahnhof a~** meet s.o. at the station

abhorchen *vt sep* (*Med*) sound

abhör|en *vt sep* listen to; (*überwachen*) tap; **jdn** *od* **jdm Vokabeln a~en** test s.o. on vocabulary. **A~gerät** *nt* bugging device

Abitur *nt* -s ≈ A levels *pl*. **A~ient(in)** *m* -**en**,-**en** (*f* -,-**nen**) pupil taking the '*Abitur*'

abkanzeln *vt sep* (*fam*) reprimand

abkaufen *vt sep* buy (*dat* from)

abkehren (**sich**) *vr sep* turn away

abkette[l]n *vt/i sep* (*haben*) cast off

abklingen† *vi sep* (*sein*) die away; (*nachlassen*) subside

abkochen *vt sep* boil

abkommen† *vi sep* (*sein*) **a~ von** stray from; (*aufgeben*) give up; **vom Thema a~** digress. **A~** *nt* -s,- agreement

abkömmlich *a* available

Abkömmling *m* -s,-**e** descendant

abkratzen *v sep* □ *vt* scrape off □ *vi* (*sein*) (*sl*) die

abkühlen *vt/i sep* (*sein*) cool; **sich a~** cool [down]; (*Wetter:*) turn cooler

Abkunft f - origin

abkuppeln vt sep uncouple

abkürz|en vt sep shorten; abbreviate 〈Wort〉. **A~ung** f short cut; 〈Wort〉 abbreviation

abladen† vt sep unload

Ablage f shelf; 〈für Akten〉 tray

ablager|n vt sep deposit; **sich a~n** be deposited. **A~ung** f -,-en deposit

ablassen† v sep □ vt drain [off]; let off 〈Dampf〉; 〈vom Preis〉 knock off □ vi 〈haben〉 **a~ von** give up; **von jdm a~** leave s.o. alone

Ablauf m drain; 〈Verlauf〉 course; 〈Ende〉 end; 〈einer Frist〉 expiry. **a~en†** v sep □ vi 〈sein〉 run or drain off; 〈verlaufen〉 go off; 〈enden〉 expire; 〈Zeit:〉 run out; 〈Uhrwerk:〉 run down □ vt walk along; 〈absuchen〉 scour 〈nach for〉; 〈abnutzen〉 wear down

ableg|en v sep □ vt put down; discard 〈Karte〉; 〈abheften〉 file; 〈ausziehen〉 take off; 〈aufgeben〉 give up; sit, take 〈Prüfung〉. **abgelegte Kleidung** cast-offs pl □ vi 〈haben〉 take off one's coat; 〈Naut〉 cast off. **A~er** m -s,- 〈Bot〉 cutting; 〈Schössling〉 shoot

ablehn|en vt sep refuse; 〈missbilligen〉 reject. **A~ung** f -,-en refusal; rejection

ableit|en vt sep divert; **sich a~en** be derived 〈von/aus from〉. **A~ung** f derivation; 〈Wort〉 derivative

ablenk|en vt sep deflect; divert 〈Aufmerksamkeit〉; 〈zerstreuen〉 distract. **A~ung** f -,-en distraction

ablesen† vt sep read; 〈absuchen〉 pick off

ableugnen vt sep deny

ablicht|en vt sep photocopy. **A~ung** f photocopy

abliefern vt sep deliver

ablös|en vt sep detach; 〈abwechseln〉 relieve; **sich a~en** come off; 〈sich abwechseln〉 take turns. **A~ung** f relief

abmach|en vt sep remove; 〈ausmachen〉 arrange; 〈vereinbaren〉 agree; **abgemacht!** agreed! **A~ung** f -,-en agreement

abmager|n vi sep 〈sein〉 lose weight. **A~ungskur** f slimming diet

abmarschieren vi sep 〈sein〉 march off

abmelden vt sep cancel 〈Zeitung〉; **sich a~** report that one is leaving; 〈im Hotel〉 check out

abmess|en† vt sep measure. **A~ungen** fpl measurements

abmühen (sich) vr sep struggle

abnäh|en vt sep take in. **A~er** m -s,- dart

Abnahme f - removal; 〈Kauf〉 purchase; 〈Verminderung〉 decrease

abnehm|en† v sep □ vt take off, remove; pick up 〈Hörer〉; **jdm etw a~en** take/

〈kaufen〉 buy sth from s.o. □ vi 〈haben〉 decrease; 〈nachlassen〉 decline; 〈Person:〉 lose weight; 〈Mond:〉 wane. **A~er** m -s,- buyer

Abneigung f dislike 〈gegen of〉

abnorm a abnormal, adv -ly

abnutz|en vt sep wear out; **sich a~en** wear out. **A~ung** f - wear [and tear]

Abon|nement /abɔnəˈmãː/ nt -s,-s subscription. **A~nent** m -en,-en subscriber. **a~nieren** vt take out a subscription to

Abordnung f -,-en deputation

abpassen vt sep wait for; **gut a~** time well

abprallen vi sep 〈sein〉 rebound; 〈Geschoss:〉 ricochet

abraten† vt sep 〈haben〉 **jdm von etw a~** advise s.o. against sth

abräumen vt/i 〈haben〉 clear away; clear 〈Tisch〉

abrechn|en v sep □ vt deduct □ vi 〈haben〉 settle up; 〈fig〉 get even. **A~ung** f settlement [of accounts]; 〈Rechnung〉 account

Abreise f departure. **a~n** vi sep 〈sein〉 leave

abreißen† v sep □ vt tear off; 〈demolieren〉 pull down □ vi 〈sein〉 come off; 〈fig〉 break off

abrichten vt sep train

abriegeln vt sep bolt; 〈absperren〉 seal off

Abriss (**Abriß**) m demolition; 〈Übersicht〉 summary

abrufen† vt sep call away; 〈Computer〉 retrieve

abrunden vt sep round off; **nach unten/oben a~** round down/up

abrupt a abrupt, adv -ly

abrüst|en vi sep 〈haben〉 disarm. **A~ung** f disarmament

abrutschen vi sep 〈sein〉 slip

Absage f -,-n cancellation; 〈Ablehnung〉 refusal. **a~n** v sep □ vt cancel □ vi 〈haben〉 [jdm] **a~n** cancel an appointment [with s.o.]; 〈auf Einladung〉 refuse [s.o.'s invitation]

absägen vt sep saw off; 〈fam〉 sack

Absatz m heel; 〈Abschnitt〉 paragraph; 〈Verkauf〉 sale

abschaff|en vt sep abolish; get rid of 〈Auto, Hund〉. **A~ung** f abolition

abschalten vt/i sep 〈haben〉 switch off

abschätzig a disparaging, adv -ly

Abschaum m 〈fig〉 scum

Abscheu m - revulsion

abscheulich a revolting; 〈fam〉 horrible, adv -bly

abschicken vt sep send off

Abschied m -[e]s,-e farewell; 〈Trennung〉 parting; **A~ nehmen** say goodbye 〈von to〉

abschießen† *vt sep* shoot down; (*abtrennen*) shoot off; (*abfeuern*) fire; launch ⟨*Rakete*⟩

abschirmen *vt sep* shield

abschlagen† *vt sep* knock off; (*verweigern*) refuse; (*abwehren*) repel

abschlägig *a* negative; **a∼e Antwort** refusal

Abschlepp|dienst *m* breakdown service. **a∼en** *vt sep* tow away. **A∼seil** *nt* tow-rope. **A∼wagen** *m* breakdown vehicle

abschließen† *v sep* □ *vt* lock; (*beenden*, *abmachen*) conclude; make ⟨*Wette*⟩; balance ⟨*Bücher*⟩; **sich a∼** (*fig*) cut oneself off □ *vi* (*haben*) lock up; (*enden*) end. **a∼d** *adv* in conclusion

Abschluss (**Abschluß**) *m* conclusion. **A∼prüfung** *f* final examination. **A∼zeugnis** *nt* diploma

abschmecken *vt sep* season

abschmieren *vt sep* lubricate

abschneiden† *v sep* □ *vt* cut off; **den Weg a∼** take a short cut □ *vi* (*haben*) **gut/schlecht a∼** do well/badly

Abschnitt *m* section; (*Stadium*) stage; (*Absatz*) paragraph; (*Kontroll-*) counterfoil

abschöpfen *vt sep* skim off

abschrauben *vt sep* unscrew

abschreck|en *vt sep* deter; (*Culin*) put in cold water ⟨*Ei*⟩. **a∼end** *a* repulsive, *adv* -ly; **a∼endes Beispiel** warning. **A∼ungsmittel** *nt* deterrent

abschreib|en† *v sep* □ *vt* copy; (*Comm & fig*) write off □ *vi* (*haben*) copy. **A∼ung** *f* (*Comm*) depreciation

Abschrift *f* copy

Abschuss (**Abschuß**) *m* shooting down; (*Abfeuern*) firing; (*Raketen-*) launch

abschüssig *a* sloping; (*steil*) steep

abschwächen *vt sep* lessen; **sich a∼** lessen; (*schwächer werden*) weaken

abschweifen *vi sep* (*sein*) digress

abschwellen† *vi sep* (*sein*) go down

abschwören† *vi sep* (*haben*) (+ *dat*) renounce

abseh|bar *a* **in a∼barer Zeit** in the foreseeable future. **a∼en**† *vt/i sep* (*haben*) copy; (*voraussehen*) foresee; **a∼en von** disregard; (*aufgeben*) refrain from; **es abgesehen haben auf** (+ *acc*) have one's eye on; (*schikanieren*) have it in for

absein† *vi sep* (*sein*) NEW **ab sein**, *s*. **ab**

abseits *adv* apart; (*Sport*) offside □ *prep* (+ *gen*) away from. **A∼** *nt* - (*Sport*) offside

absend|en† *vt sep* send off. **A∼er** *m* sender

absetzen *v sep* □ *vt* put *or* set down; (*ablagern*) deposit; (*abnehmen*) take off; (*absagen*) cancel; (*abbrechen*) stop; (*entlassen*) dismiss; (*verkaufen*) sell; (*abziehen*) deduct; **sich a∼** be deposited; (*fliehen*) flee □ *vi* (*haben*) pause

Absicht *f* -,-en intention; **mit A∼** intentionally, on purpose

absichtlich *a* intentional, *adv* -ly, deliberate, *adv* -ly

absitzen† *v sep* □ *vi* (*sein*) dismount □ *vt* (*fam*) serve ⟨*Strafe*⟩

absolut *a* absolute, *adv* -ly

Absolution /-'tsio:n/ *f* - absolution

absolvieren *vt* complete; (*bestehen*) pass

absonderlich *a* odd

absonder|n *vt sep* separate; (*ausscheiden*) secrete; **sich a∼n** keep apart (**von** from). **A∼ung** *f* -,-en secretion

absor|bieren *vt* absorb. **A∼ption** /-'tsio:n/ *f* - absorption

abspeisen *vt sep* fob off (**mit** with)

abspenstig *a* **a∼ machen** take (**jdm** from s.o.)

absperr|en *vt sep* cordon off; (*abstellen*) turn off; (*SGer*) lock. **A∼ung** *f* -,-en barrier

abspielen *vt sep* play; (*Fußball*) pass; **sich a∼** take place

Absprache *f* agreement

absprechen† *vt sep* arrange; **sich a∼** agree; **jdm etw a∼** deny s.o. sth

abspringen† *vi sep* (*sein*) jump off; (*mit Fallschirm*) parachute; (*abgehen*) come off; (*fam: zurücktreten*) back out

Absprung *m* jump

abspülen *vt sep* rinse; (*entfernen*) rinse off

abstamm|en *vi sep* be descended (**von** from). **A∼ung** *f* - descent

Abstand *m* distance; (*zeitlich*) interval; **A∼ halten** keep one's distance; **A∼ nehmen von** (*fig*) refrain from

abstatten *vt sep* **jdm einen Besuch a∼** pay s.o. a visit

abstauben *vt sep* dust

abstech|en† *vi sep* (*haben*) stand out. **A∼er** *m* -s,- detour

abstehen† *vi sep* (*haben*) stick out; **a∼ von** be away from

absteigen† *vi sep* (*sein*) dismount; (*niedersteigen*) descend; (*Fußball*) be relegated

abstell|en *vt sep* put down; (*lagern*) store; (*parken*) park; (*abschalten*) turn off; (*fig: beheben*) remedy. **A∼gleis** *nt* siding. **A∼raum** *m* box-room

absterben† *vi sep* (*sein*) die; (*gefühllos werden*) go numb

Abstieg *m* -[e]s,-e descent; (*Fußball*) relegation

abstimm|en *v sep* □ *vi* (haben) vote (**über** + *acc* on) □ *vt* coordinate (**auf** + *acc* with). **A~ung** *f* vote

Abstinenz /-st-/ *f* - abstinence. **A~ler** *m* -s,- teetotaller

abstoßen† *vt sep* knock off; (*abschieben*) push off; (*verkaufen*) sell; (*fig: ekeln*) repel. **a~d** *a* repulsive, *adv* -ly

abstrakt /-st-/ *a* abstract

abstreifen *vt sep* remove; slip off ⟨*Kleidungsstück, Schuhe*⟩

abstreiten† *vt sep* deny

Abstrich *m* (*Med*) smear; (*Kürzung*) cut

abstufen *vt sep* grade

Absturz *m* fall; (*Aviat*) crash

abstürzen *vi sep* (sein) fall; (*Aviat*) crash

absuchen *vt sep* search; (*ablesen*) pick off

absurd *a* absurd

Abszess *m* -es,-e (**Abszeß** *m* -sses,-sse) abscess

Abt *m* -[e]s,-̈e abbot

abtasten *vt sep* feel; (*Techn*) scan

abtauen *vt/i sep* (sein) thaw; (*entfrosten*) defrost

Abtei *f* -,-en abbey

Abteil *nt* compartment

abteilen *vt sep* divide off

Abteilung *f* -,-en section; (*Admin, Comm*) department

abtragen† *vt sep* clear; (*einebnen*) level; (*abnutzen*) wear out; (*abzahlen*) pay off

abträglich *a* detrimental (**dat** to)

abtreib|en *v sep* □ *vt* (*Naut*) drive off course; **ein Kind a~en lassen** have an abortion □ *vi* (sein) drift off course. **A~ung** *f* -,-en abortion

abtrennen *vt sep* detach; (*abteilen*) divide off

abtret|en† *v sep* □ *vt* cede (**an** + *acc* to); **sich** (*dat*) **die Füße a~en** wipe one's feet □ *vi* (sein) (*Theat*) exit; (*fig*) resign. **A~er** *m* -s,- doormat

abtrocknen *vt/i sep* (haben) dry; **sich a~** dry oneself

abtropfen *vi sep* (sein) drain

abtrünnig *a* renegade; **a~ werden** (+ *dat*) desert

abtun† *vt sep* (*fig*) dismiss

abverlangen *vt sep* demand (**dat** from)

abwägen† *vt sep* (*fig*) weigh

abwandeln *vt sep* modify

abwandern *vi sep* (sein) move away

abwarten *v sep* □ *vt* wait for □ *vi* (haben) wait [and see]

abwärts *adv* down[wards]

Abwasch *m* -[e]s washing-up; (*Geschirr*) dirty dishes *pl.* **a~en†** *v sep* □ *vt* wash;

wash up ⟨*Geschirr*⟩; (*entfernen*) wash off □ *vi* (haben) wash up. **A~lappen** *m* dishcloth

Abwasser *nt* -s,-̈ sewage. **A~kanal** *m* sewer

abwechseln *vi/r sep* (haben) **[sich] a~** alternate; ⟨*Personen:*⟩ take turns. **a~d** *a* alternate, *adv* -ly

Abwechslung *f* -,-en change; **zur A~ for** a change. **a~sreich** *a* varied

Abweg *m* **auf A~e geraten** (*fig*) go astray. **a~ig** *a* absurd

Abwehr *f* - defence; (*Widerstand*) resistance; (*Pol*) counter-espionage. **a~en** *vt sep* ward off; (*Mil*) repel; (*zurückweisen*) dismiss. **A~system** *nt* immune system

abweich|en† *vi sep* (sein) deviate/(*von Regel*) depart (**von** from); (*sich unterscheiden*) differ (**von** from). **a~end** *a* divergent; (*verschieden*) different. **A~ung** *f* -,-en deviation; difference

abweis|en† *vt sep* turn down; turn away ⟨*Person*⟩; (*abwehren*) repel. **a~end** *a* unfriendly. **A~ung** *f* rejection; (*Abfuhr*) rebuff

abwenden† *vt sep* turn away; (*verhindern*) avert; **sich a~** turn away; **den Blick a~** look away

abwerfen† *vt sep* throw off; throw ⟨*Reiter*⟩; (*Aviat*) drop; (*Kartenspiel*) discard; shed ⟨*Haut, Blätter*⟩; yield ⟨*Gewinn*⟩

abwert|en *vt sep* devalue. **a~end** *a* pejorative, *adv* -ly. **A~ung** *f* -,-en devaluation

abwesen|d *a* absent; (*zerstreut*) absent-minded. **A~heit** *f* - absence; absent-mindedness

abwickeln *vt sep* unwind; (*erledigen*) settle

abwischen *vt sep* wipe; (*entfernen*) wipe off

abwürgen *vt sep* stall ⟨*Motor*⟩

abzahlen *vt sep* pay off

abzählen *vt sep* count

Abzahlung *f* instalment

abzapfen *vt sep* draw

Abzeichen *nt* badge

abzeichnen *vt sep* copy; (*unterzeichnen*) initial; **sich a~** stand out

Abzieh|bild *nt* transfer. **a~en†** *v sep* □ *vt* pull off; take off ⟨*Laken*⟩; strip ⟨*Bett*⟩; (*häuten*) skin; (*Phot*) print; run off ⟨*Kopien*⟩; (*zurückziehen*) withdraw; (*abrechnen*) deduct □ *vi* (sein) go away; ⟨*Rauch:*⟩ escape

abzielen *vi sep* (haben) **a~ auf** (+ *acc*) (*fig*) be aimed at

Abzug *m* withdrawal; (*Abrechnung*) deduction; (*Phot*) print; (*Korrektur-*) proof;

(*am Gewehr*) trigger; (*A~söffnung*) vent; **A~e** *pl* deductions

abzüglich *prep* (+ *gen*) less

Abzugshaube *f* [cooker] hood

abzweig|en *v sep* □*vi* (*sein*) branch off □*vt* divert. **A~ung** *f* -,-en junction; (*Gabelung*) fork

ach *int* oh; **a~ je!** oh dear! **a~ so** I see; **mit A~ und Krach** (*fam*) by the skin of one's teeth

Achse *f* -,-n axis; (*Rad-*) axle

Achsel *f* -,-n shoulder; **die A~n zucken** shrug one's shoulders. **A~höhle** *f* armpit. **A~zucken** *nt* -s shrug

acht¹ *inv a*, **A~¹** *f* -,-en eight; **heute in a~ Tagen** a week today

acht² **außer a~ lassen/sich in a~ nehmen** (NEW) **außer Acht lassen/sich in Acht nehmen**, s. **Acht²**

Acht² *f* **A~ geben** be careful; **A~ geben auf** (+ *acc*) look after; **außer A~ lassen** disregard; **sich in A~ nehmen** be careful

acht|e(r,s) *a* eighth. **a~eckig** *a* octagonal. **a~el** *inv a* eighth. **A~el** *nt* -s,- eighth. **A~elnote** *f* quaver, (*Amer*) eighth note

achten *vt* respect □*vi* (*haben*) **~ auf** (+ *acc*) pay attention to; (*aufpassen*) look after; **darauf a~, dass** take care that

ächten *vt* ban; ostracize (*Person*)

Achter|bahn *f* roller-coaster. **a~n** *adv* (*Naut*) aft

achtgeben† *vi sep* (*haben*) (NEW) **Acht geben**, s. **Acht²**

achtlos *a* careless, *adv* -ly

achtsam *a* careful, *adv* -ly

Achtung *f* - respect (**vor** + *dat* for); **A~!** look out! (*Mil*) attention! '**A~ Stufe**' 'mind the step'

acht|zehn *inv a* eighteen. **a~zehnte(r,s)** *a* eighteenth. **a~zig** *a inv* eighty. **a~zigste(r,s)** *a* eightieth

ächzen *vi* (*haben*) groan

Acker *m* -s,: field. **A~bau** *m* agriculture. **A~land** *nt* arable land

addieren *vt/i* (*haben*) add; (*zusammenzählen*) add up

Addition /-'tsi̯o:n/ *f* -,-en addition

ade *int* goodbye

Adel *m* -s nobility

Ader *f* -,-n vein; **künstlerische A~** artistic bent

Adjektiv *nt* -s,-e adjective

Adler *m* -s,- eagle

adlig *a* noble. **A~e(r)** *m* nobleman

Administration /-'tsi̯o:n/ *f* - administration

Admiral *m* -s,:e admiral

adop|tieren *vt* adopt. **A~tion** /-'tsi̯o:n/ *f* -,-en adoption. **A~tiveltern** *pl* adoptive parents. **A~tivkind** *nt* adopted child

Adrenalin *nt* -s adrenalin

Adres|se *f* -,-n address. **a~sieren** *vt* address

adrett *a* neat, *adv* -ly

Adria *f* - Adriatic

Advent *m* -s Advent. **A~skranz** *m* Advent wreath

Adverb *nt* -s,-ien /-i̯ə:n/ adverb

Affäre *f* -,-n affair

Affe *m* -n,-n monkey; (*Menschen-*) ape

Affekt *m* -[e]s,-e **im A~** in the heat of the moment

affektiert *a* affected. **A~heit** *f* - affectation

affig *a* affected; (*eitel*) vain

Afrika *nt* -s Africa

Afrikan|er(in) *m* -s,- (*f* -,-nen) African. **a~isch** *a* African

After *m* -s,- anus

Agen|t(in) *m* -en,-en (*f* -,-nen) agent. **A~tur** *f* -,-en agency

Aggres|sion *f* -,-en aggression. **a~siv** *a* aggressive, *adv* -ly. **A~sivität** *f* - aggressiveness

Agitation /-'tsi̯o:n/ *f* - agitation

Agnostiker *m* -s,- agnostic

Ägypt|en /ɛ'gyptən/ *nt* -s Egypt. **Ä~er(in)** *m* -s,- (*f* -,-nen) Egyptian. **ä~isch** *a* Egyptian

ähneln *vi* (*haben*) (+ *dat*) resemble; **sich ä~** be alike

ahnen *vt* have a presentiment of; (*vermuten*) suspect

Ahnen *mpl* ancestors. **A~forschung** *f* genealogy. **A~tafel** *f* family tree

ähnlich *a* similar, *adv* -ly; **jdm ä~ sehen** resemble s.o.; (*typisch sein*) be just like s.o. **Ä~keit** *f* -,-en similarity; resemblance

Ahnung *f* -,-en premonition; (*Vermutung*) idea, hunch; **keine A~** (*fam*) no idea. **a~slos** *a* unsuspecting

Ahorn *m* -s,-e maple

Ähre *f* -,-n ear [of corn]

Aids /e:ts/ *nt* - Aids

Akademie *f* -,-n academy

Akadem|iker(in) *m* -s,- (*f* -,-nen) university graduate. **a~isch** *a* academic, *adv* -ally

akklimatisieren (sich) *vr* become acclimatized

Akkord *m* -[e]s,-e (*Mus*) chord; **im A~ arbeiten** be on piece-work. **A~arbeit** *f* piece-work

Akkordeon *nt* -s,-s accordion

Akkumulator *m* -s,-en /-'to:rən/ (*Electr*) accumulator

Akkusativ *m* -s,-e accusative. **A~objekt** *nt* direct object

Akrobat|(in) *m* -en,-en (*f* -,-nen) acrobat. **a~isch** *a* acrobatic

Akt *m* -[e]s,-e act; (*Kunst*) nude

Akte *f* -,-n file; **A~n** documents. **A~ndeckel** *m* folder. **A~nkoffer** *m* attaché case. **A~nschrank** *m* filing cabinet. **A~ntasche** *f* briefcase

Aktie /'aktsiə/ *f* -,-n (*Comm*) share. **A~ngesellschaft** *f* joint-stock company

Aktion /ak'tsio:n/ *f* -,-en action; (*Kampagne*) campaign. **A~är** *m* -s,-e shareholder

aktiv *a* active, *adv* -ly. **a~ieren** *vt* activate. **A~ität** *f* -,-en activity

Aktualität *f* -,-en topicality; **A~en** current events

aktuell *a* topical; (*gegenwärtig*) current; **nicht mehr a~** no longer relevant

Akupunktur *f* - acupuncture

Akust|ik *f* - acoustics *pl.* **a~isch** *a* acoustic, *adv* -ally

akut *a* acute

Akzent *m* -[e]s,-e accent

akzept|abel *a* acceptable. **a~ieren** *vt* accept

Alarm *m* -s alarm; (*Mil*) alert; **A~schlagen** raise the alarm. **a~ieren** *vt* alert; (*beunruhigen*) alarm. **a~ierend** *a* alarming

Albdruck *m* = **Alpdruck**

albern *a* silly □ *adv* in a silly way □ *vi* (*haben*) play the fool

Albtraum *m* = **Alptraum**

Album *nt* -s,-ben album

Algebra *f* - algebra

Algen *fpl* algae

Algerien /-jən/ *nt* -s Algeria

Alibi *nt* -s,-s alibi

Alimente *pl* maintenance *sg*

Alkohol *m* -s alcohol. **a~frei** *a* non-alcoholic

Alkohol|iker(in) *m* -s,- (*f* -,-nen) alcoholic. **a~isch** *a* alcoholic. **A~ismus** *m* - alcoholism

all *inv pron* **all das/mein Geld** all the/my money; **all dies** all this

All *nt* -s universe

alle *pred a* finished, (*fam*) all gone; **a~ machen** finish up

all|e(r,s) *pron* all; (*jeder*) every; **a~es** everything, all; (*alle Leute*) everyone; **a~e** *pl* all; **a~es Geld** all the money; **a~e meine Freunde** all my friends; **a~e beide** both [of them/us]; **wir a~e** we all;

a~e Tage every day; **a~e drei Jahre** every three years; **in a~er Unschuld** in all innocence; **ohne a~en Grund** without any reason; **vor a~em** above all; **a~es in a~em** all in all; **a~es aussteigen!** all change! **a~edem** *pron* **bei/trotz a~edem** with/despite all that

Allee *f* -,-n avenue

Alleg|orie *f* -,-n allegory. **a~orisch** *a* allegorical

allein *adv* alone; (*nur*) only; **a~ stehend** single; **a~ der Gedanke** the mere thought; **von a~[e]** of its/(*Person*) one's own accord; (*automatisch*) automatically; **einzig und a~** solely □ *conj* but. **A~erziehende(r)** *m/f* single parent. **a~ig** *a* sole. **a~stehend** *a* (NEW) **a~ stehend,** *s.* **allein. A~stehende** *pl* single people

allemal *adv* every time; (*gewiss*) certainly; **ein für a~** (NEW) **ein für alle Mal,** *s.* **Mal¹**

allenfalls *adv* at most; (*eventuell*) possibly

aller|beste(r,s) *a* very best; **am a~besten** best of all. **a~dings** *adv* indeed; (*zwar*) admittedly. **a~erste(r,s)** *a* very first

Allergie *f* -,-n allergy

allergisch *a* allergic (**gegen** to)

aller|hand *inv* □ *pron* all sorts of □ *pron* all sorts of things; **das ist a~hand!** that's quite something! (*empört*) that's a bit much! **A~heiligen** *nt* -s All Saints Day. **a~höchstens** *adv* at the very most. **a~lei** *inv* □ *a* all sorts of □ *pron* all sorts of things. **a~letzte(r,s)** *a* very last. **a~liebst** *a* enchanting. **a~liebste(r,s)** *a* favourite □ *adv* **am a~liebsten** for preference; **am a~liebsten haben** like best of all. **a~meiste(r,s)** *a* most □ *adv* **am a~meisten** most of all. **A~seelen** *nt* -s All Souls Day. **a~seits** *adv* generally; **guten Morgen a~seits!** good morning everyone! **a~wenigste(r,s)** *a* very least □ *adv* **am a~wenigsten** least of all

alle|s *s.* **alle(r,s). a~samt** *adv* all. **A~swisser** *m* -s,- (*fam*) know-all

allgemein *a* general, *adv* -ly; **im A~en** (**a~en**) in general. **A~heit** *f* - community; (*Öffentlichkeit*) general public

Allheilmittel *nt* panacea

Allianz *f* -,-en alliance

Alligator *m* -s,-en /-'to:rən/ alligator

alliiert *a* allied; **die A~en** *pl* the Allies

all|jährlich *a* annual, *adv* -ly. **a~mächtig** *a* almighty; **der A~mächtige** the Almighty. **a~mählich** *a* gradual, *adv* -ly

Alltag *m* working day; **der A~** (*fig*) everyday life

alltäglich *a* daily; (*gewöhnlich*) everyday; (*Mensch*) ordinary □ *adv* daily

alltags *adv* on weekdays

allzu adv [far] too; **a~ bald/oft** all too soon/often; **a~ sehr/viel** far too much; **a~ vorsichtig** over-cautious. **a~bald** adv (NEW) **a~ bald**, s. allzu. **a~ oft** adv (NEW) **a~ oft**, s. allzu. **a~sehr** adv (NEW) **a~ sehr**, s. allzu. **a~viel** adv (NEW) **a~ viel**, s. allzu

Alm f -,-en alpine pasture

Almosen ntpl alms

Alpdruck m nightmare

Alpen pl Alps. **A~veilchen** nt cyclamen

Alphabet nt -[e]s,-e alphabet. **a~isch** a alphabetical, adv -ly

Alptraum m nightmare

als conj as; (zeitlich) when; (mit Komparativ) than; **nichts als** nothing but; **als ob** as if or though; **so tun als ob** (fam) pretend

also adv & conj so; **a~ gut** all right then; **na a~!** there you are!

alt a (älter, ältest) old; (gebraucht) second-hand; (ehemalig) former; **alt werden** grow old; **alles beim A~en (a~en) lassen** leave things as they are

Alt m -s (Mus) contralto

Altar m -s,-̈e altar

Alt|e(r) m/f old man/woman; **die A~en** old people. **A~eisen** nt scrap iron. **A~enheim** nt old people's home

Alter nt -s,- age; (Bejahrtheit) old age; **im A~ von** at the age of; **im A~** in old age

älter a older; **mein ä~er Bruder** my elder brother

altern vi (sein) age

Alternative f -,-n alternative

Alters|grenze f age limit. **A~heim** nt old people's home. **A~rente** f old-age pension. **a~schwach** a old and infirm; ⟨Ding⟩ decrepit

Alter|tum nt -s,-̈er antiquity. **a~tümlich** a old; (altmodisch) old-fashioned

ältest|e(r,s) a oldest; **der ä~e Sohn** the eldest son

althergebracht a traditional

altklug a precocious, adv -ly

ältlich a elderly

alt|modisch old-fashioned □ adv in an old-fashioned way. **A~papier** nt waste paper. **A~stadt** f old [part of a] town. **A~warenhändler** m second-hand dealer. **A~weibermärchen** nt old wives' tale. **A~weibersommer** m Indian summer; (Spinnfäden) gossamer

Alufolie f [aluminium] foil

Aluminium nt -s aluminium, (Amer) aluminum

am prep = an dem; **am Montag** on Monday; **am Morgen** in the morning; **am besten/meisten** [the] best/most; **am teuersten sein** be the most expensive

Amateur /-'tø:ɐ/ m -s,-e amateur

Ambition /-'tsjo:n/ f -,-en ambition

Amboss m -es,-e (Amboß m -sses,-sse) anvil

ambulan|t a out-patient ... □ adv **a~t behandeln** treat as an out-patient. **A~z** f -,-en out-patients' department; (Krankenwagen) ambulance

Ameise f -,-n ant

amen int, **A~** nt -s amen

Amerika nt -s America

Amerikan|er(in) m -s,- (f -,-nen) American. **a~isch** a American

Ami m -s,-s (fam) Yank

Ammoniak nt -s ammonia

Amnestie f -,-n amnesty

amoralisch a amoral

Ampel f -,-n traffic lights pl; (Blumen-) hanging basket

Amphib|ie /-jə/ f -,-n amphibian. **a~isch** a amphibious

Amphitheater nt amphitheatre

Amput|ation /-'tsjo:n/ f -,-en amputation. **a~ieren** vt amputate

Amsel f -,-n blackbird

Amt nt -[e]s,-̈er office; (Aufgabe) task; (Teleph) exchange. **a~ieren** vi (haben) hold office; **a~ierend** acting. **a~lich** a official, adv -ly. **A~szeichen** nt dialling tone

Amulett nt -[e]s,-e [lucky] charm

amüs|ant a amusing, adv -ly. **a~ieren** vt amuse; **sich a~ieren** be amused (über + acc at); (sich vergnügen) enjoy oneself

an prep (+ dat/acc) at; (haftend, berührend) on; (gegen) against; (+ acc) (schicken) to; **an der/die Universität** at/to university; **an dem Tag** on that day; **es ist an mir** it is up to me; **an [und für] sich** actually; **die Arbeit an sich** the work as such □ adv (angeschaltet) on; (auf Fahrplan) arriving; **an die zwanzig Mark/Leute** about twenty marks/people; **von heute an** from today

analog a analogous; (Computer) analog. **A~ie** f -,-n analogy

Analphabet m -en,-en illiterate person. **A~entum** nt -s illiteracy

Analy|se f -,-n analysis. **a~sieren** vt analyse. **a~tiker** m -s,- analyst. **a~tisch** a analytical

Anämie f - anaemia

Ananas f -,-[se] pineapple

Anarch|ie f - anarchy. **A~ist** m -en,-en anarchist

Anat|omie f - anatomy. **a~omisch** a anatomical, adv -ly

anbahnen (sich) vr sep develop

Anbau *m* cultivation; *(Gebäude)* extension. **a~en** *vt sep* build on; *(anpflanzen)* cultivate, grow

anbehalten† *vt sep* keep on

anbei *adv* enclosed

anbeißen† *v sep* □ *vt* take a bite of □ *vi* *(haben)* *(Fisch:)* bite; *(fig)* take the bait

anbelangen *vt sep* = anbetreffen

anbellen *vt sep* bark at

anbeten *vt sep* worship

Anbetracht *m* in A~ (+ *gen*) in view of

anbetreffen† *vt sep* **was mich/das anbetrifft** as far as I am/that is concerned

Anbetung *f* - worship

anbiedern (sich) *vr sep* ingratiate oneself **(bei** with)

anbieten† *vt sep* offer; **sich a~** offer **(zu** to)

anbinden† *vt sep* tie up

Anblick *m* sight. **a~en** *vt sep* look at

anbrechen† *v sep* □ *vt* start on; break into *(Vorräte)* □ *vi (sein)* begin; *(Tag:)* break; *(Nacht:)* fall

anbrennen† *v sep* □ *vt* light □ *vi (sein)* burn; *(Feuer fangen)* catch fire

anbringen† *vt sep* bring [along]; *(befestigen)* fix

Anbruch *m (fig)* dawn; **bei A~ des Tages/der Nacht** at daybreak/nightfall

anbrüllen *vt sep (fam)* bellow at

Andacht *f* -,-en reverence; *(Gottesdienst)* prayers *pl*

andächtig *a* reverent, *adv* -ly; *(fig)* rapt, *adv* -ly

andauern *vi sep (haben)* last; *(anhalten)* continue. **a~d** *a* persistent, *adv* -ly; *(ständig)* constant, *adv* -ly

Andenken *nt* -s,- memory; *(Souvenir)* souvenir; **zum A~ an** (+ *acc*) in memory of

ander|e(r,s) *a* other; *(verschieden)* different; *(nächste)* next; **ein a~er, eine a~e** another □ *pron* **der a~e/die a~en** the other/others; **ein a~er** another [one]; *(Person)* someone else; **kein a~er** no one else; **einer nach dem a~en** one after the other; **alles a~e/nichts a~es** everything/nothing else; **etwas ganz a~es** something quite different; **alles a~e als** anything but; **unter a~em** among other things. **a~enfalls** *adv* otherwise. **a~erseits** *adv* on the other hand. **a~mal** *adv* **ein a~mal** another time

ändern *vt* alter; *(wechseln)* change; **sich ä~** change

andernfalls *adv* otherwise

anders *pred a* different; **a~ werden** change □ *adv* differently; *(riechen, schmecken)* different; *(sonst)* else; **jemand/niemand/irgendwo a~** someone/no one/somewhere else

anderseits *adv* on the other hand

anders|herum *adv* the other way round. **a~wo** *adv (fam)* somewhere else

anderthalb *inv a* one and a half; **a~ Stunden** an hour and a half

Änderung *f* -,-en alteration; *(Wechsel)* change

anderweitig *a* other □ *adv* otherwise; *(anderswo)* elsewhere

andeut|en *vt sep* indicate; *(anspielen)* hint at. **A~ung** *f* -,-en indication; hint

andicken *vt sep (Culin)* thicken

Andrang *m* rush **(nach** for); *(Gedränge)* crush

andre *a & pron* = andere

andrehen *vt sep* turn on; **jdm etw a~** *(fam)* palm sth off on s.o.

andrerseits *adv* = andererseits

androhen *vt sep* **jdm etw a~** threaten s.o. with sth

aneignen *vt sep* **sich** *(dat)* **a~** appropriate; *(lernen)* learn

aneinander *adv & pref* together; *(denken)* of one another; **a~ vorbei** past one another; **a~ geraten** quarrel. **a~geraten†** *vi sep (sein)* (NEW) **a~ geraten**, *s.* aneinander

Anekdote *f* -,-n anecdote

anekeln *vt sep* nauseate

anerkannt *a* acknowledged

anerkenn|en† *vt sep* acknowledge, recognize; *(würdigen)* appreciate. **a~end** *a* approving, *adv* -ly. **A~ung** *f* - acknowledgement, recognition; appreciation

anfahren† *v sep* □ *vt* deliver; *(streifen)* hit; *(schimpfen)* snap at □ *vi (sein)* start; **angefahren kommen** drive up

Anfall *m* fit, attack. **a~en†** *v sep* □ *vt* attack □ *vi (sein)* arise; *(Zinsen:)* accrue

anfällig *a* susceptible **(für** to); *(zart)* delicate. **A~keit** *f* - susceptibility **(für** to)

Anfang *m* -s,-e beginning, start; **zu od am A~** at the beginning; *(anfangs)* at first. **a~en†** *vt/i sep (haben)* begin, start; *(tun)* do

Anfäng|er(in) *m* -s,- *(f* -,-nen) beginner. **a~lich** *a* initial, *adv* -ly

anfangs *adv* at first. **A~buchstabe** *m* initial letter. **A~gehalt** *nt* starting salary. **A~gründe** *mpl* rudiments

anfassen *v sep* □ *vt* touch; *(behandeln)* treat; tackle *(Arbeit)*; **jdn a~** take s.o.'s hand; **sich a~** hold hands; **sich weich a~**

feel soft □ *vi* (*haben*) **mit a~** lend a hand

anfechten† *vt sep* contest; (*fig: beun-ruhigen*) trouble

anfeinden *vt sep* be hostile to

anfertigen *vt sep* make

anfeuchten *vt sep* moisten

anfeuern *vt sep* spur on

anflehen *vt sep* implore, beg

Anflug *m* (*Aviat*) approach; (*fig: Spur*) trace

anforder|n *vt sep* demand; (*Comm*) order. **A~ung** *f* demand

Anfrage *f* enquiry. **a~n** *vi sep* (*haben*) enquire, ask

anfreunden (sich) *vr sep* make friends (**mit** with); (*miteinander*) become friends

anfügen *vt sep* add

anfühlen *vt sep* feel; **sich weich a~** feel soft

anführ|en *vt sep* lead; (*zitieren*) quote; (*angeben*) give; **jdn a~en** (*fam*) have s.o. on. **A~er** *m* leader. **A~ungszeichen** *ntpl* quotation marks

Angabe *f* statement; (*Anweisung*) instruction; (*Tennis*) service; (*fam: Angeberei*) showing-off; **nähere A~n** particulars

angeb|en *v sep* □ *vt* state; give (*Namen, Grund*); (*anzeigen*) indicate; set (*Tempo*) □ *vi* (*haben*) (*Tennis*) serve; (*fam: protzen*) show off. **A~er(in)** *m* -s,- (*f* -,-nen) (*fam*) show-off. **A~erei** *f* - (*fam*) showing-off

angeblich *a* alleged, *adv* -ly

angeboren *a* innate; (*Med*) congenital

Angebot *nt* offer; (*Auswahl*) range; **A~ und Nachfrage** supply and demand

angebracht *a* appropriate

angebunden *a* **kurz a~** curt

angegriffen *a* worn out; (*Gesundheit*) poor

angeheiratet *a* (*Onkel, Tante*) by marriage

angeheitert *a* (*fam*) tipsy

angehen† *v sep* □ *vi* (*sein*) begin, start; (*Licht, Radio:*) come on; (*anwachsen*) take root; **a~ gegen** fight □ *vt* attack; tackle (*Arbeit*); (*bitten*) ask (**um** for); (*betreffen*) concern; **das geht dich nichts an** it's none of your business. **a~d** *a* future; (*Künstler*) budding

angehör|en *vi sep* (*haben*) (+ *dat*) belong to. **A~ige(r)** *m/f* relative; (*Mitglied*) member

Angeklagte(r) *m/f* accused

Angel *f* -,-n fishing-rod; (*Tür-*) hinge

Angelegenheit *f* matter; **auswärtige A~en** foreign affairs

Angel|haken *m* fish-hook. **a~n** *vi* (*haben*) fish (**nach** for); **a~n gehen** go

fishing □ *vt* (*fangen*) catch. **A~rute** *f* fishing-rod

angelsächsisch *a* Anglo-Saxon

angemessen *a* commensurate (*dat* with); (*passend*) appropriate, *adv* -ly

angenehm *a* pleasant, *adv* -ly; (*bei Vorstellung*) **a~!** delighted to meet you!

angenommen *a* (*Kind*) adopted; (*Name*) assumed

angeregt *a* animated, *adv* -ly

angesehen *a* respected; (*Firma*) reputable

angesichts *prep* (+ *gen*) in view of

angespannt *a* intent, *adv* -ly; (*Lage*) tense

Angestellte(r) *m/f* employee

angetan *a* **a~ sein von** be taken with

angetrunken *a* slightly drunk

angewandt *a* applied

angewiesen *a* dependent (**auf** + *acc* on); **auf sich selbst a~** on one's own

angewöhnen *vt sep* **jdm etw a~** get s.o. used to sth; **sich** (*dat*) **etw a~** get into the habit of doing sth

Angewohnheit *f* habit

Angina *f* - tonsillitis

angleichen† *vt sep* adjust (*dat* to)

Angler *m* -s,- angler

anglikanisch *a* Anglican

Anglistik *f* - English [language and literature]

Angorakatze *f* Persian cat

angreif|en† *vt sep* attack; tackle (*Arbeit*); (*schädigen*) damage; (*anbrechen*) break into; (*anfassen*) touch. **A~er** *m* -s,- attacker; (*Pol*) aggressor

angrenzen *vi sep* (*haben*) adjoin (**an etw** *acc* sth). **a~d** *a* adjoining

Angriff *m* attack; **in A~ nehmen** tackle. **a~slustig** *a* aggressive

Angst *f* -,̈e fear; (*Psych*) anxiety; (*Sorge*) worry (**um** about); **A~ haben** be afraid (**vor** + *dat* of); (*sich sorgen*) be worried (**um** about); **jdm A~ machen** frighten s.o. □ **mir ist a~** I am frightened; I am worried (**um** about); **jdm a~ machen** (NEW) **jdm A~ machen**

ängstigen *vt* frighten; (*Sorge machen*) worry; **sich ä~** be frightened; be worried (**um** about)

ängstlich *a* nervous, *adv* -ly; (*scheu*) timid, *adv* -ly; (*verängstigt*) frightened, scared; (*besorgt*) anxious, *adv* -ly. **Ä~keit** *f* - nervousness; timidity; anxiety

angstvoll *a* anxious, *adv* -ly; (*verängstigt*) frightened

angucken *vt sep* (*fam*) look at

angurten (sich) *vr sep* fasten one's seatbelt

anhaben† *vt sep* have on; **er/es kann mir nichts a~** (*fig*) he/it cannot hurt me

anhalt|en *v sep* □ *vt* stop; hold ⟨*Atem*⟩; **jdn zur Arbeit/Ordnung a~en** urge s.o. to work/be tidy □ *vi* (*haben*) stop; (*andauern*) continue. **a~end** *a* persistent, *adv* -ly; (*Beifall*) prolonged. **A~er(in)** *m* **-s,-** (*f* **-,-nen**) hitchhiker; **per A~er fahren** hitchhike. **A~spunkt** *m* clue

anhand *prep* (+ *gen*) with the aid of

Anhang *m* appendix; (*fam: Angehörige*) family

anhängen[1] *vt sep* (*reg*) hang up; (*befestigen*) attach; (*hinzufügen*) add

anhäng|en[2]† *vi* (*haben*) be a follower (*dat*). **A~er** *m* **-s,-** follower; (*Auto*) trailer; (*Schild*) [tie-on] label; (*Schmuck*) pendant; (*Aufhänger*) loop. **A~erin** *f* **-,-nen** follower. **A~erschaft** *f* **-** following, followers *pl*. **a~lich** *a* affectionate. **A~sel** *nt* **-s,-** appendage

anhäufen *vt sep* pile up; **sich a~** pile up, accumulate

anheben† *vt sep* lift; (*erhöhen*) raise

Anhieb *m* **auf A~** straight away

Anhöhe *f* hill

anhören *vt sep* listen to; **mit a~** overhear; **sich gut a~** sound good

animieren *vt* encourage (**zu** to)

Anis *m* **-es** aniseed

Anker *m* **-s,-** anchor; **vor A~ gehen** drop anchor. **a~n** *vi* (*haben*) anchor; (*liegen*) be anchored

anketten *vt sep* chain up

Anklage *f* accusation; (*Jur*) charge; (*Ankläger*) prosecution. **A~bank** *f* dock. **a~n** *vt sep* accuse (*gen* of); (*Jur*) charge (*gen* with)

Ankläger *m* accuser; (*Jur*) prosecutor

anklammern *vt sep* clip on; peg on the line ⟨*Wäsche*⟩; **sich a~** cling (**an** + *acc* to)

Anklang *m* **bei jdm A~ finden** meet with s.o.'s approval

ankleben *v sep* □ *vt* stick on □ *vi* (*sein*) stick (**an** + *dat* to)

Ankleide|kabine *f* changing cubicle; (*zur Anprobe*) fitting-room. **a~n** *vt sep* dress; **sich a~n** dress

anklopfen *vi sep* (*haben*) knock

anknipsen *vt sep* (*fam*) switch on

anknüpfen *v sep* □ *vt* tie on; (*fig*) enter into ⟨*Gespräch, Beziehung*⟩ □ *vi* (*haben*) refer (**an** + *acc* to)

ankommen† *vi sep* (*sein*) arrive; (*sich nähern*) approach; **gut a~** arrive safely; (*fig*) go down well (**bei** with); **nicht a~ gegen** (*fig*) be no match for; **a~ auf** (+ *acc*) depend on; **es a~ lassen auf** (+ *acc*)

risk; **das kommt darauf an** it [all] depends

ankreuzen *vt sep* mark with a cross

ankündig|en *vt sep* announce. **A~ung** *f* announcement

Ankunft *f* **-** arrival

ankurbeln *vt sep* (*fig*) boost

anlächeln *vt sep* smile at

anlachen *vt sep* smile at

Anlage *f* **-,-n** installation; (*Industrie-*) plant; (*Komplex*) complex; (*Geld-*) investment; (*Plan*) layout; (*Beilage*) enclosure; (*Veranlagung*) aptitude; (*Neigung*) predisposition; **[öffentliche] A~n** [public] gardens; **als A~** enclosed

Anlass *m* **-es,ˉe** (**Anlaß** *m* **-sses,ˉsse**) reason; (*Gelegenheit*) occasion; **A~ geben zu** give cause for

anlass|en† *vt sep* (*Auto*) start; (*fam*) leave on ⟨*Licht*⟩; keep on ⟨*Mantel*⟩; **sich gut/schlecht a~en** start off well/badly. **A~er** *m* **-s,-** starter

anlässlich (**anläßlich**) *prep* (+ *gen*) on the occasion of

Anlauf *m* (*Sport*) run-up; (*fig*) attempt. **a~en**† *v sep* □ *vi* (*sein*) start; (*beschlagen*) mist up; ⟨*Metall:*⟩ tarnish; **rot a~en** go red; (*erröten*) blush; **angelaufen kommen** come running up □ *vt* (*Naut*) call at

anlegen *v sep* □ *vt* put (**an** + *acc* against); put on ⟨*Kleidung, Verband*⟩; lay back ⟨*Ohren*⟩; aim ⟨*Gewehr*⟩; (*investieren*) invest; (*ausgeben*) spend (**für** on); (*erstellen*) build; (*gestalten*) lay out; draw up ⟨*Liste*⟩; **[mit] Hand a~** lend a hand; **es darauf a~** (*fig*) aim (**zu** to); **sich a~ mit** quarrel with □ *vi* (*haben*) ⟨*Schiff:*⟩ moor; **a~ auf** (+ *acc*) aim at

anlehnen *vt sep* lean (**an** + *acc* against); **sich a~** lean (**an** + *acc* on); **eine Tür angelehnt lassen** leave a door ajar

Anleihe *f* **-,-n** loan

anleinen *vt sep* put on a lead

anleit|en *vt sep* instruct. **A~ung** *f* instructions *pl*

anlernen *vt sep* train

Anliegen *nt* **-s,-** request; (*Wunsch*) desire

anlieg|en† *vi sep* (*haben*) **[eng] a~en** fit closely; **[eng] a~end** close-fitting. **A~er** *mpl* residents; **'A~er frei'** 'access for residents only'

anlocken *vt sep* attract

anlügen† *vt sep* lie to

anmachen *vt sep* (*fam*) fix; (*anschalten*) turn on; (*anzünden*) light; (*Culin*) dress ⟨*Salat*⟩

anmalen *vt sep* paint

Anmarsch *m* (*Mil*) approach

anmaß|en *vt sep* sich *(dat)* a∼en presume
(**zu** to); **sich** *(dat)* **ein Recht** a∼en claim
a right. **a∼end** *a* presumptuous, *adv* -ly;
(arrogant) arrogant, *adv* -ly. **A∼ung** *f* -
presumption; arrogance

anmeld|en *vt sep* announce; *(Admin)* re-
gister; **sich** a∼en say that one is coming;
(Admin) register; *(Sch)* enrol; *(im Hotel)*
check in; *(beim Arzt)* make an appointment. **A∼ung** *f* announcement; *(Admin)*
registration; *(Sch)* enrolment; *(Termin)*
appointment

anmerk|en *vt sep* mark; **sich** *(dat)* **etw**
a∼en **lassen** show sth. **A∼ung** *f* -,-en
note

Anmut *f* - grace; *(Charme)* charm

anmuten *vt sep* **es mutet mich seltsam/**
vertraut an it seems odd/familiar to me

anmutig *a* graceful, *adv* -ly; *(lieblich)*
charming, *adv* -ly

annähen *vt sep* sew on

annäher|nd *a* approximate, *adv* -ly.
A∼ungsversuche *mpl* advances

Annahme *f* -,-n acceptance; *(Adoption)*
adoption; *(Vermutung)* assumption

annehm|bar *a* acceptable. **a∼en†** *vt sep*
accept; *(adoptieren)* adopt; acquire *(Gewohnheit)*; *(sich zulegen, vermuten)* assume; **sich** a∼en (+ *gen*) take care of;
angenommen, dass assuming that. **A∼-
lichkeiten** *fpl* comforts

annektieren *vt* annex

Anno *adv* A∼ 1920 in the year 1920

Annon|ce /a'nõ:sə/ *f* -,-n advertisement.
a∼cieren /-'si:-/ *vt/i (haben)* advertise

annullieren *vt* annul; cancel *(Flug)*

anöden *vt sep (fam)* bore

Anomalie *f* -,-n anomaly

anonym *a* anonymous, *adv* -ly

Anorak *m* -s,-s anorak

anordn|en *vt sep* arrange; *(befehlen)*
order. **A∼ung** *f* arrangement; order

anorganisch *a* inorganic

anormal *a* abnormal

anpacken *v sep* □ *vt* grasp; tackle *(Arbeit,
Problem)* □ *vi (haben)* **mit** a∼ lend a hand

anpass|en *vt sep* try on; *(angleichen)* adapt
(dat to); **sich** a∼ adapt *(dat* to). **A∼ung** *f*
- adaptation. **a∼ungsfähig** *a* adaptable.
A∼ungsfähigkeit *f* adaptability

Anpfiff *m (Sport)* kick-off; *(fam: Rüge)* reprimand

anpflanzen *vt sep* plant; *(anbauen)* grow

Anprall *m* -[e]s impact. **a∼en** *vi sep (sein)*
strike (**an etw** *acc* sth)

anprangern *vt sep* denounce

anpreisen† *vt sep* commend

Anprob|e *f* fitting. **a∼ieren** *vt sep* try on

anrechnen *vt sep* count (**als** as); *(berechnen)* charge for; *(verrechnen)* allow
(Summe); **ich rechne ihm seine Hilfe**
hoch an I very much appreciate his help

Anrecht *nt* right (**auf** + *acc* to)

Anrede *f* [form of] address. **a∼n** *vt sep*
address; *(ansprechen)* speak to

anreg|en *vt sep* stimulate; *(ermuntern)* en-
courage (**zu** to); *(vorschlagen)* suggest.
a∼end *a* stimulating. **A∼ung** *f* stimula-
tion; *(Vorschlag)* suggestion

anreichern *vt sep* enrich

Anreise *f* journey; *(Ankunft)* arrival. **a∼n**
vi sep (sein) arrive

Anreiz *m* incentive

anrempeln *vt sep* jostle

Anrichte *f* -,-n sideboard. **a∼n** *vt sep (Culin)* prepare; *(garnieren)* garnish (**mit**
with); *(verursachen)* cause

anrüchig *a* disreputable

Anruf *m* call. **A∼beantworter** *m* -s,- an-
swering machine. **a∼en†** *v sep* □ *vt* call
to; *(bitten)* call on (**um** for); *(Teleph)* ring
□ *vi (haben)* ring (**bei jdm** s.o.)

anrühren *vt sep* touch; *(verrühren)* mix

ans *prep* = **an das**

Ansage *f* announcement. **a∼n** *vt sep* announce; **sich** a∼n say that one is coming.
A∼r(in) *m* -s,- *(f* -,-nen) announcer

ansamm|eln *vt sep* collect; *(anhäufen)* ac-
cumulate; **sich** a∼eln collect; *(sich
häufen)* accumulate; *(Leute:)* gather. **A∼-
lung** *f* collection; *(Menschen-)* crowd

ansässig *a* resident

Ansatz *m* beginning; *(Haar-)* hairline;
(Versuch) attempt; *(Techn)* extension

anschaff|en *vt sep* [**sich** *dat*] **etw** a∼en
acquire/*(kaufen)* buy sth. **A∼ung** *f* -,-en
acquisition; *(Kauf)* purchase

anschalten *vt sep* switch on

anschau|en *vt sep* look at. **a∼lich** *a* vivid,
adv -ly. **A∼ung** *f* -,-en *(fig)* view

Anschein *m* appearance; **den** A∼ **haben**
seem. **a∼end** *adv* apparently

anschicken (sich) *vr sep* be about (**zu** to)

anschirren *vt sep* harness

Anschlag *m* notice; *(Vor-)* estimate; *(Überfall)* attack (**auf** + *acc* on); *(Mus)* touch;
(Techn) stop; **240** A∼e **in der Minute** ≈
50 words per minute. **A∼brett** *nt* notice
board. **a∼en†** *v sep* □ *vt* put up *(Aushang)*;
strike *(Note, Taste)*; cast on *(Masche)*; *(beschädigen)* chip □ *vi (haben)*
strike/*(stoßen)* knock (**an** + *acc* against);
(Hund:) bark; *(wirken)* be effective □ *vi
(sein)* knock (**an** + *acc* against); **mit dem**
Kopf a∼en hit one's head. **A∼zettel** *m*
notice

anschließen† *v sep* ▢ *vt* connect (**an** + *acc* to); (*zufügen*) add; **sich a~ an** (+ *acc*) (*anstoßen*) adjoin; (*folgen*) follow; (*sich anfreunden*) become friendly with; **sich jdm a~** join s.o. ▢ *vi* (*haben*) **a~ an** (+ *acc*) adjoin; (*folgen*) follow. **a~d a** adjoining; (*zeitlich*) following ▢ *adv* afterwards; **a~d an** (+ *acc*) after

Anschluss (**Anschluß**) *m* connection; (*Kontakt*) contact; **A~ finden** make friends; **im A~ an** (+ *acc*) after

anschmieg|en (sich) *vr sep* snuggle up/ (*Kleid:*) cling (**an** + *acc* to). **a~sam a** affectionate

anschmieren *vt sep* smear; (*fam: täuschen*) cheat

anschnallen *vt sep* strap on; **sich a~** fasten one's seat-belt

anschneiden† *vt sep* cut into; broach (*Thema*)

anschreiben† *vt sep* write (**an** + *acc* on); (*Comm*) put on s.o.'s account; (*sich wenden*) write to; **bei jdm gut/schlecht angeschrieben sein** be in s.o.'s good/bad books

anschreien† *vt sep* shout at

Anschrift *f* address

anschuldig|en *vt sep* accuse. **A~ung** *f* -,-en accusation

anschwellen† *vi sep* (*sein*) swell

anschwemmen *vt sep* wash up

anschwindeln *vt sep* (*fam*) lie to

ansehen† *vt sep* look at; (*einschätzen*) regard (**als** as); [**sich** *dat*] **etw a~** look at sth; (*TV*) watch sth. **A~** *nt* -s respect; (*Ruf*) reputation

ansehnlich *a* considerable

ansetzen *v sep* ▢ *vt* join (**an** + *acc* to); (*festsetzen*) fix; (*veranschlagen*) estimate; **Rost a~** get rusty; **sich a~** form ▢ *vi* (*haben*) (*anbrennen*) burn; **zum Sprung a~** get ready to jump

Ansicht *f* view; **meiner A~ nach** in my view; **zur A~** (*Comm*) on approval. **A~s[post]karte** *f* picture postcard. **A~ssache** *f* matter of opinion

ansiedeln (sich) *vr sep* settle

ansonsten *adv* apart from that

anspannen *vt sep* hitch up; (*anstrengen*) strain; tense (*Muskel*)

anspiel|en *vi sep* (*haben*) **a~en auf** (+ *acc*) allude to; (*versteckt*) hint at. **A~ung** *f* -,-en allusion; hint

Anspitzer *m* -s,- pencil-sharpener

Ansporn *m* (*fig*) incentive. **a~en** *vt sep* spur on

Ansprache *f* address

ansprechen† *v sep* ▢ *vt* speak to; (*fig*) appeal to ▢ *vi* (*haben*) respond (**auf** + *acc* to). **a~d a** attractive

anspringen† *v sep* ▢ *vt* jump at ▢ *vi* (*sein*) (*Auto*) start

Anspruch *m* claim/(*Recht*) right (**auf** + *acc* to); **A~ haben** be entitled (**auf** + *acc* to); **in A~ nehmen** make use of; (*erfordern*) demand; take up (*Zeit*); occupy (*Person*); **hohe A~e stellen** be very demanding. **a~slos a** undemanding; (*bescheiden*) unpretentious. **a~svoll a** demanding; (*kritisch*) discriminating; (*vornehm*) up-market

anspucken *vt sep* spit at

anstacheln *vt sep* (*fig*) spur on

Anstalt *f* -,-en institution; **A~en/keine A~en machen** prepare/make no move (**zu** to)

Anstand *m* decency; (*Benehmen*) [good] manners *pl*

anständig *a* decent, *adv* -ly; (*ehrbar*) respectable, *adv* -bly; (*fam: beträchtlich*) considerable, *adv* -bly; (*richtig*) proper, *adv* -ly

Anstands|dame *f* chaperon. **a~los** *adv* without any trouble; (*bedenkenlos*) without hesitation

anstarren *vt sep* stare at

anstatt *conj & prep* (+ *gen*) instead of; **a~ zu arbeiten** instead of working

anstechen† *vt sep* tap (*Fass*)

ansteck|en *v sep* ▢ *vt* pin (**an** + *acc* to/on); put on (*Ring*); (*anzünden*) light; (*in Brand stecken*) set fire to; (*Med*) infect; **sich a~en** catch an infection (**bei** from) ▢ *vi* (*haben*) be infectious. **a~end a** infectious, (*fam*) catching. **A~ung** *f* -,-en infection

anstehen† *vi sep* (*haben*) queue, (*Amer*) stand in line

ansteigen† *vi sep* (*sein*) climb; (*Gelände, Preise:*) rise

anstelle *prep* (+ *gen*) instead of

anstell|en *vt sep* put, stand (**an** + *acc* against); (*einstellen*) employ; (*anschalten*) turn on; (*tun*) do; **sich a~en** queue [up], (*Amer*) stand in line; (*sich haben*) make a fuss. **A~ung** *f* employment; (*Stelle*) job

Anstieg *m* -[e]s,-e climb; (*fig*) rise

anstift|en *vt sep* cause; (*anzetteln*) instigate; **jdn a~en** put s.o. up (**zu** to). **A~er** *m* instigator

Anstoß *m* (*Anregung*) impetus; (*Stoß*) knock; (*Fußball*) kick-off; **A~ erregen/nehmen** give/take offence (**an** + *dat* at). **a~en†** *v sep* ▢ *vt* knock; (*mit dem Ellbogen*) nudge ▢ *vi* (*sein*) knock (**an** + *acc* against) ▢ *vi* (*haben*) adjoin (**an etw** *acc* sth); [**mit den Gläsern**] **a~en** clink glasses; **a~en auf** (+ *acc*) drink to; **mit der Zunge a~en** lisp

anstößig *a* offensive, *adv* -ly

anstrahlen *vt sep* floodlight; (*anlachen*) beam at

anstreiche|n† *vt sep* paint; (*anmerken*) mark. **A~r** *m* -s,- painter

anstreng|en *vt sep* strain; (*ermüden*) tire; **sich a~en** exert oneself; (*sich bemühen*) make an effort (**zu** to). **a~end** *a* strenuous; (*ermüdend*) tiring. **A~ung** *f* -,-en strain; (*Mühe*) effort

Anstrich *m* coat [of paint]

Ansturm *m* rush; (*Mil*) assault

Ansuchen *nt* -s,- request

Antagonismus *m* - antagonism

Antarktis *f* - Antarctic

Anteil *m* share; **A~ nehmen** take an interest (**an** + *dat* in); (*mitfühlen*) sympathize. **A~nahme** *f* - interest (**an** + *dat* in); (*Mitgefühl*) sympathy

Antenne *f* -,-n aerial

Anthologie *f* -,-n anthology

Anthropologie *f* - anthropology

Anti|alkoholiker *m* teetotaller. **A~biotikum** *nt* -s,-ka antibiotic

antik *a* antique. **A~e** *f* - [classical] antiquity

Antikörper *m* antibody

Antilope *f* -,-n antelope

Antipathie *f* - antipathy

Anti|quariat *nt* -[e]s,-e antiquarian bookshop. **a~quarisch** *a* & *adv* secondhand

Antiquitäten *fpl* antiques. **A~händler** *m* antique dealer

Antisemitismus *m* - anti-Semitism

Antisept|ikum *nt* -s,-ka antiseptic. **a~isch** *a* antiseptic

Antrag *m* -[e]s,-e proposal; (*Pol*) motion; (*Gesuch*) application. **A~steller** *m* -s,- applicant

antreffen† *vt sep* find

antreiben† *v sep* □ *vt* urge on; (*Techn*) drive; (*anschwemmen*) wash up □ *vi* (*sein*) be washed up

antreten† *v sep* □ *vt* start; take up (*Amt*) □ *vi* (*sein*) line up; (*Mil*) fall in

Antrieb *m* urge; (*Techn*) drive; **aus eigenem A~** of one's own accord

antrinken† *vt sep* **sich** (*dat*) **einen Rausch a~** get drunk; **sich** (*dat*) **Mut a~** give oneself Dutch courage

Antritt *m* start; **bei A~ eines Amtes** when taking office. **A~srede** *f* inaugural address

antun† *vt sep* **jdm etw a~** do sth to s.o.; **sich** (*dat*) **etwas a~** take one's own life; **es jdm angetan haben** appeal to s.o.

Antwort *f* -,-en answer, reply (**auf** + *acc* to). **a~en** *vt/i* (*haben*) answer (**jdm** s.o.)

anvertrauen *vt sep* entrust/(*mitteilen*) confide (**jdm** to s.o.); **sich jdm a~** confide in s.o.

anwachsen† *vi sep* (*sein*) take root; (*zunehmen*) grow

Anwalt *m* -[e]s,-e, **Anwältin** *f* -,-nen lawyer; (*vor Gericht*) counsel

Anwandlung *f* -,-en fit (**von** of)

Anwärter(in) *m(f)* candidate

anweis|en† *vt sep* assign (*dat* to); (*beauftragen*) instruct. **A~ung** *f* instruction; (*Geld-*) money order

anwend|en *vt sep* apply (**auf** + *acc* to); (*gebrauchen*) use. **A~ung** *f* application; use

anwerben† *vt sep* recruit

Anwesen *nt* -s,- property

anwesen|d *a* present (**bei** at); **die A~den** those present. **A~heit** *f* - presence

anwidern *vt sep* disgust

Anwohner *mpl* residents

Anzahl *f* number

anzahl|en *vt sep* pay a deposit on; pay on account (*Summe*). **A~ung** *f* deposit

anzapfen *vt sep* tap

Anzeichen *nt* sign

Anzeige *f* -,-n announcement; (*Inserat*) advertisement; **A~ erstatten gegen jdn** report s.o. to the police. **a~n** *vt sep* announce; (*inserieren*) advertise; (*melden*) report [to the police]; (*angeben*) indicate, show. **A~r** *m* indicator

anzieh|en† *vt sep* □ *vt* attract; (*festziehen*) tighten; put on (*Kleider, Bremse*); draw up (*Beine*); (*ankleiden*) dress; **sich a~en** get dressed; **was soll ich a~en?** what shall I wear? **gut angezogen** well-dressed □ *vi* (*haben*) start pulling; (*Preise:*) go up. **a~end** *a* attractive. **A~ung** *f* - attraction. **A~ungskraft** *f* attraction; (*Phys*) gravity

Anzug *m* suit; **im A~ sein** (*fig*) be imminent

anzüglich *a* suggestive; (*Bemerkung*) personal

anzünden *vt sep* light; (*in Brand stecken*) set fire to

anzweifeln *vt sep* question

apart *a* striking, *adv* -ly

Apathie *f* - apathy

apathisch *a* apathetic, *adv* -ally

Aperitif *m* -s,-s aperitif

Apfel *m* -s,- apple. **A~mus** *nt* apple purée

Apfelsine *f* -,-n orange

Apostel *m* -s,- apostle

Apostroph *m* -s,-e apostrophe

Apothek|e f -,-n pharmacy. **A~er(in)** m -s,- (f -,-nen) pharmacist, [dispensing] chemist

Apparat m -[e]s,-e device; (*Phot*) camera; (*Radio, TV*) set; (*Teleph*) telephone; **am A~!** speaking! **A~ur** f -,-en apparatus

Appell m -s,-e appeal; (*Mil*) roll-call. **a~ieren** vi (*haben*) appeal (**an** + acc to)

Appetit m -s appetite; **guten A~!** enjoy your meal! **a~lich** a appetizing, adv -ly

applaudieren vi (*haben*) applaud

Applaus m -es applause

Aprikose f -,-n apricot

April m -[s] April; **in den A~ schicken** (*fam*) make an April fool of

Aquarell n -s,-e water-colour

Aquarium nt -s,-ien aquarium

Äquator m -s equator

Ära f - era

Araber(in) m -s,- (f -,-nen) Arab

arabisch a Arab; (*Geog*) Arabian; ⟨*Ziffer*⟩ Arabic

Arbeit f -,-en work; (*Anstellung*) employment, job; (*Aufgabe*) task; (*Sch*) [written] test; (*Abhandlung*) treatise; (*Qualität*) workmanship; **bei der A~** at work; **zur A~ gehen** go to work; **an die A~ gehen, sich an die A~ machen** set to work; **sich** (*dat*) **viel A~ machen** go to a lot of trouble. **a~en** v sep □ vi (*haben*) work (**an** + dat on) □ vt make; **einen Anzug a~en lassen** have a suit made; **sich durch etw a~en** work one's way through sth. **A~er(in)** m -s,- (f -,-nen) worker; (*Land-, Hilfs-*) labourer. **A~erklasse** f working class

Arbeit|geber m -s,- employer. **A~nehmer** m -s,- employee. **a~sam** a industrious

Arbeits|amt nt employment exchange. **A~erlaubnis, A~genehmigung** f work permit. **A~kraft** f worker; **Mangel an A~kräften** shortage of labour. **a~los** a unemployed; **a~los sein** be out of work. **A~lose(r)** m/f unemployed person; **die A~losen** the unemployed pl. **A~losenunterstützung** f unemployment benefit. **A~losigkeit** f - unemployment

arbeitsparend a labour-saving

Arbeits|platz m job. **A~tag** m working day. **A~zimmer** nt study

Archäo|loge m -n,-n archaeologist. **A~logie** f - archaeology. **a~logisch** a archaeological

Arche f - die A~ Noah's Ark

Architek|t(in) m -en,-en (f -,-nen) architect. **a~tonisch** a architectural. **A~tur** f - architecture

Archiv nt -s,-e archives pl

Arena f -,-nen arena

arg a (ärger, ärgst) bad; (*groß*) terrible; **sein ärgster Feind** his worst enemy □ adv badly; (*sehr*) terribly

Argentin|ien /-jən/ nt -s Argentina. **a~isch** a Argentinian

Ärger m -s annoyance; (*Unannehmlichkeit*) trouble. **ä~lich** a annoyed; (*leidig*) annoying; **ä~lich sein** be annoyed. **ä~n** vt annoy; (*necken*) tease; **sich ä~n** get annoyed (**über jdn/etw** with s.o./ about sth). **Ä~nis** nt -ses, -se annoyance; **öffentliches Ä~nis** public nuisance

Arglist f - malice. **a~ig** a malicious, adv -ly

arglos a unsuspecting; (*unschuldig*) innocent, adv -ly

Argument nt -[e]s,-e argument. **a~ieren** vi (*haben*) argue (**dass** that)

Argwohn m -s suspicion

argwöhn|en vt suspect. **a~isch** a suspicious, adv -ly

Arie /'a:rjə/ f -,-n aria

Aristo|krat m -en,-en aristocrat. **A~kratie** f - aristocracy. **a~kratisch** a aristocratic

Arithmetik f - arithmetic

Arkt|is f - Arctic. **a~isch** a Arctic

arm a (ärmer, ärmst) poor; **Arm und Reich (arm und reich)** rich and poor

Arm m -[e]s,-e arm; **jdn auf den Arm nehmen** (*fam*) pull s.o.'s leg

Armaturenbrett nt instrument panel; (*Auto*) dashboard

Armband nt (pl -bänder) bracelet; (*Uhr-*) watch-strap. **A~uhr** f wrist-watch

Arm|e(r) m/f poor man/woman; **die A~en** the poor pl; **du A~e** od **Ärmste!** you poor thing!

Armee f -,-n army

Ärmel m -s,- sleeve. **Ä~kanal** m [English] Channel. **ä~los** a sleeveless

Arm|lehne f arm. **A~leuchter** m candelabra

ärmlich a poor, adv -ly; (*elend*) miserable, adv -bly

armselig a miserable, adv -bly

Armut f - poverty

Arom|a nt -s,-men & -mas aroma; (*Culin*) essence. **a~atisch** a aromatic

Arran|gement /arãʒə'mã:/ nt -s,-s arrangement. **a~gieren** /-'ʒi:rən/ vt arrange; **sich a~gieren** come to an arrangement

Arrest m -[e]s (*Mil*) detention

arrogan|t a arrogant, adv -ly. **A~z** f - arrogance

Arsch m -[e]s,-e (*vulg*) arse

Arsen *nt* -s arsenic

Art *f* -,-en manner; (*Weise*) way; (*Natur*) nature; (*Sorte*) kind; (*Biol*) species; **auf diese Art** in this way. **a~en** *vi* (*sein*) **a~en nach** take after

Arterie /-jə/ *f* -,-n artery

Arthritis *f* - arthritis

artig *a* well-behaved; (*höflich*) polite, *adv* -ly; **sei a~!** be good!

Artikel /-ʃlə/ *f* -,-n article

Artillerie *f* - artillery

Artischocke *f* -,-n artichoke

Artist(in) *m* -en,-en (*f* -,-nen) [circus] artiste

Arznei *f* -,-en medicine. **A~mittel** *nt* drug

Arzt *m* -[e]s,ᵋe doctor

Ärzt|in *f* -,-nen [woman] doctor. **ä~lich** *a* medical

As *nt* -ses,-se (NEW) **Ass**

Asbest *m* -[e]s asbestos

Asche *f* - ash. **A~nbecher** *m* ashtray. **A~rmittwoch** *m* Ash Wednesday

Asiat|(in) *m* -en,-en (*f* -,-nen) Asian. **a~isch** *a* Asian

Asien /'a:zjən/ *nt* -s Asia

asozial *a* antisocial

Aspekt *m* -[e]s,-e aspect

Asphalt *m* -[e]s asphalt. **a~ieren** *vt* asphalt

Ass *nt* -es,-e ace

Assistent(in) *m* -en,-en (*f* -,-nen) assistant

Ast *m* -[e]s,ᵋe branch

ästhetisch *a* aesthetic

Asth|ma *nt* -s asthma. **a~matisch** *a* asthmatic

Astro|loge *m* -n,-n astrologer. **A~logie** *f* - astrology. **A~naut** *m* -en,-en astronaut. **A~nom** *m* -en,-en astronomer. **A~nomie** *f* - astronomy. **a~nomisch** *a* astronomical

Asyl *nt* -s,-e home; (*Pol*) asylum. **A~ant** *m* -en,-en asylum-seeker

Atelier /-'lje:/ *nt* -s,-s studio

Atem *m* -s breath; **tief A~ holen** take a deep breath. **a~beraubend** *a* breath-taking. **a~los** *a* breathless, *adv* -ly. **A~pause** *f* breather. **A~zug** *m* breath

Atheist *m* -en,-en atheist

Äther *m* -s ether

Äthiopien /-jən/ *nt* -s Ethiopia

Athlet|(in) *m* -en,-en (*f* -,-nen) athlete. **a~isch** *a* athletic

Atlant *m* -s Atlantic. **a~isch** *a* Atlantic; **der A~ische Ozean** the Atlantic Ocean

Atlas *m* -lasses,-lanten atlas

atmen *vt/i* (*haben*) breathe

Atmosphär|e *f* -,-n atmosphere. **a~isch** *a* atmospheric

Atmung *f* - breathing

Atom *nt* -s,-e atom. **a~ar** *a* atomic. **A~bombe** *f* atom bomb. **A~krieg** *m* nuclear war

Atten|tat *nt* -[e]s,-e assassination attempt. **A~täter** *m* [would-be] assassin

Attest *nt* -[e]s,-e certificate

Attrak|tion /-'tsjo:n/ *f* -,-en attraction. **a~tiv** *a* attractive, *adv* -ly

Attrappe *f* -,-n dummy

Attribut *nt* -[e]s,-e attribute. **a~iv** *a* attributive, *adv* -ly

ätzen *vt* corrode; (*Med*) cauterize; (*Kunst*) etch. **ä~d** *a* corrosive; (*Spott*) caustic

au *int* ouch; **au fein!** oh good!

Aubergine /obɛr'ʒi:nə/ *f* -,-n aubergine

auch *adv* & *conj* also, too; (*außerdem*) what's more; (*selbst*) even; **a~ wenn** even if; **ich mag ihn—ich a~** I like him—so do I; **ich bin nicht müde—ich a~ nicht** I'm not tired—nor *or* neither am I; **sie weiß es a~ nicht** she doesn't know either; **wer/wie/was a~ immer** whoever/however/whatever; **ist das a~ wahr?** is that really true?

Audienz *f* -,-en audience

audiovisuell *a* audiovisual

Auditorium *nt* -s,-ien (*Univ*) lecture hall

auf *prep* (+ *dat*) on; (+ *acc*) on [to]; (*bis*) until, till; (*Proportion*) to; **auf Deutsch/ Englisch** in German/English; **auf einer/ eine Party** at/to a party; **auf der Straße** in the street; **auf seinem Zimmer** in one's room; **auf einem Ohr taub** deaf in one ear; **auf einen Stuhl steigen** climb on [to] a chair; **auf die Toilette gehen** go to the toilet; **auf ein paar Tage verreisen** go away for a few days; **auf 10 Kilometer zu sehen** visible for 10 kilometres □ *adv* open; (*in die Höhe*) up; **auf sein** be open; (*Person:*) be up; **auf und ab** up and down; **sich auf und davon machen** make off; **Tür auf!** open the door!

aufarbeiten *vt sep* do up; **Rückstände a~** clear arrears [of work]

aufatmen *vi sep* (*haben*) heave a sigh of relief

aufbahren *vt sep* lay out

Aufbau *m* construction; (*Struktur*) structure. **a~en** *v sep* □ *vt* construct, build; (*errichten*) erect; (*schaffen*) build up; (*arrangieren*) arrange; **wieder a~en** reconstruct; **sich a~en** (*fig*) be based (**auf** + *dat* on) □ *vi* (*haben*) be based (**auf** + *dat* on)

aufbäumen (**sich**) *vr sep* rear [up]; (*fig*) rebel

aufbauschen vt sep puff out; (fig) exaggerate

aufbehalten† vt sep keep on

aufbekommen† vt sep get open; (Sch) be given [as homework]

aufbessern vt sep improve; (erhöhen) increase

aufbewahr|en vt sep keep; (lagern) store. A~ung f - safe keeping; storage; (Gepäck-) left-luggage office

aufbieten† vt sep mobilize; (fig) summon up

aufblas|bar a inflatable. a~en† vt sep inflate; sich a~en (fig) give oneself airs

aufbleiben† vi sep (sein) stay open; (Person:) stay up

aufblenden vt/i sep (haben) (Auto) switch to full beam

aufblicken vi sep (haben) look up (zu at/(fig) to)

aufblühen vi sep (sein) flower; (Knospe:) open

aufbocken vt sep jack up

aufbraten† vt sep fry up

aufbrauchen vt sep use up

aufbrausen vi sep (sein) (fig) flare up. a~d a quick-tempered

aufbrechen† v sep □ vt break open □ vi (sein) (Knospe:) open; (sich aufmachen) set out, start

aufbringen† vt sep raise (Geld); find (Kraft); (wütend machen) infuriate

Aufbruch m start, departure

aufbrühen vt sep make (Tee)

aufbürden vt sep jdm etw a~ (fig) burden s.o. with sth

aufdecken vt sep (auflegen) put on; (abdecken) uncover; (fig) expose

aufdrängen vt sep force (dat on); sich jdm a~ force one's company on s.o.

aufdrehen vt sep turn on

aufdringlich a persistent

aufeinander adv one on top of the other; (schießen) at each other; (warten) for each other; a~ folgen follow one another; a~folgend successive; (Tage) consecutive. a~folgen vi sep (sein) (NEW) a~ folgen, s. aufeinander. a~folgend a (NEW) a~ folgend, s. aufeinander

Aufenthalt m stay; 10 Minuten A~ haben (Zug:) stop for 10 minutes. A~serlaubnis, A~sgenehmigung f residence permit. A~sraum m recreation room; (im Hotel) lounge

auferlegen vt sep impose (dat on)

aufersteh|en† vi sep (sein) rise from the dead. A~ung f - resurrection

aufessen† vt sep eat up

auffahr|en† vi sep (sein) drive up; (aufprallen) crash, run (auf + acc into); (aufschrecken) start up; (aufbrausen) flare up. A~t f drive; (Autobahn-) access road, slip road; (Bergfahrt) ascent

auffallen† vi sep (sein) be conspicuous; unangenehm a~ make a bad impression; jdm a~ strike s.o. a~d a striking, adv -ly

auffällig a conspicuous, adv -ly; (grell) gaudy, adv -ily

auffangen† vt sep catch; pick up (Funkspruch)

auffass|en vt sep understand; (deuten) take; falsch a~en misunderstand. A~ung f understanding; (Ansicht) view. A~ungsgabe f grasp

aufforder|n vt sep ask; (einladen) invite; jdn zum Tanz a~n ask s.o. to dance. A~ung f request; invitation

auffrischen v sep □ vt freshen up; revive (Erinnerung); seine Englischkenntnisse a~ brush up one's English

aufführ|en vt sep perform; (angeben) list; sich a~en behave. A~ung f performance

auffüllen vt sep fill up; [wieder] a~ replenish

Aufgabe f task; (Rechen-) problem; (Verzicht) giving up; A~n (Sch) homework sg

Aufgang m way up; (Treppe) stairs pl; (Astr) rise

aufgeben† v sep □ vt give up; post (Brief); send (Telegramm); place (Bestellung); register (Gepäck); put in the paper (Annonce); jdm eine Aufgabe/ein Rätsel a~ set s.o. a task/a riddle; jdm Suppe a~ serve s.o. with soup □ vi (haben) give up

aufgeblasen a (fig) conceited

Aufgebot nt contingent (an + dat of); (Relig) banns pl; unter A~ aller Kräfte with all one's strength

aufgebracht a (fam) angry

aufgedunsen a bloated

aufgehen† vi sep (sein) open; (sich lösen) come undone; (Teig, Sonne:) rise; (Saat:) come up; (Math) come out exactly; in Flammen a~ go up in flames; in etw (dat) a~ (fig) be wrapped up in sth; ihm ging auf (fam) he realized (dass that)

aufgelegt a a~ sein zu be in the mood for; gut/schlecht a~ sein be in a good/bad mood

aufgelöst a (fig) distraught; in Tränen a~ in floods of tears

aufgeregt a excited, adv -ly; (erregt) agitated, adv -ly

aufgeschlossen a (fig) openminded

aufgesprungen a chapped

aufgeweckt *a* (*fig*) bright

aufgießen† *vt sep* pour on; (*aufbrühen*) make ⟨*Tee*⟩

aufgreifen† *vt sep* pick up; take up ⟨*Vorschlag, Thema*⟩

aufgrund *prep* (+ *gen*) on the strength of

Aufguss (**Aufguß**) *m* infusion

aufhaben† *v sep* □ *vt* have on; **den Mund a~** have one's mouth open; **viel a~** (*Sch*) have a lot of homework □ *vi* (*haben*) be open

aufhalsen *vt sep* (*fam*) saddle with

aufhalten† *vt sep* hold up; (*anhalten*) stop; (*abhalten*) keep, detain; (*offen halten*) hold open; hold out ⟨*Hand*⟩; **sich a~** stay; (*sich befassen*) spend one's time (**mit** on)

aufhäng|en *vt/i sep* (*haben*) hang up; (*henken*) hang; **sich a~en** hang oneself. **A~er** *m* -s,- loop. **A~ung** *f* - (*Auto*) suspension

aufheben† *vt sep* pick up; (*hochheben*) raise; (*aufbewahren*) keep; (*beenden*) end; (*rückgängig machen*) lift; (*abschaffen*) abolish; (*Jur*) quash ⟨*Urteil*⟩; repeal ⟨*Gesetz*⟩; (*ausgleichen*) cancel out; **sich a~** cancel each other out; **gut aufgehoben sein** be well looked after. **A~** *nt* -s viel **A~s machen** make a great fuss (**von** about)

aufheitern *vt sep* cheer up; **sich a~** ⟨*Wetter:*⟩ brighten up

aufhellen *vt sep* lighten; **sich a~** ⟨*Himmel:*⟩ brighten

aufhetzen *vt sep* incite

aufholen *v sep* □ *vt* make up □ *vi* (*haben*) catch up; (*zeitlich*) make up time

aufhorchen *vi sep* (*haben*) prick up one's ears

aufhören *vi sep* (*haben*) stop; **mit der Arbeit a~, a~ zu arbeiten** stop working

aufklappen *vt/i sep* (*sein*) open

aufklär|en *vt sep* solve; **jdn a~en** enlighten s.o.; (*sexuell*) tell s.o. the facts of life; **sich a~en** be solved; ⟨*Wetter:*⟩ clear up. **A~ung** *f* solution; enlightenment; (*Mil*) reconnaissance; **sexuelle A~ung** sex education

aufkleb|en *vt sep* stick on. **A~er** *m* -s,- sticker

aufknöpfen *vt sep* unbutton

aufkochen *v sep* □ *vt* bring to the boil □ *vi* (*sein*) come to the boil

aufkommen† *vi sep* (*sein*) start; ⟨*Wind:*⟩ spring up; ⟨*Mode:*⟩ come in; **a~ für** pay for

aufkrempeln *vt sep* roll up

aufladen† *vt sep* load; (*Electr*) charge

Auflage *f* impression; (*Ausgabe*) edition; (*Zeitungs-*) circulation; (*Bedingung*) condition; (*Überzug*) coating

auflassen† *vt sep* leave open; leave on ⟨*Hut*⟩

auflauern *vi sep* (*haben*) **jdm a~** lie in wait for s.o.

Auflauf *m* crowd; (*Culin*) ≈ soufflé. **a~en**† *vi sep* (*sein*) (*Naut*) run aground

auflegen *v sep* □ *vt* apply (**auf** + *acc* to); put down ⟨*Hörer*⟩; **neu a~** reprint □ *vi* (*haben*) ring off

auflehn|en (**sich**) *vr sep* (*fig*) rebel. **A~ung** *f* - rebellion

auflesen† *vt sep* pick up

aufleuchten *vi sep* (*haben*) light up

aufliegen† *vi sep* (*haben*) rest (**auf** + *dat* on)

auflisten *vt sep* list

auflockern *vt sep* break up; (*entspannen*) relax; (*fig*) liven up

auflös|en *vt sep* dissolve; close ⟨*Konto*⟩; **sich a~en** dissolve; ⟨*Nebel:*⟩ clear. **A~ung** dissolution; (*Lösung*) solution

aufmach|en *v sep* □ *vt* open; (*lösen*) undo; **sich a~en** set out (**nach** for); (*sich schminken*) make oneself up □ *vi* (*haben*) open; **jdm a~en** open the door to s.o. **A~ung** *f* -,-en get-up; (*Comm*) presentation

aufmerksam *a* attentive, *adv* -ly; **a~ werden auf** (+ *acc*) notice; **jdn a~ machen auf** (+ *acc*) draw s.o.'s attention to. **A~keit** *f* -,-en attention; (*Höflichkeit*) courtesy

aufmucken *vi sep* (*haben*) rebel

aufmuntern *vt sep* cheer up

Aufnahme *f* -,-n acceptance; (*Empfang*) reception; (*in Klub, Krankenhaus*) admission; (*Einbeziehung*) inclusion; (*Beginn*) start; (*Foto*) photograph; (*Film-*) shot; (*Mus*) recording; (*Band-*) tape recording. **a~fähig** a receptive. **A~prüfung** *f* entrance examination

aufnehmen† *vt sep* pick up; (*absorbieren*) absorb; take ⟨*Nahrung, Foto*⟩; (*fassen*) hold; (*annehmen*) accept; (*leihen*) borrow; (*empfangen*) receive; (*in Klub, Krankenhaus*) admit; (*beherbergen, geistig erfassen*) take in; (*einbeziehen*) include; (*beginnen*) take up; (*niederschreiben*) take down; (*filmen*) film, shoot; (*Mus*) record; **auf Band a~** tape[-record]; **etw gelassen a~** take sth calmly; **es a~ können mit** (*fig*) be a match for

aufopfer|n *vt sep* sacrifice; **sich a~n** sacrifice oneself. **a~nd** *a* devoted, *adv* -ly. **A~ung** *f* self-sacrifice

aufpassen *vi sep* (*haben*) pay attention; (*sich vorsehen*) take care; **a~ auf** (+ *acc*) look after

aufpflanzen (**sich**) *vr sep* (*fam*) plant oneself

aufplatzen *vi sep* (*sein*) split open

aufplustern (**sich**) *vr sep* ⟨*Vogel:*⟩ ruffle up its feathers

Aufprall *m* -[e]s impact. **a~en** *vi sep* (*sein*) **a~en auf** (+ *acc*) hit

aufpumpen *vt sep* pump up, inflate

aufputsch|en *vt sep* incite; **sich a~en** take stimulants. **A~mittel** *nt* stimulant

aufquellen† *vi sep* (*sein*) swell

aufraffen *vt sep* pick up; **sich a~** pick oneself up; (*fig*) pull oneself together; (*sich aufschwingen*) find the energy (**zu** for)

aufragen *vi sep* (*sein*) rise [up]

aufräumen *vt/i sep* (*haben*) tidy up; (*wegräumen*) put away; **a~ mit** (*fig*) get rid of

aufrecht *a & adv* upright. **a~erhalten**† *vt sep* (*fig*) maintain

aufreg|en *vt* excite; (*beunruhigen*) upset; (*ärgern*) annoy; **sich a~en** get excited; (*sich erregen*) get worked up. **a~end** *a* exciting. **A~ung** *f* excitement

aufreiben† *vt sep* chafe; (*fig*) wear down; **sich a~** wear oneself out. **a~d** *a* trying, wearing

aufreißen† *v sep* □ *vt* tear open; dig up ⟨*Straße*⟩; open wide ⟨*Augen, Mund*⟩ □ *vi* (*sein*) split open

aufreizend *a* provocative, *adv* -ly

aufrichten *vt sep* erect; (*fig: trösten*) comfort; **sich a~** straighten up; (*sich setzen*) sit up

aufrichtig *a* sincere, *adv* -ly. **A~keit** *f* -sincerity

aufriegeln *vt sep* unbolt

aufrollen *vt sep* roll up; (*entrollen*) unroll

aufrücken *vi sep* (*sein*) move up; (*fig*) be promoted

Aufruf *m* appeal (**an** + *dat* to). **a~en**† *vt sep* call out ⟨*Namen*⟩; **jdn a~en** call s.o.'s name; (*fig*) call on s.o. (**zu** to)

Aufruhr *m* -s,-e turmoil; (*Empörung*) revolt

aufrühr|en *vt sep* stir up. **A~er** *m* -s,-rebel. **a~erisch** *a* inflammatory; (*rebellisch*) rebellious

aufrunden *vt sep* round up

aufrüsten *vi sep* (*haben*) arm

aufs *prep* = **auf das**

aufsagen *vt sep* recite

aufsammeln *vt sep* gather up

aufsässig *a* rebellious

Aufsatz *m* top; (*Sch*) essay

aufsaugen† *vt sep* soak up

aufschauen *vi sep* (*haben*) look up (**zu** at/(*fig*) to)

aufschichten *vt sep* stack up

aufschieben† *vt sep* slide open; (*verschieben*) put off, postpone

Aufschlag *m* impact; (*Tennis*) service; (*Hosen-*) turn-up; (*Ärmel-*) upturned cuff; (*Revers*) lapel; (*Comm*) surcharge. **a~en**† *v sep* □ *vt* open; crack ⟨*Ei*⟩; (*hochschlagen*) turn up; (*errichten*) put up; (*erhöhen*) increase; cast on ⟨*Masche*⟩; **sich** ⟨*dat*⟩ **das Knie a~en** cut [open] one's knee □ *vi* (*haben*) hit (**auf etw** *acc/dat* sth); (*Tennis*) serve; (*teurer werden*) go up

aufschließen† *v sep* □ *vt* unlock □ *vi* (*haben*) unlock the door

aufschlitzen *vt sep* slit open

Aufschluss (**Aufschluß**) *m* **A~ geben** give information (**über** + *acc* on). **a~reich** *a* revealing; (*lehrreich*) informative

aufschneid|en† *v sep* □ *vt* cut open; (*in Scheiben*) slice; carve ⟨*Braten*⟩ □ *vi* (*haben*) (*fam*) exaggerate. **A~er** *m* -s,-(*fam*) showoff

Aufschnitt *m* sliced sausage, cold meat [and cheese]

aufschrauben *vt sep* screw on; (*abschrauben*) unscrew

aufschrecken *v sep* □ *vt* startle □ *vi*† (*sein*) startle; **aus dem Schlaf a~** wake up with a start

Aufschrei *m* [sudden] cry

aufschreiben† *vt sep* write down; (*fam: verschreiben*) prescribe; **jdn a~** ⟨*Polizist:*⟩ book s.o.

aufschreien† *vi sep* (*haben*) cry out

Aufschrift *f* inscription; (*Etikett*) label

Aufschub *m* delay; (*Frist*) grace

aufschürfen *vt sep* **sich** ⟨*dat*⟩ **das Knie a~** graze one's knee

aufschwatzen *vt sep* **jdm etw a~** talk s.o. into buying sth

aufschwingen† (**sich**) *vr sep* find the energy (**zu** for)

Aufschwung *m* (*fig*) upturn

aufsehen† *vi sep* (*haben*) look up (**zu** at/(*fig*) to). **A~** *nt* -s **A~ erregen** cause a sensation; **A~ erregend** sensational. **a~erregend** *a* NEW **A~ erregend**, *s.* **Aufsehen**

Aufseher(in) *m* -s,-(*f* -,-nen) supervisor; (*Gefängnis-*) warder

aufsein† *vi sep* (*sein*) NEW **auf sein**, *s.* **auf**

aufsetzen *vt sep* put on; (*verfassen*) draw up; (*entwerfen*) draft; **sich a~** sit up

Aufsicht *f* supervision; (*Person*) supervisor. **A~srat** *m* board of directors

aufsitzen† *vi sep* (*sein*) mount

aufspannen *vt sep* put up

aufsparen *vt sep* save, keep

aufsperren *vt sep* open wide

aufspielen *v sep* □ *vi* (*haben*) play □ *vr* **sich a~** show off; **sich als Held a~** play the hero

aufspießen *vt sep* spear

aufspringen† *vi sep* ⟨*sein*⟩ jump up; ⟨*aufprallen*⟩ bounce; ⟨*sich öffnen*⟩ burst open; ⟨*Haut:*⟩ become chapped; a~ auf (+ *acc*) jump on

aufspüren *vt sep* track down

aufstacheln *vt sep* incite

aufstampfen *vi sep* ⟨*haben*⟩ mit dem Fuß a~ stamp one's foot

Aufstand *m* uprising, rebellion

aufständisch *a* rebellious. A~e(r) *m* rebel, insurgent

aufstapeln *vt sep* stack up

aufstauen *vt sep* dam [up]

aufstehen† *vi sep* ⟨*sein*⟩ get up; ⟨*offen sein*⟩ be open; ⟨*fig*⟩ rise up

aufsteigen† *vi sep* ⟨*sein*⟩ get on; ⟨*Reiter:*⟩ mount; ⟨*Bergsteiger:*⟩ climb up; ⟨*hochsteigen*⟩ rise [up]; ⟨*fig: befördert werden*⟩ rise (zu to); ⟨*Sport*⟩ be promoted

aufstell|en *vt sep* put up; ⟨*Culin*⟩ put on; ⟨*postieren*⟩ post; ⟨*in einer Reihe*⟩ line up; ⟨*nominieren*⟩ nominate; ⟨*Sport*⟩ select ⟨*Mannschaft*⟩; make out ⟨*Liste*⟩; lay down ⟨*Regel*⟩; make ⟨*Behauptung*⟩; set up ⟨*Rekord*⟩; sich a~en rise [up]; ⟨*in einer Reihe*⟩ line up. A~ung *f* nomination; ⟨*Liste*⟩ list

Aufstieg *m* -[e]s, -e ascent; ⟨*fig*⟩ rise; ⟨*Sport*⟩ promotion

aufstöbern *vt sep* flush out; ⟨*fig*⟩ track down

aufstoßen† *v sep* □ *vt* push open □ *vi* ⟨*haben*⟩ burp; a~ auf (+ *acc*) strike. A~ *nt* -s burping

aufstrebend *a* ⟨*fig*⟩ ambitious

Aufstrich *m* [sandwich] spread

aufstützen *vt sep* rest (auf + *acc* on); sich a~ lean (auf + *acc* on)

aufsuchen *vt sep* look for; ⟨*besuchen*⟩ go to see

Auftakt *m* ⟨*fig*⟩ start

auftauchen *vi sep* ⟨*sein*⟩ emerge; ⟨*U-Boot:*⟩ surface; ⟨*fig*⟩ turn up; ⟨*Frage:*⟩ crop up

auftauen *vt/i sep* ⟨*sein*⟩ thaw

aufteil|en *vt sep* divide [up]. A~ung *f* division

auftischen *vt sep* serve [up]

Auftrag *m* -[e]s, -̈e task; ⟨*Kunst*⟩ commission; ⟨*Comm*⟩ order; im A~ (+ *gen*) on behalf of. a~en† *v sep* □ *vt* apply; ⟨*servieren*⟩ serve; ⟨*abtragen*⟩ wear out; jdm a~en instruct s.o. (zu to) □ *vi* ⟨*haben*⟩ dick a~en ⟨*fam*⟩ exaggerate. A~ geber *m* -s,- client

auftreiben† *vt sep* distend; ⟨*fam: beschaffen*⟩ get hold of

auftrennen *vt sep* unpick, undo

auftreten† *v sep* □ *vi* ⟨*sein*⟩ tread; ⟨*sich benehmen*⟩ behave, act; ⟨*Theat*⟩ appear; ⟨*die Bühne betreten*⟩ enter; ⟨*vorkommen*⟩ occur □ *vt* kick open. A~ *nt* -s occurrence; ⟨*Benehmen*⟩ manner

Auftrieb *m* buoyancy; ⟨*fig*⟩ boost

Auftritt *m* ⟨*Theat*⟩ appearance; ⟨*auf die Bühne*⟩ entrance; ⟨*Szene*⟩ scene

auftun† *vt sep* jdm Suppe a~ serve s.o. with soup; sich ⟨*dat*⟩ etw a~ help oneself to sth; sich a~ open

aufwachen *vi sep* ⟨*sein*⟩ wake up

aufwachsen† *vi sep* ⟨*sein*⟩ grow up

Aufwand *m* -[e]s expenditure; ⟨*Luxus*⟩ extravagance; ⟨*Mühe*⟩ trouble; A~ treiben be extravagant

aufwändig *a* = aufwendig

aufwärmen *vt sep* heat up; ⟨*fig*⟩ rake up; sich a~ warm oneself; ⟨*Sport*⟩ warm up

Aufwartefrau *f* cleaner

aufwärts *adv* upwards; ⟨*bergauf*⟩ uphill; es geht a~ mit jdm/etw s.o./sth is improving. a~gehen† *vi sep* ⟨*sein*⟩ (NEW) a~ gehen, s. aufwärts

Aufwartung *f* - cleaner; jdm seine A~ machen call on s.o.

aufwaschen† *vt/i sep* ⟨*haben*⟩ wash up

aufwecken *vt sep* wake up

aufweichen *v sep* □ *vt* soften □ *vi* ⟨*sein*⟩ become soft

aufweisen† *vt sep* have, show

aufwend|en† *vt sep* spend; Mühe a~en take pains. a~ig *a* lavish, *adv* -ly; ⟨*teuer*⟩ expensive, *adv* -ly

aufwerfen† *vt sep* ⟨*fig*⟩ raise

aufwert|en *vt sep* revalue. A~ung *f* revaluation

aufwickeln *vt sep* roll up; ⟨*auswickeln*⟩ unwrap

aufwiegeln *vt sep* stir up

aufwiegen† *vt sep* compensate for

Aufwiegler *m* -s,- agitator

aufwirbeln *vt sep* Staub a~ stir up dust; ⟨*fig*⟩ cause a stir

aufwisch|en *vt sep* wipe up; wash ⟨*Fußboden*⟩. A~lappen *m* floorcloth

aufwühlen *vt sep* churn up; ⟨*fig*⟩ stir up

aufzähl|en *vt sep* enumerate, list. A~ung *f* list

aufzeichn|en *vt sep* record; ⟨*zeichnen*⟩ draw. A~ung *f* recording; A~ungen notes

aufziehen† *v sep* □ *vt* pull up; hoist ⟨*Segel*⟩; ⟨*öffnen*⟩ open; draw ⟨*Vorhang*⟩; ⟨*auftrennen*⟩ undo; ⟨*großziehen*⟩ bring up; rear ⟨*Tier*⟩; mount ⟨*Bild*⟩; thread ⟨*Perlen*⟩; wind up ⟨*Uhr*⟩; ⟨*arrangieren*⟩ organize; ⟨*fam: necken*⟩ tease □ *vi* ⟨*sein*⟩ approach

Aufzucht *f* rearing

Aufzug *m* hoist; *(Fahrstuhl)* lift, *(Amer)* elevator; *(Prozession)* procession; *(Theat)* act; *(fam: Aufmachung)* get-up

Augapfel *m* eyeball

Auge *nt* -s,-n eye; *(Punkt)* spot; **vier A∼n werfen** throw a four; **gute A∼n** good eyesight; **unter vier A∼n** in private; **aus den A∼n verlieren** lose sight of; **im A∼ behalten** keep in sight; *(fig)* bear in mind

Augenblick *m* moment; **im/jeden A∼** at the/at any moment; **A∼!** just a moment! **a∼lich** *a* immediate; *(derzeitig)* present □ *adv* immediately; *(derzeit)* at present

Augen|braue *f* eyebrow. **A∼höhle** *f* eye socket. **A∼licht** *nt* sight. **A∼lid** *nt* eyelid. **A∼schein** *m* in **A∼schein nehmen** inspect. **A∼zeuge** *m* eyewitness

August *m* -[s] August

Auktion /'tsjo:n/ *f* -,-en auction. **A∼ator** *m* -s,-en /-'to:rən/ auctioneer

Aula *f* -,-len *(Sch)* [assembly] hall

Aupairmädchen /o'pɛ:r-/ *nt* au pair

aus *prep* (+ *dat*) out of; *(von)* from; *(bestehend)* [made] of; **aus Angst** from *or* out of fear; **aus Spaß** for fun □ *adv* out; *(Licht, Radio)* off; **aus sein** be out; *(Licht, Radio:)* be off; *(zu Ende sein)* be over; **aus sein auf** (+ *acc*) be after; **mit ihm ist es aus** he's had it; **aus und ein** in and out; **nicht mehr aus noch ein wissen** be at one's wits' end; **von ... aus** from ...; **von sich aus** of one's own accord; **von mir aus** as far as I'm concerned

ausarbeiten *vt sep* work out

ausarten *vi sep (sein)* degenerate (**in** + *acc* into)

ausatmen *vt/i sep (haben)* breathe out

ausbaggern *vt sep* excavate; dredge *(Fluss)*

ausbauen *vt sep* remove; *(vergrößern)* extend; *(fig)* expand

ausbedingen† *vt sep* **sich** *(dat)* **a∼** insist on; *(zur Bedingung machen)* stipulate

ausbesser|n *vt sep* mend, repair. **A∼ung** *f* repair

ausbeulen *vt sep* remove the dents from; *(dehnen)* make baggy

Ausbeut|e *f* yield. **a∼en** *vt sep* exploit. **A∼ung** *f* - exploitation

ausbild|en *vt sep* train; *(formen)* form; *(entwickeln)* develop; **sich a∼en** train (**als/zu** as); *(entstehen)* develop. **A∼er** *m* -s,- instructor. **A∼ung** *f* training; *(Sch)* education

ausbitten† *vt sep* **sich** *(dat)* **a∼** ask for; *(verlangen)* insist on

ausblasen† *vt sep* blow out

ausbleiben† *vi sep (sein)* fail to appear/ *(Erfolg:)* materialize; *(nicht heimkommen)*

stay out; **es konnte nicht a∼** it was inevitable. **A∼** *nt* -s absence

Ausblick *m* view

ausbrech|en† *vi sep (sein)* break out; *(Vulkan:)* erupt; *(fliehen)* escape; **in Tränen a∼en** burst into tears. **A∼er** *m* runaway

ausbreit|en *vt sep* spread [out]; **sich a∼en** spread. **A∼ung** *f* spread

ausbrennen† *v sep* □ *vt* cauterize □ *vi (sein)* burn out; *(Haus:)* be gutted [by fire]

Ausbruch *m* outbreak; *(Vulkan-)* eruption; *(Wut-)* outburst; *(Flucht)* escape, break-out

ausbrüten *vt sep* hatch

Ausbund *m* **A∼ der Tugend** paragon of virtue

ausbürsten *vt sep* brush; *(entfernen)* brush out

Ausdauer *f* perseverance; *(körperlich)* stamina. **a∼nd** *a* persevering; *(unermüdlich)* untiring; *(Bot)* perennial □ *adv* with perseverance; untiringly

ausdehn|en *vt sep* stretch; *(fig)* extend; **sich a∼en** stretch; *(Phys & fig)* expand; *(dauern)* last. **A∼ung** *f* expansion; *(Umfang)* extent

ausdenken† *vt sep* **sich** *(dat)* **a∼** think up; *(sich vorstellen)* imagine

ausdrehen *vt sep* turn off

Ausdruck *m* expression; *(Fach-)* term; *(Computer)* printout. **a∼en** *vt sep* print

ausdrück|en *vt sep* squeeze out; squeeze *(Zitrone)*; stub out *(Zigarette)*; *(äußern)* express; **sich a∼en** express oneself. **a∼lich** *a* express, *adv* -ly

ausdrucks|los *a* expressionless. **a∼voll** *a* expressive, *adv* -ly

auseinander *adv* apart; *(entzwei)* in pieces; **a∼ falten** unfold; **a∼ gehen** part; *(Linien, Meinungen:)* diverge; *(Menge:)* disperse; *(Ehe:)* break up; *(entzweigehen)* come apart; **a∼ halten** tell apart; **a∼ nehmen** take apart *or* to pieces; **a∼ setzen** place apart; *(erklären)* explain (**jdm** to s.o.); **sich a∼ setzen** sit apart; *(sich aussprechen)* have it out (**mit jdm** with s.o.); come to grips (**mit einem Problem** with a problem). **a∼falten** *vt sep* **a∼falten**, *s.* auseinander. **a∼gehen**† *vi sep (sein)* (NEW) **a∼ gehen**, *s.* auseinander. **a∼halten**† *vt sep* (NEW) **a∼ halten**, *s.* auseinander. **a∼nehmen**† *vt sep* (NEW) **a∼ nehmen**, *s.* auseinander. **a∼setzen** *vt sep* (NEW) **a∼ setzen**, *s.* auseinander. **A∼setzung** *f* -,-en discussion; *(Streit)* argument

auserlesen *a* select, choice

ausfahr|en† *v sep* □ *vt* take for a drive; take out *(Baby)* [in the pram] □ *vi (sein)* go for a drive. **A∼t** *f* drive; ⟨*Autobahn-, Garagen-*⟩ exit

Ausfall *m* failure; (*Absage*) cancellation; (*Comm*) loss. **a∼en†** *vi sep* (*sein*) fall out; (*versagen*) fail; (*abgesagt werden*) be cancelled; **gut/schlecht a∼en** turn out to be good/poor

ausfallend, ausfällig *a* abusive

ausfertig|en *vt sep* make out. **A∼ung** *f* -,-en **in doppelter/dreifacher A∼ung** in duplicate/triplicate

ausfindig *a* **a∼ machen** find

ausflippen *vi* (*sein*) freak out

Ausflucht *f* -,͏̈e excuse

Ausflug *m* excursion, outing

Ausflügler *m* -s,- [day-]tripper

Ausfluss (**Ausfluß**) *m* outlet; (*Abfluss*) drain; (*Med*) discharge

ausfragen *vt sep* question

ausfransen *vi sep* (*sein*) fray

Ausfuhr *f* -,-en (*Comm*) export

ausführ|en *vt sep* take out; (*Comm*) export; (*durchführen*) carry out; (*erklären*) explain. **a∼lich** *a* detailed □ *adv* in detail. **A∼ung** *f* execution; (*Comm*) version; (*äußere*) finish; (*Qualität*) workmanship; (*Erklärung*) explanation

Ausgabe *f* issue; (*Buch-*) edition; (*Comm*) version

Ausgang *m* way out, exit; (*Flugsteig*) gate; (*Ende*) end; (*Ergebnis*) outcome, result; **A∼ haben** have time off. **A∼spunkt** *m* starting-point. **A∼ssperre** *f* curfew

ausgeben† *vt sep* hand out; issue ⟨*Fahrkarten*⟩; spend ⟨*Geld*⟩; buy ⟨*Runde Bier*⟩; **sich a∼ als** pretend to be

ausgebeult *a* baggy

ausgebildet *a* trained

ausgebucht *a* fully booked; ⟨*Vorstellung*⟩ sold out

ausgedehnt *a* extensive; (*lang*) long

ausgedient *a* worn out; ⟨*Person*⟩ retired

ausgefallen *a* unusual

ausgefranst *a* frayed

ausgeglichen *a* [well-]balanced; (*gelassen*) even-tempered

ausgeh|en† *vi sep* (*sein*) go out; ⟨*Haare:*⟩ fall out; ⟨*Vorräte, Geld:*⟩ run out; (*verblassen*) fade; (*herrühren*) come (**von** from); (*abzielen*) aim (**auf** + *acc* at); **gut/schlecht a∼en** end well/badly; **leer a∼en** come away empty-handed; **davon a∼en, dass** assume that. **A∼verbot** *nt* curfew

ausgelassen *a* high-spirited; **a∼ sein** be in high spirits

ausgelernt *a* [fully] trained

ausgemacht *a* agreed; (*fam: vollkommen*) utter

ausgenommen *conj* except; **a∼ wenn** unless

ausgeprägt *a* marked

ausgerechnet *adv* **a∼ heute** today of all days; **a∼er/Rom** he of all people/Rome of all places

ausgeschlossen *pred a* out of the question

ausgeschnitten *a* low-cut

ausgesprochen *a* marked □ *adv* decidedly

ausgestorben *a* extinct; **[wie] a∼** ⟨*Straße:*⟩ deserted

Ausgestoßene(r) *m/f* outcast

ausgewachsen *a* fully-grown

ausgewogen *a* [well-]balanced

ausgezeichnet *a* excellent, *adv* -ly

ausgiebig *a* extensive, *adv* -ly; (*ausgedehnt*) long; **a∼ Gebrauch machen von** make full use of; **a∼ frühstücken** have a really good breakfast

ausgießen† *vt sep* pour out; (*leeren*) empty

Ausgleich *m* -[e]s balance; (*Entschädigung*) compensation. **a∼en†** *v sep* □ *vt* balance; even out ⟨*Höhe*⟩; (*wettmachen*) compensate for; **sich a∼en** balance out □ *vi* (*haben*) (*Sport*) equalize. **A∼sgymnastik** *f* keep-fit exercises *pl.* **A∼streffer** *m* equalizer

ausgleiten† *vi sep* (*sein*) slip

ausgrab|en† *vt sep* dig up; (*Archaeol*) excavate. **A∼ung** *f* -,-en excavation

Ausguck *m* -[e]s,-e look-out post; (*Person*) look-out

Ausguss (**Ausguß**) *m* [kitchen] sink

aushaben† *vt sep* have finished ⟨*Buch*⟩; **wann habt ihr Schule aus?** when do you finish school?

aushalten† *v sep* □ *vt* bear, stand; hold ⟨*Note*⟩; (*Unterhalt zahlen für*) keep; **nicht auszuhalten, nicht zum A∼** unbearable □ *vi* (*haben*) hold out

aushandeln *vt sep* negotiate

aushändigen *vt sep* hand over

Aushang *m* [public] notice

aushängen¹ *vt sep* (*reg*) display; take off its hinges ⟨*Tür*⟩

aushäng|en²† *vi sep* (*haben*) be displayed. **A∼eschild** *nt* sign

ausharren *vi sep* (*haben*) hold out

ausheben† *vt sep* excavate; take off its hinges ⟨*Tür*⟩

aushecken *vt sep* (*fig*) hatch

aushelfen† *vi sep* (*haben*) help out (**jdm** s.o.)

Aushilf|e *f* [temporary] assistant; **zur A∼e** to help out. **A∼skraft** *f* temporary worker. **a∼sweise** *adv* temporarily

aushöhlen *vt sep* hollow out

ausholen *vi sep* (*haben*) [zum Schlag] a~ raise one's arm [ready to strike]

aushorchen *vt sep* sound out

auskennen† (sich) *vr sep* know one's way around; **sich mit/in etw** (*dat*) a~ know all about sth

auskleiden *vt sep* undress; (*Techn*) line; **sich a~** undress

ausknipsen *vi sep* switch off

auskommen† *vi sep* (*sein*) manage (**mit/ohne** with/without); (*sich vertragen*) get on (**gut** well). **A~** *nt* -s sein A~/ **ein gutes A~haben** get by/be well off

auskosten *vt sep* enjoy [to the full]

auskugeln *vt sep* **sich** (*dat*) **den Arm a~** dislocate one's shoulder

auskühlen *vt/i sep* (*sein*) cool

auskundschaften *vt sep* spy out; (*erfahren*) find out

Auskunft *f* -,-̈e information; (*A~sstelle*) information desk/ (*Büro*) bureau; (*Teleph*) enquiries *pl*; **eine A~** a piece of information. **A~sbüro** *nt* information bureau

auslachen *vt sep* laugh at

ausladen† *vt sep* unload; (*fam: absagen*) put off (*Gast*). **a~d** *a* projecting

Auslage *f* [window] display; **A~n** expenses

Ausland *nt* im/ins A~ abroad

Ausländ|er(in) *m* -s,- (*f* -,-nen) foreigner. **a~isch** *a* foreign

Auslandsgespräch *nt* international call

auslass|en† *vt sep* let out; let down (*Saum*); (*weglassen*) leave out; (*versäumen*) miss; (*Culin*) melt; (*fig*) vent (*Ärger*) (**an** + *dat* on); **sich a~en über** (+ *acc*) go on about. **A~ungszeichen** *nt* apostrophe

Auslauf *m* run. **a~en†** *vi sep* (*sein*) run out; (*Farbe:*) run; (*Naut*) put to sea; (*leer laufen*) run dry; (*enden*) end; (*Modell:*) be discontinued

Ausläufer *m* (*Geog*) spur; (*Bot*) runner, sucker

ausleeren *vt sep* empty [out]

ausleg|en *vt sep* lay out; display (*Waren*); (*bedecken*) cover/ (*auskleiden*) line (**mit** with); (*bezahlen*) pay; (*deuten*) interpret. **A~ung** *f* -,-en interpretation

ausleihen† *vt sep* lend; **sich** (*dat*) **a~** borrow

auslernen *vi sep* (*haben*) finish one's training

Auslese *f* - selection; (*fig*) pick; (*Elite*) élite. **a~n†** *vt sep* finish reading (*Buch*); (*auswählen*) pick out, select

ausliefer|n *vt sep* hand over; (*Jur*) extradite; **ausgeliefert sein** (+ *dat*) be at the mercy of. **A~ung** *f* handing over; (*Jur*) extradition; (*Comm*) distribution

ausliegen† *vi sep* (*haben*) be on display

auslöschen *vt sep* extinguish; (*abwischen*) wipe off; (*fig*) erase

auslosen *vt sep* draw lots for

auslös|en *vt sep* set off, trigger; (*fig*) cause; arouse (*Begeisterung*); (*einlösen*) redeem; pay a ransom for (*Gefangene*). **A~er** *m* -s,- trigger; (*Phot*) shutter release

Auslosung *f* draw

auslüften *vt/i sep* (*haben*) air

ausmachen *vt sep* put out; (*abschalten*) turn off; (*abmachen*) arrange; (*erkennen*) make out; (*betragen*) amount to; (*darstellen*) represent; (*wichtig sein*) matter; **das macht mir nichts aus** I don't mind

ausmalen *vt sep* paint; (*fig*) describe; **sich** (*dat*) **a~** imagine

Ausmaß *nt* extent; **A~e** dimensions

ausmerzen *vt sep* eliminate

ausmessen† *vt sep* measure

Ausnahm|e *f* -,-n exception. **A~ezustand** *m* state of emergency. **a~slos** *adv* without exception. **a~sweise** *adv* as an exception

ausnehmen† *vt sep* take out; gut (*Fisch*); draw (*Huhn*); (*ausschließen*) exclude; (*fam: schröpfen*) fleece; **sich gut a~** look good. **a~d** *adv* exceptionally

ausnutz|en, **ausnütz|en** *vt sep* exploit; make the most of (*Gelegenheit*). **A~ung** *f* exploitation

auspacken *v sep* □ *vt* unpack; (*auswickeln*) unwrap □ *vi* (*haben*) (*fam*) talk

auspeitschen *vt sep* flog

auspfeifen† *vt sep* whistle and boo

ausplaudern *vt sep* let out, blab

ausplündern *vt sep* loot; rob (*Person*)

ausprobieren *vt sep* try out

Auspuff *m* -s exhaust [system]. **A~gase** *ntpl* exhaust fumes. **A~rohr** *nt* exhaust pipe

auspusten *vt sep* blow out

ausradieren *vt sep* rub out

ausrangieren *vt sep* (*fam*) discard

ausrauben *vt sep* rob

ausräuchern *vt sep* smoke out; fumigate (*Zimmer*)

ausräumen *vt sep* clear out

ausrechnen *vt sep* work out, calculate

Ausrede *f* excuse. **a~n** *v sep* □ *vi* (*haben*) finish speaking; **lass mich a~n!** let me finish! □ *vt* **jdm etw a~n** talk s.o. out of sth

ausreichen *vi sep* (*haben*) be enough; **a~ mit** have enough. **a~d** a adequate, *adv* -ly; (*Sch*) ⟨*pass*⟩

Ausreise *f* departure [from a country]. **a~n** *vi sep* (*sein*) leave the country. **A~visum** *nt* exit visa

ausreiß|en† *v sep* □ *vt* pull *or* tear out □ *vi* (*sein*) (*fam*) run away. **A~er** *m* (*fam*) runaway

ausrenken *vt sep* dislocate; **sich** (*dat*) **den Arm a~** dislocate one's shoulder

ausrichten *vt sep* align; (*bestellen*) deliver; (*erreichen*) achieve; **jdm a~** tell s.o. (**dass** that); **kann ich etwas a~?** can I take a message? **ich soll Ihnen Grüße von X a~** X sends [you] his regards

ausrotten *vt sep* exterminate; (*fig*) eradicate

ausrücken *vi sep* (*sein*) (*Mil*) march off; (*fam*) run away

Ausruf *m* exclamation. **a~en**† *vt sep* exclaim; call out (*Namen*); (*verkünden*) proclaim; call (*Streik*); **jdn a~en lassen** have s.o. paged. **A~ezeichen** *nt* exclamation mark

ausruhen *vt/i sep* (*haben*) rest; **sich a~** have a rest

ausrüst|en *vt sep* equip. **A~ung** *f* equipment; (*Mil*) kit

ausrutschen *vi sep* (*sein*) slip

Aussage *f* -,-n statement; (*Jur*) testimony, evidence; (*Gram*) predicate. **a~n** *vt/i sep* (*haben*) state; (*Jur*) give evidence, testify

Aussatz *m* leprosy

Aussätzige(r) *m/f* leper

ausschachten *vt sep* excavate

ausschalten *vt sep* switch *or* turn off; (*fig*) eliminate

Ausschank *m* sale of alcoholic drinks; (*Bar*) bar

Ausschau *f* - **A~ halten nach** look out for. **a~en** *vi sep* (*haben*) (*SGer*) look; **a~en nach** look out for

ausscheiden† *v sep* □ *vi* (*sein*) leave; (*Sport*) drop out; (*nicht in Frage kommen*) be excluded; **aus dem Dienst a~** retire □ *vt* eliminate; (*Med*) excrete

ausschenken *vt sep* pour out; (*verkaufen*) sell

ausscheren *vi sep* (*sein*) (*Auto*) pull out

ausschildern *vt sep* signpost

ausschimpfen *vt sep* tell off

ausschlachten *vt sep* (*fig*) exploit

ausschlafen† *v sep* □ *vi/r* (*haben*) [**sich**] **a~** get enough sleep; (*morgens*) sleep late; **nicht ausgeschlafen haben** *od* **sein** be still tired □ *vt* sleep off (*Rausch*)

Ausschlag *m* (*Med*) rash; **den A~ geben** (*fig*) tip the balance. **a~en**† *v sep* □ *vi*

(*haben*) kick [out]; (*Bot*) sprout; ⟨*Baum:*⟩ come into leaf □ *vt* knock out; (*auskleiden*) line; (*ablehnen*) refuse. **a~gebend** *a* decisive

ausschließ|en† *vt sep* lock out; (*fig*) exclude; (*entfernen*) expel. **a~lich** *a* exclusive, *adv* -ly

ausschlüpfen *vi sep* (*sein*) hatch

Ausschluss (**Ausschluß**) *m* exclusion; expulsion; **unter A~ der Öffentlichkeit** in camera

ausschmücken *vt sep* decorate; (*fig*) embellish

ausschneiden† *vt sep* cut out

Ausschnitt *m* excerpt, extract; (*Zeitungs-*) cutting; (*Hals-*) neckline

ausschöpfen *vt sep* ladle out; (*Naut*) bail out; exhaust ⟨*Möglichkeiten*⟩

ausschreiben† *vt sep* write out; (*ausstellen*) make out; (*bekanntgeben*) announce; put out to tender ⟨*Auftrag*⟩

Ausschreitungen *fpl* riots; (*Exzesse*) excesses

Ausschuss (**Ausschuß**) *m* committee; (*Comm*) rejects *pl*

ausschütten *vt sep* tip out; (*verschütten*) spill; (*leeren*) empty; **sich vor Lachen a~** (*fam*) be in stitches

ausschweif|end *a* dissolute. **A~ung** *f* -,-en debauchery; **A~ungen** excesses

ausschwenken *vt sep* rinse [out]

aussehen† *vi sep* (*haben*) look; **es sieht nach Regen aus** it looks like rain; **wie sieht er/es aus?** what does he/it look like? **ein gut a~der Mann** a good-looking man. **A~** *nt* -s appearance

aussein† *vi sep* (*sein*) (NEW) **aus sein**, *s*. **aus**

außen *adv* [on the] outside; **nach a~** outwards. **A~bordmotor** *m* outboard motor. **A~handel** *m* foreign trade. **A~minister** *m* Foreign Minister. **A~politik** *f* foreign policy. **A~seite** *f* outside. **A~seiter** *m* -s,- outsider; (*fig*) misfit. **A~stände** *mpl* outstanding debts. **A~stehende(r)** *m/f* outsider

außer *prep* (+ *dat*) except [for], apart from; (*außerhalb*) out of; **a~ Atem/Sicht** out of breath/sight; **a~ sich** (*fig*) beside oneself □ *conj* except; **a~ wenn** unless. **a~dem** *adv* in addition, as well □ *conj* moreover

äußer|e(r,s) *a* external; ⟨*Teil, Schicht*⟩ outer. **Ä~e(s)** *nt* exterior; (*Aussehen*) appearance

außer|ehelich *a* extramarital. **a~gewöhnlich** *a* exceptional, *adv* -ly. **a~halb** *prep* (+ *gen*) outside □ *adv* **a~halb wohnen** live outside town

äußer|lich *a* external, *adv* -ly; (*fig*) outward, *adv* -ly. **ä~n** *vt* express; **sich ä~n** comment; (*sich zeigen*) manifest itself

außerordentlich *a* extraordinary, *adv* -ily; *(außergewöhnlich)* exceptional, *adv* -ly

äußerst *adv* extremely

außerstande *pred a* unable (**zu** to)

äußerste|(r,s) *a* outermost; *(weiteste)* furthest; *(höchste)* utmost, extreme; *(letzte)* last; *(schlimmste)* worst; **am ä~n Ende** at the very end; **aufs ä~ = aufs Ä~,** *s.* **Äußerste(s). Ä~(s)** *nt* **das Ä~** the limit; *(Schlimmste)* the worst; **sein Ä~s tun** do one's utmost; **aufs Ä~** extremely

Äußerung *f* -,-en comment; *(Bemerkung)* remark

aussetzen *v sep* □ *vt* expose *(dat* to); abandon *(Kind, Hund)*; launch *(Boot)*; offer *(Belohnung)*; **etwas auszusetzen haben an** (+ *dat*) find fault with □ *vi (haben)* stop; *(Motor:)* cut out

Aussicht *f* -,-en view/*(fig)* prospect **(auf** + *acc* of); **in A~ stellen** promise; **weitere A~en** *(Meteorol)* further outlook *sg.* **a~slos** *a* hopeless, *adv* -ly. **a~sreich** *a* promising

aussöhnen *vt sep* reconcile; **sich a~** become reconciled

aussortieren *vt sep* pick out; *(ausscheiden)* eliminate

ausspann|en *v sep* □ *vt* spread out; unhitch *(Pferd)*; *(fam: wegnehmen)* take *(dat* from) □ *vi (haben)* rest. **A~ung** *f* rest

aussperr|en *vt sep* lock out. **A~ung** *f* -,-en lock-out

ausspielen *v sep* □ *vt* play *(Karte)*; *(fig)* play off **(gegen** against) □ *vi (haben) (Kartenspiel)* lead

Aussprache *f* pronunciation; *(Sprechweise)* diction; *(Gespräch)* talk

aussprechen† *v sep* □ *vt* pronounce; *(äußern)* express; **sich a~** talk; come out **(für/gegen** in favour of/against) □ *vi (haben)* finish [speaking]

Ausspruch *m* saying

ausspucken *v sep* □ *vt* spit out □ *vi (haben)* spit

ausspülen *vt sep* rinse out

ausstaffieren *vt sep (fam)* kit out

Ausstand *m* strike; **in den A~ treten** go on strike

ausstatt|en *vt sep* equip; **mit Möbeln a~en** furnish. **A~ung** *f* -,-en equipment; *(Innen-)* furnishings *pl*; *(Theat)* scenery and costumes *pl*; *(Aufmachung)* get-up

ausstehen† *v sep* □ *vt* suffer; **Angst a~** be frightened; **ich kann sie nicht a~** I can't stand her □ *vi (haben)* be outstanding

aussteig|en† *vi sep (sein)* get out; *(aus Bus, Zug)* get off; *(fam: ausscheiden)* opt out;

(aus einem Geschäft) back out; **alles a~en!** all change! **A~er(in)** *m* -s,- *(f* -,-nen) *(fam)* drop-out

ausstell|en *vt sep* exhibit; *(Comm)* display; *(ausfertigen)* make out; issue *(Pass)*. **A~er** *m* -s,- exhibitor. **A~ung** *f* exhibition; *(Comm)* display. **A~ungsstück** *nt* exhibit

aussterben† *vi sep (sein)* die out; *(Biol)* become extinct. **A~** *nt* -s extinction

Aussteuer *f* trousseau

Ausstieg *m* -[e]s,-e exit

ausstopfen *vt sep* stuff

ausstoßen† *vt sep* emit; utter *(Fluch)*; heave *(Seufzer)*; *(ausschließen)* expel

ausstrahl|en *vt/i sep (sein)* radiate, emit; *(Radio, TV)* broadcast. **A~ung** *f* radiation; *(fig)* charisma

ausstrecken *vt sep* stretch out; put out *(Hand)*; **sich a~** stretch out

ausstreichen† *vt sep* cross out

ausstreuen *vt sep* scatter; spread *(Gerüchte)*

ausströmen *v sep* □ *vi (sein)* pour out; *(entweichen)* escape □ *vt* emit; *(ausstrahlen)* radiate

aussuchen *vt sep* pick, choose

Austausch *m* exchange. **a~bar** *a* interchangeable. **a~en** *vt sep* exchange; *(auswechseln)* replace

austeilen *vt sep* distribute; *(ausgeben)* hand out

Auster *f* -,-n oyster

austoben (sich) *vr sep (Sturm:)* rage; *(Person:)* let off steam; *(Kinder:)* romp about

austragen† *vt sep* deliver; hold *(Wettkampf)*; play *(Spiel)*

Austral|ien /-jən/ *nt* -s Australia. **A~ier(in)** *m* -s,- *(f* -,-nen) Australian. **a~isch** *a* Australian

austreiben† *v sep* □ *vt* drive out; *(Relig)* exorcize □ *vi (haben) (Bot)* sprout

austreten† *v sep* □ *vt* stamp out; *(abnutzen)* wear down □ *vi (sein)* come out; *(ausscheiden)* leave **(aus etw** sth); [mal] **a~** *(fam)* go to the loo; *(Sch)* be excused

austrinken† *vt/i sep (haben)* drink up; *(leeren)* drain

Austritt *m* resignation

austrocknen *vt/i sep (sein)* dry out

ausüben *vt sep* practise; carry on *(Handwerk)*; exercise *(Recht)*; exert *(Druck, Einfluss)*; have *(Wirkung)*

Ausverkauf *m* [clearance] sale. **a~t** *a* sold out; **a~tes Haus** full house

auswachsen† *vt sep* outgrow

Auswahl *f* choice, selection; *(Comm)* range; *(Sport)* team

auswählen *vt sep* choose, select

Auswander|er *m* emigrant. **a~n** *vi sep* (sein) emigrate. **A~ung** *f* emigration

auswärt|ig *a* non-local; (ausländisch) foreign. **a~s** *adv* outwards; (Sport) away; **a~s essen** eat out; **a~s arbeiten** not work locally. **A~sspiel** *nt* away game

auswaschen† *vt sep* wash out

auswechseln *vt sep* change; (ersetzen) replace; (Sport) substitute

Ausweg *m* (fig) way out. **a~los** *a* (fig) hopeless

ausweich|en† *vi sep* (sein) get out of the way; **jdm/etw a~en** avoid/ (sich entziehen) evade s.o./sth. **a~end** *a* evasive, *adv* -ly

ausweinen *vt sep* **sich** (dat) **die Augen a~** cry one's eyes out; **sich a~** have a good cry

Ausweis *m* -es,-e pass; (Mitglieds-, Studenten-) card. **a~en**† *vt sep* deport; **sich a~en** prove one's identity. **A~papiere** *ntpl* identification papers. **A~ung** *f* deportation

ausweiten *vt sep* stretch; (fig) expand

auswendig *adv* by heart

auswerten *vt sep* evaluate; (nutzen) utilize

auswickeln *vt sep* unwrap

auswirk|en (sich) *vr sep* have an effect (**auf** + acc on). **A~ung** *f* effect; (Folge) consequence

auswischen *vt sep* wipe out; **jdm eins a~** (fam) play a nasty trick on s.o.

auswringen *vt sep* wring out

Auswuchs *m* excrescence; **Auswüchse** (fig) excesses

auszahlen *vt sep* pay out; (entlohnen) pay off; (abfinden) buy out; **sich a~** (fig) pay off

auszählen *vt sep* count; (Boxen) count out

Auszahlung *f* payment

auszeichn|en *vt sep* (Comm) price; (ehren) honour; (mit einem Preis) award a prize to; (Mil) decorate; **sich a~en** distinguish oneself. **A~ung** *f* honour; (Preis) award; (Mil) decoration; (Sch) distinction

ausziehen† *v sep* □ *vt* pull out; (auskleiden) undress; take off ⟨Mantel, Schuhe⟩; **sich a~** take off one's coat; (sich entkleiden) undress □ *vi* (sein) move out; (sich aufmachen) set out

Auszubildende(r) *m/f* trainee

Auszug *m* departure; (Umzug) move; (Ausschnitt) extract, excerpt; (Bank-) statement

authentisch *a* authentic

Auto *nt* -s,-s car; **A~ fahren** drive; (mitfahren) go in the car. **A~bahn** *f* motorway, (Amer) freeway

Autobiographie *f* autobiography

Auto|bus *m* bus. **A~fähre** *f* car ferry. **A~fahrer(in)** *m(f)* driver, motorist. **A~fahrt** *f* drive

Autogramm *nt* -s,-e autograph

autokratisch *a* autocratic

Automat *m* -en,-en automatic device; (Münz-) slot-machine; (Verkaufs-) vending-machine; (Fahrkarten-) machine; (Techn) robot. **A~ik** *f* - automatic mechanism; (Auto) automatic transmission

Auto|mation /-'tsi̯oːn/ *f* - automation. **a~matisch** *a* automatic, *adv* -ally

autonom *a* autonomous. **A~ie** *f* - autonomy

Autonummer *f* registration number

Autopsie *f* -,-n autopsy

Autor *m* -s,-en /-'toːrən/ author

Auto|reisezug *m* Motorail. **A~rennen** *nt* motor race

Autorin *f* -,-nen author[ess]

Autori|sation /-'tsi̯oːn/ *f*-authorization. **a~sieren** *vt* authorize. **a~tär** *a* authoritarian. **A~tät** *f* -,-en authority

Auto|schlosser *m* motor mechanic. **A~skooter** /-skuːtɐ/ *m* -s,- dodgem. **A~stopp** *m* -s **per A~stopp fahren** hitchhike. **A~verleih** *m* car hire [firm]. **A~waschanlage** *f* car wash

autsch *int* ouch

Aversion *f* -,-en aversion (**gegen** to)

Axt *f* -,-̈e axe

B

B, b /beː/ *nt* - (Mus) B flat

Baby /'beːbi/ *nt* -s,-s baby. **B~ausstattung** *f* layette. **B~-sitter** /-sɪtɐ/ *m* -s,- babysitter

Bach *m* -[e]s,-̈e stream

Backbord *nt* -[e]s port [side]

Backe *f* -,-n cheek

backen *v* □ *vt/i*† (haben) bake; (braten) fry □ *vi* (reg) (haben) (kleben) stick (**an** + dat to)

Backenzahn *m* molar

Bäcker *m* -s,- baker. **B~ei** *f* -,-en, **B~laden** *m* baker's shop

Back|form *f* baking tin. **B~obst** *nt* dried fruit. **B~ofen** *m* oven. **B~pfeife** *f* (fam) slap in the face. **B~pflaume** *f* prune.

B~**pulver** nt baking-powder. B~**rohr** nt oven. B~**stein** m brick. B~**werk** nt cakes and pastries pl

Bad nt -[e]s,⁻er bath; (im Meer) bathe; (Zimmer) bathroom; (Schwimm-) pool; (Ort) spa

Bade|anstalt f swimming baths pl. B~**anzug** m swim-suit. B~**hose** f swimming trunks pl. B~**kappe** f bathing-cap. B~**mantel** m bathrobe. B~**matte** f bath-mat. B~**mütze** f bathing-cap. b~n vi (haben) have a bath; (im Meer) bathe □ vt bath; (waschen) bathe. B~**ort** m seaside resort; (Kurort) spa. B~**tuch** nt bath-towel. B~**wanne** f bath. B~**zimmer** nt bathroom

Bagatelle f -,-n trifle; (Mus) bagatelle

Bagger m -s,- excavator; (Nass-) dredger. b~n vt/i (haben) excavate; dredge. B~**see** m flooded gravel-pit

Bahn f -,-en path; (Astr) orbit; (Sport) track; (einzelne) lane; (Rodel-) run; (Stoff-, Papier-) width; (Rock-) panel; (Eisen-) railway; (Zug) train; (Straßen-) tram; **auf die schiefe B~ kommen** (fig) get into bad ways. b~**brechend** a (fig) pioneering. b~en vt sich (dat) **einen Weg b~en** clear a way (**durch** through). B~**hof** m [railway] station. B~**steig** m -[e]s,-e platform. B~**übergang** m level crossing, (Amer) grade crossing

Bahre f -,-n stretcher; (Toten-) bier

Baiser /bɛ'ze:/ nt -s,-s meringue

Bajonett nt -[e]s,-e bayonet

Bake f -,-n (Naut, Aviat) beacon

Bakterien /-jən/ fpl bacteria

Balance /ba'lã:sə/ f - balance; **die B~e halten/verlieren** keep/lose one's balance. b~**ieren** vt/i (haben/sein) balance

bald adv soon; (fast) almost; **b~ ... b~ ...** now ... now ...

Baldachin /-xi:n/ m -s,-e canopy

bald|ig a early; (Besserung) speedy. b~**möglichst** adv as soon as possible

Balg nt & m -[e]s,⁻er (fam) brat. b~en (sich) vr tussle. B~**erei** f -,-en tussle

Balkan m -s Balkans pl

Balken m -s,- beam

Balkon /bal'kõ:/ m -s,-s balcony; (Theat) circle

Ball¹ m -[e]s,⁻e ball

Ball² m -[e]s,⁻e (Tanz) ball

Ballade f -,-n ballad

Ballast m -[e]s ballast. B~**stoffe** mpl roughage sg

ballen vt **die [Hand zur] Faust b~** clench one's fist; **sich b~** gather, mass. B~ m -s,- bale; (Anat) ball of the hand/(Fuß-) foot; (Med) bunion

Ballerina f -,-nen ballerina

Ballett nt -s,-e ballet

Balletttänzer(in) (**Ballettänzer(in)**) m(f) ballet dancer

ballistisch a ballistic

Ballon /ba'lõ:/ m -s,-s balloon

Ball|saal m ballroom. B~**ungsgebiet** nt conurbation. B~**wechsel** m (Tennis) rally

Balsam m -s balm

Balt|ikum nt -s Baltic States pl. b~**isch** a Baltic

Balustrade f -,-n balustrade

Bambus m -ses,-se bamboo

banal a banal. B~**ität** f -,-en banality

Banane f -,-n banana

Banause m -n,-n philistine

Band¹ nt -[e]s,⁻er ribbon; (Naht-, Ton-, Ziel-) tape; (Anat) ligament; **auf B~ aufnehmen** tape; **laufendes B~** conveyor belt; **am laufenden B~** (fam) non-stop

Band² m -[e]s,⁻e volume

Band³ nt -[e]s,-e (fig) bond; B~e der Freundschaft bonds of friendship

Band⁴ /bɛnt/ f -,-s [jazz] band

Bandag|e /ban'da:ʒə/ f -,-n bandage. b~**ieren** vt bandage

Bande f -,-n gang

bändigen vt control, restrain; (zähmen) tame

Bandit m -en,-en bandit

Band|maß nt tape-measure. B~**nudeln** fpl noodles. B~**scheibe** f (Anat) disc. B~**scheibenvorfall** m slipped disc. B~**wurm** m tapeworm

bang|[e] a (bänger, bängst) anxious; **jdm b~e machen** (NEW) jdm B~e machen, s. Bange. B~e f B~e haben be afraid; **jdm B~e machen** frighten s.o. b~en vi (haben) fear (**um** for); **mir b~t davor** I dread it

Banjo nt -s,-s banjo

Bank¹ f -,⁻e bench

Bank² f -,-en (Comm) bank. B~**einzug** m direct debit

Bankett nt -s,-e banquet

Bankier /baŋ'kje:/ m -s,-s banker

Bank|konto nt bank account. B~**note** f banknote

Bankrott m -s,-s bankruptcy; B~ **machen** od **gehen** go bankrupt. b~ a bankrupt

Bankwesen nt banking

Bann m -[e]s,-e (fig) spell; **in jds B~** under s.o.'s spell. b~en vt exorcize; (abwenden) avert; [**wie**] **gebannt** spellbound

Banner nt -s,- banner

Baptist(in) m -en,-en (f -,-nen) Baptist

bar *a* (*rein*) sheer; (*Gold*) pure; **b∼es Geld** cash; **[in] bar bezahlen** pay cash; **etw für b∼e Münze nehmen** (*fig*) take sth as gospel

Bar *f* -,-s bar

Bär *m* -en,-en bear; **jdm einen B∼en aufbinden** (*fam*) pull s.o.'s leg

Baracke *f* -,-n (*Mil*) hut

Barb|ar *m* -en,-en barbarian. **b∼arisch** *a* barbaric

bar|fuß *adv* barefoot. **B∼geld** *nt* cash

Bariton *m* -s,-e /-'to:nə/ baritone

Barkasse *f* -,-n launch

Barmann *m* (*pl* -**männer**) barman

barmherzig *a* merciful. **B∼keit** *f* - mercy

barock *a* baroque. **B∼** *nt & m* -**[s]** baroque

Barometer *nt* -s,- barometer

Baron *m* -s,-e baron. **B∼in** *f* -,-nen baroness

Barren *m* -s,- (*Gold-*) bar, ingot; (*Sport*) parallel bars *pl*. **B∼gold** *nt* gold bullion

Barriere *f* -,-n barrier

Barrikade *f* -,-n barricade

barsch *a* gruff, *adv* -ly; (*kurz*) curt, *adv* -ly

Barsch *m* -[e]s,-e (*Zool*) perch

Barschaft *f* - **meine ganze B∼** all I have/had on me

Bart *m* -[e]s,-̈e beard; (*der Katze*) whiskers *pl*

bärtig *a* bearded

Barzahlung *f* cash payment

Basar *m* -s,-e bazaar

Base[1] *f* -,-n [female] cousin

Base[2] *f* -,-n (*Chem*) alkali, base

Basel *nt* -s Basle

basieren *vi* (*haben*) be based (**auf** + *dat* on)

Basilikum *nt* -s basil

Basis *f* -,**Basen** base; (*fig*) basis

basisch *a* (*Chem*) alkaline

Bask|enmütze *f* beret. **b∼isch** *a* Basque

Bass *m* -es,-̈e (Baß *m* -sses,-̈sse) bass; (*Kontra-*) double-bass

Bassin /ba'sɛ̃:/ *nt* -s,-s pond; (*Brunnen-*) basin; (*Schwimm-*) pool

Bassist *m* -en,-en bass player; (*Sänger*) bass

Bassstimme (Baßstimme) *f* bass voice

Bast *m* -[e]s raffia

basta *int* [**und damit**] **b∼!** and that's that!

bast|eln *vt* make □ *vi* (*haben*) do handicrafts; (*herum-*) tinker (**an** + *dat* with). **B∼ler** *m* -s,- amateur craftsman; (*Heim-*) do-it-yourselfer

Bataillon /batal'jo:n/ *nt* -s,-e battalion

Batterie *f* -,-n battery

Bau[1] *m* -[e]s,-e burrow; (*Fuchs-*) earth

Bau[2] *m* -[e]s,-ten construction; (*Gebäude*) building; (*Auf-*) structure; (*Körper-*) build; (*B∼stelle*) building site; **im Bau** under construction. **B∼arbeiten** *fpl* building work *sg*; (*Straßen-*) road-works. **B∼art** *f* design; (*Stil*) style

Bauch *m* -[e]s, Bäuche abdomen, belly; (*Magen*) stomach; (*Schmer-*) paunch; (*Bauchung*) bulge. **b∼ig** *a* bulbous. **B∼nabel** *m* navel. **B∼redner** *m* ventriloquist. **B∼schmerzen** *mpl* stomach-ache *sg*. **B∼speicheldrüse** *f* pancreas. **B∼weh** *nt* stomach-ache

bauen *vt* build; (*konstruieren*) construct; (*an-*) grow; **einen Unfall b∼** (*fam*) have an accident □ *vi* (*haben*) build (**an etw** *dat* sth); **b∼ auf** (+ *acc*) (*fig*) rely on

Bauer[1] *m* -s,-n farmer; (*Schach*) pawn

Bauer[2] *nt* -s,- [bird]cage

Bäuer|in *f* -,-nen farmer's wife. **b∼lich** *a* rustic

Bauern|haus *nt* farmhouse. **B∼hof** *m* farm

bau|fällig *a* dilapidated. **B∼genehmigung** *f* planning permission. **B∼gerüst** *nt* scaffolding. **B∼jahr** *nt* year of construction; **B∼jahr 1985** (*Auto*) 1985 model. **B∼kasten** *m* box of building bricks; (*Modell-*) model kit. **B∼klotz** *m* building brick. **B∼kunst** *f* architecture. **b∼lich** *a* structural, *adv* -ly. **B∼lichkeiten** *fpl* buildings

Baum *m* -[e]s, Bäume tree

baumeln *vi* (*haben*) dangle; **die Beine b∼ lassen** dangle one's legs

bäumen (sich) *vr* rear [up]

Baum|schule *f* [tree] nursery. **B∼stamm** *m* tree-trunk. **B∼wolle** *f* cotton. **b∼wollen** *a* cotton

Bauplatz *m* building plot

bäurisch *a* rustic; (*plump*) uncouth

Bausch *m* -[e]s, Bäusche wad; **in B∼ und Bogen** (*fig*) wholesale. **b∼en** *vt* puff out; **sich b∼en** billow [out]. **b∼ig** *a* puffed [out]; (*Ärmel*) full

Bau|sparkasse *f* building society. **B∼stein** *m* building brick; (*fig*) element. **B∼stelle** *f* building site; (*Straßen-*) roadworks *pl*. **B∼unternehmer** *m* building contractor. **B∼werk** *nt* building. **B∼zaun** *m* hoarding

Bayer|(in) *m* -s,-n (*f* -,-nen) Bavarian. **B∼n** *nt* -s Bavaria

bay[e]risch *a* Bavarian

Bazillus *m* -,-len bacillus; (*fam: Keim*) germ

beabsichtig|en *vt* intend. **b∼t** *a* intended; (*absichtlich*) intentional

beacht|en vt take notice of; (einhalten) observe; (folgen) follow; **nicht b~en** ignore. **b~lich** a considerable. **B~ung** f - observance; **etw** (dat) **keine B~ung schenken** take no notice of sth

Beamte(r) m, **Beamtin** f -,-nen official; (Staats-) civil servant; (Schalter-) clerk

beängstigend a alarming

beanspruchen vt claim; (erfordern) demand; (brauchen) take up; (Techn) stress; **die Arbeit beansprucht ihn sehr** his work is very demanding

beanstand|en vt find fault with; (Comm) make a complaint about. **B~ung** f -,-en complaint

beantragen vt apply for

beantworten vt answer

bearbeiten vt work; (weiter-) process; (behandeln) treat (mit with); (Admin) deal with; (redigieren) edit; (Theat) adapt; (Mus) arrange; (fam: bedrängen) pester; (fam: schlagen) pummel

Beatmung f künstliche **B~** artificial respiration. **B~gerät** nt ventilator

beaufsichtig|en vt supervise. **B~ung** f - supervision

beauftrag|en vt instruct; commission (Künstler); **jdn mit einer Arbeit b~en** assign a task to s.o. **B~te(r)** m/f representative

bebauen vt build on; (bestellen) cultivate

beben vi (haben) tremble

bebildert a illustrated

Becher m -s,- beaker; (Henkel-) mug; (Joghurt-, Sahne-) carton

Becken nt -s,- basin; (Schwimm-) pool; (Mus) cymbals pl; (Anat) pelvis

bedacht a careful; **b~ auf** (+ acc) concerned about; **darauf b~** anxious (**zu** to)

bedächtig a careful, adv -ly; (langsam) slow, adv -ly

bedanken (sich) vr thank (**bei jdm** s.o.)

Bedarf m -s need/(Comm) demand (**an** + dat for); **bei B~** if required. **B~sartikel** mpl requisites. **B~shaltestelle** f request stop

bedauer|lich a regrettable. **b~licherweise** adv unfortunately. **b~n** vt regret; (bemitleiden) feel sorry for; **bedaure!** sorry! **B~n** nt -s regret; (Mitgefühl) sympathy. **b~nswert** a pitiful; (bedauerlich) regrettable

bedeck|en vt cover; **sich b~en** (Himmel:) cloud over. **b~t** a covered; (Himmel) overcast

bedenken† vt consider; (überlegen) think over; **jdn b~** give s.o. a present; **sich b~** consider. **B~** pl misgivings; **ohne B~**

without hesitation. **b~los** a unhesitating, adv -ly

bedenklich a doubtful; (verdächtig) dubious; (bedrohlich) worrying; (ernst) serious

bedeut|en vi (haben) mean; **jdm viel/nichts b~en** mean a lot/nothing to s.o.; **es hat nichts zu b~en** it is of no significance. **b~end** a important; (beträchtlich) considerable. **b~sam** a = **b~ungsvoll**. **B~ung** f -,-en meaning; (Wichtigkeit) importance. **b~ungslos** a meaningless; (unwichtig) unimportant. **b~ungsvoll** a significant; (vielsagend) meaningful, adv -ly

bedien|en vt serve; (betätigen) operate; **sich [selbst] b~en** help oneself. **B~ung** f -,-en service; (Betätigung) operation; (Kellner) waiter; (Kellnerin) waitress. **B~ungsgeld** nt, **B~ungszuschlag** m service charge

bedingt a conditional; (eingeschränkt) qualified

Bedingung f -,-en condition; **B~en** conditions; (Comm) terms. **b~slos** a unconditional, adv -ly; (unbedingt) unquestioning, adv -ly

bedrängen vt press; (belästigen) pester

bedroh|en vt threaten. **b~lich** a threatening. **B~ung** f threat

bedrück|en vt depress. **b~end** a depressing. **b~t** a depressed

bedruckt a printed

bedürf|en† vi (haben) (+ gen) need. **B~nis** nt -ses,-se need. **B~nisanstalt** f public convenience. **b~tig** a needy

Beefsteak /'bi:fste:k/ nt -s,-s steak; **deutsches B~** hamburger

beeilen (sich) vr hurry; hasten (**zu** to); **beeilt euch!** hurry up!

beeindrucken vt impress

beeinflussen vt influence

beeinträchtigen vt mar; (schädigen) impair

beend[ig]en vt end

beengen vt restrict; **beengt wohnen** live in cramped conditions

beerben vt **jdn b~** inherit s.o.'s property

beerdig|en vt bury. **B~ung** f -,-en funeral

Beere f -,-n berry

Beet nt -[e]s,-e (Hort) bed

Beete f -,-n rote **B~** beetroot

befähig|en vt enable; (qualifizieren) qualify. **B~ung** f - qualification; (Fähigkeit) ability

befahr|bar a passable. **b~en†** vt drive along; **stark b~ene Straße** busy road

befallen† vt attack; (Angst:) seize

befangen *a* shy; (*gehemmt*) self-conscious; (*Jur*) biased. **B~heit** *f* - shyness; self-consciousness; bias

befassen (sich) *vr* concern oneself/ (*behandeln*) deal (**mit** with)

Befehl *m* -[e]s,-e order; (*Leitung*) command (**über** + *acc* of). **b~en†** *vt* jdm etw **b~en** order s.o. to do sth □ *vi* (*haben*) give the orders. **b~igen** *vt* (*Mil*) command. **B~sform** *f* (*Gram*) imperative. **B~shaber** *m* -s,- commander

befestig|en *vt* fasten (**an** + *dat* to); (*stärken*) strengthen; (*Mil*) fortify. **B~ung** *f* -,-en fastening; (*Mil*) fortification

befeuchten *vt* moisten

befinden† (**sich**) *vr* be. **B~** *nt* -s [state of] health

beflecken *vt* stain

beflissen *a* assiduous, *adv* -ly

befolgen *vt* follow

beförder|n *vt* transport; (*im Rang*) promote. **B~ung** *f* -,-en transport; promotion

befragen *vt* question

befrei|en *vt* free; (*räumen*) clear (**von** of); (*freistellen*) exempt (**von** from); **sich b~en** free oneself. **B~er** *m* -s,- liberator. **b~t** *a* (*erleichtert*) relieved. **B~ung** *f* - liberation; exemption

befremd|en *vt* disconcert. **B~en** *nt* -s surprise. **b~lich** *a* strange

befreunden (**sich**) *vr* make friends; **befreundet sein** be friends

befriedig|en *vt* satisfy. **b~end** *a* satisfying; (*zufrieden stellend*) satisfactory. **B~ung** *f* - satisfaction

befrucht|en *vt* fertilize. **B~ung** *f* - fertilization; **künstliche B~ung** artificial insemination

Befug|nis *f* -,-se authority. **b~t** *a* authorized

Befund *m* result

befürcht|en *vt* fear. **B~ung** *f* -,-en fear

befürworten *vt* support

begab|t *a* gifted. **B~ung** *f* -,-en gift, talent

begatten (sich) *vr* mate

begeben† (**sich**) *vr* go; (*liter: geschehen*) happen; **sich in Gefahr b~** expose oneself to danger. **B~heit** *f* -,-en incident

begegn|en *vi* (*sein*) jdm/etw **b~en** meet s.o./sth; **sich b~en** meet. **B~ung** *f* -,-en meeting; (*Sport*) encounter

begehen† *vt* walk along; (*verüben*) commit; (*feiern*) celebrate

begehr|en *vt* desire. **b~enswert** *a* desirable. **b~t** *a* sought-after

begeister|n *vt* jdn **b~n** arouse s.o.'s enthusiasm; **sich b~n** be enthusiastic (**für**

about). **b~t** *a* enthusiastic, *adv* -ally; (*eifrig*) keen. **B~ung** *f* - enthusiasm

Begier|de *f* -,-n desire. **b~ig** *a* eager (**auf** + *acc* for)

begießen† *vt* water; (*Culin*) baste; (*fam: feiern*) celebrate

Beginn *m* -s beginning; **zu B~** at the beginning. **b~en†** *vt/i* (*haben*) start, begin; (*anstellen*) do

beglaubigen *vt* authenticate

begleichen† *vt* settle

begleit|en *vt* accompany. **B~er** *m* -s,-, **B~erin** *f* -,-nen companion; (*Mus*) accompanist. **B~ung** *f* -,-en company; (*Gefolge*) entourage; (*Mus*) accompaniment

beglück|en *vt* make happy. **b~t** *a* happy. **b~wünschen** *vt* congratulate (**zu** on)

begnadig|en *vt* (*Jur*) pardon. **B~ung** *f* -,-en (*Jur*) pardon

begnügen (**sich**) *vr* content oneself (**mit** with)

Begonie /-jə/ *f* -,-n begonia

begraben† *vt* bury

Begräbnis *n* -ses,-se burial; (*Feier*) funeral

begreif|en† *vt* understand; **nicht b~en** incomprehensible. **b~lich** *a* understandable; **jdm etw b~lich machen** make s.o. understand sth. **b~licherweise** *adv* understandably

begrenz|en *vt* form the boundary of; (*beschränken*) restrict. **b~t** *a* limited. **B~ung** *f* -,-en restriction; (*Grenze*) boundary

Begriff *m* -[e]s,-e concept; (*Ausdruck*) term; (*Vorstellung*) idea; **für meine B~e** to my mind; **im B~sein** *od* **stehen** be about (**zu** to); **schwer von B~** (*fam*) slow on the uptake. **b~sstutzig** *a* obtuse

begründ|en *vt* give one's reason for; (*gründen*) establish. **b~et** *a* justified. **B~ung** *f* -,-en reason

begrüß|en *vt* greet; (*billigen*) welcome. **b~enswert** *a* welcome. **B~ung** *f* - greeting; welcome

begünstigen *vt* favour; (*fördern*) encourage

begutachten *vt* give an opinion on; (*fam: ansehen*) look at

begütert *a* wealthy

begütigen *vt* placate

behaart *a* hairy

behäbig *a* portly; (*gemütlich*) comfortable, *adv* -bly

behag|en *vi* (*haben*) please (**jdm** s.o.). **B~en** *nt* -s contentment; (*Genuss*) enjoyment. **b~lich** *a* comfortable, *adv* -bly. **B~lichkeit** *f* - comfort

behalten† vt keep; (sich merken) remember; **etw für sich b~** (verschweigen) keep sth to oneself

Behälter m -s,- container

behände a nimble, adv -bly

behand|eln vt treat; (sich befassen) deal with. **B~lung** f treatment

beharr|en vi (haben) persist (**auf** + dat in). **b~lich** a persistent, adv -ly; (hartnäckig) dogged, adv -ly. **B~lichkeit** f - persistence

behaupt|en vt maintain; (vorgeben) claim; (sagen) say; (bewahren) retain; **sich b~en** hold one's own. **B~ung** f -,-en assertion; claim; (Äußerung) statement

beheben† vt remedy; (beseitigen) remove

behelf|en† (sich) vr make do (mit with). **b~smäßig** a make-shift □ adv provisionally

behelligen vt bother

behende a (NEW) **behände**

beherbergen vt put up

beherrsch|en vt rule over; (dominieren) dominate; (meistern, zügeln) control; (können) know; **sich b~en** control oneself. **b~t** a self-controlled. **B~ung** f - control; (Selbst-) self-control; (Können) mastery

beherz|igen vt heed. **b~t** a courageous, adv -ly

behilflich a jdm **b~ sein** help s.o.

behinder|n vt hinder; (blockieren) obstruct. **b~t** a handicapped; (schwer) disabled. **B~te(r)** m/f handicapped/disabled person. **B~ung** f -,-en obstruction; (Med) handicap; disability

Behörde f -,-n [public] authority

behüte|n vt protect; **Gott behüte!** heaven forbid! **b~t** a sheltered

behutsam a careful, adv -ly; (zart) gentle, adv -ly

bei prep (+ dat) near; (dicht) by; at (Firma, Veranstaltung); **bei der Hand nehmen** take by the hand; **bei sich haben** have with one; **bei mir** at my place; (in meinem Fall) in my case; **Herr X bei Meyer** Mr X c/o Meyer; **bei Regen** when/(falls) if it rains; **bei Feuer** in case of fire; **bei Tag/Nacht** by day/night; **bei der Ankunft** on arrival; **bei Tisch/der Arbeit** at table/work; **bei guter Gesundheit** in good health; **bei der hohen Miete** [what] with the high rent; **bei all seiner Klugheit** for all his cleverness

beibehalten† vt sep keep

beibringen† vt sep jdm etw **b~** teach s.o. sth; (mitteilen) break sth to s.o.; (zufügen) inflict sth on s.o.

Beicht|e f -,-n confession. **b~en** vt/i (haben) confess. **B~stuhl** m confessional

beide a & pron both; **die b~n Brüder** the two brothers; **b~s** both; **dreißig b~** (Tennis) thirty all. **b~rseitig** a mutual. **b~rseits** adv & prep (+ gen) on both sides (of)

beidrehen vi sep (haben) heave to

beieinander adv together

Beifahrer|(in) m(f) [front-seat] passenger; (Lkw) driver's mate; (Motorrad) pillion passenger. **B~sitz** m passenger seat

Beifall m -[e]s applause; (Billigung) approval; **B~ klatschen** applaud

beifällig a approving, adv -ly

beifügen vt sep add; (beilegen) enclose

beige /bɛːʒ/ inv a beige

beigeben† v sep □ vt add □ vi (haben) **klein b~** give in

Beigeschmack m [slight] taste

Beihilfe f financial aid; (Studien-) grant; (Jur) aiding and abetting

beikommen† vi sep (sein) jdm **b~** get the better of s.o.

Beil nt -[e]s,-e hatchet, axe

Beilage f supplement; (Gemüse) vegetable; **als B~ Reis** (Culin) served with rice

beiläufig a casual, adv -ly

beilegen vt sep enclose; (schlichten) settle

beileibe adv **b~ nicht** by no means

Beileid nt condolences pl. **B~sbrief** m letter of condolence

beiliegend a enclosed

beim prep = **bei dem; b~ Militär** in the army; **b~ Frühstück** at breakfast; **b~ Lesen** when reading; **b~ Lesen sein** be reading

beimessen† vt sep (fig) attach (dat to)

Bein nt -[e]s,-e leg; **jdm ein B~ stellen** trip s.o. up

beinah[e] adv nearly, almost

Beiname m epithet

beipflichten vi sep (haben) agree (dat with)

Beirat m advisory committee

beirren vt sich nicht **b~ lassen** not let oneself be put off

beisammen adv together; **b~ sein** be together. **B~sein†** vi sep (NEW) **b~ sein**, s. **beisammen. B~sein** nt -s gettogether

Beisein nt presence

beiseite adv aside; (abseits) apart; **b~ legen** put aside; (sparen) put by; **Spaß od Scherz b~** joking apart

beisetz|en vt sep bury. **B~ung** f -,-en funeral

Beispiel nt example; **zum B~** for example. **b~haft** a exemplary. **b~los** a unprecedented. **b~sweise** adv for example

beispringen† *vi sep* (*sein*) jdm b~ come to s.o.'s aid

beiß|en† *vt*/*i* (*haben*) bite; (*brennen*) sting; **sich b~en** (*Farben:*) clash. **b~end** *a* (*fig*) biting; (*Bemerkung*) caustic. **B~zange** *f* pliers *pl*

Bei|stand *m* -[e]s help; **jdm B~stand leisten** help s.o. **b~stehen**† *vi sep* (*haben*) **jdm b~stehen** help s.o.

beisteuern *vt sep* contribute

beistimmen *vi sep* (*haben*) agree

Beistrich *m* comma

Beitrag *m* -[e]s,⸚e contribution; (*Mitglieds-*) subscription; (*Versicherungs-*) premium; (*Zeitungs-*) article. **b~en**† *vt*/*i sep* (*haben*) contribute

bei|treten† *vi sep* (*sein*) (+ *dat*) join. **B~tritt** *m* joining

beiwohnen *vi sep* (*haben*) (+ *dat*) be present at

Beize *f* -,-n (*Holz-*) stain; (*Culin*) marinade

beizeiten *adv* in good time

beizen *vt* stain (*Holz*)

bejahen *vt* answer in the affirmative; (*billigen*) approve of

bejahrt *a* aged, old

bejubeln *vt* cheer

bekämpf|en *vt* fight. **B~ung** *f* fight (*gen* against)

bekannt *a* well-known; (*vertraut*) familiar; **jdm b~ sein** be known to s.o.; **jdn b~ machen** introduce s.o.; **etw b~ machen** *od* **geben** announce sth; **b~ werden** become known. **B~e(r)** *m*/*f* acquaintance; (*Freund*) friend. **B~gabe** *f* announcement. **b~geben**† *vt sep* (NEW) **b~ geben, s. bekannt. b~lich** *adv* as is well known. **b~machen** *vt sep* (NEW) **b~ machen, s. bekannt. B~machung** *f* -,-en announcement; (*Anschlag*) notice. **B~schaft** *f* - acquaintance; (*Leute*) acquaintances *pl*; (*Freunde*) friends *pl*. **b~werden†** *vi sep* (*sein*) (NEW) **b~ werden, s. bekannt**

bekehr|en *vt* convert; **sich b~en** become converted. **B~ung** *f* -,-en conversion

bekenn|en† *vt* confess, profess (*Glauben*); **sich [für] schuldig b~en** admit one's guilt; **sich b~en zu** confess to (*Tat*); **profess** (*Glauben*); (*stehen zu*) stand by. **B~tnis** *nt* -ses,-se confession; (*Konfession*) denomination

beklag|en *vt* lament; (*bedauern*) deplore; **sich b~en** complain. **b~enswert** *a* unfortunate. **B~te(r)** *m*/*f* (*Jur*) defendant

beklatschen *vt* applaud

bekleid|en *vt* hold (*Amt*). **b~et** *a* dressed (**mit** in). **B~ung** *f* clothing

Beklemmung *f* -,-en feeling of oppression

beklommen *a* uneasy; (*ängstlich*) anxious, *adv* -ly

bekommen† *vt* get; have (*Baby*); catch (*Erkältung*); **Angst/Hunger b~** get frightened/hungry; **etw geliehen b~** be lent sth □ *vi* (*sein*) **jdm gut b~** do s.o. good; (*Essen:*) agree with s.o.

bekömmlich *a* digestible

beköstig|en *vt* feed; **sich selbst b~en** cater for oneself. **B~ung** *f* - board; (*Essen*) food

bekräftigen *vt* reaffirm; (*bestätigen*) confirm

bekreuzigen (sich) *vr* cross oneself

bekümmert *a* troubled; (*besorgt*) worried

bekunden *vt* show; (*bezeugen*) testify

belächeln *vt* laugh at

beladen† *vt* load □ *a* laden

Belag *m* -[e]s,⸚e coating; (*Fußboden-*) covering; (*Brot-*) topping; (*Zahn-*) tartar; (*Brems-*) lining

belager|n *vt* besiege. **B~ung** *f* -,-en siege

Belang *m* **von/ohne B~** of/of no importance; **B~e** *pl* interests. **b~en** *vt* (*Jur*) sue. **b~los** *a* irrelevant; (*unwichtig*) trivial. **B~losigkeit** *f* -,-en triviality

belassen† *vt* leave; **es dabei b~** leave it at that

belasten *vt* load; (*fig*) burden; (*beanspruchen*) put a strain on; (*Comm*) debit; (*Jur*) incriminate

belästigen *vt* bother; (*bedrängen*) pester; (*unsittlich*) molest

Belastung *f* -,-en load; (*fig*) strain; (*Last*) burden; (*Comm*) debit. **B~smaterial** *nt* incriminating evidence. **B~szeuge** *m* prosecution witness

belaufen† **(sich)** *vr* amount (**auf** + *acc* to)

belauschen *vt* eavesdrop on

beleb|en *vt* (*fig*) revive; (*lebhaft machen*) enliven; **wieder b~en** (*Med*) revive, resuscitate; (*fig*) revive (*Handel*); **sich b~en** revive; (*Stadt:*) come to life. **b~t** *a* lively; (*Straße*) busy

Beleg *m* -[e]s,-e evidence; (*Beispiel*) instance (**für** of); (*Quittung*) receipt. **b~en** *vt* cover/(*garnieren*) garnish (**mit** with); (*besetzen*) reserve; (*Univ*) enrol for; (*nachweisen*) provide evidence for; **den ersten Platz b~en** (*Sport*) take first place. **B~schaft** *f* -,-en work-force. **b~t** *a* occupied; (*Zunge*) coated; (*Stimme*) husky; **b~te Brote** open sandwiches; **der Platz ist b~t** this seat is taken

belehren *vt* instruct; (*aufklären*) inform

beleibt *a* corpulent

beleidig|en *vt* offend; *(absichtlich)* insult. **B~ung** *f* -,-en insult

belesen *a* well-read

beleucht|en *vt* light; *(anleuchten)* illuminate. **B~ung** *f* -,-en illumination; *(elektrisch)* lighting; *(Licht)* light

Belg|ien /-jən/ *nt* -s Belgium. **B~ier(in)** *m* -s,- *(f~,-nen)* Belgian. **b~isch** *a* Belgian

belicht|en *vt (Phot)* expose. **B~ung** *f* -exposure

Belieb|en *nt* -s nach **B~en** [just] as one likes; *(Culin)* if liked. **b~ig** *a* eine **b~ige Zahl/Farbe** any number/colour you like □ *adv* **b~ig lange/oft** as long/often as one likes. **b~t** *a* popular. **B~theit** *f* - popularity

beliefern *vt* supply **(mit** with)

bellen *vi (haben)* bark

belohn|en *vt* reward. **B~ung** *f* -,-en reward

belüften *vt* ventilate

belügen† *vt* lie to; **sich [selbst] b~** deceive oneself

belustig|en *vt* amuse. **B~ung** *f* -,-en amusement

bemächtigen (sich) *vr* (+ *gen)* seize

bemalen *vt* paint

bemängeln *vt* criticize

bemannt *a* manned

bemerk|bar *a* **sich b~bar machen** attract attention; *⟨Ding:⟩* become noticeable. **b~en** *vt* notice; *(äußern)* remark. **b~** enswert *a* remarkable, *adv* -bly. **B~ung** *f* -,-en remark

bemitleiden *vt* pity

bemittelt *a* well-to-do

bemüh|en *vt* trouble; **sich b~en** try (zu to; **um etw** to get sth); *(sich kümmern)* attend **(um** to); **b~t sein** endeavour (zu to). **B~ung** *f* -,-en effort; *(Mühe)* trouble

bemuttern *vt* mother

benachbart *a* neighbouring

benachrichtig|en *vt* inform; *(amtlich)* notify. **B~ung** *f* -,-en notification

benachteilig|en *vt* discriminate against; *(ungerecht sein)* treat unfairly. **B~ung** *f* -,-en discrimination *(gen* against)

benehmen† (sich) *vr* behave. **B~** *nt* -s behaviour

beneiden *vt* envy **(um etw** sth). **b~swert** *a* enviable

Bengel *m* -s,- boy; *(Rüpel)* lout

benommen *a* dazed

benötigen *vt* need

benutz|en, *(SGer)* **benütz|en** *vt* use; take *⟨Bahn⟩*. **B~er** *m* -s,- user. **b~erfreundlich** *a* user-friendly. **B~ung** *f* use

Benzin *nt* -s petrol, *(Amer)* gasoline. **B~tank** *m* petrol tank

beobacht|en *vt* observe. **B~er** *m* -s,- observer. **B~ung** *f* -,-en observation

bepacken *vt* load **(mit** with)

bepflanzen *vt* plant **(mit** with)

bequem *a* comfortable, *adv* -bly; *(mühelos)* easy, *adv* -ily; *(faul)* lazy. **b~en (sich)** *vr* deign **(zu** to). **B~lichkeit** *f* -,-en comfort; *(Faulheit)* laziness

berat|en† *vt* advise; *(überlegen)* discuss; **sich b~en** confer; **sich b~en lassen** get advice □ *vi (haben)* discuss **(über etw** *acc* sth); *(beratschlagen)* confer. **B~er(in)** *m* -s,-, *(f* -,-nen) adviser. **b~schlagen** *vi (haben)* confer. **B~ung** *f* -,-en guidance; *(Rat)* advice; *(Besprechung)* discussion; *(Med, Jur)* consultation. **B~ungsstelle** *f* advice centre

berauben *vt* rob *(gen* of)

berauschen *vt* intoxicate. **b~d** *a* intoxicating, heady

berechn|en *vt* calculate; *(anrechnen)* charge for; *(abfordern)* charge. **b~end** *a* *(fig)* calculating. **B~ung** *f* calculation

berechtig|en *vt* entitle; *(befugen)* authorize; *(fig)* justify. **b~t** *a* justified, justifiable. **B~ung** *f* -,-en authorization; *(Recht)* right; *(Rechtmäßigkeit)* justification

bered|en *vt* talk about; *(klatschen)* gossip about; *(überreden)* talk round; **sich b~en** talk. **B~samkeit** *f* - eloquence

beredt *a* eloquent, *adv* -ly

Bereich *m* -[e]s,-e area; *(fig)* realm; *(Fach-)* field

bereichern *vt* enrich; **sich b~** grow rich **(an** + *dat* on)

Bereifung *f* - tyres *pl*

bereinigen *vt (fig)* settle

bereit *a* ready. **b~en** *vt* prepare; *(verursachen)* cause; give *⟨Überraschung⟩*. **b~halten†** *vt sep* have/*⟨ständig⟩* keep ready. **b~legen** *vt sep* put out [ready]. **b~machen** *vt sep* get ready; **sich b~machen** get ready. **b~s** *adv* already

Bereitschaft *f* -,-en readiness; *(Einheit)* squad. **B~sdienst** *m* **B~sdienst haben** *(Mil)* be on call; *⟨Arzt:⟩* be on duty; *⟨Apotheke:⟩* be open for out-of-hours dispensing. **B~spolizei** *f* riot police

bereit|stehen† *vi sep (haben)* be ready. **b~stellen** *vt sep* put out ready; *(verfügbar machen)* make available. **B~ung** *f* - preparation. **b~willig** *a* willing, *adv* -ly. **B~willigkeit** *f* - willingness

bereuen *vt* regret

Berg *m* -[e]s,-e mountain; *(Anhöhe)* hill; **in den B~en** in the mountains. **b~ab** *adv* downhill. **b~an** *adv* uphill. **B~arbeiter**

m miner. **b~auf** *adv* uphill; **es geht b~auf** (*fig*) things are looking up. **B~bau** *m* **-[e]s** mining

bergen† *vt* recover; (*Naut*) salvage; (*retten*) rescue

Berg|führer *m* mountain guide. **b~ig** *a* mountainous. **B~kette** *f* mountain range. **B~mann** *m* (*pl* **-leute**) miner. **B~steigen** *nt* **-s** mountaineering. **B~steiger(in)** *m* **-s,-** (*f* **-,-nen**) mountaineer, climber. **B~und-Talbahn** *f* roller-coaster

Bergung *f* **-** recovery; (*Naut*) salvage; (*Rettung*) rescue

Berg|wacht *f* mountain rescue service. **B~werk** *nt* mine

Bericht *m* **-[e]s,-e** report; (*Reise-*) account; **B~ erstatten** report (**über** + *acc* on). **b~en** *vt/i* (*haben*) report; (*erzählen*) tell (**von** of). **B~erstatter(in)** *m* **-s,-** (*f* **-,-nen**) reporter; (*Korrespondent*) correspondent

berichtig|en *vt* correct. **B~ung** *f* **-,-en** correction

beriesel|n *vt* irrigate. **B~ungsanlage** *f* sprinkler system

beritten *a* ⟨*Polizei*⟩ mounted

Berlin *nt* **-s** Berlin. **B~er** *m* **-s,-** Berliner; (*Culin*) doughnut □ *a* Berlin ...

Bernhardiner *m* **-s,-** St Bernard

Bernstein *m* amber

bersten† *vi* (*sein*) burst

berüchtigt *a* notorious

berückend *a* entrancing

berücksichtig|en *vt* take into consideration. **B~ung** *f* **-** consideration

Beruf *m* profession; (*Tätigkeit*) occupation; (*Handwerk*) trade. **b~en**† *vt* appoint; **sich b~en** refer (**auf** + *acc* to); (*vorgeben*) plead (**auf etw** *acc* sth) □ *a* competent; **b~en sein** be destined (**zu** to). **b~lich** *a* professional; ⟨*Ausbildung*⟩ vocational □ *adv* professionally; **b~lich tätig sein** work, have a job. **B~saussichten** *fpl* career prospects. **B~sberater(in)** *m*(*f*) careers officer. **B~sberatung** *f* vocational guidance. **b~smäßig** *adv* professionally. **B~sschule** *f* vocational school. **B~ssoldat** *m* regular soldier. **b~stätig** *a* working; **b~stätig sein** work, have a job. **B~stätige(r)** *m/f* working man/woman. **B~sverkehr** *m* rush-hour traffic. **B~ung** *f* **-,-en** appointment; (*Bestimmung*) vocation; (*Jur*) appeal; **B~ung einlegen** appeal. **B~ungsgericht** *nt* appeal court

beruhen *vi* (*haben*) be based (**auf** + *dat* on); **eine Sache auf sich b~ lassen** let a matter rest

beruhig|en *vt* calm [down]; (*zuversichtlich machen*) reassure; **sich b~en** calm

---

down. **b~end** *a* calming; (*tröstend*) reassuring; (*Med*) sedative. **B~ung** *f* **-** calming; reassurance; (*Med*) sedation. **B~ungsmittel** *nt* sedative; (*bei Psychosen*) tranquillizer

berühmt *a* famous. **B~heit** *f* **-,-en** fame; (*Person*) celebrity

berühr|en *vt* touch; (*erwähnen*) touch on; (*beeindrucken*) affect; **sich b~en** touch. **B~ung** *f* **-,-en** touch; (*Kontakt*) contact

besag|en *vt* say; (*bedeuten*) mean. **b~t** *a* [afore]said

besänftigen *vt* soothe; **sich b~** calm down

Besatz *m* **-es,-̈e** trimming

Besatzung *f* **-,-en** crew; (*Mil*) occupying force

besaufen† (**sich**) *vr* (*sl*) get drunk

beschädig|en *vt* damage. **B~ung** *f* **-,-en** damage

beschaffen *vt* obtain, get □ *a* **so b~ sein, dass** be such that; **wie ist es b~ mit?** what about? **B~heit** *f* **-** consistency; (*Art*) nature

beschäftig|en *vt* occupy; ⟨*Arbeitgeber:*⟩ employ; **sich b~en** occupy oneself. **b~t** *a* busy; (*angestellt*) employed (**bei** at). **B~te(r)** *m/f* employee. **B~ung** *f* **-,-en** occupation; (*Anstellung*) employment. **b~ungslos** *a* unemployed. **B~ungstherapie** *f* occupational therapy

beschäm|en *vt* make ashamed. **b~end** *a* shameful; (*demütigend*) humiliating. **b~t** *a* ashamed; (*verlegen*) embarrassed

beschatten *vt* shade; (*überwachen*) shadow

beschau|en *vt* (*SGer*) [**sich** (*dat*)] **etw b~en** look at sth. **b~lich** *a* tranquil; (*Relig*) contemplative

Bescheid *m* **-[e]s** information; **jdm B~ sagen** *od* **geben** let s.o. know; **B~ wissen** know

bescheiden *a* modest, *adv* **-ly.** **B~heit** *f* **-** modesty

bescheinen† *vt* shine on; **von der Sonne beschienen** sunlit

bescheinig|en *vt* certify. **B~ung** *f* **-,-en** [written] confirmation; (*Schein*) certificate

beschenken *vt* give a present/presents to

bescher|en *vt* **jdn b~en** give s.o. presents; **jdm etw b~en** give s.o. sth. **B~ung** *f* **-,-en** distribution of Christmas presents; (*fam: Schlamassel*) mess

beschießen† *vt* fire at; (*mit Artillerie*) shell, bombard

beschildern *vt* signpost

beschimpf|en *vt* abuse, swear at. **B~ung** *f* **-,-en** abuse

beschirmen *vt* protect

Beschlag *m* in **B~ nehmen, mit B~ belegen** monopolize. **b~en†** *vt* shoe □ *vi* (*sein*) steam *or* mist up □ *a* steamed *or* misted up; (*erfahren*) knowledgeable (**in** + *dat* about). **B~nahme** *f* -,-n confiscation; (*Jur*) seizure. **b~nahmen** *vt* confiscate; (*Jur*) seize; (*fam*) monopolize

beschleunig|en *vt* hasten; (*schneller machen*) speed up; quicken ⟨*Schritt, Tempo*⟩; **sich b~en** speed up; quicken □ *vi* (*haben*) accelerate. **B~ung** *f* - acceleration

beschließen† *vt* decide; (*beenden*) end □ *vi* (*haben*) decide (**über** + *acc* about)

Beschluss (**Beschluß**) *m* decision

beschmieren *vt* smear/(*bestreichen*) spread (**mit** with)

beschmutzen *vt* make dirty; **sich b~** get [oneself] dirty

beschneid|en† *vt* trim; (*Hort*) prune; (*fig: kürzen*) cut back; (*Relig*) circumcise. **B~ung** *f* - circumcision

beschneit *a* snow-covered

beschnüffeln, beschnuppern *vt* sniff at

beschönigen *vt* (*fig*) gloss over

beschränken *vt* limit, restrict; **sich b~ auf** (+ *acc*) confine oneself to; ⟨*Sache:*⟩ be limited to

beschrankt *a* ⟨*Bahnübergang*⟩ with barrier[s]

beschränk|t *a* limited; (*geistig*) dull-witted; (*borniert*) narrow-minded. **B~ung** *f* -,-en limitation, restriction

beschreib|en† *vt* describe; (*schreiben*) write on. **B~ung** *f* -,-en description

beschuldig|en *vt* accuse. **B~ung** *f* -,-en accusation

beschummeln *vt* (*fam*) cheat

Beschuss (**Beschuß**) *m* (*Mil*) fire; (*Artillerie-*) shelling

beschütz|en *vt* protect. **B~er** *m* -s,- protector

Beschwer|de *f* -,-n complaint; **B~den** (*Med*) trouble *sg*. **b~en** *vt* weight down; **sich b~en** complain. **b~lich** *a* difficult

beschwichtigen *vt* placate

beschwindeln *vt* cheat (**um** out of); (*belügen*) lie to

beschwingt *a* elated; (*munter*) lively

beschwipst *a* (*fam*) tipsy

beschwören† *vt* swear to; (*anflehen*) implore; (*herauf-*) invoke

besehen† *vt* look at

beseitig|en *vt* remove. **B~ung** *f* - removal

Besen *m* -s,- broom. **B~ginster** *m* (*Bot*) broom. **B~stiel** *m* broomstick

besessen *a* obsessed (**von** by)

besetz|en *vt* occupy; fill ⟨*Posten*⟩; (*Theat*) cast ⟨*Rolle*⟩; (*verzieren*) trim (**mit** with). **b~t** *a* occupied; ⟨*Toilette, Leitung*⟩ engaged; ⟨*Zug, Bus*⟩ full up; **der Platz ist b~t** this seat is taken; **mit Perlen b~t** set with pearls. **B~tzeichen** *nt* engaged tone. **B~ung** *f* -,-en occupation; (*Theat*) cast

besichtig|en *vt* look round ⟨*Stadt, Museum*⟩; (*prüfen*) inspect; (*besuchen*) visit. **B~ung** *f* -,-en visit; (*Prüfung*) inspection; (*Stadt-*) sightseeing

besiedelt *a* **dünn/dicht b~** sparsely/densely populated

besiegeln *vt* (*fig*) seal

besieg|en *vt* defeat; (*fig*) overcome. **B~te(r)** *m/f* loser

besinn|en† (**sich**) *vr* think, reflect; (*sich erinnern*) remember (**auf jdn/etw** s.o./sth); **sich anders b~en** change one's mind. **b~lich** *a* contemplative; (*nachdenklich*) thoughtful. **B~ung** *f* - reflection; (*Bewusstsein*) consciousness; **bei/ohne B~ung** conscious/unconscious; **zur B~ung kommen** regain consciousness; (*fig*) come to one's senses. **b~ungslos** *a* unconscious

Besitz *m* possession (*Eigentum, Land-*) property; (*Gut*) estate. **b~anzeigend** *a* (*Gram*) possessive. **b~en†** *vt* own, possess; (*haben*) have. **B~er(in)** *m* -s,- (*f* -,-nen) owner; (*Comm*) proprietor. **B~ung** *f* -,-en [landed] property; (*Gut*) estate

besoffen *a* (*sl*) drunken; **b~ sein** be drunk

besohlen *vt* sole

besold|en *vt* pay. **B~ung** *f* - pay

besonder|e(r,s) *a* special; (*bestimmt*) particular; (*gesondert*) separate; **nichts B~es** nothing special. **B~heit** *f* -,-en peculiarity. **b~s** *adv* [e]specially, particularly; (*gesondert*) separately

besonnen *a* calm, *adv* -ly

besorg|en† *vt* get; (*kaufen*) buy; (*erledigen*) attend to; (*versorgen*) look after. **B~nis** *f* -,-se anxiety; (*Sorge*) worry. **b~niserregend** *a* worrying. **b~t** *a* worried/(*bedacht*) concerned (**um** about). **B~ung** *f* -,-en errand; **B~ungen machen** do shopping

bespielt *a* recorded

bespitzeln *vt* spy on

besprech|en† *vt* discuss; (*rezensieren*) review; **sich b~en** confer; **ein Tonband b~en** make a tape recording. **B~ung** *f* -,-en discussion; review; (*Konferenz*) meeting

bespritzen *vt* splash

besser *a & adv* better. **b~n** *vt* improve; sich b~n get better, improve. **B~ung** *f* - improvement; **gute B~ung!** get well soon! **B~wisser** *m* -s,- know-all

Bestand *m* -[e]s,ˉe existence; (*Vorrat*) stock (**an** + *dat* of); **B~haben, von B~ sein** last

beständig *a* constant, *adv* -ly; (*Wetter*) settled; **b~ gegen** resistant to

Bestand|saufnahme *f* stocktaking. **B~teil** *m* part

bestärken *vt* (*fig*) strengthen

bestätig|en *vt* confirm; acknowledge (*Empfang*); **sich b~en** prove to be true. **B~ung** *f* -,-en confirmation

bestatt|en *vt* bury. **B~ung** *f* -,-en funeral. **B~ungsinstitut** *nt* [firm of] undertakers *pl*, (*Amer*) funeral home

bestäuben *vt* pollinate

bestaubt *a* dusty

Bestäubung *f* - pollination

bestaunen *vt* gaze at in amazement; (*bewundern*) admire

best|e(r,s) *a* best; **b~en Dank!** many thanks! **am b~en sein** be best; **zum b~en geben/halten** (NEW) **zum B~en geben/halten**, *s.* **Beste(r,s)**. **B~e(r,s)** *m/f/nt* best; **sein B~es tun** do one's best; **zum B~en der Armen** for the benefit of the poor; **zum B~n geben** recite (*Gedicht*); tell (*Geschichte, Witz*); sing (*Lied*); **jdn zum B~n halten** (*fam*) pull s.o.'s leg

bestech|en† *vt* bribe; (*bezaubern*) captivate. **b~end** *a* captivating. **b~lich** *a* corruptible. **B~ung** *f* - bribery. **B~ungsgeld** *nt* bribe

Besteck *nt* -[e]s,-e [set of] knife, fork and spoon; (*coll*) cutlery

bestehen† *vi* (*haben*) exist; (*fortdauern*) last; (*bei Prüfung*) pass; **~ aus** consist/(*gemacht sein*) be made of; **~ auf** (+ *dat*) insist on □ *vt* pass (*Prüfung*). **B~** *nt* -s existence

bestehlen† *vt* rob

besteig|en† *vt* climb; (*einsteigen*) board; (*aufsteigen*) mount; ascend (*Thron*). **B~ung** *f* ascent

bestell|en *vt* order; (*vor-*) book; (*ernennen*) appoint; (*bebauen*) cultivate; (*ausrichten*) tell; **zu sich b~en** send for; **b~t sein** have an appointment; **kann ich etwas b~en?** can I take a message? **b~en Sie Ihrer Frau Grüße von mir** give my regards to your wife. **B~schein** *m* order form. **B~ung** *f* order; (*Botschaft*) message; (*Bebauung*) cultivation

besten|falls *adv* at best. **b~s** *adv* very well

besteuer|n *vt* tax. **B~ung** *f* - taxation

bestialisch /-st-/ *a* bestial

Bestie /'bɛstjə/ *f* -,-n beast

bestimm|en *vt* fix; (*entscheiden*) decide; (*vorsehen*) intend; (*ernennen*) appoint; (*ermitteln*) determine; (*definieren*) define; (*Gram*) qualify □ *vi* (*haben*) be in charge (**über** + *acc* of). **~t** *a* definite, *adv* -ly; (*gewiss*) certain, *adv* -ly; (*fest*) firm, *adv* -ly. **B~theit** *f* - firmness; **mit B~theit** for certain. **B~ung** *f* fixing; (*Vorschrift*) regulation; (*Ermittlung*) determination; (*Definition*) definition; (*Zweck*) purpose; (*Schicksal*) destiny. **B~ungsort** *m* destination

Bestleistung *f* (*Sport*) record

bestraf|en *vt* punish. **B~ung** *f* -,-en punishment

bestrahl|en *vt* shine on; (*Med*) treat with radiotherapy; irradiate (*Lebensmittel*). **B~ung** *f* radiotherapy

Bestreb|en *nt* -s endeavour; (*Absicht*) aim. **b~t** *a* **b~t sein** endeavour (**zu** to). **B~ung** *f* -,-en effort

bestreichen† *vt* spread (**mit** with)

bestreikt *a* strike-hit

bestreiten† *vt* dispute; (*leugnen*) deny; (*bezahlen*) pay for

bestreuen *vt* sprinkle (**mit** with)

bestürmen *vt* (*fig*) besiege

bestürz|t *a* dismayed; (*erschüttert*) stunned. **B~ung** *f* - dismay, consternation

Bestzeit *f* (*Sport*) record [time]

Besuch *m* -[e]s,-e visit; (*kurz*) call; (*Schul-*) attendance; (*Gast*) visitor; (*Gäste*) visitors *pl*; **B~ haben** have a visitor/visitors; **bei jdm zu od auf B~ sein** be staying with s.o. **b~en** *vt* visit; (*kurz*) call on; (*teilnehmen*) attend; go to (*Schule, Ausstellung*); **gut b~t** well attended. **B~er(in)** *m* -s,- (*f* -,-nen) visitor; caller; (*Theat*) patron. **B~szeit** *f* visiting hours *pl*

betagt *a* aged, old

betasten *vt* feel

betätig|en *vt* operate; **sich b~en** work (**als** as); **sich politisch b~en** engage in politics. **B~ung** *f* -,-en operation; (*Tätigkeit*) activity

betäub|en *vt* stun; (*Lärm:*) deafen; (*Med*) anaesthetize; (*lindern*) ease; deaden (*Schmerz*); **wie b~t** dazed. **B~ung** *f* - daze; (*Med*) anaesthesia; **unter örtlicher B~ung** under local anaesthetic. **B~ungsmittel** *nt* anaesthetic

Bete *f* -,-n **rote B~** beetroot

beteilig|en *vt* give a share to; **sich b~en** take part (**an** + *dat* in); (*beitragen*) contribute (**an** + *dat* to). **b~t an b~t sein** take part/(*an Unfall*) be involved/(*Comm*) have a share (**an** + *dat* in); **alle B~ten**

all those involved. **B∼ung** f -,-en participation; involvement; (*Anteil*) share

beten vi (haben) pray; (*bei Tisch*) say grace □ vt say

beteuer|n vt protest. **B∼ung** f -,-en protestation

Beton /be'tɔŋ/ m -s concrete

betonen vt stressed, emphasize

betonieren vt concrete

beton|t a stressed; (*fig*) pointed, adv -ly. **B∼ung** f -,-en stress, emphasis

betören vt bewitch

betr., **Betr.** abbr (**betreffs**) re

Betracht m in **B∼ ziehen** consider; **außer B∼ lassen** disregard; **nicht in B∼ kommen** be out of the question. **b∼en** vt look at; (*fig*) regard (**als** as)

beträchtlich a considerable, adv -bly

Betrachtung f -,-en contemplation; (*Überlegung*) reflection

Betrag m -[e]s,⸚e amount. **b∼en†** vt amount to; **sich b∼en** behave. **B∼en** nt -s behaviour; (*Sch*) conduct

betrauen vt entrust (**mit** with)

betrauern vt mourn

betreff|en† vt affect; (*angehen*) concern; **was mich betrifft** as far as I am concerned. **b∼end** a relevant; **der b∼ende Brief** the letter in question. **b∼s** prep (+ gen) concerning

betreiben† vt (*leiten*) run; (*ausüben*) carry on; (*vorantreiben*) pursue; (*antreiben*) run (**mit** on)

betreten† vt step on; (*eintreten*) enter; '**B∼ verboten**' 'no entry'; (*bei Rasen*) 'keep off [the grass]' □ a embarrassed □ adv in embarrassment

betreu|en vt look after. **B∼er(in)** m -s,- (f -,-nen) helper; (*Kranken-*) nurse. **B∼ung** f -care

Betrieb m business; (*Firma*) firm; (*Treiben*) activity; (*Verkehr*) traffic; **in B∼** working; (*in Gebrauch*) in use; **außer B∼** not in use; (*defekt*) out of order

Betriebs|anleitung, **B∼anweisung** f operating instructions pl. **B∼ferien** pl firm's holiday; '**B∼ferien**' 'closed for the holidays'. **B∼leitung** f management. **B∼rat** m works committee. **B∼ruhe** f 'montags B∼ruhe' 'closed on Mondays'. **B∼störung** f breakdown

betrinken† (sich) vr get drunk

betroffen a disconcerted; **b∼ sein** be affected (**von** by); **die B∼en** those affected in consternation

betrüb|en vt sadden. **b∼lich** a sad. **b∼t** a sad, adv -ly

Betrug m -[e]s deception; (*Jur*) fraud

betrüg|en† vt cheat, swindle; (*Jur*) defraud; (*in der Ehe*) be unfaithful to; **sich selbst b∼en** deceive oneself. **B∼er(in)** m -s,- (f -,-nen) swindler. **B∼erei** f -,-en fraud. **b∼erisch** a fraudulent; (*Person*) deceitful

betrunken a drunken; **b∼ sein** be drunk. **B∼e(r)** m drunk

Bett nt -[e]s,-en bed; **im B∼** in bed; **ins od zu B∼ gehen** go to bed. **B∼couch** f sofabed. **B∼decke** f blanket; (*Tages-*) bedspread

bettel|arm a destitute. **B∼ei** f - begging. **b∼n** vi (haben) beg

bett|en vt lay, put; **sich b∼en** lie down. **b∼lägerig** a bedridden. **B∼laken** nt sheet

Bettler(in) m -s,- (f -,-nen) beggar

Bettpfanne f bedpan

Betttuch (**Bettuch**) nt sheet

Bett|vorleger m bedside rug. **B∼wäsche** f bed linen. **B∼zeug** nt bedding

betupfen vt dab (**mit** with)

beug|en vt bend; (*Gram*) decline; conjugate (*Verb*); **sich b∼en** bend; (*lehnen*) lean; (*sich fügen*) submit (**dat** to). **B∼ung** f -,-en (*Gram*) declension; conjugation

Beule f -,-n bump; (*Delle*) dent

beunruhig|en vt worry; **sich b∼en** worry. **B∼ung** f - worry

beurlauben vt give leave to; (*des Dienstes entheben*) suspend

beurteil|en vt judge. **B∼ung** f -,-en judgement; (*Ansicht*) opinion

Beute f - booty, haul; (*Jagd-*) bag; (*B∼tier*) quarry; (*eines Raubtiers*) prey

Beutel m -s,- bag; (*Geld-*) purse; (*Tabak- & Zool*) pouch. **B∼tier** nt marsupial

bevölker|n vt populate. **B∼ung** f -,-en population

bevollmächtig|en vt authorize. **B∼te(r)** m/f [authorized] agent

bevor conj before; **b∼ nicht** until

bevormunden vt treat like a child

bevorstehen† vi sep (haben) approach; (*unmittelbar*) be imminent; **jdm b∼** be in store for s.o. **b∼d** a approaching, forthcoming; **unmittelbar b∼d** imminent

bevorzug|en vt prefer; (*begünstigen*) favour. **b∼t** a privileged; (*Behandlung*) preferential; (*beliebt*) favoured

bewachen vt guard; **bewachter Parkplatz** car park with an attendant

bewachsen a covered (**mit** with)

Bewachung f - guard; **unter B∼** under guard

bewaffn|en vt arm. **b∼et** a armed. **B∼ung** f - armament; (*Waffen*) arms pl

bewahren vt protect (**vor** + dat from); (behalten) keep; **die Ruhe b~** keep calm; **Gott bewahre!** heaven forbid!

bewähren (sich) vr prove one's/⟨Ding:⟩ its worth; (erfolgreich sein) prove a success

bewahrheiten (sich) vr prove to be true

bewähr|t a reliable; (erprobt) proven. **B~ung** f - (Jur) probation. **B~ungsfrist** f [period of] probation. **B~ungsprobe** f (fig) test

bewaldet a wooded

bewältigen vt cope with; (überwinden) overcome; (schaffen) manage

bewandert a knowledgeable

bewässer|n vt irrigate. **B~ung** f - irrigation

bewegen[1] vt (reg) move; **sich b~** move; (körperlich) take exercise

bewegen[†2] vt **jdn dazu b~, etw zu tun** induce s.o. to do sth

Beweg|grund m motive. **b~lich** a movable, mobile; (wendig) agile. **B~lichkeit** f - mobility; agility. **b~t** a moved; (ereignisreich) eventful; ⟨See⟩ rough. **B~ung** f -,-en movement; (Phys) motion; (Rührung) emotion; (Gruppe) movement; **körperliche B~ung** physical exercise; **sich in B~ung setzen** [start to] move. **B~ungsfreiheit** f freedom of movement/(fig) of action. **b~ungslos** a motionless

beweinen vt mourn

Beweis m -es,-e proof; (Zeichen) token; **B~e** evidence sg. **b~en**† vt prove; (zeigen) show; **sich b~en** prove oneself/⟨Ding:⟩ itself. **B~material** nt evidence

bewenden vi **es dabei b~lassen** leave it at that

bewerb|en† (**sich**) vr apply (**um** for; **bei** to). **B~er(in)** m -s,- (f -,-nen) applicant. **B~ung** f -,-en application

bewerkstelligen vt manage

bewerten vt value; (einschätzen) rate; (Sch) mark, grade

bewilligen vt grant

bewirken vt cause; (herbeiführen) bring about; (erreichen) achieve

bewirt|en vt entertain. **B~ung** f - hospitality

bewohn|bar a habitable. **b~en** vt inhabit, live in. **B~er(in)** m -s,- (f -,-nen) resident, occupant; (Einwohner) inhabitant

bewölk|en (sich) vr cloud over; **b~t** a cloudy. **B~ung** f - clouds pl

bewunder|n vt admire. **b~nswert** a admirable. **B~ung** f - admiration

bewusst (bewußt) a conscious (gen of); (absichtlich) deliberate, adv -ly; (besagt) said; **sich** (dat) **etw** (gen) **b~ sein/werden** be/become aware of sth. **b~los** a unconscious. **B~losigkeit** f - unconsciousness; **B~sein** n -s consciousness; (Gewissheit) awareness; **bei [vollem] B~sein** [fully] conscious; **mir kam zum B~sein** I realized (**dass** that)

bez. abbr (bezahlt) paid; (bezüglich) re

bezahl|en vt/i (haben) pay; pay for ⟨Ware, Essen⟩; **gut b~te Arbeit** well-paid work; **sich b~t machen** (fig) pay off. **B~ung** f - payment; (Lohn) pay

bezähmen vt control; (zügeln) restrain; **sich b~** restrain oneself

bezaubern vt enchant. **b~d** a enchanting

bezeichn|en vt mark; (bedeuten) denote; (beschreiben, nennen) describe (**als** as). **b~end** a typical. **B~ung** f marking; (Beschreibung) description (**als** as); (Ausdruck) term; (Name) name

bezeugen vt testify to

bezichtigen vt accuse (gen of)

bezieh|en† vt cover; (einziehen) move into; (beschaffen) obtain; (erhalten) get, receive; take ⟨Zeitung⟩; (in Verbindung bringen) relate (**auf** + acc to); **sich b~en** (bewölken) cloud over; **sich b~en auf** (+ acc) refer to; **das Bett frisch b~en** put clean sheets on the bed. **B~ung** f -,-en relation; (Verhältnis) relationship; (Bezug) respect; **in dieser B~ung** in this respect; **[gute] B~ungen haben** have [good] connections. **b~ungsweise** adv respectively; (vielmehr) or rather

beziffern (sich) vr amount (**auf** + acc to)

Bezirk m -[e]s,-e district

Bezug m cover; (Kissen-) case; (Beschaffung) obtaining; (Kauf) purchase; (Zusammenhang) reference; **B~e** pl earnings; **B~ nehmen** refer (**auf** + acc to); **in B~ (b~) auf** (+ acc) regarding, concerning

bezüglich prep (+ gen) regarding, concerning □ a relating (**auf** + acc to); (Gram) relative

bezwecken vt (fig) aim at

bezweifeln vt doubt

bezwingen† vt conquer

BH /be:'ha:/ m -[s],-[s] bra

bibbern vi (haben) tremble; (vor Kälte) shiver

Bibel f -,-n Bible

Biber[1] m -s,- beaver

Biber[2] m & nt -s flannelette

Biblio|graphie, **B~grafie** f -,-n bibliography. **B~thek** f -,-en library. **B~thekar(in)** m -s,- (f -,-nen) librarian

biblisch *a* biblical

bieder *a* honest, upright; *(ehrenwert)* worthy; *(einfach)* simple

bieg|en† *vt* bend; **sich b~en** bend; **sich vor Lachen b~en** *(fam)* double up with laughter □ *vi (sein)* curve **(nach to)**; **um die Ecke b~en** turn the corner. **b~sam** *a* flexible, supple. **B~ung** *f* -,-en bend

Biene *f* -,-n bee. **B~nhonig** *m* natural honey. **B~nstock** *m* beehive. **B~nwabe** *f* honeycomb

Bier *nt* -s,-e beer. **B~deckel** *m* beer-mat. **B~krug** *m* beer-mug

Biest *nt* -[e]s,-er *(fam)* beast

bieten† *vt* offer; *(bei Auktion)* bid; *(zeigen)* present; **das lasse ich mir nicht b~** I won't stand for that

Bifokalbrille *f* bifocals *pl*

Biga|mie *f* - bigamy. **B~ mist** *m* -en,-en bigamist

bigott *a* over-pious

Bikini *m* -s,-s bikini

Bilanz *f* -,-en balance sheet; *(fig)* result; **die B~ ziehen** *(fig)* draw conclusions (aus from)

Bild *nt* -[e]s,-er picture; *(Theat)* scene; **jdn ins B~ setzen** put s.o. in the picture

bilden *vt* form; *(sein)* be; *(erziehen)* educate; **sich b~** form; *(geistig)* educate oneself

Bild|erbuch *nt* picture-book. **B~erga-lerie** *f* picture gallery. **B~fläche** *f* screen; **von der B~fläche verschwinden** disappear from the scene. **B~hauer** *m* -s,- sculptor. **B~hauerei** *f* - sculpture. **b~hübsch** *a* very pretty. **b~lich** *a* pictorial; *(figurativ)* figurative, *adv* -ly. **B~nis** *nt* -ses,-se portrait. **B~schirm** *m* *(TV)* screen. **B~schirmgerät** *nt* visual display unit, VDU. **b~schön** *a* very beautiful

Bildung *f* - formation; *(Erziehung)* education; *(Kultur)* culture

Billard /'bɪljart/ *nt* -s billiards *sg.* **B~tisch** *m* billiard table

Billett /bɪl'jɛt/ *nt* -[e]s,-e & -s ticket

Billiarde *f* -,-n thousand million million

billig *a* cheap, *adv* -ly; *(dürftig)* poor; *(gerecht)* just; **recht und b~** right and proper. **b~en** *vt* approve. **B~ung** *f* - approval

Billion /bɪljoːn/ *f* -,-en million million, billion

bimmeln *vi (haben)* tinkle

Bimsstein *m* pumice stone

bin *s.* sein; **ich bin** I am

Binde *f* -,-n band; *(Verband)* bandage; *(Damen-)* sanitary towel. **B~haut-entzündung** *f* conjunctivitis. **b~n†** *vt* tie

(an + *acc* to); make ⟨Strauß⟩; bind ⟨Buch⟩; *(fesseln)* tie up; *(Culin)* thicken; **sich b~n** commit oneself. **b~nd** *a (fig)* binding. **B~strich** *m* hyphen. **B~wort** *nt* (*pl* -wörter) *(Gram)* conjunction

Bind|faden *m* string; **ein B~faden** a piece of string. **B~ung** *f* -,-en *(fig)* tie, bond; *(Beziehung)* relationship; *(Verpflichtung)* commitment; *(Ski-)* binding; *(Tex)* weave

binnen *prep* (+ *dat*) within; **b~ kurzem** shortly. **B~handel** *m* home trade

Binse *f* -,-n *(Bot)* rush. **B~nwahrheit, B~nweisheit** *f* truism

Bio- *pref* organic

Bio|chemie *f* biochemistry. **b~dyna-misch** *m* organic. **B~graphie, B~grafie** *f* -,-n biography

Bio|hof *m* organic farm. **B~laden** *m* health-food store

Biolog|e *m* -n,-n biologist. **B~ie** *f* - biology. **b~isch** *a* biological, *adv* -ly; **b~ischer Anbau** organic farming; **b~isch angebaut** organically grown

Birke *f* -,-n birch [tree]

Birm|a *nt* -s Burma. **b~anisch** *a* Burmese

Birn|baum *m* pear-tree. **B~e** *f* -,-n pear; *(Electr)* bulb

bis *prep* (+ *acc*) as far as, [up] to; *(zeitlich)* until, till; *(spätestens)* by; **bis zu** up to; **bis jetzt** up to now, so far; **bis dahin** until/ *(spätestens)* by then; **bis auf** (+ *acc*) *(einschließlich)* [down] to; *(ausgenommen)* except [for]; **drei bis vier Mark** three to four marks; **bis morgen!** see you tomorrow! □ *conj* until

Bischof *m* -s,-̈e bishop

bisher *adv* so far, up to now. **b~ig** *attrib a* ⟨Präsident⟩ outgoing; **meine b~igen Erfahrungen** my experiences so far

Biskuit|rolle /bɪs'kviːt-/ *f* Swiss roll. **B~teig** *m* sponge mixture

bislang *adv* so far, up to now

Biss *m* -es,-e (Biß *m* -sses,-sse) bite

bisschen (bißchen) *inv pron* **ein b~** a bit, a little; **ein b~ Brot** a bit of bread; **kein b~** not a bit

Bissen *m* -s,- bite, mouthful. **b~ig** *a* vicious; *(fig)* caustic

bist *s.* sein; **du b~** you are

Bistum *nt* -s,-̈er diocese, see

bisweilen *adv* from time to time

bitt|e *adv* please; *(nach Klopfen)* come in; *(als Antwort auf 'danke')* don't mention it, you're welcome; **wie b~e?** pardon? *(empört)* I beg your pardon? **möchten Sie Kaffee?—ja b~e** would you like some coffee?—yes please. **B~e** *f* -,-n request/*(dringend)* plea (**um** for). **b~en†** *vt/i (haben)* ask/(*dringend*) beg (**um** for); (*einladen*) invite, ask; **ich b~e dich!** I beg [of] you! (*empört*) I ask you! **b~end** *a* pleading, *adv* -ly

bitter *a* bitter, *adv* -ly. **B~keit** *f* - bitterness. **b~lich** *adv* bitterly

Bittschrift *f* petition

bizarr *a* bizarre, *adv* -ly

bläh|en *vt* swell; puff out (*Vorhang*); **sich b~en** swell; (*Vorhang, Segel.*) billow □ *vi* (*haben*) cause flatulence. **B~ungen** *fpl* flatulence *sg*, (*fam*) wind *sg*

Blamage /bla'ma:ʒə/ *f* -,-n humiliation; (*Schande*) disgrace

blamieren *vt* disgrace; **sich b~** disgrace oneself; (*sich lächerlich machen*) make a fool of oneself

blanchieren /blã'ʃiːrən/ *vt* (*Culin*) blanch

blank *a* shiny; (*nackt*) bare; **b~ sein** (*fam*) be broke. **B~oscheck** *m* blank cheque

Blase *f* -,-n bubble; (*Med*) blister; (*Anat*) bladder. **B~balg** *m* -[e]s,-̈e bellows *pl*. **b~n†** *vt/i* (*haben*) blow; play (*Flöte*). **B~nentzündung** *f* cystitis

Bläser *m* -s,- (*Mus*) wind player; **die B~** the wind section *sg*

blasiert *a* blasé

Blas|instrument *nt* wind instrument. **B~kapelle** *f* brass band

Blasphemie *f* - blasphemy

blass (**blaß**) *a* (**blasser, blassest**) pale; (*schwach*) faint; **b~ werden** turn pale

Blässe *f* - pallor

Blatt *nt* -[e]s,-̈er (*Bot*) leaf; (*Papier*) sheet; (*Zeitung*) paper; **kein B~ vor den Mund nehmen** (*fig*) not mince one's words

blätter|n *vi* (*haben*) **b~n in** (+ *dat*) leaf through. **B~teig** *m* puff pastry

Blattlaus *f* greenfly

blau *a* **b~,~** *nt* -s,- blue; **b~er Fleck** bruise; **b~es Auge** black eye; **b~ sein** (*fam*) be tight; **Fahrt ins B~e** mystery tour. **B~beere** *f* bilberry. **B~licht** *nt* blue flashing light. **b~machen** *vi sep* (*haben*) (*fam*) skive off work

Blech *nt* -[e]s,-e sheet metal; (*Weiß-*) tin; (*Platte*) metal sheet; (*Back-*) baking sheet; (*Mus*) brass; (*fam: Unsinn*) rubbish. **b~en** *vt/i* (*haben*) (*fam*) pay. **B~[blas]instrument** *nt* brass instrument. **B~schaden** *m* (*Auto*) damage to the bodywork

Blei *nt* -[e]s lead

Bleibe *f* - place to stay. **b~n†** *vi* (*sein*) remain, stay; (*übrig-*) be left; **ruhig b~n** keep calm; **bei etw b~n** (*fig*) stick to sth; **b~n Sie am Apparat** hold the line; **etw b~n lassen** not do sth; (*aufhören*) stop

doing sth. **b~nd** *a* permanent; (*anhaltend*) lasting. **b~nlassen†** *vt sep* (NEW) **b~n lassen, s. bleiben**

bleich *a* pale. **b~en†** *vi* (*sein*) bleach; (*ver-*) fade □ *vt* (*reg*) bleach. **B~mittel** *nt* bleach

blei|ern *a* leaden. **b~frei** *a* unleaded. **B~stift** *m* pencil. **B~stiftabsatz** *m* stiletto heel. **B~stiftspitzer** *m* -s,- pencil-sharpener

Blende *f* -,-n shade, shield; (*Sonnen-*) [sun] visor; (*Phot*) diaphragm; (*Öffnung*) aperture; (*an Kleid*) facing. **b~n** *vt* dazzle, blind. **b~nd** *a* (*fig*) dazzling; (*prima*) marvellous, *adv* -ly

Blick *m* -[e]s,-e look; (*kurz*) glance; (*Aussicht*) view; **auf den ersten B~** at first sight; **einen B~ für etw haben** (*fig*) have an eye for sth. **b~en** *vi* (*haben*) look/ (*kurz*) glance (**auf** + *acc* at). **B~punkt** *m* (*fig*) point of view

blind *a* blind; (*trübe*) dull; **b~er Alarm** false alarm; **b~er Passagier** stowaway. **B~darm** *m* appendix. **B~darmentzündung** *f* appendicitis. **B~e(r)** *m/f* blind man/woman; **die B~en** the blind *pl*. **B~enhund** *m* guidedog. **B~enschrift** *f* braille. **B~gänger** *m* -s,- (*Mil*) dud. **B~heit** *f* - blindness. **b~lings** *adv* (*fig*) blindly

blink|en *vi* (*haben*) flash; (*funkeln*) gleam; (*Auto*) indicate. **B~er** *m* -s,- (*Auto*) indicator. **B~licht** *nt* flashing light

blinzeln *vi* (*haben*) blink

Blitz *m* -es,-e [flash of] lightning; (*Phot*) flash; **ein B~ aus heiterem Himmel** (*fig*) a bolt from the blue. **B~ableiter** *m* lightning-conductor. **b~artig** *a* lightning . . . □ *adv* like lightning. **B~birne** *f* flashbulb. **b~en** *vi* (*haben*) flash; (*funkeln*) sparkle; **es hat geblitzt** there was a flash of lightning. **B~gerät** *nt* flash [unit]. **B~licht** *nt* (*Phot*) flash. **b~sauber** *a* spick and span. **b~schnell** *a* lightning . . . □ *adv* like lightning. **B~strahl** *m* flash of lightning

Block *m* -[e]s,-̈e block □ -[e]s,-s & -̈e (*Schreib-*) [note-]pad; (*Häuser-*) block; (*Pol*) bloc

Blockade *f* -,-n blockade

Blockflöte *f* recorder

blockieren *vt* block; (*Mil*) blockade

Blockschrift *f* block letters *pl*

blöd[e] *a* feeble-minded; (*dumm*) stupid, *adv* -ly

Blödsinn *m* -[e]s idiocy; (*Unsinn*) nonsense. **b~ig** *a* feeble-minded; (*verrückt*) idiotic

blöken *vi* (*haben*) bleat

blond *a* fair-haired; (*Haar*) fair. **B~ine** *f* -,-n blonde

bloß *a* bare; *(alleinig)* mere; **mit b~em Auge** with the naked eye □ *adv* only, just; **was mache ich b~?** whatever shall I do?

Blöße *f* -,-n nakedness; **sich** *(dat)* **eine B~ geben** *(fig)* show a weakness

bloß|legen *vt sep* uncover. **b~stellen** *vt sep* compromise; **sich b~stellen** show oneself up

Bluff *m* -s,-s bluff. **b~en** *vt/i (haben)* bluff

blühen *vi (haben)* flower; *(fig)* flourish. **b~d** *a* flowering; *(fig)* flourishing, thriving; *(Phantasie)* fertile

Blume *f* -,-n flower; *(vom Wein)* bouquet. **B~nbeet** *n* flower-bed. **B~ngeschäft** *nt* flower-shop, florist's [shop]. **B~nkohl** *m* cauliflower. **B~nmuster** *nt* floral design. **B~nstrauß** *m* bunch of flowers. **B~ntopf** *m* flowerpot; *(Pflanze)* [flowering] pot plant. **B~nzwiebel** *f* bulb

blumig *a (fig)* flowery

Bluse *f* -,-n blouse

Blut *nt* -[e]s blood. **b~arm** *a* anaemic. **B~bahn** *f* blood-stream. **b~befleckt** *a* blood-stained. **B~bild** *nt* blood count. **B~buche** *f* copper beech. **B~druck** *m* blood pressure. **b~dürstig** *a* bloodthirsty

Blüte *f* -,-n flower, bloom; *(vom Baum)* blossom; *(B~zeit)* flowering period; *(Baum-)* blossom time; *(fig)* flowering; *(Höhepunkt)* peak, prime; *(fam: Banknote)* forged note, *(fam)* dud

Blut|egel *m* -s,- leech. **b~en** *vi (haben)* bleed

Blüten|blatt *nt* petal. **B~staub** *m* pollen

Blut|er *m* -s,- haemophiliac. **B~erguss** (B~erguß) *m* bruise. **B~gefäß** *nt* blood-vessel. **B~gruppe** *f* blood group. **B~hund** *m* bloodhound. **b~ig** *a* bloody. **b~jung** *a* very young. **B~körperchen** *nt* -s,- [blood] corpuscle. **B~probe** *f* blood test. **b~rünstig** *a (fig)* bloody, gory; *(Person)* blood-thirsty. **B~schande** *f* incest. **B~spender** *m* blood donor. **B~sturz** *m* haemorrhage. **B~sverwandte(r)** *m/f* blood relation. **B~transfusion**, **B~übertragung** *f* blood transfusion. **B~ung** *f* -,-en bleeding; *(Med)* haemorrhage; *(Regel-)* period. **b~unterlaufen** *a* bruised; *(Auge)* bloodshot. **B~vergießen** *nt* -s bloodshed. **B~vergiftung** *f* blood-poisoning. **B~wurst** *f* black pudding

Bö *f* -,-en gust; *(Regen-)* squall

Bob *m* -s,-s bob[-sleigh]

Bock *m* -[e]s,¨e buck; *(Ziege)* billy goat; *(Schaf)* ram; *(Gestell)* support; **einen B~ schießen** *(fam)* make a blunder. **b~en** *vi (haben) (Pferd:)* buck; *(Kind:)* be stubborn. **b~ig** *a (fam)* stubborn. **B~springen** *nt* leap-frog

Boden *m* -s,¨ ground; *(Erde)* soil; *(Fuß-)* floor; *(Grundfläche)* bottom; *(Dach-)* loft, attic. **B~kammer** *f* attic [room]. **b~los** *a* bottomless; *(fam)* incredible. **B~satz** *m* sediment. **B~schätze** *mpl* mineral deposits. **B~see (der)** Lake Constance

Bogen *m* -s,- & ¨ curve; *(Geom)* arc; *(beim Skilauf)* turn; *(Archit)* arch; *(Waffe, Geigen-)* bow; *(Papier)* sheet; **einen großen B~um jdn/etw machen** *(fig)* give s.o./sth a wide berth. **B~gang** *m* arcade. **B~schießen** *nt* archery

Bohle *f* -,-n [thick] plank

Böhm|en *nt* -s Bohemia. **b~isch** *a* Bohemian

Bohne *f* -,-n bean; **grüne B~n** French beans. **B~nkaffee** *m* real coffee

bohner|n *vt* polish. **B~wachs** *nt* floor-polish

bohr|en *vt/i (haben)* drill **(nach** for); drive *(Tunnel)*; sink *(Brunnen)*; *(Insekt:)* bore; **in der Nase b~en** pick one's nose. **B~er** *m* -s,- drill. **B~insel** *f* [offshore] drilling rig. **B~maschine** *f* electric drill. **B~turm** *m* derrick

Boje *f* -,-n buoy

Böllerschuss *m* gun salute

Bolzen *m* -s,- bolt; *(Stift)* pin

bombardieren *vt* bomb; *(fig)* bombard **(mit** with)

bombastisch *a* bombastic

Bombe *f* -,-n bomb. **B~nangriff** *m* bombing raid. **B~nerfolg** *m* huge success. **B~r** *m* -s,- *(Aviat)* bomber

Bon /bɔŋ/ *m* -s,-s voucher; *(Kassen-)* receipt

Bonbon /bɔŋ'bɔŋ/ *m & nt* -s,-s sweet

Bonus *m* -[sses],-[sse] bonus

Boot *nt* -[e]s,-e boat. **B~ssteg** *m* landing-stage

Bord¹ *nt* -[e]s,-e shelf

Bord² *m (Naut)* **an B~** aboard, on board; **über B~** overboard. **B~buch** *nt* log [-book]

Bordell *nt* -s,-e brothel

Bord|karte *f* boarding-pass. **B~stein** *m* kerb

borgen *vt* borrow; **jdm etw b~** lend s.o. sth

Borke *f* -,-n bark

borniert *a* narrow-minded

Börse *f* -,-n purse; *(Comm)* stock exchange. **B~nmakler** *m* stockbroker

Borst|e *f* -,-n bristle. **b~ig** *a* bristly

Borte *f* -,-n braid

bösartig *a* vicious; *(Med)* malignant

Böschung *f* -,-en embankment; *(Hang)* slope

böse *a* wicked, evil; (*unartig*) naughty; (*schlimm*) bad, *adv* -ly; (*zornig*) cross; **jdm od auf jdn b~ sein** be cross with s.o. **B~wicht** *m* -[e]s,-e villain; (*Schlingel*) rascal

bos|haft *a* malicious, *adv* -ly; (*gehässig*) spiteful, *adv* -ly. **B~heit** *f* -,-en malice; spite; (*Handlung*) spiteful act/(*Bemerkung*) remark

böswillig *a* malicious, *adv* -ly. **B~keit** *f* - malice

Botani|k *f* - botany. **B~ker(in)** *m* -s,- (*f* -,-nen) botanist. **b~sch** *a* botanical

Bot|e *m* -n,-n messenger. **B~engang** *m* errand. **B~schaft** *f* -,-en message; (*Pol*) embassy. **B~schafter** *m* -s,- ambassador

Bottich *m* -[e]s,-e vat; (*Wasch-*) tub

Bouillon /bʊlˈjɔŋ/ *f* -,-s clear soup. **B~würfel** *m* stock cube

Bowle /ˈboːlə/ *f* -,-n punch

box|en *vi* (*haben*) box □ *vt* punch. **B~en** *nt* -s boxing. **B~er** *m* -s,- boxer. **B~kampf** *m* boxing match; (*Boxen*) boxing

Boykott *m* -[e]s,-s boycott. **b~ieren** *vt* boycott; (*Comm*) black

brachliegen† *vi sep* (*haben*) lie fallow

Branche /ˈbrãːʃə/ *f* -,-n [line of] business. **B~nverzeichnis** *nt* (*Teleph*) classified directory

Brand *m* -[e]s,ˉe fire; (*Med*) gangrene; (*Bot*) blight; **in B~ geraten** catch fire; **in B~ setzen** *od* **stecken** set on fire. **B~bombe** *f* incendiary bomb

branden *vi* (*haben*) surge; (*sich brechen*) break

Brand|geruch *m* smell of burning. **b~marken** *vt* (*fig*) brand. **B~stifter** *m* arsonist. **B~stiftung** *f* arson

Brandung *f* - surf. **B~sreiten** *nt* surfing

Brand|wunde *f* burn. **B~zeichen** *nt* brand

Branntwein *m* spirit; (*coll*) spirits *pl*. **B~brennerei** *f* distillery

brasilianisch *a* Brazilian. **B~ilien** /-jən/ *nt* -s Brazil

Brat|apfel *m* baked apple. **b~en†** *vt/i* (*haben*) roast; (*in der Pfanne*) fry. **B~en** *m* -s,- roast; (*B~stück*) joint. **B~ensoße** *f* gravy. **b~fertig** *a* oven-ready. **B~hähnchen, B~huhn** *nt* roast/(*zum Braten*) roasting chicken. **B~kartoffeln** *fpl* fried potatoes. **B~klops** *m* rissole. **B~pfanne** *f* frying-pan

Bratsche /-ʃ-/ *f* -,-n (*Mus*) viola

Brat|spieß *m* spit. **B~wurst** *f* sausage for frying; (*gebraten*) fried sausage

Brauch *m* -[e]s,Bräuche custom. **b~bar** *a* usable; (*nützlich*) useful. **b~en** *vt* need; (*ge-, verbrauchen*) use; take (*Zeit*); **er b~t**

es nur zu sagen he only has to say; **du b~st nicht zu gehen** you needn't go

Braue *f* -,-n eyebrow

brau|en *vt* brew. **B~er** *m* -s,- brewer. **B~erei** *f* -,-en brewery

braun *a*, **B~** *nt* -s,- brown; **b~werden** (*Person:*) get a tan; **b~ [gebrannt] sein** be [sun-]tanned

Bräune *f* - [sun-]tan. **b~n** *vt/i* (*haben*) brown; (*in der Sonne*) tan

braungebrannt *a* (NEW) **braun gebrannt**, s. **braun**

Braunschweig *nt* -s Brunswick

Brause *f* -,-n (*Dusche*) shower; (*an Gießkanne*) rose; (*B~limonade*) fizzy drink. **b~n** *vi* (*haben*) roar; (*duschen*) shower □ *vi* (*sein*) rush [along] □ *vr* **sich b~n** shower. **b~nd** *a* roaring; (*sprudelnd*) effervescent

Braut *f* -,ˉe bride; (*Verlobte*) fiancée

Bräutigam *m* -s,-e bridegroom; (*Verlobter*) fiancé

Brautkleid *nt* wedding dress

bräutlich *a* bridal

Brautpaar *nt* bridal couple; (*Verlobte*) engaged couple

brav *a* good, well-behaved; (*redlich*) honest □ *adv* dutifully; (*redlich*) honestly

bravo *int* bravo!

BRD *abbr* (**Bundesrepublik Deutschland**) FRG

Brech|eisen *nt* jemmy; (*B~stange*) crowbar. **b~en†** *vt* break; (*Phys*) refract (*Licht*); (*erbrechen*) vomit; **sich b~en** (*Wellen:*) break; (*Licht:*) be refracted; **sich** (*dat*) **den Arm b~en** break one's arm □ *vi* (*sein*) break □ *vi* (*haben*) vomit, be sick; **mit jdm b~en** (*fig*) break with s.o. **B~er** *m* -s,- breaker. **B~reiz** *m* nausea. **B~stange** *f* crowbar

Brei *m* -[e]s,-e paste; (*Culin*) purée; (*Grieß-*) pudding; (*Hafer-*) porridge. **b~ig** *a* mushy

breit *a* wide; (*Schultern, Grinsen*) broad □ *adv* **b~ grinsen** grin broadly. **b~beinig** *a* & *adv* with legs apart. **B~e** *f* -,-n width; breadth; (*Geog*) latitude. **b~en** *vt* spread (**über** + *acc* over). **B~engrad** *m* [degree of] latitude. **B~enkreis** *m* parallel. **B~seite** *f* long side; (*Naut*) broadside

Bremse¹ *f* -,-n horsefly

Bremse² *f* -,-n brake. **b~n** *vt* slow down; (*fig*) restrain □ *vi* (*haben*) brake

Bremslicht *nt* brake-light

brenn|bar *a* combustible; **leicht b~bar** highly [in]flammable. **b~en†** *vi* (*haben*) burn; (*Licht:*) be on; (*Zigarette:*) be alight; (*weh tun*) smart, sting; **es b~t in X** there's a fire in X; **darauf b~en, etw zu tun** be dying to do sth □ *vt* burn; (*rösten*) roast;

(*im Brennofen*) fire; (*destillieren*) distil. **b~end** *a* burning; (*angezündet*) lighted; (*fig*) fervent □ *adv* **ich würde b~end gern** ... I'd love to ... **B~erei** *f* -,-en distillery

Brennessel *f* (NEW) **Brennnessel**

Brenn|holz *nt* firewood. **B~nessel** *f* stinging nettle. **B~ofen** *m* kiln. **B~punkt** *m* (*Phys*) focus; **im B~punkt des Interesses stehen** be the focus of attention. **B~spiritus** *m* methylated spirits. **B~stoff** *m* fuel

brenzlig *a* (*fam*) risky; **b~er Geruch** smell of burning

Bresche *f* -,-n (*fig*) breach

Bretagne /bre'tanjə/ (**die**) - Brittany

Brett *nt* -[e]s,-er board; (*im Regal*) shelf; **schwarzes B~** notice board. **B~chen** *nt* -s,- slat; (*Frühstücks-*) small board (*used as plate*). **B~spiel** *nt* board game

Brezel *f* -,-n pretzel

Bridge /brɪtʃ/ *nt* - (*Spiel*) bridge

Brief *m* -[e]s,-e letter. **B~beschwerer** *m* -s,- paperweight. **B~block** *m* writing pad. **B~freund(in)** *m(f)* pen-friend. **B~kasten** *m* letter-box, (*Amer*) mailbox. **B~kopf** *m* letter-head. **b~lich** *a & adv* by letter. **B~marke** *f* [postage] stamp. **B~öffner** *m* paper-knife. **B~papier** *nt* notepaper. **B~porto** *nt* letter rate. **B~tasche** *f* wallet. **B~träger** *m* postman, (*Amer*) mailman. **B~umschlag** *m* envelope. **B~wahl** *f* postal vote. **B~wechsel** *m* correspondence

Brigade *f* -,-n brigade

Brikett *nt* -s,-s briquette

brillan|t /brɪl'jant/ *a* brilliant, *adv* -ly. **B~t** *m* -en,-en [cut] diamond. **B~z** *f* - brilliance

Brille *f* -,-n glasses *pl*, spectacles *pl*; (*Schutz-*) goggles *pl*; (*Klosett-*) toilet seat

bringen† *vt* bring; (*fort-*) take; (*ein-*) yield; (*veröffentlichen*) publish; (*im Radio*) broadcast; show (*Film*); **ins Bett b~** put to bed; **jdn nach Hause b~** take/(*begleiten*) see s.o. home; **an sich** (*acc*) **b~** get possession of; **mit sich b~** entail; **um etw b~** deprive of sth; **etw hinter sich** (*acc*) **b~** get sth over [and done] with; **jdn dazu b~, etw zu tun** get s.o. to do sth; **es weit b~** (*fig*) go far

brisant *a* explosive

Brise *f* -,-n breeze

Brit|e *m* -n,-n, **B~in** *f* -,-nen Briton. **b~isch** *a* British

Bröck|chen *nt* -s,- (*Culin*) crouton. **b~elig** *a* crumbly; (*Gestein*) friable. **b~eln** *vt/i* (*haben/sein*) crumble

Brocken *m* -s,- chunk; (*Erde, Kohle*) lump; **ein paar B~ Englisch** (*fam*) a smattering of English

Brokat *m* -[e]s,-e brocade

Brokkoli *pl* broccoli *sg*

Brombeer|e *f* blackberry. **B~strauch** *m* bramble [bush]

Bronchitis *f* - bronchitis

Bronze /'brõːsə/ *f* -,-n bronze

Brosch|e *f* -,-n brooch. **b~iert** *a* paperback. **B~üre** *f* -,-n brochure; (*Heft*) booklet

Brösel *mpl* (*Culin*) breadcrumbs

Brot *n* -[e]s,-e bread; **ein B~** a loaf [of bread]; (*Scheibe*) a slice of bread; **sein B~ verdienen** (*fig*) earn one's living (**mit** by)

Brötchen *n* -s,- [bread] roll

Brot|krümel *m* breadcrumb. **B~verdiener** *m* breadwinner

Bruch *m* -[e]s,¨e break; (*Brechen*) breaking; (*Rohr-*) burst; (*Med*) fracture; (*Eingeweide-*) rupture, hernia; (*Math*) fraction; (*fig*) breach; (*in Beziehung*) break-up

brüchig *a* brittle

Bruch|landung *f* crash-landing. **B~rechnung** *f* fractions *pl*. **B~stück** *nt* fragment. **b~stückhaft** *a* fragmentary. **B~teil** *m* fraction

Brücke *f* -,-n bridge; (*Teppich*) rug

Bruder *m* -s,¨ brother

brüderlich *a* brotherly, fraternal

Brügge *nt* -s Bruges

Brüh|e *f* -,-n broth; (*Knochen-*) stock; **klare B~e** clear soup. **b~en** *vt* scald; (*auf-*) make (*Kaffee*). **B~würfel** *m* stock cube

brüllen *vt/i* (*haben*) roar; (*Kuh:*) moo; (*fam: schreien*) bawl

brumm|eln *vt/i* (*haben*) mumble. **b~en** *vi* (*haben*) (*Insekt:*) buzz; (*Bär:*) growl; (*Motor:*) hum; (*murren*) grumble □ *vt* mutter. **B~er** *m* -s,- (*fam*) bluebottle. **b~ig** *a* (*fam*) grumpy, *adv* -ily

brünett *a* dark-haired. **B~e** *f* -,-n brunette

Brunnen *m* -s,- well; (*Spring-*) fountain; (*Heil-*) spa water. **B~kresse** *f* watercress

brüsk *a* brusque, *adv* -ly. **b~ieren** *vt* snub

Brüssel *nt* -s Brussels

Brust *f* -,¨e chest; (*weibliche, Culin: B~stück*) breast. **B~bein** *nt* breastbone. **B~beutel** *m* purse worn round the neck

brüsten (sich) *vr* boast

Brust|fellentzündung *f* pleurisy. **B~schwimmen** *nt* breaststroke

Brüstung *f* -,-en parapet

Brustwarze *f* nipple

Brut f -,-en incubation; (*Junge*) brood; (*Fisch-*) fry

brutal a brutal, adv -ly. **B~ität** f -,-en brutality

brüten vi (haben) sit (*on eggs*); (*fig*) ponder (**über** + dat over); **b~de Hitze** oppressive heat

Brutkasten m (*Med*) incubator

brutto adv, **B~-** pref gross

brutzeln vi (haben) sizzle □ vt fry

Bub m -en,-en (*SGer*) boy. **B~e** m -n,-n (*Karte*) jack, knave

Bubikopf m bob

Buch nt -[e]s,¨er book; **B~ führen** keep a record (**über** + acc of); **die B~er führen** keep the accounts. **B~drucker** m printer

Buche f -,-n beech

buchen vt book; (*Comm*) enter

Bücher|bord, **B~brett** nt bookshelf. **B~ei** f -,-en library. **B~regal** nt bookcase, bookshelves pl. **B~schrank** m bookcase. **B~wurm** m bookworm

Buchfink m chaffinch

Buch|führung f bookkeeping. **B~halter(in)** m -s,- (f -,-nen) bookkeeper, accountant. **B~haltung** f bookkeeping, accountancy; (*Abteilung*) accounts department. **B~händler(in)** m(f) bookseller. **B~handlung** f bookshop. **B~macher** m -s,- bookmaker. **B~prüfer** m auditor

Büchse f -,-n box; (*Konserven-*) tin, can; (*Gewehr*) [sporting] gun. **B~nmilch** f evaporated milk. **B~nöffner** m tin or can opener

Buch|stabe m -n,-n letter. **b~stabieren** vt spell [out]. **b~stäblich** adv literally

Buchstützen fpl book-ends

Bucht f -,-en (*Geog*) bay

Buchung f -,-en booking, reservation; (*Comm*) entry

Buckel m -s,- hump; (*Beule*) bump; (*Hügel*) hillock; **einen B~ machen** ⟨*Katze:*⟩ arch its back

bücken (sich) vr bend down

bucklig a hunchbacked. **B~e(r)** m/f hunchback

Buckling m -s,-e smoked herring; (*fam: Verbeugung*) bow

buddeln vt/i (haben) (*fam*) dig

Buddhis|mus m - Buddhism. **B~t(in)** m -en,-en (f -,-nen) Buddhist. **b~tisch** a Buddhist

Bude f -,-n hut; (*Kiosk*) kiosk; (*Markt-*) stall; (*fam: Zimmer*) room; (*Studenten-*) digs pl

Budget /by'dʒe:/ nt -s,-s budget

Büfett nt -[e]s,-e sideboard; (*Theke*) bar; **kaltes B~** cold buffet

Büffel m -s,- buffalo. **b~n** vt/i (haben) (*fam*) swot

Bug m -[e]s,-e (*Naut*) bow[s pl]

Bügel m -s,- frame; (*Kleider-*) coathanger; (*Steig-*) stirrup; (*Brillen-*) sidepiece. **B~brett** nt ironing-board. **B~eisen** nt iron. **B~falte** f crease. **b~frei** a non-iron. **b~n** vt/i (haben) iron

bugsieren vt (*fam*) manœuvre

buhen vi (haben) (*fam*) boo

Buhne f -,-n breakwater

Bühne f -,-n stage. **B~nbild** nt set. **B~neingang** m stage door

Buhrufe mpl boos

Bukett nt -[e]s,-e bouquet

Bulette f -,-n [meat] rissole

Bulgarien /-jən/ nt -s Bulgaria

Bull|auge nt (*Naut*) porthole. **B~dogge** f bulldog. **B~dozer** /-do:zɐ/ m -s,- bulldozer. **B~e** m -n,-n bull; (*sl: Polizist*) cop

Bummel|l m -s,- (*fam*) stroll. **B~lant** m -en,-en (*fam*) dawdler; (*Faulenzer*) loafer. **B~lei** f - (*fam*) dawdling; (*Nachlässigkeit*) carelessness

bummel|ig a (*fam*) slow; (*nachlässig*) careless. **b~n** vi (sein) (*fam*) stroll □ vi (haben) (*fam*) dawdle. **B~streik** m goslow. **B~zug** m (*fam*) slow train

Bums m -es,-e (*fam*) bump, thump

Bund¹ nt -[e]s,-e bunch; (*Stroh-*) bundle

Bund² m -[e]s,¨e association; (*Bündnis*) alliance; (*Pol*) federation; (*Rock-, Hosen-*) waistband; **im B~e sein** be in league (**mit** with); **der B~** the Federal Government; (*fam: Bundeswehr*) the [German] Army

Bündel nt -s,- bundle. **b~n** vt bundle [up]

Bundes|- pref Federal. **B~genosse** m ally. **B~kanzler** m Federal Chancellor. **B~land** nt [federal] state; (*Aust*) province. **B~liga** f German national league. **B~rat** m Upper House of Parliament. **B~regierung** f Federal Government. **B~republik** f **die B~republik Deutschland** the Federal Republic of Germany. **B~straße** f ≈ A road. **B~tag** m Lower House of Parliament. **B~wehr** f [Federal German] Army

bünd|ig a & adv **kurz und b~ig** short and to the point. **B~nis** nt -sses,-sse alliance

Bunker m -s,- bunker; (*Luftschutz-*) shelter

bunt a coloured; (*farbenfroh*) colourful; (*grell*) gaudy; (*gemischt*) varied; (*wirr*) confused; **b~er Abend** social evening; **b~e Platte** assorted cold meats □ adv **b~ durcheinander** higgledy-piggledy; **es zu b~ treiben** (*fam*) go too far. **B~stift** m crayon

Bürde *f* -,-n *(fig)* burden

Burg *f* -,-en castle

Bürge *m* -n,-n guarantor. **b∼n** *vi (haben)* **b∼n für** vouch for; *(fig)* guarantee

Bürger|(in) *m* -s,- *(f* -,-nen) citizen. **B∼krieg** *m* civil war. **b∼lich** *a* civil; *(Pflicht)* civic; *(mittelständisch)* middle-class; **b∼liche Küche** plain cooking. **B∼liche(r)** *m/f* commoner. **B∼meister** *m* mayor. **B∼rechte** *npl* civil rights. **B∼steig** *m* -[e]s, -e pavement, *(Amer)* sidewalk

Burggraben *m* moat

Bürgschaft *f* -,-en surety; **B∼ leisten** stand surety

Burgunder *m* -s,- *(Wein)* Burgundy

Burleske *f* -,-n burlesque

Büro *nt* -s,-s office. **B∼angestellte(r)** *m/f* office-worker. **B∼klammer** *f* paper-clip. **B∼krat** *m* -en,-en bureaucrat. **B∼kratie** *f* -,-n bureaucracy. **b∼kratisch** *a* bureaucratic

Bursch|e *m* -n,-n lad, youth; *(fam: Kerl)* fellow. **b∼ikos** *a* hearty; *(männlich)* mannish

Bürste *f* -,-n brush. **b∼n** *vt* brush. **B∼nschnitt** *m* crew cut

Bus *m* -ses,-se bus; *(Reise-)* coach. **B∼bahnhof** *m* bus and coach station

Busch *m* -[e]s,-e bush

Büschel *nt* -s,- tuft

buschig *a* bushy

Busen *m* -s,- bosom

Bussard *m* -s,-e buzzard

Buße *f* -,-n penance; *(Jur)* fine

büßen *vt/i (haben)* **[für] etw b∼** atone for sth; *(fig: bezahlen)* pay for sth

buß|fertig *a* penitent. **B∼geld** *nt (Jur)* fine

Büste *f* -,-n bust; *(Schneider-)* dummy. **B∼nhalter** *m* -s,- bra

Butter *f* - butter. **B∼blume** *f* buttercup. **B∼brot** *nt* slice of bread and butter. **B∼brotpapier** *nt* grease-proof paper. **B∼fass (B∼faß)** *nt* churn. **B∼milch** *f* buttermilk. **b∼n** *vi (haben)* make butter. □ *vt* butter

b.w. *abbr* (bitte wenden) P.T.O.

bzgl. *abbr* s. bezüglich

bzw. *abbr* s. beziehungsweise

C

ca. *abbr* (circa) about

Café /ka'fe:/ *nt* -s,-s café

Cafeteria /kafete'ri:a/ *f* -,-s cafeteria

camp|en /'kɛmpən/ *vi (haben)* go camping. **C∼ing** *nt* -s camping. **C∼ingplatz** *m* campsite

Cape /ke:p/ *nt* -s,-s cape

Caravan /'ka[:]ravan/ *m* -s,-s *(Auto)* caravan; *(Kombi)* estate car

Cassette /ka'sɛtə/ *f* -,-n cassette. **C∼nrecorder** /-rekɔrdɐ/ *m* -s,- cassette recorder

CD /tse:'de:/ *f* -,-s compact disc, CD

Cell|ist(in) /tʃɛ'lɪst(ɪn)/ *m* -en, -en *(f* -,-nen) cellist. **C∼o** /'tʃɛlo/ *nt* -,-los & -li cello

Celsius /'tsɛlzjʊs/ *inv* Celsius, centigrade

Cembalo /'tʃɛmbalo/ *nt* -s,-los & -li harpsichord

Champagner /ʃam'panjɐ/ *m* -s champagne

Champignon /'ʃampɪnjɔŋ/ *m* -s,-s [field] mushroom

Chance /'ʃã:s[ə]/ *f* -,-n chance

Chaos /'ka:ɔs/ *nt* - chaos

chaotisch /ka'o:tıʃ/ *a* chaotic

Charakter /ka'raktɐ/ *m* -s,-e /-'te:rə/ character. **c∼isieren** *vt* characterize. **c∼istisch** *a* characteristic (für of), *adv* -ally

Charism|a /ka'rɪsma/ *nt* -s charisma. **c∼atisch** *a* charismatic

charm|ant /ʃar'mant/ *a* charming, *adv* -ly. **C∼e** /ʃarm/ *m* -s charm

Charter|flug /'tʃ-, 'ʃartɐ-/ *m* charter flight. **c∼n** *vt* charter

Chassis /ʃa'si:/ *nt* -,- /-'si:[s], -'si:s/ chassis

Chauffeur /ʃɔ'føːɐ/ *m* -s,-e chauffeur; *(Taxi-)* driver

Chauvinis|mus /ʃovi'nɪsmʊs/ *m* - chauvinism. **C∼t** *m* -en,-en chauvinist

Chef /ʃɛf/ *m* -s,-s head; *(fam)* boss

Chem|ie /çe'mi:/ *f* - chemistry. **C∼ikalien** /-jən/ *fpl* chemicals

Chem|iker(in) /'çe:-/ *m* -s,- *(f* -,-nen) chemist. **c∼isch** *a* chemical, *adv* -ly; **c∼ische Reinigung** dry-cleaning; *(Geschäft)* dry-cleaner's

Chicorée /'ʃikore:/ *m* -s chicory

Chiffr|e /'ʃɪfɐ, 'ʃɪfrə/ *f* -,-n cipher; *(bei Annonce)* box number. **c∼iert** *a* coded

Chile /'çi:le/ *nt* -s Chile

Chin|a /'çi:na/ *nt* -s China. **C∼ese** *m* -n, -n, **C∼esin** *f* -,-nen Chinese. **c∼esisch** *a* Chinese. **C∼esisch** *nt* -[s] *(Lang)* Chinese

Chip /tʃɪp/ *m* -s,-s [micro]chip. **C∼s** *pl* crisps, *(Amer)* chips

Chirurg /çi'rʊrk/ *m* -en,-en surgeon. **C∼ie** /-'gi:/ *f* - surgery. **c∼isch** /-g-/ *a* surgical, *adv* -ly

Chlor /kloːɐ̯/ nt -s chlorine. **C~oform** /kloroˈfɔrm/ nt -s chloroform

Choke /tʃoːk/ m -s,-s (*Auto*) choke

Cholera /ˈkoːlera/ f - cholera

cholerisch /koˈleːrɪʃ/ a irascible

Cholesterin /ço-, koleste'riːn/ nt -s cholesterol

Chor /koːɐ̯/ m -[e]s,ːe choir; (*Theat*) chorus; **im C~** in chorus

Choral /koˈraːl/ m -[e]s,ːe chorale

Choreographie, Choreografie /koreogra'fiː/ f -,-n choreography

Chor|knabe /ˈkoːɐ̯-/ m choirboy. **C~musik** f choral music

Christ /krɪst/ m -en,-en Christian. **C~baum** m Christmas tree. **C~entum** nt -s Christianity. **C~in** f -,-nen Christian. **C~kind** nt Christ-child; (*als Geschenkbringer*) ≈ Father Christmas. **c~lich** a Christian

Christus /ˈkrɪstus/ m -ti Christ

Chrom /kroːm/ nt -s chromium

Chromosom /kromoˈzoːm/ nt -s,-en chromosome

Chronik /ˈkroːnɪk/ f -,-en chronicle

chron|isch /ˈkroːnɪʃ/ a chronic, adv -ally. **c~ologisch** a chronological, adv -ly

Chrysantheme /kryzanˈteːmə/ f -,-n chrysanthemum

circa /ˈtsɪrka/ adv about

Clique /ˈklɪkə/ f -,-n clique

Clou /kluː/ m -s,-s highlight, (*fam*) high spot

Clown /klaʊn/ m -s,-s clown. **c~en** vi (*haben*) clown

Club /klʊp/ m -s,-s club

Cocktail /ˈkɔkteːl/ m -s,-s cocktail

Code /ˈkoːt/ m -s,-s code

Cola /ˈkoːla/ f -,- (*fam*) Coke (P)

Comic-Heft /ˈkɔmɪk-/ nt comic

Computer /kɔmˈpjuːtɐ/ m -s,- computer. **c~isieren** vt computerize

Conférencier /kõˈferãˈsje:/ m -s,- compère

Cord /kɔrt/ m -s, **C~samt** m corduroy. **C~[samt]hose** f cords pl

Couch /kaʊtʃ/ f -,-es settee. **C~tisch** m coffee-table

Coupon /kuˈpõ:/ m -s,-s = **Kupon**

Cousin /kuˈzɛ̃:/ m -s,-s [male] cousin. **C~e** /-ˈziːnə/ f -,-n [female] cousin

Crem|e /kreːm/ f -,-s cream; (*Speise*) cream dessert. **c~efarben** a cream. **c~ig** a creamy

Curry /ˈkari, ˈkœri/ nt & m -s curry powder □ nt -s,-s (*Gericht*) curry

D

da adv there; (*hier*) here; (*zeitlich*) then; (*in dem Fall*) in that case; **von da an** from then on; **da sein** be there/(*hier*) here; (*existieren*) exist; **wieder da sein** be back; **noch nie da gewesen** unprecedented □ conj as, since

dabehalten† vt sep keep there

dabei (*emphatic:* **dabei**) adv nearby; (*daran*) with it; (*eingeschlossen*) included; (*hinsichtlich*) about it; (*währenddem*) during this; (*gleichzeitig*) at the same time; (*doch*) and yet; **dicht d~** close by; **d~ sein** be present; (*mitmachen*) be involved; **d~ sein, etw zu tun** be just doing sth; **d~ bleiben** (*fig*) remain adamant; **was ist denn d~?** (*fam*) so what? **d~sein†** vi sep (*sein*) s. **dabei**

dableiben† vi sep (*sein*) stay there

Dach nt -[e]s,ːer roof. **D~boden** m loft. **D~gepäckträger** m roof-rack. **D~kammer** f attic room. **D~luke** f skylight. **D~rinne** f gutter

Dachs m -es,-e badger

Dach|sparren m -s,- rafter. **D~ziegel** m [roofing] tile

Dackel m -s,- dachshund

dadurch (*emphatic:* **dadurch**) adv through it/them; (*Ursache*) by it; (*deshalb*) because of that; **d~, dass** because

dafür (*emphatic:* **dafür**) adv for it/them; (*anstatt*) instead; (*als Ausgleich*) but [on the other hand]; (*jedoch*) considering that; **ich kann nichts dafür** it's not my fault. **d~können†** vi sep (*haben*) NEW **d~ können**, s. **dafür**

dagegen (*emphatic:* **dagegen**) adv against it/them; (*Mittel, Tausch*) for it; (*verglichen damit*) by comparison; (*jedoch*) however; **hast du was d~?** do you mind? **d~halten†** vt sep argue (**dass** that)

daheim adv at home

daher (*emphatic:* **daher**) adv from there; (*deshalb*) for that reason; **das kommt d~, weil** that's because; **d~ meine Eile** hence my hurry □ conj that is why

dahin (*emphatic:* **dahin**) adv there; **bis d~** up to there; (*bis dann*) until/(*Zukunft*) by then; **jdn d~ bringen, dass er etw tut** get s.o. to do sth; **d~ sein** (*fam*) be gone. **d~gehen†** vi sep (*sein*) walk along; ⟨*Zeit.*⟩ pass. **d~gestellt** a **d~gestellt lassen** (*fig*) leave open; **das bleibt d~gestellt** that remains to be seen

dahinten adv back there

dahinter (emphatic: **dahinter**) adv behind it/them; **d~ kommen** (fig) get to the bottom of it. **d~kommen†** vi sep (sein) NEW **d~ kommen**, s. **dahinter**

Dahlie /-ə/ f -,-n dahlia

dalassen† vt sep leave there

daliegen† vi sep (haben) lie there

damalig a at that time; **der d~e Minister** the then minister

damals adv at that time

Damast m -es,-e damask

Dame f -,-n lady; (Karte, Schach) queen; (D~spiel) draughts sg, (Amer) checkers sg; (Doppelstein) king. **D~n- pref** ladies'/lady's ... **d~nhaft** a ladylike

damit (emphatic: **damit**) adv with it/them; (dadurch) by it; **hör auf d~!** stop it! □ conj so that

dämlich a (fam) stupid, adv -ly

Damm m -[e]s,-e dam; (Insel-) causeway; **nicht auf dem D~** (fam) under the weather

dämmer|ig a dim; **es wird d~ig** dusk is falling. **D~licht** nt twilight. **d~n** vi (haben) (Morgen:) dawn; **der Abend d~t** dusk is falling; **es d~t** it is getting light/(abends) dark. **D~ung** f dawn; (Abend-) dusk

Dämon m -s,-en /-'mo:nən/ demon

Dampf m -es,-e steam; (Chem) vapour. **d~en** vi (haben) steam

dämpfen vt (Culin) steam; (fig) muffle (Ton); lower (Stimme); dampen (Enthusiasmus)

Dampf|er m -s,- steamer. **D~kochtopf** m pressure-cooker. **D~maschine** f steam engine. **D~walze** f steamroller

Damwild nt fallow deer pl

danach (emphatic: **danach**) adv after it/them; (suchen) for it/them; (riechen) of it; (später) afterwards; (entsprechend) accordingly; **es sieht d~ aus** it looks like it

Däne m -n,-n Dane

daneben (emphatic: **daneben**) adv beside it/them; (außerdem) in addition; (verglichen damit) by comparison. **d~gehen†** vi sep (sein) miss; (scheitern) fail

Dän|emark nt -s Denmark. **D~in** f -,-nen Dane. **d~isch** a Danish

Dank m -es thanks pl; **vielen D~!** thank you very much! **d~ prep** (+ dat or gen) thanks to. **d~bar** a grateful, adv -ly; (erleichtert) thankful, adv -ly; (lohnend) rewarding. **D~barkeit** f - gratitude. **d~e** adv **d~e [schön** or **sehr]!** thank you [very much]! **[nein] d~e!** no thank you! **d~en** vi (haben) thank (jdm s.o.); (ablehnen) decline; **ich d~e!** no thank you! **nichts zu d~en!** don't mention it!

dann adv then; **d~ und wann** now and then; **nur/selbst d~, wenn** only/even if

daran (emphatic: **daran**) adv on it/them; at it/them; (denken) of it; **nahe d~** on the point (etw zu tun of doing sth); **denkt d~!** remember! **d~gehen†** vi sep (sein), **d~machen (sich)** vr sep set about (etw zu tun doing sth). **d~setzen** vt sep **alles d~setzen** do one's utmost (zu to)

darauf (emphatic: **darauf**) adv on it/them; (warten) for it; (antworten) to it; (danach) after that; (d~hin) as a result; **am Tag d~** the day after; **am d~ folgenden Tag** the following or next day. **d~folgend** a NEW **d~ folgend**, s. **darauf**. **d~hin** adv as a result

daraus (emphatic: **daraus**) adv out of or from it/them; **er macht sich nichts d~** he doesn't care for it; **was ist d~ geworden?** what has become of it?

Darbietung f -,-en performance; (Nummer) item

darin (emphatic: **darin**) adv in it/them

darlegen vt sep expound; (erklären) explain

Darlehen nt -s,- loan

Darm m -[e]s,-e intestine; (Wurst-) skin. **D~grippe** f gastric flu

darstell|en vt sep represent; (bildlich) portray; (Theat) interpret; (spielen) play; (schildern) describe. **D~er** m -s,- actor. **D~erin** f -,-nen actress. **D~ung** f representation; interpretation; description; (Bericht) account

darüber (emphatic: **darüber**) adv over it/them; (höher) above it/them; (sprechen, lachen, sich freuen) about it; (mehr) more; (inzwischen) in the meantime; **d~ hinaus** beyond [it]; (dazu) on top of that

darum (emphatic: **darum**) adv round it/them; (bitten, kämpfen) for it; (deshalb) that is why; **d~, weil** because

darunter (emphatic: **darunter**) adv under it/them; (tiefer) below it/them; (weniger) less; (dazwischen) among them

das def art & pron s. **der**

dasein† vi sep (sein) NEW **da sein**, s. **da**. **D~** nt -s existence

dasitzen† vi sep (haben) sit there

dasjenige pron s. **derjenige**

dass (daß) conj that; **d~ du nicht fällst!** mind you don't fall!

dasselbe pron s. **derselbe**

dastehen† vi sep (haben) stand there; **allein d~** (fig) be alone

Daten|sichtgerät nt visual display unit, VDU. **D~verarbeitung** f data processing

datieren vt/i (haben) date

Dativ m -s,-e dative. **D~objekt** nt indirect object

Dattel f -,-n date

Datum nt s,-ten date; **Daten** dates; (Angaben) data

Dauer f - duration, length; (*Jur*) term; **von D~** lasting; **auf die D~** in the long run. **D~auftrag** m standing order. **d~haft** a lasting, enduring; (*fest*) durable. **D~karte** f season ticket. **D~lauf** m im **D~lauf** at a jog. **D~milch** f long-life milk. **d~n** vi (*haben*) last; **lange d~n** take a long time. **d~nd** a lasting; (*ständig*) constant, adv -ly; **d~nd fragen** keep asking. **D~stellung** f permanent position. **D~welle** f perm. **D~wurst** f salami-type sausage

Daumen m -s,- thumb; **jdm den D~ drücken** od **halten** keep one's fingers crossed for s.o.

Daunen fpl down sg. **D~decke** f [down-filled] duvet

davon (*emphatic:* **davon**) adv from it/them; (*dadurch*) by it; (*damit*) with it/them; (*darüber*) about it; (*Menge*) of it/them; **die Hälfte d~** half of it/them; **das kommt d~!** it serves you right! **d~kommen†** vi sep (*sein*) escape (**mit dem Leben** with one's life). **d~laufen†** vi sep (*sein*) run away. **d~machen** (**sich**) vr sep (*fam*) make off. **d~tragen†** vt sep carry off; (*erleiden*) suffer; (*gewinnen*) win

davor (*emphatic:* **davor**) adv in front of it/them; (*sich fürchten*) of it; (*zeitlich*) before it/them

dazu (*emphatic:* **dazu**) adv to it/them; (*damit*) with it/them; (*dafür*) for it; **noch d~** in addition to that; **jdn d~ bringen, etw zu tun** get s.o. to do sth; **ich kam nicht d~** I didn't get round to [doing] it. **d~gehören** vi sep (*haben*) belong to it/them; **alles, was d~gehört** everything that goes with it. **d~kommen†** vi sep (*sein*) arrive [on the scene]; (*hinzukommen*) be added; **d~ kommt, dass er krank ist** on top of that he is ill. **d~rechnen** vt sep add to it/them

dazwischen (*emphatic:* **dazwischen**) adv between them; in between; (*darunter*) among them. **d~fahren†** vi sep (*sein*) (*fig*) intervene. **d~kommen†** vi sep (*sein*) (*fig*) crop up; **wenn nichts d~kommt** if all goes well. **d~reden** vi sep (*haben*) interrupt. **d~treten†** vi sep (*sein*) (*fig*) intervene

DDR f - abbr (**Deutsche Demokratische Republik**) GDR

Debatte f -,-n debate; **zur D~te stehen** be at issue. **d~tieren** vt/i (*haben*) debate

Debüt /de'by:/ nt -s,-s début

dechiffrieren /deʃɪ'fri:rən/ vt decipher

Deck nt -[e]s,-s (*Naut*) deck; **an D~** on deck. **D~bett** nt duvet

Decke f -,-n cover; (*Tisch-*) table-cloth; (*Bett-*) blanket; (*Reise-*) rug; (*Zimmer-*) ceiling; **unter einer D~stecken** (*fam*) be in league

Deckel m -s,- lid; (*Flaschen-*) top; (*Buch-*) cover

decken vt cover; tile (*Dach*); lay (*Tisch*); (*schützen*) shield; (*Sport*) mark; meet (*Bedarf*); **jdn d~** (*fig*) cover up for s.o.; **sich d~** (*fig*) cover oneself (**gegen** against); (*übereinstimmen*) coincide

Deck|mantel m (*fig*) pretence. **D~name** m pseudonym

Deckung f - (*Mil*) cover; (*Sport*) defence; (*Mann-*) marking; (*Boxen*) guard; (*Sicherheit*) security; **in D~ gehen** take cover

Defekt m -[e]s,-e defect. **d~** a defective

defensiv a defensive. **D~e** f - defensive

defilieren vi (*sein/haben*) file past

defin|ieren vt define. **D~ition** /-'tsio:n/ f -,-en definition. **d~itiv** a definite, adv -ly

Defizit nt -s,-e deficit

Deflation /-'tsio:n/ f - deflation

deformiert a deformed

deftig a (*fam*) (*Mahlzeit*) hearty; (*Witz*) coarse

Degen m -s,- sword; (*Fecht-*) épée

degenerieren vi (*sein*) degenerate. **d~t** a (*fig*) degenerate

degradieren vt (*Mil*) demote; (*fig*) degrade

dehn|bar a elastic. **d~en** vt stretch; lengthen (*Vokal*); **sich d~en** stretch

Deich m -[e]s,-e dike

Deichsel f -,-n pole; (*Gabel-*) shafts pl

dein poss pron your. **d~e(r,s)** poss pron yours; **die D~en** od **d~en** pl your family sg. **d~erseits** adv for your part. **d~etwegen** adv for your sake; (*wegen dir*) because of you, on your account. **d~etwillen** adv um **d~etwillen** for your sake. **d~ige** poss pron **der/die/das d~ige** yours. **d~s** poss pron yours

Deka nt -[s],- (*Aust*) = **Dekagramm**

dekaden|t a decadent. **D~z** f - decadence

Dekagramm nt (*Aust*) 10 grams; **10 D~** 100 grams

Dekan m -s,-e dean

Deklin|ation /-'tsio:n/ f -,-en declension. **d~ieren** vt decline

Dekolleté, Dekolletee /dekɔl'te:/ nt -s,-s low neckline

Dekor m & nt -s decoration. **D~ateur** /-'tø:ɐ/ m -s,-e interior decorator; (*Schaufenster-*) window-dresser. **D~ation** /-'tsio:n/ f -,-en decoration; (*Schaufenster-*) window-dressing; (*Auslage*) display; **D~ationen** (*Theat*) scenery sg. **d~ativ** a decorative. **d~ieren** vt decorate; dress (*Schaufenster*)

Delegation /-'tsio:n/ f -,-en delegation. **d~ieren** vt delegate. **D~ierte(r)** m/f delegate

Delfin *m* -s,-e = Delphin

delikat *a* delicate; (*lecker*) delicious; (*taktvoll*) tactful, *adv* -ly. **D~esse** *f* -,-n delicacy. **D~essengeschäft** *nt* delicatessen

Delikt *nt* -[e]s,-e offence

Delinquent *m* -en,-en offender

Delirium *nt* -s delirium

Delle *f* -,-n dent

Delphin *m* -s,-e dolphin

Delta *nt* -s,-s delta

dem *def art & pron s.* der

Dement|i *nt* -s,-s denial. **d~ieren** *vt* deny

dem|entsprechend *a* corresponding; (*passend*) appropriate □ *adv* accordingly; (*passend*) appropriately. **d~gemäß** *adv* accordingly. **d~nach** *adv* according to that; (*folglich*) consequently. **d~nächst** *adv* soon; (*in Kürze*) shortly

Demokrat *m* -en,-en democrat. **D~ie** *f* -,-n democracy. **d~isch** *a* democratic, *adv* -ally

demolieren *vt* wreck

Demonstr|ant *m* -en,-en demonstrator. **D~ation** /-'tsjo:n/ *f* -,-en demonstration. **d~ativ** *a* pointed, *adv* -ly; (*Gram*) demonstrative. **D~ativpronomen** *nt* demonstrative pronoun. **d~ieren** *vt/i* (*haben*) demonstrate

demontieren *vt* dismantle

demoralisieren *vt* demoralize

Demoskopie *f* - opinion research

Demut *f* - humility

demütig *a* humble, *adv* -bly. **d~en** *vt* humiliate; **sich d~en** humble oneself. **D~ung** *f* -,-en humiliation

demzufolge *adv* = demnach

den *def art & pron s.* der. **d~en** *pron s.* der

denk|bar *a* conceivable. **d~en†** *vt/i* (*haben*) think (**an** + *acc* of); (*sich erinnern*) remember (**an etw** *acc* sth); **für jdn gedacht** meant for s.o.; **das kann ich mir d~en** I can imagine [that]; **ich d~e nicht daran** I have no intention of doing it; **d~t daran!** don't forget! **D~mal** *nt* memorial; (*Monument*) monument. **d~würdig** *a* memorable. **D~zettel** *m* jdm einen **D~zettel geben** (*fam*) teach s.o. a lesson

denn *conj* for; **besser/mehr d~ je** better/more than ever □ *adv* **wie/wo d~?** but how/where? **warum d~ nicht?** why ever not? **es sei d~ [, dass]** unless

dennoch *adv* nevertheless

Denunz|iant *m* -en,-en informer. **d~ieren** *vt* denounce

Deodorant *nt* -s,-s deodorant

deplaciert, deplatziert (deplaziert) /-'tsi:ɐt/ *a* (*fig*) out of place

Deponie *f* -,-n dump. **d~ren** *vt* deposit

deportieren *vt* deport

Depot /de'po:/ *nt* -s,-s depot; (*Lager*) warehouse; (*Bank-*) safe deposit

Depression *f* -,-en depression

deprimieren *vt* depress. **d~d** *a* depressing

Deputation /-'tsjo:n/ *f* -,-en deputation

der, die, das, *pl* **die** *def art* (*acc* **den, die, das,** *pl* **die;** *gen* **des, der, des,** *pl* **der;** *dat* **dem, der, dem,** *pl* **den**) the; **der Mensch** man; **die Natur** nature; **das Leben** life; **das Lesen/Tanzen** reading/dancing; **sich** (*dat*) **das Gesicht/die Hände waschen** wash one's face/hands; **5 Mark das Pfund** 5 marks a pound □ *pron* (*acc* **den, die, das,** *pl* **die;** *gen* **dessen, deren, dessen,** *pl* **deren;** *dat* **dem, der, dem,** *pl* **denen**) □ *dem pron* that; (*pl*) those; (*substantivisch*) he, she, it; (*Ding*) it; (*betont*) that; (*d~jenige*) the one; (*pl*) they, those; (*Dinge*) those; (*diejenigen*) the ones; **der und der** such and such; **um die und die Zeit** at such and such a time; **das waren Zeiten!** those were the days! □ *rel pron* who; (*Ding*) which, that

derart *adv* so; (*so sehr*) so much. **d~ig** *a* such □ *adv* = derart

derb *a* tough; (*kräftig*) strong; (*grob*) coarse, *adv* -ly; (*unsanft*) rough, *adv* -ly

deren *pron s.* der

dergleichen *inv a* such □ *pron* such a thing/such things; **nichts d~** nothing of the kind; **und d~** and the like

der-/die-/dasjenige, *pl* **diejenigen** *pron* the one; (*Person*) he, she; (*Ding*) it; (*pl*) those, the ones

dermaßen *adv* = derart

der-/die-/dasselbe, *pl* **dieselben** *pron* the same; **ein- und dasselbe** one and the same thing

derzeit *adv* at present

des *def art s.* der

Desert|eur /-'tø:ɐ/ *m* -s,-e deserter. **d~ieren** *vi* (*sein/haben*) desert

desgleichen *adv* likewise □ *pron* the like

deshalb *adv* for this reason; (*also*) therefore

Designer(in) /di'zaɪnɐ, -nərɪn/ *m* -s,- (*f* -,-nen) designer

Desin|fektion /dɛsʔɪnfɛk'tsjo:n/ *f* disinfecting. **D~fektionsmittel** *nt* disinfectant. **d~fizieren** *vt* disinfect

Desodorant *nt* -s,-s deodorant

Despot *m* -en,-en despot

dessen *pron s.* der

Dessert /dɛ'se:ɐ/ *nt* -s,-s dessert, sweet. **D~löffel** *m* dessertspoon

Destill|ation /-'tsjo:n/ *f* - distillation. **d~ieren** *vt* distil

desto *adv* **je mehr/eher, d~ besser** the more/sooner the better

destruktiv *a* (*fig*) destructive

deswegen *adv* = **deshalb**

Detail /de'taj/ *nt* -s,-s detail

Detektiv *m* -s,-e detective. **D~roman** *m* detective story

Deton|ation /-'tsjo:n/ *f* -,-en explosion. **d~ieren** *vi* (*sein*) explode

deut|en *vt* interpret; predict ⟨*Zukunft*⟩ □ *vi* (*haben*) point (**auf** + *acc* at/⟨*fig*⟩ to). **d~lich** *a* clear, *adv* -ly; (*eindeutig*) plain, *adv* -ly. **D~lichkeit** *f* - clarity

deutsch *a* German; **auf d~** NEW **auf D~**, *s.* Deutsch. **D~** *nt* -[s] (*Lang*) German; **auf D~** in German. **D~e(r)** *m*/*f* German. **D~land** *nt* -s Germany

Deutung *f* -,-en interpretation

Devise *f* -,-n motto. **D~n** *pl* foreign currency or exchange *sg*

Dezember *m* -s,- December

dezent *a* unobtrusive, *adv* -ly; (*diskret*) discreet, *adv* -ly

Dezernat *nt* -[e]s,-e department

Dezimal|system *nt* decimal system. **D~zahl** *f* decimal

dezimieren *vt* decimate

dgl. *abbr s.* **dergleichen**

d.h. *abbr* (*das heißt*) i.e.

Dia *nt* -s,-s (*Phot*) slide

Diabet|es *m* - diabetes. **D~iker** *m* -s,- diabetic

Diadem *nt* -s,-e tiara

Diagnos|e *f* -,-n diagnosis. **d~tizieren** *vt* diagnose

diagonal *a* diagonal, *adv* -ly. **D~e** *f* -,-n diagonal

Diagramm *nt* -s,-e diagram; (*Kurven-*) graph

Diakon *m* -s,-e deacon

Dialekt *m* -[e]s,-e dialect

Dialog *m* -[e]s,-e dialogue

Diamant *m* -en,-en diamond

Diameter *m* -s,- diameter

Diapositiv *nt* -s,-e (*Phot*) slide

Diaprojektor *m* slide projector

Diät *f* -,-en (*Med*) diet; **D~ leben** be on a diet. **d~** *adv* **d~ leben** NEW **D~ leben**, *s.* Diät. **D~assistent(in)** *m*(*f*) dietician

dich *pron* (*acc of* **du**) you; (*refl*) yourself

dicht *a* dense; (*dick*) thick; (*undurchlässig*) airtight; (*wasser-*) watertight □ *adv* densely; thickly; (*nahe*) close (**bei** to). **D~e** *f* - density. **d~en¹** *vt* make watertight; (*ab-*) seal

dicht|en² *vi* (*haben*) write poetry □ *vt* write, compose. **D~er(in)** *m* -s,- (*f* -,-en)

poet. **d~erisch** *a* poetic. **D~ung¹** *f* -,-en poetry; (*Gedicht*) poem

Dichtung² *f* -,-en seal; (*Ring*) washer; (*Auto*) gasket

dick *a* thick, *adv* -ly; (*beleibt*) fat; (*geschwollen*) swollen; (*fam; eng*) close; **d~ werden** get fat; **d~ machen** be fattening; **ein d~es Fell haben** (*fam*) be thick-skinned. **D~e** *f* -,-n thickness; (*D~leibigkeit*) fatness. **d~fellig** *a* (*fam*) thick-skinned. **d~flüssig** *a* thick; (*Phys*) viscous. **D~kopf** *m* (*fam*) stubborn person; **einen D~kopf haben** be stubborn. **d~köpfig** *a* (*fam*) stubborn

didaktisch *a* didactic

die *def art & pron s.* **der**

Dieb|(in) *m* -[e]s,-e (*f* -,-nen) thief. **d~isch** *a* thieving; ⟨*Freude*⟩ malicious. **D~stahl** *m* -[e]s,-̈e theft; (*geistig*) plagiarism

diejenige *pron s.* **derjenige**

Diele *f* -,-n floorboard; (*Flur*) hall

dien|en *vi* (*haben*) serve. **D~er** *m* -s,- servant; (*Verbeugung*) bow. **D~erin** *f* -,-nen maid, servant. **d~lich** *a* helpful

Dienst *m* -[e]s,-e service; (*Arbeit*) work; (*Amtsausübung*) duty; **außer D~** off duty; (*pensioniert*) retired; **D~ haben** work; ⟨*Soldat, Arzt:*⟩ be on duty; **der D~ habende Arzt** the duty doctor; **jdm einen schlechten D~ erweisen** do s.o. a disservice

Dienstag *m* Tuesday. **d~s** *adv* on Tuesdays

Dienst|alter *nt* seniority. **d~bereit** *a* obliging; ⟨*Apotheke*⟩ open. **D~bote** *m* servant. **d~eifrig** *a* zealous, *adv* -ly. **d~frei** *a* **d~freier Tag** day off; **d~frei haben** have time off; ⟨*Soldat, Arzt:*⟩ be off duty. **D~grad** *m* rank. **d~habend** *a* NEW **D~ habend**, *s.* Dienst. **D~leistung** *f* service. **d~lich** *a* official □ *adv* **d~lich verreist** away on business. **D~mädchen** *nt* maid. **D~reise** *f* business trip. **D~stelle** *f* office. **D~stunden** *fpl* office hours. **D~weg** *m* official channels *pl*

dies *inv pron* this. **d~bezüglich** *a* relevant □ *adv* regarding this matter. **d~e(r,s)** *pron* this; (*pl*) these; (*substantivisch*) this [one]; (*pl*) these; **d~e Nacht** tonight; (*letzte*) last night

Diesel *m* -[s],- (*fam*) diesel

dieselbe *pron s.* **derselbe**

Diesel|kraftstoff *m* diesel [oil]. **D~motor** *m* diesel engine

diesig *a* hazy, misty

dies|mal *adv* this time. **d~seits** *adv* & *prep* (+ *gen*) this side (of)

Dietrich *m* -s,-e skeleton key

Diffam|ation /-'tsjo:n/ f - defamation. **d~ierend** a defamatory

Differential /-'tsja:l/ nt -s,-e (NEW) Differenzial

Differenz f -,-en difference. **D~ial** nt -s,-e differential. **d~ieren** vt/i (haben) differentiate (**zwischen** + dat between)

Digital- pref digital. **D~uhr** f digital clock/watch

Dikt|at nt -[e]s,-e dictation. **D~ator** m -s,-en /-'to:rən/ dictator. **d~atorisch** a dictatorial. **D~atur** f -,-en dictatorship. **d~ieren** vt/i (haben) dictate

Dilemma nt -s,-s dilemma

Dilettant|(in) m -en,-en (f -,-nen) dilettante. **d~isch** a amateurish

Dill m -s dill

Dimension f -,-en dimension

Ding nt -[e]s,-e & (fam) -er thing; **guter D~e sein** be cheerful; **vor allen D~en** above all

Dinghi /'dɪŋi/ nt -s,-s dinghy

Dinosaurier /-jɐ/ m -s,- dinosaur

Diözese f -,-n diocese

Diphtherie f - diphtheria

Diplom nt -s,-e diploma; (Univ) degree

Diplomat m -en,-en diplomat. **D~ie** f - diplomacy. **d~isch** a diplomatic, adv -ally

dir pron (dat of **du**) [to] you; (refl) yourself; **ein Freund von dir** a friend of yours

direkt a direct □ adv directly; (wirklich) really. **D~ion** /-'tsjo:n/ f - management; (Vorstand) board of directors. **D~or** m -s,-en /-'to:rən/, **D~orin** f -,-nen director; (Bank-, Theater-) manager; (Sch) head; (Gefängnis) governor. **D~übertragung** f live transmission

Dirig|ent m -en,-en (Mus) conductor. **d~ieren** vt direct; (Mus) conduct

Dirndl nt -s,- dirndl [dress]

Dirne f -,-n prostitute

Diskant m -s,-e (Mus) treble

Diskette f -,-n floppy disc

Disko f -,-s (fam) disco. **D~thek** f -,-en discothèque

Diskrepanz f -,-en discrepancy

diskret a discreet, adv -ly. **D~ion** /-'tsjo:n/ f discretion

diskriminier|en vt discriminate against. **D~ung** f - discrimination

Diskus m -,-se & **Disken** discus

Disku|ssion f -,-en discussion. **d~tieren** vt/i (haben) discuss

disponieren vi (haben) make arrangements; **d~ [können] über** (+ acc) have at one's disposal

Disput m -[e]s,-e dispute

Disqualifi|kation /-'tsjo:n/ f disqualification. **d~zieren** vt disqualify

Dissertation /-'tsjo:n/ f -,-en dissertation

Dissident m -en,-en dissident

Dissonanz f -,-en dissonance

Distanz f -,-en distance. **d~ieren (sich)** vr dissociate oneself (**von** from). **d~iert** a aloof

Distel f -,-n thistle

distinguiert /dɪstɪŋ'gi:ɐt/ a distinguished

Disziplin f -,-en discipline. **d~arisch** a disciplinary. **d~iert** a disciplined

dito adv ditto

diverse attrib a pl various

Divid|ende f -,-en dividend. **d~ieren** vt divide (**durch** by)

Division f -,-en division

DJH abbr (**Deutsche Jugendherberge**) [German] youth hostel

DM abbr (**Deutsche Mark**) DM

doch conj & adv but; (dennoch) yet; (trotzdem) after all; **wenn d~ ...!** if only ...! **nicht d~!** don't [do that]! **er kommt d~?** he is coming, isn't he? **kommst du nicht?** —**d~!** aren't you coming?—yes, I am!

Docht m -[e]s,-e wick

Dock nt -s,-s dock. **d~en** vt/i (haben) dock

Dogge f -,-n Great Dane

Dogm|a nt -s,-men dogma. **d~atisch** a dogmatic, adv -ally

Dohle f -,-n jackdaw

Doktor m -s,-en /-'to:rən/ doctor. **D~arbeit** f [doctoral] thesis. **D~würde** f doctorate

Doktrin f -,-en doctrine

Dokument nt -[e]s,-e document. **D~arbericht** m documentary. **D~arfilm** m documentary film

Dolch m -[e]s,-e dagger

doll a (fam) fantastic; (schlimm) awful □ adv beautifully; (sehr) very; (schlimm) badly

Dollar m -s,- dollar

dolmetsch|en vt/i (haben) interpret. **D~er(in)** m -s,- (f -,-nen) interpreter

Dom m -[e]s,-e cathedral

domin|ant a dominant. **d~ieren** vi (haben) dominate; (vorherrschen) predominate

Domino nt -s,-s dominoes sg. **D~stein** m domino

Dompfaff m -en,-en bullfinch

Donau f - Danube

Donner m -s thunder. **d~n** vi (haben) thunder

Donnerstag *m* Thursday. **d~s** *adv* on Thursdays

Donnerwetter *nt* (*fam*) telling-off; (*Krach*) row □ *int* /'--'--/ wow! (*Fluch*) damn it!

doof *a* (*fam*) stupid, *adv* -ly

Doppel *nt* -s,- duplicate; (*Tennis*) doubles *pl*. **D~bett** *nt* double bed. **D~decker** *m* -s,- doubledecker [bus]. **d~deutig** *a* ambiguous. **D~gänger** *m* -s,- double. **D~kinn** *nt* double chin. **D~name** *m* double-barrelled name. **D~punkt** *m* (*Gram*) colon. **D~schnitte** *f* sandwich. **d~sinnig** *a* ambiguous. **D~stecker** *m* two-way adaptor. **d~t** *a* double; (*Boden*) false; **in d~ter Ausfertigung** in duplicate; **die d~te Menge** twice the amount □ *adv* doubly; (*zweimal*) twice; **d~t so viel** twice as much. **D~zimmer** *nt* double room

Dorf *nt* -[e]s,¨er village. **D~bewohner** *m* villager

dörflich *a* rural

Dorn *m* -[e]s,-en thorn. **d~ig** *a* thorny

Dörrobst *nt* dried fruit

Dorsch *m* -[e]s,-e cod

dort *adv* there; **d~ drüben** over there. **d~her** *adv* [von] **d~her** from there. **d~hin** *adv* there. **d~ig** *a* local

Dose *f* -,-n tin, can; (*Schmuck-*) box

dösen *vi* (*haben*) doze

Dosen|milch *f* evaporated milk. **D~öffner** *m* tin or can opener

dosieren *vt* measure out

Dosis *f* -, Dosen dose

Dotter *m & nt* -s,- [egg] yolk

Dozent(in) *m* -en,-en *f* (*-,-nen*) (*Univ*) lecturer

Dr. *abbr* (**Doktor**) Dr

Drache *m* -n,-n dragon. **D~n** *m* -s,- kite; (*fam: Frau*) dragon. **D~nfliegen** *nt* hanggliding. **D~nflieger** *m* hang-glider

Draht *m* -[e]s,¨e wire; **auf D~** (*fam*) on the ball. **d~ig** *a* (*fig*) wiry. **D~seilbahn** *f* cable railway

drall *a* plump; (*Frau*) buxom

Dram|a *nt* -s,-men drama. **D~atik** *f* - drama. **D~atiker** *m* -s,- dramatist. **d~a-tisch** *a* dramatic, *adv* -ally. **d~atisieren** *vt* dramatize

dran *adv* (*fam*) = **daran**; **gut/schlecht d~sein** be well off/in a bad way; **ich bin d~** it's my turn

Dränage /-'na:ʒə/ *f* - drainage

Drang *m* -[e]s urge; (*Druck*) pressure

dräng|eln *vt/i* (*haben*) push; (*bedrängen*) pester. **d~en** *vt* push; (*bedrängen*) urge; **sich d~en** crowd (**um** round) □ *vi* (*haben*)

push; (*eilen*) be urgent; ⟨*Zeit:*⟩ press; **d~en auf** (+ *acc*) press for

dran|halten† (**sich**) *vr sep* hurry. **d~kommen†** *vi sep* (*sein*) have one's turn; **wer kommt dran?** whose turn is it?

drapieren *vt* drape

drastisch *a* drastic, *adv* -ally

drauf *adv* (*fam*) = **darauf; d~ und dran sein** be on the point (**etw zu tun** of doing sth). **D~gänger** *m* -s,- daredevil. **d~gän-gerisch** *a* reckless

draus *adv* (*fam*) = **daraus**

draußen *adv* outside; (*im Freien*) out of doors

drechseln *vt* (*Techn*) turn

Dreck *m* -s dirt; (*Morast*) mud; (*fam: Kleinigkeit*) trifle; **in den D~ ziehen** (*fig*) denigrate. **d~ig** *a* dirty; muddy

Dreh *m* -s (*fam*) knack; **den D~ heraus-haben** have got the hang of it. **D~bank** *f* lathe. **D~bleistift** *m* propelling pencil. **D~buch** *nt* screenplay, script. **d~en** *vt* turn; (*im Kreis*) rotate; (*verschlingen*) twist; roll ⟨*Zigarette*⟩; shoot ⟨*Film*⟩; **lauter/leiser d~en** turn up/down; **sich d~en** turn; (*im Kreis*) rotate; (*schnell*) spin; ⟨*Wind:*⟩ change; **sich d~en um** revolve around; (*sich handeln*) be about □ *vi* (*haben*) turn; ⟨*Wind:*⟩ change; **an etw** (*dat*) **d~en** turn sth. **D~orgel** *f* barrel organ. **D~stuhl** *m* swivel chair. **D~tür** *f* revolving door. **D~ung** *f* -,-en turn; (*im Kreis*) rotation. **D~zahl** *f* number of revolutions

drei *inv a*, **D~** *f* -,-en three; (*Sch*) ≈ pass. **D~eck** *nt* -[e]s,-e triangle. **d~eckig** *a* triangular. **D~einigkeit** *f* - **die [Heilige] D~einigkeit** the [Holy] Trinity. **d~erlei** *inv a* three kinds of □ *pron* three things. **d~fach** *a* triple; **in d~facher Ausferti-gung** in triplicate. **D~faltigkeit** *f* - = **D~einigkeit. d~mal** *adv* three times. **D~rad** *nt* tricycle

dreißig *inv a* thirty. **d~ste(r,s)** *a* thirtieth

dreist *a* impudent, *adv* -ly; (*verwegen*) audacious, *adv* -ly. **D~igkeit** *f* - impudence; audacity

dreiviertel *inv a* ⟨NEW⟩ **drei viertel**, *s.* **viertel. D~stunde** *f* three-quarters of an hour

dreizehn *inv a* thirteen. **d~te(r,s)** *a* thirteenth

dreschen† *vt* thresh

dress|ieren *vt* train. **D~ur** *f* - training

dribbeln *vi* (*haben*) dribble

Drill *m* -[e]s (*Mil*) drill. **d~en** *vt* drill

Drillinge *mpl* triplets

drin *adv* (*fam*) = **darin**; (*drinnen*) inside

dring|en† *vi* (*sein*) penetrate (**in** + *acc* into; **durch etw** sth); (*heraus-*) come (**aus**

out of); **d~en auf** (+ *acc*) insist on. **d~end**
a urgent, *adv* -ly. **d~lich** *a* urgent.
D~lichkeit *f* - urgency

Drink *m* -[s],-s [alcoholic] drink

drinnen *adv* inside; (*im Haus*) indoors

dritt *adv* **zu d~** in threes; **wir waren zu
d~** there were three of us. **d~e(r,s)** *a*
third; **ein D~er** a third person. **d~el** *inv*
a third; **ein d~el Apfel** a third of an apple.
D~el *nt* -s,- third. **d~ens** *adv* thirdly.
d~rangig *a* third-rate

Drog|e *f* -,-n drug. **D~enabhängige(r)**
m/f drug addict. **D~erie** *f* -,-n chemist's
shop, (*Amer*) drugstore. **D~ist** *m* -en,-en
chemist

drohen *vi* (*haben*) threaten (**jdm** s.o.).
d~d *a* threatening; (*Gefahr*) imminent

dröhnen *vi* (*haben*) resound; (*tönen*) boom

Drohung *f* -,-en threat

drollig *a* funny; (*seltsam*) odd

Drops *m* -,- [fruit] drop

Droschke *f* -,-n cab

Drossel *f* -,-n thrush

drosseln *vt* (*Techn*) throttle; (*fig*) cut back

drüb|en *adv* over there. **d~er** *adv* (*fam*) =
darüber

Druck¹ *m* -[e]s,-̈e pressure; **unter D~
setzen** (*fig*) pressurize

Druck² *m* -[e]s,-e printing; (*Schrift, Repro-
duktion*) print. **D~buchstabe** *m* block letter

Drückeberger *m* -s,- shirker

drucken *vt* print

drücken *vt/i* (*haben*) press; (*aus-*)
squeeze; (*Schuh:*) pinch; (*umarmen*) hug;
(*fig: belasten*) weigh down; **Preise d~**
force down prices; (*an Tür*) **d~** push; **sich
d~** (*fam*) make oneself scarce; **sich d~
vor** (+ *dat*) (*fam*) shirk. **d~d** *a* heavy;
(*schwül*) oppressive

Drucker *m* -s,- printer

Drücker *m* -s,- push-button; (*Tür-*) door
knob

Druckerei *f* -,-en printing works

Druck|fehler *m* misprint. **D~knopf** *m*
press-stud; (*Drücker*) push-button.
D~luft *f* compressed air. **D~sache** *f*
printed matter. **D~schrift** *f* type; (*Veröffentlichung*) publication; **in D~schrift** in
block letters *pl*

drucksen *vi* (*haben*) hum and haw

Druck|stelle *f* bruise. **D~taste** *f* push-
button. **D~topf** *m* pressure-cooker

drum *adv* (*fam*) = darum

drunter *adv* (*fam*) = darunter; **alles
geht d~ und drüber** (*fam*) everything is
topsy-turvy

Drüse *f* -,-n (*Anat*) gland

Dschungel *m* -s,- jungle

du *pron* (*familiar address*) you; **auf Du und
Du** (*auf du und du*) on familiar terms

Dübel *m* -s,- plug

duck|en *vt* duck; (*fig: demütigen*) humili-
ate; **sich d~en** duck; (*fig*) cringe.
D~mäuser *m* -s,- moral coward

Dudelsack *m* bagpipes *pl*

Duell *nt* -s,-e duel

Duett *nt* -s,-e [vocal] duet

Duft *m* -[e]s,-̈e fragrance, scent; (*Aroma*)
aroma. **d~en** *vi* (*haben*) smell (**nach** of).
d~ig *a* fine; (*zart*) delicate

duld|en *vt* tolerate; (*erleiden*) suffer □ *vi*
(*haben*) suffer. **d~sam** *a* tolerant

dumm *a* (**dümmer, dümmst**) stupid, *adv*
-ly; (*unklug*) foolish, *adv* -ly; (*fam: lästig*)
awkward; **wie d~!** what a nuisance! **der
D~e sein** (*fig*) be the loser. **d~erweise**
adv stupidly; (*leider*) unfortunately.
D~heit *f* -,-en stupidity; (*Torheit*) fool-
ishness; (*Handlung*) folly. **D~kopf** *m*
(*fam*) fool.

dumpf *a* dull, *adv* -y; (*muffig*) musty. **d~ig**
a musty

Düne *f* -,-n dune

Dung *m* -s manure

Düng|emittel *nt* fertilizer. **d~en** *vt* fertil-
ize. **D~er** *m* -s,- fertilizer

dunk|el *a* dark; (*vage*) vague, *adv* -ly;
(*fragwürdig*) shady; **d~les Bier** brown
ale; **im D~eln** in the dark

Dünkel *m* -s conceit

dunkel|blau *a* dark blue. **d~braun** *a*
dark brown

dünkelhaft *a* conceited

Dunkel|heit *f* - darkness. **D~kammer** *f*
dark-room. **d~n** *vi* (*haben*) get dark.
d~rot *a* dark red

dünn *a* thin, *adv* -ly; (*Buch*) slim; (*spärlich*)
sparse; (*schwach*) weak

Dunst *m* -es,-̈e mist, haze; (*Dampf*) vapour

dünsten *vt* steam

dunstig *a* misty, hazy

Dünung *f* - swell

Duo *nt* -s,-s [instrumental] duet

Duplikat *nt* -[e]s,-e duplicate

Dur *nt* - (*Mus*) major [key]; **in A-Dur** in A
major

durch *prep* (+ *acc*) through; (*mittels*) by;
[**geteilt**] **d~** (*Math*) divided by □ *adv* **die
Nacht d~** throughout the night; **sechs
Uhr d~** (*fam*) gone six o'clock; **d~ und
d~ nass** wet through

durcharbeiten *vt sep* work through; **sich
d~** work one's way through

durchaus *adv* absolutely; **d~ nicht** by no
means

durchbeißen† *vt sep* bite through

durchblättern *vt sep* leaf through

durchblicken *vi sep* (*haben*) look through; **d~ lassen** (*fig*) hint at

Durchblutung *f* circulation

durchbohren *vt insep* pierce

durchbrechen†[1] *vt/i sep* (*haben*) break [in two]

durchbrechen†[2] *vt insep* break through; break ⟨*Schallmauer*⟩

durchbrennen† *vi sep* (*sein*) burn through; ⟨*Sicherung:*⟩ blow; (*fam: weglaufen*) run away

durchbringen† *vt sep* get through; (*verschwenden*) squander; (*versorgen*) support; **sich d~ mit** make a living by

Durchbruch *m* breakthrough

durchdacht *a* **gut d~** well thought out

durchdrehen *v sep* ⟡ *vt* mince ⟡ *vi* (*haben/sein*) (*fam*) go crazy

durchdringen†[1] *vt insep* penetrate

durchdringen†[2] *vi sep* (*sein*) penetrate; (*sich durchsetzen*) get one's way. **d~d** *a* penetrating; ⟨*Schrei*⟩ piercing

durcheinander *adv* in a muddle; ⟨*Person*⟩ confused; **d~ bringen** muddle [up]; confuse ⟨*Person*⟩; **d~ geraten** get mixed up; **d~ reden** all talk at once. **D~** *nt* -s muddle. **d~bringen**† *vt sep* NEW **d~ bringen**, *s.* **durcheinander. d~geraten**† *vi sep* (*sein*) NEW **d~ geraten**, *s.* **durcheinander. d~reden** *vi sep* (*haben*) NEW **d~ reden**, *s.* **durcheinander**

durchfahren[1] *vi sep* (*sein*) drive through; ⟨*Zug:*⟩ go through

durchfahren†[2] *vt insep* drive/go through; **jdn d~** ⟨*Gedanke:*⟩ flash through s.o.'s mind

Durchfahrt *f* journey/drive through; **auf der D~** passing through; '**D~ verboten**' 'no thoroughfare'

Durchfall *m* diarrhoea; (*fam: Versagen*) flop. **d~en**/*vi sep* (*sein*) fall through; (*fam: versagen*) flop; (*bei Prüfung*) fail

durchfliegen†[1] *vi sep* (*sein*) fly through; (*fam: durchfallen*) fail

durchfliegen†[2] *vt insep* fly through; (*lesen*) skim through

durchfroren *a* frozen

Durchfuhr *f* - (*Comm*) transit

durchführ|bar *a* feasible. **d~en** *vt sep* carry out

Durchgang *m* passage; (*Sport*) round; '**D~ verboten**' 'no entry'. **D~sverkehr** *m* through traffic

durchgeben† *vt sep* pass through; (*übermitteln*) transmit; (*Radio, TV*) broadcast

durchgebraten *a* **gut d~** well done

durchgehen† *v sep* ⟡ *vi* (*sein*) go through; (*davonlaufen*) run away; ⟨*Pferd:*⟩ bolt; **jdm etw d~ lassen** let s.o. get away with sth ⟡ *vt* go through. **d~d** *a* continuous, *adv* -ly; **d~d geöffnet** open all day; **d~der Wagen/Zug** through carriage/train

durchgreifen† *vi sep* (*haben*) reach through; (*vorgehen*) take drastic action. **d~d** *a* drastic

durchhalte|n† *v sep* (*fig*) ⟡ *vi* (*haben*) hold out ⟡ *vt* keep up. **D~vermögen** *nt* stamina

durchhängen† *vi sep* (*haben*) sag

durchkommen† *vi sep* (*sein*) come through; (*gelangen, am Telefon*) get through; (*bestehen*) pass; (*überleben*) pull through; (*finanziell*) get by (**mit** on)

durchkreuzen *vt insep* thwart

durchlassen† *vt sep* let through

durchlässig *a* permeable; (*undicht*) leaky

durchlaufen†[1] *v sep* ⟡ *vi* (*sein*) run through ⟡ *vt* wear out

durchlaufen†[2] *vt insep* pass through

Durchlauferhitzer *m* -s,- geyser

durchleben *vt insep* live through

durchlesen† *vt sep* read through

durchleuchten *vt insep* X-ray

durchlöchert *a* riddled with holes

durchmachen *vt sep* go through; (*erleiden*) undergo; have ⟨*Krankheit*⟩

Durchmesser *m* -s,- diameter

durchnässt (**durchnäßt**) *a* wet through

durchnehmen† *vt sep* (*Sch*) do

durchnummeriert (**durchnumeriert**) *a* numbered consecutively

durchpausen *vt sep* trace

durchqueren *vt insep* cross

Durchreiche *f* -,-n (*serving*) hatch. **d~n** *vt sep* pass through

Durchreise *f* journey through; **auf der D~** passing through. **d~n** *vi sep* (*sein*) pass through

durchreißen† *vt/i sep* (*sein*) tear

durchs *adv* = **durch das**

Durchsage *f* -,-n announcement. **d~n** *vt sep* announce

durchschauen *vt insep* (*fig*) see through

durchscheinend *a* translucent

Durchschlag *m* carbon copy; (*Culin*) colander. **d~en**†[1] *v sep* ⟡ *vt* (*Culin*) rub through a sieve; **sich d~en** (*fig*) struggle through ⟡ *vi* (*sein*) ⟨*Sicherung:*⟩ blow

durchschlagen†[2] *vt insep* smash

durchschlagend *a* (*fig*) effective; (*Erfolg*) resounding

durchschneiden† *vt sep* cut

Durchschnitt *m* average; **im D~** on average. **d~lich** *a* average □ *adv* on average. **D~s-** *pref* average

Durchschrift *f* carbon copy

durchsehen† *v sep* □ *vi* (*haben*) see through □ *vt* look through

durchseihen *vt sep* strain

durchsetzen[1] *vt sep* force through; **sich d~** assert oneself; ⟨*Mode:*⟩ catch on

durchsetzen[2] *vt insep* intersperse; (*infiltrieren*) infiltrate

Durchsicht *f* check

durchsichtig *a* transparent

durchsickern *vi sep* (*sein*) seep through; ⟨*Neuigkeit:*⟩ leak out

durchsprechen† *vt sep* discuss

durchstehen† *vt sep* (*fig*) come through

durchstreichen† *vt sep* cross out

durchsuch|en *vt insep* search. **D~ung** *f* -,-en search

durchtrieben *a* cunning

durchwachsen *a* ⟨*Speck*⟩ streaky; (*fam: gemischt*) mixed

durchwacht *a* sleepless ⟨*Nacht*⟩

durchwählen *vi sep* (*haben*) (*Teleph*) dial direct

durchweg *adv* without exception

durchweicht *a* soggy

durchwühlen *vt insep* rummage through; ransack ⟨*Haus*⟩

durchziehen† *v sep* □ *vt* pull through □ *vi* (*sein*) pass through

durchzucken *vt insep* (*fig*) shoot through; **jdn d~** ⟨*Gedanke:*⟩ flash through s.o.'s mind

Durchzug *m* through draught

dürfen† *vt & v aux* **etw [tun] d~** be allowed to do sth; **darf ich?** may I? **sie darf es nicht sehen** she must not see it; **ich hätte es nicht tun/sagen d~** I ought not to have done/said it; **das dürfte nicht allzu schwer sein** that should not be too difficult

dürftig *a* poor; ⟨*Mahlzeit*⟩ scanty

dürr *a* dry; ⟨*Boden*⟩ arid; (*mager*) skinny. **D~e** *f* -,-n drought

Durst *m* -[e]s thirst; **D~ haben** be thirsty. **d~en** *vi* (*haben*) be thirsty. **d~ig** *a* thirsty

Dusche *f* -,-n shower. **d~n** *vi/r* (*haben*) [sich] **d~n** have a shower

Düse *f* -,-n nozzle. **D~nflugzeug** *nt* jet

düster *a* gloomy, *adv* -ily; (*dunkel*) dark

Dutzend *nt* -s,-e dozen. **d~weise** *adv* by the dozen

duzen *vt* **jdn d~** call s.o. 'du'

Dynam|ik *f* - dynamics *sg*; (*fig*) dynamism. **d~isch** *a* dynamic; ⟨*Rente*⟩ index-linked

Dynamit *nt* -es dynamite

Dynamo *m* -s,-s dynamo

Dynastie *f* -,-n dynasty

D-Zug /'de:-/ *m* express [train]

E

Ebbe *f* -,-n low tide

eben *a* level; (*glatt*) smooth; **zu e~er Erde** on the ground floor □ *adv* just; (*genau*) exactly; **e~ noch** only just; (*gerade vorhin*) just now; **das ist es e~!** that's just it! **[na] e~** exactly! **E~bild** *nt* image. **e~bürtig** *a* equal; **jdm e~bürtig sein** be s.o.'s equal

Ebene *f* -,-n (*Geog*) plain; (*Geom*) plane; (*fig: Niveau*) level

eben|falls *adv* also; **danke, e~falls** thank you, [the] same to you. **E~holz** *nt* ebony. **e~mäßig** *a* regular, *adv* -ly. **e~so** *adv* just the same; (*ebenso sehr*) just as much; **e~so schön/teuer** just as beautiful/expensive; **e~so gut** just as good; *adv* just as well; **e~so sehr** just as much; **e~so viel** just as much/many; **e~so wenig** just as little/few; (*noch*) no more. **e~sogut** *adv* NEW **e~so gut**, *s.* ebenso. **e~sosehr** *adv* NEW **e~so sehr**, *s.* ebenso. **e~soviel** *adv* NEW **e~so viel**, *s.* ebenso. **e~sowenig** *adv* NEW **e~so wenig**, *s.* ebenso

Eber *m* -s,- boar. **E~esche** *f* rowan

ebnen *vt* level; (*fig*) smooth

Echo *nt* -s,-s echo. **e~en** *vt/i* (*haben*) echo

echt *a* genuine, real; (*authentisch*) authentic; ⟨*Farbe*⟩ fast; (*typisch*) typical □ *adv* (*fam*) really; typically. **E~heit** *f* - authenticity

Eck|ball *m* (*Sport*) corner. **E~e** *f* -,-n corner; **um die E~e bringen** (*fam*) bump off. **e~ig** *a* angular; ⟨*Klammern*⟩ square; (*unbeholfen*) awkward. **E~stein** *m* corner-stone. **E~stoß** *m* = **E~ball**. **E~zahn** *m* canine tooth

Ecu, ECU /e'ky:/ *m* -[s],-[s] ecu

edel *a* noble, *adv* -bly; (*wertvoll*) precious; (*fein*) fine. **E~mann** *m* (*pl* -leute) nobleman. **E~mut** *m* magnanimity. **e~mütig** *a* magnanimous, *adv* -ly. **E~stahl** *m* stainless steel. **E~stein** *m* precious stone

Efeu *m* -s ivy

Effekt *m* -[e]s,-e effect. **E~en** *pl* securities. **e~iv** *a* actual, *adv* -ly; (*wirksam*) effective, *adv* -ly. **e~voll** *a* effective

EG f - abbr (Europäische Gemeinschaft) EC

egal a das ist mir e~ (fam) it's all the same to me □ adv e~ wie/wo no matter how/where. **e~itär** a egalitarian

Egge f -,-n harrow

Ego|ismus m - selfishness. **E~ist(in)** m -en,-en (f -,-nen) egoist. **e~istisch** a selfish, adv -ly. **e~zentrisch** a egocentric

eh adv (Aust fam) anyway; **seit eh und je** from time immemorial

ehe conj before; **ehe nicht** until

Ehe f -,-n marriage. **E~bett** nt double bed. **E~bruch** m adultery. **E~frau** f wife. **E~leute** pl married couple sg. **e~lich** a marital; ⟨Recht⟩ conjugal; ⟨Kind⟩ legitimate

ehemal|ig a former. **e~s** adv formerly

Ehe|mann m (pl -männer) husband. **E~paar** nt married couple

eher adv earlier, sooner; (lieber, vielmehr) rather; (mehr) more

Ehering m wedding ring

ehr|bar a respectable. **E~e** f -,-n honour; **jdm E~e machen** do credit to s.o. **e~en** vt honour. **e~enamtlich** a honorary □ adv in an honorary capacity. **E~endoktorat** nt honorary doctorate. **E~engast** m guest of honour. **e~enhaft** a honourable, adv -bly. **e~enmann** m (pl -männer) man of honour. **E~enmitglied** nt honorary member. **e~enrührig** a defamatory. **E~enrunde** f lap of honour. **E~ensache** f point of honour. **e~enwert** a honourable. **E~enwort** nt word of honour. **e~erbietig** a deferential, adv -ly. **E~erbietung** f - deference. **E~erfurcht** f reverence; ⟨Scheu⟩ awe. **e~erfürchtig** a reverent, adv -ly. **E~egefühl** nt sense of honour. **E~egeiz** m ambition. **e~egeizig** a ambitious. **e~elich** a honest, adv -ly; **e~lich gesagt** to be honest. **E~elichkeit** f - honesty. **e~elos** a dishonourable. **e~esam** a respectable. **e~ewürdig** a venerable; (als Anrede) Reverend

Ei nt -[e]s,-er egg

Eibe f -,-n yew

Eiche f -,-n oak. **E~l** f -,-n acorn. **E~lhäher** m -s,- jay

eichen vt standardize

Eichhörnchen nt -s,- squirrel

Eid m -[e]s,-e oath

Eidechse f -,-n lizard

eidlich a sworn □ adv on oath

Eidotter m & nt egg yolk

Eier|becher m egg-cup. **E~kuchen** m pancake; (Omelett) omelette. **E~schale** f eggshell. **E~schnee** m beaten egg-white. **E~stock** m ovary. **E~uhr** f egg-timer

Eifer m -s eagerness; (Streben) zeal. **E~sucht** f jealousy. **e~süchtig** a jealous, adv -ly

eiförmig a egg-shaped; (oval) oval

eifrig a eager, adv -ly; (begeistert) keen, adv -ly

Eigelb nt -[e]s,-e [egg] yolk

eigen a own; (typisch) characteristic (dat of); (seltsam) odd, adv -ly; (genau) particular. **E~art** f peculiarity. **e~artig** a peculiar, adv -ly; (seltsam) odd. **E~brötler** m -s,- crank. **e~händig** a personal, adv -ly; ⟨Unterschrift⟩ own. **E~heit** f -,-en peculiarity. **e~mächtig** a high-handed; (unbefugt) unauthorized □ adv high-handedly; without authority. **E~name** m proper name. **E~nutz** m self-interest. **e~nützig** a selfish, adv -ly. **e~s** adv specially. **E~schaft** f -,-en quality; (Phys) property; (Merkmal) characteristic; (Funktion) capacity. **E~schaftswort** nt (pl -wörter) adjective. **E~sinn** m obstinacy. **e~sinnig** a obstinate, adv -ly

eigentlich a actual, real; (wahr) true □ adv actually, really; (streng genommen) strictly speaking; **wie geht es ihm e~?** by the way, how is he?

Eigen|tor nt own goal. **E~tum** nt -s property. **E~tümer(in)** m -s,- (f -,-nen) owner. **e~tümlich** a odd, adv -ly; (typisch) characteristic. **E~tumswohnung** f freehold flat. **e~willig** a self-willed; ⟨Stil⟩ highly individual

eign|en (sich) vr be suitable. **E~ung** f - suitability

Eil|brief m express letter. **E~e** f - hurry; **E~e haben** be in a hurry; ⟨Sache:⟩ be urgent. **e~en** vi (sein) hurry □ (haben) (drängen) be urgent. **e~ends** adv hurriedly. **e~ig** a hurried, adv -ly; (dringend) urgent, adv -ly; **es e~ig haben** be in a hurry. **E~zug** m semi-fast train

Eimer m -s,- bucket; (Abfall-) bin

ein¹ adj one; **e~es Tages/ Abends** one day/ evening; **mit jdm in einem Zimmer schlafen** sleep in the same room as s.o. □ indef art a, (vor Vokal) an; **so ein** such a; **was für ein** (Frage) what kind of a? (Ausruf) what a!

ein² adv **ein und aus** in and out; **nicht mehr ein noch aus wissen** (fam) be at one's wits' end

einander pron one another

einarbeiten vt sep train

einäscher|n vt sep reduce to ashes; cremate ⟨Leiche⟩. **E~ung** f -,-en cremation

einatmen vt/i sep (haben) inhale, breathe in

ein|äugig a one-eyed. **E~bahnstraße** f one-way street

einbalsamieren *vt sep* embalm

Einband *m* binding

Einbau *m* installation; (*Montage*) fitting. **e~en** *vt sep* install; (*montieren*) fit. **E~küche** *f* fitted kitchen

einbegriffen *pred a* included

einberuf|en† *vt sep* convene; (*Mil*) call up, (*Amer*) draft. **E~ung** *f* call-up, (*Amer*) draft

Einbettzimmer *nt* single room

einbeulen *vt sep* dent

einbeziehen† *vt sep* [mit] **e~** include; (*berücksichtigen*) take into account

einbiegen† *vi sep* (*sein*) turn

einbild|en *vt sep* sich (*dat*) etw **e~en** imagine sth; **sich** (*dat*) **viel e~en** be conceited. **E~ung** *f* imagination; (*Dünkel*) conceit. **E~ungskraft** *f* imagination

einbläuen *vt sep* **jdm etw e~** (*fam*) drum sth into s.o.

einblenden *vt sep* fade in

einbleuen *vt sep* (NEW) einbläuen

Einblick *m* insight

einbrech|en† *vi sep* (*haben/sein*) break in; **bei uns ist eingebrochen worden** we have been burgled □ (*sein*) set in; (*Nacht:*) fall. **E~er** *m* burglar

einbring|en† *vt sep* get in; bring in (*Geld*); **das bringt nichts ein** it's not worth while. **e~lich** *a* profitable

Einbruch *m* burglary; bei **E~ der Nacht** at nightfall

einbürger|n *vt sep* naturalize; **sich e~n** become established. **E~ung** *f* - naturalization

Ein|buße *f* loss (an + *dat* of). **e~büßen** *vt sep* lose

einchecken /-tʃɛkən/ *vt/i sep* (*haben*) check in

eindecken (sich) *vr sep* stock up

eindeutig *a* unambiguous; (*deutlich*) clear, *adv* -ly

eindicken *vt sep* (*Culin*) thicken

eindring|en† *vi sep* (*sein*) **e~en in** (+ *acc*) penetrate into; (*mit Gewalt*) force one's/ (*Wasser:*) its way into; (*Mil*) invade; **auf jdn e~en** (*fig*) press s.o.; (*bittend*) plead with s.o. **e~lich** *a* urgent, *adv* -ly. **E~ling** *m* -s,-e intruder

Eindruck *m* impression; **E~ machen** impress (**auf jdn** s.o.)

eindrücken *vt sep* crush

eindrucksvoll *a* impressive

ein|e(r,s) *pron* one; (*jemand*) someone; (*man*) one, you; **e~er von uns** one of us; **es macht e~en müde** it makes you tired

einebnen *vt sep* level

eineiig *a* (*Zwillinge*) identical

eineinhalb *inv a* one and a half; **e~ Stunden** an hour and a half

Einelternfamilie *f* one-parent family

einengen *vt sep* restrict

Einer *m* -s,- (*Math*) unit. **e~** *pron s.* **eine(r,s)**. **e~lei** *inv a* □ *attrib a* one kind of; (*eintönig, einheitlich*) the same □ *pred a* (*fam*) immaterial; **es ist mir e~lei** it's all the same to me. **E~lei** *nt* -s monotony. **e~seits** *adv* on the one hand

einfach *a* simple, *adv* -ly; (*Essen*) plain; (*Faden, Fahrt, Fahrkarte*) single; **e~er Soldat** private. **E~heit** *f* - simplicity

einfädeln *vt sep* thread; (*fig: arrangieren*) arrange; **sich e~** (*Auto*) filter in

einfahr|en *v sep* □ *vi* (*sein*) arrive; (*Zug:*) pull in □ *vt* (*Auto*) run in; **die Ernte e~en** get in the harvest. **E~t** *f* arrival; (*Eingang*) entrance, way in; (*Auffahrt*) drive; (*Autobahn-*) access road; **keine E~t** no entry

Einfall *m* idea; (*Mil*) invasion. **e~en**† *vi sep* (*sein*) collapse; (*eindringen*) invade; (*einstimmen*) join in; **jdm e~en** occur to s.o.; **sein Name fällt mir nicht ein** I can't think of his name; **was fällt ihm ein!** what does he think he is doing! **e~sreich** *a* imaginative

Einfalt *f* - naïvety

einfältig *a* simple; (*naiv*) naïve

Einfaltspinsel *m* simpleton

einfangen† *vt sep* catch

einfarbig *a* of one colour; (*Stoff, Kleid*) plain

einfass|en *vt sep* edge; set (*Edelstein*). **E~ung** *f* border, edging

einfetten *vt sep* grease

einfinden† **(sich)** *vr sep* turn up

einfließen† *vi sep* (*sein*) flow in

einflößen *vt sep* **jdm etw e~** give s.o. sips of sth; **jdm Angst e~** (*fig*) frighten s.o.

Einfluss (**Einfluß**) *m* influence. **e~reich** *a* influential

einförmig *a* monotonous, *adv* -ly. **E~keit** *f* - monotony

einfried[ig]en *vt sep* enclose. **E~ung** *f* -,-en enclosure

einfrieren† *vt/i sep* (*sein*) freeze

einfügen *vt sep* insert; (*einschieben*) interpolate; **sich e~** fit in

einfühl|en (sich) *vr sep* empathize (**in** + *acc* with). **e~sam** *a* sensitive

Einfuhr *f* -,-en import

einführ|en *vt sep* introduce; (*einstecken*) insert; (*einweisen*) initiate; (*Comm*) import. **e~end** *a* introductory. **E~ung** *f* introduction; (*Einweisung*) initiation

Eingabe *f* petition; (*Computer*) input

Eingang *m* entrance, way in; ⟨*Ankunft*⟩ arrival

eingebaut *a* built-in; ⟨*Schrank*⟩ fitted

eingeben† *vt sep* hand in; ⟨*einflößen*⟩ give ⟨jdm s.o.⟩; ⟨*Computer*⟩ feed in

eingebildet *a* imaginary; ⟨*überheblich*⟩ conceited

Eingeborene(r) *m/f* native

Eingebung *f* -,-en inspiration

eingedenk *prep* (+ *gen*) mindful of

eingefleischt *a* **e~er Junggeselle** confirmed bachelor

eingehakt *adv* arm in arm

eingehen† *v sep* □ *vi* (*sein*) come in; ⟨*ankommen*⟩ arrive; ⟨*einlaufen*⟩ shrink; ⟨*sterben*⟩ die; ⟨*Zeitung, Firma:*⟩ fold; **auf etw** (*acc*) **e~** go in to sth; ⟨*annehmen*⟩ agree to sth □ *vt* enter into; contract ⟨*Ehe*⟩; make ⟨*Wette*⟩; take ⟨*Risiko*⟩. **e~d** *a* detailed; ⟨*gründlich*⟩ thorough, *adv* -ly

eingelegt *a* inlaid; ⟨*Culin*⟩ pickled; ⟨*mariniert*⟩ marinaded

eingemacht *a* ⟨*Culin*⟩ bottled

eingenommen *pred a* ⟨*fig*⟩ taken (**von** with); prejudiced (**gegen** against); **von sich e~** conceited

eingeschneit *a* snowbound

eingeschrieben *a* registered

Einge|ständnis *nt* admission. **e~stehen†** *vt sep* admit

eingetragen *a* registered

Eingeweide *pl* bowels, entrails

eingewöhnen (sich) *vr sep* settle in

eingießen† *vt sep* pour in; ⟨*einschenken*⟩ pour

eingleisig *a* single-track

einglieder|n *vt sep* integrate. **E~ung** *f* integration

eingraben† *vt sep* bury

eingravieren *vt sep* engrave

eingreifen† *vi sep* (*haben*) intervene. **E~** *nt* -s intervention

Eingriff *m* intervention; ⟨*Med*⟩ operation

einhaken *vt/r sep* **jdn e~** *od* **sich bei jdm e~** take s.o.'s arm

einhalten† *v sep* □ *vt* keep; ⟨*befolgen*⟩ observe □ *vi* (*haben*) stop

einhändigen *vt sep* hand in

einhängen *v sep* □ *vt* hang; put down ⟨*Hörer*⟩; **sich bei jdm e~** take s.o.'s arm □ *vi* (*haben*) hang up

einheimisch *a* local; ⟨*eines Landes*⟩ native; ⟨*Comm*⟩ home-produced. **E~e(r)** *m/f* local; native

Einheit *f* -,-en unity; ⟨*Maß*, *Mil*⟩ unit. **e~lich** *a* uniform, *adv* -ly; ⟨*vereinheitlicht*⟩ standard. **E~spreis** *m* standard price; ⟨*Fahrpreis*⟩ flat fare

einhellig *a* unanimous, *adv* -ly

einholen *vt sep* catch up with; ⟨*aufholen*⟩ make up for; ⟨*erbitten*⟩ seek; ⟨*einkaufen*⟩ buy; **e~ gehen** go shopping

einhüllen *vt sep* wrap

einhundert *inv a* one hundred

einig *a* united; [**sich** (*dat*)] **e~ werden/ sein** come to an/be in agreement

einig|e(r,s) *pron* some; ⟨*ziemlich viel*⟩ quite a lot of; ⟨*substantivisch*⟩ **e~e** *pl* some; ⟨*mehrere*⟩ several; ⟨*ziemlich viele*⟩ quite a lot; **e~es** *sg* some things; **vor e~er Zeit** some time ago. **e~emal** *adv* ⟨NEW⟩ **e~e Mal, s. Mal**[1]

einigen *vt* unite; unify ⟨*Land*⟩; **sich e~** come to an agreement; ⟨*ausmachen*⟩ agree (**auf** + *acc* on)

einigermaßen *adv* to some extent; ⟨*ziemlich*⟩ fairly; ⟨*ziemlich gut*⟩ fairly well

Einig|keit *f* - unity; ⟨*Übereinstimmung*⟩ agreement. **E~ung** *f* - unification; ⟨*Übereinkunft*⟩ agreement

einjährig *a* one-year-old; ⟨*ein Jahr dauernd*⟩ one year's ...; **e~e Pflanze** annual

einkalkulieren *vt sep* take into account

einkassieren *vt sep* collect

Einkauf *m* purchase; ⟨*Einkaufen*⟩ shopping; **Einkäufe machen** do some shopping. **e~en** *vt sep* buy; **e~en gehen** go shopping. **E~skorb** *m* shopping/⟨*im Geschäft*⟩ wire basket. **E~stasche** *f* shopping bag. **E~swagen** *m* shopping trolley. **E~szentrum** *nt* shopping centre

einkehren *vi sep* (*sein*) **[in einem Lokal] e~** stop for a meal/drink [at an inn]

einklammern *vt sep* bracket

Einklang *m* harmony; **in E~ stehen** be in accord (**mit** with)

einkleben *vt sep* stick in

einkleiden *vt sep* fit out

einklemmen *vt sep* clamp; **sich** (*dat*) **den Finger in der Tür e~** catch one's finger in the door

einkochen *v sep* □ *vi* (*sein*) boil down □ *vt* preserve, bottle

Einkommen *nt* -s income. **E~[s]steuer** *f* income tax

einkreisen *vt sep* encircle; **rot e~** ring in red

Einkünfte *pl* income *sg*; ⟨*Einnahmen*⟩ revenue *sg*

einlad|en† *vt sep* load; ⟨*auffordern*⟩ invite; ⟨*bezahlen für*⟩ treat. **e~end** *a* inviting. **E~ung** *f* invitation

Einlage *f* enclosure; ⟨*Schuh-*⟩ arch support; ⟨*Zahn-*⟩ temporary filling;

(*Programm-*) interlude; (*Comm*) invest-ment; (*Bank-*) deposit; **Suppe mit E~** soup with noodles/dumplings

Ein|lass *m* -es (**Einlaß** *m* -sses) admit-tance. **e~lassen†** *vt sep* let in; run ⟨*Bad, Wasser*⟩; **sich auf etw** (*acc*)/**mit jdm e~ lassen** get involved in sth/with s.o.

einlaufen† *vi sep* (*sein*) come in; (*ankom-men*) arrive; ⟨*Wasser*⟩ run in; (*schrumpfen*) shrink; **[in den Hafen] e~** enter port

einleben (sich) *vr sep* settle in

Einlege|arbeit *f* inlaid work. **e~n** *vt sep* put in; lay in (*Vorrat*); lodge ⟨*Protest, Beru-fung*⟩; (*einfügen*) insert; (*Auto*) engage ⟨*Gang*⟩; (*verzieren*) inlay; (*Culin*) pickle; (*marinieren*) marinade; **eine Pause e~n** have a break. **E~sohle** *f* insole

einleit|en *vt sep* initiate; (*eröffnen*) begin. **e~end** *a* introductory. **E~ung** *f* intro-duction

einlenken *vi sep* (*haben*) (*fig*) relent

einleuchten *vi sep* (*haben*) be clear (*dat* to). **e~d** *a* convincing

einliefer|n *vt sep* take (**ins Krankenhaus** to hospital). **E~ung** *f* admission

einlösen *vt sep* cash ⟨*Scheck*⟩; redeem ⟨*Pfand*⟩; (*fig*) keep

einmachen *vt sep* preserve

einmal *adv* once; (*eines Tages*) one *or* some day; **noch/schon e~** again/before; **noch e~ so teuer** twice as expensive; **auf e~** at the same time; (*plötzlich*) suddenly; **nicht e~** not even; **es geht nun e~ nicht** it's just not possible. **E~eins** *nt* - [multiplica-tion] tables *pl*. **e~ig** *a* single; (*einzigartig*) unique; (*fam: großartig*) fantastic, *adv* -ally

einmarschieren *vi sep* (*sein*) march in

einmisch|en (sich) *vr sep* interfere. **E~ung** *f* interference

einmütig *a* unanimous, *adv* -ly

Einnahme *f* -,-n taking; (*Mil*) capture; **E~n** *pl* income *sg*; (*Einkünfte*) revenue *sg*; (*Comm*) receipts; (*eines Ladens*) takings

einnehmen† *vt sep* take; have ⟨*Mahlzeit*⟩; (*Mil*) capture; take up ⟨*Platz*⟩; (*fig*) preju-dice (**gegen** against); **jdn für sich e~** win s.o. over. **e~d** *a* engaging

einnicken *vi sep* (*sein*) nod off

Einöde *f* wilderness

einordnen *vt sep* put in its proper place; (*klassifizieren*) classify; **sich e~** fit in; (*Auto*) get in lane

einpacken *vt sep* pack; (*einhüllen*) wrap

einparken *vt sep* park

einpauken *vt sep* **jdm etw e~** (*fam*) drum sth into s.o.

einpflanzen *vt sep* plant; implant ⟨*Organ*⟩

einplanen *vt sep* allow for

einpräg|en *vt sep* impress (**jdm** [up]on s.o.); **sich** (*dat*) **etw e~en** memorize sth. **e~sam** *a* easy to remember; ⟨*Melodie*⟩ cat-chy

einquartieren *vt sep* (*Mil*) billet (**bei** on); **sich in einem Hotel e~** put up at a hotel

einrahmen *vt sep* frame

einrasten *vi sep* (*sein*) engage

einräumen *vt sep* put away; (*zugeben*) ad-mit; (*zugestehen*) grant

einrechnen *vt sep* include

einreden *v sep* □ *vt* **jdm/sich** (*dat*) **etw e~** persuade s.o./oneself of sth □ *vi* (*haben*) **auf jdn e~** talk insistently to s.o.

einreib|en† *vt sep* rub (**mit** with). **E~mit-tel** *nt* liniment

einreichen *vt sep* submit; **die Scheidung e~** file for divorce

Einreih|er *m* -s,- single-breasted suit. **e~ig** *a* single-breasted

Einreise *f* entry. **e~n** *vi sep* (*sein*) enter (**nach Irland** Ireland). **E~visum** *nt* entry visa

einreißen† *v sep* □ *vt* tear; (*abreißen*) pull down □ *vi* (*sein*) tear; ⟨*Sitte*⟩ become a habit

einrenken *vt sep* (*Med*) set

einricht|en *vt sep* fit out; (*möblieren*) fur-nish; (*anordnen*) arrange; (*Med*) set ⟨*Bruch*⟩; (*eröffnen*) set up; **sich e~en** fur-nish one's home; (*sich einschränken*) econ-omize; (*sich vorbereiten*) prepare (**auf** + *acc* for). **E~ung** *f* furnishing; ⟨*Möbel*⟩ fur-nishings *pl*; (*Techn*) equipment; (*Vorrich-tung*) device; (*Eröffnung*) setting up; (*Institution*) institution; (*Gewohnheit*) practice. **E~ungsgegenstand** *m* piece of equipment/⟨*Möbelstück*⟩ furniture

einrollen *vt sep* roll up; put in rollers ⟨*Haare*⟩

einrosten *vi sep* (*sein*) rust; (*fig*) get rusty

einrücken *v sep* □ *vi* (*sein*) (*Mil*) be called up; (*einmarschieren*) move in □ *vt* indent

eins *inv a & pron* one; **noch e~** one other thing; **mir ist alles e~** (*fam*) it's all the same to me. **E~** *f* -,-en one; (*Sch*) ≈ A

einsam *a* lonely; (*allein*) solitary; (*abge-legen*) isolated. **E~keit** *f* - loneliness; soli-tude; isolation

einsammeln *vt sep* collect

Einsatz *m* use; (*Mil*) mission; (*Wett-*) stake; (*E~teil*) insert; **im E~** in action. **e~be-reit** *a* ready for action

einschalt|en *vt sep* switch on; (*einschie-ben*) interpolate; (*fig: beteiligen*) call in; **sich e~en** (*fig*) intervene. **E~quote** *f* (*TV*) viewing figures *pl*; ≈ ratings *pl*

einschärfen *vt sep* **jdm etw e~** impress sth [up]on s.o.

einschätz|en *vt sep* assess; (*bewerten*) rate. **E~ung** *f* assessment; estimation

einschenken *vt sep* pour

einscheren *vi sep* (*sein*) pull in

einschicken *vt sep* send in

einschieben† *vt sep* push in; (*einfügen*) insert; (*fig*) interpolate

einschiff|en (**sich**) *vr sep* embark. **E~ung** *f* - embarkation

einschlafen† *vi sep* (*sein*) go to sleep; (*aufhören*) peter out

einschläfern *vt sep* lull to sleep; (*betäuben*) put out; (*töten*) put to sleep. **e~d** *a* soporific

Einschlag *m* impact; (*fig: Beimischung*) element. **e~en**† *v sep* □ *vt* knock in; (*zerschlagen*) smash; (*einwickeln*) wrap; (*falten*) turn up; (*drehen*) turn; take ⟨*Weg*⟩; take up ⟨*Laufbahn*⟩ □ *vi* (*haben*) hit/ (*Blitz:*) strike (**in etw** *acc* sth); (*zustimmen*) shake hands [on a deal]; (*Erfolg haben*) be a hit; **auf jdn e~en** beat s.o.

einschlägig *a* relevant

einschleusen *vt sep* infiltrate

einschließ|en† *vt sep* lock in; (*umgeben*) enclose; (*einkreisen*) surround; (*einbeziehen*) include; **sich e~en** lock oneself in; **Bedienung eingeschlossen** service included. **e~lich** *adv* inclusive □ *prep* (+ *gen*) including

einschmeicheln (**sich**) *vr sep* ingratiate oneself (**bei** with)

einschnappen *vi sep* (*sein*) click shut; **eingeschnappt sein** (*fam*) be in a huff

einschneiden† *vt/i sep* (*haben*) [**in**] **etw** *acc* **e~** cut into sth. **e~d** *a* (*fig*) drastic, *adv* -ally

Einschnitt *m* cut; (*Med*) incision; (*Lücke*) gap; (*fig*) decisive event

einschränk|en *vt sep* restrict; (*reduzieren*) cut back; **sich e~en** economize. **E~ung** *f* -,-en restriction; (*Reduzierung*) reduction; (*Vorbehalt*) reservation

Einschreib|e[e]brief *m* registered letter. **e~en**† *vt sep* enter; register ⟨*Brief*⟩; **sich e~en** put one's name down; (*sich anmelden*) enrol. **E~en** *nt* registered letter/packet; **als** *od* **per E~en** by registered post

einschreiten† *vi sep* (*sein*) intervene

einschüchter|n *vt sep* intimidate. **E~ung** *f* - intimidation

einsegn|en *vt sep* (*Relig*) confirm. **E~ung** *f* -,-en confirmation

einsehen† *vt sep* inspect; (*lesen*) consult; (*begreifen*) see. **E~** *nt* **-s ein E~ haben** show some understanding; (*vernünftig sein*) see reason

einseitig *a* one-sided; (*Pol*) unilateral □ *adv* on one side; (*fig*) one-sidedly; (*Pol*) unilaterally

einsenden† *vt sep* send in

einsetzen *v sep* □ *vt* put in; (*einfügen*) insert; (*verwenden*) use; put on ⟨*Zug*⟩; call out ⟨*Truppen*⟩; (*Mil*) deploy; (*ernennen*) appoint; (*wetten*) stake; (*riskieren*) risk; **sich e~ für** support □ *vi* (*haben*) start; ⟨*Winter, Regen:*⟩ set in

Einsicht *f* insight; (*Verständnis*) understanding; (*Vernunft*) reason; **zur E~ kommen** see reason. **e~ig** *a* understanding; (*vernünftig*) sensible

Einsiedler *m* hermit

einsilbig *a* monosyllabic; (*Person*) taciturn

einsinken† *vi sep* (*sein*) sink in

einspannen *vt sep* harness; **jdn e~** (*fam*) rope s.o. in; **sehr eingespannt** (*fam*) very busy

einsparen *vt sep* save

einsperren *vt sep* shut/(*im Gefängnis*) lock up

einspielen (**sich**) *vr sep* warm up; **gut aufeinander eingespielt sein** work well together

einsprachig *a* monolingual

einspringen† *vi sep* (*sein*) step in (**für** for)

einspritzen *vt sep* inject

Einspruch *m* objection; **E~ erheben** object; (*Jur*) appeal

einspurig *a* single-track; (*Auto*) single-lane

einst *adv* once; (*Zukunft*) one day

Einstand *m* (*Tennis*) deuce

einstecken *vt sep* put in; post ⟨*Brief*⟩; (*Electr*) plug in; (*fam: behalten*) pocket; (*fam: hinnehmen*) take; suffer ⟨*Niederlage*⟩; **etw e~** put sth in one's pocket

einstehen† *vi sep* (*haben*) **e~ für** vouch for; answer for ⟨*Folgen*⟩

einsteigen† *vi sep* (*sein*) get in; (*in Bus/Zug*) get on

einstell|en *vt sep* put in; (*anstellen*) employ; (*aufhören*) stop; (*regulieren*) adjust, set; (*Optik*) focus; tune ⟨*Motor, Zündung*⟩; tune to ⟨*Sender*⟩; **sich e~en** turn up; (*ankommen*) arrive; (*eintreten*) occur; ⟨*Schwierigkeiten:*⟩ arise; **sich e~en auf** (+ *acc*) adjust to; (*sich vorbereiten*) prepare for. **E~ung** *f* employment; (*Aufhören*) cessation; (*Regulierung*) adjustment; (*Optik*) focusing; (*TV, Auto*) tuning; (*Haltung*) attitude

Einstieg *m* **-[e]s,-e** entrance

einstig *a* former

einstimmen *vi sep* (*haben*) join in

einstimmig *a* unanimous, *adv* -ly. **E~keit** *f* - unanimity

einstöckig *a* single-storey

einstudieren *vt sep* rehearse

einstufen *vt sep* classify

Ein|sturz *m* collapse. **e~stürzen** *vi sep* (*sein*) collapse

einstweil|en *adv* for the time being; (*inzwischen*) meanwhile. **e~ig** *a* temporary

eintasten *vt sep* key in

eintauchen *vt/i sep* (*sein*) dip in; (*heftiger*) plunge in

eintauschen *vt sep* exchange

eintausend *inv a* one thousand

einteil|en *vt sep* divide (**in** + *acc* into); (*Biol*) classify; **sich** (*dat*) **seine Zeit gut e~en** organize one's time well. **e~ig** *a* one-piece. **E~ung** *f* division; classification

eintönig *a* monotonous, *adv* -ly. **E~keit** *f* - monotony

Eintopf *m*, **E~gericht** *nt* stew

Ein|tracht *f* - harmony. **e~trächtig** *a* harmonious □ *adv* in harmony

Eintrag *m* -[e]s,⸚e entry. **e~en†** *vt sep* enter; (*Admin*) register; (*einbringen*) bring in; **sich e~en** put one's name down

einträglich *a* profitable

Eintragung *f* -,-en registration; (*Eintrag*) entry

eintreffen† *vi sep* (*sein*) arrive; (*fig*) come true; (*geschehen*) happen. **E~** *nt* -s arrival

eintreiben† *vt sep* drive in; (*einziehen*) collect

eintreten† *v sep* □ *vi* (*sein*) enter; (*geschehen*) occur; **in einen Klub e~** join a club; **e~ für** (*fig*) stand up for □ *vt* kick in

Eintritt *m* entrance; (*zu Veranstaltung*) admission; (*Beitritt*) joining; (*Beginn*) beginning. **E~skarte** *f* [admission] ticket

eintrocknen *vi sep* (*sein*) dry up

einüben *vt sep* practise

einundachtzig *inv a* eighty-one

einverleiben *vt sep* incorporate (*dat* into); **sich** (*dat*) **etw e~** (*fam*) consume sth

Einvernehmen *nt* -s understanding; (*Übereinstimmung*) agreement; **in bestem E~** on the best of terms

einverstanden *a* **e~ sein** agree

Einverständnis *nt* agreement; (*Zustimmung*) consent

Einwand *m* -[e]s,⸚e objection

Einwander|er *m* immigrant. **e~n** *vi sep* (*sein*) immigrate. **E~ung** *f* immigration

einwandfrei *a* perfect, *adv* -ly; (*untadelig*) impeccable, *adv* -bly; (*eindeutig*) indisputable, *adv* -bly

einwärts *adv* inwards

einwechseln *vt sep* change

einwecken *vt sep* preserve, bottle

Einweg- *pref* non-returnable; (*Feuerzeug*) throw-away

einweichen *vt sep* soak

einweih|en *vt sep* inaugurate; (*Relig*) consecrate; (*einführen*) initiate; (*fam*) use for the first time; **in ein Geheimnis e~en** let into a secret. **E~ung** *f* -,-en inauguration; consecration; initiation

einweisen† *vt sep* direct; (*einführen*) initiate; **ins Krankenhaus e~** send to hospital

einwenden† *vt sep* **etwas e~** object (**gegen** to); **dagegen hätte ich nichts einzuwenden** (*fam*) I wouldn't say no

einwerfen† *vt sep* insert; post (*Brief*); (*Sport*) throw in; (*vorbringen*) interject; (*zertrümmern*) smash

einwickeln *vt sep* wrap [up]

einwillig|en *vi sep* (*haben*) consent, agree (**in** + *acc* to). **E~ung** *f* - consent

einwirken *vi sep* (*haben*) **e~ auf** (+ *acc*) have an effect on; (*beeinflussen*) influence

Einwohner|(in) *m* -s,- (*f* -,-nen) inhabitant. **E~zahl** *f* population

Einwurf *m* interjection; (*Einwand*) objection; (*Sport*) throw-in; (*Münz-*) slot

Einzahl *f* (*Gram*) singular

einzahl|en *vt sep* pay in. **E~ung** *f* payment; (*Einlage*) deposit

einzäunen *vt sep* fence in

Einzel *nt* -s,- (*Tennis*) singles *pl*. **E~bett** *nt* single bed. **E~fall** *m* individual/(*Sonderfall*) isolated case. **E~gänger** *m* -s,- loner. **E~haft** *f* solitary confinement. **E~handel** *m* retail trade. **E~händler** *m* retailer. **E~haus** *nt* detached house. **E~heit** *f* -,-en detail. **E~karte** *f* single ticket. **E~kind** *nt* only child

einzeln *a* single, *adv* -gly; (*individuell*) individual, *adv* -ly; (*gesondert*) separate, *adv* -ly; odd (*Handschuh, Socken*); **e~e Fälle** some cases. **E~e(r,s)** (**e~e(r,s)**) *pron* **der/die E~e** (**e~e**) the individual; **ein E~er** (**e~er**) a single one; (*Person*) one individual; **jeder E~e** (**e~e**) every single one; (*Person*) each individual; **E~e** (**e~e**) *pl* some; **im E~en** (**e~en**) in detail; **ins E~e** (**e~e**) **gehen** go into detail

Einzel|person *f* single person. **E~teil** *nt* [component] part. **E~zimmer** *nt* single room

einziehen† *v sep* □ *vt* move in; draw in (*Atem, Krallen*); (*Zool, Techn*) retract; indent (*Zeile*); (*aus dem Verkehr ziehen*) withdraw; (*beschlagnahmen*) confiscate; (*eintreiben*) collect; make (*Erkundigungen*); (*Mil*) call up; (*einfügen*) insert; (*einbauen*) put in; **den Kopf e~** duck [one's head] □ *vi* (*sein*) enter; (*umziehen*) move in; (*eindringen*) penetrate

einzig *a* only; (*einmalig*) unique; **eine/keine e~e Frage** a/not a single question; **ein e~es Mal** only once □ *adv* only; **e~ und allein** solely. **e~artig** *a* unique (*unvergleichlich*) unparalleled. **E~e(r,s)** (**e~e(r,s)**) *pron* **der/die/das E~e** (**e~e**) the only one; **ein/kein E~er** (**e~er**) a/not a single one; **das E~e** (**e~e**), **was mich stört** the only thing that bothers me

Einzug *m* entry; (*Umzug*) move (**in +** *acc* into). **E~sgebiet** *nt* catchment area

Eis *nt* -es ice; (*Speise-*) ice-cream; **Eis am Stiel** ice lolly; **Eis laufen** skate. **E~bahn** *f* ice rink. **E~bär** *m* polar bear. **E~becher** *m* ice-cream sundae. **E~bein** *nt* (*Culin*) knuckle of pork. **E~berg** *m* iceberg. **E~diele** *f* ice-cream parlour

Eisen *nt* -s,- iron. **E~bahn** *f* railway. **E~bahner** *m* -s,- railwayman

eisern *a* iron; (*fest*) resolute, *adv* -ly; **e~er Vorhang** (*Theat*) safety curtain; (*Pol*) Iron Curtain

Eis|fach *nt* freezer compartment. **e~gekühlt** *a* chilled. **e~ig** *a* icy. **E~kaffee** *m* iced coffee. **e~kalt** *a* ice cold; (*fig*) icy, *adv* -ily. **E~kunstlauf** *m* figure skating. **E~lauf** *m* skating. **e~laufen†** *vi sep* (*sein*) ⟨NEW⟩ **Eis laufen, s. Eis. E~läufer(in)** *m(f)* skater. **E~pickel** *m* ice-axe. **E~scholle** *f* ice-floe. **E~schrank** *m* refrigerator. **E~vogel** *m* kingfisher. **E~würfel** *m* icecube. **E~zapfen** *m* icicle. **E~zeit** *f* ice age

eitel *a* vain; (*rein*) pure. **E~keit** *f* - vanity

Eiter *m* -s pus. **e~n** *vi* (*haben*) discharge pus

Eiweiß *nt* -es,-e egg-white; (*Chem*) protein

Ekel[1] *m* -s disgust; (*Widerwille*) revulsion

Ekel[2] *nt* -s,- (*fam*) beast

ekel|erregend *a* nauseating. **e~haft** *a* nauseating; (*widerlich*) repulsive. **e~n** *vt/i* (*haben*) **mich** *od* **mir e~t** [**es**] **davor** it makes me feel sick □ *vr* **sich e~n vor** (**+** *dat*) find repulsive

eklig *a* disgusting, repulsive

Eksta|se *f* - ecstasy. **e~tisch** *a* ecstatic, *adv* -ally

Ekzem *nt* -s,-e eczema

elasti|sch *a* elastic; (*federnd*) springy; (*fig*) flexible. **E~zität** *f* - elasticity; flexibility

Elch *m* -[e]s,-e elk

Elefant *m* -en,-en elephant

elegan|t *a* elegant, *adv* -ly. **E~z** *f* - elegance

elektrifizieren *vt* electrify

Elektri|ker *m* -s,- electrician. **e~sch** *a* electric, *adv* -ally

elektrisieren *vt* electrify; **sich e~** get an electric shock

Elektrizität *f* - electricity. **E~swerk** *nt* power station

Elektr|oartikel *mpl* electrical appliances. **E~ode** *f* -,-n electrode. **E~oherd** *m* electric cooker. **E~on** *nt* -s,-en /-'tro:nən/ electron. **E~onik** *f* - electronics *sg*. **e~onisch** *a* electronic

Element *nt* -[e]s,-e element; (*Anbau-*) unit. **e~ar** *a* elementary

Elend *nt* -s misery; (*Armut*) poverty. **e~** *a* miserable, *adv* -bly, wretched, *adv* -ly; (*krank*) poorly; (*gemein*) contemptible; (*fam: schrecklich*) dreadful, *adv* -ly. **E~sviertel** *nt* slum

elf *inv* *a*, **E~** *f* -,-en eleven

Elfe *f* -,-n fairy

Elfenbein *nt* ivory

Elfmeter *m* (*Fußball*) penalty

elfte(r,s) *a* eleventh

eliminieren *vt* eliminate

Elite *f* -,-n élite

Elixier *nt* -s,-e elixir

Ell[en]bogen *m* elbow

Ellip|se *f* -,-n ellipse. **e~tisch** *a* elliptical

Elsass (**Elsaß**) *nt* - Alsace

elsässisch *a* Alsatian

Elster *f* -,-n magpie

elter|lich *a* parental. **E~n** *pl* parents. **E~nhaus** *nt* [parental] home. **e~nlos** *a* orphaned. **E~nteil** *m* parent

Email /e'mai/ *nt* -s,-s, **E~le** /e'maljə/ *f* -,-n enamel. **e~lieren** /ema[l]'ji:rən/ *vt* enamel

Emanzi|pation /-'tsio:n/ *f* - emancipation. **e~piert** *a* emancipated

Embargo *nt* -s,-s embargo

Emblem *nt* -s,-e emblem

Embryo *m* -s,-s embryo

Emigr|ant(in) *m* -en,-en (*f* -,-nen) emigrant. **E~ation** /-'tsio:n/ *f* - emigration. **e~ieren** *vi* (*sein*) emigrate

eminent *a* eminent, *adv* -ly

Emission *f* -,-en emission; (*Comm*) issue

Emotion /-'tsio:n/ *f* -,-en emotion. **e~al** *a* emotional

Empfang *m* -[e]s,-e reception; (*Erhalt*) receipt; **in E~ nehmen** receive; (*annehmen*) accept. **e~en†** *vt* receive; (*Biol*) conceive

Empfäng|er *m* -s,- recipient; (*Post-*) addressee; (*Zahlungs-*) payee; (*Radio, TV*)

receiver. e~lich *a* receptive/(*Med*) susceptible (**für** to). **E~nis** *f* - (*Biol*) conception

Empfängnisverhütung *f* contraception. **E~smittel** *nt* contraceptive

Empfangs|bestätigung *f* receipt. **E~chef** *m* reception manager. **E~dame** *f* receptionist. **E~halle** *f* [hotel] foyer

empfehl|en† *vt* recommend; **sich e~en** be advisable; (*verabschieden*) take one's leave. **e~enswert** *a* to be recommended; (*ratsam*) advisable. **E~ung** *f* -,-en recommendation; (*Gruß*) regards *pl*

empfind|en† *vt* feel. **e~lich** *a* sensitive (**gegen** to); (*zart*) delicate; (*wund*) tender; (*reizbar*) touchy; (*hart*) severe, *adv* -ly. **E~lichkeit** *f* - sensitivity; delicacy; tenderness; touchiness. **e~sam** *a* sensitive; (*sentimental*) sentimental. **E~ung** *f* -,-en sensation; (*Regung*) feeling

emphatisch *a* emphatic, *adv* -ally

empor *adv* (*liter*) up[wards]

empören *vt* incense; **sich e~** be indignant; (*sich auflehnen*) rebel. **e~d** *a* outrageous

Empor|kömmling *m* -s,-e upstart. **e~ragen** *vi sep* (*haben*) rise [up]

empör|t *a* indignant, *adv* -ly. **E~ung** *f* - indignation; (*Auflehnung*) rebellion

emsig *a* busy, *adv* -ily

Ende *nt* -s,-n end; (*eines Films, Romans*) ending; (*fam: Stück*) bit; **E~ Mai** at the end of May; **zu E~sein/gehen** be finished/come to an end; **etw zu E~ schreiben** finish writing sth; **am E~** at the end; (*schließlich*) in the end; (*fam: vielleicht*) perhaps; (*fam: erschöpft*) at the end of one's tether

end|en *vi* (*haben*) end. **e~gültig** *a* final, *adv* -ly; (*bestimmt*) definite, *adv* -ly

Endivie /-jə/ *f* -,-n endive

end|lich *adv* at last, finally; (*schließlich*) in the end. **e~los** *a* endless, *adv* -ly. **E~resultat** *nt* final result. **E~spiel** *nt* final. **E~spurt** *m* -[e]s final spurt. **E~station** *f* terminus. **E~ung** *f* -,-en (*Gram*) ending

Energie *f* - energy

energisch *a* resolute, *adv* -ly; (*nachdrücklich*) vigorous, *adv* -ly; **e~ werden** put one's foot down

eng *a* narrow; (*beengt*) cramped; (*anliegend*) tight; (*nah*) close, *adv* -ly; **e~ anliegend** tight-fitting

Enga|gement /ãgaʒəˈmãː/ *nt* -s,-s (*Theat*) engagement; (*fig*) commitment. **e~gieren** /-ˈʒiːrən/ *vt* (*Theat*) engage; **sich e~gieren** become involved; **e~giert** committed

eng|anliegend *a* (NEW) **e~ anliegend**, *s.* **eng. E~e** *f* - narrowness; **in die E~e treiben** (*fig*) drive into a corner

Engel *m* -s,- angel. **e~haft** *a* angelic

engherzig *a* petty

England *nt* -s England

Engländer *m* -s,- Englishman; (*Techn*) monkey-wrench; **die E~** the English *pl*. **E~in** *f* -,-nen Englishwoman

englisch *a* English; **auf e~** (NEW) **auf E~**, *s.* **Englisch. E~** *nt* -[s] (*Lang*) English; **auf E~** in English

Engpass (**Engpaß**) *m* (*fig*) bottle-neck

en gros /ãˈgroː/ *adv* wholesale

engstirnig *a* (*fig*) narrowminded

Enkel *m* -s,- grandson; **E~** *pl* grandchildren. **E~in** *f* -,-nen granddaughter. **E~kind** *nt* grandchild. **E~sohn** *m* grandson. **E~tochter** *f* granddaughter

enorm *a* enormous, *adv* -ly; (*fam: großartig*) fantastic

Ensemble /ãˈsãːbəl/ *nt* -s,-s ensemble; (*Theat*) company

entart|en *vi* (*sein*) degenerate. **e~et** *a* degenerate

entbehr|en *vt* do without; (*vermissen*) miss. **e~lich** *a* dispensable; (*überflüssig*) superfluous. **E~ung** *f* -,-en privation

entbind|en† *vt* release (**von** from); (*Med*) deliver (**von** of) □ *vi* (*haben*) give birth. **E~ung** *f* delivery. **E~ungsstation** *f* maternity ward

entblöß|en *vt* bare. **e~t** *a* bare

entdeck|en *vt* discover. **E~er** *m* -s,- discoverer; (*Forscher*) explorer. **E~ung** *f* -,-en discovery

Ente *f* -,-n duck

entehren *vt* dishonour

enteignen *vt* dispossess; expropriate (*Eigentum*)

enterben *vt* disinherit

Enterich *m* -s,-e drake

entfachen *vt* kindle

entfallen† *vi* (*sein*) not apply; **jdm e~** slip from s.o.'s hand; (*aus dem Gedächtnis*) slip s.o.'s mind; **auf jdn e~** be s.o.'s share

entfalt|en *vt* unfold; (*entwickeln*) develop; (*zeigen*) display; **sich e~en** unfold; develop. **E~ung** *f* - development

entfern|en *vt* remove; **sich e~en** leave. **e~t** *a* distant; (*schwach*) vague, *adv* -ly; **2 Kilometer e~t** 2 kilometres away; **e~t verwandt** distantly related; **nicht im E~testen** not in the least. **E~ung** *f* -,-en removal; (*Abstand*) distance; (*Reichweite*) range. **E~ungsmesser** *m* range-finder

entfesseln *vt* (*fig*) unleash

entfliehen† *vi* (*sein*) escape

entfremd|en vt alienate. **E~ung** f - alienation

entfrosten vt defrost

entführ|en vt abduct, kidnap; hijack ⟨Flugzeug⟩. **E~er** m abductor, kidnapper; hijacker. **E~ung** f abduction, kidnapping; hijacking

entgegen adv towards □ prep (+ dat) contrary to. **e~gehen†** vi sep (sein) (+ dat) go to meet; ⟨fig⟩ be heading for. **e~gesetzt** a opposite; ⟨gegensätzlich⟩ opposing. **e~halten†** vt sep ⟨fig⟩ object. **e~kommen†** vi sep (sein) (+ dat) come to meet; ⟨zukommen auf⟩ come towards; ⟨fig⟩ oblige. **E~kommen** nt -s helpfulness; ⟨Zugeständnis⟩ concession. **e~kommend** a approaching; ⟨Verkehr⟩ oncoming; ⟨fig⟩ obliging. **e~nehmen†** vt sep accept. **e~sehen†** vi sep (haben) (+ dat) ⟨fig⟩ await; ⟨freudig⟩ look forward to. **e~setzen** vt sep Widerstand **e~setzen** (+ dat) resist. **e~treten†** vi sep (sein) (+ dat) ⟨fig⟩ confront; ⟨bekämpfen⟩ fight. **e~wirken** vi sep (haben) (+ dat) counteract; ⟨fig⟩ oppose

entgegn|en vt reply (**auf** + acc to). **E~ung** f -,-en reply

entgehen† vi sep (sein) (+ dat) escape; **jdm e~** ⟨unbemerkt bleiben⟩ escape s.o.'s notice; **sich** (dat) **etw e~ lassen** miss sth

entgeistert a flabbergasted

Entgelt nt -[e]s payment; **gegen E~** for money. **e~en** vt **jdn etw e~en lassen** ⟨fig⟩ make s.o. pay for sth

entgleis|en vi (sein) be derailed; ⟨fig⟩ make a gaffe. **E~ung** f -,-en derailment; ⟨fig⟩ gaffe

entgleiten† vi (sein) **jdm e~** slip from s.o.'s grasp

entgräten vt fillet, bone

Enthaarungsmittel nt depilatory

enthalt|en† vt contain; **in etw** (dat) **e~en sein** be contained/ ⟨eingeschlossen⟩ included in sth; **sich der Stimme e~en** ⟨Pol⟩ abstain. **e~sam** a abstemious. **E~samkeit** f -abstinence. **E~ung** f ⟨Pol⟩ abstention

enthaupten vt behead

enthaben† vt **jdn seines Amtes e~** relieve s.o. of his post

enthüll|en vt unveil; ⟨fig⟩ reveal. **E~ung** f -,-en revelation

Enthusias|mus m - enthusiast. **E~t** m -en,-en enthusiast. **e~tisch** a enthusiastic, adv -ally

entkernen vt stone; core ⟨Apfel⟩

entkleid|en vt undress; **sich e~en** undress. **E~ungsnummer** f strip-tease [act]

entkommen† vi (sein) escape

entkorken vt uncork

entkräft|en vt weaken; ⟨fig⟩ invalidate. **E~ung** f - debility

entkrampfen vt relax; **sich e~** relax

entladen† vt unload; ⟨Electr⟩ discharge; **sich e~** discharge; ⟨Gewitter:⟩ break; ⟨Zorn:⟩ explode

entlang adv & prep (+ preceding acc or following dat) along; **die Straße e~, e~ der Straße** along the road; **an etw** (dat) **e~** along sth. **e~fahren†** vi sep (sein) drive along. **e~gehen†** vi sep (sein) walk along

entlarven vt unmask

entlass|en† vt dismiss; ⟨aus Krankenhaus⟩ discharge; ⟨aus der Haft⟩ release; **aus der Schule e~en werden** leave school. **E~ung** f -,-en dismissal; discharge; release

entlast|en vt relieve the strain on; ease ⟨Gewissen, Verkehr⟩; relieve (**von** of); ⟨Jur⟩ exonerate. **E~ung** f - relief; exoneration. **E~ungszug** m relief train

entlaufen† vi (sein) run away

entledigen (sich) vr (+ gen) rid oneself of; ⟨ausziehen⟩ take off; ⟨erfüllen⟩ discharge

entleeren vt empty

entlegen a remote

entleihen† vt borrow (**von** from)

entlocken vt coax (dat from)

entlohnen vt pay

entlüft|en vt ventilate. **E~er** m -s,- extractor fan. **E~ung** f ventilation

entmündigen vt declare incapable of managing his own affairs

entmutigen vt discourage

entnehmen† vt take (dat from); ⟨schließen⟩ gather (dat from)

Entomologie f - entomology

entpuppen (sich) vr ⟨fig⟩ turn out (**als** etw to be sth)

entrahmt a skimmed

entreißen† vt snatch (dat from)

entrichten vt pay

entrinnen† vi (sein) escape

entrollen vt unroll; unfurl ⟨Fahne⟩; **sich e~** unroll; unfurl

entrüst|en vt fill with indignation; **sich e~en** be indignant (**über** + acc at). **e~et** a indignant, adv -ly. **E~ung** f - indignation

entsaft|en vt extract the juice from. **E~er** m -s,- juice extractor

entsag|en vi (haben) (+ dat) renounce. **E~ung** f - renunciation

entschädig|en vt compensate. **E~ung** f -,-en compensation

entschärfen vt defuse

entscheid|en† *vt/i* (haben) decide; **sich e~en** decide; ⟨Sache:⟩ be decided. **e~end** *a* decisive, *adv* -ly; (kritisch) crucial. **E~ung** *f* decision.

entschieden *a* decided, *adv* -ly; (fest) firm, *adv* -ly

entschlafen† *vi* (sein) (liter) pass away

entschließen† (sich) *vr* decide, make up one's mind; **sich anders e~** change one's mind

entschlossen *a* determined; (energisch) resolute, *adv* -ly; **kurz e~** without hesitation; (spontan) on the spur of the moment. **E~heit** *f* - determination

Entschluss (**Entschluß**) *m* decision; **einen E~ fassen** make a decision

entschlüsseln *vt* decode

entschuld|bar *a* excusable. **e~igen** *vt* excuse; **sich e~igen** apologize (**bei** to); **e~igen Sie [bitte]!** sorry! (bei Frage) excuse me. **E~igung** *f* -,-en apology; (Ausrede) excuse; [jdn] **um E~igung bitten** apologize [to s.o.]; **E~igung!** sorry! (bei Frage) excuse me

entsetz|en *vt* horrify. **E~en** *nt* -s horror. **e~lich** *a* horrible, *adv* -bly, (schrecklich) terrible, *adv* -bly. **e~t** *a* horrified

entsinnen† (sich) *vr* (+ gen) remember

Entsorgung *f* - waste disposal

entspann|en *vt* relax; **sich e~en** relax; ⟨Lage:⟩ ease. **E~ung** *f* - relaxation; easing; (Pol) détente

entsprech|en† *vi* (haben) (+ dat) correspond to; (übereinstimmen) agree with; (nachkommen) comply with. **e~end** *a* corresponding; (angemessen) appropriate; (zuständig) relevant □ *adv* correspondingly; appropriately; (demgemäß) accordingly □ *prep* (+ dat) in accordance with. **E~ung** *f* -,-en equivalent

entspringen† *vi* (sein) ⟨Fluss:⟩ rise; (fig) arise, spring (dat from); (entfliehen) escape

entstammen *vi* (sein) come /(abstammen) be descended (dat from)

entsteh|en† *vi* (sein) come into being; (sich bilden) form; (sich entwickeln) develop; ⟨Brand:⟩ start; (stammen) originate /(sich ergeben) result (aus from). **E~ung** *f* - origin; formation; development; (fig) birth

entsteinen *vt* stone

entstell|en *vt* disfigure; (verzerren) distort. **E~ung** *f* disfigurement; distortion

entstört *a* (Electr) suppressed

enttäusch|en *vt* disappoint. **E~ung** *f* disappointment

entvölkern *vt* depopulate

entwaffnen *vt* disarm. **e~d** *a* (fig) disarming

Entwarnung *f* all-clear [signal]

entwässer|n *vt* drain. **E~ung** *f* - drainage

entweder *conj* & *adv* either

entweichen† *vi* (sein) escape

entweih|en *vt* desecrate. **E~ung** *f* - desecration

entwenden *vt* steal (dat from)

entwerfen† *vt* design; (aufsetzen) draft; (skizzieren) sketch

entwert|en *vt* devalue; (ungültig machen) cancel. **E~er** *m* -s,- ticket-cancelling machine. **E~ung** *f* devaluation; cancelling

entwick|eln *vt* develop; **sich e~eln** develop. **E~lung** *f* -,-en development; (Biol) evolution. **E~lungsland** *nt* developing country

entwinden† *vt* wrench (dat from)

entwirren *vt* disentangle; (fig) unravel

entwischen *vi* (sein) **jdm e~** (fam) give s.o. the slip

entwöhnen *vt* wean (gen from); cure ⟨Süchtige⟩

entwürdigend *a* degrading

Entwurf *m* design; (Konzept) draft; (Skizze) sketch

entwurzeln *vt* uproot

entzie|hen† *vt* take away (dat from); **jdm den Führerschein e~hen** disqualify s.o. from driving; **sich e~hen** (+ dat) withdraw from; (entgehen) evade. **E~hungskur** *f* treatment for drug/alcohol addiction

entziffern *vt* decipher

entzücken *vt* delight. **E~** *nt* -s delight. **e~d** *a* delightful

Entzug *m* withdrawal; (Vorenthaltung) deprivation. **E~serscheinungen** *fpl* withdrawal symptoms

entzünd|en *vt* ignite; (anstecken) light; (fig: erregen) inflame; **sich e~en** ignite; (Med) become inflamed. **e~et** *a* (Med) inflamed. **e~lich** *a* inflammable. **E~ung** *f* (Med) inflammation

entzwei *a* broken. **e~en** (sich) *vr* quarrel. **e~gehen**† *vi sep* (sein) break

Enzian *m* -s,-e gentian

Enzyklo|pädie *f* -,-en encyclopaedia. **e~pädisch** *a* encyclopaedic

Enzym *nt* -s,-e enzyme

Epidemie *f* -,-n epidemic

Epi|lepsie *f* - epilepsy. **E~leptiker(in)** *m* -s,- (*f* -,-nen) epileptic. **e~leptisch** *a* epileptic

Epilog *m* -s,-e epilogue

episch *a* epic

Episode *f* -,-n episode

Epitaph *nt* -s,-e epitaph

Epoche *f* -,-n epoch. **e~machend** *a* epoch-making

Epos *nt* -/**Epen** epic

er *pron* he; (*Ding, Tier*) it

erachten *vt* consider (**für nötig** necessary). **E~ nt-s meines E~s** in my opinion

erbarmen (sich) *vr* have pity/⟨*Gott:*⟩ mercy (*gen* on). **E~** *nt* -s pity; mercy

erbärmlich *a* wretched, *adv* -ly; (*stark*) terrible, *adv* -bly

erbarmungslos *a* merciless, *adv* -ly

erbau|en *vt* build; (*fig*) edify; **sich e~en** be edified (**an** + *dat* by); **nicht e~t von** (*fam*) not pleased about. **e~lich** *a* edifying

Erbe[1] *m* -n,-n heir

Erbe[2] *nt*-s inheritance; (*fig*) heritage. **e~n** *vt* inherit

erbeuten *vt* get; (*Mil*) capture

Erbfolge *f* (*Jur*) succession

erbieten† (**sich**) *vr* offer (**zu** to)

Erbin *f* -,-nen heiress

erbitten† *vt* ask for

erbittert *a* bitter; (*heftig*) fierce, *adv* -ly

erblassen *vi* (*sein*) turn pale

erblich *a* hereditary

erblicken *vt* catch sight of

erblinden *vi* (*sein*) go blind

erbost *a* angry, *adv* -ily

erbrechen† *vt* vomit □*vi/r* [**sich**] **e~** vomit. **E~** *nt* -s vomiting

Erbschaft *f* -,-en inheritance

Erbse *f* -,-n pea

Erb|stück *nt* heirloom. **E~teil** *nt* inheritance

Erd|apfel *m* (*Aust*) potato. **E~beben** *nt* -s,- earthquake. **E~beere** *f* strawberry. **E~boden** *m* ground

Erde *f* -,-n earth; (*Erdboden*) ground; (*Fußboden*) floor; **auf der E~** on earth; (*auf dem Boden*) on the ground/floor. **e~n** *vt* (*Electr*) earth

erdenklich *a* imaginable

Erd|gas *nt* natural gas. **E~geschoss** (**E~geschoß**) *nt* ground floor, (*Amer*) first floor. **e~ig** *a* earthy. **E~kugel** *f* globe. **E~kunde** *f* geography. **E~nuss** (**E~nuß**) *f* peanut. **E~öl** *nt* [mineral] oil. **E~reich** *nt* soil

erdreisten (sich) *vr* have the audacity (**zu** to)

erdrosseln *vt* strangle

erdrücken *vt* crush to death. **e~d** *a* (*fig*) overwhelming

Erd|rutsch *m* landslide. **E~teil** *m* continent

erdulden *vt* endure

ereifern (sich) *vr* get worked up

ereignen (sich) *vr* happen

Ereignis *nt* -ses,-se event. **e~los** *a* uneventful. **e~reich** *a* eventful

Eremit *m* -en,-en hermit

ererbt *a* inherited

erfahr|en† *vt* learn, hear; (*erleben*) experience □ *a* experienced. **E~ung** *f* -,-en experience; **in E~ung bringen** find out

erfassen *vt* seize; (*begreifen*) grasp; (*einbeziehen*) include; (*aufzeichnen*) record; **von einem Auto erfasst werden** be struck by a car

erfind|en† *vt* invent. **E~er** *m* -s,- inventor. **e~erisch** *a* inventive. **E~ung** *f* -,-en invention

Erfolg *m* -[e]s,-e success; (*Folge*) result; **E~ haben** be successful; **E~ versprechend** promising. **e~en** *vi* (*sein*) take place; (*geschehen*) happen. **e~los** *a* unsuccessful, *adv* -ly. **e~reich** *a* successful, *adv* -ly. **e~versprechend** *a* (NEW) **E~versprechend**, *s.* **Erfolg**

erforder|lich *a* required, necessary. **e~n** *vt* require, demand. **E~nis** *nt* -ses,-se requirement

erforsch|en *vt* explore; (*untersuchen*) investigate. **E~ung** *f* exploration; investigation

erfreu|en *vt* please; **sich guter Gesundheit e~en** enjoy good health. **e~lich** *a* pleasing, gratifying; (*willkommen*) welcome. **e~licherweise** *adv* happily. **e~t** *a* pleased

erfrier|en† *vi* (*sein*) freeze to death; ⟨*Glied:*⟩ become frostbitten; (*Pflanze:*) be killed by the frost. **E~ung** *f* -,-en frostbite

erfrisch|en *vt* refresh; **sich e~en** refresh oneself. **e~end** *a* refreshing. **E~ung** *f* -,-en refreshment

erfüll|en *vt* fill; (*nachkommen*) fulfil; serve ⟨*Zweck*⟩; discharge ⟨*Pflicht:*⟩; **sich e~en** come true. **E~ung** *f* fulfilment; **in E~ung gehen** come true

erfunden *a* invented; (*fiktiv*) fictitious

ergänz|en *vt* complement; (*nachtragen*) supplement; (*auffüllen*) replenish; (*vervollständigen*) complete; (*hinzufügen*) add; **sich e~en** complement each other. **E~ung** *f* complement; supplement; (*Zusatz*) addition. **E~ungsband** *m* supplement

ergeb|en† *vt* produce; (*zeigen*) show, establish; **sich e~en** result; ⟨*Schwierigkeit:*⟩ arise; (*kapitulieren*) surrender; (*sich fügen*) submit; **es ergab sich** it turned out (**dass** that) □ *a* devoted, *adv* -ly; (*resigniert*) resigned, *adv* -ly. **E~enheit** *f* -devotion

Ergebnis *nt* **-ses,-se** result. **e~los** *a* fruitless, *adv* **-ly**

ergehen† *vi* (*sein*) be issued; **etw über sich** (*acc*) **e~ lassen** submit to sth; **wie ist es dir ergangen?** how did you get on? □ *vr* **sich e~ in** (+ *dat*) indulge in

ergiebig *a* productive; (*fig*) rich

ergötzen *vt* amuse

ergreifen† *vt* seize; take ⟨*Maßnahme, Gelegenheit*⟩; take up ⟨*Beruf*⟩; (*rühren*) move; **die Flucht e~** flee. **e~d** *a* moving

ergriffen *a* deeply moved. **E~heit** *f* - emotion

ergründen *vt* (*fig*) get to the bottom of

erhaben *a* raised; (*fig*) sublime; **über etw** (*acc*) **e~ sein** (*fig*) be above sth

Erhalt *m* **-[e]s** receipt. **e~en†** *vt* receive, get; (*gewinnen*) obtain; (*bewahren*) preserve, keep; (*instand halten*) maintain; (*unterhalten*) support; **am Leben e~en** keep alive □ *a* **gut/schlecht e~en** in good/bad condition; **e~en bleiben** survive

erhältlich *a* obtainable

Erhaltung *f* - (*s.* **erhalten**) preservation; maintenance

erhängen (sich) *vr* hang oneself

erhärten *vt* (*fig*) substantiate

erheben† *vt* raise; levy ⟨*Steuer*⟩; charge ⟨*Gebühr*⟩; **Anspruch e~en** lay claim (**auf** + *acc* to); **Protest e~en** protest; **sich e~en** rise; ⟨*Frage:*⟩ arise; (*sich empören*) rise up. **e~lich** *a* considerable, *adv* -bly. **E~ung** *f* -,-en elevation; (*Anhöhe*) rise; (*Aufstand*) uprising; (*Ermittlung*) survey

erheiter|n *vt* amuse. **E~ung** *f* - amusement

erhitzen *vt* heat; **sich e~** get hot; (*fig*) get heated

erhoffen *vt* **sich** (*dat*) **etw e~** hope for sth

erhöh|en *vt* raise; (*fig*) increase. **E~en** rise, increase. **E~ung** *f* -,-en increase. **E~ungszeichen** *nt* (*Mus*) sharp

erhol|en (sich) *vr* recover (**von** from); (*nach Krankheit*) convalesce, recuperate; (*sich ausruhen*) have a rest. **e~sam** *a* restful. **E~ung** *f* - recovery; convalescence; (*Ruhe*) rest. **E~ungsheim** *nt* convalescent home

erhören *vt* (*fig*) answer

erinner|n *vt* remind (**an** + *acc* of); **sich e~n** remember (**an jdn/etw** s.o./sth). **E~ung** *f* -,-en memory; (*Andenken*) souvenir

erkält|en (sich) *vr* catch a cold; **e~et sein** have a cold. **E~ung** *f* -,-en cold

erkenn|bar *a* recognizable; (*sichtbar*) visible. **e~en†** *vt* recognize; (*wahrnehmen*) distinguish; (*einsehen*) realize. **e~tlich** *a*

sich e~tlich zeigen show one's appreciation. **E~tnis** *f* -,-se recognition; realization; (*Wissen*) knowledge; **die neuesten E~tnisse** the latest findings

Erker *m* **-s,-** bay

erklär|en *vt* declare; (*erläutern*) explain; **sich bereit e~en** agree (**zu** to); **ich kann es mir nicht e~en** I can't explain it. **e~end** *a* explanatory. **e~lich** *a* explicable; (*verständlich*) understandable. **e~licherweise** *adv* understandably. **e~t** *attrib a* declared. **E~ung** *f* -,-en declaration; explanation; **öffentliche E~ung** public statement

erklingen† *vi* (*sein*) ring out

erkrank|en *vi* (*sein*) fall ill; be taken ill (**an** + *dat* with). **E~ung** *f* -,-en illness

erkunden *vt* explore; (*Mil*) reconnoitre

erkundig|en (sich) *vr* enquire (**nach jdm/etw** after s.o./about sth). **E~ung** *f* -,-en enquiry

erlahmen *vi* (*sein*) tire; ⟨*Kraft, Eifer:*⟩ flag

erlangen *vt* attain, get

Erlass *m* **-es,-̈e** (**Erlaß** *m* **-sses,-̈sse**) (*Admin*) decree; (*Befreiung*) exemption; (*Straf-*) remission

erlassen† *vt* (*Admin*) issue; **jdm etw e~** exempt s.o. from sth; let s.o. off ⟨*Strafe*⟩

erlauben *vt* allow, permit; **sich e~, etw zu tun** take the liberty of doing sth; **ich kann es mir nicht e~** I can't afford it

Erlaubnis *f* - permission. **E~schein** *m* permit

erläuter|n *vt* explain. **E~ung** *f* -,-en explanation

Erle *f* -,-n alder

erleb|en *vt* experience; (*mit-*) see; have ⟨*Überraschung, Enttäuschung*⟩; **etw nicht mehr e~en** not live to see sth. **E~nis** *nt* -ses,-se experience

erledig|en *vt* do; (*sich befassen mit*) deal with; (*beenden*) finish; (*entscheiden*) settle; (*töten*) kill; **e~t sein** be done/settled / ⟨*fam: müde*⟩ worn out / ⟨*fam: ruiniert*⟩ finished

erleichter|n *vt* lighten; (*vereinfachen*) make easier; (*befreien*) relieve; (*lindern*) ease; **sich e~n** (*fig*) unburden oneself. **e~t** *a* relieved. **E~ung** *f* - relief

erleiden† *vt* suffer

erlernen *vt* learn

erlesen *a* exquisite; (*auserlesen*) choice, select

erleucht|en *vt* illuminate; **hell e~et** brightly lit. **E~ung** *f* -,-en (*fig*) inspiration

erliegen† *vi* (*sein*) succumb (*dat* to); **seinen Verletzungen e~** die of one's injuries

erlogen *a* untrue, false

Erlös *m* -es proceeds *pl*

erlöschen† *vi* (*sein*) go out; (*vergehen*) die; (*aussterben*) die out; (*ungültig werden*) expire; **erloschener Vulkan** extinct volcano

erlös|en *vt* save; (*befreien*) release (**von** from); (*Relig*) redeem. **e~t** *a* relieved. **E~ung** *f* release; (*Erleichterung*) relief; (*Relig*) redemption

ermächtig|en *vt* authorize. **E~ung** *f* -,-en authorization

ermahn|en *vt* exhort; (*zurechtweisen*) admonish. **E~ung** *f* exhortation; admonition

ermäßig|en *vt* reduce. **E~ung** *f* -,-en reduction

ermatt|en *vi* (*sein*) grow weary □ *vt* weary. **E~ung** *f* - weariness

ermessen† *vt* judge; (*begreifen*) appreciate. **E~** *nt* -s discretion; (*Urteil*) judgement; **nach eigenem E~** at one's own discretion

ermitt|eln *vt* establish; (*herausfinden*) find out □ *vi* (*haben*) investigate (**gegen jdn** s.o.). **E~lungen** *fpl* investigations. **E~lungsverfahren** *nt* (*Jur*) preliminary inquiry

ermöglichen *vt* make possible

ermord|en *vt* murder. **E~ung** *f* -,-en murder

ermüd|en *vt* tire □ *vi* (*sein*) get tired. **E~ung** *f* - tiredness

ermunter|n *vt* encourage; **sich e~n** rouse oneself. **E~ung** *f* - encouragement

ermutigen *vt* encourage. **e~d** *a* encouraging

ernähr|en *vt* feed; (*unterhalten*) support, keep; **sich e~en von** live/⟨*Tier:*⟩ feed on. **E~er** *m* -s,- breadwinner. **E~ung** *f* - nourishment; nutrition; (*Kost*) diet

ernenn|en† *vt* appoint. **E~ung** *f* -,-en appointment

erneu|ern *vt* renew; (*auswechseln*) replace; change (*Verband*); (*renovieren*) renovate. **E~erung** *f* renewal; replacement; renovation. **e~t** *a* renewed; (*neu*) new □ *adv* again

erniedrig|en *vt* degrade; **sich e~en** lower oneself. **e~end** *a* degrading. **E~ungszeichen** *nt* (*Mus*) flat

ernst *a* serious, *adv* -ly; **e~ nehmen** take seriously. **E~** *m* -es seriousness; **im E~** seriously; **mit einer Drohung E~ machen** carry out a threat; **ist das dein E~?** are you serious? **E~fall** *m* **im E~fall** when the real thing happens. **e~haft** *a* serious, *adv* -ly. **e~lich** *a* serious, *adv* -ly

Ernte *f* -,-n harvest; (*Ertrag*) crop. **E~dankfest** *nt* harvest festival. **e~n** *vt* harvest; (*fig*) reap, win

ernüchter|n *vt* sober up; (*fig*) bring down to earth; (*enttäuschen*) disillusion. **e~nd** *a* (*fig*) sobering. **E~ung** *f* - disillusionment

Erober|er *m* -s,- conqueror. **e~n** *vt* conquer. **E~ung** *f* -,-en conquest

eröffn|en *vt* open; **jdm etw e~en** announce sth to s.o.; **sich jdm e~en** ⟨*Aussicht:*⟩ present itself to s.o. **E~ung** *f* opening; (*Mitteilung*) announcement. **E~ungsansprache** *f* opening address

erörter|n *vt* discuss. **E~ung** *f* -,-en discussion

Erosion *f* -,-en erosion

Erot|ik *f* - eroticism. **e~isch** *a* erotic

Erpel *m* -s,- drake

erpicht *a* **e~ auf** (+ *acc*) keen on

erpress|en *vt* extort; blackmail ⟨*Person*⟩. **E~er** *m* -s,- blackmailer. **E~ung** *f* - extortion; blackmail

erprob|en *vt* test. **e~t** *a* proven

erquicken *vt* refresh

erraten† *vt* guess

erreg|bar *a* excitable. **e~en** *vt* excite; (*hervorrufen*) arouse; **sich e~en** get worked up. **e~end** *a* exciting. **E~er** *m* -s,- (*Med*) germ. **e~t** *a* agitated; (*hitzig*) heated. **E~ung** *f* - excitement; (*Erregtheit*) agitation

erreich|bar *a* within reach; ⟨*Ziel*⟩ attainable; ⟨*Person*⟩ available. **e~en** *vt* reach; catch ⟨*Zug*⟩; live to ⟨*Alter*⟩; (*durchsetzen*) achieve

erretten *vt* save

errichten *vt* erect

erringen† *vt* gain, win

erröten *vi* (*sein*) blush

Errungenschaft *f* -,-en achievement; (*fam: Anschaffung*) acquisition; **E~en der Technik** technical advances

Ersatz *m* -es replacement, substitute; (*Entschädigung*) compensation. **E~dienst** *m* = Zivildienst. **E~reifen** *m* spare tyre. **E~spieler(in)** *m(f)* substitute. **E~teil** *nt* spare part

ersäufen *vt* drown

erschaffen† *vt* create

erschallen† *vi* (*sein*) ring out

erschein|en† *vi* (*sein*) appear; ⟨*Buch:*⟩ be published; **jdm merkwürdig e~en** seem odd to s.o. **E~en** *nt* -s appearance; publication. **E~ung** *f* -,-en appearance; (*Person*) figure; (*Phänomen*) phenomenon; (*Symptom*) symptom; (*Geist*) apparition

erschieß|en† *vt* shoot [dead]. **E~ungskommando** *nt* firing squad

erschlaffen *vi* (*sein*) go limp; ⟨*Haut, Muskeln:*⟩ become flabby

erschlagen† *vt* beat to death; (*tödlich treffen*) strike dead; **vom Blitz e~ werden** be killed by lightning □ *a* (*fam*) (*erschöpft*) worn out; (*fassungslos*) stunned

erschließen† *vt* develop; (*zugänglich machen*) open up; (*nutzbar machen*) tap

erschöpf|en *vt* exhaust. **e~end** *a* exhausting; (*fig: vollständig*) exhaustive. **e~t** *a* exhausted. **E~ung** *f* - exhaustion

erschreck|en *vi* (*sein*) get a fright □ *vt* (*reg*) startle; (*beunruhigen*) alarm; **du hast mich e~t** you gave me a fright □ *vr* (*reg & irreg*) **sich e~en** get a fright. **e~end** *a* alarming, *adv* -ly

erschrocken *a* frightened; (*erschreckt*) startled; (*bestürzt*) dismayed

erschütter|n *vt* shake; (*ergreifen*) upset deeply. **E~ung** *f* -,-en shock

erschweren *vt* make more difficult

erschwinglich *a* affordable

ersehen† *vt* (*fig*) see (aus from)

ersetzen *vt* replace; make good ⟨*Schaden*⟩; refund ⟨*Kosten*⟩; **jdm etw e~** compensate s.o. for sth

ersichtlich *a* obvious, apparent

erspar|en *vt* save; **jdm etw e~en** save/(*fern halten*) spare s.o. sth. **E~nis** *f* -,-se saving; **E~nisse** savings

erst *adv* (*zuerst*) first; (*noch nicht mehr als*) only; (*nicht vor*) not until; **e~ dann** only then; **eben od gerade e~** [only] just; **das machte ihn e~ recht wütend** it made him all the more angry

erstarren *vi* (*sein*) solidify; (*gefrieren*) freeze; (*steif werden*) go stiff; (*vor Schreck*) be paralysed

erstatten *vt* (*zurück-*) refund; **Bericht e~** report (**jdm** to s.o.)

Erstaufführung *f* first performance, première

erstaun|en *vt* amaze, astonish. **E~en** *nt* amazement, astonishment. **e~lich** *a* amazing, *adv* -ly. **e~licherweise** *adv* amazingly

Erst|ausgabe *f* first edition. **e~e(r,s)** *a* first; (*beste*) best; **e~e** (**E~e**) **Hilfe** first aid; **der e~e Beste** (**beste**) the first one to come along; (*fam*) any Tom, Dick or Harry; **als e~es/fürs e~e** NEW **als E~es/fürs E~e**, *s.* **Erste(r,s)**. **E~e(r)** *m/f* first; (*Beste*) best; **fürs E~e** for the time being; **als E~es** first of all; **er kam als E~er** he arrived first; **er ist der/sie ist die E~e in Latein** he/she is top in Latin

erstechen† *vt* stab to death

erstehen† *vt* buy

ersteigern *vt* buy at an auction

erst|emal *adv* **das e~emal/zum e~enmal** NEW **das erste Mal/zum ersten Mal**, *s.* **Mal**[1]. **e~ens** *adv* firstly, in the first place. **e~ere(r,s)** *a* the former; **der/die/das E~ere** (**e~ere**) the former

ersticken *vt* suffocate; smother ⟨*Flammen*⟩; (*unterdrücken*) suppress □ *vi* (*sein*) suffocate. **E~ nt -s** suffocation; **zum E~** stifling

erst|klassig *a* first-class. **e~mals** *adv* for the first time

erstreben *vt* strive for. **e~swert** *a* desirable

erstrecken (**sich**) *vr* stretch; **sich e~ auf** (+ *acc*) (*fig*) apply to

ersuchen *vt* ask, request. **E~ nt -s** request

ertappen *vt* (*fam*) catch

erteilen *vt* give (**jdm** s.o.)

ertönen *vi* (*sein*) sound; (*erschallen*) ring out

Ertrag *m* -[e]s,⁻e yield. **e~en†** *vt* bear

erträglich *a* bearable; (*leidlich*) tolerable

ertränken *vt* drown

ertrinken† *vi* (*sein*) drown

erübrigen (**sich**) *vr* be unnecessary

erwachen *vi* (*sein*) awake

erwachsen *a* grown-up. **E~e(r)** *m/f* adult, grown-up

erwäg|en† *vt* consider. **E~ung** *f* -,-en consideration; **in E~ung ziehen** consider

erwähn|en *vt* mention. **E~ung** *f* -,-en mention

erwärmen *vt* warm; **sich e~** warm up; (*fig*) warm (**für** to)

erwart|en *vt* expect; (*warten auf*) wait for. **E~ung** *f* -,-en expectation. **e~ungsvoll** *a* expectant, *adv* -ly

erwecken *vt* (*fig*) arouse; give ⟨*Anschein*⟩

erweichen *vt* soften; (*fig*) move; **sich e~ lassen** (*fig*) relent

erweisen† *vt* prove; (*bezeigen*) do ⟨*Gefallen, Dienst, Ehre*⟩; **sich e~ als** prove to be

erweitern *vt* widen; dilate ⟨*Pupille*⟩; (*fig*) extend, expand

Erwerb *m* -[e]s acquisition; (*Kauf*) purchase; (*Brot-*) livelihood; (*Verdienst*) earnings *pl.* **e~en†** *vt* acquire; (*kaufen*) purchase; (*fig: erlangen*) gain. **e~slos** *a* unemployed. **e~stätig** *a* [gainfully] employed. **E~ung** *f* -,-en acquisition

erwider|n *vt* reply; return ⟨*Besuch, Gruß*⟩. **E~ung** *f* -,-en reply

erwirken *vt* obtain

erwischen *vt* (*fam*) catch

erwünscht *a* desired

erwürgen *vt* strangle

Erz nt -es,-e ore

erzähl|en vt tell (jdm s.o.) ◻ vi (haben) talk (von about). **E~er** m -s,- narrator. **E~ung** f -,-en story, tale

Erzbischof m archbishop

erzeug|en vt produce; (Electr) generate; (fig) create. **E~er** m -s,- producer; (Vater) father. **E~nis** nt -ses,-se product; **landwirtschaftliche E~nisse** farm produce sg. **E~ung** f - production; generation

Erz|feind m arch-enemy. **E~herzog** m archduke

erzieh|en† vt bring up; (Sch) educate. **E~er** m -s,- [private] tutor. **E~erin** f -,-nen governess. **E~ung** f - upbringing; education

erzielen vt achieve; score ⟨Tor⟩

erzogen a **gut/schlecht e~** well/badly brought up

erzürnt a angry

erzwingen† vt force

es pron it; (Mädchen) she; (acc) her; impers **es regnet** it is raining; **es gibt** there is/(pl) are; **ich hoffe es** I hope so

Esche f -,-n ash

Esel m -s,- donkey; (fam: Person) ass. **E~sohr** nt **E~sohren haben** ⟨Buch:⟩ be dog-eared

Eskal|ation /-'tsio:n/ f - escalation. **e~ieren** vt/i (haben) escalate

Eskimo m -[s],-[s] Eskimo

Eskort|e f -,-n (Mil) escort. **e~ieren** vt escort

essbar (eßbar) a edible. **Essecke** (Eßecke) f dining area

essen† vt/i (haben) eat; **zu Mittag/Abend e~** have lunch/supper; **[auswärts] e~ gehen** eat out; **chinesisch e~** have a Chinese meal. **E~** nt -s,- food; (Mahl) meal; (festlich) dinner

Essenz f -,-en essence

Esser(in) m -s,- (f -,-nen) eater

Essig m -s vinegar. **E~gurke** f [pickled] gherkin

Esskastanie (Eßkastanie) f sweet chestnut. **Esslöffel** (Eßlöffel) m ≈ dessertspoon. **Essstäbchen** (Eßstäbchen) ntpl chopsticks. **Esstisch** (Eßtisch) m dining-table. **Esswaren** (Eßwaren) fpl food sg; (Vorräte) provisions. **Esszimmer** (Eßzimmer) nt diningroom

Estland nt -s Estonia

Estragon m -s tarragon

etablieren (sich) vr establish oneself/ ⟨Geschäft:⟩ itself

Etage /e'ta:ʒə/ f -,-n storey. **E~nbett** nt bunk-beds pl. **E~nwohnung** f flat, (Amer) apartment

Etappe f -,-n stage

Etat /e'ta:/ m -s,-s budget

etepetete a (fam) fussy

Eth|ik f - ethic; (Sittenlehre) ethics sg. **e~isch** a ethical

Etikett nt -[e]s,-e[n] label; (Preis-) tag. **E~e** f -,-n etiquette; (Aust) = Etikett. **e~ieren** vt label

etlich|e(r,s) pron some; (mehrere) several; **e~e Mal** several times; **e~es** a number of things; (ziemlich viel) quite a lot. **e~emal** adv (NEW) **e~e Mal**, s. etliche(r,s)

Etui /e'tvi:/ nt -s,-s case

etwa adv (ungefähr) about; (zum Beispiel) for instance; (womöglich) perhaps; **nicht e~, dass** ... not that ...; **denkt nicht e~** ... don't imagine ...; **du hast doch nicht e~ Angst?** you're not afraid, are you? **e~ig** a possible

etwas pron something; (fragend/verneint) anything; (ein bisschen) some, a little; **ohne e~ zu sagen** without saying anything; **sonst noch e~?** anything else? **noch e~ Tee?** some more tea? **so e~ Ärgerliches!** what a nuisance! ◻ adv a bit

Etymologie f - etymology

euch pron (acc of ihr pl) you; (dat) [to] you; (refl) yourselves; (einander) each other; **ein Freund von e~** a friend of yours

euer poss pron pl your. **e~e, e~t-** s. **eure, euret-**

Eule f -,-n owl

Euphorie f - euphoria

eur|e poss pron pl your. **e~e(r,s)** poss pron yours. **e~erseits** adv for your part. **e~etwegen** adv for your sake; (wegen euch) because of you, on your account. **e~etwillen** adv **um e~etwillen** for your sake. **e~ige** poss pron **der/die/das e~ige** yours

Euro m -[s]/-[s] Euro. **E~** pref Euro-

Europa nt -s Europe. **E~-** pref European

Europä|er(in) m -s,- (f-,-nen) European. **e~isch** a European; **E~ische Gemeinschaft** European Community

Euro|paß m Europassport. **E~scheck** m Eurocheque

Euter nt -s,- udder

evakuier|en vt evacuate. **E~ung** f - evacuation

evan|gelisch a Protestant. **E~gelist** m -en,-en evangelist. **E~gelium** nt -s,-ien gospel

evaporieren vt/i (sein) evaporate

Eventu|alität f -,-en eventuality. **e~ell** a possible ◻ adv possibly; (vielleicht) perhaps

Evolution /-'tsio:n/ f - evolution

evtl. *abbr s.* **eventuell**

ewig *a* eternal, *adv* -ly; *(fam: ständig)* constant, *adv* -ly; *(endlos)* never-ending; **e~ dauern** *(fam)* take ages. **E~keit** *f* - eternity; **eine E~keit** *(fam)* ages

exakt *a* exact, *adv* -ly. **E~heit** *f* - exactitude

Examen *nt* -s,- & -mina *(Sch)* examination

Exekutive *f* - *(Pol)* executive

Exempel *nt* -s,- example; **ein E~ an jdm statuieren** make an example of s.o.

Exemplar *nt* -s,-e specimen; *(Buch)* copy. **e~isch** *a* exemplary

exerzieren *vt/i (haben) (Mil)* drill; *(üben)* practise

exhumieren *vt* exhume

Exil *nt* -s exile

Existenz *f* -,-en existence; *(Lebensgrundlage)* livelihood; *(pej: Person)* individual

existieren *vi (haben)* exist

exklusiv *a* exclusive. **e~e** *prep (+ gen)* excluding

exkommunizieren *vt* excommunicate

Exkremente *npl* excrement *sg*

exotisch *a* exotic

expan|dieren *vt/i (haben)* expand. **E~sion** *f* - expansion

Expedition /-'tsio:n/ *f* -,-en expedition

Experiment *nt* -[e]s,-e experiment. **e~ell** *a* experimental. **e~ieren** *vi (haben)* experiment

Experte *m* -n,-n expert

explo|dieren *vi (sein)* explode. **E~sion** *f* -,-en explosion. **e~siv** *a* explosive

Expor|t *m* -[e]s,-e export. **E~teur** /-'tø:ɐ̯/ *m* -s,-e exporter. **e~tieren** *vt* export

Express *m* -es,-e **(Expreß** *m* -sses,-sse)** express

extra *adv* separately; *(zusätzlich)* extra; *(eigens)* specially; *(fam: absichtlich)* on purpose

Extrakt *m* -[e]s,-e extract

Extras *ntpl (Auto)* extras

extravagan|t *a* flamboyant, *adv* -ly; *(übertrieben)* extravagant. **E~z** *f* -,-en flamboyance; extravagance; *(Überspanntheit)* folly

extravertiert *a* extrovert

extrem *a* extreme, *adv* -ly. **E~** *nt* -s,-e extreme. **E~ist** *m* -en,-en extremist. **E~itäten** *fpl* extremities

Exzellenz *f* - *(title)* Excellency

Exzen|triker *m* -s,- eccentric. **e~isch** *a* eccentric

Exzess *m* -es,-e **(Exzeß** *m* -sses, -sse)** excess

F

Fabel *f* -,-n fable. **f~haft** *a (fam)* fantastic, *adv* -ally

Fabrik *f* -,-en factory. **F~ant** *m* -en,-en manufacturer. **F~at** *nt* -[e]s,-e product; *(Marke)* make. **F~ation** /-'tsio:n/ *f* - manufacture

Facette /fa'sɛtə/ *f* -,-n facet

Fach *nt* -[e]s,-̈er compartment; *(Schub-)* drawer; *(Gebiet)* field; *(Sch)* subject. **F~arbeiter** *m* skilled worker. **F~arzt** *m*, **F~ärztin** *f* specialist. **F~ausdruck** *m* technical term

fäch|eln (sich) *vr* fan oneself. **F~er** *m* -s,- fan

Fach|gebiet *nt* field. **f~gemäß, f~gerecht** *a* expert, *adv* -ly. **F~hochschule** *f* ≈ technical university. **f~kundig** *a* expert, *adv* -ly. **f~lich** *a* technical, *adv* -ly; *(beruflich)* professional. **F~mann** *m (pl* -leute) expert. **f~männisch** *a* expert, *adv* -ly. **F~schule** *f* technical college. **f~simpeln** *vi (haben) (fam)* talk shop. **F~werkhaus** *nt* half-timbered house. **F~wort** *nt (pl* -wörter) technical term

Fackel *f* -,-n torch. **F~zug** *m* torchlight procession

fade *a* insipid; *(langweilig)* dull

Faden *m* -s,-̈ thread; *(Bohnen-)* string; *(Naut)* fathom. **f~scheinig** *a* threadbare; *(Grund)* flimsy

Fagott *nt* -[e]s,-e bassoon

fähig *a* capable **(zu/gen** of); *(tüchtig)* able, competent. **F~keit** *f* -,-en ability; competence

fahl *a* pale

fahnd|en *vi (haben)* search **(nach** for). **F~ung** *f* -,-en search

Fahne *f* -,-n flag; *(Druck-)* galley [proof]; **eine F~ haben** *(fam)* reek of alcohol. **F~nflucht** *f* desertion. **f~nflüchtig** *a* **f~nflüchtig werden** desert

Fahr|ausweis *m* ticket. **F~bahn** *f* carriageway; *(Straße)* road. **f~bar** *a* mobile

Fähre *f* -,-n ferry

fahr|en† *vi (sein)* go, travel; *(Fahrer:)* drive; *(Radfahrer:)* ride; *(verkehren)* run, *(ab-)* leave; *(Schiff:)* sail; **mit dem Auto/ Zug f~en** go by car/train; **in die Höhe f~en** start up; **in die Kleider f~en** throw on one's clothes; **mit der Hand über etw** *(acc)* **f~en** run one's hand over sth; **was ist in ihn gefahren?** *(fam)* what has got into him? □ *vt* drive; ride *(Fahrrad)*; take

⟨Kurve⟩. f∼end a moving; ⟨f∼bar⟩ mobile; ⟨nicht sesshaft⟩ travelling, itinerant. F∼er m -s,- driver. F∼erflucht f failure to stop after an accident. F∼erhaus nt driver's cab. F∼erin f -,-nen woman driver. F∼gast m passenger; ⟨im Taxi⟩ fare. F∼geld nt fare. F∼gestell nt chassis; ⟨Aviat⟩ undercarriage. f∼ig a nervy; ⟨zerstreut⟩ distracted. F∼karte f ticket. F∼kartenausgabe f, F∼kartenschalter m ticket office. f∼lässig a negligent, adv -ly. F∼lässigkeit f - negligence. F∼lehrer m driving instructor. F∼plan m timetable. f∼planmäßig a scheduled □ adv according to/⟨pünktlich⟩ on schedule. F∼preis m fare. F∼prüfung f driving test. F∼rad nt bicycle. F∼schein m ticket

Fährschiff nt ferry

Fahr|schule f driving school. F∼schüler(in) m(f) learner driver. F∼spur f [traffic] lane. F∼stuhl m lift, ⟨Amer⟩ elevator. F∼stunde f driving lesson

Fahrt f -,-en journey; ⟨Auto⟩ drive; ⟨Ausflug⟩ trip; ⟨Tempo⟩ speed; **in voller F∼** at full speed. **F∼ausweis** m ticket

Fährte f -,-n track; ⟨Witterung⟩ scent; **auf der falschen F∼** ⟨fig⟩ on the wrong track

Fahr|tkosten pl travelling expenses. F∼werk nt undercarriage. F∼zeug nt -[e]s,-e vehicle; ⟨Wasser-⟩ craft, vessel

fair /fɛːɐ̯/ a fair, adv -ly. F∼ness (F∼neß) f - fairness

Fakten pl facts

Faktor m -s,-en /-'toːrən/ factor

Fakul|tät f -,-en faculty. f∼tativ a optional

Falke m -n,-n falcon

Fall m -[e]s,ːe fall; ⟨Jur, Med, Gram⟩ case; **im F∼[e]** in case ⟨gen of⟩; **auf jeden F∼**, **auf alle Fːe** in any case; ⟨bestimmt⟩ definitely; **für alle Fːe** just in case; **auf keinen F∼** on no account

Falle f -,-n trap; **eine F∼ stellen** set a trap ⟨dat for⟩

fallen vi (sein) fall; ⟨sinken⟩ go down; [im Krieg] f∼ be killed in the war; f∼ lassen drop ⟨etw, fig: Plan, jdn⟩; make ⟨Bemerkung⟩

fällen vt fell; ⟨fig⟩ pass ⟨Urteil⟩; make ⟨Entscheidung⟩

fallenlassen† vt sep (NEW) **fallen lassen**, s. **fallen**

fällig a due; ⟨Wechsel⟩ mature; **längst f∼** long overdue. F∼keit f - ⟨Comm⟩ maturity

Fallobst nt windfalls pl

falls conj in case; ⟨wenn⟩ if

Fallschirm m parachute. F∼jäger m paratrooper. F∼springer m parachutist

Falltür f trapdoor

falsch a wrong; ⟨nicht echt, unaufrichtig⟩ false; ⟨gefälscht⟩ forged; ⟨Geld⟩ counterfeit; ⟨Schmuck⟩ fake □ adv wrongly; falsely; ⟨singen⟩ out of tune; **f∼ gehen** ⟨Uhr:⟩ be wrong

fälsch|en vt forge, fake. F∼er m -s,- forger

Falsch|geld nt counterfeit money. F∼heit f - falseness

fälschlich a wrong, adv -ly; ⟨irrtümlich⟩ mistaken, adv -ly. f∼erweise adv by mistake

Falsch|meldung f false report; ⟨absichtlich⟩ hoax report. F∼münzer m -s,- counterfeiter

Fälschung f -,-en forgery; fake; ⟨Fälschen⟩ forging

Falte f -,-n fold; ⟨Rock-⟩ pleat; ⟨Knitter-⟩ crease; ⟨im Gesicht⟩ line; ⟨Runzel⟩ wrinkle

falten vt fold; **sich f∼** ⟨Haut:⟩ wrinkle. F∼rock m pleated skirt

Falter m -s,- butterfly; ⟨Nacht-⟩ moth

faltig a creased; ⟨Gesicht⟩ lined; ⟨runzlig⟩ wrinkled

familiär a family ...; ⟨vertraut, zudringlich⟩ familiar; ⟨zwanglos⟩ informal

Familie /-ᵢə/ f -,-n family. F∼nanschluss (F∼nanschluß) m F∼nanschluss haben live as one of the family. F∼nforschung f genealogy. F∼nleben nt family life. F∼nname m surname. F∼nplanung f family planning. F∼nstand m marital status

Fan /fɛn/ m -s,-s fan

Fana|tiker m -s,- fanatic. f∼tisch a fanatical, adv -ly. F∼tismus m - fanaticism

Fanfare f -,-n trumpet; ⟨Signal⟩ fanfare

Fang m -[e]s,ːe capture; ⟨Beute⟩ catch; Fːe ⟨Krallen⟩ talons; ⟨Zähne⟩ fangs. F∼arm m tentacle. f∼en† vt catch; ⟨ein-⟩ capture; **sich f∼en** get caught ⟨in + dat in⟩; ⟨fig⟩ regain one's balance/⟨seelisch⟩ composure; **gefangen nehmen** take prisoner; **gefangen halten** hold prisoner; keep in captivity ⟨Tier⟩. F∼en nt -s F∼en spielen play tag. F∼frage f catch question. F∼zahn m fang

Fantasie f -,-n = **Phantasie**

fantastisch a = **phantastisch**

Farb|aufnahme f colour photograph. F∼band nt (pl -bänder) typewriter ribbon. F∼e f -,-n colour; ⟨Maler-⟩ paint; ⟨zum Färben⟩ dye; ⟨Karten⟩ suit. f∼echt a colour-fast

färben vt colour; dye ⟨Textilien, Haare⟩; ⟨fig⟩ slant ⟨Bericht⟩; **sich [rot] f∼** turn [red] □ vi (haben) not be colour-fast

farb|enblind a colour-blind. f∼enfroh a colourful. F∼fernsehen nt colour television. F∼film m colour film. F∼foto nt colour photo. **f~ig** *a* coloured □ *adv* in colour. **F~ige(r)** *m/f* coloured man/woman. **F~kasten** *m* box of paints. **f~los** *a* colourless. **F~stift** *m* crayon. **F~stoff** *m* dye; (*Lebensmittel-*) colouring. **F~ton** *m* shade

Färbung *f* -,-en colouring; (*fig: Anstrich*) bias

Farce /'farsə/ *f* -,-n farce; (*Culin*) stuffing

Farn *m* -[e]s,-e, **F~kraut** *nt* fern

Färse *f* -,-n heifer

Fasan *m* -[e]s,-e[n] pheasant

Faschierte(s) *nt* (*Aust*) mince

Fasching *m* -s (*SGer*) carnival

Faschis|mus *m* - fascism. **F~t** *m* -en,-en fascist. **f~tisch** *a* fascist

faseln *vt/i* (*haben*) (*fam*) [Unsinn] f~ talk nonsense

Faser *f* -,-n fibre. **f~n** *vi* (*haben*) fray

Fass *nt* -es,-̈er (**Faß** *nt* -sses,-̈sser) barrel, cask; **Bier vom F~** draught beer; **F~ ohne Boden** (*fig*) bottomless pit

Fassade *f* -,-n façade

fassbar (**faßbar**) *a* comprehensible; (*greifbar*) tangible

fassen *vt* take [hold of], grasp; (*ergreifen*) seize; (*fangen*) catch; (*ein-*) set; (*enthalten*) hold; (*fig: begreifen*) take in, grasp; conceive (*Plan*); make (*Entschluss*); **sich f~** compose oneself; **sich kurz/in Geduld f~** be brief/patient; **in Worte f~** put into words; **nicht zu f~** (*fig*) unbelievable □ *vi* (*haben*) **f~ an** (+ *acc*) touch; **f~ nach** reach for

fasslich (**faßlich**) *a* comprehensible

Fasson /fa'sõ:/ *f* - style; (*Form*) shape; (*Weise*) way

Fassung *f* -,-en mount; (*Edelstein-*) setting; (*Electr*) socket; (*Version*) version; (*Beherrschung*) composure; **aus der F~ bringen** disconcert. **f~slos** *a* shaken; (*erstaunt*) flabbergasted. **F~svermögen** *nt* capacity

fast *adv* almost, nearly; **f~ nie** hardly ever

fast|en *vi* (*haben*) fast. **F~enzeit** *f* Lent. **F~nacht** *f* Shrovetide; (*Karneval*) carnival. **F~nachtsdienstag** *m* Shrove Tuesday. **F~tag** *m* fast-day

Faszin|ation /-'tsjo:n/ *f* - fascination. **f~ieren** *vt* fascinate; **f~ierend** fascinating

fatal *a* fatal; (*peinlich*) embarrassing. **F~ismus** *m* - fatalism. **F~ist** *m* -en,-en fatalist

Fata Morgana *f* --, - -nen mirage

fauchen *vi* (*haben*) spit, hiss □ *vt* snarl

faul *a* lazy; (*verdorben*) rotten, bad; (*Ausrede*) lame; (*zweifelhaft*) bad; (*verdächtig*) fishy

Fäule *f* - decay

faul|en *vi* (*sein*) rot; (*Zahn:*) decay; (*verwesen*) putrefy. **f~enzen** *vi* (*haben*) be lazy. **F~enzer** *m* -s,- lazy-bones *sg.* **F~heit** *f* - laziness. **f~ig** *a* rotting; (*Geruch*) putrid

Fäulnis *f* - decay

Faulpelz *m* (*fam*) lazy-bones *sg*

Fauna *f* - fauna

Faust *f* -,Fäuste fist; **auf eigene F~** (*fig*) off one's own bat. **F~handschuh** *m* mitten. **F~schlag** *m* punch

Fauxpas /fo'pa/ *m* -,- /-[s],-s/ gaffe

Favorit(in) /favo'ri:t(in)/ *m* -en, -en (*f* -,-nen) (*Sport*) favourite

Fax *nt* -,-[e] fax. **f~en** *vt* fax

Faxen *fpl* (*fam*) antics; **F~ machen** fool about; **F~ schneiden** pull faces

Faxgerät *nt* fax machine

Feber *m* -s,- (*Aust*) February

Februar *m* -s,-e February

fecht|en† *vi* (*haben*) fence. **F~er** *m* -s,- fencer

Feder *f* -,-n feather; (*Schreib-*) pen; (*Spitze*) nib; (*Techn*) spring. **F~ball** *m* shuttlecock; (*Spiel*) badminton. **F~busch** *m* plume. **f~leicht** *a* as light as a feather. **F~messer** *nt* penknife. **f~nd** *vi* (*haben*) be springy; (*nachgeben*) give; (*hoch-*) bounce. **f~nd** *a* springy; (*elastisch*) elastic. **F~ung** *f* - (*Techn*) springs *pl*; (*Auto*) suspension

Fee *f* -,-n fairy

Fegefeuer *nt* purgatory

fegen *vt* sweep □ *vi* (*sein*) (*rasen*) tear

Fehde *f* -,-n feud

fehl *a* **f~ am Platze** out of place. **F~betrag** *m* deficit. **f~en** *vi* (*haben*) be missing/(*Sch*) absent; (*mangeln*) be lacking; **es f~t an** (+ *dat*) there is a shortage of; **mir f~t die Zeit** I haven't got the time; **sie/es f~t mir sehr** I miss her/it very much; **was f~t ihm?** what's the matter with him? **es f~te nicht viel und er ...** he very nearly ...; **das hat uns noch gefehlt!** that's all we need! **f~end** *a* missing; (*Sch*) absent

Fehler *m* -s,- mistake, error; (*Sport & fig*) fault; (*Makel*) flaw. **f~frei** *a* faultless, adv -ly. **f~haft** *a* faulty. **f~los** *a* flawless, adv -ly

Fehl|geburt *f* miscarriage. **f~gehen†** *vi* sep (*sein*) go wrong; (*Schuss:*) miss; (*fig*) be mistaken. **F~griff** *m* mistake. **F~kalkulation** *f* miscalculation. **F~schlag** *m* failure. **f~schlagen†** *vi* sep (*sein*) fail. **F~start** *m* (*Sport*) false start. **F~tritt** *m* false step; (*fig*) [moral] lapse. **F~zündung** *f* (*Auto*) misfire

Feier f -,-n celebration; (*Zeremonie*) ceremony; (*Party*) party. F~abend m end of the working day; F~abend machen stop work, (*fam*) knock off; nach F~abend after work. f~lich a solemn, adv -ly; (*förmlich*) formal, adv -ly. F~lichkeit f -,-en solemnity; F~lichkeiten festivities. f~n vt celebrate; hold ⟨*Fest*⟩; (*ehren*) fête □ vi (*haben*) celebrate; (*lustig sein*) make merry. F~tag m [public] holiday; (*kirchlicher*) feast-day; erster/zweiter F~tag Christmas Day / Boxing Day. f~tags adv on public holidays

feige a cowardly; f~ sein be a coward □ adv in a cowardly way

Feige f -,-n fig. F~nbaum m fig tree

Feig|heit f - cowardice. F~ling m -s,-e coward

Feile f -,-n file. f~n vt/i (*haben*) file

feilschen vi (*haben*) haggle

Feilspäne mpl filings

fein a fine, adv -ly; (*zart*) delicate, adv -ly; (*Strümpfe*) sheer; ⟨*Unterschied*⟩ subtle; (*scharf*) keen; (*vornehm*) refined; (*elegant*) elegant; (*prima*) great; sich f~ machen dress up. F~arbeit f precision work

feind a jdm f~ sein NEW jdm F~ sein, s. Feind. F~(in) m -es,-e (f -,-nen) enemy; jdm F~ sein be hostile towards s.o. f~lich a enemy; (*feindselig*) hostile. F~schaft f -,-en enmity. f~selig a hostile. F~seligkeit f -,-en hostility

fein|fühlig a sensitive. F~gefühl nt sensitivity; (*Takt*) delicacy. F~heit f -,-en (s. fein) fineness; delicacy; subtlety; keenness; refinement; F~heiten subtleties. F~kostgeschäft nt delicatessen [shop]. F~schmecker m -s,- gourmet

feist a fat

feixen vi (*haben*) smirk

Feld nt -[e]s,-er field; (*Fläche*) ground; (*Sport*) pitch; (*Schach-*) square; (*auf Formular*) box. F~bau m agriculture. F~bett nt camp-bed, (*Amer*) cot. F~forschung f fieldwork. F~herr m commander. F~marschall m Field Marshal. F~stecher m -s,- field-glasses pl. F~webel m -s,- (*Mil*) sergeant. F~zug m campaign

Felge f -,-n [wheel] rim

Fell nt -[e]s,-e (*Zool*) coat; (*Pelz*) fur; (*abgezogen*) skin, pelt; ein dickes F~ haben (*fam*) be thick-skinned

Fels m -en,-en rock. F~block m boulder. F~en m -s,- rock. f~enfest a (*fig*) firm, adv -ly. f~ig a rocky

feminin a feminine; (*weibisch*) effeminate

Femininum nt -s,-na (*Gram*) feminine

Feminist|(in) m -en,-en (f -,-nen) feminist. f~isch a feminist

Fenchel m -s fennel

Fenster nt -s,- window. F~brett nt window-sill. F~laden m [window] shutter. F~leder nt chamois[-leather]. F~putzer m -s,- window-cleaner. F~scheibe f [window-]pane

Ferien /ˈfeːrjən/ pl holidays; (*Univ*) vacation sg; F~ haben be on holiday. F~ort m holiday resort

Ferkel nt -s,- piglet

fern a distant; der F~e Osten the Far East; f~ halten keep away; sich f~ halten keep away □ adv far away; von f~ from a distance □ prep (+ dat) far [away] from. F~bedienung f remote control. f~bleiben† vi sep (*sein*) stay away (*dat* from). F~e f - distance; in/aus der F~e in the/ from a distance; in weiter F~e far away; (*zeitlich*) in the distant future. f~er a further □ adv (*außerdem*) furthermore; (*in Zukunft*) in future. f~gelenkt a remote-controlled; ⟨*Rakete*⟩ guided. F~gespräch nt long-distance call. f~gesteuert a = f~gelenkt. F~glas nt binoculars pl. f~halten† vt sep NEW f~ halten, s. fern. F~kopierer m -s,- fax machine. F~kurs[us] m correspondence course. F~lenkung f remote control. F~licht nt (*Auto*) full beam. F~meldewesen nt telecommunications pl. F~rohr nt telescope. F~schreiben nt telex. F~schreiber m -s,- telex [machine]

Fernseh|apparat m television set. f~en† vi sep (*haben*) watch television. F~en nt -s television. F~er m -s,- [television] viewer; (*Gerät*) television set. F~gerät nt television set

Fernsprech|amt nt telephone exchange, (*Amer*) central. F~er m telephone. F~nummer f telephone number. F~zelle f telephone box

Fernsteuerung f remote control

Ferse f -,-n heel. F~ngeld nt F~ngeld geben (*fam*) take to one's heels

fertig a finished; (*bereit*) ready; (*Comm*) ready-made; ⟨*Gericht*⟩ ready-to-serve; f~ werden mit finish; (*bewältigen*) cope with; f~ sein have finished; (*fig*) be through (mit jdm with s.o.); (*fam: erschöpft*) be all in/(*seelisch*) shattered; etw f~ bringen od (*fam*) kriegen manage to do sth; (*beenden*) finish sth; ich bringe od (*fam*) kriege es nicht f~ I can't bring myself to do it; etw/jdn f~ machen finish sth; (*bereitmachen*) get sth/s.o. ready; (*fam: erschöpfen*) wear s.o. out; (*seelisch*) shatter s.o.; (*fam: abkanzeln*) carpet s.o.; sich f~ machen get ready; etw f~ stellen complete sth □ adv (*fam: essen/lesen*) finish eating/reading. F~bau m (pl -bauten) prefabricated building.

f~bringen† *vt sep* NEW **f~ bringen**, *s.* **fertig.** **f~en** *vt* make. **F~gericht** *nt* ready-to-serve meal. **F~haus** *nt* prefabricated house. **F~keit** *f* -,-en skill. **f~kriegen** *vt sep* (*fam*) NEW **f~ kriegen**, *s.* **fertig.** **f~machen** *vt sep* NEW **f~ machen**, *s.* **fertig.** **f~stellen** *vt sep* NEW **f~ stellen**, *s.* **fertig.** **F~stellung** *f* completion. **F~ung** *f* - manufacture

fesch *a* (*fam*) attractive; (*flott*) smart; (*Aust: nett*) kind

Fessel *f* -,-n ankle

fesseln *vt* tie up; tie (**an** + *acc* to); (*fig*) fascinate; **ans Bett gefesselt** confined to bed. **F~** *fpl* bonds. **f~d** *a* (*fig*) fascinating; (*packend*) absorbing

fest *a* firm; (*nicht flüssig*) solid; (*erstarrt*) set; (*haltbar*) strong; (*nicht locker*) tight; (*feststehend*) fixed; (*ständig*) steady; (*Anstellung*) permanent; (*Schlaf*) sound; (*Blick, Stimme*) steady; **f~ werden** harden; (*Gelee:*) set; **f~e Nahrung** solids *pl* □ *adv* firmly; tightly; steadily; soundly; (*kräftig, tüchtig*) hard; **f~ schlafen** be fast asleep; **f~ angestellt** permanent

Fest *nt* -[e]s,-e celebration; (*Party*) party; (*Relig*) festival; **frohes F~!** happy Christmas!

fest|angestellt *a* NEW **f~ angestellt**, *s.* **fest.** **f~binden†** *vt sep* tie (**an** + *dat* to). **f~bleiben†** *vi sep* (*sein*) remain firm. **f~e** *adv* (*fam*) hard. **F~essen** *nt* = **F~mahl. f~fahren†** *vi*/*r sep* (*sein*) **[sich] f~fahren** get stuck; (*Verhandlungen:*) reach deadlock. **f~halten†** *v sep* □ *vt* hold on to; (*aufzeichnen*) record; **sich f~halten** hold on □ *vi* (*haben*) **f~halten an** (+ *dat*) (*fig*) stick to; cling to (*Tradition*). **f~igen** *vt* strengthen; **sich f~igen** grow stronger. **F~iger** *m* -s,- styling lotion/(*Schaum-*) mousse. **F~igkeit** *f* - (*s. fest*) firmness; solidity; strength; steadiness. **f~klammern** *vt sep* clip (**an** + *dat* to); **sich f~klammern** cling (**an** + *dat* to). **F~land** *nt* mainland; (*Kontinent*) continent. **f~legen** *vt sep* (*fig*) fix, settle; lay down (*Regeln*); tie up (*Geld*); **sich f~legen** commit oneself

festlich *a* festive, *adv* -ly. **F~keiten** *fpl* festivities

fest|liegen† *vi sep* (*haben*) be fixed, settled. **f~machen** *v sep* □ *vt* fasten/ (*binden*) tie (**an** + *dat* to); (*f~legen*) fix, settle □ *vi* (*haben*) (*Naut*) moor. **F~mahl** *nt* feast; (*Bankett*) banquet. **F~nahme** *f* -,-n arrest. **f~nehmen†** *vt sep* arrest. **F~ordner** *m* steward. **f~setzen** *vt sep* fix, settle; (*inhaftieren*) gaol; **sich f~setzen** collect. **f~sitzen†** *vi sep* (*haben*) be firm/(*Schraube:*) tight; (*haften*) stick; (*nicht weiterkommen*) be stuck. **F~spiele**

npl festival *sg.* **f~stehen†** *vi sep* (*haben*) be certain. **f~stellen** *vt sep* fix; (*ermitteln*) establish; (*bemerken*) notice; (*sagen*) state. **F~stellung** *f* establishment; (*Aussage*) statement; (*Erkenntnis*) realization. **F~tag** *m* special day

Festung *f* -,-en fortress

Fest|zelt *nt* marquee. **f~ziehen†** *vt sep* pull tight. **F~zug** *m* [grand] procession

Fete /ˈfeːtə, ˈfɛːtə/ *f* -,-n party

fett *a* fat; (*f~reich*) fatty; (*fettig*) greasy; (*üppig*) rich; (*Druck*) bold; **f~ gedruckt** bold. **F~** *nt* -[e]s,-e fat; (*flüssig*) grease. **f~arm** *a* low-fat. **f~en** *vt* grease □ *vi* (*haben*) be greasy. **F~fleck** *m* grease mark. **f~ig** *a* greasy. **f~leibig** *a* obese. **F~näpfchen** *nt* **ins F~näpfchen treten** (*fam*) put one's foot in it

Fetzen *m* -s,- scrap; (*Stoff*) rag; **in F~** in shreds

feucht *a* damp, moist; (*Luft*) humid. **f~heiß** *a* humid. **F~igkeit** *f* - dampness; (*Nässe*) moisture; (*Luft-*) humidity. **F~igkeitscreme** *f* moisturizer

feudal *a* (*fam: vornehm*) sumptuous, *adv* -ly. **F~ismus** *m* - feudalism

Feuer *nt* -s,- fire; (*für Zigarette*) light; (*Begeisterung*) passion; **F~ machen** light a fire; **F~ fangen** catch fire; (*fam: sich verlieben*) be smitten; **jdm F~ geben** give s.o. a light; **F~ speiender Berg** volcano. **F~alarm** *m* fire alarm. **F~bestattung** *f* cremation. **f~gefährlich** *a* [in]flammable. **F~leiter** *f* fire-escape. **F~löscher** *m* -s,- fire extinguisher. **F~melder** *m* -s,- fire alarm. **f~n** *vi* (*haben*) fire (**auf** + *acc* on) □ *vt* (*fam*) (*schleudern*) fling; (*entlassen*) fire. **F~probe** *f* (*fig*) test. **f~rot** *a* crimson. **F~speiend** *a* NEW **F~ speiend**, *s.* **Feuer.** **F~stein** *m* flint. **F~stelle** *f* hearth. **F~treppe** *f* fire-escape. **F~wache** *f* fire station. **F~waffe** *f* firearm. **F~wehr** *f* -,-en fire brigade. **F~wehrauto** *nt* fire-engine. **F~wehrmann** *m* (*pl* -männer & -leute) fireman. **F~werk** *nt* firework display, fireworks *pl.* **F~werkskörper** *m* firework. **F~zeug** *nt* lighter

feurig *a* fiery; (*fig*) passionate

Fiaker *m* -s,- (*Aust*) horse-drawn cab

Fichte *f* -,-n spruce

fidel *a* cheerful

Fieber *nt* -s [raised] temperature; **F~ haben** have a temperature. **F~haft** *a* (*fig*) feverish, *adv* -ly. **f~n** *vi* (*haben*) be feverish. **F~thermometer** *nt* thermometer

fiebrig *a* feverish

fies *a* (*fam*) nasty, *adv* -ily

Figur *f* -,-en figure; (*Roman-, Film-*) character; (*Schach-*) piece

Fik|tion /-'tsjo:n/ *f* -,-en fiction. **f~tiv** *a* fictitious

Filet /fi'le:/ *nt* -s,-s fillet

Filia|le *f* -,-n, **F~geschäft** *nt* (*Comm*) branch

Filigran *nt* -s filigree

Film *m* -[e]s,-e film; (*Kino-*) film, (*Amer*) movie; (*Schicht*) coating. **f~en** *vt/i* (*haben*) film. **F~kamera** *f* cine-/(*für Kinofilm*) film camera

Filt|er *m* & (*Techn*) *nt* -s,- filter; (*Zigaretten-*) filter-tip. **f~ern** *vt* filter. **F~erzigarette** *f* filter-tipped cigarette. **f~rieren** *vt* filter

Filz *m* -es felt. **f~en** *vi* (*haben*) become matted □ *vt* (*fam*) (*durchsuchen*) frisk; (*stehlen*) steal. **F~schreiber** *m* -s,-, **F~stift** *m* felt-tipped pen

Fimmel *m* -s,- (*fam*) obsession

Fina|le *nt* -s,- (*Mus*) finale; (*Sport*) final. **F~list(in)** *m* -en,-en (*f* -,-nen) finalist

Finanz *f* -,-en finance. **F~amt** *nt* tax office. **f~iell** *a* financial, *adv* -ly. **f~ieren** *vt* finance. **F~minister** *m* minister of finance

find|en† *vt* find; (*meinen*) think; **den Tod f~en** meet one's death; **wie f~est du das?** what do you think of that? **f~est du?** do you think so? **es wird sich f~en** it'll turn up; (*fig*) it'll be all right □ *vi* (*haben*) find one's way. **F~er** *m* -s,- finder. **F~erlohn** *m* reward. **f~ig** *a* resourceful. **F~ling** *m* -s,-e boulder

Finesse *f* -,-n (*Kniff*) trick; **F~n** (*Techn*) refinements

Finger *m* -s,- finger; **die F~ lassen von** (*fam*) leave alone; **etw im kleinen F~ haben** (*fam*) have sth at one's fingertips. **F~abdruck** *m* finger-mark; (*Admin*) fingerprint. **F~hut** *m* thimble. **F~nagel** *m* finger-nail. **F~ring** *m* ring. **F~spitze** *f* finger-tip. **F~zeig** *m* -[e]s,-e hint

fingier|en *vt* fake. **f~t** *a* fictitious

Fink *m* -en,-en finch

Finn|e *m* -n,-n, **F~in** *f* -,-nen Finn. **f~isch** *a* Finnish. **F~land** *nt* -s Finland

finster *a* dark; (*düster*) gloomy; (*unheildrohend*) sinister; **im F~n** in the dark. **F~nis** *f* - darkness; (*Astr*) eclipse

Finte *f* -,-n trick; (*Boxen*) feint

Firma *f* -,-men firm, company

firmen *vt* (*Relig*) confirm

Firmen|wagen *m* company car. **F~zeichen** *nt* trade mark, logo

Firmung *f* -,-en (*Relig*) confirmation

Firnis *m* -ses,-se varnish. **f~sen** *vt* varnish

First *m* -[e]s,-e [roof] ridge

Fisch *m* -[e]s,-e fish; **F~e** (*Astr*) Pisces. **F~dampfer** *m* trawler. **f~en** *vt/i* (*haben*) fish; **aus dem Wasser f~en** (*fam*) fish out of the water. **F~er** *m* -s,- fisherman. **F~erei** *f* -, **F~fang** *m* fishing. **F~gräte** *f* fishbone. **F~händler** *m* fishmonger. **F~otter** *m* otter. **F~reiher** *m* heron. **F~stäbchen** *nt* -s,- fish finger. **F~teich** *m* fish-pond

Fiskus *m* - **der F~** the Treasury

Fisole *f* -,-n (*Aust*) French bean

fit *a* fit. **Fitness (Fitneß)** *f* - fitness

fix *a* (*fam*) quick, *adv* -ly; (*geistig*) bright; **f~e Idee** obsession; **fix und fertig** all finished; (*bereit*) all ready; (*fam: erschöpft*) shattered. **F~er** *m* -s,- (*sl*) junkie

fixieren *vt* stare at; (*Phot*) fix

Fjord *m* -[e]s,-e fiord

FKK *abbr* (*Freikörperkultur*) naturism

flach *a* flat; (*eben*) level; (*niedrig*) low; (*nicht tief*) shallow; **f~er Teller** dinner plate; **die f~e Hand** the flat of the hand

Fläche *f* -,-n area; (*Ober-*) surface; (*Seite*) face. **F~nmaß** *nt* square measure

Flachs *m* -es flax. **f~blond** *a* flaxen-haired; (*Haar*) flaxen

flackern *vi* (*haben*) flicker

Flagge *f* -,-n flag

flagrant *a* flagrant

Flair /flɛ:ɐ̯/ *nt* -s air, aura

Flak *f* -,-[s] anti-aircraft artillery/(*Geschütz*) gun

flämisch *a* Flemish

Flamme *f* -,-n flame; (*Koch-*) burner; **in F~n** in flames

Flanell *m* -s (*Tex*) flannel

Flank|e *f* -,-n flank. **f~ieren** *vt* flank

Flasche *f* -,-n bottle. **F~nbier** *nt* bottled beer. **F~nöffner** *m* bottle-opener

flatter|haft *a* fickle. **f~n** *vi* (*sein/haben*) flutter; (*Segel:*) flap

flau *a* (*schwach*) faint; (*Comm*) slack; **mir ist f~** I feel faint

Flaum *m* -[e]s down. **f~ig** *a* downy; **f~ig rühren** (*Aust Culin*) cream

flauschig *a* fleecy; (*Spielzeug*) fluffy

Flausen *fpl* (*fam*) silly ideas; (*Ausflüchte*) silly excuses

Flaute *f* -,-n (*Naut*) calm; (*Comm*) slack period; (*Schwäche*) low

fläzen (sich) *vr* (*fam*) sprawl

Flechte *f* -,-n (*Med*) eczema; (*Bot*) lichen; (*Zopf*) plait. **f~n†** *vt* plait; weave (*Korb*)

Fleck *m* -[e]s,-e[n] spot; (*größer*) patch; (*Schmutz-*) stain, mark; **blauer F~** bruise; **nicht vom F~ kommen** (*fam*) make no progress. **f~en** *vi* (*haben*) stain. **F~en** *m* -s,- = **Fleck**; (*Ortschaft*) small town. f~enlos a spotless. F~entferner m -s,- stain remover. f~ig a stained; ⟨Haut⟩ blotchy

Fledermaus f bat

Flegel m -s,- lout. f~haft a loutish. F~jahre npl ⟨fam⟩ awkward age sg. f~n (sich) vr loll

flehen vi ⟨haben⟩ beg (um for). f~tlich a pleading, adv -ly

Fleisch nt -[e]s flesh; ⟨Culin⟩ meat; ⟨Frucht-⟩ pulp; F~ fressend carnivorous. F~er m -s,- butcher. F~erei f -,-en, F~erladen m butcher's shop. f~fressend a (NEW) F~ fressend, s. Fleisch. F~fresser m -s,- carnivore. F~hauer m -s,- ⟨Aust⟩ butcher. f~ig a fleshy. f~lich a carnal. F~wolf m mincer. F~wunde f flesh-wound

Fleiß m -es diligence; mit F~ diligently; ⟨absichtlich⟩ on purpose. f~ig a diligent, adv -ly; ⟨arbeitsam⟩ industrious, adv -ly

flektieren vt ⟨Gram⟩ inflect

fletschen vt die Zähne f~ ⟨Tier:⟩ bare its teeth

flex|ibel a flexible; ⟨Einband⟩ limp. F~ibilität f - flexibility. F~ion f -,-en ⟨Gram⟩ inflexion

flicken vt mend; ⟨mit Flicken⟩ patch. F~ m -s,- patch

Flieder m -s lilac. f~farben a lilac

Fliege f -,-n fly; ⟨Schleife⟩ bow-tie; zwei F~n mit einer Klappe schlagen kill two birds with one stone. f~n† vi ⟨sein⟩ fly; ⟨geworfen werden⟩ be thrown; ⟨fam: fallen⟩ fall; ⟨fam: entlassen werden⟩ be fired/⟨von der Schule⟩ expelled; in die Luft f~n blow up □ vt fly. f~nd a flying; ⟨Händler⟩ itinerant; in F~nder Eile in great haste. F~r m -s,- airman; ⟨Pilot⟩ pilot; ⟨fam: Flugzeug⟩ plane. F~rangriff m air raid

flieh|en† vi ⟨sein⟩ flee (vor + dat from); ⟨entweichen⟩ escape □ vt shun. f~end a fleeing; ⟨Kinn, Stirn⟩ receding. F~kraft f centrifugal force

Fliese f -,-n tile

Fließ|band nt assembly line. f~en† vi ⟨sein⟩ flow; ⟨aus Wasserhahn⟩ run. f~end a flowing; ⟨Wasser⟩ running; ⟨Verkehr⟩ moving; ⟨geläufig⟩ fluent, adv -ly. F~heck nt fastback. F~wasser nt running water

flimmern vi ⟨haben⟩ shimmer; ⟨TV⟩ flicker; es flimmert mir vor den Augen everything is dancing in front of my eyes

flink a nimble, adv -bly; ⟨schnell⟩ quick, adv -ly

Flinte f -,-n shotgun

Flirt /flœrt/ m -s,-s flirtation. f~en vi ⟨haben⟩ flirt

Flitter m -s sequins pl; ⟨F~schmuck⟩ tinsel. F~wochen fpl honeymoon sg

flitzen vi ⟨sein⟩ ⟨fam⟩ dash; ⟨Auto:⟩ whizz

Flock|e f -,-n flake; ⟨Wolle⟩ tuft. f~ig a fluffy

Floh m -[e]s,ˉe flea. F~markt m flea market. F~spiel nt tiddly-winks sg

Flor m -s gauze; ⟨Trauer-⟩ crape; ⟨Samt-, Teppich-⟩ pile

Flora f - flora

Florett nt -[e]s,-e foil

florieren vi ⟨haben⟩ flourish

Floskel f -,-n [empty] phrase

Floß nt -es,ˉe raft

Flosse f -,-n fin; ⟨Seehund-, Gummi-⟩ flipper; ⟨sl: Hand⟩ paw

Flöt|e f -,-n flute; ⟨Block-⟩ recorder. f~en vi ⟨haben⟩ play the flute/recorder; ⟨fam: pfeifen⟩ whistle □ vt play on the flute/recorder. F~ist(in) m -en,-en ⟨f -,-nen⟩ flautist

flott a quick, adv -ly; ⟨lebhaft⟩ lively; ⟨schick⟩ smart, adv -ly; f~ leben live it up

Flotte f -,-n fleet

flottmachen vt sep wieder f~ ⟨Naut⟩ refloat; get going again ⟨Auto⟩; put back on its feet ⟨Unternehmen⟩

Flöz nt -es,-e [coal] seam

Fluch m -[e]s,ˉe curse. f~en vi ⟨haben⟩ curse, swear

Flucht¹ f -,-en ⟨Reihe⟩ line; ⟨Zimmer-⟩ suite

Flucht² f - flight; ⟨Entweichen⟩ escape; die F~ ergreifen take flight. f~artig a hasty, adv -ily

flücht|en vi ⟨sein⟩ flee (vor + dat from); ⟨entweichen⟩ escape □ vr sich f~en take refuge. f~ig a fugitive; ⟨kurz⟩ brief, adv -ly; ⟨Blick, Gedanke⟩ fleeting; ⟨Bekanntschaft⟩ passing; ⟨oberflächlich⟩ cursory, adv -ily; ⟨nicht sorgfältig⟩ careless, adv -ly; ⟨Chem⟩ volatile; f~ig sein be on the run; f~ig kennen know slightly. F~igkeitsfehler m slip. F~ling m -s,-e fugitive; ⟨Pol⟩ refugee

Fluchwort nt ⟨pl -wörter⟩ swear-word

Flug m -[e]s,ˉe flight. F~abwehr f anti-aircraft defence. F~ball m ⟨Tennis⟩ volley. F~blatt nt pamphlet

Flügel m -s,- wing; ⟨Fenster-⟩ casement; ⟨Mus⟩ grand piano

Fluggast m [air] passenger

flügge a fully-fledged

Flug|gesellschaft f airline. F~hafen m airport. F~lotse m air-traffic controller. F~platz m airport; ⟨klein⟩ airfield. F~preis m air fare. F~schein m air ticket. F~schneise f flight path. F~schreiber m -s,- flight recorder. F~

schrift f pamphlet. **F~steig** m -[e]s,-e gate. **F~wesen** nt aviation. **F~zeug** nt -[e]s,-e aircraft, plane

Fluidum nt -s aura

Flunder f -,-n flounder

flunkern vi (haben) (fam) tell fibs; (aufschneiden) tell tall stories

Flunsch m -[e]s,-e pout

fluoreszierend a fluorescent

Flur m -[e]s,-e [entrance] hall; (Gang) corridor

Flusen fpl fluff sg

Fluss m -es,ˉe (**Fluß** m -sses,ˉsse) river; (Fließen) flow; **im F~** (fig) in a state of flux. **f~abwärts** adv down-stream. **f~aufwärts** adv up-stream. **F~bett** nt river-bed

flüssig a liquid; (Lava) molten; (fließend) fluent, adv -ly; (Verkehr) freely moving. **F~keit** f -,-en liquid; (Anat) fluid

Flusspferd (**Flußpferd**) nt hippopotamus

flüstern vt/i (haben) whisper

Flut f -,-en high tide; (fig) flood; **F~en** waters. **F~licht** nt flood-light. **F~welle** f tidal wave

Föderation /-'tsio:n/ f -,-en federation

Fohlen nt -s,- foal

Föhn m -s föhn [wind]; (Haartrockner) hair-drier. **f~en** vt [blow-]dry

Folg|e f -,-n consequence; (Reihe) succession; (Fortsetzung) instalment; (Teil) part; **F~e leisten** (+ dat) accept (Einladung); obey (Befehl). **f~en** vi (sein) follow (jdm/etw s.o./sth); (zuhören) listen (dat to); **daraus f~t, dass** it follows that; **wie f~t** as follows □ (haben) (gehorchen) obey (jdm s.o.). **f~end** a following; **F~endes** (f~endes) the following. **f~endermaßen** adv as follows

folger|n vt conclude (**aus** from). **F~ung** f -,-en conclusion

folg|lich adv consequently. **f~sam** a obedient, adv -ly

Folie /'fo:liə/ f -,-n foil; (Plastik-) film

Folklore f - folklore

Folter f -,-n torture; **auf die F~ spannen** (fig) keep on tenterhooks. **f~n** vt torture

Fön (P) m -s,-e hair-drier

Fonds /fõ:/ m -,- //-[s],-s// fund

fönen vt (NEW) föhnen

Fontäne f -,-n jet; (Brunnen) fountain

Förder|band nt (pl -bänder) conveyor belt. **f~lich** a beneficial

fordern vt demand; (beanspruchen) claim; (zum Kampf) challenge; **gefordert werden** (fig) be stretched

fördern vt promote; (unterstützen) encourage; (finanziell) sponsor; (gewinnen) extract

Forderung f -,-en demand; (Anspruch) claim

Förderung f - (s. fördern) promotion; encouragement; (Techn) production

Forelle f -,-n trout

Form f -,-en form; (Gestalt) shape; (Culin, Techn) mould; (Back-) tin; [gut] in F~ in good form

Formalität f -,-en formality

Format nt -[e]s,-e format; (Größe) size; (fig: Bedeutung) stature

Formation /-'tsio:n/ f -,-en formation

Formel f -,-n formula

formell a formal, adv -ly

formen vt shape, mould; (bilden) form; **sich f~** take shape

förmlich a formal, adv -ly; (regelrecht) virtual, adv -ly. **F~keit** f -,-en formality

form|los a shapeless; (zwanglos) informal, adv -ly. **F~sache** f formality

Formular nt -s,-e [printed] form

formulier|en vt formulate, word. **F~ung** f -,-en wording

forsch a brisk, adv -ly; (schneidig) dashing, adv -ly

forsch|en vi (haben) search (**nach** for). **f~end** a searching. **F~er** m -s,- research scientist; (Reisender) explorer. **F~ung** f -,-en research. **F~ungsreisende(r)** m explorer

Forst m -[e]s,-e forest

Förster m -s,- forester

Forstwirtschaft f forestry

Forsythie /-tsiə/ f -,-n forsythia

Fort nt -s,-s (Mil) fort

fort adv away; **f~ sein** be away; (gegangen/verschwunden) have gone; **und so f~** and so on; **in einem f~** continuously. **f~bewegen** vt sep move; **sich f~bewegen** move. **F~bewegung** f locomotion. **F~bildung** f further education/training. **f~bleiben†** vi sep (sein) stay away. **f~bringen†** vt sep take away. **f~fahren†** vi sep (sein) go away □ (haben/sein) continue (**zu** to). **f~fallen†** vi sep (sein) be dropped/ (ausgelassen) omitted; (entfallen) no longer apply; (aufhören) cease. **f~führen** vt sep continue. **F~gang** m departure; (Verlauf) progress. **f~gehen†** vi sep (sein) leave, go away; (ausgehen) go out; (andauern) go on. **f~geschritten** a advanced; (spät) late. **F~geschrittene(r)** m/f advanced student. **f~gesetzt** a constant, adv -ly. **f~jagen** vt sep chase away. **f~lassen†** vt *sep* let go; *(auslassen)* omit. **f~laufen†** *vi sep (sein)* run away; *(sich f~setzen)* continue. **f~laufend** *a* consecutive, *adv* -ly. **f~nehmen†** *vt sep* take away. **f~pflanzen (sich)** *vr sep* reproduce; ⟨*Ton, Licht:*⟩ travel. **F~pflanzung** *f* - reproduction. **F~pflanzungsorgan** *nt* reproductive organ. **f~reißen†** *vt sep* carry away; *(entreißen)* tear away. **f~schaffen** *vt sep* take away. **f~schicken** *vt sep* send away; *(abschicken)* send off. **f~schreiten†** *vi sep (sein)* continue; *(Fortschritte machen)* progress, advance. **f~schreitend** *a* progressive; ⟨*Alter*⟩ advancing. **F~schritt** *m* progress; **F~schritte machen** make progress. **f~schrittlich** *a* progressive. **f~setzen** *vt sep* continue; **sich f~setzen** continue. **F~setzung** *f* -,-en continuation; *(Folge)* instalment; **F~setzung folgt** to be continued. **F~setzungsroman** *m* serialized novel, serial. **f~während** *a* constant, *adv* -ly. **f~werfen†** *vt sep* throw away. **f~ziehen†** *v sep* ▯ *vt* pull away ▯ *vi (sein)* move away

Fossil *nt* -,-ien /-jən/ fossil

Foto *nt* -s,-s photo. **F~apparat** *m* camera. **f~gen** *a* photogenic

Fotograf(in) *m* -en,-en *(f* -,-nen) photographer. **F~ie** *f* -,-n photography; *(Bild)* photograph. **f~ieren** *vt* take a photo [graph] of; **sich f~ieren lassen** have one's photo[graph] taken ▯ *vi (haben)* take photographs. **f~isch** *a* photographic

Fotokopie *f* photocopy. **f~ren** *vt* photocopy. **F~rgerät** *nt* photocopier

Fötus *m* -,- foetus

Foul /faul/ *nt* -s,-s *(Sport)* foul. **f~en** *vt* foul

Foyer /fŏa'je:/ *nt* -s,-s foyer

Fracht *f* -,-en freight. **F~er** *m* -s,- freighter. **F~gut** *nt* freight. **F~schiff** *nt* cargo boat

Frack *m* -[e]s,¨e & -s tailcoat; **im F~** in tails *pl*

Frage *f* -,-n question; **ohne F~** undoubtedly; **eine F~ stellen** ask a question; **etw in F~ stellen** = **etw infrage stellen**, *s.* **infrage**; **nicht in F~ kommen** = **nicht infrage kommen**, *s.* **infrage**. **F~bogen** *m* questionnaire. **f~n** *vt (haben)* ask; **sich f~n** wonder *(ob* whether). **f~nd** *a* questioning, *adv* -ly; *(Gram)* interrogative. **F~zeichen** *nt* question mark

frag|lich *a* doubtful; ⟨*Person, Sache*⟩ in question. **f~los** *adv* undoubtedly

Fragment *nt* -[e]s,-e fragment. **f~arisch** *a* fragmentary

fragwürdig *a* questionable; *(verdächtig)* dubious

fraisefarben /'frɛ:s-/ *a* strawberry-pink

Fraktion /-'tsĭo:n/ *f* -,-en parliamentary party

Franken¹ *m* -s,- *(Swiss)* franc

Franken² *nt* -s Franconia

Frankfurter *f* -,- frankfurter

frankieren *vt* stamp, frank

Frankreich *nt* -s France

Fransen *fpl* fringe *sg*

Franz|ose *m* -n,-n Frenchman; **die F~osen** the French *pl.* **F~ösin** *f* -,-nen Frenchwoman. **f~ösisch** *a* French. **F~ösisch** *nt* -[s] *(Lang)* French

frapp|ant *a* striking. **f~ieren** *vt (fig)* strike; **f~ierend** striking

fräsen *vt (Techn)* mill

Fraß *m* -es feed; *(pej: Essen)* muck

Fratze *f* -,-n grotesque face; *(Grimasse)* grimace; *(pej: Gesicht)* face; **F~n schneiden** pull faces

Frau *f* -,-en woman; *(Ehe:)* wife; **F~ Thomas** Mrs/*(unverheiratet)* Miss/ *(Admin)* Ms Thomas; **Unsere Liebe F~** *(Relig)* Our Lady. **F~chen** *nt* -s,- mistress

Frauen|arzt *m*, **F~ärztin** *f* gynaecologist. **F~rechtlerin** *f* -,-nen feminist. **F~zimmer** *nt* woman

Fräulein *nt* -s,- single woman; *(jung)* young lady; *(Anrede)* Miss

fraulich *a* womanly

frech *a* cheeky, *adv* -ily; *(unverschämt)* impudent, *adv* -ly. **F~dachs** *m (fam)* cheeky monkey. **F~heit** *f* -,-en cheekiness; impudence; *(Äußerung, Handlung)* impertinence

frei *a* free; *(freischaffend)* freelance; ⟨*Künstler*⟩ independent; *(nicht besetzt)* vacant; *(offen)* open; *(bloß)* bare; **f~er Tag** day off; **sich (dat) f~ nehmen** take time off; **f~ machen** *(räumen)* clear; vacate ⟨*Platz*⟩; *(befreien)* liberate; **f~ lassen** leave free; **jdm f~e Hand lassen** give s.o. a free hand; **ist dieser Platz f~?** is this seat taken? **'Zimmer f~'** 'vacancies' ▯ *adv* freely; *(ohne Notizen)* without notes; *(umsonst)* free

Frei|bad *nt* open-air swimming pool. **f~bekommen†** *vt sep* get released; **einen Tag f~bekommen** get a day off. **f~beruflich** *a* & *adv* freelance. **F~e** *nt* im **F~en** in the open air, out of doors. **F~frau** *f* baroness. **F~gabe** *f* release. **f~geben†** *v sep* ▯ *vt* release; *(eröffnen)* open; **jdm einen Tag f~geben** give s.o. a day off ▯ *vi (haben)* **jdm f~geben** give s.o. time off. **f~gebig** *a* generous, *adv* -ly. **F~gebigkeit** *f* - generosity. **f~haben†** *v sep* ▯ *vt* **eine Stunde f~haben** have an hour off; *(Sch)* have a free period ▯ *vi (haben)* be off work/*(Sch)* school; *(beurlaubt sein)* have time off. **f~halten†** *vt sep* keep clear;

(*belegen*) keep; **einen Tag/sich f~halten** keep a day/oneself free; **jdn f~halten** treat s.o. [to a meal/drink]. **F~handelszone** f free-trade area. **f~händig** adv without holding on

Freiheit f -,-en freedom, liberty; **sich** (*dat*) **f~en erlauben** take liberties. **F~sstrafe** f prison sentence

freiheraus adv frankly

Frei|herr m baron. **F~karte** f free ticket. **F~körperkultur** f naturism. **f~lassen†** vt sep release, set free. **F~lassung** f - release. **F~lauf** m free-wheel. **f~legen** vt sep expose. **f~lich** adv admittedly; (*natürlich*) of course. **F~lichttheater** nt open-air theatre. **f~machen** v sep ⊃ vt (*frankieren*) frank; (*entkleiden*) bare; **einen Tag f~machen** take a day off ⊃ vi/r (*haben*) [**sich**] **f~machen** take time off. **F~marke** f [postage] stamp. **F~maurer** m Freemason. **f~mütig** a candid, adv -ly. **F~platz** m free seat; (*Sch*) free place. **f~schaffend** a freelance. **f~schwimmen†** (**sich**) v sep pass one's swimming test. **f~setzen** vt sep release; (*entlassen*) make redundant. **f~sprechen†** vt sep acquit. **F~spruch** m acquittal. **f~stehen†** vi sep (*haben*) stand empty; **es steht ihm f~** (*fig*) he is free (**zu** to). **f~stellen** vt sep exempt (**von** from); **jdm etw f~stellen** leave sth up to s.o. **f~stempeln** vt sep frank. **F~stil** m freestyle. **F~stoß** m free kick. **F~stunde** f (*Sch*) free period

Freitag m Friday. **f~s** adv on Fridays

Frei|tod m suicide. **F~übungen** fpl [physical] exercises. **F~umschlag** m stamped envelope. **f~weg** adv freely; (*offen*) openly. **f~willig** a voluntary, adv -ily. **F~willige(r)** m/f volunteer. **F~zeichen** nt ringing tone; (*Rufzeichen*) dialling tone. **F~zeit** f free or spare time; (*Muße*) leisure; (*Tagung*) [weekend/holiday] course. **F~zeit-** pref leisure ... **F~zeitbekleidung** f casual wear. **f~zügig** a unrestricted; (*großzügig*) liberal; (*moralisch*) permissive

fremd a foreign; (*unbekannt, ungewohnt*) strange; (*nicht das eigene*) other people's; **ein f~er Mann** a stranger; **f~e Leute** strangers; **unter f~em Namen** under an assumed name; **jdm f~ sein** be unknown/(*wesens-*) alien to s.o.; **ich bin hier f~** I'm a stranger here. **f~artig** a strange, adv -ly; (*exotisch*) exotic. **F~e** f - **in der F~e** away from home; (*im Ausland*) in a foreign country. **F~e(r)** m/f stranger; (*Ausländer*) foreigner; (*Tourist*) tourist. **F~enführer** m [tourist] guide. **F~enverkehr** m tourism. **F~enzimmer** nt room [to let]; (*Gäste-*) guest room.

f~gehen† vi sep (*sein*) (*fam*) be unfaithful. **F~körper** m foreign body. **f~ländisch** a foreign; (*exotisch*) exotic. **F~ling** m -s,-e stranger. **F~sprache** f foreign language. **F~wort** nt (pl -wörter) foreign word

frenetisch a frenzied

frequen|tieren vt frequent. **F~enz** f -,-en frequency

Freske f -,-n, **Fresko** nt -s,-ken fresco

Fresse f -,-n (*sl*) (*Mund*) gob; (*Gesicht*) mug; **halt die F~!** shut your trap! **f~n†** vt/i (*haben*) eat. **F~n** nt -s feed; (*sl: Essen*) grub

Fressnapf (**Freßnapf**) m feeding bowl

Freud|e f -,-n pleasure; (*innere*) joy; **mit F~en** with pleasure; **jdm eine F~e machen** please s.o. **f~ig** a joyful, adv -ly; **f~iges Ereignis** (*fig*) happy event. **f~los** a cheerless; (*traurig*) sad

freuen vt please; **sich f~** be pleased (**über** + acc about); **sich f~ auf** (+ acc) look forward to; **es freut mich, ich freue mich** I'm glad or pleased (**dass** that)

Freund m -es,-e friend; (*Verehrer*) boyfriend; (*Anhänger*) lover (*gen* of). **F~in** f -,-nen friend; (*Liebste*) girlfriend; (*Anhängerin*) lover (*gen* of). **f~lich** a kind, adv -ly; (*umgänglich*) friendly; (*angenehm*) pleasant; **wären Sie so f~lich?** would you be so kind? **f~licherweise** adv kindly. **F~lichkeit** f -,-en kindness; friendliness; pleasantness

Freundschaft f -,-en friendship; **F~ schließen** become friends. **f~lich** a friendly

Frevel /'fre:fəl/ m -s,- (*liter*) outrage. **f~haft** a (*liter*) wicked

Frieden m -s peace; **F~ schließen** make peace; **im F~** in peace-time; **laß mich in F~!** leave me alone! **F~srichter** m ≈ magistrate. **F~svertrag** m peace treaty

fried|fertig a peaceable. **F~hof** m cemetery. **f~lich** a peaceful, adv -ly; (*verträglich*) peaceable. **f~liebend** a peace-loving

frieren† vi (*haben*) (*Person:*) be cold; *impers* **es friert/hat gefroren** it is freezing/there has been a frost; **frierst du? friert [es] dich?** are you cold? □ (*sein*) (*gefrieren*) freeze

Fries m -es,-e frieze

Frikadelle f -,-n [meat] rissole

frisch a fresh; (*sauber*) clean; (*leuchtend*) bright; (*munter*) lively; (*rüstig*) fit; **sich f~machen** freshen up □ adv freshly, newly; **f~ gelegte Eier** new-laid eggs; **ein Bett f~ beziehen** put clean sheets on a bed; **f~ gestrichen!** wet paint! **F~e** f - freshness; brightness; liveliness; fitness. **F~haltepackung** f vacuum pack.

F~käse m ≈ cottage cheese. **f~weg** adv
freely

Fri|seur /fri'zø:ɐ/ m -s,-e hairdresser;
(Herren-) barber. **F~seursalon** m hair-
dressing salon. **F~seuse** /-'zø:zə/ f -,-n
hairdresser

frisier|en vt jdn/sich f~en do s.o.'s/one's
hair; **die Bilanz/einen Motor f~en**
(fam) fiddle the accounts/soup up an engine. **F~kommode** f dressing-table.
F~salon m = Friseursalon. **F~tisch** m
dressing-table

Frisör m -s,-e = Friseur

Frist f -,-en period; (Termin) deadline;
(Aufschub) time; **drei Tage F~** three
days' grace. **f~en** vt **sein Leben f~en** eke
out an existence. **f~los** a instant, adv -ly

Frisur f -,-en hairstyle

frittieren (fritieren) vt deep-fry

frivol /fri'vo:l/ a frivolous, adv -ly; (schlüpfrig) smutty

froh a happy; (freudig) joyful; (erleichtert)
glad; **f~e Ostern!** happy Easter!

fröhlich a cheerful, adv -ly; (vergnügt)
merry, adv -ily; **f~e Weihnachten!** merry
Christmas! **F~keit** f - cheerfulness; merriment

frohlocken vi (haben) rejoice; (schadenfroh) gloat

Frohsinn m - cheerfulness

fromm a (frömmer, frömmst) devout,
adv -ly; (gutartig) docile, adv -ly; **f~er
Wunsch** idle wish

Frömm|igkeit f - devoutness, piety.
f~lerisch a sanctimonious, adv -ly

frönen vi (haben) indulge (dat in)

Fronleichnam m Corpus Christi

Front f -,-en front. **f~al** a frontal; ⟨Zusam-
menstoß⟩ head-on □ adv from the front;
⟨zusammenstoßen⟩ head-on. **F~alzusam-
menstoß** m head-on collision

Frosch m -[e]s,ẽe frog. **F~laich** m frog-
spawn. **F~mann** m (pl -männer) frog-
man

Frost m -[e]s,ẽe frost. **F~beule** f chilblain

frösteln vi (haben) shiver; **mich fröstelte
[es]** I shivered/(fror) felt chilly

frostig a frosty, adv -ily. **F~schutzmittel**
nt antifreeze

Frottee nt & m -s towelling

frottier|en vt rub down. **F~[hand]tuch**
nt terry towel

frotzeln vt/i (haben) [über] jdn f~ make
fun of s.o.

Frucht f -,ẽe fruit; **F~ tragen** bear fruit.
f~bar a fertile; (fig) fruitful. **F~barkeit**
f - fertility. **f~en** vi (haben) **wenig/nichts
f~en** have little/no effect. **f~ig** a fruity.

f~los a fruitless, adv -ly. **F~saft** m fruit
juice

frugal a frugal, adv -ly

früh a early □ adv early; (morgens) in the
morning; **heute/gestern/morgen f~**
this/yesterday/tomorrow morning; **von
f~ an** □ adv from an early age. **f~auf**
adv von **f~auf** (NEW) von **f~ auf,** s. früh.
F~aufsteher m -s,- early riser. **F~e** f -
in aller F~e bright and early; **in der F~e**
(SGer) in the morning. **f~er** adv earlier;
(eher) sooner; (ehemals) formerly; (vor
langer Zeit) in the old days; **f~er oder
später** sooner or later; **ich wohnte f~er
in X** I used to live in X. **f~ere(r,s)** a earlier; (ehemalig) former; (vorige) previous;
in f~eren Zeiten in former times. **f~es-
tens** adv at the earliest. **F~geburt** f
premature birth/(Kind) baby. **F~jahr** nt
spring. **F~jahrsputz** m spring-cleaning.
F~kartoffeln fpl new potatoes. **F~ling**
m -s,-e spring. **f~morgens** adv early in
the morning. **f~reif** a precocious

Frühstück nt breakfast. **f~en** vi (haben)
have breakfast

frühzeitig a & adv early; (vorzeitig)
premature, adv -ly

Frustr|ation /-'tsio:n/ f -,-en frustration.
f~ieren vt frustrate; **f~ierend** frus-
trating

Fuchs m -es,ẽe fox; (Pferd) chestnut. **f~en**
vt (fam) annoy

Füchsin f -,-nen vixen

fuchteln vi (haben) **mit etw f~** (fam)
wave sth about

Fuder nt -s,- cart-load

Fuge¹ f -,-n joint; **aus den F~n gehen** fall
apart

Fuge² f -,-n (Mus) fugue

füg|en vt fit (in + acc into); (an-) join (an
+ acc on to); (dazu-) add (zu to); (fig: bewirken) ordain; **sich f~en** fit (in + acc
into); adjoin/(folgen) follow (an etw acc
sth); (fig: gehorchen) submit (dat to); **sich
in sein Schicksal f~en** resign oneself to
one's fate; **es f~te sich** it so happened
(dass that). **f~sam** a obedient, adv -ly.
F~ung f -,-en **eine F~ung des Schick-
sals** a stroke of fate

fühl|bar a noticeable. **f~en** vt/i (haben)
feel; **sich f~en** feel (krank/einsam
ill/lonely); (fam: stolz sein) fancy oneself;
sich [nicht] wohl f~en feel [not] feel well.
F~er m -s,- feeler. **F~ung** f - contact;
F~ung aufnehmen get in touch

Fuhre f -,-n load

führ|en vt lead; guide ⟨Tourist⟩; (geleiten)
take; (leiten) run; (befehligen) command;
(verkaufen) stock; bear ⟨Namen, Titel⟩;
keep ⟨Liste, Bücher, Tagebuch⟩; **bei od mit**

sich f~en carry; sich gut/schlecht f~en conduct oneself well/badly □ vi (haben) lead; (verlaufen) go, run; zu etw f~en lead to sth. f~end a leading. F~er m -s,- leader; (Fremden-) guide; (Buch) guide[book]. F~erhaus nt driver's cab. F~erschein m driving licence; den F~erschein machen take one's driving test. F~erscheinentzug m disqualification from driving. F~ung f -,-en leadership; (Leitung) management; (Mil) command; (Betragen) conduct; (Besichtigung) guided tour; (Vorsprung) lead; in F~ung gehen go into the lead

Fuhr|unternehmer m haulage contractor. F~werk nt cart

Fülle f -,-n abundance, wealth (an + dat of); (Körper-) plumpness. f~n vt fill; (Culin) stuff; sich f~n fill [up]

Füllen nt -s,- foal

Füll|er m -s,- (fam), F~federhalter m fountain pen. f~ig a plump; (Busen) ample. F~ung f -,-en filling; (Kissen-, Braten-) stuffing; (Pralinen-) centre

fummeln vi (haben) fumble (an + dat with)

Fund m -[e]s,-e find

Fundament nt -[e]s,-e foundations pl. f~al a fundamental

Fund|büro nt lost-property office. F~grube f (fig) treasure trove. F~sachen fpl lost property sg

fünf inv a, F~ f -,-en five; (Sch) ≈ fail mark. F~linge mpl quintuplets. f~te(r,s) a fifth. f~zehn inv a fifteen. f~zehnte(r,s) a fifteenth. f~zig inv a fifty. F~ziger m -s,- man in his fifties; (Münze) 50-pfennig piece. f~zigste(r,s) a fiftieth

fungieren vi (haben) act (als as)

Funk m -s radio; über F~ over the radio. F~e m -n,-n spark. f~eln vi (haben) sparkle; (Stern:) twinkle. f~elnagelneu a (fam) brand-new. F~en m -s,- spark. f~en vi radio. F~er m -s,- radio operator. F~sprechgerät nt walkie-talkie. F~spruch m radio message. F~streife f [police] radio patrol

Funktion /-'tsjo:n/ f -,-en function; (Stellung) position; (Funktionieren) working; außer F~ out of action. F~är m -s,-e official. f~ieren vi (haben) work

für prep (+ acc) for; Schritt für Schritt step by step; was für [ein] what [a]! (fragend) what sort of [a]? für sich by oneself/(Ding:) itself. Für nt das Für und Wider the pros and cons pl. F~bitte f intercession

Furche f -,-n furrow

Furcht f - fear (vor + dat of); F~ erregend terrifying. f~bar a terrible, adv -bly

fürcht|en vt/i (haben) fear; sich f~en be afraid (vor + dat of); ich f~e, das geht nicht I'm afraid that's impossible. f~erlich a dreadful, adv -ly

furcht|erregend a (NEW) F~ erregend, s. Furcht. f~los a fearless, adv -ly. f~sam a timid, adv -ly

füreinander adv for each other

Furnier nt -s,-e veneer. f~t a veneered

fürs prep = für das

Fürsorg|e f care; (Admin) welfare; (fam: Geld) ≈ social security. F~er(in) m (f -,-nen) social worker. f~lich a solicitous

Fürsprache f intercession; F~ einlegen intercede

Fürsprecher m (fig) advocate

Fürst m -en,-en prince. F~entum nt -s, ¨-er principality. F~in f -,-nen princess. f~lich a princely; (üppig) lavish, adv -ly

Furt f -,-en ford

Furunkel m -s,- (Med) boil

Fürwort nt (pl -wörter) pronoun

Furz m -es,-e (vulg) fart. f~en vi (haben) (vulg) fart

Fusion f -,-en fusion; (Comm) merger. f~ieren vi (haben) (Comm) merge

Fuß m -es,¨-e foot; (Aust: Bein) leg; (Lampen-) base; (von Weinglas) stem; zu Fuß on foot; zu Fuß gehen walk; auf freiem Fuß free; auf freundschaftlichem/großem Fuß on friendly terms/in grand style. F~abdruck m footprint. F~abtreter m -s,- doormat. F~bad nt footbath. F~ball m football. F~ballspieler m footballer. F~balltoto nt football pools pl. F~bank f footstool. F~boden m floor. F~bremse f footbrake

Fussel f -,-n & m -s,-[n] piece of fluff; F~n fluff sg. f~n vi (haben) shed fluff

fuß|en vi (haben) be based (auf + dat on). F~ende nt foot

Fußgänger|(in) m -s,- (f -,-nen) pedestrian. F~brücke f footbridge. F~überweg m pedestrian crossing. F~zone f pedestrian precinct

Fuß|geher m -s,- (Aust) = F~gänger. F~gelenk nt ankle. F~hebel m pedal. F~nagel m toenail. F~note f footnote. F~pflege f chiropody. F~pfleger(in) m(f) chiropodist. F~rücken m instep. F~sohle f sole of the foot. F~stapfen pl in jds F~stapfen treten (fig) follow in s.o.'s footsteps. F~tritt m kick. F~weg m footpath; eine Stunde F~weg an hour's walk

futsch pred a (fam) gone

Futter[1] nt -s feed; (Trocken-) fodder

Futter² nt -s,- (*Kleider-*) lining

Futteral nt -s,-e case

füttern¹ vt feed

füttern² vt line

Futur nt -s (*Gram*) future; **zweites F~** future perfect. **f~istisch** a futuristic

G

Gabe f -,-n gift; (*Dosis*) dose

Gabel f -,-n fork. **g~n (sich)** vr fork. **G~stapler** m -s,- fork-lift truck. **G~ung** f -,-en fork

gackern vi (*haben*) cackle

gaffen vi (*haben*) gape, stare

Gag /gɛk/ m -s,-s (*Theat*) gag

Gage /ˈgaːʒə/ f -,-n (*Theat*) fee

gähnen vi (*haben*) yawn. **G~** nt -s yawn; (*wiederholt*) yawning

Gala f - ceremonial dress

galant a gallant, adv -ly

Galavorstellung f gala performance

Galerie f -,-n gallery

Galgen m -s,- gallows sg. **G~frist** f (*fam*) reprieve

Galionsfigur f figurehead

Galle f - bile; (*G~nblase*) gall-bladder. **G~nblase** f gall-bladder. **G~nstein** m gallstone

Gallert nt -[e]s,-e, **Gallerte** f -,-n [meat] jelly

Galopp m -s gallop; **im G~** at a gallop. **g~ieren** vi (*sein*) gallop

galvanisieren vt galvanize

gammeln vi (*haben*) (*fam*) loaf around. **G~ler(in)** m -s,- (f -,-nen) drop-out

Gams f -,-en (*Aust*) chamois

Gämse f -,-n chamois

gang pred a **g~ und gäbe** quite usual

Gang m -[e]s,ᵉe walk; (*G~art*) gait; (*Boten-*) errand; (*Funktionieren*) running; (*Verlauf, Culin*) course; (*Durch-*) passage; (*Korridor*) corridor; (*zwischen Sitzreihen*) aisle, gangway; (*Anat*) duct; (*Auto*) gear; **in G~ bringen/halten** get/keep going; **in G~ kommen** get going/(*fig*) under way; **im G~e/in vollem G~e sein** be in progress/in full swing; **Essen mit vier G~en** four-course meal. **G~art** f gait

gängig a common; (*Comm*) popular

Gangschaltung f gear change

Gangster /ˈgɛnstɐ/ m -s,- gangster

Gangway /ˈgɛnweː/ f -,-s gangway

Ganove m -n,-n (*fam*) crook

Gans f -,ᵉe goose

Gänse|blümchen nt -s,- daisy. **G~füßchen** ntpl inverted commas. **G~haut** f goose-pimples pl. **G~marsch** m **im G~marsch** in single file. **G~rich** m -s,-e gander

ganz a whole, entire; (*vollständig*) complete; (*fam: heil*) undamaged, intact; **die g~e Zeit** all the time, the whole time; **eine g~e Weile/Menge** quite a while/lot; **g~e zehn Mark** all of ten marks; **meine g~en Bücher** all my books; inv **g~ Deutschland** the whole of Germany; **g~ bleiben** (*fam*) remain intact; **wieder g~ machen** (*fam*) mend; **im g~en** (**in G~en**) in all, altogether; **im Großen und G~en** (**im großen und g~en**) on the whole □ adv quite; (*völlig*) completely, entirely; (*sehr*) very; **nicht g~** not quite; **g~ allein** all on one's own; **ein g~ alter Mann** a very old man; **g~ wie du willst** just as you like; **es war g~ nett** it was quite nice; **g~ und gar** completely, totally; **g~ und gar nicht** not at all. **G~e(s)** nt whole; **es geht ums G~e** it's all or nothing. **g~jährig** adv all the year round

gänzlich adv completely, entirely

ganz|tägig a & adv full-time; (*geöffnet*) all day. **g~tags** adv all day; (*arbeiten*) full-time

gar¹ a done, cooked

gar² adv **gar nicht/nichts/niemand** not/nothing/no one at all; **oder gar** or even

Garage /gaˈraːʒə/ f -,-n garage

Garantie f -,-n guarantee. **g~ren** vt/i (*haben*) **[für] etw g~ren** guarantee sth; **er kommt g~rt zu spät** (*fam*) he's sure to be late. **G~schein** m guarantee

Garbe f -,-n sheaf

Garderobe f -,-n (*Kleider*) wardrobe; (*Ablage*) cloakroom, (*Amer*) checkroom; (*Flur-*) coat-rack; (*Künstler-*) dressing-room. **G~nfrau** f cloakroom attendant

Gardine f -,-n curtain. **G~nstange** f curtain rail

garen vt/i (*haben*) cook

gären† vi (*haben*) ferment; (*fig*) seethe

Garn nt -[e]s,-e yarn; (*Näh-*) cotton

Garnele f -,-n shrimp; (*rote*) prawn

garnieren vt decorate; (*Culin*) garnish

Garnison f -,-en garrison

Garnitur f -,-en set; (*Wäsche*) set of matching underwear; (*Möbel-*) suite; **erste/zweite G~ sein** (*fam*) be first-rate/second-best

garstig a nasty

Garten m -s,ᵉ garden; **botanischer G~** botanical gardens pl. **G~arbeit** f gardening. **G~bau** m horticulture. **G~haus** nt, **G~laube** f summerhouse. **G~lokal**

nt open-air café. **G∼schere** *f* secateurs *pl*

Gärtner|(in) *m* -s,- (*f* -,-nen) gardener. **G∼ei** *f* -,-en nursery; (*fam: Gartenarbeit*) gardening

Gärung *f* - fermentation

Gas *nt* -es,-e gas; **Gas geben** (*fam*) accelerate. **G∼herd** *m* gas cooker. **G∼maske** *f* gas mask. **G∼pedal** *nt* (*Auto*) accelerator

Gasse *f* -,-n alley; (*Aust*) street

Gast *m* -[e]s,-e guest; (*Hotel-, Urlaubs-*) visitor; (*im Lokal*) patron; **zum Mittag G∼e haben** have people to lunch; **bei jdm zu G∼ sein** be staying with s.o. **G∼arbeiter** *m* foreign worker. **G∼bett** *nt* spare bed

Gäste|bett *nt* spare bed. **G∼buch** *nt* visitors' book. **G∼zimmer** *nt* [hotel] room; (*privat*) spare room; (*Aufenthaltsraum*) residents' lounge

gast|frei, **g∼freundlich** *a* hospitable, *adv* -bly. **G∼freundschaft** *f* hospitality. **G∼geber** *m* -s,- host. **G∼geberin** *f* -,-nen hostess. **G∼haus** *nt*, **G∼hof** *m* inn, hotel

gastieren *vi* (*haben*) make a guest appearance; ⟨*Truppe, Zirkus:*⟩ perform (**in** + *dat* in)

gastlich *a* hospitable, *adv* -bly. **G∼keit** *f* - hospitality

Gastro|nomie *f* - gastronomy. **g∼nomisch** *a* gastronomic

Gast|spiel *nt* guest performance. **G∼spielreise** *f* (*Theat*) tour. **G∼stätte** *f* restaurant. **G∼stube** *f* bar; (*Restaurant*) restaurant. **G∼wirt** *m* landlord. **G∼wirtin** *f* landlady. **G∼wirtschaft** *f* restaurant

Gas|werk *nt* gasworks *sg*. **G∼zähler** *m* gas-meter

Gatte *m* -n,-n husband

Gatter *nt* -s,- gate; (*Gehege*) pen

Gattin *f* -,-nen wife

Gattung *f* -,-en kind; (*Biol*) genus; (*Kunst*) genre. **G∼sbegriff** *m* generic term

Gaudi *f* - (*Aust, fam*) fun

Gaul *m* -[e]s, **Gäule** [old] nag

Gaumen *m* -s,- palate

Gauner *m* -s,- crook, swindler. **G∼ei** *f* -,-en swindle

Gaze /ˈgaːzə/ *f* - gauze

Gazelle *f* -,-n gazelle

geachtet *a* respected

geädert *a* veined

geartet *a* **gut g∼** good-natured; **anders g∼** different

Gebäck *nt* -s [cakes and] pastries *pl*; (*Kekse*) biscuits *pl*

Gebälk *nt* -s timbers *pl*

geballt *a* (*Faust*) clenched

Gebärde *f* -,-n gesture. **g∼n (sich)** *vr* behave (**wie** like)

Gebaren *nt* -s behaviour

gebär|en† *vt* give birth to, bear; **geboren werden** be born. **G∼mutter** *f* womb, uterus

Gebäude *nt* -s,- building

Gebeine *ntpl* [mortal] remains

Gebell *nt* -s barking

geben† *vt* give; (*tun, bringen*) put; (*Karten*) deal; (*aufführen*) perform; (*unterrichten*) teach; **etw verloren g∼** give sth up as lost; **von sich g∼** utter; (*fam: erbrechen*) bring up; **viel/wenig g∼ auf** (+ *acc*) set great/little store by; **sich g∼** (*nachlassen*) wear off; (*besser werden*) get better; (*sich verhalten*) behave; **sich geschlagen g∼** admit defeat □ *impers* **es gibt** there is/are; **was gibt es Neues/zum Mittag/im Kino?** what's the news/for lunch/on at the cinema? **es wird Regen g∼** it's going to rain; **das gibt es nicht** there's no such thing □ *vi* (*haben*) (*Karten*) deal

Gebet *nt* -[e]s,-e prayer

Gebiet *nt* -[e]s,-e area; (*Hoheits-*) territory; (*Sach-*) field

gebiet|en† *vt* command; (*erfordern*) demand □ *vi* (*haben*) rule. **G∼er** *m* -s,- master; (*Herrscher*) ruler. **g∼erisch** *a* imperious, *adv* -ly; ⟨*Ton*⟩ peremptory

Gebilde *nt* -s,- structure

gebildet *a* educated; (*kultiviert*) cultured

Gebirg|e *nt* -s,- mountains *pl.* **g∼ig** *a* mountainous

Gebiss *nt* -es,-e (*Gebiß nt* -sses, -sse) teeth *pl*; (*künstliches*) false teeth *pl*, dentures *pl*; (*des Zaumes*) bit

geblümt *a* floral, flowered

gebogen *a* curved

geboren *a* born; **g∼er Deutscher** German by birth; **Frau X, g∼e Y** Mrs X, née Y

geborgen *a* safe, secure. **G∼heit** *f* - security

Gebot *nt* -[e]s,-e rule; (*Relig*) commandment; (*bei Auktion*) bid

gebraten *a* fried

Gebrauch *m* use; (*Sprach-*) usage; **Gebräuche** customs; **in G∼** in use; **G∼ machen von** make use of. **g∼en** *vt* use; **ich kann es nicht/gut g∼en** I have no use for/can make good use of it; **zu nichts zu g∼en** useless

gebräuchlich *a* common; ⟨*Wort*⟩ in common use

Gebrauch|sanleitung, **G∼sanweisung** *f* directions *pl* for use. **g∼t** *a* used; (*Comm*) secondhand. **G∼twagen** *m* used car

gebrechlich *a* frail, infirm

gebrochen *a* broken □ *adv* **g~ Englisch sprechen** speak broken English

Gebrüll *nt* -s roaring; *(fam: Schreien)* bawling

Gebrumm *nt* -s buzzing; *(Motoren-)* humming

Gebühr *f* -,-en charge, fee; **über G~** excessively. **g~en** *vi (haben)* **ihm g~t Respekt** he deserves respect; **wie es sich g~t** as is right and proper. **g~end** *a* due, *adv* duly; *(geziemend)* proper, *adv* -ly. **g~enfrei** *a* free □ *adv* free of charge. **g~enpflichtig** *a* & *adv* subject to a charge; **g~enpflichtige Straße** toll road

gebunden *a* bound; *(Suppe)* thickened

Geburt *f* -,-en birth; **von G~** by birth. **G~enkontrolle, G~enregelung** *f* birthcontrol. **G~enziffer** *f* birth-rate

gebürtig *a* a native **(aus** of); **g~er Deutscher** German by birth

Geburts|datum *nt* date of birth. **G~helfer** *m* obstetrician. **G~hilfe** *f* obstetrics *sg*. **G~ort** *m* place of birth. **G~tag** *m* birthday. **G~urkunde** *f* birth certificate

Gebüsch *nt* -[e]s,-e bushes *pl*

Gedächtnis *nt* -ses memory; **aus dem G~** from memory

gedämpft *a* *(Ton)* muffled; *(Stimme)* hushed; *(Musik)* soft; *(Licht, Stimmung)* subdued

Gedanke *m* -ns,-n thought **(an** + *acc* of); *(Idee)* idea; **sich** *(dat)* **G~n machen** worry **(über** + *acc* about). **G~nblitz** *m* brainwave. **g~nlos** *a* thoughtless, *adv* -ly; *(zerstreut)* absent-minded, *adv* -ly. **G~nstrich** *m* dash. **G~nübertragung** *f* telepathy. **g~nvoll** *a* pensive, *adv* -ly

Gedärme *ntpl* intestines; *(Tier-)* entrails

Gedeck *nt* -[e]s,-e place setting; *(auf Speisekarte)* set meal; **ein G~ auflegen** set a place. **g~t** *a* covered; *(Farbe)* muted

gedeihen† *vi (sein)* thrive, flourish

gedenken† *vi (haben)* propose **(etw zu tun** to do sth); **jds/etw g~** remember s.o./sth. **G~** *nt* -s memory; **zum G~ an (**+ *acc*) in memory of

Gedenk|feier *f* commemoration. **G~gottesdienst** *m* memorial service. **G~stätte** *f* memorial. **G~tafel** *f* commemorative plaque. **G~tag** *m* day of remembrance; *(Jahrestag)* anniversary

Gedicht *nt* -[e]s,-e poem

gediegen *a* quality . . .; *(solide)* well-made; *(Charakter)* upright; *(Gold)* pure □ *adv* **g~ gebaut** well built

Gedräng|e *nt* -s crush, crowd. **g~t** *a* *(knapp)* concise □ *adv* **g~t voll** packed

gedrückt *a* depressed

gedrungen *a* stocky

Geduld *f* - patience; **G~ haben** be patient. **g~en (sich)** *vr* be patient. **g~ig** *a* patient, *adv* -ly. **G~[s]spiel** *nt* puzzle

gedunsen *a* bloated

geehrt *a* honoured; **Sehr g~er Herr X** Dear Mr X

geeignet *a* suitable; **im g~en Moment** at the right moment

Gefahr *f* -,-en danger; **in/außer G~** in/ out of danger; **auf eigene G~** at one's own risk; **G~ laufen** run the risk **(etw zu tun** of doing sth)

gefähr|den *vt* endanger; *(fig)* jeopardize. **g~lich** *a* dangerous, *adv* -ly; *(riskant)* risky

gefahrlos *a* safe

Gefährt *nt* -[e]s,-e vehicle

Gefährte *m* -n,-n, **Gefährtin** *f* -,-nen companion

gefahrvoll *a* dangerous, perilous

Gefälle *nt* -s,- slope; *(Straßen-)* gradient

gefallen† *vi (haben)* **jdm g~** please s.o.; **er/es gefällt mir** I like him/it; **sich** *(dat)* **etw g~ lassen** put up with sth

Gefallen[1] *m* -s,- favour

Gefallen[2] *nt* -s pleasure **(an** + *dat* in); **G~ finden an (**+ *dat*) like; **dir zu G~** to please you

Gefallene(r) *m* soldier killed in the war

gefällig *a* pleasing; *(hübsch)* attractive, *adv* -ly; *(hilfsbereit)* obliging; **jdm g~ sein** do s.o. a good turn; **[sonst] noch etwas g~?** will there be anything else? **G~keit** *f* -,-en favour; *(Freundlichkeit)* kindness. **g~st** *adv (fam)* kindly

Gefangen|e(r) *m/f* prisoner. **g~halten†** *vt sep* ~NEW~ **g~ halten,** *s.* **fangen.** **G~nahme** *f* - capture. **g~nehmen†** *vt sep* ~NEW~ **g~ nehmen,** *s.* **fangen.** **G~schaft** *f* - captivity; **in G~schaft geraten** be taken prisoner

Gefängnis *nt* -ses,-se prison; *(Strafe)* imprisonment. **G~strafe** *f* imprisonment; *(Urteil)* prison sentence. **G~wärter** *m* [prison] warder, *(Amer)* guard

Gefäß *nt* -es,-e container, receptacle; *(Blut-)* vessel

gefasst **(gefaßt)** *a* composed; *(ruhig)* calm, *adv* -ly; **g~ sein auf (**+ *acc*) be prepared for

Gefecht *nt* -[e]s,-e fight; *(Mil)* engagement; **außer G~ setzen** put out of action

gefedert *a* sprung

gefeiert *a* celebrated

Gefieder *nt* -s plumage. **g~t** *a* feathered

Geflecht *nt* -[e]s,-e network; *(Gewirr)* tangle; *(Korb-)* wicker-work

gefleckt *a* spotted

geflissentlich *adv* studiously

Geflügel *nt* -s poultry. **G~klein** *nt* -s giblets *pl.* **g~t** *a* winged; **g~tes Wort** familiar quotation

Geflüster *nt* -s whispering

Gefolg|e *nt* -s retinue, entourage. **G~schaft** *f* - followers *pl,* following; ⟨*Treue*⟩ allegiance

gefragt *a* popular; **g~ sein** be in demand

gefräßig *a* voracious; ⟨*Mensch*⟩ greedy

Gefreite(r) *m* lance-corporal

gefrier|en† *vi* (*sein*) freeze. **G~fach** *nt* freezer compartment. **G~punkt** *m* freezing point. **G~schrank** *m* upright freezer. **G~truhe** *f* chest freezer

gefroren *a* frozen. **G~e(s)** *nt* (*Aust*) ice-cream

Gefüge *nt* -s,- structure; (*fig*) fabric

gefügig *a* compliant; (*gehorsam*) obedient

Gefühl *nt* -[e]s,-e feeling; (*Empfindung*) sensation; (*G~sregung*) emotion; **im G~ haben** know instinctively. **g~los** *a* insensitive; (*herzlos*) unfeeling; (*taub*) numb. **g~betont** *a* emotional. **g~skalt** *a* (*fig*) cold. **g~smäßig** *a* emotional, *adv* -ly; (*instinktiv*) instinctive, *adv* -ly. **G~sregung** *f* emotion. **g~voll** *a* sensitive, *adv* -ly; (*sentimental*) sentimental, *adv* -ly

gefüllt *a* filled; (*voll*) full; (*Bot*) double; (*Culin*) stuffed; ⟨*Schokolade*⟩ with a filling

gefürchtet *a* feared, dreaded

gefüttert *a* lined

gegeben *a* given; (*bestehend*) present; (*passend*) appropriate; **zu g~er Zeit** at the proper time. **g~enfalls** *adv* if need be. **G~heiten** *fpl* realities, facts

gegen *prep* (+ *acc*) against; (*Sport*) versus; (*g~über*) to[wards]; (*Vergleich*) compared with; (*Richtung, Zeit*) towards; (*ungefähr*) around; **ein Mittel g~** a remedy for □ *adv* **g~ 100 Leute** about 100 people. **G~angriff** *m* counter-attack

Gegend *f* -,-en area, region; (*Umgebung*) neighbourhood

gegeneinander *adv* against/(*gegenüber*) towards one another

Gegen|fahrbahn *f* opposite carriageway. **G~gift** *nt* antidote. **G~leistung** *f* als **G~leistung** in return. **G~maßnahme** *f* countermeasure. **G~satz** *m* contrast; (*Widerspruch*) contradiction; (*G~teil*) opposite; **im G~satz zu** unlike. **g~sätzlich** *a* contrasting; (*widersprüchlich*) opposing. **g~seitig** *a* mutual, *adv* -ly; **sich g~seitig hassen** hate one another. **G~spieler** *m* opponent. **G~sprechanlage** *f* intercom. **G~stand** *m* object; (*Gram, Gesprächs-*) subject. **g~standslos** *a* unfounded; (*überflüssig*) irrelevant; (*abstrakt*) abstract. **G~stück** *nt* counterpart; (*G~teil*) opposite. **G~teil** *nt* opposite, contrary; **im G~teil** on the contrary. **g~teilig** *a* opposite

gegenüber *prep* (+ *dat*) opposite; (*Vergleich*) compared with; **jdm g~ höflich sein** be polite to s.o. □ *adv* opposite. **G~** *nt* -s person opposite. **g~liegen†** *vi sep* (*haben*) be opposite (*etw dat* sth). **g~liegend** *a* opposite. **g~stehen†** *vi sep* (*haben*) (+ *dat*) face; **feindlich g~stehen** (+ *dat*) be hostile to. **g~stellen** *vt sep* confront; (*vergleichen*) compare. **g~treten†** *vi sep* (*sein*) (+ *dat*) face

Gegen|verkehr *m* oncoming traffic. **G~vorschlag** *m* counter-proposal. **G~wart** *f* - present; (*Anwesenheit*) presence. **g~wärtig** *a* present □ *adv* at present. **G~wehr** *f* - resistance. **G~wert** *m* equivalent. **G~wind** *m* head wind. **g~zeichnen** *vt sep* countersign

geglückt *a* successful

Gegner|(in) *m* -s,- (*f* -,-nen) opponent. **g~isch** *a* opposing

Gehabe *nt* -s affected behaviour

Gehackte(s) *nt* mince, (*Amer*) ground meat

Gehalt¹ *m* -[e]s content

Gehalt² *nt* -[e]s,-̈er salary. **G~serhöhung** *f* rise, (*Amer*) raise

gehaltvoll *a* nourishing

gehässig *a* spiteful, *adv* -ly

gehäuft *a* heaped

Gehäuse *nt* -s,- case; (*TV, Radio*) cabinet; (*Schnecken-*) shell; (*Kern-*) core

Gehege *nt* -s,- enclosure

geheim *a* secret; **g~ halten** keep secret; **im G~en** (**g~en**) secretly. **G~dienst** *m* Secret Service. **g~halten†** *vt sep* NEW **g~ halten,** s. **geheim. G~nis** *nt* -ses,-se secret. **g~nisvoll** *a* mysterious, *adv* -ly. **G~polizei** *f* secret police

gehemmt *a* (*fig*) inhibited

gehen† *vi* (*sein*) go; (*zu Fuß*) walk; (*fort-*) leave; (*funktionieren*) work; ⟨*Teig:*⟩ rise; **tanzen/einkaufen g~** go dancing/shopping; **an die Arbeit g~** set to work; **in Schwarz [gekleidet] g~** dress in black; **nach Norden g~** ⟨*Fenster:*⟩ face north; **wenn es nach mir ginge** if I had my way; **über die Straße g~** cross the road; **was geht hier vor sich?** what is going on here? **das geht zu weit** (*fam*) that's going too far; *impers* **wie geht es [Ihnen]?** how are you? **es geht ihm gut/besser/schlecht** he is well/better/not well; (*geschäftlich*) he is doing well/badly; **ein gut g~des Geschäft** a flourishing *or* thriving business; **es geht nicht/nicht anders** it's impossible/there is no other way; **es ging ganz schnell** it was very quick; **es geht um** it concerns; **es geht ihr nur ums Geld** she is only interested in the money; **es geht [so]** (fam) not too bad; **sich g~ lassen** lose one's self-control; (sich vernachlässigen) let oneself go □ vt walk. **g~lassen†** (**sich**) vr sep (NEW) **g~ lassen (sich)**, s. **gehen**

geheuer a **nicht g~** eerie; (verdächtig) suspicious; **mir ist nicht g~** I feel uneasy

Geheul nt -s howling

Gehilfe m -n,-n, **Gehilfin** f -,-nen trainee; (Helfer) assistant

Gehirn nt -s brain; (Verstand) brains pl. **G~erschütterung** f concussion. **G~hautentzündung** f meningitis. **G~wäsche** f brainwashing

gehoben a (fig) superior; (Sprache) elevated

Gehöft nt -[e]s,-e farm

Gehölz nt -es,-e coppice, copse

Gehör nt -s hearing; **G~ schenken** (+ dat) listen to

gehorchen vi (haben) (+ dat) obey

gehören vi (haben) belong (dat to); **zu den Besten g~** be one of the best; **dazu gehört Mut** that takes courage; **sich g~** be [right and] proper; **es gehört sich nicht** it isn't done

gehörig a proper, adv -ly; **jdn g~ verprügeln** give s.o. a good hiding

gehörlos a deaf

Gehörn nt -s,-e horns pl; (Geweih) antlers pl

gehorsam a obedient, adv -ly. **G~** m -s obedience

Geh|steig m -[e]s,-e pavement, (Amer) sidewalk. **G~weg** m = **Gehsteig**; (Fußweg) footpath

Geier m -s,- vulture

Geig|e f -,-n violin. **g~en** vi (haben) play the violin □ vt play on the violin. **G~er(in)** m -s,- (f -,-nen) violinist

geil a lecherous; (fam) randy; (fam: toll) great

Geisel f -,-n hostage

Geiß f -,-en (SGer) [nanny-]goat. **G~blatt** nt honeysuckle

Geißel f -,-n scourge

Geist m -[e]s,-er mind; (Witz) wit; (Gesinnung) spirit; (Gespenst) ghost; **der Heilige G~** the Holy Ghost or Spirit; **im G~** in one's mind. **g~erhaft** a ghostly

geistes|abwesend a absent-minded, adv -ly. **G~blitz** m brainwave. **G~gegenwart** f presence of mind. **g~gegenwärtig** adv with great presence of mind. **g~gestört** a [mentally] deranged. **g~krank** a mentally ill. **G~krankheit** f mental illness. **G~wissenschaften** fpl arts. **G~zustand** m mental state

geist|ig a mental, adv -ly; (intellektuell) intellectual, adv -ly; **g~ige Getränke** spirits. **g~lich** a spiritual, adv -ly; (religiös) religious; (Musik) sacred; (Tracht) clerical. **G~liche(r)** m clergyman. **G~lichkeit** f - clergy. **g~los** a uninspired. **g~reich** a clever; (witzig) witty

Geiz m -es meanness. **g~en** vi (haben) be mean (**mit** with). **G~hals** m (fam) miser. **g~ig** a mean, miserly. **G~kragen** m (fam) miser

Gekicher nt -s giggling

geknickt a (fam) dejected, adv -ly

gekonnt a accomplished □ adv expertly

Gekrakel nt -s scrawl

gekränkt a offended, hurt

Gekritzel nt -s scribble

gekünstelt a affected, adv -ly

Gelächter nt -s laughter

geladen a loaded; (fam: wütend) furious

Gelage nt -s,- feast

gelähmt a paralysed

Gelände nt -s,- terrain; (Grundstück) site. **G~lauf** m cross-country run

Geländer nt -s,- railings pl; (Treppen-) banisters pl; (Brücken-) parapet

gelangen vi (sein) reach/(fig) attain (**zu etw/an etw** acc sth); **in jds Besitz g~** come into s.o.'s possession

gelassen a composed; (ruhig) calm, adv -ly. **G~heit** f - equanimity; (Fassung) composure

Gelatine /ʒela-/ f - gelatine

geläufig a common, current; (fließend) fluent, adv -ly; **jdm g~ sein** be familiar to s.o.

gelaunt a **gut/schlecht g~e Leute** good-humoured/bad-tempered people; **gut/schlecht g~ sein** be in a good/bad mood

gelb a yellow; (bei Ampel) amber; **g~e Rübe** (SGer) carrot; **das G~e vom Ei** the yolk of the egg. **G~** nt -s,- yellow; **bei G~** (Auto) on [the] amber. **g~lich** a yellowish. **G~sucht** f jaundice

Geld nt -es,-er money; **öffentliche G~er** public funds. **G~beutel** m, **G~börse** f purse. **G~geber** m -s,- backer. **g~lich** a financial, adv -ly. **G~mittel** ntpl funds. **G~schein** m banknote. **G~schrank** m safe. **G~strafe** f fine. **G~stück** nt coin

Gelee /ʒe'le:/ nt -s,-s jelly

gelegen a situated; (passend) convenient; **jdm sehr g~ sein** od **kommen** suit s.o. well; **mir ist viel/wenig daran g~** I'm very/not keen on it; (es ist wichtig) it matters a lot/little to me

Gelegenheit *f* -,-en opportunity, chance; (*Anlass*) occasion; (*Comm*) bargain; **bei G~** some time. **G~sarbeit** *f* casual work. **G~sarbeiter** *m* casual worker. **G~skauf** *m* bargain

gelegentlich *a* occasional □ *adv* occasionally; (*bei Gelegenheit*) some time □ *prep* (+ *gen*) on the occasion of

gelehrt *a* learned. **G~e(r)** *m/f* scholar

Geleise *nt* -s,- = **Gleis**

Geleit *nt* -[e]s escort; **freies G~** safe conduct. **g~en** *vt* escort. **G~zug** *m* (*Naut*) convoy

Gelenk *nt* -[e]s,-e joint. **g~ig** *a* supple; (*Techn*) flexible

gelernt *a* skilled

Geliebte(r) *m/f* lover; (*liter*) beloved

gelieren /ʒe-/ *vi* (*haben*) set

gelinde *a* mild, *adv* -ly; **g~ gesagt** to put it mildly

gelingen† *vi* (*sein*) succeed, be successful; **es gelang ihm, zu entkommen** he succeeded in escaping. **G~** *nt* -s success

gell *int* (*SGer*) = **gelt**

gellend *a* shrill, *adv* -y

geloben *vt* promise [solemnly]; **sich** (*dat*) **g~** vow (**zu** to); **das Gelobte Land** the Promised Land

Gelöbnis *nt* -ses,-se vow

gelöst *a* (*fig*) relaxed

Gelse *f* -,-n (*Aust*) mosquito

gelt *nt* (*SGer*) **das ist schön, g~?** it's nice, isn't it? **ihr kommt doch, g~?** you are coming, aren't you?

gelten† *vi* (*haben*) be valid; (*Regel:*) apply; **g~ als** be regarded as; **etw nicht g~ lassen** not accept sth; **wenig/viel g~** be worth-/(*fig*) count for little/a lot; **jdm g~** be meant for s.o.; **das gilt nicht** that doesn't count. **g~d** *a* valid; (*Preise*) current; (*Meinung*) prevailing; **g~d machen** assert (*Recht, Forderung*); bring to bear (*Einfluss*)

Geltung *f* - validity; (*Ansehen*) prestige; **G~ haben** be valid; **zur G~ bringen/kommen** set off/show to advantage

Gelübde *nt* -s,- vow

gelungen *a* successful

Gelüst *nt* -[e]s,-e desire-/(*stark*) craving (**nach** for)

gemächlich *a* leisurely □ *adv* in a leisurely manner

Gemahl *m* -s,-e husband. **G~in** *f* -,-nen wife

Gemälde *nt* -s,- painting. **G~galerie** *f* picture gallery

gemäß *prep* (+ *dat*) in accordance with □ *a* **etw** (*dat*) **g~ sein** be in keeping with sth

gemäßigt *a* moderate; (*Klima*) temperate

gemein *a* common; (*unanständig*) vulgar; (*niederträchtig*) mean; **g~er Soldat** private; **etw g~ haben** have sth in common □ *adv* shabbily; (*fam: schrecklich*) terribly

Gemeinde *f* -,-n [local] community; (*Admin*) borough; (*Pfarr~*) parish; (*bei Gottesdienst*) congregation. **G~rat** *m* local council-/(*Person*) councillor. **G~wahlen** *fpl* local elections

gemein|gefährlich *a* dangerous. **G~heit** *f* -,-en (*s.* gemein) commonness; vulgarity; meanness; (*Bemerkung, Handlung*) mean thing [to say/do]; **so eine G~heit!** how mean! (*wie ärgerlich*) what a nuisance! **G~kosten** *pl* overheads. **g~nützig** *a* charitable. **G~platz** *m* platitude. **g~sam** *a* common; **etw g~sam haben** have sth in common □ *adv* together

Gemeinschaft *f* -,-en community. **g~lich** *a* joint; (*Besitz*) communal □ *adv* jointly; (*zusammen*) together. **G~sarbeit** *f* team-work

Gemenge *nt* -s,- mixture

gemessen *a* measured; (*würdevoll*) dignified

Gemetzel *nt* -s,- carnage

Gemisch *nt* -[e]s,-e mixture. **g~t** *a* mixed

Gemme *f* -,-n engraved gem

Gemse *f* -,-n (NEW) **Gämse**

Gemurmel *nt* -s murmuring

Gemüse *nt* -s,- vegetable; (*coll*) vegetables *pl*. **G~händler** *m* greengrocer

gemustert *a* patterned

Gemüt *nt* -[e]s,-er nature, disposition; (*Gefühl*) feelings *pl*; (*Person*) soul

gemütlich *a* cosy; (*gemächlich*) leisurely; (*zwanglos*) informal; (*Person*) genial; **es sich** (*dat*) **g~ machen** make oneself comfortable □ *adv* cosily; in a leisurely manner; informally. **G~keit** *f* - cosiness; leisureliness

Gemüts|art *f* nature, disposition. **G~mensch** *m* (*fam*) placid person. **G~ruhe** *f* **in aller G~ruhe** (*fam*) calmly. **G~verfassung** *f* frame of mind

Gen *nt* -s,-e gene

genau *a* exact, *adv* -ly, precise, *adv* -ly; (*Waage, Messung*) accurate, *adv* -ly; (*sorgfältig*) meticulous, *adv* -ly; (*ausführlich*) detailed; **nichts G~es wissen** not know any details; **es nicht so g~ nehmen** not be too particular; **g~ genommen** strictly speaking; **g~!** exactly! **g~genommen** *adv* (NEW) **g~ genommen**, *s.* **genau**. **G~igkeit** *f* - exactitude; precision; accuracy; meticulousness

genauso *adv* just the same; (*g~ sehr*) just as much; **g~ schön/teuer** just as beautiful/expensive; **g~ gut** just as good; *adv* just as well; **g~ sehr** just as much; **g~ viel** just as much/many; **g~ wenig** just as little/few; (*noch*) no more. **g~gut** *adv* (NEW) **g~ gut**, *s.* **genauso**. **g~sehr** *adv* (NEW) **g~ sehr**, *s.* **genauso**. **g~viel** *adv* (NEW) **g~ viel**, *s.* **genauso**. **g~wenig** *adv* (NEW) **g~ wenig**, *s.* **genauso**

Gendarm /ʒãˈdarm/ *m* -en,-en (*Aust*) policeman

Genealogie *f* - genealogy

genehmig|en *vt* grant; approve (*Plan*). **G~ung** *f* -,-en permission; (*Schein*) permit

geneigt *a* sloping, inclined; (*fig*) well-disposed (*dat* towards); **[nicht] g~ sein** (*fig*) [not] feel inclined (**zu** to)

General *m* -s,-e general. **G~direktor** *m* managing director. **g~isieren** *vi* (*haben*) generalize. **G~probe** *f* dress rehearsal. **G~streik** *m* general strike. **g~überholen** *vt insep* (*inf & pp only*) completely overhaul

Generation /-ˈtsi̯oːn/ *f* -,-en generation

Generator *m* -s,-en /-ˈtoːrən/ generator

generell *a* general, *adv* -ly

genes|en† *vi* (*sein*) recover. **G~ung** *f* - recovery; (*Erholung*) convalescence

Genet|ik *f* - genetics *sg*. **g~isch** *a* genetic, *adv* -ally

Genf *nt* -s Geneva. **G~er** *a* Geneva ...; **G~er See** Lake Geneva

genial *a* brilliant, *adv* -ly; **ein g~er Mann** a man of genius. **G~ität** *f* - genius

Genick *nt* -s,-e [back of the] neck; **sich** (*dat*) **das G~ brechen** break one's neck

Genie /ʒeˈniː/ *nt* -s,-s genius

genieren /ʒeˈniːrən/ *vt* embarrass; **sich g~** feel *or* be embarrassed

genieß|bar *a* fit to eat/drink. **g~en†** *vt* enjoy; (*verzehren*) eat/drink. **G~er** *m* -s,- gourmet. **g~erisch** *a* appreciative □ *adv* with relish

Genitiv *m* -s,-e genitive

Genosse *m* -n,-n (*Pol*) comrade. **G~nschaft** *f* -,-en cooperative

Genre /ˈʒãːrə/ *nt* -s,-s genre

Gentechnologie *f* genetic engineering

genug *inv a & adv* enough

Genüge *f* **zur G~** sufficiently. **g~n** *vi* (*haben*) be enough; **jds Anforderungen g~n** meet s.o.'s requirements. **g~nd** *inv a* sufficient, enough; (*Sch*) fair □ *adv* sufficiently, enough

genügsam *a* frugal, *adv* -ly; (*bescheiden*) modest, *adv* -ly

Genugtuung *f* - satisfaction

Genuss *m* -es,-̈e (**Genuß** *m* -sses,-̈sse) enjoyment; (*Vergnügen*) pleasure; (*Verzehr*) consumption. **genüsslich** (**genüßlich**) *a* pleasurable □ *adv* with relish

geöffnet *a* open

Geo|graphie, **G~grafie** *f* - geography. **g~graphisch**, **g~grafisch** *a* geographical, *adv* -ly. **G~loge** *m* -n,-n geologist. **G~logie** *f* - geology. **g~logisch** *a* geological. *adv* -ly. **G~meter** *m* -s,- surveyor. **G~metrie** *f* - geometry. **g~metrisch** *a* geometric[al]

geordnet *a* well-ordered; (*stabil*) stable; **alphabetisch g~** in alphabetical order

Gepäck *nt* -s luggage, baggage. **G~ablage** *f* luggage-rack. **G~aufbewahrung** *f* left-luggage office. **G~schalter** *m* luggage office. **G~schein** *m* left-luggage ticket; (*Aviat*) baggage check. **G~stück** *nt* piece of luggage. **G~träger** *m* porter; (*Fahrrad-*) luggage carrier; (*Dach-*) roof-rack. **G~wagen** *m* luggage-van

Gepard *m* -s,-e cheetah

gepflegt *a* well-kept; (*Person*) well-groomed; (*Hotel*) first-class

Gepflogenheit *f* -,-en practice; (*Brauch*) custom

Gepolter *nt* -s [loud] noise

gepunktet *a* spotted

gerade *a* straight; (*direkt*) direct; (*aufrecht*) upright; (*aufrichtig*) straightforward; (*Zahl*) even; **etw g~ biegen** straighten sth; **sich g~ halten** hold oneself straight □ *adv* straight; directly; (*eben*) just; (*genau*) exactly; (*besonders*) especially; **g~ sitzen/stehen** sit/stand [up] straight; **nicht g~ billig** not exactly cheap; **g~ erst** only just; **g~ an dem Tag** on that very day. **G~** *f* -,-n straight line. **g~aus** *adv* straight ahead/on

gerade|biegen† *vt sep* (NEW) **g~ biegen**, *s.* **gerade**. **g~halten†** (**sich**) *vr sep* (NEW) **sich g~ halten**, *s.* **gerade**. **g~heraus** *adv* (*fig*) straight out. **g~sitzen†** *vi sep* (*haben*) (NEW) **g~ sitzen**, *s.* **gerade**. **g~so** *adv* just the same; **g~so gut** just as good; *adv* just as well. **g~sogut** *adv* (NEW) **g~so gut**, *s.* **geradeso**. **g~stehen†** *vi sep* (*haben*) (*fig*) accept responsibility (**für** for); (*aufrecht stehen*) (NEW) **g~ stehen**, *s.* **gerade**. **g~wegs** *adv* directly, straight. **g~zu** *adv* virtually; (*wirklich*) absolutely

Geranie /-i̯ə/ *f* -,-n geranium

Gerät *nt* -[e]s,-e tool; (*Acker-*) implement; (*Küchen-*) utensil; (*Elektro-*) appliance; (*Radio-, Fernseh-*) set; (*Turn-*) piece of apparatus; (*coll*) equipment

geraten† *vi* (*sein*) get; **in Brand g~** catch fire; **in Wut g~** get angry; **in Streit g~** start quarrelling; **gut/schlecht g~** turn

Geratewohl *nt* **aufs G~** at random

geräuchert *a* smoked

geräumig *a* spacious, roomy

Geräusch *nt* -[e]s,-e noise. **g~los** *a* noiseless, *adv* -ly. **g~voll** *a* noisy, *adv* -ily

gerben *vt* tan

gerecht *a* just, *adv* -ly; *(fair)* fair, *adv* -ly; **g~ werden** (+ *dat*) do justice to. **g~fertigt** *a* justified. **G~igkeit** *f* - justice; fairness

Gerede *nt* -s talk; *(Klatsch)* gossip

geregelt *a* regular

gereift *a* mature

gereizt *a* irritable, *adv* -bly. **G~heit** *f* - irritability

gereuen *vt* **es gereut mich nicht** I don't regret it

Geriatrie *f* - geriatrics *sg*

Gericht[1] *nt* -[e]s,-e *(Culin)* dish

Gericht[2] *nt* -[e]s,-e court [of law]; **vor G~** in court; **das Jüngste G~** the Last Judgement; **mit jdm ins G~ gehen** take s.o. to task. **g~lich** *a* judicial; ⟨*Verfahren*⟩ legal □ *adv* **g~lich vorgehen** take legal action. **G~sbarkeit** *f* - jurisdiction. **G~shof** *m* court of justice. **G~smedizin** *f* forensic medicine. **G~ssaal** *m* court-room. **G~svollzieher** *m* -s,- bailiff

gerieben *a* grated; *(fam: schlau)* crafty

gering *a* small; *(niedrig)* low; *(g~fügig)* slight; **jdn/etw g~ achten** have little regard for s.o./sth; *(verachten)* despise s.o./sth. **g~achten** *vt* *sep* (NEW) **g~achten**, *s.* **gering**. **g~fügig** *a* slight, *adv* -ly. **g~schätzig** *a* contemptuous, *adv* -ly; *(Bemerkung)* disparaging. **g~ste(r,s)** *a* least; **nicht im G~sten** (g~sten) not in the least

gerinnen† *vi* *(sein)* curdle; ⟨*Blut:*⟩ clot

Gerippe *nt* -s,- skeleton; *(fig)* framework

gerissen *a* *(fam)* crafty

Germ *m* -[e]s & *(Aust)* *f* - yeast

German|**e** *m* -n,-n [ancient] German. **g~isch** *a* Germanic. **G~ist(in)** *m* -en,-en *(f* -,-nen) Germanist. **G~istik** *f* - German [language and literature]

gern[e] *adv* gladly; **g~ haben** like; *(lieben)* be fond of; **ich tanze/schwimme g~** I like dancing/swimming; **das kannst du g~ tun** you're welcome to do that; **willst du mit?—g~!** do you want to come?—I'd love to!

gerötet *a* red

Gerste *f* - barley. **G~nkorn** *nt* *(Med)* stye

Geruch *m* -[e]s,-e smell *(von/nach* of). **g~los** *a* odourless. **G~ssinn** *m* sense of smell

Gerücht *nt* -[e]s,-e rumour

geruhen *vi* *(haben)* deign *(zu* to)

gerührt *a* *(fig)* moved, touched

Gerümpel *nt* -s lumber, junk

Gerüst *nt* -[e]s,-e scaffolding; *(fig)* framework

gesalzen *a* salted; *(fam: hoch)* steep

gesammelt *a* collected; *(gefasst)* composed

gesamt *a* entire, whole. **G~ausgabe** *f* complete edition. **G~betrag** *m* total amount. **G~eindruck** *m* overall impression. **G~heit** *f* - whole. **G~schule** *f* comprehensive school. **G~summe** *f* total

Gesandte(r) *m/f* envoy

Gesang *m* -[e]s,-e singing; *(Lied)* song; *(Kirchen-)* hymn. **G~buch** *nt* hymn-book. **G~verein** *m* choral society

Gesäß *nt* -es buttocks *pl.* **G~tasche** *f* hip pocket

Geschäft *nt* -[e]s,-e business; *(Laden)* shop, *(Amer)* store; *(Transaktion)* deal; *(fam: Büro)* office; **schmutzige G~e** shady dealings; **ein gutes G~machen** do very well **(mit** out of); **sein G~ verstehen** know one's job. **g~ehalber** *adv* on business. **g~ig** *a* busy, *adv* -ily; ⟨*Treiben*⟩ bustling. **G~igkeit** *f* - activity. **g~lich** *a* business . . . □ *adv* on business

Geschäfts|**brief** *m* business letter. **G~führer** *m* manager; *(Vereins-)* secretary. **G~mann** *m* *(pl* -leute) businessman. **G~reise** *f* business trip. **G~stelle** *f* office; *(Zweigstelle)* branch. **g~tüchtig** *a* **g~tüchtig sein** be a good businessman/-woman. **G~viertel** *nt* shopping area. **G~zeiten** *fpl* hours of business

geschehen† *vi* *(sein)* happen *(dat* to); **es ist ein Unglück g~** there has been an accident; **es ist um uns g~** we are done for; **das geschieht dir recht!** it serves you right! **gern g~!** you're welcome! **G~** *nt* -s events *pl*

gescheit *a* clever; **daraus werde ich nicht g~** I can't make head or tail of it

Geschenk *nt* -[e]s,-e present, gift. **G~korb** *m* gift hamper

Geschicht|**e** *f* -,-n history; *(Erzählung)* story; *(fam: Sache)* business. **g~lich** *a* historical, *adv* -ly

Geschick *nt* -[e]s fate; *(Talent)* skill; **G~ haben** be good *(zu* at). **G~lichkeit** *f* - skilfulness, skill. **g~t** *a* skilful, *adv* -ly; *(klug)* clever, *adv* -ly

geschieden *a* divorced. **G~e(r)** *m/f* divorcee

Geschirr *nt* -s,-e *(coll)* crockery; *(Porzellan)* china; *(Service)* service; *(Pferde-)* harness; **schmutziges G~** dirty dishes *pl.*

G~spülmaschine *f* dishwasher. G~tuch *nt* tea-towel

Geschlecht *nt* -[e]s,-er sex; (*Gram*) gender; (*Familie*) family; (*Generation*) generation. g~lich *a* sexual, *adv* -ly. G~skrankheit *f* venereal disease. G~steile *ntpl* genitals. G~sverkehr *m* sexual intercourse. G~swort *nt* (*pl* -wörter) article

geschliffen *a* (*fig*) polished

geschlossen *a* closed □ *adv* unanimously; (*vereint*) in a body

Geschmack *m* -[e]s,-̈e taste; (*Aroma*) flavour; (*G~ssinn*) sense of taste; einen guten G~ haben (*fig*) have good taste; G~ finden an (+ *dat*) acquire a taste for. g~los *a* tasteless, *adv* -ly; g~los sein (*fig*) be in bad taste. G~ssache *f* matter of taste. g~voll *a* (*fig*) tasteful, *adv* -ly

geschmeidig *a* supple; (*weich*) soft

Geschöpf *nt* -[e]s,-e creature

Geschoss *nt* -es,-e (Geschoß *nt* -sses,-sse) missile; (*Stockwerk*) storey, floor

geschraubt *a* (*fig*) stilted

Geschrei *nt* -s screaming; (*fig*) fuss

Geschütz *nt* -es,-e gun, cannon

geschützt *a* protected; (*Stelle*) sheltered

Geschwader *nt* -s,- squadron

Geschwätz *nt* -es talk. g~ig *a* garrulous

geschweift *a* curved

geschweige *conj* g~ denn let alone

geschwind *a* quick, *adv* -ly

Geschwindigkeit *f* -,-en speed; (*Phys*) velocity. G~sbegrenzung, G~sbeschränkung *f* speed limit

Geschwister *pl* brother[s] and sister[s]; siblings

geschwollen *a* swollen; (*fig*) pompous, *adv* -ly

Geschworene|(r) *m/f* juror; die G~n the jury *sg*

Geschwulst *f* -,-̈e swelling; (*Tumor*) tumour

geschwungen *a* curved

Geschwür *nt* -s,-e ulcer

Geselle *m* -n,-n fellow; (*Handwerks-*) journeyman

gesellig *a* sociable; (*Zool*) gregarious; (*unterhaltsam*) convivial; g~er Abend social evening. G~keit *f* -,-en entertaining; die G~keit lieben love company

Gesellschaft *f* -,-en company; (*Veranstaltung*) party; die G~ society; jdm G~ leisten keep s.o. company. g~lich *a* social, *adv* -ly. G~sreise *f* group tour. G~sspiel *nt* party game

Gesetz *nt* -es,-e law. G~entwurf *m* bill. g~gebend *a* legislative. G~gebung *f* - legislation. g~lich *a* legal, *adv* -ly. g~los

a lawless. g~mäßig *a* lawful, *adv* -ly; (*gesetzlich*) legal, *adv* -ly

gesetzt *a* staid; (*Sport*) seeded □ *conj* g~ den Fall supposing

gesetzwidrig *a* illegal, *adv* -ly

gesichert *a* secure

Gesicht *nt* -[e]s,-er face; (*Aussehen*) appearance; zu G~ bekommen set eyes on. G~sausdruck *m* [facial] expression. G~sfarbe *f* complexion. G~spunkt *m* point of view. G~szüge *mpl* features

Gesindel *nt* -s riff-raff

gesinnt *a* gut/übel g~ well/ill disposed (*dat* towards)

Gesinnung *f* -,-en mind; (*Einstellung*) attitude; politische G~ political convictions *pl*

gesittet *a* well-mannered; (*zivilisiert*) civilized

gesondert *a* separate, *adv* -ly

Gespann *nt* -[e]s,-e team; (*Wagen*) horse and cart/carriage

gespannt *a* taut; (*fig*) tense, *adv* -ly; ⟨Beziehungen⟩ strained; (*neugierig*) eager, *adv* -ly; (*erwartungsvoll*) expectant, *adv* -ly; g~ sein, ob wonder whether; auf etw/jdn g~ sein look forward eagerly to sth/to seeing s.o.

Gespenst *nt* -[e]s,-er ghost. g~isch *a* ghostly; (*unheimlich*) eerie

Gespött *nt* -[e]s mockery; zum G~ werden become a laughing-stock

Gespräch *nt* -[e]s-e conversation; (*Telefon-*) call; ins G~ kommen get talking; im G~ sein be under discussion. g~ig *a* talkative. G~sgegenstand *m*, G~sthema *nt* topic of conversation

gesprenkelt *a* speckled

Gespür *nt* -s feeling; (*Instinkt*) instinct

Gestalt *f* -,-en figure; (*Form*) shape, form; G~ annehmen (*fig*) take shape. g~en *vt* shape; (*organisieren*) arrange; (*schaffen*) create; (*entwerfen*) design; sich g~en turn out

geständ|ig *a* confessed; g~ig sein have confessed. G~nis *nt* -ses,-se confession

Gestank *m* -s stench, [bad] smell

gestatten *vt* allow, permit; nicht gestattet prohibited; g~ Sie? may I?

Geste /'gɛ-, 'gɛːstə/ *f* -,-n gesture

Gesteck *nt* -[e]s,-e flower arrangement

gestehen† *vt/i* (*haben*) confess; confess to ⟨Verbrechen⟩; offen gestanden to tell the truth

Gestein *nt* -[e]s,-e rock

Gestell *nt* -[e]s,-e stand; (*Flaschen-*) rack; (*Rahmen*) frame

gestellt *a* **gut/schlecht g~** well/badly off; **auf sich** *(acc)* **selbst g~ sein** be thrown on one's own resources

gestelzt *a* *(fig)* stilted

gesteppt *a* quilted

gestern *adv* yesterday; **g~ Nacht (nacht)** last night

Gestik /'gɛstɪk/ *f* - gestures *pl.* **g~ulieren** *vi (haben)* gesticulate

gestrandet *a* stranded

gestreift *a* striped

gestrichelt *a* ⟨Linie⟩ dotted

gestrichen *a* **g~er Teelöffel** level teaspoon[ful]

gestrig /'gɛstrɪç/ *a* yesterday's; **am g~en Tag** yesterday

Gestrüpp *nt* -s,-e undergrowth

Gestüt *nt* -[e]s,-e stud [farm]

Gesuch *nt* -[e]s,-e request; *(Admin)* application. **g~t** *a* sought-after; *(gekünstelt)* contrived

gesund *a* healthy, *adv* -ily; **g~ sein** be in good health; *(Sport, Getränk:)* be good for one; **wieder g~ werden** get well again

Gesundheit *f* - health; **G~!** *(bei Niesen)* bless you! **g~lich** *a* health . .; **gesundheitlicher Zustand** state of health □ *adv* **es geht ihm g~lich gut/schlecht** he is in good/poor health. **g~shalber** *adv* for health reasons. **g~sschädlich** *a* harmful. **G~szustand** *m* state of health

getäfelt *a* panelled

getigert *a* tabby

Getöse *nt* -s racket, din

getragen *a* solemn, *adv* -ly

Getränk *nt* -[e]s,-e drink. **G~ekarte** *f* wine-list

getrauen *vt* sich *(dat)* etw **g~** dare [to] do sth; **sich g~** dare

Getreide *nt* -s *(coll)* grain

getrennt *a* separate, *adv* -ly; **g~ leben** live apart; **g~ schreiben** write as two words. **g~schreiben†** *vt sep* NEW **g~ schreiben**, *s.* **getrennt**

getreu *a* faithful, *adv* -ly □ *prep* (+ *dat*) true to; **der Wahrheit g~** truthfully. **g~lich** *adv* faithfully

Getriebe *nt* -s,- bustle; *(Techn)* gear; *(Auto)* transmission; *(Gehäuse)* gearbox

getrost *adv* with confidence

Getto *nt* -s,-s ghetto

Getue *nt* -s *(fam)* fuss

Getümmel *nt* -s tumult

getüpfelt *a* spotted

geübt *a* skilled; ⟨Auge, Hand⟩ practised

Gewächs *nt* -es,-e plant; *(Med)* growth

gewachsen *a* jdm/etw **g~ sein** *(fig)* be a match for s.o./be equal to sth

Gewächshaus *nt* greenhouse; *(Treibhaus)* hothouse

gewagt *a* daring

gewählt *a* refined

gewahr *a* **g~ werden** become aware *(acc/gen* of)

Gewähr *f* - guarantee

gewahren *vt* notice

gewähr|en *vt* grant; *(geben)* offer; **jdn g~en lassen** let s.o. have his way. **g~leisten** *vt* guarantee

Gewahrsam *m* -s safekeeping; *(Haft)* custody

Gewährsmann *m* (*pl* **-männer** & **-leute**) informant, source

Gewalt *f* -,-en power; *(Kraft)* force; *(Brutalität)* violence; **mit G~** by force; **G~ anwenden** use force; **sich in der G~ haben** be in control of oneself. **G~herrschaft** *f* tyranny. **g~ig** *a* powerful; *(fam: groß)* enormous, *adv* -ly; *(stark)* tremendous, *adv* -ly. **g~sam** *a* forcible, *adv* -bly; ⟨Tod⟩ violent. **g~tätig** *a* violent. **G~tätigkeit** *f* -,-en violence; *(Handlung)* act of violence

Gewand *nt* -[e]s,-̈er robe

gewandt *a* skilful, *adv* -ly; *(flink)* nimble, *adv* -bly. **G~heit** *f* - skill; nimbleness

Gewässer *nt* -s,- body of water; **G~** *pl* waters

Gewebe *nt* -s,- fabric; *(Anat)* tissue

Gewehr *nt* -s,-e rifle, gun

Geweih *nt* -[e]s,-e antlers *pl*

Gewerb|e *nt* -s,- trade. **g~lich** *a* commercial, *adv* -ly. **g~smäßig** *a* professional, *adv* -ly

Gewerkschaft *f* -,-en trade union. **G~ler(in)** *m* -s,- *(f* -,-nen) trade unionist

Gewicht *nt* -[e]s,-e weight; *(Bedeutung)* importance. **G~heben** *nt* -s weight-lifting. **g~ig** *a* important

gewieft *a* *(fam)* crafty

gewillt *a* **g~ sein** be willing

Gewinde *nt* -s,- [screw] thread

Gewinn *m* -[e]s,-e profit; *(fig)* gain, benefit; *(beim Spiel)* winnings *pl*; *(Preis)* prize; *(Los)* winning ticket; **G~ bringend** profitable, *adv* -bly. **G~beteiligung** *f* profit-sharing. **g~bringend** *a* NEW **G~ bringend**, *s.* **Gewinn**. **g~en†** *vt* win; *(erlangen)* gain; *(fördern)* extract; **jdn für sich g~en** win s.o. over □ *vi (haben)* win; **g~en an** (+ *dat*) gain in. **g~end** *a* engaging. **G~er(in)** *m* -s,- *(f* -,-nen) winner

Gewirr *nt* -s,-e tangle; *(Straßen-)* maze; **G~ von Stimmen** hubbub of voices

gewiss *(gewiß)* *a* **(gewisser, gewissest)** certain, *adv* -ly

Gewissen *nt* -s,- conscience. **g~haft** *a* conscientious, *adv* -ly. **g~los** *a* unscrupulous. **G~sbisse** *mpl* pangs of conscience

gewissermaßen *adv* to a certain extent; *(sozusagen)* as it were

Gewissheit (Gewißheit) *f* - certainty

Gewitter *nt* -s,- thunderstorm. **g~ern** *vi* *(haben)* es **g~ert** it is thundering. **g~rig** *a* thundery

gewogen *a* *(fig)* well-disposed *(dat* towards)

gewöhnen *vt* jdn/sich **g~ an** (+ *acc)* get s.o. used to/get used to; [an] jdn/etw **gewöhnt sein** be used to s.o./sth

Gewohnheit *f* -,-en habit. **g~smäßig** *a* habitual, *adv* -ly. **g~srecht** *nt* common law

gewöhnlich *a* ordinary, *adv* -ily; *(üblich)* usual, *adv* -ly; *(ordinär)* common

gewohnt *a* customary; *(vertraut)* familiar; *(üblich)* usual; etw *(acc)* **g~** sein be used to sth

Gewöhnung *f* - getting used (an + *acc* to); *(Süchtigkeit)* addiction

Gewölbe *nt* -s,- vault. **g~t** *a* curved; *(Archit)* vaulted

gewollt *a* forced

Gewühl *nt* -[e]s crush

gewunden *a* winding

gewürfelt *a* check[ed]

Gewürz *nt* -es,-e spice. **G~nelke** *f* clove

gezackt *a* serrated

gezähnt *a* serrated; *(Säge)* toothed

Gezeiten *fpl* tides

gezielt *a* specific; *(Frage)* pointed

geziemend *a* proper, *adv* -ly

geziert *a* affected, *adv* -ly

gezwungen *a* forced □ *adv* **g~** lachen give a forced laugh. **g~ermaßen** *adv* of necessity; etw **g~ermaßen tun** be forced to do sth

Gicht *f* - gout

Giebel *m* -s,- gable

Gier *f* - greed (nach for). **g~ig** *a* greedy, *adv* -ily

gieß|en† *vt* pour; water *(Blumen, Garten)*; *(Techn)* cast □ *v impers* es **g~t** it is pouring [with rain]. **G~erei** *f* -,-en foundry. **G~kanne** *f* watering-can

Gift *nt* -[e]s,-e poison; *(Schlangen-)* venom; *(Biol, Med)* toxin. **g~ig** *a* poisonous; *(Schlange)* venomous; *(Med, Chem)* toxic; *(fig)* spiteful, *adv* -ly. **G~müll** *m* toxic waste. **G~pilz** *m* poisonous fungus, toadstool. **G~zahn** *m* [poison] fang

gigantisch *a* gigantic

Gilde *f* -,-n guild

Gimpel *m* -s,- bullfinch; *(fam: Tölpel)* simpleton

Gin /dʒɪn/ *m* -s gin

Ginster *m* -s *(Bot)* broom

Gipfel *m* -s,- summit, top; *(fig)* peak. **G~konferenz** *f* summit conference. **g~n** *vi* *(haben)* culminate (in + *dat* in)

Gips *m* -es plaster. **G~abguss (G~abguß)** *m* plaster cast. **G~er** *m* -s,- plasterer. **G~verband** *m (Med)* plaster cast

Giraffe *f* -,-n giraffe

Girlande *f* -,-n garland

Girokonto /ˈʒiːro-/ *nt* current account

Gischt *m* -[e]s & *f* - spray

Gitar|re *f* -,-n guitar. **G~rist(in)** *m* -en, -en *(f* -,-nen) guitarist

Gitter *nt* -s,- bars *pl*; *(Rost)* grating, grid; *(Geländer, Zaun)* railings *pl*; *(Fenster-)* grille; *(Draht-)* wire screen; hinter **G~n** *(fam)* behind bars. **G~netz** *nt* grid

Glanz *m* -es shine; *(von Farbe, Papier)* gloss; *(Seiden-)* sheen; *(Politur)* polish; *(fig)* brilliance; *(Pracht)* splendour

glänzen *vi* *(haben)* shine. **g~d** *a* shining, bright; *(Papier, Haar)* glossy; *(fig)* brilliant, *adv* -ly

glanz|los *a* dull. **G~stück** *nt* masterpiece; *(einer Sammlung)* show-piece. **g~voll** *a* *(fig)* brilliant, *adv* -ly; *(prachtvoll)* splendid, *adv* -ly. **G~zeit** *f* heyday

Glas *nt* -es,-̈er glass; *(Brillen-)* lens; *(Fern-)* binoculars *pl*; *(Marmeladen-)* [glass] jar. **G~er** *m* -s,- glazier

gläsern *a* glass ...

Glashaus *nt* greenhouse

glasieren *vt* glaze; ice *(Kuchen)*

glas|ig *a* glassy; *(durchsichtig)* transparent. **G~scheibe** *f* pane

Glasur *f* -,-en glaze; *(Culin)* icing

glatt *a* smooth; *(eben)* even; *(Haar)* straight; *(rutschig)* slippery; *(einfach)* straightforward; *(eindeutig)* downright; *(Absage)* flat; **g~ streichen** smooth out □ *adv* smoothly; evenly; *(fam: völlig)* completely; *(gerade)* straight; *(leicht)* easily; *(ablehnen)* flatly; **g~ rasiert** clean-shaven; **g~ gehen** *od* **verlaufen** go off smoothly; **das ist g~ gelogen** it's a downright lie

Glätte *f* - smoothness; *(Rutschigkeit)* slipperiness

Glatteis *nt* [black] ice; **aufs G~ führen** *(fam)* take for a ride

glätten *vt* smooth; **sich g~** become smooth; *(Wellen:)* subside

glatt|gehen† *vi sep (sein)* ⟨NEW⟩ **g~ gehen**, *s.* glatt. **g~rasiert** *a* ⟨NEW⟩ **g~ rasiert**, *s.* glatt. **g~streichen†** *vt sep* ⟨NEW⟩ **g~**

streichen, *s.* glatt. **g~weg** *adv* (*fam*) outright

Glatz|e *f* -,-**n** bald patch; (*Voll-*) bald head; **eine G~e bekommen** go bald. **g~köpfig** *a* bald

Glaube *m* -**ns** belief (**an** + *acc* in); (*Relig*) faith; **in gutem G~n** in good faith; **G~n schenken** (+ *dat*) believe. **g~n** *vt/i* (*haben*) believe (**an** + *acc* in); (*vermuten*) think; **jdm g~n** believe s.o; **nicht zu g~n** unbelievable, incredible. **G~nsbekenntnis** *nt* creed

glaubhaft *a* credible; (*überzeugend*) convincing, *adv* -ly

gläubig *a* religious; (*vertrauend*) trusting, *adv* -ly. **G~e(r)** *m*/*f* (*Relig*) believer; **die G~en** the faithful. **G~er** *m* -**s**,- (*Comm*) creditor

glaub|lich *a* **kaum g~lich** scarcely believable. **g~würdig** *a* credible; (*Person*) reliable. **G~würdigkeit** *f* - credibility; reliability

gleich *a* same; (*identisch*) identical; (*g~wertig*) equal; **g~ bleibend** constant; **2 mal 5 [ist] g~ 10** two times 5 equals 10; **das ist mir g~** it's all the same to me; **ganz g~, wo/wer** no matter where/who □ *adv* equally; (*übereinstimmend*) identically, the same; (*sofort*) immediately; (*in Kürze*) in a minute; (*fast*) nearly; (*direkt*) right; **g~ gesinnt** like-minded; **g~ alt/schwer sein** be the same age/weight. **g~altrig** *a* [of] the same age. **g~artig** *a* similar. **g~bedeutend** *a* synonymous. **g~berechtigt** *a* equal. **G~berechtigung** *f* equality. **g~bleibend** *a* (NEW) **g~ bleibend**, *s.* gleich

gleichen† *vi* (*haben*) **jdm/etw g~** be like *or* resemble s.o./sth; **sich g~** be alike

gleich|ermaßen *adv* equally. **g~falls** *adv* also, likewise; **danke g~falls** thank you, the same to you. **g~förmig** *a* uniform, *adv* -ly; (*eintönig*) monotonous, *adv* -ly. **G~förmigkeit** *f* uniformity; monotony. **g~gesinnt** *a* (NEW) **g~ gesinnt**, *s.* gleich. **G~gewicht** *nt* balance; (*Phys & fig*) equilibrium. **g~gültig** *a* indifferent, *adv* -ly; (*unwichtig*) unimportant. **G~gültigkeit** *f* indifference. **G~heit** *f* - equality; (*Ähnlichkeit*) similarity. **g~machen** *vt sep* make equal; **dem Erdboden g~machen** raze to the ground. **g~mäßig** *a* even, *adv* -ly, regular, *adv* -ly; (*beständig*) constant, *adv* -ly. **G~mäßigkeit** *f* - regularity. **G~mut** *m* equanimity. **g~mütig** *a* calm, *adv* -ly

Gleichnis *nt* -**ses**,-**se** parable

gleich|sam *adv* as it were. **G~schritt** *m* **im G~schritt** in step. **g~sehen†** *vi sep* (*haben*) **jdm g~sehen** look like s.o.; (*fam: typisch sein*) be just like s.o. **g~setzen** *vt*

sep equate/(*g~stellen*) place on a par (*dat*/ **mit** with). **g~stellen** *vt sep* place on a par (*dat* with). **G~strom** *m* direct current. **g~tun†** *vi sep* (*haben*) **es jdm g~tun** emulate s.o.

Gleichung *f* -,-**en** equation

gleich|viel *adv* no matter (**ob/wer** whether/who). **g~wertig** *a* of equal value. **g~zeitig** *a* simultaneous, *adv* -ly

Gleis *nt* -**es**,-**e** track; (*Bahnsteig*) platform; **G~ 5** platform 5

gleiten† *vi* (*sein*) glide; (*rutschen*) slide. **g~d** *a* sliding; **g~de Arbeitszeit** flexitime

Gleitzeit *f* flexitime

Gletscher *m* -**s**,- glacier. **G~spalte** *f* crevasse

Glied *nt* -[**e**]**s**,-**er** limb; (*Teil*) part; (*Ketten-*) link; (*Mitglied*) member; (*Mil*) rank. **g~ern** *vt* arrange; (*einteilen*) divide; **sich g~ern** be divided (**in** + *acc* into). **G~maßen** *fpl* limbs

glimmen† *vi* (*haben*) glimmer

glimpflich *a* lenient, *adv* -ly; **g~ davonkommen** get off lightly

glitschig *a* slippery

glitzern *vi* (*haben*) glitter

global *a* global, *adv* -ly

Globus *m* - & -**busses**,-**ben** & -**busse** globe

Glocke *f* -,-**n** bell. **G~nturm** *m* bell-tower, belfry

glorifizieren *vt* glorify

glorreich *a* glorious

Glossar *nt* -**s**,-**e** glossary

Glosse *f* -,-**n** comment

glotzen *vi* (*haben*) stare

Glück *nt* -[**e**]**s** [good] luck; (*Zufriedenheit*) happiness; **G~ bringend** lucky; **G~/kein G~ haben** be lucky/unlucky; **zum G~** luckily, fortunately; **auf gut G~** on the off chance; (*wahllos*) at random. **g~bringend** *a* (NEW) **G~ bringend**, *s.* Glück. **g~en** *vi* (*sein*) succeed; **es ist mir geglückt** I succeeded

gluckern *vi* (*haben*) gurgle

glücklich *a* lucky, fortunate; (*zufrieden*) happy; (*sicher*) safe □ *adv* happily; safely; (*fam: endlich*) finally. **g~erweise** *adv* luckily, fortunately

glückselig *a* blissfully happy. **G~keit** *f* bliss

glucksen *vi* (*haben*) gurgle

Glücksspiel *nt* game of chance; (*Spielen*) gambling

Glückwunsch *m* good wishes *pl*; (*Gratulation*) congratulations *pl*; **herzlichen G~!** congratulations! (*zum Geburtstag*) happy birthday! **G~karte** *f* greetings card

Glüh|birne f light-bulb. **g~en** vi (haben) glow. **g~end** a glowing; (rot-) red-hot; (Hitze) scorching; (leidenschaftlich) fervent, adv -ly. **G~faden** m filament. **G~wein** m mulled wine. **G~würmchen** nt -s,- glow-worm

Glukose f - glucose

Glut f - embers pl; (Röte) glow; (Hitze) heat; (fig) ardour

Glyzinie /-jə/ f -,-n wisteria

GmbH abbr (Gesellschaft mit beschränkter Haftung) ≈ plc

Gnade f - mercy; (Gunst) favour; (Relig) grace. **G~nfrist** f reprieve. **g~nlos** a merciless, adv -ly

gnädig a gracious, adv -ly; (mild) lenient, adv -ly; **g~e Frau** Madam

Gnom m -en,-en gnome

Gobelin /gobə'lɛ̃-/ m -s,-s tapestry

Gold nt -[e]s gold. **g~en** a gold ...; (g~farben) golden; **g~ene Hochzeit** golden wedding. **G~fisch** m goldfish. **G~grube** f gold-mine. **g~ig** a sweet, lovely. **G~lack** m wallflower. **G~regen** m laburnum. **G~schmied** m goldsmith

Golf[1] m -[e]s,-e (Geog) gulf

Golf[2] nt -s golf. **G~platz** m golf-course. **G~schläger** m golf-club. **G~spieler(in)** m(f) golfer

Gondel f -,-n gondola; (Kabine) cabin

Gong m -s,-s gong

gönnen vt **jdm etw g~** not begrudge s.o. sth; **jdm etw nicht g~** begrudge s.o. sth; **sie gönnte sich** (dat) **keine Ruhe** she allowed herself no rest

Gönner m -s,- patron. **g~haft** a patronizing, adv -ly

Gör nt -s,-en, **Göre** f -,-n (fam) kid

Gorilla m -s,-s gorilla

Gosse f -,-n gutter

Got|ik f - Gothic. **g~isch** a Gothic

Gott m -[e]s,⁻er God; (Myth) god

Götterspeise f jelly

Gottes|dienst m service. **g~lästerlich** a blasphemous, adv -ly. **G~lästerung** f blasphemy

Gottheit f -,-en deity

Göttin f -,-nen goddess

göttlich a divine, adv -ly

gott|los a ungodly; (atheistisch) godless; **g~ verlassen** a God-forsaken

Götze m -n,-n, **G~nbild** nt idol

Gouver|nante /guvər'nantə/ f -,-n governess. **G~neur** /-'nøːg/ m -s,-e governor

Grab nt -[e]s,⁻er grave

graben† vi (haben) dig

Graben m -s,⁻ ditch; (Mil) trench

Grab|mal nt tomb. **G~stein** m gravestone, tombstone

Grad m -[e]s,-e degree

Graf m -en,-en count

Grafik f -,-en graphics sg; (Kunst) graphic arts pl; (Druck) print

Gräfin f -,-nen countess

grafisch a graphic; **g~e Darstellung** diagram

Grafschaft f -,-en county

Gram m -s grief

grämen (sich) vr grieve

grämlich a morose, adv -ly

Gramm nt -s,-e gram

Gram|matik f -,-en grammar. **g~matikalisch**, **g~matisch** a grammatical, adv -ly

Granat m -[e]s,-e (Miner) garnet. **G~apfel** m pomegranate. **G~e** f -,-n shell; (Hand-) grenade

Granit m -s,-e granite

Graph|ik f, **g~isch** a = Grafik, grafisch

Gras nt -es,⁻er grass. **g~en** vi (haben) graze. **G~hüpfer** m -s,- grasshopper

grassieren vi (haben) be rife

grässlich (gräßlich) a dreadful, adv -ly

Grat m -[e]s,-e [mountain] ridge

Gräte f -,-n fishbone

Gratifikation /-'tsio:n/ f -,-en bonus

gratis adv free [of charge]. **G~probe** f free sample

Gratu|lant(in) m -en,-en (f -,-nen) wellwisher. **G~lation** /-'tsio:n/ f -,-en congratulations pl; (Glückwünsche) best wishes pl. **g~lieren** vi (haben) **jdm g~lieren** congratulate s.o. (zu on); (zum Geburtstag) wish s.o. happy birthday; **[ich] g~liere!** congratulations!

grau a, **G~** nt -s,- grey. **G~brot** nt mixed rye and wheat bread

Gräuel m -s,- horror. **G~tat** f atrocity

grauen[1] vi (haben) **der Morgen** od **es graut** dawn is breaking

grauen[2] v impers **mir graut [es] davor** I dread it. **G~** nt -s dread. **g~haft**, **g~voll** a gruesome; (grässlich) horrible, adv -bly

gräulich[1] a greyish

gräulich[2] a horrible, adv -bly

Graupeln fpl soft hail sg

grausam a cruel, adv -ly. **G~keit** f -,-en cruelty

graus|en v impers **mir graust davor** I dread it. **G~en** nt -s horror, dread. **g~ig** a gruesome

gravieren vt engrave. **g~d** a (fig) serious

Grazie /'gra:tsjə/ f - grace

graziös a graceful, adv -ly

greifbar *a* tangible; **in g~er Nähe** within reach

greifen† *vt* take hold of; *(fangen)* catch □ *vi (haben)* reach **(nach** for); **g~ zu** *(fig)* turn to; **um sich g~** *(fig)* spread. **G~** *nt* **G~ spielen** play tag

Greis *m* **-es,-e** old man. **G~enalter** *nt* extreme old age. **g~enhaft** *a* old. **G~in** *f* **-,-nen** old woman

grell *a* glaring; *(Farbe)* garish; *(schrill)* shrill, *adv* -y

Gremium *nt* **-s,-ien** committee

Grenz|e *f* **-,-n** border; *(Staats-)* frontier; *(Grundstücks-)* boundary; *(fig)* limit. **g~en** *vi (haben)* border **(an** + *acc* on). **g~enlos** *a* boundless; *(maßlos)* infinite, *adv* -ly. **G~fall** *m* borderline case

Greu|el *m* **-s,-** NEW **Gräuel. g~lich** *a* NEW **gräulich**[2]

Griech|e *m* **-n,-n** Greek. **G~enland** *nt* **-s** Greece. **G~in** *f* **-,-nen** Greek woman. **g~isch** *a* Greek. **G~isch** *nt* **-[s]** *(Lang)* Greek

griesgrämig *a (fam)* grumpy

Grieß *m* **-es** semolina

Griff *m* **-[e]s,-e** grasp, hold; *(Hand-)* movement of the hand; *(Tür-, Messer-)* handle; *(Schwert-)* hilt. **g~bereit** *a* handy

Grill *m* **-s,-s** grill; *(Garten-)* barbecue

Grille *f* **-,-n** *(Zool)* cricket; *(fig: Laune)* whim

grill|en *vt* grill; *(im Freien)* barbecue □ *vi (haben)* have a barbecue. **G~fest** *nt* barbecue. **G~gericht** *nt* grill

Grimasse *f* **-,-n** grimace; **G~n schneiden** pull faces

grimmig *a* furious; *(Kälte)* bitter

grinsen *vi (haben)* grin. **G~** *nt* **-s** grin

Grippe *f* **-,-n** influenza, *(fam)* flu

grob *a* **(gröber, gröbst)** coarse, *adv* -ly; *(unsanft, ungefähr)* rough, *adv* -ly; *(un-höflich)* rude, *adv* -ly; *(schwer)* gross, *adv* -ly; *(Fehler)* bad; **g~e Arbeit** rough work; **g~ geschätzt** roughly. **G~ian** *m* **-s,-e** brute

gröblich *a* gross, *adv* -ly

grölen *vt/i (haben)* bawl

Groll *m* **-[e]s** resentment; **einen G~ gegen jdn hegen** bear s.o. a grudge. **g~en** *vi (haben)* be angry *(dat* with); *(Donner:)* rumble

Grönland *nt* **-s** Greenland

Gros[1] *nt* **-ses,-** *(Maß)* gross

Gros[2] /groː/ *nt* - majority, bulk

Groschen *m* **-s,-** *(Aust)* groschen; *(fam)* ten-pfennig piece; **der G~ ist gefallen** *(fam)* the penny's dropped

groß *a* **(größer, größt)** big; *(Anzahl, Summe)* large; *(bedeutend, stark)* great; *(g~artig)* grand; *(Buchstabe)* capital; **g~e Ferien** summer holidays; **g~e Angst haben** be very frightened; **der größte Teil** the majority *or* bulk; **g~ werden** *(Person:)* grow up; **g~ in etw** *(dat)* **sein** be good at sth; **g~ geschrieben werden** *(fig)* be very important **(bei jdm** to s.o.); **G~ und Klein (g~ und klein)** young and old; **im G~en und Ganzen (im g~en und ganzen)** on the whole □ *adv (feiern)* in style; *(fam: viel)* much; **jdn g~ ansehen** look at s.o. in amazement

groß|artig *a* magnificent, *adv* -ly. **G~aufnahme** *f* close-up. **G~britannien** *nt* **-s** Great Britain. **G~buchstabe** *m* capital letter. **G~e(r)** *m/f* **unser G~er** our eldest; **die G~en** the grown-ups; *(fig)* the great *pl*

Größe *f* **-,-n** size; *(Ausmaß)* extent; *(Körper-)* height; *(Bedeutsamkeit)* greatness; *(Math)* quantity; *(Person)* great figure

Groß|eltern *pl* grandparents. **g~enteils** *adv* largely

Größenwahnsinn *m* megalomania

Groß|handel *m* wholesale trade. **G~händler** *m* wholesaler. **g~herzig** *a* magnanimous, *adv* -ly. **G~macht** *f* superpower. **G~mut** *f* - magnanimity. **g~mütig** *a* magnanimous, *adv* -ly. **G~mutter** *f* grandmother. **G~onkel** *m* great-uncle. **G~reinemachen** *nt* **-s** spring-clean. **g~schreiben**† *vt sep* write with a capital [initial] letter; **g~geschrieben werden** *(fig)* NEW **g~ geschrieben werden,** *s.* **groß. G~schreibung** *f* capitalization. **g~sprecherisch** *a* boastful. **g~spurig** *a* pompous, *adv* -ly; *(überheblich)* arrogant, *adv* -ly. **G~stadt** *f* [large] city. **g~städtisch** *a* city ... **G~tante** *f* great-aunt. **G~teil** *m* large proportion; *(Hauptteil)* bulk

größtenteils *adv* for the most part

groß|tun† *(sich)* *vr sep* brag. **G~vater** *m* grandfather. **g~ziehen**† *vt sep* bring up; rear *(Tier:)*. **g~zügig** *a* generous, *adv* -ly; *(weiträumig)* spacious. **G~zügigkeit** *f* - generosity

grotesk *a* grotesque, *adv* -ly

Grotte *f* **-,-n** grotto

Grübchen *nt* **-s,-** dimple

Grube *f* **-,-n** pit

grübeln *vi (haben)* brood

Gruft *f* **-,-e** [burial] vault

grün *a* green; **im G~en** out in the country; **die G~en** the Greens. **G~** *nt* **-s,-** green; *(Laub, Zweige)* greenery

Grund *m* **-[e]s,-e** ground; *(Boden)* bottom; *(Hinter-)* background; *(Ursache)* reason; **aus diesem G~e** for this reason; **von G~**

auf (*fig*) radically; **im G~e [genommen]** basically; **auf G~ laufen** (*Naut*) run aground; **auf G~** (+ *gen*) = **aufgrund**; **zu G~e richten/gehen/liegen** = **zugrunde richten/gehen/liegen**, *s.* **zugrunde**. **G~begriffe** *mpl* basics. **G~besitz** *m* landed property. **G~besitzer** *m* landowner

gründ|en *vt* found, set up; start ⟨*Familie*⟩; (*fig*) base (**auf** + *acc* on); **sich g~en** be based (**auf** + *acc* on). **G~er(in)** *m* -s,- (*f* -,-nen) founder

Grund|farbe *f* primary colour. **G~form** *f* (*Gram*) infinitive. **G~gesetz** *nt* (*Pol*) constitution. **G~lage** *f* basis, foundation. **g~legend** *a* fundamental, *adv* -ly

gründlich *a* thorough, *adv* -ly. **G~keit** *f* - thoroughness

grund|los *a* bottomless; (*fig*) groundless □ *adv* without reason. **G~mauern** *fpl* foundations

Gründonnerstag *m* Maundy Thursday

Grund|regel *f* basic rule. **G~riss** (**G~riß**) *m* ground-plan; (*fig*) outline. **G~satz** *m* principle. **g~sätzlich** *a* fundamental, *adv* -ly; (*im Allgemeinen*) in principle; (*prinzipiell*) on principle; **G~schule** *f* primary school. **G~stein** *m* foundation-stone. **G~stück** *nt* plot [of land]

Gründung *f* -,-en foundation

grün|en *vi* (*haben*) become green. **G~gürtel** *m* green belt. **G~span** *m* verdigris. **G~streifen** *m* grass verge; (*Mittel-*) central reservation, (*Amer*) median strip

grunzen *vi* (*haben*) grunt

Gruppe *f* -,-n group; (*Reise-*) party

gruppieren *vt* group; **sich g~** form a group/groups

Grusel|geschichte *f* horror story. **g~ig** *a* creepy

Gruß *m* -es,-̈e greeting; (*Mil*) salute; **einen schönen G~ an X** give my regards to X; **viele/herzliche G~̈e** regards; **Mit freundlichen G~̈en** Yours sincerely/(*Comm*) faithfully

grüßen *vt/i* (*haben*) say hallo (**jdn** to s.o.); (*Mil*) salute; **g~ Sie X von mir** give my regards to X; **jdn g~ lassen** send one's regards to s.o.; **grüß Gott!** (*SGer, Aust*) good morning/afternoon/evening!

guck|en *vi* (*haben*) (*fam*) look. **G~loch** *nt* peep-hole

Guerilla /ge'rılja/ *f* - guerrilla warfare. **G~kämpfer** *m* guerrilla

Gulasch *nt & m* -[e]s goulash

gültig *a* valid, *adv* -ly. **G~keit** *f* - validity

Gummi *m & nt* -s,-[s] rubber; (*Harz*) gum. **G~band** *nt* (*pl* -bänder) elastic *or* rubber band; (*G~zug*) elastic

gummiert *a* gummed

Gummi|knüppel *m* truncheon. **G~stiefel** *m* gumboot, wellington. **G~zug** *m* elastic

Gunst *f* - favour; **zu jds G~en** in s.o.'s favour; **zu G~** (+ *gen*) = **zugunsten**

günstig *a* favourable, *adv* -bly; (*passend*) convenient, *adv* -ly

Günstling *m* -s,-e favourite

Gurgel *f* -,-n throat. **g~n** *vi* (*haben*) gargle. **G~wasser** *nt* gargle

Gurke *f* -,-n cucumber; (*Essig-*) gherkin

gurren *vi* (*haben*) coo

Gurt *m* -[e]s,-e strap; (*Gürtel*) belt; (*Auto*) safety-belt. **G~band** *nt* (*pl* -bänder) waistband

Gürtel *m* -s,- belt. **G~linie** *f* waistline. **G~rose** *f* shingles *sg*

GUS *abbr* (**Gemeinschaft Unabhängiger Staaten**) CIS

Guss *m* -es,-̈e (**Guß** *m* -sses,-̈sse) (*Techn*) casting; (*Strom*) stream; (*Regen-*) downpour; (*Torten-*) icing. **G~eisen** *nt* cast iron. **g~eisern** *a* cast-iron

gut *a* (**besser, best**) good; (*Gewissen*) clear; (*gütig*) kind (**zu** to); **jdm gut sein** be fond of s.o.; **im G~en (g~en)** amicably; **zu g~er Letzt** in the end; **schon gut** that's all right □ *adv* well; (*schmecken, riechen*) good; (*leicht*) easily; **es gut haben** be well off; (*Glück haben*) be lucky; **gut zu sehen** clearly visible; **gut drei Stunden** a good three hours; **du hast gut reden** it's easy for you to talk

Gut *nt* -[e]s,-̈er possession, property; (*Land-*) estate; **Gut und Böse** good and evil; **Güter** (*Comm*) goods

Gutachten *nt* -s,- expert's report. **G~er** *m* -s,- expert

gut|artig *a* good-natured; (*Med*) benign. **g~aussehend** *a* (NEW) **gut aussehend**, *s.* **aussehen**. **g~bezahlt** *a* (NEW) **gut bezahlt**, *s.* **bezahlen**. **G~dünken** *nt* -s **nach eigenem G~dünken** at one's own discretion

Gute|(s) *nt* **etwas/nichts G~s** something/nothing good; **G~s tun** do good; **das G~ daran** the good thing about it all; **alles G~!** all the best!

Güte *f* -,-n goodness, kindness; (*Qualität*) quality; **du meine G~!** my goodness!

Güterzug *m* goods/(*Amer*) freight train

gut|gehen† *vi sep* (*sein*) (NEW) **gut gehen**, *s.* **gehen**. **g~gehend** *a* (NEW) **gut gehend**, *s.* **gehen**. **g~gemeint** *a* (NEW) **gut gemeint**, *s.* **meinen**. **g~gläubig** *a* trusting. **g~haben†** *vt sep* **fünfzig Mark g~haben** have fifty marks credit (**bei** with). **G~haben** *nt* -s,- [credit] balance;

(*Kredit*) credit. **g~heißen†** *vt sep* approve of

gütig *a* kind, *adv* -ly

gütlich *a* amicable, *adv* -bly

gut|machen *vt sep* make up for; make good 〈*Schaden*〉. **g~mütig** *a* good-natured, *adv* -ly. **G~mütigkeit** *f* - good nature. **G~schein** *m* credit note; (*Bon*) voucher; (*Geschenk-*) gift token. **g~schreiben†** *vt sep* credit. **G~schrift** *f* credit

Guts|haus *nt* manor house. **G~hof** *m* manor

gut|situiert *a* (NEW) gut situiert, *s.* situiert. **g~tun†** *vi sep* (*haben*) (NEW) gut tun, *s.* tun. **g~willig** *a* willing, *adv* -ly

Gymnasium *nt* -s,-ien ≈ grammar school

Gymnast|ik *f* - [keep-fit] exercises *pl*; (*Turnen*) gymnastics *sg.* **g~isch** *a* **g~ische Übung** exercise

Gynäko|loge *m* -n,-n gynaecologist. **G~logie** *f* - gynaecology. **g~logisch** *a* gynaecological

H

H, h /ha:/ *nt*, -,- (*Mus*) B, b

Haar *nt* -[e]s,-e hair; **sich** (*dat*) **die Haare** *od* **das H~ waschen** wash one's hair; **um ein H~** (*fam*) very nearly. **H~bürste** *f* hairbrush. **h~en** *vi* (*haben*) shed hairs; 〈*Tier:*〉 moult □ *vr* **sich h~en** moult. **h~ig** *a* hairy; (*fam*) tricky. **H~klammer, H~klemme** *f* hair-grip. **H~nadel** *f* hairpin. **H~nadelkurve** *f* hairpin bend. **H~schleife** *f* bow. **H~schnitt** *m* haircut. **H~spange** *f* slide. **h~sträubend** *a* hair-raising; (*empörend*) shocking. **H~trockner** *m* -s,- hair-drier. **H~waschmittel** *nt* shampoo

Habe *f* - possessions *pl*

haben† *vt* have; **Angst/Hunger/Durst h~** be frightened/hungry/thirsty; **ich hätte gern** I'd like; **sich h~** (*fam*) make a fuss; **es gut/schlecht h~** be well/badly off; **etw gegen jdn h~** have sth against s.o.; **was hat er?** what's the matter with him? □ *v aux* have; **ich habe/hatte geschrieben** I have/had written; **er hätte ihr geholfen** he would have helped her

Habgier *f* greed. **h~ig** *a* greedy

Habicht *m* -[e]s,-e hawk

Hab|seligkeiten *fpl* belongings. **H~sucht** *f* = Habgier

Hachse *f* -,-n (*Culin*) knuckle

Hack|beil *nt* chopper. **H~braten** *m* meat loaf

Hacke¹ *f* -,-n hoe; (*Spitz-*) pick

Hacke² *f* -,-n, **Hacken** *m* -s,- heel

hack|en *vt* hoe; (*schlagen, zerkleinern*) chop; 〈*Vogel:*〉 peck; **gehacktes Rindfleisch** minced/ (*Amer*) ground beef. **H~fleisch** *nt* mince, (*Amer*) ground meat

Hafen *m* -s,-˙ harbour; (*See-*) port. **H~arbeiter** *m* docker. **H~damm** *m* mole. **H~stadt** *f* port

Hafer *m* -s oats *pl.* **H~flocken** *fpl* [rolled] oats. **H~mehl** *nt* oatmeal

Haft *f* - (*Jur*) custody; (*H~strafe*) imprisonment. **h~bar** *a* (*Jur*) liable. **H~befehl** *m* warrant [of arrest]

haften *vi* (*haben*) cling; (*kleben*) stick; (*bürgen*) vouch /(*Jur*) be liable (**für** for)

Häftling *m* -s,-e detainee

Haftpflicht *f* (*Jur*) liability. **H~versicherung** *f* (*Auto*) third-party insurance

Haftstrafe *f* imprisonment

Haftung *f* - (*Jur*) liability

Hagebutte *f* -,-n rose-hip

Hagel *m* -s hail. **H~korn** *nt* hailstone. **h~n** *vi* (*haben*) hail

hager *a* gaunt

Hahn *m* -[e]s,-˙e cock; (*Techn*) tap, (*Amer*) faucet

Hähnchen *nt* -,-s- (*Culin*) chicken

Hai[fisch] *m* -[e]s,-e shark

Häkchen *nt* -s,- tick

häkel|n *vt/i* (*haben*) crochet. **H~nadel** *f* crochet-hook

Haken *m* -s,- hook; (*Häkchen*) tick; (*fam: Schwierigkeit*) snag. **h~** *vt* hook (**an** + *acc* to). **H~kreuz** *nt* swastika. **H~nase** *f* hooked nose

halb *a* half; **eine h~e Stunde** half an hour; **zum h~en Preis** at half price; **auf h~em Weg** half-way □ *adv* half; **h~ drei** half past two; **fünf [Minuten] vor/nach h~ vier** twenty-five [minutes] past three/to four; **h~ und h~** half and half; (*fast ganz*) more or less. **H~blut** *nt* half-breed. **H~dunkel** *nt* semi-darkness. **H~e(r,s)** *f*/*m*/*nt* half [a litre]

halber *prep* (+ *gen*) for the sake of; **Geschäfte h~** on business

Halb|finale *nt* semifinal. **H~heit** *f* -,-en (*fig*) half-measure

halbieren *vt* halve, divide in half; (*Geom*) bisect

Halb|insel *f* peninsula. **H~kreis** *m* semicircle. **H~kugel** *f* hemisphere. **h~laut** *a* low □ *adv* in an undertone. **h~mast** *adv* at half-mast. **H~messer** *m* -s,- radius. **H~mond** *m* half moon. **H~pension** *f* half-board. **h~rund** *a* semicircular.

H~schuh m [flat] shoe. **h~stündlich** a & adv half-hourly. **h~tags** adv [for] half a day; **h~tags arbeiten** ≈ work part-time. **H~ton** m semitone. **h~wegs** adv halfway; (ziemlich) more or less. **h~wüchsig** a adolescent. **H~zeit** f (Sport) half-time; (Spielzeit) half

Halde f -,-n dump, tip

Hälfte f -,-n half; **zur H~** half

Halfter¹ m & nt -s,- halter

Halfter² f -,-n & nt -s,- holster

Hall m -[e]s,-e sound

Halle f -,-n hall; (Hotel-) lobby; (Bahnhofs-) station concourse

hallen vi (haben) resound; (wider-) echo

Hallen- pref indoor

hallo int hallo

Halluzination /-'tsjo:n/ f -,-en hallucination

Halm m -[e]s,-e stalk; (Gras-) blade

Hals m -es,⁻e neck; (Kehle) throat; **aus vollem H~e** at the top of one's voice; ⟨lachen⟩ out loud. **H~ausschnitt** m neckline. **H~band** nt (pl -bänder) collar. **H~kette** f necklace. **H~schmerzen** mpl sore throat; **sg. h~starrig** a stubborn. **H~tuch** nt scarf

halt¹ adv (SGer) just; **es geht h~ nicht** it's just not possible

halt² int stop! (Mil) halt! (fam) wait a minute!

Halt m -[e]s,-e hold; (Stütze) support; (innerer) stability; (Anhalten) stop; **H~ machen** stop. **h~bar** a durable; (Tex) hard-wearing; (fig) tenable; **h~bar bis . . .** (Comm) use by . . .

halten† vt hold; make ⟨Rede⟩; give ⟨Vortrag⟩; (einhalten, bewahren) keep; [sich (dat)] **etw h~** keep ⟨Hund⟩; take ⟨Zeitung⟩; run ⟨Auto⟩; **warm h~** keep warm; **h~ für** regard as; **viel/nicht viel h~ von** think highly/little of; **sich h~** hold on (**an** + dat to); (fig) hold out; ⟨Geschäft:⟩ keep going; ⟨haltbar sein⟩ keep; ⟨Wetter:⟩ hold; ⟨Blumen:⟩ last; **sich links h~** keep left; **sich gerade h~** hold oneself upright; **sich h~ an** (+ acc) (fig) keep to □ vi (haben) hold; ⟨haltbar sein, bestehen bleiben⟩ keep; ⟨Freundschaft, Blumen:⟩ last; ⟨Halt machen⟩ stop; **h~ auf** (+ acc) (fig) set great store by; **auf sich** (acc) **h~** take pride in oneself; **an sich** (acc) **h~** contain oneself; **zu jdm h~** be loyal to s.o.

Halter m -s,- holder

Halte|stelle f stop. **H~verbot** nt waiting restriction; **'H~verbot'** 'no waiting'

halt|los a (fig) unstable; (unbegründet) unfounded. **h~machen** vi sep (haben) (NEW) **H~ machen**, s. Halt

Haltung f -,-en (Körper-) posture; (Verhalten) manner; (Einstellung) attitude; (Fassung) composure; (Halten) keeping; **H~ annehmen** (Mil) stand to attention

Halunke m -n,-n scoundrel

Hamburger m -s,- hamburger

hämisch a malicious, adv -ly

Hammel m -s,- ram; (Culin) mutton. **H~fleisch** nt mutton

Hammer m -s,⁻ hammer

hämmern vt/i (haben) hammer; ⟨Herz:⟩ pound

Hämorrhoiden /hɛmɔro'iːdən/, **Hämorriden** /hɛmɔ'riːdən/ fpl haemorrhoids

Hamster m -s,- hamster. **h~n** vt/i (haben) (fam) hoard

Hand f -,⁻e hand; **eine H~ voll Kirschen** a handful of cherries; **jdm die H~ geben** shake hands with s.o.; **rechter/linker H~** on the right/left; [**aus**] **zweiter H~** second-hand; **unter der H~** unofficially; (geheim) secretly; **an H~** (+ gen) = **anhand**; **H~ und Fuß haben** (fig) be sound. **H~arbeit** f manual work; (handwerklich) handicraft; (Nadelarbeit) needlework; (Gegenstand) hand-made article. **H~ball** m [German] handball. **H~besen** m brush. **H~bewegung** f gesture. **H~bremse** f handbrake. **H~buch** nt handbook, manual

Händedruck m handshake

Handel m -s trade, commerce; (Unternehmen) business; (Geschäft) deal; **H~ treiben** trade. **h~n** vi (haben) act; (Handel treiben) trade (**mit** in); **von etw** od **über etw** (acc) **h~n** deal with sth; **sich h~n um** be about, concern. **H~smarine** f merchant navy. **H~sschiff** nt merchant vessel. **H~sschule** f commercial college. **h~süblich** a customary. **H~sware** f merchandise

Hand|feger m -s,- brush. **H~fertigkeit** f dexterity. **h~fest** a sturdy; (fig) solid. **H~fläche** f palm. **h~gearbeitet** a handmade. **H~gelenk** nt wrist. **h~gemacht** a handmade. **H~gemenge** nt -s,- scuffle. **H~gepäck** nt hand-luggage. **h~geschrieben** a hand-written. **H~granate** f hand-grenade. **h~greiflich** a tangible; **h~greiflich werden** become violent. **H~griff** m handle; **mit einem H~griff** with a flick of the wrist

handhaben vt insep (reg) handle

Handikap /'hɛndikɛp/ nt -s,-s handicap

Hand|kuss (**Handkuß**) m kiss on the hand. **H~lauf** m handrail

Händler m -s,- dealer, trader

handlich a handy

Handlung f -,-en act; (*Handeln*) action; (*Roman-*) plot; (*Geschäft*) shop. **H~sweise** f conduct

Hand|schellen fpl handcuffs. **H~schlag** m handshake. **H~schrift** f handwriting; (*Text*) manuscript. **H~schuh** m glove. **H~schuhfach** nt glove compartment. **H~stand** m handstand. **H~tasche** f handbag. **H~tuch** nt towel. **H~voll** f -,- eine **H~voll** (NEW) eine **H~ voll**, s. **Hand**

Handwerk nt craft, trade; sein **H~** verstehen know one's job. **H~er** m -s,- craftsman; (*Arbeiter*) workman

Handy /'hɛndi/ nt -s,-s mobile phone

Hanf m -[e]s hemp

Hang m -[e]s,-e slope; (*fig*) inclination, tendency

Hänge|brücke f suspension bridge. **H~lampe** f [light] pendant. **H~matte** f hammock

hängen[1] vt (*reg*) hang

hängen[2] vi (*haben*) hang; **h~ an** (+ *dat*) (*fig*) be attached to; **h~ bleiben** stick (**an** + *dat* to); ⟨*Kleid:*⟩ catch (**an** + *dat* on); **h~ lassen** leave; **den Kopf h~ lassen** be downcast. **H~bleiben**† vi sep (*sein*) (NEW) **h~ bleiben**, s. **hängen**. **h~lassen**† vt sep (NEW) **h~ lassen**, s. **hängen**

Hannover nt -s Hanover

hänseln vt tease

hantieren vi (*haben*) busy oneself

hapern vi (*haben*) es **hapert** there's a lack (**an** + *dat* of)

Happen m -s,- mouthful; einen **H~ essen** have a bite to eat

Harfe f -,-n harp

Harke f -,-n rake. **h~n** vt/i (*haben*) rake

harmlos a harmless; (*arglos*) innocent, adv -ly. **H~igkeit** f - harmlessness; innocence

Harmonie f -,-n harmony. **h~ren** vi (*haben*) harmonize; (*gut auskommen*) get on well

Harmonika f -,-s accordion; (*Mund-*) mouth-organ

harmonisch a harmonious, adv -ly

Harn m -[e]s urine. **H~blase** f bladder

Harpune f -,-n harpoon

hart (härter, härtest) a hard; (*heftig*) violent; (*streng*) harsh □ adv hard; (*streng*) harshly

Härte f -,-n hardness; (*Strenge*) harshness; (*Not*) hardship. **h~n** vt harden

Hart|faserplatte f hardboard. **h~gekocht** a (NEW) **h~ gekocht**, s. **kochen**. **h~herzig** a hard-hearted. **h~näckig** a stubborn, adv -ly; (*ausdauernd*) persistent, adv -ly. **H~näckigkeit** f - stubbornness; persistence

Harz nt -es,-e resin

Haschee nt -s,-s (*Culin*) hash

haschen vi (*haben*) **h~ nach** try to catch

Haschisch nt & m -[s] hashish

Hase m -n,-n hare; **falscher H~** meat loaf

Hasel f -,-n hazel. **H~maus** f dormouse. **H~nuss** (**H~nuß**) f hazel-nut

Hasenfuß m (*fam*) coward

Hass m -es (**Haß** m -sses) hatred

hassen vt hate

hässlich (**häßlich**) a ugly; (*unfreundlich*) nasty, adv -ily. **H~keit** f - ugliness; nastiness

Hast f -haste. **h~en** vi (*sein*) hasten, hurry. **h~ig** a hasty, adv -ily, hurried, adv -ly

hast, hat, hatte, hätte s. **haben**

Haube f -,-n cap; (*Trocken-*) drier; (*Kühler-*) bonnet, (*Amer*) hood

Hauch m -[e]s breath; (*Luft-*) breeze; (*Duft*) whiff; (*Spur*) tinge. **h~dünn** a very thin; ⟨*Strümpfe*⟩ sheer. **h~en** vt/i (*haben*) breathe

Haue f -,-n pick; (*fam: Prügel*) beating. **h~n**† vt beat; (*hämmern*) knock; (*meißeln*) hew; **sich h~n** fight; **übers Ohr h~n** (*fam*) cheat □ vi (*haben*) bang (**auf** + *acc* on); **jdm ins Gesicht h~n** hit s.o. in the face

Haufen m -s,- heap, pile; (*Leute*) crowd

häufen vt heap or pile [up]; **sich h~** pile up; (*zunehmen*) increase

haufenweise adv in large numbers; **h~ Geld** pots of money

häufig a frequent, adv -ly. **H~keit** f - frequency

Haupt nt -[e]s, Häupter head. **H~bahnhof** m main station. **H~darsteller** m, **H~darstellerin** f male/female lead. **H~fach** nt main subject. **H~gericht** nt main course. **H~hahn** m mains tap; (*Wasser-*) stopcock

Häuptling m -s,-e chief

Haupt|mahlzeit f main meal. **H~mann** m (pl -leute) captain. **H~person** f most important person; (*Theat*) principal character. **H~post** f main post office. **H~quartier** nt headquarters pl. **H~rolle** f lead; (*fig*) leading role. **H~sache** f main thing; **in der H~sache** in the main. **h~sächlich** a main, adv -ly. **H~satz** m main clause. **H~schlüssel** m master key. **H~stadt** f capital. **H~straße** f main street. **H~verkehrsstraße** f main road. **H~verkehrszeit** f rush-hour. **H~wort** nt (pl -wörter) noun

Haus nt -es, Häuser house; (Gebäude) building; (Schnecken-) shell; zu H~e at home; nach H~e home; H~ halten = haushalten. H~angestellte(r) m/f domestic servant. H~arbeit f housework; (Sch) homework. H~arzt m family doctor. H~aufgaben fpl homework sg. H~besetzer m -s,- squatter. H~besuch m house-call

hausen vi (haben) live; (wüten) wreak havoc

Haus|frau f housewife. H~gehilfin f domestic help. h~gemacht a homemade. H~halt m -[e]s,-e household; (Pol) budget. h~halten† vi sep (haben) h~halten mit manage carefully; conserve (Kraft). H~hälterin f -,-nen housekeeper. H~haltsgeld nt housekeeping [money]. H~haltsplan m budget. H~herr m head of the household; (Gastgeber) host. h~hoch a huge; (fam) big ▪ adv (fam) vastly; (verlieren) by a wide margin

hausier|en vi (haben) h~en mit hawk. H~er m -s,- hawker

Hauslehrer m [private] tutor. H~in f governess

häuslich a domestic, (Person) domesticated

Haus|meister m caretaker. H~nummer f house number. H~ordnung f house rules pl. H~putz m cleaning. H~rat m -[e]s household effects pl. H~schlüssel m front-door key. H~schuh m slipper. H~stand m household. H~suchung f [police] search. H~suchungsbefehl m search-warrant. H~tier nt domestic animal; (Hund, Katze) pet. H~tür f front door. H~wart m -[e]s,-e caretaker. H~wirt m landlord. H~wirtin f landlady

Haut f -,Häute skin; (Tier-) hide; aus der H~ fahren (fam) fly off the handle. H~arzt m dermatologist

häuten vt skin; sich h~ moult

haut|eng a skin-tight. H~farbe f colour; (Teint) complexion

Haxe f -,-n = Hachse

Hbf. abbr s. Hauptbahnhof

Hebamme f -,-n midwife

Hebel m -s,- lever. H~kraft, H~wirkung f leverage

heben† vt lift; (hoch-, steigern) raise; sich h~ rise; (Nebel:) lift; (sich verbessern) improve

hebräisch a Hebrew

hecheln vi (haben) pant

Hecht m -[e]s,-e pike

Heck nt -s,-s (Naut) stern; (Aviat) tail; (Auto) rear

Hecke f -,-n hedge. H~nschütze m sniper

Heck|fenster nt rear window. H~motor m rear engine. H~tür f hatchback

Heer nt -[e]s,-e army

Hefe f - yeast. H~teig m yeast dough. H~teilchen nt Danish pastry

Heft¹ nt -[e]s,-e haft, handle

Heft² nt -[e]s,-e booklet; (Sch) exercise book; (Zeitschrift) issue. h~en vt (nähen) tack; (stecken) pin/(klammern) clip/(mit Heftmaschine) staple (an + acc to). H~er m -s,- file

heftig a fierce, adv -ly, violent, adv -ly; (Schlag, Regen) heavy, adv -ily; (Schmerz, Gefühl) intense, adv -ly; (Person) quick-tempered. H~keit f -fierceness, violence; intensity

Heft|klammer f staple; (Büro-) paper-clip. H~maschine f stapler. H~pflaster nt sticking plaster. H~zwecke f -,-n drawing-pin

hegen vt care for; (fig) cherish (Hoffnung); harbour (Verdacht)

Hehl nt & m kein[en] H~ machen aus make no secret of. H~er m -s,- receiver, fence

Heide¹ m -n,-n heathen

Heide² f -,-n heath; (Bot) heather. H~kraut nt heather

Heidelbeere f bilberry, (Amer) blueberry

Heid|in f -,-nen heathen. h~nisch a heathen

heikel a difficult, tricky; (delikat) delicate; (dial) (Person) fussy

heil a undamaged, intact; (Person) unhurt; (gesund) well; mit h~er Haut (fam) unscathed

Heil nt -s salvation; sein H~ versuchen try one's luck

Heiland m -s (Relig) Saviour

Heil|anstalt f sanatorium; (Nerven-) mental hospital. H~bad nt spa. h~bar a curable

Heilbutt m -[e]s,-e halibut

heilen vt cure; heal (Wunde) ▪ vi (sein) heal

heilfroh a (fam) very relieved

Heilgymnastik f physiotherapy

heilig a holy; (geweiht) sacred; der H~e Abend Christmas Eve; die h~e Anna Saint Anne; h~ halten hold sacred; keep (Feiertag); h~ sprechen canonize. H~abend m Christmas Eve. H~e(r) m/f saint. h~en vt keep, observe. H~enschein m halo. h~halten† vt sep (NEW) h~ halten, s. halten. H~keit f - sanctity, holiness. h~sprechen† vt sep (NEW) h~ sprechen, s. heilig. H~tum nt -s,-er shrine

heil|kräftig a medicinal. H~kräuter ntpl medicinal herbs. h~los a unholy.

H∼**mittel** nt remedy. **H∼praktiker** m
-s,- practitioner of alternative medicine.
h∼**sam** a (fig) salutary. **H∼sarmee** f
Salvation Army. **H∼ung** f - cure

Heim nt -[e]s,-e home; (Studenten-) hostel.
h∼ adv home

Heimat f -,-en home; (Land) native land.
H∼abend m folk evening. **h∼los** a homeless. **H∼stadt** f home town

heim|begleiten vt sep see home.
h∼bringen† vt sep bring home; (begleiten) see home. **H∼computer** m home
computer. **h∼fahren**† v sep □ vi (sein)
go/drive home □ vt take/drive home.
H∼fahrt f way home. **h∼gehen**† vi sep
(sein) go home; (sterben) die

heimisch a native, indigenous; (Pol)
domestic; **h∼ sein/sich h∼fühlen** be/
feel at home

Heim|kehr f - return [home]. **h∼kehren**
vi sep (sein) return home. **h∼kommen**†
vi sep (sein) come home

heimlich a secret, adv -ly; **h∼ tun** be secretive; **etw h∼ tun** do sth secretly or in
secret. **H∼keit** f -,-en secrecy; **H∼keiten**
secrets. **H∼tuerei** f - secretiveness

Heim|reise f journey home. **h∼reisen** vi
sep (sein) go home. **H∼spiel** nt home
game. **h∼suchen** vt sep afflict. **h∼tü-
ckisch** a treacherous; (Krankheit) insidious. **h∼wärts** adv home. **H∼weg** m
way home. **H∼weh** nt -s homesickness;
H∼weh haben be homesick. **H∼werker**
m -s,- [home] handyman. **h∼zahlen** vt sep
jdm etw h∼zahlen (fig) pay s.o. back for
sth

Heirat f -,-en marriage. **h∼en** vt/i (haben)
marry. **H∼santrag** m proposal; **jdm
einen H∼santrag machen** propose to
s.o. **h∼sfähig** a marriageable

heiser a hoarse, adv -ly. **H∼keit** f - hoarse-
ness

heiß a hot, adv -ly; (hitzig) heated; (leidenschaftlich) fervent, adv -ly; **mein h∼ ge-
liebter Sohn** my beloved son; **mir ist h∼**
I am hot

heißen† vi (haben) be called; (bedeuten)
mean; **ich heiße ...** my name is ...; **wie
h∼ Sie?** what is your name? **wie heißt
... auf Englisch?** what's the English for
...? **es heißt** it says; (man sagt) it is said;
das heißt that is [to say]; **was soll das
h∼?** what does it mean? (empört) what is
the meaning of this? □ vt call; **jdn etw tun
h∼** tell s.o. to do sth

heiß|geliebt a (NEW) **h∼ geliebt,** s. **heiß.**
h∼hungrig a ravenous. **H∼wasserbe-
reiter** m -s,- water heater

heiter a cheerful, adv -ly; (Wetter) bright;
(amüsant) amusing; **aus h∼em Himmel**

(fig) out of the blue. **H∼keit** f - cheerfulness; (Gelächter) mirth

Heiz|anlage f heating; (Auto) heater.
H∼decke f electric blanket. **h∼en** vt
heat; light (Ofen) □ vi (haben) put the heating on; (Ofen:) give out heat. **H∼gerät** nt
heater. **H∼kessel** m boiler. **H∼körper**
m radiator. **H∼lüfter** m -s,- fan heater.
H∼material nt fuel. **H∼ofen** m heater.
H∼ung f -,-en heating; (Heizkörper) radiator

Hektar nt & m -s,- hectare

hektisch a hectic

Held m -en,-en hero. **h∼enhaft** a heroic,
adv -ally. **H∼enmut** m heroism. **h∼en-
mütig** a heroic, adv -ally. **H∼entum** nt -s
heroism. **H∼in** f -,-nen heroine

helfen† vi (haben) help (jdm s.o.);
(nützen) be effective; **sich (dat) nicht zu
h∼en wissen** not know what to do; **es
hilft nichts** it's no use. **H∼er(in)** m -s,-
(f -,-nen) helper, assistant. **H∼ershelfer**
m accomplice

hell a light; (Licht ausstrahlend, klug)
bright; (Stimme) clear; (fam: völlig) utter;
h∼es Bier ≈ lager □ adv brightly; **h∼
begeistert** absolutely delighted. **h∼hö-
rig** a poorly soundproofed; **h∼hörig
werden** (fig) sit up and take notice

hellicht a (NEW) **helllicht**

Hell|igkeit f - brightness. **h∼licht** a
h∼lichter Tag broad daylight.
H∼seher(in) m -s,- (f -,-nen) clairvoyant.
h∼wach a wide awake

Helm m -[e]s,-e helmet

Hemd nt -[e]s,-en vest, (Amer) undershirt;
(Ober-) shirt. **H∼bluse** f shirt

Hemisphäre f -,-n hemisphere

hemm|en vt check; (verzögern) impede;
(fig) inhibit. **H∼ung** f -,-en (fig) in-
hibition; (Skrupel) scruple; **H∼ungen
haben** be inhibited. **h∼ungslos** a unre-
strained, adv -ly

Hendl nt -s,-[n] (Aust) chicken

Hengst m -[e]s,-e stallion. **H∼fohlen** nt
colt

Henkel m -s,- handle

henken vt hang

Henne f -,-n hen

her adv here; (zeitlich) ago; **her mit ...!**
give me ...! **von oben unten/Nor-
den/weit her** from above/below/
the north/far away; **von der Farbe/vom
Thema her** as far as the colour/subject
is concerned; **vor/hinter jdm/etw her**
in front of/behind s.o./sth; **her sein** come
(von from); **hinter jdm/etw her sein** be
after s.o./sth; **es ist schon lange/drei
Tage her** it was a long time/three days
ago

herab adv down [here]; **von oben h~** from above; (fig) condescending, adv -ly. **h~blicken** vi sep (haben) = **h~sehen**

herablass|en† vt sep let down; **sich h~en** condescend (**zu** to). **h~end** a condescending, adv -ly. **H~ung** f - condescension

herab|sehen† vi sep (haben) look down (**auf** + acc on). **h~setzen** vt sep reduce, cut; (fig) belittle. **h~setzend** a disparaging, adv -ly. **h~würdigen** vt sep belittle, disparage

Heraldik f - heraldry

heran adv near; [**bis] h~ an** (+ acc) up to. **h~bilden** vt sep train. **h~gehen†** vi sep (sein) **h~gehen an** (+ acc) go up to; get down to ⟨Arbeit⟩. **h~kommen** vi sep (sein) approach; **h~kommen an** (+ acc) come up to; (erreichen) get at; (fig) measure up to. **h~machen (sich)** vr sep **sich h~machen an** (+ acc) approach; get down to ⟨Arbeit⟩. **h~reichen** vi sep (haben) **h~reichen an** (+ acc) reach; (fig) measure up to. **h~wachsen** vi sep (sein) grow up. **h~ziehen†** v sep □ vt pull up (**an** + acc to); ⟨züchten⟩ raise; (h~bilden) train; (hinzuziehen) call in □ vi (sein) approach

herauf adv up [here]; **die Treppe h~** up the stairs. **h~beschwören†** vt sep evoke; (verursachen) cause. **h~kommen†** vi sep (sein) come up. **h~setzen** vt sep raise, increase

heraus adv out (**aus** of); **h~ damit** od **mit der Sprache!** out with it! **h~ sein** be out; **aus dem Gröbsten h~ sein** be over the worst; **fein h~ sein** be sitting pretty. **h~bekommen†** vt sep get out; (ausfindig machen) find out; (lösen) solve; **Geld h~bekommen** get change. **h~bringen†** vt sep bring out; (fam) get out. **h~finden†** v sep □ vt find out □ vi (haben) find one's way out. **H~forderer** m -s,- challenger. **h~fordern** vt sep provoke; challenge ⟨Person⟩. **H~forderung** f provocation; challenge. **H~gabe** f handing over; (Admin) issue; (Veröffentlichung) publication. **h~geben†** vt sep hand over; (Admin) issue; (veröffentlichen) publish; edit ⟨Zeitschrift⟩; **jdm Geld h~geben** give s.o. change □ vi (haben) give change (**auf** + acc for). **H~geber** m -s,- publisher; editor. **h~gehen†** vi sep (sein) ⟨Fleck:⟩ come out; **aus sich h~gehen** (fig) come out of one's shell. **h~halten (sich)** vr sep (fig) keep out (**aus** of). **h~holen** vt sep get out. **h~kommen** vi sep (sein) come out; (aus Schwierigkeit, Takt) get out; **auf eins** od **dasselbe h~kommen** come to the same thing. **h~lassen†** vt sep let out. **h~machen** vt sep get out; **sich gut**

h~machen (fig) do well. **h~nehmen†** vt sep take out; **sich zu viel h~nehmen** (fig) take liberties. **h~platzen** vi sep (fam) burst out laughing. **h~putzen (sich)** vr sep doll oneself up. **h~ragen** vi sep (haben) jut out; (fig) stand out. **h~reden (sich)** vr sep make excuses. **h~rücken** v sep □ vt move out; (hergeben) hand over □ vi (sein) **h~rücken mit** hand over; (fig: sagen) come out with. **h~rutschen** vi sep (sein) slip out. **h~schlagen†** vt sep knock out; (fig) gain. **h~stellen** vt sep put out; **sich h~stellen** turn out (**als** to be; **daß** that). **h~suchen** vt sep pick out. **h~wollen** vi sep (haben) **nicht mit der Sprache h~wollen** hum and haw. **h~ziehen†** vt sep pull out

herb a sharp; ⟨Wein⟩ dry; ⟨Landschaft⟩ austere; (fig) harsh

herbei adv here. **h~führen** vt sep (fig) bring about. **h~lassen† (sich)** vr sep condescend (**zu** to). **h~schaffen** vt sep get. **h~sehnen** vt sep long for

Herberg|e f -,-n [youth] hostel; (Unterkunft) lodging. **H~svater** m warden

herbestellen vt sep summon

herbitten† vt sep ask to come

herbringen† vt sep bring [here]

Herbst m -[e]s,-e autumn. **h~lich** a autumnal

Herd m -[e]s,-e stove, cooker; (fig) focus

Herde f -,-n herd; ⟨Schaf-⟩ flock

herein adv in [here]; **h~!** come in! **h~bitten†** vt sep ask in. **h~brechen†** vi sep (sein) burst in; (fig) set in; ⟨Nacht:⟩ fall; **h~brechen über** (+ acc) (fig) overtake. **h~fallen†** vi sep (sein) (fam) be taken in (**auf** + acc by). **h~kommen†** vi sep (sein) come in. **h~lassen†** vt sep let in. **h~legen** vt sep (fam) take for a ride. **h~rufen†** vt sep call in

Herfahrt f journey/drive here

herfallen† vi sep (sein) **h~ über** (+ acc) attack; fall upon ⟨Essen⟩

hergeben† vt sep hand over; (fig) give up; **sich h~ zu** (fig) be a party to

hergebracht a traditional

hergehen† vi sep (sein) **h~ vor/neben/hinter** (+ dat) walk along in front of/beside/behind; **es ging lustig her** (fam) there was a lot of merriment

herhalten† vi sep (haben) hold out; **h~ müssen** be the one to suffer

herholen vt sep fetch; **weit hergeholt** (fig) far-fetched

Hering m -s,-e herring; (Zeltpflock) tentpeg

her|kommen† vi sep (sein) come here; **wo kommt das her?** where does it come

from? **h~kömmlich** *a* traditional.
H~kunft *f* - origin

herlaufen† *vi sep* (*sein*) **h~ vor/ne-ben/hinter** (+ *dat*) run/(*gehen*) walk along in front of/beside/behind

herleiten *vt sep* derive

hermachen *vt sep* **viel/wenig h~** be impressive/unimpressive; (*wichtig nehmen*) make a lot of/little fuss (**von** of); **sich h~ über** (+ *acc*) fall upon; tackle ⟨*Arbeit*⟩

Hermelin[1] *nt* -s,-e ⟨*Zool*⟩ stoat

Hermelin[2] *m* -s,-e ⟨*Pelz*⟩ ermine

hermetisch *a* hermetic, *adv* -ally

Hernie /ˈhɛrnjə/ *f* -,-n hernia

Heroin *nt* -s heroin

heroisch *a* heroic, *adv* -ally

Herr *m* -n,-en gentleman; ⟨*Gebieter*⟩ master (**über** + *acc* of); **[Gott,] der H~** the Lord [God]; **H~ Meier** Mr Meier; **Sehr geehrte H~en** Dear Sirs. **H~chen** *nt* -s,- master. **H~enhaus** *nt* manor [house]. **h~enlos** *a* ownerless; ⟨*Tier*⟩ stray. **H~ensitz** *m* manor

Herrgott *m* **der H~** the Lord; **H~ [noch mal]!** damn it!

herrichten *vt sep* prepare; **wieder h~** renovate

Herrin *f* -,-nen mistress

herrisch *a* imperious, *adv* -ly; ⟨*Ton*⟩ peremptory; (*herrschsüchtig*) overbearing

herrlich *a* marvellous, *adv* -ly; (*großartig*) magnificent, *adv* -ly. **H~keit** *f* -,-en splendour

Herrschaft *f* -,-en rule; (*Macht*) power; (*Kontrolle*) control; **meine H~en!** ladies and gentlemen!

herrsch|en *vi* (*haben*) rule; (*verbreitet sein*) prevail; **es h~te Stille/große Aufregung** there was silence/great excitement. **H~er(in)** *m* -s,- (*f* -,-nen) ruler. **h~süchtig** *a* domineering

herrühren *vi sep* (*haben*) stem (**von** from)

hersein† *vi sep* (*sein*) NEW **her sein**, *s.* **her**

herstammen *vi sep* (*haben*) come (**aus/von** from)

herstell|en *vt sep* establish; (*Comm*) manufacture, make. **H~er** *m* -s,- manufacturer, maker. **H~ung** *f* - establishment; manufacture

herüber *adv* over [here]. **h~kommen**† *vi sep* (*sein*) come over [here]

herum *adv* **im Kreis h~** [round] in a circle; **falsch h~** the wrong way round; **um ... h~** round ...; (*ungefähr*) [round] about ...; **h~ sein** be over. **h~albern** *vi sep* (*haben*) fool around. **h~drehen** *vt sep* turn round/(*wenden*) over; turn ⟨*Schlüssel*⟩; **sich h~drehen** turn round/over. **h~gehen**† *vi sep* (*sein*) walk around;

⟨*Zeit:*⟩ pass; **h~gehen um** go round. **h~kommen**† *vi sep* (*sein*) get about; **h~kommen um** get round; come round ⟨*Ecke*⟩; **um etw [nicht] h~kommen** ⟨*fig*⟩ [not] get out of sth. **h~kriegen** *vt sep* jdn **h~kriegen** (*fam*) talk s.o. round. **h~liegen**† *vi sep* (*sein*) lie around. **h~lungern** *vi sep* (*haben*) loiter. **h~schnüffeln** *vi sep* (*haben*) nose about. **h~sitzen**† *vi sep* (*haben*) sit around; **h~sitzen um** sit round. **h~sprechen**† (**sich**) *vr sep* ⟨*Gerücht:*⟩ get about. **h~stehen**† *vi sep* (*haben*) stand around; **h~stehen um** stand round. **h~treiben** (**sich**) *vr sep* hang around. **h~ziehen**† *vi sep* (*sein*) move around; (*ziellos*) wander about

herunter *adv* down [here]; **die Treppe h~** down the stairs; **h~ sein** be down; (*körperlich*) be run down. **h~fallen** *vi* fall off. **h~fahren** *vi sep* (*sein*) come down; (*sinken*) go/come down. **h~gekommen** *a* (*fig*) run-down; ⟨*Gebäude*⟩ dilapidated; ⟨*Person*⟩ down-at-heel. **h~kommen**† *vi sep* (*sein*) come down; (*fig*) go to rack and ruin; ⟨*Firma, Person:*⟩ go downhill; (*gesundheitlich*) get run down. **h~lassen**† *vt sep* let down, lower. **h~machen** *vt sep* (*fam*) reprimand; (*herabsetzen*) run down. **h~spielen** *vt sep* (*fig*) play down. **h~ziehen**† *vt sep* pull down

hervor *adv* out (**aus** of). **h~bringen**† *vt sep* produce; utter ⟨*Wort*⟩. **h~gehen** *vi sep* (*sein*) come/(*sich ergeben*) emerge/(*folgen*) follow (**aus** from). **h~heben** *vt sep* (*fig*) stress, emphasize. **h~quellen**† *vi sep* (*sein*) stream out; (*h~treten*) bulge. **h~ragen** *vi sep* (*haben*) jut out; (*fig*) stand out. **h~ragend** *a* (*fig*) outstanding. **h~rufen**† *vt sep* (*fig*) cause. **h~stehen**† *vi sep* (*haben*) protrude. **h~treten**† *vi sep* (*sein*) protrude, bulge; (*fig*) stand out. **h~tun**† (**sich**) *vr sep* (*fig*) distinguish oneself; (*angeben*) show off

Herweg *m* way here

Herz *nt* -ens,-en heart; (*Kartenspiel*) hearts *pl*; **sich** ⟨*dat*⟩ **ein H~ fassen** pluck up courage. **H~anfall** *m* heart attack

herzeigen *vt sep* show

herz|en *vt* hug. **H~enslust** *f* **nach H~enslust** to one's heart's content. **h~haft** *a* hearty, *adv* -ily; (*würzig*) savoury

herziehen† *v sep* □ *vt* **hinter sich** (*dat*) **h~** pull along [behind one] □ *vi* (*sein*) **hinter jdm h~** follow along behind s.o.; **über jdn h~** (*fam*) run s.o. down

herz|ig *a* sweet, adorable. **H~infarkt** *m* heart attack. **H~klopfen** *nt* -s palpitations *pl*; **ich hatte H~klopfen** my heart was pounding

herzlich *a* cordial, *adv* -ly; (*warm*) warm, *adv* -ly; (*aufrichtig*) sincere, *adv* -ly; **h~en Dank!** many thanks! **h~e Grüße** kind regards; **h~ wenig** precious little. **H~keit** *f* - cordiality; warmth; sincerity

herzlos *a* heartless

Herzog *m* -s,-̈e duke. **H~in** *f* -,-nen duchess. **H~tum** *nt* -s,-̈er duchy

Herz|schlag *m* heartbeat; (*Med*) heart failure. **h~zerreißend** *a* heart-breaking

Hessen *nt* -s Hesse

heterosexuell *a* heterosexual

Hetze *f* - rush; (*Kampagne*) virulent campaign (**gegen** against). **h~n** *vt* chase; **sich h~n** hurry □ *vi* (*haben*) agitate; (*sich beeilen*) hurry □ *vi* (*sein*) rush

Heu *nt* -s hay; **Geld wie Heu haben** (*fam*) have pots of money

Heuchelei *f* - hypocrisy

heuch|eln *vt* feign □ *vi* (*haben*) pretend. **H~ler(in)** *m* -s,- (*f* -,-nen) hypocrite. **h~lerisch** *a* hypocritical, *adv* -ly

heuer *adv* (*Aust*) this year

Heuer *f* -,-n (*Naut*) pay. **h~n** *vt* hire; sign on (*Matrosen*)

heulen *vi* (*haben*) howl; (*fam: weinen*) cry; (*Sirene:*) wail

Heurige(r) *m* (*Aust*) new wine

Heu|schnupfen *m* hay fever. **H~schober** *m* -s,- haystack. **H~schrecke** *f* -,-n grasshopper; (*Wander-*) locust

heut|e *adv* today; (*heutzutage*) nowadays; **h~e früh** *od* **Morgen** (**morgen**) this morning; **von h~e auf morgen** from one day to the next. **h~ig** *a* today's ...; (*gegenwärtig*) present; **der h~ige Tag** today. **h~zutage** *adv* nowadays

Hexe *f* -,-n witch. **h~n** *vi* (*haben*) work magic; **ich kann nicht h~n** (*fam*) I can't perform miracles. **H~njagd** *f* witchhunt. **H~nschuss** (**H~nschuß**) *m* lumbago. **H~rei** *f* - witchcraft

Hieb *m* -[e]s,-e blow; (*Peitschen-*)lash; **H~e** hiding *sg*

hier *adv* here; **h~ sein/bleiben/lassen/ behalten** be/stay/leave/keep here; **h~ und da** here and there; (*zeitlich*) now and again

Hierarchie /hjerar̩çi:/ *f* -,-n hierarchy

hier|auf *adv* on this/these; (*antworten*) to this; (*zeitlich*) after this. **h~aus** *adv* out of *or* from this/these. **h~behalten†** *vt sep* (NEW) **h~ behalten**, *s.* hier. **h~bleiben†** *vi sep* (*sein*) (NEW) **h~ bleiben**, *s.* hier. **h~durch** *adv* through this/these; (*Ursache*) as a result of this. **h~für** *adv* for this/these. **h~her** *adv* here. **h~hin** *adv* here. **h~in** *adv* in this/these. **h~lassen†** *vt sep* (NEW) **h~ lassen**, *s.* hier.

h~mit *adv* with this/these; (*Comm*) herewith; (*Admin*) hereby. **h~nach** *adv* after this/these; (*demgemäß*) according to this/these. **h~sein†** *vi sep* (*sein*) (NEW) **h~ sein**, *s.* hier. **h~über** *adv* over/(*höher*) above this/these; (*sprechen, streiten*) about this/these. **h~unter** *adv* under/ (*tiefer*) below this/these; (*dazwischen*) among these. **h~von** *adv* from this/these; (*h~über*) about this/these; (*Menge*) of this/these. **h~zu** *adv* to this/these; (*h~für*) for this/these. **h~zulande** *adv* here

hiesig *a* local. **H~e(r)** *m/f* local

Hilf|e *f* -,-n help, aid; **um H~e rufen** call for help; **jdm zu H~e kommen** come to s.o.'s aid; **mit H~e** (+ *gen*) (NEW) **mithilfe**. **h~los** *a* helpless, *adv* -ly. **H~losigkeit** *f* - helplessness. **h~reich** *a* helpful

Hilfs|arbeiter *m* unskilled labourer. **h~bedürftig** *a* needy; **h~bedürftig sein** be in need of help. **h~bereit** *a* helpful, *adv* -ly. **H~kraft** *f* helper. **H~mittel** *nt* aid. **H~verb, H~zeitwort** *nt* auxiliary verb

Himbeere *f* raspberry

Himmel *m* -s,- sky; (*Relig & fig*) heaven; (*Bett-*) canopy; **am H~** in the sky; **unter freiem H~** in the open air. **H~bett** *nt* four-poster [bed]. **H~fahrt** *f* Ascension; **Mariä H~fahrt** Assumption. **h~schreiend** *a* scandalous. **H~srichtung** *f* compass point; **in alle H~srichtungen** in all directions. **h~weit** *a* (*fam*) vast

himmlisch *a* heavenly

hin *adv* there; **hin und her** to and fro; **hin und zurück** there and back; (*Rail*) return; **hin und wieder** now and again; **an** (+ *dat*) ... **hin** along; **auf** (+ *acc*) ... **hin** in reply to (*Brief, Anzeige*); on (*jds Rat*); **zu** *od* **nach** ... **hin** towards; **vor sich hin reden** talk to oneself; **hin sein** (*fam*) be gone; (*kaputt, tot*) have had it; **[ganz] hin sein von** be overwhelmed by; **es ist noch/ nicht mehr lange hin** it's a long time yet/not long to go

hinab *adv* down [there]

hinauf *adv* up [there]; **die Treppe/Straße h~** up the stairs/road. **h~gehen†** *vi sep* (*sein*) go up. **h~setzen** *vt sep* raise

hinaus *adv* out [there]; (*nach draußen*) outside; **zur Tür h~** out of the door; **auf Jahre h~** for years to come; **über etw** (*acc*) **h~** beyond sth; (*Menge*) [over and] above sth; **über etw** (*acc*) **h~ sein** (*fig*) be past sth. **h~fliegen†** *v sep* □ *vi* (*sein*) fly out; (*fam*) get the sack □ *vt* out fly out. **h~gehen†** *vi sep* (*sein*) go out; (*Zimmer:*) face (**nach Norden** north); **h~gehen über** (+ *acc*) go beyond, exceed. **h~kommen†** *vi sep* (*sein*) get out; **h~kommen über** (+ *acc*) get beyond. **h~laufen†** *vi* *sep* (*sein*) run out; **h~laufen auf** (+ *acc*) (*fig*) amount to. **h~lehnen (sich)** *vr sep* lean out. **h~ragen** *vi sep* (*haben*) **h~ragen über** (+ *acc*) project beyond; (*in der Höhe*) rise above; (*fig*) stand out above. **h~schicken** *vt sep* send out. **h~schieben** *vt sep* push out; (*fig*) put off. **h~sehen†** *vi sep* (*haben*) look out. **h~sein†** *vi sep* (*sein*) (NEW) **h~ sein**, *s.* **hinaus. h~werfen†** *vt sep* throw out; (*fam: entlassen*) fire. **h~wollen†** *vi sep* (*haben*) want to go out; **h~wollen auf** (+ *acc*) (*fig*) aim at; **hoch h~wollen** (*fig*) be ambitious. **h~ziehen†** *v sep □ vt* pull out; (*in die Länge ziehen*) drag out; (*verzögern*) delay; **sich h~ziehen** drag on; be delayed □ *vi* (*sein*) move out. **h~zögern** *vt* delay; **sich h~zögern** be delayed

Hinblick *m* im **H~ auf** (+ *acc*) in view of; (*hinsichtlich*) regarding

hinbringen† *vt sep* take there; (*verbringen*) spend

hinder|lich *a* awkward; **jdm h~lich sein** hamper s.o. **h~n** *vt* hamper; (*verhindern*) prevent. **H~nis** *nt* **-ses,-se** obstacle. **H~nisrennen** *nt* steeplechase

hindeuten *vi sep* (*haben*) point (**auf** + *acc* to)

Hindu *m* -s,-s Hindu. **H~ismus** *m* - Hinduism

hindurch *adv* through it/them; **den Sommer h~** throughout the summer

hinein *adv* in [there]; (*nach drinnen*) inside; **h~ in** (+ *acc*) into. **h~fallen†** *vi sep* (*sein*) fall in. **h~gehen†** *vi sep* (*sein*) go in; **h~gehen in** (+ *acc*) go into. **h~laufen†** *vi sep* (*sein*) run in; **h~laufen in** (+ *acc*) run into. **h~reden** *vi sep* (*haben*) **jdm h~reden** interrupt s.o.; (*sich einmischen*) interfere in s.o.'s affairs. **h~versetzen (sich)** *vr sep* **sich in jds Lage h~versetzen** put oneself in s.o.'s position. **h~ziehen†** *vt sep* pull in; **h~ziehen in** (+ *acc*) pull into; **in etw** (*acc*) **h~gezogen werden** (*fig*) become involved in sth

hin|fahren† *v sep □ vi* (*sein*) go/drive there □ *vt* take/drive there. **H~fahrt** *f* journey/drive there; (*Rail*) outward journey. **h~fallen†** *vi sep* (*sein*) fall. **h~fällig** *a* (*gebrechlich*) frail; (*ungültig*) invalid. **h~fliegen†** *v sep □ vi* (*sein*) fly there; (*fam*) fall □ *vt* fly there. **H~flug** *m* flight there; (*Admin*) outward flight. **H~gabe** *f* - devotion; (*Eifer*) dedication

hingeb|en† *vt sep* give up; **sich h~en** (*fig*) devote oneself (**einer Aufgabe** to a task); abandon oneself (**dem Vergnügen** to pleasure). **H~ung** *f* - devotion. **h~ungsvoll** *a* devoted, *adv* -ly

hingegen *adv* on the other hand

hingehen† *vi sep* (*sein*) go/(*zu Fuß*) walk there; (*vergehen*) pass; **h~ zu** go up to; **wo gehst du hin**? where are you going? **etw h~ lassen** (*fig*) let sth pass

hingerissen *a* rapt, *adv* -ly; **h~ sein** be carried away (**von** by)

hin|halten† *vt sep* hold out; (*warten lassen*) keep waiting. **h~hocken (sich)** *vr sep* squat down. **h~kauern (sich)** *vr sep* crouch down

hinken *vi* (*haben/sein*) limp

hin|knien (sich) *vr sep* kneel down. **h~kommen** *vi sep* (*sein*) get there; (*h~gehören*) belong, go; (*fam: auskommen*) manage (**mit** with); (*fam: stimmen*) be right. **h~länglich** *a* adequate, *adv* -ly. **h~laufen†** *vi sep* (*sein*) run/(*gehen*) walk there. **h~legen** *vt sep* lay *or* put down; **sich h~legen** lie down. **h~nehmen†** *vt sep* (*fig*) accept

hinreichen *v sep □ vt* hand (*dat* to) □ *vi* (*haben*) extend (**bis** to); (*ausreichen*) be equate. **h~d** *a* adequate, *adv* -ly

Hinreise *f* journey there; (*Rail*) outward journey

hinreißen† *vt sep* (*fig*) carry away; **sich h~ lassen** get carried away. **h~d** *a* ravishing, *adv* -ly

hinricht|en *vt sep* execute. **H~ung** *f* execution

hinschicken *vt sep* send there

hinschleppen *vt sep* drag there; (*fig*) drag out; **sich h~** drag oneself along; (*fig*) drag on

hinschreiben† *vt sep* write there; (*aufschreiben*) write down

hinsehen† *vi sep* (*haben*) look

hinsein† *vi sep* (*sein*) (*fam*) (NEW) **hin sein**, *s.* **hin**

hinsetzen *vt sep* put down; **sich h~** sit down

Hinsicht *f* - in dieser/gewisser **H~** in this respect/in a certain sense; **in finanzieller H~** financially. **h~lich** *prep* (+ *gen*) regarding

hinstellen *vt sep* put *or* set down; park ⟨*Auto*⟩; (*fig*) make out (**als** to be); **sich h~** stand

hinstrecken *vt sep* hold out; **sich h~** extend

hintan|setzen, h~stellen *vt sep* ignore; (*vernachlässigen*) neglect

hinten *adv* at the back; **dort h~** back there; **nach/von h~** to the back/from behind. **h~herum** *adv* round the back; (*fam*) by devious means; ⟨*erfahren*⟩ in a roundabout way

hinter *prep* (+ *dat/acc*) behind; (*nach*) after; **h~ jdm/etw herlaufen** run after s.o./sth; **h~ etw** (*dat*) **stecken** (*fig*) be behind sth; **h~ etw** (*acc*) **kommen** (*fig*) get to the bottom of sth; **etw h~ sich** (*acc*) **bringen** get sth over [and done] with. **H~bein** *nt* hind leg

Hinterbliebene *pl* (*Admin*) surviving dependants; **die H~n** the bereaved family *sg*

hinterbringen† *vt* tell (*jdm* s.o.)

hintere|(r,s) *a* back, rear; **h~s Ende** far end

hintereinander *adv* one behind/(*zeitlich*) after the other; **dreimal h~** three times in succession *or* (*fam*) in a row

Hintergedanke *m* ulterior motive

hintergehen† *vt* deceive

Hinter|grund *m* background. **H~halt** *m* -[e]s,-e ambush; **aus dem H~halt überfallen** ambush. **h~hältig** *a* underhand

hinterher *adv* behind, after; (*zeitlich*) afterwards. **h~gehen†** *vi sep* (*sein*) follow (*jdm* s.o.). **h~kommen†** *vi sep* (*sein*) follow [behind]. **h~laufen†** *vi sep* (*sein*) run after (*jdm* s.o.)

Hinter|hof *m* back yard. **H~kopf** *m* back of the head

hinterlassen† *vt* leave [behind]; (*Jur*) leave, bequeath (*dat* to). **H~schaft** *f* -,-en (*Jur*) estate

hinterlegen *vt* deposit

Hinter|leib *m* (*Zool*) abdomen. **H~list** *f* deceit. **h~listig** *a* deceitful, *adv* -ly. **h~m** *prep* = **hinter dem. H~mann** *m* (*pl* -männer) person behind. **h~n** *prep* = **hinter den. H~n** *m* -s,- (*fam*) bottom, backside. **H~rad** *nt* rear *or* back wheel. **h~rücks** *adv* from behind. **h~s** *prep* = **hinter das. h~ste(r,s)** *a* last; **h~ste Reihe** back row. **H~teil** *nt* (*fam*) behind

hintertreiben† *vt* (*fig*) block

Hinter|treppe *f* back stairs *pl*. **H~tür** *f* back door; (*fig*) loophole

hinterziehen† *vt* (*Admin*) evade

Hinterzimmer *nt* back room

hinüber *adv* over or across [there]; **h~ sein** (*fam: unbrauchbar, tot*) have had it; (*betrunken*) be gone. **h~gehen†** *vi sep* (*sein*) go over or across; **h~gehen über** (+ *acc*) cross

hinunter *adv* down [there]; **die Treppe/Straße h~** down the stairs/road. **h~gehen†** *vi sep* (*sein*) go down. **h~schlucken** *vt sep* swallow

Hinweg *m* way there

hinweg *adv* away, off; **h~ über** (+ *acc*) over; **über eine Zeit h~** over a period. **h~gehen†** *vi sep* (*sein*) **h~gehen über** (+ *acc*) (*fig*) pass over. **h~kommen†** *vt sep* (*sein*) **h~kommen über** (+ *acc*) (*fig*) get over. **h~sehen†** *vi sep* (*haben*) **h~sehen über** (+ *acc*) see over; (*fig*)

overlook. **h~setzen (sich)** *vr sep* sich **h~setzen über** (+ *acc*) ignore

Hinweis *m* -es,-e reference; (*Andeutung*) hint; (*Anzeichen*) indication; **unter H~ auf** (+ *acc*) with reference to. **h~en†** *v sep* ▫ *vi* (*haben*) point (**auf** + *acc* to) ▫ *vt* **jdn auf etw** (*acc*) **h~en** point sth out to s.o. **h~end** *a* (*Gram*) demonstrative

hin|wenden† *vt sep* turn; **sich h~wenden** turn (**zu** to). **h~werfen†** *vt sep* throw down; drop (*Bemerkung*); (*schreiben*) jot down; (*zeichnen*) sketch; (*fam: aufgeben*) pack in

hinwieder *adv* on the other hand

hin|zeigen *vi sep* (*haben*) point (**auf** + *acc* to). **h~ziehen†** *vt sep* pull; (*fig: in die Länge ziehen*) drag out; (*verzögern*) delay; **sich h~ziehen** drag on; be delayed; **sich h~gezogen fühlen zu** (*fig*) feel drawn to

hinzu *adv* in addition. **h~fügen** *vt sep* add. **h~kommen†** *vt sep* (*sein*) be added; (*ankommen*) arrive [on the scene]; join (**zu** *jdm* s.o.). **h~rechnen** *vt sep* add. **h~ziehen†** *vt sep* call in

Hiobsbotschaft *f* bad news *sg*

Hirn *nt* -s brain; (*Culin*) brains *pl*. **H~gespinst** *nt* -[e]s,-e figment of the imagination. **H~hautentzündung** *f* meningitis. **h~verbrannt** *a* (*fam*) crazy

Hirsch *m* -[e]s,-e deer; (*männlich*) stag; (*Culin*) venison

Hirse *f* - millet

Hirt *m* -en,-en, **Hirte** *m* -n,-n shepherd

hissen *vt* hoist

Histor|iker *m* -s,- historian. **h~isch** *a* historical; (*bedeutend*) historic

Hit *m* -s,-s (*Mus*) hit

Hitz|e *f* - heat. **H~ewelle** *f* heatwave. **h~ig** *a* (*fig*) heated, *adv* -ly; (*Person*) hotheaded; (*jähzornig*) hot-tempered. **H~kopf** *m* hothead. **H~schlag** *m* heatstroke

H-Milch /'ha:-/ *f* long-life milk

Hobby *nt* -s,-s hobby

Hobel *m* -s,- (*Techn*) plane; (*Culin*) slicer. **h~n** *vt*/*i* (*haben*) plane; (*Culin*) slice. **H~späne** *mpl* shavings

hoch *a* (**höher, höchst**; *attrib* **hohe(r,s)**) high; (*Baum, Mast*) tall; (*Offizier*) high-ranking; (*Alter*) great; (*Summe*) large; (*Strafe*) heavy; **hohe Schuhe** ankle boots ▫ *adv* high; (*sehr*) highly; **h~gewachsen** tall; **h~ begabt** highly gifted; **h~ gestellte Persönlichkeit** important person; **die Treppe/den Berg h~** up the stairs/hill; **sechs Mann h~** six of us/them. **H~** *nt* -s,-s cheer; (*Meteorol*) high

Hoch|achtung *f* high esteem. **H~achtungsvoll** *adv* Yours faithfully. **H~amt** *nt* High Mass. **h~arbeiten (sich)** *vr sep*

work one's way up. **h~begabt** *attrib a* (NEW)**h~ begabt**, *s.* **hoch**. **H~betrieb** *m* great activity; **in den Geschäften herrscht H~betrieb** the shops are terribly busy. **H~burg** *f* (*fig*) stronghold. **H~deutsch** *nt* High German. **H~druck** *m* high pressure. **H~ebene** *f* plateau. **h~fahren†** *vi sep* (*sein*) go up; (*auffahren*) start up; (*aufbrausen*) flare up. **h~fliegend** *a* (*fig*) ambitious. **h~gehen†** *vi sep* (*sein*) go up; (*explodieren*) blow up; (*aufbrausen*) flare up. **h~gestellt** *attrib a* ⟨*Zahl*⟩ superior; (*fig*) (NEW)**h~ gestellt**, *s.* **hoch**. **h~gewachsen** *a* (NEW)**h~ gewachsen**, *s.* **hoch**. **H~glanz** *m* high gloss. **h~gradig** *a* extreme, *adv* -ly. **h~hackig** *a* high-heeled. **h~halten†** *vt sep* hold up; (*fig*) uphold. **H~haus** *nt* high-rise building. **h~heben†** *vt sep* lift up; raise ⟨*Kopf, Hand*⟩. **h~herzig** *a* magnanimous, *adv* -ly. **h~kant** *adv* on end. **h~kommen†** *vi sep* (*sein*) come up; (*aufstehen*) get up; (*fig*) get on [in the world]. **H~konjunktur** *f* boom. **h~krempeln** *vt sep* roll up. **h~leben** *vi sep* (*haben*) **h~leben lassen** give three cheers for; **... lebe hoch!** three cheers for ...! **H~mut** *m* pride, arrogance. **h~mütig** *a* arrogant, *adv* -ly. **h~näsig** *a* (*fam*) snooty. **h~nehmen†** *vt sep* pick up; (*fam*) tease. **H~ofen** *m* blast-furnace. **h~ragen** *vi sep* rise [up]; ⟨*Turm:*⟩ soar. **H~ruf** *m* cheer. **H~saison** *f* high season. **H~schätzung** *f* high esteem. **h~schlagen†** *vt sep* turn up ⟨*Kragen*⟩. **h~schrecken†** *vi sep* (*sein*) start up. **H~schule** *f* university; (*Musik-, Kunst-*) academy. **h~sehen†** *vi sep* (*haben*) look up. **H~sommer** *m* midsummer. **H~spannung** *f* high/(*fig*) great tension. **h~spielen** *vt sep* (*fig*) magnify. **H~sprache** *f* standard language. **H~sprung** *m* high jump

höchst *adv* extremely, most

Hochstapler *m* -s,- confidence trickster

höchst|e(r,s) *a* highest; ⟨*Baum, Turm*⟩ tallest; (*oberste, größte*) top; **es ist h~e Zeit** it is high time. **h~ens** *adv* at most; (*es sei denn*) except perhaps. **H~fall** *m* **im H~fall** at most. **H~geschwindigkeit** *f* top *or* maximum speed. **H~maß** *nt* maximum. **h~persönlich** *adv* in person. **H~preis** *m* top price. **H~temperatur** *f* maximum temperature. **h~wahrscheinlich** *adv* most probably

hoch|trabend *a* pompous, *adv* -ly. **h~treiben†** *vt sep* push up ⟨*Preis*⟩. **H~verrat** *m* high treason. **H~wasser** *nt* high tide; (*Überschwemmung*) floods *pl.* **H~würden** *m* -s Reverend; (*Anrede*) Father

Hochzeit *f* -,-en wedding; **H~ feiern** get married. **H~skleid** *nt* wedding dress.

H~sreise *f* honeymoon [trip]. **H~stag** *m* wedding day/(*Jahrestag*) anniversary

hochziehen† *vt sep* pull up; (*hissen*) hoist; raise ⟨*Augenbrauen*⟩

Hocke *f* - **in der H~ sitzen** squat; **in die H~ gehen** squat down. **h~n** *vi* (*haben*) squat ▫ *vr* **sich h~n** squat down

Hocker *m* -s,- stool

Höcker *m* -s,- bump; (*Kamel-*) hump

Hockey /hɔki/ *nt* -s hockey

Hode *f* -,-n, **Hoden** *m* -s,- testicle

Hof *m* -[e]s,ᵉe [court]yard; (*Bauern-*) farm; (*Königs-*) court; (*Schul-*) playground; (*Astr*) halo; **Hof halten** hold court

hoffen *vt/i* (*haben*) hope (**auf** + *acc* for). **h~tlich** *adv* I hope, let us hope; (*als Antwort*) **h~tlich/h~tlich nicht** let's hope so/not

Hoffnung *f* -,-en hope. **h~slos** *a* hopeless, *adv* -ly. **h~svoll** *a* hopeful, *adv* -ly

höflich *a* polite, *adv* -ly, courteous, *adv* -ly. **H~keit** *f* -,-en politeness, courtesy; (*Äußerung*) civility

hohe(r,s) *a s.* **hoch**

Höhe *f* -,-n height; (*Aviat, Geog*) altitude; (*Niveau*) level; (*einer Summe*) size; (*An-*) hill; **in die H~ gehen** rise, go up; **nicht auf der H~** (*fam*) under the weather; **das ist die H~!** (*fam*) that's the limit!

Hoheit *f* -,-en (*Staats-*) sovereignty; (*Titel*) Highness. **H~sgebiet** *nt* [sovereign] territory. **H~szeichen** *nt* national emblem

Höhe|nlinie *f* contour line. **H~nsonne** *f* sun-lamp. **H~nzug** *m* mountain range. **H~punkt** *m* (*fig*) climax, peak; (*einer Vorstellung*) highlight. **h~r** *a & adv* higher; **h~re Schule** secondary school

hohl *a* hollow; (*leer*) empty

Höhle *f* -,-n cave; (*Tier-*) den; (*Hohlraum*) cavity; (*Augen-*) socket

Hohl|maß *nt* measure of capacity. **H~raum** *m* cavity

Hohn *m* -s scorn, derision

höhn|en *vt* deride ▫ *vi* (*haben*) jeer. **h~isch** *a* scornful, *adv* -ly

holen *vt* fetch, get; (*kaufen*) buy; (*nehmen*) take (**aus** from); **h~ lassen** send for; **[tief] Atem** *od* **Luft h~** take a [deep] breath; **sich** (*dat*) **etw h~** get sth; catch (*Erkältung*)

Holland *nt* -s Holland

Holländ|er *m* -s,- Dutchman; **die H~er** the Dutch *pl.* **H~erin** *f* -,-nen Dutchwoman. **h~isch** *a* Dutch

Höll|e *f* - hell. **h~isch** *a* infernal; (*schrecklich*) terrible, *adv* -bly

holpern *vi* (*sein*) jolt *or* bump along ▫ *vi* (*haben*) be bumpy

holp[e]rig *a* bumpy

Holunder *m* -s (*Bot*) elder

Holz *nt* -es,-̈er wood; (*Nutz-*) timber. **H~blasinstrument** *nt* woodwind instrument

hölzern *a* wooden

Holz|hammer *m* mallet. **h~ig** *a* woody. **H~kohle** *f* charcoal. **H~schnitt** *m* woodcut. **H~schuh** *m* [wooden] clog. **H~wolle** *f* wood shavings *pl*. **H~wurm** *m* woodworm

homogen *a* homogeneous

Homöopathie *f* - homoeopathy

homosexuell *a* homosexual. **H~e(r)** *m/f* homosexual

Honig *m* -s honey. **H~wabe** *f* honeycomb

Hono|rar *nt* -s,-e fee. **h~rieren** *vt* remunerate; (*fig*) reward

Hopfen *m* -s hops *pl*; (*Bot*) hop

hopsen *vi* (*sein*) jump

Hör|apparat *m* hearing-aid. **h~bar** *a* audible, *adv* -bly

horchen *vi* (*haben*) listen (**auf** + *acc* to); (*heimlich*) eavesdrop

Horde *f* -,-n horde; (*Gestell*) rack

hören *vt* hear; (*an-*) listen to □ *vi* (*haben*) hear; (*horchen*) listen; (*gehorchen*) obey; **h~auf**(+ *acc*) listen to. **H~sagen** *nt* **vom H~sagen** from hearsay

Hör|er *m* -s,- listener; (*Teleph*) receiver. **H~funk** *m* radio. **H~gerät** *nt* hearing-aid

Horizon|t *m* -[e]s horizon. **h~tal** *a* horizontal, *adv* -ly

Hormon *nt* -s,-e hormone

Horn *nt* -s,-̈er horn. **H~haut** *f* hard skin; (*Augen-*) cornea

Hornisse *f* -,-n hornet

Horoskop *nt* -[e]s,-e horoscope

Hörrohr *nt* stethoscope

Horrorfilm *m* horror film

Hör|saal *m* (*Univ*) lecture hall. **H~spiel** *nt* radio play

Hort *m* -[e]s,-e (*Schatz*) hoard; (*fig*) refuge. **h~en** *vt* hoard

Hortensie /-ɪə/ *f* -,-n hydrangea

Hörweite *f* **in/außer H~** within/out of earshot

Hose *f* -,-n, **Hosen** *pl* trousers *pl*. **H~nrock** *m* culottes *pl*. **H~nschlitz** *m* fly, flies *pl*. **H~nträger** *mpl* braces, (*Amer*) suspenders

Hostess (**Hosteß**) *f* -,-tessen hostess; (*Aviat*) air hostess

Hostie /ˈhɔstjə/ *f* -,-n (*Relig*) host

Hotel *nt* -s,-s hotel; **H~ garni** /~ garˈniː/ bed-and-breakfast hotel. **H~ier** /-ˈljeː/ *m* -s,-s hotelier

hübsch *a* pretty, *adv* -ily; (*nett*) nice, *adv* -ly; (*Summe*) tidy

Hubschrauber *m* -s,- helicopter

huckepack *adv* **jdn h~ tragen** give s.o. a piggyback

Huf *m* -[e]s,-e hoof. **H~eisen** *nt* horseshoe

Hüft|e *f* -,-n hip. **H~gürtel**, **H~halter** *m* -s,- girdle

Hügel *m* -s,- hill. **h~ig** *a* hilly

Huhn *nt* -s,-̈er chicken; (*Henne*) hen

Hühn|chen *nt* -s,- chicken. **H~erauge** *nt* corn. **H~erbrühe** *f* chicken broth. **H~erstall** *m* henhouse, chicken-coop

huldig|en *vi* (*haben*) pay homage (*dat* to). **H~ung** *f* - homage

Hülle *f* -,-n cover; (*Verpackung*) wrapping; (*Platten-*) sleeve; **in H~ und Fülle** in abundance. **h~n** *vt* wrap

Hülse *f* -,-n (*Bot*) pod; (*Etui*) case. **H~nfrüchte** *fpl* pulses

human *a* humane, *adv* -ly. **h~itär** *a* humanitarian. **H~ität** *f* - humanity

Hummel *f* -,-n bumble-bee

Hummer *m* -s,- lobster

Hum|or *m* -s humour; **H~or haben** have a sense of humour. **h~oristisch** *a* humorous. **h~orvoll** *a* humorous, *adv* -ly

humpeln *vi* (*sein/haben*) hobble

Humpen *m* -s,- tankard

Hund *m* -[e]s,-e dog; (*Jagd-*) hound. **H~ehalsband** *nt* dog-collar. **H~ehütte** *f* kennel. **H~eleine** *f* dog lead

hundert *inv a* one/a hundred. **H~** *nt* -s,-e hundred; **H~e od h~e von** hundreds of. **H~jahrfeier** *f* centenary, (*Amer*) centennial. **h~prozentig** *a* & *adv* one hundred per cent. **h~ste(r,s)** *a* hundredth. **H~stel** *nt* -s,- hundredth

Hündin *f* -,-nen bitch

Hüne *m* -n,-n giant

Hunger *m* -s hunger; **H~ haben** be hungry. **h~n** *vi* (*haben*) starve; **h~n nach** (*fig*) hunger for. **H~snot** *f* famine

hungrig *a* hungry, *adv* -ily

Hupe *f* -,-n (*Auto*) horn. **h~n** *vi* (*haben*) sound one's horn

hüpf|en *vi* (*sein*) skip; (*Vogel, Frosch:*) hop; (*Grashüpfer:*) jump. **H~er** *m* -s,- skip, hop

Hürde *f* -,-n (*Sport & fig*) hurdle; (*Schaf-*) pen, fold

Hure *f* -,-n whore

hurra *int* hurray. **H~** *nt* -s,-s hurray; (*Beifallsruf*) cheer

Husche *f* -,-n [short] shower. **h~n** *vi* (*sein*) slip; (*Eidechse:*) dart; (*Maus:*) scurry; (*Lächeln:*) flit

hüsteln *vi* (*haben*) give a slight cough

husten *vi* (*haben*) cough. **H∼** *m* -s cough. **H∼saft** *m* cough mixture

Hut¹ *m* -[e]s,-̈e hat; (*Pilz-*) cap

Hut² *f* - **auf der H∼ sein** be on one's guard (**vor** + *dat* against)

hüten *vt* watch over; tend (*Tiere*); (*aufpassen*) look after; **das Bett h∼ müssen** be confined to bed; **sich h∼** be on one's guard (**vor** + *dat* against); **sich h∼, etw zu tun** take care not to do sth

Hütte *f* -,-n hut; (*Hunde-*) kennel; (*Techn*) iron and steel works. **H∼nkäse** *m* cottage cheese. **H∼nkunde** *f* metallurgy

Hyäne *f* -,-n hyena

Hybride *f* -,-n hybrid

Hydrant *m* -en,-en hydrant

hydraulisch *a* hydraulic, *adv* -ally

hydroelektrisch /hydro-e'lɛktrɪʃ/ *a* hydroelectric

Hygien|e /hy'gie:nə/ *f* - hygiene. **h∼isch** *a* hygienic, *adv* -ally

hypermodern *a* ultra-modern

Hypno|se *f* - hypnosis. **h∼tisch** *a* hypnotic. **H∼tiseur** /-'zø:ɐ̯/ *m* -s,-e hypnotist. **h∼tisieren** *vt* hypnotize

Hypochonder /hypo'xɔndɐ/ *m* -s,- hypochondriac

Hypothek *f* -,-en mortgage

Hypothe|se *f* -,-n hypothesis. **h∼tisch** *a* hypothetical, *adv* -ly

Hys|terie *f* - hysteria. **h∼terisch** *a* hysterical, *adv* -ly

I

ich *pron* I; **ich bin's** it's me. **Ich** *nt* -[s],-[s] self; (*Psych*) ego

IC-Zug /i'tse:-/ *m* inter-city train

ideal *a* ideal. **I∼** *nt* -s,-e ideal. **i∼isieren** *vt* idealize. **I∼ismus** *m* - idealism. **I∼ist(in)** *m* -en, -en (*f* -,-nen) idealist. **i∼istisch** *a* idealistic

Idee *f* -,-n idea; **fixe I∼** obsession; **eine I∼** (*fam: wenig*) a tiny bit

identifizieren *vt* identify

identi|sch *a* identical. **I∼tät** *f* -,-en identity

Ideo|logie *f* -,-n ideology. **i∼logisch** *a* ideological

idiomatisch *a* idiomatic

Idiot *m* -en,-en idiot. **i∼isch** *a* idiotic, *adv* -ally

Idol *nt* -s,-e idol

idyllisch /i'dʏlɪʃ/ *a* idyllic

Igel *m* -s,- hedgehog

ignorieren *vt* ignore

ihm *pron* (*dat of* **er, es**) [to] him; (*Ding, Tier*) [to] it; **Freunde von ihm** friends of his

ihn *pron* (*acc of* **er**) him; (*Ding, Tier*) it. **i∼en** *pron* (*dat of* **sie** *pl*) [to] them; **Freunde von i∼en** friends of theirs. **I∼en** *pron* (*dat of* **Sie**) [to] you; **Freunde von I∼en** friends of yours

ihr *pron* (*2nd pers pl*) you □ (*dat of* **sie** *sg*) [to] her; (*Ding, Tier*) [to] it; **Freunde von ihr** friends of hers □ *poss pron* her; (*Ding, Tier*) its; (*pl*) their. **Ihr** *poss pron* your. **i∼e(r,s)** *poss pron* hers; (*pl*) theirs. **I∼e(r,s)** *poss pron* yours. **I∼erseits** *adv* for her/(*pl*) their part. **I∼erseits** *adv* on your part. **i∼etwegen** *adv* for her/(*Ding, Tier*) its/(*pl*) their sake; (*wegen*) because of her/it/them, on her/its/their account. **I∼etwegen** *adv* for your sake; (*wegen*) because of you, on your account. **i∼etwillen** *adv* **um i∼etwillen** for her/(*Ding, Tier*) its/(*pl*) their sake. **I∼etwillen** *adv* **um I∼etwillen** for your sake. **i∼ige** *poss pron* **der/die/das i∼ige** hers; (*pl*) theirs. **I∼ige** *poss pron* **der/die/das I∼ige** yours. **i∼s** *poss pron* hers; (*pl*) theirs. **I∼s** *poss pron* yours

Ikone *f* -,-n icon

illegal *a* illegal, *adv* -ly

Illus|ion *f* -,-en illusion; **sich** (*dat*) **I∼ionen machen** delude oneself. **i∼orisch** *a* illusory

Illustr|ation /-'tsi̯o:n/ *f* -,-en illustration. **i∼ieren** *vt* illustrate. **I∼ierte** *f* -n,-[n] [illustrated] magazine

Iltis *m* -ses,-se polecat

im *prep* = **in dem; im Mai** in May; **im Kino** at the cinema

Image /'ɪmɪdʒ/ *nt* -[s],-s /-ɪs/ [public] image

Imbiss (**Imbiß**) *m* snack. **I∼halle, I∼stube** *f* snack-bar

Imit|ation /-'tsi̯o:n/ *f* -,-en imitation. **i∼ieren** *vt* imitate

Imker *m* -s,- bee-keeper

Immatrikul|ation /-'tsi̯o:n/ *f* - (*Univ*) enrolment. **i∼ieren** *vt* (*Univ*) enrol; **sich i∼ieren** enrol

immer *adv* always; **für i∼** for ever; (*endgültig*) for good; **i∼ noch** still; **i∼ mehr/weniger/wieder** more and more/less and less/again and again; **wer/was [auch] i∼** whoever/whatever. **i∼fort** *adv* = **i∼zu. i∼grün** *a* evergreen. **i∼hin** *adv* (*wenigstens*) at least; (*trotzdem*) all the same; (*schließlich*) after all. **i∼zu** *adv* all the time

Immobilien /-jən/ *pl* real estate *sg*. **I~händler**, **I~makler** *m* estate agent, (*Amer*) realtor

immun *a* immune (**gegen** to). **i~isieren** *vt* immunize. **I~ität** *f* - immunity

Imperativ *m* -s,-e imperative

Imperfekt *nt* -s,-e imperfect

Imperialismus *m* - imperialism

impf|en *vt* vaccinate, inoculate. **I~stoff** *m* vaccine. **I~ung** *f* -,-en vaccination, inoculation

Implantat *nt* -[e]s,-e implant

imponieren *vi* (*haben*) impress (**jdm** s.o.)

Impor|t *m* -[e]s,-e import. **I~teur** /-'tø:ɐ̯/ *m* -s,-e importer. **i~tieren** *vt* import

imposant *a* imposing

impoten|t *a* (*Med*) impotent. **I~z** *f* - (*Med*) impotence

imprägnieren *vt* waterproof

Impressionismus *m* - impressionism

improvisieren *vt/i* (*haben*) improvise

Impuls *m* -es,-e impulse. **i~iv** *a* impulsive, *adv* -ly

imstande *pred a* able (**zu** to); capable (**etw zu tun** of doing sth)

in *prep* (+ *dat*) in; (+ *acc*) into, in; (*bei Bus, Zug*) on; **in der Schule/Oper** at school/the opera; **in die Schule** to school □ *a* **in sein** be in

Inbegriff *m* embodiment. **i~en** *pred a* included

Inbrunst *f* - fervour

inbrünstig *a* fervent, *adv* -ly

indem *conj* (*während*) while; (*dadurch*) by (+ -ing)

Inder(in) *m* -s,- (*f* -,-nen) Indian

indessen *conj* while □ *adv* (*unterdessen*) meanwhile; (*jedoch*) however

Indian *m* -s,-e (*Aust*) turkey

Indian|er(in) *m* -s,- (*f* -,-nen) (American) Indian. **i~isch** *a* Indian

Indien /'ɪndjən/ *nt* -s India

indigniert *a* indignant, *adv* -ly

Indikativ *m* -s,-e indicative

indirekt *a* indirect, *adv* -ly

indisch *a* Indian

indiskre|t *a* indiscreet. **I~tion** /-'tsjo:n/ *f* -,-en indiscretion

indiskutabel *a* out of the question

indisponiert *a* indisposed

Individu|alist *m* -en,-en individualist. **I~alität** *f* - individuality. **i~ell** *a* individual, *adv* -ly. **I~um** /-'vi:duʊm/ *nt* -s,-duen individual

Indizienbeweis /ɪn'di:tsjən-/ *m* circumstantial evidence

indoktrinieren *vt* indoctrinate

industr|ialisiert *a* industrialized. **I~ie** *f* -,-n industry. **i~iell** *a* industrial. **I~ielle(r)** *m* industrialist

ineinander *adv* in/into one another

Infanterie *f* - infantry

Infektion /-'tsjo:n/ *f* -,-en infection. **I~skrankheit** *f* infectious disease

Infinitiv *m* -s,-e infinitive

infizieren *vt* infect; **sich i~** become/⟨*Person:*⟩ be infected

Inflation /-'tsjo:n/ *f* - inflation. **i~är** *a* inflationary

infolge *prep* (+ *gen*) as a result of. **i~dessen** *adv* consequently

Inform|atik *f* - information science. **I~ation** /-'tsjo:n/ *f* -,-en information; **I~ationen** information *sg*. **i~ieren** *vt* inform; **sich i~ieren** find out (**über** + *acc* about)

infrage *adv* **etw i~ stellen** question sth; (*ungewiss machen*) make sth doubtful; **nicht i~ kommen** be out of the question

infrarot *a* infra-red

Ingenieur /ɪnʒe'njø:ɐ̯/ *m* -s,-e engineer

Ingwer *m* -s ginger

Inhaber(in) *m* -s,- (*f* -,-nen) holder; (*Besitzer*) proprietor; (*Scheck-*) bearer

inhaftieren *vt* take into custody

inhalieren *vt/i* (*haben*) inhale

Inhalt *m* -[e]s,-e contents *pl*; (*Bedeutung, Gehalt*) content; (*Geschichte*) story. **I~sangabe** *f* summary. **I~sverzeichnis** *nt* list/(*in Buch*) table of contents

Initiale /-'tsja:lə/ *f* -,-n initial

Initiative /ɪnitsja'ti:və/ *f* -,-n initiative

Injektion /-'tsjo:n/ *f* -,-en injection.

injizieren *vt* inject

inklusive *prep* (+ *gen*) including □ *adv* inclusive

inkognito *adv* incognito

inkonsequen|t *a* inconsistent, *adv* -ly. **I~z** *f* -,-en inconsistency

inkorrekt *a* incorrect, *adv* -ly

Inkubationszeit /-'tsjo:ns-/ *f* (*Med*) incubation period

Inland *nt* -[e]s home country; (*Binnenland*) interior. **I~sgespräch** *nt* inland call

inmitten *prep* (+ *gen*) in the middle of; (*unter*) amongst □ *adv* **i~ von** amongst, amidst

inne|haben† *vt sep* hold, have. **i~halten†** *vi sep* (*haben*) pause

innen *adv* inside; **nach i~** inwards. **I~architekt(in)** *m(f)* interior designer. **I~minister** *m* Minister of the Interior; (*in UK*) Home Secretary. **I~politik** *f* domestic policy. **I~stadt** *f* town centre

inner|e(r,s) *a* inner; (*Med, Pol*) internal. **I~e(s)** *nt* interior; (*Mitte*) centre; (*fig: Seele*) inner being. **I~eien** *fpl* (*Culin*) offal *sg.* **i~halb** *prep* (+ *gen*) inside; (*zeitlich & fig*) within; (*während*) during □ *adv* **i~halb von** within. **i~lich** *a* internal; (*seelisch*) inner; (*besinnlich*) introspective □ *adv* internally; (*im Inneren*) inwardly. **i~ste(r,s)** innermost; **im I~sten** (*fig*) deep down

innig *a* sincere, *adv* -ly; (*tief*) deep, *adv* -ly; (*eng*) intimate, *adv* -ly

Innung *f* -,-en guild

inoffiziell *a* unofficial, *adv* -ly

ins *prep* = **in das**; **ins Kino/Büro** to the cinema/office

Insasse *m* -n,-n inmate; (*im Auto*) occupant; (*Passagier*) passenger

insbesondere *adv* especially

Inschrift *f* inscription

Insekt *nt* -[e]s,-en insect. **I~envertilgungsmittel** *nt* insecticide

Insel *f* -,-n island

Inser|at *nt* -[e]s,-e [newspaper] advertisement. **I~ent** *m* -en,-en advertiser. **i~ieren** *vt/i* (*haben*) advertise

insge|heim *adv* secretly. **i~samt** *adv* [all] in all

Insignien /-jən/ *pl* insignia

insofern, **insoweit** *adv* /-'zo:-/ in this respect; **i~ als** in as much as □ *conj* /-zo-'fɛrn, -'vait/ **i~ als** in so far as

Insp|ektion /ɪnspɛk'tsjo:n/ *f* -,-en inspection. **I~ektor** *m* -en,-en /-'to:rən/ inspector

Inspir|ation /ɪnspira'tsjo:n/ *f* -,-en inspiration. **i~ieren** *vt* inspire

inspizieren /-sp-/ *vt* inspect

Install|ateur /ɪnstala'tø:ɐ/ *m* -s,-e fitter; (*Klempner*) plumber. **i~ieren** *vt* install

instand *adv* **i~ halten** maintain; (*pflegen*) look after; **i~ setzen** restore; (*reparieren*) repair. **I~haltung** *f* - maintenance, upkeep

instängig *a* urgent, *adv* -ly

Instandsetzung *f* - repair

Instant- /'ɪnstənt-/ *pref* instant

Instanz /-st-/ *f* -,-en authority

Instinkt /-st-/ *m* -[e]s,-e instinct. **i~iv** *a* instinctive, *adv* -ly

Institu|t /-st-/ *nt* -[e]s,-e institute. **I~tion** /-'tsjo:n/ *f* -,-en institution

Instrument /-st-/ *nt* -[e]s,-e instrument. **I~almusik** *f* instrumental music

Insulin *nt* -s insulin

inszenier|en *vt* (*Theat*) produce. **I~ung** *f* -,-en production

Integr|ation /-'tsjo:n/ *f* - integration. **i~ieren** *vt* integrate; **sich i~ieren** integrate. **I~ität** *f* - integrity

Intellekt *m* -[e]s intellect. **i~uell** *a* intellectual

intelligen|t *a* intelligent, *adv* -ly. **I~z** *f* - intelligence; (*Leute*) intelligentsia

Intendant *m* -en,-en director

Intens|ität *f* - intensity. **i~iv** *a* intensive, *adv* -ly. **i~ivieren** *vt* intensify. **I~ivstation** *f* intensive-care unit

inter|essant *a* interesting. **I~esse** *nt* -s,-n interest. **I~esse haben** be interested (**an** + *dat* in). **I~essengruppe** *f* pressure group. **I~essent** *m* -en,-en interested party; (*Käufer*) prospective buyer. **i~essieren** *vt* interest; **sich i~essieren** be interested (**für** in)

intern *a* (*fig*) internal, *adv* -ly

Inter|nat *nt* -[e]s,-e boarding school. **i~national** *a* international, *adv* -ly. **i~nieren** *vt* intern. **I~nierung** *f* - internment. **I~nist** *m* -en,-en specialist in internal diseases. **I~pretation** /-'tsjo:n/ *f* -,-en interpretation. **i~pretieren** *vt* interpret. **I~punktion** /-'tsjo:n/ *f* - punctuation. **I~rogativpronomen** *nt* interrogative pronoun. **I~vall** *nt* -s,-e interval. **I~vention** /-'tsjo:n/ *f* -,-en intervention

Interview /'ɪntɐvju:/ *nt* -s,-s interview. **i~en** /-'vju:ən/ *vt* interview

intim *a* intimate, *adv* -ly. **I~ität** *f* -,-en intimacy

intoleran|t *a* intolerant. **I~z** *f* - intolerance

intransitiv *a* intransitive, *adv* -ly

intravenös *a* intravenous, *adv* -ly

Intrig|e *f* -,-n intrigue. **i~ieren** *vi* (*haben*) plot

introvertiert *a* introverted

Intui|tion /-'tsjo:n/ *f* -,-en intuition. **i~tiv** *a* intuitive, *adv* -ly

Invalidenrente *f* disability pension

Invasion *f* -,-en invasion

Inven|tar *nt* -s,-e furnishings and fittings *pl*; (*Techn*) equipment; (*Bestand*) stock; (*Liste*) inventory. **I~tur** *f* -,-en stock-taking

investieren *vt* invest

inwendig *a & adv* inside

inwie|fern *adv* in what way. **i~weit** *adv* how far, to what extent

Inzest *m* -[e]s incest

inzwischen *adv* in the meantime

Irak (der) -[s] Iraq. **i~isch** *a* Iraqi

Iran (der) -[s] Iran. **i~isch** *a* Iranian

irdisch *a* earthly

Ire *m* -n,-n Irishman; **die I~n** the Irish *pl*

irgend adv wer/was/wann i∼ whoever/whatever/whenever; wenn i∼ möglich if at all possible; i∼ etwas (NEW) i∼etwas; i∼ jemand (NEW) i∼jemand. i∼ein indef art some/any; i∼ein anderer someone/anyone else. i∼eine(r,s) pron any one; (jemand) someone/anyone. i∼etwas pron something; (fragend, verneint) anything. i∼jemand pron someone; (fragend, verneint) anyone. i∼wann pron at some time [or other]/at any time. i∼was pron (fam) something [or other]/anything. i∼welche(r,s) pron any. i∼wer pron someone/anyone. i∼wie adv somehow [or other]. i∼wo adv somewhere/anywhere; i∼wo anders somewhere else

Irin f -,-nen Irishwoman

Iris f -,- (Anat, Bot) iris

irisch a Irish

Irland nt -s Ireland

Ironie f - irony

ironisch a ironic, adv -ally

irr a = irre

irrational a irrational

irre a mad, crazy; (fam: gewaltig) incredible, adv -bly; i∼ werden (NEW) i∼werden. I∼(r) m/f lunatic. i∼führen vt sep (fig) mislead. i∼gehen† vi sep (sein) lose one's way; (sich täuschen) be wrong

irrelevant a irrelevant

irre|machen vt sep confuse. i∼n vi/r (haben) [sich] i∼n be mistaken; wenn ich mich nicht i∼ if I am not mistaken □ vi (sein) wander. I∼nanstalt f, I∼nhaus nt lunatic asylum. i∼reden vi sep (haben) ramble. i∼werden† vi sep (sein) get confused

Irr|garten m maze. i∼ig a erroneous

irritieren vt irritate

Irr|sinn m madness, lunacy. i∼sinnig a mad; (fam: gewaltig) incredible, adv -bly. I∼tum m -s,-̈er mistake. i∼tümlich a mistaken, adv -ly

Ischias m & nt - sciatica

Islam (der) -[s] Islam. islamisch a Islamic

Island nt -s Iceland

Isolier|band nt insulating tape. i∼en vt isolate; (Phys, Electr) insulate; (gegen Schall) soundproof. I∼ung f - isolation; insulation; soundproofing

Israel nt /'ɪsraːl/ nt -s Israel. I∼eli m -[s], -s & f -,-[s] Israeli. i∼elisch a Israeli

ist s. sein; er ist he is

Ital|ien /-jən/ nt -s Italy. I∼iener(in) m -s,- (f -,-nen) Italian. i∼ienisch a Italian. I∼ienisch nt -[s] (Lang) Italian

J

ja adv, Ja nt -[s] yes; ich glaube ja I think so; ja nicht! not on any account! seid ja vorsichtig! whatever you do, be careful! da seid ihr ja! there you are! das ist es ja that's just it; das mag ja wahr sein that may well be true

Jacht f -,-en yacht

Jacke f -,-n jacket; (Strick-) cardigan

Jackett /ʒa'kɛt/ nt -s,-s jacket

Jade m -[s] & f - jade

Jagd f -,-en hunt; (Schießen) shoot; (Jagen) hunting; shooting; (fig) pursuit (nach of); auf die J∼ gehen go hunting/shooting. J∼flugzeug nt fighter aircraft. J∼gewehr nt sporting gun. J∼hund m gun-dog; (Hetzhund) hound

jagen vt hunt; (schießen) shoot; (verfolgen, wegjagen) chase; (treiben) drive; sich j∼ chase each other; in die Luft j∼ blow up □ vi (haben) hunt, go hunting/shooting; (fig) chase (nach after) □ vi (sein) race, dash

Jäger m -s,- hunter

jäh a sudden, adv -ly; (steil) steep, adv -ly

Jahr nt -[e]s,-e year. J∼buch nt year-book. j∼elang adv for years. J∼estag m anniversary. J∼eszahl f year. J∼eszeit f season. J∼gang m year; (Wein) vintage. J∼hundert nt century. J∼hundertfeier f centenary, (Amer) centennial

jährlich a annual, yearly □ adv annually, yearly

Jahr|markt m fair. J∼tausend nt millenium. J∼zehnt nt -[e]s,-e decade

Jähzorn m violent temper. j∼ig a hot-tempered

Jalousie /ʒalu'zi:/ f -,-n venetian blind

Jammer m -s misery; (Klagen) lamenting; es ist ein J∼ it is a shame

jämmerlich a miserable, adv -bly; (Mitleid erregend) pitiful, adv -ly

jammer|n vi (haben) lament □ vt jdn j∼n arouse s.o.'s pity. j∼schade a j∼schade sein (fam) be a terrible shame

Jänner m -s,- (Aust) January

Januar m -s,-e January

Jap|an nt -s Japan. J∼aner(in) m -s,- (f -,-nen) Japanese. j∼anisch a Japanese. J∼anisch nt -[s] (Lang) Japanese

Jargon /ʒar'gõ:/ m -s jargon

jäten vt/i (haben) weed

jauchzen vi (haben) (liter) exult

jaulen vi (haben) yelp

Jause f -,-n (Aust) snack

jawohl *adv* yes

Jawort *nt* **jdm sein J~ geben** accept s.o.'s proposal [of marriage]

Jazz /jatș, dȝɛs/ *m* - jazz

je *adv* (*jemals*) ever; (*jeweils*) each; (*pro*) per; **je nach** according to; **seit eh und je** always; **besser denn je** better than ever □ *conj* **je mehr, desto** *od* **umso besser** the more the better □ *prep* (+ *acc*) per

Jeans /dȝiːns/ *pl* jeans

jed|e(r,s) *pron* every; (*j~er Einzelne*) each; (*j~er Beliebige*) any; (*substantivisch*) everyone; each one; anyone; **ohne j~en Grund** without any reason. **j~enfalls** *adv* in any case; (*wenigstens*) at least. **j~ermann** *pron* everyone. **j~erzeit** *adv* at any time. **j~esmal** *adv* (NEW) **jedes Mal**, s. **Mal¹**

jedoch *adv & conj* however

jeher *adv* **von** *od* **seit j~** always

jemals *adv* ever

jemand *pron* someone, somebody; (*fragend, verneint*) anyone, anybody

jen|e(r,s) *pron* that; (*pl*) those; (*substantivisch*) that one; (*pl*) those. **j~seits** *prep* (+ *gen*) [on] the other side of

jetzig *a* present; (*Preis*) current

jetzt *adv* now. **J~zeit** *f* present

jeweil|ig *a* respective. **j~s** *adv* at a time

jiddisch *a*, **J~** *nt* -[s] Yiddish

Job /dȝɔp/ *m* -s,-s job. **j~ben** *vi* (*haben*) (*fam*) work

Joch *nt* -[e]s,-e yoke

Jockei, Jockey /'dȝɔki/ *m* -s,-s jockey

Jod *nt* -[e]s iodine

jodeln *vi* (*haben*) yodel

Joga *m & nt* -[s] yoga

jogg|en /'dȝɔgən/ *vi* (*haben/sein*) jog. **J~ing** *nt* -[s] jogging

Joghurt, Jogurt *m & nt* -[s] yoghurt

Johannisbeere *f* redcurrant; **schwarze J~** blackcurrant

johlen *vi* (*haben*) yell; (*empört*) jeer

Joker *m* -s,- (*Karte*) joker

Jolle *f* -,-n dinghy

Jongl|eur /ȝõˈgløːɐ̯/ *m* -s,-e juggler. **j~ieren** *vi* (*haben*) juggle

Joppe *f* -,-n [thick] jacket

Jordanien /-jən/ *nt* -s Jordan

Journalis|mus /ȝʊrnaˈlɪsmʊs/ *m* - journalism. **J~t(in)** *m* -en,-en (*f* -,-nen) journalist

Jubel *m* -s rejoicing, jubilation. **j~n** *vi* (*haben*) rejoice

Jubil|ar(in) *m* -s,-e (*f* -,-nen) person celebrating an anniversary. **J~äum** *nt* -s,-äen jubilee; (*Jahrestag*) anniversary

juck|en *vi* (*haben*) itch; **sich j~en** scratch; **es j~t mich** I have an itch; (*fam: möchte*) I'm itching (**zu** to). **J~reiz** *m* itch[ing]

Jude *m* -n,-n Jew. **J~ntum** *nt* -s Judaism; (*Juden*) Jewry

Jüd|in *f* -,-nen Jewess. **j~isch** *a* Jewish

Judo *nt* -[s] judo

Jugend *f* - youth; (*junge Leute*) young people *pl*. **J~herberge** *f* youth hostel. **J~klub** *m* youth club. **J~kriminalität** *f* juvenile delinquency. **j~lich** *a* youthful. **J~liche(r)** *m/f* young man/woman; (*Admin*) juvenile; **J~liche** *pl* young people. **J~stil** *m* art nouveau. **J~zeit** *f* youth

Jugoslaw|ien /-jən/ *nt* -s Yugoslavia. **j~isch** *a* Yugoslav

Juli *m* -[s],-s July

jung *a* (jünger, jüngst) young; (*Wein*) new □ *pron* **J~ und Alt** (j~ und alt) young and old. **J~e** *m* -n,-n boy. **J~e(s)** *nt* young animal/bird; (*Katzen-*) kitten; (*Bären-, Löwen-*) cub; (*Hunde-, Seehund-*) pup; **die J~en** the young *pl*. **j~enhaft** *a* boyish

Jünger *m* -s,- disciple

Jungfer *f* -,-n **alte J~** old maid. **J~nfahrt** *f* maiden voyage

Jung|frau *f* virgin; (*Astr*) Virgo. **j~fräulich** *a* virginal. **J~geselle** *m* bachelor

Jüngling *m* -s,-e youth

jüngst|e(r,s) *a* youngest; (*neueste*) latest; **in j~er Zeit** recently

Juni *m* -[s],-s June

Junior *m* -s,-en /-ˈoːrən/ junior

Jura *pl* law *sg*

Jurist|(in) *m* -en,-en (*f* -,-nen) lawyer. **j~isch** *a* legal, *adv* -ly

Jury /ȝyˈriː/ *f* -,-s jury; (*Sport*) judges *pl*

justieren *vt* adjust

Justiz *f* - **die J~** justice. **J~irrtum** *m* miscarriage of justice. **J~minister** *m* Minister of Justice

Juwel *nt* -s,-en *& (fig)* -e jewel. **J~ier** *m* -s,-e jeweller

Jux *m* -es,-e (*fam*) joke; **aus Jux** for fun

K

Kabarett *nt* -s,-s *& -e* cabaret

kabbelig *a* choppy

Kabel *nt* -s,- cable. **K~fernsehen** *nt* cable television

Kabeljau *m* -s,-e *& -s* cod

Kabine *f* -,-n cabin; (*Umkleide-*) cubicle; (*Telefon-*) booth; (*einer K~nbahn*) car. **K~nbahn** *f* cable-car

Kabinett *nt* -s,-e (*Pol*) Cabinet

Kabriolett *nt* -s,-s convertible

Kachel *f* -,-n tile. **k~n** *vt* tile

Kadaver *m* -s,- carcass

Kadenz *f* -,-en (*Mus*) cadence; (*für Solisten*) cadenza

Kadett *m* -en,-en cadet

Käfer *m* -s,- beetle

Kaff *nt* -s,-s (*fam*) dump

Kaffee /'kafe:, ka'fe:/ *m* -s,-s coffee; (*Mahlzeit*) afternoon coffee. **K~grund** *m* = **K~satz**. **K~kanne** *f* coffee-pot. **K~maschine** *f* coffee-maker. **K~mühle** *f* coffee-grinder. **K~satz** *m* coffee-grounds *pl*

Käfig *m* -s,-e cage

kahl *a* bare; (*haarlos*) bald; **k~ geschoren** shaven. **k~geschoren** *a* (NEW) **k~ geschoren**, *s.* **kahl**. **k~köpfig** *a* bald-headed

Kahn *m* -s,-e boat; (*Last-*) barge

Kai *m* -s,-e quay

Kaiser *m* -s,- emperor. **K~in** *f* -,-nen empress. **k~lich** *a* imperial. **K~reich** *nt* empire. **K~schnitt** *m* Caesarean [section]

Kajüte *f* -,-n (*Naut*) cabin

Kakao /ka'kau/ *m* -s cocoa

Kakerlak *m* -s & -en,-en cockroach

Kaktee /kak'te:ə/ *f* -,-n, **Kaktus** *m* -,-teen /-'te:ən/ cactus

Kalb *nt* -[e]s,-er calf. **K~fleisch** *nt* veal

Kalender *m* -s,- calendar; (*Taschen-, Termin-*) diary

Kaliber *nt* -s,- calibre; (*Gewehr-*) bore

Kalium *nt* -s potassium

Kalk *m* -[e]s,-e lime; (*Kalzium*) calcium. **k~en** *vt* whitewash. **K~stein** *m* limestone

Kalkulation /-'tsjo:n/ *f* -,-en calculation. **k~ieren** *vt/i* (*haben*) calculate

Kalorie *f* -,-n calorie

kalt *a* (kälter, kältest) cold; **es ist k~** it is cold; **mir ist k~** I am cold. **k~blütig** *a* cold-blooded, *adv* -ly; (*ruhig*) cool, *adv* -ly

Kälte *f* - cold; (*Gefühls-*) coldness; **10 Grad K~** 10 degrees below zero. **K~welle** *f* cold spell

kalt|herzig *a* cold-hearted. **k~schnäuzig** *a* (*fam*) cold, *adv* -ly

Kalzium *nt* -s calcium

Kamel *nt* -s,-e camel; (*fam: Idiot*) fool

Kamera *f* -,-s camera

Kamerad(in) *m* -en,-en (*f* -,-nen) companion; (*Freund*) mate; (*Mil, Pol*) comrade. **K~schaft** *f* - comradeship

Kameramann *m* (*pl* -männer & -leute) cameraman

Kamille *f* - camomile

Kamin *m* -s,-e fireplace; (*SGer: Schornstein*) chimney. **K~feger** *m* -s,- (*SGer*) chimney-sweep

Kamm *m* -[e]s,-e comb; (*Berg-*) ridge; (*Zool, Wellen-*) crest

kämmen *vt* comb; **jdn/sich k~** comb s.o.'s/one's hair

Kammer *f* -,-n small room; (*Techn, Biol, Pol*) chamber. **K~diener** *m* valet. **K~musik** *f* chamber music

Kammgarn *nt* (*Tex*) worsted

Kampagne /kam'panjə/ *f* -,-n (*Pol, Comm*) campaign

Kampf *m* -es,-e fight; (*Schlacht*) battle; (*Wett-*) contest; (*fig*) struggle; **schwere K~e** heavy fighting *sg*; **den K~ ansagen** (+ *dat*) (*fig*) declare war on

kämpf|en *vi* (*haben*) fight; **sich k~en durch** fight one's way through. **K~er(in)** *m* -s,- (*f* -,-nen) fighter

kampf|los *adv* without a fight. **K~richter** *m* (*Sport*) judge

kampieren *vi* (*haben*) camp

Kanada *nt* -s Canada

Kanad|ier(in) /-jɐ, -jərɪn/ *m* -s,- (*f* -,-nen) Canadian. **k~isch** *a* Canadian

Kanal *m* -s,-e canal; (*Abfluss-*) drain, sewer; (*Radio, TV*) channel; **der K~** the [English] Channel

Kanalis|ation /-'tsjo:n/ *f* - sewerage system, drains *pl*. **k~ieren** *vt* canalize; (*fig: lenken*) channel

Kanarienvogel /-jən-/ *m* canary

Kanarisch *a* **K~e Inseln** Canaries

Kandi|dat(in) *m* -en,-en (*f* -,-nen) candidate. **k~dieren** *vi* (*haben*) stand (**für** for)

kandiert *a* candied

Känguru (**Känguruh**) *nt* -s,-s kangaroo

Kaninchen *nt* -s,- rabbit

Kanister *m* -s,- canister; (*Benzin-*) can

Kännchen *nt* -s,- [small] jug; (*Kaffee-*) pot

Kanne *f* -,-n jug; (*Kaffee-, Tee-*) pot; (*Öl-*) can; (*große Milch-*) churn; (*Gieß-*) watering-can

Kannibal|e *m* -n,-n cannibal. **K~ismus** *m* - cannibalism

Kanon *m* -s,-s canon; (*Lied*) round

Kanone *f* -,-n cannon, gun; (*fig: Könner*) ace

kanonisieren *vt* canonize

Kantate *f* -,-n cantata

Kante *f* -,-n edge; **auf die hohe K~ legen** (*fam*) put by

Kanten *m* -s,- crust [of bread]

Kanter *m* -s,- canter

kantig *a* angular

Kantine *f* -,-n canteen

Kanton *m* -s,-e (*Swiss*) canton

Kantor *m* -s,-en /-'to:rən/ choir-master and organist

Kanu *nt* -s,-s canoe

Kanzel *f* -,-n pulpit; (*Aviat*) cockpit

Kanzleistil *m* officialese

Kanzler *m* -s,- chancellor

Kap *nt* -s,-s (*Geog*) cape

Kapazität *f* -,-en capacity; (*Experte*) authority

Kapelle *f* -,-n chapel; (*Mus*) band

Kaper *f* -,-n (*Culin*) caper

kapern *vt* (*Naut*) seize

kapieren *vt* (*fam*) understand, (*fam*) get

Kapital *nt* -s capital; K~ schlagen aus (*fig*) capitalize on. **K~ismus** *m* - capitalism. **K~ist** *m* -en,-en capitalist. **k~istisch** *a* capitalist

Kapitän *m* -s,-e captain

Kapitel *nt* -s,- chapter

Kapitulation /-'tsjo:n/ *f* - capitulation. **k~ieren** *vi* (*haben*) capitulate

Kaplan *m* -s,-e curate

Kappe *f* -,-n cap. **k~n** *vt* cut

Kapsel *f* -,-n capsule; (*Flaschen-*) top

kaputt *a* (*fam*) broken; (*zerrissen*) torn; (*defekt*) out of order; (*ruiniert*) ruined; (*erschöpft*) worn out. **k~gehen†** *vi sep* (*sein*) (*fam*) break; (*zerreißen*) tear; (*defekt werden*) pack up; (*Ehe, Freundschaft:*) break up. **k~lachen (sich)** *vr sep* (*fam*) be in stitches. **k~machen** *vt sep* (*fam*) break; (*zerreißen*) tear; (*defekt machen*) put out of order; (*erschöpfen*) wear out; **sich k~machen** wear oneself out

Kapuze *f* -,-n hood

Kapuzinerkresse *f* nasturtium

Karaffe *f* -,-n carafe; (*mit Stöpsel*) decanter

Karambolage /karambo'la:ʒə/ *f* -,-n collision

Karamell (**Karamel**) *m* -s caramel. **K~bonbon** *m & nt* ≈ toffee

Karat *nt* -[e]s,-e carat

Karawane *f* -,-n caravan

Kardinal *m* -s,-e cardinal. **K~zahl** *f* cardinal number

Karfiol *m* -s (*Aust*) cauliflower

Karfreitag *m* Good Friday

karg *a* (*kärger, kärgst*) meagre; (*frugal*) frugal; (*spärlich*) sparse; (*unfruchtbar*) barren; (*gering*) scant. **k~en** *vi* (*haben*) be sparing (**mit** with)

kärglich *a* poor, meagre; (*gering*) scant

Karibik *f* - Caribbean

kariert *a* check[ed]; (*Papier*) squared; **schottisch k~** tartan

Karikatur *f* -,-en caricature; (*Journ*) cartoon. **k~ieren** *vt* caricature

karitativ *a* charitable

Karneval *m* -s,-e & -s carnival

Karnickel *nt* -s,- (*dial*) rabbit

Kärnten *nt* -s Carinthia

Karo *nt* -s,-s (*Raute*) diamond; (*Viereck*) square; (*Muster*) check; (*Kartenspiel*) diamonds *pl*. **K~muster** *nt* check

Karosserie *f* -,-n bodywork

Karotte *f* -,-n carrot

Karpfen *m* -s,- carp

Karre *f* -,-n = Karren

Karree *nt* -s,-s square; **ums K~** round the block

Karren *m* -s,- cart; (*Hand-*) barrow. **k~** *vt* cart

Karriere /ka'rje:rə/ *f* -,-n career; **K~ machen** get to the top

Karte *f* -,-n card; (*Eintritts-, Fahr-*) ticket; (*Speise-*) menu; (*Land-*) map

Kartei *f* -,-en card index. **K~karte** *f* index card

Kartenspiel *nt* card-game; (*Spielkarten*) pack/(*Amer*) deck of cards. **K~vorverkauf** *m* advance booking

Kartoffel *f* -,-n potato. **K~brei** *m*, **K~püree** *nt* mashed potatoes *pl*. **K~salat** *m* potato salad

Karton /kar'tɔŋ/ *m* -s,-s cardboard; (*Schachtel*) carton, cardboard box

Karussell *nt* -s,-s & -e roundabout

Karwoche *f* Holy Week

Käse *m* -s,- cheese. **K~kuchen** *m* cheesecake

Kaserne *f* -,-n barracks *pl*

Kasino *nt* -s,-s casino

Kasperle *nt & m* -s,- Punch. **K~theater** *nt* Punch and Judy show

Kasse *f* -,-n till; (*Registrier-*) cash register; (*Zahlstelle*) cash desk; (*im Supermarkt*) check-out; (*Theater-*) box-office; (*Geld*) pool [of money], (*fam*) kitty; (*Kranken-*) health insurance scheme; (*Spar-*) savings bank; **knapp/gut bei K~ sein** (*fam*) be short of cash/be flush. **K~npatient** *m* ≈ NHS patient. **K~nschlager** *m* box-office hit. **K~nwart** *m* -[e]s,-e treasurer. **K~nzettel** *m* receipt

Kasserolle *f* -,-n saucepan [with one handle]

Kassette *f* -,-n cassette; (*Film-, Farbband-*) cartridge; (*Geld-*) money-box; (*Schmuck-*) case. **K~nrecorder** /-rəkɔrdɐ/ *m* -s,- cassette recorder

kassieren *vi* (*haben*) collect the money/(*im Bus*) the fares □ *vt* collect. **K~er(in)** *m* -s,- (*f* -,-nen) cashier

Kastagnetten /kastan'jɛtən/ *pl* castanets

Kastanie /kas'ta:njə/ *f* -,-n [horse] chestnut, (*fam*) conker. **k~nbraun** *a* chestnut

Kaste *f* -,-n caste

Kasten *m* -s,: box; (*Brot-*) bin; (*Flaschen-*) crate; (*Brief-*) letter-box; (*Aust: Schrank*) cupboard; (*Kleider-*) wardrobe

kastrieren *vt* castrate; neuter ⟨*Tier*⟩

Kasus *m* -,- /-u:s/ (*Gram*) case

Katalog *m* -[e]s,-e catalogue. **k~isieren** *vt* catalogue

Katalysator *m* -s,-en /-'to:rən/ catalyst; (*Auto*) catalytic converter

Katapult *nt* -[e]s,-e catapult. **k~ieren** *vt* catapult

Katarrh, Katarr *m* -s,-e catarrh

katastrophal *a* catastrophic. **K~ophe** *f* -,-n catastrophe

Katechismus *m* - catechism

Kategorie *f* -,-n category. **k~orisch** *a* categorical, *adv* -ly

Kater *m* -s,- tom-cat; (*fam: Katzenjammer*) hangover

Katheder *nt* -s,- [teacher's] desk

Kathedrale *f* -,-n cathedral

Kath|olik(in) *m* -en,-en (*f* -,-nen) Catholic. **k~olisch** *a* Catholic. **K~olizismus** *m* - Catholicism

Kätzchen *nt* -s,- kitten; (*Bot*) catkin

Katze *f* -,-n cat. **K~njammer** *m* (*fam*) hangover. **K~nsprung** *m* ein **K~nsprung** (*fam*) a stone's throw

Kauderwelsch *nt* -[s] gibberish

kauen *vt/i* (*haben*) chew; bite ⟨*Nägel*⟩

kauern *vi* (*haben*) crouch; **sich k~** crouch down

Kauf *m* -[e]s, Käufe purchase; **guter K~** bargain; **in K~ nehmen** (*fig*) put up with. **k~en** *vt/i* (*haben*) buy; **k~en bei** shop at

Käufer(in) *m* -s,- (*f* -,-nen) buyer; (*im Geschäft*) shopper

Kauf|haus *nt* department store. **K~kraft** *f* purchasing power. **K~laden** *m* shop

käuflich *a* saleable; (*bestechlich*) corruptible; **k~ sein** be for sale; **k~ erwerben** buy

Kauf|mann *m* (*pl* -leute) businessman; (*Händler*) dealer; (*dial*) grocer. **k~männisch** *a* commercial. **K~preis** *m* purchase price

Kaugummi *m* chewing-gum

Kaulquappe *f* -,-n tadpole

kaum *adv* hardly; **k~ glaublich** *od* **zu glauben** hard to believe

kauterisieren *vt* cauterize

Kaution /-'tsjo:n/ *f* -,-en surety; (*Jur*) bail; (*Miet-*) deposit

Kautschuk *m* -s rubber

Kauz *m* -es, Käuze owl; **komischer K~** (*fam*) odd fellow

Kavalier *m* -s,-e gentleman

Kavallerie *f* - cavalry

Kaviar *m* -s caviare

keck *a* bold; (*frech*) cheeky

Kegel *m* -s,- skittle; (*Geom*) cone; **mit Kind und K~** (*fam*) with all the family. **K~bahn** *f* skittle-alley. **k~förmig** *a* conical. **k~n** *vi* (*haben*) play skittles

Kehl|e *f* -,-n throat; **aus voller K~e** at the top of one's voice; **etw in die falsche K~e bekommen** (*fam*) take sth the wrong way. **K~kopf** *m* larynx. **K~kopfentzündung** *f* laryngitis

Kehr|e *f* -,-n [hairpin] bend. **k~en** *vi* (*haben*) (*fegen*) sweep □ *vt* sweep; (*wenden*) turn; **den Rücken k~en** turn one's back (*dat* on); **sich k~en** turn; **sich nicht k~en an** (+ *acc*) not care about. **K~icht** *m* -[e]s sweepings *pl*. **K~reim** *m* refrain. **K~seite** *f* (*fig*) drawback; **die K~seite der Medaille** the other side of the coin. **k~tmachen** *vi sep* (*haben*) turn back; (*sich umdrehen*) turn round. **K~twendung** *f* about-turn; (*fig*) U-turn

keifen *vi* (*haben*) scold

Keil *m* -[e]s,-e wedge

Keil|e *f* - (*fam*) hiding. **k~n (sich)** *vr* (*fam*) fight. **K~rei** *f* -,-en (*fam*) punch-up

Keil|kissen *nt* [wedge-shaped] bolster. **K~riemen** *m* fan belt

Keim *m* -[e]s,-e (*Bot*) sprout; (*Med*) germ; **im K~ ersticken** (*fig*) nip in the bud. **k~en** *vi* (*haben*) germinate; (*austreiben*) sprout. **k~frei** *a* sterile

kein *pron* no; not a; **auf k~en Fall** on no account; **k~e fünf Minuten** less than five minutes. **k~e(r,s)** *pron* no one, nobody; (*Ding*) none, not one. **k~esfalls** *adv* on no account. **k~eswegs** *adv* by no means. **k~mal** *adv* not once. **k~s** *pron* none, not one

Keks *m* -[es],-[e] biscuit, (*Amer*) cookie

Kelch *m* -[e]s,-e goblet, cup; (*Relig*) chalice; (*Bot*) calyx

Kelle *f* -,-n ladle; (*Maurer-, Pflanz-*) trowel

Keller *m* -s,- cellar. **K~ei** *f* -,-en winery. **K~geschoss (K~geschoß)** *nt* cellar; (*bewohnbar*) basement. **K~wohnung** *f* basement flat

Kellner *m* -s,- waiter. **K~in** *f* -,-nen waitress

keltern *vt* press

keltisch *a* Celtic

Kenia *nt* -s Kenya

kennen† *vt* know; **k~en lernen** get to know; (*treffen*) meet; **sich k~en lernen**

meet; (*näher*) get to know one another.
k~enlernen *vt sep* ⟨NEW⟩ **k~en lernen,**
s. **kennen. K~er** *m* -s,-, **K~erin** *f* -,-nen
connoisseur; (*Experte*) expert. **K~melo-**
die *f* signature tune. **k~tlich** *a* recogniz-
able; **k~tlich machen** mark. **K~tnis** *f*
-,-se knowledge; **zur K~tnis nehmen**
take note of; **in K~tnis setzen** inform
(**von** of). **K~wort** *nt* (*pl* -wörter) reference; (*geheimes*) password. **K~zeichen** *nt*
distinguishing mark or feature; (*Merk-*
mal) characteristic, (*Markierung*) mark,
marking; (*Abzeichen*) badge; (*Auto*)
registration. **k~zeichnen** *vt* distinguish;
(*markieren*) mark. **k~zeichnend** *a* typical (**für** of). **K~ziffer** *f* reference number

kentern *vi* (*sein*) capsize

Keramik *f* -,-en pottery, ceramics *sg*;
(*Gegenstand*) piece of pottery

Kerbe *f* -,-n notch

Kerbholz *nt* etwas auf dem **K~ haben**
(*fam*) have a record

Kerker *m* -s,- dungeon; (*Gefängnis*) prison

Kerl *m* -s,-e & -s (*fam*) fellow, bloke

Kern *m* -s,-e pip; (*Kirsch-*) stone; (*Nuss-*)
kernel; (*Techn*) core; (*Atom-, Zell- & fig*)
nucleus; (*Stadt-*) centre; (*einer Sache*)
heart. **K~energie** *f* nuclear energy.
K~gehäuse *nt* core. **k~gesund** *a* perfectly healthy. **k~ig** *a* robust; ⟨*Ausspruch*⟩
pithy. **K~los** *a* seedless. **K~physik** *f* nuclear physics *sg*

Kerze *f* -,-n candle. **k~ngerade** *a & adv*
straight. **K~nhalter** *m* -s,- candlestick

kess (**keß**) *a* (**kesser, kessest**) pert

Kessel *m* -s,- kettle; (*Heiz-*) boiler.
K~stein *m* fur

Ketschup (**Ketchup**) /'kɛtʃap/ *m* -[s],-s
ketchup

Kette *f* -,-n chain; (*Hals-*) necklace. **k~n**
vt chain (**an** + *acc* to). **K~nladen** *m* chain
store. **K~nraucher** *m* chain-smoker.
K~nreaktion *f* chain reaction

Ketze|r(in) *m* -s, (*f* -,-nen) heretic.
K~rei *f* - heresy

keuch|en *vi* (*haben*) pant. **K~husten** *m*
whooping cough

Keule *f* -,-n club; (*Culin*) leg; (*Hühner-*)
drumstick

keusch *a* chaste. **K~heit** *f* - chastity

Kfz *abbr s.* **Kraftfahrzeug**

Khaki *nt* - khaki. **k~farben** *a* khaki

kichern *vi* (*haben*) giggle

Kiefer[1] *f* -,-n pine[-tree]

Kiefer[2] *m* -s,- jaw

Kiel *m* -s,-e (*Naut*) keel. **K~wasser** *nt*
wake

Kiemen *fpl* gills

Kies *m* -es gravel. **K~el** *m* -s,-, **K~elstein**
m pebble. **K~grube** *f* gravel pit

Kilo *nt* -s,-[s] kilo. **K~gramm** *nt* kilogram.
K~hertz *nt* kilohertz. **K~meter** *m* kilo-
metre. **K~meterstand** *m* ≈ mileage.
K~watt *nt* kilowatt

Kind *nt* -es,-er child; **von K~ auf** from
childhood

Kinder|arzt *m*, **K~ärztin** *f* paediatri-
cian. **K~bett** *nt* child's cot. **K~ei** *f*
-,-en childish prank. **K~garten** *m* nursery school. **K~gärtnerin** *f* nursery-
school teacher. **K~geld** *nt* child benefit.
K~gottesdienst *m* Sunday school.
K~lähmung *f* polio. **k~leicht** *a* very
easy. **k~los** *a* childless. **K~mädchen** *nt*
nanny. **k~reich** *a* **k~reiche Familie**
large family. **K~reim** *m* nursery rhyme.
K~spiel *nt* children's game; **das ist**
ein/kein K~spiel that is dead easy/not
easy. **K~tagesstätte** *f* day nursery.
K~teller *m* children's menu. **K~wagen**
m pram, (*Amer*) baby carriage.
K~zimmer *nt* child's/children's room;
(*für Baby*) nursery

Kind|heit *f* - childhood. **k~isch** *a* child-
ish, puerile. **k~lich** *a* childlike

kinetisch *a* kinetic

Kinn *nt* -[e]s,-e chin. **K~lade** *f* jaw

Kino *nt* -s,-s cinema

Kiosk *m* -[e]s,-e kiosk

Kippe *f* -,-n (*Müll-*) dump; (*fam:*
Zigaretten-) fag-end; **auf der K~ stehen**
(*fam*) be in a precarious position; (*un-*
sicher sein) hang in the balance. **k~lig** *a*
wobbly. **K~ln** *vi* (*haben*) wobble. **k~n** *vt*
tilt; (*schütten*) tip (**in** + *acc* into) □ *vi* (*sein*)
topple

Kirch|e *f* -,-n church. **K~enbank** *f* pew.
K~endiener *m* verger. **K~enlied** *nt*
hymn. **K~enschiff** *nt* nave. **K~hof** *m*
churchyard. **k~lich** *a* church ... □ *adv*
k~lich getraut werden be married in
church. **K~turm** *m* church tower,
steeple. **K~weih** *f* -,-en [village] fair

Kirmes *f* -,-sen = **Kirchweih**

Kirsch|e *f* -,-n cherry. **K~wasser** *nt*
kirsch

Kissen *nt* -s,- cushion; (*Kopf-*) pillow

Kiste *f* -,-n crate; (*Zigarren-*) box

Kitsch *m* -es sentimental rubbish; (*Kunst*)
kitsch. **k~ig** *a* slushy; (*Kunst*) kitschy

Kitt *m* -s [adhesive] cement; (*Fenster-*) putty

Kittel *m* -s,- overall, smock; (*Arzt-, Labor-*)
white coat

kitten *vt* stick; (*fig*) cement

Kitz *nt* -es,-e (*Zool*) kid

Kitz|el *m* -s,- tickle; (*Nerven-*) thrill. **k~eln**
vt/i (*haben*) tickle. **k~lig** *a* ticklish

Kladde *f* -,-n notebook

klaffen *vi* (*haben*) gape

kläffen *vi* (*haben*) yap

Klage *f* -,-n lament; (*Beschwerde*) complaint; (*Jur*) action. **k~n** *vi* (*haben*) lament; (*sich beklagen*) complain; (*Jur*) sue

Kläger(in) *m* -s,- (*f* -,-nen) (*Jur*) plaintiff

kläglich *a* pitiful, *adv* -ly; (*erbärmlich*) miserable, *adv* -bly

klamm *a* cold and damp; (*steif*) stiff. **K~** *f* -,-en (*Geog*) gorge

Klammer *f* -,-n (*Wäsche-*) peg; (*Büro-*) paper-clip; (*Heft-*) staple; (*Haar-*) grip; (*für Zähne*) brace; (*Techn*) clamp; (*Typ*) bracket. **k~n** (**sich**) *vr* cling (**an** + *acc* to)

Klang *m* -[e]s,-̈e sound; (*K~farbe*) tone. **k~voll** *a* resonant; ⟨*Stimme*⟩ sonorous

Klapp|bett *nt* folding bed. **K~e** *f* -,-n flap; (*fam: Mund*) trap. **k~en** *vt* fold; (*hoch-*) tip up □ *vi* (*haben*) (*fam*) work out. **K~entext** *m* blurb

Klapper *f* -,-n rattle. **k~n** *vi* (*haben*) rattle. **K~schlange** *f* rattlesnake

klapp|rig *a* rickety; (*schwach*) decrepit. **K~stuhl** *m* folding chair. **K~tisch** *m* folding table

Klaps *m* -es,-̈e pat; (*strafend*) smack. **k~en** *vt* smack

klar *a* clear; **k~ werden** clear; (*fig*) become clear (**dat** to); **sich** (*dat*) **k~ werden** make up one's mind; (*erkennen*) realize (**dass** that); **sich** (*dat*) **k~** *od* **im K~en** (**k~en**) **sein** realize (**dass** that) □ *adv* clearly; (*fam: natürlich*) of course. **K~e(r)** *m* (*fam*) schnapps

klären *vt* clarify; **sich k~** clear; (*fig: sich lösen*) resolve itself

Klarheit *f* - clarity

Klarinette *f* -,-n clarinet

klar|machen *vt sep* make clear (*dat* to); **sich** (*dat*) **etw k~machen** understand sth. **K~sichtfolie** *f* transparent/(*haftend*) cling film. **k~stellen** *vt sep* clarify

Klärung *f* - clarification

klarwerden† *vi sep* (*sein*) ⟨NEW⟩ **klar werden**, s. **klar**

Klasse *f* -,-n class; (*Sch*) class, form, (*Amer*) grade; (*Zimmer*) classroom; **erster/zweiter K~ reisen** travel first/second class. **k~** *inv a* (*fam*) super. **K~narbeit** *f* [written] test. **K~nbuch** *nt* ≈ register. **K~nkamerad(in)** *m*(*f*) classmate. **K~nkampf** *m* class struggle. **K~nzimmer** *nt* classroom

klassifizier|en *vt* classify. **K~ung** *f* -,-en classification

Klass|ik *f* - classicism; (*Epoche*) classical period. **K~iker** *m* -s,- classical author/(*Mus*) composer. **k~isch** *a* classical; (*mustergültig, typisch*) classic

Klatsch *m* -[e]s gossip. **K~base** *f* (*fam*) gossip. **k~en** *vt* slap; **Beifall k~en** applaud □ *vi* (*haben*) make a slapping sound; (*im Wasser*) splash; (*tratschen*) gossip; (*applaudieren*) clap; [**in die Hände**] **k~en** clap one's hands □ *vi* (*haben/sein*) slap (**gegen** against). **K~maul** *nt* gossip. **k~nass** (*k~naß*) *a* (*fam*) soaking wet

klauben *vt* pick

Klaue *f* -,-n claw; (*fam: Schrift*) scrawl. **k~n** *vt/i* (*haben*) (*fam*) steal

Klausel *f* -,-n clause

Klaustrophobie *f* - claustrophobia

Klausur *f* -,-en (*Univ*) [examination] paper; (*Sch*) written test

Klaviatur *f* -,-en keyboard

Klavier *nt* -s,-e piano. **K~spieler(in)** *m*(*f*) pianist

kleb|en *vt* stick/(*mit Klebstoff*) glue (**an** + *acc* to) □ *vi* (*haben*) stick (**an** + *dat* to). **k~rig** *a* sticky. **K~stoff** *m* adhesive, glue. **K~streifen** *m* adhesive tape

kleckern *vi* (*haben*) (*fam*) = **klecksen**

Klecks *m* -es,-e stain; (*Tinten-*) blot; (*kleine Menge*) dab. **k~en** *vi* (*haben*) make a mess

Klee *m* -s clover. **K~blatt** *nt* clover leaf

Kleid *nt* -[e]s,-er dress; **K~er** dresses; (*Kleidung*) clothes. **k~en** *vt* dress; (*gut stehen*) suit; **sich k~en** dress. **K~erbügel** *m* coat-hanger. **K~erbürste** *f* clothesbrush. **K~erhaken** *m* coat-hook. **K~errock** *m* pinafore dress. **K~erschrank** *m* wardrobe, (*Amer*) clothes closet. **k~sam** *a* becoming. **K~ung** *f* - clothes *pl*, clothing. **K~ungsstück** *nt* garment

Kleie *f* - bran

klein *a* small, little; (*von kleinem Wuchs*) short; **k~ hacken/schneiden** chop/cut up small *or* into small pieces; **k~ geschrieben werden** (*fig*) count for very little (**bei jdm** with s.o.); **von k~ auf** from childhood. **K~arbeit** *f* painstaking work. **K~bus** *m* minibus. **K~e(r,s)** *m*/*f*/*nt* little one. **K~geld** *nt* [small] change. **k~hacken** *vt sep* ⟨NEW⟩ **k~ hacken**, s. **klein**. **K~handel** *m* retail trade. **K~heit** *f* - smallness; (*Wuchs*) short stature. **K~holz** *nt* firewood. **K~igkeit** *f* -,-en trifle; (*Mahl*) snack. **K~kind** *nt* infant. **K~kram** *m* (*fam*) odds and ends *pl*; (*Angelegenheiten*) trivia *pl*. **k~laut** *a* subdued. **k~lich** *a* petty. **K~lichkeit** *f* - pettiness. **k~mütig** *a* faint-hearted

Kleinod *nt* -[e]s,-e jewel

klein|schneiden† *vt sep* ⟨NEW⟩ **k~ schneiden**, s. **klein**. **k~schreiben**† *vt sep* write with a small [initial] letter; **k~geschrieben werden** (*fig*) ⟨NEW⟩ **k~ geschrieben werden**, s. **klein**. **K~stadt**

f small town. **k~städtisch** *a* provincial. **K~wagen** *m* small car

Kleister *m* -s paste. **k~n** *vt* paste

Klemme *f* -,-n [hair-]grip; **in der K~sitzen** (*fam*) be in a fix. **k~n** *vt* jam; **sich** (*dat*) **den Finger k~n** get one's finger caught □ *vi* (*haben*) jam, stick

Klempner *m* -s,- plumber

Klerus (der) - the clergy

Klette *f* -,-n burr; **wie eine K~** (*fig*) like a limpet

kletter|n *vi* (*sein*) climb. **K~pflanze** *f* climber. **K~rose** *f* climbing rose

Klettverschluss (**Klettverschluß**) *m* Velcro (P) fastening

klicken *vi* (*haben*) click

Klient(in) /kli'ɛnt(ɪn)/ *m* -en,-en (*f* -,-nen) (*Jur*) client

Kliff *nt* -[e]s,-e cliff

Klima *nt* -s climate. **K~anlage** *f* air-conditioning

klimat|isch *a* climatic. **k~isiert** *a* air-conditioned

klimpern *vi* (*haben*) jingle; **k~ auf** (+ *dat*) tinkle on 〈*Klavier*〉; strum 〈*Gitarre*〉

Klinge *f* -,-n blade

Klingel *f* -,-n bell. **k~n** *vi* (*haben*) ring; **es k~t** there's a ring at the door

klingen† *vi* (*haben*) sound

Klini|k *f* -,-en clinic. **k~sch** *a* clinical, *adv* -ly

Klinke *f* -,-n [door] handle

klipp *pred a* **k~ und klar** quite plain, *adv* -ly

Klipp *m* -s,-s = **Klips**

Klippe *f* -,-n [submerged] rock

Klips *m* -es,-e clip; (*Ohr-*) clip-on ear-ring

klirren *vi* (*haben*) rattle; 〈*Geschirr, Glas:*〉 chink

Klischee *nt* -s,-s cliché

Klo *nt* -s,-s (*fam*) loo, (*Amer*) john

klobig *a* clumsy

klönen *vi* (*haben*) (*NGer fam*) chat

klopf|en *vi* (*haben*) knock; (*leicht*) tap; 〈*Herz:*〉 pound; **es k~te** there was a knock at the door □ *vt* beat; (*ein-*) knock

Klops *m* -es,-e meatball; (*Brat-*) rissole

Klosett *nt* -s,-s lavatory

Kloß *m* -es,¨e dumpling; **ein K~ im Hals** (*fam*) a lump in one's throat

Kloster *nt* -s,¨ monastery; (*Nonnen-*) convent

klösterlich *a* monastic

Klotz *m* -es,¨e block

Klub *m* -s,-s club

Kluft¹ *f* -,¨e cleft; (*fig: Gegensatz*) gulf

Kluft² *f* -,-en outfit; (*Uniform*) uniform

klug *a* (**klüger, klügst**) intelligent, *adv* -ly; (*schlau*) clever, *adv* -ly; **nicht k~ werden aus** not understand. **K~heit** *f* - cleverness

Klump|en *m* -s,- lump. **k~en** *vi* (*haben*) go lumpy

knabbern *vt/i* (*haben*) nibble

Knabe *m* -n,-n boy. **k~nhaft** *a* boyish

Knäckebrot *nt* crispbread

knack|en *vt/i* (*haben*) crack. **K~s** *m* -es,-e crack; **einen K~s haben** be cracked/(*fam: verrückt sein*) crackers

Knall *m* -[e]s,-e bang. **K~bonbon** *m* cracker. **k~en** *vi* (*haben*) go bang; 〈*Peitsche:*〉 crack □ *vt* (*fam: werfen*) chuck; **jdm eine k~en** (*fam*) clout s.o. **k~ig** *a* (*fam*) gaudy. **k~rot** *a* bright red

knapp *a* (*gering*) scant; (*kurz*) short; (*mangelnd*) scarce; (*gerade ausreichend*) bare; (*eng*) tight; **ein k~es Pfund** just under a pound; **jdn k~ halten** (*fam*) keep s.o. short (*mit of*). **k~halten†** *vt sep* (NEW) **k~ halten, s. knapp. K~heit** *f* - scarcity

Knarre *f* -,-n rattle. **k~n** *vi* (*haben*) creak

Knast *m* -[e]s (*fam*) prison

knattern *vi* (*haben*) crackle; 〈*Gewehr:*〉 stutter

Knäuel *m & nt* -s,- ball

Knauf *m* -[e]s, **Knäufe** knob

knauser|ig *a* (*fam*) stingy. **k~n** *vi* (*haben*) (*fam*) be stingy

knautschen *vt* (*fam*) crumple □ *vi* (*haben*) crease

Knebel *m* -s,- gag. **k~n** *vt* gag

Knecht *m* -[e]s,-e farm-hand; (*fig*) slave. **k~en** *vt* (*fig*) enslave. **K~schaft** *f* - (*fig*) slavery

kneif|en† *vt* pinch □ *vi* (*haben*) pinch; (*fam: sich drücken*) chicken out. **K~zange** *f* pincers *pl*

Kneipe *f* -,-n (*fam*) pub, (*Amer*) bar

knet|en *vt* knead; (*formen*) mould. **K~masse** *f* Plasticine (P)

Knick *m* -[e]s,-e bend; (*im Draht*) kink; (*Kniff*) crease. **k~en** *vt* bend; (*kniffen*) fold; **geknickt sein** (*fam*) be dejected. **k~[e]rig** *a* (*fam*) stingy

Knicks *m* -es,-e curtsy. **k~en** *vi* (*haben*) curtsy

Knie *nt* -s,- /'kni:ə/ knee. **K~bundhose** *f* knee-breeches *pl*. **K~kehle** *f* hollow of the knee

knien /'kni:ən/ *vi* (*haben*) kneel □ *vr* **sich k~** kneel [down]

Knie|scheibe *f* kneecap. **K~strumpf** *m* knee-length sock

Kniff *m* -[e]s,-e pinch; (*Falte*) crease; (*fam: Trick*) trick. **k~en** *vt* fold. **k~[e]lig** *a* (*fam*) tricky

knipsen vt (lochen) punch; (Phot) photograph □ vi (haben) take a photograph/photographs

Knirps m -es,-e (fam) little chap; (P) (Schirm) telescopic umbrella

knirschen vi (haben) grate; ⟨Schnee, Kies:⟩ crunch; **mit den Zähnen k~** grind one's teeth

knistern vi (haben) crackle; ⟨Papier:⟩ rustle

Knitter|falte f crease. **k~frei** a crease-resistant. **k~n** vi (haben) crease

knobeln vi (haben) toss (**um** for); (fam: überlegen) puzzle

Knoblauch m -s garlic

Knöchel m -s,- ankle; (Finger-) knuckle

Knochen m -s,- bone. **K~mark** nt bone marrow. **k~trocken** a bone-dry

knochig a bony

Knödel m -s,- (SGer) dumpling

Knoll|e f -,-n tuber. **k~ig** a bulbous

Knopf m -[e]s,⁈e button; (Kragen-) stud; (Griff) knob

knöpfen vt button

Knopfloch nt buttonhole

Knorpel m -s gristle; (Anat) cartilage

knorrig a gnarled

Knospe f bud

Knötchen nt -s,- nodule

Knoten m -s,- knot; (Med) lump; (Haar-) bun, chignon. **k~** vt knot. **K~punkt** m junction

knotig a knotty; ⟨Hände⟩ gnarled

knuffen vt poke

knüll|en vt crumple □ vi (haben) crease. **K~er** m -s,- (fam) sensation

knüpfen vt knot; (verbinden) attach (**an** + acc to)

Knüppel m -s,- club; (Gummi-) truncheon

knurr|en vi (haben) growl; (Magen:) rumble; (fam: schimpfen) grumble. **k~ig** a grumpy

knusprig a crunchy, crisp

knutschen vi (haben) (fam) smooch

k.o. /ka'⁈oː/ a **k.o. schlagen** knock out; **k.o. sein** (fam) be worn out. **K.o.** m -s,-s knock-out

Koalition /koaliˈtsjoːn/ f -,-en coalition

Kobold m -[e]s,-e goblin, imp

Koch m -[e]s,⁈e cook; (im Restaurant) chef. **K~buch** nt cookery book, (Amer) cookbook. **k~en** vt cook; (sieden) boil; make ⟨Kaffee, Tee⟩; **hart gekochtes Ei** hard-boiled egg □ vi (haben) cook; (sieden) boil; (fam) seethe (**vor** + dat with). **K~en** nt -s cooking; (Sieden) boiling; **zum K~n bringen/kommen** bring/come to the boil. **k~end** a boiling □ adv **k~end heiß** boiling hot. **K~er** m -s,- cooker. **K~gelegenheit** f cooking facilities pl. **K~herd** m cooker, stove

Köchin f -,-nen [woman] cook

Koch|kunst f cookery. **K~löffel** m wooden spoon. **K~nische** f kitchenette. **K~platte** f hotplate. **K~topf** m saucepan

Kode /koːt/ m -s,-s code

Köder m -s,- bait

Koexist|enz /ˈkoːˀɛksɪstɛntš/ f coexistence. **k~ieren** vi (haben) coexist

Koffein /kɔfeˈiːn/ nt -s caffeine. **k~frei** a decaffeinated

Koffer m -s,- suitcase. **K~kuli** m luggage trolley. **K~radio** nt portable radio. **K~raum** m (Auto) boot, (Amer) trunk

Kognak /ˈkɔnjak/ m -s,-s brandy

Kohl m -[e]s cabbage

Kohle f -,-n coal. **K~[n]hydrat** nt -[e]s,-e carbohydrate. **K~nbergwerk** nt coal-mine, colliery. **K~ndioxid** nt carbon dioxide. **K~ngrube** f = K~nbergwerk. **K~nherd** m [kitchen] range. **K~nsäure** f carbon dioxide. **K~nstoff** m carbon. **K~papier** nt carbon paper

Kohl|kopf m cabbage. **K~rabi** m -[s],-[s] kohlrabi. **K~rübe** f swede

Koje f -,-n (Naut) bunk

Kokain /kokaˈiːn/ nt -s cocaine

kokett a flirtatious. **k~ieren** vi (haben) flirt

Kokon /koˈkõː/ m -s,-s cocoon

Kokosnuss (Kokosnuß) f coconut

Koks m -es coke

Kolben m -s,- (Gewehr-) butt; (Mais-) cob; (Techn) piston; (Chem) flask

Kolibri m -s,-s humming-bird

Kolik f -,-en colic

Kollabora|teur /-ˈtøːɐ̯/ m -s,-e collaborator. **K~tion** /-ˈtsjoːn/ f - collaboration

Kolleg nt -s,-s & -ien /-jən/ (Univ) course of lectures

Kolleg|e m -n,-n, **K~in** f -,-nen colleague. **K~ium** nt -s,-ien staff

Kollekt|e f -,-en (Relig) collection. **K~tion** /-ˈtsjoːn/ f -,-en collection. **k~tiv** a collective. **K~tivum** nt -s,-va collective noun

kolli|dieren vi (sein) collide. **K~sion** f -,-en collision

Köln nt -s Cologne. **K~ischwasser, K~isch Wasser** nt eau-de-Cologne

Kolonialwaren fpl groceries

Kolon|ie f -,-n colony. **k~isieren** vt colonize

Kolonne f -,-n column; (Mil) convoy

Koloss m -es,-e (Koloß m -sses,-sse) giant

kolossal *a* enormous, *adv* -ly

Kolumne *f* -,-n (*Journ*) column

Koma *nt* -s,-s coma

Kombi *m* -s,-s = K∼wagen. K∼nation /-'tsi̯o:n/ *f* -,-en combination; (*Folgerung*) deduction; (*Kleidung*) co-ordinating outfit. k∼nieren *vt* combine; (*fig*) reason; (*folgern*) deduce. K∼wagen *m* estate car, (*Amer*) station-wagon

Kombüse *f* -,-n (*Naut*) galley

Komet *m* -en,-en comet. k∼enhaft *a* (*fig*) meteoric

Komfort /kɔm'fo:ɐ̯/ *m* -s comfort; (*Luxus*) luxury. k∼abel /-'ta:bəl/ *a* comfortable, *adv* -bly; (*luxuriös*) luxurious, *adv* -ly

Komik *f* - humour. K∼er *m* -s,- comic, comedian

komisch *a* funny; (*Oper*) comic; (*sonderbar*) odd, funny □ *adv* funnily; oddly. k∼erweise *adv* funnily enough

Komitee *nt* -s,-s committee

Komma *nt* -s,-s & -ta comma; (*Dezimal-*) decimal point; **drei K∼ fünf** three point five

Komman|dant *m* -en,-en commanding officer. K∼deur /-'dø:ɐ̯/ *m* -s,-e commander. k∼dieren *vt* command; (*befehlen*) order; (*fam: herum-*) order about □ *vi* (*haben*) give the orders

Kommando *nt* -s,-s order; (*Befehlsgewalt*) command; (*Einheit*) detachment. K∼brücke *f* bridge

kommen† *vi* (*sein*) come; (*eintreffen*) arrive; (*gelangen*) get (**nach** to); k∼ **lassen** send for; **auf/hinter etw** (*acc*) k∼ think of/find out about sth; **um/zu etw** k∼ lose/acquire sth; **wieder zu sich** k∼ come round; **wie kommt das?** why is that? **K∼** *nt* -s coming; **K∼ und Gehen** coming and going. k∼d *a* coming; k∼den **Montag** next Monday

Kommen|tar *m* -s,-e commentary; (*Bemerkung*) comment. K∼tator *m* -s,-en /-'to:rən/ commentator. k∼tieren *vt* comment on

kommer|zialisieren *vt* commercialize. k∼ziell *a* commercial, *adv* -ly

Kommili|tone *m* -n,-n, K∼tonin *f* -,-nen fellow student

Kommiss *m* -es (Kommiß *m* -sses) (*fam*) army

Kommissar *m* -s,-e commissioner; (*Polizei-*) superintendent

Kommission *f* -,-en commission; (*Gremium*) committee

Kommode *f* -,-n chest of drawers

Kommunalwahlen *fpl* local elections

Kommunikation /-'tsi̯o:n/ *f* -,-en communication

Kommunikee /kɔmyni'ke:/ *nt* -s,-s = Kommuniqué

Kommunion *f* -,-en [Holy] Communion

Kommuniqué /kɔmyni'ke:/ *nt* -s,-s communiqué

Kommun|ismus *m* - Communism. K∼ist(in) *m* -en,-en (*f* -,-nen) Communist. k∼istisch *a* Communist

kommunizieren *vi* (*haben*) receive [Holy] Communion

Komödie /ko'mø:di̯ə/ *f* -,-n comedy

Kompagnon /'kɔmpanjɔ:/ *m* -s,-s (*Comm*) partner

kompakt *a* compact. K∼schallplatte *f* compact disc

Kompanie *f* -,-n (*Mil*) company

Komparativ *m* -s,-e comparative

Komparse *m* -n,-n (*Theat*) extra

Kompass *m* -es,-e (Kompaß *m* -sses,-sse) compass

kompatibel *a* compatible

kompeten|t *a* competent. K∼z *f* -,-en competence

komplett *a* complete, *adv* -ly

Komplex *m* -es,-e complex. k∼ *a* complex

Komplikation /-'tsi̯o:n/ *f* -,-en complication

Kompliment *nt* -[e]s,-e compliment

Komplize *m* -n,-n accomplice

komplizier|en *vt* complicate. k∼t *a* complicated

Komplott *nt* -[e]s,-e plot

kompo|nieren *vt/i* (*haben*) compose. K∼nist *m* -en,-en composer. K∼sition /-'tsi̯o:n/ *f* -,-en composition

Kompositum *nt* -s,-ta compound

Kompost *m* -[e]s compost

Kompott *nt* -[e]s,-e stewed fruit

Kompresse *f* -,-n compress

komprimieren *vt* compress

Kompromiss *m* -es,-e (Kompromiß *m* -sses,-sse) compromise; **einen** K∼ **schließen** compromise. k∼los *a* uncompromising

kompromittieren *vt* compromise

Konden|sation /-'tsi̯o:n/ *f* - condensation. k∼sieren *vt* condense

Kondensmilch *f* evaporated/(*gesüßt*) condensed milk

Kondition /-'tsi̯o:n/ *f* - (*Sport*) fitness; **in** K∼ in form. K∼al *m* -s,-e (*Gram*) conditional

Konditor *m* -s,-en /-'to:rən/ confectioner. K∼ei *f* -,-en patisserie

Kondo|lenzbrief *m* letter of condolence. k∼lieren *vi* (*haben*) express one's condolences

Kondom *nt* & *m* -s,-e condom

Konfekt nt -[e]s confectionery; (Pralinen) chocolates pl

Konfektion /-'tsio:n/ f - ready-to-wear clothes pl

Konferenz f -,-en conference; (Besprechung) meeting

Konfession f -,-en [religious] denomination. **k~ell** a denominational. **k~slos** a non-denominational

Konfetti nt -s confetti

Konfirm|and(in) m -en,-en (f -,-nen) candidate for confirmation. **K~ation** /-'tsio:n/ f -,-en confirmation. **k~ieren** vt (Relig) confirm

Konfitüre f -,-n jam

Konflikt m -[e]s,-e conflict

Konföderation /-'tsio:n/ f confederation

Konfront|ation /-'tsio:n/ f -,-en confrontation. **k~ieren** vt confront

konfus a confused

Kongress m -es,-e (**Kongreß** m -sses,-sse) congress

König m -s,-e king. **K~in** f -,-nen queen. **k~lich** a royal, adv -ly; (hoheitsvoll) regal, adv -ly; (großzügig) handsome, adv -ly; (fam: groß) tremendous, adv -ly. **K~reich** nt kingdom

konisch a conical

Konjug|ation /-'tsio:n/ f -,-en conjugation. **k~ieren** vt conjugate

Konjunktion /-'tsio:n/ f -,-en (Gram) conjunction

Konjunktiv m -s,-e subjunctive

Konjunktur f - economic situation; (Hoch-) boom

konkav a concave

konkret a concrete

Konkurren|t(in) m -en,-en (f -,-nen) competitor, rival. **K~z** f - competition; **jdm K~z machen** compete with s.o. **k~zfähig** a (Comm) competitive. **K~zkampf** m competition, rivalry

konkurrieren vi (haben) compete

Konkurs m -es,-e bankruptcy; **K~ machen** go bankrupt

können† vt/i (haben) etw **k~** be able to do sth; (beherrschen) know sth; **k~ Sie Deutsch?** do you know any German? **das kann ich nicht** I can't do that; **er kann nicht mehr** he can't go on; **für etw nichts k~** not to be to blame for sth □ v aux lesen/schwimmen **k~** be able to read/swim; **er kann/konnte es tun** he can/could do it; **das kann** od **könnte [gut] sein** that may [well] be. **K~** nt -s ability; (Wissen) knowledge.

Könner(in) m -s,- (f -,-nen) expert

konsequen|t a consistent, adv -ly; (logisch) logical, adv -ly. **K~z** f -,-en consequence

konservativ a conservative

Konserv|en fpl tinned or canned food sg. **K~enbüchse, K~endose** f tin, can. **k~ieren** vt preserve; (in Dosen) tin, can. **K~ierungsmittel** nt preservative

Konsistenz f - consistency

konsolidieren vt consolidate

Konsonant m -en,-en consonant

konsterniert a dismayed

Konstitution /-'tsio:n/ f -,-en constitution. **k~ell** a constitutional

konstruieren vt construct; (entwerfen) design

Konstruk|tion /-'tsio:n/ f -,-en construction; (Entwurf) design. **k~tiv** a constructive

Konsul m -s,-n consul. **K~at** nt -[e]s,-e consulate

Konsult|ation /-'tsio:n/ f -,-en consultation. **k~ieren** vt consult

Konsum m -s consumption. **K~ent** m -en,-en consumer. **K~güter** ntpl consumer goods

Kontakt m -[e]s,-e contact. **K~linsen** fpl contact lenses. **K~person** f contact

kontern vt/i (haben) counter

Kontinent /'kɔn-, kɔnti'nɛnt/ m -[e]s,-e continent

Kontingent nt -[e]s,-e (Comm) quota; (Mil) contingent

Kontinuität f - continuity

Konto nt -s,-s account. **K~auszug** m [bank] statement. **K~nummer** f account number. **K~stand** m [bank] balance

Kontrabass (**Kontrabaß**) m double-bass

Kontrast m -[e]s,-e contrast

Kontroll|abschnitt m counterfoil. **K~e** f -,-n control; (Prüfung) check. **K~eur** /-'lø:ɐ/ m -s,-e [ticket] inspector. **k~ieren** vt check; inspect ⟨Fahrkarten⟩; (beherrschen) control

Kontroverse f -,-n controversy

Kontur f -,-en contour

Konvention /-'tsio:n/ f -,-en convention. **k~ell** a conventional, adv -ly

Konversation /-'tsio:n/ f -,-en conversation. **K~slexikon** nt encyclopaedia

konvert|ieren vi (haben) (Relig) convert. **K~it** m -en,-en convert

konvex a convex

Konvoi /kɔn'vɔy/ m -s,-s convoy

Konzentration /-'tsio:n/ f -,-en concentration. **K~slager** nt concentration camp

konzentrieren vt concentrate; **sich k~** concentrate (auf + acc on)

Konzept nt -[e]s,-e [rough] draft; **jdn aus dem K~ bringen** put s.o. off his stroke. **K~papier** nt rough paper

Konzern m -s,-e (Comm) group [of companies]

Konzert nt -[e]s,-e concert; (Klavier-, Geigen-) concerto. **K~meister** m leader, (Amer) concertmaster

Konzession f -,-en licence; (Zugeständnis) concession

Konzil nt -s,-e (Relig) council

Kooperation /ko?opera'tsjo:n/ f co-operation

Koordin|ation /ko?ordina'tsjo:n/ f - co-ordination. **k~ieren** vt co-ordinate

Kopf m -[e]s,ˑe head; **ein K~ Kohl/Salat** a cabbage/lettuce; **aus dem K~** from memory; (auswendig) by heart; **auf dem K~** (verkehrt) upside down; **K~ an K~** neck and neck; ⟨stehen⟩ shoulder to shoulder; **K~ stehen** stand on one's head; **sich** (dat) **den K~ waschen** wash one's hair; **sich** (dat) **den K~ zerbrechen** rack one's brains. **K~ball** m header. **K~bedeckung** f head-covering

Köpf|chen nt -s,- little head; **K~chen haben** (fam) be clever. **k~en** vt behead; (Fußball) head

Kopf|ende nt head. **K~haut** f scalp. **K~hörer** m headphones pl. **K~kissen** nt pillow. **K~kissenbezug** m pillow-case. **k~los** a panic-stricken. **K~nicken** nt -s nod. **K~rechnen** nt mental arithmetic. **K~salat** m lettuce. **K~schmerzen** mpl headache sg. **K~schütteln** nt -s shake of the head. **K~sprung** m header, dive. **K~stand** m headstand. **K~steinpflaster** nt cobble-stones pl. **K~stütze** f head-rest. **K~tuch** nt headscarf. **k~über** adv head first; (fig) headlong. **K~wäsche** f shampoo. **K~weh** nt headache. **K~zerbrechen** nt -s sich (dat) **K~zerbrechen machen** rack one's brains; (sich sorgen) worry

Kopie f -,-n copy. **k~ren** vt copy

Koppel[1] f -,-n enclosure; (Pferde-) paddock

Koppel[2] nt -s,- (Mil) belt. **k~n** vt couple

Koralle f -,-n coral

Korb m -[e]s,ˑe basket; **jdm einen K~ geben** (fig) turn s.o. down. **K~ball** m [kind of] netball. **K~stuhl** m wicker chair

Kord m -s (Tex) corduroy

Kordel f -,-n cord

Korinthe f -,-n currant

Kork m -s,- cork. **K~en** m -s,- cork. **K~enzieher** m -s,- corkscrew

Korn[1] nt -[e]s,ˑer grain, (Samen-) seed; (coll: Getreide) grain, corn; (am Visier) front sight

Korn[2] m -[e]s,- (fam) grain schnapps

Körn|chen nt -s,- granule. **k~ig** a granular

Körper m -s,- body; (Geom) solid. **K~bau** m build, physique. **k~behindert** a physically disabled. **k~lich** a physical, adv -ly; ⟨Strafe⟩ corporal. **K~pflege** f personal hygiene. **K~puder** m talcum powder. **K~schaft** f -,-en corporation, body. **K~strafe** f corporal punishment. **K~teil** m part of the body

Korps /ko:ɐ̯/ nt -,- /-[s],-s/ corps

korpulent a corpulent

korrekt a correct, adv -ly. **K~or** m -s,-en /-'to:rən/ proof-reader. **K~ur** f -,-en correction. **K~urabzug, K~urbogen** m proof

Korrespon|dent(in) m -en,-en (f -,-nen) correspondent. **K~denz** f -,-en correspondence. **k~dieren** vi (haben) correspond

Korridor m -s,-e corridor

korrigieren vt correct

Korrosion f - corrosion

korrumpieren vt corrupt

korrup|t a corrupt. **K~tion** /-'tsjo:n/ f - corruption

Korsett nt -[e]s,-e corset

koscher a kosher

Kose|name m pet name. **K~wort** nt (pl -wörter) term of endearment

Kosmet|ik f - beauty culture. **K~ika** ntpl cosmetics. **K~ikerin** f -,-nen beautician. **k~isch** a cosmetic; ⟨Chirurgie⟩ plastic

kosm|isch a cosmic. **K~onaut(in)** m -en,-en (f -,-nen) cosmonaut. **k~opolitisch** a cosmopolitan

Kosmos m - cosmos

Kost f - food; (Ernährung) diet; (Verpflegung) board

kostbar a precious. **K~keit** f -,-en treasure

kosten[1] vt/i (haben) [von] etw k~ taste sth

kosten[2] vt cost; (brauchen) take; **wie viel kostet es?** how much is it? **K~** pl expense sg, cost sg; (Jur) costs; **auf meine K~** at my expense. **K~[vor]anschlag** m estimate. **k~los** a free ◻ adv free [of charge]

Kosthappen m taste

köstlich a delicious; (entzückend) delightful. **K~keit** f -,-en (fig) gem; (Culin) delicacy

Kost|probe f taste; (fig) sample. **k~spielig** a expensive, costly

Kostüm nt -s,-e (Theat) costume; (Verkleidung) fancy dress; (Schneider-) suit. **K~fest** nt fancy-dress party. **k~iert** a **k~iert sein** be in fancy dress

Kot *m* -[e]s excrement; (*Schmutz*) dirt

Kotelett /kɔt'lɛt/ *nt* -s,-s chop, cutlet. **K~en** *pl* sideburns

Köter *m* -s,- (*pej*) dog

Kotflügel *m* (*Auto*) wing, (*Amer*) fender

kotzen *vi* (*haben*) (*sl*) throw up; **es ist zum K~** it makes you sick

Krabbe *f* -,-n crab; (*Garnele*) shrimp; (*rote*) prawn

krabbeln *vi* (*sein*) crawl

Krach *m* -[e]s,ᵉ din, racket; (*Knall*) crash; (*fam: Streit*) row; (*fam: Ruin*) crash. **k~en** *vi* (*haben*) crash; **es hat gekracht** there was a bang/(*fam: Unfall*) a crash □ (*sein*) break, crack; (*auftreffen*) crash (*gegen* into)

krächzen *vi* (*haben*) croak

Kraft *f* -,ᵉe strength; (*Gewalt*) force; (*Arbeits-*) worker; **in/außer K~** in/no longer in force; **in K~ treten** come into force. **k~** *prep* (+ *gen*) by virtue of. **K~ausdruck** *m* swear-word. **K~fahrer** *m* driver. **K~fahrzeug** *nt* motor vehicle. **K~fahrzeugbrief** *m* [vehicle] registration document

kräftig *a* strong; (*gut entwickelt*) sturdy; (*nahrhaft*) nutritious; (*heftig*) hard □ *adv* strongly; (*heftig*) hard. **k~en** *vt* strengthen

kraft|los *a* weak. **K~post** *f* post bus service. **K~probe** *f* trial of strength. **K~rad** *nt* motorcycle. **K~stoff** *m* (*Auto*) fuel. **k~voll** *a* strong, powerful. **K~wagen** *m* motor car. **K~werk** *nt* power station

Kragen *m* -s,- collar

Krähe *f* -,-n crow

krähen *vi* (*haben*) crow

krakeln *vt/i* (*haben*) scrawl

Kralle *f* -,-n claw. **k~n (sich)** *vr* clutch (**an** jdn/etw s.o./sth); (*Katze:*) dig its claws (**in** + *acc* into)

Kram *m* -s (*fam*) things *pl*, (*fam*) stuff; (*Angelegenheiten*) business; **wertloser K~** junk. **k~en** *vi* (*haben*) rummage about (**in** + *dat* in; **nach** for). **K~laden** *m* [small] general store

Krampf *m* -[e]s,ᵉe cramp. **K~adern** *fpl* varicose veins. **k~haft** *a* convulsive, *adv* -ly; (*verbissen*) desperate, *adv* -ly

Kran *m* -[e]s,ᵉe (*Techn*) crane

Kranich *m* -s,-e (*Zool*) crane

krank *a* (kränker, kränkst) sick; (*Knie, Herz*) bad; **k~ sein/werden/machen** be/fall/make ill; **jdn k~ melden/schreiben** ⟨NEW⟩ jdn **k~melden/k~schreiben** krank melden, krankschreiben. **K~e(r)** *m/f* sick man/woman, invalid; **die K~en** the sick *pl*

kränkeln *vi* (*haben*) be in poor health. **k~d** *a* ailing

kranken *vi* (*haben*) (*fig*) suffer (**an** + *dat* from)

kränken *vt* offend, hurt

Kranken|bett *nt* sick-bed. **K~geld** *nt* sickness benefit. **K~gymnast(in)** *m* -en,-en (*f* -,-nen) physiotherapist. **K~gymnastik** *f* physiotherapy. **K~haus** *nt* hospital. **K~kasse** *f* health insurance scheme/(*Amt*) office. **K~pflege** *f* nursing. **K~pfleger(in)** *m(f)* nurse. **K~saal** *m* [hospital] ward. **K~schein** *m* certificate of entitlement to medical treatment. **K~schwester** *f* nurse. **K~urlaub** *m* sick-leave. **K~versicherung** *f* health insurance. **K~wagen** *m* ambulance. **K~zimmer** *nt* sick-room

krank|haft *a* morbid; (*pathologisch*) pathological. **K~heit** *f* -,-en illness, disease

kränklich *a* sickly

krank|melden *vt sep* jdn **k~melden** report s.o. sick; **sich k~melden** report sick. **k~schreiben†** *vt sep* jdn **k~schreiben** give s.o. a medical certificate; **sich k~schreiben lassen** get a medical certificate

Kränkung *f* -,-en slight

Kranz *m* -es,ᵉe wreath; (*Ring*) ring

Krapfen *m* -s,- doughnut

krass (kraß) *a* (krasser, krassest) glaring; (*offensichtlich*) blatant; (*stark*) gross; rank ⟨Außenseiter⟩

Krater *m* -s,- crater

kratz|bürstig *a* (*fam*) prickly. **k~en** *vt/i* (*haben*) scratch; **sich k~en** scratch oneself/⟨Tier:⟩ itself. **K~er** *m* -s,- scratch; (*Werkzeug*) scraper

Kraul *nt* -s (*Sport*) crawl. **k~en¹** *vi* (*haben/sein*) (*Sport*) do the crawl

kraulen *vt* tickle; **sich am Kopf k~** scratch one's head

kraus *a* wrinkled; ⟨Haar⟩ frizzy; (*verworren*) muddled; **k~ ziehen** wrinkle. **K~e** *f* -,-n frill, ruffle; (*Haar-*) frizziness

kräuseln *vt* wrinkle; frizz ⟨Haar⟩; gather ⟨Stoff⟩; ripple ⟨Wasser⟩; **sich k~** wrinkle; (*sich kringeln*) curl; ⟨Haar:⟩ go frizzy; ⟨Wasser:⟩ ripple

krausen *vt* wrinkle; frizz ⟨Haar⟩; gather ⟨Stoff⟩; **sich k~** wrinkle; ⟨Haar:⟩ go frizzy

Kraut *nt* -[e]s, Kräuter herb; (*SGer*) cabbage; (*Sauer-*) sauerkraut; **wie K~ und Rüben** (*fam*) higgledy-piggledy

Krawall *m* -s,-e riot; (*Lärm*) row

Krawatte *f* -,-n [neck]tie

kraxeln *vi* (*sein*) (*fam*) clamber

krea|tiv /krea'ti:f/ *a* creative. **K~tur** *f* -,-en creature

Krebs *m* -es,-e crayfish; (*Med*) cancer; (*Astr*) Cancer. **k~ig** *a* cancerous

Kredit *m* -s,-e credit; (*Darlehen*) loan; **auf K~** on credit. **K~karte** *f* credit card

Kreid|e *f* - chalk. **k~ebleich** *a* deathly pale. **k~ig** a chalky

kreieren /kre'i:rən/ *vt* create

Kreis *m* -es,-e circle; (*Admin*) district

kreischen *vt/i* (*haben*) screech; (*schreien*) shriek

Kreisel *m* -s,- [spinning] top; (*fam: Kreisverkehr*) roundabout

kreis|en *vi* (*haben*) circle; revolve (**um** around). **k~förmig** *a* circular. **K~lauf** *m* cycle; (*Med*) circulation. **k~rund** *a* circular. **K~säge** *f* circular saw. **K~verkehr** *m* [traffic] roundabout, (*Amer*) traffic circle

Krem *f* -,-s & *m* -s,-e cream

Krematorium *nt* -s,-ien crematorium

Krempe *f* -,-n [hat] brim

Krempel *m* -s (*fam*) junk

krempeln *vt* turn (**nach oben** up)

Kren *m* -[e]s (*Aust*) horseradish

krepieren *vi* (*sein*) explode; (*sl: sterben*) die

Krepp *m* -s,-s & -e crêpe

Krepppapier (**Kreppapier**) *nt* crêpe paper

Kresse *f* -,-n cress; (*Kapuziner-*) nasturtium

Kreta *nt* -s Crete

Kreuz *nt* -es,-e cross; (*Kreuzung*) intersection; (*Mus*) sharp; (*Kartenspiel*) clubs *pl*; (*Anat*) small of the back; **über K~** crosswise; **das K~ schlagen** cross oneself. **k~** *adv* **k~ und quer** in all directions. **k~en** *vt* cross; **sich k~en** cross; ⟨*Straßen:*⟩ intersect; ⟨*Meinungen:*⟩ clash □ *vi* (*haben/sein*) cruise; ⟨*Segelschiff:*⟩ tack. **K~er** *m* -s,- cruiser. **K~fahrt** *f* (*Naut*) cruise; (*K~zug*) crusade. **K~feuer** *nt* crossfire. **K~gang** *m* cloister

kreuzig|en *vt* crucify. **K~ung** *f* -,-en crucifixion

Kreuz|otter *f* adder, common viper. **K~ung** *f* -,-en intersection; (*Straßen-*) crossroads *sg*; (*Hybride*) cross. **K~verhör** *nt* cross-examination; **ins K~verhör nehmen** cross-examine. **K~weg** *m* crossroads *sg*; (*Relig*) Way of the Cross. **k~weise** *adv* crosswise. **K~worträtsel** *nt* crossword [puzzle]. **K~zug** *m* crusade

kribbel|ig *a* (*fam*) edgy. **k~n** *vi* (*haben*) tingle; (*kitzeln*) tickle

kriech|en† *vi* (*sein*) crawl; (*fig*) grovel (**vor** + *dat* to). **k~erisch** *a* grovelling. **K~spur** *f* (*Auto*) crawler lane. **K~tier** *nt* reptile

Krieg *m* -[e]s,-e war; **K~ führen** wage war (**gegen** on)

kriegen *vt* (*fam*) get; **ein Kind k~** have a baby

Krieger|denkmal *nt* war memorial. **k~isch** *a* warlike; (*militärisch*) military

kriegs|beschädigt *a* war-disabled. **K~dienstverweigerer** *m* -s,- conscientious objector. **K~gefangene(r)** *m* prisoner of war. **K~gefangenschaft** *f* captivity. **K~gericht** *nt* court martial. **K~list** *f* stratagem. **K~rat** *m* council of war. **K~recht** *nt* martial law. **K~schiff** *nt* warship. **K~verbrechen** *nt* war crime

Krimi *m* -s,-s (*fam*) crime story/film. **K~nalität** *f* - crime; (*Vorkommen*) crime rate. **K~nalpolizei** *f* criminal investigation department. **K~nalroman** *m* crime novel. **k~nell** *a* criminal. **K~nelle(r)** *m* criminal

kringeln (**sich**) *vr* curl [up]; (*vor Lachen*) fall about

Kripo *f* - = Kriminalpolizei

Krippe *f* -,-n manger; (*Weihnachts-*) crib; (*Kinder-*) crèche. **K~nspiel** *nt* Nativity play

Krise *f* -,-n crisis

Kristall[1] *nt* -s (*Glas*) crystal; (*geschliffen*) cut glass

Kristall[2] *m* -s,-e crystal. **k~isieren** *vi/r* (*haben*) [**sich**] **k~isieren** crystallize

Kriterium *nt* -s,-ien criterion

Kritik *f* -,-en criticism; (*Rezension*) review; **unter aller K~** (*fam*) abysmal

Kriti|ker *m* -s,- critic; (*Rezensent*) reviewer. **k~sch** *a* critical, *adv* -ly. **k~sieren** *vt* criticize; review

kritteln *vi* (*haben*) find fault (**an** + *acc* with)

kritzeln *vt/i* (*haben*) scribble

Krokette *f* -,-n (*Culin*) croquette

Krokodil *nt* -s,-e crocodile

Krokus *m* -,-[se] crocus

Krone *f* -,-n crown; (*Baum-*) top

krönen *vt* crown

Kron|leuchter *m* chandelier. **K~prinz** *m* crown prince

Krönung *f* -,-en coronation; (*fig: Höhepunkt*) crowning event/(*Leistung*) achievement

Kropf *m* -[e]s,-e (*Zool*) crop; (*Med*) goitre

Kröte *f* -,-n toad

Krücke *f* -,-n crutch; (*Stock-*) handle; **an K~n** on crutches

Krug *m* -[e]s,-e jug; (*Bier-*) tankard

Krume f -,-n soft part [of loaf]; (Krümel) crumb; (Acker-) topsoil

Krümel m -s,- crumb. **k~ig** a crumbly. **k~n** vt crumble □ vi (haben) be crumbly; ⟨Person:⟩ drop crumbs

krumm a crooked; (gebogen) curved; (verbogen) bent; **etw k~ nehmen** (fam) take sth amiss. **k~beinig** a bow-legged

krümmen vt bend; crook ⟨Finger⟩; **sich k~** bend; (sich winden) writhe; (vor Schmerzen/Lachen) double up

krummnehmen† vt sep (NEW) **krumm nehmen**, s. krumm

Krümmung f -,-en bend; (Kurve) curve

Krüppel m -s,- cripple

Kruste f -,-n crust; (Schorf) scab

Kruzifix nt -es,-e crucifix

Krypta /'krypta/ f -,-ten crypt

Kub|a nt -s Cuba. **k~anisch** a Cuban

Kübel m -s,- tub; (Eimer) bucket; (Techn) skip

Kubik -pref cubic. **K~meter** m & nt cubic metre

Küche f -,-n kitchen; (Kochkunst) cooking; **kalte/warme K~** cold/hot food; **französische K~** French cuisine

Kuchen m -s,- cake

Küchen|herd m cooker, stove. **K~maschine** f food processor, mixer. **K~schabe** f -,-n cockroach. **K~zettel** m menu

Kuckuck m -s,-e cuckoo; **zum K~!** (fam) hang it! **K~suhr** f cuckoo clock

Kufe f -,-n [sledge] runner

Kugel f -,-n ball; (Geom) sphere; (Gewehr-) bullet; (Sport) shot. **k~förmig** a spherical. **K~lager** nt ball-bearing. **k~n** vt/i (haben) roll; **sich k~n** roll/(vor Lachen) fall about. **k~rund** a spherical; (fam: dick) tubby. **K~schreiber** m -s,-, ballpoint [pen]. **k~sicher** a bullet-proof. **K~stoßen** nt -s shot-putting

Kuh f -,-e cow

kühl a cool, adv -ly; (kalt) chilly. **K~box** f -,-en cool-box. **K~e** f - coolness; chilliness. **k~en** vt cool; refrigerate (Lebensmittel); chill (Wein). **K~er** m -s,- icebucket; (Auto) radiator. **K~erhaube** f bonnet, (Amer) hood. **K~fach** nt frozen-food compartment. **K~raum** m cold store. **K~schrank** m refrigerator. **K~truhe** f freezer. **K~ung** f - cooling; (Frische) coolness. **K~wasser** nt [radiator] water

Kuhmilch f cow's milk

kühn a bold, adv -ly; (wagemutig) daring. **K~heit** f - boldness

Kuhstall m cowshed

Küken nt -s,- chick; (Enten-) duckling

Kukuruz m -[es] (Aust) maize

kulant a obliging

Kuli m -s,- (fam: Kugelschreiber) ballpoint [pen], Biro (P)

kulinarisch a culinary

Kulissen fpl (Theat) scenery sg; (seitlich) wings; **hinter den K~** (fig) behind the scenes

kullern vt/i (sein) (fam) roll

Kult m -[e]s,-e cult

kultivieren vt cultivate. **k~t** a cultured

Kultur f -,-en culture; **K~en** plantations. **K~beutel** m toiletbag. **k~ell** a cultural. **K~film** m documentary film

Kultusminister m Minister of Education and Arts

Kümmel m -s caraway; (Getränk) kümmel

Kummer m -s sorrow, grief; (Sorge) worry; (Ärger) trouble

kümmer|lich a puny; (dürftig) meagre; (armselig) wretched. **k~n** vt concern; **sich k~n um** look after; (sich befassen) concern oneself with; (beachten) take notice of; **ich werde mich darum k~n** I shall see to it; **k~e dich um deine eigenen Angelegenheiten!** mind your own business!

kummervoll a sorrowful

Kumpel m -s,- (fam) mate

Kunde m -n,-n customer. **K~ndienst** m [after-sales] service

Kund|gebung f -,-en (Pol) rally. **k~ig** a knowledgeable; (sach-) expert

kündig|en vt cancel ⟨Vertrag⟩; give notice of withdrawal for ⟨Geld⟩; give notice to quit ⟨Wohnung⟩; **seine Stellung k~en** give [in one's] notice □ vi (haben) give [in one's] notice; **jdm k~en** give s.o. notice [of dismissal/⟨Vermieter:⟩ to quit]. **K~ung** f -,-en cancellation; notice [of withdrawal/dismissal/to quit]; (Entlassung) dismissal. **K~ungsfrist** f period of notice

Kund|in f -,-nen [woman] customer. **K~machung** f -,-en (Aust) [public] notice. **K~schaft** f - clientele, customers pl

künftig a future □ adv in future

Kunst f -,-e art; (Können) skill. **K~dünger** m artificial fertilizer. **K~faser** f synthetic fibre. **k~fertig** a skilful. **K~fertigkeit** f skill. **K~galerie** f art gallery. **k~gerecht** a expert, adv -ly. **K~geschichte** f history of art. **K~gewerbe** nt arts and crafts pl. **K~griff** m trick. **K~händler** m art dealer

Künstler m -s,- artist; (Könner) master. **K~in** f -,-nen [woman] artist. **k~isch** a artistic, adv -ally. **K~name** m pseudonym; (Theat) stage name

künstlich *a* artificial, *adv* -ly

kunst|los *a* simple. **K~maler** *m* painter. **K~stoff** *m* plastic. **K~stopfen** *nt* invisible mending. **K~stück** *nt* trick; (*große Leistung*) feat. **k~voll** *a* artistic; (*geschickt*) skilful, *adv* -ly; (*kompliziert*) elaborate, *adv* -ly. **K~werk** *nt* work of art

kunterbunt *a* multicoloured; (*gemischt*) mixed □ *adv* **k~ durcheinander** higgledy-piggledy

Kupfer *nt* -s copper. **k~n** *a* copper

kupieren *vt* crop

Kupon /ku'põ:/ *m* -s,-s voucher; (*Zins-*) coupon; (*Stoff-*) length

Kuppe *f* -,-n [rounded] top; (*Finger-*) end, tip

Kuppel *f* -,-n dome

kupp|eln *vt* couple (**an** + *acc* to) □ *vi* (*haben*) (*Auto*) operate the clutch. **K~lung** *f* -,-en coupling; (*Auto*) clutch

Kur *f* -,-en course of treatment; (*im Kurort*) cure

Kür *f* -,-en (*Sport*) free exercise; (*Eislauf*) free programme

Kurbel *f* -,-n crank. **k~n** *vt* wind (**nach oben/unten** up/down). **K~welle** *f* crankshaft

Kürbis *m* -ses,-se pumpkin; (*Flaschen-*) marrow

Kurgast *m* health-resort visitor

Kurier *m* -s,-e courier

kurieren *vt* cure

kurios *a* curious, odd. **K~ität** *f* -,-en oddness; (*Objekt*) curiosity; (*Kunst*) curio

Kur|ort *m* health resort; (*Badeort*) spa. **K~pfuscher** *m* quack

Kurs *m* -es,-e course; (*Aktien-*) price. **K~buch** *nt* timetable

kursieren *vi* (*haben*) circulate

kursiv *a* italic □ *adv* in italics. **K~schrift** *f* italics *pl*

Kursus *m* -,**Kurse** course

Kurswagen *m* through carriage

Kurtaxe *f* visitors' tax

Kurve *f* -,-n curve; (*Straßen-*) bend

kurz *a* (**kürzer, kürzest**) short; (*knapp*) brief; (*rasch*) quick; (*schroff*) curt; **k~e Hosen** shorts; **vor k~em** a short time ago; **seit k~em** lately; **binnen k~em** shortly; **den Kürzeren (kürzeren) ziehen** get the worst of it □ *adv* briefly, quickly; curtly; **k~ vor/nach** a little way/ (*zeitlich*) shortly before/after; **sich k~ fassen** be brief; **k~ und gut** in short; **über k~ oder lang** sooner or later; **zu k~ kommen** get less than one's fair share. **K~arbeit** *f* short-time working. **k~ärmelig** *a* short-sleeved. **k~atmig** *a* **k~atmig sein** be short of breath

Kürze *f* - shortness; (*Knappheit*) brevity; **in K~** shortly. **k~n** *vt* shorten; (*verringern*) cut

kurz|erhand *adv* without further ado. **k~fristig** *a* short-term □ *adv* at short notice. **K~geschichte** *f* short story. **k~lebig** *a* short-lived

kürzlich *adv* recently

Kurz|meldung *f* newsflash. **K~nachrichten** *fpl* news headlines. **K~schluss** (**K~schluß**) *m* short circuit; (*fig*) brainstorm. **K~schrift** *f* shorthand. **k~sichtig** *a* short-sighted. **K~sichtigkeit** *f* - short-sightedness. **K~streckenrakete** *f* short-range missile. **k~um** *adv* in short

Kürzung *f* -,-en shortening; (*Verringerung*) cut (**gen** in)

Kurz|waren *fpl* haberdashery *sg*, (*Amer*) notions. **k~weilig** *a* amusing. **K~welle** *f* short wave

kuscheln (sich) *vr* snuggle (**an** + *acc* up to)

Kusine *f* -,-n [female] cousin

Kuss *m* -es,¨e (**Kuß** *m* -sses,¨-sse) kiss

küssen *vt/i* (*haben*) kiss; **sich k~** kiss

Küste *f* -,-n coast. **K~nwache** *f*, **K~nwacht** *f* coastguard

Küster *m* -s,- verger

Kustos *m* -,-**toden** /-'to:-/ curator

Kutsch|e *f* -,-n [horse-drawn] carriage/ (*geschlossen*) coach. **K~er** *m* -s,- coachman, driver. **k~ieren** *vt/i* (*haben*) drive

Kutte *f* -,-n (*Relig*) habit

Kutter *m* -s,- (*Naut*) cutter

Kuvert /ku've:ɐ/ *nt* -s,-s envelope

KZ /ka:'tsɛt/ *nt* -[s],-s concentration camp

L

labil *a* unstable

Labor *nt* -s,-s & -e laboratory. **L~ant(in)** *m* -en,-en (*f* -,-nen) laboratory assistant. **L~atorium** *nt* -s,-ien laboratory

Labyrinth *nt* -[e]s,-e maze, labyrinth

Lache *f* -,-n puddle; (*Blut-*) pool

lächeln *vi* (*haben*) smile. **L~** *nt* -s smile. **l~d** *a* smiling

lachen *vi* (*haben*) laugh. **L~** *nt* -s laugh; (*Gelächter*) laughter

lächerlich *a* ridiculous, *adv* -ly; **sich l~ machen** make a fool of oneself. **L~keit** *f* -,-en ridiculousness; (*Kleinigkeit*) triviality

lachhaft *a* laughable

Lachs *m* -es,-e salmon. **l~farben, l~rosa** *a* salmon-pink

Lack *m* -[e]s,-e varnish; (*Japan-*) lacquer; (*Auto*) paint. **l~en** *vt* varnish. **l~ieren** *vt* varnish; (*spritzen*) spray. **L~schuhe** *mpl* patent-leather shoes

Lade *f* -,-n drawer

laden† *vt* load; (*Electr*) charge; (*Jur: vor-*) summons

Laden *m* -s,- shop, (*Amer*) store; (*Fenster-*) shutter. **L~dieb** *m* shop-lifter. **L~diebstahl** *m* shop-lifting. **L~schluß** (**L~schluss**) *m* [shop] closing-time. **L~tisch** *m* counter

Laderaum *m* (*Naut*) hold

lädieren *vt* damage

Ladung *f* -,-en load; (*Naut, Aviat*) cargo; (*elektrische, Spreng-*) charge; (*Jur: Vor-*) summons

Lage *f* -,-n position; (*Situation*) situation; (*Schicht*) layer; (*fam: Runde*) round; **nicht in der L~ sein** not be in a position (**zu** to)

Lager *nt* -s,- camp; (*L~haus*) warehouse; (*Vorrat*) stock; (*Techn*) bearing; (*Erz-, Ruhe-*) bed; (*eines Tieres*) lair; **[nicht] auf L~** [not] in stock. **L~haus** *nt* warehouse. **l~n** *vt* store; (*legen*) lay; **sich l~n** settle; (*sich legen*) lie down □ *vi* (*haben*) camp; (*liegen*) lie; (*Waren:*) be stored. **L~raum** *m* store-room. **L~stätte** *f* (*Geol*) deposit. **L~ung** *f* - storage

Lagune *f* -,-n lagoon

lahm *a* lame; **l~ legen** (*fig*) paralyse. **l~en** *vi* (*haben*) be lame

lähmen *vt* paralyse

lahmlegen *vt sep* (NEW) **lahm legen**, *s.* **lahm**

Lähmung *f* -,-en paralysis

Laib *m* -[e]s,-e loaf

Laich *m* -[e]s (*Zool*) spawn. **l~en** *vi* (*haben*) spawn

Laie *m* -n,-n layman; (*Theat*) amateur. **l~nhaft** *a* amateurish. **L~nprediger** *m* lay preacher

Lake *f* -,-n brine

Laken *nt* -s,- sheet

lakonisch *a* laconic, *adv* -ally

Lakritze *f* - liquorice

lallen *vt/i* (*haben*) mumble; (*Baby:*) babble

Lametta *nt* -s tinsel

Lamm *nt* -[e]s,-er lamb

Lampe *f* -,-n lamp; (*Decken-, Wand-*) light; (*Glüh-*) bulb. **L~nfieber** *nt* stage fright. **L~nschirm** *m* lampshade

Lampion /lamˈpi̯ɔŋ/ *m* -s,-s Chinese lantern

lancieren /lãˈsiːrən/ *vt* (*Comm*) launch

Land *nt* -[e]s,ˍer country; (*Fest-*) land; (*Bundes-*) state, Land; (*Aust*) province; **Stück L~** piece of land; **auf dem L~e** in the country; **an L~ gehen** (*Naut*) go ashore; **hier zu L~e = hierzulande.** **L~arbeiter** *m* agricultural worker. **L~ebahn** *f* runway. **l~einwärts** *adv* inland. **l~en** *vt/i* (*sein*) land; (*fam: gelangen*) end up

Ländereien *pl* estates

Länderspiel *nt* international

Landesteg *m* landing-stage

Landesverrat *m* treason

Land|karte *f* map. **l~läufig** *a* popular

ländlich *a* rural

Land|maschinen *fpl* agricultural machinery *sg.* **L~schaft** *f* -,-en scenery; (*Geog, Kunst*) landscape; (*Gegend*) country[side]. **l~schaftlich** *a* scenic; (*regional*) regional. **L~smann** *m* (*pl* -leute) fellow countryman, compatriot. **L~smännin** *f* -,-nen fellow countrywoman. **L~straße** *f* country road; (*Admin*) ≈ B road. **L~streicher** *m* -s,- tramp. **L~tag** *m* state/(*Aust*) provincial parliament

Landung *f* -,-en landing. **L~sbrücke** *f* landing-stage

Land|vermesser *m* -s,- surveyor. **L~weg** *m* country lane; **auf dem L~weg** overland. **L~wirt** *m* farmer. **L~wirtschaft** *f* agriculture; (*Hof*) farm. **l~wirtschaftlich** *a* agricultural

lang¹ *adv & prep* (+ *preceding acc or preceding an* + *dat*) along; **den** *od* **am Fluss l~** along the river

lang² *a* (**länger, längst**) long; (*groß*) tall; **seit l~em** for a long time □ *adv* **eine Stunde/Woche l~** for an hour/a week; **mein Leben l~** all my life. **l~ärmelig** *a* long-sleeved. **l~atmig** *a* long-winded. **l~e** *adv* a long time; (*schlafen*) late; **wie/zu l~e** how/too long; **schon l~e** [for] a long time; (*zurückliegend*) a long time ago; **so l~e wie möglich** as long as possible; **l~e nicht** not for a long time; (*bei weitem nicht*) nowhere near

Länge *f* -,-n length; (*Geog*) longitude; **der L~ nach** lengthways; (*liegen, fallen*) full length

langen *vt* hand (*dat* to) □ *vi* (*haben*) reach (**an etw** *acc* sth; **nach** for); (*genügen*) be enough

Läng|engrad *m* degree of longitude. **L~enmaß** *nt* linear measure. **l~er** *a & adv* longer; (*längere Zeit*) [for] some time

Langeweile *f* - boredom; **L~ haben** be bored

lang|fristig *a* long-term; ⟨*Vorhersage*⟩ long-range. **l~jährig** *a* long-standing; ⟨*Erfahrung*⟩ long. **l~lebig** *a* long-lived

länglich *a* oblong; **l~ rund** oval

langmütig *a* long-suffering

längs *adv* & *prep* (+ *gen/dat*) along; ⟨*der Länge nach*⟩ lengthways

lang|sam *a* slow, *adv* -ly. **L~samkeit** *f* - slowness. **L~schläfer(in)** *m(f)* (*fam*) late riser. **L~schrift** *f* longhand

längst *adv* [**schon**] **l~** for a long time; ⟨*zurückliegend*⟩ a long time ago; **l~ nicht** nowhere near

Lang|strecken- *pref* long-distance; ⟨*Mil, Aviat*⟩ long-range. **l~weilen** *vt* bore; **sich l~weilen** be bored. **l~weilig** *a* boring, *adv* -ly. **L~welle** *f* long wave. **l~wierig** *a* lengthy

Lanze *f* -,-n lance

Lappalie /la'pa:ljə/ *f* -,-n trifle

Lappen *m* -s,- cloth; ⟨*Anat*⟩ lobe

läppisch *a* silly

Lapsus *m* -,- slip

Lärche *f* -,-n larch

Lärm *m* -s noise. **l~en** *vi* (*haben*) make a noise. **l~end** *a* noisy

Larve /'larfə/ *f* -,-n larva; ⟨*Maske*⟩ mask

lasch *a* listless; ⟨*schlaff*⟩ limp; ⟨*fade*⟩ insipid

Lasche *f* -,-n tab; ⟨*Verschluss-*⟩ flap; ⟨*Zunge*⟩ tongue

Laser /'le:-, 'la:zɐ/ *m* -s,- laser

lassen† *vt* leave; ⟨*zulassen*⟩ let; **jdm etw l~** let s.o. keep sth; **sein Leben l~** lose one's life; **etw [sein** *od* **bleiben] l~** not do sth; ⟨*aufhören*⟩ stop [doing] sth; **lass das!** stop it! **jdn schlafen/gewinnen l~** let s.o. sleep/win; **jdn warten l~** keep s.o. waiting; **etw machen/reparieren l~** have sth done/repaired; **etw verschwinden l~** make sth disappear; **sich [leicht] biegen/öffnen l~** bend/open [easily]; **sich gut waschen l~** wash well; **es lässt sich nicht leugnen** it is undeniable; **lasst uns gehen!** let's go!

lässig *a* casual, *adv* -ly. **L~keit** *f* - casualness

Lasso *nt* -s,-s lasso

Last *f* -,-en load; ⟨*Gewicht*⟩ weight; ⟨*fig*⟩ burden; **L~en** charges; ⟨*Steuern*⟩ taxes; **jdm zur L~ fallen** be a burden on s.o. **L~auto** *nt* lorry. **l~en** *vi* (*haben*) weigh heavily/⟨*liegen*⟩ rest (**auf** + *dat* on). **L~enaufzug** *m* goods lift

Laster¹ *m* -s,- (*fam*) lorry, (*Amer*) truck

Laster² *nt* -s,- vice. **l~haft** *a* depraved; ⟨*zügellos*⟩ dissolute

läster|lich *a* blasphemous. **l~n** *vt* blaspheme ▫ *vi* (*haben*) make disparaging remarks (**über** + *acc* about). **L~ung** *f* -,-en blasphemy

lästig *a* troublesome; **l~ sein/werden** be/become a nuisance

Last|kahn *m* barge. **L~[kraft]wagen** *m* lorry, (*Amer*) truck. **L~zug** *m* lorry with trailer[s]

Latein *nt* -[s] Latin. **L~amerika** *nt* Latin America. **l~isch** *a* Latin

latent *a* latent

Laterne *f* -,-n lantern; ⟨*Straßen-*⟩ street lamp. **L~npfahl** *m* lamp-post

latschen *vi* (*sein*) (*fam*) traipse; ⟨*schlurfen*⟩ shuffle

Latte *f* -,-n slat; ⟨*Tor-, Hoch- sprung-*⟩ bar

Latz *m* -es,¨e bib

Lätzchen *nt* -s,- [baby's] bib

Latzhose *f* dungarees *pl*

lau *a* lukewarm; ⟨*mild*⟩ mild

Laub *nt* -[e]s leaves *pl*; ⟨*L~werk*⟩ foliage. **L~baum** *m* deciduous tree

Laube *f* -,-n summer-house; ⟨*gewachsen*⟩ arbour. **L~ngang** *m* pergola; ⟨*Archit*⟩ arcades *pl*

Laub|säge *f* fretsaw. **L~wald** *m* deciduous forest

Lauch *m* -[e]s leeks *pl*

Lauer *f* **auf der L~ liegen** lie in wait. **l~n** *vi* (*haben*) lurk; **l~n auf** (+ *acc*) lie in wait for

Lauf *m* -[e]s, Läufe run; ⟨*Laufen*⟩ running; ⟨*Verlauf*⟩ course; ⟨*Wett-*⟩ race; ⟨*Sport: Durchgang*⟩ heat; ⟨*Gewehr-*⟩ barrel; **im L~[e]** (+ *gen*) in the course of. **L~bahn** *f* career. **l~en†** *vi* (*sein*) run; ⟨*zu Fuß gehen*⟩ walk; ⟨*gelten*⟩ be valid; **Ski/Schlittschuh l~en** ski/skate; **jdn l~en lassen** (*fam*) let s.o. go. **l~end** *a* running; ⟨*gegenwärtig*⟩ current; ⟨*regelmäßig*⟩ regular; **l~ende Nummer** serial number; **auf dem L~enden (l~enden) sein/jdn auf dem L~enden (l~enden) halten** be/keep s.o. up to date ▫ *adv* continually. **l~enlassen†** *vt sep* ⟨NEW⟩ **l~en lassen,** *s.* **laufen**

Läufer *m* -s,- (*Person, Teppich*) runner; ⟨*Schach*⟩ bishop

Lauf|gitter *nt* play-pen. **L~masche** *f* ladder. **L~rolle** *f* castor. **L~schritt** *m* **im L~schritt** at a run; ⟨*Mil*⟩ at the double. **L~stall** *m* play-pen. **L~zettel** *m* circular

Lauge *f* -,-n soapy water

Laun|e *f* -,-n mood; ⟨*Einfall*⟩ whim; **guter L~e sein, gute L~e haben** be in a good mood. **l~enhaft** *a* capricious. **l~isch** *a* moody

Laus f -,Läuse louse; (*Blatt-*) greenfly. **L~bub** m (*fam*) rascal

lauschen vi (*haben*) listen; (*heimlich*) eavesdrop

lausig a (*fam*) lousy □ adv terribly

laut a loud, adv -ly; (*geräuschvoll*) noisy, adv -ily; **l~ lesen** read aloud; **l~er stellen** turn up □ prep (+ gen/dat) according to. **L~** m **-es,-e** sound

Laute f -,-n (*Mus*) lute

lauten vi (*haben*) ⟨*Text:*⟩ run, read; **auf jds Namen l~** be in s.o.'s name

läuten vt/i (*haben*) ring

lauter a pure; (*ehrlich*) honest; ⟨*Wahrheit*⟩ plain □ a inv sheer; (*nichts als*) nothing but. **L~keit** f - integrity

läutern vt purify

laut|hals adv at the top of one's voice; ⟨*lachen*⟩ out loud. **l~los** a silent, adv -ly; ⟨*Stille*⟩ hushed. **L~schrift** f phonetics pl. **L~sprecher** m loudspeaker. **l~stark** a vociferous, adv -ly. **L~stärke** f volume

lauwarm a lukewarm

Lava f -,-ven lava

Lavendel m -s lavender

lavieren vi (*haben*) manœuvre

Lawine f -,-n avalanche

lax a lax. **L~heit** f - laxity

Lazarett nt -[e]s,-e military hospital

leasen /'li:sən/ vt rent

Lebehoch nt cheer

leben vt/i (*haben*) live (**von** on); **leb wohl!** farewell! **L~** nt -s,- life, (*Treiben*) bustle; **am L~** alive. **l~d** a living

lebendig a live; (*lebhaft*) lively; (*anschaulich*) vivid, adv -ly; **l~ sein** be alive. **L~keit** f - liveliness; vividness

Lebens|abend m old age. **L~alter** nt age. **L~art** f manners pl. **l~fähig** a viable. **L~gefahr** f mortal danger; **in L~gefahr** in mortal danger; ⟨*Patient*⟩ critically ill. **l~gefährlich** a extremely dangerous; ⟨*Verletzung*⟩ critical □ adv critically. **L~größe** f life-size; **in L~größe** life-sized. **L~haltungskosten** pl cost of living sg. **l~lang** a lifelong. **l~länglich** a life ... □ adv for life. **L~lauf** m curriculum vitae. **L~mittel** ntpl food sg. **L~mittelgeschäft** nt food shop. **L~mittelhändler** m grocer. **l~notwendig** a vital. **L~retter** m rescuer; (*beim Schwimmen*) life-guard. **L~standard** m standard of living. **L~unterhalt** m livelihood; **seinen L~unterhalt verdienen** earn one's living. **L~versicherung** f life assurance. **L~wandel** m conduct. **l~wichtig** a vital. **L~zeichen** nt sign of life. **L~zeit** f **auf L~zeit** for life

Leber f -,-n liver. **L~fleck** m mole. **L~wurst** f liver sausage

Lebe|wesen nt living being. **L~wohl** nt -s,-s & -e farewell

leb|haft a lively; ⟨*Farbe*⟩ vivid. **L~haftigkeit** f - liveliness. **L~kuchen** m gingerbread. **l~los** a lifeless. **L~tag** m **mein/dein L~tag** all my/your life. **L~zeiten** fpl **zu jds L~zeiten** in s.o.'s lifetime

leck a leaking. **L~** nt -s,-s leak. **l~en**[1] vi (*haben*) leak

lecken[2] vi (*haben*) lick

lecker a tasty. **L~bissen** m delicacy. **L~ei** f -,-en sweet

Leder nt -s,- leather. **l~n** a leather; (*wie Leder*) leathery

ledig a single. **l~lich** adv merely

Lee f & nt - **nach Lee** (*Naut*) to leeward

leer a empty; (*unbesetzt*) vacant; **l~ laufen** (*Auto*) idle. **L~e** f - emptiness; (*leerer Raum*) void. **l~en** vt empty; **sich l~en** empty. **L~lauf** m (*Auto*) neutral. **L~ung** f -,-en (*Post*) collection

legal a legal, adv -ly. **l~isieren** vt legalize. **L~ität** f - legality

Legas|thenie f - dyslexia. **L~theniker** m -s,- dyslexic

legen vt put; (*hin-, ver-*) lay; set ⟨*Haare*⟩; **Eier l~** lay eggs; **sich l~** lie down; ⟨*Staub:*⟩ settle; (*nachlassen*) subside

legendär a legendary

Legende f -,-n legend

leger /le'ʒeːɐ̯/ a casual, adv -ly

legier|en vt alloy; (*Culin*) thicken. **L~ung** f -,-en alloy

Legion f -,-en legion

Legislative f - legislature

legitim a legitimate, adv -ly. **l~ieren (sich)** vr prove one's identity. **L~ität** f - legitimacy

Lehm m -s clay. **l~ig** a clayey

Lehn|e f -,-n (*Rücken-*) back; (*Arm-*) arm. **l~en** vt lean (**an** + acc against); **sich l~en** lean (**an** + acc against) □ vi (*haben*) be leaning (**an** + dat against). **L~sessel, L~stuhl** m armchair

Lehr|buch nt textbook. **L~e** f -,-n apprenticeship; (*Anschauung*) doctrine; (*Theorie*) theory; (*Wissenschaft*) science; (*Ratschlag*) advice; (*Erfahrung*) lesson; **jdm eine L~e erteilen** (*fig*) teach s.o. a lesson. **l~en** vt/i (*haben*) teach. **L~er** m -s,- teacher; (*Fahr-, Ski-*) instructor. **L~erin** f -,-nen teacher. **L~erzimmer** nt staff-room. **L~fach** nt (*Sch*) subject. **L~gang** m course. **L~kraft** f teacher. **L~ling** m -s,-e apprentice; (*Auszubildender*) trainee. **L~plan** m syllabus. **l~**

reich *a* instructive. **L~stelle** *f* apprenticeship. **L~stuhl** *m* (*Univ*) chair. **L~zeit** *f* apprenticeship

Leib *m* **-es,-er** body; (*Bauch*) belly. **L~es-erziehung** *f* (*Sch*) physical education. **L~eskraft** *f* **aus L~eskräften** as hard/(*schreien*) loud as one can. **L~gericht** *nt* favourite dish. **l~haftig** *a* **der l~haftige Satan** the devil incarnate □ *adv* in the flesh. **l~lich** *a* physical; (*blutsverwandt*) real, natural. **L~speise** *f* = **L~gericht**. **L~wache** *f* (*coll*) bodyguard. **L~wächter** *m* bodyguard. **L~wäsche** *f* underwear

Leiche *f* **-,-n** [dead] body; corpse. **L~nbegängnis** *nt* **-ses,-se** funeral. **L~nbestatter** *m* **-s,-** undertaker. **l~nblass** (**l~nblaß**) *a* deathly pale. **L~nhalle** *f* mortuary. **L~nwagen** *m* hearse. **L~nzug** *m* funeral procession, cortège

Leichnam *m* **-s,-e** [dead] body

leicht *a* light, *adv* -ly; (*Stoff, Anzug*) lightweight; (*gering*) slight, *adv* -ly; (*mühelos*) easy, *adv* -ily; **jdm l~ fallen** be easy for s.o.; **etw l~ machen** make sth easy (**dat** for); **es sich (*dat*) l~ machen** take the easy way out; **etw l~ nehmen** (*fig*) take sth lightly. **L~athletik** *f* [track and field] athletics *sg*. **l~fallen†** *vi sep* (*sein*) NEW **l~ fallen, s. leicht**. **l~fertig** *a* thoughtless, *adv* -ly; (*vorschnell*) rash, *adv* -ly; (*frivol*) frivolous, *adv* -ly. **L~gewicht** *nt* (*Boxen*) lightweight. **l~gläubig** *a* gullible. **l~hin** *adv* casually. **L~igkeit** *f* lightness; (*Mühelosigkeit*) ease; (*L~sein*) easiness; **mit L~igkeit** with ease. **l~lebig** *a* happy-go-lucky. **l~machen** *vt sep* NEW **l~ machen, s. leicht**. **l~nehmen†** *vt sep* NEW **l~ nehmen, s. leicht**. **L~sinn** *m* carelessness; recklessness; (*Frivolität*) frivolity. **l~sinnig** *a* careless, *adv* -ly; (*unvorsichtig*) reckless, *adv* -ly; (*frivol*) frivolous, *adv* -ly

Leid *nt* **-[e]s** sorrow, grief; (*Böses*) harm; **es tut mir L~** I am sorry; **er tut mir L~** I feel sorry for him; **jdm etw zu L~e tun = jdm etw zuleide tun, s. zuleide**. **l~** *a* **jdn/etw l~ sein/werden** be/get tired of s.o./sth; **jdm l~ tun** NEW **jdm L~ tun, s. Leid**

Leide|form *f* passive. **l~n†** *vt/i* (*haben*) suffer (**an** + *dat* from); **jdn [gut] l~n können** like s.o.; **jdn/etw nicht l~n können** dislike s.o./sth. **L~n** *nt* **-s,-** suffering; (*Med*) complaint; (*Krankheit*) disease. **l~nd** *a* suffering; **l~nd sein** be in poor health. **L~nschaft** *f* **-,-en** passion. **l~nschaftlich** *a* passionate, *adv* -ly

leid|er *adv* unfortunately; **l~er ja/nicht** I'm afraid so/not. **l~ig** *a* wretched,

l~lich *a* tolerable, *adv* -bly. **L~tragende(r)** *m/f* person who suffers; (*Trauernde*) mourner. **L~wesen** *nt* **zu meinem L~wesen** to my regret

Leier *f* **-,-n die alte L~** (*fam*) the same old story. **L~kasten** *m* barrel-organ. **l~n** *vt/i* (*haben*) wind; (*herunter-*) drone out

Leih|bibliothek *f*, **L~bücherei** *f* lending library. **L~e** *f* **-,-n** loan. **l~en†** *vt* lend; **sich** (*dat*) **etw l~en** borrow sth. **L~gabe** *f* loan. **L~gebühr** *f* rental; (*für Bücher*) lending charge. **L~haus** *nt* pawnshop. **L~wagen** *m* hire-car. **l~weise** *adv* on loan

Leim *m* **-s** glue. **l~en** *vt* glue

Leine *f* **-,-n** rope; (*Wäsche-*) line; (*Hunde-*) lead, leash

Lein|en *nt* **-s** linen. **l~en** *a* linen. **l~tuch** *nt* sheet. **l~wand** *f* linen; (*Kunst*) canvas; (*Film-*) screen

leise *a* quiet, *adv* -ly; (*Stimme, Musik, Berührung*) soft, *adv* -ly; (*schwach*) faint, *adv* -ly; (*leicht*) light, *adv* -ly; **l~r stellen** turn down

Leiste *f* **-,-n** strip; (*Holz-*) batten; (*Zier-*) moulding; (*Anat*) groin

Leisten *m* **-s,-** [shoemaker's] last

leist|en *vt* achieve, accomplish; **sich** (*dat*) **etw l~en** treat oneself to sth; (*fam: anstellen*) get up to sth; **ich kann es mir nicht l~en** I can't afford it. **L~ung** *f* **-,-en** achievement; (*Sport, Techn*) performance; (*Produktion*) output; (*Zahlung*) payment. **L~ungsfähig** *a* efficient. **L~ungsfähigkeit** *f* efficiency

Leit|artikel *m* leader, editorial. **L~bild** *nt* (*fig*) model. **l~en** *vt* run, manage; (*an-/hinführen*) lead; (*Mus, Techn, Phys*) conduct; (*lenken, schicken*) direct. **l~end** *a* leading; (*Posten*) executive

Leiter[1] *f* **-,-n** ladder

Leit|er[2] *m* **-s,-** director; (*Comm*) manager; (*Führer*) leader; (*Sch*) head; (*Mus, Phys*) conductor. **L~erin** *f* **-,-nen** director; manageress; leader; head. **L~faden** *m* manual. **L~kegel** *m* [traffic] cone. **L~planke** *f* crash barrier. **L~spruch** *m* motto. **L~ung** *f* **-,-en** (*Führung*) direction; (*Comm*) management; (*Aufsicht*) control; (*Electr: Schnur*) lead, flex; (*Kabel*) cable; (*Telefon-*) line; (*Rohr-*) pipe; (*Haupt-*) main. **L~ungswasser** *nt* tap water

Lektion /-'tsjo:n/ *f* **-,-en** lesson

Lekt|or *m* **-s,-en** /-'to:rən/, **L~orin** *f* **-,-nen** (*Univ*) assistant lecturer; (*Verlags-*) editor. **L~üre** *f* **-,-n** reading matter; (*Lesen*) reading

Lende *f* **-,-n** loin

lenk|bar *a* steerable; (*fügsam*) tractable. **l~en** *vt* guide; (*steuern*) steer; (*Aust*) drive; (*regeln*) control; **jds Aufmerksamkeit auf sich** (*acc*) **l~en** attract s.o.'s attention. **L~er** *m* -s,- driver; (*L~stange*) handlebars *pl*. **L~rad** *nt* steering-wheel. **L~stange** *f* handlebars *pl*. **L~ung** *f* - steering

Leopard *m* -en,-en leopard

Lepra *f* - leprosy

Lerche *f* -,-n lark

lernen *vt/i* (*haben*) learn; (*für die Schule*) study; **schwimmen l~** learn to swim

lesbar *a* readable; (*leserlich*) legible

Lesb|ierin /'lɛsbjərɪn/ *f* -,-nen lesbian. **l~isch** *a* lesbian

Lese *f* -,-n harvest. **L~buch** *nt* reader. **l~n†** *vt/i* (*haben*) read; (*Univ*) lecture ◻ *vt* pick, gather. **L~n** *nt* -s reading. **L~r(in)** *m* -s,- (*f* -,-nen) reader. **L~ratte** *f* (*fam*) bookworm. **l~rlich** *a* legible, *adv* -bly. **L~zeichen** *nt* bookmark

Lesung *f* -,-en reading

lethargisch *a* lethargic, *adv* -ally

Lettland *nt* -s Latvia

letzt|e(r,s) *a* last; (*neueste*) latest; **in l~er Zeit** recently; **l~en Endes** in the end; **er kam als L~er (l~er)** he arrived last. **l~emal** *adv* **das l~emal/zum l~enmal** NEW **das l~e Mal/zum l~en Mal**, *s.* **Mal**[1]. **l~ens** *adv* recently; (*zuletzt*) lastly. **l~ere(r,s)** *a* the latter; **der/die/das L~ere (l~ere)** the latter

Leucht|e *f* -,-n light. **l~en** *vi* (*haben*) shine. **l~end** *a* shining. **L~er** *m* -s,- candlestick. **L~feuer** *nt* beacon. **L~kugel, L~rakete** *f* flare. **L~reklame** *f* neon sign. **L~[stoff]röhre** *f* fluorescent tube. **L~turm** *m* lighthouse. **L~zifferblatt** *nt* luminous dial

leugnen *vt* deny

Leukämie *f* - leukaemia

Leumund *m* -s reputation

Leute *pl* people; (*Mil*) men; (*Arbeiter*) workers

Leutnant *m* -s,-s second lieutenant

leutselig *a* affable, *adv* -bly

Levkoje /lɛfˈkoːjə/ *f* -,-n stock

Lexikon *nt* -s,-ka encyclopaedia; (*Wörterbuch*) dictionary

Libanon (der) -s Lebanon

Libelle *f* -,-n dragonfly; (*Techn*) spirit-level; (*Haarspange*) slide

liberal *a* (*Pol*) Liberal

Libyen *nt* -s Libya

Licht *nt* -[e]s,-er light; (*Kerze*) candle; **L~ machen** turn on the light; **hinters L~ führen** (*fam*) dupe. **l~** *a* bright; (*Med*) lucid; (*spärlich*) sparse. **L~bild** *nt* [passport] photograph; (*Dia*) slide. **L~bildervortrag** *m* slide lecture. **L~blick** *m* (*fig*)

ray of hope. **l~en** *vt* thin out; **den Anker l~en** (*Naut*) weigh anchor; **sich l~en** become less dense; (*Haare:*) thin. **L~hupe** *f* headlight flasher; **die L~hupe betätigen** flash one's headlights. **L~maschine** *f* dynamo. **L~schalter** *m* light-switch. **L~ung** *f* -,-en clearing

Lid *nt* -[e]s,-er [eye]lid. **L~schatten** *m* eye-shadow

lieb *a* dear; (*nett*) nice; (*artig*) good; **jdn l~ haben** be fond of s.o.; (*lieben*) love s.o.; **jdn l~ gewinnen** grow fond of s.o.; **es ist mir l~** I'm glad (*dass* that); **es wäre mir l~er** I should prefer it (*wenn* if). **l~äugeln** *vi* (*haben*) **l~äugeln mit** fancy; toy with (*Gedanken*)

Liebe *f* -,-n love. **L~lei** *f* -,-en flirtation. **l~n** *vt* love; (*mögen*) like; **sich l~n** love each other; (*körperlich*) make love. **l~nd** *a* loving ◻ *adv* **etw l~nd gern tun** love to do sth. **l~nswert** *a* lovable. **l~nswürdig** *a* kind. **l~nswürdigerweise** *adv* very kindly. **L~nswürdigkeit** *f* -,-en kindness

lieber *adv* rather; (*besser*) better; **l~ mögen** like better; **ich trinke l~ Tee** I prefer tea

Liebes|brief *m* love letter. **L~dienst** *m* favour. **L~geschichte** *f* love story. **L~kummer** *m* heartache; **L~kummer haben** be depressed over an unhappy love-affair. **L~paar** *nt* [pair of] lovers *pl*

lieb|evoll *a* loving, *adv* -ly, (*zärtlich*) affectionate, *adv* -ly; **l~gewinnen†** *vt* sep NEW **l~ gewinnen**, *s.* **lieb**. **l~haben†** *vt* sep NEW **l~ haben**, *s.* **lieb**. **L~haber** *m* -s,- lover; (*Sammler*) collector. **L~haberei** *f* -,-en hobby. **l~kosen** *vt* caress. **L~kosung** *f* -,-en caress. **l~lich** *a* lovely; (*sanft*) gentle; (*süß*) sweet. **L~ling** *m* -s,-e darling; (*Bevorzugte*) favourite. **L~lings-** *pref* favourite. **l~los** *a* loveless; (*Eltern*) uncaring; (*unfreundlich*) unkind ◻ *adv* unkindly; (*ohne Sorgfalt*) without care. **L~schaft** *f* -,-en [love] affair. **l~ste(r,s)** *a* dearest; (*bevorzugt*) favourite ◻ *adv* **am l~sten** best [of all]; **jdn/etw am l~sten mögen** like s.o./sth best [of all]; **ich hätte am l~sten geweint** I felt like crying. **L~ste(r)** *m/f* beloved; (*Schatz*) sweetheart

Lied *nt* -[e]s,-er song

liederlich *a* slovenly; (*unordentlich*) untidy; (*ausschweifend*) dissolute. **L~keit** *f* - slovenliness; untidiness; dissoluteness

Lieferant *m* -en,-en supplier

liefer|bar *a* (*Comm*) available. **l~n** *vt* supply; (*zustellen*) deliver; (*hervorbringen*) yield. **L~ung** *f* -,-en delivery; (*Sendung*) consignment; (*per Schiff*) shipment. **L~wagen** *m* delivery van

Liege *f* -,-n couch. **l~n†** *vi* (*haben*) lie; (*gelegen sein*) be situated; **l~n bleiben** remain lying [there]; (*im Bett*) stay in bed; ⟨*Ding:*⟩ be left; ⟨*Schnee:*⟩ settle; ⟨*Arbeit:*⟩ remain undone; (*zurückgelassen werden*) be left behind; (*Panne haben*) break down; **l~n lassen** leave [lying there]; (*zurücklassen*) leave behind; (*nicht fortführen*) leave undone; **l~n an** (+ *dat*) (*fig*) be due to; (*abhängen*) depend on; **jdm [nicht] l~n** [not] suit s.o.; (*ansprechen*) [not] appeal to s.o.; **mir liegt viel/nicht daran** it is very/ not important to me. **l~nbleiben†** *vi sep* (*sein*) (NEW) **l~n bleiben**, s. **liegen. l~nlassen†** *vt sep* (NEW) **l~n lassen**, s. **liegen. L~sitz** *m* reclining seat. **L~stuhl** *m* deck-chair. **L~stütz** *m* -es,-e press-up, (*Amer*) push-up. **L~wagen** *m* couchette car. **L~wiese** *f* lawn for sunbathing

Lift *m* -[e]s,-e & -s lift, (*Amer*) elevator

Liga *f* -,-gen league

Likör *m* -s,-e liqueur

lila *inv a* mauve; (*dunkel*) purple

Lilie /ˈliːli̯ə/ *f* -,-n lily

Liliputaner(in) *m* -s,- (*f* -,-nen) dwarf

Limo *f* -,-[s] (*fam*), **L~nade** *f* -,-n fizzy drink, (*Amer*) soda; (*Zitronen-*) lemonade

Limousine /limuˈziːnə/ *f* -,-n saloon, (*Amer*) sedan; (*mit Trennscheibe*) limousine

lind *a* mild; (*sanft*) gentle

Linde *f* -,-n lime tree

linder|n *vt* relieve, ease. **L~ung** *f* - relief

Line|al *nt* -s,-e ruler. **l~ar** *a* linear

Linguistik *f* - linguistics *sg*

Linie /-i̯ə/ *f* -,-n line; (*Zweig*) branch; (*Bus-*) route; **L~ 4** number 4 [bus/tram]; **in erster L~** primarily. **L~nflug** *m* scheduled flight. **L~nrichter** *m* linesman

lin[i]iert *a* lined, ruled

Link|e *f* -n,-n left side; (*Hand*) left hand; (*Boxen*) left; **die L~e** (*Pol*) the left; **zu meiner L~en** on my left. **l~e(r,s)** *a* left; (*Pol*) left-wing; **l~e Seite** left[-hand] side; (*von Stoff*) wrong side; **l~e Masche** purl. **l~isch** *a* awkward, *adv* -ly

links *adv* on the left; (*bei Stoff*) on the wrong side; (*verkehrt*) inside out; **von/ nach l~** from/to the left; **l~ stricken** purl. **L~händer(in)** *m* -s,- (*f* -,-nen) lefthander. **l~händig** *a & adv* left-handed. **L~verkehr** *m* driving on the left

Linoleum /-leʊm/ *nt* -s lino, linoleum

Linse *f* -,-n lens; (*Bot*) lentil

Lippe *f* -,-n lip. **L~nstift** *m* lipstick

Liquid|ation /-ˈtsi̯oːn/ *f* -,-en liquidation. **l~ieren** *vt* liquidate

lispeln *vt*/*i* (*haben*) lisp

List *f* -,-en trick, ruse; (*Listigkeit*) cunning

Liste *f* -,-n list

listig *a* cunning, *adv* -ly, crafty, *adv* -ily

Litanei *f* -,-en litany

Litauen *nt* -s Lithuania

Liter *m & nt* -s,- litre

liter|arisch *a* literary. **L~atur** *f* - literature

Litfaßsäule *f* advertising pillar

Liturgie *f* -,-n liturgy

Litze *f* -,-n braid; (*Electr*) flex

live /laif/ *adv* (*Radio, TV*) live

Lizenz *f* -,-en licence

Lkw /ɛlkaˈveː/ *m* -[s],-s = **Lastkraftwagen**

Lob *nt* -[e]s praise

Lobby /ˈlɔbi/ *f* - (*Pol*) lobby

loben *vt* praise. **l~swert** *a* praiseworthy, laudable

löblich *a* praiseworthy

Lobrede *f* eulogy

Loch *nt* -[e]s,-̈er hole. **l~en** *vt* punch a hole/holes in; punch ⟨*Fahrkarte*⟩. **L~er** *m* -s,- punch

löcher|ig *a* full of holes. **l~n** *vt* (*fam*) pester

Locke *f* -,-n curl. **l~n¹** *vt* curl; **sich l~n** curl

locken² *vt* lure, entice; (*reizen*) tempt. **l~d** *a* tempting

Lockenwickler *m* -s,- curler; (*Rolle*) roller

locker *a* loose, *adv* -ly; ⟨*Seil:*⟩ slack; ⟨*Erde, Kuchen*⟩ light; (*zwanglos*) casual; (*zu frei*) lax; (*unmoralisch*) loose. **l~n** *vt* loosen; slacken ⟨*Seil, Zügel*⟩; break up ⟨*Boden*⟩; relax ⟨*Griff*⟩; **sich l~n** become loose; ⟨*Seil:*⟩ slacken; (*sich entspannen*) relax. **L~ungsübungen** *fpl* limbering-up exercises

lockig *a* curly

Lock|mittel *nt* bait. **L~ung** *f* -,-en lure; (*Versuchung*) temptation. **L~vogel** *m* decoy

Loden *m* -s (*Tex*) loden

lodern *vi* (*haben*) blaze

Löffel *m* -s,- spoon; (*L~ voll*) spoonful. **l~n** *vt* spoon up

Logarithmus *m* -,-men logarithm

Logbuch *nt* (*Naut*) log-book

Loge /ˈloːʒə/ *f* -,-n lodge; (*Theat*) box

Logierbesuch /loˈʒiːɐ̯-/ *m* house guest/guests *pl*

Log|ik *f* - logic. **l~isch** *a* logical, *adv* -ly

Logo *nt* -s,-s logo

Lohn *m* -[e]s,-̈e wages *pl*, pay; (*fig*) reward. **L~empfänger** *m* wage-earner. **l~en** *vi/r* (*haben*) [sich] **l~en** be worth it *or* worth

while □ *vt* be worth; **jdm etw l∼en re-**
ward s.o. for sth. **l∼end** *a* worthwhile;
(befriedigend) rewarding. **L∼erhöhung** *f*
[pay] rise; *(Amer)* raise. **L∼steuer** *f* income tax

Lok *f* -,-s *(fam)* = **Lokomotive**

Lokal *nt* -s,-e restaurant; *(Trink-)* bar. **l∼**
a local. **l∼sieren** *vt* locate; *(begrenzen)*
localize

Lokomotiv|e *f* -,-n engine, locomotive.
L∼führer *m* engine driver

London *nt* -s London. **L∼er** *a* London ...
□ *m* -s,- Londoner

Lorbeer *m* -s,-en laurel; **echter L∼** bay.
L∼blatt *nt (Culin)* bay-leaf

Lore *f* -,-n *(Rail)* truck

Los *nt* -es,-e lot; *(Lotterie-)* ticket; *(Schick-*
sal) fate; **das große Los ziehen** hit the
jackpot

los *pred a* **los sein** be loose; **jdn/etw los**
sein be rid of s.o./sth; **was ist [mit ihm]**
los? what's the matter [with him]? □ *adv*
los! go on! **Achtung, fertig, los!** ready,
steady, go!

lösbar *a* soluble

losbinden† *vt sep* untie

Lösch|blatt *nt* sheet of blotting-paper. **l∼**
vt put out, extinguish; quench ⟨Durst⟩; blot
⟨Tinte⟩; *(tilgen)* cancel; *(streichen)* delete;
erase ⟨Aufnahme⟩

löschen² *vt (Naut)* unload

Lösch|fahrzeug *nt* fire-engine. **L∼gerät**
nt fire extinguisher. **L∼papier** *nt* blotting-paper

lose *a* loose, *adv* -ly

Lösegeld *nt* ransom

losen *vt (haben)* draw lots *(um* for)

lösen *vt* undo; *(lockern)* loosen; *(entfernen)*
detach; *(klären)* solve; *(auflösen)* dissolve;
cancel ⟨Vertrag⟩; break off ⟨Beziehung,
Verlobung⟩; *(kaufen)* buy; **sich l∼** come
off; *(sich trennen)* detach oneself/itself;
(lose werden) come undone; *(sich ent-*
spannen) relax; *(sich klären)* resolve itself;
(sich auflösen) dissolve

los|fahren† *vi sep (sein)* start; ⟨Auto:⟩
drive off; **l∼fahren auf** *(+ acc)* head for;
(fig: angreifen) go for. **l∼gehen**† *vi sep*
(sein) set off; *(fam: anfangen)* start; *(fam:*
abgehen) come off; ⟨Bombe, Gewehr:⟩ go
off; **l∼gehen auf** *(+ acc)* head for; *(fig:*
angreifen) go for. **l∼kommen**† *vi sep*
(sein) get away *(von* from); **l∼kommen**
auf *(+ acc)* come towards. **l∼lachen** *vi*
sep *(haben)* burst out laughing. **l∼lassen**†
vt sep let go of; *(freilassen)* release

löslich *a* soluble

los|lösen *vt sep* detach; **sich l∼lösen** be-
come detached; *(fig)* break away *(von*

from). **l∼machen** *vt sep* detach; *(los-*
binden) untie; **sich l∼machen** free one-
self/itself. **l∼platzen** *vi sep (sein) (fam)*
burst out laughing. **l∼reißen**† *vt sep* tear
off; **sich l∼reißen** break free; *(fig)* tear
oneself away. **l∼sagen (sich)** *vr sep* renounce **(von etw** sth). **l∼schicken** *vt sep*
send off. **l∼sprechen**† *vt sep* absolve **(von**
from). **l∼steuern** *vi sep (sein)* head **(auf**
+ acc for)

Losung *f* -,-en *(Pol)* slogan; *(Mil)*
password

Lösung *f* -,-en solution. **L∼smittel** *nt*
solvent

los|werden† *vt sep* get rid of. **l∼ziehen**†
vi sep (sein) set off; **l∼ziehen gegen** *od*
über *(+ acc) (beschimpfen)* run down

Lot *nt* -[e]s,-e perpendicular; *(Blei-)*
plumb[-bob]; **im Lot sein** *(fig)* be all right.
l∼en *vt* plumb

löt|en *vt* solder. **L∼lampe** *f* blow-lamp,
(Amer) blowtorch. **L∼metall** *nt* solder

lotrecht *a* perpendicular, *adv* -ly

Lotse *m* -n,-n *(Naut)* pilot. **l∼n** *vt (Naut)*
pilot; *(fig)* guide

Lotterie *f* -,-n lottery

Lotto *nt* -s,-s lotto; *(Lotterie)* lottery

Löw|e *m* -n,-n lion; *(Astr)* Leo. **L∼enanteil**
m (fig) lion's share. **L∼enzahn** *m (Bot)*
dandelion. **L∼in** *f* -,-nen lioness

loyal /lɔa'ja:l/ *a* loyal. **L∼ität** *f* - loyalty

Luchs *m* -es,-e lynx

Lücke *f* -,-n gap. **L∼nbüßer** *m* -s,- stop-
gap. **l∼nhaft** *a* incomplete; ⟨Wissen⟩ patchy. **l∼nlos** *a* complete; ⟨Folge⟩ unbroken

Luder *nt* -s,- *(sl) (Frau)* bitch; **armes L∼**
poor wretch

Luft *f* -,-e air; **tief L∼ holen** take a deep
breath; **in die L∼ gehen** explode. **L∼an-**
griff *m* air raid. **L∼aufnahme** *f* aerial
photograph. **L∼ballon** *m* balloon.
L∼bild *nt* aerial photograph. **L∼blase** *f*
air bubble

Lüftchen *nt* -s,- breeze

luft|dicht *a* airtight. **L∼druck** *m* atmos-
pheric pressure

lüften *vt* air; raise ⟨Hut⟩; reveal
⟨Geheimnis⟩

Luft|fahrt *f* aviation. **L∼fahrt-**
gesellschaft *f* airline. **L∼gewehr** *nt* air-
gun. **L∼hauch** *m* breath of air. **l∼ig** *a*
airy; ⟨Kleid⟩ light. **L∼kissenfahrzeug** *nt*
hovercraft. **L∼krieg** *m* aerial warfare.
L∼kurort *m* climatic health resort.
l∼leer *a* **l∼leerer Raum** vacuum. **L∼li-**
nie *f* 100 km *a* **L∼linie** 100 km as the crow
flies. **L∼loch** *nt* air-hole; *(Aviat)* air pocket. **L∼matratze** *f* air-bed, inflatable mattress. **L∼pirat** *m* [aircraft] hijacker.
L∼post *f* airmail. **L∼pumpe** *f* air pump;

M

(*Fahrrad-*) bicycle-pump. **L∼röhre** *f* windpipe. **L∼schiff** *nt* airship. **L∼schlange** *f* [paper] streamer. **L∼schlösser** *ntpl* castles in the air. **L∼schutzbunker** *m* air-raid shelter

Lüftung *f* - ventilation

Luft|veränderung *f* change of air. **L∼waffe** *f* air force. **L∼weg** *m* **auf dem L∼weg** by air. **L∼zug** *m* draught

Lüg|e *f* -,-n lie. **l∼en†** *vt/i* (*haben*) lie. **L∼ner(in)** *m* -s,- (*f* -,-nen) liar. **l∼nerisch** *a* untruthful; ⟨*Person*⟩ untruthful

Luke *f* -,-n hatch; (*Dach-*) skylight

Lümmel *m* -s,- lout; (*fam: Schelm*) rascal. **l∼n (sich)** *vr* loll

Lump *m* -en,-en scoundrel. **L∼en** *m* -s,- rag; **in L∼en** in rags. **l∼en** *vt* **sich nicht l∼en lassen** be generous. **L∼engesindel, L∼enpack** *nt* riff-raff. **L∼ensammler** *m* rag-and-bone man. **l∼ig** *a* mean, shabby; (*gering*) measly

Lunchpacket /'lan[t]ʃ-/ *nt* packed lunch

Lunge *f* -,-n lungs *pl*; (L∼*nflügel*) lung. **L∼nentzündung** *f* pneumonia

lungern *vi* (*haben*) loiter

Lunte *f* **L∼ riechen** (*fam*) smell a rat

Lupe *f* -,-n magnifying glass

Lurch *m* -[e]s,-e amphibian

Lust *f* -,·̈e pleasure; (*Verlangen*) desire; (*sinnliche Begierde*) lust; **L∼ haben** feel like (**auf etw** *acc* sth); **ich habe keine L∼** I don't feel like it; (*will nicht*) I don't want to

Lüster *m* -s,- lustre; (*Kronleuchter*) chandelier

lüstern *a* greedy (**auf** + *acc* for); (*sinnlich*) lascivious; (*geil*) lecherous

lustig *a* jolly; (*komisch*) funny; **sich l∼ machen über** (+ *acc*) make fun of

Lüstling *m* -s,-e lecher

lust|los *a* listless, *adv* -ly. **L∼mörder** *m* sex killer. **L∼spiel** *nt* comedy

lutherisch *a* Lutheran

lutsch|en *vt/i* (*haben*) suck. **L∼er** *m* -s,- lollipop; (*Schnuller*) dummy, (*Amer*) pacifier

lütt *a* (*NGer*) little

Lüttich *nt* -s Liège

Luv *f* & *nt* - **nach Luv** (*Naut*) to windward

luxuriös *a* luxurious, *adv* -ly

Luxus *m* - luxury. **L∼artikel** *m* luxury article. **L∼ausgabe** *f* de luxe edition. **L∼hotel** *nt* luxury hotel

Lymph|drüse /'lymf-/ *f*, **L∼knoten** *m* lymph gland

lynchen /'lynçən/ *vt* lynch

Lyr|ik *f* - lyric poetry. **L∼iker** *m* -s,- lyric poet. **l∼isch** *a* lyrical; ⟨*Dichtung*⟩ lyric

Mach|art *f* style. **m∼bar** *a* feasible. **m∼en** *vt* make; get ⟨*Mahlzeit*⟩; take ⟨*Foto*⟩; (*ausführen, tun, in Ordnung bringen*) do; (*Math: ergeben*) be; (*kosten*) come to; **sich** (*dat*) **etw m∼en lassen** have sth made; **was m∼st du da?** what are you doing? **was m∼t die Arbeit?** how is work? **das m∼t 6 Mark [zusammen]** that's 6 marks [altogether]; **das m∼t nichts** it doesn't matter; **sich** (*dat*) **wenig/nichts m∼en aus** care little/ nothing for ▫ *vr* **sich m∼en** do well; **sich an die Arbeit m∼en** get down to work ▫ *vi* (*haben*) **ins Bett m∼en** (*fam*) wet the bed; **schnell m∼en** hurry. **M∼enschaften** *fpl* machinations

Macht *f* -,·̈e power; **mit aller M∼** with all one's might. **M∼haber** *m* -s,- ruler

mächtig *a* powerful; (*groß*) enormous ▫ *adv* (*fam*) terribly

macht|los *a* powerless. **M∼wort** *nt* **ein M∼wort sprechen** put one's foot down

Mädchen *nt* -s,- girl; (*Dienst-*) maid. **m∼haft** *a* girlish. **M∼name** *m* girl's name; (*vor der Ehe*) maiden name

Made *f* -,-n maggot

Mädel *nt* -s,- girl

madig *a* maggoty; **jdn m∼ machen** (*fam*) run s.o. down

Madonna *f* -,-nen madonna

Magazin *nt* -s,-e magazine; (*Lager*) warehouse; (*Raum*) store-room

Magd *f* -,·̈e maid

Magen *m* -s,·̈ stomach. **M∼schmerzen** *mpl* stomachache *sg*. **M∼verstimmung** *f* stomach upset

mager *a* thin; ⟨*Fleisch*⟩ lean; ⟨*Boden*⟩ poor; (*dürftig*) meagre. **M∼keit** *f* - thinness; leanness. **M∼sucht** *f* anorexia

Magie *f* - magic

Mag|ier /'ma:giɐ/ *m* -s,- magician. **m∼isch** *a* magic; (*geheimnisvoll*) magical

Magistrat *m* -s,-e city council

Magnesia *f* - magnesia

Magnet *m* -en & -[e]s,-e magnet. **m∼isch** *a* magnetic. **m∼isieren** *vt* magnetize. **M∼ismus** *m* - magnetism

Mahagoni *nt* -s mahogany

Mäh|drescher *m* -s,- combine harvester. **m∼en** *vt/i* (*haben*) mow

Mahl *nt* -[e]s,·̈er & -e meal

mahlen† *vt* grind

Mahlzeit *f* meal; **M∼!** enjoy your meal!

Mähne *f* -,-n mane

mahn|en *vt/i* (*haben*) remind (**wegen** about); (*ermahnen*) admonish; (*auffordern*) urge (**zu** to); **zur Vorsicht/Eile m~en** urge caution/haste. **M~ung** *f* -,-en reminder; admonition; (*Aufforderung*) exhortation

Mai *m* -[e]s,-e May; **der Erste Mai** May Day. **M~glöckchen** *nt* -s,- lily of the valley. **M~käfer** *m* cockchafer

Mailand *nt* -s Milan

Mais *m* -es maize, (*Amer*) corn; (*Culin*) sweet corn. **M~kolben** *m* corn-cob

Majestät *f* -,-en majesty. **m~isch** *a* majestic, *adv* -ally

Major *m* -s,-e major

Majoran *m* -s marjoram

Majorität *f* -,-en majority

makaber *a* macabre

Makel *m* -s,- blemish; (*Defekt*) flaw; (*fig*) stain. **m~los** *a* flawless; (*fig*) unblemished

mäkeln *vi* (*haben*) grumble

Makkaroni *pl* macaroni *sg*

Makler *m* -s,- (*Comm*) broker

Makrele *f* -,-n mackerel

Makrone *f* -,-n macaroon

mal *adv* (*Math*) times; (*bei Maßen*) by; (*fam: einmal*) once; (*eines Tages*) one day; **schon mal** once before; (*jemals*) ever; **nicht mal** not even; **hört/seht mal!** listen!/look!

Mal¹ *nt* -[e]s,-e time; **das erste/zweite/letzte/nächste Mal** the first/second/last/next time; **zum ersten/ letzten Mal** for the first/last time; **mit einem Mal** all at once; **ein für alle Mal** once and for all; **jedes Mal** every time; **jedes Mal, wenn** whenever; **einige/ mehrere Mal** a few/several times

Mal² *nt* -[e]s,-e mark; (*auf der Haut*) mole; (*Mutter-*) birthmark

Mal|buch *nt* colouring book. **m~en** *vt/i* (*haben*) paint. **M~er** *m* -s,- painter. **M~erei** *f* -,-en painting. **M~erin** *f* -,-nen painter. **m~erisch** *a* picturesque

Malheur /maˈløːɐ/ *nt* -s,-e & -s (*fam*) mishap; (*Ärger*) trouble

Mallorca /maˈlɔrka, -ˈjɔrka/ *nt* -s Majorca

malnehmen† *vt sep* multiply (**mit** by)

Malz *nt* -es malt. **M~bier** *nt* malt beer

Mama /ˈmama, maˈmaː/ *f* -s,-s mummy

Mammut *nt* -s,-e & -s mammoth

mampfen *vt* (*fam*) munch

man *pron* one, you; (*die Leute*) people, they; **man sagt** they say, it is said

Manager /ˈmɛnɪdʒɐ/ *m* -s,- manager

manch *inv pron* **m~ ein(e)** many a; **m~ einer/eine** many a man/woman. **m~e(r,s)** *pron* many a; [**so**] **m~es Mal**

many a time; **m~e Leute** some people □ (*substantivisch*) **m~er/m~e** many a man/woman; **m~e** *pl* some; (*Leute*) some people; (*viele*) many [people]; **m~es** some things; (*vieles*) many things. **m~erlei** *inv a* various □ *pron* various things

manchmal *adv* sometimes

Mandant(in) *m* -en,-en (*f* -,-nen) (*Jur*) client

Mandarine *f* -,-n mandarin

Mandat *nt* -[e]s,-e mandate; (*Jur*) brief; (*Pol*) seat

Mandel *f* -,-n almond; (*Anat*) tonsil. **M~entzündung** *f* tonsillitis

Manege /maˈneːʒə/ *f* -,-n ring; (*Reit-*) arena

Mangel¹ *m* -s,- lack; (*Knappheit*) shortage; (*Med*) deficiency; (*Fehler*) defect; **M~ leiden** go short

Mangel² *f* -,-n mangle

mangel|haft *a* faulty, defective; (*Sch*) unsatisfactory. **m~n¹** *vi* (*haben*) **es m~t an** (+ *dat*) there is a lack/(*Knappheit*) shortage of

mangeln² *vt* put through the mangle

mangels *prep* (+ *gen*) for lack of

Mango *f* -,-s mango

Manie *f* -,-n mania; (*Sucht*) obsession

Manier *f* -,-en manner; **M~en** manners. **m~lich** *a* well-mannered □ *adv* properly

Manifest *nt* -[e]s,-e manifesto. **m~ieren (sich)** *vr* manifest itself

Maniküre *f* -,-n manicure; (*Person*) manicurist. **m~n** *vt* manicure

Manipul|ation /-ˈtsjoːn/ *f* -,-en manipulation. **m~ieren** *vt* manipulate

Manko *nt* -s,-s disadvantage; (*Fehlbetrag*) deficit

Mann *m* -[e]s,-̈er man; (*Ehe-*) husband

Männchen *nt* -s,- little man; (*Zool*) male; **M~ machen** (*Hund:*) sit up

Mannequin /ˈmanəkɛ̃/ *nt* -s,-s model

Männerchor *m* male voice choir

Mannes|alter *nt* manhood. **M~kraft** *f* virility

mannhaft *a* manful, *adv* -ly

mannigfaltig *a* manifold; (*verschieden*) diverse

männlich *a* male; (*Gram* & *fig*) masculine; (*mannhaft*) manly; (*Frau*) mannish. **M~keit** *f* - masculinity; (*fig*) manhood

Mannschaft *f* -,-en team; (*Naut*) crew. **M~sgeist** *m* team spirit

Manöv|er *nt* -s,- manoeuvre; (*Winkelzug*) trick. **m~rieren** *vt/i* (*haben*) manoeuvre

Mansarde *f* -,-n attic room; (*Wohnung*) attic flat

Manschette f -,-n cuff; (*Blumentopf-*) paper frill. **M∼knopf** m cuff-link

Mantel m -s,: coat; (*dick*) overcoat; (*Reifen-*) outer tyre

Manuskript nt -[e]s,-e manuscript

Mappe f -,-n folder; (*Akten-*) briefcase; (*Schul-*) bag

Marathon m -s,-s marathon

Märchen nt -s,- fairy-tale. **m∼haft** a fairy-tale . . .; (*phantastisch*) fabulous

Margarine f - margarine

Marienkäfer /ma'ri:ən-/ m lady-bird, (*Amer*) ladybug

Marihuana nt -s marijuana

Marille f -,-n (*Aust*) apricot

Marinade f -,-n marinade

Marine f marine; (*Kriegs-*) navy. **m∼blau** a navy [blue]. **M∼infanterist** m marine

marinieren vt marinade

Marionette f -,-n puppet, marionette

Mark[1] f -,- mark; **drei M∼** three marks

Mark[2] nt -[e]s (*Knochen-*) marrow; (*Bot*) pith; (*Frucht-*) pulp; **bis ins M∼ getroffen** (*fig*) cut to the quick

markant a striking

Marke f -,-n token; (*rund*) disc; (*Erkennungs-*) tag; (*Brief-*) stamp; (*Lebensmittel-*) coupon; (*Spiel-*) counter; (*Markierung*) mark; (*Fabrikat*) make; (*Tabak-*) brand. **M∼nartikel** m branded article

markier|en vt mark; (*fam: vortäuschen*) fake. **M∼ung** f -,-en marking

Markise f -,-n awning

Markstück nt one-mark piece

Markt m -[e]s,:e market; (*M∼platz*) market-place. **M∼forschung** f market research. **M∼platz** m market-place

Marmelade f -,-n jam; (*Orangen-*) marmalade

Marmor m -s marble

Marokko nt -s Morocco

Marone f -,-n [sweet] chestnut

Marotte f -,-n whim

Marsch[1] f -,-en marsh

Marsch[2] m -[e]s,:e march. **m∼** int (*Mil*) march! **m∼ ins Bett!** off to bed!

Marschall m -s,:e marshal

marschieren vi (*sein*) march

Marter f - torture. **m∼n** vt torture

Martinshorn nt [police] siren

Märtyrer(in) m -s,- (f -,-nen) martyr

Martyrium nt -s martyrdom

Mar|xismus m - Marxism. **m∼xistisch** a Marxist

März m -,-e March

Marzipan nt -s marzipan

Masche f -,-n stitch; (*im Netz*) mesh; (*fam: Trick*) dodge. **M∼ndraht** m wire netting

Maschin|e f -,-n machine; (*Flugzeug*) plane; (*Schreib-*) typewriter; **M∼e schreiben** type. **m∼egeschrieben** a typewritten, typed. **m∼ell** a machine . . . □ adv by machine. **M∼enbau** m mechanical engineering. **M∼engewehr** nt machine-gun. **M∼enpistole** f submachine-gun. **M∼erie** f - machinery. **M∼eschreiben** nt typing. **M∼ist** m -en,-en machinist; (*Naut*) engineer

Masern pl measles sg

Maserung f -,-en [wood] grain

Maske f -,-n mask; (*Theat*) make-up. **M∼rade** f -,-n disguise; (*fig: Heuchelei*) masquerade

maskieren vt mask; **sich m∼** dress up (**als** as)

Maskottchen nt -s,- mascot

maskulin a masculine

Maskulinum nt -s,-na (*Gram*) masculine

Masochis|mus /mazo'xɪsmus/ m - masochism. **M∼t** m -en,-en masochist

Maß[1] nt -es,-e measure; (*Abmessung*) measurement; (*Grad*) degree; (*Mäßigung*) moderation; **Maß halten** exercise moderation; **in od mit Maß[en]** in moderation; **in hohem Maße** to a high degree

Maß[2] f -,- (*SGer*) litre [of beer]

Massage /ma'sa:ʒə/ f -,-n massage

Massaker nt -s,- massacre

Maß|anzug m made-to-measure suit. **M∼band** nt (pl -bänder) tape-measure

Masse f -,-n mass; (*Culin*) mixture; (*Menschen-*) crowd; **eine M∼ Arbeit** (*fam*) masses of work. **M∼nartikel** m mass-produced article. **m∼nhaft** adv in huge quantities. **M∼nmedien** pl mass media. **M∼nproduktion** f mass production. **m∼nweise** adv in huge numbers

Masseu|r /ma'sø:ɐ̯/ m -s,-e masseur. **M∼rin** f -,-nen, **M∼se** /-'sø:zə/ f -,-n masseuse

maß|gebend a authoritative; (*einflussreich*) influential. **m∼geblich** a decisive, adv -ly. **m∼geschneidert** a made-to-measure. **m∼halten†** vi sep (*haben*) (NEW) **Maß halten**, s. **Maß**[1]

massieren[1] vt massage

massieren[2] (sich) vr mass

massig a massive

mäßig a moderate, adv -ly; (*mittelmäßig*) indifferent. **m∼en** vt moderate; **sich m∼en** moderate; (*sich beherrschen*) restrain oneself. **M∼keit** f - moderation. **M∼ung** f - moderation

massiv a solid; (*stark*) heavy

Maß|krug m beer mug. **m∼los** a excessive; (*grenzenlos*) boundless; (*äußerst*) extreme, adv -ly. **M∼nahme** f -,-n measure. **m∼regeln** vt reprimand

Maßstab m scale; (*Norm & fig*) standard. **m∼gerecht, m∼sgetreu** a scale ... □ adv to scale

maßvoll a moderate

Mast[1] m -[e]s,-en pole; (*Überland-*) pylon; (*Naut*) mast

Mast[2] f - fattening. **M∼darm** m rectum

mästen vt fatten

Masturb|ation /-'tsjo:n/ f - masturbation. **m∼ieren** vi (*haben*) masturbate

Material nt -s,-ien /-jən/ material; (*coll*) materials pl. **M∼ismus** m - materialism. **m∼istisch** a materialistic

Mater|ie /ma'te:rjə/ f -,-n matter; (*Thema*) subject. **m∼iell** a material

Mathe f - (*fam*) maths sg

Mathe|matik f - mathematics sg. **M∼matiker** m -s,- mathematician. **m∼matisch** a mathematical

Matinee f -,-n (*Theat*) morning performance

Matratze f -,-n mattress

Mätresse f -,-n mistress

Matrose m -n,-n sailor

Matsch m -[e]s mud; (*Schnee-*) slush. **m∼ig** a muddy; slushy; (*weich*) mushy

matt a weak; (*gedämpft*) dim; (*glanzlos*) dull; (*Politur, Farbe*) matt; **jdn m∼ setzen** checkmate s.o. **M∼** nt -s (*Schach*) mate

Matte f -,-n mat

Mattglas nt frosted glass

Matt|igkeit f - weakness; (*Müdigkeit*) weariness. **M∼scheibe** f (*fam*) television screen

Matura f - (*Aust*) ≈ A levels pl

Mauer f -,-n wall. **m∼n** vt build □ vi (*haben*) lay bricks. **M∼werk** nt masonry

Maul nt -[e]s, Mäuler (*Zool*) mouth; **halt's M∼!** (*fam*) shut up! **m∼en** vi (*haben*) (*fam*) grumble. **M∼korb** m muzzle. **M∼tier** nt mule. **M∼wurf** m mole. **M∼wurfshaufen, M∼wurfshügel** m molehill

Maurer m -s,- bricklayer

Maus f -,Mäuse mouse. **M∼efalle** f mousetrap

mausern (sich) vr moult; (*fam*) turn (**zu** into)

Maut f -,-en (*Aust*) toll. **M∼straße** f toll road

maximal a maximum

Maximum nt -s,-ma maximum

Mayonnaise /majo'nɛ:zə/ f -,-n mayonnaise

Mäzen m -s,-e patron

Mechan|ik /me'ça:nɪk/ f - mechanics sg; (*Mechanismus*) mechanism. **M∼iker** m -s,- mechanic. **m∼isch** a mechanical, adv -ly. **m∼isieren** vt mechanize. **M∼ismus** m -,-men mechanism

meckern vi (*haben*) bleat; (*fam: nörgeln*) grumble

Medaill|e /me'daljə/ f -,-n medal. **M∼on** /-'jõ:/ nt -s,-s medallion; (*Schmuck*) locket

Medikament nt -[e]s,-e medicine

Medit|ation /-'tsjo:n/ f -,-en meditation. **m∼ieren** vi (*haben*) meditate

Medium nt -s,-ien medium; **die Medien** the media

Medizin f -,-en medicine. **M∼er** m -s,- doctor; (*Student*) medical student. **m∼isch** a medical; (*heilkräftig*) medicinal

Meer nt -[e]s,-e sea. **M∼busen** m gulf. **M∼enge** f strait. **M∼esspiegel** m sealevel. **M∼jungfrau** f mermaid. **M∼rettich** m horseradish. **M∼schweinchen** nt -s,- guinea-pig

Megaphon, Megafon nt -s,-e megaphone

Mehl nt -[e]s flour. **m∼ig** a floury. **M∼schwitze** f (*Culin*) roux. **M∼speise** f (*Aust*) dessert; (*Kuchen*) pastry. **M∼tau** m (*Bot*) mildew

mehr pron & adv more; **nicht m∼** no more; (*zeitlich*) no longer; **nichts m∼** no more; (*nichts weiter*) nothing else; **nie m∼** never again. **m∼deutig** a ambiguous. **m∼en** vt increase; **sich m∼en** increase. **m∼ere** pron several. **m∼eremal** adv (NEW) **m∼ere Mal,** s. Mal[1]. **m∼eres** pron several things pl. **m∼fach** a multiple; (*mehrmalig*) repeated □ adv several times. **M∼fahrtenkarte** f book of tickets. **m∼farbig** a [multi]coloured. **M∼heit** f -,-en majority. **m∼malig** a repeated. **m∼mals** adv several times. **m∼sprachig** a multilingual. **m∼stimmig** a (*Mus*) for several voices □ adv **m∼stimmig singen** sing in harmony. **M∼wertsteuer** f value-added tax, VAT. **M∼zahl** f majority; (*Gram*) plural. **M∼zweck-** pref multi-purpose

meiden† vt avoid, shun

Meierei f -,-en (*dial*) dairy

Meile f -,-n mile. **M∼nstein** m milestone. **m∼nweit** adv [for] miles

mein poss pron my. **m∼e(r,s)** poss pron mine; **die M∼en** od **m∼en** pl my family sg

Meineid m perjury; **einen M∼ leisten** perjure oneself

meinen vt mean; (*glauben*) think; (*sagen*) say; **gut gemeinter Rat** wel-meant advice; **es gut m∼** mean well

mein|erseits *adv* for my part.
m~etwegen *adv* for my sake; (*wegen mir*)
because of me, on my account; (*fam: von
mir aus*) as far as I'm concerned. **m~et-
willen** *adv* um m~etwillen for my sake.
m~ige *poss pron* der/die/das m~ige
mine. **m~s** *poss pron* mine

Meinung *f* -,-en opinion; **jdm die M~
sagen** give s.o. a piece of one's mind.
M~sumfrage *f* opinion poll

Meise *f* -,-n (*Zool*) tit

Meißel *m* -s,- chisel. **m~n** *vt/i* (*haben*)
chisel

meist *adv* mostly; (*gewöhnlich*) usually.
m~e *a* der/die/das **m~e** most; **die
m~en Leute** most people; **die m~e Zeit**
most of the time; **am m~en** [the] most
□ *pron* **das m~e** most [of it]; **die m~en**
most. **m~ens** *adv* mostly; (*gewöhnlich*)
usually

Meister *m* -s,- master craftsman; (*Könner*)
master; (*Sport*) champion. **m~haft** *a* masterly □ *adv* in masterly fashion. **m~n** *vt*
master. **M~schaft** *f* -,-en mastery;
(*Sport*) championship. **M~stück,
M~werk** *nt* masterpiece

Melanch|olie /melaŋkoˈliː/ *f* - melan-
choly. **m~olisch** *a* melancholy

meld|en *vt* report; (*anmelden*) register;
(*ankündigen*) announce; **sich m~en** report (**bei** to); (*zum Militär*) enlist;
(*freiwillig*) volunteer; (*Teleph*) answer;
(*Sch*) put up one's hand; (*von sich hören
lassen*) get in touch (**bei** with); **sich krank
m~en** (NEW) **sich krankmelden**. **M~ung**
f -,-en report; (*Anmeldung*) registration

meliert† *a* mottled; **grau m~es Haar** hair
flecked with grey

melken† *vt* milk

Melod|ie *f* -,-n tune, melody. **m~iös** *a*
melodious

melodisch *a* melodic; (*melodiös*) melodious, tuneful

melodramatisch *a* melodramatic, *adv*
-ally

Melone *f* -,-n melon; **[schwarze] M~**
(*fam*) bowler [hat]

Membran *f* -,-en membrane

Memoiren /meˈmo̯aːrən/ *pl* memoirs

Menge *f* -,-n amount, quantity; (*Men-
schen-*) crowd; (*Math*) set; **eine M~ Geld**
a lot of money. **m~n** *vt* mix

Mensa *f* -,-sen (*Univ*) refectory

Mensch *m* -en,-en human being; **der M~**
man; **die M~en** people; **jeder/kein M~**
everybody/nobody. **M~enaffe** *m* ape.
M~enfeind *m* misanthropist. **m~en-
feindlich** *a* antisocial. **M~enfresser** *m*
-s,- cannibal; (*Zool*) man-eater; (*fam*) ogre.
m~enfreundlich *a* philanthropic.

M~enleben *nt* human life; (*Lebenszeit*)
lifetime. **m~enleer** *a* deserted. **M~en-
menge** *f* crowd. **M~enraub** *m* kidnap-
ping. **M~enrechte** *ntpl* human rights.
m~enscheu *a* unsociable. **M~enskind**
int (*fam*) good heavens! **M~enverstand**
m gesunder **M~enverstand** common
sense. **m~enwürdig** *a* humane, *adv* -ly.
M~heit *f* - die **M~heit** mankind, humanity. **m~lich** *a* human; (*human*) humane, *adv* -ly. **M~lichkeit** *f* - humanity

Menstru|ation /-ˈtsi̯oːn/ *f* - menstru-
ation. **m~ieren** *vi* (*haben*) menstruate

Mentalität *f* -,-en mentality

Menü *nt* -s,-s menu; (*festes M~*) set meal

Menuett *nt* -[e]s,-e minuet

Meridian *m* -s,-e meridian

merk|bar *a* noticeable. **M~blatt** *nt* [ex-
planatory] leaflet. **m~en** *vt* notice; **sich**
(*dat*) etw m~en remember sth. **m~lich**
a noticeable, *adv* -bly. **M~mal** *nt* feature

merkwürdig *a* odd, *adv* -ly, strange, *adv*
-ly. **m~erweise** *adv* oddly enough

mess|bar (**meß|bar**) *a* measurable.
M~becher *m* (*Culin*) measure

Messe¹ *f* -,-n (*Relig*) mass; (*Comm*) [trade]
fair

Messe² *f* -,-n (*Mil*) mess

messen† *vt/i* (*haben*) measure; (*ansehen*)
look at; **[bei jdm] Fieber m~** take s.o.'s
temperature; **sich m~** compete (**mit**
with); **sich mit jdm m~/nicht m~
können** be a/no match for s.o.

Messer *nt* -s,- knife

Messias *m* - Messiah

Messing *nt* -s brass

Messung *f* -,-en measurement

Metabolismus *m* - metabolism

Metall *nt* -s,-e metal. **m~en** *a* metal;
(*metallisch*) metallic. **m~isch** *a* metallic

Metallurgie *f* - metallurgy

Metamorphose *f* -,-n metamorphosis

Metaph|er *f* -,-n metaphor. **m~orisch** *a*
metaphorical, *adv* -ly

Meteor *m* -s,-e meteor. **M~ologe** *m* -n,-n
meteorologist. **M~ologie** *f* - meteorology.
m~ologisch *a* meteorological

Meter *m & nt* -s,- metre, (*Amer*) meter.
M~maß *nt* tape-measure

Method|e *f* -,-n method. **m~isch** *a* meth-
odical

metrisch *a* metric

Metropole *f* -,-n metropolis

metzeln *vt* (*fig*) massacre

Metzger *m* -s,- butcher. **M~ei** *f* -,-en butcher's shop

Meute *f* -,-n pack [of hounds]; (*fig: Menge*)
mob

Meuterei f -,-en mutiny

meutern vi (haben) mutiny; (fam: schimpfen) grumble

Mexikan|er(in) m -s,- (f -,-nen) Mexican. **m~isch** a Mexican

Mexiko nt -s Mexico

miauen vi (haben) mew, miaow

mich pron (acc of **ich**) me; (refl) myself

Mieder nt -s,- bodice; (Korsett) corset

Miene f -,-n expression; **M~ machen** make as if (zu to)

mies a (fam) lousy; **mir ist m~** I feel rotten

Miet|e f -,-n rent; (Mietgebühr) hire charge; **zur M~e wohnen** live in rented accommodation. **m~en** vt rent (Haus, Zimmer); hire (Auto, Boot, Fernseher). **M~er(in)** m -s,- (f-,-nen) tenant. **m~frei** a & adv rent-free. **M~shaus** nt block of rented flats. **M~vertrag** m lease. **M~wagen** m hire-car. **M~wohnung** f rented flat; (zu vermieten) flat to let

Mieze f -,-n (fam) puss[y]

Migräne f -,-n migraine

Mikrobe f -,-n microbe

Mikro|chip m microchip. **M~computer** m microcomputer. **M~film** m microfilm

Mikro|fon, M~phon nt -s,-e microphone. **M~prozessor** m -s,-en /-'so:rən/ microprocessor. **M~skop** nt -s,-e microscope. **m~skopisch** a microscopic

Mikrowelle f microwave. **M~ngerät** nt, **M~nherd** m microwave oven

Milbe f -,-n mite

Milch f - milk. **M~bar** f milk bar. **M~geschäft** nt dairy. **M~glas** nt opal glass. **m~ig** a milky. **M~kuh** f dairy cow. **M~mann** m (pl -männer) milkman. **M~mixgetränk** nt milk shake. **M~straße** f Milky Way. **M~zahn** m milk tooth

mild a mild; (nachsichtig) lenient; **m~e Gaben** alms. **M~e** f - mildness; leniency. **m~ern** vt make milder; (mäßigen) moderate; (lindern) alleviate, ease; **sich m~ern** become milder; (sich mäßigen) moderate; (nachlassen) abate; (Schmerz:) ease; **m~ernde Umstände** mitigating circumstances. **m~tätig** a charitable

Milieu /mi'ljø:/ nt -s,-s [social] environment

militant a militant

Militär nt -s army; (Soldaten) troops pl; **beim M~** in the army. **m~isch** a military

Miliz f -,-en militia

Milliarde /mi'ljardə/ f -,-n thousand million, billion

Milli|gramm nt milligram. **M~meter** m & nt millimetre. **M~meterpapier** nt graph paper

Million /mɪ'ljo:n/ f -,-en million. **M~är** m -s,-e millionaire. **M~ärin** f -,-nen millionairess

Milz f - (Anat) spleen

mim|en vt (fam: vortäuschen) act. **M~ik** f - [expressive] gestures and facial expressions pl

Mimose f -,-n mimosa

minder a lesser □ adv less; **mehr oder m~** more or less. **M~heit** f -,-en minority

minderjährig a (Jur) under-age; **m~ sein** be under age. **M~e(r)** m/f (Jur) minor. **M~keit** f - (Jur) minority

minder|n vt diminish; decrease (Tempo). **M~ung** f - decrease

minderwertig a inferior. **M~keit** f - inferiority. **M~keitskomplex** m inferiority complex

Mindest- pref minimum. **m~e** a & pron **der/die/das M~e** od **m~e** the least; **zum M~en** od **m~en** at least; **nicht im M~en** od **m~en** not in the least. **m~ens** adv at least. **M~lohn** m minimum wage. **M~maß** nt minimum

Mine f -,-n mine; (Bleistift-) lead; (Kugelschreiber-) refill. **M~nfeld** nt minefield. **M~nräumboot** nt minesweeper

Mineral nt -s,-e & -ien /-jən/ mineral. **m~isch** a mineral. **M~ogie** f - mineralogy. **M~wasser** nt mineral water

Miniatur f -,-en miniature

Minigolf nt miniature golf

minimal a minimal

Minimum nt -s,-ma minimum

Minirock m miniskirt

Mini|ster m -s,- minister. **m~steriell** a ministerial. **M~sterium** nt -s,-ien ministry

Minorität f -,-en minority

minus conj, adv & prep (+ gen) minus. **M~** nt - deficit; (Nachteil) disadvantage. **M~zeichen** nt minus [sign]

Minute f -,-n minute

mir pron (dat of **ich**) [to] me; (refl) myself; **mir nichts, dir nichts** without so much as a 'by your leave'

Misch|ehe f mixed marriage. **m~en** vt mix; blend (Tee, Kaffee); toss (Salat); shuffle (Karten); **sich m~en** mix; (Person:) mingle (unter + acc with); **sich m~en in** (+ acc) join in (Gespräch); meddle in (Angelegenheit) □ vi (haben) shuffle the cards. **M~ling** m -s,-e halfcaste; (Hund) cross. **M~masch** m -[e]s,-e (fam) hotchpotch. **M~ung** f -,-en mixture; blend

miserabel a abominable; (erbärmlich) wretched

missachten (mißachten) *vt* disregard

Miss|achtung (Miß|achtung) *f* disregard. **M~behagen** *nt* [feeling of] unease. **M~bildung** *f* deformity

missbilligen (mißbilligen) *vt* disapprove of

Miss|billigung (Miß|billigung) *f* disapproval. **M~brauch** *m* abuse; **M~brauch treiben mit** abuse

miss|brauchen (miß|brauchen) *vt* abuse; (*vergewaltigen*) rape. **m~deuten** *vt* misinterpret

missen *vt* do without; **ich möchte es nicht m~** I should not like to be without it

Miss|erfolg (Miß|erfolg) *m* failure. **M~ernte** *f* crop failure

Misse|tat *f* misdeed. **M~täter** *m* (*fam*) culprit

missfallen† (mißfallen†) *vi* (*haben*) displease (**jdm** s.o.)

Miss|fallen (Miß|fallen) *nt* -s displeasure; (*Missbilligung*) disapproval. **m~gebildet** *a* deformed. **M~geburt** *f* freak; (*fig*) monstrosity. **M~geschick** *nt* mishap; (*Unglück*) misfortune. **m~gestimmt** *a* **m~gestimmt sein** be in a bad mood

miss|glücken (miß|glücken) *vi* (*sein*) fail. **m~gönnen** *vt* begrudge

Miss|griff (Miß|griff) *m* mistake. **M~gunst** *f* resentment. **m~günstig** *a* resentful

misshandeln (mißhandeln) *vt* ill-treat

Miss|handlung (Miß|handlung) *f* ill-treatment. **M~helligkeit** *f* -,-en disagreement

Mission *f* -,-en mission

Missionar(in) *m* -s,-e (*f* -,-nen) missionary

Miss|klang (Miß|klang) *m* discord. **M~kredit** *m* discredit; **in M~kredit bringen** discredit. **m~lich** *a* awkward. **m~liebig** *a* unpopular

misslingen† (mißlingen†) *vi* (*sein*) fail; **es misslang ihr** she failed. **M~** *nt* -s failure

Missmut (Mißmut) *m* ill humour. **m~ig** *a* morose, *adv* -ly

missraten† (mißraten†) *vi* (*sein*) turn out badly

Miss|stand (Miß|stand) *m* abuse; (*Zustand*) undesirable state of affairs. **M~stimmung** *f* discord; (*Laune*) bad mood. **M~ton** *m* discordant note

misstrauen (mißtrauen) *vi* (*haben*) **jdm/etw m~** mistrust s.o./sth; (*Argwohn hegen*) distrust s.o./sth

Misstrau|en (Mißtrau|en) *nt* -s mistrust; (*Argwohn*) distrust. **M~ensvotum** *nt* vote of no confidence. **m~isch** *a* distrustful; (*argwöhnisch*) suspicious

Miss|verhältnis (Miß|verhältnis) *nt* disproportion. **M~verständnis** *nt* misunderstanding. **m~verstehen†** *vt* misunderstand. **M~wirtschaft** *f* mismanagement

Mist *m* -[e]s manure; (*fam*) rubbish

Mistel *f* -,-n mistletoe

Misthaufen *m* dungheap

mit *prep* (+ *dat*) with; (*sprechen*) to; (*mittels*) by; (*inklusive*) including; (*bei*) at; **mit Bleistift** in pencil; **mit lauter Stimme** in a loud voice; **mit drei Jahren** at the age of three □ *adv* (*auch*) as well; **mit anfassen** (*fig*) lend a hand; **es ist mit das ärmste Land der Welt** it is among the poorest countries in the world

Mitarbeit *f* collaboration. **m~en** *vi sep* collaborate (**an** + *dat* on). **M~er(in)** *m(f)* collaborator; (*Kollege*) colleague; (*Betriebsangehörige*) employee

Mitbestimmung *f* co-determination

mitbring|en† *vt sep* bring [along]; **jdm Blumen m~en** bring/(*hinbringen*) take s.o. flowers. **M~sel** *nt* -s,- present (*brought back from holiday etc*)

Mitbürger *m* fellow citizen

miteinander *adv* with each other

miterleben *vt sep* witness

Mitesser *m* (*Med*) blackhead

mitfahren† *vi sep* (*sein*) go/come along; **mit jdm m~** go with s.o.; (*mitgenommen werden*) be given a lift by s.o.

mitfühlen *vi sep* (*haben*) sympathize. **m~d** *a* sympathetic; (*mitleidig*) compassionate

mitgeben† *vt sep* **jdm etw m~** give s.o. sth to take with him

Mitgefühl *nt* sympathy

mitgehen† *vi sep* (*sein*) **mit jdm m~** go with s.o.; **etw m~ lassen** (*fam*) pinch sth

mitgenommen *a* worn; **m~ sein** be in a sorry state; (*erschöpft*) be exhausted

Mitgift *f* -,-en dowry

Mitglied *nt* member. **M~schaft** *f* - membership

mithalten† *vi sep* (*haben*) join in; **mit jdm nicht m~ können** not be able to keep up with s.o.

Mithilfe *f* assistance

mithilfe *prep* (+ *gen*) with the aid of

mitkommen† *vi sep* (*sein*) come [along] too; (*fig: folgen können*) keep up; (*verstehen*) follow

Mitlaut *m* consonant

Mitleid *nt* pity, compassion; **M~ erregend** pitiful. **M~enschaft** *f* in **M~enschaft ziehen** affect. **m~erregend** *a* =

M∼ **erregend**, *s.* **Mitleid. m∼ig** *a* pitying; (*mitfühlend*) compassionate. **m∼slos** *a* pitiless

mitmachen *v sep* ▫ *vt* take part in; (*erleben*) go through ▫ *vi* (*haben*) join in

Mitmensch *m* fellow man

mitnehmen† *vt sep* take along; (*mitfahren lassen*) give a lift to; (*fig: schädigen*) affect badly; (*erschöpfen*) exhaust; '**zum M∼**' 'to take away', (*Amer*) 'to go'

mitnichten *adv* not at all

mitreden *vi sep* (*haben*) join in [the conversation]; (*mit entscheiden*) have a say (**bei** in)

mitreißen† *vt sep* sweep along; (*fig: begeistern*) carry away; **m∼d** rousing

mitsamt *prep* (+ *dat*) together with

mitschneiden† *vt sep* record

mitschreiben† *vt sep* (*haben*) take down

Mitschuld *f* partial blame. **m∼ig** *a* **m∼ig sein** be partly to blame

Mitschüler(in) *m(f)* fellow pupil

mitspiel|en *vi sep* (*haben*) join in; (*Theat*) be in the cast; (*beitragen*) play a part; **jdm übel m∼en** treat s.o. badly. **M∼er** *m* fellow player; (*Mitwirkender*) participant

Mittag *m* midday, noon; (*Mahlzeit*) lunch; (*Pause*) lunch-break; **heute/gestern M∼** at lunch-time today/yesterday; [**zu**] **M∼ essen** have lunch. **m∼** *adv* heute/gestern **m∼** (NEW) **heute/gestern M∼**, *s.* **Mittag. M∼essen** *nt* lunch. **m∼s** *adv* at noon; (*als Mahlzeit*) for lunch; **um 12 Uhr m∼s** at noon. **M∼spause** *f* lunch-hour; (*Pause*) lunch-break. **M∼schlaf** *m* after-lunch nap. **M∼stisch** *m* lunch table; (*Essen*) lunch. **M∼szeit** *f* lunch-time

Mittäter|(in) *m(f)* accomplice. **M∼schaft** *f* - complicity

Mitte *f* -,-n middle; (*Zentrum*) centre; **die goldene M∼** the golden mean; **M∼ Mai** in mid-May; **in unserer M∼** in our midst

mitteil|en *vt sep* **jdm etw m∼en** tell s.o. sth; (*amtlich*) inform s.o. of sth. **m∼sam** *a* communicative. **M∼ung** *f* -,-en communication; (*Nachricht*) piece of news

Mittel *nt* -s,- means *sg*; (*Heil*) remedy; (*Medikament*) medicine; (*M∼wert*) mean; (*Durchschnitt*) average; **M∼** *pl* (*Geld-*) funds, resources. **m∼** *pred* *a* medium; (*m∼mäßig*) middling. **M∼alter** *nt* Middle Ages *pl*. **m∼alterlich** *a* medieval. **m∼bar** *a* indirect, *adv* -ly. **M∼ding** *nt* (*fig*) cross. **m∼europäisch** *a* Central European. **M∼finger** *m* middle finger. **m∼groß** *a* medium-sized; (*Person*) of medium height. **M∼klasse** *f* middle range. **m∼los** *a* destitute. **m∼mäßig** *a* middling; [**nur**] **m∼mäßig** mediocre.

M∼**meer** *nt* Mediterranean. **M∼punkt** *m* centre; (*fig*) centre of attention

mittels *prep* (+ *gen*) by means of

Mittel|schule *f* = **Realschule. M∼smann** *m* (*pl* -**männer**), **M∼sperson** *f* intermediary, go-between. **M∼stand** *m* middle class. **m∼ste(r,s)** *a* middle. **M∼streifen** *m* (*Auto*) central reservation, (*Amer*) median strip. **M∼stürmer** *m* centre-forward. **M∼weg** *m* (*fig*) middle course; **goldener M∼weg** happy medium. **M∼welle** *f* medium wave. **M∼wort** *nt* (*pl* -**wörter**) participle

mitten *adv* **m∼ in/auf** (*dat/acc*) in the middle of; **m∼ unter** (*dat/acc*) amidst. **m∼durch** *adv* [right] through the middle

Mitternacht *f* midnight

mittler|e(r,s) *a* middle; (*Größe, Qualität*) medium; (*durchschnittlich*) mean, average. **m∼weile** *adv* meanwhile; (*seitdem*) by now

Mittwoch *m* -s,-e Wednesday. **m∼s** *adv* on Wednesdays

mitunter *adv* now and again

mitwirk|en *vi sep* (*haben*) take part; (*helfen*) contribute. **M∼ung** *f* participation

mix|en *vt* mix. **M∼er** *m* -s,- (*Culin*) liquidizer, blender. **M∼tur** *f* -,-en (*Med*) mixture

Möbel *pl* furniture *sg*. **M∼stück** *nt* piece of furniture. **M∼tischler** *m* cabinetmaker. **M∼wagen** *m* removal van

mobil *a* mobile; (*fam: munter*) lively; (*nach Krankheit*) fit [and well]; **m∼ machen** mobilize

Mobile *nt* -s,-s mobile

Mobiliar *nt* -s furniture

mobilisier|en *vt* mobilize. **M∼ung** *f* - mobilization

Mobil|machung *f* - mobilization. **M∼telefon** *nt* mobile phone

möblier|en *vt* furnish; **m∼tes Zimmer** furnished room

mochte, möchte *s.* **mögen**

Modalverb *nt* modal auxiliary

Mode *f* -,-n fashion; **M∼ sein** be fashionable

Modell *nt* -s,-e model; **M∼ stehen** pose (**jdm** for s.o.). **m∼ieren** *vt* model

Modenschau *f* fashion show

Modera|tor *m* -s,-en /-'to:rən/, **M∼torin** *f* -,-nen (*TV*) presenter

modern¹ *vi* (*haben*) decay

modern² *a* modern; (*modisch*) fashionable. **m∼isieren** *vt* modernize

Mode|schmuck *m* costume jewellery. **M∼schöpfer** *m* fashion designer

Modifi|kation /-'tsjo:n/ f -,-en modification. **m~zieren** vt modify

modisch a fashionable

Modistin f -,-nen milliner

modrig a musty

modulieren vt modulate

Mofa nt -s,-s moped

mogeln vi (haben) (fam) cheat

mögen† vt like; **lieber m~** prefer □ v aux **ich möchte I'd like; möchtest du nach Hause?** do you want to go home? **ich mag nicht mehr** I've had enough; **ich hätte weinen m~** I could have cried; **ich mag mich irren** I may be wrong; **wer/was mag das sein?** whoever/whatever can it be? **wie mag es ihm ergangen sein?** I wonder how he got on; **[das] mag sein** that may well be; **mag kommen, was da will** come what may

möglich a possible; **alle m~en** all sorts of; **über alles M~e (m~e)** sprechen talk about all sorts of things; **sein M~stes (m~stes) tun** do one's utmost. **m~erweise** adv possibly. **M~keit** f -,-en possibility. **M~keitsform** f subjunctive. **m~st** adv if possible; **m~st viel/früh** as much/early as possible

Mohammedan|er(in) m -s,- (f -,-nen) Muslim. **m~isch** a Muslim

Mohn m -s poppy; (Culin) poppyseed. **M~blume** f poppy

Möhre, Mohrrübe f -,-n carrot

mokieren (sich) vr make fun (**über** + acc of)

Mokka m -s mocha; (Geschmack) coffee

Molch m -[e]s,-e newt

Mole f -,-n (Naut) mole

Molekül nt -s,-e molecule

Molkerei f -,-en dairy

Moll nt - (Mus) minor

mollig a cosy; (warm) warm; (rundlich) plump

Moment m -s,-e moment; **im/jeden M~** at the/any moment; **M~ [mal]!** just a moment! **m~an** a momentary, adv -ily; (gegenwärtig) at the moment

Momentaufnahme f snapshot

Monarch m -en,-en monarch. **M~ie** f -,-n monarchy

Monat m -s,-e month. **m~elang** adv for months. **m~lich** a & adv monthly. **M~skarte** f monthly season ticket

Mönch m -[e]s,-e monk

Mond m -[e]s,-e moon

mondän a fashionable, adv -bly

Mond|finsternis f lunar eclipse. **m~hell** a moonlit. **M~sichel** f crescent moon. **M~schein** m moonlight

monieren vt criticize

Monitor m -s,-en /-'to:rən/ (Techn) monitor

Monogramm nt -s,-e monogram

Mono|log m -s,-e monologue. **M~pol** nt -s,-e monopoly. **m~polisieren** vt monopolize. **m~ton** a monotonous, adv -ly. **M~tonie** f - monotony

Monster nt -s,- monster

monstr|ös a monstrous **M~osität** f -,-en monstrosity

Monstrum nt -s,-stren monster

Monsun m -s,-e monsoon

Montag m Monday

Montage /mɔn'ta:ʒə/ f -,-n fitting; (Zusammenbau) assembly; (Film-) editing; (Kunst) montage

montags adv on Mondays

Montanindustrie f coal and steel industry

Monteur /mɔn'tø:ɐ/ m -s,-e fitter. **M~anzug** m overalls pl

montieren vt fit; (zusammenbauen) assemble

Monument nt -[e]s,-e monument. **m~al** a monumental

Moor nt -[e]s,-e bog; (Heide-) moor

Moos nt es,-e moss. **m~ig** a mossy

Mop m -s,-s (NEW) **Mopp**

Moped nt -s,-s moped

Mopp m -s,-s mop

Mops m -s,ːe pug [dog]

Moral f - morals pl; (Selbstvertrauen) morale; (Lehre) moral. **m~isch** a moral, adv -ly. **m~isieren** vi (haben) moralize

Morast m -[e]s,-e morass; (Schlamm) mud

Mord m -[e]s,-e murder, (Pol) assassination. **M~anschlag** m murder/assassination attempt. **m~en** vt/i (haben) murder, kill

Mörder m -s,- murderer, (Pol) assassin. **M~in** f -,-nen murderess. **m~isch** a murderous; (fam: schlimm) dreadful

Mords- pref (fam) terrific. **m~mäßig** a (fam) frightful, adv -ly

morgen adv tomorrow; **m~ Abend (abend)/Nachmittag (nachmittag)** tomorrow evening/afternoon; **heute/gestern/Montag m~** (NEW) **heute/gestern/Montag M~,** s. **Morgen**

Morgen m -s,- morning; (Maß) ≈ acre; **am M~** in the morning; **heute/gestern/Montag M~** this/yesterday/Monday morning. **M~dämmerung** f dawn. **m~dlich** a morning ... **M~grauen** nt -s dawn; **im M~grauen** at dawn. **M~mantel, M~rock** m dressing-gown. **M~rot** nt red sky in the morning. **m~s** a in the morning

morgig *a* tomorrow's; **der m~e Tag** tomorrow

Morphium *nt* -s morphine

morsch *a* rotten

Morsealphabet *nt* Morse code

Mörtel *m* -s mortar

Mosaik /moza'i:k/ *nt* -s,-e[n] mosaic

Moschee *f* -,-n mosque

Mosel *f* - Moselle. **M~wein** *m* Moselle [wine]

Moskau *nt* -s Moscow

Moskito *m* -s,-s mosquito

Mos|lem *m* -s,-s Muslim. **m~lemisch** *a* Muslim

Most *m* -[e]s must; (*Apfel-*) ≈ cider

Mostrich *m* -s (*NGer*) mustard

Motel *nt* -s,-s motel

Motiv *nt* -s,-e motive; (*Kunst*) motif. **M~ation** /-'tsjo:n/ *f* - motivation. **m~ieren** *vt* motivate

Motor /'mo:tɔr,mo'to:ɐ̯/ *m* -s,-en /-'to:rən/ engine; (*Elektro-*) motor. **M~boot** *nt* motor boat

motorisieren *vt* motorize

Motor|rad *nt* motor cycle. **M~radfahrer** *m* motor-cyclist. **M~roller** *m* motor scooter

Motte *f* -,-n moth. **M~nkugel** *f* mothball

Motto *nt* -s,-s motto

Möwe *f* -,-n gull

Mücke *f* -,-n gnat; (*kleine*) midge; (*Stech-*) mosquito

mucksen (sich) *vr* sich nicht m~ (*fam*) keep quiet

müd|e *a* tired; **nicht m~e werden/es m~e sein** not tire/be tired (etw zu tun of doing sth). **M~igkeit** *f* - tiredness

Muff *m* -s,-e muff

muffig *a* musty; (*fam: mürrisch*) grumpy

Mühe *f* -,-n effort; (*Aufwand*) trouble; sich (*dat*) **M~ geben** make an effort; (*sich bemühen*) try; **nicht der M~ wert** not worth while; **mit M~ und Not** with great difficulty; (*gerade noch*) only just. **m~los** *a* effortless, *adv* -ly

muhen *vi* (*haben*) moo

mühe|n (sich) *vr* struggle. **m~voll** *a* laborious; (*anstrengend*) arduous

Mühl|e *f* -,-n mill; (*Kaffee-*) grinder. **M~stein** *m* millstone

Müh|sal *f* -,-e (*liter*) toil; (*Mühe*) trouble. **m~sam** *a* laborious, *adv* -ly; (*beschwerlich*) difficult, *adv* with difficulty. **m~selig** *a* laborious, *adv* -ly

Mulde *f* -,-n hollow

Müll *m* -s refuse, (*Amer*) garbage. **M~abfuhr** *f* refuse collection

Mullbinde *f* gauze bandage

Mülleimer *m* waste bin; (*Mülltonne*) dustbin, (*Amer*) garbage can

Müller *m* -s,- miller

Müll|halde *f* [rubbish] dump. **M~schlucker** *m* refuse chute. **M~tonne** *f* dustbin, (*Amer*) garbage can. **M~wagen** *m* dustcart, (*Amer*) garbage truck

mulmig *a* (*fam*) dodgy; ⟨*Gefühl*⟩ uneasy; **ihm war m~ zumute** he felt uneasy/ (*übel*) queasy

multi|national *a* multinational. **M~plikation** /-'tsjo:n/ *f* -,-en multiplication. **m~plizieren** *vt* multiply

Mumie /'mu:mjə/ *f* -,-n mummy

mumifiziert *a* mummified

Mumm *m* -s (*fam*) energy

Mumps *m* - mumps

Mund *m* -[e]s,ᐨer mouth; **ein M~ voll Suppe** a mouthful of soup; **halt den M~!** be quiet! (*sl*) shut up! **M~art** *f* dialect. **m~artlich** *a* dialect

Mündel *nt* & *m* -s,- (*Jur*) ward. **m~sicher** *a* gilt-edged

münden *vi* (*sein*) flow/⟨*Straße:*⟩ lead (**in** + *acc* into)

mund|faul *a* taciturn. **M~geruch** *m* bad breath. **M~harmonika** *f* mouth-organ

mündig *a* **m~ sein/werden** (*Jur*) be/ come of age. **M~keit** *f* - (*Jur*) majority

mündlich *a* verbal, *adv* -ly; **m~e Prüfung** oral

Mund|stück *nt* mouthpiece; (*Zigaretten-*) tip. **m~tot** *a* **m~tot machen** (*fig*) gag

Mündung *f* -,-en (*Fluss-*) mouth; (*Gewehr-*) muzzle

Mund|voll *m* -,- **ein M~voll** (NEW) **ein M~ voll**, s. **Mund**. **M~wasser** *nt* mouthwash. **M~werk** *nt* **ein gutes M~werk haben** (*fam*) be very talkative. **M~winkel** *m* corner of the mouth

Munition /-'tsjo:n/ *f* - ammunition

munkeln *vt/i* (*haben*) talk (**von** of); **es wird gemunkelt** rumour has it (**dass** that)

Münster *nt* -s,- cathedral

munter *a* lively; (*heiter*) merry; **m~ sein** (*wach*) be wide awake/(*aufgestanden, gesund*) up and about; **gesund und m~** fit and well □ *adv* [*immer*] **m~** merrily

Münz|e *f* -,-n coin; (*M~stätte*) mint. **m~en** *vt* mint; **das war auf dich gemünzt** (*fam*) that was aimed at you. **M~fernsprecher** *m* coin-box telephone, payphone. **M~wäscherei** *f* launderette

mürbe *a* crumbly; ⟨*Obst*⟩ mellow; ⟨*Fleisch*⟩ tender; **jdn m~ machen** (*fig*) wear s.o. down. **M~teig** *m* short pastry

Murmel *f* -,-n marble

murmeln *vt/i (haben)* murmur; *(undeutlich)* mumble, mutter. **M~** *nt* -s murmur

Murmeltier *nt* marmot

murren *vt/i (haben)* grumble

mürrisch *a* surly

Mus *nt* -es purée

Muschel *f* -,-n mussel; *(Schale)* [sea] shell

Museum /mu'ze:ʊm/ *nt* -s,-seen /-'ze:ən/ museum

Musik *f* - music. **M~alien** /-jən/ *pl* [printed] music *sg.* **m~alisch** *a* musical

Musikbox *f* juke-box

Musiker(in) *m* -s,- *(f* -,-nen) musician

Musik|instrument *nt* musical instrument. **M~kapelle** *f* band. **M~pavillon** *m* bandstand

musisch *a* artistic

musizieren *vi (haben)* make music

Muskat *m* -[e]s nutmeg

Muskel *m* -s,-n muscle. **M~kater** *m* stiff and aching muscles *pl*

Musku|latur *f* - muscles *pl.* **m~lös** *a* muscular

Müsli *nt* -s muesli

muss (muß) *s.* **müssen. Muss (Muß)** *nt* - ein **M~** a must

Muße *f* - leisure; **mit M~** at leisure

müssen† *v aux* etw tun m~ have to/*(fam)* have got to do sth; **ich muss jetzt gehen** I have to *or* must go now; **ich musste lachen** I had to laugh; **ich muss es wissen** I need to know; **du müsstest es mal versuchen** you ought to *or* should try it; **muss das sein?** is that necessary?

müßig *a* idle; *(unnütz)* futile. **M~gang** *m* - idleness

musste (mußte), müsste (müßte) *s.* **müssen**

Muster *nt* -s,- pattern; *(Probe)* sample; *(Vorbild)* model. **M~beispiel** *nt* typical example; *(Vorbild)* perfect example. **M~betrieb** *m* model factory. **m~gültig, m~haft** *a* exemplary. **m~n** *vt* eye; *(inspizieren)* inspect. **M~schüler(in)** *m(f)* model pupil. **M~ung** *f* -,-en inspection; *(Mil)* medical; *(Muster)* pattern

Mut *m* -[e]s courage; **jdm Mut machen** encourage s.o.; **zu M~e sein = zumute sein,** *s.* **zumute**

Mutation /-'tsio:n/ *f* -,-en *(Biol)* mutation

mut|ig *a* courageous, *adv* -ly. **m~los** *a* despondent; *(entmutigt)* disheartened

mutmaß|en *vt* presume; *(Vermutungen anstellen)* speculate. **m~lich** *a* probable, *adv* -bly; **der m~liche Täter** the suspect. **M~ung** *f* -,-en speculation, conjecture

Mutprobe *f* test of courage

Mutter[1] *f* -,- mother; **werdende M~** mother-to-be

Mutter[2] *f* -,-n *(Techn)* nut

Muttergottes *f* -,- madonna

Mutter|land *nt* motherland. **M~leib** *m* womb

mütterlich *a* maternal; *(fürsorglich)* motherly. **m~erseits** *adv* on one's/the mother's side

Mutter|mal *nt* birthmark; *(dunkel)* mole. **M~schaft** *f* - motherhood. **M~seelenallein** *a* & *adv* all alone. **M~sprache** *f* mother tongue. **M~tag** *m* Mother's Day

Mutti *f* -,-s *(fam)* mummy

Mutwill|e *m* wantonness. **m~ig** *a* wanton, *adv* -ly

Mütze *f* -,-n cap; **wollene M~** woolly hat

MwSt. *abbr* **(Mehrwertsteuer)** VAT

mysteriös *a* mysterious, *adv* -ly

Myst|ik /'mʏstɪk/ *f* - mysticism. **m~isch** *a* mystical

myth|isch *a* mythical. **M~ologie** *f* - mythology. **M~os** *m* -,-then myth

N

na *int* well; **na gut** all right then; **na ja** oh well; **na und?** so what?

Nabe *f* -,-n hub

Nabel *m* -s,- navel. **N~schnur** *f* umbilical cord

nach *prep* (+ *dat*) after; *(Uhrzeit)* past; *(Richtung)* to; *(greifen, rufen, sich sehnen)* for; *(gemäß)* according to; **meiner Meinung n~** in my opinion; **n~ oben** upwards ▫ *adv* **n~ und n~** gradually, bit by bit; **n~ wie vor** still

nachäffen *vt sep* mimic

nachahm|en *vt sep* imitate. **N~ung** *f* -,-en imitation

nacharbeiten *vt sep* make up for

nacharten *vi sep (sein)* jdm n~ take after s.o.

Nachbar|(in) *m* -n,-n *(f* -,-nen) neighbour. **N~haus** *nt* house next door. **N~land** *nt* neighbouring country. **n~lich** *a* neighbourly; *(Nachbar-)* neighbouring. **N~schaft** *f* - neighbourhood; **gute N~schaft** neighbourliness

nachbestell|en *vt sep* reorder. **N~ung** *f* repeat order

nachbild|en *vt sep* copy, reproduce. **N~ung** *f* copy, reproduction

nachdatieren *vt sep* backdate

nachdem *conj* after; **je n~** it depends

nachdenk|en† *vi sep* (*haben*) think (**über** + *acc* about). **N~en** *nt* -s reflection, thought. **n~lich** *a* thoughtful, *adv* -ly

Nachdruck *m* (*pl* -e) reproduction; (*unveränderter*) reprint; (*Betonung*) emphasis

nachdrücklich *a* emphatic, *adv* -ally

nacheifern *vi sep* (*haben*) jdm n~ emulate s.o.

nacheilen *vi sep* (*sein*) (+ *dat*) hurry after

nacheinander *adv* one after the other

Nachfahre *m* -n,-n descendant

Nachfolg|e *f* succession. **n~en** *vi sep* (*sein*) (+ *dat*) follow; (*im Amt*) succeed. **N~er(in)** *m* -s,(-/ -,-nen) successor

nachforsch|en *vi sep* (*haben*) make enquiries. **N~ung** *f* enquiry; **N~ungen** anstellen make enquiries

Nachfrage *f* (*Comm*) demand. **n~n** *vi sep* (*haben*) enquire

nachfüllen *vt sep* refill (*Behälter*); **Wasser n~** fill up with water

nachgeben† *v sep* □ *vi* (*haben*) give way; (*sich fügen*) give in, yield □ *vt* jdm Suppe n~ give s.o. more soup

Nachgebühr *f* surcharge

nachgehen† *vi sep* (*sein*) (*Uhr:*) be slow; jdm/etw n~ follow s.o./sth; follow up (*Spur, Angelegenheit*); pursue (*Angelegenheit, Tätigkeit*); go about (*Arbeit*)

nachgeraten† *vi sep* (*sein*) jdm n~ take after s.o.

Nachgeschmack *m* after-taste

nachgiebig *a* indulgent; (*gefällig*) compliant. **N~keit** *f* - indulgence; compliance

nachgrübeln *vi sep* (*haben*) ponder (**über** + *acc* on)

nachhallen *vi sep* (*haben*) reverberate

nachhaltig *a* lasting

nachhause *adv* = nach Hause, *s.* Haus

nachhelfen† *vi sep* (*haben*) help

nachher *adv* later; (*danach*) afterwards; bis n~! see you later!

Nachhilfeunterricht *m* coaching

Nachhinein (**nachhinein**) *adv* im N~ (n~) afterwards

nachhinken *vi sep* (*sein*) (*fig*) lag behind

nachholen *vt sep* (*später holen*) fetch later; (*mehr holen*) get more; (*später machen*) do later; (*aufholen*) catch up on; make up for (*Zeit*)

nachjagen *vi sep* (*haben*) (+ *dat*) chase after

Nachkomme *m* -n,-n† descendant. **n~n**† *vi sep* (*sein*) follow [later], come later; (*Schritt halten*) keep up; etw (*dat*) n~n (*fig*) comply with (*Bitte, Wunsch*); carry out (*Versprechen, Pflicht*). **N~nschaft** *f* - descendants *pl*, progeny

Nachkriegszeit *f* post-war period

Nachlass *m* -es,-̈e (**Nachlaß** *m* -sses,-̈sse) discount; (*Jur*) [deceased's] estate

nachlassen† *v sep* □ *vi* (*haben*) decrease; (*Regen, Hitze:*) let up; (*Schmerz:*) ease; (*Sturm:*) abate; (*Augen, Kräfte, Leistungen:*) deteriorate; **er ließ nicht nach [mit Fragen]** he persisted [with his questions] □ *vt* etw vom Preis n~ take sth off the price

nachlässig *a* careless, *adv* -ly; (*leger*) casual, *adv* -ly; (*unordentlich*) sloppy, *adv* -ily. **N~keit** *f* - carelessness; sloppiness

nachlaufen† *vi sep* (*sein*) (+ *dat*) run after

nachlegen *vt sep* Holz/Kohlen n~ put more wood/coal on the fire

nachlesen† *vt sep* look up

nachlöse|n *vi sep* (*haben*) pay one's fare on the train/on arrival. **N~schalter** *m* excess-fare office

nachmachen *vt sep* (*später machen*) do later; (*imitieren*) imitate, copy; (*fälschen*) forge; jdm etw n~ copy sth from s.o.; repeat (*Übung*) after s.o.

Nachmittag *m* afternoon; heute/gestern N~ this/yesterday afternoon. **n~** *adv* heute/gestern n~ (NEW) heute/gestern N~, *s.* Nachmittag. **n~s** *adv* in the afternoon

Nachnahme *f* etw per N~ schicken send sth cash on delivery *or* COD

Nachname *m* surname

Nachporto *nt* excess postage

nachprüfen *vt sep* check, verify

nachrechnen *vt sep* work out; (*prüfen*) check

Nachrede *f* üble N~ defamation

Nachricht *f* -,-en [piece of] news *sg*; **N~en** news *sg*; **eine N~ hinterlassen** leave a message; jdm N~ geben inform, notify s.o. **N~endienst** *m* (*Mil*) intelligence service. **N~ensendung** *f* news bulletin. **N~enwesen** *nt* communications *pl*

nachrücken *vi sep* (*sein*) move up

Nachruf *m* obituary

nachsagen *vt sep* repeat (jdm after s.o.); jdm Schlechtes/Gutes n~ speak ill/well of s.o.; **man sagt ihm nach, dass er geizig ist** he is said to be stingy

Nachsaison *f* late season

Nachsatz *m* postscript

nachschicken *vt sep* (*später schicken*) send later; (*hinterher-*) send after (jdm s.o.); send on (*Post*) (jdm to s.o.)

nachschlag|en† *v sep* □ *vt* look up □ *vi* (*haben*) in einem Wörterbuch n~en consult a dictionary; jdm n~en take after s.o. **N~ewerk** *nt* reference book

Nachschlüssel *m* duplicate key

Nachschrift f transcript; (*Nachsatz*) postscript

Nachschub m (*Mil*) supplies pl

nachsehen† v sep ▫ vt (*prüfen*) check; (*nachschlagen*) look up; (*hinwegsehen über*) overlook ▫ vi (*haben*) have a look; (*prüfen*) check; **im Wörterbuch n∼** consult a dictionary; **jdm/etw n∼** gaze after s.o./sth. **N∼** nt das **N∼** haben (*fam*) go empty-handed

nachsenden† vt sep forward (*Post*) (**jdm** to s.o.); **'bitte n∼'** 'please forward'

Nachsicht f forbearance; (*Milde*) leniency; (*Nachgiebigkeit*) indulgence. **n∼ ig** a forbearing; lenient; indulgent

Nachsilbe f suffix

nachsitzen† vi sep (*haben*) **n∼ müssen** be kept in [after school]; **jdn n∼ lassen** give s.o. detention. **N∼** nt **-s** (*Sch*) detention

Nachspeise f dessert, sweet

Nachspiel nt (*fig*) sequel

nachspionieren vi sep (*haben*) **jdm n∼** spy on s.o.

nachsprechen† vt sep repeat (**jdm** after s.o.)

nachspülen vt sep rinse

nächst /-çst/ prep (+ dat) next to. **n∼beste(r,s)** a first [available]; (*zweitbeste*) next best. **n∼e(r,s)** a next; (*nächstgelegene*) nearest; (*Verwandte*) closest; **n∼e Woche** next week; **in n∼er Nähe** close by; **am n∼en sein** be nearest or closest ▫ pron **der/die/das n∼e (n∼e)** the next; **der N∼e (n∼e) bitte** next please; **als N∼es (n∼es)** next; **fürs N∼e (n∼e)** for the time being. **N∼e(r)** m fellow man

nachstehend a following ▫ adv below

nachstellen v sep ▫ vt readjust; put back (*Uhr*) ▫ vi (*haben*) (+ dat) pursue

nächst|emal adv **das n∼emal** (NEW) **das nächste Mal**, s. **Mal¹**. **N∼enliebe** f charity. **n∼ens** adv shortly. **n∼gelegen** a nearest. **n∼liegend** a most obvious

nachstreben vi sep (*haben*) **jdm n∼** emulate s.o.

nachsuchen vi sep (*haben*) search; **n∼ um** request

Nacht f -,⸚e night; **über/bei N∼** overnight/at night; **Montag/morgen N∼** Monday/tomorrow night; **heute N∼** tonight; (*letzte Nacht*) last night; **gestern N∼** last night; (*vorletzte Nacht*) the night before last. **n∼** adv **morgen/heute/gestern n∼** (NEW) **morgen/heute/gestern N∼**, s. **Nacht**. **N∼dienst** m night duty

Nachteil m disadvantage; **zum N∼** to the detriment (*gen* of). **n∼ig** a adverse, adv -ly

Nacht|essen nt (*SGer*) supper. **N∼falter** m moth. **N∼hemd** nt night-dress; (*Männer-*) night-shirt

Nachtigall f -,-en nightingale

Nachtisch m dessert

Nacht|klub m night-club. **N∼leben** nt night-life

nächtlich a nocturnal, night ...

Nacht|lokal nt night-club. **N∼mahl** nt (*Aust*) supper

Nachtrag m postscript; (*Ergänzung*) supplement. **n∼en†** vt sep add; **jdm etw n∼en** walk behind s.o. carrying sth; (*fig*) bear a grudge against s.o. for sth. **n∼end** a vindictive; **n∼end sein** bear grudges

nachträglich a subsequent, later; (*verspätet*) belated ▫ adv later; (*nachher*) afterwards; (*verspätet*) belatedly

nachtrauern vi sep (*haben*) (+ dat) mourn the loss of

Nacht|ruhe f night's rest; **angenehme N∼ruhe!** sleep well! **n∼s** adv at night; **2 Uhr n∼s** 2 o'clock in the morning. **N∼schicht** f night-shift. **N∼tisch** m bedside table. **N∼tischlampe** f bedside lamp. **N∼topf** m chamber-pot. **N∼wächter** m night-watchman. **N∼zeit** f night-time

Nachuntersuchung f check-up

nachwachsen† vi sep (*sein*) grow again

Nachwahl f by-election

Nachweis m -es,-e proof. **n∼bar** a demonstrable. **n∼en†** vt sep prove; (*aufzeigen*) show; (*vermitteln*) give details of; **jdm nichts n∼en können** have no proof against s.o. **n∼lich** a demonstrable, adv -bly

Nachwelt f posterity

Nachwirkung f after-effect

Nachwort nt (pl -e) epilogue

Nachwuchs m new generation; (*fam: Kinder*) offspring. **N∼spieler** m young player

nachzahlen vt/i sep (*haben*) pay extra; (*später zahlen*) pay later; **Steuern n∼** pay tax arrears

nachzählen vt/i sep (*haben*) count again; (*prüfen*) check

Nachzahlung f extra/later payment; (*Gehalts-*) back-payment

nachzeichnen vt sep copy

Nachzügler m -s,- late-comer; (*Zurückgebliebener*) straggler

Nacken m -s,- nape or back of the neck

nackt a naked; (*bloß, kahl*) bare; (*Wahrheit*) plain. **N∼baden** nt nude bathing. **N∼heit** f - nakedness, nudity. **N∼kultur** f nudism. **N∼schnecke** f slug

Nadel *f* -,-n needle; (*Häkel-*) hook; (*Schmuck-, Hut-*) pin. **N~arbeit** *f* needlework. **N~baum** *m* conifer. **N~kissen** *nt* pincushion. **N~stich** *m* stitch; (*fig*) pinprick. **N~wald** *m* coniferous forest

Nagel *m* -s,-̈ nail. **N~bürste** *f* nail-brush. **N~feile** *f* nail-file. **N~haut** *f* cuticle. **N~lack** *m* nail varnish. **n~n** *vt* nail. **n~neu** *a* brand-new. **N~schere** *f* nail scissors *pl*

nagen *vt/i* (*haben*) gnaw (**an** + *dat* at); **n~d** (*fig*) nagging

Nagetier *nt* rodent

nah *a, adv & prep* = **nahe; von nah und fern** from far and wide

Näharbeit *f* sewing; **eine N~** a piece of sewing

Nahaufnahme *f* close-up

nahe *a* (**näher, nächst**) nearby; (*zeitlich*) imminent; (*eng*) close; **der N~ Osten** the Middle East; **in n~r Zukunft** in the near future; **von n~m** [from] close to; **n~ sein** be close (*dat* to); **den Tränen n~** close to tears □ *adv* near, close; (*verwandt*) closely; **n~ an** (+ *acc/dat*) near [to], close to; **n~ daran sein, etw zu tun** nearly do sth; **n~ liegen** be close; (*fig*) be highly likely; **n~ liegende Lösung** obvious solution; **n~ legen** (*fig*) recommend (*dat* to); **jdm n~ legen, etw zu tun** urge s.o. to do sth; **jdm n~ stehen** (*fig*) be close to s.o.; **etw** (*dat*) **n~ kommen** (*fig*) come close to sth; **jdm n~ kommen** (*fig*) get close to s.o.; **jdm n~ gehen** (*fig*) affect s.o. deeply; **jdm zu n~ treten** (*fig*) offend s.o. □ *prep* (+ *dat*) near [to], close to

Nähe *f* - nearness, proximity; **aus der N~** [from] close to; **in der N~** near or close by; **in der N~ der Kirche** near the church

nahebei *adv* near or close by

nahe|gehen† *vi sep* (*sein*) (NEW) **n~ gehen**, *s.* **nahe. n~kommen**† *vi sep* (*sein*) (NEW) **n~ kommen**, *s.* **nahe. n~legen** *vt sep* (NEW) **n~ legen**, *s.* **nahe. n~liegen**† *vi sep* (*haben*) (NEW) **n~ liegen**, *s.* **nahe. n~liegend** *a* (NEW) **n~ liegend**, *s.* **nahe**

nahen *vi* (*sein*) (*liter*) approach

nähen *vt/i* (*haben*) sew; (*anfertigen*) make; (*Med*) stitch [up]

näher *a* closer; (*Weg*) shorter; (*Einzelheiten*) further □ *adv* closer; (*genauer*) more closely; **n~ kommen** come closer, approach; (*fig*) get closer (*dat* to); **sich n~ erkundigen** make further enquiries; **n~an** (+ *acc/dat*) nearer [to], closer to □ *prep* (+ *dat*) nearer [to], closer to. **N~e[s]** *nt* [further] details *pl*. **n~kommen**† *vi sep* (*sein*) (NEW) **n~ kommen**, *s.* **näher. n~n (sich)** *vr* approach

nahestehen† *vi sep* (*haben*) (NEW) **nahe stehen**, *s.* **nahe**

nahezu *adv* almost

Nähgarn *nt* [sewing] cotton

Nahkampf *m* close combat

Näh|maschine *f* sewing machine. **N~nadel** *f* sewing-needle

nähren *vt* feed; (*fig*) nurture; **sich n~ von** live on □ *vi* (*haben*) be nutritious

nahrhaft *a* nutritious

Nährstoff *m* nutrient

Nahrung *f* - food, nourishment. **N~smittel** *nt* food

Nährwert *m* nutritional value

Naht *f* -,-̈e seam; (*Med*) suture. **n~los** *a* seamless

Nahverkehr *m* local service. **N~szug** *m* local train

Nähzeug *nt* sewing; (*Zubehör*) sewing kit

naiv /na'i:f/ *a* naïve, *adv* -ly. **N~ität** /-vi'tɛ:t/ *f* - naïvety

Name *m* -ns,-n name; **im N~n** (+ *gen*) in the name of; (*handeln*) on behalf of; **das Kind beim rechten N~n nennen** (*fam*) call a spade a spade. **n~nlos** *a* nameless; (*unbekannt*) unknown, anonymous. **n~ns** *adv* by the name of □ *prep* (+ *gen*) on behalf of. **N~nstag** *m* name-day. **N~nsvetter** *m* namesake. **N~nszug** *m* signature. **n~ntlich** *adv* by name; (*besonders*) especially

namhaft *a* noted; (*ansehnlich*) considerable; **n~ machen** name

nämlich *adv* (*und zwar*) namely; (*denn*) because

nanu *int* hallo

Napf *m* -[e]s,-̈e bowl

Narbe *f* -,-n scar

Narkose *f* -,-n general anaesthetic. **N~arzt** *m* anaesthetist. **N~mittel** *nt* anaesthetic

Narkot|ikum *nt* -s,-ka narcotic; (*Narkosemittel*) anaesthetic. **n~isieren** *vt* anaesthetize

Narr *m* -en,-en fool; **zum N~en haben** *od* **halten** make a fool of. **n~en** *vt* fool. **n~ensicher** *a* foolproof. **N~heit** *f* -,-en folly

Närr|in *f* -,-nen fool. **n~isch** *a* foolish; (*fam: verrückt*) crazy (**auf** + *acc* about)

Narzisse *f* -,-n narcissus; **gelbe N~** daffodil

nasal *a* nasal

nasch|en *vt/i* (*haben*) nibble (**an** + *dat* at); **wer hat vom Kuchen genascht?** who's been at the cake? **n~haft** *a* sweet-toothed

Nase *f* -,-n nose; **an der N~ herumführen** (*fam*) dupe

näseln vi (haben) speak through one's nose; **n~d** nasal

Nasen|bluten nt -s nosebleed. **N~loch** nt nostril. **N~rücken** m bridge of the nose

Naseweis m -es,-e (fam) know-all

Nashorn nt rhinoceros

nass (naß) a (nasser, nassest) wet

Nässe f - wet; (Nasssein) wetness. **n~n** vt wet

nasskalt (naßkalt) a cold and wet

Nation /naˈtsi̯oːn/ f -,-en nation. **n~al** a national. **N~alhymne** f national anthem. **N~alismus** m - nationalism. **N~alität** f -,-en nationality. **N~alsozialismus** m National Socialism. **N~alspieler** m international

Natrium nt -s sodium

Natron nt -s doppeltkohlensaures **N~** bicarbonate of soda

Natter f -,-n snake; (Gift-) viper

Natur f -,-en nature; **von N~ aus** by nature. **N~alien** /-i̯ən/ pl natural produce sg. **n~alisieren** vt naturalize. **N~alisierung** f -,-en naturalization

Naturell nt -s,-e disposition

Natur|erscheinung f natural phenomenon. **n~farben** a natural[-coloured]. **N~forscher** m naturalist. **N~kunde** f natural history. **N~lehrpfad** m nature trail

natürlich a natural □ adv naturally; (selbstverständlich) of course. **N~keit** f - naturalness

natur|rein a pure. **N~schutz** m nature conservation; **unter N~schutz stehen** be protected. **N~schutzgebiet** nt nature reserve. **N~wissenschaft** f [natural] science. **N~wissenschaftler** m scientist. **n~wissenschaftlich** a scientific; (Sch) science ...

nautisch a nautical

Navigation /-ˈtsi̯oːn/ f - navigation

Nazi m -s,-s Nazi

n.Chr. abbr (nach Christus) AD

Nebel m -s,- fog; (leicht) mist. **n~haft** a hazy. **N~horn** nt foghorn. **n~ig** a = neblig

neben prep (+ dat/acc) next to, beside; (+ dat) (außer) apart from; **n~ mir** next to me. **n~an** adv next door

Neben|anschluss (**Nebenanschluß**) m (Teleph) extension. **N~ausgaben** fpl incidental expenses

nebenbei adv in addition; (beiläufig) casually; **n~ bemerkt** incidentally

Neben|bemerkung f passing remark. **N~beruf** m second job. **N~beschäftigung** f spare-time occupation. **N~buhler(in)** m -s,- (f -,-nen) rival

nebeneinander adv next to each other, side by side

Neben|eingang m side entrance. **N~fach** nt (Univ) subsidiary subject. **N~fluss** (**N~fluß**) m tributary. **N~gleis** nt siding. **N~haus** nt house next door

nebenher adv in addition. **n~gehen†** vi sep (sein) walk alongside

nebenhin adv casually

Neben|höhle f sinus. **N~kosten** pl additional costs. **N~mann** m (pl -männer) person next to one. **N~produkt** nt byproduct. **N~rolle** f supporting role; (kleine) minor role; **eine N~rolle spielen** (fig) be unimportant. **N~sache** f unimportant matter. **n~sächlich** a unimportant. **N~satz** m subordinate clause. **N~straße** f minor road; (Seiten-) side street. **N~verdienst** m additional earnings pl. **N~wirkung** f side-effect. **N~zimmer** nt room next door

neblig a foggy; (leicht) misty

nebst prep (+ dat) [together] with

Necessaire /nesɛˈsɛːʀ/ nt -s,-s toilet bag; (Näh-, Nagel-) set

neck|en vt tease. **N~erei** f - teasing. **n~isch** a teasing; (kess) saucy

nee adv (fam) no

Neffe m -n,-n nephew

negativ a negative. **N~** nt -s,-e (Phot) negative

Neger m -s,- Negro

nehmen† vt take (dat from); **sich** (dat) **etw n~** take sth; help oneself to (Essen); **jdn zu sich n~** have s.o. to live with one

Neid m -[e]s envy, jealousy. **n~en** vt jdm den Erfolg **n~en** be jealous of s.o.'s success. **n~isch** a envious, jealous (auf + acc of); **auf jdn n~isch sein** envy s.o.

neig|en vt incline; (zur Seite) tilt; (beugen) bend; **sich n~en** incline; (Boden:) slope; (Person:) bend (über + acc over) □ vi (haben) **n~en zu** (fig) have a tendency towards; be prone to (Krankheit); incline towards (Ansicht); **dazu n~en, etw zu tun** tend to do sth. **N~ung** f -,-en inclination; (Gefälle) slope; (fig) tendency; (Hang) leaning; (Herzens-) affection

nein adv, **N~** nt -s no

Nektar m -s nectar

Nelke f -,-n carnation; (Feder-) pink; (Culin) clove

nenn|en† vt call; (taufen) name; (angeben) give; (erwähnen) mention; **sich n~en** call oneself. **n~enswert** a significant. **N~ung** f -,-en mention; (Sport) entry. **N~wert** m face value

Neofaschismus m neofascism

Neon nt -s neon. **N~beleuchtung** f fluorescent lighting

neppen vt (fam) rip off

Nerv m -s,-en /-fən/ nerve; **die N~en verlieren** lose control of oneself. **n~en** vt jdn **n~en** (sl) get on s.o.'s nerves. **N~enarzt** m neurologist. **n~enaufreibend** a nerve-racking. **N~enbündel** nt (fam) bundle of nerves. **N~enkitzel** m (fam) thrill. **N~ensystem** nt nervous system. **N~enzusammenbruch** m nervous breakdown

nervös a nervy, edgy; (Med) nervous; **n~ sein** be on edge

Nervosität f -, nerviness, edginess

Nerz m -es,-e mink

Nessel f -,-n nettle

Nessessär nt -s,-s = Necessaire

Nest nt -[e]s,-er nest; (fam: Ort) small place

nesteln vi (haben) fumble (**an** + dat with)

Nesthäkchen nt -s,- (fam) baby of the family

nett a nice, adv -ly; (freundlich) kind, adv -ly

netto adv net. **N~gewicht** nt net weight

Netz nt -es,-e net; (Einkaufs-) string bag; (Spinnen-) web; (auf Landkarte) grid; (System) network; (Electr) mains pl. **N~haut** f retina. **N~karte** f area season ticket. **N~werk** nt network

neu a new; (modern) modern; **wie neu** as good as new; **das ist mir neu** it's news to me; **aufs N~e** (n~e) [once] again; **von n~em** all over again □ adv newly; (gerade erst) only just; (erneut) again; **etw neu schreiben/streichen** rewrite/repaint sth; **neu vermähltes Paar** newly-weds pl. **N~ankömmling** m -s,-e newcomer. **N~anschaffung** f recent acquisition. **n~artig** a new [kind of]. **N~auflage** f new edition; (unverändert) reprint. **N~bau** m (pl -ten) new house/building

Neu|e(r) m/f new person, newcomer; (Schüler) new boy/girl. **N~e(s)** nt das **N~e** the new; **etwas N~es** something new; (Neuigkeit) a piece of news; **was gibt's N~es?** what's the news?

neuer|dings adv [just] recently. **n~lich** a renewed, new □ adv again. **N~ung** f -,-en innovation

neuest|e(r,s) a newest; (letzte) latest; **seit n~em** just recently. **N~e** nt das **N~e** the latest thing; (Neuigkeit) the latest news sg

neugeboren a newborn

Neugier, **Neugierde** f - curiosity; (Wissbegierde) inquisitiveness

neugierig a curious (**auf** + acc about), adv -ly; (wissbegierig) inquisitive, adv -ly

Neuheit f -,-en novelty; (Neusein) newness; **die letzte N~** the latest thing

Neuigkeit f -,-en piece of news; **N~en** news sg

Neujahr nt New Year's Day; **über N~** over the New Year

neulich adv the other day

Neu|ling m -s,-e novice. **n~modisch** a newfangled. **N~mond** m new moon

neun inv a, **N~** f -,-en nine. **N~malkluge(r)** m (fam) clever Dick. **n~te(r,s)** a ninth. **n~zehn** inv a nineteen. **n~zehnte(r,s)** a nineteenth. **n~zig** inv a ninety. **n~zigste(r,s)** a ninetieth

Neuralgie f -,-n neuralgia

neureich a nouveau riche

Neurologe m -n,-n neurologist

Neuro|se f -,-n neurosis. **n~tisch** a neurotic

Neuschnee m fresh snow

Neuseeland nt -s New Zealand

neuste(r,s) a = neueste(r,s)

neutral a neutral. **n~isieren** vt neutralize. **N~ität** f - neutrality

Neutrum nt -s,-tra neuter noun

neu|vermählt a (NEW) **n~ vermählt**, s. **neu**. **N~zeit** f modern times pl

nicht adv not; **ich kann n~** I cannot or can't; **er ist n~ gekommen** he hasn't come; **n~ mehr/besser als** no more/better than; **bitte n~!** please don't! **n~ berühren!** do not touch! **du kommst doch auch, ~ [wahr]?** you are coming too, aren't you? **du kennst ihn doch, n~?** you know him, don't you?

Nichtachtung f disregard; (Geringschätzung) disdain

Nichte f -,-n niece

nichtig a trivial; (Jur) [null and] void

Nichtraucher m non-smoker. **N~abteil** nt non-smoking compartment

nichts pron & a nothing; **n~ anderes/Besseres** nothing else/better; **n~ mehr** no more; **ich weiß n~** I know nothing or don't know anything; **n~ ahnend** unsuspecting; **n~ sagend** meaningless; (uninteressant) nondescript. **N~** nt - nothingness; (fig: Leere) void; (Person) nonentity. **n~ahnend** a (NEW) **n~ ahnend**, s. **nichts**

Nichtschwimmer m non-swimmer

nichtsdesto|trotz adv all the same. **n~weniger** adv nevertheless

nichts|nutzig a good-for-nothing; (fam: unartig) naughty. **n~sagend** a (NEW) **n~ sagend**, s. **nichts**. **N~tun** nt -s idleness

Nickel nt -s nickel

nicken vi (haben) nod. **N~** nt -s nod

Nickerchen nt -s,- (fam) nap; **ein N~ machen** have forty winks

nie adv never

nieder a low □ adv down. **n~brennen†** vt/i sep (sein) burn down. **N~deutsch** nt

Low German. **N~gang** *m* (*fig*) decline. **n~gedrückt** *a* (*fig*) depressed. **n~gehen†** *vi sep* (*sein*) come down. **n~geschlagen** *a* dejected, despondent. **N~geschlagenheit** *f* - dejection, despondency. **N~kunft** *f* -,⁝e confinement. **N~lage** *f* defeat

Niederlande (die) *pl* the Netherlands

Niederländ|er *m* -s,- Dutchman; **die N~er** the Dutch *pl*. **N~erin** *f* -,-nen Dutchwoman. **n~isch** *a* Dutch

nieder|lassen† *vt sep* let down; **sich n~lassen** settle; (*sich setzen*) sit down. **N~lassung** *f* -,-en settlement; (*Zweigstelle*) branch. **n~legen** *vt sep* put *or* lay down; resign (*Amt*); **die Arbeit n~legen** go on strike; **sich n~legen** lie down. **n~machen, n~metzeln** *vt sep* massacre. **n~reißen†** *vt sep* tear down. **N~sachsen** *nt* Lower Saxony. **N~schlag** *m* precipitation; (*Regen*) rainfall; (*radioaktiver*) fallout; (*Boxen*) knock-down; **n~schlagen†** *vt sep* knock down; lower (*Augen*); (*unterdrücken*) crush. **n~schmettern** *vt sep* (*fig*) shatter. **n~schreiben†** *vt sep* write down. **n~schreien†** *vt sep* shout down. **n~setzen** *vt sep* put *or* set down; **sich n~setzen** sit down. **n~strecken** *vt sep* fell; (*durch Schuss*) gun down

niederträchtig *a* base, vile

Niederung *f* -,-en low ground

nieder|walzen *vt sep* flatten. **n~werfen†** *vt sep* throw down; (*unterdrücken*) crush; **sich n~werfen** prostrate oneself

niedlich *a* pretty; (*goldig*) sweet; (*Amer*) cute

niedrig *a* low; (*fig: gemein*) base □ *adv* low

niemals *adv* never

niemand *pron* nobody, no one

Niere *f* -,-n kidney; **künstliche N~** kidney machine

nieseln *vi* (*haben*) drizzle; **es n~t** it is drizzling. **N~regen** *m* drizzle

niesen *vi* (*haben*) sneeze. **N~** *nt* -s sneezing; (*Nieser*) sneeze

Niet *m* & *nt* -[e]s,e, **Niete¹** *f* -,-n rivet; (*an Jeans*) stud

Niete² *f* -,-n blank; (*fam*) failure

nieten *vt* rivet

Nikotin *nt* -s nicotine

Nil *m* -[s] Nile. **N~pferd** *nt* hippopotamus

nimmer *adv* (*SGer*) not any more; **nie und n~** never. **n~müde** *a* tireless. **n~satt** *a* insatiable. **N~wiedersehen n auf N~wiedersehen** (*fam*) for good

nippen *vi* (*haben*) take a sip (**an** + *dat* of)

nirgends, nirgendwo *adv* nowhere

Nische *f* -,-n recess, niche

nisten *vi* (*haben*) nest

Nitrat *nt* -[e]s,-e nitrate

Niveau /ni'vo:/ *nt* -s,-s level; (*geistig, künstlerisch*) standard

nix *adv* (*fam*) nothing

Nixe *f* -,-n mermaid

nobel *a* noble; (*fam: luxuriös*) luxurious; (*fam: großzügig*) generous

noch *adv* still; (*zusätzlich*) as well; (*mit Komparativ*) even; **n~ nicht** not yet; **gerade n~** only just; **n~ immer** *od* **immer n~** still; **n~ letzte Woche** only last week; **es ist n~ viel Zeit** there's plenty of time yet; **wer/was/wo n~?** who/what/where else? **n~ jemand/etwas** someone/something else; (*Frage*) anyone/anything else? **n~ einmal** again; **n~ einmal so viel** as much again; **n~ ein Bier** another beer; **n~ größer** even bigger; **n~ so sehr/schön** however much/beautiful □ *conj* **weder ... n~** neither ... nor

nochmal|ig *a* further. **n~s** *adv* again

Nomad|e *m* -n,-n nomad. **n~isch** *a* nomadic

Nominativ *m* -s,-e nominative

nominell *a* nominal, *adv* -ly

nominier|en *vt* nominate. **N~ung** *f* -,-en nomination

nonchalant /nõʃa'lã:/ *a* nonchalant, *adv* -ly

Nonne *f* -,-n nun. **N~nkloster** *nt* convent

Nonstopflug *m* direct flight

Nord *m* -[e]s north. **N~amerika** *nt* North America. **n~deutsch** *a* North German

Norden *m* -s north; **nach N~** north

nordisch *a* Nordic

nördlich *a* northern; (*Richtung*) northerly □ *adv & prep* (+ *gen*) **n~ [von] der Stadt** [to the] north of the town

Nordosten *m* north-east

Nord|pol *m* North Pole. **N~see** *f* - North Sea. **n~wärts** *adv* northwards. **N~westen** *m* north-west

Nörgelei *f* -,-en grumbling

nörgeln *vi* (*haben*) grumble

Norm *f* -,-en norm; (*Techn*) standard; (*Soll*) quota

normal *a* normal, *adv* -ly. **n~erweise** *adv* normally. **n~isieren** *vt* normalize; **sich n~isieren** return to normal

normen, normieren *vt* standardize

Norwe|gen *nt* -s Norway. **N~ger(in)** *m* -s,- (*f* -,-nen) Norwegian. **n~gisch** *a* Norwegian

Nost|algie *f* - nostalgia. **n~algisch** *a* nostalgic

Not *f* -,-̈e need; (*Notwendigkeit*) necessity; (*Entbehrung*) hardship; (*seelisch*) trouble; **Not leiden** be in need, suffer hardship; **Not leidende Menschen** needy people; **mit knapper Not** only just; **zur Not** if need be; (*äußerstenfalls*) at a pinch

Notar *m* -s,-e notary public

Not|arzt *m* emergency doctor. **N~ausgang** *m* emergency exit. **N~behelf** *m* -[e]s,-e makeshift. **N~bremse** *f* emergency brake. **N~dienst** *m* **N~dienst haben** be on call. **n~dürftig** *a* scant; (*behelfsmäßig*) makeshift

Note *f* -,-n note; (*Zensur*) mark; **ganze/halbe N~** (*Mus*) semi-breve/minim, (*Amer*) whole/half note; **N~n lesen** read music; **persönliche N~** personal touch. **N~nblatt** *nt* sheet of music. **N~nschlüssel** *m* clef. **N~nständer** *m* musicstand

Notfall *m* emergency; **im N~** in an emergency; (*notfalls*) if need be; **für den N~** just in case. **n~s** *adv* if need be

not|gedrungen *adv* of necessity. **N~groschen** *m* nest-egg

notieren *vt* note down; (*Comm*) quote; **sich** (*dat*) **etw n~** make a note of sth

nötig *a* necessary; **n~ haben** need; **das N~ste** the essentials *pl* □ *adv* urgently. **n~en** *vt* force; (*auffordern*) press; **laßt euch nicht n~en** help yourselves. **n~enfalls** *adv* if need be. **N~ung** *f* - coercion

Notiz *f* -,-en note; (*Zeitungs-*) item; **[keine] N~ nehmen von** take [no] notice of. **N~buch** *nt* notebook. **N~kalender** *m* diary

Not|lage *f* plight. **n~landen** *vi* (*sein*) make a forced landing. **N~landung** *f* forced landing. **n~leidend** *a* ⟨NEW⟩ **Not leidend**, s. **Not**. **N~lösung** *f* stopgap. **N~lüge** *f* white lie

notorisch *a* notorious

Not|ruf *m* emergency call; (*Naut, Aviat*) distress call; (*Nummer*) emergency services number. **N~signal** *nt* distress signal. **N~stand** *m* state of emergency. **N~unterkunft** *f* emergency accommodation. **N~wehr** *f* - (*Jur*) self-defence

notwendig *a* necessary; (*unerlässlich*) essential □ *adv* urgently. **N~keit** *f* -,-en necessity

Notzucht *f* - (*Jur*) rape

Nougat /'nu:gat/ *m* & *nt* -s nougat

Novelle *f* -,-n novella; (*Pol*) amendment

November *m* -s,- November

Novität *f* -,-en novelty

Novize *m* -n,-n, **Novizin** *f* -,-nen (*Relig*) novice

Nu *m* **im Nu** (*fam*) in a flash

Nuance /'nyã:sə/ *f* -,-n nuance; (*Spur*) shade

nüchtern *a* sober; (*sachlich*) matter-of-fact; (*schmucklos*) bare; (*ohne Würze*) bland; **auf n~en Magen** on an empty stomach □ *adv* soberly

Nudel *f* -,-n piece of pasta; **N~n** pasta *sg*; (*Band-*) noodles. **N~holz** *nt* rolling-pin

Nudist *m* -en,-en nudist

nuklear *a* nuclear

null *inv a* zero, nought; (*Teleph*) O; (*Sport*) nil; (*Tennis*) love; **n~ Fehler** no mistakes; **n~ und nichtig** (*Jur*) null and void. **N~** *f* -,-en nought, zero; (*fig: Person*) nonentity; **drei Grad unter N~** three degrees below zero. **N~punkt** *m* zero

numerieren *vt* ⟨NEW⟩ **nummerieren**

numerisch *a* numerical

Nummer *f* -,-n number; (*Ausgabe*) issue; (*Darbietung*) item; (*Zirkus-*) act; (*Größe*) size. **n~ieren** *vt* number. **N~nschild** *nt* number-/(*Amer*) license-plate

nun *adv* now; (*na*) well; (*halt*) just; **von nun an** from now on; **nun gut!** very well then! **das Leben ist nun mal so** life's like that

nur *adv* only, just; **wo kann sie nur sein?** wherever can she be? **alles, was ich nur will** everything I could possibly want; **er soll es nur versuchen!** (*drohend*) just let him try! **könnte/hätte ich nur ...!** if only I could/had ...! **nur Geduld!** just be patient!

Nürnberg *nt* -s Nuremberg

nuscheln *vt/i* (*fam*) mumble

Nuss *f* -,-̈e (**Nuß** *f* -;-̈sse) nut. **N~baum** *m* walnut tree. **N~knacker** *m* -s,- nutcrackers *pl*. **N~schale** *f* nutshell

Nüstern *fpl* nostrils

Nut *f* -,-en, **Nute** *f* -,-n groove

Nutte *f* -,-n (*sl*) tart (*sl*)

Nutz **zu N~e machen** = **zunutze machen**, *s.* **zunutze**. **n~bar** *a* usable; **n~bar machen** utilize; cultivate ⟨Boden⟩. **n~bringend** *a* profitable, *adv* -bly

nütze *a* **zu etwas/nichts n~ sein** be useful/useless

nutzen *vt* use, utilize; (*aus-*) take advantage of □ *vi* (*haben*) = **nützen**. **N~** *m* -s benefit; (*Comm*) profit; **N~ ziehen aus** benefit from; **von N~ sein** be useful

nützen *vi* (*haben*) be useful *or* of use (*dat* to); ⟨Mittel:⟩ be effective; **nichts n~** be useless *or* no use; **was nützt mir das?** what good is that to me? □ *vt* = **nutzen**

Nutzholz *nt* timber

nützlich *a* useful; **sich n~ machen** make oneself useful. **N~keit** *f* - usefulness

nutz|los *a* useless; (*vergeblich*) vain. **N∼losigkeit** *f* - uselessness. **N∼nießer** *m* -s,- beneficiary. **N∼ung** *f* - use, utilization

Nylon /'nailɔn/ *nt* -s nylon

Nymphe /'nʏmfə/ *f* -,-n nymph

O

o *int* o **ja/nein!** oh yes/no! **o weh!** oh dear!

Oase *f* -,-n oasis

ob *conj* whether; **ob reich, ob arm** rich or poor; **ob sie wohl krank ist?** I wonder whether she is ill; **und ob!** (*fam*) you bet!

Obacht *f* **O∼ geben** pay attention; **O∼ geben auf** (+ *acc*) look after; **O∼!** look out!

Obdach *nt* -[e]s shelter. **o∼los** *a* homeless. **O∼lose(r)** *m/f* homeless person; **die O∼losen** the homeless *pl*

Obduktion /-'tsi̯oːn/ *f* -,-en post-mortem

O-Beine *ntpl* (*fam*) bow-legs, bandy legs. **O-beinig, o-beinig** *a* bandy-legged

oben *adv* at the top; (*auf der Oberseite*) on top; (*eine Treppe hoch*) upstairs; (*im Text*) above; **da o∼** up there; **o∼ im Norden** up in the north; **siehe o∼** see above; **o∼ auf** (+ *acc/dat*) on top of; **nach o∼** up[wards]; (*die Treppe hinauf*) upstairs; **von o∼** from above/upstairs; **von o∼ bis unten** from top to bottom/(*Person*) to toe; **jdn von o∼ bis unten mustern** look s.o. up and down; **o∼ erwähnt** *od* **genannt** above-mentioned. **o∼an** *adv* at the top. **o∼auf** *adv* on top; **o∼auf sein** (*fig*) be cheerful. **o∼drein** *adv* on top of that. **o∼erwähnt, o∼genannt** *a* (NEW) **o∼ erwähnt** *od* **genannt**, *s.* **oben. o∼hin** *adv* casually

Ober *m* -s,- waiter

Ober|arm *m* upper arm. **O∼arzt** *m* ≈ senior registrar. **O∼befehlshaber** *m* commander-in-chief. **O∼begriff** *m* generic term. **O∼deck** *nt* upper deck. **o∼e(r,s)** *a* upper; (*höhere*) higher. **O∼fläche** *f* surface. **o∼flächlich** *a* superficial, *adv* -ly. **O∼geschoss** (**O∼geschoß**) *nt* upper storey. **o∼halb** *adv & prep* (+ *gen*) above; **o∼halb vom Dorf** *od* **des Dorfes** above the village. **O∼hand** *f* **die O∼hand gewinnen** gain the upper hand. **O∼haupt** *nt* (*fig*) head. **O∼haus** *nt* (*Pol*) upper house; (*in UK*) House of Lords. **O∼hemd** *nt* [man's] shirt

Oberin *f* -,-nen matron; (*Relig*) mother superior

ober|irdisch *a* surface ... □ *adv* above ground. **O∼kellner** *m* head waiter. **O∼kiefer** *m* upper jaw. **O∼körper** *m* upper part of the body. **O∼leutnant** *m* lieutenant. **O∼licht** *nt* overhead light; (*Fenster*) skylight; (*über Tür*) fanlight. **O∼lippe** *f* upper lip

Obers *nt* - (*Aust*) cream

Ober|schenkel *m* thigh. **O∼schicht** *f* upper class. **O∼schule** *f* grammar school. **O∼schwester** *f* (*Med*) sister. **O∼seite** *f* upper/(*rechte Seite*) right side

Oberst *m* -en & -s,-en colonel

oberste(r,s) *a* top; (*höchste*) highest; (*Befehlshaber, Gerichtshof*) supreme; (*wichtigste*) first

Ober|stimme *f* treble. **O∼stufe** *f* upper school. **O∼teil** *nt* top. **O∼weite** *f* chest/(*der Frau*) bust size

obgleich *conj* although

Obhut *f* - care; **in guter O∼ sein** be well looked after

obig *a* above

Objekt *nt* -[e]s,-e object; (*Haus, Grundstück*) property; **O∼ der Forschung** subject of research

Objektiv *nt* -s,-e lens. **o∼** *a* objective, *adv* -ly. **O∼ität** *f* - objectivity

Oblate *f* -,-n (*Relig*) wafer

obliga|t *a* (*fam*) inevitable. **O∼tion** /-'tsi̯oːn/ *f* -,-en obligation; (*Comm*) bond. **o∼torisch** *a* obligatory

Obmann *m* (*pl* -männer) [jury] foreman; (*Sport*) referee

Oboe /o'boːə/ *f* -,-n oboe

Obrigkeit *f* - authorities *pl*

obschon *conj* although

Observatorium *nt* -s,-ien observatory

obskur *a* obscure; (*zweifelhaft*) dubious

Obst *nt* -es (*coll*) fruit. **O∼baum** *m* fruit-tree. **O∼garten** *m* orchard. **O∼händler** *m* fruiterer. **O∼kuchen** *m* fruit flan. **O∼salat** *m* fruit salad

obszön *a* obscene. **O∼ität** *f* -,-en obscenity

O-Bus *m* trolley bus

obwohl *conj* although

Ochse *m* -n,-n ox. **o∼n** *vi* (*haben*) (*fam*) swot. **O∼nschwanzsuppe** *f* oxtail soup

öde *a* desolate; (*unfruchtbar*) barren; (*langweilig*) dull. **Öde** *f* - desolation; barrenness; dullness; (*Gegend*) waste

oder *conj* or; **du kennst ihn doch, o∼?** you know him, don't you?

Ofen *m* -s,- stove; (*Heiz-*) heater; (*Back-*) oven; (*Techn*) furnace

offen *a* open, *adv* -ly; (*Haar*) loose; (*Flamme*) naked; (*o∼herzig*) frank, *adv*

-ly; (o~ *gezeigt*) overt, *adv* -ly; (*unentschieden*) unsettled; o~e Stelle vacancy; Tag der o~en Tür open day; Wein o~ verkaufen sell wine by the glass; o~ bleiben remain open; o~ halten hold open ⟨*Tür*⟩; keep open ⟨*Mund, Augen*⟩; o~ lassen leave open; leave vacant ⟨*Stelle*⟩; o~ stehen be open; ⟨*Rechnung:*⟩ be outstanding; jdm o~ stehen (*fig*) be open to s.o.; *adv* o~ gesagt *od* gestanden to be honest. o~bar *a* obvious □ *adv* apparently. o~baren *vt* reveal. O~barung *f* -,-en revelation. o~bleiben† *vi sep* (*sein*) (NEW) o~ bleiben, *s.* offen. o~halten† *vt sep* (NEW) o~ halten, *s.* offen. O~heit *f* - frankness, openness. o~herzig *a* frank, *adv* -ly. O~herzigkeit *f* - frankness. o~kundig *a* manifest, *adv* -ly. o~lassen† *vt sep* (NEW) o~ lassen, *s.* offen. o~sichtlich *a* obvious, *adv* -ly

offensiv *a* offensive. O~e *f* -,-n offensive. offenstehen† *vi sep* (*haben*) (NEW) offen stehen, *s.* offen

öffentlich *a* public, *adv* -ly. Ö~keit *f* - public; an die Ö~keit gelangen become public; in aller Ö~keit in public, publicly

Offerte *f* -,-n (*Comm*) offer

offiziell *a* official, *adv* -ly

Offizier *m* -s,-e (*Mil*) officer

öffn|en *vt/i* (*haben*) open; sich ö~en open. Ö~er *m* -s,- opener. Ö~ung *f* -,-en opening. Ö~ungszeiten *fpl* opening hours

oft *adv* often

öfter *adv* quite often. ö~e(r,s) *a* frequent; des Ö~en (ö~en) frequently. ö~s *adv* (*fam*) quite often

oftmals *adv* often

oh *int* oh!

ohne *prep* (+ *acc*) without; o~ mich! count me out! oben o~ topless; nicht o~ sein (*fam*) be not bad; (*nicht harmlos*) be quite nasty □ *conj* o~ zu überlegen without thinking; o~ dass ich es merkte without my noticing it. o~dies *adv* anyway. o~gleichen *pred a* unparalleled; eine Frechheit o~gleichen a piece of unprecedented insolence. o~hin *adv* anyway

Ohn|macht *f* -,-en faint; (*fig*) powerlessness; in O~macht fallen faint. o~mächtig *a* unconscious; (*fig*) powerless; o~mächtig werden faint

Ohr *nt* -[e]s,-en ear; übers Ohr hauen (*fam*) cheat

Öhr *nt* -[e]s,-e eye

ohren|betäubend *a* deafening. O~schmalz *nt* ear-wax. O~schmerzen *mpl* earache *sg*. O~sessel *m* wing-chair. O~tropfen *mpl* ear drops

Ohrfeige *f* slap in the face; jdm eine O~ geben slap s.o.'s face. o~n *vt* jdn o~n slap s.o.'s face

Ohr|läppchen *nt* -s,- ear-lobe. O~ring *m* ear-ring. O~wurm *m* earwig

oje *int* oh dear!

okay /o'ke:/ *a & adv* (*fam*) OK

okkult *a* occult

Öko|logie *f* - ecology. ö~logisch *a* ecological. Ö~nomie *f* - economy; (*Wissenschaft*) economics *sg.* ö~nomisch *a* economic; (*sparsam*) economical

Oktave *f* -,-n octave

Oktober *m* -s,- October

Okular *nt* -s,-e eyepiece

okulieren *vt* graft

ökumenisch *a* ecumenical

Öl *nt* -[e]s,-e oil; in Öl malen paint in oils. Ölbaum *m* olivetree. ölen *vt* oil; wie ein geölter Blitz (*fam*) like greased lightning. Ölfarbe *f* oil-paint. Ölfeld *nt* oilfield. Ölgemälde *nt* oil-painting. ölig *a* oily

Oliv|e *f* -,-n olive. O~enöl *nt* olive oil. o~grün *a* olive[-green]

oll *a* (*fam*) old; (*fam: hässlich*) nasty

Ölmessstab (Ölmeßstab) *m* dip-stick. Ölsardinen *fpl* sardines in oil. Ölstand *m* oil-level. Öltanker *m* oil-tanker. Ölteppich *m* oil-slick

Olympiade *f* -,-n Olympic Games *pl,* Olympics *pl*

Olymp|iasieger(in) /o'lympia-/ *m(f)* Olympic champion. o~isch *a* Olympic; O~ische Spiele Olympic Games

Ölzeug *nt* oilskins *pl*

Oma *f* -,-s (*fam*) granny

Omelett *nt* -[e]s,-e & -s omelette

Omen *nt* -s,- omen

ominös *a* ominous

Omnibus *m* bus; (*Reise-*) coach

onanieren *vi* (*haben*) masturbate

Onkel *m* -s,- uncle

Opa *m* -s,-s (*fam*) grandad

Opal *m* -s,-e opal

Oper *f* -,-n opera

Operation /-'tsio:n/ *f* -,-en operation. O~ssaal *m* operating theatre

Operette *f* -,-n operetta

operieren *vt* operate on ⟨*Patient, Herz*⟩; sich o~ lassen have an operation □ *vi* (*haben*) operate

Opern|glas *nt* opera-glasses *pl.* O~haus *nt* opera-house. O~sänger(in) *m(f)* opera-singer

Opfer *nt* -s,- sacrifice; (*eines Unglücks*) victim; ein O~ bringen make a sacrifice; jdm/etw zum O~ fallen fall victim to s.o./sth. o~n *vt* sacrifice. **O~ung** *f* -,-en sacrifice

Opium *nt* -s opium

opponieren *vi* (*haben*) **o~ gegen** oppose

Opportunist *m* -en,-en opportunist. **o~isch** *a* opportunist

Opposition /-'tsio:n/ *f* - opposition. **O~spartei** *f* opposition party

Optik *f* - optics *sg* (*fam: Objektiv*) lens. **O~er** *m* -s,- optician

optimal *a* optimum

Optimis|mus *m* - optimism. **O~t** *m* -en, -en optimist. **o~tisch** *a* optimistic, *adv* -ally

Optimum *nt* -s,-ma optimum

Option /ɔp'tsio:n/ *f* -,-en option

optisch *a* optical; (*Eindruck*) visual

Orakel *nt* -s,- oracle

Orange /o'rã:ʒə/ *f* -,-n orange. **o~** *inv a* orange. **O~ade** /orã'ʒa:də/ *f* -,-n orangeade. **O~nmarmelade** *f* [orange] marmalade. **O~nsaft** *m* orange juice

Oratorium *nt* -s,-ien oratorio

Orchest|er /ɔr'kɛstɐ/ *nt* -s,- orchestra. **o~rieren** *vt* orchestrate

Orchidee /ɔrçi'de:ə/ *f* -,-n orchid

Orden *m* -s,- (*Ritter-, Kloster-*) order; (*Auszeichnung*) medal, decoration; **jdm einen O~ verleihen** decorate s.o. **O~stracht** *f* (*Relig*) habit

ordentlich *a* neat. tidy; (*anständig*) respectable; (*ordnungsgemäß, fam: richtig*) proper; (*Mitglied, Versammlung*) ordinary; (*fam: gut*) decent; (*fam: gehörig*) good □ *adv* neatly, tidily; respectably; properly; (*fam: gut, gehörig*) well; (*sehr*) very; (*regelrecht*) really

Order *f* -,-s & -n order

ordinär *a* common

Ordin|ation /-'tsio:n/ *f* -,-en (*Relig*) ordination; (*Aust*) surgery. **o~ieren** *vt* (*Relig*) ordain

ordn|en *vt* put in order; (*aufräumen*) tidy; (*an-*) arrange; **sich zum Zug o~en** form a procession. **O~er** *m* -s,- steward; (*Akten-*) file

Ordnung *f* - order; **O~ halten** keep order; **O~ machen** tidy up; **in O~ bringen** put in order; (*aufräumen*) tidy; (*reparieren*) mend; (*fig*) put right; **in O~ sein** be in order; (*ordentlich sein*) be tidy; (*fig*) be all right; **ich bin mit dem Magen** *od* **mein Magen ist nicht ganz in O~** I have a slight stomach upset; **[geht] in O~!** OK! **o~sgemäß** *a* proper, *adv* -ly. **O~sstrafe** *f* (*Jur*) fine. **o~swidrig** *a* improper, *adv* -ly

Ordonnanz, Ordonanz *f* -,-en (*Mil*) orderly

Organ *nt* -s,-e organ; (*fam: Stimme*) voice

Organi|sation /-'tsio:n/ *f* -,-en organization. **O~sator** *m* -s,-en /-'to:rən/ organizer

organisch *a* organic, *adv* -ally

organisieren *vt* organize; (*fam: beschaffen*) get [hold of]

Organis|mus *m* -,-men organism; (*System*) system. **O~t** *m* -en,-en organist

Organspenderkarte *f* donor card

Orgasmus *m* -,-men orgasm

Orgel *f* -,-n (*Mus*) organ. **O~pfeife** *f* organ-pipe

Orgie /'ɔrgiə/ *f* -,-n orgy

Orien|t /'o:riɛnt/ *m* -s Orient. **o~talisch** *a* Oriental

orientier|en /oriɛn'ti:rən/ *vt* inform (**über** + *acc* about); **sich o~en** get one's bearings, orientate oneself; (*unterrichten*) inform oneself (**über** + *acc* about). **O~ung** *f* - orientation; **die O~ung verlieren** lose one's bearings

original *a* original. **O~** *nt* -s,-e original; (*Person*) character. **O~ität** *f* - originality. **O~übertragung** *f* live transmission

originell *a* original; (*eigenartig*) unusual

Orkan *m* -s,-e hurricane

Ornament *nt* -[e]s,-e ornament

Ornat *m* -[e]s,-e robes *pl*

Ornithologie *f* - ornithology

Ort *m* -[e]s,-e place; (*Ortschaft*) [small] town; **am Ort** locally; **am Ort des Verbrechens** at the scene of the crime; **an Ort und Stelle** in the right place; (*sofort*) on the spot. **o~en** *vt* locate

ortho|dox *a* orthodox. **O~graphie, O~grafie** *f* - spelling. **o~graphisch, o~grafisch** *a* spelling ... **O~päde** *m* -n,-n orthopaedic specialist. **o~pädisch** *a* orthopaedic

örtlich *a* local, *adv* -ly. **Ö~keit** *f* -,-en locality

Ortschaft *f* -,-en [small] town; (*Dorf*) village; **geschlossene O~** (*Auto*) built-up area

orts|fremd *a* **o~fremd sein** be a stranger. **O~gespräch** *nt* (*Teleph*) local call. **O~name** *m* place-name. **O~sinn** *m* sense of direction. **O~verkehr** *m* local traffic. **O~zeit** *f* local time

Öse *f* -,-n eyelet; (*Schlinge*) loop; **Haken und Öse** hook and eye

Ost *m* -[e]s east. **o~deutsch** *a* Eastern/(*Pol*) East German

Osten *m* -s east; **nach O~** east

ostentativ *a* pointed, *adv* -ly

Osteopath *m* -en,-en osteopath

Oster|ei /'o:stɐʔaɪ/ *nt* Easter egg. **O~fest** *nt* Easter. **O~glocke** *f* daffodil. **O~montag** *m* Easter Monday. **O~n** *nt* -,- Easter; **frohe O~n!** happy Easter!

Österreich *nt* -s Austria. **Ö~er** *m,* -s,-, **Ö~erin** *f* -,-nen Austrian. **ö~isch** *a* Austrian

östlich *a* eastern; ⟨*Richtung*⟩ easterly □ *adv & prep* (+ *gen*) **ö~ [von] der Stadt** [to the] east of the town

Ost|see *f* Baltic [Sea]. **o~wärts** *adv* eastwards

oszillieren *vi* (*haben*) oscillate

Otter[1] *m* -s,- otter

Otter[2] *f* -,-n adder

Ouverture /uver'ty:rə/ *f* -,-n overture

oval *a* oval. **O~** *nt* -s,-e oval

Ovation /-'tsi̯o:n/ *f* -,-en ovation

Ovulation /-'tsi̯o:n/ *f* -,-en ovulation

Oxid, Oxyd *nt* -[e]s,-e oxide

Ozean *m* -s,-e ocean

Ozon *nt* -s ozone. **O~loch** *nt* hole in the ozone layer. **O~schicht** *f* ozone layer

P

paar *pron inv* **ein p~** a few; **ein p~ Mal** a few times; **alle p~ Tage** every few days. **P~** *nt* -[e]s,-e pair; (*Ehe-, Liebes-, Tanz-*) couple. **p~en** *vt* mate; (*verbinden*) combine; **sich p~en** mate. **p~mal** *adv* **ein p~mal** (NEW) **ein p~ Mal,** *s.* **paar. P~ung** *f* -,-en mating. **p~weise** *adv* in pairs, in twos

Pacht *f* -,-en lease; (*P~summe*) rent. **p~en** *vt* lease

Pächter *m* -s,- lessee; (*eines Hofes*) tenant

Pachtvertrag *m* lease

Pack[1] *m* -[e]s,-e bundle

Pack[2] *nt* -[e]s (*sl*) rabble

Päckchen *nt* -s,- package, small packet

pack|en *vt/i* (*haben*) pack; (*ergreifen*) seize; (*fig:fesseln*) grip; **p~ dich!** (*sl*) beat it! **P~en** *m* -s,- bundle. **p~end** *a* (*fig*) gripping. **P~papier** *nt* [strong] wrapping paper. **P~ung** *f* -,-en packet; (*Med*) pack

Pädagog|e *m* -n,-n educationalist; (*Lehrer*) teacher. **P~ik** *f* educational science. **p~isch** *a* educational

Paddel *nt* -s,- paddle. **P~boot** *nt* canoe. **p~n** *vt/i* (*haben/sein*) paddle. **P~sport** *m* canoeing

Page /'pa:ʒə/ *m* -n,-n page

Paillette /paɪ'jɛtə/ *f* -,-n sequin

Paket *nt* -[e]s,-e packet; (*Post-*) parcel

Pakist|an *nt* -s Pakistan. **P~aner(in)** *m* -s,- (*f* -,-nen) Pakistani. **p~anisch** *a* Pakistani

Pakt *m* -[e]s,-e pact

Palast *m* -[e]s,-̈e palace

Palästin|a *nt* -s Palestine. **P~enser(in)** *m* -s,- (*f* -,-nen) Palestinian. **p~ensisch** *a* Palestinian

Palette *f* -,-n palette

Palm|e *f* -,-n palm[-tree]; **jdn auf die P~e bringen** (*fam*) drive s.o. up the wall. **P~sonntag** *m* Palm Sunday

Pampelmuse *f* -,-n grapefruit

Panier|mehl *nt* (*Culin*) breadcrumbs *pl*. **p~t** *a* (*Culin*) breaded

Panik *f* - panic; **in P~ geraten** panic

panisch *a* **p~e Angst** panic

Panne *f* -,-n breakdown; (*Reifen-*) flat tyre; (*Missgeschick*) mishap. **P~ndienst** *m* breakdown service

Panorama *nt* -s panorama

panschen *vt* adulterate □ *vi* (*haben*) splash about

Panther, Panter *m* -s,- panther

Pantine *f* -,-n [wooden] clog

Pantoffel *m* -s,-n slipper; (*ohne Ferse*) mule. **P~held** *m* (*fam*) henpecked husband

Pantomime[1] *f* -,-n mime

Pantomime[2] *m* -n,-n mime artist

pantschen *vt/i* = **panschen**

Panzer *m* -s,- armour; (*Mil*) tank; (*Zool*) shell. **p~n** *vt* armourplate. **P~schrank** *m* safe

Papa /'papa, pa'pa:/ *m* -s,-s daddy

Papagei *m* -s & -en,-en parrot

Papier *nt* -[e]s,-e paper. **P~korb** *m* wastepaper basket. **P~schlange** *f* streamer. **P~waren** *fpl* stationery *sg*

Pappe *f* - cardboard; (*dial: Kleister*) glue

Pappel *f* -,-n poplar

pappen *vt/i* (*haben*) (*fam*) stick

pappig *a* (*fam*) sticky

Papp|karton *m,* **P~schachtel** *f* cardboard box

Paprika *m* -s,-[s] [sweet] pepper; (*Gewürz*) paprika □ *f* -,- [s] (*P~schote*) pepper

Papst *m* -[e]s,-̈e pope

päpstlich *a* papal

Parade *f* -,-n parade

Paradeiser *m* -s,- (*Aust*) tomato

Paradies *nt* -es,-e paradise. **p~isch** *a* heavenly

Paradox *nt* -es,-e paradox. **p~** *a* paradoxical

Paraffin *nt* -s paraffin

Paragraph, Paragraf *m* -en,-en section

parallel *a & adv* parallel. **P~e** *f* -,-n parallel

Paranuss (Paranuß) *f* Brazil nut

Parasit *m* -en,-en parasite

parat *a* ready

Pärchen *nt* -s,- pair; (*Liebes-*) couple

Parcours /par'kuːɐ̯/ *m* -,- /-[s],-s/ (*Sport*) course

Pardon /par'dõ/ *int* sorry!

Parfüm *nt* -s,-e & -s perfume, scent. **p~iert** *a* perfumed, scented

parieren[1] *vt* parry

parieren[2] *vi* (*haben*) (*fam*) obey

Parität *f* - parity; (*in Ausschuss*) equal representation

Park *m* -s,-s park. **p~en** *vt/i* (*haben*) park. **P~en** *nt* -s parking; 'P~en verboten' 'no parking'

Parkett *nt* -[e]s,-e parquet floor; (*Theat*) stalls *pl*

Park|haus *nt* multi-storey car park. **P~lücke** *f* parking space. **P~platz** *m* car park, (*Amer*) parking-lot; (*für ein Auto*) parking space; (*Autobahn-*) lay-by. **P~scheibe** *f* parking-disc. **P~schein** *m* car-park ticket. **P~uhr** *f* parking-meter. **P~verbot** *nt* parking ban; 'P~verbot' 'no parking'

Parlament *nt* -[e]s,-e parliament. **p~a-risch** *a* parliamentary

Parodie *f* -,-n parody. **p~ren** *vt* parody

Parole *f* -,-n slogan; (*Mil*) password

Part *m* -s,-s (*Theat, Mus*) part

Partei *f* -,-en (*Pol, Jur*) party; (*Miet-*) tenant; **für jdn P~ ergreifen** take s.o.'s part. **p~isch** *a* biased. **p~los** *a* independent

Parterre /par'ter/ *nt* -s,-s ground floor, (*Amer*) first floor; (*Theat*) rear stalls *pl*. **p~** *adv* on the ground floor

Partie *f* -,-n part; (*Tennis, Schach*) game; (*Golf*) round; (*Comm*) batch; **eine gute P~ machen** marry well

Partikel[1] *nt* -s,- particle

Partikel[2] *f* -,-n (*Gram*) particle

Partitur *f* -,-en (*Mus*) full score

Partizip *nt* -s,-ien /-jən/ participle; **erstes/zweites P~** present/past participle

Partner|(in) *m* -s,- (*f* -,-nen) partner. **P~schaft** *f* -,-en partnership. **P~stadt** *f* twin town

Party /'paːɐ̯ti/ *f* -,-s party

Parzelle *f* -,-n plot [of ground]

Pass *m* -es,ˑe (**Paß** *m* -sses,ˑsse) passport; (*Geog, Sport*) pass

passabel *a* passable

Passage /pa'saːʒə/ *f* -,-n passage; (*Einkaufs-*) shopping arcade

Passagier /pasa'ʒiːɐ̯/ *m* -s,-e passenger

Passamt (Paßamt) *nt* passport office

Passant(in) *m* -en,-en (*f* -,-nen) passer-by

Passbild (Paßbild) *nt* passport photograph

Passe *f* -,-n yoke

passen *vi* (*haben*) fit; (*geeignet sein*) be right (**für** for); (*Sport*) pass the ball; (*aufgeben*) pass; **p~ zu** go [well] with; (*übereinstimmen*) match; **jdm p~** fit s.o.; (*gelegen sein*) suit s.o.; **seine Art passt mir nicht** I don't like his manner; **[ich] passe** pass. **p~d** *a* suitable; (*angemessen*) appropriate; (*günstig*) convenient; (*übereinstimmend*) matching

passier|bar *a* passable. **p~en** *vt* pass; cross ⟨*Grenze*⟩; (*Culin*) rub through a sieve □ *vi* (*sein*) happen (**jdm** to s.o.); **es ist ein Unglück p~t** there has been an accident. **P~schein** *m* pass

Passion *f* -,-en passion. **p~iert** *a* very keen ⟨*Jäger, Angler*⟩

passiv *a* passive. **P~** *nt* -s,-e (*Gram*) passive

Pass|kontrolle (Paßkontrolle) *f* passport control. **P~straße** *f* pass

Paste *f* -,-n paste

Pastell *nt* -[e]s,-e pastel. **P~farbe** *f* pastel colour

Pastet|chen *nt* -s,- [individual] pie; (*Königin-*) vol-au-vent. **P~e** *f* -,-n pie; (*Gänseleber-*) pâté

pasteurisieren /pastøri'ziːrən/ *vt* pasteurize

Pastille *f* -,-n pastille

Pastinake *f* -,-n parsnip

Pastor *m* -s,-en /-'toːrən/ pastor

Pate *m* -n,-n godfather; (*fig*) sponsor; **P~n** godparents. **P~nkind** *nt* godchild. **P~nschaft** *f* - sponsorship. **P~nsohn** *m* godson

Patent *nt* -[e]s,-e patent; (*Offiziers-*) commission. **p~** *a* (*fam*) clever, *adv* -ly; ⟨*Person*⟩ resourceful. **p~ieren** *vt* patent

Patentochter *f* god-daughter

Pater *m* -s,- (*Relig*) Father

pathetisch *a* emotional □ *adv* with emotion

Patholog|e *m* -n,-n pathologist. **p~isch** *a* pathological, *adv* -ly

Pathos *nt* - emotion, feeling

Patience /pa'sjãːs/ *f* -,-n patience

Patient(in) /pa'tsjɛnt(ɪn)/ *m* -en, -en (*f* -,-nen) patient

Patin *f* -,-nen godmother

Patriot(in) *m* -en,-en (*f* -,-nen) patriot. **p~isch** *a* patriotic. **P~ismus** *m* - patriotism

Patrone *f* -,-n cartridge

Patrouill|e /pa'trʊljə/ *f* -,-n patrol. **p~ieren** /-'ji:rən/ *vi* (*haben/sein*) patrol

Patsch|e *f* in der **P~e sitzen** (*fam*) be in a jam. **p~en** *vi* (*haben/sein*) splash □ *vt* slap. **p~nass** (**p~naß**) *a* (*fam*) soaking wet

Patt *nt* -s stalemate

Patz|er *m* -s,- (*fam*) slip. **p~ig** *a* (*fam*) insolent

Pauk|e *f* -,-n kettledrum; **auf die P~e hauen** (*fam*) have a good time; (*prahlen*) boast. **p~en** *vt/i* (*haben*) (*fam*) swot. **P~er** *m* -s,- (*fam: Lehrer*) teacher

pausbäckig *a* chubby-cheeked

pauschal *a* all-inclusive; (*einheitlich*) flat-rate; (*fig*) sweeping ⟨*Urteil*⟩; **p~e Summe** lump sum □ *adv* in a lump sum; (*fig*) wholesale. **P~e** *f* -,-n lump sum. **P~reise** *f* package tour. **P~summe** *f* lump sum

Pause[1] *f* -,-n break; (*beim Sprechen*) pause; (*Theat*) interval; (*im Kino*) intermission; (*Mus*) rest; **P~ machen** have a break

Pause[2] *f* -,-n tracing. **p~n** *vt* trace

pausenlos *a* incessant, *adv* -ly

pausieren *vi* (*haben*) have a break; (*ausruhen*) rest

Pauspapier *nt* tracing-paper

Pavian *m* -s,-e baboon

Pavillon /'pavɪljõ/ *m* -s,-s pavilion

Pazifi|k *m* -s Pacific [Ocean]. **p~sch** *a* Pacific

Pazifist *m* -en,-en pacifist

Pech *nt* -s pitch; (*Unglück*) bad luck; **P~ haben** be unlucky. **p~schwarz** *a* pitch-black; ⟨*Haare, Augen*⟩ jet-black. **P~strähne** *f* run of bad luck. **P~vogel** *m* (*fam*) unlucky devil

Pedal *nt* -s,-e pedal

Pedant *m* -en,-en pedant. **p~isch** *a* pedantic, *adv* -ally

Pediküre *f* -,-n pedicure

Pegel *m* -s,- level; (*Gerät*) water-level indicator. **P~stand** *m* [water] level

peilen *vt* take a bearing on; **über den Daumen gepeilt** (*fam*) at a rough guess

Pein *f* - (*liter*) torment. **p~igen** *vt* torment

peinlich *a* embarrassing, awkward; (*genau*) scrupulous, *adv* -ly; **es war mir sehr p~** I was very embarrassed

Peitsche *f* -,-n whip. **p~n** *vt* whip; (*fig*) lash □ *vi* (*sein*) lash (**an** + *acc* against). **P~nhieb** *m* lash

pekuniär *a* financial, *adv* -ly

Pelikan *m* -s,-e pelican

Pell|e *f* -,-n skin. **p~en** *vt* peel; shell ⟨*Ei*⟩; **sich p~en** peel. **P~kartoffeln** *fpl* potatoes boiled in their skins

Pelz *m* -es,-e fur. **P~mantel** *m* fur coat

Pendel *nt* -s,- pendulum. **p~n** *vi* (*haben*) swing □ *vi* (*sein*) commute. **P~verkehr** *m* shuttle-service; (*für Pendler*) commuter traffic

Pendler *m* -s,- commuter

penetrant *a* penetrating; (*fig*) obtrusive, *adv* -ly

penibel *a* fastidious, fussy; (*pedantisch*) pedantic

Penis *m* -,-se penis

Penne *f* -,-n (*fam*) school. **p~n** *vi* (*haben*) (*fam*) sleep. **P~r** *m* -s,- (*sl*) tramp

Pension /pã'zjo:n/ *f* -,-en pension; (*Hotel*) guest-house; **bei voller/halber P~** with full/half board. **P~är(in)** *m* -s,-e (*f*-,-nen) pensioner. **P~at** *nt* -[e]s,-e boarding-school. **p~ieren** *vt* retire. **p~iert** *a* retired. **P~ierung** *f* - retirement

Pensum *nt* -s [allotted] work

Peperoni *f* -,- chilli

per *prep* (+ *acc*) by; **per Luftpost** by airmail

perfekt *a* perfect, *adv* -ly; **p~ sein** ⟨*Vertrag:*⟩ be settled

Perfekt *nt* -s (*Gram*) perfect

Perfektion /-'tsjo:n/ *f* - perfection

perforiert *a* perforated

Pergament *nt* -[e]s,-e parchment. **P~papier** *nt* grease-proof paper

Period|e *f* -,-n period. **p~isch** *a* periodic, *adv* -ally

Perl|e *f* -,-n pearl; (*Glas-, Holz-*) bead; ⟨*Sekt-*⟩ bubble; (*fam: Hilfe*) treasure. **p~en** *vi* (*haben*) bubble. **P~mutt** *m* -s, **P~mutter** *f* - & *nt* -s mother-of-pearl

perplex *a* (*fam*) perplexed

Perserkatze *f* Persian cat

Pers|ien /-jən/ *nt* -s Persia. **p~isch** *a* Persian

Person *f* -,-en person; (*Theat*) character; **ich für meine P~** [I] for my part; **für vier P~en** for four people

Personal *nt* -s personnel, staff. **P~ausweis** *m* identity card. **P~chef** *m* personnel manager. **P~ien** /-jən/ *pl* personal particulars. **P~mangel** *m* staff shortage. **P~pronomen** *nt* personal pronoun

Personen|kraftwagen *m* private car. **P~zug** *m* stopping train

personifizieren *vt* personify

persönlich *a* personal □ *adv* personally, in person. **P~keit** *f* -,-en personality

Perspektive *f* -,-n perspective; (*Zukunfts-*) prospect

Perücke *f* -,-n wig

pervers *a* [sexually] perverted. **P~ion** *f* -,-en perversion

Pessimis|mus *m* - pessimism. **P~t** *m* -en,-en pessimist. **p~tisch** *a* pessimistic, *adv* -ally

Pest *f* - plague

Petersilie /-jə/ *f* - parsley

Petroleum /-leʊm/ *nt* -s paraffin, (*Amer*) kerosene

Petze *f* -,-n (*fam*) sneak. **p~n** *vi* (*haben*) (*fam*) sneak

Pfad *m* -[e]s,-e path. **P~finder** *m* -s,- [Boy] Scout. **P~finderin** *f* -,-nen [Girl] Guide

Pfahl *m* -[e]s,ˉe stake, post

Pfalz (die) - the Palatinate

Pfand *nt* -[e]s,ˉer pledge; (*beim Spiel*) forfeit; (*Flaschen-*) deposit

pfänd|en *vt* (*Jur*) seize. **P~erspiel** *nt* game of forfeits

Pfand|haus *nt* pawnshop. **P~leiher** *m* -s,- pawnbroker

Pfändung *f* -,-en (*Jur*) seizure

Pfann|e *f* -,-n [frying-]pan. **P~kuchen** *m* pancake; Berliner **P~kuchen** doughnut

Pfarr|er *m* -s,- vicar, parson; (*katholischer*) priest. **P~haus** *nt* vicarage

Pfau *m* -s,-en peacock

Pfeffer *m* -s pepper. **P~kuchen** *m* gingerbread. **P~minzbonbon** *m* & *nt* [pepper-]mint. **P~minze** *f* - (*Bot*) peppermint. **P~minztee** *m* [pepper]mint tea. **p~n** *vt* pepper; (*fam: schmeißen*) chuck. **P~streuer** *m* -s,- pepperpot

Pfeif|e *f* -,-n whistle; (*Tabak-, Orgel-*) pipe. **p~en†** *vt/i* (*haben*) whistle; (*als Signal*) blow the whistle; **ich p~e darauf!** (*fam*) I couldn't care less [about it]!

Pfeil *m* -[e]s,-e arrow

Pfeiler *m* -s,- pillar; (*Brücken-*) pier

Pfennig *m* -s,-e pfennig; **10 P~** 10 pfennigs

Pferch *m* -[e]s,-e [sheep] pen. **p~en** *vt* (*fam*) cram (**in** + *acc* into)

Pferd *nt* -es,-e horse; **zu P~e** on horseback; **das P~ beim Schwanz aufzäumen** put the cart before the horse. **P~erennen** *nt* horse-race; (*als Sport*) [horse-]racing. **P~eschwanz** *m* horse's tail; (*Frisur*) pony-tail. **P~estall** *m* stable. **P~estärke** *f* horsepower. **P~ewagen** *m* horse-drawn cart

Pfiff *m* -[e]s,-e whistle; **P~ haben** (*fam*) have style

Pfifferling *m* -s,-e chanterelle

pfiffig *a* smart

Pfingst|en *nt* -s Whitsun. **P~montag** *m* Whit Monday. **P~rose** *f* peony

Pfirsich *m* -s,-e peach. **p~farben** *a* peach[-coloured]

Pflanz|e *f* -,-n plant. **p~en** *vt* plant. **P~enfett** *nt* vegetable fat. **p~lich** *a* vegetable; (*Mittel*) herbal. **P~ung** *f* -,-en plantation

Pflaster *nt* -s,- pavement; (*Heft-*) plaster. **p~n** *vt* pave. **P~stein** *m* paving-stone

Pflaume *f* -,-n plum

Pflege *f* - care; (*Kranken-*) nursing; **in P~ nehmen** look after; (*Admin*) foster (*Kind*). **p~bedürftig** *a* in need of care. **P~eltern** *pl* foster-parents. **P~kind** *nt* foster-child. **p~leicht** *a* easy-care. **P~mutter** *f* foster-mother. **p~n** *vt* look after, care for; nurse (*Kranke*); cultivate (*Künste, Freundschaft*). **P~r(in)** *m* -s,- (*f* -,-nen) nurse; (*Tier-*) keeper

Pflicht *f* -,-en duty; (*Sport*) compulsory exercise/routine. **p~bewusst** (**p~bewußt**) *a* conscientious, *adv* -ly. **p~eifrig** *a* zealous, *adv* -ly. **P~fach** *nt* (*Sch*) compulsory subject. **P~gefühl** *nt* sense of duty. **p~gemäß** *a* due □ *adv* duly

Pflock *m* -[e]s,ˉe peg

pflücken *vt* pick

Pflug *m* -[e]s,ˉe plough

pflügen *vt/i* (*haben*) plough

Pforte *f* -,-n gate

Pförtner *m* -s,- porter

Pfosten *m* -s,- post

Pfote *f* -,-n paw

Pfropfen *m* -s,- stopper; (*Korken*) cork. **p~** *vt* graft (**auf** + *acc* on [to]); (*fam: pressen*) cram (**in** + *acc* into)

pfui *int* ugh; **p~ schäm dich!** you should be ashamed of yourself!

Pfund *nt* -[e]s,-e & - pound

Pfusch|arbeit *f* (*fam*) shoddy work. **p~en** *vi* (*haben*) (*fam*) botch one's work. **P~er** *m* -s,- (*fam*) shoddy worker. **P~erei** *f* -,-en (*fam*) botch-up

Pfütze *f* -,-n puddle

Phänomen *nt* -s,-e phenomenon. **p~al** *a* phenomenal

Phantasie *f* -,-n imagination; **P~n** fantasies; (*Fieber-*) hallucinations. **p~los** *a* unimaginative. **p~ren** *vi* (*haben*) fantasize; (*im Fieber*) be delirious. **p~voll** *a* imaginative, *adv* -ly

phant|astisch *a* fantastic, *adv* -ally. **P~om** *nt* -s,-e phantom

pharma|zeutisch *a* pharmaceutical. **P~zie** *f* - pharmacy

Phase *f* -,-n phase

Philanthrop *m* -en,-en philanthropist. **p~isch** *a* philanthropic

Philolo|ge *m* -n,-n teacher/student of language and literature. **P~gie** *f* - [study of] language and literature

Philosoph *m* -en,-en philosopher. **P~ie** *f* -,-n philosophy. **p~ieren** *vi* (*haben*) philosophize

philosophisch *a* philosophical, *adv* -ly

phlegmatisch *a* phlegmatic

Phobie *f* -,-n phobia

Phonet|ik *f* - phonetics *sg.* **p~isch** *a* phonetic, *adv* -ally

Phonotypistin *f* -,-nen audio typist

Phosphor *m* -s phosphorus

Photo *nt,* **Photo-** = Foto, Foto-

Phrase *f* -,-n empty phrase

Physik *f* - physics *sg.* **p~alisch** *a* physical; *⟨Experiment, Forschung⟩* physics ...

Physiker(in) *m* -s,- (*f* -,-nen) physicist

Physio|logie *f* - physiology. **P~therapie** *f* physiotherapy

physisch *a* physical, *adv* -ly

Pianist(in) *m* -en,-en (*f* -,-nen) pianist

Pickel *m* -s,- pimple, spot; *⟨Spitzhacke⟩* pick. **p~ig** *a* spotty

picken *vt/i* (*haben*) peck (**nach** at); *⟨fam: nehmen⟩* pick (**aus** out of); *⟨Aust fam: kleben⟩* stick

Picknick *nt* -s,-s picnic. **p~en** *vi* (*haben*) picnic

piep[s]|en *vi* (*haben*) *⟨Vogel:⟩* cheep; *⟨Maus:⟩* squeak; *⟨Techn⟩* bleep. **P~er** *m* -s,- bleeper

Pier *m* -s,-e [harbour] pier

Pietät /pie'tɛ:t/ *f* - reverence. **p~los** *a* irreverent, *adv* -ly

Pigment *nt* -[e]s,-e pigment. **P~ierung** *f* - pigmentation

Pik *nt* -s,-s *⟨Karten⟩* spades *pl*

pikant *a* piquant; *⟨gewagt⟩* racy

piken *vt* (*fam*) prick

pikiert *a* offended, hurt

piksen *vt* (*fam*) prick

Pilger|(in) *m* -s,- (*f* -,-nen) pilgrim. **P~fahrt** *f* pilgrimage. **p~n** *vi* (*sein*) make a pilgrimage

Pille *f* -,-n pill

Pilot *m* -en,-en pilot

Pilz *m* -es,-e fungus; *⟨essbarer⟩* mushroom; **wie P~e aus dem Boden schießen** *⟨fig⟩* mushroom

pingelig *a* (*fam*) fussy

Pinguin *m* -s,-e penguin

Pinie /-iə/ *f* -,-n stone-pine

pink *pred a* shocking pink

pinkeln *vi* (*haben*) (*fam*) pee

Pinsel *m* -s,- [paint]brush

Pinzette *f* -,-n tweezers *pl*

Pionier *m* -s,-e *⟨Mil⟩* sapper; *⟨fig⟩* pioneer. **P~arbeit** *f* pioneering work

Pirat *m* -en,-en pirate

pirschen *vi* (*haben*) **p~ auf** (+ *acc*) stalk □ *vr* **sich p~** creep (**an** + *acc* up to)

pissen *vi* (*haben*) (*sl*) piss

Piste *f* -,-n *⟨Ski-⟩* run, piste; *⟨Renn-⟩* track; *⟨Aviat⟩* runway

Pistole *f* -,-n pistol

pitschnass (**pitschnaß**) *a* (*fam*) soaking wet

pittoresk *a* picturesque

Pizza *f* -,-s pizza

Pkw /'pe:kave:/ *m* -s,-s (= **Personenkraftwagen**) [private] car

placieren /-'tsi:rən/ *vt* = platzieren

Plackerei *f* - (*fam*) drudgery

plädieren *vi* (*haben*) plead (**für** for); **auf Freispruch p~** *⟨Jur⟩* ask for an acquittal

Plädoyer /plɛdoa'je:/ *nt* -s,-s *⟨Jur⟩* closing speech; *⟨fig⟩* plea

Plage *f* -,-n [hard] labour; *⟨Mühe⟩* trouble; *⟨Belästigung⟩* nuisance. **p~n** *vt* torment, plague; *⟨bedrängen⟩* pester; **sich p~n** struggle; *⟨arbeiten⟩* work hard

Plagi|at *nt* -[e]s,-e plagiarism. **p~ieren** *vt* plagiarize

Plakat *nt* -[e]s,-e poster

Plakette *f* -,-n badge

Plan *m* -[e]s,-̈e plan

Plane *f* -,-n tarpaulin; *⟨Boden-⟩* groundsheet

planen *vt/i* (*haben*) plan

Planet *m* -en,-en planet

planier|en *vt* level. **P~raupe** *f* bulldozer

Planke *f* -,-n plank

plan|los *a* unsystematic, *adv* -ally. **p~mäßig** *a* systematic; *⟨Ankunft⟩* scheduled □ *adv* systematically; *⟨nach Plan⟩* according to plan; *⟨ankommen⟩* on schedule

Plansch|becken *nt* paddling pool. **p~en** *vi* (*haben*) splash about

Plantage /plan'ta:ʒə/ *f* -,-n plantation

Planung *f* - planning

Plapper|maul *nt* (*fam*) chatter-box. **p~n** *vi* (*haben*) chatter □ *vt* talk *⟨Unsinn⟩*

plärren *vi* (*haben*) bawl; *⟨Radio:⟩* blare

Plasma *nt* -s plasma

Plastik[1] *f* -,-en sculpture

Plast|ik[2] *nt* -s plastic. **p~isch** *a* three-dimensional; *⟨formbar⟩* plastic; *⟨anschaulich⟩* graphic, *adv* -ally; **p~ische Chirurgie** plastic surgery

Platane *f* -,-n plane [tree]

Plateau /pla'to:/ *nt* -s,-s plateau

Platin *nt* -s platinum

Platitüde *f* -,-n (NEW) Plattitüde

platonisch *a* platonic

platschen *vi* (*sein*) splash

plätschern *vi* (*haben*) splash; *⟨Bach:⟩* babble □ *vi* (*sein*) *⟨Bach:⟩* babble along

platt *a & adv* flat; *⟨fam⟩* **p~ sein** be flabbergasted. **P~** *nt* -[s] *⟨Lang⟩* Low German

Plättbrett *nt* ironing-board

Platte *f* -,-n slab; (*Druck*-) plate; (*Metall*-, *Glas*-) sheet; (*Fliese*) tile; (*Koch*-) hotplate; (*Tisch*-) top; (*Auszieh*-) leaf; (*Schall*-) record, disc; (*zum Servieren*) [flat] dish, platter; **kalte P~** assorted cold meats and cheeses *pl*

Plätt|eisen *nt* iron. **p~en** *vt/i* (*haben*) iron

Plattenspieler *m* record-player

Platt|form *f* -,-en platform. **P~füße** *mpl* flat feet. **P~heit** *f* -,-en platitude

Plattitüde *f* -,-n platitude

Platz *m* -es,ᵉe place; (*von Häusern umgeben*) square; (*Sitz*-) seat; (*Sport*-) ground; (*Fußball*-) pitch; (*Tennis*-) court; (*Golf*-) course; (*freier Raum*) room, space; **P~ nehmen** take a seat; **P~ machen/lassen** make/leave room; **vom P~ stellen** (*Sport*) send off. **P~angst** *f* agoraphobia; (*Klaustrophobie*) claustrophobia. **P~anweiserin** *f* -,-nen usherette

Plätzchen *nt* -s,- spot; (*Culin*) biscuit

platzen *vi* (*sein*) burst; (*auf*-) split; (*fam: scheitern*) fall through; (*Verlobung:*) be off; **vor Neugier p~** be bursting with curiosity

platzieren *vt* place, put; **sich p~** (*Sport*) be placed

Platz|karte *f* seat reservation ticket. **P~konzert** *nt* open-air concert. **P~mangel** *m* lack of space. **P~patrone** *f* blank. **P~regen** *m* downpour. **P~verweis** *m* (*Sport*) sending off. **P~wunde** *f* laceration

Plauderei *f* -,-en chat

plaudern *vi* (*haben*) chat

Plausch *m* -[e]s,-e (*SGer*) chat. **p~en** *vi* (*haben*) (*SGer*) chat

plausibel *a* plausible

plazieren *vt* (NEW) **platzieren**

pleite *a* (*fam*) **p~ sein** be broke; (*Firma:*) be bankrupt; **p~ gehen** (NEW) **P~ gehen**, *s.* Pleite. **P~** *f* -,-n (*fam*) bankruptcy; (*Misserfolg*) flop; **P~ gehen** *od* **machen** go bankrupt

plissiert *a* [finely] pleated

Plomb|e *f* -,-n seal; (*Zahn*-) filling. **p~ieren** *vt* seal; fill (*Zahn*)

plötzlich *a* sudden, *adv* -ly

plump *a* plump; (*ungeschickt*) clumsy, *adv* -ily

plumpsen *vi* (*sein*) (*fam*) fall

Plunder *m* -s (*fam*) junk, rubbish

plündern *vt/i* (*haben*) loot

Plunderstück *nt* Danish pastry

Plural *m* -s,-e plural

plus *adv, conj & prep* (+ *dat*) plus. **P~** *nt* - surplus; (*Gewinn*) profit; (*Vorteil*) advantage, plus. **P~punkt** *m* (*Sport*) point; (*fig*)

plus. **P~quamperfekt** *nt* pluperfect. **P~zeichen** *nt* plus sign

Po *m* -s,-s (*fam*) bottom

Pöbel *m* -s mob, rabble. **p~haft** *a* loutish

pochen *vi* (*haben*) knock; (*Herz:*) pound; **p~ auf** (+ *acc*) (*fig*) insist on

pochieren /pɔˈʃiːrən/ *vt* (*Culin*) poach

Pocken *pl* smallpox *sg*

Podest *nt* -[e]s,-e rostrum

Podium *nt* -s,-ien /-jən/ platform; (*Podest*) rostrum

Poesie /poeˈziː/ *f* - poetry

poetisch *a* poetic

Pointe /ˈpo̯ɛ̃ːtə/ *f* -,-n point (*of a joke*)

Pokal *m* -s,-e goblet; (*Sport*) cup

pökeln *vt* (*Culin*) salt

Poker *nt* -s poker

Pol *m* -s,-e pole. **p~ar** *a* polar

polarisieren *vt* polarize

Polarstern *m* pole-star

Pole *m* -,-n,-n Pole. **P~n** *nt* -s Poland

Police /poˈliːsə/ *f* -,-n policy

Polier *m* -s,-e foreman

polieren *vt* polish

Polin *f* -,-nen Pole

Politesse *f* -,-n [woman] traffic warden

Politik *f* - politics *sg*; (*Vorgehen, Maßnahme*) policy

Polit|iker(in) *m* -s,- (*f*, -,-nen) politician. **p~isch** *a* political, *adv* -ly

Politur *f* -,-en polish

Polizei *f* - police *pl*. **P~beamte(r)** *m* police officer. **p~lich** *a* police ... □ *adv* by the police; (*sich anmelden*) with the police. **P~streife** *f* police patrol. **P~stunde** *f* closing time. **P~wache** *f* police station

Polizist *m* -en,-en policeman **P~in** *f* -,-nen policewoman

Pollen *m* -s pollen

polnisch *a* Polish

Polohemd *nt* polo shirt

Polster *nt* -s,- pad; (*Kissen*) cushion; (*Möbel*-) upholstery; (*fam: Rücklage*) reserves *pl*. **P~er** *m* -s,- upholsterer. **P~möbel** *pl* upholstered furniture *sg*. **p~n** *vt* pad; upholster (*Möbel*). **P~ung** *f* - padding; upholstery

Polter|abend *m* wedding-eve party. **p~n** *vi* (*haben*) thump, bang; (*schelten*) bawl □ *vi* (*sein*) crash down; (*gehen*) clump [along]; (*fahren*) rumble [along]

Polyäthylen *nt* -s polythene

Polyester *m* -s polyester

Polyp *m* -en,-en polyp; (*sl: Polizist*) copper; **P~en** adenoids *pl*

Pomeranze *f* -,-n Seville orange

Pommes pl (fam) French fries

Pommes frites /pɔmˈfriːt/ pl chips; (dünner) French fries

Pomp m -s pomp

Pompon /põˈpõː/ m -s,-s pompon

pompös a ostentatious, adv -ly

Pony¹ nt -s,-s pony

Pony² m -s,-s fringe

Pop m -[s] pop. **P~musik** f pop music

Popo m -s,-s (fam) bottom

popul|är a popular. **P~arität** f - popularity

Pore f -,-n pore

Porno|graphie, Pornografie f - pornography. **p~graphisch, p~grafisch** a pornographic

porös a porous

Porree m -s leeks pl; **eine Stange P~** a leek

Portal nt -s,-e portal

Portemonnaie /pɔrtmoˈneː/ nt -s,-s purse

Portier /pɔrˈtjeː/ m -s,-s doorman, porter

Portion /-ˈtsi̯oːn/ f -,-en helping, portion

Portmonee nt -s,-s = Portemonnaie

Porto nt -s postage. **p~frei** adv post free, post paid

Porträt /pɔrˈtrɛː/ nt -s,-s portrait. **p~tieren** vt paint a portrait of

Portugal nt -s Portugal

Portugies|e m -n,-n, **P~in** f -,-nen Portuguese. **p~isch** a Portuguese

Portwein m port

Porzellan nt -s china, porcelain

Posaune f -,-n trombone

Pose f -,-n pose

posieren vi (haben) pose

Position /-ˈtsi̯oːn/ f -,-en position

positiv a positive, adv -ly. **P~** nt -s,-e (Phot) positive

Posse f -,-n (Theat) farce. **P~n** m -s,- prank; **P~n** pl tomfoolery sg

Possessivpronomen nt possessive pronoun

possierlich a cute

Post f - post office; (Briefe) mail, post; **mit der P~** by post

postalisch a postal

Post|amt nt post office. **P~anweisung** f postal money order. **P~bote** m postman

Posten m -s,- post; (Wache) sentry; (Waren-) batch; (Rechnungs-) item, entry; **P~ stehen** stand guard; **nicht auf dem P~** (fam) under the weather

Poster nt & m -s,- poster

Postfach nt post-office or PO box

postieren vt post, station; **sich p~** station oneself

Post|karte f postcard. **p~lagernd** adv poste restante. **P~leitzahl** f postcode, (Amer) Zip code. **P~scheckkonto** nt ≈ National Girobank account. **P~stempel** m postmark

postum a posthumous, adv -ly

post|wendend adv by return of post. **P~wertzeichen** nt [postage] stamp

Poten|tial /-ˈtsi̯aːl/ nt -s,-e = Potenzial. **p~tiell** /-ˈtsi̯ɛl/ a = potenziell

Potenz f -,-en potency; (Math & fig) power. **P~ial** nt -s,-e potential. **p~iell** a potential, adv -ly

Pracht f - magnificence, splendour. **P~exemplar** nt magnificent specimen

prächtig a magnificent, adv -ly; (prima) splendid, adv -ly

prachtvoll a magnificent, adv -ly

Prädikat nt -[e]s,-e rating; (Comm) grade; (Gram) predicate. **p~iv** a (Gram) predicative, adv -ly. **P~swein** m high-quality wine

präge|n vt stamp (auf + acc on); emboss (Leder, Papier); mint (Münze); coin (Wort, Ausdruck); (fig) shape. **P~stempel** m die

pragmatisch a pragmatic, adv -ally

prägnant a succinct, adv -ly

prähistorisch a prehistoric

prahl|en vi (haben) boast, brag (mit about). **p~erisch** a boastful, adv -ly

Prakti|k f -,-en practice. **P~kant(in)** m -en,-en (f -,-nen) trainee

Prakti|kum nt -s,-ka practical training. **p~sch** a practical; (nützlich) handy; (tatsächlich) virtual; **p~scher Arzt** general practitioner □ adv practically; virtually; (in der Praxis) in practice; **p~sch arbeiten** do practical work. **p~zieren** vt/i (haben) practise; (anwenden) put into practice; (fam: bekommen) get

Praline f -,-n chocolate; **Schachtel P~n** box of chocolates

prall a bulging; (dick) plump; (Sonne) blazing □ adv **p~ gefüllt** full to bursting. **p~en** vi (sein) **p~ auf** (+ acc)/**gegen** collide with, hit; (Sonne:) blaze down on

Prämie /-i̯ə/ f -,-n premium; (Preis) award

präm[i]ieren vt award a prize to

Pranger m -s,- pillory

Pranke f -,-n paw

Präpar|at nt -[e]s,-e preparation. **p~ieren** vt prepare; (zerlegen) dissect; (ausstopfen) stuff

Präposition /-ˈtsi̯oːn/ f -,-en preposition

Präsens nt - (Gram) present

präsentieren vt present; **sich p~** present itself/(Person:) oneself

Präsenz *f* - presence

Präservativ *nt* -s,-e condom

Präsident|(in) *m* -en,-en (*f* -,-nen) president. **P∼schaft** *f* - presidency

Präsidium *nt* -s presidency; (*Gremium*) executive committee; (*Polizei-*) headquarters *pl*

prasseln *vi* (*haben*) ⟨*Regen:*⟩ beat down; ⟨*Feuer:*⟩ crackle □ *vi* (*sein*) **p∼ auf** (+ *acc*)/**gegen** beat down on/beat against

prassen *vi* (*haben*) live extravagantly; (*schmausen*) feast

Präteritum *nt* -s imperfect

präventiv *a* preventive

Praxis *f* -,-xen practice; (*Erfahrung*) practical experience; (*Arzt-*) surgery; **in der P∼** in practice

Präzedenzfall *m* precedent

präzis[e] *a* precise, *adv* -ly

Präzision *f* - precision

predig|en *vt/i* (*haben*) preach. **P∼er** *m* -s,- preacher. **P∼t** *f* -,-en sermon

Preis *m* -es,-e price; (*Belohnung*) prize; **um jeden/keinen P∼** at any/not at any price. **P∼ausschreiben** *nt* competition

Preiselbeere *f* (*Bot*) cowberry; (*Culin*) ≈ cranberry

preisen† *vt* praise; **sich glücklich p∼** count oneself lucky

preisgeben† *vt sep* abandon (*dat* to); reveal ⟨*Geheimnis*⟩

preis|gekrönt *a* award-winning. **P∼gericht** *nt* jury. **p∼günstig** *a* reasonably priced □ *adv* at a reasonable price. **P∼lage** *f* price range. **p∼lich** *a* price . . . □ *adv* in price. **P∼richter** *m* judge. **P∼schild** *nt* price-tag. **P∼träger(in)** *m(f)* prize-winner. **p∼wert** *a* reasonable, *adv* -bly; (*billig*) inexpensive, *adv* -ly

prekär *a* difficult; (*heikel*) delicate

Prell|bock *m* buffers *pl*. **p∼en** *vt* bounce; (*verletzen*) bruise; (*fam: betrügen*) cheat. **P∼ung** *f* -,-en bruise

Premiere /prə'mjɛ:rə/ *f* -,-n première

Premierminister(in) /prə'mje:-/ *m(f)* Prime Minister

Presse *f* -,-n press. **p∼n** *vt* press; **sich p∼n** press (**an** + *acc* against)

pressieren *vi* (*haben*) (*SGer*) be urgent

Pressluft (**Preßluft**) *f* compressed air. **P∼bohrer** *m* pneumatic drill

Prestige /prɛs'ti:ʒə/ *nt* -s prestige

Preuß|en *nt* -s Prussia. **p∼isch** *a* Prussian

prickeln *vi* (*haben*) tingle

Priester *m* -s,- priest

prima *inv a* first-class, first-rate; (*fam:toll*) fantastic, *adv* fantastically well

primär *a* primary, *adv* -ily

Primel *f* -,-n primula; (*Garten-*) polyanthus

primitiv *a* primitive

Prinz *m* -en,-en prince. **P∼essin** *f* -,-nen princess

Prinzip *nt* -s,-ien /-jən/ principle; **im/aus P∼** in/on principle. **p∼iell** *a* ⟨*Frage*⟩ of principle □ *adv* on principle; (*im Prinzip*) in principle

Priorität *f* -,-en priority

Prise *f* -,-n **P∼ Salz** pinch of salt

Prisma *nt* -s,-men prism

privat *a* private, *adv* -ly; (*persönlich*) personal. **P∼adresse** *f* home address. **p∼isieren** *vt* privatize

Privat|leben *nt* private life. **P∼lehrer** *m* private tutor. **P∼lehrerin** *f* governess. **P∼patient(in)** *m(f)* private patient

Privileg *nt* -[e]s,-ien /-jən/ privilege. **p∼iert** *a* privileged

pro *prep* (+ *dat*) per. **Pro** *nt* - **das Pro und Kontra** the pros and cons *pl*

Probe *f* -,-n test, trial; (*Menge, Muster*) sample; (*Theat*) rehearsal; **auf die P∼ stellen** put to the test; **ein Auto P∼ fahren** test-drive a car. **P∼fahrt** *f* test drive. **p∼n** *vt/i* (*haben*) (*Theat*) rehearse. **p∼weise** *adv* on a trial basis. **P∼zeit** *f* probationary period

probieren *vt/i* (*haben*) try; (*kosten*) taste; (*proben*) rehearse

Problem *nt* -s,-e problem. **p∼atisch** *a* problematic

problemlos *a* problem-free □ *adv* without any problems

Produkt *nt* -[e]s,-e product

Produk|tion /-'tsjo:n/ *f* -,-en production. **p∼tiv** *a* productive. **P∼tivität** *f* - productivity

Produ|zent *m* -en,-en producer. **p∼zieren** *vt* produce; **sich p∼zieren** (*fam*) show off

professionell *a* professional, *adv* -ly

Professor *m* -s,-en /-'so:rən/ professor

Profi *m* -s,-s (*Sport*) professional

Profil *nt* -s,-e profile; (*Reifen-*) tread; (*fig*) image. **p∼iert** *a* (*fig*) distinguished

Profit *m* -[e]s,-e profit. **p∼ieren** *vi* (*haben*) profit (**von** from)

Prognose *f* -,-n forecast; (*Med*) prognosis

Programm *nt* -s,-e programme; (*Computer-*) program; (*TV*) channel; (*Comm: Sortiment*) range. **p∼ieren** *vt/i* (*haben*) (*Computer*) program. **P∼ierer(in)** *m* -s, (*f* -,-nen) [computer] programmer

progressiv *a* progressive

Projekt *nt* -[e]s,-e project

Projektor *m* -s,-en /-'to:rən/ projector

projizieren *vt* project

Proklam|ation /-'tsjo:n/ *f* -,-en proclamation. **p~ieren** *vt* proclaim

Prolet *m* -en,-en boor. **P~ariat** *nt* -[e]s proletariat. **P~arier** /-jɐ/ *m* -s,- proletarian

Prolog *m* -s,-e prologue

Promenade *f* -,-n promenade. **P~nmischung** *f (fam)* mongrel

Promille *pl (fam)* alcohol level *sg* in the blood; **zu viel P~ haben** *(fam)* be over the limit

prominen|t *a* prominent. **P~z** *f* -prominent figures *pl*

Promiskuität *f* - promiscuity

promovieren *vi (haben)* obtain one's doctorate

prompt *a* prompt, *adv* -ly; *(fam: natürlich)* of course

Pronomen *nt* -s,- pronoun

Propag|anda *f* - propaganda; *(Reklame)* publicity. **p~ieren** *vt* propagate

Propeller *m* -s,- propeller

Prophet *m* -en,-en prophet. **p~isch** *a* prophetic

prophezei|en *vt* prophesy. **P~ung** *f* -,-en prophecy

Proportion /-'tsjo:n/ *f* -,-en proportion. **p~al** *a* proportional. **p~iert** *a* **gut p~iert** well proportioned

Prosa *f* - prose

prosaisch *a* prosaic, *adv* -ally

prosit *int* cheers!

Prospekt *m* -[e]s,-e brochure; *(Comm)* prospectus

prost *int* cheers!

Prostitu|ierte *f* -n,-n prostitute. **P~tion** /-'tsjo:n/ *f* - prostitution

Protest *m* -[e]s,-e protest

Protestant|(in) *m* -en,-en *(f* -,-nen) *(Relig)* Protestant. **p~isch** *a (Relig)* Protestant

protestieren *vi (haben)* protest

Prothese *f* -,-n artificial limb; *(Zahn-)* denture

Protokoll *nt* -s,-e record; *(Sitzungs-)* minutes *pl*; *(diplomatisches)* protocol; *(Strafzettel)* ticket

Prototyp *m* -s,-en prototype

protz|en *vi (haben)* show off **(mit etw** sth). **p~ig** *a* ostentatious

Proviant *m* -s provisions *pl*

Provinz *f* -,-en province. **p~iell** *a* provincial

Provision *f* -,-en *(Comm)* commission

provisorisch *a* provisional, *adv* -ly, temporary, *adv* -ily

Provokation /-'tsjo:n/ *f* -,-en provocation

provozieren *vt* provoke. **p~d** *a* provocative, *adv* -ly

Prozedur *f* -,-en [lengthy] business

Prozent *nt* -[e]s,-e & - per cent; **5 P~** 5 per cent. **P~satz** *m* percentage. **p~ual** *a* percentage ...

Prozess *m* -es,-e **(Prozeß** *m* -sses,-sse) process; *(Jur)* lawsuit; *(Kriminal-)* trial

Prozession *f* -,-en procession

prüde *a* prudish

prüf|en *vt* test/*(über-)* check **(auf** + *acc* for); audit *(Bücher)*; *(Sch)* examine; **p~ender Blick** searching look. **P~er** *m* -s,- inspector; *(Buch-)* auditor; *(Sch)* examiner. **P~ling** *m* -s,-e examination candidate. **P~ung** *f* -,-en examination; *(Test)* test; *(Bücher-)* audit; *(fig)* trial

Prügel *m* -s,- cudgel; **P~** *pl* hiding *sg*, beating *sg*. **P~ei** *f* -,-en brawl, fight. **p~n** *vt* beat, thrash; **sich p~n** fight, brawl

Prunk *m* -[e]s magnificence, splendour. **p~en** *vi (haben)* show off **(mit etw** sth). **p~voll** *a* magnificent, *adv* -ly

prusten *vi (haben)* splutter; *(schnauben)* snort

Psalm *m* -s,-en psalm

Pseudonym *nt* -s,-e pseudonym

pst *int* shush!

Psychi|ater *m* -s,- psychiatrist. **P~atrie** *f* - psychiatry. **p~atrisch** *a* psychiatric

psychisch *a* psychological, *adv* -ly; *(Med)* mental, *adv* -ly

Psycho|analyse *f* psychoanalysis. **P~loge** *m* -n,-n psychologist. **P~logie** *f* - psychology. **p~logisch** *a* psychological, *adv* -ly

Pubertät *f* - puberty

publik *a* **p~ werden/machen** become/make public

Publi|kum *nt* -s public; *(Zuhörer)* audience; *(Zuschauer)* spectators *pl*. **p~zieren** *vt* publish

Pudding *m* -s blancmange; *(im Wasserbad gekocht)* pudding

Pudel *m* -s,- poodle

Puder *m & (fam)* nt -s,- powder; *(Körper-)* talcum [powder]. **P~dose** *f* [powder] compact. **p~n** *vt* powder. **P~zucker** *m* icing sugar

Puff¹ *m* -[e]s,ˉe push, poke

Puff² *m & nt* -s,-s *(sl)* brothel

puffen *vt (fam)* poke □ *vi (sein)* puff along

Puffer *m* -s,- *(Rail)* buffer; *(Culin)* pancake. **P~zone** *f* buffer zone

Pull|i *m* -s,-s jumper. **P~over** *m* -s,- jumper; *(Herren-)* pullover

Puls *m* -es pulse. **P~ader** *f* artery. **p~ieren** *vi* (*haben*) pulsate

Pult *nt* -[e]s,-e desk; (*Lese-*) lectern

Pulver *nt* -s,- powder. **p~ig** *a* powdery. **p~isieren** *vt* pulverize

Pulver|kaffee *m* instant coffee. **P~schnee** *m* powder snow

pummelig *a* (*fam*) chubby

Pump *m* auf **P~** on tick

Pumpe *f* -,-n pump. **p~n** *vt/i* (*haben*) pump; (*fam: leihen*) lend; [**sich** (*dat*)] **etw p~n** (*fam: borgen*) borrow sth

Pumps /pœmps/ *pl* court shoes

Punkt *m* -[e]s,-e dot; (*Tex*) spot; (*Geom, Sport & fig*) point; (*Gram*) full stop, period; **P~ sechs Uhr** at six o'clock sharp; **nach P~en siegen** win on points. **p~iert** *a* (*Linie, Note*) dotted

pünktlich *a* punctual, *adv* -ly. **P~keit** *f* - punctuality

Punsch *m* -[e]s,-e [hot] punch

Pupille *f* -,-n (*Anat*) pupil

Puppe *f* -,-n doll; (*Marionette*) puppet; (*Schaufenster-, Schneider-*) dummy; (*Zool*) chrysalis

pur *a* pure; (*fam: bloß*) sheer; **Whisky pur** neat whisky

Püree *nt* -s,-s purée; (*Kartoffel-*) mashed potatoes *pl*

puritanisch *a* puritanical

purpurrot *a* crimson

Purzel|baum *m* (*fam*) somersault. **p~n** *vi* (*sein*) (*fam*) tumble

pusseln *vi* (*haben*) (*fam*) potter

Puste *f* - (*fam*) breath; **aus der P~** out of breath. **p~n** *vt/i* (*haben*) (*fam*) blow

Pute *f* -,-n turkey; (*Henne*) turkey hen. **P~r** *m* -s,- turkey cock

Putsch *m* -[e]s,-e coup

Putz *m* -es plaster; (*Staat*) finery. **p~en** *vt* clean; (*Aust*) dry-clean; (*zieren*) adorn; **sich p~en** dress up; **sich** (*dat*) **die Zähne/Nase p~en** clean one's teeth/blow one's nose. **P~frau** *f* cleaner, charwoman. **p~ig** *a* (*fam*) amusing, cute; (*seltsam*) odd. **P~macherin** *f* -,-nen milliner

Puzzlespiel /'pazl-/ *nt* jigsaw

Pyramide *f* -,-n pyramid

Q

Quacksalber *m* -s,- quack

Quadrat *nt* -[e]s,-e square. **q~isch** *a* square. **Q~meter** *m & nt* square metre

quaken *vi* (*haben*) quack; (*Frosch:*) croak

quäken *vi* (*haben*) screech; (*Baby:*) whine

Quäker(in) *m* -s,- (*f* -,-nen) Quaker

Qual *f* -,-en torment; (*Schmerz*) agony

quälen *vt* torment; (*foltern*) torture; (*bedrängen*) pester; **sich q~** torment oneself; (*leiden*) suffer; (*sich mühen*) struggle. **q~d** *a* agonizing

Quälerei *f* -,-en torture; (*Qual*) agony

Quälgeist *m* (*fam*) pest

Qualifi|kation /-'tsio:n/ *f* -,-en qualification. **q~zieren** *vt* qualify; **sich q~zieren** qualify. **q~ziert** *a* qualified; (*fähig*) competent; (*Arbeit*) skilled

Qualität *f* -,-en quality

Qualle *f* -,-n jellyfish

Qualm *m* -s [thick] smoke. **q~en** *vi* (*haben*) smoke

qualvoll *a* agonizing

Quantität *f* -,-en quantity

Quantum *nt* -s,-ten quantity; (*Anteil*) share, quota

Quarantäne *f* - quarantine

Quark *m* -s quark, ≈ curd cheese; (*fam: Unsinn*) rubbish

Quartal *nt* -s,-e quarter

Quartett *nt* -[e]s,-e quartet

Quartier *nt* -s,-e accommodation; (*Mil*) quarters *pl*; **ein Q~ suchen** look for accommodation

Quarz *m* -es quartz

quasseln *vi* (*haben*) (*fam*) jabber

Quaste *f* -,-n tassel

Quatsch *m* -[e]s (*fam*) nonsense, rubbish; **Q~ machen** (*Unfug machen*) fool around; (*etw falsch machen*) do a silly thing. **q~en** (*fam*) *vi* (*haben*) talk; (*schwatzen*) natter; (*Wasser, Schlamm:*) squelch □ *vt* talk. **q~nass** (*q~naß*) *a* (*fam*) soaking wet

Quecksilber *nt* mercury

Quelle *f* -,-n spring; (*Fluss- & fig*) source. **q~n†** *vi* (*sein*) well [up]/(*fließen*) pour (*aus* from); (*aufquellen*) swell; (*hervortreten*) bulge

quengeln *vi* (*fam*) whine; (*Baby:*) grizzle

quer *adv* across, crosswise; (*schräg*) diagonally; **q~ gestreift** horizontally striped

Quere *f* - **der Q~ nach** across, crosswise; **jdm in die Q~ kommen** get in s.o.'s way

querfeldein *adv* across country

quer|gestreift *a* (NEW) **Q~ gestreift**, s. **quer**. **q~köpfig** *a* (*fam*) awkward. **Q~latte** *f* crossbar. **Q~schiff** *nt* transept. **Q~schnitt** *m* cross-section. **q~schnittsgelähmt** *a* paraplegic. **Q~straße** *f* side-street; **die erste Q~straße links** the first turning on the left. **Q~verweis** *m* cross-reference

quetsch|en *vt* squash; (*drücken*) squeeze; (*zerdrücken*) crush; (*Culin*) mash; **sich q~en in** (+ *acc*) squeeze into; **sich** (*dat*) **den Arm q~en** bruise one's arm. **Q~ung** *f* -,-en, **Q~wunde** *f* bruise

Queue /køː/ *nt* -s,-s cue

quicklebendig *a* very lively

quieken *vi* (*haben*) squeak; (*Maus:*) squeak

quietschen *vi* (*haben*) squeal; (*Tür, Dielen:*) creak

Quintętt *nt* -[e]s,-e quintet

Quirl *m* -[e]s,-e blender with a star-shaped head. **q~en** *vt* mix

quitt *a* **q~ sein** (*fam*) be quits

Quitte *f* -,-n quince

quittieren *vt* receipt (*Rechnung*); sign for (*Geldsumme, Sendung*); (*reagieren auf*) greet (mit with); **den Dienst q~** resign

Quittung *f* -,-en receipt

Quiz /kvɪs/ *nt* -,- quiz

Quote *f* -,-n proportion

R

Rabatt *m* -[e]s,-e discount

Rabatte *f* -,-n (*Hort*) border

Rabattmarke *f* trading stamp

Rabbiner *m* -s,- rabbi

Rabe *m* -n,-n raven. **r~nschwarz** *a* pitch-black

rabiat *a* violent, *adv* -ly; (*wütend*) furious, *adv* -ly

Rache *f* - revenge, vengeance

Rachen *m* -s,- pharynx; (*Maul*) jaws *pl*

rächen *vt* avenge; **sich r~** take revenge (**an** + *dat* on); (*Fehler, Leichtsinn:*) cost s.o. dear

Racker *m* -s,- (*fam*) rascal

Rad *nt* -[e]s,¨er wheel; (*Fahr-*) bicycle, (*fam*) bike; **Rad fahren** cycle

Radar *m* & *nt* -s radar

Radau *m* -s (*fam*) din, racket

radebrechen *vt/i* (*haben*) [**Deutsch/ Englisch**] **r~** speak broken German/ English

radeln *vi* (*sein*) (*fam*) cycle

Rädelsführer *m* ringleader

radfahr|en† *vi sep* (*sein*) (NEW) **Rad fahren**, *s.* **Rad. R~er(in)** *m(f)* -s,- (*f* -,-nen) cyclist

radier|en *vt/i* (*haben*) rub out; (*Kunst*) etch. **R~gummi** *m* eraser, rubber. **R~ung** *f* -,-en etching

Radieschen /-'diːsçən/ *nt* -s,- radish

radikal *a* radical, *adv* -ly; (*drastisch*) drastic, *adv* -ally. **R~e(r)** *m/f* (*Pol*) radical

Radio *nt* -s,-s radio

radioaktiv *a* radioactive. **R~ität** *f* - radioactivity

Radioapparat *m* radio [set]

Radius *m* -,-ien /-jən/ radius

Rad|kappe *f* hub-cap. **R~ler** *m* -s,- cyclist; (*Getränk*) shandy. **R~weg** *m* cycle track

raff|en *vt* grab; (*kräuseln*) gather; (*kürzen*) condense. **r~gierig** *a* avaricious

Raffin|ade *f* - refined sugar. **R~erie** *f* -,-n refinery. **R~esse** *f* -,-n refinement; (*Schlauheit*) cunning. **r~ieren** *vt* refine. **r~iert** *a* ingenious, *adv* -ly; (*durchtrieben*) crafty, *adv* -ily

Rage /'raːʒə/ *f* - (*fam*) fury

ragen *vi* (*haben*) rise [up]

Rahm *m* -s (*SGer*) cream

rahmen *vt* frame. **R~** *m* -s,- frame; (*fig*) framework; (*Grenze*) limits *pl*; (*einer Feier*) setting

Rain *m* -[e]s,-e grass verge

räkeln *v* = rekeln

Rakete *f* -,-n rocket; (*Mil*) missile

Rallye /'rali/ *nt* -s,-s rally

rammen *vt* ram

Rampe *f* -,-n ramp; (*Theat*) front of the stage. **R~nlicht** *nt* **im R~nlicht stehen** (*fig*) be in the limelight

ramponier|en *vt* (*fam*) damage; (*ruinieren*) ruin; **r~t** battered

Ramsch *m* -[e]s junk. **R~laden** *m* junk-shop

ran *adv* = heran

Rand *m* -[e]s,¨er edge; (*Teller-, Gläser-, Brillen-*) rim; (*Zier-*) border, edging; (*Buch-, Brief-*) margin; (*Stadt-*) outskirts *pl*; (*Ring*) ring; **am R~e des Ruins** on the brink of ruin; **am R~e erwähnen** mention in passing; **zu R~e kommen mit** = **zurande kommen mit**, *s.* **zurande**; **außer R~ und Band** (*fam: ausgelassen*) very boisterous

randalieren *vi* (*haben*) rampage

Rand|bemerkung *f* marginal note. **R~streifen** *m* (*Auto*) hard shoulder

Rang *m* -[e]s,¨e rank; (*Theat*) tier; **erster/zweiter R~** (*Theat*) dress/upper circle; **ersten R~es** first-class

rangieren /raŋ'ʒiːrən/ *vt* shunt □ *vi* (*haben*) rank (**vor** + *dat* before); **an erster Stelle r~** come first

Rangordnung *f* order of importance; (*Hierarchie*) hierarchy

Ranke *f* -,-n tendril; (*Trieb*) shoot

ranken (sich) *vr* (*Bot*) trail; (*in die Höhe*) climb; **sich r~ um** twine around

Ranzen *m* -s,- (*Sch*) satchel

ranzig *a* rancid

Rappe *m* -n,-n black horse

rappeln *v* (*fam*) □ *vi* (*haben*) rattle □ *vr* **sich r~** pick oneself up; (*fig*) rally

Raps *m* -es (*Bot*) rape

rar *a* rare; **er macht sich rar** (*fam*) we don't see much of him. **R~ität** *f* -,-en rarity

rasant *a* fast; (*schnittig, schick*) stylish □ *adv* fast; stylishly

rasch *a* quick, *adv* -ly

rascheln *vi* (*haben*) rustle

Rasen *m* -s,- lawn

rasen *vi* (*sein*) tear [along]; ⟨*Puls:*⟩ race; ⟨*Zeit:*⟩ fly; **gegen eine Mauer r~** career into a wall □ *vi* (*haben*) rave; ⟨*Sturm:*⟩ rage; **vor Begeisterung r~** go wild with enthusiasm. **r~d** *a* furious; (*tobend*) raving; ⟨*Sturm, Durst*⟩ raging; ⟨*Schmerz*⟩ excruciating; ⟨*Beifall*⟩ tumultuous □ *adv* terribly

Rasenmäher *m* lawn-mower

Raserei *f* - speeding; (*Toben*) frenzy

Rasier|apparat *m* razor. **r~en** *vt* shave; **sich r~en** shave. **R~klinge** *f* razor blade. **R~pinsel** *m* shaving-brush. **R~wasser** *nt* aftershave [lotion]

Raspel *f* -,-n rasp; (*Culin*) grater. **r~n** *vt* grate

Rasse *f* -,-n race. **R~hund** *m* pedigree dog

Rassel *f* -,-n rattle. **r~n** *vi* (*haben*) rattle; ⟨*Schlüssel:*⟩ jangle; ⟨*Kette:*⟩ clank □ *vi* (*sein*) rattle [along]

Rassen|diskriminierung *f* racial discrimination. **R~trennung** *f* racial segregation

Rassepferd *nt* thoroughbred. **rassisch** *a* racial

Rassis|mus *m* - racism. **r~tisch** *a* racist

Rast *f* -,-en rest. **r~en** *vi* (*haben*) rest. **R~haus** *nt* motorway restaurant. **r~los** *a* restless, *adv* -ly; (*ununterbrochen*) ceaseless, *adv* -ly. **R~platz** *m* picnic area. **R~stätte** *f* motorway restaurant [and services]

Rasur *f* -,-en shave

Rat[1] *m* -[e]s [piece of] advice; **guter Rat** good advice; **sich** (*dat*) **keinen Rat wissen** not know what to do; **zu Rat[e] ziehen** = **zurate ziehen**, *s.* **zurate**

Rat[2] *m* -[e]s,-̈e (*Admin*) council; (*Person*) councillor

Rate *f* -,-n instalment

raten† *vt* guess; (*empfehlen*) advise □ *vi* (*haben*) guess; **jdm r~** advise s.o.

Ratenzahlung *f* payment by instalments

Rat|geber *m* -s,- adviser; (*Buch*) guide. **R~haus** *nt* town hall

ratifizier|en *vt* ratify. **R~ung** *f* -,-en ratification

Ration /ra'tsi̯o:n/ *f* -,-en ration; **eiserne R~** iron rations *pl.* **r~al** *a* rational, *adv* -ly. **r~alisieren** *vt/i* (*haben*) rationalize. **r~ell** *a* efficient, *adv* -ly. **r~ieren** *vt* ration

rat|los *a* helpless, *adv* -ly; **r~los sein** not know what to do. **r~sam** *pred a* advisable; (*klug*) prudent. **R~schlag** *m* piece of advice; **R~schläge** advice *sg*

Rätsel *nt* -s,- riddle; (*Kreuzwort-*) puzzle; (*Geheimnis*) mystery. **r~haft** *a* puzzling, mysterious. **r~n** *vi* (*haben*) puzzle

Ratte *f* -,-n rat

rattern *vi* (*haben*) rattle □ *vi* (*sein*) rattle [along]

rau *a* rough, *adv* -ly; (*unfreundlich*) gruff, *adv* -ly; ⟨*Klima, Wind*⟩ harsh, raw; ⟨*Landschaft*⟩ rugged; (*heiser*) husky; ⟨*Hals*⟩ sore

Raub *m* -[e]s robbery; (*Menschen-*) abduction; (*Beute*) loot, booty. **r~en** *vt* steal; abduct ⟨*Menschen*⟩; **jdm etw r~en** rob s.o. of sth

Räuber *m* -s,- robber

Raub|mord *m* robbery with murder. **R~tier** *nt* predator. **R~überfall** *m* robbery. **R~vogel** *m* bird of prey

Rauch *m* -[e]s smoke. **r~en** *vt/i* (*haben*) smoke. **R~en** *nt* -s smoking; '**R~en verboten**' 'no smoking'. **R~er** *m* -s,-smoker. **R~erabteil** *nt* smoking compartment

Räucher|lachs *m* smoked salmon. **r~n** *vt* (*Culin*) smoke

Rauch|fang *m* (*Aust*) chimney. **r~ig** *a* smoky. **R~verbot** *nt* smoking ban

räudig *a* mangy

rauf *adv* = **herauf, hinauf**

rauf|en *vt* pull; **sich** (*dat*) **die Haare r~en** (*fig*) tear one's hair □ *vr/i* (*haben*) [**sich**] **r~en** fight. **R~erei** *f* -,-en fight

rauh *a* NEW **rau**

rau|haarig *a* wire-haired. **R~heit** *f* - (*s.* **rau**) roughness; gruffness; harshness; ruggedness

rauh|haarig *a* NEW **rauhaarig. R~reif** *m* NEW **Raureif**

Raum *m* -[e]s,**Räume** room; (*Gebiet*) area; (*Welt-*) space

räumen *vt* clear; vacate ⟨*Wohnung*⟩; evacuate ⟨*Gebäude, Gebiet, (Mil Stellung)*⟩; (*bringen*) put (**in/auf** + *acc* into/on); (*holen*) get (**aus** out of); **beiseite r~** move/put to one side; **aus dem Weg r~** (*fam*) get rid of

Raum|fahrer *m* astronaut. **R~fahrt** *f* space travel. **R~fahrzeug** *nt* spacecraft.

R~flug m space flight. R~inhalt m volume

räumlich a spatial. R~keiten fpl rooms

Raum|pflegerin f cleaner. R~schiff nt spaceship

Räumung f - (s. räumen) clearing; vacating; evacuation. R~sverkauf m clearance/closing-down sale

raunen vt/i (haben) whisper

Raupe f -,-n caterpillar

Raureif m hoar-frost

raus adv = heraus, hinaus

Rausch m -[e]s, Räusche intoxication; (fig) exhilaration; einen R~ haben be drunk

rauschen vi (haben) ⟨Wasser, Wind:⟩ rush; ⟨Bäume Blätter:⟩ rustle □ vi (sein) rush [along]; aus dem Zimmer r~ sweep out of the room. r~d a rushing; rustling; ⟨Applaus⟩ tumultuous

Rauschgift nt [narcotic] drug; (coll) drugs pl. R~süchtige(r) m/f drug addict

räuspern (sich) vr clear one's throat

rausschmeiß|en† vt sep (fam) throw out; (entlassen) sack. R~er m -s,- (fam) bouncer

Raute f -,-n diamond

Razzia f -,-ien /-jən/ [police] raid

Reagenzglas nt test-tube

reagieren vi (haben) react (auf + acc to)

Reaktion /-'tsjo:n/ f -,-en reaction. r~är a reactionary

Reaktor m -s,-en /-'to:rən/ reactor

real a real; (gegenständlich) tangible; (realistisch) realistic, adv -ally. r~isieren vt realize

Realis|mus m - realism. R~t m -en,-en realist. r~tisch a realistic, adv -ally

Realität f -,-en reality

Realschule f ≈ secondary modern school

Rebe f -,-n vine

Rebell m -en,-en rebel. r~ieren vi (haben) rebel. R~ion f -,-en rebellion

rebellisch a rebellious

Rebhuhn nt partridge

Rebstock m vine

Rechen m -s- rake. r~ vt/i (haben) rake

Rechen|aufgabe f arithmetical problem; (Sch) sum. R~fehler m arithmetical error. R~maschine f calculator

Rechenschaft f - R~ ablegen give account (über + acc of); jdn zur R~ ziehen call s.o. to account

recherchieren /reʃɛr'ʃi:rən/ vt/i (haben) investigate; (Journ) research

rechnen vi (haben) do arithmetic; (schätzen) reckon; (zählen) count (zu among; auf + acc on); r~ mit reckon with; (erwarten) expect; gut r~ können be good at figures □ vt calculate, work out; do ⟨Aufgabe⟩; (dazu-) add (zu to); (fig) count (zu among). R~ nt -s arithmetic

Rechner m -s,- calculator; (Computer) computer; ein guter R~ sein be good at figures

Rechnung f -,-en bill; (Amer) check; (Comm) invoice; (Berechnung) calculation; R~ führen über (+ acc) keep account of; etw (dat) R~ tragen (fig) take sth into account. R~sjahr nt financial year. R~sprüfer m auditor

Recht nt -[e]s,-e law; (Berechtigung) right (auf + acc to): im R~ sein be in the right; R~ haben/behalten be right; R~ bekommen be proved right; jdm R~ geben agree with s.o.; mit od zu R~ rightly; von R~s wegen by right; (eigentlich) by rights

recht a right; (wirklich) real; ich habe keine r~e Lust I don't really feel like it; es jdm r~ machen please s.o.; jdm r~ sein be all right with s.o.; r~ haben/ behalten/bekommen (NEW) Recht haben/behalten/bekommen, s. Recht; jdm r~ geben (NEW) jdm Recht geben, s. Recht □ adv correctly; (ziemlich) quite; (sehr) very; r~ vielen Dank many thanks

Recht|e f -n,-[n] right side; (Hand) right hand; (Boxen) right; die R~e (Pol) the right; zu meiner R~en on my right. r~e(r,s) a right; (Pol) right-wing; r~e Masche plain stitch. R~e(r) m/f der/die R~e the right man/woman; du bist mir der/die R~e! you're a fine one! R~e(s) nt das R~e the right thing; etwas R~es lernen learn something useful; nach dem R~en sehen see that everything is all right

Rechteck nt -[e]s,-e rectangle. r~ig a rectangular

rechtfertig|en vt justify; sich r~en justify oneself. R~ung f - justification

recht|haberisch a opinionated. r~lich a legal, adv -ly. r~mäßig a legitimate, adv -ly.

rechts adv on the right; (bei Stoff) on the right side; von/nach r~ from/to the right; zwei r~, zwei links stricken knit two, purl two. R~anwalt m, R~anwältin f lawyer

rechtschaffen a upright; (ehrlich) honest, adv -ly. r~ müde thoroughly tired

rechtschreib|en vi (inf only) spell correctly. R~fehler m spelling mistake. R~ung f - spelling

Rechts|händer(in) m -s,- (f -,-nen) right-hander. r~händig a & adv right-handed. r~kräftig a legal, adv -ly.

R~streit *m* law suit. **R~verkehr** *m* driving on the right. **r~widrig** *a* illegal, *adv* -ly. **R~wissenschaft** *f* jurisprudence

recht|winklig *a* right-angled. **r~zeitig** *a* & *adv* in time

Reck *nt* -[e]s,-e horizontal bar

recken *vt* stretch; **sich r~** stretch; **den Hals r~** crane one's neck

Redakteur /redak'tøːɐ̯/ *m* -s,-e editor; (*Radio, TV*) producer

Redaktion /-'tsi̯oːn/ *f* -,-en editing; (*Radio, TV*) production; (*Abteilung*) editorial/production department. **r~ell** *a* editorial

Rede *f* -,-n speech; **zur R~ stellen** demand an explanation from; **davon ist keine R~** there's no question of it; **nicht der R~ wert** not worth mentioning. **r~gewandt** *a* eloquent, *adv* -ly

reden *vi* (*haben*) talk (**von** about; **mit** to); (*eine Rede halten*) speak □ *vt* talk; speak ⟨*Wahrheit*⟩; **kein Wort r~** not say a word. **R~sart** *f* saying; (*Phrase*) phrase

Redewendung *f* idiom

redigieren *vt* edit

redlich *a* honest, *adv* -ly

Red|ner *m* -s,- speaker. **r~selig** *a* talkative

reduzieren *vt* reduce

Reeder *m* -s,- shipowner. **R~ei** *f* -,-en shipping company

reell *a* real; (*ehrlich*) honest, *adv* -ly; ⟨*Preis, Angebot*⟩ fair

Refer|at *nt* -[e]s,-e report; (*Abhandlung*) paper; (*Abteilung*) section. **R~ent(in)** *m* -en,-en (*f* -,-nen) speaker; (*Sachbearbeiter*) expert. **R~enz** *f* -,-en reference. **r~ieren** *vi* (*haben*) deliver a paper; (*berichten*) report (**über** + *acc* on)

reflektieren *vt/i* (*haben*) reflect (**über** + *acc* on)

Reflex *m* -es,-e reflex; (*Widerschein*) reflection. **R~ion** *f* -,-en reflection. **r~iv** *a* reflexive. **R~ivpronomen** *nt* reflexive pronoun

Reform *f* -,-en reform. **R~ation** /-'tsi̯oːn/ *f* - (*Relig*) Reformation

Reform|haus *nt* health-food shop. **r~ieren** *vt* reform

Refrain /rə'frɛ̃ː/ *m* -s,-s refrain

Regal *nt* -s,-e [set of] shelves *pl*

Regatta *f* -,-ten regatta

rege *a* active; (*lebhaft*) lively; (*geistig*) alert; ⟨*Handel*⟩ brisk □ *adv* actively

Regel *f* -,-n rule; (*Monats-*) period; **in der R~** as a rule. **r~mäßig** *a* regular, *adv* -ly. **r~n** *vt* regulate; direct ⟨*Verkehr*⟩; (*erledigen*) settle. **r~recht** *a* real, proper □ *adv*

really. **R~ung** *f* -,-en regulation; settlement. **r~widrig** *a* irregular, *adv* -ly

regen *vt* move; **sich r~** move; (*wach werden*) stir

Regen *m* -s,- rain. **R~bogen** *m* rainbow. **R~bogenhaut** *f* iris

Regener|ation /-'tsi̯oːn/ *f* - regeneration. **r~ieren** *vt* regenerate; **sich r~ieren** regenerate

Regen|mantel *m* raincoat. **R~schirm** *m* umbrella. **R~tag** *m* rainy day. **R~tropfen** *m* raindrop. **R~wetter** *nt* wet weather. **R~wurm** *m* earthworm

Regie /re'ʒiː/ *f* - direction; **R~ führen** direct

regier|en *vt/i* (*haben*) govern, rule; ⟨*Monarch:*⟩ reign [over]; (*Gram*) take. **r~end** *a* ruling; reigning. **R~ung** *f* -,-en government; (*Herrschaft*) rule; (*eines Monarchen*) reign

Regime /re'ʒiːm/ *nt* -s,- /-mə/ regime

Regiment[1] *nt* -[e]s,-er regiment

Regiment[2] *nt* -[e]s,-e rule

Region *f* -,-en region. **r~al** *a* regional, *adv* -ly

Regisseur /reʒɪ'søːɐ̯/ *m* -s,-e director

Register *nt* -s,- register; (*Inhaltsverzeichnis*) index; (*Orgel-*) stop

registrier|en *vt* register; (*Techn*) record. **R~kasse** *f* cash register

Regler *m* -s,- regulator

reglos *a* & *adv* motionless

regn|en *vi* (*haben*) rain; **es r~et** it is raining. **r~erisch** *a* rainy

regul|är *a* normal, *adv* -ly; (*rechtmäßig*) legitimate, *adv* -ly. **r~ieren** *vt* regulate

Regung *f* -,-en movement; (*Gefühls-*) emotion. **r~slos** *a* & *adv* motionless

Reh *nt* -[e]s,-e roe-deer; (*Culin*) venison

Rehabilit|ation /-'tsi̯oːn/ *f* - rehabilitation. **r~ieren** *vt* rehabilitate

Rehbock *m* roebuck

Reib|e *f* -,-n grater. **r~en**† *vt* rub; (*Culin*) grate; **blank r~en** polish □ *vi* (*haben*) rub. **R~ereien** *fpl* (*fam*) friction *sg*. **R~ung** *f* - friction. **r~ungslos** *a* (*fig*) smooth, *adv* -ly

reich *a* rich (**an** + *dat* in), *adv* -ly; (*r~haltig*) abundant, *adv* -ly; **Arm und R~** (**arm und r~**) rich and poor

Reich *nt* -[e]s,-e empire; (*König-*) kingdom; (*Bereich*) realm

Reich|e(r) *m/f* rich man/woman; **die R~en** the rich *pl*

reichen *vt* hand; (*anbieten*) offer □ *vi* (*haben*) be enough; (*in der Länge*) be long enough; **r~ bis zu** reach [up to]; (*sich erstrecken*) extend to; **mit dem Geld r~**

have enough money; **mir reicht's!** I've had enough!

reich|haltig *a* extensive, large; ⟨*Mahlzeit*⟩ substantial. **r~lich** *a* ample; ⟨*Vorrat*⟩ abundant, plentiful; **eine r~liche Stunde** a good hour □ *adv* amply; abundantly; (*fam: sehr*) very. **R~tum** *m* -s,-tümer wealth (**an** + *dat* of); **R~tümer** riches. **R~weite** *f* reach; (*Techn, Mil*) range

Reif *m* -[e]s [hoar-]frost

reif *a* ripe; (*fig*) mature; **r~ für** ready for. **R~e** *f* - ripeness; (*fig*) maturity. **r~en** *vi* (*sein*) ripen; ⟨*Wein, Käse & fig*⟩ mature

Reifen *m* -s,- hoop; (*Arm-*) bangle; (*Auto-*) tyre. **R~druck** *m* tyre pressure. **R~panne** *f* puncture, flat tyre

Reifeprüfung *f* ≈ A Levels *pl*

reiflich *a* careful, *adv* -ly

Reihe *f* -,-n row; (*Anzahl & Math*) series; **der R~ nach** in turn; **außer der R~** out of turn; **wer ist an der** *od* **kommt an die R~?** whose turn is it? **r~n (sich)** *vr* sich **r~n an** (+ *acc*) follow. **R~nfolge** *f* order. **R~nhaus** *nt* terraced house. **R~nweise** *adv* in rows; (*fam*) in large numbers

Reiher *m* -s,- heron

Reim *m* -[e]s,-e rhyme. **r~en** *vt* rhyme; **sich r~en** rhyme

rein[1] *a* pure; (*sauber*) clean; ⟨*Unsinn, Dummheit*⟩ sheer; **ins R~e (r~e) schreiben** make a fair copy of; **ins R~e (r~e) bringen** (*fig*) sort out □ *adv* purely; (*fam*) absolutely

rein[2] *adv* = **herein, hinein**

Reineclaude /rɛ:nə'klo:də/ *f* -,-n greengage

Reinfall *m* (*fam*) let-down; (*Misserfolg*) flop. **r~en**† *vi sep* (*sein*) fall in; (*fam*) be taken in (**auf** + *acc* by)

Rein|gewinn *m* net profit. **R~heit** *f* - purity

reinig|en *vt* clean; (*chemisch*) dry-clean. **R~ung** *f* -,-en cleaning; (*chemische*) dry-cleaning; ⟨*Geschäft*⟩ dry cleaner's

Reinkarnation /re͜ɪnkarna'tsjo:n/ *f* -,-en reincarnation

reinlegen *vt sep* put in; (*fam*) dupe; (*betrügen*) take for a ride

reinlich *a* clean. **R~keit** *f* - cleanliness

Rein|machefrau *f* cleaner. **R~schrift** *f* fair copy. **r~seiden** *a* pure silk

Reis *m* -es rice

Reise *f* -,-n journey; (*See-*) voyage; (*Urlaubs-, Geschäfts-*) trip. **R~andenken** *nt* souvenir. **R~büro** *nt* travel agency. **R~bus** *m* coach. **R~führer** *m* tourist guide; (*Buch*) guide. **R~gesellschaft** *f* tourist group. **R~leiter(in)** *m(f)* courier.

r~n *vi* (*sein*) travel. **R~nde(r)** *m/f* traveller. **R~pass (R~paß)** *m* passport. **R~scheck** *m* traveller's cheque. **R~unternehmer, R~veranstalter** *m* -s,- tour operator. **R~ziel** *nt* destination

Reisig *nt* -s brushwood

Reißaus *m* **R~ nehmen** (*fam*) run away

Reißbrett *nt* drawing-board

reißen† *vt* tear; (*weg-*) snatch; (*töten*) kill; **Witze r~** crack jokes; **aus dem Schlaf r~** awaken rudely; **an sich** (*acc*) **r~** snatch; seize ⟨*Macht*⟩; **mit sich r~** sweep away; **sich r~ um** (*fam*) fight for; (*gern mögen*) be keen on; **hin und her gerissen sein** (*fig*) be torn □ *vi* (*sein*) tear; ⟨*Seil, Faden-*⟩ break □ *vi* (*haben*) **r~ an** (+ *dat*) pull at. **r~d** *a* raging; ⟨*Tier*⟩ ferocious; ⟨*Schmerz*⟩ violent

Reißer *m* -s,- (*fam*) thriller; (*Erfolg*) big hit. **r~isch** *a* (*fam*) sensational

Reiß|nagel *m* = **R~zwecke**. **R~verschluss (R~verschluß)** *m* zip [fastener]. **R~wolf** *m* shredder. **R~zwecke** *f* -,-n drawing-pin, (*Amer*) thumbtack

reit|en† *vt/i* (*sein*) ride. **R~er(in)** *m* -s,- (*f* -,-nen) rider. **R~hose** *f* riding breeches *pl*. **R~pferd** *nt* saddle-horse. **R~schule** *f* riding-school. **R~weg** *m* bridle-path

Reiz *m* -es,-e stimulus; (*Anziehungskraft*) attraction, appeal; (*Charme*) charm. **r~bar** *a* irritable. **R~barkeit** *f* - irritability. **r~en** *vt* provoke; (*Med*) irritate; (*interessieren, locken*) appeal to, attract; arouse ⟨*Neugier*⟩; (*beim Kartenspiel*) bid. **r~end** *a* charming, *adv* -ly; (*entzückend*) delightful. **R~ung** *f* -,-en (*Med*) irritation. **r~voll** *a* attractive

rekapitulieren *vt/i* (*haben*) recapitulate

rekeln (sich) *vr* stretch; (*lümmeln*) sprawl

Reklamation /-'tsjo:n/ *f* -,-en (*Comm*) complaint

Reklam|e *f* -,-n advertising, publicity; (*Anzeige*) advertisement; (*TV, Radio*) commercial; **R~e machen** advertise (**für etw** sth). **r~ieren** *vt* complain about; (*fordern*) claim □ *vi* (*haben*) complain

rekonstru|ieren *vt* reconstruct. **R~ktion** /-'tsjo:n/ *f* -,-en reconstruction

Rekonvaleszenz *f* - convalescence

Rekord *m* -[e]s,-e record

Rekrut *m* -en,-en recruit. **r~ieren** *vt* recruit

Rek|tor *m* -s,-en /-'to:rən/ (*Sch*) head[master]; (*Univ*) vice-chancellor. **R~torin** *f* -,-nen head[mistress]; vice-chancellor

Relais /rə'lɛ:/ *nt* -,- /-s,-s/ (*Electr*) relay

relativ *a* relative, *adv* -ly. **R~pronomen** *nt* relative pronoun

relevan|t *a* relevant (**für** to). **R~z** *f* - relevance

Relief /rə'liːf/ nt -s,-s relief
Religi|on f -,-en religion; (Sch) religious education. **r~ös** a religious
Reling f -,-s (Naut) rail
Reliquie /re'liːkvjə/ f -,-n relic
Remouladensoße /remu'laːdən-/ f ≈ tartar sauce
rempeln vt jostle; (stoßen) push
Ren nt -s,-s reindeer
Reneklode f -,-n greengage
Renn|auto nt racing car. **R~bahn** f racetrack; (Pferde-) racecourse. **R~boot** nt speed-boat. **r~en†** vt/i (sein) run; **um die Wette r~en** have a race. **R~en** nt -s,- race. **R~pferd** nt racehorse. **R~sport** m racing. **R~wagen** m racing car
renommiert a renowned; (Hotel, Firma) of repute
renovier|en vt renovate; redecorate (Zimmer). **R~ung** f - renovation; redecoration
rentabel a profitable, adv -bly
Rente f -,-n pension; **in R~ gehen** (fam) retire. **R~nversicherung** f pension scheme
Rentier nt reindeer
rentieren (sich) vr be profitable; (sich lohnen) be worth while
Rentner(in) m -s,- (f -,-nen) [old-age] pensioner
Reparatur f -,-en repair. **R~werkstatt** f repair workshop; (Auto) garage
reparieren vt repair, mend
repatriieren vt repatriate
Repertoire /reper'toaːɐ/ nt -s,-s repertoire
Reportage /-'taːʒə/ f -,-n report
Reporter(in) m -s,- (f -,-nen) reporter
repräsent|ativ a representative (für of); (eindrucksvoll) imposing; (Prestige verleihend) prestigious. **r~ieren** vt represent □ vi (haben) perform official/social duties
Repress|alie /-ljə/ f -,-n reprisal. **r~iv** a repressive
Reprodu|ktion /-'tsjoːn/ f -,-en reproduction. **r~zieren** vt reproduce
Reptil nt -s,-ien /-jən/ reptile
Republik f -,-en republic. **r~anisch** a republican
requirieren vt (Mil) requisition
Requisiten pl (Theat) properties, (fam) props
Reservat nt -[e]s,-e reservation
Reserve f -,-n reserve; (Mil, Sport) reserves pl. **R~rad** nt spare wheel. **R~spieler** m reserve. **R~tank** m reserve tank

reservier|en vt reserve; **r~en lassen** book. **r~t** a reserved. **R~ung** f -,-en reservation
Reservoir /rezɛr'voaːɐ/ nt -s,-s reservoir
Resid|enz f -,-en residence. **r~ieren** vi (haben) reside
Resign|ation /-'tsjoːn/ f - resignation. **r~ieren** vi (haben) (fig) give up. **r~iert** a resigned, adv -ly
resolut a resolute, adv -ly
Resolution /-'tsjoːn/ f -,-en resolution
Resonanz f -,-en resonance; (fig: Widerhall) response
Respekt m -sp-, -ʃp-/ m -[e]s respect (vor + dat for). **r~abel** a respectable. **r~ieren** vt respect
respekt|los a disrespectful, adv -ly. **r~voll** a respectful, adv -ly
Ressort /rɛ'soːɐ/ nt -s,-s department
Rest m -[e]s,-e remainder, rest; **R~e** remains; (Essens-) leftovers
Restaurant /rɛsto'raː/ nt -s,-s restaurant
Restaur|ation /rɛstaura'tsjoːn/ f - restoration. **r~ieren** vt restore
Rest|betrag m balance. **r~lich** a remaining. **r~los** a utter, adv -ly
Resultat nt -[e]s,-e result
Retorte f -,-n (Chem) retort. **R~nbaby** nt (fam) test-tube baby
Rettich m -s,-e white radish
rett|en vt save (vor + dat from); (aus Gefahr befreien) rescue; **sich r~en** save oneself; (flüchten) escape. **R~er** m -s,- rescuer; (fig) saviour
Rettung f -,-en rescue; (fig) salvation; **jds letzte R~** s.o.'s last hope. **R~sboot** nt lifeboat. **R~sdienst** m rescue service. **R~sgürtel** m lifebelt. **r~slos** adv hopelessly. **R~sring** m lifebelt. **R~swagen** m ambulance
retuschieren vt (Phot) retouch
Reu|e f - remorse; (Relig) repentance. **r~en** vt fill with remorse; **es reut mich nicht** I don't regret it. **r~ig** a penitent. **r~mütig** a contrite, adv -ly
Revanch|e /re'vãːʃə/ f -,-n revenge; **R~e fordern** (Sport) ask for a return match. **r~ieren (sich)** vr take revenge; (sich erkenntlich zeigen) reciprocate (mit with); **sich für eine Einladung r~ieren** return an invitation
Revers /re've:ɐ/ nt -,- /-[s],-s/ lapel
revidieren vt revise; (prüfen) check
Revier nt -s,-e district; (Zool & fig) territory; (Polizei-) [police] station
Revision /-'zjoːn/ f -,-en revision; (Prüfung) check; (Bücher-) audit; (Jur) appeal
Revolte f -,-n revolt

Revolution /-'tsjo:n/ f -,-en revolution. **r~är** a revolutionary. **r~ieren** vt revolutionize

Revolver m -s,- revolver

Revue /rə'vy:/ f -,-n revue

Rezen|sent m -en,-en reviewer. **r~sieren** vt review. **R~sion** f -,-en review

Rezept nt -[e]s,-e prescription; (Culin) recipe

Rezeption /-'tsjo:n/ f -,-en reception

Rezession f -,-en recession

rezitieren vt recite

R-Gespräch nt reverse-charge call, (Amer) collect call

Rhabarber m -s rhubarb

Rhapsodie f -,-n rhapsody

Rhein m -s Rhine. **R~land** nt -s Rhineland. **R~wein** m hock

Rhetori|k f -rhetoric. **r~sch** a rhetorical

Rheum|a nt -s rheumatism. **r~atisch** a rheumatic. **R~atismus** m - rheumatism

Rhinozeros nt -[ses],-se rhinoceros

rhyth|misch /'rʏt-/ a rhythmic[al], adv -ally. **R~mus** m -,-men rhythm

Ribisel f -,-n (Aust) redcurrant

richten vt direct (**auf** + acc at); address ⟨Frage, Briefe⟩ (**an** + acc to); aim, train ⟨Waffe⟩ (**auf** + acc at); (einstellen) set; (vorbereiten) prepare; (reparieren) mend; (hinrichten) execute; (SGer: ordentlich machen) tidy; **in die Höhe r~** raise [up]; **das Wort an jdn r~** address s.o.; **sich r~** be directed (**auf** + acc at; **gegen** against); ⟨Blick:⟩ turn (**auf** + acc on); **sich r~ nach** comply with ⟨Vorschrift, jds Wünschen⟩; fit in with ⟨jds Plänen⟩; (befolgen) go by; (abhängen) depend on □ vi (haben) **r~ über** (+ acc) judge

Richter m -s,- judge

Richtfest nt topping-out ceremony

richtig a right, correct; (wirklich, echt) real; **das R~e (r~e)** the right thing □ adv correctly; really; **r~ stellen** put right ⟨Uhr⟩; (fig) correct ⟨Irrtum⟩; **die Uhr geht r~** the clock is right. **R~keit** f - correctness. **r~stellen** vt sep (NEW) **r~ stellen**, s. richtig

Richtlinien fpl guidelines

Richtung f -,-en direction; (fig) trend

riechen† vt/i (haben) smell (**nach** of; **an** **etw** dat sth)

Riegel m -s,- bolt; (Seife) bar

Riemen m -s,- strap; (Ruder) oar

Riese m -n,-n giant

rieseln vi (sein) trickle; ⟨Schnee:⟩ fall lightly

Riesen|erfolg m huge success. **r~groß** a huge, enormous

riesig a huge; (gewaltig) enormous □ adv (fam) terribly

Riff nt -[e]s,-e reef

rigoros a rigorous, adv -ly

Rille f -,-n groove

Rind nt -es,-er ox; (Kuh) cow; (Stier) bull; (R~fleisch) beef; **R~er** cattle pl

Rinde f -,-n bark; (Käse-) rind; (Brot-) crust

Rinderbraten m roast beef

Rind|fleisch nt beef. **R~vieh** nt cattle pl; (fam: Idiot) idiot

Ring m -[e]s,-e ring

ringeln (sich) vr curl; ⟨Schlange:⟩ coil itself (**um** round)

ring|en† vi (haben) wrestle; (fig) struggle (**um/nach** for) □ vt wring ⟨Hände⟩. **R~en** nt -s wrestling. **R~er** m -s,- wrestler. **R~kampf** m wrestling match; (als Sport) wrestling. **R~richter** m referee

rings adv **r~ im Kreis** in a circle; **r~ um** **jdn/etw** all around s.o./sth. **r~herum**, **r~um** adv all around

Rinn|e f -,-n channel; (Dach-) gutter. **r~en**† vi (sein) run; ⟨Sand:⟩ trickle. **R~stein** m gutter

Rippe f -,-n rib. **R~nfellentzündung** f pleurisy. **R~nstoß** m dig in the ribs

Risiko nt -s,-s & -ken risk; **ein R~ eingehen** take a risk

risk|ant a risky. **r~ieren** vt risk

Riss m -es,-e (Riß m -sses,-sse) tear; (Mauer-) crack; (fig) rift

rissig a cracked; ⟨Haut:⟩ chapped

Rist m -[e]s,-e instep

Ritt m -[e]s,-e ride

Ritter m -s,- knight. **r~lich** a chivalrous, adv -ly. **R~lichkeit** f - chivalry

rittlings adv astride

Ritu|al nt -s,-e ritual. **r~ell** a ritual

Ritz m -es,-e scratch. **R~e** f -,-n crack; (Fels-) cleft; (zwischen Betten, Vorhängen) gap. **r~en** vt scratch

Rival|e m -n,-n, **R~in** f -,-nen rival. **r~isieren** vi (haben) compete (**mit** with). **r~isierend** a rival ... **R~ität** f -,-en rivalry

Robbe f -,-n seal. **r~n** vi (sein) crawl

Robe f -,-n gown; (Talar) robe

Roboter m -s,- robot

robust a robust

röcheln vi (haben) breathe stertorously

Rochen m -s,- (Zool) ray

Rock¹ m -[e]s,-e skirt; (Jacke) jacket

Rock² m -[s] (Mus) rock

Rodel|bahn f toboggan run. **r~n** vi (sein/haben) toboggan. **R~schlitten** m toboggan

roden vt clear ⟨Land⟩; grub up ⟨Stumpf⟩

Rogen *m* -s,- [hard] roe

Roggen *m* -s rye

roh *a* rough; (*ungekocht*) raw; (*Holz*) bare; (*brutal*) brutal; **r~e Gewalt** brute force □ *adv* roughly; brutally. **R~bau** *m* -[e]s, -ten shell. **R~heit** *f* -,-en brutality. **R~kost** *f* raw [vegetarian] food. **R~ling** *m* -s,-e brute. **R~material** *nt* raw material. **R~öl** *nt* crude oil

Rohr *nt* -[e]s,-e pipe; (*Geschütz-*) barrel; (*Bot*) reed; (*Zucker-, Bambus-*) cane

Röhr|chen *nt* -s,- [drinking] straw; (*Auto, fam*) breathalyser (P). **R~e** *f* -,-n tube; (*Radio-*) valve; (*Back-*) oven

Rohstoff *m* raw material

Rokoko *nt* -s rococo

Rollladen *m* (NEW) **Rollladen**

Rollbahn *f* taxiway; (*Start-/Landebahn*) runway

Rolle *f* -,-n roll; (*Garn-*) reel; (*Draht-*) coil; (*Techn*) roller; (*Seil-*) pulley; (*Wäsche-*) mangle; (*Lauf-*) castor; (*Schrift-*) scroll; (*Theat*) part, role; **das spielt keine R~** (*fig*) that doesn't matter. **r~n** *vt* roll; (*auf-*) roll up; roll out (*Teig*); put through the mangle (*Wäsche*); **sich r~n** roll; (*sich ein-*) curl up □ *vi* (*sein*) roll; (*Flugzeug:*) taxi □ *vi* (*haben*) (*Donner:*) rumble. **R~r** *m* -s,- scooter

Roll|feld *nt* airfield. **R~kragen** *m* polo-neck. **R~laden** *m* roller shutter. **R~mops** *m* rollmop[s] *sg*

Rollo *nt* -s,-s [roller] blind

Roll|schuh *m* roller-skate; **R~schuh laufen** roller-skate. **R~splitt** *m* -s loose chippings *pl*. **R~stuhl** *m* wheelchair. **R~treppe** *f* escalator

Rom *nt* -s Rome

Roman *m* -s,-e novel. **r~isch** *a* Romanesque; (*Sprache*) Romance. **R~schriftsteller(in)** *m(f)* novelist

Romant|ik *f* - romanticism. **r~isch** *a* romantic, *adv* -ally

Romanze *f* -,-n romance

Röm|er(in) *m* -s,- (*f* -,-nen) Roman. **r~isch** *a* Roman

Rommé, Rommee /'rɔme:/ *nt* -s rummy

röntgen *vt* X-ray. **R~aufnahme** *f*, **R~bild** *nt* X-ray. **R~strahlen** *mpl* X-rays

rosa *inv a*, **R~** *nt* -[s],- pink

Rose *f* -,-n rose. **R~nkohl** *m* [Brussels] sprouts *pl*. **R~n-kranz** *m* (*Relig*) rosary. **R~nmontag** *m* Monday before Shrove Tuesday

Rosette *f* -,-n rosette

rosig *a* rosy

Rosine *f* -,-n raisin

Rosmarin *m* -s rosemary

Ross *nt* -es,ˉer (Roß *nt* -sses,ˉsser). horse. **R~kastanie** *f* horse-chestnut

Rost¹ *m* -[e]s,-e grating; (*Kamin-*) grate; (*Brat-*) grill

Rost² *m* -[e]s rust. **r~en** *vi* (*haben*) rust; **nicht r~end** stainless

röst|en *vt* roast; toast (*Brot*). **R~er** *m* -s,- toaster

rostfrei *a* stainless

rostig *a* rusty

rot *a* (röter, rötest), **Rot** *nt* -s,- red; **rot werden** turn red; (*erröten*) go red, blush

Rotation /-'tsio:n/ *f* -,-en rotation

Röte *f* - redness; (*Scham-*) blush

Röteln *pl* German measles *sg*

röten *vt* redden; **sich r~** turn red

rothaarig *a* red-haired

rotieren *vi* (*haben*) rotate

Rot|kehlchen *nt* -s,- robin. **R~kohl** *m* red cabbage

rötlich *a* reddish

Rot|licht *nt* red light. **R~wein** *m* red wine

Rou|lade /ru'la:də/ *f* -,-n beef olive. **R~leau** /-'lo:/ *nt* -s,-s [roller] blind

Route /'ru:tə/ *f* -,-n route

Routin|e /ru'ti:nə/ *f* -,-n routine; (*Erfahrung*) experience. **r~emäßig** *a* routine ... □ *adv* routinely. **r~iert** *a* experienced

Rowdy /'raʊdi/ *m* -s,-s hooligan

Rübe *f* -,-n beet; **rote R~** beetroot; **gelbe R~** (*SGer*) carrot

rüber *adv* = herüber, hinüber

Rubin *m* -s,-e ruby

Rubrik *f* -,-en column; (*Kategorie*) category

Ruck *m* -[e]s,-e jerk

Rückantwort *f* reply

ruckartig *a* jerky, *adv* -ily

rück|bezüglich *a* (*Gram*) reflexive. **R~blende** *f* flashback. **R~blick** *m* (*fig*) review (**auf** + *acc* of). **r~blickend** *adv* in retrospect. **r~datieren** *vt* (*inf & pp only*) backdate

rücken *vt/i* (*sein/haben*) move; **an etw** (*dat*) **r~** move sth

Rücken *m* -s,- back; (*Buch-*) spine; (*Berg-*) ridge. **R~lehne** *f* back. **R~mark** *nt* spinal cord. **R~schwimmen** *nt* backstroke. **R~wind** *m* following wind; (*Aviat*) tail wind

rückerstatten *vt* (*inf & pp only*) refund

Rückfahr|karte *f* return ticket. **R~t** *f* return journey

Rück|fall *m* relapse. **r~fällig** *a* **r~fällig werden** (*Jur*) re-offend. **R~flug** *m* return flight. **R~frage** *f* [further] query. **r~fragen** *vi* (*haben*) (*inf & pp only*) check (**bei** with). **R~gabe** *f* return. **R~gang** *m* decline; (*Preis-*) drop, fall. **r~gängig** *a* r~gängig machen cancel; break off ⟨*Verlobung*⟩. R~grat *nt* -[e]s, -e spine, backbone. R~halt *m* (*fig*) support. R~hand *f* backhand. R~kehr return. R~lagen *fpl* reserves. R~licht *nt* rear-light. r~lings *adv* backwards; (*von hinten*) from behind. R~reise *f* return journey

Rucksack *m* rucksack

Rück|schau *f* review. R~schlag *m* (*Sport*) return; (*fig*) set-back. R~schluss (R~schluß) *m* conclusion. R~schritt *m* (*fig*) retrograde step. r~schrittlich *a* retrograde. R~seite *f* back; (*einer Münze*) reverse

Rücksicht *f* -,-en consideration; R~ nehmen auf (+ *acc*) show consideration for; (*berücksichtigen*) take into consideration. R~nahme *f* consideration. r~slos *a* inconsiderate, *adv* -ly; (*schonungslos*) ruthless, *adv* -ly. r~svoll *a* considerate, *adv* -ly

Rück|sitz *m* back seat; (*Sozius*) pillion. R~spiegel *m* rear-view mirror. R~spiel *nt* return match. R~sprache *f* consultation; R~sprache nehmen mit consult. R~stand *m* (*Chem*) residue; (*Arbeits-*) backlog; R~stände arrears; im R~stand sein be behind. r~ständig *a* (*fig*) backward. R~stau *m* (*Auto*) tailback. R~strahler *m* -s,- reflector. R~tritt *m* resignation; (*Fahrrad*) back pedalling. r~vergüten *vt* (*inf & pp only*) refund. R~wanderer *m* repatriate

rückwärt|ig *a* back ..., rear ... r~s *adv* backwards. R~sgang *m* reverse [gear]

Rückweg *m* way back

ruckweise *adv* jerkily

rück|wirkend *a* retrospective, *adv* -ly. R~wirkung *f* retrospective force; mit R~wirkung vom backdated to. R~zahlung *f* repayment. R~zug *m* retreat

Rüde *m* -n,-n [male] dog

Rudel *nt* -s,- herd; (*Wolfs-*) pack; (*Löwen-*) pride

Ruder *nt* -s,- oar; (*Steuer-*) rudder; am R~ (*Naut & fig*) at the helm. R~boot *nt* rowing boat. R~er *m* -s,- oarsman. r~n *vt/i* (*haben/sein*) row

Ruf *m* -[e]s,-e call; (*laut*) shout; (*Telefon*) telephone number; (*Ansehen*) reputation; Künstler von Ruf artist of repute. r~en† *vt/i* (*haben*) call (nach for); r~en lassen send for

Rüffel *m* -s,- (*fam*) telling-off. r~n *vt* (*fam*) tell off

Ruf|name *m* forename by which one is known. R~nummer *f* telephone number. R~zeichen *nt* dialling tone

Rüge *f* -,-n reprimand. r~n *vt* reprimand; (*kritisieren*) criticize

Ruhe *f* -rest; (*Stille*) quiet; (*Frieden*) peace; (*innere*) calm; (*Gelassenheit*) composure; die R~ bewahren keep calm; in R~ lassen leave in peace; sich zur R~ setzen retire; R~ [da]! quiet! R~gehalt *nt* [retirement] pension. r~los *a* restless, *adv* -ly. r~n *vi* (*haben*) rest (auf + *dat* on); (*Arbeit, Verkehr:*) have stopped; hier ruht ... here lies ... R~pause *f* rest, break. R~stand *m* retirement; in den R~stand treten retire; im R~stand retired. R~störung *f* disturbance of the peace. R~tag *m* day of rest; 'Montag R~tag' 'closed on Mondays'

ruhig *a* quiet, *adv* -ly; (*erholsam*) restful; (*friedlich*) peaceful, *adv* -ly; (*unbewegt, gelassen*) calm, *adv* -ly; r~ bleiben remain calm; sehen Sie sich r~ um you're welcome to look round; man kann r~ darüber sprechen there's no harm in talking about it

Ruhm *m* -[e]s fame; (*Ehre*) glory

rühmen *vt* praise; sich r~ boast (*gen* about)

ruhmreich *a* glorious

Ruhr *f* - (*Med*) dysentery

Rühr|ei *nt* scrambled eggs *pl*. r~en *vt* move; (*Culin*) stir; sich r~en move; zu Tränen r~en move to tears; r~t euch! (*Mil*) at ease! □ *vi* (*haben*) stir; r~en an (+ *acc*) touch; (*fig*) touch on; r~en von (*fig*) come from. r~end *a* touching, *adv* -ly

rühr|ig *a* active. r~selig *a* sentimental. R~ung *f* - emotion

Ruin *m* -s ruin. R~e *f* -,-n ruin; ruins *pl* (*gen* of). r~ieren *vt* ruin

rülpsen *vi* (*haben*) (*fam*) belch

Rum *m* -s rum

rum *adv* = herum

Rumän|ien /-jən/ *nt* -s Romania. r~isch *a* Romanian

Rummel *m* -s (*fam*) hustle and bustle; (*Jahrmarkt*) funfair. R~platz *m* fairground

rumoren *vi* (*haben*) make a noise; (*Magen:*) rumble

Rumpel|kammer *f* junk-room. r~n *vi* (*haben/sein*) rumble

Rumpf *m* -[e]s,-̈e body, trunk; (*Schiffs-*) hull; (*Aviat*) fuselage

rümpfen *vt* die Nase r~ turn up one's nose (über + *acc* at)

rund *a* round □ *adv* approximately; r~ um [a]round. R~blick *m* panoramic view. R~brief *m* circular [letter]

Runde *f* -,-n round; (*Kreis*) circle; (*eines Polizisten*) beat; (*beim Rennen*) lap; eine R~ Bier a round of beer. r~n *vt* round; sich r~n become round; (*Backen:*) fill out

Rund|fahrt *f* tour. **R∼frage** *f* poll

Rundfunk *m* radio; **im R∼** on the radio. **R∼gerät** *nt* radio [set]

Rund|gang *m* round; (*Spaziergang*) walk (**durch** round). **r∼heraus** *adv* straight out. **r∼herum** *adv* all around. **r∼lich** *a* rounded; (*mollig*) plump. **R∼reise** *f* [circular] tour. **R∼schreiben** *nt* circular. **r∼um** *adv* all round. **R∼ung** *f* -,-en curve. **r∼weg** *adv* ⟨*ablehnen*⟩ flatly

runter *adv* = **herunter, hinunter**

Runzel *f* -,-n wrinkle. **r∼n** *vt* die Stirn **r∼n** frown

runzlig *a* wrinkled

Rüpel *m* -s,- (*fam*) lout. **r∼haft** *a* (*fam*) loutish

rupfen *vt* pull out; pluck ⟨*Geflügel*⟩; (*fam*: *schröpfen*) fleece

ruppig *a* rude, *adv* -ly

Rüsche *f* -,-n frill

Ruß *m* -es soot

Russe *m* -n,-n Russian

Rüssel *m* -s,- ⟨*Zool*⟩ trunk

ruß|en *vi* (*haben*) smoke. **r∼ig** *a* sooty

Russ|in *f* -,-nen Russian. **r∼isch** *a* Russian. **R∼isch** *nt* -[s] ⟨*Lang*⟩ Russian

Russland (Rußland) *nt* -s Russia

rüsten *vi* (*haben*) prepare (**zu/für** for) □ *vr* **sich r∼** get ready; **gerüstet sein** be ready

rüstig *a* sprightly

rustikal *a* rustic

Rüstung *f* -,-en armament; (*Harnisch*) armour. **R∼skontrolle** *f* arms control

Rute *f* -,-n twig; (*Angel-, Wünschel-*) rod; (*zur Züchtigung*) birch; (*Schwanz*) tail

Rutsch *m* -[e]s,-e slide. **R∼bahn** *f* slide. **R∼e** *f* -,-n chute. **r∼en** *vt* slide; (*rücken*) move □ *vi* (*sein*) slide; (*aus-, ab-*) slip; (*Auto*) skid; (*rücken*) move [along]. **r∼ig** *a* slippery

rütteln *vt* shake □ *vi* (*haben*) **r∼ an** (+ *dat*) rattle

S

Saal *m* -[e]s,Säle hall; (*Theat*) auditorium; (*Kranken-*) ward

Saat *f* -,-en seed; (*Säen*) sowing; (*Gesätes*) crop. **S∼gut** *nt* seed

sabbern *vi* (*haben*) (*fam*) slobber; ⟨*Baby:*⟩ dribble; (*reden*) jabber

Säbel *m* -s,- sabre

Sabo|tage /zabo'ta:ʒə/ *f* - sabotage. **S∼teur** /-'tø:ɐ̯/ *m* -s,-e saboteur. **s∼tieren** *vt* sabotage

Sach|bearbeiter *m* expert. **S∼buch** *nt* non-fiction book. **s∼dienlich** *a* relevant

Sache *f* -,-n matter, business; (*Ding*) thing; (*fig*) cause; **zur S∼ kommen** come to the point

Sach|gebiet *nt* (*fig*) area, field. **s∼gemäß** *a* proper, *adv* -ly. **S∼kenntnis** *f* expertise. **s∼kundig** *a* expert, *adv* -ly. **s∼lich** *a* factual, *adv* -ly; (*nüchtern*) matter-of-fact, *adv* -ly; (*objektiv*) objective, *adv* -ly; (*schmucklos*) functional

sächlich *a* (*Gram*) neuter

Sachse *m* -n,-n Saxon. **S∼n** *nt* -s Saxony

sächsisch *a* Saxon

sacht *a* gentle, *adv* -ly

Sach|verhalt *m* -[e]s facts *pl*. **s∼verständig** *a* expert, *adv* -ly. **S∼verständige(r)** *mf* expert

Sack *m* -[e]s,ⸯe sack; **mit S∼ und Pack** with all one's belongings

sacken *vi* (*sein*) sink; (*zusammen-*) go down; ⟨*Person:*⟩ slump

Sack|gasse *f* cul-de-sac; (*fig*) impasse. **S∼leinen** *nt* sacking

Sadis|mus *m* - sadism. **S∼t** *m* -en,-en sadist. **s∼tisch** *a* sadistic, *adv* -ally

säen *vt/i* (*haben*) sow

Safe /ze:f/ *m* -s,-s safe

Saft *m* -[e]s,ⸯe juice; (*Bot*) sap. **s∼ig** *a* juicy; ⟨*Wiese*⟩ lush; ⟨*Preis, Rechnung*⟩ hefty; ⟨*Witz*⟩ coarse. **s∼los** *a* dry

Sage *f* -,-n legend

Säge *f* -,-n saw. **S∼mehl** *nt* sawdust

sagen *vt* say; (*mitteilen*) tell; (*bedeuten*) mean; **das hat nichts zu s∼** it doesn't mean anything; **ein viel s∼der Blick** a meaningful look

sägen *vt/i* (*haben*) saw

sagenhaft *a* legendary; (*fam: unglaublich*) fantastic, *adv* -ally

Säge|späne *mpl* wood shavings. **S∼werk** *nt* sawmill

Sahn|e *f* - cream. **S∼ebonbon** *m* & *nt* ≈ toffee. **s∼ig** *a* creamy

Saison /zɛ'zõ:/ *f* -,-s season

Saite *f* -,-n ⟨*Mus, Sport*⟩ string. **S∼ninstrument** *nt* stringed instrument

Sakko *m* & *nt* -s,-s sports jacket

Sakrament *nt* -[e]s,-e sacrament

Sakrileg *nt* -s,-e sacrilege

Sakrist|an *m* -s,-e verger. **S∼ei** *f* -,-en vestry

Salat *m* -[e]s,-e salad; **ein Kopf S∼** a lettuce. **S∼soße** *f* salad-dressing

Salbe *f* -,-n ointment

Salbei *m* -s & *f* - sage

salben *vt* anoint

Saldo *m* -s,-dos & -den balance

Salon /za'lõ:/ *m* -s,-s salon; (*Naut*) saloon

salopp *a* casual, *adv* -ly; ⟨Benehmen⟩ informal, *adv* -ly; ⟨Ausdruck⟩ slangy

Salto *m* -s,-s somersault

Salut *m* -[e]s,-e salute. **s~ieren** *vi* (haben) salute

Salve *f* -,-n volley; (Geschütz-) salvo; (von Gelächter) burst

Salz *nt* -es,-e salt. **s~en**† *vt* salt. **S~fass** (**S~faß**) *nt* salt-cellar. **s~ig** *a* salty. **S~kartoffeln** *fpl* boiled potatoes. **S~säure** *f* hydrochloric acid

Samen *m* -s,- seed; (Anat) semen, sperm

sämig *a* (Culin) thick

Sämling *m* -s,-e seedling

Sammel|becken *nt* reservoir. **S~begriff** *m* collective term. **s~n** *vt/i* (haben) collect; (suchen, versammeln) gather; **sich s~n** collect; (sich versammeln) gather; (sich fassen) collect oneself. **S~name** *m* collective noun

Samm|ler(in) *m* -s,- (f -,-nen) collector. **S~lung** *f* -,-en collection; (innere) composure

Samstag *m* -s,-e Saturday. **s~s** *adv* on Saturdays

samt *prep* (+ dat) together with □ *adv* **s~ und sonders** without exception

Samt *m* -[e]s velvet. **s~ig** *a* velvety

sämtlich *indef pron inv* all. **s~e(r,s)** *indef pron* all the; **s~e Werke** complete works; **meine s~en Bücher** all my books

Sanatorium *nt* -s,-ien sanatorium

Sand *m* -[e]s sand

Sandal|e *f* -,-n sandal. **S~ette** *f* -,-n high-heeled sandal

Sand|bank *f* sandbank. **S~burg** *f* sandcastle. **s~ig** *a* sandy. **S~kasten** *m* sandpit. **S~kuchen** *m* Madeira cake. **S~papier** *nt* sandpaper. **S~stein** *m* sandstone

sanft *a* gentle, *adv* -ly. **s~mütig** *a* meek

Sänger(in) *m* -s,-,(f -,-nen) singer

sanieren *vt* clean up; redevelop ⟨Gebiet⟩; (modernisieren) modernize; make profitable ⟨Industrie, Firma⟩; **sich s~** become profitable

sanitär *a* sanitary

Sanität|er *m* -s,- first-aid man; (Fahrer) ambulance man; (Mil) medical orderly. **S~swagen** *m* ambulance

Sanktion /zaŋk'tsjo:n/ *f* -,-en sanction. **s~ieren** *vt* sanction

Saphir *m* -s,-e sapphire

Sardelle *f* -,-n anchovy

Sardine *f* -,-n sardine

Sarg *m* -[e]s,-e coffin

Sarkas|mus *m* - sarcasm. **s~tisch** *a* sarcastic, *adv* -ally

Sat|an *m* -s Satan; (fam: Teufel) devil. **s~anisch** *a* satanic

Satellit *m* -en,-en satellite. **S~enfernsehen** *nt* satellite television

Satin /za'tɛŋ/ *m* -s satin

Satir|e *f* -,-n satire. **s~isch** *a* satirical, *adv* -ly

satt *a* full; ⟨Farbe⟩ rich; **s~ sein** have had enough [to eat]; **sich s~ essen** eat as much as one wants; **s~ machen** feed; ⟨Speise:⟩ be filling; **etw s~ haben** (fam) be fed up with sth

Sattel *m* -s,- saddle. **s~n** *vt* saddle. **S~schlepper** *m* tractor unit. **S~zug** *m* articulated lorry

sättigen *vt* satisfy; (Chem & fig) saturate □ *vi* (haben) be filling. **s~d** a filling

Satz *m* -es,-e sentence; (Teil-) clause; (These) proposition; (Math) theorem; (Mus) movement; (Tennis, Zusammengehöriges) set; (Boden-) sediment; (Kaffee-) grounds *pl*; (Steuer-, Zins-) rate; (Druck-) setting; (Schrift-) type; (Sprung-) leap, bound. **S~aussage** *f* predicate. **S~gegenstand** *m* subject. **S~zeichen** *nt* punctuation mark

Sau *f* -,Säue sow; (sl: schmutziger Mensch) dirty pig

sauber *a* clean; (ordentlich) neat, *adv* -ly; (anständig) decent, *adv* -ly; (fam: nicht anständig) fine; **s~ halten** keep clean; **s~ machen** clean. **s~halten**† *vt sep* (NEW) **halten, s. sauber. S~keit** *f* - cleanliness; neatness; decency

säuberlich *a* neat, *adv* -ly

saubermachen *vt/i sep* (haben) (NEW) **sauber machen, s. sauber**

säuber|n *vt* clean; (befreien) rid/ (Pol) purge (**von** of). **S~ungsaktion** *f* (Pol) purge

Sauce /'zo:sə/ *f* -,-n sauce; (Braten-) gravy

Saudi-Arabien /-jən/ *nt* -s Saudi Arabia

sauer *a* sour; (Chem) acid; (eingelegt) pickled; (schwer) hard; **saurer Regen** acid rain; **s~ sein** (fam) be annoyed

Sauerei *f* -,-en = **Schweinerei**

Sauerkraut *nt* sauerkraut

säuerlich *a* slightly sour

Sauer|stoff *m* oxygen

saufen† *vt/i* (haben) drink; (sl) booze

Säufer *m* -s,- (sl) boozer

saugen† *vt/i* (haben) suck; (staub-) vacuum, hoover; **sich voll Wasser s~** soak up water

säugen *vt* suckle

Sauger *m* -s,- [baby's] dummy, (Amer) pacifier; (Flaschen-) teat

Säugetier *nt* mammal

saugfähig *a* absorbent

Säugling m -s,-e infant

Säule f -,-n column

Saum m -[e]s,Säume hem; (Rand) edge

säumen[1] vt hem; (fig) line

säum|en[2] vi (haben) delay. s~ig a dilatory

Sauna f -,-nas & -nen sauna

Säure f -,-n acidity; (Chem) acid

säuseln vi (haben) rustle [softly]

sausen vi (haben) rush; (Ohren:) buzz □ vi (sein) rush [along]

Sauwetter nt (sl) lousy weather

Saxophon, Saxofon nt -s,-e saxophone

SB- /εs'be:-/ pref (= **Selbstbedienung**) self-service ...

S-Bahn f city and suburban railway

sch int shush! (fort) shoo!

Schabe f -,-n cockroach

schaben vt/i (haben) scrape

schäbig a shabby, adv -ily

Schablone f -,-n stencil; (Muster) pattern; (fig) stereotype

Schach nt -s chess; S~! check! **in S~ halten** (fig) keep in check. S~**brett** nt chessboard

schachern vi (haben) haggle

Schachfigur f chess-man

schachmatt a s~ **setzen** checkmate; s~! checkmate!

Schachspiel nt game of chess

Schacht m -[e]s,-e shaft

Schachtel f -,-n box; (Zigaretten-) packet

Schachzug m move

schade a s~ **sein** be a pity or shame: **zu s~ für** too good for; **[wie] s~!** [what a] pity or shame!

Schädel m -s, skull. S~**bruch** m fractured skull

schaden vi (haben) (+ dat) damage; (nachteilig sein) hurt; **das schadet nichts** that doesn't matter. S~ m -s,- damage; (Defekt) defect; (Nachteil) disadvantage; **zu S~ kommen** be hurt. S~**ersatz** m damages pl. S~**freude** f malicious glee. s~**froh** a gloating

schadhaft a defective

schädig|en vt damage, harm. S~**ung** f -,-en damage

schädlich a harmful

Schädling m -s,-e pest. S~**sbekämpfungsmittel** nt pesticide

Schaf nt -[e]s,-e sheep; (fam: Idiot) idiot. S~**bock** m ram

Schäfchen nt -s,- lamb

Schäfer m -s,- shepherd. S~**hund** m sheepdog; **Deutscher S~hund** German shepherd, alsatian

Schaffell nt sheepskin

schaffen[†1] vt create; (herstellen) establish; make (Platz); **wie geschaffen für** made for

schaffen[2] v (reg) □ vt manage [to do]; pass (Prüfung); catch (Zug); (bringen) take; **jdm zu s~ machen** trouble s.o.; **sich** (dat) **zu s~ machen** busy oneself (**an** + dat with) □ vi (haben) (SGer: arbeiten) work. S~ nt -s work

Schaffner m -s,- conductor; (Zug-) ticket-inspector

Schaffung f - creation

Schaft m -[e]s,-e shaft; (Gewehr-) stock; (Stiefel-) leg. S~**stiefel** m high boot

Schal m -s,-s scarf

schal a insipid; (abgestanden) flat; (fig) stale

Schale f -,-n skin; (abgeschält) peel; (Eier-, Nuss-, Muschel-) shell; (Schüssel) dish

schälen vt peel; **sich s~** peel

schalkhaft a mischievous, adv -ly

Schall m -[e]s sound. S~**dämpfer** m silencer. s~**dicht** a soundproof. s~**en** vi (haben) ring out; (nachhallen) resound; **s~end lachen** roar with laughter. S~**mauer** f sound barrier. S~**platte** f record, disc

schalt|en vt switch □ vi (haben) switch/ (Ampel:) turn (**auf** + acc to); (Auto) change gear; (fam: begreifen) catch on. S~**er** m -s,- switch; (Post-, Bank-) counter; (Fahrkarten-) ticket window. S~**hebel** m switch; (Auto) gear lever. S~**jahr** nt leap year. S~**kreis** m circuit. S~**ung** f -,-en circuit; (Auto) gear change

Scham f - shame; (Anat) private parts pl; **falsche S~** false modesty

schämen (sich) vr be ashamed; **schämt euch!** you should be ashamed of yourselves!

scham|haft a modest, adv -ly; (schüchtern) bashful, adv -ly. s~**los** a shameless, adv -ly

Schampon nt -s shampoo. s~**ieren** vt shampoo

Schande f - disgrace, shame; S~ **machen** (+ dat) bring shame on; **zu S~n machen/werden** = **zuschanden machen/werden**, s. **zuschanden**

schänd|en vt dishonour; (fig) defile (Relig) desecrate; (sexuell) violate. s~**lich** a disgraceful, adv -ly. S~**ung** f -,-en defilement, desecration; violation

Schänke f -,-n = **Schenke**

Schanktisch m bar

Schanze f -,-n (ski-)jump

Schar f -,-en crowd; (Vogel-) flock; **in [hellen] S~en** in droves

Scharade f -,-n charade

scharen *vt* **um sich s~** gather round one; **sich s~ um** flock round. **s~weise** *adv* in droves

scharf *a* (**schärfer, schärfst**) sharp; *(stark)* strong; *(stark gewürzt)* hot; *⟨Geruch⟩* pungent; *⟨Frost, Wind, Augen, Verstand⟩* keen; *(streng)* harsh; *⟨Galopp, Ritt⟩* hard; *⟨Munition⟩* live; *⟨Hund⟩* fierce; **s~ einstellen** *(Phot)* focus; **s~ sein** *(Phot)* be in focus; **s~ sein auf** (+ *acc*) *(fam)* be keen on ☐ *adv* sharply; *(hinsehen, nachdenken, bremsen, reiten)* hard; *(streng)* harshly; **s~ schießen** fire live ammunition

Scharfblick *m* perspicacity

Schärfe *f* - (*s.* **scharf**) sharpness; strength; hotness; pungency; keenness; harshness. **s~n** *vt* sharpen

scharf|machen *vt sep* *(fam)* incite. **S~richter** *m* executioner. **S~schütze** *m* marksman. **s~sichtig** *a* perspicacious. **S~sinn** *m* astuteness. **s~sinnig** *a* astute, *adv* -ly

Scharlach *m* -s scarlet fever

Scharlatan *m* -s,-e charlatan

Scharnier *nt* -s,-e hinge

Schärpe *f* -,-n sash

scharren *vi* *(haben)* scrape; *⟨Huhn⟩* scratch; *⟨Pferd:⟩* paw the ground ☐ *vt* scrape

Schart|e *f* -,-n nick. **s~ig** *a* jagged

Schaschlik *m & nt* -s,-s kebab

Schatten *m* -s,- shadow; *(schattige Stelle)* shade; **im S~** in the shade. **s~haft** *a* shadowy. **S~riss** (**S~riß**) *m* silhouette. **S~seite** *f* shady side; *(fig)* disadvantage

schattier|en *vt* shade. **S~ung** *f* -,-en shading; *(fig: Variante)* shade

schattig *a* shady

Schatz *m* -es,¨e treasure; *(Freund, Freundin)* sweetheart; *(Anrede)* darling

Schätzchen *nt* -s,- darling

schätzen *vt* estimate; *(taxieren)* value; *(achten)* esteem; *(würdigen)* appreciate; *(fam: vermuten)* reckon; **sich glücklich s~** consider oneself lucky

Schätzung *f* -,-en estimate; *(Taxierung)* valuation. **s~sweise** *adv* approximately

Schau *f* -,-en show; **zur S~ stellen** display. **S~bild** *nt* diagram

Schauder *m* -s shiver; *(vor Abscheu)* shudder. **s~haft** *a* dreadful, *adv* -ly. **s~n** *vi* *(haben)* shiver; *(vor Abscheu)* shudder; **mich s~te** I shivered/shuddered

schauen *vi* *(haben)* *(SGer, Aust)* look; **s~, dass** make sure that

Schauer *m* -s,- shower; *(Schauder)* shiver. **S~geschichte** *f* horror story. **s~lich** *a*

ghastly. **s~n** *vi* *(haben)* shiver; **mich s~te** I shivered

Schaufel *f* -,-n shovel; *(Kehr-)* dustpan. **s~n** *vt* shovel; *(graben)* dig

Schaufenster *nt* shop-window. **S~bummel** *m* window-shopping. **S~puppe** *f* dummy

Schaukasten *m* display case

Schaukel *f* -,-n swing. **s~n** *vt* rock ☐ *vi* *(haben)* rock; *(auf einer Schaukel)* swing; *(schwanken)* sway. **S~pferd** *nt* rocking-horse. **S~stuhl** *m* rocking-chair

schaulustig *a* curious

Schaum *m* -[e]s foam; *(Seifen-)* lather; *(auf Bier)* froth; *(als Frisier-, Rasiermittel)* mousse

schäumen *vi* *(haben)* foam, froth; *⟨Seife:⟩* lather

Schaum|gummi *m* foam rubber. **s~ig** *a* frothy; **s~ig rühren** *(Culin)* cream. **S~krone** *f* white crest; *(auf Bier)* head. **S~speise** *f* mousse. **S~stoff** *m* [synthetic] foam. **S~wein** *m* sparkling wine

Schauplatz *m* scene

schaurig *a* dreadful, *adv* -ly; *(unheimlich)* eerie, *adv* eerily

Schauspiel *nt* play; *(Anblick)* spectacle. **S~er** *m* actor. **S~erin** *f* actress. **s~ern** *vi* *(haben)* act; *(sich verstellen)* play-act

Scheck *m* -s,-s cheque, *(Amer)* check. **S~buch, S~heft** *nt* cheque-book. **S~karte** *f* cheque card

Scheibe *f* -,-n disc; *(Schieß-)* target; *(Glas-)* pane; *(Brot-, Wurst-)* slice. **S~nwaschanlage** *f* windscreen washer. **S~nwischer** *m* -s,- windscreen-wiper

Scheich *m* -s,-e & -s sheikh

Scheide *f* -,-n sheath; *(Anat)* vagina

scheid|en† *vt* separate; *(unterscheiden)* distinguish; dissolve *⟨Ehe⟩*; **sich s~en lassen** get divorced; **sich s~en** diverge; *⟨Meinungen:⟩* differ ☐ *vi* *(sein)* leave; *(voneinander)* part. **S~ung** *f* -,-en divorce

Schein *m* -[e]s,-e light; *(Anschein)* appearance; *(Bescheinigung)* certificate; *(Geld-)* note; **etw nur zum S~ tun** only pretend to do sth. **s~bar** *a* apparent, *adv* -ly. **s~en†** *vi* *(haben)* shine; *(den Anschein haben)* seem, appear; **mir s~t** it seems to me

scheinheilig *a* hypocritical, *adv* -ly. **S~keit** *f* hypocrisy

Scheinwerfer *m* -s,- floodlight; *(Such-)* searchlight; *(Auto)* headlight; *(Theat)* spotlight

Scheiß-, scheiß- *pref* *(vulg)* bloody. **S~e** *f* - *(vulg)* shit. **s~en†** *vi* *(haben)* *(vulg)* shit

Scheit *nt* -[e]s,-e log

Scheitel *m* -s,- parting. **s~n** *vt* part *⟨Haar⟩*

scheitern *vi (sein)* fail

Schelle *f -,-n* bell. **s~n** *vi (haben)* ring

Schellfisch *m* haddock

Schelm *m -s,-e* rogue. **s~isch** *a* mischievous, *adv* -ly

Schelte *f* - scolding. **s~n†** *vi (haben)* grumble (**über** + *acc* about); **mit jdm s~n** scold s.o. □ *vt* scold; *(bezeichnen)* call

Schema *nt -s,-mata* model, pattern; *(Skizze)* diagram

Schemel *m -s,-* stool

Schenke *f -,-n* tavern

Schenkel *m -s,-* thigh; *(Geom)* side

schenken *vt* give [as a present]; **jdm Vertrauen/Glauben s~** trust/believe s.o.; **sich** (*dat*) **etw s~** give sth a miss

scheppern *vi (haben)* clank

Scherbe *f -,-n* [broken] piece

Schere *f -,-n* scissors *pl*; *(Techn)* shears *pl*; *(Hummer-)* claw. **s~n†** *vt* shear; crop *(Haar)*; clip *(Hund)*

scheren² *vt (reg) (fam)* bother; **sich nicht s~ um** not care about; **scher dich zum Teufel!** go to hell!

Scherenschnitt *m* silhouette

Scherereien *fpl (fam)* trouble *sg*

Scherz *m -es,-e* joke; **im/zum S~** as a joke. **s~en** *vi (haben)* joke. **S~frage** *f* riddle. **s~haft** *a* humorous

scheu *a* shy, *adv* -ly; *(Tier)* timid; **s~ werden** *(Pferd:)* shy; **s~ machen** startle. **S~** *f* - shyness; timidity; *(Ehrfurcht)* awe

scheuchen *vt* shoo

scheuen *vt* be afraid of; *(meiden)* shun; **keine Mühe/Kosten s~** spare no effort/expense; **sich s~** be afraid (**vor** + *dat* of); shrink (**etw zu tun** from doing sth) □ *vi (haben) (Pferd:)* shy

Scheuer|lappen *m* floor-cloth. **s~n** *vt* scrub; *(mit Scheuerpulver)* scour; *(reiben)* rub; **[wund] s~n** chafe □ *vi (haben)* rub, chafe. **S~tuch** *nt* floor-cloth

Scheuklappen *fpl* blinkers

Scheune *f -,-n* barn

Scheusal *nt -s,-e* monster

scheußlich *a* horrible, *adv* -bly

Schi *m -s,-er* ski; **S~ fahren** *od* **laufen** ski

Schicht *f -,-en* layer; *(Geol)* stratum; *(Gesellschafts-)* class; *(Arbeits-)* shift. **S~arbeit** *f* shift work. **s~en** *vt* stack [up]

schick *a* stylish, *adv* -ly; *(Pferd:)* chic; *(fam: prima)* great. **S~** *m* -[e]s style

schicken *vt/i (haben)* send; **s~ nach** send for; **sich s~ in** (+ *acc*) resign oneself to

schicklich *a* fitting, proper

Schicksal *nt -s,-e* fate. **s~haft** *a* fateful. **S~sschlag** *m* misfortune

Schieb|edach *nt (Auto)* sun-roof. **s~en†** *vt* push; *(gleitend)* slide; *(fam: handeln mit)* traffic in; **etw s~en auf** (+ *acc*) *(fig)* put sth down to; shift *(Schuld, Verantwortung)* on to □ *vi (haben)* push. **S~er** *m -s,-* slide; *(Person)* black marketeer. **S~etür** *f* sliding door. **S~ung** *f -,-en (fam)* illicit deal; *(Betrug)* rigging, fixing

Schieds|gericht *nt* panel of judges; *(Jur)* arbitration tribunal. **S~richter** *m* referee; *(Tennis)* umpire; *(Jur)* arbitrator

schief *a* crooked; *(unsymmetrisch)* lopsided; *(geneigt)* slanting, sloping; *(nicht senkrecht)* leaning; *(Winkel)* oblique; *(fig)* false; *(misstrauisch)* suspicious □ *adv* not straight; **jdn s~ ansehen** look at s.o. askance; **s~ gehen** *(fam)* go wrong

Schiefer *m -s* slate

schief|gehen† *vi sep (sein)* (NEW) **s~ gehen**, *s. schief*. **s~lachen (sich)** *vr sep* double up with laughter

schielen *vi (haben)* squint

Schienbein *nt* shin; *(Knochen)* shinbone

Schiene *f -,-n* rail; *(Gleit-)* runner; *(Med)* splint. **s~n** *vt (Med)* put in a splint

schier¹ *adv* almost

schier² *a* pure; *(Fleisch)* lean

Schieß|bude *f* shooting-gallery. **s~en†** *vt* shoot; fire *(Kugel)*; score *(Tor)* □ *vi (haben)* shoot, fire (**auf** + *acc* at) □ *vi (sein)* shoot [along]; *(strömen)* gush; **in die Höhe s~en** shoot up. **S~erei** *f -,-en* shooting. **S~scheibe** *f* target. **S~stand** *m* shooting-range

Schifahr|en *nt* skiing. **S~er(in)** *m(f)* skier

Schiff *nt -[e]s,-e* ship; *(Kirchen-)* nave; *(Seiten-)* aisle

Schiffahrt *f* (NEW) **Schifffahrt**

schiff|bar *a* navigable. **S~bau** *m* shipbuilding. **S~bruch** *m* shipwreck. **s~brüchig** *a* shipwrecked. **S~chen** *nt -s,-* small boat; *(Tex)* shuttle. **S~er** *m -s,-* skipper. **S~fahrt** *f* shipping

Schikan|e *f -,-n* harassment; **mit allen S~en** with every refinement. **s~ieren** *vt* harass; *(tyrannisieren)* bully

Schi|laufen *nt* -s skiing. **S~läufer(in)** *m(f) -s,- (f -,-nen)* skier

Schild¹ *m -[e]s,-e* shield; **etw im S~e führen** *(fam)* be up to sth

Schild² *nt -[e]s,-er* sign; *(Namens-, Nummern-)* plate; *(Mützen-)* badge; *(Etikett)* label

Schilddrüse *f* thyroid [gland]

schilder|n *vt* describe. **S~ung** *f -,-en* description

Schild|kröte *f* tortoise; *(See-)* turtle. **S~patt** *nt -[e]s* tortoiseshell

Schilf nt -[e]s reeds pl

schillern vi (haben) shimmer

Schimmel m -s,- mould; (Pferd) white horse. **s~ig** a mouldy. **s~n** vi (haben/sein) go mouldy

Schimmer m -s gleam; (Spur) glimmer. **s~n** vi (haben) gleam

Schimpanse m -n,-n chimpanzee

schimpf|en vi (haben) grumble (**mit** at; **über** + acc about); scold (**mit jdm** s.o.) □ vt call. **S~name** m term of abuse. **S~wort** nt (pl -wörter) swear-word; (Beleidigung) insult

schind|en† vt work or drive hard; (quälen) ill-treat; **sich s~en** slave [away]; **Eindruck s~en** (fam) try to impress. **S~er** m -s,- slave-driver. **S~erei** f - slave-driving; (Plackerei) hard slog

Schinken m -s,- ham. **S~speck** m bacon

Schippe f -,-n shovel. **s~n** vt shovel

Schirm m -[e]s,-e umbrella; (Sonnen-) sun-shade; (Lampen-) shade; (Mützen-) peak; (Ofen-, Bild-) screen; (fig: Schutz) shield. **S~herr** m patron. **S~herrschaft** f patronage. **S~mütze** f peaked cap

schizophren a schizophrenic. **S~ie** f - schizophrenia

Schlacht f -,-en battle

schlachten vt slaughter, kill

Schlachter, Schlächter m -s,- (NGer) butcher

Schlacht|feld nt battlefield. **S~haus** nt, **S~hof** m abattoir. **S~platte** f plate of assorted cooked meats and sausages. **S~schiff** nt battleship

Schlacke f -,-n slag

Schlaf m -[e]s sleep; **im S~** in one's sleep. **S~anzug** m pyjamas pl, (Amer) pajamas pl. **S~couch** f sofa bed

Schläfe f -,-n (Anat) temple

schlafen† vi (haben) sleep; (fam: nicht aufpassen) be asleep; **s~ gehen** go to bed; **er schläft noch** he is still asleep. **S~zeit** f bedtime

Schläfer(in) m -s,- (f -,-nen) sleeper

schlaff a limp, adv -ly; (Seil) slack; (Muskel) flabby

Schlaf|lied nt lullaby. **s~los** a sleepless. **S~losigkeit** f - insomnia. **S~mittel** nt sleeping drug

schläfrig a sleepy, adv -ily

Schlaf|saal m dormitory. **S~sack** m sleeping-bag. **S~tablette** f sleeping-pill. **s~trunken** a [still] half asleep. **S~wagen** m sleeping-car, sleeper. **s~wandeln** vi (haben/sein) sleep-walk. **s~zimmer** nt bedroom

Schlag m -[e]s,-̈e blow; (Faust-) punch; (Herz-, Puls-, Trommel-) beat; (einer Uhr) chime; (Glocken-, Gong- & Med) stroke; (elektrischer) shock; (Portion) helping; (Art) type; (Aust) whipped cream; **S~e bekommen** get a beating; **S~ auf S~** in rapid succession. **S~ader** f artery. **S~anfall** m stroke. **S~artig** a sudden, adv -ly. **S~baum** m barrier

Schlägel m -s,- mallet; (Trommel-) stick

schlagen† vt hit, strike; (fällen) fell; knock (Loch, Nagel) (**in** + acc into); (prügeln, besiegen) beat; (Culin) whisk (Eiweiß); whip (Sahne); (legen) throw; (wickeln) wrap; (hinzufügen) add (**zu** to); **sich s~** fight; **sich geschlagen geben** admit defeat □ vi (haben) beat; (Tür:) bang; (Uhr:) strike; (melodisch) chime; **mit den Flügeln s~** flap its wings; **um sich s~** lash out; **es schlug sechs** the clock struck six □ vi (sein) **in etw** (acc) **s~** (Blitz, Kugel:) strike sth; **s~ an** (+ acc) knock against; **nach jdm s~** (fig) take after s.o. **s~d** a (fig) conclusive, adv -ly

Schlager m -s,- popular song; (Erfolg) hit

Schläger m -s,- racket; (Tischtennis-) bat; (Golf-) club; (Hockey-) stick; (fam: Raufbold) thug. **S~ei** f -,-en fight, brawl

schlag|fertig a quick-witted. **S~instrument** nt percussion instrument. **S~loch** nt pothole. **S~sahne** f whipped cream; (ungeschlagen) whipping cream. **S~seite** f (Naut) list. **S~stock** m truncheon. **S~wort** nt (pl -worte) slogan. **S~zeile** f headline. **S~zeug** nt (Mus) percussion. **S~zeuger** m -s,- percussionist; (in Band) drummer

schlaksig a gangling

Schlamassel m & nt -s (fam) mess

Schlamm m -[e]s mud. **s~ig** a muddy

Schlamp|e f -,-n (fam) slut. **s~en** vi (haben) (fam) be sloppy (**bei** in). **S~erei** f -,-en sloppiness; (Unordnung) mess. **s~ig** a slovenly; (Arbeit) sloppy □ adv in a slovenly way; sloppily

Schlange f -,-n snake; (Menschen-, Auto-) queue; **S~ stehen** queue, (Amer) stand in line

schlängeln (sich) vr wind; (Person:) weave (**durch** through)

Schlangen|biss (Schlangenbiß) m snakebite. **S~linie** f wavy line

schlank a slim. **S~heit** f - slimness. **S~heitskur** f slimming diet

schlapp a tired; (schlaff) limp, adv -ly. **S~e** f -,-n (fam) setback

schlau a clever, adv -ly; (gerissen) crafty, adv -ily; **ich werde nicht s~ daraus** I can't make head or tail of it

Schlauch m -[e]s,Schläuche tube; (Wasser-) hose[pipe]. S~boot nt rubber dinghy. s~en vt (fam) exhaust

Schlaufe f -,-n loop

schlecht a bad; (böse) wicked; (unzulänglich) poor; s~ werden go bad; ⟨Wetter:⟩ turn bad; s~er werden get worse; s~ aussehen look bad/⟨Person:⟩ unwell; mir ist s~ I feel sick; s~ machen (fam) run down □ adv badly; poorly; (kaum) not really. s~gehen† vi sep (sein) NEW s~ gehen, s. gehen. s~gelaunt a NEW s~ gelaunt, s. gelaunt. s~hin adv quite simply. S~igkeit f - wickedness. s~machen vt sep NEW s~ machen, s. schlecht

schlecken vt/i (haben) lick (an etw dat sth); (auf-) lap up

Schlegel m -s,- ⟨SGer: Keule⟩ leg; ⟨Hühner-⟩ drumstick; (Techn, Mus) NEW Schlägel

schleichen† vi (sein) creep; (langsam gehen/fahren) crawl □ vr sich s~ creep. s~d a creeping; ⟨Krankheit⟩ insidious

Schleier m -s,- veil; (fig) haze. s~haft a es ist mir s~haft (fam) it's a mystery to me

Schleife f -,-n bow; (Fliege) bow-tie; (Biegung) loop

schleifen¹ v (reg) □ vt drag; (zerstören) raze to the ground □ vi (haben) trail, drag

schleifen†² vt grind; (schärfen) sharpen; cut ⟨Edelstein, Glas⟩; (drillen) drill

Schleim m -[e]s slime; (Anat) mucus; (Med) phlegm. s~ig a slimy

schlemm|en vi (haben) feast □ vt feast on. S~er m -s,- gourmet

schlendern vi (sein) stroll

schlenkern vt/i (haben) swing; s~ mit swing; dangle ⟨Beine⟩

Schlepp|dampfer m tug. S~e f -,-n train. s~en vt drag; (tragen) carry; (ziehen) tow; sich s~en drag oneself; (sich hinziehen) drag on; sich s~en mit carry. s~end a slow, adv -ly. S~er m -s,- tug; (Traktor) tractor. S~kahn m barge. S~lift m T-bar lift. S~tau nt tow-rope; ins S~tau nehmen take in tow

Schleuder f -,-n catapult; (Wäsche-) spin-drier. s~n vt hurl; spin ⟨Wäsche⟩; extract ⟨Honig⟩ □ vi (sein) skid; ins S~n geraten skid. S~preise mpl knock-down prices. S~sitz m ejector seat

schleunigst adv hurriedly; (sofort) at once

Schleuse f -,-n lock; (Sperre) sluice[-gate]. s~n vt steer

Schliche pl tricks; jdm auf die S~ kommen (fam) get on to s.o.

schlicht a plain, adv -ly; (einfach) simple, adv -ply

schlicht|en vt settle □ vi (haben) arbitrate. S~ung f - settlement; (Jur) arbitration

Schlick m -[e]s silt

Schließe f -,-n clasp; (Schnalle) buckle

schließen† vt close (ab-) lock; fasten ⟨Kleid, Verschluss⟩; (stilllegen) close down; (beenden, folgern) conclude; enter into ⟨Vertrag⟩; sich s~ close; in die Arme s~ embrace; etw s~ an (+ acc) connect sth to; sich s~ an (+ acc) follow □ vi (haben) close, (den Betrieb einstellen) close down; (den Schlüssel drehen) turn the key; (enden, folgern) conclude; s~ lassen auf (+ acc) suggest

Schließ|fach nt locker. s~lich adv finally, in the end; (immerhin) after all. S~ung f -,-en closure

Schliff m -[e]s cut; (Schleifen) cutting; (fig) polish; der letzte S~ the finishing touches pl

schlimm a bad, adv -ly; s~er werden get worse; nicht so s~! it doesn't matter! s~stenfalls adv if the worst comes to the worst

Schlinge f -,-n loop; (Henkers-) noose; (Med) sling; (Falle) snare

Schlingel m -s,- (fam) rascal

schling|en† vt wind, wrap; tie ⟨Knoten⟩; sich s~en um coil around □ vi (haben) bolt one's food. S~pflanze f climber

Schlips m -es,-e tie

Schlitten m -s,- sledge; (Rodel-) toboggan; (Pferde-) sleigh; S~ fahren toboggan

schlittern vi (haben/ sein) slide

Schlittschuh m skate; S~ laufen skate. S~läufer(in) m(f) -s,- (f -,-nen) skater

Schlitz m -es,-e slit; (für Münze) slot; (Jacken-) vent; (Hosen-) flies pl. s~en vt slit

Schloss nt -es,¨er (Schloß nt -sses,-sser) lock; (Vorhänge-) padlock; (Verschluss) clasp; (Gebäude) castle; (Palast) palace

Schlosser m -s,- locksmith; (Auto-) mechanic; (Maschinen-) fitter

Schlot m -[e]s,-e chimney

schlottern vi (haben) shake, tremble; ⟨Kleider:⟩ hang loose

Schlucht f -,-en ravine, gorge

schluchz|en vi (haben) sob. S~er m -s,- sob

Schluck m -[e]s,-e mouthful; (klein) sip

Schluckauf m -s hiccups pl

schlucken vt/i (haben) swallow. S~ m -s hiccups pl

schlud|ern vi (haben) be sloppy (bei in). s~rig a sloppy, adv -ily; ⟨Arbeit⟩ slipshod

Schlummer m -s slumber. s~n vi (haben) slumber

Schlund *m* -[e]s [back of the] throat; *(fig)* mouth

schlüpf|en *vi (sein)* slip; [aus dem Ei] s~en hatch. **S~er** *m* -s,- knickers *pl.* s~rig *a* slippery; *(anstößig)* smutty

schlurfen *vi (sein)* shuffle

schlürfen *vt/i (haben)* slurp

Schluss *m* -es,-̈e (**Schluß** *m* -sses,-̈sse) end; *(S~folgerung)* conclusion; **zum S~** finally; **S~ machen** stop (mit etw sth); finish (mit jdm with s.o.)

Schlüssel *m* -s,- key; *(Schrauben-)* spanner; *(Geheim-)* code; *(Mus)* clef. **S~bein** *nt* collar-bone. **S~bund** *m & nt* bunch of keys. **S~loch** *nt* keyhole. **S~ring** *m* key-ring

Schlussfolgerung (**Schlußfolgerung**) *f* conclusion

schlüssig *a* conclusive, *adv* -ly; **sich** *(dat)* s~ werden make up one's mind

Schluss|licht (**Schluß|licht**) *nt* rear-light. **S~verkauf** *m* [end of season] sale

Schmach *f* - disgrace

schmachten *vi (haben)* languish

schmächtig *a* slight

schmackhaft *a* tasty

schmal *a* narrow; *(dünn)* thin; *(schlank)* slender; *(karg)* meagre

schmälern *vt* diminish; *(herabsetzen)* belittle

Schmalz[1] *nt* -es lard; *(Ohren-)* wax

Schmalz[2] *m* -es *(fam)* schmaltz. **s~ig** *a* *(fam)* schmaltzy, slushy

schmarotz|en *vi (haben)* be parasitic (auf + *acc* on); *(Person:)* sponge (bei on). **S~er** *m* -s,- parasite; *(Person)* sponger

Schmarren *m* -s,- *(Aust)* pancake [torn into strips]; *(fam: Unsinn)* rubbish

schmatzen *vi (haben)* eat noisily

schmausen *vi (haben)* feast

schmecken *vi (haben)* taste (nach of); [gut] s~ taste good; hat es dir geschmeckt? did you enjoy it? □ *vt* taste

Schmeichelei *f* -,-en flattery; *(Kompliment)* compliment

schmeichel|haft *a* complimentary, flattering. **s~n** *vi (haben)* (+ *dat*) flatter

schmeißen† *vt/i (haben)* s~ [mit] *(fam)* chuck

Schmeißfliege *f* bluebottle

schmelz|en† *vt/i (sein)* melt; smelt *(Erze)*. **S~wasser** *nt* melted snow and ice

Schmerbauch *m (fam)* paunch

Schmerz *m* -es,-en pain; *(Kummer)* grief; **S~en haben** be in pain. **s~en** *vt* hurt; *(fig)* grieve □ *vi (haben)* hurt, be painful. **S~ensgeld** *nt* compensation for pain and suffering. **s~haft** *a* painful. **s~lich** *a (fig)*

painful; *(traurig)* sad, *adv* -ly. **s~los** *a* painless, *adv* -ly. **s~stillend** *a* pain-killing; **s~stillendes Mittel** analgesic, pain-killer. **S~tablette** *f* pain-killer

Schmetterball *m (Tennis)* smash

Schmetterling *m* -s,-e butterfly

schmettern *vt* hurl; *(Tennis)* smash; *(singen)* sing; *(spielen)* blare out □ *vi (haben)* sound; *(Trompeten:)* blare

Schmied *m* -[e]s,-e blacksmith

Schmiede *f* -,-n forge. **S~eisen** *nt* wrought iron. **s~n** *vt* forge; *(fig)* hatch; **Pläne s~n** make plans

schmieg|en *vt* press; **sich s~en an** (+ *acc*) nestle *or* snuggle up to; *(Kleid:)* cling to. **s~sam** *a* supple

Schmier|e *f* -,-n grease; *(Schmutz)* mess. **s~en** *vt* lubricate; *(streichen)* spread; *(schlecht schreiben)* scrawl; *(sl: bestechen)* bribe □ *vi (haben)* smudge; *(schreiben)* scrawl. **S~fett** *nt* grease. **S~geld** *nt (fam)* bribe. **s~ig** *a* greasy; *(schmutzig)* grubby; *(anstößig)* smutty; *(Person)* slimy. **S~mittel** *nt* lubricant

Schminke *f* -,-n make-up. **s~n** *vt* make up; **sich s~n** put on make-up; **sich** *(dat)* **die Lippen s~n** put on lipstick

schmirgel|n *vt* sand down. **S~papier** *nt* emery-paper

schmökern *vt/i (haben) (fam)* read

schmollen *vi (haben)* sulk; *(s~d den Mund verziehen)* pout

schmor|en *vt/i (haben)* braise; *(fam: schwitzen)* roast. **S~topf** *m* casserole

Schmuck *m* -[e]s jewellery; *(Verzierung)* ornament, decoration

schmücken *vt* decorate, adorn; **sich s~** adorn oneself

schmuck|los *a* plain. **S~stück** *nt* piece of jewellery; *(fig)* jewel

schmuddelig *a* grubby

Schmuggel *m* -s smuggling. **s~n** *vt* smuggle. **S~ware** *f* contraband

Schmuggler *m* -s,- smuggler

schmunzeln *vi (haben)* smile

schmusen *vi (haben)* cuddle

Schmutz *m* -es dirt; **in den S~ziehen** *(fig)* denigrate. **s~en** *vi (haben)* get dirty. **S~fleck** *m* dirty mark. **s~ig** *a* dirty

Schnabel *m* -s,-̈ beak, bill; *(eines Kruges)* lip; *(Tülle)* spout

Schnake *f* -,-n mosquito; *(Kohl-)* daddy-long-legs

Schnalle *f* -,-n buckle. **s~n** *vt* strap; *(zu-)* buckle; **den Gürtel enger s~n** tighten one's belt

schnalzen *vi (haben)* **mit der Zunge/den Fingern s~** click one's tongue/snap one's fingers

schnapp|en vi (haben) **s~en nach** snap
at; gasp for ⟨Luft⟩ □ vt snatch, grab; (fam:
festnehmen) nab. **S~schloss (S~schloß)**
nt spring lock. **S~schuss (S~schuß)** m
snapshot

Schnaps m -es,ːe schnapps

schnarchen vi (haben) snore

schnarren vi (haben) rattle; ⟨Klingel:⟩
buzz

schnattern vi (haben) cackle

schnauben vi (haben) snort □ vt **sich**
(dat) **die Nase s~** blow one's nose

schnaufen vi (haben) puff, pant

Schnauze f -,-n muzzle; (eines Kruges) lip;
(Tülle) spout

schnäuzen (sich) vr blow one's nose

Schnecke f -,-n snail; (Nackt-) slug; (Spirale) scroll; (Gebäck) ≈ Chelsea bun.
S~nhaus nt snail-shell

Schnee m -s snow; (Eier-) beaten egg-
white. **S~ball** m snowball. **S~besen** m
whisk. **S~brille** f snow-goggles pl.
S~fall m snow-fall. **S~flocke** f snow-
flake. **S~glöckchen** nt -s,- snowdrop.
S~kette f snow chain. **S~mann** m (pl
-männer) snowman. **S~pflug** m snow-
plough. **S~schläger** m whisk. **S~sturm**
m snowstorm, blizzard. **S~wehe** f -,-n
snowdrift

Schneid m -[e]s (SGer) courage

Schneide f -,-n [cutting] edge; (Klinge)
blade

schneiden† vt cut; (in Scheiben) slice;
(kreuzen) cross; (nicht beachten) cut dead;
Gesichter s~ pull faces; **sich s~** cut oneself; (über-) intersect; **sich** (dat/acc) **in
den Finger s~** cut one's finger. **s~d** a
cutting; (kalt) biting

Schneider m -s,- tailor. **S~in** f -,-nen
dressmaker. **s~n** vt make ⟨Anzug, Kos-
tüm⟩

Schneidezahn m incisor

schneidig a dashing, adv -ly

schneien vi (haben) snow; **es schneit** it is
snowing

Schneise f -,-n path; (Feuer-) firebreak

schnell a quick; ⟨Auto, Tempo⟩ fast □ adv
quickly; (in s~em Tempo) fast; (bald)
soon; **mach s~!** hurry up! **s~en** vi (sein)
in die Höhe s~en shoot up. **S~igkeit** f
- rapidity; ⟨Tempo⟩ speed. **S~imbiss
(S~imbiß)** m snack-bar. **S~kochtopf** m
pressure-cooker. **S~reinigung** f express
cleaners. **s~stens** adv as quickly as possible. **S~zug** m express [train]

schnetzeln vt cut into thin strips

schneuzen (sich) vr (NEW) **schnäuzen
(sich)**

schnippen vt flick

schnippisch a pert, adv -ly

Schnipsel m & nt -s,- scrap

Schnitt m -[e]s,-e cut; (Film-) cutting;
(S~muster) [paper] pattern; **im S~**
(durchschnittlich) on average

Schnitte f -,-n slice [of bread]; (belegt)
open sandwich

schnittig a stylish; (stromlinienförmig)
streamlined

Schnitt|käse m hard cheese. **S~lauch** m
chives pl. **S~muster** nt [paper] pattern.
S~punkt m [point of] intersection.
S~wunde f cut

Schnitzel nt -s,- scrap; (Culin) escalope.
s~n vt shred

schnitz|en vt/i (haben) carve. **S~er** m -s,-
carver; (fam: Fehler) blunder. **S~erei** f
-,-en carving

schnodderig a (fam) brash

schnöde a despicable, adv -bly; (verächtlich) contemptuous, adv -ly

Schnorchel m -s,- snorkel

Schnörkel m -s,- flourish; (Kunst) scroll.
s~ig a ornate

schnorren vt/i (haben) (fam) scrounge

schnüffeln vi (haben) sniff (**an etw** dat
sth); (fam: spionieren) snoop [around]

Schnuller m -s,- [baby's] dummy, (Amer)
pacifier

schnupf|en vt sniff; **Tabak s~en** take
snuff. **S~en** m -s,- [head] cold. **S~tabak**
m snuff

schnuppern vt/i (haben) sniff (**an etw**
dat sth)

Schnur f -,ːe string; (Kordel) cord;
(Besatz-) braid; (Electr) flex; **eine S~** a
piece of string

Schnür|chen nt -s,- **wie am S~chen**
(fam) like clockwork. **s~en** vt tie; lace
[up] ⟨Schuhe⟩

schnurgerade a & adv dead straight

Schnurr|bart m moustache. **s~en** vi
(haben) hum; ⟨Katze:⟩ purr

Schnür|schuh m lace-up shoe. **S~sen-
kel** m [shoe-]lace

schnurstracks adv straight

Schock m -[e]s,-s shock. **s~en** vt (fam)
shock; **geschockt sein** be shocked.
s~ieren vt shock; **s~ierend** shocking

Schöffe m -n,-n lay judge

Schokolade f - chocolate

Scholle f -,-n clod [of earth]; (Eis-) [ice-]
floe; (Fisch) plaice

schon adv already; (allein) just; (sogar)
even; (ohnehin) anyway; **s~ einmal** before; (jemals) ever; **s~ immer/oft/wie-
der** always/often/again; **hast du ihn s~
gesehen?** have you seen him yet? **s~ der
Gedanke daran** the mere thought of it;

s~ **deshalb** for that reason alone; **das ist s~ möglich** that's quite possible; **ja s~, aber** well yes, but; **nun geh/komm s~!** go/come on then!

schön *a* beautiful; ⟨*Wetter*⟩ fine; ⟨*angenehm, nett*⟩ nice; ⟨*gut*⟩ good; ⟨*fam: beträchtlich*⟩ pretty; **s~en Dank!** thank you very much! **na s~** all right then □ *adv* beautifully; nicely; ⟨*gut*⟩ well; **s~ langsam** nice and slowly

schonen *vt* spare; ⟨*gut behandeln*⟩ look after; **sich s~** take things easy. **s~d** *a* gentle, *adv* -tly

Schönheit *f* -,-en beauty. **S~sfehler** *m* blemish. **S~skonkurrenz** *f*, **S~swettbewerb** *m* beauty contest

schönmachen *vt sep* smarten up; **sich s~** make oneself look nice

Schonung *f* -,-en gentle care; ⟨*nach Krankheit*⟩ rest; ⟨*Baum-*⟩ plantation. **s~slos** *a* ruthless, *adv* -ly

Schonzeit *f* close season

Schöpf|en *vt* scoop [up]; ladle ⟨*Suppe*⟩; **Mut s~en** take heart; **frische Luft s~en** get some fresh air. **S~er** *m* -s,- creator; ⟨*Kelle*⟩ ladle. **S~erisch** *a* creative. **S~kelle** *f*, **S~löffel** *m* ladle. **S~ung** *f* -,-en creation

Schoppen *m* -s,- ⟨*SGer*⟩ ≈ pint

Schorf *m* -[e]s scab

Schornstein *m* chimney. **S~feger** *m* -s,- chimney-sweep

Schoß *m* -es,ⸯe lap; ⟨*Frack-*⟩ tail

Schössling (**Schößling**) *m* -s,-e ⟨*Bot*⟩ shoot

Schote *f* -,-n pod; ⟨*Erbse*⟩ pea

Schotte *m* -n,-n Scot, Scotsman

Schotter *m* -s gravel; ⟨*für Gleise*⟩ ballast

schott|isch *a* Scottish, Scots. **S~land** *nt* -s Scotland

schraffieren *vt* hatch

schräg *a* diagonal, *adv* -ly; ⟨*geneigt*⟩ sloping; **s~ halten** tilt. **S~e** *f* -,-n slope. **S~strich** *m* oblique stroke

Schramme *f* -,-n scratch. **s~n** *vt* scrape, scratch

Schrank *m* -[e]s,ⸯe cupboard; ⟨*Kleider-*⟩ wardrobe; ⟨*Akten-, Glas-*⟩ cabinet

Schranke *f* -,-n barrier

Schraube *f* -,-n screw; ⟨*Schiffs-*⟩ propeller. **s~n** *vt* screw; ⟨*ab-*⟩ unscrew; ⟨*drehen*⟩ turn; **sich in die Höhe s~n** spiral upwards. **S~nmutter** *f* nut. **S~nschlüssel** *m* spanner. **S~nzieher** *m* -s,- screwdriver

Schraubstock *m* vice

Schrebergarten *m* ≈ allotment

Schreck *m* -[e]s,-e fright; **jdm einen S~ einjagen** give s.o. a fright. **S~en** *m* -s,- fright; ⟨*Entsetzen*⟩ horror. **s~en** *vt* ⟨*reg*⟩ frighten; ⟨*auf-*⟩ startle □ *vi*† ⟨*sein*⟩ **in die Höhe s~en** start up

Schreck|gespenst *nt* spectre. **s~haft** *a* easily frightened; ⟨*nervös*⟩ jumpy. **s~lich** *a* terrible, *adv* -bly. **S~schuss** (**S~schuß**) *m* warning shot

Schrei *m* -[e]s,-e cry, shout; ⟨*gellend*⟩ scream; **der letzte S~** ⟨*fam*⟩ the latest thing

Schreib|block *m* writing-pad. **s~en†** *vt/i* ⟨*haben*⟩ write; ⟨*auf der Maschine*⟩ type; **richtig/falsch s~en** spell right/wrong; **sich s~en** ⟨*Wort:*⟩ be spelt; ⟨*korrespondieren*⟩ correspond; **krank s~en** (NEW) **krankschreiben**. **S~en** *nt* -s,- writing; ⟨*Brief*⟩ letter. **S~fehler** *m* spelling mistake. **S~heft** *nt* exercise book. **S~kraft** *f* clerical assistant; ⟨*für Maschineschreiben*⟩ typist. **S~maschine** *f* typewriter. **S~papier** *nt* writing-paper. **S~schrift** *f* script. **S~tisch** *m* desk. **S~ung** *f* -,-en spelling. **S~waren** *fpl* stationery *sg*. **S~weise** *f* spelling

schreien† *vt/i* ⟨*haben*⟩ cry; ⟨*gellend*⟩ scream; ⟨*rufen, laut sprechen*⟩ shout; **zum S~ sein** ⟨*fam*⟩ be a scream. **s~d** *a* ⟨*fig*⟩ glaring; ⟨*grell*⟩ garish

Schreiner *m* -s,- joiner

schreiten† *vi* ⟨*sein*⟩ walk

Schrift *f* -,-en writing; ⟨*Druck-*⟩ type; ⟨*Abhandlung*⟩ paper; **die Heilige S~** the Scriptures *pl*. **S~führer** *m* secretary. **s~lich** *a* written □ *adv* in writing. **S~sprache** *f* written language. **S~steller(in)** *m* -s,- ⟨*f* -,-nen⟩ writer. **S~stück** *nt* document. **S~zeichen** *nt* character

schrill *a* shrill, *adv* -y

Schritt *m* -[e]s,-e step; ⟨*Entfernung*⟩ pace; ⟨*Gangart*⟩ walk; ⟨*der Hose*⟩ crotch; **im S~** in step; ⟨*langsam*⟩ at walking pace; **S~ halten mit** ⟨*fig*⟩ keep pace with. **S~macher** *m* -s,- pace-maker. **S~weise** *adv* step by step

schroff *a* precipitous, *adv* -ly; ⟨*abweisend*⟩ brusque, *adv* -ly; ⟨*unvermittelt*⟩ abrupt, *adv* -ly; ⟨*Gegensatz*⟩ stark

schröpfen *vt* ⟨*fam*⟩ fleece

Schrot *m* & *nt* -[e]s coarse meal; ⟨*Blei-*⟩ small shot. **s~en** *vt* grind coarsely. **S~flinte** *f* shotgun

Schrott *m* -[e]s scrap[-metal]; **zu S~ fahren** ⟨*fam*⟩ write off. **S~platz** *m* scrapyard. **s~reif** *a* ready for the scrap-heap

schrubb|en *vt/i* ⟨*haben*⟩ scrub. **S~er** *m* -s,- [long-handled] scrubbing-brush

Schrull|e *f* -,-n whim; **alte S~e** ⟨*fam*⟩ old crone. **s~ig** *a* cranky

schrumpfen *vi* ⟨*sein*⟩ shrink; ⟨*Obst:*⟩ shrivel

schrump[e]lig *a* wrinkled

Schrunde *f* -,-n crack; (*Spalte*) crevasse

Schub *m* -[e]s,-̈e (*Phys*) thrust; (*S~fach*) drawer; (*Menge*) batch. **S~fach** *nt* drawer. **S~karre** *f*, **S~karren** *m* wheelbarrow. **S~lade** *f* drawer

Schubs *m* -es,-e push, shove. **s~en** *vt* push, shove

schüchtern *a* shy, *adv* -ly; (*zaghaft*) tentative, *adv* -ly. **S~heit** *f* - shyness

Schuft *m* -[e]s,-e (*pej*) swine. **s~en** *vi* (*haben*) (*fam*) slave away

Schuh *m* -[e]s,-e shoe. **S~anzieher** *m* -s,-shoehorn. **S~band** *nt* (*pl* -bänder) shoelace. **S~creme** *f* shoe-polish. **S~löffel** *m* shoehorn. **S~macher** *m* -s,- shoemaker; (*zum Flicken*) [shoe] mender. **S~werk** *nt* shoes *pl*

Schul|abgänger *m* -s,- schoolleaver. **S~arbeiten**, **S~aufgaben** *fpl* homework *sg*. **S~buch** *nt* school-book

Schuld *f* -,-en guilt; (*Verantwortung*) blame; (*Geld-*) debt; **S~en machen** get into debt; **S~ haben** be to blame (**an** + *dat* for); **jdm S~ geben** blame s.o.; **sich** (*dat*) **etwas zu S~en kommen lassen** = **sich etwas zuschulden kommen lassen**, s. **zuschulden □ s~ sein** be to blame (**an** + *dat* for); **s~ haben/jdm s~ geben** (NEW) **S~ haben/jdm S~ geben**, s. **Schuld. s~en** *vt* owe

schuldig *a* guilty (*gen* of); (*gebührend*) due; **jdm etw s~ sein** owe s.o. sth. **S~keit** *f* - duty

schuld|los *a* innocent. **S~ner** *m* -s,- debtor. **S~spruch** *m* guilty verdict

Schule *f* -,-n school; **in der/die S~** at/to school. **s~n** *vt* train

Schüler|(in) *m* -s,- (*f* -,-nen) pupil. **S~lotse** *m* pupil acting as crossing warden

schul|frei *a* **s~freier Tag** day without school; **wir haben morgen s~frei** there's no school tomorrow. **S~hof** *m* [school] playground. **S~jahr** *nt* school year; (*Klasse*) form. **S~junge** *m* schoolboy. **S~kind** *nt* schoolchild. **S~leiter(in)** *m(f)* head [teacher]. **S~mädchen** *nt* schoolgirl. **S~stunde** *f* lesson

Schulter *f* -,-n shoulder. **S~blatt** *nt* shoulder-blade. **s~n** *vt* shoulder. **S~tuch** *nt* shawl

Schulung *f* - training

schummeln *vi* (*haben*) (*fam*) cheat

Schund *m* -[e]s trash. **S~roman** *m* trashy novel

Schuppe *f* -,-n scale; **S~n** *pl* dandruff *sg*. **s~n** (**sich**) *vr* flake [off]

Schuppen *m* -s,- shed

Schur *f* - shearing

Schür|eisen *nt* poker. **s~en** *vt* poke; (*fig*) stir up

schürf|en *vt* mine; **sich** (*dat*) **das Knie s~en** graze one's knee □ *vi* (*haben*) **s~en nach** prospect for. **S~wunde** *f* abrasion, graze

Schürhaken *m* poker

Schurke *m* -n,-n villain

Schürze *f* -,-n apron. **s~n** *vt* (*raffen*) gather [up]; tie (*Knoten*); purse (*Lippen*). **S~njäger** *m* (*fam*) womanizer

Schuss *m* -es,-̈e (**Schuß** *m* -sses,-̈sse) shot; (*kleine Menge*) dash

Schüssel *f* -,-n bowl; (*TV*) dish

schusselig *a* (*fam*) scatter-brained

Schuss|fahrt (**Schußfahrt**) *f* (*Ski*) schuss. **S~waffe** *f* firearm

Schuster *m* -s,- = **Schuhmacher**

Schutt *m* -[e]s rubble. **S~abladeplatz** *m* rubbish dump

Schüttel|frost *m* shivering fit. **s~n** *vt* shake; **sich s~n** shake oneself/itself; (*vor Ekel*) shudder; **jdm die Hand s~n** shake s.o.'s hand

schütten *vt* pour; (*kippen*) tip; (*ver-*) spill □ *vi* (*haben*) **es schüttet** it is pouring [with rain]

Schutthaufen *m* pile of rubble

Schutz *m* -es protection; (*Zuflucht*) shelter; (*Techn*) guard; **S~ suchen** take refuge; **unter dem S~ der Dunkelheit** under cover of darkness. **S~anzug** *m* protective suit. **S~blech** *nt* mudguard. **S~brille** goggles *pl*

Schütze *m* -n,-n marksman; (*Tor-*) scorer; (*Astr*) Sagittarius; **guter S~** good shot

schützen *vt* protect/(*Zuflucht gewähren*) shelter (**vor** + *dat* from) □ *vi* (*haben*) give protection/shelter (**vor** + *dat* from). **s~d** *a* protective, *adv* -ly

Schützenfest *nt* fair with shooting competition

Schutz|engel *m* guardian angel. **S~heilige(r)** *m/f* patron saint

Schützling *m* -s,-e charge; (*Protegé*) protégé

schutz|los *a* defenceless, helpless. **S~mann** *m* (*pl* -männer & -leute) policeman. **S~umschlag** *m* dust-jacket

Schwaben *nt* -s Swabia

schwäbisch *a* Swabian

schwach *a* (**schwächer, schwächst**) weak, *adv* -ly; (*nicht gut; gering*) poor, *adv* -ly; (*leicht*) faint, *adv* -ly

Schwäche *f* -,-n weakness. **s~n** *vt* weaken

Schwach|heit *f* - weakness. **S~kopf** *m* (*fam*) idiot

schwäch|lich *a* delicate. **S~ling** *m* -s,-e weakling

Schwachsinn *m* mental deficiency. **s~ig** *a* mentally deficient; (*fam*) idiotic

Schwächung *f* - weakening

schwafeln (*fam*) *vi* (*haben*) waffle □ *vt* talk

Schwager *m* -s,- brother-in-law

Schwägerin *f* -,-nen sister-in-law

Schwalbe *f* -,-n swallow

Schwall *m* -[e]s torrent

Schwamm *m* -[e]s,-e sponge; (*SGer: Pilz*) fungus; (*fam*) mushroom. **s~ig** *a* spongy; (*aufgedunsen*) bloated

Schwan *m* -[e]s,-e swan

schwanen *vi* (*haben*) (*fam*) **mir schwante, dass** I had a nasty feeling that

schwanger *a* pregnant

schwängern *vt* make pregnant

Schwangerschaft *f* -,-en pregnancy

Schwank *m* -[e]s,-e (*Theat*) farce

schwank|en *vi* (*haben*) sway; (*Boot:*) rock; (*sich ändern*) fluctuate; (*unentschieden sein*) be undecided □ (*sein*) stagger. **S~ung** *f* -,-en fluctuation

Schwanz *m* -es,-e tail

schwänzen *vt* (*fam*) skip; **die Schule s~** play truant

Schwarm *m* -[e]s,-e swarm; (*Fisch-*) shoal; (*fam: Liebe*) idol

schwärmen *vi* (*haben*) swarm; **s~ für** (*fam*) adore; (*verliebt sein*) have a crush on; **s~ von** (*fam*) rave about

Schwarte *f* -,-n (*Speck-*) rind; (*fam: Buch*) tome

schwarz *a* (**schwärzer, schwärzest**) black; (*fam: illegal*) illegal, *adv* -ly; **s~er Markt** black market; **s~ gekleidet** dressed in black; **s~ auf weiß** in black and white; **s~ sehen** (*fig*) be pessimistic; **ins S~e treffen** score a bull's-eye. **S~** *nt* -[e]s,- black. **S~arbeit** *f* moonlighting. **s~arbeiten** *vi sep* (*haben*) moonlight. **S~brot** *nt* black bread. **S~e(r)** *m/f* black

Schwärze *f* - blackness. **s~n** *vt* blacken

Schwarz|fahrer *m* fare-dodger. **S~handel** *m* black market (**mit in**). **S~händler** *m* black marketeer. **s~markt** *m* black market. **s~sehen†** *vi sep* (*haben*) watch television without a licence; (*fig*) (NEW) **s~ sehen, s. schwarz. S~wald** *m* Black Forest. **s~weiß** *a* black and white

Schwatz *m* -es (*fam*) chat

schwatzen *vi*, (*SGer*) **schwätzen** *vi* (*haben*) chat; (*klatschen*) gossip; (*Sch*) talk [in class] □ *vt* talk

schwatzhaft *a* garrulous

Schwebe *f* - **in der S~** (*fig*) undecided. **S~bahn** *f* cable railway. **s~n** *vi* (*haben*) float; (*fig*) be undecided; (*Verfahren:*) be pending; **in Gefahr s~n** be in danger □ (*sein*) float

Schwed|e *m* -n,-n Swede. **S~en** *nt* -s Sweden. **S~in** *f* -,-nen Swede. **s~isch** *a* Swedish

Schwefel *m* -s sulphur. **S~säure** *f* sulphuric acid

schweigen† *vi* (*haben*) be silent; **ganz zu s~ von** to say nothing of, let alone. **S~** *nt* -s silence; **zum S~ bringen** silence. **s~d** *a* silent, *adv* -ly

schweigsam *a* silent; (*wortkarg*) taciturn

Schwein *nt* -[e]s,-e pig; (*Culin*) pork; (*sl*) (*schmutziger Mensch*) dirty pig; (*Schuft*) swine; **s~ haben** (*fam*) be lucky. **S~ebraten** *m* roast pork. **S~efleisch** *nt* pork. **S~ehund** *m* (*sl*) swine. **S~erei** *f* -,-en (*sl*) [dirty] mess; (*Gemeinheit*) dirty trick. **S~estall** *m* pigsty. **s~isch** *a* lewd. **S~sleder** *nt* pigskin

Schweiß *m* -es sweat

schweiß|en *vt* weld. **S~er** *m* -s,- welder

Schweiz (die) - Switzerland. **S~er** *a & m* -s,-, **S~erin** *f* -,-nen Swiss. **s~erisch** *a* Swiss

schwelen *vi* (*haben*) smoulder

schwelgen *vi* (*haben*) feast; **s~ in** (+ *dat*) wallow in

Schwelle *f* -,-n threshold; (*Eisenbahn-*) sleeper

schwell|en† *vi* (*sein*) swell. **S~ung** *f* -,-en swelling

Schwemme *f* -,-n watering-place; (*fig: Überangebot*) glut. **s~n** *vt* wash; **an Land s~n** wash up

Schwenk *m* -[e]s swing. **s~en** *vt* swing; (*schwingen*) wave; (*spülen*) rinse; **in Butter s~en** toss in butter □ *vi* (*sein*) turn

schwer *a* heavy; (*schwierig*) difficult; (*mühsam, streng*) hard; (*ernst*) serious; (*schlimm*) bad; **3 Pfund s~** sein weigh 3 pounds □ *adv* heavily; with difficulty; (*mühsam, streng*) hard; (*schlimm, sehr*) badly, seriously; **s~ krank/verletzt** seriously ill/injured; **s~ arbeiten** work hard; **s~ hören** be hard of hearing; **etw s~ nehmen** take sth seriously; **jdm s~ fallen** be hard for s.o.; **es jdm s~ machen** make it *or* things difficult for s.o.; **sich s~ tun** have difficulty (**mit with**); **s~ zu sagen** difficult *or* hard to say

Schwere *f* - heaviness; (*Gewicht*) weight; (*Schwierigkeit*) difficulty; (*Ernst*) gravity. **S~losigkeit** *f* - weightlessness

schwer|fallen† *vi sep* (*sein*) (NEW) **s~ fallen, s. schwer. s~fällig** *a* ponderous, *adv* -ly; (*unbeholfen*) clumsy, *adv* -ily. **S~gewicht** *nt* heavyweight. **s~hörig** *a* **s~hörig sein** be hard of hearing.

S~kraft *f* (*Phys*) gravity. s~krank *a* (NEW) s~ krank, *s.* schwer. s~lich *adv* hardly. s~machen *vt sep* (NEW) s~ machen, *s.* schwer. s~mütig *a* melancholic. s~nehmen† *vt sep* (NEW) s~ nehmen, *s.* schwer. S~punkt *m* centre of gravity; (*fig*) emphasis

Schwert *nt* -[e]s,-er sword. S~lilie *f* iris

schwer|tun† (sich) *vr sep* (NEW) s~ tun (sich), *s.* schwer. S~verbrecher *m* serious offender. s~verdaulich *a* (NEW) s~ verdaulich, *s.* verdaulich. s~verletzt *a* (NEW) s~ verletzt, *s.* schwer. s~wiegend *a* weighty

Schwester *f* -,-n sister; (*Kranken-*) nurse. s~lich *a* sisterly

Schwieger|eltern *pl* parents-in-law. S~mutter *f* mother-in-law. S~sohn *m* son-in-law. S~tochter *f* daughter-in-law. S~vater *m* father-in-law

Schwiele *f* -,-n callus

schwierig *a* difficult. S~keit *f* -,-en difficulty

Schwimm|bad *nt* swimming-baths *pl*. S~becken *nt* swimming-pool. s~en† *vi/i* (*sein/haben*) swim; (*auf dem Wasser treiben*) float. S~er *m* -s,- swimmer; (*Techn*) float. S~weste *f* life-jacket

Schwindel *m* -s dizziness, vertigo; (*fam: Betrug*) fraud; (*Lüge*) lie. S~anfall *m* dizzy spell. s~frei *a* s~frei sein have a good head for heights. s~n *vi* (*haben*) (*lügen*) lie; mir od mich s~t I feel dizzy

schwinden† *vi* (*sein*) dwindle; (*vergehen*) fade; (*nachlassen*) fail

Schwindl|er *m* -s,- liar; (*Betrüger*) fraud, con-man. s~ig *a* dizzy; mir ist od wird s~ig I feel dizzy

schwing|en† *vi* (*haben*) swing; (*Phys*) oscillate; (*vibrieren*) vibrate □ *vt* swing; wave (*Fahne*); (*drohend*) brandish. S~tür *f* swing-door. S~ung *f* -,-en oscillation; vibration

Schwips *m* -es,-e einen S~ haben (*fam*) be tipsy

schwirren *vi* (*haben/sein*) buzz; (*surren*) whirr

Schwitz|e *f* -,-n (*Culin*) roux. s~en *vi* (*haben*) sweat; ich s~e od mich s~t I am hot □ *vt* (*Culin*) sweat

schwören† *vt/i* (*haben*) swear (auf + *acc* by); Rache s~ swear revenge

schwul *a* (*fam: homosexuell*) gay

schwül *a* close. S~e *f* - closeness

schwülstig *a* bombastic, *adv* -ally

Schwung *m* -[e]s,-̈e swing; (*Bogen*) sweep; (*Schnelligkeit*) momentum; (*Kraft*) vigour; (*Feuer*) verve; (*fam: Anzahl*) batch; in S~ kommen gather momentum; (*fig*) get going. s~haft *a* brisk, *adv* -ly. s~los

a dull. s~voll *a* vigorous, *adv* -ly; (*Bogen, Linie*) sweeping; (*mitreißend*) spirited, lively

Schwur *m* -[e]s,-̈e vow; (*Eid*) oath. S~gericht *nt* jury [court]

sechs *inv a*, S~ *f* -,-en six; (*Sch*) ≈ fail mark. s~eckig *a* hexagonal. s~te(r,s) *a* sixth

sech|zehn *inv a* sixteen. s~zehnte(r,s) *a* sixteenth. s~zig *inv a* sixty. s~zigste(r,s) *a* sixtieth

sedieren *vt* sedate

See¹ *m* -s,-n /'ze:ən/ lake

See² *f* - sea; an die/der See to/at the seaside; auf See at sea. S~bad *nt* seaside resort. S~fahrt *f* [sea] voyage; (*Schiffahrt*) navigation. S~gang *m* schwerer S~gang rough sea. S~hund *m* seal. s~krank *a* seasick

Seele *f* -,-n soul. s~nruhig *a* calm, *adv* -ly

seelisch *a* psychological, *adv* -ly; (*geistig*) mental, *adv* -ly

Seelsorger *m* -s,- pastor

See|luft *f* sea air. S~macht *f* maritime power. S~mann *m* (*pl* -leute) seaman, sailor. S~not *f* in S~not in distress. S~räuber *m* pirate. S~reise *f* [sea] voyage. S~rose *f* water-lily. S~sack *m* kitbag. S~stern *m* starfish. S~tang *m* seaweed. s~tüchtig *a* seaworthy. S~weg *m* sea route; auf dem S~weg by sea. S~zunge *f* sole

Segel *nt* -s,- sail. S~boot *nt* sailing-boat. S~fliegen *nt* gliding. S~flieger *m* glider pilot. S~flugzeug *nt* glider. s~n *vt/i* (*sein/haben*) sail. S~schiff *nt* sailing-ship. S~sport *m* sailing. S~tuch *nt* canvas

Segen *m* -s blessing. s~sreich *a* beneficial; (*gesegnet*) blessed

Segler *m* -s,- yachtsman

Segment *nt* -[e]s,-e segment

segnen *vt* bless; gesegnet mit blessed with

sehen† *vt* see; watch (*Fernsehsendung*); jdn/etw wieder s~ see s.o./sth again; sich s~ lassen show oneself □ *vi* (*haben*) see; (*blicken*) look (auf + *acc* at); (*ragen*) show (aus above); gut/schlecht s~ have good/bad eyesight; vom S~ kennen know by sight; s~ nach keep an eye on; (*betreuen*) look after; (*suchen*) look for; darauf s~, dass see [to it] that. s~swert, s~swürdig *a* worth seeing. S~swürdigkeit *f* -,-en sight

Sehkraft *f* sight, vision

Sehne *f* -,-n tendon; (*eines Bogens*) string

sehnen (sich) *vr* long (nach for)

sehnig *a* sinewy; (*zäh*) stringy

sehn|lich[st] *a* (*Wunsch*) dearest □ *adv* longingly. S~sucht *f* - longing (nach for).

s~süchtig *a* longing, *adv* -ly; ⟨*Wunsch*⟩ dearest

sehr *adv* very; (*mit Verb*) very much; **so s~, dass** so much that

seicht *a* shallow

seid *s.* **sein¹**; **ihr s~** you are

Seide *f -,-n* silk

Seidel *nt -s,-* beer-mug

seiden *a* silk ... **S~papier** *nt* tissue paper. **S~raupe** *f* silk-worm. **s~weich** *a* silky-soft

seidig *a* silky

Seife *f -,-n* soap. **S~npulver** *nt* soap powder. **S~nschaum** *m* lather

seifig *a* soapy

seihen *vt* strain

Seil *nt -[e]s,-e* rope; (*Draht-*) cable. **S~bahn** *f* cable railway. **s~springen†** *vi* (*sein*) (*inf & pp only*) skip. **S~tänzer(in)** *m(f)* tightrope walker

sein¹† *vi* (*sein*) be; **er ist Lehrer** he is a teacher; **sei still!** be quiet! **mir ist kalt/schlecht** I am cold/feel sick; **wie dem auch sei** be that as it may; **etw s~ lassen** (*aufhören mit*) stop sth □ *v aux* have; **angekommen/gestorben s~** have arrived/died; **er war/wäre gefallen** he had/would have fallen; **es ist/war viel zu tun/nichts zu sehen** there is/was a lot to be done/nothing to be seen

sein² *poss pron* his; (*Ding, Tier*) its; (*nach man*) one's; **sein Glück versuchen** try one's luck. **s~e(r,s)** *poss pron* his; (*nach man*) one's own; **das S~e tun** do one's share. **s~erseits** *adv* for his part. **s~erzeit** *adv* in those days. **s~etwegen** *adv* for his sake; (*wegen ihm*) because of him, on his account. **s~etwillen** *adv* **um s~etwillen** for his sake. **s~ige** *poss pron* **der/die/das s~ige** his

seinlassen† *vt sep* NEW sein lassen, *s.* sein¹

seins *poss pron* his; (*nach man*) one's own

seit *conj & prep* (+ *dat*) since; **s~ wann?** since when? **s~ einiger Zeit** for some time [past]; **ich wohne s~ zehn Jahren hier** I've lived here for ten years. **s~dem** *conj adv* since then

Seite *f -,-n* side; (*Buch-*) page; **S~ an S~** side by side; **zur S~ legen/treten** put/step aside; **jds starke S~** s.o.'s strong point; **auf der einen/anderen S~** (*fig*) on the one/other hand; **von S~n (s~n)** (+ *gen*) = vonseiten

seitens *prep* (+ *gen*) on the part of

Seiten|schiff *nt* [side] aisle. **S~sprung** *m* infidelity; **einen S~sprung machen** be unfaithful. **S~stechen** *nt -s* (*Med*) stitch.

S~straße *f* side-street. **S~streifen** *m* verge; (*Autobahn-*) hard shoulder

seither *adv* since then

seit|lich *a* side ... □ *adv* at/on the side; **s~lich von** to one side of □ *prep* (+ *gen*) to one side of. **s~wärts** *adv* on/to one side; (*zur Seite*) sideways

Sekret *nt -[e]s,-e* secretion

Sekret|är *m -s,-e* secretary; (*Schrank-*) bureau. **S~ariat** *nt -[e]s,-e* secretary's office. **S~ärin** *f -,-nen* secretary

Sekt *m -[e]s* [German] sparkling wine

Sekte *f -,-n* sect

Sektion /'tsio:n/ *f -,-en* section; (*Sezierung*) autopsy

Sektor *m -s,-en* /-'to:rən/ sector

Sekundant *m -en,-en* (*Sport*) second

sekundär *a* secondary

Sekunde *f -,-n* second

selber *pron* (*fam*) = selbst

selbst *pron* oneself; **ich/du/er/sie s~** I myself/you yourself/he himself/she herself; **wir/ihr/sie s~** we ourselves/you yourselves/they themselves; **ich schneide mein Haar s~** I cut my own hair; **von s~** of one's own accord; (*automatisch*) automatically; **s~ gemacht** home-made □ *adv* even. **S~achtung** *f* self-esteem, self-respect

selbständig *a* = selbstständig. **S~keit** *f* - = Selbstständigkeit

Selbstaufopferung *f* self-sacrifice

Selbstbedienung *f* self-service. **S~srestaurant** *nt* self-service restaurant, cafeteria

Selbst|befriedigung *f* masturbation. **S~beherrschung** *f* self-control. **S~bestimmung** *f* self-determination. **s~bewusst (s~bewußt)** *a* self-confident. **S~bewusstsein (S~bewußtsein)** *nt* self-confidence. **S~bildnis** *nt* self-portrait. **S~erhaltung** *f* self-preservation. **s~gefällig** *a* self-satisfied, smug, *adv* -ly. **s~gemacht** *a* NEW s~ gemacht, *s.* selbst. **s~gerecht** *a* self-righteous. **S~gespräch** *nt* soliloquy; **S~gespräche führen** talk to oneself. **s~haftend** *a* self-adhesive. **s~herrlich** *a* autocratic, *adv* -ally. **S~hilfe** *f* self-help. **s~klebend** *a* self-adhesive. **S~kostenpreis** *m* cost price. **S~laut** *m* vowel. **s~los** *a* selfless, *adv* -ly. **S~mitleid** *nt* self-pity. **S~mord** *m* suicide. **S~mörder(in)** *m(f)* suicide. **s~mörderisch** *a* suicidal. **S~porträt** *nt* self-portrait. **s~sicher** *a* self-assured. **S~sicherheit** *f* self-assurance. **s~ständig** *a* independent, *adv* -ly; self-employed ⟨*Handwerker*⟩; **sich s~ständig machen** set up on one's own. **S~ständigkeit** *f* - independence. **s~süchtig** *a* selfish, *adv*

-ly. **S~tanken** nt self-service (*for petrol*).
s~tätig a automatic, adv -ally. **S~versorgung** f self-catering
selbstverständlich a natural, adv -ly;
etw für s~ halten take sth for granted;
das ist s~ that goes without saying; **s~!**
of course! **S~keit** f - matter of course; **das
ist eine S~keit** that goes without saying
Selbst|verteidigung f self-defence.
S~vertrauen nt self-confidence. **S~verwaltung** f self-government. **s~zufrieden** a complacent, adv -ly
selig a blissfully happy; (*Relig*) blessed;
(*verstorben*) late. **S~keit** f - bliss
Sellerie m -s,-s & f -,- celeriac; (*Stangen-*)
celery
selten a rare □ adv rarely, seldom; (*besonders*) exceptionally. **S~heit** f -,-en rarity
Selterswasser nt seltzer [water]
seltsam a odd, adv -ly, strange, adv -ly.
s~erweise adv oddly/strangely enough
Semester nt -s,- (*Univ*) semester
Semikolon nt -s,-s semicolon
Seminar nt -s,-e seminar; (*Institut*) department; (*Priester-*) seminary
Semmel f -,-n [bread] roll. **S~brösel** pl
breadcrumbs
Senat m -[e]s,-e senate. **S~or** m -s,-en
/-'to:rən/ senator
senden¹ vt send
senden² vt (reg) broadcast; (*über Funk*)
transmit, send. **S~r** m -s,- [broadcasting]
station; (*Anlage*) transmitter. **S~reihe** f
series
Sendung f -,-en consignment, shipment;
(*Auftrag*) mission; (*Radio, TV*) programme
Senf m -s mustard
sengend a scorching
senil a senile. **S~ität** f - senility
Senior m -s,-en /-'o:rən/ senior; **S~en**
senior citizens. **S~enheim** nt old people's
home. **S~enteller** m senior citizen's
menu
Senke f -,-n dip, hollow
Senkel m -s,- [shoe-]lace
senken vt lower; bring down (*Fieber,
Preise*); bow (*Kopf*); **sich s~** come down,
fall; (*absinken*) subside; (*abfallen*) slope
down
senkrecht a vertical, adv -ly. **S~e** f -n,-n
perpendicular
Sensation /-'tsjo:n/ f -,-en sensation.
s~ell a sensational, adv -ly
Sense f -,-n scythe
sensibel a sensitive, adv -ly. **S~ilität** f -
sensitivity
sentimental a sentimental. **S~ität** f -
sentimentality

separat a separate, adv -ly
September m -s,- September
Serenade f -,-n serenade
Serie /'ze:rjə/ f -,-n series; (*Briefmarken*)
set; (*Comm*) range. **S~nnummer** f serial
number
seriös a respectable, adv -bly; (*zuverlässig*)
reliable, adv -bly; (*ernst gemeint*) serious
Serpentine f -,-n winding road; (*Kehre*)
hairpin bend
Serum nt -s,Sera serum
Service¹ /zɛr'vi:s/ nt -[s],- /-'vi:s[əs], -'vi:-
sə/ service, set
Service² /'zø:gvis/ m & nt -s /-vis[əs]/
(*Comm, Tennis*) service
servier|en vt/i (haben) serve. **S~erin** f
-,-nen waitress. **S~wagen** m trolley
Serviette f -,-n napkin, serviette
Servus int (Aust) cheerio; (*Begrüßung*)
hallo
Sessel m -s,- armchair. **S~bahn** f, **S~lift**
m chair-lift
sesshaft (seßhaft) a settled; **s~ werden**
settle down
Set /zɛt/ nt & m -[s],-s set; (*Deckchen*) place-
mat
setz|en vt put; (*abstellen*) set down; (*hin-*)
sit down (*Kind*); move (*Spielstein*);
(*pflanzen*) plant; (*schreiben, wetten*) put;
sich s~en sit down; (*sinken*) settle □ vi
(*sein*) leap □ vi (haben) **s~en auf** (+ acc)
back. **S~ling** m -s,-e seedling
Seuche f -,-n epidemic
seufz|en vt/i (haben) sigh. **S~er** m -s,- sigh
Sex /zɛks/ m -[es] sex. **s~istisch** a sexist
Sexu|alität f - sexuality. **s~ell** a sexual,
adv -ly
sexy /'zɛksi/ inv a sexy
sezieren vt dissect
Shampoo /ʃam'pu:/, **Shampoon** /ʃam'po:
n/ nt -s shampoo
siamesisch a Siamese
sich refl pron oneself; (*mit er/sie/es*) himself/herself/itself; (*mit sie pl*) themselves;
(*mit Sie*) yourself; (*pl*) yourselves; (*einander*) each other; **s~ kennen** know
oneself/(*einander*) each other; **s~
waschen** have a wash; **s~** (dat) **die
Zähne putzen/die Haare kämmen** clean
one's teeth/comb one's hair; **s~** (dat) **das
Bein brechen** break a leg; **s~ wundern/schämen** be surprised/ashamed;
s~ gut lesen/verkaufen read/sell well;
von s~ aus of one's own accord
Sichel f -,-n sickle
sicher a safe; (*gesichert*) secure; (*gewiss*)
certain; (*zuverlässig*) reliable; sure (*Urteil, Geschmack*); steady (*Hand*);
(*selbstbewusst*) self-confident; **sich** (dat)

etw (*gen*) **s~ sein** be sure of sth; **bist du s~?** are you sure? □ *adv* safely; securely; certainly; reliably; self-confidently; (*wahrscheinlich*) most probably; **er kommt s~** he is sure to come; **s~!** certainly! **s~gehen†** *vi sep* (*sein*) (*fig*) be sure

Sicherheit *f* - safety; (*Pol, Psych, Comm*) security; (*Gewissheit*) certainty; (*Zuverlässigkeit*) reliability; (*des Urteils, Geschmacks*) surety; (*Selbstbewusstsein*) self-confidence. **S~gurt** *m* safety-belt; (*Auto*) seat-belt. **s~shalber** *adv* to be on the safe side. **S~snadel** *f* safety-pin

sicherlich *adv* certainly; (*wahrscheinlich*) most probably

sicher|n *vt* secure; (*garantieren*) safeguard; (*schützen*) protect; put the safety-catch on (*Pistole*); **sich** (*dat*) **etw s~n** secure sth. **s~stellen** *vt sep* safeguard; (*beschlagnahmen*) seize. **S~ung** *f* -,-en safeguard, protection; (*Gewehr-*) safety-catch; (*Electr*) fuse

Sicht *f* - view; (*S~weite*) visibility; **in S~ kommen** come into view; **auf lange S~** in the long term. **s~bar** *a* visible, *adv* -bly. **s~en** *vt* sight; (*durchsehen*) sift through. **s~lich** *a* obvious, *adv* -ly. **S~vermerk** *m* visa. **S~weite** *f* visibility; **in/außer S~weite** within/out of sight

sickern *vi* (*sein*) seep

sie *pron* (*nom*) (*sg*) she; (*Ding, Tier*) it; (*pl*) they; (*acc*) (*sg*) her; (*Ding, Tier*) it; (*pl*) them

Sie *pron* you; **gehen/warten Sie!** go/wait!

Sieb *nt* -[e]s,-e sieve; (*Tee-*) strainer. **s~en¹** *vt* sieve, sift

sieben² *inv a*, **S~** *f* -,-en seven. **S~sachen** *fpl* (*fam*) belongings. **s~te(r,s)** *a* seventh

sieb|te(r,s) *a* seventh. **s~zehn** *inv a* seventeen. **s~zehnte(r,s)** *a* seventeenth. **s~zig** *inv a* seventy. **s~zigste(r,s)** *a* seventieth

siede|n† *vt/i* (*haben*) boil; **s~nd heiß** boiling hot. **S~punkt** *m* boiling point

Siedl|er *m* -s,- settler. **S~ung** *f* -,-en [housing] estate; (*Niederlassung*) settlement

Sieg *m* -[e]s,-e victory

Siegel *nt* -s,- seal. **S~ring** *m* signet-ring

sieg|en *vi* (*haben*) win. **S~er(in)** *m* -s,- (*f* -,-nen) winner. **s~reich** *a* victorious

siezen *vt* jdn s~ call s.o. 'Sie'

Signal *nt* -s,- signal. **s~isieren** *vt* signal

signieren *vt* sign

Silbe *f* -,-n syllable. **S~ntrennung** *f* word-division

Silber *nt* -s silver. **S~hochzeit** *f* silver wedding. **s~n** *a* silver. **S~papier** *nt* silver paper

Silhouette /zɪ'lu̯ɛtə/ *f* -,-n silhouette

Silizium *nt* -s silicon

Silo *m & nt* -s,-s silo

Silvester *nt* -s New Year's Eve

simpel *a* simple, *adv* -ply; (*einfältig*) simple-minded

Simplex *nt* -,-e simplex

Sims *m & nt* -es,-e ledge; (*Kamin-*) mantelpiece

Simul|ant *m* -en,-en malingerer. **s~ieren** *vt* feign; (*Techn*) simulate □ *vi* (*haben*) pretend; (*sich krank stellen*) malinger

simultan *a* simultaneous, *adv* -ly

sind *s.* **sein¹**; **wir/sie s~** we/they are

Sinfonie *f* -,-n symphony

singen† *vt/i* (*haben*) sing

Singular *m* -s,-e singular

Singvogel *m* songbird

sinken† *vi* (*sein*) sink; (*nieder-*) drop; (*niedriger werden*) go down, fall; **den Mut s~ lassen** lose courage

Sinn *m* -[e]s,-e sense; (*Denken*) mind; (*Zweck*) point; **im S~ haben** have in mind; **in gewissem S~e** in a sense; **es hat keinen S~** it is pointless; **nicht bei S~en sein** be out of one's mind. **S~bild** *nt* symbol. **s~en†** *vi* (*haben*) think; **auf Rache s~en** plot one's revenge

sinnlich *a* sensory; (*sexuell*) sensual; (*Genüsse*) sensuous. **S~keit** *f* - sensuality; sensuousness

sinn|los *a* senseless, *adv* -ly; (*zwecklos*) pointless, *adv* -ly. **s~voll** *a* meaningful; (*vernünftig*) sensible, *adv* -bly

Sintflut *f* flood

Siphon /'zi:fõ/ *m* -s,-s siphon

Sipp|e *f* -,-n clan. **S~schaft** *f* - clan; (*Pack*) crowd

Sirene *f* -,-n siren

Sirup *m* -s,-e syrup; (*schwarzer*) treacle

Sitte *f* -,-n custom; **S~n** manners. **s~nlos** *a* immoral

sittlich *a* moral, *adv* -ly. **S~keit** *f* - morality. **S~keitsverbrecher** *m* sex offender

sittsam *a* well-behaved; (*züchtig*) demure, *adv* -ly

Situ|ation /-'tsi̯o:n/ *f* -,-en situation. **s~iert** *a* gut/schlecht **s~iert** well/badly off

Sitz *m* -es,-e seat; (*Passform*) fit

sitzen† *vi* (*haben*) sit; (*sich befinden*) be; (*passen*) fit; (*fam: treffen*) hit home; **[im Gefängnis] s~** (*fam*) be in jail; **s~ bleiben** remain seated; (*fam*) (*Sch*) stay or be kept down; (*nicht heiraten*) be left on the shelf; **s~ bleiben auf** (+ *dat*) be left with; **jdn s~ lassen** let s.o. sit down; (*fam*) (*Sch*) keep s.o. down; (*nicht heiraten*) jilt s.o.; (*im Stich lassen*) leave s.o. in the lurch. **s~bleiben†** *vi sep* (*sein*) (NEW) **s~ bleiben**, *s.* sitzen. **s~d** *a* seated; ⟨*Tätigkeit*⟩ sedentary. **s~lassen†** *vt sep* (NEW) **s~ lassen,** *s.* sitzen

Sitz|gelegenheit *f* seat. **S~platz** *m* seat. **S~ung** *f* -,-en session

Sizilien /-jən/ *nt* -s Sicily

Skala *f* -,-len scale; ⟨*Reihe*⟩ range

Skalpell *nt* -s,-e scalpel

skalpieren *vt* scalp

Skandal *m* -s,-e scandal. **s~ös** *a* scandalous

skandieren *vt* scan ⟨*Verse*⟩; chant ⟨*Parolen*⟩

Skandinav|ien /-jən/ *nt* -s Scandinavia. **s~isch** *a* Scandinavian

Skat *m* -s skat

Skelett *nt* -[e]s,-e skeleton

Skep|sis *f* - scepticism. **s~tisch** *a* sceptical, *adv* -ly; ⟨*misstrauisch*⟩ doubtful, *adv* -ly

Ski /ʃiː/ *m* -s,-er ski; **Ski fahren** *od* **laufen** ski. **S~fahrer(in), S~läufer(in)** *m(f)* -s,- (*f* -,-nen) skier. **S~sport** *m* skiing

Skizze *f* -,-n sketch. **s~nhaft** *a* sketchy, *adv* -ily. **s~ieren** *vt* sketch

Sklav|e *m* -n,-n slave. **s~erei** *f* - slavery. **S~in** *f* -,-nen slave. **s~isch** *a* slavish, *adv* -ly

Skorpion *m* -s,-e scorpion; ⟨*Astr*⟩ Scorpio

Skrupel *m* -s,- scruple. **s~los** *a* unscrupulous

Skulptur *f* -,-en sculpture

skurril *a* absurd, *adv* -ly

Slalom *m* -s,-s slalom

Slang /slɛŋ/ *m* -s slang

Slaw|e *m* -n,-n, **S~in** *f* -,-nen Slav. **s~isch** *a* Slav; ⟨*Lang*⟩ Slavonic

Slip *m* -s,-s briefs *pl*

Smaragd *m* -[e]s,-e emerald

Smoking *m* -s,-s dinner jacket, (*Amer*) tuxedo

Snob *m* -s,-s snob. **S~ismus** *m* - snobbery. **s~istisch** *a* snobbish

so *adv* so; (*so sehr*) so much; (*auf diese Weise*) like this/that; (*solch*) such; (*fam: sowieso*) anyway; (*fam: umsonst*) free; (*fam: ungefähr*) about; **nicht so schnell/viel** not so fast/much; **so gut/bald wie** as good/soon as; **so ein Mann** a man like that; **so ein Zufall!** what a coincidence! **so nicht** not like that; **mir ist so, als ob** I feel as if; **so oder so** in any case; **eine Stunde oder so** an hour or so; **so um zehn Mark** (*fam*) about ten marks; **[es ist] gut so** that's fine; **so, das ist geschafft** there, that's done; **so?** really? **so kommt doch!** come on then! □ *conj* (*also*) so; (*dann*) then; **so gern ich auch käme** as much as I would like to come; **so dass (daß)** = **sodass**

sobald *conj* as soon as

Söckchen *nt* -s,- [ankle] sock

Socke *f* -,-n sock

Sockel *m* -s,- plinth, pedestal

Socken *m* -s,- sock

Soda *nt* -s soda

sodass *conj* so that

Sodawasser *nt* soda water

Sodbrennen *nt* -s heartburn

soeben *adv* just [now]

Sofa *nt* -s,-s settee, sofa

sofern *adv* provided [that]

sofort *adv* at once, immediately; (*auf der Stelle*) instantly. **s~ig** *a* immediate

Software /ˈzɔftvɛːɐ̯/ *f* - software

sogar *adv* even

sogenannt *a* so-called

sogleich *adv* at once

Sohle *f* -,-n sole; (*Tal-*) bottom

Sohn *m* -[e]s,¨e son

Sojabohne *f* soya bean

solange *conj* as long as

solch *inv pron* such; **s~ ein(e)** such a; **s~ einer/eine/eins** one/(*Person*) someone like that. **s~e(r,s)** *pron* such; **ein s~er Mann/eine s~e Frau** a man/woman like that; **ich habe s~e Angst** I am so afraid □ (*substantivisch*) **ein s~er/eine s~e/ ein s~es** one/(*Person*) someone like that; **s~e** (*pl*) those; (*Leute*) people like that

Sold *m* -[e]s (*Mil*) pay

Soldat *m* -en,-en soldier

Söldner *m* -s,- mercenary

solidarisch *a* **s~e Handlung** act of solidarity; **sich s~ erklären** declare one's solidarity

Solidarität *f* - solidarity

solide *a* solid, *adv* -ly; (*haltbar*) sturdy, *adv* -ily; (*sicher*) sound, *adv* -ly; (*anständig*) respectable, *adv* -bly

Solist(in) *m* -en,-en (*f* -,-nen) soloist

Soll *nt* -s (*Comm*) debit; (*Produktions-*) quota

sollen† *v aux* **er soll warten** he is to wait; (*möge*) let him wait; **was soll ich machen?** what shall I do? **du sollst nicht lügen** you shouldn't tell lies; **du sollst nicht töten** (*liter*) thou shalt not kill; **ihr sollt jetzt still sein!** will you be quiet now! **du solltest dich schämen** you ought to *or* should be ashamed of yourself; **es hat nicht sein s~** it was not to be; **ich hätte es nicht tun s~** I ought not to *or* should not have done it; **er soll sehr nett/ reich sein** he is supposed to be very nice/rich; **sollte es regnen, so . . .** if it should rain then . . .; **das soll man nicht [tun]** you're not supposed to [do that]; **soll**

ich [mal versuchen]? shall I [try]? **soll er doch!** let him! **was soll's!** so what!

Solo *nt* -s,-los & -li solo. **s~** *adv* solo

somịt *adv* therefore, so

Sommer *m* -s,- summer. **S~ferien** *pl* summer holidays. **s~lich** *a* summery; *(Sommer-)* summer ... □ *adv* **s~lich warm** as warm as summer. **S~schlussverkauf (S~schlußverkauf)** *m* summer sale. **S~sprossen** *fpl* freckles. **s~sprossig** *a* freckled

Sonate *f* -,-n sonata

Sonde *f* -,-n probe

Sonder|angebot *nt* special offer. **s~bar** *a* odd, *adv* -ly. **S~fahrt** *f* special excursion. **S~fall** *m* special case. **s~gleichen** *adv* **eine Gemeinheit/Grausamkeit s~gleichen** unparalleled meanness/cruelty. **s~lich** *a* particular, *adv* -ly; *(sonderbar)* odd, *adv* -ly. **S~ling** *m* -s,-e crank. **S~marke** *f* special stamp

sondern *conj* but; **nicht nur ... s~ auch** not only ... but also

Sonder|preis *m* special price. **S~schule** *f* special school. **S~zug** *m* special train

sondieren *ut* sound out

Sonett *nt* -[e]s,-e sonnet

Sonnabend *m* -s,-e Saturday. **s~s** *adv* on Saturdays

Sonne *f* -,-n sun. **s~n (sich)** *vr* sun oneself; *(fig)* bask *(in + dat in)*

Sonnen|aufgang *m* sunrise. **s~baden** *vi (haben)* sunbathe. **S~bank** *f* sun-bed. **S~blume** *f* sunflower. **S~brand** *m* sunburn. **S~brille** *f* sun-glasses *pl*. **S~energie** *f* solar energy. **S~finsternis** *f* solar eclipse. **S~milch** *f* sun-tan lotion. **S~öl** *nt* sun-tan oil. **S~schein** *m* sunshine. **S~schirm** *m* sunshade. **S~stich** *m* sunstroke. **S~uhr** *f* sundial. **S~untergang** *m* sunset. **S~wende** *f* solstice

sonnig *a* sunny

Sonntag *m* -s,-e Sunday. **s~s** *adv* on Sundays

sonst *adv* *(gewöhnlich)* usually; *(im Übrigen)* apart from that; *(andernfalls)* otherwise, or [else]; **wer/was/wie/wo s~?** who/what/how/where else? **s~ niemand/nichts** no one/nothing else; **s~ noch jemand/etwas?** anyone/anything else? **s~ noch Fragen?** any more questions? **s~** jemand *od* **wer** someone/*(fragend, verneint)* anyone else; *(irgendjemand)* [just] anyone; **s~ wie** some/*(fragend, verneint)* any other way; **s~ wo** somewhere/*(fragend, verneint)* anywhere else; *(irgendwo)* [just] anywhere. **s~ig** *a* other. **s~jemand** *pron* (NEW) **s~ jemand**, *s*. **sonst. s~wer** *pron* (NEW) **s~ wer**, *s*. **sonst. s~wie**

adv (NEW) **s~ wie**, *s*. **sonst. s~wo** *adv* (NEW) **s~ wo**, *s*. **sonst**

sooft *conj* whenever

Sopran *m* -s,-e soprano

Sorge *f* -,-n worry **(um** about); *(Fürsorge)* care; **in S~ sein** be worried; **sich** *(dat)* **S~n machen** worry; **keine S~!** don't worry! **s~n** *vi (haben)* **s~n für** look after, care for; *(vorsorgen)* provide for; **(sich kümmern)** see to; **dafür s~n, dass** see [to it] *or* make sure that □ *vr* **sich s~n** worry. **s~nfrei** *a* carefree. **s~nvoll** *a* worried, *adv* -ly. **S~recht** *nt* *(Jur)* custody

Sorg|falt *f* - care. **s~fältig** *a* careful, *adv* -ly. **s~los** *a* careless, *adv* -ly; *(unbekümmert)* carefree. **s~sam** *a* careful, *adv* -ly

Sorte *f* -,-n kind, sort; *(Comm)* brand

sort|ieren *vt* sort [out]; *(Comm)* grade. **S~iment** *nt* -[e]s,-e range

sosehr *conj* however much

Soße *f* -,-n sauce; *(Braten-)* gravy; *(Salat-)* dressing

Souffl|eur /zu'flø:ɐ/ *m* -s,-e, **S~euse** /-ø:zə/ *f* -,-n prompter. **s~ieren** *vi (haben)* prompt

Souvenir /zuvə'ni:ɐ/ *nt* -s,-s souvenir

souverän /zuvə'rɛ:n/ *a* sovereign; *(fig: überlegen)* expert, *adv* -ly. **S~ität** *f* - sovereignty

soviel *conj* however much; **s~ ich weiß** as far as I know □ *adv* (NEW) **so viel**, *s*. **viel**

soweit *conj* as far as; *(insoweit)* [in] so far as □ *adv* (NEW) **so weit**, *s*. **weit**

sowenig *conj* however little □ *adv* (NEW) **so wenig**, *s*. **wenig**

sowie *conj* as well as; *(sobald)* as soon as

sowieso *adv* anyway, in any case

sowjet|isch *a* Soviet. **S~union** *f* - Soviet Union

sowohl *adv* **s~ ... als** *od* **wie auch ...... as** well as ...; **s~ er als auch seine Frau** both he and his wife

sozial *a* social, *adv* -ly; *(Einstellung, Beruf)* caring. **S~arbeit** *f* social work. **S~arbeiter(in)** *m(f)* social worker. **S~demokrat** *m* social democrat. **S~hilfe** *f* social security

Sozialis|mus *m* - socialism. **S~t** *m* -en, -en socialist. **s~tisch** *a* socialist

Sozial|versicherung *f* National Insurance. **S~wohnung** *f* ≈ council flat

Soziol|oge *m* -n,-n sociologist. **S~ogie** *f* - sociology

Sozius *m* -,-se *(Comm)* partner; *(Beifahrersitz)* pillion

sozusagen *adv* so to speak

Spachtel *m* -s,- & *f* -,-n spatula

Spagat *m* -[e]s,-e *(Aust)* string; **S~ machen** do the splits *pl*

Spaghetti, **Spagetti** pl spaghetti sg

spähen vi (haben) peer

Spalier nt -s,-e trellis; **S~ stehen** line the route

Spalt m -[e]s,-e crack; (im Vorhang) chink

Spalt|e f -,-n crack, crevice; (Gletscher-) crevasse; (Druck-) column; (Orangen-) segment. **s~en†** vt split; **sich s~en** split. **S~ung** f -,-en splitting; (Kluft) split; (Phys) fission

Span m -[e]s,-̈e [wood] chip; (Hobel-) shaving

Spange f -,-n clasp; (Haar-) slide; (Zahn-) brace; (Arm-) bangle

Span|ien /-jən/ nt -s Spain. **S~ier** m -s,-, **S~ierin** f -,-nen Spaniard. **s~isch** a Spanish. **S~isch** nt -[s] (Lang) Spanish

Spann m -[e]s instep

Spanne f -,-n span; (Zeit-) space; (Comm) margin

spann|en vt stretch; put up (Leine); (straffen) tighten; (an-) harness (an + acc to); **den Hahn s~en** cock the gun; **sich s~en** tighten □ vi (haben) be too tight. **s~end** a exciting. **S~er** m -s,- (fam) Peeping Tom. **S~ung** f -,-en tension; (Erwartung) suspense; (Electr) voltage

Spar|buch nt savings book. **S~büchse** f money-box. **s~en** vt/i (haben) save; (sparsam sein) economize (**mit/an** + dat on); **sich** (dat) **die Mühe s~en** save oneself the trouble. **S~er** m -s,- saver

Spargel m -s,- asparagus

Spar|kasse f savings bank. **S~konto** nt deposit account

spärlich a sparse, adv -ly; (dürftig) meagre; (knapp) scanty, adv -ily

Sparren m -s,- rafter

sparsam a economical, adv -ly; (Person) thrifty. **S~keit** f - economy; thrift

Sparschwein nt piggy bank

spartanisch a Spartan

Sparte f -,-n branch; (Zeitungs-) section; (Rubrik) column

Spaß m -es,-̈e fun; (Scherz) joke; **im/aus/zum S~** for fun; **S~ machen** be fun; (Person:) be joking; **es macht mir keinen S~** I don't enjoy it; **viel S~!** have a good time! **s~en** vi (haben) joke. **s~ig** a amusing, funny. **S~vogel** m joker

Spast|iker m -s,- spastic. **s~isch** a spastic

spät a & adv late; **wie s~ ist es?** what time is it? **zu s~** too late; **zu s~ kommen** be late. **s~abends** adv late at night

Spatel m -s,- & f -,-n spatula

Spaten m -s,- spade

später a later; (zukünftig) future □ adv later

spätestens adv at the latest

Spatz m -en,-en sparrow

Spätzle pl (Culin) noodles

spazieren vi (sein) stroll; **s~ gehen** go for a walk. **s~gehen†** vi sep (sein) (NEW) **s~ gehen**, s. **spazieren**

Spazier|gang m walk; **einen S~gang machen** go for a walk. **S~gänger(in)** m -s,- (f -,-nen) walker. **S~stock** m walking-stick

Specht m -[e]s,-e woodpecker

Speck m -s bacon; (fam: Fettpolster) fat. **s~ig** a greasy

Spedi|teur /ʃpediˈtøːɐ̯/ m -s,-e haulage/(für Umzüge) removals contractor. **S~tion** /-ˈtsi̯oːn/ f -,-en carriage, haulage; (Firma) haulage/(für Umzüge) removals firm

Speer m -[e]s,-e spear; (Sport) javelin

Speiche f -,-n spoke

Speichel m -s saliva

Speicher m -s,- warehouse; (dial: Dachboden) attic; (Computer) memory. **s~n** vt store

speien† vt spit; (erbrechen) vomit

Speise f -,-n food; (Gericht) dish; (Pudding) blancmange. **S~eis** nt ice-cream. **S~kammer** f larder. **S~karte** f menu. **s~n** vi (haben) eat; **zu Abend s~n** have dinner □ vt feed. **S~röhre** f oesophagus. **S~saal** m dining-room. **S~wagen** m dining-car

Spektakel m -s (fam) noise

spektakulär a spectacular

Spektrum nt -s,-tra spectrum

Spekul|ant m -en,-en speculator. **S~ation** /-ˈtsi̯oːn/ f -,-en speculation. **s~ieren** vi (haben) speculate; **s~ieren auf** (+ acc) (fam) hope to get

Spelze f -,-n husk

spendabel a generous

Spende f -,-n donation. **s~n** vt donate; give (Blut, Schatten); **Beifall s~n** applaud. **S~r** m -s,- donor; (Behälter) dispenser

spendieren vt pay for; **jdm etw/ein Bier s~** treat s.o. to sth/stand s.o. a beer

Spengler m -s,- (SGer) plumber

Sperling m -s,-e sparrow

Sperre f -,-n barrier; (Verbot) ban; (Comm) embargo. **s~n** vt close; (ver-) block; (verbieten) ban; cut off (Strom, Telefon); stop (Scheck, Kredit); **s~n in** (+ acc) put in (Gefängnis, Käfig); **sich s~n** balk (gegen at); **gesperrt gedruckt** (Typ) spaced

Sperr|holz nt plywood. **s~ig** a bulky. **S~müll** m bulky refuse. **S~stunde** f closing time

Spesen pl expenses

spezial|isieren (sich) vr specialize (**auf** + acc in). **S~ist** m -en,-en specialist. **S~i-tät** f -,-en speciality

speziell a special, adv -ly

spezifisch a specific, adv -ally

Sphäre /'sfɛːrə/ f -,-n sphere

spicken vt (Culin) lard; **gespickt mit** (fig) full of □ vi (haben) (fam) crib (**bei** from)

Spiegel m -s,- mirror; (Wasser-, Alkohol-) level. **S~ei** nt fried egg. **s~n** vt reflect; **sich s~n** be reflected □ vi (haben) reflect [the light]; (glänzen) gleam. **S~ung** f -,-en reflection

Spiel nt -[e]s,-e game; (Spielen) playing; (Glücks-) gambling; (Schau-) play; (Satz) set; **ein S~ Karten** a pack/(Amer) deck of cards; **auf dem S~ stehen** be at stake; **aufs S~ setzen** risk. **S~art** f variety. **S~automat** m fruit machine. **S~bank** f casino. **S~dose** f musical box. **s~en** vt/i (haben) play; (im Glücksspiel) gamble; (vortäuschen) act; (Roman:) be set (**in** + dat in); **s~en mit** (fig) toy with. **s~end** a (mühelos) effortless, adv -ly

Spieler|(in) m -s,- (f -,-nen) player; (Glücks-) gambler. **S~ei** f -,-en amusement; (Kleinigkeit) trifle

Spiel|feld nt field, pitch. **S~gefährte** m, **S~gefährtin** f playmate. **S~karte** f playing-card. **S~marke** f chip. **S~plan** m programme. **S~platz** m playground. **S~raum** m (fig) scope; (Techn) clearance. **S~regeln** fpl rules [of the game]. **S~sachen** fpl toys. **S~verderber** m -s,- spoilsport. **S~waren** fpl toys. **S~waren-geschäft** nt toyshop. **S~zeug** nt toy; (S~sachen) toys pl

Spieß m -es,-e spear; (Brat-) spit; (für Schaschlik) skewer; (Fleisch-) kebab; **den S~ umkehren** turn the tables on s.o. **S~bürger** m [petit] bourgeois. **s~bür-gerlich** a bourgeois. **s~en** vt etw auf etw (acc) **s~en** spear sth with sth. **S~er** m -s,- [petit] bourgeois. **s~ig** a bourgeois. **S~ruten** fpl **S~ruten laufen** run the gauntlet

Spike[s]reifen /'ʃpaik[s]-/ m studded tyre

Spinat m -s spinach

Spind m & nt -[e]s,-e locker

Spindel f -,-n spindle

Spinne f -,-n spider

spinn|en† vt/i (haben) spin; **er spinnt** (fam) he's crazy. **S~ennetz** nt spider's web. **S~[en]gewebe** nt, **S~webe** f -,-n cobweb

Spion m -s,-e spy

Spionage /ʃpio'naːʒə/ f - espionage, spy-ing; **S~ treiben** spy. **S~abwehr** f coun-ter-espionage

spionieren vi (haben) spy

Spionin f -,-nen [woman] spy

Spiral|e f -,-n spiral. **s~ig** a spiral

Spiritis|mus m - spiritualism. **s~tisch** a spiritualist

Spirituosen pl spirits

Spiritus m - alcohol; (Brenn-) methylated spirits pl. **S~kocher** m spirit stove

Spital nt -s,⸚er (Aust) hospital

spitz a pointed; (scharf) sharp; (schrill) shrill; (Winkel) acute; **s~e Bemerkung** dig. **S~bube** m scoundrel; (Schlingel) ras-cal. **s~bübisch** a mischievous, adv -ly

Spitze f -,-n point; (oberer Teil) top; (vor-derer Teil) front; (Pfeil-, Finger-, Nasen-) tip; (Schuh-, Strumpf-) toe; (Zigarren-, Zigaretten-) holder; (Höchstleistung) max-imum; (Tex) lace; (fam: Anspielung) dig; **an der S~ liegen** be in the lead

Spitzel m -s,- informer

spitzen vt sharpen; purse (Lippen); prick up (Ohren); **sich s~ auf** (+ acc) (fam) look forward to. **S~geschwindigkeit** f top speed

spitz|findig a over-subtle. **S~hacke** f pickaxe. **S~name** m nickname

Spleen /ʃpliːn/ m -s,-e obsession; **einen S~ haben** be crazy. **s~ig** a eccentric

Splitter m -s,- splinter. **s~n** vi (sein) shatter. **s~[faser]nackt** a (fam) stark naked

sponsern vt sponsor

spontan a spontaneous, adv -ly

sporadisch a sporadic, adv -ally

Spore f -,-n (Biol) spore

Sporn m -[e]s, **Sporen** spur; **einem Pferd die Sporen geben** spur a horse

Sport m -[e]s sport; (Hobby) hobby. **S~art** f sport. **S~fest** nt sports day. **S~ler** m -s,- sportsman. **S~lerin** f -,-nen sports-woman. **s~lich** a sports ...; (fair) sport-ing, adv -ly; (flott, schlank) sporty. **S~platz** m sports ground. **S~verein** m sports club. **S~wagen** m sports car; (Kinder-) push-chair, (Amer) stroller

Spott m -[e]s mockery. **s~billig** a & adv dirt cheap

spötteln vi (haben) mock; **s~ über** (+ acc) poke fun at

spotten vi (haben) mock; **s~ über** (+ acc) make fun of; (höhnend) ridicule

spöttisch a mocking, adv -ly

Sprach|e f -,-n language; (Sprechfähig-keit) speech; **zur S~e bringen** bring up. **S~fehler** m speech defect. **S~labor** nt language laboratory. **s~lich** a linguistic, adv -ally. **s~los** a speechless

Spray /ʃpreː/ nt & m -s,-s spray. **S~dose** f aerosol [can]

Sprech|anlage f intercom. **S~chor** m chorus; **im S~chor rufen** chant

sprechen† vi (haben) speak/(sich unterhalten) talk (über + acc/von about/of); **Deutsch/Englisch s~** speak German/English ◻ vt speak; (sagen, aufsagen) say; pronounce (Urteil); **schuldig s~** find guilty; **jdn s~** speak to s.o.; **Herr X ist nicht zu s~** Mr X is not available

Sprecher(in) m -s,- (f -,-nen) speaker; (Radio, TV) announcer; (Wortführer) spokesman, f spokeswoman

Sprechstunde f consulting hours pl; (Med) surgery. **S~nhilfe** f (Med) receptionist

Sprechzimmer nt consulting room

spreizen vt spread

Sprengel m -s,- parish

spreng|en vt blow up; blast (Felsen); (fig) burst; (begießen) water; (mit Sprenger) sprinkle; dampen (Wäsche). **S~er** m -s,- sprinkler. **S~kopf** m warhead. **S~körper** m explosive device. **S~stoff** m explosive

Spreu f - chaff

Sprich|wort nt (pl -wörter) proverb. **s~wörtlich** a proverbial

sprießen† vi (sein) sprout

Springbrunnen m fountain

spring|en† vi (sein) jump; (Schwimmsport) dive; (Ball:) bounce; (spritzen) spurt; (zer-) break; (rissig werden) crack; (SGer: laufen) run. **S~er** m -s,- jumper; (Kunst-) diver; (Schach) knight. **S~reiten** nt show-jumping. **S~seil** nt skipping-rope

Sprint m -s,-s sprint

Sprit m -s (fam) petrol

Spritz|e f -,-n syringe; (Injektion) injection; (Feuer-) hose. **s~en** vt spray; (be-, ver-) splash; (Culin) pipe; (Med) inject ◻ vi (haben) splash; (Fett:) spit ◻ vi (sein) splash; (hervor-) spurt; (fam: laufen) dash. **S~er** m -s,- splash; (Schuss) dash. **s~ig** a lively; (Wein, Komödie) sparkling. **S~tour** f (fam) spin

spröde a brittle; (trocken) dry; (rissig) chapped; (Stimme) harsh; (abweisend) aloof

Spross m -es,-e (Sproß m -sses, -sse) shoot

Sprosse f -,-n rung. **S~nkohl** m (Aust) Brussels sprouts pl

Sprössling (Sprößling) m -s,-e (fam) offspring

Sprotte f -,-n sprat

Spruch m -[e]s,-̈e saying; (Denk-) motto; (Zitat) quotation. **S~band** nt (pl -bänder) banner

Sprudel m -s,- sparkling mineral water. **s~n** vi (haben/sein) bubble

Sprüh|dose f aerosol [can]. **s~en** vt spray ◻ vi (sein) (Funken:) fly; (fig) sparkle. **S~regen** m fine drizzle

Sprung m -[e]s,-̈e jump, leap; (Schwimmsport) dive; (Riss) crack; **auf einen S~** (fam) for a moment. **S~brett** nt springboard. **s~haft** a erratic; (plötzlich) sudden, adv -ly. **S~schanze** f ski-jump. **S~seil** nt skipping-rope

Spucke f - spit. **s~n** vt/i (haben) spit; (sich übergeben) be sick

Spuk m -[e]s,-e [ghostly] apparition. **s~en** vi (haben) (Geist:) walk; **in diesem Haus s~t es** this house is haunted

Spülbecken nt sink

Spule f -,-n spool

Spüle f -,-n sink unit; (Becken) sink

spulen vt spool

spül|en vt rinse; (schwemmen) wash; Geschirr **s~en** wash up ◻ vi (haben) flush [the toilet]. **S~kasten** m cistern. **S~mittel** nt washing-up liquid. **S~tuch** nt dishcloth

Spur f -,-en track; (Fahr-) lane; (Fährte) trail; (Anzeichen) trace; (Hinweis) lead; **keine** od **nicht die S~** (fam) not in the least

spürbar a noticeable, adv -bly

spuren vi (haben) (fam) toe the line

spür|en vt feel; (seelisch) sense. **S~hund** m tracker dog

spurlos adv without trace

spurten vi (sein) put on a spurt; (fam: laufen) sprint

sputen (sich) vr hurry

Staat m -[e]s,-en state; (Land) country; (Putz) finery. **s~lich** a state ... ◻ adv by the state

Staatsangehörig|e(r) m/f national. **S~keit** f - nationality

Staats|anwalt m state prosecutor. **S~beamte(r)** m civil servant. **S~besuch** m state visit. **S~bürger(in)** m(f) national. **S~mann** m (pl -männer) statesman. **S~streich** m coup

Stab m -[e]s,-̈e rod; (Gitter-) bar; (Sport) baton; (Mitarbeiter-) team; (Mil) staff

Stäbchen ntpl chopsticks

Stabhochsprung m pole-vault

stabil a stable; (gesund) robust; (solide) sturdy, adv -ily. **s~isieren** vt stabilize; sich **s~isieren** stabilize. **S~ität** f - stability

Stachel m -s,- spine; (Gift-) sting; (Spitze) spike. **S~beere** f goose-berry. **S~draht**

m barbed wire. **s~ig** *a* prickly. **S~schwein** *nt* porcupine

Stadion *nt* **-s,-ien** stadium

Stadium *nt* **-s,-ien** stage

Stadt *f* **-,-̈e** town; (*Groß-*) city

Städt|chen *nt* **-s,-** small town. **s~isch** *a* urban; (*kommunal*) municipal

Stadt|mauer *f* city wall. **S~mitte** *f* town centre. **S~plan** *m* street map. **S~teil** *m* district. **S~zentrum** *nt* town centre

Staffel *f* **-,-n** team; (*S~lauf*) relay; (*Mil*) squadron

Staffelei *f* **-,-en** easel

Staffel|lauf *m* relay race. **s~n** *vt* stagger; (*abstufen*) grade

Stagn|ation /-'tsjo:n/ *f* **-** stagnation. **s~ieren** *vi* (*haben*) stagnate

Stahl *m* **-s** steel. **S~beton** *m* reinforced concrete

Stall *m* **-[e]s,-̈e** stable; (*Kuh-*) shed; (*Schweine-*) sty; (*Hühner-*) coop; (*Kaninchen-*) hutch

Stamm *m* **-[e]s,-̈e** trunk; (*Sippe*) tribe; (*Kern*) core; (*Wort-*) stem. **S~baum** *m* family tree; (*eines Tieres*) pedigree

stammeln *vt/i* (*haben*) stammer

stammen *vi* (*haben*) come/(*zeitlich*) date (*von/aus* from); **das Zitat stammt von Goethe** the quotation is from Goethe

Stamm|gast *m* regular. **S~halter** *m* son and heir

stämmig *a* sturdy

Stamm|kundschaft *f* regulars *pl.* **S~lokal** *nt* favourite pub. **S~tisch** *m* table reserved for the regulars; (*Treffen*) meeting of the regulars

stampf|en *vi* (*haben*) stamp; (*Maschine:*) pound; **mit den Füßen s~en** stamp one's feet □ *vi* (*sein*) tramp □ *vt* pound; mash (*Kartoffeln*). **S~kartoffeln** *fpl* mashed potatoes

Stand *m* **-[e]s,-̈e** standing position; (*Zustand*) state; (*Spiel-*) score; (*Höhe*) level; (*gesellschaftlich*) class; (*Verkaufs-*) stall; (*Messe-*) stand; (*Taxi-*) rank; **auf den neuesten S~ bringen** up-date; **in S~ halten/setzen = instand halten/setzen,** *s.* **instand; im/außer S~e sein = imstande/außerstande sein,** *s.* **imstande, außerstande; zu S~e bringen/kommen = zustande bringen/kommen,** *s.* **zustande**

Standard *m* **-s,-s** standard. **s~isieren** *vt* standardize

Standarte *f* **-,-n** standard

Standbild *nt* statue

Ständchen *nt* **-s,-** serenade; **jdm ein S~ bringen** serenade s.o.

Ständer *m* **-s,-** stand; (*Geschirr-, Platten-*) rack; (*Kerzen-*) holder

Standes|amt *nt* registry office. **S~beamte(r)** *m* registrar. **S~unterschied** *m* class distinction

stand|haft *a* steadfast, *adv* **-ly. s~halten**† *vi sep* (*haben*) stand firm; **etw** (*dat*) **s~halten** stand up to sth

ständig *a* constant, *adv* **-ly;** (*fest*) permanent, *adv* **-ly**

Stand|licht *nt* sidelights *pl.* **S~ort** *m* position; (*Firmen-*) location; (*Mil*) garrison. **S~pauke** *f* (*fam*) dressing-down. **S~punkt** *m* point of view. **S~spur** *f* hard shoulder. **S~uhr** *f* grandfather clock

Stange *f* **-,-n** bar; (*Holz-*) pole; (*Gardinen-*) rail; (*Hühner-*) perch; (*Zimt-*) stick; **von der S~** (*fam*) off the peg

Stängel *m* **-s,-** stalk, stem

Stangen|bohne *f* runner bean. **S~brot** *nt* French bread

Stanniol *nt* **-s** tin foil. **S~papier** *nt* silver paper

stanzen *vt* stamp; (*aus-*) stamp out; punch (*Loch*)

Stapel *m* **-s,-** stack, pile; **vom S~ laufen** be launched. **S~lauf** *m* launch[ing]. **s~n** *vt* stack or pile up; **sich s~n** pile up

stapfen *vi* (*sein*) tramp, trudge

Star[1] *m* **-[e]s,-e** starling

Star[2] *m* **-[e]s** (*Med*) **[grauer] S~** cataract; **grüner S~** glaucoma

Star[3] *m* **-s,-s** (*Theat, Sport*) star

stark *a* (**stärker, stärkst**) strong; (*Motor*) powerful; (*Verkehr, Regen*) heavy; (*Hitze, Kälte*) severe; (*groß*) big; (*schlimm*) bad; (*dick*) thick; (*korpulent*) stout □ *adv* strongly; heavily; badly; (*sehr*) very much

Stärk|e *f* **-,-n** (*s.* **stark**) strength; power; thickness; stoutness; (*Größe*) size; (*Mais-, Wäsche-*) starch. **S~emehl** *nt* cornflour. **s~en** *vt* strengthen; starch (*Wäsche*); **sich s~en** fortify oneself. **S~ung** *f* **-,-en** strengthening; (*Erfrischung*) refreshment

starr *a* rigid, *adv* **-ly;** (*steif*) stiff, *adv* **-ly;** (*Blick*) fixed; (*unbeugsam*) inflexible, *adv* **-bly**

starren *vi* (*haben*) stare; **vor Schmutz s~** be filthy

starr|köpfig *a* stubborn. **S~sinn** *m* obstinacy. **s~sinnig** *a* obstinate, *adv* **-ly**

Start *m* **-s,-s** start; (*Aviat*) take-off. **S~bahn** *f* runway. **s~en** *vi* (*sein*) start; (*Aviat*) take off; (*aufbrechen*) set off; (*teilnehmen*) compete □ *vt* start; (*fig*) launch

Station /-'tsjo:n/ *f* **-,-en** station; (*Haltestelle*) stop; (*Abschnitt*) stage; (*Med*) ward; **S~ machen** break one's journey; **bei freier S~** all found. **s~är** *adv* as an inpatient. **s~ieren** *vt* station

statisch *a* static

Statist(in) *m* -en,-en (*f* -,-nen) (*Theat*) extra

Statisti|k *f* -,-en statistics *sg*; (*Aufstellung*) statistics *pl*. **s~sch** *a* statistical, *adv* -ly

Stativ *nt* -s,-e (*Phot*) tripod

statt *prep* (+ *gen*) instead of; **an seiner s~** in his place; **an Kindes s~ annehmen** adopt; **s~ dessen** (NEW) **s~dessen □** *conj* **s~ etw zu tun** instead of doing sth. **s~dessen** *adv* instead

Stätte *f* -,-n place

statt|finden† *vi sep* (*haben*) take place. **s~haft** *a* permitted

stattlich *a* imposing; (*beträchtlich*) considerable

Statue /ˈʃtaːtuə/ *f* -,-n statue

Statur *f* - build, stature

Status *m* - status. **S~symbol** *nt* status symbol

Statut *nt* -[e]s,-en statute

Stau *m* -[e]s,-s congestion; (*Auto*) [traffic] jam; (*Rück-*) tailback

Staub *m* -[e]s dust; **S~ wischen** dust; **S~ saugen** vacuum, hoover

Staubecken *nt* reservoir

staub|en *vi* (*haben*) raise dust; **es s~t** it's dusty. **s~ig** *a* dusty. **s~saugen** *vt/i* (*haben*) vacuum, hoover. **S~sauger** *m* vacuum cleaner, Hoover (P). **S~tuch** *nt* duster

Staudamm *m* dam

Staude *f* -,-n shrub

stauen *vt* dam up; **sich s~** accumulate; (*Autos:*) form a tailback

staunen *vi* (*haben*) be amazed *or* astonished. **S~** *nt* -s amazement, astonishment

Stau|see *m* reservoir. **S~ung** *f* -,-en congestion; (*Auto*) [traffic] jam

Steak /ʃteːk, steːk/ *nt* -s,-s steak

stechen† *vt* stick (**in** + *acc* in); (*verletzen*) prick; (*mit Messer*) stab; (*Insekt:*) sting; (*Mücke:*) bite; (*gravieren*) engrave **□** *vi* (*haben*) prick; (*Insekt:*) sting; (*Mücke:*) bite; (*mit Stechuhr*) clock in/out; **in See s~** put to sea. **s~d** *a* stabbing; (*Geruch*) pungent

Stech|ginster *m* gorse. **S~kahn** *m* punt. **S~mücke** *f* mosquito. **S~palme** *f* holly. **S~uhr** *f* time clock

Steck|brief *m* 'wanted' poster. **S~dose** *f* socket. **s~en** *vt* put; (*mit Nadel, Reißzwecke*) pin; (*pflanzen*) plant **□** *vi* (*haben*) be; (*fest-*) be stuck; **s~ bleiben** get stuck; **den Schlüssel s~ lassen** leave the key in the lock; **hinter etw** (*dat*) **s~en** (*fig*) be behind sth

Stecken *m* -s,- (*SGer*) stick

stecken|bleiben† *vi sep* (*sein*) (NEW) **s~ bleiben**, *s.* **stecken**. **s~lassen†** *vt sep* (NEW) **s~ lassen**, *s.* **stecken**. **S~pferd** *nt* hobby-horse

Steck|er *m* -s,- (*Electr*) plug. **S~ling** *m* -s,-e cutting. **S~nadel** *f* pin. **S~rübe** *f* swede

Steg *m* -[e]s,-e foot-bridge; (*Boots-*) landing-stage; (*Brillen-*) bridge. **S~reif** *m* **aus dem S~reif** extempore

stehen† *vi* (*haben*) stand; (*sich befinden*) be; (*still-*) be stationary; (*Maschine, Uhr:*) have stopped; **s~ bleiben** remain standing; (*Gebäude:*) be left standing; (*anhalten*) stop; (*Motor:*) stall; (*Zeit:*) stand still; **s~ lassen** leave [standing]; **sich** (*dat*) **einen Bart s~ lassen** grow a beard; **vor dem Ruin s~** face ruin; **zu jdm/etw s~** (*fig*) stand by s.o./sth; **gut s~** (*Getreide, Aktien:*) be doing well; (*Chancen:*) be good; **jdm [gut] s~** suit s.o.; **sich gut s~** be on good terms; **es steht 3 zu 1** the score is 3–1; **es steht schlecht um ihn** he is in a bad way. **S~** *nt* -s standing; **zum S~ bringen/kommen** bring/come to a standstill. **s~bleiben†** *vi sep* (*sein*) (NEW) **s~ bleiben**, *s.* **stehen**. **s~d** *a* standing; (*sich nicht bewegend*) stationary; (*Gewässer:*) stagnant. **s~lassen†** *vt sep* (NEW) **s~ lassen**, *s.* **stehen**

Steh|lampe *f* standard lamp. **S~leiter** *f* step-ladder

stehlen† *vt/i* (*haben*) steal; **sich s~** steal, creep

Steh|platz *m* standing place. **S~vermögen** *nt* stamina, staying-power

steif *a* stiff, *adv* -ly. **S~heit** *f* - stiffness

Steig|bügel *m* stirrup. **S~eisen** *nt* crampon

steigen† *vi* (*sein*) climb; (*hochgehen*) rise, go up; (*Schulden, Spannung:*) mount; **s~ auf** (+ *acc*) climb on [to] (*Stuhl*); climb (*Berg, Leiter*); get on (*Pferd, Fahrrad*); **s~ in** (+ *acc*) climb into; get in (*Auto*); get on (*Bus, Zug*); **s~ aus** climb out of; get out of (*Bett, Auto*); get off (*Bus, Zug*); **einen Drachen s~ lassen** fly a kite; **s~de Preise** rising prices

steiger|n *vt* increase; **sich s~n** increase; (*sich verbessern*) improve. **S~ung** *f* -,-en increase; improvement; (*Gram*) comparison

Steigung *f* -,-en gradient; (*Hang*) slope

steil *a* steep, *adv* -ly. **S~küste** *f* cliffs *pl*

Stein *m* -[e]s,-e stone; (*Ziegel-*) brick; (*Spiel-*) piece. **s~alt** *a* ancient. **S~bock** *m* ibex; (*Astr*) Capricorn. **S~bruch** *m* quarry. **S~garten** *m* rockery. **S~gut** *nt* earthenware. **s~hart** *a* rock-hard. **s~ig** *a* stony. **s~igen** *vt* stone. **S~kohle** *f* [hard] coal. **s~reich** *a* (*fam*) very rich. **S~schlag** *m* rock fall

Stelle *f* -,-n place; (*Fleck*) spot; (*Abschnitt*) passage; (*Stellung*) job, post; (*Büro*) office; (*Behörde*) authority; **kahle S~** bare patch; **auf der S~** immediately; **an deiner S~** in your place

stellen *vt* put; (*aufrecht*) stand; set (*Wecker, Aufgabe*); ask (*Frage*); make (*Antrag, Forderung, Diagnose*); **zur Verfügung s~** provide; **lauter/leiser s~** turn up/down; **kalt/warm s~** chill/keep hot; **sich s~** [go and] stand; give oneself up (**der Polizei** to the police); **sich tot/schlafend s~** pretend to be dead/asleep; **gut gestellt sein** be well off

Stellen|anzeige *f* job advertisement. **S~vermittlung** *f* employment agency. **s~weise** *adv* in places

Stellung *f* -,-en position; (*Arbeit*) job; **S~nehmen** make a statement (**zu** on). **s~slos** *a* jobless. **S~suche** *f* job-hunting

stellvertret|end *a* deputy ... □ *adv* as a deputy; **s~end für jdn** on s.o.'s behalf. **S~er** *m* deputy

Stellwerk *nt* signal-box

Stelzen *fpl* stilts. **s~** *vi* (*sein*) stalk

stemmen *vt* press; lift (*Gewicht*); **sich s~ gegen** brace oneself against

Stempel *m* -s,- stamp; (*Post-*) post-mark; (*Präge-*) die; (*Feingehalts-*) hallmark. **s~n** *vt* stamp; hallmark (*Silber*); cancel (*Marke*)

Stengel *m* -s,- (NEW) **Stängel**

Steno *f* - (*fam*) shorthand

Steno|gramm *nt* -[e]s,-e shorthand text. **S~graphie**, **S~grafie** *f* - shorthand. **s~graphieren**, **s~grafieren** *vt* take down in shorthand □ *vi* (*haben*) do shorthand. **S~typistin** *f* -,-nen shorthand typist

Steppdecke *f* quilt

Steppe *f* -,-n steppe

Stepptanz (**Steptanz**) *m* tap-dance

sterben† *vi* (*sein*) die (**an** + *dat* of); **im S~ liegen** be dying

sterblich *a* mortal. **S~e(r)** *m/f* mortal. **S~keit** *f* - mortality

stereo *adv* in stereo. **S~anlage** *f* stereo [system]

stereotyp *a* stereotyped

steril *a* sterile. **s~isieren** *vt* sterilize. **S~ität** *f* - sterility

Stern *m* -[e]s,-e star. **S~bild** *nt* constellation. **S~chen** *nt* -s,- asterisk. **S~kunde** *f* astronomy. **S~schnuppe** *f* -,-n shooting star. **S~warte** *f* -,-n observatory

stetig *a* steady, *adv* -ily

stets *adv* always

Steuer[1] *nt* -s,- steering-wheel; (*Naut*) helm; **am S~** at the wheel

Steuer[2] *f* -,-n tax

Steuer|bord *nt* -[e]s starboard [side]. **S~erklärung** *f* tax return. **s~frei** *a* & *adv* tax-free. **S~mann** *m* (*pl* -leute) helmsman; (*beim Rudern*) cox. **s~n** *vt* steer; (*Aviat*) pilot; (*Techn*) control □ *vi* (*haben*) be at the wheel/(*Naut*) helm □ (*sein*) head (**nach** for). **s~pflichtig** *a* taxable. **S~rad** *nt* steering-wheel. **S~ruder** *nt* helm. **S~ung** *f* - steering; (*Techn*) controls *pl*. **S~zahler** *m* -s,- tax-payer

Stewardess /'stju:ɐdɛs/ *f* -,-en (**Stewardeß** *f* -,-ssen) air hostess, stewardess

Stich *m* -[e]s,-e prick; (*Messer-*) stab; (*S~wunde*) stab wound; (*Bienen-*) sting; (*Mücken-*) bite; (*Schmerz*) stabbing pain; (*Näh-*) stitch; (*Kupfer-*) engraving; (*Kartenspiel*) trick; **S~ ins Rötliche** tinge of red; **jdn im S~ lassen** leave s.o. in the lurch; (*Gedächtnis:*) fail s.o. **s~eln** *vi* (*haben*) make snide remarks

Stich|flamme *f* jet of flame. **s~haltig** *a* valid. **S~probe** *f* spot check. **S~wort** *nt* (*pl* -wörter) headword; (*pl* -worte) (*Theat*) cue; **S~worte** notes

stick|en *vt/i* (*haben*) embroider. **S~erei** *f* - embroidery

stickig *a* stuffy

Stickstoff *m* nitrogen

Stiefbruder *m* stepbrother

Stiefel *m* -s,- boot

Stief|kind *nt* stepchild. **S~mutter** *f* stepmother. **S~mütterchen** *nt* -s,- pansy. **S~schwester** *f* stepsister. **S~sohn** *m* stepson. **S~tochter** *f* stepdaughter. **S~vater** *m* stepfather

Stiege *f* -,-n stairs *pl*

Stiel *m* -[e]s,-e handle; (*Blumen-, Gläser-*) stem; (*Blatt-*) stalk

Stier *m* -[e]s,-e bull; (*Astr*) Taurus

stieren *vi* (*haben*) stare

Stier|kampf *m* bullfight

Stift[1] *m* -[e]s,-e pin; (*Nagel*) tack; (*Blei-*) pencil; (*Farb-*) crayon

Stift[2] *nt* -[e]s,-e [endowed] foundation. **s~en** *vt* endow; (*spenden*) donate; create (*Unheil, Verwirrung*); bring about (*Frieden*). **S~er** *m* -s,- founder; (*Spender*) donor. **S~ung** *f* -,-en foundation; (*Spende*) donation

Stigma *nt* -s (*fig*) stigma

Stil *m* -[e]s,-e style; **in großem S~** in style. **s~isiert** *a* stylized. **s~istisch** *a* stylistic, *adv* -ally

still *a* quiet, *adv* -ly; (*reglos; ohne Kohlensäure*) still; (*heimlich*) secret, *adv* -ly; **der**

S∼e Ozean the Pacific; im S∼en (s∼en) secretly; (bei sich) inwardly. S∼e f - quiet; (Schweigen) silence

Stilleben nt (NEW) Stillleben

stillegen vt sep (NEW) stilllegen

stillen vt satisfy; quench (Durst); stop (Schmerzen, Blutung); breast-feed (Kind)

still|halten† vi sep (haben) keep still. S∼leben nt still life. s∼legen vt sep close down. S∼legung f -,-en closure

Stillschweigen nt silence. s∼d a silent, adv -ly; (fig) tacit, adv -ly

still|sitzen† vi sep (haben) sit still. S∼stand m standstill; zum S∼stand bringen/kommen stop. s∼stehen† vi sep (haben) stand still; (anhalten) stop; (Verkehr:) be at a standstill

Stil|möbel pl reproduction furniture sg. s∼voll a stylish, adv -ly

Stimm|bänder ntpl vocal cords. s∼berechtigt a entitled to vote. S∼bruch m er ist im S∼bruch his voice is breaking

Stimme f -,-n voice; (Wahl-) vote

stimmen vi (haben) be right; (wählen) vote; stimmt das? is that right/(wahr) true? □ vt tune; jdn traurig/fröhlich s∼ make s.o. feel sad/happy

Stimm|enthaltung f abstention. S∼recht nt right to vote

Stimmung f -,-en mood; (Atmosphäre) atmosphere. s∼svoll a full of atmosphere

Stimmzettel m ballot-paper

stimulieren vt stimulate

stink|en† vi (haben) smell/(stark) stink (nach of). S∼tier nt skunk

Stipendium nt -s,-ien scholarship; (Beihilfe) grant

Stirn f -,-en forehead; die S∼ bieten (+ dat) (fig) defy. S∼runzeln nt -s frown

stöbern vi (haben) rummage

stochern vi (haben) s∼ in (+ dat) poke (Feuer); pick at (Essen); pick (Zähne)

Stock¹ m -[e]s,-e stick; (Ski-) pole; (Bienen-) hive; (Rosen-) bush; (Reb-) vine

Stock² m -[e]s,- storey, floor. S∼bett nt bunk-beds pl. s∼dunkel a (fam) pitch-dark

stock|en vi (haben) stop; (Verkehr:) come to a standstill; (Person:) falter. s∼end a hesitant, adv -ly. s∼taub a (fam) stone-deaf. S∼ung f -,-en hold-up

Stockwerk nt storey, floor

Stoff m -[e]s,-e substance; (Tex) fabric, material; (Thema) subject [matter]; (Gesprächs-) topic. S∼tier nt soft toy. S∼wechsel m metabolism

stöhnen vi (haben) groan, moan. S∼ nt -s groan, moan

stoisch a stoic, adv -ally

Stola f -,-len stole

Stollen m -s,- gallery; (Kuchen) stollen

stolpern vi (sein) stumble; s∼ über (+ acc) trip over

stolz a proud (auf + acc of), adv -ly. S∼ m -es pride

stolzieren vi (sein) strut

stopfen vt stuff; (stecken) put; (ausbessern) darn □ vi (haben) be constipating; (fam: essen) guzzle

Stopp m -s,-s stop. s∼ int stop!

stoppel|ig a stubbly. S∼n fpl stubble sg

stopp|en vt stop; (Sport) time □ vi (haben) stop. S∼schild nt stop sign. S∼uhr f stop-watch

Stöpsel m -s,- plug; (Flaschen-) stopper

Storch m -[e]s,-e stork

Store /ʃtoːɐ/ m -s,-s net curtain

stören vt disturb; disrupt (Rede, Sitzung); jam (Sender); (missfallen) bother; stört es Sie, wenn ich rauche? do you mind if I smoke? □ vi (haben) be a nuisance; entschuldigen Sie, dass ich störe I'm sorry to bother you

stornieren vt cancel

störrisch a stubborn, adv -ly

Störung f -,-en (s. stören) disturbance; disruption; (Med) trouble; (Radio) interference; technische S∼ technical fault

Stoß m -es,-e push, knock; (mit Ellbogen) dig; (Hörner-) butt; (mit Waffe) thrust; (Schwimm-) stroke; (Ruck) jolt; (Erd-) shock; (Stapel) stack, pile. S∼dämpfer m -s,- shock absorber

stoßen† vt push, knock; (mit Füßen) kick; (mit Kopf, Hörnern) butt; (an-) poke, nudge; (treiben) thrust; sich s∼ knock oneself; sich (dat) den Kopf s∼ hit one's head □ vi (haben) push; s∼ an (+ acc) knock against; (angrenzen) adjoin □ vi (sein) s∼ gegen knock against; bump into (Tür); s∼ auf (+ acc) bump into; (entdecken) come across; strike (Öl); (fig) meet with (Ablehnung)

Stoß|stange f bumper. S∼verkehr m rush-hour traffic. S∼zahn m tusk. S∼zeit f rush-hour

stottern vt/i (haben) stutter, stammer

Str. abbr (Straße) St

Straf|anstalt f prison. S∼arbeit f (Sch) imposition. s∼bar a punishable; sich s∼bar machen commit an offence

Strafe f -,-n punishment; (Jur & fig) penalty; (Geld-) fine; (Freiheits-) sentence. s∼n vt punish

straff a tight, taut. s∼en vt tighten; sich s∼en tighten

Strafgesetz nt criminal law

sträf|lich *a* criminal, *adv* -ly. **S∼ling** *m* -s,-e prisoner

Straf|mandat *nt* (*Auto*) [parking/speeding] ticket. **S∼porto** *nt* excess postage. **S∼predigt** *f* (*fam*) lecture. **S∼raum** *m* penalty area. **S∼stoss** (**S∼stoß**) *m* penalty. **S∼tat** *f* crime. **S∼zettel** *m* (*fam*) = **S∼mandat**

Strahl *m* -[e]s,-en ray; (*einer Taschenlampe*) beam; (*Wasser-*) jet. **s∼en** *vi* (*haben*) shine; (*funkeln*) sparkle; (*lächeln*) beam. **S∼enbehandlung** *f* radiotherapy. **s∼end** *a* shining; sparkling; beaming; radiant (*Schönheit*). **S∼entherapie** *f* radiotherapy. **S∼ung** *f* - radiation

Strähn|e *f* -,-n strand. **s∼ig** *a* straggly

stramm *a* tight, *adv* -ly; (*kräftig*) sturdy; (*gerade*) upright

Strampel|höschen /-sç-/ *nt* -s,- rompers *pl*. **s∼n** *vi* (*haben*) (*Baby:*) kick

Strand *m* -[e]s,-e beach. **s∼en** *vi* (*sein*) run aground; (*fig*) fail. **S∼korb** *m* wicker beach-chair. **S∼promenade** *f* promenade

Strang *m* -[e]s,-e rope

Strapaz|e *f* -,-n strain. **s∼ieren** *vt* be hard on; tax (*Nerven, Geduld*). **s∼ierfähig** *a* hard-wearing. **s∼iös** *a* exhausting

Strass *m* - & -es (**Straß** *m* - & -sses) paste

Straße *f* -,-n road; (*in der Stadt auch*) street; (*Meeres-*) strait; **auf der S∼** in the road/street. **S∼nbahn** *f* tram, (*Amer*) streetcar. **S∼nkarte** *f* road-map. **S∼nlaterne** *f* street lamp. **S∼nsperre** *f* roadblock

Strat|egie *f* -,-n strategy. **s∼egisch** *a* strategic, *adv* -ally

sträuben *vt* ruffle up (*Federn*); **sich s∼** (*Fell, Haar:*) stand on end; (*fig*) resist

Strauch *m* -[e]s, Sträucher bush

straucheln *vi* (*sein*) stumble

Strauß¹ *m* -es, Sträuße bunch [of flowers]; (*Bukett*) bouquet

Strauß² *m* -es,-e ostrich

Strebe *f* -,-n brace, strut

streben *vi* (*haben*) strive (**nach** for) □ *vi* (*sein*) head (**nach/zu** for)

Streb|er *m* -s,- pushy person; (*Sch*) swot. **s∼sam** *a* industrious

Strecke *f* -,-n stretch, section; (*Entfernung*) distance; (*Rail*) line; (*Route*) route

strecken *vt* stretch; (*aus-*) stretch out; (*gerade machen*) straighten; (*Culin*) thin down; **sich s∼** stretch; (*sich aus-*) stretch out; **den Kopf aus dem Fenster s∼** put one's head out of the window

Streich *m* -[e]s,-e prank, trick; **jdm einen S∼ spielen** play a trick on s.o.

streicheln *vt* stroke

streichen† *vt* spread; (*weg-*) smooth; (*an-*) paint; (*aus-*) delete; (*kürzen*) cut □ *vi* (*haben*) **s∼ über** (+ *acc*) stroke

Streicher *m* -s,- string-player; **die S∼** the strings

Streichholz *nt* match. **S∼schachtel** *f* matchbox

Streich|instrument *nt* stringed instrument. **S∼käse** *m* cheese spread. **S∼orchester** *nt* string orchestra. **S∼ung** *f* -,-en deletion; (*Kürzung*) cut

Streife *f* -,-n patrol

streifen *vt* brush against; (*berühren*) touch; (*verletzen*) graze; (*fig*) touch on (*Thema*); (*ziehen*) slip (**über** + *acc* over); **mit dem Blick s∼** glance at □ *vi* (*sein*) roam

Streifen *m* -s,- stripe; (*Licht-*) streak; (*auf der Fahrbahn*) line; (*schmales Stück*) strip

Streifenwagen *m* patrol car. **s∼ig** *a* streaky. **S∼schuss** (**S∼schuß**) *m* glancing shot; (*Wunde*) graze

Streik *m* -s,-s strike; **in den S∼ treten** go on strike. **S∼brecher** *m* strike-breaker, (*pej*) scab. **s∼en** *vi* (*haben*) strike; (*fam*) refuse; (*versagen*) pack up. **S∼ende(r)** *m* striker. **S∼posten** *m* picket

Streit *m* -[e]s,-e quarrel; (*Auseinandersetzung*) dispute. **s∼en†** *vr/i* (*haben*) [**sich**] **s∼en** quarrel. **s∼ig** *a* **jdm etw s∼ig machen** dispute s.o.'s right to sth. **S∼igkeiten** *fpl* quarrels. **S∼kräfte** *fpl* armed forces. **s∼süchtig** *a* quarrelsome

streng *a* strict, *adv* -ly; (*Blick, Ton*) stern, *adv* -ly; (*rau, nüchtern*) severe, *adv* -ly; (*Geschmack*) sharp; **s∼ genommen** strictly speaking. **S∼e** *f* - strictness; sternness; severity. **s∼genommen** *adv* (NEW) **s∼ genommen,** *s.* **streng**. **s∼gläubig** *a* strict; (*orthodox*) orthodox. **s∼stens** *adv* strictly

Stress *m* -es,-e (**Streß** *m* -sses,-sse) stress

stressig *a* (*fam*) stressful

streuen *vt* spread; (*ver-*) scatter; sprinkle (*Zucker, Salz*); **die Straßen s∼** grit the roads

streunen *vi* (*sein*) roam; **s∼der Hund** stray dog

Strich *m* -[e]s,-e line; (*Feder-, Pinsel-*) stroke; (*Morse-, Gedanken-*) dash; **gegen den S∼** the wrong way; (*fig*) against the grain. **S∼kode** *m* bar code. **S∼punkt** *m* semicolon

Strick *m* -[e]s,-e cord; (*Seil*) rope; (*fam: Schlingel*) rascal

strick|en *vt/i* (*haben*) knit. **S∼jacke** *f* cardigan. **S∼leiter** *f* rope-ladder. **S∼nadel** *f* knitting-needle. **S∼waren** *fpl* knitwear *sg*. **S∼zeug** *nt* knitting

striegeln vt groom

strikt a strict, adv -ly

strittig a contentious

Stroh nt -[e]s straw. **S~blumen** fpl everlasting flowers. **S~dach** nt thatched roof. **s~gedeckt** a thatched. **S~halm** m straw

Strolch m -[e]s,-e (fam) rascal

Strom m -[e]s,-e river; (Menschen-, Auto-, Blut-) stream; (Tränen-) flood; (Schwall) torrent; (Electr) current, power; **gegen den S~** (fig) against the tide; **es regnet in Strömen** it is pouring with rain. **s~abwärts** adv downstream. **s~aufwärts** adv upstream

strömen vi (sein) flow; (Menschen, Blut:) stream, pour; **s~der Regen** pouring rain

Strom|kreis m circuit. **s~linienförmig** a streamlined. **S~sperre** f power cut

Strömung f -,-en current

Strophe f -,-n verse

strotzen vi (haben) be full (vor + dat of); **vor Gesundheit s~d** bursting with health

Strudel m -s,- whirlpool; (SGer Culin) strudel

Struktur f -,-en structure; (Tex) texture

Strumpf m -[e]s,-e stocking; (Knie-) sock. **S~band** nt (pl -bänder) suspender, (Amer) garter. **S~bandgürtel** m suspender/(Amer) garter belt. **S~halter** m = **S~band. S~hose** f tights pl, (Amer) pantyhose

Strunk m -[e]s,-e stalk; (Baum-) stump

struppig a shaggy

Stube f -,-n room. **s~nrein** a house-trained

Stuck m -s stucco

Stück nt -[e]s,-e piece; (Zucker-) lump; (Seife) tablet; (Theater-) play; (Gegenstand) item; (Exemplar) specimen; **20 S~ Vieh** 20 head of cattle; **ein S~** (Entfernung) some way; **aus freien S~en** voluntarily. **S~chen** nt -s,- [little] bit. **s~weise** adv bit by bit; (einzeln) singly

Student|(in) m -en,-en (f -,-nen) student. **s~isch** a student ...

Studie /-jə/ f -,-n study

studier|en vt/i (haben) study. **S~zimmer** nt study

Studio nt -s,-s studio

Studium nt -s,-ien studies pl

Stufe f -,-n step; (Treppen-) stair; (Raketen-) stage; (Niveau) level. **s~n** vt terrace; (staffeln) grade

Stuhl m -[e]s,-e chair; (Med) stools pl. **S~gang** m bowel movement

stülpen vt put (über + acc over)

stumm a dumb; (schweigsam) silent, adv -ly

Stummel m -s,- stump; (Zigaretten-) butt; (Bleistift-) stub

Stümper m -s,- bungler. **s~haft** a incompetent, adv -ly

stumpf a blunt; (Winkel) obtuse; (glanzlos) dull; (fig) apathetic, adv -ally. **S~** m -[e]s, -e stump

Stumpfsinn m apathy; (Langweiligkeit) tedium. **s~ig** a apathetic, adv -ally; (langweilig) tedious

Stunde f -,-n hour; (Sch) lesson

stunden vt jdm eine Schuld s~ give s.o. time to pay a debt

Stunden|kilometer mpl kilometres per hour. **s~lang** adv for hours. **S~lohn** m hourly rate. **S~plan** m timetable. **s~weise** adv by the hour

stündlich a & adv hourly

Stups m -es,-e nudge; (Schubs) push. **s~en** vt nudge; (schubsen) push. **S~nase** f snub nose

stur a pigheaded; (phlegmatisch) stolid, adv -ly; (unbeirrbar) dogged, adv -ly

Sturm m -[e]s,-e gale; (schwer) storm; (Mil) assault

stürm|en vi (haben) (Wind:) blow hard; **es s~t** it's blowing a gale □ vi (sein) rush □ vt storm; (bedrängen) besiege. **S~er** m -s,- forward. **s~isch** a stormy; (Überfahrt) rough; (fig) tumultuous, adv -ly; (ungestüm) tempestuous, adv -ly

Sturz m -es,-e [heavy] fall; (Preis-, Kurs-) sharp drop; (Pol) overthrow

stürzen vi (sein) fall [heavily]; (in die Tiefe) plunge; (Preise, Kurse:) drop sharply; (Regierung:) fall; (eilen) rush □ vt throw; (umkippen) turn upside down; turn out (Speise, Kuchen); (Pol) overthrow, topple; **sich s~** throw oneself (aus/in + acc out of/into); **sich s~ auf** (+ acc) pounce on

Sturz|flug m (Aviat) dive. **S~helm** m crash-helmet

Stute f -,-n mare

Stütze f -,-n support; (Kopf-, Arm-) rest

stutzen vi (haben) stop short □ vt trim; (Hort) cut back; (kupieren) crop

stützen vt support; (auf-) rest; **sich s~ auf** (+ acc) lean on; (beruhen) be based on

Stutzer m -s,- dandy

stutzig a puzzled; (misstrauisch) suspicious

Stützpunkt m (Mil) base

Subjekt nt -[e]s,-e subject. **s~iv** a subjective, adv -ly

Subskription /-'tsjo:n/ f -,-en subscription

Substantiv nt -s,-e noun

Substanz f -,-en substance

subtil *a* subtle, *adv* -tly

subtra|hieren *vt* subtract. **S~ktion** /-'tsjo:n/ *f* -,-en subtraction

Subvention /-'tsjo:n/ *f* -,-en subsidy. **s~ieren** *vt* subsidize

subversiv *a* subversive

Such|e *f* - search; **auf der S~e nach** looking for. **s~en** *vt* look for; *(intensiv)* search for; seek *(Hilfe, Rat)* **'Zimmer gesucht'** 'room wanted' □ *vi (haben)* look, search (**nach** for). **S~er** *m* -s,- *(Phot)* viewfinder

Sucht *f* -,-e addiction; *(fig)* mania

süchtig *a* addicted. **S~e(r)** *m/f* addict

Süd *m* -[e]s south. **S~afrika** *nt* South Africa. **S~amerika** *nt* South America. **s~deutsch** *a* South German

Süden *m* -s south; **nach S~** south

Süd|frucht *f* tropical fruit. **s~lich** *a* southern; *(Richtung)* southerly □ *adv & prep* (+ *gen*) **s~lich [von] der Stadt** [to the] south of the town. **S~osten** *m* southeast. **S~pol** *m* South Pole. **s~wärts** *adv* southwards. **S~westen** *m* south-west

süffisant *a* smug, *adv* -ly

suggerieren *vt* suggest (*dat* to)

Suggest|ion /-'tsjo:n/ *f* -,-en suggestion. **s~iv** *a* suggestive

Sühne *f* -,-n atonement; *(Strafe)* penalty. **s~n** *vt* atone for

Sultanine *f* -,-n sultana

Sülze *f* -,-n [meat] jelly; *(Schweinskopf-)* brawn

Summe *f* -,-n sum

summ|en *vi (haben)* hum; *(Biene:)* buzz □ *vt* hum. **S~er** *m* -s,- buzzer

summieren (sich) *vr* add up; *(sich häufen)* increase

Sumpf *m* -[e]s,-e marsh, swamp. **s~ig** *a* marshy

Sünd|e *f* -,-n sin. **S~enbock** *m* scapegoat. **S~er(in)** *m* -s,- *(f* -,-nen) sinner. **s~haft** *a* sinful. **s~igen** *vi (haben)* sin

super *inv a (fam)* great. **S~lativ** *m* -s,-e superlative. **S~markt** *m* supermarket

Suppe *f* -,-n soup. **S~nlöffel** *m* soup-spoon. **S~nteller** *m* soup-plate. **S~nwürfel** *m* stock cube

Surf|brett /'sœːɐ̯f-/ *nt* surfboard. **S~en** *nt* -s surfing

surren *vi (haben)* whirr

süß *a* sweet, *adv* -ly. **S~e** *f* - sweetness. **s~en** *vt* sweeten. **S~igkeit** *f* -,-en sweet. **s~lich** *a* sweetish; *(fig)* sugary. **S~speise** *f* sweet. **S~stoff** *m* sweetener. **S~waren** *fpl* confectionery *sg*, sweets *pl*. **S~wasser-** *pref* freshwater ...

Sylvester *nt* -s = Silvester

Symbol *nt* -s,-e symbol. **S~ik** *f* - symbolism. **s~isch** *a* symbolic, *adv* -ally. **s~isieren** *vt* symbolize

Sym|metrie *f* - symmetry. **s~metrisch** *a* symmetrical, *adv* -ly

Sympathie *f* -,-n sympathy

sympath|isch *a* agreeable; *(Person)* likeable. **s~isieren** *vi (haben)* be sympathetic (**mit** to)

Symphonie *f* -,-n = Sinfonie

Symptom *nt* -s,-e symptom. **s~atisch** *a* symptomatic

Synagoge *f* -,-n synagogue

synchronisieren /zynkroni'zi:rən/ *vt* synchronize; dub *(Film)*

Syndikat *nt* -[e]s,-e syndicate

Syndrom *nt* -s,-e syndrome

synonym *a* synonymous, *adv* -ly. **S~** *nt* -s,-e synonym

Syntax /'zyntaks/ *f* - syntax

Synthe|se *f* -,-n synthesis. **S~tik** *nt* -s synthetic material. **s~tisch** *a* synthetic, *adv* -ally

Syrien /-jən/ *nt* -s Syria

System *nt* -s,-e system. **s~atisch** *a* systematic, *adv* -ally

Szene *f* -,-n scene. **S~rie** *f* - scenery

T

Tabak *m* -s,-e tobacco

Tabelle *f* -,-n table; *(Sport)* league table

Tablett *nt* -[e]s,-s tray

Tablette *f* -,-n tablet

tabu *a* taboo. **T~** *nt* -s,-s taboo

Tacho *m* -s,-s, **Tachometer** *m & nt* speedometer

Tadel *m* -s,- reprimand; *(Kritik)* censure; *(Sch)* black mark. **t~los** *a* impeccable, *adv* -bly. **t~n** *vt* reprimand; censure. **t~nswert** *a* reprehensible

Tafel *f* -,-n *(Tisch, Tabelle)* table; *(Platte)* slab; *(Anschlag-, Hinweis-)* board; *(Gedenk-)* plaque; *(Schiefer-)* slate; *(Wand-)* blackboard; *(Bild-)* plate; *(Schokolade)* bar. **t~n** *vi (haben)* feast

Täfelung *f* - panelling

Tag *m* -[e]s,-e day; **Tag für Tag** day by day; **am T~e** in the daytime; **eines T~es** one day; **unter T~e** underground; **es wird Tag** it is getting light; **guten Tag!** good morning/afternoon! **zu T~e treten** *od* **kommen/bringen** = zutage treten *od* kommen/bringen, *s.* zutage. **t~aus** *adv* **t~aus, t~ein** day in, day out

Tage|buch *nt* diary. **t~lang** *adv* for days

tagen *vi* (*haben*) meet; (*Gericht:*) sit; **es tagt** day is breaking

Tages|anbruch *m* daybreak. **T~ausflug** *m* day trip. **T~decke** *f* bedspread. **T~karte** *f* day ticket; (*Speise-*) menu of the day. **T~licht** *nt* daylight. **T~mutter** *f* child-minder. **T~ordnung** *f* agenda. **T~rückfahrkarte** *f* day return [ticket]. **T~zeit** *f* time of the day. **T~zeitung** *f* daily [news]paper

täglich *a* & *adv* daily; **zweimal t~** twice a day

tags *adv* by day; **t~ zuvor/darauf** the day before/after

tagsüber *adv* during the day

tag|täglich *a* daily □ *adv* every single day. **T~traum** *m* day-dream. **T~undnachtgleiche** *f* -,-n equinox. **T~ung** *f* -,-en meeting; (*Konferenz*) conference

Taill|e /'taljə/ *f* -,-n waist. **t~iert** /ta'ji:ɐt/ *a* fitted

Takt *m* -[e]s,-e tact; (*Mus*) bar; (*Tempo*) time; (*Rhythmus*) rhythm; **im T~** in time [to the music]. **T~gefühl** *nt* tact

Takt|ik *f* - tactics *pl.* **t~isch** *a* tactical, *adv* -ly

takt|los *a* tactless, *adv* -ly. **T~losigkeit** *f* - tactlessness. **T~stock** *m* baton. **t~voll** *a* tactful, *adv* -ly

Tal *nt* -[e]s,-e valley

Talar *m* -s,-e robe; (*Univ*) gown

Talent *nt* -[e]s,-e talent. **t~iert** *a* talented

Talg *m* -s tallow; (*Culin*) suet

Talsperre *f* dam

Tampon /tam'põ:/ *m* -s,-s tampon

Tang *m* -s seaweed

Tangente *f* -,-n tangent; (*Straße*) bypass

Tank *m* -s,-s tank. **t~en** *vt* fill up with (*Benzin*) □ *vi* (*haben*) fill up with petrol; (*Aviat*) refuel; **ich muss t~en** I need petrol. **T~er** *m* -s,- tanker. **T~stelle** *f* petrol/(*Amer*) gas station. **T~wart** *m* -[e]s,-e petrol-pump attendant

Tanne *f* -,-n fir [tree]. **T~nbaum** *m* fir tree; (*Weihnachtsbaum*) Christmas tree. **T~nzapfen** *m* fir cone

Tante *f* -,-n aunt

Tantiemen /tan'tje:mən/ *pl* royalties

Tanz *m* -es,-e dance. **t~en** *vt/i* (*haben*) dance

Tänzer(in) *m* -s,- (*f* -,-nen) dancer

Tanz|lokal *nt* dance-hall. **T~musik** *f* dance music

Tapete *f* -,-n wallpaper. **T~nwechsel** *m* (*fam*) change of scene

tapezier|en *vt* paper. **T~er** *m* -s,- paperhanger, decorator

tapfer *a* brave, *adv* -ly. **T~keit** *f* - bravery

tappen *vi* (*sein*) walk hesitantly; (*greifen*) grope (**nach** for)

Tarif *m* -s,-e rate; (*Verzeichnis*) tariff

tarn|en *vt* disguise; (*Mil*) camouflage; **sich t~en** disguise/camouflage oneself. **T~ung** *f* - disguise; camouflage

Tasche *f* -,-n bag; (*Hosen-, Mantel-*) pocket. **T~nbuch** *nt* paperback. **T~ndieb** *m* pickpocket. **T~ngeld** *nt* pocket-money. **T~nlampe** *f* torch, (*Amer*) flashlight. **T~nmesser** *nt* penknife. **T~ntuch** *nt* handkerchief

Tasse *f* -,-n cup

Tastatur *f* -,-en keyboard

tast|bar *a* palpable. **T~e** *f* -,-n key; (*Druck-*) push-button. **t~en** *vi* (*haben*) feel, grope (**nach** for) □ *vt* key in (*Daten*); **sich t~en** feel one's way (**zu** to). **t~end** *a* tentative, *adv* -ly

Tat *f* -,-en action; (*Helden-*) deed; (*Straf-*) crime; **in der Tat** indeed; **auf frischer Tat ertappt** caught in the act. **t~enlos** *adv* passively

Täter(in) *m* -s,- (*f* -,-nen) culprit; (*Jur*) offender

tätig *a* active, *adv* -ly; **t~ sein** work. **T~keit** *f* -,-en activity; (*Funktionieren*) action; (*Arbeit*) work, job

Tatkraft *f* energy

tätlich *a* physical, *adv* -ly; **t~ werden** become violent. **T~keiten** *fpl* violence *sg*

Tatort *m* scene of the crime

tätowier|en *vt* tattoo. **T~ung** *f* -,-en tattooing; (*Bild*) tattoo

Tatsache *f* fact. **T~nbericht** *m* documentary

tatsächlich *a* actual, *adv* -ly

tätscheln *vt* pat

Tatze *f* -,-n paw

Tau¹ *m* -[e]s dew

Tau² *nt* -[e]s,-e rope

taub *a* deaf; (*gefühllos*) numb; (*Nuss*) empty; (*Gestein*) worthless

Taube *f* -,-n pigeon; (*Turtel- & fig*) dove. **T~nschlag** *m* pigeon-loft

Taub|heit *f* - deafness; (*Gefühllosigkeit*) numbness. **t~stumm** *a* deaf and dumb

tauch|en *vt* dip, plunge; (*unter-*) duck □ *vi* (*haben/sein*) dive/(*ein-*) plunge (**in** + *acc* into); (*auf-*) appear (**aus** out of). **T~er** *m* -s,- diver. **T~eranzug** *m* diving-suit. **T~sieder** *m* -s,- [small, portable] immersion heater

tauen *vi* (*sein*) melt, thaw □ *impers* **es taut** it is thawing

Tauf|becken *nt* font. **T~e** *f* -,-n christening, baptism. **t~en** *vt* christen, baptize. **T~pate** *m* godfather. **T~stein** *m* font

tauge|n vi (haben) etwas/nichts t~n be good/no good; zu etw t~n/nicht t~n be good/no good for sth. T~nichts m -es,-e good-for-nothing

tauglich a suitable; (Mil) fit. T~keit f - suitability; fitness

Taumel m -s daze; **wie im T~** in a daze. **t~n** vi (sein) stagger

Tausch m -[e]s,-e exchange, (fam) swap. **t~en** vt exchange/(handeln) barter (**gegen** for); **die Plätze t~en** change places □ vi (haben) swap (**mit etw** sth; **mit jdm** with s.o.)

täuschen vt deceive, fool; betray (Vertrauen); **sich t~** delude oneself; (sich irren) be mistaken □ vi (haben) be deceptive. **t~d** a deceptive; (Ähnlichkeit) striking

Tausch|geschäft nt exchange. **T~handel** m barter; (T~geschäft) exchange

Täuschung f -,-en deception; (Irrtum) mistake; (Illusion) delusion

tausend inv a one/a thousand. **T~** nt -s, -e thousand. **T~e** od **t~e von** thousands of. **T~füßler** m -s,- centipede. **t~ste(r, s)** a thousandth. **T~stel** nt -s,- thousandth

Tau|tropfen m dewdrop. **T~wetter** nt thaw. **T~ziehen** nt -s tug of war

Taxe f -,-n charge; (Kur-) tax; (Taxi) taxi

Taxi nt -s,-s taxi, cab

taxieren vt estimate/(im Wert) value (**auf** + acc at); (fam: mustern) size up

Taxi|fahrer m taxi driver. **T~stand** m taxi rank

Teakholz /'tiːk-/ nt teak

Team /tiːm/ nt -s,-s team

Techni|k f -,-en technology; (Methode) technique. **T~ker** m -s,- technician. **t~sch** a technical, adv -ly; (technologisch) technological, adv -ly; **T~sche Hochschule** Technical University

Techno|logie f -,-n technology. **t~logisch** a technological

Teckel m -s,- dachshund

Teddybär m teddy bear

Tee m -s,-s tea. **T~beutel** m tea-bag. **T~kanne** f teapot. **T~kessel** m kettle. **T~löffel** m teaspoon

Teer m -s tar. **t~en** vt tar

Tee|sieb nt tea-strainer. **T~tasse** f teacup. **T~wagen** m [tea] trolley

Teich m -[e]s,-e pond

Teig m -[e]s,-e pastry; (Knet-) dough; (Rühr-) mixture; (Pfannkuchen-) batter. **T~rolle** f, **T~roller** m rolling-pin. **T~waren** fpl pasta sg

Teil m -[e]s,-e part; (Bestand-) component; (Jur) party; **der vordere T~** the front part; **zum T~** partly; **zum großen/**größten **T~** for the most part □ m & nt -[e]s (Anteil) share; **sein[en] T~ beitragen** do one's share; **ich für mein[en] T~** for my part □ nt -[e]s,-e part; (Ersatz-) spare part; (Anbau-) unit

teil|bar a divisible. **T~chen** nt -s,- particle. **t~en** vt divide; (auf-) share out; (gemeinsam haben) share; (Pol) partition (Land); **sich** (dat) **etw [mit jdm] t~en** share sth [with s.o.]; **sich t~en** divide; (sich gabeln) fork; (Vorhang:) open; (Meinungen:) differ □ vi (haben) share

teilhab|en† vi sep (haben) share (**an etw** dat sth). **T~er** m -s,- (Comm) partner

Teilnahm|e f - participation; (innere) interest; (Mitgefühl) sympathy. **t~slos** a apathetic, adv -ally

teilnehm|en† vi sep (haben) **t~en an** (+ dat) take part in; (mitfühlen) share [in]. **T~er(in)** m -s,- (f -,-nen) participant; (an Wettbewerb) competitor

teil|s adv partly. **T~ung** f -,-en division; (Pol) partition. **t~weise** a partial □ adv partially, partly; (manchmal) in some cases. **T~zahlung** f part-payment; (Rate) instalment. **T~zeitbeschäftigung** f part-time job

Teint /tɛː/ m -s,-s complexion

Telefax nt fax

Telefon nt -s,-e [tele]phone. **T~anruf** m, **T~at** nt -[e]s,-e [tele]phone call. **T~buch** nt [tele]phone book. **t~ieren** vi (haben) [tele]phone

telefon|isch a [tele]phone ... □ adv by [tele]phone. **T~ist(in)** m -en,-en (f -,-nen) telephonist. **T~karte** f phone card. **T~nummer** f [tele]phone number. **T~zelle** f [tele]phone box

Telegraf m -en,-en telegraph. **T~enmast** m telegraph pole. **t~ieren** vi (haben) send a telegram. **t~isch** a telegraphic □ adv by telegram

Telegramm nt -s,-e telegram

Telegraph m -en,-en = Telegraf

Teleobjektiv nt telephoto lens

Telepathie f - telepathy

Telephon nt -s,-e = Telefon

Teleskop nt -s,-e telescope. **t~isch** a telescopic

Telex nt -,-[e] telex. **t~en** vt telex

Teller m -s,- plate

Tempel m -s,- temple

Temperament nt -s,-e temperament; (Lebhaftigkeit) vivacity. **t~los** a dull. **t~voll** a vivacious; (Pferd) spirited

Temperatur f -,-en temperature

Tempo nt -s,-s speed; (Mus: pl -pi) tempo; **T~ [T~]!** hurry up!

Tend|enz f -,-en trend; (*Neigung*) tendency. **t~ieren** vi (*haben*) tend (**zu** towards)

Tennis nt - tennis. **T~platz** m tenniscourt. **T~schläger** m tennis-racket

Tenor m -s,⸚e (*Mus*) tenor

Teppich m -s,-e carpet. **T~boden** m fitted carpet

Termin m -s,-e date; (*Arzt-*) appointment; [letzter] **T~** deadline. **T~kalender** m [appointments] diary

Terminologie f -,-n terminology

Terpentin nt -s turpentine

Terrain /tɛ'rɛ̃:/ nt -s,-s terrain

Terrasse f -,-n terrace

Terrier /'tɛrɪ̯ɐ/ m -s,- terrier

Terrine f -,-n tureen

Territorium nt -s,-ien territory

Terror m -s terror. **t~isieren** vt terrorize. **T~ismus** m - terrorism. **T~ist** m -en,-en terrorist

Terzett nt -[e]s,-e [vocal] trio

Tesafilm (P) m ≈ Sellotape (P)

Test m -[e]s,-s & -e test

Testament nt -[e]s,-e will; **Altes/Neues T~** Old/New Testament. **T~svollstrecker** m -s,- executor

testen vt test

Tetanus m - tetanus

teuer a expensive, adv -ly; (*lieb*) dear; **wie t~?** how much? **T~ung** f -,-en rise in prices

Teufel m -s,- devil; **zum T~!** (*sl*) damn [it]! **T~skreis** m vicious circle

teuflisch a fiendish

Text m -[e]s,-e text; (*Passage*) passage; (*Bild-*) caption; (*Lied-*) lyrics pl, words pl; (*Opern-*) libretto. **T~er** m -s,- copy-writer; (*Schlager-*) lyricist

Textil|ien /-i̯ən/ pl textiles; (*Textilwaren*) textile goods. **T~industrie** f textile industry

Textverarbeitungssystem nt word processor

TH abbr = **Technische Hochschule**

Theater nt -s,- theatre; (*fam: Getue*) fuss, to-do; **T~ spielen** act; (*fam*) put on an act. **T~kasse** f box-office. **T~stück** nt play

theatralisch a theatrical, adv -ly

Theke f -,-n bar; (*Ladentisch*) counter

Thema nt -s,-men subject; (*Mus*) theme

Themse f - Thames

Theolo|ge m -n,-n theologian. **T~gie** f - theology

theor|etisch a theoretical, adv -ly. **T~ie** f -,-n theory

Therapeut|(in) m -en,-en (f -,-nen) therapist. **t~isch** a therapeutic

Therapie f -,-n therapy

Thermal|bad nt thermal bath; (*Ort*) thermal spa. **T~quelle** f thermal spring

Thermometer nt -s,- thermometer

Thermosflasche (P) f Thermos flask (P)

Thermostat m -[e]s,-e thermostat

These f -,-n thesis

Thrombose f -,-n thrombosis

Thron m -[e]s,-e throne. **t~en** vi (*haben*) sit [in state]. **T~folge** f succession. **T~folger** m -s,- heir to the throne

Thunfisch m tuna

Thymian m -s thyme

Tick m -s,-s (*fam*) quirk; **einen T~ haben** be crazy

ticken vi (*haben*) tick

tief a deep; (*t~ liegend, niedrig*) low; (*t~gründig*) profound; **t~er Teller** soupplate; **im t~sten Winter** in the depths of winter □ adv deep; low; (*sehr*) deeply, profoundly; (*schlafen*) soundly; **t~ greifend** (*fig*) radical, adv -ly; **t~ schürfend** (*fig*) profound. **T~** nt -s,-s (*Meteorol*) depression. **T~bau** m civil engineering. **T~e** f -,-n depth

Tief|ebene f [lowland] plain. **T~garage** f underground car park. **t~gekühlt** a [deep-]frozen. **t~greifend** a (NEW) **t~ greifend, s. tief. t~gründig** a (*fig*) profound

Tiefkühl|fach nt freezer compartment. **T~kost** f frozen food. **T~truhe** f deep-freeze

Tief|land nt lowlands pl. **T~punkt** m (*fig*) low. **t~schürfend** a (NEW) **t~ schürfend, s. tief. t~sinnig** (*fig*) profound; (*trübsinnig*) melancholy. **T~stand** m (*fig*) low

Tiefsttemperatur f minimum temperature

Tier nt -[e]s,-e animal. **T~arzt** m, **T~ärztin** f vet, veterinary surgeon. **T~garten** m zoo. **t~isch** a animal ...; (*fig: roh*) bestial. **T~kreis** m zodiac. **T~kreiszeichen** nt sign of the zodiac. **T~kunde** f zoology. **T~quälerei** f cruelty to animals

Tiger m -s,- tiger

tilgen vt pay off (*Schuld*); (*streichen*) delete; (*fig: auslöschen*) wipe out

Tinte f -,-n ink. **T~nfisch** m squid

Tipp (Tip) m -s,-s (*fam*) tip

tipp|en vt (*fam*) type □ vi (*haben*) (*berühren*) touch (**auf/an etw** acc sth); (*fam: Maschine schreiben*) type; **t~en auf** (+ acc) (*fam: wetten*) bet on. **T~fehler** m (*fam*) typing error. **T~schein** m pools/lottery coupon

tipptopp a (*fam*) immaculate, adv -ly

Tirol nt -s [the] Tyrol

Tisch m -[e]s,-e table; (*Schreib-*) desk; **nach T~** after the meal. **T~decke** f table-cloth. **T~gebet** nt grace. **T~ler** m -s,- joiner; (*Möbel-*) cabinet-maker. **T~rede** f after-dinner speech. **T~tennis** nt table tennis. **T~tuch** nt table-cloth

Titel m -s,- title. **T~rolle** f title-role

Toast /to:st/ m -[e]s,-e toast; (*Scheibe*) piece of toast; **einen T~ ausbringen** propose a toast (**auf** + acc to). **T~er** m -s,- toaster

tob|en vi (*haben*) rave; ⟨*Sturm:*⟩ rage; ⟨*Kinder:*⟩ play boisterously □ vi (*sein*) rush. **t~süchtig** a raving mad

Tochter f -,: daughter. **T~gesellschaft** f subsidiary

Tod m -es death. **t~blass** (**t~blaß**) n deathly pale. **t~ernst** a deadly serious, adv -ly

Todes|angst f mortal fear. **T~anzeige** f death announcement; (*Zeitungs-*) obituary. **T~fall** m death. **T~opfer** nt fatality, casualty. **T~strafe** f death penalty. **T~urteil** nt death sentence

Tod|feind m mortal enemy. **t~krank** a dangerously ill

tödlich a fatal, adv -ly; ⟨*Gefahr*⟩ mortal, adv -ly; ⟨*groß*⟩ deadly; **t~ gelangweilt** bored to death

tod|müde a dead tired. **t~sicher** a (*fam*) dead certain □ adv for sure. **T~sünde** f deadly sin. **t~unglücklich** a desperately unhappy

Toilette /tɔa'lɛtə/ f -,-n toilet. **T~npapier** nt toilet paper

toler|ant a tolerant. **T~anz** f - tolerance. **t~ieren** vt tolerate

toll a crazy, mad; (*fam: prima*) fantastic; (*schlimm*) awful □ adv beautifully; (*sehr*) very; (*schlimm*) badly. **t~en** vi (*haben/sein*) romp. **t~kühn** a foolhardy. **t~patschig** a clumsy, adv -ily. **T~wut** f rabies. **t~wütig** a rabid

tolpatschig a (NEW) **tollpatschig**

Tölpel m -s,- fool

Tomate f -,-n tomato. **T~nmark** nt tomato purée

Tombola f -,-s raffle

Ton¹ m -[e]s clay

Ton² m -[e]s,:e tone; (*Klang*) sound; (*Note*) note; (*Betonung*) stress; (*Farb-*) shade; **der gute Ton** (*fig*) good form. **T~abnehmer** m -s,- pick-up. **t~angebend** a (*fig*) leading. **T~art** f tone [of voice]; (*Mus*) key. **T~band** nt (*pl* -bänder) tape. **T~bandgerät** nt tape recorder

tönen vi (*haben*) sound □ vt tint

Ton|fall m tone [of voice]: (*Akzent*) intonation. **T~leiter** f scale. **t~los** a toneless, adv -ly

Tonne f -,-n barrel, cask: (*Müll-*) bin; (*Maß*) tonne, metric ton

Topf m -[e]s,:e pot; (*Koch-*) pan

Topfen m -s (Aust) ≈ curd cheese

Töpfer(in) m -s,- (f -,-nen) potter. **T~ei** f -,-en pottery

Töpferwaren fpl pottery sg

Topf|lappen m oven-cloth. **T~pflanze** f potted plant

Tor¹ m -en,-en fool

Tor² nt -[e]s,-e gate; (*Einfahrt*) gateway; (*Sport*) goal. **T~bogen** m archway

Torf m -s peat

Torheit f -,-en folly

Torhüter m -s,- goalkeeper

töricht a foolish, adv -ly

torkeln vi (*sein/habe*) stagger

Tornister m -s,- knapsack; (*Sch*) satchel

torp|edieren vt torpedo. **T~edo** m -s,-s torpedo

Torpfosten m goal-post

Torte f -,-n gateau; (*Obst-*) flan

Tortur f -,-en torture

Torwart m -s,-e goalkeeper

tosen vi (*haben*) roar; ⟨*Sturm:*⟩ rage

tot a dead; **tot geboren** stillborn; **sich tot stellen** pretend to be dead; **einen t~en Punkt haben** (*fig*) be at a low ebb

total a total, adv -ly. **t~itär** a totalitarian. **T~schaden** m ≈ write-off

Tote(r) m/f dead man/woman; (*Todesopfer*) fatality; **die T~n** the dead pl

töten vt kill

toten|blass (**totenblaß**) a deathly pale. **T~gräber** m -s,- grave-digger. **T~kopf** m skull. **T~schein** m death certificate. **T~stille** f deathly silence

tot|fahren† vt sep run over and kill. **t~geboren** a (NEW) **tot geboren**, s. **tot**. **t~lachen (sich)** vt sep (*fam*) be in stitches

Toto nt & m -s football pools pl. **T~schein** m pools coupon

tot|schießen† vt sep shoot dead. **T~schlag** m (*Jur*) manslaughter. **t~schlagen†** vt sep kill. **t~schweigen†** vt sep (*fig*) hush up. **t~stellen (sich)** vr sep (NEW) **tot stellen (sich)**, s. **tot**

Tötung f -,-en killing; **fahrlässige T~** (*Jur*) manslaughter

Toup|et /tu'pe:/ nt -s,-s toupee. **t~ieren** vt back-comb

Tour /tu:ɐ/ f -,-en tour; (*Ausflug*) trip; (*Auto-*) drive; (*Rad-*) ride; (*Strecke*) distance; (*Techn*) revolution; (*fam: Weise*) way; **auf vollen T~en** at full speed; (*fam*) flat out

Touris|mus /tu'rɪsmʊs/ m - tourism. **T~t** m -en,-en tourist

Tournee /tʊr'ne:/ f -,-n tour

Trab m -[e]s trot

Trabant m -en,-en satellite

traben vi (haben/sein) trot

Tracht f -,-en [national] costume; **eine T~** Prügel a good hiding

trachten vi (haben) strive (**nach** for); **jdm nach dem Leben t~** be out to kill s.o

trächtig a pregnant

Tradition /-'tsio:n/ f -,-en tradition. **t~ell** a traditional, adv -ly

Trafik f -,-en (Aust) tobacconist's

Trag|bahre f stretcher. **t~bar** a portable; ⟨Kleidung⟩ wearable; (erträglich) bearable

träge a sluggish, adv -ly; (faul) lazy, adv -ily; (Phys) inert

tragen† vt carry; (an-/ aufhaben) wear; (fig) bear □ vi (haben) carry; **gut t~** ⟨Baum:⟩ produce a good crop; **schwer t~** carry a heavy load; (fig) be deeply affected (**an** + dat by). **t~d** a (Techn) load-bearing; (trächtig) pregnant

Träger m -s,- porter; (Inhaber) bearer; (eines Ordens) holder; (Bau-) beam; (Stahl-) girder; (Achsel-) [shoulder] strap. **T~kleid** nt pinafore dress

Trag|etasche f carrier bag. **T~fläche** f (Aviat) wing; (Naut) hydrofoil. **T~flächenboot, T~flügelboot** nt hydrofoil

Trägheit f - sluggishness; (Faulheit) laziness; (Phys) inertia

Trag|ik f - tragedy. **t~isch** a tragic, adv -ally

Tragödie /-jə/ f -,-n tragedy

Tragweite f range; (fig) consequence

Train|er /'trɛːnɐ/ m -s,- trainer; (Tennis-) coach. **t~ieren** vt/i (haben) train

Training /'trɛːnɪŋ/ nt -s training. **T~san-zug** m tracksuit. **T~s-schuhe** mpl trainers

Trakt m -[e]s,-e section; (Flügel) wing

traktieren vi (haben) **mit Schlägen/ Tritten t~** hit/kick

Traktor m -s,-en /-'to:rən/ tractor

trampeln vi (haben) stamp one's feet □ vi (sein) trample (**auf** + acc on) □ vt trample

trampen /'trɛmpən/ vi (sein) (fam) hitch-hike

Trance /'trãːsə/ f -,-n trance

Tranchier|messer /trã'ʃiːɐ̯-/ nt carving-knife. **t~en** vt carve

Träne f -,-n tear. **t~n** vi (haben) water. **T~ngas** nt tear-gas

Tränke f -,-n watering-place; (Trog) drinking-trough. **t~n** vt water ⟨Pferd⟩; (nässen) soak (mit with)

Trans|aktion f transaction. **T~fer** m -s,-s transfer. **T~formator** m -s,-en

/-'to:rən/ transformer. **T~fusion** f -,-en [blood] transfusion

Transistor m -,-en /-'to:rən/ transistor

Transit /tran'zi:t/ m -s transit

transitiv a transitive, adv -ly

Transparent nt -[e]s,-e banner; (Bild) transparency

transpirieren vi (haben) perspire

Transplantation /-'tsio:n/ f -,-en transplant

Transport m -[e]s,-e transport; (Güter-) consignment. **t~ieren** vt transport. **T~mittel** nt means of transport

Trapez nt -es,-e trapeze; (Geom) trapezium

Tratsch m -[e]s (fam) gossip. **t~en** vi (haben) (fam) gossip

Tratte f -,-n (Comm) draft

Traube f -,-n bunch of grapes; (Beere) grape; (fig) cluster. **T~nzucker** m glucose

trauen vi (haben) (+ dat) trust; **ich traute kaum meinen Augen** I could hardly believe my eyes □ vt marry; **sich t~** dare (**etw zu tun** [to] do sth); venture (**in** + acc/**aus** into/out of)

Trauer f - mourning; (Schmerz) grief (**um** for); **T~ tragen** be [dressed] in mourning. **T~fall** m bereavement. **T~feier** f funeral service. **T~marsch** m funeral march. **t~n** vi (haben) grieve; **t~n um** mourn [for]. **T~spiel** nt tragedy. **T~weide** f weeping willow

traulich a cosy, adv -ily

Traum m -[e]s, Träume dream

Trau|ma nt -s,-men trauma. **t~matisch** a traumatic

träumen vt/i (haben) dream

traumhaft a dreamlike; (schön) fabulous, adv -ly

traurig a sad, adv -ly; (erbärmlich) sorry. **T~keit** f - sadness

Trau|ring m wedding-ring. **T~schein** m marriage certificate. **T~ung** f -,-en wedding [ceremony]

Treck m -s,-s trek

Trecker m -s,- tractor

Treff nt -s,-s (Karten) spades pl

treff|en† vt hit; ⟨Blitz:⟩ strike; (fig: verletzen) hurt; (zusammenkommen mit) meet; take ⟨Maßnahme⟩; **sich t~en** meet (**mit jdm** s.o.); **sich gut t~en** be convenient; **es traf sich, dass** it so happened that; **es gut/schlecht t~en** be lucky/unlucky □ vi (haben) hit the target; **t~en auf** (+ acc) meet; (fig) meet with. **T~en** nt -s,- meeting. **t~end** a apt, adv -ly; ⟨Ähnlichkeit⟩ striking. **T~er** m -s,- hit; (Los) winner. **T~punkt** m meeting-place

treiben† vt drive; (sich befassen mit) do; carry on (Gewerbe); indulge in (Luxus); get up to (Unfug); **Handel t~** trade; **Blüten/Blätter t~** come into flower/leaf; **zur Eile t~** hurry [up]; **was treibt ihr da?** (fam) what are you up to? □ vi (sein) drift; (schwimmen) float □ vi (haben) (Bot) sprout. **T~** nt -s activity; (Getriebe) bustle

Treib|haus nt hothouse. **T~hauseffekt** m greenhouse effect. **T~holz** nt driftwood. **T~riemen** m transmission belt. **T~sand** m quicksand. **T~stoff** m fuel

Trend m -s,-s trend

trenn|bar a separable. **t~en** vt separate/(abmachen) detach (von from); divide, split (Wort); **sich t~en** separate; (auseinander gehen) part; **sich t~en von** leave; (fortgeben) part with. **T~ung** f -,-en separation; (Silben-) division. **T~ungsstrich** m hyphen. **T~wand** f partition

trepp|ab adv downstairs. **t~auf** adv upstairs

Treppe f -,-n stairs pl; (Außen-) steps pl; **eine T~** a flight of stairs/steps. **T~nflur** m landing. **T~ngeländer** nt banisters pl. **T~nhaus** nt stairwell. **T~nstufe** f stair, step

Tresor m -s,-e safe

Tresse f -,-n braid

Treteimer m pedal bin

treten† vi (sein/haben) step; (versehentlich) tread; (ausschlagen) kick (nach at); **in Verbindung t~** get in touch □ vt tread; (mit Füßen) kick

treu a faithful, adv -ly; (fest) loyal, adv -ly. **T~e** f - faithfulness; loyalty; (eheliche) fidelity. **T~händer** m -s,- trustee. **t~herzig** a trusting, adv -ly; (arglos) innocent, adv -ly. **t~los** a disloyal, adv -ly; (untreu) unfaithful

Tribüne f -,-n platform; (Zuschauer-) stand

Tribut m -[e]s,-e tribute; (Opfer) toll

Trichter m -s,- funnel; (Bomben-) crater

Trick m -s,-s trick. **T~film** m cartoon. **t~reich** a clever

Trieb m -[e]s,-e drive, urge; (Instinkt) instinct; (Bot) shoot. **T~täter**, **T~verbrecher** m sex offender. **T~werk** nt (Aviat) engine; (Uhr-) mechanism

triefen|en vi (haben) drip; (nass sein) be dripping (von/vor + dat with). **t~nass** (t~naß) a dripping wet

triftig a valid

Trigonometrie f - trigonometry

Trikot[1] /tri'ko:/ m -s (Tex) jersey

Trikot[2] nt -s,-s (Sport) jersey; (Fußball-) shirt

Trimester nt -s,- term

Trimm-dich nt -s keep-fit

trimmen vt trim; (fam) train; tune (Motor); **sich t~** keep fit

trink|bar a drinkable. **t~en**† vt/i (haben) drink. **T~er(in)** m -s,- (f -,-nen) alcoholic. **T~geld** nt tip. **T~halm** m [drinking-]straw. **T~spruch** m toast. **T~wasser** nt drinking-water

Trio nt -s,-s trio

trippeln vi (sein) trip along

trist a dreary

Tritt m -[e]s,-e step; (Fuß-) kick. **T~brett** nt step. **T~leiter** f step-ladder

Triumph m -s,-e triumph. **t~ieren** vi (haben) rejoice; **t~ieren über** (+ acc) triumph over. **t~ierend** a triumphant, adv -ly

trocken a dry, adv drily. **T~haube** f drier. **T~heit** f -,-en dryness; (Dürre) drought. **t~legen** vt sep change (Baby); drain (Sumpf). **T~milch** f powdered milk

trockn|en vt/i (sein) dry. **T~er** m -s,- drier

Troddel f -,-n tassel

Trödel m -s (fam) junk. **T~laden** m (fam) junk-shop. **T~markt** m (fam) flea market. **t~n** vi (haben) dawdle

Trödler m -s,- (fam) slowcoach; (Händler) junk-dealer

Trog m -[e]s,-e trough

Trommel f -,-n drum. **T~fell** nt ear-drum. **t~n** vi (haben) drum

Trommler m -s,- drummer

Trompete f -,-n trumpet. **T~r** m -s,- trumpeter

Tropen pl tropics

Tropf m -[e]s,-e (Med) drip

tröpfeln vt/i (sein/haben) drip; **es tröpfelt** it's spitting with rain

tropfen vt/i (sein/haben) drip. **T~** m -s,- drop; (fallend) drip. **t~weise** adv drop by drop

tropf|nass (**tropfnaß**) a dripping wet. **T~stein** m stalagmite; (hängend) stalactite

Trophäe /tro'fɛ:ə/ f -,-n trophy

tropisch a tropical

Trost m -[e]s consolation, comfort

tröst|en vt console, comfort; **sich t~en** console oneself. **t~lich** a comforting

trost|los a desolate; (elend) wretched; (reizlos) dreary. **T~preis** m consolation prize. **t~reich** a comforting

Trott m -s amble; (fig) routine

Trottel m -s,- (fam) idiot

trotten vi (sein) traipse; (Tier:) amble

Trottoir /tro'toa:ɐ/ nt -s,-s pavement, (Amer) sidewalk

trotz *prep* (+ *gen*) despite, in spite of. **T~** *m* **-es** defiance. **t~dem** *adv* nevertheless. **t~en** *vi* (*haben*) (+ *dat*) defy. **t~ig** *a* defiant, *adv* -ly; ⟨*Kind*⟩ stubborn

trübe *a* dull; ⟨*Licht*⟩ dim; ⟨*Flüssigkeit*⟩ cloudy; ⟨*fig*⟩ gloomy

Trubel *m* **-s** bustle

trüben *vt* dull; make cloudy ⟨*Flüssigkeit*⟩; ⟨*fig*⟩ spoil; strain ⟨*Verhältnis*⟩; **sich t~** ⟨*Flüssigkeit:*⟩ become cloudy; ⟨*Himmel:*⟩ cloud over; ⟨*Augen:*⟩ dim; ⟨*Verhältnis, Erinnerung:*⟩ deteriorate

Trüb|sal *f* - misery; **T~sal blasen** ⟨*fam*⟩ mope. **t~selig** *a* miserable; ⟨*trübe*⟩ gloomy, *adv* -ily. **T~sinn** *m* melancholy. **t~sinnig** *a* melancholy

Trugbild *nt* illusion

trüg|en† *vt* deceive □ *vi* (*haben*) be deceptive. **t~erisch** *a* false; ⟨*täuschend*⟩ deceptive

Trugschluss (**Trugschluß**) *m* fallacy

Truhe *f* **-,-n** chest

Trümmer *pl* rubble *sg*; ⟨*T~teile*⟩ wreckage *sg*; ⟨*fig*⟩ ruins. **T~haufen** *m* pile of rubble

Trumpf *m* **-[e]s,-̈e** trump [card]; **T~ sein** be trumps. **t~en** *vi* (*haben*) play trumps

Trunk *m* **-[e]s** drink. **T~enbold** *m* **-[e]s, -e** drunkard. **T~enheit** *f* - drunkenness; **T~enheit am Steuer** drink-driving. **T~sucht** *f* alcoholism

Trupp *m* **-s,-s** group; ⟨*Mil*⟩ squad. **T~e** *f* **-, -n** ⟨*Mil*⟩ unit; ⟨*Theat*⟩ troupe; **T~en** troops

Truthahn *m* turkey

Tschech|e *m* **-n,-n, T~in** *f* **-,-nen** Czech. **t~isch** *a* Czech. **T~oslowakei (die)** - Czechoslovakia

tschüs, tschüss *int* bye, cheerio

Tuba *f* **-,-ben** ⟨*Mus*⟩ tuba

Tube *f* **-,-n** tube

Tuberkulose *f* - tuberculosis

Tuch[1] *nt* **-[e]s,-̈er** cloth; ⟨*Hals-, Kopf-*⟩ scarf; ⟨*Schulter-*⟩ shawl

Tuch[2] *nt* **-[e]s,-e** ⟨*Stoff*⟩ cloth

tüchtig *a* competent; ⟨*reichlich, beträchtlich*⟩ good; ⟨*groß*⟩ big □ *adv* competently; ⟨*ausreichend*⟩ well; ⟨*regnen, schneien*⟩ hard. **T~keit** *f* - competence

Tück|e *f* **-,-n** malice; **T~en haben** be temperamental; ⟨*gefährlich sein*⟩ be treacherous. **t~isch** *a* malicious, *adv* -ly; ⟨*gefährlich*⟩ treacherous

tüfteln *vi* (*haben*) ⟨*fam*⟩ fiddle (**an** + *dat* with); ⟨*geistig*⟩ puzzle (**an** + *dat* over)

Tugend *f* **-,en** virtue. **t~haft** *a* virtuous

Tülle *f* **-,-n** spout

Tulpe *f* **-,-n** tulip

tummeln (sich) *vr* romp [about]; ⟨*sich beeilen*⟩ hurry [up]

Tümmler *m* **-s,-** porpoise

Tumor† *m* **-s,-en** /-'moːrən/ tumour

Tümpel *m* **-[e]s,-** pond

Tumult *m* **-[e]s,-e** commotion; ⟨*Aufruhr*⟩ riot

tun† *vt* do; take ⟨*Schritt, Blick*⟩; work ⟨*Wunder*⟩; ⟨*bringen*⟩ put (**in** + *acc* into); **sich tun** happen; **jdm etwas tun** hurt s.o.; **viel zu tun haben** have a lot to do; **das tut man nicht** it isn't done; **das tut nichts** it doesn't matter □ *vi* (*haben*) act (**als ob** as if); **überrascht tun** pretend to be surprised; **er tut nur so** he's just pretending; **jdm/etw gut tun** do s.o./sth good; **zu tun haben** have things/work to do; **[es] zu tun haben mit** have to deal with; **[es] mit dem Herzen zu tun haben** have heart trouble. **Tun** *nt* **-s** actions *pl*

Tünche *f* **-,-n** whitewash; ⟨*fig*⟩ veneer. **t~n** *vt* whitewash

Tunesien /-jən/ *nt* **-s** Tunisia

Tunfisch *m* = **Thunfisch**

Tunke *f* **-,-n** sauce. **t~n** *vt/i* (*haben*) ⟨*fam*⟩ dip (**in** + *acc* into)

Tunnel *m* **-s,-** tunnel

tupf|en *vt* dab □ *vi* (*haben*) **t~en an/auf** (+ *acc*) touch. **T~en** *m* **-s,-** spot. **T~er** *m* **-s,-** spot; ⟨*Med*⟩ swab

Tür *f* **-,-en** door

Turban *m* **-s,-e** turban

Turbine *f* **-,-n** turbine

turbulen|t *a* turbulent. **T~z** *f* **-,-en** turbulence

Türk|e *m* **-n,-n** Turk. **T~ei (die)** - Turkey. **T~in** *f* **-,-nen** Turk

türkis *inv* *a* turquoise. **T~** *m* **-es,-e** turquoise

türkisch *a* Turkish

Turm *m* **-[e]s,-̈e** tower; ⟨*Schach*⟩ rook, castle

Türm|chen *nt* **-s,-** turret. **t~en** *vt* pile [up]; **sich t~en** pile up □ *vi* (*sein*) ⟨*fam*⟩ escape

Turmspitze *f* spire

turn|en *vi* (*haben*) do gymnastics. **T~en** *nt* **-s** gymnastics *sg*; ⟨*Sch*⟩ physical education, ⟨*fam*⟩ gym. **T~er(in)** *m* **-s,-** ⟨*f-,-nen*⟩ gymnast. **T~halle** *f* gymnasium

Turnier *nt* **-s,-e** tournament; ⟨*Reit-*⟩ show

Turnschuhe *mpl* gym shoes; ⟨*Trainingsschuhe*⟩ trainers

Türschwelle *f* doorstep, threshold

Tusch *m* **-[e]s,-e** fanfare

Tusche *f* **-,-n** [drawing] ink; ⟨*Wasserfarbe*⟩ watercolour

tuscheln *vt/i* (*haben*) whisper

Tüte *f* **-,-n** bag; ⟨*Comm*⟩ packet; ⟨*Eis-*⟩ cornet; **in die T~ blasen** ⟨*fam*⟩ be breathalysed

tuten *vi* (*haben*) hoot; ⟨*Schiff:*⟩ sound its hooter; ⟨*Sirene:*⟩ sound

TÜV *m* - ≈ MOT [test]

Typ *m* -s,-en type; (*fam: Kerl*) bloke. **T~e** *f* -,-n type; (*fam: Person*) character

Typhus *m* - typhoid

typisch *a* typical, *adv* -ly (für of)

Typographie, Typografie *f* - typography

Typus *m* -, **Typen** type

Tyrann *m* -en,-en tyrant. **T~ei** *f* - tyranny. **t~isch** *a* tyrannical. **t~isieren** *vt* tyrannize

U

u.a. *abbr* (**unter anderem**) amongst other things

U-Bahn *f* underground, (*Amer*) subway

übel *a* bad; (*hässlich*) nasty, *adv* -ily; **mir ist/wird ü~** I feel sick; **etw ü~ nehmen** take sth amiss; **jdm etw ü~ nehmen** hold sth against s.o. **Ü~** *nt* -s,- evil. **Ü~keit** *f* - nausea. **ü~nehmen†** *vt sep* (NEW) **ü~ nehmen, s. übel. Ü~täter** *m* culprit

üben *vt/i* (*haben*) practise; **sich in etw** (*dat*) **ü~** practise sth

über *prep* (+ *dat/acc*) over; (*höher als*) above; (*betreffend*) about; ⟨*Buch, Vortrag*⟩ on; ⟨*Scheck, Rechnung*⟩ for; (*quer ü~*) across; **ü~ Köln fahren** go via Cologne; **ü~ Ostern** over Easter; **die Woche ü~** during the week; **heute ü~ eine Woche** a week today; **Fehler ü~ Fehler** mistake after mistake □ *adv* **ü~ und ü~** all over; **jdm ü~ sein** be better/(*stärker*) stronger than s.o. □ *a* (*fam*) **ü~ sein** be left over; **etw ü~ sein** be fed up with sth

überall *adv* everywhere

überanstrengen *vt insep* overtax; strain ⟨*Augen*⟩; **sich ü~** overexert oneself

überarbeit|en *vt insep* revise; **sich ü~en** overwork. **Ü~ung** *f* - revision; overwork

überaus *adv* extremely

überbewerten *vt insep* overrate

überbieten† *vt insep* outbid; (*fig*) outdo; (*übertreffen*) surpass

Überblick *m* overall view; (*Abriss*) summary

überblicken *vt insep* overlook; (*abschätzen*) assess

überbringen† *vt insep* deliver

überbrücken *vt insep* (*fig*) bridge

überdauern *vt insep* survive

überdenken† *vt insep* think over

überdies *adv* moreover

überdimensional *a* oversized

Überdosis *f* overdose

Überdruss *m* -es (**Überdruß** *m* -sses) surfeit; **bis zum Ü~** ad nauseam

überdrüssig *a* **ü~ sein/werden** be/ grow tired (*gen* of)

übereignen *vt insep* transfer

übereilt *a* over-hasty, *adv* -ily

übereinander *adv* one on top of/above the other; ⟨*sprechen*⟩ about each other; **die Arme/Beine ü~ schlagen** fold one's arms/cross one's legs. **ü~schlagen†** *vt sep* (NEW) **ü~ schlagen, s. übereinander**

überein|kommen† *vi sep* (*sein*) agree. **Ü~kunft** *f* - agreement. **ü~stimmen** *vi sep* (*haben*) agree; ⟨*Zahlen:*⟩ tally; ⟨*Ansichten:*⟩ coincide; ⟨*Farben:*⟩ match. **Ü~stimmung** *f* agreement

überempfindlich *a* over-sensitive; (*Med*) hypersensitive

überfahren† *vt insep* run over

Überfahrt *f* crossing

Überfall *m* attack; (*Bank-*) raid

überfallen† *vt insep* attack; raid ⟨*Bank*⟩; (*bestürmen*) bombard (**mit** with); (*überkommen*) come over; (*fam: besuchen*) surprise

überfällig *a* overdue

überfliegen† *vt insep* fly over; (*lesen*) skim over

überflügeln *vt insep* outstrip

Überfluss (**Überfluß**) *m* abundance; (*Wohlstand*) affluence

überflüssig *a* superfluous

überfluten *vt insep* flood

überfordern *vt insep* overtax

überführ|en *vt insep* transfer; (*Jur*) convict (*gen* of). **Ü~ung** *f* transfer; (*Straße*) flyover; (*Fußgänger-*) foot-bridge

überfüllt *a* overcrowded

Übergabe *f* (*s.* **übergeben**) handing over; transfer

Übergang *m* crossing; (*Wechsel*) transition. **Ü~sstadium** *nt* transitional stage

übergeben† *vt insep* hand over; (*übereignen*) transfer; **sich ü~** be sick

übergehen†[1] *vi sep* (*sein*) pass (**an** + *acc* to); (*überwechseln*) go over (**zu** to); (*werden zu*) turn (**in** + *acc* into); **zum Angriff ü~** start the attack

übergehen†[2] *vt insep* (*fig*) pass over; (*nicht beachten*) ignore; (*auslassen*) leave out

Übergewicht *nt* excess weight; (*fig*) predominance; **Ü~ haben** be overweight

übergießen† *vt insep* **mit Wasser ü~** pour water over

überglücklich *a* overjoyed

über|greifen† vi sep (haben) spread (auf + acc to). **Ü~griff** m infringement

über|groß a outsize; (übertrieben) exaggerated. **Ü~größe** f outsize

überhaben† vt sep have on; (fam: satthaben) be fed up with

überhand adv **ü~ nehmen** increase alarmingly. **ü~nehmen**† vi sep (haben) (NEW) **ü~ nehmen**, s. **überhand**

überhängen v sep □ vi† (haben) overhang □ vt (reg) **sich** (dat) **etw ü~** sling over one's shoulder (Gewehr); put round one's shoulders (Jacke)

überhäufen vt insep inundate (mit with)

überhaupt adv (im Allgemeinen) altogether; (eigentlich) anyway; (überdies) besides; **ü~ nicht/nichts** not/nothing at all

überheblich a arrogant, adv -ly. **Ü~keit** f - arrogance

überhol|en vt insep overtake; (reparieren) overhaul. **ü~t** a out-dated. **Ü~ung** f -,-en overhaul. **Ü~verbot** nt 'Ü~verbot' 'no overtaking'

überhören vt insep fail to hear; (nicht beachten) ignore

überirdisch a supernatural

überkochen vi sep (sein) boil over

überladen† vt insep overload □ a overornate

überlassen† vt insep **jdm etw ü~** leave sth to s.o.; (geben) let s.o. have sth; **sich seinem Schmerz ü~** abandon oneself to one's grief; **sich** (dat) **selbst ü~ sein** be left to one's own devices

überlasten vt insep overload; overtax (Person)

Überlauf m overflow

überlaufen†[1] vi sep (sein) overflow; (Mil, Pol) defect

überlaufen†[2] vt insep **jdn ü~** (Gefühl:) come over s.o. □ a over-run;(Kursus:) oversubscribed

Überläufer m defector

überleben vt/i insep (haben) survive. **Ü~de(r)** m/f survivor

überlegen[1] vt sep put over

überlegen[2] v insep □ vt [sich dat] **ü~** think over, consider; **es sich** (dat) **anders ü~** change one's mind □ vi (haben) think, reflect; **ohne zu ü~** without thinking

überlegen[3] a superior; (herablassend) supercilious, adv -ly. **Ü~heit** f - superiority

Überlegung f -,-en reflection

überliefer|n vt insep hand down. **Ü~ung** f tradition

überlisten vt insep outwit

überm prep = über dem

Über|macht f superiority. **ü~mächtig** a superior; (Gefühl) overpowering

übermannen vt insep overcome

Über|maß nt excess. **ü~mäßig** a excessive, adv -ly

Übermensch m superman. **ü~lich** a superhuman

übermitteln vt insep convey; (senden) transmit

übermorgen adv the day after tomorrow

übermüdet a overtired

Über|mut m high spirits pl. **ü~mütig** a high-spirited □ adv in high spirits

übern prep = über den

übernächst|e(r,s) a next ... but one; **ü~es Jahr** the year after next

übernacht|en vi insep (haben) stay overnight. **Ü~ung** f -,-en overnight stay; **Ü~ung und Frühstück** bed and breakfast

Übernahme f - taking over; (Comm) takeover

übernatürlich a supernatural

übernehmen† vt insep take over; (annehmen) take on; **sich ü~** overdo things; (finanziell) over-reach oneself

überprüf|en vt insep check. **Ü~ung** f check

überqueren vt insep cross

überragen vt insep tower above; (fig) surpass. **ü~d** a outstanding

überrasch|en vt insep surprise. **ü~end** a surprising, adv -ly; (unerwartet) unexpected, adv -ly. **Ü~ung** f -,-en surprise

überreden vt insep persuade

überreichen vt insep present

überreizt a overwrought

überrennen† vt insep overrun

Überreste mpl remains

überrumpeln vt insep take by surprise

übers prep = über das

Überschall- pref supersonic

überschatten vt insep overshadow

überschätzen vt insep overestimate

Überschlag m rough estimate; (Sport) somersault

überschlagen†[1] vt sep cross (Beine)

überschlagen†[2] vt insep estimate roughly; (auslassen) skip; **sich ü~** somersault; (Ereignisse:) happen fast □ a tepid

überschnappen vi sep (sein) (fam) go crazy

überschneiden† (sich) vr insep intersect, cross; (zusammenfallen) overlap

überschreiben† vt insep entitle; (übertragen) transfer

überschreiten† vt insep cross; (fig) exceed

Überschrift f heading; (*Zeitungs-*) headline

Über|schuss (**Überschuß**) m surplus. **ü~schüssig** a surplus

überschütten vt insep **ü~ mit** cover with; (*fig*) shower with

überschwänglich a effusive, adv -ly

überschwemm|en vt insep flood; (*fig*) inundate. **Ü~ung** f -,-en flood

überschwenglich a (NEW) **überschwänglich**

Übersee in/nach **Ü~** overseas; **aus/von Ü~** from overseas. **Ü~dampfer** m ocean liner. **ü~isch** a overseas

übersehen† vt insep look out over; (*abschätzen*) assess; (*nicht sehen*) overlook, miss; (*ignorieren*) ignore

übersenden† vt insep send

übersetzen[1] vi sep (*haben/sein*) cross [over]

übersetz|en[2] vt insep translate. **Ü~er(in)** m -s,- (f -,-nen) translator. **Ü~ung** f -,-en translation

Übersicht f overall view; (*Abriss*) summary; (*Tabelle*) table. **ü~lich** a clear, adv -ly

übersied|eln vi sep (*sein*), **übersied|eln** vi insep (*sein*) move (**nach** to). **Ü~lung** f move

übersinnlich a supernatural

überspannt a exaggerated; (*verschroben*) eccentric

überspielen vt insep (*fig*) cover up; **auf Band ü~** tape

überspitzt a exaggerated

überspringen† vt insep jump [over]; (*auslassen*) skip

überstehen†[1] vi sep (*haben*) project, jut out

überstehen†[2] vt insep come through; get over (*Krankheit*); (*überleben*) survive

übersteigen† vt insep climb [over]; (*fig*) exceed

überstimmen vt insep outvote

überstreifen vt sep slip on

Überstunden fpl overtime sg; **Ü~ machen** work overtime

überstürz|en vt insep rush; **sich ü~en** (*Ereignisse:*) happen fast; (*Worte:*) tumble out. **ü~t** a hasty, adv -ily

übertölpeln vt insep dupe

übertönen vt insep drown [out]

übertrag|bar a transferable; (*Med*) infectious. **ü~en†** vt insep transfer; (*übergeben*) assign (**dat** to); (*Techn, Med*) transmit; (*Radio, TV*) broadcast; (*übersetzen*) translate; (*anwenden*) apply (**auf** + acc to). □ a transferred, figurative.

Ü~ung f -,-en transfer; transmission; broadcast; translation; application

übertreffen† vt insep surpass; (*übersteigen*) exceed; **sich selbst ü~** excel oneself

übertreib|en† vt insep exaggerate; (*zu weit treiben*) overdo. **Ü~ung** f -,-en exaggeration

übertret|en†[1] vi sep (*sein*) step over the line; (*Pol*) go over/(*Relig*) convert (**zu** to)

übertret|en†[2] vt insep infringe; break (*Gesetz*). **Ü~ung** f -,-en infringement; breach

übertrieben a exaggerated; (*übermäßig*) excessive, adv -ly

übervölkert a overpopulated

übervorteilen vt insep cheat

überwachen vt insep supervise; (*kontrollieren*) monitor; (*bespitzeln*) keep under surveillance

überwachsen a overgrown

überwältigen vt insep overpower; (*fig*) overwhelm. **ü~d** a overwhelming

überweis|en† vt insep transfer; refer (*Patienten*). **Ü~ung** f transfer; (*ärztliche*) referral

überwerfen†[1] vt sep throw on (*Mantel*)

überwerfen†[2] (**sich**) vr insep fall out (**mit** with)

überwiegen† v insep □ vi (*haben*) predominate □ vt outweigh. **ü~d** a predominant, adv -ly

überwind|en† vt insep overcome; **sich ü~en** force oneself. **Ü~ung** f effort

Überwurf m wrap; (*Bett-*) bedspread

Über|zahl f majority. **ü~zählig** a spare

überzeug|en vt insep convince; **sich [selbst] ü~en** satisfy oneself. **ü~end** a convincing, adv -ly. **Ü~ung** f -,-en conviction

überziehen†[1] vt sep put on

überziehen†[2] vt insep cover; overdraw (*Konto*)

Überzug m cover; (*Schicht*) coating

üblich a usual; (*gebräuchlich*) customary

U-Boot nt submarine

übrig a remaining; (*andere*) other; **alles Ü~e** (**ü~e**) [all] the rest; **im Ü~en** (**ü~en**) besides; (*ansonsten*) apart from that; **ü~ sein** od **bleiben** be left [over]; **etw ü~ haben** od **behalten** have sth left [over]; **etw ü~ lassen** leave sth [over]; **uns blieb nichts anderes ü~** we had no choice. **ü~behalten†** vt sep (NEW) **ü~ behalten**, s. **übrig**. **ü~bleiben†** vi sep (*sein*) (NEW) **ü~ bleiben**, s. **übrig**. **ü~ens** adv by the way. **ü~lassen†** vt sep (NEW) **ü~ lassen**, s. **übrig**

Übung f -,-en exercise; (*Üben*) practice; **außer od aus der Ü~** out of practice

UdSSR f - USSR

Ufer nt -s,- shore; (*Fluss-*) bank

Uhr f -,-en clock; (*Armband-*) watch; (*Zähler-*) meter; **um ein U~** at one o'clock; **wie viel U~ ist es?** what's the time? **U~armband** nt watch-strap. **U~macher** m -s,- watch and clockmaker. **U~werk** nt clock/watch mechanism. **U~zeiger** m [clock-/watch-]hand. **U~zeigersinn** m **im/entgegen dem U~zeigersinn** clockwise/anticlockwise. **U~zeit** f time

Uhu m -s,-s eagle owl

UKW abbr (*Ultrakurzwelle*) VHF

Ulk m -s fun; (*Streich*) trick. **u~en** vi (*haben*) joke. **u~ig** a funny; (*seltsam*) odd, adv -ly

Ulme f -,-n elm

Ultimatum nt -s,-ten ultimatum

Ultrakurzwelle f very high frequency

Ultraschall m ultrasound

ultraviolett a ultraviolet

um prep (+ acc) [a]round; (*Uhrzeit*) at; (*bitten, kämpfen*) for; (*streiten*) over; (*sich sorgen*) about; (*betrügen*) out of; (*bei Angabe einer Differenz*) by; **um [... herum]** around, [round] about; **Tag um Tag** day after day; **einen Tag um den andern** every other day; **um seinetwillen** for his sake o adv (*ungefähr*) around, about; **um sein** (*fam*) be over; (*Zeit*) be up o conj **um zu** to; (*Absicht*) [in order] to; **zu müde, um zu . . .** too tired to . . .; **um so besser** (NEW) **umso besser**, s. **umso**

umändern vt sep alter

umarbeiten vt sep alter; (*bearbeiten*) revise

umarm|en vt insep embrace, hug. **U~ung** f -,-en embrace, hug

Umbau m rebuilding; conversion (**zu** into). **u~en** vt sep rebuild; convert (**zu** into)

umbild|en vt sep change; (*umgestalten*) reorganize; reshuffle (*Kabinett*). **U~ung** f reorganization; (*Pol*) reshuffle

umbinden† vt sep put on

umblättern v sep o vt turn [over] o vi (*haben*) turn the page

umblicken (sich) vr sep look round; (*zurück*) look back

umbringen† vt sep kill; **sich u~** kill oneself

Umbruch m (*fig*) radical change

umbuchen v sep o vt change; (*Comm*) transfer o vi (*haben*) change one's booking

umdrehen v sep o vt turn round/(*wenden*) over; turn (*Schlüssel*);

(*umkrempeln*) turn inside out; **sich u~** turn round; (*im Liegen*) turn over o vi (*haben/sein*) turn back

Umdrehung f turn; (*Motor-*) revolution

umeinander adv around each other; **sich u~ sorgen** worry about each other

umfahren†[1] vt sep run over

umfahren†[2] vt insep go round; bypass (*Ort*)

umfallen† vi sep (*sein*) fall over; (*Person:*) fall down

Umfang m girth; (*Geom*) circumference; (*Größe*) size; (*Ausmaß*) extent; (*Mus*) range

umfangen† vt insep embrace; (*fig*) envelop

umfangreich a extensive; (*dick*) big

umfassen vt insep consist of, comprise; (*umgeben*) surround. **u~d** a comprehensive

Umfrage f survey, poll

umfüllen vt sep transfer

umfunktionieren vt sep convert

Umgang m [social] contact; (*Umgehen*) dealing (**mit** with): **U~ haben mit** associate with

umgänglich a sociable

Umgangs|formen fpl manners. **U~sprache** f colloquial language. **u~sprachlich** a colloquial, adv -ly

umgeb|en† vt/i insep (*haben*) surround o a **u~en von** surrounded by. **U~ung** f -,-en surroundings pl

umgehen†[1] vi sep (*sein*) go round; **u~ mit** treat, handle; (*verkehren*) associate with; **in dem Schloss geht ein Gespenst um** the castle is haunted

umgehen†[2] vt insep avoid; (*nicht beachten*) evade; (*Straße:*) bypass

umgehend a immediate, adv -ly

Umgehungsstraße f bypass

umgekehrt a inverse; (*Reihenfolge*) reverse; **es war u~** it was the other way round o adv conversely; **und u~** and vice versa

umgraben† vt sep dig [over]

umhaben† vt sep have on

Umhang m cloak

umhauen† vt sep knock down; (*fällen*) chop down

umher adv weit **u~** all around. **u~gehen†** vi sep (*sein*) walk about

umhören (sich) vr sep ask around

Umkehr f - turning back. **u~en** v sep o vi (*sein*) turn back o vt turn round; turn inside out (*Tasche*); (*fig*) reverse. **U~ung** f - reversal

umkippen *v sep* □ *vt* tip over; *(versehentlich)* knock over □ *vi (sein)* fall over; *⟨Boot:⟩* capsize; *(fam: ohnmächtig werden)* faint

Umkleide|kabine *f* changing-cubicle. **u~n (sich)** *vr sep* change. **U~raum** *m* changing-room

umknicken *v sep* □ *vt* bend; *(falten)* fold □ *vi (sein)* bend; *(mit dem Fuß)* go over on one's ankle

umkommen† *vi sep (sein)* perish; **u~ lassen** waste *⟨Lebensmittel⟩*

Umkreis *m* surroundings *pl*; **im U~ von** within a radius of

umkreisen *vt insep* circle; *⟨Astr⟩* revolve around; *⟨Satellit:⟩* orbit

umkrempeln *vt sep* turn up; *(von innen nach außen)* turn inside out; *(ändern)* change radically

Umlauf *m* circulation; *⟨Astr⟩* revolution. **U~bahn** *f* orbit

Umlaut *m* umlaut

umlegen *vt sep* lay *or* put down; flatten *⟨Getreide⟩*; turn down *⟨Kragen⟩*; put on *⟨Schal⟩*; throw *⟨Hebel⟩*; *⟨verlegen⟩* transfer; *(fam: niederschlagen)* knock down; *(töten)* kill

umleit|en *vt sep* divert. **U~ung** *f* diversion

umliegend *a* surrounding

umpflanzen *vt sep* transplant

umrahmen *vt insep* frame

umranden *vt insep* edge

umräumen *vt sep* rearrange

umrechn|en *vt sep* convert. **U~ung** *f* conversion

umreißen†¹ *vt sep* tear down; knock down *⟨Person⟩*

umreißen†² *vt insep* outline

umringen *vt insep* surround

Umriss (Umriß) *m* outline

umrühren *vt/i sep (haben)* stir

ums *pron* = um das; **u~ Leben kommen** lose one's life

Umsatz *m* *⟨Comm⟩* turnover

umschalten *vt sep (haben)* switch over; **auf Rot u~** *⟨Ampel:⟩* change to red

Umschau *f* **U~ halten nach** look out for. **u~en (sich)** *vr sep* look round/*(zurück)* back

Umschlag *m* cover; *⟨Schutz-⟩* jacket; *⟨Brief-⟩* envelope; *⟨Med⟩* compress; *⟨Hosen-⟩* turn-up; *⟨Wechsel⟩* change. **u~en†** *v sep* □ *vt* turn up; turn over *⟨Seite⟩*; *⟨fällen⟩* chop down □ *vi (sein)* topple over; *⟨Boot:⟩* capsize; *⟨Wetter:⟩* change; *⟨Wind:⟩* veer

umschließen† *vt insep* enclose

umschnallen *vt sep* buckle on

umschreiben†¹ *vt sep* rewrite

umschreib|en² *vt insep* define; *(anders ausdrücken)* paraphrase. **U~ung** *f* definition; paraphrase

umschulen *vt sep* retrain; *⟨Sch⟩* transfer to another school

Umschweife *pl* **keine U~ machen** come straight out with it; **ohne U~** straight out

Umschwung *m* *⟨fig⟩* change; *⟨Pol⟩* U-turn

umsehen† **(sich)** *vr sep* look round; *(zurück)* look back; **sich u~ nach** look for

umsein† *vi sep (sein)* NEW **um sein**, *s.* um

umseitig *a & adv* overleaf

umsetzen *vt sep* move; *(umpflanzen)* transplant; *⟨Comm⟩* sell

Umsicht *f* circumspection. **u~ig** *a* circumspect, *adv* -ly

umsied|eln *v sep* □ *vt* resettle □ *vi (sein)* move. **U~lung** *f* resettlement

umso *conj* **~ besser/mehr** all the better/more; **je mehr, ~ besser** the more the better

umsonst *adv* in vain; *(grundlos)* without reason; *(gratis)* free

umspringen† *vi sep (sein)* change; *⟨Wind:⟩* veer; **übel u~ mit** treat badly

Umstand *m* circumstance; *(Tatsache)* fact; *(Aufwand)* fuss; *(Mühe)* trouble; **unter U~en** possibly; **U~e machen** make a fuss; **jdm U~e machen** put s.o. to trouble; **in andern U~en** pregnant

umständlich *a* laborious, *adv* -ly; *(kompliziert)* involved; *⟨Person⟩* fussy

Umstands|kleid *nt* maternity dress. **U~wort** *nt (pl* -wörter*)* adverb

umstehen† *vi insep* surround

Umstehende *pl* bystanders

umsteigen† *vi sep (sein)* change

umstellen¹ *vt insep* surround

umstell|en² *vt sep* rearrange; transpose *⟨Wörter⟩*; *(anders einstellen)* reset; *⟨Techn⟩* convert; *(ändern)* change; **sich u~en** adjust. **U~ung** *f* rearrangement; transposition; resetting; conversion; change; adjustment

umstimmen *vt sep* **jdn u~** change s.o.'s mind

umstoßen† *vt sep* knock over; *⟨fig⟩* overturn; upset *⟨Plan⟩*

umstritten *a* controversial; *(ungeklärt)* disputed

umstülpen *vt sep* turn upside down; *(von innen nach außen)* turn inside out

Um|sturz *m* coup. **u~stürzen** *v sep* □ *vt* overturn; *⟨Pol⟩* overthrow □ *vi (sein)* fall over

umtaufen *vt sep* rename

Umtausch *m* exchange. **u~en** *vt sep* change; exchange (**gegen** for)

umwälzend *a* revolutionary

umwandeln *vt sep* convert; (*fig*) transform

umwechseln *vt sep* change

Umweg *m* detour; **auf U~en** (*fig*) in a roundabout way

Umwelt *f* environment. **u~freundlich** *a* environmentally friendly. **U~schutz** *m* protection of the environment. **U~schützer** *m* environmentalist

umwenden† *vt sep* turn over; **sich u~** turn round

umwerfen† *vt sep* knock over; (*fig*) upset ⟨*Plan*⟩; (*fam*) bowl over ⟨*Person*⟩

umziehen† *v sep* □ *vi* (*sein*) move □ *vt* change; **sich u~** change

umzingeln *vt insep* surround

Umzug *m* move; (*Prozession*) procession

unabänderlich *a* irrevocable; ⟨*Tatsache*⟩ unalterable

unabhängig *a* independent, *adv* -ly; **u~ davon, ob** irrespective of whether. **U~keit** *f* - independence

unabkömmlich *pred a* busy

unablässig *a* incessant, *adv* -ly

unabsehbar *a* incalculable

unabsichtlich *a* unintentional, *adv* -ly

unachtsam *a* careless, *adv* -ly. **U~keit** *f* - carelessness

unangebracht *a* inappropriate

unangemeldet *a* unexpected, *adv* -ly

unangemessen *a* inappropriate, *adv* -ly

unangenehm *a* unpleasant, *adv* -ly; (*peinlich*) embarrassing

Unannehmlichkeiten *fpl* trouble *sg*

unansehnlich *a* shabby; ⟨*Person*⟩ plain

unanständig *a* indecent, *adv* -ly

unantastbar *a* inviolable

unappetitlich *a* unappetizing

Unart *f* -,-en bad habit. **u~ig** *a* naughty

unauffällig *a* inconspicuous, *adv* -ly, unobtrusive, *adv* -ly

unauffindbar *a* **u~ sein** be nowhere to be found

unaufgefordert *adv* without being asked

unaufhaltsam *a* inexorable, *adv* -bly. **u~hörlich** *a* incessant, *adv* -ly

unaufmerksam *a* inattentive

unaufrichtig *a* insincere

unausbleiblich *a* inevitable

unausgeglichen *a* unbalanced; ⟨*Person*⟩ unstable

unaus|löschlich *a* (*fig*) indelible, *adv* -bly. **u~sprechlich** *a* indescribable, *adv* -bly. **u~stehlich** *a* insufferable

unbarmherzig *a* merciless, *adv* -ly

unbeabsichtigt *a* unintentional, *adv* -ly

unbedacht *a* rash, *adv* -ly

unbedenklich *a* harmless □ *adv* without hesitation

unbedeutend *a* insignificant; (*geringfügig*) slight, *adv* -ly

unbedingt *a* absolute, *adv* -ly; **nicht u~** not necessarily

unbefangen *a* natural, *adv* -ly; (*unparteiisch*) impartial

unbefriedig|end *a* unsatisfactory. **u~t** *a* dissatisfied

unbefugt *a* unauthorized □ *adv* without authorization

unbegreiflich *a* incomprehensible

unbegrenzt *a* unlimited □ *adv* indefinitely

unbegründet *a* unfounded

Unbehag|en *nt* unease; (*körperlich*) discomfort. **u~lich** *a* uncomfortable, *adv* -bly

unbeholfen *a* awkward, *adv* -ly

unbekannt *a* unknown; (*nicht vertraut*) unfamiliar. **U~e(r)** *m/f* stranger

unbekümmert *a* unconcerned; (*unbeschwert*) carefree

unbeliebt *a* unpopular. **U~heit** *f* unpopularity

unbemannt *a* unmanned

unbemerkt *a & adv* unnoticed

unbenutzt *a* unused

unbequem *a* uncomfortable, *adv* -bly; (*lästig*) awkward

unberechenbar *a* unpredictable

unberechtigt *a* unjustified; (*unbefugt*) unauthorized

unberufen *int* touch wood!

unberührt *a* untouched; (*fig*) virgin; ⟨*Landschaft*⟩ unspoilt

unbescheiden *a* presumptuous

unbeschrankt *a* unguarded

unbeschränkt *a* unlimited □ *adv* without limit

unbeschreiblich *a* indescribable, *adv* -bly

unbeschwert *a* carefree

unbesiegbar *a* invincible

unbesiegt *a* undefeated

unbesonnen *a* rash, *adv* -ly

unbespielt *a* blank

unbeständig *a* inconsistent; ⟨*Wetter*⟩ unsettled

unbestechlich *a* incorruptible

unbestimmt *a* indefinite; ⟨*Alter*⟩ indeterminate; (*ungewiss*) uncertain; (*unklar*) vague □ *adv* vaguely

unbestreitbar *a* indisputable, *adv* -bly

unbestritten *a* undisputed □ *adv* indisputably

unbeteiligt *a* indifferent; **u~ an** (+ *dat*) not involved in

unbetont *a* unstressed

unbewacht *a* unguarded

unbewaffnet *a* unarmed

unbeweglich *a* & *adv* motionless, still

unbewohnt *a* uninhabited

unbewusst (**unbewußt**) *a* unconscious, *adv* -ly

unbezahlbar *a* priceless

unbezahlt *a* unpaid

unbrauchbar *a* useless

und *conj* and; **und so weiter** and so on; **nach und nach** bit by bit

Undank *m* ingratitude. **u~bar** *a* ungrateful; (*nicht lohnend*) thankless. **U~barkeit** *f* ingratitude

undefinierbar *a* indefinable

undenk|bar *a* unthinkable. **u~lich** *a* **seit u~lichen Zeiten** from time immemorial

undeutlich *a* indistinct, *adv* -ly; (*vage*) vague, *adv* -ly

undicht *a* leaking; **u~e Stelle** leak

Unding *nt* absurdity

undiplomatisch *a* undiplomatic, *adv* -ally

unduldsam *a* intolerant

undurch|dringlich *a* impenetrable; (*Miene*) inscrutable. **u~führbar** *a* impracticable

undurch|lässig *a* impermeable. **u~sichtig** *a* opaque; (*fig*) doubtful

uneben *a* uneven, *adv* -ly. **U~heit** *f* -,-en unevenness; (*Buckel*) bump

unecht *a* false; **u~er Schmuck/Pelz** imitation jewellery/fur

unehelich *a* illegitimate

unehr|enhaft *a* dishonourable, *adv* -bly. **u~lich** *a* dishonest, *adv* -ly. **U~lichkeit** *f* dishonesty

uneinig *a* (*fig*) divided; [**sich** (*dat*)] **u~ sein** disagree. **U~keit** *f* disagreement; (*Streit*) discord

uneins *a* **~ sein** be at odds

unempfindlich *a* insensitive (**gegen** to); (*widerstandsfähig*) tough; (*Med*) immune

unendlich *a* infinite, *adv* -ly; (*endlos*) endless, *adv* -ly. **U~keit** *f* - infinity

unentbehrlich *a* indispensable

unentgeltlich *a* free; (*Arbeit*) unpaid □ *adv* free of charge; (*arbeiten*) without pay

unentschieden *a* undecided; (*Sport*) drawn; **u~ spielen** draw. **U~** *nt* -s,- draw

unentschlossen *a* indecisive; (*unentschieden*) undecided. **U~heit** *f* indecision

unentwegt *a* persistent *adv* -ly; (*unaufhörlich*) incessant, *adv* -ly

unerbittlich *a* implacable, *adv* -bly; (*Schicksal*) inexorable

unerfahren *a* inexperienced. **U~heit** *f* - inexperience

unerfreulich *a* unpleasant, *adv* -ly

unergründlich *a* unfathomable

unerhört *a* enormous, *adv* -ly; (*empörend*) outrageous, *adv* -ly

unerklärlich *a* inexplicable

unerlässlich (**unerläßlich**) *a* essential

unerlaubt *a* unauthorized □ *adv* without permission

unermesslich (**unermeßlich**) *a* immense, *adv* -ly

unermüdlich *a* tireless, *adv* -ly

unersättlich *a* insatiable

unerschöpflich *a* inexhaustible

unerschütterlich *a* unshakeable

unerschwinglich *a* prohibitive

unersetzlich *a* irreplaceable; (*Verlust*) irreparable

unerträglich *a* unbearable, *adv* -bly

unerwartet *a* unexpected, *adv* -ly

unerwünscht *a* unwanted; (*Besuch*) unwelcome

unfähig *a* incompetent; **u~, etw zu tun** incapable of doing sth; (*nicht in der Lage*) unable to do sth. **U~keit** *f* incompetence; inability (**zu** to)

unfair *a* unfair, *adv* -ly

Unfall *m* accident. **U~flucht** *f* failure to stop after an accident. **U~station** *f* casualty department

unfassbar (**unfaßbar**) *a* incomprehensible; (*unglaublich*) unimaginable

unfehlbar *a* infallible. **U~keit** *f* - infallibility

unfolgsam *a* disobedient

unförmig *a* shapeless

unfreiwillig *a* involuntary, *adv* -ily; (*unbeabsichtigt*) unintentional, *adv* -ly

unfreundlich *a* unfriendly; (*unangenehm*) unpleasant, *adv* -ly. **U~keit** *f* unfriendliness; unpleasantness

Unfriede[n] *m* discord

unfruchtbar *a* infertile; (*fig*) unproductive. **U~keit** *f* infertility

Unfug *m* -s mischief; (*Unsinn*) nonsense

Ungar|(in) *m* -n,-n (*f* -,-nen) Hungarian. **u~isch** *a* Hungarian. **U~n** *nt* -s Hungary

ungastlich *a* inhospitable

ungeachtet *prep* (+ *gen*) in spite of; **dessen u~** notwithstanding [this]. **ungebärdig** *a* unruly. **ungebeugt** *a* (*Gram*) uninflected. **ungebraucht** *a* unused. **ungebührlich** *a* improper, *adv* -ly. **ungedeckt** *a* uncovered; (*Sport*) unmarked; ⟨*Tisch*⟩ unlaid

Ungeduld *f* impatience. **u~ig** *a* impatient, *adv* -ly

ungeeignet *a* unsuitable

ungefähr *a* approximate, *adv* -ly, rough, *adv* -ly

ungefährlich *a* harmless

ungehalten *a* angry, *adv* -ily

ungeheuer *a* enormous, *adv* -ly. **U~** *nt* -s,- monster

ungeheuerlich *a* outrageous

ungehobelt *a* uncouth

ungehörig *a* improper, *adv* -ly; ⟨*frech*⟩ impertinent, *adv* -ly

ungehorsam *a* disobedient. **U~** *m* disobedience

ungeklärt *a* unsolved; ⟨*Frage*⟩ unsettled; ⟨*Ursache*⟩ unknown

ungeladen *a* unloaded; ⟨*Gast*⟩ uninvited

ungelegen *a* inconvenient. **U~heiten** *fpl* trouble *sg*

ungelernt *a* unskilled. **ungemein** *a* tremendous, *adv* -ly

ungemütlich *a* uncomfortable, *adv* -bly; ⟨*unangenehm*⟩ unpleasant, *adv* -ly

ungenau *a* inaccurate, *adv* -ly; ⟨*vage*⟩ vague, *adv* -ly. **U~igkeit** *f* -,-en inaccuracy

ungeniert /'ʊnʒeniːɐ̯t/ *a* uninhibited ▫ *adv* openly

ungenießbar *a* inedible; ⟨*Getränk*⟩ undrinkable. **ungenügend** *a* inadequate, *adv* -ly; (*Sch*) unsatisfactory. **ungepflegt** *a* neglected; ⟨*Person*⟩ unkempt. **ungerade** *a* ⟨*Zahl*⟩ odd

ungerecht *a* unjust, *adv* -ly. **U~igkeit** *f* -,-en injustice

ungern *adv* reluctantly

ungesalzen *a* unsalted

ungeschehen *a* **u~ machen** undo

Ungeschick|lichkeit *f* clumsiness. **u~t** *a* clumsy, *adv* -ily

ungeschminkt *a* without make-up; ⟨*Wahrheit*⟩ unvarnished. **ungeschrieben** *a* unwritten. **ungesehen** *a* & *adv* unseen. **ungesellig** *a* unsociable. **ungesetzlich** *a* illegal, *adv* -ly. **ungestört** *a* undisturbed. **ungestraft** *adv* with impunity. **ungestüm** *a* impetuous, *adv* -ly. **ungesund** *a* unhealthy. **ungesüßt** *a* unsweetened. **ungetrübt** *a* perfect

Ungetüm *nt* -s,-e monster

ungewiss (**ungewiß**) *a* uncertain; **im Ungewissen** (**ungewissen**) **sein/lassen** be/leave in the dark. **U~heit** *f* uncertainty

ungewöhnlich *a* unusual, *adv* -ly. **ungewohnt** *a* unaccustomed; ⟨*nicht vertraut*⟩ unfamiliar. **ungewollt** *a* unintentional, *adv* -ly; ⟨*Schwangerschaft*⟩ unwanted

Ungeziefer *nt* -s vermin

ungezogen *a* naughty, *adv* -ily

ungezwungen *a* informal, *adv* -ly; ⟨*natürlich*⟩ natural, *adv* -ly

ungläubig *a* incredulous

unglaublich *a* incredible, *adv* -bly, unbelievable, *adv* -bly

ungleich *a* unequal, *adv* -ly; ⟨*verschieden*⟩ different. **U~heit** *f* - inequality. **u~mäßig** *a* uneven, *adv* -ly

Unglück *nt* -s,-e misfortune; (*Pech*) bad luck; (*Missgeschick*) mishap; (*Unfall*) accident; **U~ bringen** be unlucky. **u~lich** *a* unhappy, *adv* -ily; ⟨*ungünstig*⟩ unfortunate, *adv* -ly. **u~licherweise** *adv* unfortunately. **u~selig** *a* unfortunate. **U~sfall** *m* accident

ungültig *a* invalid; (*Jur*) void

ungünstig *a* unfavourable, *adv* -bly; ⟨*unpassend*⟩ inconvenient, *adv* -ly

ungut *a* ⟨*Gefühl*⟩ uneasy; **nichts für u~!** no offence!

unhandlich *a* unwieldy

Unheil *nt* -s disaster; **U~ anrichten** cause havoc

unheilbar *a* incurable, *adv* -bly

unheimlich *a* eerie; ⟨*gruselig*⟩ creepy; (*fam: groß*) terrific ▫ *adv* eerily; (*fam: sehr*) terribly

unhöflich *a* rude, *adv* -ly. **U~keit** *f* rudeness

unhörbar *a* inaudible, *adv* -bly

unhygienisch *a* unhygienic

Uni *f* -,-s (*fam*) university

uni /y'ni:/ *inv a* plain

Uniform *f* -,-en uniform

uninteress|ant *a* uninteresting. **u~iert** *a* uninterested; ⟨*unbeteiligt*⟩ disinterested

Union *f* -,-en union

universal *a* universal

universell *a* universal, *adv* -ly

Universität *f* -,-en university

Universum *nt* -s universe

unkennt|lich *a* unrecognizable. **U~nis** *f* ignorance

unklar *a* unclear; ⟨*ungewiss*⟩ uncertain; ⟨*vage*⟩ vague, *adv* -ly; **im U~en** (**u~en**) **sein/lassen** be/leave in the dark. **U~heit** *f* -,-en uncertainty

unklug *a* unwise, *adv* -ly

unkompliziert *a* uncomplicated

Unkosten *pl* expenses

Unkraut *nt* weed; (*coll*) weeds *pl*; U~jäten weed. U~vertilgungsmittel *nt* weed-killer

unkultiviert *a* uncultured

unlängst *adv* recently

unlauter *a* dishonest; (*unfair*) unfair

unleserlich *a* illegible, *adv* -bly

unleugbar *a* undeniable, *adv* -bly

unlogisch *a* illogical, *adv* -ly

unlös|bar *a* (*fig*) insoluble. u~lich *a* (*Chem*) insoluble

unlustig *a* listless, *adv* -ly

unmäßig *a* excessive, *adv* -ly; (*äußerst*) extreme, *adv* -ly

Unmenge *f* enormous amount/(*Anzahl*) number

Unmensch *m* (*fam*) brute. u~lich *a* inhuman; (*entsetzlich*) appalling, *adv* -ly

unmerklich *a* imperceptible, *adv* -bly

unmissverständlich (**unmißverständlich**) *a* unambiguous, *adv* -ly; (*offen*) unequivocal, *adv* -ly

unmittelbar *a* immediate, *adv* -ly; (*direkt*) direct, *adv* -ly

unmöbliert *a* unfurnished

unmodern *a* old-fashioned

unmöglich *a* impossible, *adv* -bly. U~keit *f* - impossibility

Unmoral *f* immorality. u~isch *a* immoral, *adv* -ly

unmündig *a* under-age

Unmut *m* displeasure

unnachahmlich *a* inimitable

unnachgiebig *a* intransigent

unnatürlich *a* unnatural, *adv* -ly

unnormal *a* abnormal, *adv* -ly

unnötig *a* unnecessary, *adv* -ily

unnütz *a* useless □ *adv* needlessly

unord|entlich *a* untidy, *adv* -ily; (*nachlässig*) sloppy, *adv* -ily. U~nung *f* disorder; (*Durcheinander*) muddle

unorganisiert *a* disorganized

unorthodox *a* unorthodox □ *adv* in an unorthodox manner

unparteiisch *a* impartial, *adv* -ly

unpassend *a* inappropriate, *adv* -ly; (*Moment*) inopportune

unpässlich (**unpäßlich**) *a* indisposed

unpersönlich *a* impersonal

unpraktisch *a* impractical

unpünktlich *a* unpunctual □ *adv* late

unrasiert *a* unshaven

Unrast *f* restlessness

unrealistisch *a* unrealistic, *adv* -ally

unrecht *a* wrong, *adv* -ly □ *n* jdm u~ tun do s.o. an injustice; u~ haben/geben ⟨NEW⟩ U~ haben/geben, s. Unrecht. U~ *nt* wrong; zu U~ wrongly; U~ haben be wrong; jdm U~ geben disagree with s.o. u~mäßig *a* unlawful, *adv* -ly

unregelmäßig *a* irregular, *adv* -ly. U~keit *f* irregularity

unreif *a* unripe; (*fig*) immature

unrein *a* impure; (*Luft*) polluted; ⟨Haut⟩ bad; ins U~e (u~e) schreiben make a rough draft of

unrentabel *a* unprofitable, *adv* -bly

unrichtig *a* incorrect

Unruh|e *f* -,-n restlessness; (*Erregung*) agitation; (*Besorgnis*) anxiety; U~en (*Pol*) unrest *sg*. u~ig *a* restless, *adv* -ly; ⟨Meer⟩ agitated; (*laut*) noisy, *adv* -ily; (*besorgt*) anxious, *adv* -ly

uns *pron* (*acc/dat* of **wir**) us; (*refl*) ourselves; (*einander*) each other; **ein Freund von uns** a friend of ours

unsagbar, **unsäglich** *a* indescribable, *adv* -bly

unsanft *a* rough, *adv* -ly

unsauber *a* dirty; (*nachlässig*) sloppy, *adv* -ily; (*unlauter*) dishonest, *adv* -ly

unschädlich *a* harmless

unscharf *a* blurred

unschätzbar *a* inestimable

unscheinbar *a* inconspicuous

unschicklich *a* improper, *adv* -ly

unschlagbar *a* unbeatable

unschlüssig *a* undecided

Unschuld *f* - innocence; (*Jungfräulichkeit*) virginity. u~ig *a* innocent, *adv* -ly

unselbstständig, **unselbständig** *a* dependent □ *adv* u~ denken not think for oneself

unser *poss pron* our. u~e(r,s) *poss pron* ours. u~erseits *adv* for our part. u~twegen *adv* for our sake; (*wegen uns*) because of us, on our account. u~twillen *adv* um u~twillen for our sake

unsicher *a* unsafe; (*ungewiss*) uncertain; (*nicht zuverlässig*) unreliable; ⟨Schritte, Hand⟩ unsteady; (*Person*) insecure □ *adv* unsteadily. U~heit *f* uncertainty; unreliability; insecurity

unsichtbar *a* invisible

Unsinn *m* nonsense. u~ig *a* nonsensical, absurd

Unsitt|e *f* bad habit. u~lich *a* indecent, *adv* -ly

unsportlich *a* not sporty; (*unfair*) unsporting, *adv* -ly

uns|re(r,s) *poss pron* = unsere(r,s). u~rige *poss pron* der/die/das u~rige ours

unsterblich *a* immortal. **U~keit** *f* immortality

unstet *a* restless, *adv* -ly; *(unbeständig)* unstable

Unstimmigkeit *f* -,-en inconsistency; *(Streit)* difference

Unsumme *f* vast sum

unsymmetrisch *a* not symmetrical

unsympathisch *a* unpleasant; **er ist mir u~** I don't like him

untätig *a* idle, *adv* idly. **U~keit** *f* - idleness

untauglich *a* unsuitable; *(Mil)* unfit

unteilbar *a* indivisible

unten *adv* at the bottom; *(auf der Unterseite)* underneath; *(eine Treppe tiefer)* downstairs; *(im Text)* below; **hier/da u~** down here/there; **nach u~** down[wards]; *(die Treppe hinunter)* downstairs; **siehe u~** see below

unter *prep* (+ *dat/acc*) under; *(niedriger als)* below; *(inmitten, zwischen)* among; **u~ anderem** among other things; **u~ der Woche** during the week; **u~ sich** by themselves; **u~ uns gesagt** between ourselves

Unter|arm *m* forearm. **U~bewusstsein** (**U~bewußtsein**) *nt* subconscious

unterbieten† *vt insep* undercut; beat ⟨Rekord⟩

unterbinden† *vt insep* stop

unterbleiben† *vi insep* (*sein*) cease; **es hat zu u~** it must stop

unterbrech|en† *vt insep* interrupt; break ⟨Reise⟩. **U~ung** *f* -,-en interruption; break

unterbreiten *vt insep* present

unterbringen† *vt sep* put; *(beherbergen)* put up

unterdessen *adv* in the meantime

unterdrück|en *vt insep* suppress; oppress ⟨Volk⟩. **U~ung** *f* - suppression; oppression

untere(r,s) *a* lower

untereinander *adv* one below the other; *(miteinander)* among ourselves/yourselves/themselves

unterernähr|t *a* undernourished. **U~ung** *f* malnutrition

Unterfangen *nt* -s,- venture

Unterführung *f* underpass; *(Fußgänger-)* subway

Untergang *m* *(Astr)* setting; *(Naut)* sinking; *(Zugrundegehen)* disappearance; *(der Welt)* end

Untergebene(r) *m/f* subordinate

untergehen† *vi sep* (*sein*) *(Astr)* set; *(versinken)* go under; ⟨Schiff:⟩ go down, sink; *(zugrunde gehen)* disappear; ⟨Welt:⟩ come to an end

untergeordnet *a* subordinate

Untergeschoss (**Untergeschoß**) *nt* basement

untergraben† *vt insep* *(fig)* undermine

Untergrund *m* foundation; *(Hintergrund)* background; *(Pol)* underground. **U~bahn** *f* underground [railway] ; *(Amer)* subway

unterhaken *vt sep* **jdn u~** take s.o.'s arm; **untergehakt** arm in arm

unterhalb *adv & prep* (+ *gen*) below

Unterhalt *m* maintenance

unterhalt|en† *vt insep* maintain; *(ernähren)* support; *(betreiben)* run; *(erheitern)* entertain; **sich u~en** talk; *(sich vergnügen)* enjoy oneself. **u~sam** *a* entertaining. **U~ung** *f* -,-en maintenance; *(Gespräch)* conversation; *(Zeitvertreib)* entertainment

unterhandeln *vi insep* *(haben)* negotiate

Unter|haus *nt* *(Pol)* lower house; *(in UK)* House of Commons. **U~hemd** *nt* vest. **U~holz** *nt* undergrowth. **U~hose** *f* underpants *pl*. **u~irdisch** *a & adv* underground

unterjochen *vt insep* subjugate

Unterkiefer *m* lower jaw

unter|kommen† *vi sep* (*sein*) find accommodation; *(eine Stellung finden)* get a job. **u~kriegen** *vt sep* *(fam)* get down

Unterkunft *f* -,-künfte accommodation

Unterlage *f* pad; **U~n** papers

Unterlass (**Unterlaß**) *m* **ohne U~** incessantly

unterlass|en† *vt insep* **etw u~en** refrain from [doing] sth; **es u~en, etw zu tun** fail or omit to do sth. **U~ung** *f* -,-en omission

unterlaufen† *vi insep* (*sein*) occur; **mir ist ein Fehler u~** I made a mistake

unterlegen¹ *vt sep* put underneath

unterlegen² *a* inferior; *(Sport)* losing; **zahlenmäßig u~** out-numbered *(dat* by). **U~e(r)** *m/f* loser

Unterleib *m* abdomen

unterliegen† *vi insep* (*sein*) lose *(dat* to); *(unterworfen sein)* be subject *(dat* to)

Unterlippe *f* lower lip

unterm *prep* = unter dem

Untermiete *f* **zur U~ wohnen** be a lodger. **U~r(in)** *m(f)* lodger

unterminieren *vt insep* undermine

untern *prep* = unter den

unternehm|en† *vt insep* undertake; take ⟨Schritte⟩; **etw/nichts u~en** do sth/nothing. **U~en** *nt* -s,- undertaking, enterprise; *(Betrieb)* concern. **u~end** *a* enterprising. **U~er** *m* -s,- employer; *(Bau-)* contractor; *(Industrieller)* industrialist. **U~ung** *f* -,-en undertaking; *(Comm)* venture. **u~ungslustig** *a* enterprising; (*abenteuerlustig*) adventurous

Unteroffizier *m* non-commissioned officer

unterordnen *vt sep* subordinate; **sich u~** accept a subordinate role

Unterredung *f* -,-en talk

Unterricht *m* -[e]s teaching; (*Privat-*) tuition; (*U~sstunden*) lessons *pl*; **U~ geben/nehmen** give/have lessons

unterrichten *vt/i insep* (*haben*) teach; (*informieren*) inform; **sich u~** inform oneself

Unterrock *m* slip

unters *prep* = **unter das**

untersagen *vt insep* forbid

Untersatz *m* mat; (*mit Füßen*) stand; (*Gläser-*) coaster

unterschätzen *vt insep* underestimate

unterscheid|en† *vt/i insep* (*haben*) distinguish; (*auseinander halten*) tell apart; **sich u~en** differ. **U~ung** *f* -,-en distinction

Unterschied *m* -[e]s,-e difference; (*Unterscheidung*) distinction; **im U~ zu ihm** unlike him. **u~lich** *a* different; (*wechselnd*) varying; **das ist u~lich** it varies. **u~slos** *a* equal, *adv* -ly

unterschlag|en† *vt insep* embezzle; (*verheimlichen*) suppress. **U~ung** *f* -,-en embezzlement; suppression

Unterschlupf *m* -[e]s shelter; (*Versteck*) hiding-place

unterschreiben† *vt/i insep* (*haben*) sign

Unter|schrift *f* signature; (*Bild-*) caption. **U~seeboot** *nt* submarine. **U~setzer** *m* -s,- = **Untersatz**

untersetzt *a* stocky

Unterstand *m* shelter

unterste(r,s) *a* lowest, bottom

unterstehen†1 *vi sep* (*haben*) shelter

unterstehen†2 *v insep* □ *vi* (*haben*) be answerable (*dat* to); (*unterliegen*) be subject (*dat* to) □ *vr* **sich u~** dare; **untersteh dich!** don't you dare!

unterstellen1 *vt sep* put underneath; (*abstellen*) store; **sich u~** shelter

unterstellen2 *vt insep* place under the control (*dat* of); (*annehmen*) assume; (*fälschlich zuschreiben*) impute (*dat* to)

unterstreichen† *vt insep* underline

unterstütz|en *vt insep* support; (*helfen*) aid. **U~ung** *f* -,-en support; (*finanziell*) aid; (*regelmäßiger Betrag*) allowance; (*Arbeitslosen-*) benefit

untersuch|en *vt insep* examine; (*Jur*) investigate; (*prüfen*) test; (*überprüfen*) check; (*durchsuchen*) search. **U~ung** *f* -,-en examination; investigation; test;

check; search. **U~ungshaft** *f* detention on remand; **in U~ungshaft** on remand. **U~ungsrichter** *m* examining magistrate

Untertan *m* -s & -en,-en subject

Untertasse *f* saucer

untertauchen *v sep* □ *vt* duck □ *vi* (*sein*) go under; (*fig*) disappear

Unterteil *nt* bottom (part)

unterteilen *vt insep* subdivide; (*aufteilen*) divide

Untertitel *m* subtitle

Unterton *m* undertone

untervermieten *vt/i insep* (*haben*) sublet

unterwandern *vt insep* infiltrate

Unterwäsche *f* underwear

Unterwasser- *pref* underwater

unterwegs *adv* on the way; (*außer Haus*) out; (*verreist*) away

unterweisen† *vt insep* instruct

Unterwelt *f* underworld

unterwerfen† *vt insep* subjugate; **sich u~** submit (*dat* to); **etw** (*dat*) **unterworfen sein** be subject to sth

unterwürfig *a* obsequious, *adv* -ly

unterzeichnen *vt insep* sign

unterziehen†1 *vt sep* put on underneath; (*Culin*) fold in

unterziehen†2 *vt insep* **etw einer Untersuchung/Überprüfung u~** examine/ check sth; **sich einer Operation/Prüfung u~** have an operation/take a test

Untier *nt* monster

untragbar *a* intolerable

untrennbar *a* inseparable

untreu *a* disloyal; (*in der Ehe*) unfaithful. **U~e** *f* disloyalty; infidelity

untröstlich *a* inconsolable

untrüglich *a* infallible

Untugend *f* bad habit

unüberlegt *a* rash, *adv* -ly

unüber|sehbar *a* obvious; (*groß*) immense. **u~troffen** *a* unsurpassed

unum|gänglich *a* absolutely necessary. **u~schränkt** *a* absolute. **u~wunden** *adv* frankly

ununterbrochen *a* incessant, *adv* -ly

unveränderlich *a* invariable; (*gleich bleibend*) unchanging

unverändert *a* unchanged

unverantwortlich *a* irresponsible, *adv* -bly

unverbesserlich *a* incorrigible

unverbindlich *a* non-committal; (*Comm*) not binding □ *adv* without obligation

unverblümt *a* blunt, *adv* -ly

unverdaulich *a* indigestible

unver|einbar *a* incompatible. **u~gesslich** (**u~geßlich**) *a* unforgettable. **u~gleichlich** *a* incomparable

unver|hältnismäßig *adv* disproportionately. **u~hofft** *a* unexpected, *adv* -ly. **u~hohlen** *a* undisguised □ *adv* openly. **u~käuflich** *a* not for sale; ⟨*Muster*⟩ free

unverkennbar *a* unmistakable, *adv* -bly

unverletzt *a* unhurt

unvermeidlich *a* inevitable

unver|mindert *a* & *adv* undiminished. **u~mittelt** *a* abrupt, *adv* -ly. **u~mutet** *a* unexpected, *adv* -ly

Unver|nunft *f* folly. **u~nünftig** *a* foolish, *adv* -ly

unverschämt *a* insolent, *adv* -ly; ⟨*fam: ungeheuer*⟩ outrageous, *adv* -ly. **U~heit** *f* -,-en insolence

unver|sehens *adv* suddenly. **u~sehrt** *a* unhurt; ⟨*unbeschädigt*⟩ intact. **u~söhnlich** *a* irreconcilable; ⟨*Gegner*⟩ implacable

unverständ|lich *a* incomprehensible; ⟨*undeutlich*⟩ indistinct. **U~nis** *nt* lack of understanding

unverträglich *a* incompatible; ⟨*Person*⟩ quarrelsome; ⟨*unbekömmlich*⟩ indigestible

unverwandt *a* fixed, *adv* -ly

unver|wundbar *a* invulnerable. **u~wüstlich** *a* indestructible; ⟨*Person, Humor*⟩ irrepressible; ⟨*Gesundheit*⟩ robust. **u~zeihlich** *a* unforgivable

unverzüglich *a* immediate, *adv* -ly

unvollendet *a* unfinished

unvollkommen *a* imperfect; ⟨*unvollständig*⟩ incomplete. **U~heit** *f* -,-en imperfection

unvollständig *a* incomplete

unvor|bereitet *a* unprepared. **u~eingenommen** *a* unbiased. **u~hergesehen** *a* unforeseen

unvorsichtig *a* careless, *adv* -ly. **U~keit** *f* - carelessness

unvorstellbar *a* unimaginable, *adv* -bly

unvorteilhaft *a* unfavourable; ⟨*nicht hübsch*⟩ unattractive; ⟨*Kleid, Frisur*⟩ unflattering

unwahr *a* untrue. **U~heit** *f* -,-en untruth. **u~scheinlich** *a* unlikely; ⟨*unglaublich*⟩ improbable; ⟨*fam: groß*⟩ incredible, *adv* -bly

unweigerlich *a* inevitable, *adv* -bly

unweit *adv* & *prep* (+ *gen*) not far; **u~ vom Fluss** *od* **des Flusses** not far from the river

unwesentlich *a* unimportant □ *adv* slightly

Unwetter *nt* -s,- storm

unwichtig *a* unimportant

unwider|legbar *a* irrefutable. **u~ruflich** *a* irrevocable, *adv* -bly. **u~stehlich** *a* irresistible

Unwill|e *m* displeasure. **u~ig** *a* angry, *adv* -ily; ⟨*widerwillig*⟩ reluctant, *adv* -ly. **u~kürlich** *a* involuntary, *adv* -ily; ⟨*instinktiv*⟩ instinctive, *adv* -ly

unwirklich *a* unreal

unwirksam *a* ineffective

unwirsch *a* irritable, *adv* -bly

unwirtlich *a* inhospitable

unwirtschaftlich *a* uneconomic, *adv* -ally

unwissen|d *a* ignorant. **U~heit** *f* - ignorance

unwohl *a* unwell; ⟨*unbehaglich*⟩ uneasy. **U~sein** *nt* -s indisposition

unwürdig *a* unworthy ⟨*gen* of⟩; ⟨*würdelos*⟩ undignified

Unzahl *f* vast number. **unzählig** *a* innumerable, countless

unzerbrechlich *a* unbreakable

unzerstörbar *a* indestructible

unzertrennlich *a* inseparable

Unzucht *f* sexual offence; **gewerbsmäßige U~** prostitution

unzüchtig *a* indecent, *adv* -ly; ⟨*Schriften*⟩ obscene

unzufrieden *a* dissatisfied; ⟨*innerlich*⟩ discontented. **U~heit** *f* dissatisfaction; ⟨*Pol*⟩ discontent

unzulänglich *a* inadequate, *adv* -ly

unzulässig *a* inadmissible

unzumutbar *a* unreasonable

unzurechnungsfähig *a* insane. **U~keit** *f* insanity

unzusammenhängend *a* incoherent

unzutreffend *a* inapplicable; ⟨*falsch*⟩ incorrect

unzuverlässig *a* unreliable

unzweckmäßig *a* unsuitable, *adv* -bly

unzweideutig *a* unambiguous

unzweifelhaft *a* undoubted, *adv* -ly

üppig *a* luxuriant, *adv* -ly; ⟨*überreichlich*⟩ lavish, *adv* -ly; ⟨*Busen, Figur*⟩ voluptuous

uralt *a* ancient

Uran *nt* -s uranium

Uraufführung *f* first performance

urbar *a* **u~ machen** cultivate

Ureinwohner *mpl* native inhabitants

Urenkel *m* great-grandson; ⟨*pl*⟩ great-grandchildren

Urgroß|mutter *f* great-grandmother. **U~vater** *m* great-grandfather

Urheber *m* -s,- originator; (*Verfasser*) author. **U∼recht** *nt* copyright

Urin *m* -s,-e urine

Urkunde *f* -,-n certificate; (*Dokument*) document

Urlaub *m* -s holiday; (*Mil, Admin*) leave; **auf U∼** on holiday/leave; **U∼ haben** be on holiday/leave. **U∼er(in)** *m* -s,- (*f* -,-nen) holiday-maker. **U∼sort** *m* holiday resort

Urne *f* -,-n urn; (*Wahl-*) ballot-box

Ursache *f* cause; (*Grund*) reason; **keine U∼!** don't mention it!

Ursprung *m* origin

ursprünglich *a* original, *adv* -ly; (*anfänglich*) initial, *adv* -ly; (*natürlich*) natural

Urteil *nt* -s,-e judgement; (*Meinung*) opinion; (*U∼sspruch*) verdict; (*Strafe*) sentence. **u∼en** *vi* (*haben*) judge. **U∼svermögen** *nt* [power of] judgement

Urwald *m* primeval forest; (*tropischer*) jungle

urwüchsig *a* natural; (*derb*) earthy

Urzeit *f* primeval times *pl*; **seit U∼en** from time immemorial

USA *pl* USA *sg*

usw. *abbr* (**und so weiter**) etc.

Utensilien /-jən/ *ntpl* utensils

utopisch *a* Utopian

V

vage /'va:gə/ *a* vague, *adv* -ly

Vakuum /'va:kuʊm/ *nt* -s vacuum. **v∼verpackt** *a* vacuum-packed

Vanille /va'nɪljə/ *f* - vanilla

vari|abel /va'rja:bəl/ *a* variable. **V∼ante** *f* -,-n variant. **V∼ation** /-'tsjo:n/ *f* -,-en variation. **v∼ieren** *vt/i* (*haben*) vary

Vase /'va:zə/ *f* -,-n vase

Vater *m* -s,- father. **V∼land** *nt* fatherland

väterlich *a* paternal; (*fürsorglich*) fatherly. **v∼erseits** *adv* on one's/the father's side

Vater|schaft *f* - fatherhood; (*Jur*) paternity. **V∼unser** *nt* -s,- Lord's Prayer

Vati *m* -s,-s (*fam*) daddy

v. Chr. *abbr* (**vor Christus**) BC

Vegetar|ier(in) /vege'ta:rjɐ, -jərɪn/ *m(f)* -s,- (*f* -,-nen) vegetarian. **v∼isch** *a* vegetarian

Vegetation /vegeta'tsjo:n/ *f* -,-en vegetation

Veilchen *nt* -s,-n violet

Vene /'ve:nə/ *f* -,-n vein

Venedig /ve'ne:dɪç/ *nt* -s Venice

Ventil /vɛn'ti:l/ *nt* -s,-e valve. **V∼ator** *m* -s,-en /-'to:rən/ fan

verabred|en *vt* arrange; **sich [mit jdm] v∼en** arrange to meet [s.o.]. **V∼ung** *f* -,-en arrangement; (*Treffen*) appointment

verabreichen *vt* administer

verabscheuen *vt* detest, loathe

verabschieden *vt* say goodbye to; (*aus dem Dienst*) retire; *pass* (*Gesetz*); **sich v∼** say goodbye

verachten *vt* despise. **v∼swert** *a* contemptible

verächtlich *a* contemptuous, *adv* -ly; (*unwürdig*) contemptible

Verachtung *f* - contempt

verallgemeiner|n *vt/i* (*haben*) generalize. **V∼ung** *f* -,-en generalization

veralte|n *vi* (*sein*) become obsolete. **v∼t** *a* obsolete

Veranda /ve'randa/ *f* -,-den veranda

veränder|lich *a* changeable; (*Math*) variable. **v∼n** *vt* change; **sich v∼n** change; (*beruflich*) change one's job. **V∼ung** *f* change

verängstigt *a* frightened, scared

verankern *vt* anchor

veranlag|t *a* **künstlerisch/musikalisch v∼t sein** have an artistic/a musical bent; **praktisch v∼t** practically minded. **V∼ung** *f* -,-en disposition; (*Neigung*) tendency; (*künstlerisch*) bent

veranlass|en *vt* (*reg*) arrange for; (*einleiten*) institute; **jdn v∼en** prompt s.o. (**zu** to). **V∼ung** *f* - reason; **auf meine V∼ung** at my suggestion; (*Befehl*) on my orders

veranschaulichen *vt* illustrate

veranschlagen *vt* (*reg*) estimate

veranstalt|en *vt* organize; hold; give (*Party*); make (*Lärm*). **V∼er** *m* -s,- organizer. **V∼ung** *f* -,-en event

verantwort|en *vt* take responsibility for; **sich v∼en** answer (**für** for). **v∼lich** *a* responsible; **v∼lich machen** hold responsible. **V∼ung** *f* - responsibility. **v∼ungsbewusst** (**v∼ungsbewußt**) *a* responsible, *adv* -bly. **v∼ungslos** *a* irresponsible, *adv* -bly. **v∼ungsvoll** *a* responsible

verarbeiten *vt* use; (*Techn*) process; (*verdauen & fig*) digest; **v∼ zu** make into

verärgern *vt* annoy

verarmt *a* impoverished

verästeln (sich) *vr* branch out

verausgaben (sich) *vr* spend all one's money; (*körperlich*) wear oneself out

veräußern *vt* sell

Verb /vɛrp/ *nt* -s,-en verb. **v~al**
/ver'ba:l/ *a* verbal, *adv* -ly

Verband *m* -[e]s,-̈e association; (*Mil*) unit;
(*Med*) bandage; (*Wund-*) dressing.
V~szeug *nt* first-aid kit

verbann|en *vt* exile; (*fig*) banish. **V~ung**
f - exile

verbarrikadieren *vt* barricade

verbeißen† *vt* suppress; **ich konnte mir
kaum das Lachen v~** I could hardly keep
a straight face

verbergen† *vt* hide; **sich v~** hide

verbesser|n *vt* improve; (*berichtigen*) cor-
rect. **V~ung** *f* -,-en improvement; correction

verbeug|en (sich) *vr* bow. **V~ung** *f* bow

verbeulen *vt* dent

verbiegen† *vt* bend; **sich v~** bend

verbieten† *vt* forbid; (*Admin*) prohibit,
ban

verbillig|en *vt* reduce [in price]. **v~t** *a*
reduced

verbinden† *vt* connect (**mit** to); (*zusammenfügen*) join; (*verknüpfen*) combine; (*in
Verbindung bringen*) associate; (*Med*)
bandage; dress (*Wunde*); **sich v~** combine; (*sich zusammentun*) join together;
jdm die Augen v~ blindfold s.o.; **jdm
verbunden sein** (*fig*) be obliged to s.o.

verbindlich *a* friendly; (*bindend*)
binding. **V~keit** *f* -,-en friendliness;
V~keiten obligations; (*Comm*) liabilities

Verbindung *f* connection; (*Ver-
knüpfung*) combination; (*Kontakt*) contact; (*Vereinigung*) association;
chemische **V~** chemical compound; **in
V~ stehen/sich in V~ setzen** be/get in
touch

verbissen *a* grim, *adv* -ly; (*zäh*) dogged,
adv -ly

verbitten† *vt* **sich** (*dat*) **etw v~** not stand
for sth

verbitter|n *vt* make bitter. **v~t** *a* bitter.
V~ung *f* - bitterness

verblassen *vi* (*sein*) fade

verbläuen *vt* (*fam*) thrash

Verbleib *m* -s whereabouts *pl*. **v~en**† *vi*
(*sein*) remain

verbleichen† *vi* (*sein*) fade

verbleit *a* ⟨*Benzin*⟩ leaded

verbleuen *vt* (NEW) verbläuen

verblüff|en *vt* amaze, astound. **V~ung** *f*
- amazement

verblühen *vi* (*sein*) wither, fade

verbluten *vi* (*sein*) bleed to death

verborgen[1] *a* hidden

verborgen[2] *vt* lend

Verbot *nt* -[e]s,-e ban. **v~en** *a* forbidden;
(*Admin*) prohibited; '**Rauchen v~en**' 'no
smoking'

Verbrauch *m* -[e]s consumption. **v~en**
vt use; consume ⟨*Lebensmittel*⟩; (*erschöpfen*) use up, exhaust. **V~er** *m* -s,-
consumer. **v~t** *a* worn; ⟨*Luft*⟩ stale

verbrechen† *vt* (*fam*) perpetrate. **V~** *nt*
-s,- crime

Verbrecher *m* -s,- criminal. **v~isch** *a*
criminal

verbreit|en *vt* spread; **sich v~en** spread.
v~ern *vt* widen; **sich v~ern** widen. **v~et**
a widespread. **V~ung** *f* - spread; (*Verbreiten*) spreading

verbrenn|en† *vt/i* (*sein*) burn; cremate
⟨*Leiche*⟩. **V~ung** *f* -,-en burning; cremation; (*Wunde*) burn

verbringen† *vt* spend

verbrühen *vt* scald

verbuchen *vt* enter; (*fig*) notch up ⟨*Erfolg*⟩

verbünd|en (sich) *vr* form an alliance.
V~ete(r) *m/f* ally

verbürgen *vt* guarantee; **sich v~ für**
vouch for

verbüßen *vt* serve ⟨*Strafe*⟩

Verdacht *m* -[e]s suspicion; **in** *or* **im V~**
haben suspect

verdächtig *a* suspicious, *adv* -ly. **v~en** *vt*
suspect (*gen* of). **V~te(r)** *m/f* suspect

verdamm|en *vt* condemn; (*Relig*) damn.
V~nis *f* - damnation; **v~t** *a* & *adv* (*sl*)
damned; **v~t!** damn!

verdampfen *vt/i* (*sein*) evaporate

verdanken *vt* owe (*dat* to)

verdau|en *vt* digest. **v~lich** *a* digestible;
schwer v~lich indigestible. **V~ung** *f* -
digestion

Verdeck *nt* -[e]s,-e hood; (*Oberdeck*) top
deck. **v~en** *vt* cover; (*verbergen*) hide,
conceal

verdenken† *vt* **das kann man ihm nicht
v~** you can't blame him for it

verderb|en† *vi* (*sein*) spoil; ⟨*Lebensmittel*:⟩
go bad □ *vt* spoil; (*zerstören*) ruin;
(*moralisch*) corrupt; **ich habe mir den
Magen verdorben** I have an upset
stomach. **V~en** *nt* -s ruin. **v~lich** *a* peri-
shable; (*schädlich*) pernicious

verdeutlichen *vt* make clear

verdichten *vt* compress; **sich v~** ⟨*Nebel*:⟩
thicken

verdien|en *vt/i* (*haben*) earn; (*fig*) de-
serve. **V~er** *m* -s,- wage-earner

Verdienst[1] *m* -[e]s earnings *pl*

Verdienst[2] *nt* -[e]s,-e merit

verdient a well-deserved; ⟨Person⟩ of outstanding merit. **v~ermaßen** adv deservedly

verdoppeln vt double; ⟨fig⟩ redouble; **sich v~** double

verdorben a spoilt, ruined; ⟨Magen⟩ upset; ⟨moralisch⟩ corrupt; ⟨verkommen⟩ depraved

verdorren vi (sein) wither

verdrängen vt force out; ⟨fig⟩ displace; ⟨psychisch⟩ repress

verdreh|en vt twist; roll ⟨Augen⟩; ⟨fig⟩ distort. **v~t** a ⟨fam⟩ crazy

verdreifachen vt treble, triple

verdreschen† vt ⟨fam⟩ thrash

verdrießlich a morose, adv -ly

verdrücken vt crumple; ⟨fam: essen⟩ polish off; **sich v~** ⟨fam⟩ slip away

Verdruss m -es (**Verdruß** m -sses) annoyance

verdunk|eln vt darken; black out ⟨Zimmer⟩; **sich v~eln** darken. **V~[e]lung** f - black-out

verdünnen vt dilute; **sich v~** taper off

verdunst|en vi (sein) evaporate. **V~ung** f - evaporation

verdursten vi (sein) die of thirst

verdutzt a baffled

veredeln vt refine; ⟨Hort⟩ graft

verehr|en vt revere; ⟨Relig⟩ worship; ⟨bewundern⟩ admire; ⟨schenken⟩ give. **V~er(in)** m -s,- (f -,-nen) admirer. **V~ung** f - veneration; worship; admiration

vereidigen vt swear in

Verein m -s,-e society; ⟨Sport-⟩ club

vereinbar a compatible; **v~en** vt arrange; **nicht zu v~en** incompatible. **V~ung** f -,-en agreement

vereinen vt unite; **sich v~** unite

vereinfachen vt simplify

vereinheitlichen vt standardize

vereinig|en vt unite; merge ⟨Firmen⟩; wieder **v~en** reunite; reunify ⟨Land⟩; **sich v~en** unite; **V~te Staaten [von Amerika]** United States sg [of America]. **V~ung** f -,-en union; ⟨Organisation⟩ organization

vereinsamt a lonely

vereinzelt a isolated □ adv occasionally

vereist a frozen; ⟨Straße⟩ icy

vereiteln vt foil, thwart

vereitert a septic

verenden vi (sein) die

verengen vt restrict; **sich v~** narrow; ⟨Pupille:⟩ contract

vererb|en vt leave (dat to); ⟨Biol & fig⟩ pass on (dat to). **V~ung** f - heredity

verewigen vt immortalize; **sich v~** ⟨fam⟩ leave one's mark

verfahren† vi (sein) proceed; **v~ mit** deal with □ vr **sich v~** lose one's way □ a muddled. **V~** nt -s,- procedure; ⟨Techn⟩ process; ⟨Jur⟩ proceedings pl

Verfall m decay; ⟨eines Gebäudes⟩ dilapidation; ⟨körperlich & fig⟩ decline; ⟨Ablauf⟩ expiry. **v~en†** vi (sein) decay; ⟨Person, Sitten:⟩ decline; ⟨ablaufen⟩ expire; **v~en in** (+ acc) lapse into; **v~en auf** (+ acc) hit on ⟨Idee⟩; **jdm/etw v~en sein** be under the spell of s.o./sth; be addicted to ⟨Alkohol⟩

verfälschen vt falsify; adulterate ⟨Wein, Lebensmittel⟩

verfänglich a awkward

verfärben (sich) vr change colour; ⟨Stoff:⟩ discolour

verfass|en vt write; ⟨Jur⟩ draw up; ⟨entwerfen⟩ draft. **V~er** m -s,- author. **V~ung** f ⟨Pol⟩ constitution; ⟨Zustand⟩ state

verfaulen vi (sein) rot, decay

verfechten† vt advocate

verfehlen vt miss

verfeinde|n (sich) vr become enemies; **v~t sein** be enemies

verfeinern vt refine; ⟨verbessern⟩ improve

verfilmen vt film

verfilzt a matted

verfliegen† vi (sein) evaporate; ⟨Zeit:⟩ fly

verflixt a ⟨fam⟩ awkward; ⟨verdammt⟩ blessed; **v~!** damn!

verfluch|en vt curse. **v~t** a & adv ⟨fam⟩ damned; **v~t!** damn!

verflüchtigen (sich) vr evaporate

verflüssigen vt liquefy

verfolg|en vt pursue; ⟨folgen⟩ follow; ⟨bedrängen⟩ pester; ⟨Pol⟩ persecute; **strafrechtlich v~en** prosecute. **V~er** m -s,- pursuer. **V~ung** f - pursuit; persecution

verfrachten vt ship

verfrüht a premature

verfügbar a available

verfüg|en vt order; ⟨Jur⟩ decree □ vi ⟨haben⟩ **v~en über** (+ acc) have at one's disposal. **V~ung** f -,-en order; ⟨Jur⟩ decree; **jdm zur V~ung stehen/stellen** be/place at s.o.'s disposal

verführ|en vt seduce; ⟨verlocken⟩ tempt. **V~er** m seducer. **v~erisch** a seductive; tempting. **V~ung** f seduction; temptation

vergammelt a rotten; ⟨Gebäude⟩ decayed; ⟨Person⟩ scruffy

vergangen a past; ⟨letzte⟩ last. **V~heit** f - past; ⟨Gram⟩ past tense

vergänglich *a* transitory

vergas|en *vt* gas. V~**er** *m* -s,- carburettor

vergeb|en† *vt* award (**an** + *dat* to); (*weg-geben*) give away; (*verzeihen*) forgive. **v~ens** *adv* in vain. **v~lich** *a* futile, vain □ *adv* in vain. **V~ung** *f* - forgiveness

vergehen *vi* (*sein*) pass; **v~ vor** (+ *dat*) nearly die of; **sich v~** violate (**gegen etw** sth); (*sexuell*) sexually assault (**an jdm** s.o.). **V~** *nt* -s,- offence

vergelt|en† *vt* repay. **V~ung** *f* - retaliation; (*Rache*) revenge. **V~ungsmaßnahme** *f* reprisal

vergessen† *vt* forget; (*liegen lassen*) leave behind. **V~heit** *f* - oblivion; **in V~heit geraten** be forgotten

vergesslich (**vergeßlich**) *a* forgetful. **V~keit** *f* - forgetfulness

vergeuden *vt* waste, squander

vergewaltig|en *vt* rape. **V~ung** *f* -,-en rape

vergewissern (sich) *vr* make sure (*gen* of)

vergießen† *vt* spill; shed ⟨*Tränen, Blut*⟩

vergift|en *vt* poison. **V~ung** *f* -,-en poisoning

Vergissmeinnicht (**Vergißmeinnicht**) *nt* -[e]s,-[e] forget-me-not

vergittert *a* barred

verglasen *vt* glaze

Vergleich *m* -[e]s,-e comparison; (*Jur*) settlement. **v~bar** *a* comparable. **v~en†** *vt* compare (**mit** with/to). **v~sweise** *adv* comparatively

vergnüg|en (sich) *vr* enjoy oneself. **V~en** *nt* -s,- pleasure; (*Spaß*) fun; **viel V~en!** have a good time! **v~lich** *a* enjoyable. **v~t** *a* cheerful, *adv* -ly; (*zufrieden*) happy, *adv* -ily; (*vergnüglich*) enjoyable. **V~ungen** *fpl* entertainments

vergolden *vt* gild; (*plattieren*) gold-plate

vergönnen *vt* grant

vergöttern *vt* idolize

vergraben† *vt* bury

vergreifen† (sich) *vr* **sich v~an** (+ *dat*) assault; (*stehlen*) steal

vergriffen *a* out of print

vergrößer|n *vt* enlarge; ⟨*Linse:*⟩ magnify; (*vermehren*) increase; (*erweitern*) extend; expand ⟨*Geschäft*⟩; **sich v~n** grow bigger; ⟨*Firma:*⟩ expand; (*zunehmen*) increase. **V~ung** *f* -,-en magnification; increase; expansion; (*Phot*) enlargement. **V~ungsglas** *nt* magnifying glass

Vergünstigung *f* -,-en privilege

vergüt|en *vt* pay for; **jdm etw v~en** reimburse s.o. for sth. **V~ung** *f* -,-en remuneration; (*Erstattung*) reimbursement

verhaft|en *vt* arrest. **V~ung** *f* -,-en arrest

verhalten† (sich) *vr* behave; (*handeln*) act; (*beschaffen sein*) be; **sich still v~** keep quiet. **V~** *nt* -s behaviour, conduct

Verhältnis *nt* -ses,-se relationship; (*Liebes-*) affair; (*Math*) ratio; **V~se** circumstances; (*Bedingungen*) conditions; **über seine V~se leben** live beyond one's means. **v~mäßig** *adv* comparatively, relatively

verhand|eln *vt* discuss; (*Jur*) try □ *vi* (*haben*) negotiate; **v~eln gegen** (*Jur*) try. **V~lung** *f* (*Jur*) trial; **V~lungen** negotiations

verhängen *vt* cover; (*fig*) impose

Verhängnis *nt* -ses fate, doom. **v~voll** *a* fatal, disastrous

verharmlosen *vt* play down

verharren *vi* (*haben*) remain

verhärten *vt/i* (*sein*) harden; **sich v~** harden

verhasst (**verhaßt**) *a* hated

verhätscheln *vt* spoil, pamper

verhauen† *vt* (*fam*) beat; make a mess of ⟨*Prüfung*⟩

verheerend *a* devastating; (*fam*) terrible

verhehlen *vt* conceal

verheilen *vi* (*sein*) heal

verheimlichen *vt* keep secret

verheirat|en (sich) *vr* get married (**mit** to); **sich wieder v~en** remarry. **v~et** *a* married

verhelfen† *vi* (*haben*) **jdm zu etw v~** help s.o. get sth

verherrlichen *vt* glorify

verhexen *vt* bewitch; **es ist wie verhext** (*fam*) there is a jinx on it

verhinder|n *vt* prevent; **v~t sein** be unable to come. **V~ung** *f* - prevention

verhöhnen *vt* deride

Verhör *nt* -s,-e interrogation; **ins V~ nehmen** interrogate. **v~en** *vt* interrogate; **sich v~en** mishear

verhüllen *vt* cover; (*fig*) disguise. **v~d** *a* euphemistic, *adv* -ally

verhungern *vi* (*sein*) starve

verhüt|en *vt* prevent. **V~ung** *f* - prevention. **V~ungsmittel** *nt* contraceptive

verhutzelt *a* wizened

verirren (sich) *vr* get lost

verjagen *vt* chase away

verjüngen *vt* rejuvenate; **sich v~** taper

verkalkt *a* (*fam*) senile

verkalkulieren (sich) *vr* miscalculate

Verkauf *m* sale; **zum V~** for sale. **v~en** *vt* sell; **zu v~en** for sale

Verkäufer(in) *m(f)* seller; (*im Geschäft*) shop assistant

Verkehr m -s traffic; (*Kontakt*) contact; (*Geschlechts-*) intercourse; **aus dem V∼ ziehen** take out of circulation. **v∼en** vi (*haben*) operate; (*Bus, Zug:*) run; (*Umgang haben*) associate, mix (**mit** with); (*Gast sein*) visit (**bei jdm** s.o.); frequent (**in einem Lokal** a restaurant); **brieflich v∼en** correspond □ vt **ins Gegenteil v∼en** turn round

Verkehrs|ampel f traffic lights pl. **V∼büro** nt = **V∼verein. V∼funk** m [radio] traffic information. **V∼unfall** m road accident. **V∼verein** m tourist office. **V∼zeichen** nt traffic sign

verkehrt a wrong, adv -ly; **v∼ herum** the wrong way round; (*links*) inside out

verkennen† vt misjudge

verklagen vt sue (**auf** + acc for)

verkleid|en vt disguise; (*Techn*) line; **sich v∼en** disguise oneself; (*für Kostümfest*) dress up. **V∼ung** f -,-en disguise; (*Kostüm*) fancy dress; (*Techn*) lining

verkleiner|n vt reduce [in size]. **V∼ung** f - reduction. **V∼ungsform** f diminutive

verklemmt a jammed; (*psychisch*) inhibited

verkneifen† vt **sich** (*dat*) **etw v∼** do without sth; (*verbeißen*) suppress sth

verknittern vt/i (*sein*) crumple

verknüpfen vt knot together; (*verbinden*) connect, link; (*zugleich tun*) combine

verkommen† vi (*sein*) be neglected; (*sittlich*) go to the bad; (*verfallen*) decay; (*Haus:*) fall into disrepair; (*Gegend:*) become run-down; (*Lebensmittel:*) go bad □ a neglected; (*sittlich*) depraved; (*Haus*) dilapidated; (*Gegend*) run-down

verkörper|n vt embody, personify. **V∼ung** f -,-en embodiment, personification

verkraften vt cope with

verkrampft a (*fig*) tense

verkriechen† (**sich**) vr hide

verkrümmt a crooked, bent

verkrüppelt a crippled; (*Glied*) deformed

verkühl|en (**sich**) vr catch a chill. **V∼ung** f -,-en chill

verkümmer|n vi (*sein*) waste/(*Pflanze:*) wither away. **v∼t** a stunted

verkünd|en vt announce; pronounce (*Urteil*). **v∼igen** vt announce; (*predigen*) preach

verkürzen vt shorten; (*verringern*) reduce; (*abbrechen*) cut short; while away (*Zeit*)

verladen† vt load

Verlag m -[e]s,-e publishing firm

verlangen vt ask for; (*fordern*) demand; (*berechnen*) charge; **am Telefon verlangt**

werden be wanted on the telephone. **V∼ nt** -s desire; (*Bitte*) request; **auf V∼** on demand

verlänger|n vt extend; lengthen (*Kleid*); (*zeitlich*) prolong; renew (*Pass, Vertrag*); (*Culin*) thin down. **V∼ung** f -,-en extension; renewal. **V∼ungsschnur** f extension cable

verlangsamen vt slow down

Verlass (**Verlaß**) m **auf ihn ist kein V∼** you cannot rely on him

verlassen† vt leave; (*im Stich lassen*) desert; **sich v∼ auf** (+ acc) rely or depend on □ a deserted. **V∼heit** f - desolation

verlässlich (**verläßlich**) a reliable

Verlauf m course; **im V∼** (+ gen) in the course of. **v∼en†** vi (*sein*) run; (*ablaufen*) go; (*zerlaufen*) melt; **gut v∼en** go [off] well □ vr **sich v∼en** lose one's way; (*Menge:*) disperse; (*Wasser:*) drain away

verleben vt spend

verlegen vt move; (*verschieben*) postpone; (*vor-*) bring forward; (*verlieren*) mislay; (*versperren*) block; (*legen*) lay (*Teppich, Rohre*); (*veröffentlichen*) publish; **sich v∼ auf** (+ acc) take up (*Beruf, Fach*); resort to (*Taktik, Bitten*) □ a embarrassed; **nie v∼ um** never at a loss for. **V∼heit** f - embarrassment

Verleger m -s,- publisher

verleihen† vt lend; (*gegen Gebühr*) hire out; (*überreichen*) award, confer; (*fig*) give

verleiten vt induce/(*verlocken*) tempt (**zu** to)

verlernen vt forget

verlesen†[1] vt read out; **ich habe mich v∼** I misread it

verlesen†[2] vt sort out

verletz|en vt injure; (*kränken*) hurt; (*verstoßen gegen*) infringe; violate (*Grenze*). **v∼end** a hurtful, wounding. **v∼lich** a vulnerable. **V∼te(r)** m/f injured person; (*bei Unfall*) casualty. **V∼ung** f -,-en injury; (*Verstoß*) infringement; violation

verleugnen vt deny; disown (*Freund*)

verleumd|en vt slander; (*schriftlich*) libel. **v∼erisch** a slanderous; libellous. **V∼ung** f -,-en slander; (*schriftlich*) libel

verlieben (**sich**) vr fall in love (**in** + acc with); **verliebt sein** be in love (**in** + acc with)

verlier|en† vt lose; shed (*Laub*); **sich v∼en** disappear; (*Weg:*) peter out □ vi (*haben*) lose (**an etw** dat sth). **V∼er** m -s,- loser

verlob|en (**sich**) vr get engaged (**mit** to); **v∼t sein** be engaged. **V∼te** f fiancée. **V∼te(r)** m fiancé. **V∼ung** f -,-en engagement

verlock|en vt tempt; **v~end** tempting. **V~ung** f -,-en temptation

verlogen a lying

verloren a lost; **v~e Eier** poached eggs; **v~ gehen** get lost. **v~gehen†** vi sep (sein) (NEW) **v~ gehen,** s. **verloren**

verlos|en vt raffle. **V~ung** f -,-en raffle; (Ziehung) draw

verlottert a run-down; (Person) scruffy; (sittlich) dissolute

Verlust m -[e]s,-e loss

vermachen vt leave, bequeath

Vermächtnis nt -ses,-se legacy

vermähl|en (sich) vr marry. **V~ung** f -,-en marriage

vermehren vt increase; propagate (Pflanzen); **sich v~** increase; (sich fortpflanzen) breed, multiply

vermeiden† vt avoid

vermeintlich a supposed, adv -ly

Vermerk m -[e]s,-e note. **v~en** vt note [down]; **übel v~en** take amiss

vermess|en† vt measure; survey (Gelände) □ a presumptuous. **V~enheit** f - presumption. **V~ung** f measurement; (Land-) survey

vermiet|en vt let, rent [out]; hire out (Boot, Auto); **zu v~en** to let; (Boot:) for hire. **V~er** m landlord. **V~erin** f landlady

vermin|der|n vt reduce, lessen. **V~ung** f - reduction, decrease

vermischen vt mix; **sich v~** mix

vermissen vt miss

vermisst a (vermißt) a missing. **V~e(r)** m missing person/(Mil) soldier

vermittel|n vi (haben) mediate □ vt arrange; (beschaffen) find; place (Arbeitskräfte); impart (Wissen); convey (Eindruck). **v~s** prep (+ gen) by means of

Vermittl|er m -s,- agent; (Schlichter) mediator. **V~ung** f -,-en arrangement; (Agentur) agency; (Teleph) exchange; (Schlichtung) mediation

vermög|en† vt be able (zu to). **V~** nt -s,- fortune. **v~d** a wealthy

vermut|en vt suspect; (glauben) presume. **v~lich** a probable □ adv presumably. **V~ung** f -,-en supposition; (Verdacht) suspicion; (Mutmaßung) conjecture

vernachlässig|en vt neglect. **V~ung** f - neglect

vernehm|en† vt hear; (verhören) question; (Jur) examine. **V~ung** f -,-en questioning

verneig|en (sich) vr bow. **V~ung** f -,-en bow

vernein|en vt answer in the negative; (ablehnen) reject. **v~end** a negative. **V~ung** f -,-en negative answer; (Gram) negative

vernicht|en vt destroy; (ausrotten) exterminate. **v~end** a devastating; (Niederlage) crushing. **V~ung** f - destruction; extermination

Vernunft f - reason; **V~ annehmen** see reason

vernünftig a reasonable, sensible; (fam: ordentlich) decent □ adv sensibly; (fam) properly

veröffentlich|en vt publish. **V~ung** f -,-en publication

verordn|en vt prescribe (dat for). **V~ung** f -,-en prescription; (Verfügung) decree

verpachten vt lease [out]

verpack|en vt pack; (einwickeln) wrap. **V~ung** f packaging; wrapping

verpassen vt miss; (fam: geben) give

verpfänden vt pawn

verpflanzen vt transplant

verpfleg|en vt feed; **sich selbst v~en** cater for oneself. **V~ung** f -; board; (Essen) food; **Unterkunft und V~ung** board and lodging

verpflicht|en vt oblige; (einstellen) engage; (Sport) sign; **sich v~en** undertake/(versprechen) promise (zu to); (vertraglich) sign a contract; **jdm v~et sein** be indebted to s.o. **V~ung** f -,-en obligation, commitment

verpfuschen vt make a mess of

verpönt a **v~ sein** be frowned upon

verprügeln vt beat up, thrash

Verputz m -es plaster. **v~en** vt plaster; (fam: essen) polish off

Verrat m -[e]s betrayal, treachery. **v~en†** vt betray; give away (Geheimnis); (fam: sagen) tell; **sich v~en** give oneself away

Verräter m -s,- traitor. **v~isch** a treacherous; (fig) revealing

verräuchert a smoky

verrech|nen vt settle; clear (Scheck); **sich v~nen** make a mistake; (fig) miscalculate. **V~nungsscheck** m crossed cheque

verregnet a spoilt by rain; (Tag) rainy, wet

verreisen vi (sein) go away; **verreist sein** be away

verreißen† vt (fam) pan, slate

verrenken vt dislocate; **sich v~** contort oneself

verricht|en vt perform, do; say (Gebet). **V~ung** f -,-en task

verriegeln vt bolt

verringer|n vt reduce; **sich v~n** decrease. **V~ung** f - reduction; decrease

verrost|en vi (sein) rust. **v~et** a rusty

verrücken vt move

verrückt *a* crazy, mad; **v~ wer-den/machen** go/drive crazy. **V~e(r)** *m/f* lunatic; **V~heit** *f* -,-en madness; (*Torheit*) folly

Verruf *m* disrepute. **v~en** *a* disreputable

verrühren *vt* mix

verrunzelt *a* wrinkled

verrutschen *vt* (*sein*) slip

Vers /fɛrs/ *m* -es,-e verse

versag|en *vi* (*haben*) fail □ *vt* **jdm/sich etw v~en** deny s.o./oneself sth. **V~en** *nt* -s,- failure. **V~er** *m* -s,- failure

versalzen† *vt* put too much salt in/on; (*fig*) spoil

versamm|eln *vt* assemble; **sich v~eln** assemble, meet. **V~lung** *f* assembly, meeting

Versand *m* -[e]s dispatch. **V~haus** *nt* mail-order firm

versäum|en *vt* miss; lose (*Zeit*); (*unterlassen*) neglect; [es] **v~en, etw zu tun** fail *or* neglect to do sth. **V~nis** *nt* -ses,-se omission

verschaffen *vt* get; **sich** (*dat*) **v~** obtain; gain (*Respekt*)

verschämt *a* bashful, *adv* -ly

verschandeln *vt* spoil

verschärfen *vt* intensify; tighten (*Kontrolle*); increase (*Tempo*); aggravate (*Lage*); **sich v~** intensify; increase; (*Lage:*) worsen

verschätzen (sich) *vr* **sich v~ in** (+ *dat*) misjudge

verschenken *vt* give away

verscheuchen *vt* shoo/(*jagen*) chase away

verschicken *vt* send; (*Comm*) dispatch

verschieb|en† *vt* move; (*aufschieben*) put off, postpone; (*sl: handeln mit*) traffic in; **sich v~en** move, shift; (*verrutschen*) slip; (*zeitlich*) be postponed. **V~ung** *f* shift; postponement

verschieden *a* different; **v~e** (*pl*) different; (*mehrere*) various; **V~es** (**v~es**) some things; (*dieses und jenes*) various things; **die v~sten Farben** a whole variety of colours; **das ist v~** it varies □ *adv* differently; **v~ groß/lang** of different sizes/lengths. **V~artig** *a* diverse. **V~heit** *f* - difference; (*Vielfalt*) diversity. **v~tlich** *adv* several times

verschimmel|n *vi* (*sein*) go mouldy. **v~t** *a* mouldy

verschlafen† *vi* (*haben mit*) oversleep □ *vt* sleep through (*Tag*); (*versäumen*) miss (*Zug, Termin*); **sich v~** oversleep □ *a* sleepy; **noch v~** still half asleep

Verschlag *m* -[e]s,-e shed

verschlagen† *vt* lose (*Seite*); **jdm die Sprache/den Atem v~** leave s.o. speechless/take s.o.'s breath away; **nach X v~ werden** end up in X □ *a* sly, *adv* -ly

verschlechter|n *vt* make worse; **sich v~n** get worse, deteriorate. **V~ung** *f* -,-en deterioration

verschleiern *vt* veil; (*fig*) hide

Verschleiß *m* -es wear and tear; (*Verbrauch*) consumption. **v~en†** *vt/i* (*sein*) wear out

verschleppen *vt* carry off; (*entführen*) abduct; spread (*Seuche*); neglect (*Krankheit*); (*hinausziehen*) delay

verschleudern *vt* sell at a loss; (*verschwenden*) squander

verschließen† *vt* close; (*abschließen*) lock; (*einschließen*) lock up

verschlimmer|n *vt* make worse; aggravate (*Lage*); **sich v~n** get worse, deteriorate. **V~ung** *f* -,-en deterioration

verschlingen† *vt* intertwine; (*fressen*) devour; (*fig*) swallow

verschlissen *a* worn

verschlossen *a* reserved. **V~heit** *f* - reserve

verschlucken *vt* swallow; **sich v~** choke (**an** + *dat* on)

Verschluss *m* -es,-̈e (**Verschluß** *m* -sses, -̈sse) fastener, clasp; (*Fenster-, Koffer-*) catch; (*Flaschen-*) top; (*luftdicht*) seal; (*Phot*) shutter; **unter v~** under lock and key

verschlüsselt *a* coded

verschmähen *vt* spurn

verschmelzen† *vt/i* (*sein*) fuse

verschmerzen *vt* get over

verschmutz|en *vt* soil; pollute (*Luft*) □ *vi* (*sein*) get dirty. **V~ung** *f* - pollution

verschnaufen *vi/r* (*haben*) **[sich] v~** get one's breath

verschneit *a* snow-covered

verschnörkelt *a* ornate

verschnüren *vt* tie up

verschollen *a* missing

verschonen *vt* spare

verschönern *vt* brighten up; (*verbessern*) improve

verschossen *a* faded

verschrammt *a* scratched

verschränken *vt* cross

verschreiben† *vt* prescribe; **sich v~** make a slip of the pen

verschrie[e]n *a* notorious

verschroben *a* eccentric

verschrotten *vt* scrap

verschulden *vt* be to blame for; **sich v~** get into debt. **V~** *nt* -s fault

verschuldet *a* v~ **sein** be in debt
verschütten *vt* spill; ⟨*begraben*⟩ bury
verschweigen† *vt* conceal, hide
verschwend|en *vt* waste. v~**erisch** *a* extravagant, *adv* -ly; ⟨*üppig*⟩ lavish, *adv* -ly. V~**ung** *f* - extravagance; ⟨*Vergeudung*⟩ waste
verschwiegen *a* discreet; ⟨*Ort*⟩ secluded. V~**heit** *f* - discretion
verschwimmen† *vi* ⟨*sein*⟩ become blurred
verschwinden† *vi* ⟨*sein*⟩ disappear; [mal] v~ ⟨*fam*⟩ spend a penny. V~ *nt* -s disappearance
verschwommen *a* blurred
verschwör|en† ⟨sich⟩ *vr* conspire. V~**ung** *f* -,-en conspiracy
versehen *vt* perform; hold ⟨*Posten*⟩; keep ⟨*Haushalt*⟩; v~ **mit** provide with; **sich v~** make a mistake; **ehe man sich's versieht** before you know where you are. V~ *nt* -s,- oversight; ⟨*Fehler*⟩ slip; **aus V~** by mistake. v~**tlich** *adv* by mistake
Versehrte(r) *m* disabled person
versenden† *vt* send [out]
versengen *vt* singe; ⟨*stärker*⟩ scorch
versenken *vt* sink; **sich v~ in** (+ *acc*) immerse oneself in
versessen *a* keen (**auf** + *acc* on)
versetz|en *vt* move; transfer ⟨*Person*⟩; ⟨*Sch*⟩ move up; ⟨*verpfänden*⟩ pawn; ⟨*verkaufen*⟩ sell; ⟨*vermischen*⟩ blend; ⟨*antworten*⟩ reply; **jdn v~en** ⟨*fam: warten lassen*⟩ stand s.o. up; **jdm einen Stoß/Schreck v~en** give s.o. a push/ fright; **jdm in Angst/Erstaunen v~en** frighten/astonish s.o.; **sich in jds Lage v~en** put oneself in s.o.'s place. V~**ung** *f* -,-en move; transfer; ⟨*Sch*⟩ move to a higher class
verseuch|en *vt* contaminate. V~**ung** *f* - contamination
versicher|n *vt* insure; ⟨*bekräftigen*⟩ affirm; **jdm v~n** assure s.o (**dass** that). V~**ung** *f* -,-en insurance; assurance
versiegeln *vt* seal
versiegen *vi* ⟨*sein*⟩ dry up
versiert /vɛrˈʒiːɐt/ *a* experienced
versilbert *a* silver-plated
versinken† ⟨*sein*⟩ sink; **in Gedanken versunken** lost in thought
Version /vɛrˈzjoːn/ *f* -,-en version
Versmaß /ˈfɛrs-/ *nt* metre
versöhn|en *vt* reconcile; **sich v~en** become reconciled. v~**lich** *a* conciliatory. V~**ung** *f* -,-en reconciliation
versorg|en *vt* provide, supply (**mit** with); provide for ⟨*Familie*⟩; ⟨*betreuen*⟩ look

after; keep ⟨*Haushalt*⟩. V~**ung** *f* - provision, supply; ⟨*Betreuung*⟩ care
verspät|en (sich) *vr* be late. v~**et** *a* late; ⟨*Zug*⟩ delayed; ⟨*Dank, Glückwunsch*⟩ belated □ *adv* late; belatedly. V~**ung** *f* - lateness; V~**ung haben** be late
versperren *vt* block; bar ⟨*Weg*⟩
verspiel|en *vt* gamble away; **sich v~en** play a wrong note. v~**t** *a* playful, *adv* -ly
verspotten *vt* mock, ridicule
versprech|en† *vt* promise; **sich v~en** make a slip of the tongue; **sich** ⟨*dat*⟩ **viel v~en von** have high hopes of; **ein viel v~ender Anfang** a promising start. V~**en** *nt* -s,- promise. V~**ungen** *fpl* promises
verspüren *vt* feel
verstaatlich|en *vt* nationalize. V~**ung** *f* - nationalization
Verstand *m* -[e]s mind; ⟨*Vernunft*⟩ reason; **den V~ verlieren** go out of one's mind. v~**esmäßig** *a* rational, *adv* -ly
verständig *a* sensible, *adv* -bly; ⟨*klug*⟩ intelligent, *adv* -ly. v~**en** *vt* notify, inform; **sich v~en** communicate; ⟨*sich verständlich machen*⟩ make oneself understood; ⟨*sich einigen*⟩ reach agreement. V~**ung** *f* - notification; communication; ⟨*Einigung*⟩ agreement
verständlich *a* comprehensible, *adv* -bly; ⟨*deutlich*⟩ clear, *adv* -ly; ⟨*begreiflich*⟩ understandable; **leicht v~** easily understood; **sich v~ machen** make oneself understood. v~**erweise** *adv* understandably
Verständnis *nt* -ses understanding. v~**los** *a* uncomprehending, *adv* -ly. v~**voll** *a* understanding, *adv* -ly
verstärk|en *vt* strengthen, reinforce; ⟨*steigern*⟩ intensify, increase; amplify ⟨*Ton*⟩; **sich v~en** intensify. V~**er** *m* -s,- amplifier. V~**ung** *f* reinforcement; increase; amplification; ⟨*Truppen*⟩ reinforcements *pl*
verstaubt *a* dusty
verstauchen *vt* sprain
verstauen *vt* stow
Versteck *nt* -[e]s,-e hiding-place; **V~ spielen** play hide-and-seek. v~**en** *vt* hide; **sich v~en** hide. v~**t** *a* hidden; ⟨*heimlich*⟩ secret; ⟨*verstohlen*⟩ furtive, *adv* -ly
verstehen† *vt* understand; ⟨*können*⟩ know; **falsch v~** misunderstand; **sich v~** understand one another; ⟨*auskommen*⟩ get on; **das versteht sich von selbst** that goes without saying
versteifen *vt* stiffen; **sich v~** stiffen; ⟨*fig*⟩ insist (**auf** + *acc* on)
versteiger|n *vt* auction. V~**ung** *f* auction

versteinert a fossilized

verstell|bar a adjustable. **v~en** vt adjust; (versperren) block; (verändern) disguise; **sich v~en** pretend. **V~ung** f - pretence

versteuern vt pay tax on

verstiegen a (fig) extravagant

verstimm|t a disgruntled; ⟨Magen⟩ upset; (Mus) out of tune. **V~ung** f - ill humour; ⟨Magen-⟩ upset

verstockt a stubborn, adv -ly

verstohlen a furtive, adv -ly

verstopf|en vt plug; (versperren) block; **v~t** blocked; ⟨Person⟩ constipated. **V~ung** f -,-en blockage; (Med) constipation

verstorben a late, deceased. **V~e(r)** m/f deceased

verstört a bewildered

Verstoß m infringement. **v~en†** vt disown □ vi (haben) **v~en gegen** contravene, infringe; offend against ⟨Anstand⟩

verstreichen† vt spread □ vi (sein) pass

verstreuen vt scatter

verstümmeln vt mutilate; garble ⟨Text⟩

verstummen vi (sein) fall silent; ⟨Gespräch, Lärm:⟩ cease

Versuch m -[e]s,-e attempt; (Experiment) experiment. **v~en** vt/i (haben) try; **sich v~en in** (+ dat) try one's hand at; **v~t sein** be tempted (zu to). **V~skaninchen** nt (fig) guinea-pig. **v~sweise** adv as an experiment. **V~ung** f -,-en temptation

versündigen (sich) vr sin (an + dat against)

vertagen vt adjourn; (aufschieben) postpone; **sich v~** adjourn

vertauschen vt exchange; (verwechseln) mix up

verteidig|en vt defend. **V~er** m -s,- defender; (Jur) defence counsel. **V~ung** f -,-en defence

verteil|en vt distribute; (zuteilen) allocate; (ausgeben) hand out; (verstreichen) spread; **sich v~en** spread out. **V~ung** f - distribution; allocation

vertief|en vt deepen; **v~t sein in** (+ acc) be engrossed in. **V~ung** f -,-en hollow, depression

vertikal /vɛrti'ka:l/ a vertical, adv -ly

vertilgen vt exterminate; kill [off] ⟨Unkraut⟩; (fam: essen) demolish

vertippen (sich) vr make a typing mistake

vertonen vt set to music

Vertrag m -[e]s,ᵉe contract; (Pol) treaty

vertragen† vt tolerate, stand; take ⟨Kritik, Spaß⟩; **sich v~** get on; (passen) go (mit with); **sich wieder v~** make it up □ a worn

verträglich a contractual

verträglich a good-natured; (bekömmlich) digestible

vertrauen vi (haben) trust (jdm/etw s.o./sth; auf + acc in). **V~** nt -s trust, confidence (zu in); **im V~** in confidence. **V~smann** m (pl -leute) representative; (Sprecher) spokesman. **v~svoll** a trusting, adv -ly. **v~swürdig** a trustworthy

vertraulich a confidential, adv -ly; (intim) familiar, adv -ly

vertraut a intimate; (bekannt) familiar; **sich v~ machen mit** familiarize oneself with. **V~heit** f - intimacy; familiarity

vertreib|en† vt drive away; drive out ⟨Feind⟩; (Comm) sell; **sich (dat) die Zeit v~en** pass the time. **V~ung** f -,-en expulsion

vertret|en† vt represent; (einspringen für) stand in or deputize for; (verfechten) support; hold ⟨Meinung⟩; **sich (dat) den Fuß v~en** twist one's ankle; **sich (dat) die Beine v~en** stretch one's legs. **V~er** m -s,- representative; deputy; ⟨Arzt-⟩ locum; (Verfechter) supporter, advocate. **V~ung** f -,-en representation; (Person) deputy; ⟨eines Arztes⟩ locum; (Handels-) agency

Vertrieb m -[e]s (Comm) sale. **V~ene(r)** m/f displaced person

vertrocknen vi (sein) dry up

vertrösten vt jdn auf später v~ put s.o. off until later

vertun† vt waste; **sich v~** (fam) make a mistake

vertuschen vt hush up

verübeln vt jdm etw v~ hold sth against s.o.

verüben vt commit

verunglimpfen vt denigrate

verunglücken vi (sein) be involved in an accident; (fam: misslücken) go wrong; **tödlich v~** be killed in an accident

verunreinigen vt pollute; (verseuchen) contaminate; (verschmutzen) soil

verunstalten vt disfigure

veruntreu|en vt embezzle. **V~ung** f - embezzlement

verursachen vt cause

verurteil|en vt condemn; (Jur) convict (wegen of); sentence (zum Tode to death). **V~ung** f - condemnation; (Jur) conviction

vervielfachen vt multiply

vervielfältigen vt duplicate

vervollkommnen vt perfect

vervollständigen vt complete

verwachsen a deformed

verwählen (sich) vr misdial

verwahren vt keep; (verstauen) put away; **sich v~** (fig) protest

verwahrlost a neglected; (Haus) dilapidated; (sittlich) depraved

Verwahrung f - keeping; **in V~ nehmen** take into safe keeping

verwaist a orphaned

verwalt|en vt administer; (leiten) manage; govern (Land). **V~er** m -s,- administrator; manager. **V~ung** f -,-en administration; management; government

verwand|eln vt transform, change (in + acc into); **sich v~eln** change, turn (in + acc into). **V~lung** f transformation

verwandt a related (mit to). **V~e(r)** m/f relative. **V~schaft** f - relationship; (Menschen) relatives pl

verwarn|en vt warn, caution. **V~ung** f warning, caution

verwaschen a washed out, faded

verwechs|eln vt mix up, confuse; (halten für) mistake (mit for). **V~lung** f -,-en mix-up

verwegen a audacious, adv -ly

Verwehung f -,-en [snow-]drift

verweichlicht a (fig) soft

verweiger|n vt/i (haben) refuse (jdm etw s.o sth); **den Gehorsam v~n** refuse to obey. **V~ung** f refusal

verweilen vi (haben) stay

Verweis m -es,-e reference (auf + acc to); (Tadel) reprimand; **v~en†** vt refer (auf/an + acc to); (tadeln) reprimand; **von der Schule v~en** expel

verwelken vi (sein) wilt

verwend|en† vt use; spend (Zeit, Mühe). **V~ung** f use

verwerf|en† vt reject; **sich v~en** warp. **v~lich** a reprehensible

verwert|en vt utilize, use; (Comm) exploit. **V~ung** f - utilization; exploitation

verwesen vi (sein) decompose

verwick|eln vt involve (in + acc in); **sich v~eln** get tangled up; **in etw** (acc) **v~elt sein** (fig) be involved or mixed up in sth. **v~elt** a complicated

verwildert a wild; (Garten) overgrown; (Aussehen) unkempt

verwinden† vt (fig) get over

verwirken vt forfeit

verwirklichen vt realize; **sich v~** be realized

verwirr|en vt tangle up; (fig) confuse; **sich v~en** get tangled; (fig) become confused. **v~t** a confused. **V~ung** f - confusion

verwischen vt smudge

verwittert a weathered; (Gesicht) weather-beaten

verwitwet a widowed

verwöhn|en vt spoil. **v~t** a spoilt; (anspruchsvoll) discriminating

verworren a confused

verwund|bar a vulnerable. **v~en** vt wound

verwunder|lich a surprising. **v~n** vt surprise; **sich v~n** be surprised. **V~ung** f - surprise

Verwund|ete(r) m wounded soldier; **die V~eten** the wounded pl. **V~ung** f -,-en wound

verwünsch|en vt curse. **v~t** a confounded

verwüst|en vt devastate, ravage. **V~ung** f -,-en devastation

verzagen vi (haben) lose heart

verzählen (sich) vr miscount

verzärteln vt mollycoddle

verzauber|n vt bewitch; (fig) enchant; **v~in** (+ acc) turn into

Verzehr m -s consumption. **v~en** vt eat; (aufbrauchen) use up; **sich v~en** (fig) pine away

verzeich|nen vt list; (registrieren) register. **V~nis** nt -ses,-se list; (Inhalts-) index

verzeih|en† vt forgive; **v~en Sie!** excuse me! **V~ung** f - forgiveness; **um V~ung bitten** apologize; **V~ung!** sorry! (bei Frage) excuse me!

verzerren vt distort; contort (Gesicht); pull (Muskel)

Verzicht m -[e]s renunciation (auf + acc of). **v~en** vi (haben) do without; **v~en auf** (+ acc) give up; renounce (Recht, Erbe)

verziehen† vt pull out of shape; (verwöhnen) spoil; **sich v~** lose shape; (Holz:) warp; (Gesicht:) twist; (verschwinden) disappear; (Nebel:) disperse; (Gewitter:) pass; **das Gesicht v~** pull a face □ vi (sein) move [away]

verzier|en vt decorate. **V~ung** f -,-en decoration

verzinsen vt pay interest on

verzöger|n vt delay; (verlangsamen) slow down; **sich v~n** be delayed. **V~ung** f -,-en delay

verzollen vt pay duty on; **haben Sie etwas zu v~?** have you anything to declare?

verzück|t a ecstatic, adv -ally. **V~ung** f - rapture, ecstasy

Verzug m delay; **in V~** in arrears

verzweif|eln vi (sein) despair. **v~elt** a desperate, adv -ly; **v~elt sein** be in despair; (ratlos) be desperate. **V~lung** f - despair; (Ratlosigkeit) desperation

verzweigen (sich) *vr* branch [out]

verzwickt *a (fam)* tricky

Veto /'ve:to/ *nt* -s,-s veto

Vetter *m* -s,-n cousin. **V~nwirtschaft** *f* nepotism

vgl. *abbr* (**vergleiche**) cf.

Viadukt /vja'dʊkt/ *nt* -[e]s,-e viaduct

vibrieren /vi'bri:rən/ *vi (haben)* vibrate

Video /'vi:deo/ *nt* -s,-s video. **V~kassette** *f* video cassette. **V~recorder** /-rəkɔrdɐ/ *m* -s,- video recorder

Vieh *nt* -[e]s livestock; *(Rinder)* cattle *pl*; *(fam: Tier)* creature. **v~isch** *a* brutal, *adv* -ly

viel *pron* a great deal/*(fam)* a lot of; *(pl)* many, *(fam)* a lot of; *(substantivisch)* **v~[es]** much, *(fam)* a lot; **nicht/so/ wie/zu v~** not/so/how/too much/ *(pl)* many; **v~e** *pl* many; **das v~e Geld** □ *adv* Lesen all that money/reading □ *adv* much, *(fam)* a lot; **v~ mehr/weniger** much more/less; **v~ zu groß/klein/viel** much *or* far too big/small/much; **so v~ wie möglich** as much as possible; **so/zu v~ arbeiten** work so/too much

viel|deutig *a* ambiguous. **v~erlei** *inv a* many kinds of □ *pron* many things. **v~fach** *a* multiple □ *adv* many times; *(fam: oft)* frequently. **V~falt** *f* - diversity, [great] variety. **v~fältig** *a* diverse, varied

vielleicht *adv* perhaps, maybe; *(fam: wirklich)* really

vielmals *adv* very much; **danke v~!** thank you very much!

viel|mehr *adv* rather; *(im Gegenteil)* on the contrary. **v~sagend** *a* (NEW) **v~ sagend,** *s.* **sagen**

vielseitig *a* varied; *(Person)* versatile □ *adv* **v~ begabt** versatile. **V~keit** *f* - versatility

vielversprechend *a* (NEW) **viel versprechend,** *s.* **versprechen**

vier *inv a,* **V~** *f* -,-en four; *(Sch)* ≈ fair. **V~eck** *nt* -[e]s,-e oblong, rectangle; *(Quadrat)* square. **v~eckig** *a* oblong, rectangular; square. **v~fach** *a* quadruple. **V~linge** *mpl* quadruplets

viertel /'fɪrtəl/ *inv a* a quarter; **eine v~ Million** a quarter of a million; **um v~ neun** at [a] quarter past eight; **um drei v~ neun** at [a] quarter to nine; **eine v~ Stunde = eine Viertelstunde. V~** *nt* -s,- quarter; *(Wein)* quarter litre; **v~ vor/ nach sechs** [a] quarter to/past six; **um V~/drei V~ neun** (NEW) **um v~/drei v~ neun,** *s.* **viertel. V~finale** *nt* quarter-final. **V~jahr** *nt* three months *pl*; *(Comm)* quarter. **v~jährlich** *a & adv* quarterly. **v~n** *vt* quarter. **V~note** *f* crotchet,

(Amer) quarter note. **V~stunde** *f* quarter of an hour

vier|zehn /'fɪr-/ *inv a* fourteen. **v~zehnte(r,s)** *a* fourteenth. **v~zig** *inv a* forty. **v~zigste(r,s)** *a* fortieth

Villa /'vɪla/ *f* -,-len villa

violett /vio'lɛt/ *a* violet

Vio|line /vio'li:nə/ *f* -,-n violin. **V~linschlüssel** *m* treble clef. **V~loncello** /-lɔn'tʃɛlo/ *nt* cello

Virtuose /vɪr'tʊo:zə/ *m* -n,-n virtuoso

Virus /'vi:rʊs/ *nt* -,-ren virus

Visier /vi'zi:ɐ/ *nt* -s,-e visor

Vision /vi'zio:n/ *f* -,-en vision

Visite /vi'zi:tə/ *f* -,-n round; **v~ machen** do one's round

visuell /vi'zʊɛl/ *a* visual, *adv* -ly

Visum /'vi:zʊm/ *nt* -s,-sa visa

vital /vi'ta:l/ *a* vital; *(Person)* energetic. **V~ität** *f* - vitality

Vitamin /vita'mi:n/ *nt* -s,-e vitamin

Vitrine /vi'tri:nə/ *f* -,-n display cabinet; *(im Museum)* case

Vizepräsident /'fi:tsə-/ *m* vice president

Vogel *m* -s,⸚ bird; **einen V~ haben** *(fam)* have a screw loose. **V~scheuche** *f* -,-n scarecrow

Vokab|eln /vo'ka:bəln/ *fpl* vocabulary *sg.* **V~ular** *nt* -s,-e vocabulary

Vokal /vo'ka:l/ *m* -s,-e vowel

Volant /vo'lã:/ *m* -s,-s flounce; *(Auto)* steering-wheel

Volk *nt* -[e]s,⸚er people *sg*; *(Bevölkerung)* people *pl*; *(Bienen-)* colony

Völker|kunde *f* ethnology. **V~mord** *m* genocide. **V~recht** *nt* international law

Volks|abstimmung *f* plebiscite. **V~fest** *nt* public festival. **V~hochschule** *f* adult education classes *pl/ (Gebäude)* centre. **V~lied** *nt* folk-song. **V~tanz** *m* folk-dance. **v~tümlich** *a* popular. **V~wirt** *m* economist. **V~wirtschaft** *f* economics *sg.* **V~zählung** *f* [national] census

voll *a* full *(von od mit* of); *(Haar)* thick; *(Erfolg, Ernst)* complete; *(Wahrheit)* whole; **v~ machen** fill up; **v~ tanken** fill up with petrol; **die Uhr schlug v~** *(fam)* the clock struck the hour □ *adv (ganz)* completely; *(arbeiten)* full-time; *(auszahlen)* in full; **v~ und ganz** completely

vollauf *adv* fully, completely

Voll|beschäftigung *f* full employment. **V~blut** *nt* thoroughbred

vollbringen† *vt insep* accomplish; work *(Wunder)*

vollende|n *vt insep* complete. **v~t a** perfect, *adv* -ly; **v~te Gegenwart/Vergangenheit** perfect/pluperfect

vollends *adv* completely

Vollendung *f* completion; (*Vollkommenheit*) perfection

voller *inv a* full of; **v~ Angst/Freude** filled with fear/joy; **v~ Flecken** covered with stains

Völlerei *f* - gluttony

Volleyball /'vɔli-/ *m* volleyball

vollführen *vt insep* perform

vollfüllen *vt sep* fill up

Vollgas *nt* **V~ geben** put one's foot down; **mit V~** flat out

völlig *a* complete, *adv* -ly

volljährig *a* **v~ sein** (*Jur*) be of age. **V~keit** *f* - (*Jur*) majority

Vollkaskoversicherung *f* fully comprehensive insurance

vollkommen *a* perfect, *adv* -ly; (*völlig*) complete, *adv* -ly. **V~heit** *f* - perfection

Voll|kornbrot *nt* wholemeal bread. **V~macht** *f* -,-en authority; (*Jur*) power of attorney. **V~mond** *m* full moon. **V~pension** *f* full board. **v~schlank** *a* with a fuller figure

vollständig *a* complete, *adv* -ly

vollstrecken *vt insep* execute; carry out ⟨*Urteil*⟩

volltanken *vi sep* (*haben*) (NEW) **voll tanken**, s. **voll**

Volltreffer *m* direct hit

vollzählig *a* complete; **sind wir v~?** are we all here?

vollziehen† *vt insep* carry out; perform ⟨*Handlung*⟩; consummate ⟨*Ehe*⟩; **sich v~** take place

Volt /vɔlt/ *nt* -[s],- volt

Volumen /vo'lu:mən/ *nt* -s,- volume

vom *prep* = **von dem**; **vom Rauchen** from smoking

von *prep* (+ *dat*) of; (*über*) about; (*Ausgangspunkt, Ursache*) from; (*beim Passiv*) by; **Musik von Mozart** music by Mozart; **einer von euch** one of you; **von hier/heute an** from here/today; **von mir aus** I don't mind

voneinander *adv* from each other; ⟨*abhängig*⟩ on each other

vonseiten *prep* (+ *gen*) on the part of

vonstatten *adv* **v~ gehen** take place; **gut v~ gehen** go [off] well

vor *prep* (+ *dat/acc*) in front of; (*zeitlich, Reihenfolge*) before; (+ *dat*) (*bei Uhrzeit*) to; ⟨*warnen, sich fürchten/schämen*⟩ of; ⟨*schützen, davonlaufen*⟩ from; ⟨*Respekt haben*⟩ for; **vor Angst/Kälte zittern** tremble with fear/cold; **vor drei Tagen/**

Jahren three days/years ago; **vor sich** (*acc*) **hin murmeln** mumble to oneself; **vor allen Dingen** above all □ *adv* forward; **vor und zurück** backwards and forwards

Vor|abend *m* eve. **V~ahnung** *f* premonition

voran *adv* at the front; (*voraus*) ahead; (*vorwärts*) forward. **v~gehen†** *vi sep* (*sein*) lead the way; (*Fortschritte machen*) make progress; **jdm/etw v~gehen** precede s.o./sth. **v~kommen†** *vi sep* (*sein*) make progress; (*fig*) get on

Vor|anschlag *m* estimate. **V~anzeige** *f* advance notice. **V~arbeit** *f* preliminary work. **V~arbeiter** *m* foreman

voraus *adv* ahead (*dat* of); (*vorn*) at the front; (*vorwärts*) forward □ **im Voraus** (**voraus**) in advance. **v~bezahlen** *vt sep* pay in advance. **v~gehen†** *vi sep* (*sein*) go on ahead; **jdm/etw v~gehen** precede s.o./sth. **V~sage** *f* -,-n prediction. **v~sagen** *vt sep* predict. **v~sehen†** *vt sep* foresee

voraussetz|en *vt sep* take for granted; (*erfordern*) require; **vorausgesetzt, dass** provided that. **V~ung** *f* -,-en assumption; (*Erfordernis*) prerequisite; **unter der V~ung, dass** on condition that

Voraussicht *f* foresight; **aller V~ nach** in all probability. **v~lich** *a* anticipated, expected □ *adv* probably

Vorbehalt *m* -[e]s,-e reservation. **v~en†** *vt sep* **sich** (*dat*) **v~en** reserve ⟨*Recht*⟩; **jdm v~en sein/bleiben** be left to s.o. **v~los** *a* unreserved, *adv* -ly

vorbei *adv* past (**an jdm/etw** s.o./sth); (*zu Ende*) over. **v~fahren†** *vi sep* (*sein*) drive/go past. **v~gehen†** *vi sep* (*sein*) go past; (*verfehlen*) miss; (*vergehen*) pass; (*fam: besuchen*) drop in (**bei** on). **v~kommen†** *vi sep* (*sein*) pass/(*v~können*) get past (**an jdm/etw** s.o./sth); (*fam: besuchen*) drop in (**bei** on)

vorbereit|en *vt sep* prepare; prepare for ⟨*Reise*⟩; **sich v~en** prepare [oneself] (**auf** + *acc* for). **V~ung** *f* -,-en preparation

vorbestellen *vt sep* order/(*im Theater, Hotel*) book in advance

vorbestraft *a* **v~ sein** have a [criminal] record

vorbeug|en *v sep* □ *vt* bend forward; **sich v~en** bend *or* lean forward □ *vi* (*haben*) prevent (**etw** *dat* sth); **v~end** preventive. **V~ung** *f* - prevention

Vorbild *nt* model. **v~lich** *a* exemplary, model □ *adv* in an exemplary manner

vorbringen† *vt sep* put forward; offer ⟨*Entschuldigung*⟩

vordatieren *vt sep* post-date

Vorder|bein *nt* foreleg. **v~e(r,s)** *a* front. **V~grund** *m* foreground. **V~mann** *m* (*pl* -männer) person in front; **auf V~mann bringen** (*fam*) lick into shape; (*aufräumen*) tidy up. **V~rad** *nt* front wheel. **V~seite** *f* front; (*einer Münze*) obverse. **V~ste(r,s)** *a* front, first. **V~teil** *nt* front

vor|drängeln (sich) *vr sep* jump the queue. **v~drängen (sich)** *vr sep* push forward. **v~dringen†** *vi sep* (*sein*) advance

vor|ehelich *a* pre-marital. **v~eilig** *a* rash, *adv* -ly

voreingenommen *a* biased, prejudiced. **V~heit** *f* - bias

vorenthalten† *vt sep* withhold

vorerst *adv* for the time being

Vorfahr *m* -en,-en ancestor

vorfahren† *vi sep* (*sein*) drive up; (*vorwärts-*) move forward; (*voraus-*) drive on ahead

Vorfahrt *f* right of way; '**V~ beachten**' 'give way'. **V~straße** *f* ≈ major road

Vorfall *m* incident. **v~en†** *vi sep* (*sein*) happen

vorfinden† *vt sep* find

Vorfreude *f* [happy] anticipation

vorführ|en *vt sep* present, show; (*demonstrieren*) demonstrate; (*aufführen*) perform. **V~ung** *f* presentation; demonstration; performance

Vor|gabe *f* (*Sport*) handicap. **V~gang** *m* occurrence; (*Techn*) process. **V~gänger(in)** *m* -s,- (*f* -,-nen) predecessor. **V~garten** *m* front garden

vorgeben† *vt sep* pretend

vor|gefasst (**vor|gefaßt**) *a* preconceived. **v~gefertigt** *a* prefabricated

vorgehen† *vi sep* (*sein*) go forward; (*voraus-*) go on ahead; ⟨*Uhr:*⟩ be fast; (*wichtig sein*) take precedence; (*verfahren*) act, proceed; (*geschehen*) happen, go on. **V~** *nt* -s action

vor|geschichtlich *a* prehistoric. **V~geschmack** *m* foretaste. **V~gesetzte(r)** *m/f* superior. **V~gestern** *adv* the day before yesterday; **v~gestern Abend/Nacht** the evening/night before last

vorhaben† *vt sep* propose, intend (zu to); **etw v~** have sth planned; **nichts v~** have no plans. **V~** *nt* -s,- plan; (*Projekt*) project

vorhalt|en† *v sep ▢ vt* hold up; **jdm etw v~en** reproach s.o. for sth ▢ *vi* (*haben*) last. **V~ungen** *fpl* **jdm v~ungen machen** reproach s.o. (**wegen** for)

Vorhand *f* (*Sport*) forehand

vorhanden *a* existing; **v~ sein** exist; (*verfügbar sein*) be available. **V~sein** *nt* -s existence

Vorhang *m* curtain

Vorhängeschloss (**Vorhängeschloß**) *nt* padlock

vorher *adv* before[hand]

vorhergehend *a* previous

vorherig *a* prior; (*vorhergehend*) previous

Vorherrsch|aft *f* supremacy. **v~en** *vi sep* (*haben*) predominate. **v~end** *a* predominant

Vorher|sage *f* -,-n prediction; (*Wetter-*) forecast. **v~sagen** *vt sep* predict; forecast ⟨*Wetter*⟩. **v~sehen†** *vt sep* foresee

vorhin *adv* just now

vorige(r,s) *a* last, previous

Vor|kämpfer *m* (*fig*) champion. **V~kehrungen** *fpl* precautions. **V~kenntnisse** *fpl* previous knowledge *sg*

vorkommen† *vi sep* (*sein*) happen; (*vorhanden sein*) occur; (*nach vorn kommen*) come forward; (*hervorkommen*) come out; (*zu sehen sein*) show; **jdm bekannt/verdächtig v~** seem familiar/suspicious to s.o.; **sich** (*dat*) **dumm/alt v~** feel stupid/old. **V~** *nt* -s,- occurrence; (*Geol*) deposit

Vorkriegszeit *f* pre-war period

vorlad|en† *vt sep* (*Jur*) summons. **V~ung** *f* summons

Vorlage *f* model; (*Muster*) pattern; (*Gesetzes-*) bill

vorlassen† *vt sep* admit; **jdn v~** (*fam*) let s.o. pass; (*den Vortritt lassen*) let s.o. go first

Vor|lauf *m* (*Sport*) heat. **V~läufer** *m* forerunner. **v~läufig** *a* provisional, *adv* -ly; (*zunächst*) for the time being. **v~laut** *a* forward. **V~leben** *nt* past

vorleg|en *vt sep* put on ⟨*Kette*⟩; (*unterbreiten*) present; (*vorzeigen*) show; **jdm Fleisch v~en** serve s.o. with meat. **V~er** *m* -s,- mat; (*Bett-*) rug

vorles|en† *vt sep* read [out]; **jdm v~en** read to s.o. **V~ung** *f* (*Univ*) lecture

vorletzt|e(r,s) *a* last ... but one; ⟨*Silbe*⟩ penultimate; **v~es Jahr** the year before last

vorlieb *adv* **v~ nehmen** make do (**mit** with). **v~nehmen†** *vt sep* (NEW) **v~ nehmen**, *s.* **vorlieb**

Vorliebe *f* preference

vorliegen† *vt sep* (*haben*) be present/(*verfügbar*) available; (*bestehen*) exist, be; **es muss ein Irrtum v~** there must be some mistake. **v~d** *a* present; ⟨*Frage*⟩ at issue

vorlügen† *vt sep* lie (*dat* to)

vorm *prep* = **vor dem**

vormachen vt sep put up; put on ⟨Kette⟩; push ⟨Riegel⟩; (zeigen) demonstrate; **jdm etwas v~** (fam: täuschen) kid s.o.

Vormacht f supremacy

vormals adv formerly

Vormarsch m (Mil & fig) advance

vormerken vt sep make a note of; (reservieren) reserve

Vormittag m morning; **gestern/heute V~** yesterday/this morning. **v~** adv **gestern/heute v~** (NEW) **gestern/heute V~**, s. **Vormittag**. **v~s** adv in the morning

Vormund m **-[e]s,-munde** & **-münder** guardian

vorn adv at the front; **nach v~** to the front; **von v~** from the front/(vom Anfang) beginning; **wieder von v~ anfangen** start afresh

Vorname m first name

vorne adv = vorn

vornehm a distinguished; (elegant) smart, adv -ly

vornehmen† vt sep carry out; **sich** (dat) **v~, etw zu tun** plan/(beschließen) resolve to do sth

vorn|herein adv **von v~herein** from the start. **v~über** adv forward

Vor|ort m suburb. **V~rang** m priority, precedence (vor + dat over). **V~rat** m **-[e]s,-e** supply, stock (an + dat of). **v~rätig** a available; **v~rätig haben** have in stock. **V~ratskammer** f larder. **V~raum** m ante-room. **V~recht** nt privilege. **V~richtung** f device

vorrücken vt/i sep (sein) move forward; (Mil) advance

Vorrunde f qualifying round

vors prep = vor das

vorsagen vt/i sep (haben) recite; **jdm [die Antwort] v~** tell s.o. the answer

Vor|satz m resolution. **v~sätzlich** a deliberate, adv -ly; (Jur) premeditated

Vorschau f preview; (Film-) trailer

Vorschein m **zum V~ kommen** appear

vorschießen† vt sep advance ⟨Geld⟩

Vorschlag m suggestion, proposal. **v~en†** vt sep suggest, propose

vorschnell a rash, adv -ly

vorschreiben† vt sep lay down; dictate (dat to); **vorgeschriebene Dosis** prescribed dose

Vorschrift f regulation; (Anweisung) instruction; **jdm V~en machen** tell s.o. what to do; **Dienst nach V~** work to rule. **v~smäßig** a correct, adv -ly

Vorschule f nursery school

Vorschuss (Vorschuß) m advance

vorschützen vt sep plead [as an excuse]; feign ⟨Krankheit⟩

vorseh|en† v sep □vt intend (für/als for/as); (planen) plan; **sich v~en** be careful (vor + dat of) □vi (haben) peep out. **V~ung** f - providence

vorsetzen vt sep move forward; **jdm etw v~** serve s.o. sth

Vorsicht f - care; (bei Gefahr) caution; **V~!** careful! (auf Schild) 'caution'. **v~ig** a careful, adv -ly; cautious, adv -ly. **v~shalber** adv to be on the safe side. **V~smaßnahme** f precaution

Vorsilbe f prefix

Vorsitz m chairmanship; **den V~ führen** be in the chair. **v~en†** vi sep (haben) preside (dat over). **V~ende(r)** m/f chair[man]

Vorsorge f **V~ treffen** take precautions; make provisions (für for). **v~n** vi sep (haben) provide (für for). **V~untersuchung** f check-up

vorsorglich adv as a precaution

Vorspeise f starter

Vorspiel nt prelude. **v~en** v sep □vt perform/ (Mus) play (dat for) □vi (haben) audition

vorsprechen† v sep □vt recite; (zum Nachsagen) say (dat to) □vi (haben) (Theat) audition; **bei jdm v~** call on s.o.

vorspringen† vi sep (sein) jut out; **v~des Kinn** prominent chin

Vor|sprung m projection; (Fels-) ledge; (Vorteil) lead (vor + dat over). **V~stadt** f suburb. **v~städtisch** a suburban. **V~stand** m board [of directors]; (Vereins-) committee; (Partei-) executive

vorsteh|en† vi sep (haben) project, protrude; **einer Abteilung v~en** be in charge of a department; **v~end** protruding; ⟨Augen⟩ bulging. **V~er** m **-s,-** head; (Gemeinde-) chairman

vorstell|bar a imaginable, conceivable. **v~en** vt sep put forward ⟨Bein, Uhr⟩; (darstellen) represent; (bekannt machen) introduce; **sich v~en** introduce oneself; (als Bewerber) go for an interview; **sich** (dat) **etw v~en** imagine sth. **V~ung** f introduction; (bei Bewerbung) interview; (Aufführung) performance; (Idee) idea; (Phantasie) imagination. **V~ungsgespräch** nt interview. **V~ungskraft** f imagination

Vorstoß m advance

Vorstrafe f previous conviction

Vortag m day before

vortäuschen vt sep feign, fake

Vorteil m advantage. **v~haft** a advantageous, adv -ly; (Kleidung, Farbe) flattering

Vortrag m **-[e]s,-e** talk; (wissenschaftlich) lecture; ⟨Klavier-, Gedicht-⟩ recital. **v~en†** vt sep perform; (aufsagen) recite; (singen)

sing; (*darlegen*) present (*dat* to); express (*Wunsch*)

vortrefflich *a* excellent, *adv* -ly

vortreten† *vi sep* (*sein*) step forward; (*hervor-*) protrude

Vortritt *m* precedence; **jdm den V~ lassen** let s.o. go first

vorüber *adv* **v~ sein** be over; **an etw** (*dat*) **v~** past sth. **v~gehen**† *vi sep* (*sein*) walk past; (*vergehen*) pass. **v~gehend** *a* temporary, *adv* -ily

Vor|urteil *nt* prejudice. **V~verkauf** *m* advance booking

vorverlegen *vt sep* bring forward

Vor|wahl[nummer] *f* dialling code. **V~wand** *m* -[e]s,-e pretext; (*Ausrede*) excuse

vorwärts *adv* forward[s]; **v~ kommen** make progress; (*fig*) get on *or* ahead. **v~kommen**† *vi sep* (*sein*) (NEW) **v~ kommen**, *s.* **vorwärts**

vorweg *adv* beforehand; (*vorn*) in front; (*voraus*) ahead. **v~nehmen**† *vt sep* anticipate

vorweisen† *vt sep* show

vorwerfen† *vt sep* throw (*dat* to); **jdm etw v~** reproach s.o. with sth; (*beschuldigen*) accuse s.o. of sth

vorwiegend *adv* predominantly

Vorwort *nt* (*pl* -worte) preface

Vorwurf *m* reproach; **jdm Vorwürfe machen** reproach s.o. **v~svoll** *a* reproachful, *adv* -ly

Vorzeichen *nt* sign; (*fig*) omen

vorzeigen *vt sep* show

vorzeitig *a* premature, *adv* -ly

vorziehen† *vt sep* pull forward; draw (*Vorhang*); (*vorverlegen*) bring forward; (*lieber mögen*) prefer; (*bevorzugen*) favour

Vor|zimmer *nt* ante-room; (*Büro*) outer office. **V~zug** *m* preference; (*gute Eigenschaft*) merit, virtue; (*Vorteil*) advantage

vorzüglich *a* excellent, *adv* -ly

vorzugsweise *adv* preferably

vulgär /vʊlˈgɛːɐ̯/ *a* vulgar ▯ *adv* in a vulgar way

Vulkan /vʊlˈkaːn/ *m* -s,-e volcano

W

Waage *f* -,-n scales *pl*; (*Astr*) Libra. **w~recht** *a* horizontal, *adv* -ly

Wabe *f* -,-n honeycomb

wach *a* awake; (*aufgeweckt*) alert; **w~ werden** wake up

Wach|e *f* -,-n guard; (*Posten*) sentry; (*Dienst*) guard duty; (*Naut*) watch; (*Polizei*) station; **W~e halten** keep watch; **W~e stehen** stand guard. **w~en** *vi* (*haben*) be awake; **w~en über** (+ *acc*) watch over. **W~hund** *m* guard-dog

Wacholder *m* -s juniper

Wachposten *m* sentry

Wachs *nt* -es wax

wachsam *a* vigilant, *adv* -ly. **W~keit** *f* - vigilance

wachsen†[1] *vi* (*sein*) grow

wachs|en[2] *vt* (*reg*) wax. **W~figur** *f* waxwork. **W~tuch** *nt* oil-cloth

Wachstum *nt* -s growth

Wächter *m* -s,- guard; (*Park-*) keeper; (*Parkplatz-*) attendant

Wacht|meister *m* [police] constable. **W~posten** *m* sentry

Wachturm *m* watch-tower

wackel|ig *a* wobbly; (*Stuhl*) rickety; (*Person*) shaky. **W~kontakt** *m* loose connection. **w~n** *vi* (*haben*) wobble; (*zittern*) shake ▯ *vi* (*sein*) totter

wacklig *a* = **wackelig**

Wade *f* -,-n (*Anat*) calf

Waffe *f* -,-n weapon; **W~n** arms

Waffel *f* -,-n waffle; (*Eis-*) wafer

Waffen|ruhe *f* cease-fire. **W~schein** *m* firearms licence. **W~stillstand** *m* armistice

Wagemut *m* daring. **w~ig** *a* daring, *adv* -ly

wagen *vt* risk; **es w~**, **etw zu tun** dare [to] do sth; **sich w~** (*gehen*) venture

Wagen *m* -s,- cart; (*Eisenbahn-*) carriage, coach; (*Güter-*) wagon; (*Kinder-*) pram; (*Auto*) car. **W~heber** *m* -s,- jack

Waggon /vaˈɡõː/ *m* -s,-s wagon

waghalsig *a* daring, *adv* -ly

Wagnis *nt* -ses,-se risk

Wagon /vaˈɡõː/ *m* -s,-s = **Waggon**

Wahl *f* -,-n choice; (*Pol, Admin*) election; (*geheime*) ballot; **zweite W~** (*Comm*) seconds *pl*

wähl|en *vt/i* (*haben*) choose; (*Pol, Admin*) elect; (*stimmen*) vote; (*Teleph*) dial; **jdn wieder w~en** re-elect s.o. **W~er(in)** *m* -s,- (*f* -,-nen) voter. **w~erisch** *a* choosy, fussy

Wahl|fach *nt* optional subject. **w~frei** *a* optional. **W~kampf** *m* election campaign. **W~kreis** *m* constituency. **W~lokal** *nt* polling-station. **w~los** *a* indiscriminate, *adv* -ly. **W~recht** *nt* [right to] vote

Wählscheibe *f* (*Teleph*) dial

Wahl|spruch *m* motto. **W~urne** *f* ballot-box

Wahn m -[e]s delusion; (*Manie*) mania

wähnen vt believe

Wahnsinn m madness. **w~ig** a mad, insane; (*fam: unsinnig*) crazy; (*fam: groß*) terrible; **w~ig werden** go mad □ *adv* (*fam*) terribly. **W~ige(r)** m/f maniac

wahr a true; (*echt*) real; **w~ werden** come true; **du kommst doch, nicht w~?** you are coming, aren't you?

wahren vt keep; (*verteidigen*) safeguard; **den Schein w~** keep up appearances

währen vi (*haben*) last

während prep (+ gen) during □ *conj* while; (*wohingegen*) whereas. **w~dessen** *adv* in the meantime

wahrhaben vt **etw nicht w~ wollen** refuse to admit sth

wahrhaftig *adv* really, truly

Wahrheit f -,-en truth. **w~sgemäß** a truthful, *adv* -ly

wahrnehm|bar a perceptible. **w~en†** vt sep notice; (*nutzen*) take advantage of; exploit (*Vorteil*); look after (*Interessen*). **W~ung** f -,-en perception

wahrsag|en v sep □ vt predict □ vi (*haben*) **jdm w~en** tell s.o.'s fortune. **W~erin** f -,-nen fortune-teller

wahrscheinlich a probable, *adv* -bly. **W~keit** f - probability

Währung f -,-en currency

Wahrzeichen nt symbol

Waise f -,-n orphan. **W~nhaus** nt orphanage. **W~nkind** nt orphan

Wal m -[e]s,-e whale

Wald m -[e]s,¨er wood; (*groß*) forest. **w~ig** a wooded

Walis|er m -s,- Welshman. **w~isch** a Welsh

Wall m -[e]s,¨e mound; (*Mil*) rampart

Wallfahr|er(in) m(f) pilgrim. **W~t** f pilgrimage

Walnuss (**Walnuß**) f walnut

Walze f -,-n roller. **w~n** vt roll

wälzen vt roll; pore over (*Bücher*); mull over (*Probleme*); **sich w~** roll [about]; (*schlaflos*) toss and turn

Walzer m -s,- waltz

Wand f -,¨e wall; (*Trenn-*) partition; (*Seite*) side; (*Fels-*) face

Wandel m -s change. **w~bar** a changeable. **w~n** vi (*sein*) stroll □ vr **sich w~n** change

Wander|er m -s,-, **W~in** f -,-nen hiker, rambler. **w~n** vi (*sein*) hike, ramble; (*ziehen*) travel; (*gemächlich gehen*) wander; (*ziellos*) roam. **W~schaft** f - travels pl. **W~ung** f -,-en hike, ramble; (*länger*) walking tour. **W~weg** m footpath

Wandgemälde nt mural

Wandlung f -,-en change, transformation

Wand|malerei f mural. **W~tafel** f blackboard. **W~teppich** m tapestry

Wange f -,-n cheek

wank|elmütig a fickle. **w~en** vi (*haben*) sway; (*Person:*) stagger; (*fig*) waver □ vi (*sein*) stagger

wann *adv* when

Wanne f -,-n tub

Wanze f -,-n bug

Wappen nt -s,- coat of arms. **W~kunde** f heraldry

war, wäre s. **sein**[1]

Ware f -,-n article; (*Comm*) commodity; (*coll*) merchandise; **W~n** goods. **W~nhaus** nt department store. **W~nprobe** f sample. **W~nzeichen** nt trademark

warm a (**wärmer, wärmst**) warm; (*Mahlzeit*) hot; **w~ machen** heat □ *adv* warmly; **w~ essen** have a hot meal

Wärm|e f - warmth; (*Phys*) heat; **10 Grad W~e** 10 degrees above zero. **w~en** vt warm; heat (*Essen, Wasser*). **W~flasche** f hot-water bottle

warmherzig a warm-hearted

Warn|blinkanlage f hazard [warning] lights pl. **w~en** vt/i (*haben*) warn (**vor** + dat of). **W~ung** f -,-en warning

Warteliste f waiting list

warten vi (*haben*) wait (**auf** + acc for); **auf sich** (acc) **w~ lassen** take one's/its time □ vt (*Techn*) service

Wärter(in) m -s,- (f -,-nen) keeper; (*Museums-*) attendant; (*Gefängnis-*) warder, (*Amer*) guard; (*Kranken-*) orderly

Warte|raum, W~saal m waiting-room. **W~zimmer** nt (*Med*) waiting-room

Wartung f - (*Techn*) service

warum *adv* why

Warze f -,-n wart

was pron what; **was für [ein]?** what kind of [a]? **was für ein Pech!** what bad luck! **das gefällt dir, was?** you like that, don't you? □ *rel pron* that; **alles, was ich brauche** all [that] I need □ *indef pron* (*fam: etwas*) something; (*fragend, verneint*) anything; **was zu essen** something to eat; **so was Ärgerliches!** what a nuisance! □ *adv* (*fam*) (*warum*) why; (*wie*) how

wasch|bar a washable. **W~becken** nt wash-basin. **W~beutel** m sponge-bag

Wäsche f - washing; (*Unter-*) underwear; **in der W~** in the wash

waschecht a colour-fast; (*fam*) genuine

Wäsche|klammer f clothes-peg. **W~leine** f clothes-line

waschen† *vt* wash; **sich w~** have a wash; **sich** (*dat*) **die Hände w~** wash one's hands; **W~ und Legen** shampoo and set □ *vi* (*haben*) do the washing

Wäscherei *f* -,-en laundry

Wäsche|schleuder *f* spin-drier. **W~trockner** *m* tumble-drier

Wasch|küche *f* laundry-room. **W~lappen** *m* face-flannel, (*Amer*) washcloth; (*fam: Feigling*) sissy. **W~maschine** *f* washing machine. **W~mittel** *nt* detergent. **W~pulver** *nt* washing-powder. **W~raum** *m* wash-room. **W~salon** *m* launderette. **W~zettel** *m* blurb

Wasser *nt* -s water; (*Haar-*) lotion; **ins W~ fallen** (*fam*) fall through; **mir lief das W~ im Mund zusammen** my mouth was watering. **W~ball** *m* beach-ball; (*Spiel*) water polo. **w~dicht** *a* watertight; (*Kleidung*) waterproof. **W~fall** *m* waterfall. **W~farbe** *f* water-colour. **W~hahn** *m* tap, (*Amer*) faucet. **W~kasten** *m* cistern. **W~kraft** *f* water-power. **W~kraftwerk** *nt* hydroelectric power-station. **W~leitung** *f* water-main; **aus der W~leitung** from the tap. **W~mann** *m* (*Astr*) Aquarius

wässern *vt* soak; (*begießen*) water □ *vi* (*haben*) water

Wasser|scheide *f* watershed. **W~ski** *nt* -s water-skiing. **W~stoff** *m* hydrogen. **W~straße** *f* waterway. **W~waage** *f* spirit-level. **W~werfer** *m* -s,- water-cannon. **W~zeichen** *nt* watermark

wässrig (**wäßrig**) *a* watery

waten *vi* (*sein*) wade

watscheln *vi* (*sein*) waddle

Watt¹ *nt* -[e]s mud-flats *pl*

Watt² *nt* -s,- (*Phys*) watt

Watt|e *f* - cotton wool. **w~iert** *a* padded; (*gesteppt*) quilted

WC /ve'tse:/ *nt* -s,-s WC

web|en *vt/i* (*haben*) weave. **W~er** *m* -s,- weaver. **W~stuhl** *m* loom

Wechsel *m* -s,- change; (*Tausch*) exchange; (*Comm*) bill of exchange. **W~geld** *nt* change. **w~haft** *a* changeable. **W~jahre** *npl* menopause *sg*. **W~kurs** *m* exchange rate. **w~n** *vt* change; (*tauschen*) exchange □ *vi* (*haben*) change; (*ab-*) alternate; (*verschieden sein*) vary. **w~nd** *a* changing; (*verschieden*) varying. **w~seitig** *a* mutual, *adv* -ly. **W~strom** *m* alternating current. **W~stube** *f* bureau de change. **w~weise** *adv* alternately. **W~wirkung** *f* interaction

weck|en *vt* wake [up]; (*fig*) awaken □ *vi* (*haben*) (*Wecker:*) go off. **W~er** *m* -s,- alarm [clock]

wedeln *vi* (*haben*) wave; **mit dem Schwanz w~** wag its tail

weder *conj* **w~ ... noch** neither ... nor

Weg *m* -[e]s,-e way; (*Fuß-*) path; (*Fahr-*) track; (*Gang*) errand; **auf dem Weg** on the way (**nach** to); **sich auf den Weg machen** set off; **im Weg sein** be in the way; **zu W~e bringen** = **zuwege bringen**, *s.* **zuwege**

weg *adv* away, off; (*verschwunden*) gone; **weg sein** be away; (*gegangen/verschwunden*) have gone; (*fam: schlafen*) be asleep; **Hände weg!** hands off! **w~bleiben†** *vi sep* (*sein*) stay away. **w~bringen†** *vt sep* take away

wegen *prep* (+ *gen*) because of; (*um ... willen*) for the sake of; (*bezüglich*) about

weg|fahren† *vi sep* (*sein*) go away; (*abfahren*) leave. **w~fallen†** *vi sep* (*sein*) be dropped/(*ausgelassen*) omitted; (*entfallen*) no longer apply; (*aufhören*) cease. **w~geben†** *vt sep* give away; send to the laundry (*Wäsche*). **w~gehen†** *vi sep* (*sein*) leave, go away; (*ausgehen*) go out; (*Fleck:*) come out. **w~jagen** *vt sep* chase away. **w~kommen†** *vi sep* (*sein*) get away; (*verloren gehen*) disappear; **schlecht w~kommen** (*fam*) get a raw deal. **w~lassen†** *vt sep* let go; (*auslassen*) omit. **w~laufen†** *vi sep* (*sein*) run away. **w~machen** *vt sep* remove. **w~nehmen†** *vt sep* take away. **w~räumen** *vt sep* put away; (*entfernen*) clear away. **w~schicken** *vt sep* send away; (*abschicken*) send off. **w~tun†** *vt sep* put away; (*wegwerfen*) throw away

Wegweiser *m* -s,- signpost

weg|werfen† *vt sep* throw away. **w~ziehen†** *v sep* □ *vt* pull away □ *vi* (*sein*) move away

weh *a* sore; **weh tun** hurt; (*Kopf, Rücken:*) ache; **jdm weh tun** hurt s.o. □ *int* **oh weh!** oh dear!

wehe *int* alas; **w~ [dir/euch]!** (*drohend*) don't you dare!

wehen *vi* (*haben*) blow; (*flattern*) flutter □ *vt* blow

Wehen *fpl* contractions; **in den W~ liegen** be in labour

weh|leidig *a* soft; (*weinerlich*) whining. **W~mut** *f* - wistfulness. **w~mütig** *a* wistful, *adv* -ly

Wehr¹ *nt* -[e]s,-e weir

Wehr² *f* **sich zur W~ setzen** resist. **W~dienst** *m* military service. **W~dienstverweigerer** *m* -s,- conscientious objector

wehren (sich) *vr* resist; (*gegen Anschuldigung*) protest; (*sich sträuben*) refuse

wehr|los *a* defenceless. **W~macht** *f* armed forces *pl*. **W~pflicht** *f* conscription

Weib *nt* -[e]s,-er woman; ⟨*Ehe-*⟩ wife. **W~chen** *nt* -s,- ⟨*Zool*⟩ female. **W~erheld** *m* womanizer. **w~isch** *a* effeminate. **w~lich** *a* feminine; ⟨*Biol*⟩ female. **W~lichkeit** *f* - femininity

weich *a* soft, *adv* -ly; ⟨*gar*⟩ done; ⟨*Ei*⟩ soft-boiled; ⟨*Mensch*⟩ soft-hearted; **w~werden** ⟨*fig*⟩ relent

Weiche *f* -,-n ⟨*Rail*⟩ points *pl*

weichen¹ *vi* (*sein*) ⟨*reg*⟩ soak

weichen†² *vi* (*sein*) give way (*dat* to); **nicht von jds Seite w~** not leave s.o.'s side

Weich|heit *f* - softness. **w~herzig** *a* soft-hearted. **w~lich** *a* soft; ⟨*Charakter*⟩ weak. **W~spüler** *m* -s,- ⟨*Tex*⟩ conditioner. **W~tier** *nt* mollusc

Weide¹ *f* -,-n ⟨*Bot*⟩ willow

Weide² *f* -,-n pasture. **w~n** *vt/i* (*haben*) graze; **sich w~n an** (+ *dat*) enjoy; ⟨*schadenfroh*⟩ gloat over

weiger|n (sich) *vr* refuse. **W~ung** *f* -,-en refusal

Weihe *f* -,-n consecration; ⟨*Priester-*⟩ ordination. **w~n** *vt* consecrate; ⟨*zum Priester*⟩ ordain; dedicate ⟨*Kirche*⟩ (*dat* to)

Weiher *m* -s,- pond

Weihnacht|en *nt* -s & *pl* Christmas. **w~lich** *a* Christmassy. **W~sbaum** *m* Christmas tree. **W~sfest** *nt* Christmas. **W~slied** *nt* Christmas carol. **W~smann** *m* (*pl* -männer) Father Christmas. **W~stag** *m* **erster/zweiter W~stag** Christmas Day/Boxing Day

Weih|rauch *m* incense. **W~wasser** *nt* holy water

weil *conj* because; ⟨*da*⟩ since

Weile *f* - while

Wein *m* -[e]s,-e wine; ⟨*Bot*⟩ vines *pl*; ⟨*Trauben*⟩ grapes *pl*. **W~bau** *m* wine-growing. **W~beere** *f* grape. **W~berg** *m* vineyard. **W~brand** *m* -[e]s brandy

wein|en *vt/i* (*haben*) cry, weep. **w~erlich** *a* tearful, *adv* -ly

Wein|glas *nt* wineglass. **W~karte** *f* wine-list. **W~keller** *m* wine-cellar. **W~lese** *f* grape harvest. **W~liste** *f* wine-list. **W~probe** *f* wine-tasting. **W~rebe** *f*, **W~stock** *m* vine. **W~stube** *f* wine-bar. **W~traube** *f* bunch of grapes; (*W~beere*) grape

weise *a* wise, *adv* -ly

Weise *f* -,-n way; ⟨*Melodie*⟩ tune; **auf diese W~** in this way

weisen† *vt* show; **von sich w~** ⟨*fig*⟩ reject □ *vi* (*haben*) point (**auf** + *acc* at)

Weisheit *f* -,-en wisdom. **W~szahn** *m* wisdom tooth

weiß *a*, **W~** *nt* -,- white

weissag|en *vt/i insep* (*haben*) prophesy. **W~ung** *f* -,-en prophecy

Weiß|brot *nt* white bread. **W~e(r)** *m/f* white man/woman. **w~en** *vt* whitewash. **W~wein** *m* white wine

Weisung *f* -,-en instruction; ⟨*Befehl*⟩ order

weit *a* wide; ⟨*ausgedehnt*⟩ extensive; ⟨*lang*⟩ long □ *adv* widely; ⟨*offen, öffnen*⟩ wide; ⟨*lang*⟩ far; **von w~em** from a distance; **bei w~em** by far; **w~ und breit** far and wide; **ist es noch w~?** is it much further? **so w~ wie möglich** as far as possible; **ich bin so w~** I'm ready; **es ist so w~** the time has come; **zu w~ gehen** ⟨*fig*⟩ go too far; **w~ verbreitet** widespread; **w~blickend** ⟨*fig*⟩ far-sighted; **w~reichende Folgen** far-reaching consequences. **w~aus** *adv* far. **W~blick** *m* ⟨*fig*⟩ far-sightedness. **w~blickend** *a* = **w~ blickend**, *s.* **weit**

Weite *f* -,-n expanse; ⟨*Entfernung*⟩ distance; ⟨*Größe*⟩ width. **w~n** *vt* widen; stretch ⟨*Schuhe*⟩; **sich w~n** widen; stretch; ⟨*Pupille*⟩ dilate

weiter *a* further □ *adv* further; ⟨*außerdem*⟩ in addition; ⟨*anschließend*⟩ then; **etw w~tun** go on doing sth; **w~ nichts/niemand** nothing/no one else; **und so w~** and so on. **w~arbeiten** *vi sep* (*haben*) go on working

weiter|e(r,s) *a* further; **im w~en Sinne** in a wider sense; **ohne w~es** just like that; ⟨*leicht*⟩ easily; **bis auf w~es** until further notice; ⟨*vorläufig*⟩ for the time being

weiter|erzählen *vt sep* go on with; ⟨*w~sagen*⟩ repeat. **w~fahren†** *vi sep* (*sein*) go on. **w~geben†** *vt sep* pass on. **w~gehen†** *vi sep* (*sein*) go on. **w~hin** *adv* ⟨*immer noch*⟩ still; ⟨*in Zukunft*⟩ in future; ⟨*außerdem*⟩ furthermore; **etw w~hin tun** go on doing sth. **w~kommen†** *vi sep* (*sein*) get on. **w~machen** *vi sep* (*haben*) carry on. **w~sagen** *vt sep* pass on; ⟨*verraten*⟩ repeat

weit|gehend *a* extensive □ *adv* to a large extent. **w~hin** *adv* a long way; ⟨*fig*⟩ widely. **w~läufig** *a* spacious; ⟨*entfernt*⟩ distant, *adv* -ly; ⟨*ausführlich*⟩ lengthy, *adv* at length. **w~reichend** *a* = **w~reichend**, *s.* **weit**. **w~schweifig** *a* long-winded. **w~sichtig** *a* long-sighted; ⟨*fig*⟩ far-sighted. **W~sprung** *m* long jump. **w~verbreitet** *a* = **w~ verbreitet**, *s.* **weit**

Weizen *m* -s wheat

welch *inv pron* what; **w~ ein(e)** what a. **w~e(r,s)** *pron* which; **um w~e Zeit?** at what time? □ *rel pron* which; *(Person)* who □ *indef pron* some; *(fragend)* any; **was für w~e?** what sort of?

welk *a* wilted; *(Laub)* dead. **w~en** *vi (haben)* wilt; *(fig)* fade

Wellblech *nt* corrugated iron

Well|e *f -,-n* wave; *(Techn)* shaft. **W~enlänge** *f* wavelength. **W~enlinie** *f* wavy line. **W~enreiten** *nt* surfing. **W~ensittich** *m -s,-e* budgerigar. **w~ig** *a* wavy

Welt *f -,-en* world; **auf der W~** in the world; **auf die** *od* **zur W~kommen** be born. **W~all** *nt* universe. **w~berühmt** *a* world-famous. **w~fremd** *a* unworldly. **w~gewandt** *a* sophisticated. **W~kugel** *f* globe. **w~lich** *a* worldly; *(nicht geistlich)* secular

Weltmeister|(in) *m(f)* world champion. **W~schaft** *f* world championship

Weltraum *m* space. **W~fahrer** *m* astronaut

Welt|rekord *m* world record. **w~weit** *a & adv* world-wide

wem *pron (dat of* **wer)** to whom

wen *pron (acc of* **wer)** whom

Wende *f -,-n* change. **W~kreis** *m (Geog)* tropic

Wendeltreppe *f* spiral staircase

wenden[1] *vt (reg)* turn; **sich zum Guten w~** take a turn for the better □ *vi (haben)* turn [round]

wenden†[2] *(& reg) vt* turn; **sich w~** turn; **sich an jdn w~** turn/*(schriftlich)* write to s.o.

Wend|epunkt *m (fig)* turning-point. **w~ig** *a* nimble; *(Auto)* manœuvrable. **W~ung** *f -,-en* turn; *(Biegung)* bend; *(Veränderung)* change; **eine W~ung zum Besseren/Schlechteren** a turn for the better/worse

wenig *pron* little; *(pl)* few; **so/zu w~** so/too little/*(pl)* few; **w~e** *pl* few □ *adv* little; *(kaum)* not much; **so/zu w~ verdienen** earn so/too little; **so w~ wie möglich** as little as possible. **w~er** *pron* less; *(pl)* fewer; **immer w~er** less and less □ *adv & conj* less. **w~ste(r,s)** *pron* least; **am w~sten** least [of all]. **w~stens** *adv* at least

wenn *conj* if; *(sobald)* when; **immer w~** whenever; **w~ nicht** *od* **außer w~** unless; **w~ auch** even though

wer *pron* who; *(fam: jemand)* someone; *(fragend)* anyone; **ist da wer?** is anyone there?

Werbe|agentur *f* advertising agency. **w~n†** *vt* recruit; attract *(Kunden, Besucher)* □ *vi (haben)* **w~n für** advertise;

canvass for *(Partei)*; **w~n um** try to attract *(Besucher)*; court *(Frau, Gunst)*. **W~spot** /-sp-/ *m* **-s,-s** commercial

Werbung *f* - advertising

werden† *vi (sein)* become; *(müde, alt, länger)* get, grow; *(blind, wahnsinnig)* go; **blass w~** turn pale; **krank w~** fall ill; **es wird warm/dunkel** it is getting warm/dark; **mir wurde schlecht/schwindlig** I felt sick/dizzy; **er will Lehrer w~** he wants to be a teacher; **was ist aus ihm geworden?** what has become of him? □ *v aux (Zukunft)* shall; **wir w~ sehen** we shall see; **es wird bald regnen** it's going to rain soon; **würden Sie so nett sein?** would you be so kind? □ *(Passiv; pp* **worden)** be; **geliebt/geboren w~** be loved/born; **es wurde gemunkelt** it was rumoured

werfen† *vt* throw; cast *(Blick, Schatten)*; **sich w~** *(Holz:)* warp □ *vi (haben)* **w~ mit** throw

Werft *f -,-en* shipyard

Werk *nt -[e]s,-e* work; *(Fabrik)* works *sg*, factory; *(Trieb-)* mechanism. **W~en** *nt* **-s** *(Sch)* handicraft. **W~statt** *f -,-̈en* workshop; *(Auto-)* garage; *(Künstler-)* studio. **W~tag** *m* weekday. **w~tags** *adv* on weekdays. **w~tätig** *a* working. **W~unterricht** *m (Sch)* handicraft

Werkzeug *nt* tool; *(coll)* tools *pl*. **W~maschine** *f* machine tool

Wermut *m* **-s** vermouth

wert *a* **viel/50 Mark w~** worth a lot/50 marks; **nichts w~ sein** be worthless; **jds/etw** *(gen)* **w~ sein** be worthy of s.o./sth. **W~** *m* **-[e]s,-e** value; *(Nenn-)* denomination; **im W~ von** worth; **W~ legen auf** (+ *acc*) set great store by. **w~en** *vt* rate

Wert|gegenstand *m* object of value; **W~gegenstände** valuables. **w~los** *a* worthless. **W~minderung** *f* depreciation. **W~papier** *nt (Comm)* security. **W~sachen** *fpl* valuables. **w~voll** *a* valuable

Wesen *nt* **-s,-** nature; *(Lebe-)* being; *(Mensch)* creature

wesentlich *a* essential; *(grundlegend)* fundamental; *(erheblich)* considerable; **im W~en (w~en)** essentially □ *adv* considerably, much

weshalb *adv* why

Wespe *f -,-n* wasp

wessen *pron (gen of* **wer)** whose

westdeutsch *a* West German

Weste *f -,-n* waistcoat, *(Amer)* vest

Westen *m* **-s** west; **nach W~** west

Western *m* **-[s],-** western

Westfalen *nt* **-s** Westphalia

Westindien *nt* West Indies *pl*

west|lich *a* western; ⟨*Richtung*⟩ westerly □ *adv* & *prep* (+ *gen*) **w~lich [von] der Stadt** [to the] west of the town. **w~wärts** *adv* westwards

weswegen *adv* why

wett *a* **w~ sein** be quits

Wett|bewerb *m* **-s,-e** competition. **W~büro** *nt* betting shop

Wette *f* **-,-n** bet; **um die W~ laufen** race **(mit jdm** s.o.)

wetteifern *vi* (*haben*) compete

wetten *vt/i* (*haben*) bet **(auf** + *acc* on); **mit jdm w~** have a bet with s.o.

Wetter *nt* **-s,-** weather; (*Un-*) storm. **W~bericht** *m* weather report. **W~hahn** *m* weathercock. **W~lage** *f* weather conditions *pl*. **W~vorhersage** *f* weather forecast. **W~warte** *f* **-,-n** meteorological station

Wett|kampf *m* contest. **W~kämpfer(in)** *m(f)* competitor. **W~lauf** *m* race. **w~machen** *vt sep* make up for. **W~rennen** *nt* race. **W~streit** *m* contest

wetzen *vt* sharpen □ *vi* (*sein*) (*fam*) dash

Whisky *m* **-s** whisky

wichsen *vt* polish

wichtig *a* important; **w~ nehmen** take seriously. **W~keit** *f* **-** importance. **w~tuerisch** *a* self-important

Wicke *f* **-,-n** sweet pea

Wickel *m* **-s,-** compress

wick|eln *vt* wind; (*ein-*) wrap; (*bandagieren*) bandage; **ein Kind frisch w~eln** change a baby. **W~ler** *m* **-s,-** curler

Widder *m* **-s,-** ram; (*Astr*) Aries

wider *prep* (+ *acc*) against; (*entgegen*) contrary to; **w~ Willen** against one's will

widerfahren† *vi insep* (*sein*) **jdm w~** happen to s.o.

widerhallen *vi sep* (*haben*) echo

widerlegen *vt insep* refute

wider|lich *a* repulsive; (*unangenehm*) nasty, *adv* -ily. **w~rechtlich** *a* unlawful, *adv* -ly. **W~rede** *f* contradiction; **keine W~rede!** don't argue!

widerrufen† *vt/i insep* (*haben*) retract; revoke ⟨*Befehl*⟩

Widersacher *m* **-s,-** adversary

widersetzen (**sich**) *vr insep* resist **(jdm/etw** s.o./sth)

wider|sinnig *a* absurd. **w~spenstig** *a* unruly; (*störrisch*) stubborn

widerspiegeln *vt sep* reflect; **sich w~** be reflected

widersprechen† *vi insep* (*haben*) contradict **(jdm/etw** s.o./sth)

Wider|spruch *m* contradiction; (*Protest*) protest. **w~sprüchlich** *a* contradictory. **w~spruchslos** *adv* without protest

Widerstand *m* resistance; **W~ leisten** resist. **w~sfähig** *a* resistant; (*Bot*) hardy

widerstehen† *vi insep* (*haben*) resist **(jdm/etw** s.o./sth); (*anwidern*) be repugnant **(jdm** to s.o.)

widerstreben *vi insep* (*haben*) **es widerstrebt mir** I am reluctant **(zu** to). **W~** *nt* **-s** reluctance. **w~d** *a* reluctant, *adv* -ly

widerwärtig *a* disagreeable, unpleasant; (*ungünstig*) adverse

Widerwill|e *m* aversion, repugnance. **w~ig** *a* reluctant, *adv* -ly

widm|en *vt* dedicate (*dat* to); (*verwenden*) devote (*dat* to); **sich w~en** (+ *dat*) devote oneself to. **W~ung** *f* **-,-en** dedication

widrig *a* adverse, unfavourable

wie *adv* how; **wie viel** how much/(*pl*) many; **um wie viel Uhr?** at what time? **wie viele?** how many? **wie ist Ihr Name?** what is your name? **wie ist das Wetter?** what is the weather like? □ *conj* as; (*gleich wie*) like; (*sowie*) as well as; (*als*) when, as; **genau wie du** just like you; **so gut/reich wie** as good/rich as; **nichts wie** nothing but; **größer wie ich** (*fam*) bigger than me

wieder *adv* again; **er ist w~ da** he is back; **jdn/etw w~ erkennen** recognize s.o./sth; **eine Tätigkeit w~ aufnehmen** resume an activity; **etw w~ verwenden/ verwerten** reuse/recycle sth; **etw w~ gutmachen** make up for ⟨*Schaden*⟩; redress ⟨*Unrecht*⟩; (*bezahlen*) pay for sth

Wiederaufbau *m* reconstruction. **w~en** *vt sep* NEW **wieder aufbauen**, *s.* aufbauen

wieder|aufnehmen† *vt sep* NEW **w~ aufnehmen**, *s.* **wieder. W~aufrüstung** *f* rearmament

wieder|bekommen† *vt sep* get back. **w~beleben** *vt sep* NEW **w~ beleben**, *s.* **beleben. W~belebung** *f* - resuscitation. **w~bringen**† *vt sep* bring back. **w~erkennen**† *vt sep* NEW **w~ erkennen**, *s.* **wieder. W~gabe** *f* (*s.* **w~geben**) return; portrayal; rendering; reproduction. **w~geben**† *vt sep* give back, return; (*darstellen*) portray; (*ausdrücken, übersetzen*) render; (*zitieren*) quote; (*Techn*) reproduce. **W~geburt** *f* reincarnation

wiedergutmach|en *vt sep* NEW **w~ gutmachen**, *s.* **wieder. W~ung** *f* - reparation; (*Entschädigung*) compensation

wiederher|stellen *vt sep* re-establish; restore ⟨*Gebäude*⟩; restore to health ⟨*Kranke*⟩; **w~gestellt sein** be fully recovered. **W~stellung** *f* re-establishment; restoration; (*Genesung*) recovery

wiederholen[1] *vt sep* get back

wiederhol|en[2] *vt insep* repeat; *(Sch)* revise; **sich w~en** recur; *(Person:)* repeat oneself. **w~t** *a* repeated, *adv* -ly. **W~ung** *f* -,-en repetition; *(Sch)* revision

Wieder|hören *nt* **auf W~hören!** goodbye! **W~käuer** *m* -s,- ruminant. **W~kehr** *f* - return; *(W~holung)* recurrence. **w~kehren** *vi sep (sein)* return; *(sich wiederholen)* recur. **w~kommen**† *vi sep (sein)* come back

wiedersehen† *vt sep* (NEW) **wieder sehen**, *s.* **sehen. W~** *nt* -s,- reunion; **auf W~!** goodbye!

wiederum *adv* again; *(andererseits)* on the other hand

wiedervereinig|en *vt sep* (NEW) **wieder vereinigen**, *s.* **vereinigen. W~ung** *f* reunification

wieder|verheiraten (sich) *vr sep* (NEW) **w~ verheiraten (sich)**, *s.* **verheiraten. w~verwenden**† *vt sep* (NEW) **w~ verwenden**, *s.* **wieder. w~verwerten** *vt sep* (NEW) **w~ verwerten**, *s.* **wieder. w~wählen** *vt sep* (NEW) **w~ wählen**, *s.* **wählen**

Wiege *f* -,-n cradle

wiegen†[1] *vt/i (haben)* weigh

wiegen[2] *vt (reg)* rock; **sich w~** sway; *(schaukeln)* rock. **W~lied** *nt* lullaby

wiehern *vi (haben)* neigh

Wien *nt* -s Vienna. **W~er** *a* Viennese; **W~er Schnitzel** Wiener schnitzel □ *m* -s,- Viennese □ *f* -,- ≈ frankfurter. **w~erisch** *a* Viennese

Wiese *f* -,-n meadow

Wiesel *nt* -s,- weasel

wieso *adv* why

wieviel *pron* (NEW) **wie viel**, *s.* **wie. w~te(r,s)** *a* which; **der W~te ist heute?** what is the date today?

wieweit *adv* how far

wild *a* wild, *adv* -ly; *(Stamm)* savage; **w~er Streik** wildcat strike; **w~ wachsen** grow wild. **W~** *nt* -[e]s game; *(Rot-)* deer; *(Culin)* venison. **W~dieb** *m* poacher. **W~e(r)** *m/f* savage

Wilder|er *m* -s,- poacher. **w~n** *vt/i (haben)* poach

wildfremd *a* totally strange; **w~e Leute** total strangers

Wild|heger, **W~hüter** *m* -s,- gamekeeper. **W~leder** *nt* suede. **w~ledern** *a* suede. **W~nis** *f* - wilderness. **W~schwein** *nt* wild boar. **W~westfilm** *m* western

Wille *m* -ns will; **letzter W~** will; **seinen W~n durchsetzen** get one's [own] way; **mit W~n** intentionally

Willen *prep* (+ *gen*) **um ... w~** for the sake of ...

Willens|kraft *f* will-power. **w~stark** *a* strong-willed

willig *a* willing, *adv* -ly

willkommen *a* welcome; **w~ heißen** welcome. **W~** *nt* -s welcome

willkürlich *a* arbitrary, *adv* -ily

wimmeln *vi (haben)* swarm

wimmern *vi (haben)* whimper

Wimpel *m* -s,- pennant

Wimper *f* -,-n [eye]lash; **nicht mit der W~ zucken** *(fam)* not bat an eyelid. **W~ntusche** *f* mascara

Wind *m* -[e]s,-e wind

Winde *f* -,-n *(Techn)* winch

Windel *f* -,-n nappy, *(Amer)* diaper

winden† *vt* wind; make *(Kranz)*; **in die Höhe w~** winch up; **sich w~** wind *(um round)*; *(sich krümmen)* writhe

Wind|hund *m* greyhound. **w~ig** *a* windy. **W~mühle** *f* windmill. **W~pocken** *fpl* chickenpox *sg.* **W~schutzscheibe** *f* windscreen, *(Amer)* windshield. **w~still** *a* calm. **W~stille** *f* calm. **W~stoß** *m* gust of wind. **W~surfen** *nt* windsurfing

Windung *f* -,-en bend; *(Spirale)* spiral

Wink *m* -[e]s,-e sign; *(Hinweis)* hint

Winkel *m* -s,- angle; *(Ecke)* corner. **W~messer** *m* -s,- protractor

winken *vi (haben)* wave; **jdm w~** wave/*(herbei -)* beckon to s.o.

winseln *vi (haben)* whine

Winter *m* -s,- winter. **w~lich** *a* wintry; *(Winter-)* winter ... **W~schlaf** *m* hibernation; **W~schlaf halten** hibernate. **W~sport** *m* winter sports *pl*

Winzer *m* -s,- winegrower

winzig *a* tiny, minute

Wipfel *m* -s,- [tree-]top

Wippe *f* -,-n see-saw. **w~n** *vi (haben)* bounce; *(auf Wippe)* play on the see-saw

wir *pron* we; **wir sind es** it's us

Wirbel *m* -s,- eddy; *(Drehung)* whirl; *(Trommel-)* roll; *(Anat)* vertebra; *(Haar-)* crown; *(Aufsehen)* fuss. **w~n** *vt/i (sein/haben)* whirl. **W~säule** *f* spine. **W~sturm** *m* cyclone. **W~tier** *nt* vertebrate. **W~wind** *m* whirlwind

wird *s.* **werden**

wirken *vi (haben)* have an effect (**auf** + *acc* on); *(zur Geltung kommen)* be effective; *(tätig sein)* work; *(scheinen)* seem □ *vt (Tex)* knit; **Wunder w~** work miracles

wirklich *a* real, *adv* -ly. **W~keit** *f* -,-en reality

wirksam *a* effective, *adv* -ly. **W~keit** *f* - effectiveness

Wirkung f -,-en effect. **w~slos** a ineffective, adv -ly. **w~svoll** a effective, adv -ly

wirr a tangled; ⟨Haar⟩ tousled; ⟨verwirrt, verworren⟩ confused. **W~warr** m -s tangle; ⟨fig⟩ confusion; ⟨von Stimmen⟩ hubbub

Wirt m -[e]s,-e landlord. **W~in** f -,-nen landlady

Wirtschaft f -,-en economy; ⟨Gast-⟩ restaurant; ⟨Kneipe⟩ pub. **w~en** vi ⟨haben⟩ manage one's finances; ⟨sich betätigen⟩ busy oneself; **sie kann nicht w~en** she's a bad manager. **W~erin** f -,-nen housekeeper. **w~lich** a economic, adv -ally; ⟨sparsam⟩ economical, adv -ly. **W~sgeld** nt housekeeping [money]. **W~sprüfer** m auditor

Wirtshaus nt inn; ⟨Kneipe⟩ pub

Wisch m -[e]s,-e ⟨fam⟩ piece of paper

wisch|en vt/i ⟨haben⟩ wipe; wash ⟨Fußboden⟩ ▫ vi ⟨sein⟩ slip; ⟨Maus:⟩ scurry. **W~lappen** m cloth; ⟨Aufwisch-⟩ floorcloth

wispern vt/i ⟨haben⟩ whisper

wissen† vt/i ⟨haben⟩ know; **weißt du noch?** do you remember? **ich wüsste gern...** I should like to know...; **nichts w~ wollen von** not want anything to do with. **W~** nt -s knowledge; **meines W~s** to my knowledge

Wissenschaft f -,-en science. **W~ler** m -s,- academic; ⟨Natur-⟩ scientist. **w~lich** a academic, adv -ally; scientific, adv -ally

wissen|swert a worth knowing. **w~tlich** a deliberate ▫ adv knowingly

witter|n vt scent; ⟨ahnen⟩ sense. **W~ung** f - scent; ⟨Wetter⟩ weather

Witwe f -,-n widow. **W~r** m -s,- widower

Witz m -es,-e joke; ⟨Geist⟩ wit. **W~bold** m -[e]s,-e joker. **w~ig** a funny; ⟨geistreich⟩ witty

wo adv where; ⟨als⟩ when; ⟨irgendwo⟩ somewhere; **wo immer** wherever ▫ conj seeing that; ⟨obwohl⟩ although; ⟨wenn⟩ if

woanders adv somewhere else

wobei adv how; ⟨relativ⟩ during the course of which

Woche f -,-n week. **W~nende** nt weekend. **W~nkarte** f weekly ticket. **w~nlang** adv for weeks. **W~ntag** m day of the week; ⟨Werktag⟩ weekday. **w~tags** adv on weekdays

wöchentlich a & adv weekly

Wodka m -s vodka

wodurch adv how; ⟨relativ⟩ through/⟨Ursache⟩ by which; ⟨Folge⟩ as a result of which

wofür adv what ... for; ⟨relativ⟩ for which

Woge f -,-n wave

wogegen adv what ... against; ⟨relativ⟩ against which ▫ conj whereas. **woher** adv where from; **woher weißt du das?** how do you know that? **wohin** adv where [to]; **wohin gehst du?** where are you going? **wohingegen** conj whereas

wohl adv well; ⟨vermutlich⟩ probably; ⟨etwa⟩ about; ⟨zwar⟩ perhaps; **w~ kaum** hardly; **w~ oder übel** willy-nilly; **sich w~ fühlen** feel well/⟨behaglich⟩ comfortable; **jdm w~ tun** do s.o. good; **der ist w~ verrückt!** he must be mad! **W~** nt -[e]s welfare, well-being; **auf jds W~ trinken** drink s.o.'s health; **zum W~** (+ gen) for the good of; **zum W~!** cheers!

wohlauf a **w~ sein** to be well

Wohl|befinden nt well-being. **W~behagen** nt feeling of well-being. **w~behalten** a safe, adv -ly. **W~ergehen** nt -s welfare. **w~erzogen** a well brought-up

Wohlfahrt f - welfare. **W~sstaat** m Welfare State

Wohl|gefallen nt -s pleasure. **W~geruch** m fragrance. **w~gesinnt** a well disposed ⟨dat towards⟩. **w~habend** a prosperous, well-to-do. **w~ig** a comfortable, adv -bly. **w~klingend** a melodious. **w~riechend** a fragrant. **w~schmeckend** a tasty

Wohlstand m prosperity. **W~sgesellschaft** f affluent society

Wohltat f [act of] kindness; ⟨Annehmlichkeit⟩ treat; ⟨Genuss⟩ bliss

Wohltät|er m benefactor. **w~ig** a charitable

wohl|tuend a agreeable, adv -bly. **w~tun**† vi sep ⟨haben⟩ (NEW) **w~ tun**, s. **wohl**. **w~verdient** a well-deserved. **w~weislich** adv deliberately

Wohlwollen nt -s goodwill; ⟨Gunst⟩ favour. **w~d** a benevolent, adv -ly

Wohn|anhänger m = **Wohnwagen**. **W~block** m block of flats. **w~en** vi ⟨haben⟩ live; ⟨vorübergehend⟩ stay. **W~gegend** f residential area. **w~haft** a resident. **W~haus** nt [dwelling-]house. **W~heim** nt hostel; ⟨Alten-⟩ home. **w~lich** a comfortable, adv -bly. **W~mobil** nt -s,-e camper. **W~ort** m place of residence. **W~raum** m living space; ⟨Zimmer⟩ living-room. **W~sitz** m place of residence

Wohnung f -,-en flat, ⟨Amer⟩ apartment; ⟨Unterkunft⟩ accommodation. **W~snot** f housing shortage

Wohn|wagen m caravan, ⟨Amer⟩ trailer. **W~zimmer** nt living-room

wölb|en vt curve; arch ⟨Rücken⟩. **W~ung** f -,-en curve; ⟨Archit⟩ vault

Wolf *m* -[e]s,⁓e wolf; (*Fleisch-*) mincer; (*Reiß-*) shredder

Wolk|e *f* -,-n cloud. **W⁓enbruch** *m* cloudburst. **W⁓enkratzer** *m* skyscraper. **w⁓enlos** *a* cloudless. **w⁓ig** *a* cloudy

Woll|decke *f* blanket. **W⁓e** *f* -,-n wool

wollen†¹ *vt/i* (*haben*) & *v aux* want; etw tun w⁓ want to do sth; (*beabsichtigen*) be going to do sth; **ich will nach Hause** I want to go home; **wir wollten gerade gehen** we were just going; **ich wollte, ich könnte dir helfen** I wish I could help you; **der Motor will nicht anspringen** the engine won't start

woll|en² *a* woollen. **w⁓ig** *a* woolly. **W⁓sachen** *fpl* woollens

wollüstig *a* sensual, *adv* -ly

womit *adv* what ... with; (*relativ*) with which. **womöglich** *adv* possibly. **wonach** *adv* what ... after/(*suchen*) for/(*riechen*) of; (*relativ*) after/for/of which

Wonne *f* -,-n bliss; (*Freude*) joy. **w⁓ig** *a* sweet

woran *adv* what ... on/(*denken, sterben*) of; (*relativ*) on/of which; **woran hast du ihn erkannt?** how did you recognize him? **worauf** *adv* what ... on/(*warten*) for; (*relativ*) on/for which; (*woraufhin*) whereupon. **woraufhin** *adv* whereupon. **woraus** *adv* what ... from; (*relativ*) from which. **worin** *adv* what ... in; (*relativ*) in which

Wort *nt* -[e]s,⁓er & -e word; **jdm ins W⁓ fallen** interrupt s.o.; **ein paar W⁓e sagen** say a few words. **w⁓brüchig** *a* **w⁓brüchig werden** break one's word

Wörterbuch *nt* dictionary

Wort|führer *m* spokesman. **w⁓getreu** *a* & *adv* word-for-word. **w⁓gewandt** *a* eloquent, *adv* -ly. **w⁓karg** *a* taciturn. **W⁓laut** *m* wording

wörtlich *a* literal, *adv* -ly; (*wortgetreu*) word-for-word

wort|los *a* silent ▫ *adv* without a word. **W⁓schatz** *m* vocabulary. **W⁓spiel** *nt* pun, play on words. **W⁓wechsel** *m* exchange of words; (*Streit*) argument. **w⁓wörtlich** *a* & *adv* = **wörtlich**

worüber *adv* what ... over/(*lachen, sprechen*) about; (*relativ*) over/about which. **worum** *adv* what ... round/(*bitten, kämpfen*) for; (*relativ*) round/for which; **worum geht es?** what is it about? **worunter** *adv* what ... under/ (*wozwischen*) among; (*relativ*) under/among which. **wovon** *adv* what ... from/(*sprechen*) about; (*relativ*) from/about which. **wovor** *adv* what ... in front of; (*sich fürchten*) what ... of; (*relativ*) in front of which; of which. **wozu** *adv* what ...

to/(*brauchen, benutzen*) for; (*relativ*) to/for which; **wozu?** what for?

Wrack *nt* -s,-s wreck

wringen† *vt* wring

wucher|n *vi* (*haben/sein*) grow profusely. **W⁓preis** *m* extortionate price. **W⁓ung** *f* -,-en growth

Wuchs *m* -es growth; (*Gestalt*) stature

Wucht *f* - force. **w⁓en** *vt* heave. **w⁓ig** *a* massive

wühlen *vi* (*haben*) rummage; (*in der Erde*) burrow ▫ *vt* dig

Wulst *m* -[e]s,⁓e bulge; (*Fett-*) roll. **w⁓ig** *a* bulging; (*Lippen*) thick

wund *a* sore; **w⁓ reiben** chafe; **sich w⁓ liegen** get bedsores. **W⁓brand** *m* gangrene

Wunde *f* -,-n wound

Wunder *nt* -s,- wonder, marvel; (*übernatürliches*) miracle; **kein W⁓!** no wonder! **w⁓bar** *a* miraculous; (*herrlich*) wonderful, *adv* -ly, marvellous, *adv* -ly. **W⁓kind** *nt* infant prodigy. **w⁓lich** *a* odd, *adv* -ly. **w⁓n** *vt* surprise; **sich w⁓n** be surprised (**über** + *acc* at). **w⁓schön** *a* beautiful, *adv* -ly. **w⁓voll** *a* wonderful, *adv* -ly

Wundstarrkrampf *m* tetanus

Wunsch *m* -[e]s,⁓e wish; (*Verlangen*) desire; (*Bitte*) request

wünschen *vt* want; **sich** (*dat*) **etw w⁓** want sth; (*bitten um*) ask for sth; **jdm Glück/gute Nacht w⁓** wish s.o. luck/ good night; **ich wünschte, ich könnte ...** I wish I could ...; **Sie w⁓?** can I help you? **zu w⁓ übrig lassen** leave something to be desired. **w⁓swert** *a* desirable

Wunsch|konzert *nt* musical request programme. **W⁓traum** *m* (*fig*) dream

wurde, würde *s*. **werden**

Würde *f* -,-n dignity; (*Ehrenrang*) honour. **w⁓los** *a* undignified. **W⁓nträger** *m* dignitary. **w⁓voll** *a* dignified ▫ *adv* with dignity

würdig *a* dignified; (*wert*) worthy. **w⁓en** *vt* recognize; (*schätzen*) appreciate; **keines Blickes w⁓en** not deign to look at

Wurf *m* -[e]s,⁓e throw; (*Junge*) litter

Würfel *m* -s,- cube; (*Spiel-*) dice; (*Zucker-*) lump. **w⁓n** *vi* (*haben*) throw the dice; **w⁓n um** play dice for ▫ *vt* throw; (*in Würfel schneiden*) dice. **W⁓zucker** *m* cube sugar

Wurfgeschoss (**Wurfgeschoß**) *nt* missile

würgen *vt* choke ▫ *vi* (*haben*) retch; choke (**an** + *dat* on)

Wurm *m* -[e]s,⁓er worm; (*Made*) maggot. **w⁓en** *vi* (*haben*) jdn w⁓en (*fam*) rankle [with s.o.]. **w⁓stichig** *a* worm-eaten

Wurst f -,-̈e sausage; **das ist mir W∼** (*fam*) I couldn't care less

Würstchen nt -s,- small sausage; **Frankfurter W∼** frankfurter

Würze f -,-n spice; (*Aroma*) aroma

Wurzel f -,-n root; **W∼n schlagen** take root. **w∼n** vi (*haben*) root

würz|en vt season. **w∼ig** a tasty; (*aromatisch*) aromatic; (*pikant*) spicy

wüst a chaotic; (*wirr*) tangled; (*öde*) desolate; (*wild*) wild, adv -ly; (*schlimm*) terrible, adv -bly

Wüste f -,-n desert

Wut f - rage, fury. **W∼anfall** m fit of rage

wüten vi (*haben*) rage. **w∼d** a furious, adv -ly; **w∼d machen** infuriate

X

x /ɪks/ inv a (*Math*) x; (*fam*) umpteen. **X-Beine** ntpl knock-knees. **x-beinig**, **X-beinig** a knock-kneed. **x-beliebig** a (*fam*) any; **eine x-beliebige Zahl** any number [you like]. **x-mal** adv (*fam*) umpteen times; **zum x-ten Mal** for the umpteenth time

Y

Yoga /ˈjoːɡa/ m & nt -[s] yoga

Z

Zack|e f -,-n point; (*Berg-*) peak; (*Gabel-*) prong. **z∼ig** a jagged; (*gezackt*) serrated; (*fam: schneidig*) smart, adv -ly

zaghaft a timid, adv -ly; (*zögernd*) tentative, adv -ly

zäh a tough; (*hartnäckig*) tenacious, adv -ly; (*zähflüssig*) viscous; (*schleppend*) sluggish, adv -ly. **z∼flüssig** a viscous; (*Verkehr*) slow-moving. **Z∼igkeit** f - toughness; tenacity

Zahl f -,-en number; (*Ziffer, Betrag*) figure

zahl|bar a payable. **z∼en** vt/i (*haben*) pay; (*bezahlen*) pay for; **bitte z∼en!** the bill please!

zählen vi (*haben*) count; **z∼ zu** (*fig*) be one/(*pl*) some of; **z∼ auf** (+ *acc*) count on □ vt count; **z∼ zu** add to; (*fig*) count among; **die Stadt zählt 5000 Einwohner** the town has 5000 inhabitants

zahlenmäßig a numerical, adv -ly

Zähler m -s,- meter

Zahl|grenze f fare-stage. **Z∼karte** f paying-in slip. **z∼los** a countless. **z∼reich** a numerous; ⟨*Anzahl, Gruppe*⟩ large □ adv in large numbers. **Z∼ung** f -,-en payment; **in Z∼ung nehmen** take in part-exchange

Zählung f -,-en count

zahlungsunfähig a insolvent

Zahlwort nt (pl -wörter) numeral

zahm a tame

zähmen vt tame; (*fig*) restrain

Zahn m -[e]s,-̈e tooth; (*am Zahnrad*) cog. **Z∼arzt** m, **Z∼ärztin** f dentist. **Z∼belag** m plaque. **Z∼bürste** f toothbrush. **z∼en** vi (*haben*) be teething. **Z∼fleisch** nt gums pl. **z∼los** a toothless. **Z∼pasta** f -,-en toothpaste. **Z∼rad** nt cog-wheel. **Z∼schmelz** m enamel. **Z∼schmerzen** mpl toothache sg. **Z∼spange** f brace. **Z∼stein** m tartar. **Z∼stocher** m -s,- toothpick

Zange f -,-n pliers pl; (*Kneif-*) pincers pl; (*Kohlen-, Zucker-*) tongs pl; (*Geburts-*) forceps pl

Zank m -[e]s squabble. **z∼en** vr sich z∼en squabble □ vi (*haben*) scold (**mit jdm** s.o.)

zänkisch a quarrelsome

Zäpfchen nt -s,- (*Anat*) uvula; (*Med*) suppository

Zapfen m -s,- (*Bot*) cone; (*Stöpsel*) bung; (*Eis-*) icicle. **z∼** vt tap, draw. **Z∼streich** m (*Mil*) tattoo

Zapf|hahn m tap. **Z∼säule** f petrol-pump

zappel|ig a fidgety; (*nervös*) jittery. **z∼n** vi (*haben*) wriggle; ⟨*Kind:*⟩ fidget

zart a delicate, adv -ly; (*weich, zärtlich*) tender, adv -ly; (*sanft*) gentle, adv -ly. **Z∼gefühl** nt tact. **Z∼heit** f - delicacy; tenderness; gentleness

zärtlich a tender, adv -ly; (*liebevoll*) loving, adv -ly. **Z∼keit** f -,-en tenderness; (*Liebkosung*) caress

Zauber m -s magic; (*Bann*) spell. **Z∼er** m -s,- magician. **z∼haft** a enchanting. **Z∼künstler** m conjuror. **Z∼kunststück** nt = **Z∼trick**. **z∼n** vi (*haben*) do magic; (*Zaubertricks ausführen*) do conjuring tricks □ vt produce as if by magic. **Z∼stab** m magic wand. **Z∼trick** m conjuring trick

zaudern vi (*haben*) delay; (*zögern*) hesitate

Zaum m -[e]s,Zäume bridle; **im Z~ halten** (fig) restrain

Zaun m -[e]s,Zäune fence. **Z~könig** m wren

z.B. abbr (**zum Beispiel**) e.g.

Zebra nt -s,-s zebra. **Z~streifen** m zebra crossing

Zeche f -,-n bill; (Bergwerk) pit

zechen vi (haben) (fam) drink

Zeder f -,-n cedar

Zeh m -[e]s,-en toe. **Z~e** f -,-n toe; (Knoblauch-) clove. **Z~ennagel** m toenail

zehn inv a, **Z~** f -,-en ten. **z~te(r,s)** a tenth. **Z~tel** nt -s,- tenth

Zeichen nt -s,- sign; (Signal) signal. **Z~setzung** f punctuation. **Z~trickfilm** m cartoon [film]

zeichn|en vt/i (haben) draw; (kenn-) mark; (unter-) sign. **Z~er** m -s,- draughtsman. **Z~ung** f -,-en drawing; (auf Fell) markings pl

Zeige|finger m index finger. **z~n** vt show; **sich z~n** appear; (sich herausstellen) become clear; **das wird sich z~n** we shall see □ vi (haben) point (**auf** + acc to). **Z~r** m -s,- pointer; (Uhr-) hand

Zeile f -,-n line; (Reihe) row

zeit prep (+ gen) **z~ meines/seines Lebens** all my/his life

Zeit f -,-en time; **sich** (dat) **Z~ lassen** take one's time; **es hat Z~** there's no hurry; **mit der Z~** in time; **in nächster Z~** in the near future; **die erste Z~** at first; **von Z~ zu Z~** from time to time; **zur Z~** (rechtzeitig) in time; (derzeit) NEW zur- **zeit**; **eine Z~ lang** for a time or while; **[ach] du liebe Z~!** (fam) good heavens!

Zeit|alter nt age, era. **Z~arbeit** f temporary work. **Z~bombe** f time bomb. **z~gemäß** a modern, up-to-date. **Z~genosse** m, **Z~genossin** f contemporary. **z~genössisch** a contemporary. **z~ig** a & adv early. **Z~lang** f **eine Z~lang** NEW **eine Z~ lang**, s. Zeit. **z~lebens** adv all one's life

zeitlich a (Dauer) in time; (Folge) chronological □ adv **z~ begrenzt** for a limited time

zeit|los a timeless. **Z~lupe** f slow motion. **Z~punkt** m time. **z~raubend** a time-consuming. **Z~raum** m period. **Z~schrift** f magazine, periodical

Zeitung f -,-en newspaper. **Z~spapier** nt newspaper

Zeit|verschwendung f waste of time. **Z~vertreib** m pastime; **zum Z~vertreib** to pass the time. **z~weilig** a temporary □ adv temporarily; (hin und wieder) at times. **z~weise** adv at times. **Z~wort** nt (pl -wörter) verb. **Z~zünder** m time fuse

Zelle f -,-n cell; (Telefon-) box

Zelt nt -[e]s,-e tent; (Fest-) marquee. **z~en** vi (haben) camp. **Z~en** nt -s camping. **Z~plane** f tarpaulin. **Z~platz** m campsite

Zement m -[e]s cement. **z~ieren** vt cement

zen|sieren vt (Sch) mark; censor (Presse, Film). **Z~sur** f -,-en (Sch) mark, (Amer) grade; (Presse-) censorship

Zentimeter m & nt centimetre. **Z~maß** nt tape-measure

Zentner m -s,- [metric] hundredweight (50 kg)

zentr|al a central, adv -ly. **Z~e** f -,-n central office; (Partei-) headquarters pl; (Teleph) exchange. **Z~heizung** f central heating. **z~isieren** vt centralize

Zentrum nt -s,-tren centre

zerbrech|en† vt/i (sein) break; **sich** (dat) **den Kopf z~en** rack one's brains. **z~lich** a fragile

zerdrücken vt crush; mash (Kartoffeln)

Zeremonie f -,-n ceremony

Zeremoniell nt -s,-e ceremonial. **z~** a ceremonial, adv -ly

Zerfall m disintegration; (Verfall) decay. **z~en†** vi (sein) disintegrate; (verfallen) decay; **in drei Teile z~en** be divided into three parts

zerfetzen vt tear to pieces

zerfließen† vi (sein) melt; (Tinte:) run

zergehen† vi (sein) melt; (sich auflösen) dissolve

zergliedern vt dissect

zerkleinern vt chop/(schneiden) cut up; (mahlen) grind

zerknirscht a contrite

zerknüllen vt crumple [up]

zerkratzen vt scratch

zerlassen† vt melt

zerlegen vt take to pieces, dismantle; (zerschneiden) cut up; (tranchieren) carve

zerlumpt a ragged

zermalmen vt crush

zermürb|en vt (fig) wear down. **Z~ungs- krieg** m war of attrition

zerplatzen vi (sein) burst

zerquetschen vt squash, crush; mash (Kartoffeln)

Zerrbild nt caricature

zerreißen† vt tear; (in Stücke) tear up; break (Faden, Seil) □ vi (sein) tear; break

zerren vt drag; pull (Muskel) □ vi (haben) pull (**an** + dat at)

zerrinnen† vi (sein) melt

zerrissen a torn

zerrütten *vt* ruin, wreck; shatter ⟨*Nerven*⟩; **zerrüttete Ehe** broken marriage

zerschlagen† *vt* smash; smash up ⟨*Möbel*⟩; **sich z~** ⟨*fig*⟩ fall through; ⟨*Hoffnung:*⟩ be dashed □ *a* ⟨*erschöpft*⟩ worn out

zerschmettern *vt/i* ⟨*sein*⟩ smash

zerschneiden† *vt* cut; ⟨*in Stücke*⟩ cut up

zersetzen *vt* corrode; undermine ⟨*Moral*⟩. **sich z~** decompose

zersplittern *vi* ⟨*sein*⟩ splinter; ⟨*Glas:*⟩ shatter □ *vt* shatter

zerspringen† *vi* ⟨*sein*⟩ shatter; ⟨*bersten*⟩ burst

Zerstäuber *m* -s,- atomizer

zerstör|en *vt* destroy; ⟨*zunichte machen*⟩ wreck. **Z~er** *m* -s,- destroyer. **Z~ung** *f* destruction

zerstreu|en *vt* scatter; disperse ⟨*Menge*⟩; dispel ⟨*Zweifel*⟩; **sich z~en** disperse; ⟨*sich unterhalten*⟩ amuse oneself. **z~t** *a* absent-minded, *adv* -ly. **Z~ung** *f* -,-en ⟨*Unterhaltung*⟩ entertainment

zerstückeln *vt* cut up into pieces

zerteilen *vt* divide up

Zertifikat *nt* -[e]s,-e certificate

zertreten† *vt* stamp on; ⟨*zerdrücken*⟩ crush

zertrümmern *vt* smash [up]; wreck ⟨*Gebäude, Stadt*⟩

zerzaus|en *vt* tousle. **z~t** *a* dishevelled; ⟨*Haar*⟩ tousled

Zettel *m* -s,- piece of paper; ⟨*Notiz*⟩ note; ⟨*Bekanntmachung*⟩ notice; ⟨*Reklame-*⟩ leaflet

Zeug *nt* -s ⟨*fam*⟩ stuff; ⟨*Sachen*⟩ things *pl*; ⟨*Ausrüstung*⟩ gear; **dummes Z~** nonsense; **das Z~ haben zu** have the makings of

Zeuge *m* -n,-n witness. **z~n** *vi* ⟨*haben*⟩ testify; **z~n von** ⟨*fig*⟩ show □ *vt* father. **Z~naussage** *f* testimony. **Z~nstand** *m* witness box/⟨*Amer*⟩ stand

Zeugin *f* -,-nen witness

Zeugnis *nt* -ses,-se certificate; ⟨*Sch*⟩ report; ⟨*Referenz*⟩ reference; ⟨*fig: Beweis*⟩ evidence

Zickzack *m* -[e]s,-e zigzag

Ziege *f* -,-n goat

Ziegel *m* -s,- brick; ⟨*Dach-*⟩ tile. **Z~stein** *m* brick

ziehen† *vt* pull; ⟨*sanfter; zücken; zeichnen*⟩ draw; ⟨*heraus-*⟩ pull out; extract ⟨*Zahn*⟩; raise ⟨*Hut*⟩; put on ⟨*Bremse*⟩; move ⟨*Schachfigur*⟩; put up ⟨*Leine, Zaun*⟩; ⟨*dehnen*⟩ stretch; make ⟨*Grimasse, Scheitel*⟩; ⟨*züchten*⟩ breed; grow ⟨*Rosen, Gemüse*⟩; **nach sich z~** ⟨*fig*⟩ entail □ *vr* **sich z~** ⟨*sich erstrecken*⟩ run; ⟨*sich verziehen*⟩

warp □ *vi* ⟨*haben*⟩ pull (**an** + *dat* on/at); ⟨*Tee, Ofen:*⟩ draw; ⟨*Culin*⟩ simmer; **es zieht** there is a draught; **solche Filme z~ nicht mehr** films like that are no longer popular □ *vi* ⟨*sein*⟩ ⟨*um-*⟩ move (**nach** to); ⟨*Menge:*⟩ march; ⟨*Vögel:*⟩ migrate; ⟨*Wolken, Nebel:*⟩ drift. **Z~** *nt* -s ache

Ziehharmonika *f* accordion

Ziehung *f* -,-en draw

Ziel *nt* -[e]s,-e destination; ⟨*Sport*⟩ finish; ⟨*Z~scheibe & Mil*⟩ target; ⟨*Zweck*⟩ aim, goal. **z~bewusst** (**z~bewußt**) *a* purposeful, *adv* -ly. **z~en** *vi* ⟨*haben*⟩ aim (**auf** + *acc* at). **z~end** *a* ⟨*Gram*⟩ transitive. **z~los** *a* aimless, *adv* -ly. **Z~scheibe** *f* target; ⟨*fig*⟩ butt. **z~strebig** *a* single-minded, *adv* -ly

ziemen (sich) *vr* be seemly

ziemlich *a* ⟨*fam*⟩ fair □ *adv* rather, fairly; ⟨*fast*⟩ pretty well

Zier|de *f* -,-n ornament. **z~en** *vt* adorn; **sich z~en** make a fuss; ⟨*sich bitten lassen*⟩ need coaxing

zierlich *a* dainty, *adv* -ily; ⟨*fein*⟩ delicate, *adv* -ly; ⟨*Frau*⟩ petite

Ziffer *f* -,-n figure, digit; ⟨*Zahlzeichen*⟩ numeral. **Z~blatt** *nt* dial

zig *inv* *a* ⟨*fam*⟩ umpteen

Zigarette *f* -,-n cigarette

Zigarre *f* -,-n cigar

Zigeuner(in) *m* -s,- ⟨*f* -,-nen⟩ gypsy

Zimmer *nt* -s,- room. **Z~mädchen** *nt* chambermaid. **Z~mann** *m* ⟨*pl* -leute⟩ carpenter. **z~n** *vt* make □ *vi* ⟨*haben*⟩ do carpentry. **Z~nachweis** *m* accommodation bureau. **Z~pflanze** *f* house plant

zimperlich *a* squeamish; ⟨*wehleidig*⟩ soft; ⟨*prüde*⟩ prudish

Zimt *m* -[e]s cinnamon

Zink *nt* -s zinc

Zinke *f* -,-n prong; ⟨*Kamm-*⟩ tooth

Zinn *m* -s tin; ⟨*Gefäße*⟩ pewter

Zins|en *mpl* interest *sg*; **Z~en tragen** earn interest. **Z~eszins** *m* -es,-en compound interest. **Z~fuß**, **Z~satz** *m* interest rate

Zipfel *m* -s,- corner; ⟨*Spitze*⟩ point; ⟨*Wurst-*⟩ [tail-]end

zirka *adv* about

Zirkel *m* -s,- [pair of] compasses *pl*; ⟨*Gruppe*⟩ circle

Zirkul|ation /-'tsjo:n/ *f* - circulation. **z~ieren** *vi* ⟨*sein*⟩ circulate

Zirkus *m* -,-se circus

zirpen *vi* ⟨*haben*⟩ chirp

zischen *vi* ⟨*haben*⟩ hiss; ⟨*Fett:*⟩ sizzle □ *vt* hiss

Zit|at *nt* -[e]s,-e quotation. **z~ieren** *vt/i* ⟨*haben*⟩ quote; ⟨*rufen*⟩ summon

Zitr|onat *nt* -[e]s candied lemon-peel. **Z~one** *f* -,-n lemon. **Z~onenlimonade** *f* lemonade

zittern *vi* (*haben*) tremble; (*vor Kälte*) shiver; (*beben*) shake

zittrig *a* shaky, *adv* -ily

Zitze *f* -,-n teat

zivil *a* civilian; ⟨*Ehe, Recht, Luftfahrt*⟩ civil; (*mäßig*) reasonable. **Z~** *nt* -s civilian clothes *pl*. **Z~courage** /-kura:ʒə/ *f* - courage of one's convictions. **Z~dienst** *m* community service

Zivili|sation /-'tsjo:n/ *f* -,-en civilization. **z~sieren** *vt* civilize. **z~siert** *a* civilized ▫ *adv* in a civilized manner

Zivilist *m* -en,-en civilian

zögern *vi* (*haben*) hesitate. **Z~** *nt* -s hesitation. **z~d** *a* hesitant, *adv* -ly

Zoll¹ *m* -[e]s,- inch

Zoll² *m* -[e]s,⁻e [customs] duty; (*Behörde*) customs *pl*. **Z~abfertigung** *f* customs clearance. **Z~beamte(r)** *m* customs officer. **z~frei** *a* & *adv* duty-free. **Z~kontrolle** *f* customs check

Zone *f* -,-n zone

Zoo *m* -s,-s zoo

Zoo|loge /tsoo'lo:gə/ *m* -n,-n zoologist. **Z~logie** *f* - zoology. **z~logisch** *a* zoological

Zopf *m* -[e]s,⁻e plait

Zorn *m* -[e]s anger. **z~ig** *a* angry, *adv* -ily

zotig *a* smutty, dirty

zottig *a* shaggy

z.T. *abbr* (**zum Teil**) partly

zu *prep* (+ *dat*) to; (*dazu*) with; (*zeitlich; preislich*) at; (*Zweck*) for; (*über*) about; zu ... hin towards; **zu Hause** at home; **zu Fuß/Pferde** on foot/horseback; **zu beiden Seiten** on both sides; **zu Ostern** at Easter; **zu diesem Zweck** for this purpose; **zu meinem Erstaunen/Entsetzen** to my surprise/horror; **zu Dutzenden** by the dozen; **eine Marke zu 60 Pfennig** a 60-pfennig stamp; **das Stück zu zwei Mark** at two marks each; **wir waren zu dritt/viert** there were three/four of us; **es steht 5 zu 3** the score is 5–3; **zu etw werden** turn into sth ▫ *adv* (*allzu*) too; (*Richtung*) towards; (*geschlossen*) closed; (*an Schalter, Hahn*) off; **zu sein** be closed: **zu groß/viel/weit** too big/much/far; **nach dem Fluss zu** towards the river; **Augen zu!** close your eyes! **Tür zu!** shut the door! **nur zu!** go on! **macht zu!** (*fam*) hurry up! ▫ *conj* to; **etwas zu essen** something to eat; **nicht zu glauben** unbelievable; **zu erörternde Probleme** problems to be discussed

zuallererst *adv* first of all. **z~letzt** *adv* last of all

Zubehör *nt* -s accessories *pl*

zubereit|en *vt sep* prepare. **Z~ung** *f* - preparation; (*in Rezept*) method

zubilligen *vt sep* grant

zubinden† *vt sep* tie [up]

zubring|en† *vt sep* spend. **Z~er** *m* -s,- access road; (*Bus*) shuttle

Zucchini /tsu'ki:ni/ *pl* courgettes

Zucht *f* -,-en breeding; (*Pflanzen-*) cultivation; (*Art, Rasse*) breed; (*von Pflanzen*) strain; (*Z~farm*) farm; (*Pferde-*) stud; (*Disziplin*) discipline

züchten *vt* breed; cultivate, grow ⟨*Rosen, Gemüse*⟩. **Z~er** *m* -s,- breeder; grower

Zuchthaus *nt* prison

züchtigen *vt* chastise

Züchtung *f* -,-en breeding; (*Pflanzen-*) cultivation; (*Art, Rasse*) breed; (*von Pflanzen*) strain

zucken *vi* (*haben*) twitch; (*sich z~d bewegen*) jerk; ⟨*Blitz:*⟩ flash; (*Flamme:*) flicker ▫ *vt* **die Achseln z~** shrug one's shoulders

zücken *vt* draw ⟨*Messer*⟩

Zucker *m* -s sugar. **Z~dose** *f* sugar basin. **Z~guss** (**Z~guß**) *m* icing. **z~krank** *a* diabetic. **Z~krankheit** *f* diabetes. **z~n** *vt* sugar. **Z~rohr** *nt* sugar cane. **Z~rübe** *f* sugar beet. **z~süß** *a* sweet; (*fig*) sugary. **Z~watte** *f* candyfloss. **Z~zange** *f* sugar tongs *pl*

zuckrig *a* sugary

zudecken *vt sep* cover up; (*im Bett*) tuck up; cover ⟨*Topf*⟩

zudem *adv* moreover

zudrehen *vt sep* turn off; **jdm den Rücken z~** turn one's back on s.o.

zudringlich *a* pushing, (*fam*) pushy

zudrücken *vt sep* press *or* push shut; close ⟨*Augen*⟩

zueinander *adv* to one another; **z~ passen** go together; **z~ halten** (*fig*) stick together. **z~halten†** *vt sep* (*haben*) NEW **z~ halten**, s. **zueinander**

zuerkennen† *vt sep* award (*dat* to)

zuerst *adv* first; (*anfangs*) at first; **mit dem Kopf z~** head first

zufahr|en† *vi sep* (*sein*) **z~en auf** (+ *acc*) drive towards. **Z~t** *f* access; (*Einfahrt*) drive

Zufall *m* chance; (*Zusammentreffen*) coincidence; **durch Z~** by chance/coincidence. **z~en†** *vi sep* (*sein*) close, shut; **jdm z~en** ⟨*Aufgabe:*⟩ fall/⟨*Erbe:*⟩ go to s.o.

zufällig *a* chance, accidental ▫ *adv* by chance; **ich war z~ da** I happened to be there

Zuflucht *f* refuge; (*Schutz*) shelter. **Z~sort** *m* refuge

zufolge *prep* (+ *dat*) according to

zufrieden *a* contented, *adv* -ly; (*befriedigt*) satisfied; **sich z~ geben** be satisfied; **jdn z~ lassen** leave s.o. in peace; **jdn z~ stellen** satisfy s.o.; **z~ stellend** satisfactory. **z~geben†** (**sich**) *vr sep* (NEW) **geben** (**sich**), *s.* **zufrieden. Z~heit** *f* - contentment; satisfaction. **z~lassen†** *vt sep* (NEW) **z~ lassen**, *s.* **zufrieden. z~stellen** *vt sep* (NEW) **z~ stellen**, *s.* **zufrieden. z~stellend** *a* (NEW) **z~ stellend**, *s.* **zufrieden**

zufrieren† *vi sep* (*sein*) freeze over

zufügen *vt sep* inflict (*dat* on); do (*Unrecht*) (*dat* to)

Zufuhr *f* - supply

zuführen *vt sep* □ *vt* supply □ *vi* (*haben*) **z~ auf** (+ *acc*) lead to

Zug *m* -[e]s,ᵉe train; (*Kolonne*) column; (*Um-*) procession; (*Mil*) platoon; (*Vogelschar*) flock; (*Ziehen, Zugkraft*) pull; (*Wandern, Ziehen*) migration; (*Schluck, Luft-*) draught; (*Atem-*) breath; (*beim Rauchen*) puff; (*Schach-*) move; (*beim Schwimmen, Rudern*) stroke; (*Gesichts-*) feature; (*Wesens-*) trait; **etw in vollen Zügen genießen** enjoy sth to the full; **in einem Zug[e]** at one go

Zugabe *f* (*Geschenk*) [free] gift; (*Mus*) encore

Zugang *m* access

zugänglich *a* accessible; (*Mensch:*) approachable; (*fig*) amenable (*dat/*für to)

Zugbrücke *f* drawbridge

zugeben† *vt sep* add; (*gestehen*) admit; (*erlauben*) allow. **zugegebenermaßen** *adv* admittedly

zugegen *a* **z~ sein** be present

zugehen† *vi sep* (*sein*) close; **jdm z~** be sent to s.o.; **z~ auf** (+ *acc*) go towards; **dem Ende z~** draw to a close; (*Vorräte:*) run low; **auf der Party ging es lebhaft zu** the party was pretty lively

Zugehörigkeit *f* - membership

Zügel *m* -s,- rein

zugelassen *a* registered

zügel|los *a* unrestrained, *adv* -ly; (*sittenlos*) licentious. **z~n** *vt* rein in; (*fig*) curb

Zuge|ständnis *nt* concession. **z~stehen†** *vt sep* grant

zugetan *a* fond (*dat* of)

zugig *a* draughty

zügig *a* quick, *adv* -ly

Zug|kraft *f* (*fig*) attraction. **z~kräftig** *a* effective; (*anreizend*) popular; (*Titel*) catchy

zugleich *adv* at the same time

Zug|luft *f* draught. **Z~pferd** *nt* draughthorse; (*fam*) draw

zugreifen† *vi sep* (*haben*) grab it/them; (*bei Tisch*) help oneself; (*bei Angebot*) jump at it; (*helfen*) lend a hand

zugrunde *adv* **z~ richten** destroy; **z~ gehen** be destroyed; (*Ehe:*) founder; (*sterben*) die; **z~ liegen** form the basis (*dat* of)

zugucken *vi sep* (*haben*) = **zusehen**

zugunsten *prep* (+ *gen*) in favour of; (*Sammlung*) in aid of

zugute *adv* **jdm/etw z~ kommen** benefit s.o./sth; **jdm seine Jugend z~ halten** make allowances for s.o.'s youth

Zugvogel *m* migratory bird

zuhalten† *v sep* □ *vt* keep closed; (*bedecken*) cover; **sich** (*dat*) **die Nase z~** hold one's nose □ *vi* (*haben*) **z~ auf** (+ *acc*) head for

Zuhälter *m* -s,- pimp

zuhause *adv* = **zu Hause**, *s.* **Haus. Z~** *nt* -s,- home

zuhör|en *vi sep* (*haben*) listen (*dat* to). **Z~er(in)** *m(f)* listener

zujubeln *vi sep* (*haben*) **jdm z~** cheer s.o.

zukehren *vt sep* turn (*dat* to)

zukleben *vt sep* seal

zuknallen *vt/i sep* (*sein*) slam

zuknöpfen *vt sep* button up

zukommen† *vi sep* (*sein*) **z~ auf** (+ *acc*) come towards; (*sich nähern*) approach; **z~ lassen** send (**jdm** s.o.); devote (*Pflege*) (*dat* to); **jdm z~** be s.o.'s right

Zukunft *f* - future. **zukünftig** *a* future □ *adv* in future

zulächeln *vi sep* (*haben*) smile (*dat* at)

Zulage *f* -,-n extra allowance

zulangen *vi sep* (*haben*) help oneself; **tüchtig z~** tuck in

zulassen† *vt sep* allow, permit; (*teilnehmen lassen*) admit; (*Admin*) license, register; (*geschlossen lassen*) leave closed; leave unopened (*Brief*)

zulässig *a* permissible

Zulassung *f* -,-en admission; registration; (*Lizenz*) licence

zulaufen† *vi sep* (*sein*) **z~en auf** (+ *acc*) run towards; **spitz z~en** taper to a point

zulegen *vt sep* add; **sich** (*dat*) **etw z~** get sth; grow (*Bart*)

zuleide *adv* **jdm etwas z~ tun** hurt s.o.

zuletzt *adv* last; (*schließlich*) in the end; **nicht z~** not least

zuliebe *adv* **jdm/etw z~** for the sake of s.o./sth

zum *prep* = **zu dem**; **zum Spaß** for fun; **etw zum Lesen** sth to read

zumachen v sep □ vt close, shut; do up ⟨Jacke⟩; seal ⟨Umschlag⟩; turn off ⟨Hahn⟩; ⟨stilllegen⟩ close down □ vi (haben) close, shut; ⟨stillgelegt werden⟩ close down

zumal adv especially □ conj especially since

zumeist adv for the most part

zumindest adv at least

zumutbar a reasonable

zumute adv mir ist traurig/elend z∼ I feel sad/wretched; mir ist nicht danach z∼ I don't feel like it

zumut|en vt sep jdm etw z∼en ask or expect sth of s.o.; sich (dat) zu viel z∼en overdo things. Z∼ung f - imposition; eine Z∼ung sein be unreasonable

zunächst adv first [of all]; ⟨anfangs⟩ at first; ⟨vorläufig⟩ for the moment □ prep (+ dat) nearest to

Zunahme f -,-n increase

Zuname m surname

zünd|en vt/i (haben) ignite; z∼ende Rede rousing speech. Z∼er m -s,- detonator, fuse. Z∼holz nt match. Z∼kerze f sparking-plug. Z∼schlüssel m ignition key. Z∼schnur f fuse. Z∼ung f -,-en ignition

zunehmen† vi sep (haben) increase (an + dat in); ⟨Mond:⟩ wax; ⟨an Gewicht⟩ put on weight. z∼d a increasing, adv -ly

Zuneigung f - affection

Zunft f -,ꞏe guild

zünftig a proper, adv -ly

Zunge f -,-n tongue. Z∼nbrecher m tongue-twister

zunichte a z∼ machen wreck; z∼ werden come to nothing

zunicken vi sep (haben) nod (dat to)

zunutze a sich (dat) etw z∼ machen make use of sth; ⟨ausnutzen⟩ take advantage of sth

zuoberst adv right at the top

zuordnen vt sep assign (dat to)

zupfen vt/i (haben) pluck (an + dat at); pull out ⟨Unkraut⟩

zur prep = zu der; zur Schule/Arbeit to school/work

zurande adv z∼ kommen mit (fam) cope with

zurate adv z∼ ziehen consult

zurechnungsfähig a of sound mind

zurecht|finden† (sich) vr sep find one's way. z∼kommen† vi sep (sein) cope (mit with); ⟨rechtzeitig kommen⟩ be in time. z∼legen vt sep put out ready; sich (dat) eine Ausrede z∼legen have an excuse all ready. z∼machen vt sep get ready; sich z∼machen get ready. z∼weisen† vt sep reprimand. Z∼weisung f reprimand

zureden vi sep (haben) jdm z∼ try to persuade s.o.

zurichten vt sep prepare; ⟨beschädigen⟩ damage; ⟨verletzen⟩ injure

zuriegeln vt sep bolt

zurück adv back; Berlin, hin und z∼ return to Berlin. z∼behalten† vt sep keep back; be left with ⟨Narbe⟩. z∼bekommen† vt sep get back; 20 Pfennig z∼bekommen get 20 pfennigs change. z∼bleiben† vi sep (sein) stay behind; ⟨nicht mithalten⟩ lag behind. z∼blicken vi sep (haben) look back. z∼bringen† vt sep bring back; ⟨wieder hinbringen⟩ take back. z∼erobern vt sep recapture; ⟨fig⟩ regain. z∼erstatten vt sep refund. z∼fahren† adv v sep □ vt drive back □ vi (sein) return, go back; ⟨im Auto⟩ drive back; ⟨z∼weichen⟩ recoil. z∼finden† vi sep (haben) find one's way back. z∼führen v sep □ vt take back; ⟨fig⟩ attribute (auf + acc to) □ vi (haben) lead back. z∼geben† vt sep give back, return. z∼geblieben a retarded. z∼gehen† vi sep (sein) go back, return; ⟨abnehmen⟩ go down; z∼gehen auf (+ acc) ⟨fig⟩ go back to

zurückgezogen a secluded. Z∼heit f - seclusion

zurückhalt|en† vt sep hold back; ⟨abhalten⟩ stop; sich z∼en restrain oneself. z∼end a reserved. Z∼ung f - reserve

zurück|kehren vi sep (sein) return. z∼kommen† vi sep (sein) come back, return; ⟨ankommen⟩ get back; z∼kommen auf (+ acc) ⟨fig⟩ come back to. z∼lassen† vt sep leave behind; ⟨z∼kehren lassen⟩ allow back. z∼legen vt sep put back; ⟨reservieren⟩ keep; ⟨sparen⟩ put by; cover ⟨Strecke⟩. z∼lehnen (sich) vr sep lean back. z∼liegen† vi sep (haben) be in the past; ⟨Sport⟩ be behind; das liegt lange zurück that was long ago. z∼melden (sich) vr sep report back. z∼nehmen† vt sep take back. z∼rufen† vt/i sep (haben) call back. z∼scheuen vi sep (sein) shrink (vor + dat from). z∼schicken vt sep send back. z∼schlagen† v sep □ vi (haben) hit back □ vt hit back; ⟨abwehren⟩ beat back; ⟨umschlagen⟩ turn back. z∼schneiden† vt sep cut back. z∼schrecken† vi sep (sein) shrink back, recoil; ⟨fig⟩ shrink (vor + dat from). z∼setzen v sep □ vt put back; ⟨Auto⟩ reverse, back; ⟨herabsetzen⟩ reduce; ⟨fig⟩ neglect □ vi (haben) reverse, back. z∼stellen vt sep put back; ⟨reservieren⟩ keep; ⟨fig⟩ put aside; ⟨aufschieben⟩ postpone. z∼stoßen† v sep □ vt push back □ vi (sein) reverse, back. z∼treten† vi sep (sein) step back; ⟨vom Amt⟩ resign; ⟨verzichten⟩ withdraw. z∼weichen† vi sep (sein) draw back; ⟨z∼schrecken⟩ shrink back. **z~weisen**† *vt sep* turn away; *(fig)* reject. **z~werfen**† *vt* throw back; *(reflektieren)* reflect. **z~zahlen** *vt sep* pay back. **z~ziehen**† *vt sep* draw back; *(fig)* withdraw; **sich z~ziehen** withdraw; *(vom Beruf)* retire; *(Mil)* retreat

Zuruf *m* shout. **z~en**† *vt sep* shout *(dat* to)

zurzeit *adv* at present

Zusage *f* -,-n acceptance; *(Versprechen)* promise. **z~n** *v sep* □ *vt* promise □ *vi (haben)* accept; **jdm z~n** appeal to s.o.

zusammen *adv* together; *(insgesamt)* altogether; **z~ sein** be together. **Z~arbeit** *f* co-operation. **z~arbeiten** *vi sep (haben)* co-operate. **z~bauen** *vt sep* assemble. **z~beißen**† *vt sep* **die Zähne z~beißen** clench/*(fig)* grit one's teeth. **z~bleiben**† *vi sep (sein)* stay together. **z~brechen**† *vi sep (sein)* collapse. **z~bringen**† *vt sep* bring together; *(beschaffen)* raise. **Z~bruch** *m* collapse; *(Nerven- & fig)* breakdown. **z~fahren**† *vi sep (sein)* collide; *(z~zucken)* start. **z~fallen**† *vi sep (sein)* collapse; *(zeitlich)* coincide. **z~falten** *vt sep* fold up. **z~fassen** *vt sep* summarize, sum up. **Z~fassung** *f* summary. **z~fügen** *vt sep* fit together. **z~führen** *vt sep* bring together. **z~gehören** *vi sep (haben)* belong together; *(z~passen)* go together. **z~gesetzt** *a (Gram)* compound. **z~halten**† *v sep* □ *vt* hold together; *(beisammenhalten)* keep together □ *vi (haben) (fig)* stick together. **Z~hang** *m* connection; *(Kontext)* context. **z~hängen**† *vi sep (haben)* be connected. **z~hanglos** *a* incoherent, *adv* -ly. **z~klappen** *v sep* □ *vt* fold up □ *vi (sein)* collapse. **z~kommen**† *vi sep (sein)* meet; *(sich sammeln)* accumulate. **Z~kunft** *f* -, :-e meeting. **z~laufen**† *vi sep (sein)* gather; *(Flüssigkeit:)* collect; *(Linien:)* converge. **z~leben** *vi sep (haben)* live together. **z~legen** *v sep* □ *vt* put together; *(z~falten)* fold up; *(vereinigen)* amalgamate; pool *(Geld)* □ *vi (haben)* club together. **z~nehmen**† *vt sep* gather up; summon up *(Mut)*; collect *(Gedanken)*; **sich z~nehmen** pull oneself together. **z~passen** *vi sep (haben)* go together, match; *(Personen:)* be well matched. **Z~prall** *m* collision. **z~prallen** *vi sep (sein)* collide. **z~rechnen** *vt sep* add up. **z~reißen**† *(sich) vr sep (fam)* pull oneself together. **z~rollen** *vt sep* roll up; **sich z~rollen** curl up. **z~schlagen**† *vt sep* smash up; *(prügeln)* beat up. **z~schließen**† *(sich) vr sep* join together; *(Firmen:)* merge. **Z~schluss (Z~schluß)** *m* union; *(Comm)* merger. **z~schreiben**† *vt sep* write as one word

zusammensein† *vi sep (sein)* ＮＥＷ **zusammen sein**, *s.* **zusammen**. **Z~** *nt* -s get-together

zusammensetz|en *vt sep* put together; *(Techn)* assemble; **sich z~en** sit [down] together; *(bestehen)* be made up **(aus** from). **Z~ung** *f* -,-en composition; *(Techn)* assembly; *(Wort)* compound

zusammen|stellen *vt sep* put together; *(gestalten)* compile. **Z~stoß** *m* collision; *(fig)* clash. **z~stoßen**† *vi sep (sein)* collide. **z~treffen**† *vi sep (sein)* meet; *(zeitlich)* coincide. **Z~treffen** *nt* meeting; coincidence. **z~zählen** *vt sep* add up. **z~ziehen**† *v sep* □ *vt* draw together; *(addieren)* add up; *(konzentrieren)* mass; **sich z~ziehen** contract; *(Gewitter:)* gather □ *vi (sein)* move in together; move in **(mit** with). **z~zucken** *vi sep (sein)* start; *(vor Schmerz)* wince

Zusatz *m* addition; *(Jur)* rider; *(Lebensmittel-)* additive. **Z~gerät** *nt* attachment. **zusätzlich** *a* additional □ *adv* in addition

zuschanden *adv* **z~ machen** ruin, wreck; **z~ werden** be wrecked *or* ruined; **z~ fahren** wreck

zuschau|en *vi sep (haben)* watch. **Z~er(in)** *m -s,- (f -,-nen)* spectator; *(TV)* viewer. **Z~erraum** *m* auditorium

zuschicken *vt sep* send *(dat* to)

Zuschlag *m* surcharge; *(D-Zug-)* supplement. **z~en**† *v sep* □ *vt* shut; *(heftig)* slam; *(bei Auktion)* knock down **(jdm** to s.o.) □ *vi (haben)* hit out; *(Feind:)* strike □ *vi (sein)* slam shut. **z~pflichtig** *a (Zug)* for which a supplement is payable

zuschließen† *v sep* □ *vt* lock □ *vi (haben)* lock up

zuschneiden† *vt sep* cut out; cut to size *(Holz)*

zuschreiben† *vt sep* attribute *(dat* to); **jdm die Schuld z~** blame s.o.

Zuschrift *f* letter; *(auf Annonce)* reply

zuschulden *adv* **sich (dat) etwas z~ kommen lassen** do wrong

Zuschuss (Zuschuß) *m* contribution; *(staatlich)* subsidy

zusehen† *vi sep (haben)* watch; **z~, dass** see [to it] that

zusehends *adv* visibly

zusein† *vi sep (sein)* ＮＥＷ **zu sein**, *s.* **zu**

zusenden† *vt sep* send *(dat* to)

zusetzen *v sep* □ *vt* add; *(einbüßen)* lose □ *vi (haben)* **jdm z~** pester s.o.; *(Hitze:)* take it out of s.o.

zusicher|n *vt sep* promise. **Z~ung** *f* promise

Zuspätkommende(r) *m/f* late-comer

zuspielen *vt sep (Sport)* pass

zuspitzen (sich) *vr sep* (*fig*) become critical

zusprechen† *v sep* □ *vt* award (jdm s.o.); **jdm Trost/Mut z~** comfort/encourage s.o. □ *vi* (*haben*) **dem Essen z~** eat heartily

Zustand *m* condition, state

zustande *adv* **z~ bringen/kommen** bring/come about

zuständig *a* competent; (*verantwortlich*) responsible. **Z~keit** *f* - competence; responsibility

zustehen† *vi sep* (*haben*) **jdm z~** be s.o.'s right; ⟨*Urlaub:*⟩ be due to s.o.; **es steht ihm nicht zu** he is not entitled to it; (*gebührt*) it is not for him (zu to)

zusteigen† *vi sep* (*sein*) get on; **noch jemand zugestiegen?** tickets please; (*im Bus*) any more fares please?

zustell|en *vt sep* block; (*bringen*) deliver. **Z~ung** *f* delivery

zusteuern *v sep* □ *vi* (*sein*) head (auf + acc for) □ *vt* contribute

zustimm|en *vi sep* (*haben*) agree; (*billigen*) approve (dat of). **Z~ung** *f* consent; approval

zustoßen† *vi sep* (*sein*) happen (dat to)

Zustrom *m* influx

zutage *adv* **z~ treten** *od* **kommen/bringen** come/bring to light

Zutat *f* (*Culin*) ingredient

zuteil|en *vt sep* allocate; assign ⟨*Aufgabe*⟩. **Z~ung** *f* allocation

zutiefst *adv* deeply

zutragen† *vt sep* carry/(*fig*) report (dat to); **sich z~** happen

zutrau|en *vt sep* **jdm etw z~** believe s.o. capable of sth. **Z~en** *nt* -s confidence. **z~lich** *a* trusting, *adv* -ly; ⟨*Tier*⟩ friendly

zutreffen† *vi sep* (*haben*) be correct; **z~ auf** (+ acc) apply to. **z~d** *a* applicable (auf + acc to); (*richtig*) correct, *adv* -ly

zutrinken† *vi sep* (*haben*) **jdm z~** drink to s.o.

Zutritt *m* admittance

zuunterst *adv* right at the bottom

zuverlässig *a* reliable, *adv* -bly. **Z~keit** *f* - reliability

Zuversicht *f* - confidence. **z~lich** *a* confident, *adv* -ly

zuviel *pron & adv* (NEW) **zu viel**, *s.* viel

zuvor *adv* before; (*erst*) first

zuvorkommen† *vi sep* (*sein*) (+ dat) anticipate; **jdm z~** beat s.o. to it. **z~d** *a* obliging, *adv* -ly

Zuwachs *m* -es increase

zuwege *adv* **z~ bringen** achieve

zuweilen *adv* now and then

zuweisen† *vt sep* assign; (*zuteilen*) allocate

zuwend|en† *vt sep* turn (dat to); **sich z~en** (+ dat) turn to; (*fig*) devote oneself to. **Z~ung** *f* donation; (*Fürsorge*) care

zuwenig *pron & adv* (NEW) **zu wenig**, *s.* wenig

zuwerfen† *vt sep* slam ⟨*Tür*⟩; **jdm etw z~** throw s.o. sth; give s.o. ⟨*Blick, Lächeln*⟩

zuwider *adv* **jdm z~ sein** be repugnant to s.o. □ *prep* (+ dat) contrary to. **z~handeln** *vi sep* (*haben*) contravene (etw *dat* sth)

zuzahlen *vt sep* pay extra

zuziehen† *v sep* □ *vt* pull tight; draw ⟨*Vorhänge*⟩; (*hinzu-*) call in; **sich** (dat) **etw z~** contract ⟨*Krankheit*⟩; sustain ⟨*Verletzung*⟩; incur ⟨*Zorn*⟩ □ *vi* (*sein*) move into the area

zuzüglich *prep* (+ gen) plus

Zwang *m* -[e]s,-̈e compulsion; (*Gewalt*) force; (*Verpflichtung*) obligation

zwängen *vt* squeeze

zwanglos *a* informal, *adv* -ly; ⟨*Benehmen*⟩ free and easy. **Z~igkeit** *f* - informality

Zwangs|jacke *f* straitjacket. **Z~lage** *f* predicament. **z~läufig** *a* inevitable, *adv* -bly

zwanzig *inv a* twenty. **z~ste(r,s)** *a* twentieth

zwar *adv* admittedly; **und z~** to be precise

Zweck *m* -[e]s,-e purpose; (*Sinn*) point; **es hat keinen Z~** there is no point. **z~dienlich** *a* appropriate; ⟨*Information*⟩ relevant. **z~los** *a* pointless. **z~mäßig** *a* suitable, *adv* -bly; (*praktisch*) functional, *adv* -ly. **z~s** *prep* (+ gen) for the purpose of

zwei *inv a*, **Z~** *f* -,-en two; (*Sch*) ≈ B. **Z~bettzimmer** *nt* twin-bedded room

zweideutig *a* ambiguous, *adv* -ly; (*schlüpfrig*) suggestive, *adv* -ly. **Z~keit** *f* -,-en ambiguity

zwei|erlei *inv a* two kinds of □ *pron* two things. **z~fach** *a* double

Zweifel *m* -s,- doubt. **z~haft** *a* doubtful; (*fragwürdig*) dubious. **z~los** *adv* undoubtedly. **z~n** *vi* (*haben*) doubt (an etw *dat* sth)

Zweig *m* -[e]s,-e branch. **Z~geschäft** *nt* branch. **Z~stelle** *f* branch [office]

Zwei|kampf *m* duel. **z~mal** *adv* twice. **z~reihig** *a* ⟨*Anzug*⟩ double-breasted. **z~sprachig** *a* bilingual

zweit *adv* **zu z~** in twos; **wir waren zu z~** there were two of us. **z~beste(r,s)** *a* second-best. **z~e(r,s)** *a* second

zwei|teilig *a* two-piece; ⟨*Film, Programm*⟩ two-part. **z~tens** *adv* secondly

zweitklassig *a* second-class

Zwerchfell *nt* diaphragm

Zwerg *m* -[e]s,-e dwarf

Zwetsch[g]e *f* -,-n quetsche

Zwickel *m* -s,- gusset

zwicken *vt/i* (*haben*) pinch

Zwieback *m* -[e]s,-̈e rusk

Zwiebel *f* -,-n onion; (*Blumen-*) bulb

Zwielicht *nt* half-light; (*Dämmerlicht*) twilight. **z~ig** *a* shady

Zwie|spalt *m* conflict. **z~spältig** *a* conflicting. **Z~tracht** *f* - discord

Zwilling *m* -s,-e twin; **Z~e** (*Astr*) Gemini

zwingen† *vt* force; **sich z~** force oneself. **z~d** *a* compelling

Zwinger *m* -s,- run; (*Zucht-*) kennels *pl*

zwinkern *vi* (*haben*) blink; (*als Zeichen*) wink

Zwirn *m* -[e]s button thread

zwischen *prep* (+ *dat/acc*) between; (*unter*) among[st]. **Z~bemerkung** *f* interjection. **Z~ding** *nt* (*fam*) cross. **z~durch**
adv in between; (*in der Z~zeit*) in the meantime; (*ab und zu*) now and again. **Z~fall** *m* incident. **Z~händler** *m* middleman. **Z~landung** *f* stop over. **Z~raum** *m* gap, space. **Z~ruf** *m* interjection. **Z~stecker** *m* adaptor. **Z~wand** *f* partition. **Z~zeit** *f* **in der Z~zeit** in the meantime

Zwist *m* -[e]s,-e discord; (*Streit*) feud. **Z~igkeiten** *fpl* quarrels

zwitschern *vi* (*haben*) chirp

zwo *inv a* two

zwölf *inv a* twelve. **z~te(r,s)** *a* twelfth

zwote(r,s) *a* second

Zyklus *m* -,-klen cycle

Zylind|er *m* -s,- cylinder; (*Hut*) top hat. **z~risch** *a* cylindrical

Zyn|iker *m* -s,- cynic. **z~isch** *a* cynical, *adv* -ly. **Z~ismus** *m* - cynicism

Zypern *nt* -s Cyprus

Zypresse *f* -,-n cypress

Zyste /ˈtsʏstə/ *f* -,-n cyst

A

a /ə, *betont* eɪ/ (*vor einem Vokal* an) *indef art* ein(e); (*each*) pro; **not a** kein(e)

aback /ə'bæk/ *adv* **be taken ~** verblüfft sein

abandon /ə'bændən/ *vt* verlassen; (*give up*) aufgeben □ *n* Hingabe *f*. **~ed** *a* verlassen; (*behaviour*) hemmungslos

abase /ə'beɪs/ *vt* demütigen

abashed /ə'bæʃt/ *a* beschämt, verlegen

abate /ə'beɪt/ *vi* nachlassen

abattoir /'æbətwɑː(r)/ *n* Schlachthof *m*

abb|ey /'æbɪ/ *n* Abtei *f*. **~ot** /-ət/ *n* Abt *m*

abbreviat|e /ə'briːvɪeɪt/ *vt* abkürzen. **~ion** /-'eɪʃn/ *n* Abkürzung *f*

abdicat|e /'æbdɪkeɪt/ *vi* abdanken. **~ion** /-'keɪʃn/ *n* Abdankung *f*

abdom|en /'æbdəmən/ *n* Unterleib *m*. **~i-nal** /-'dɒmɪnl/ *a* Unterleibs-

abduct /əb'dʌkt/ *vt* entführen. **~ion** /-ʌkʃn/ *n* Entführung *f*. **~or** *n* Entführer *m*

aberration /æbə'reɪʃn/ *n* Abweichung *f*; (*mental*) Verwirrung *f*

abet /ə'bet/ *vt* (*pt/pp* abetted) **aid and ~** (*Jur*) Beihilfe leisten (+ *dat*)

abeyance /ə'beɪəns/ *n* **in ~** [zeitweilig] außer Kraft; **fall into ~** außer Kraft kommen

abhor /əb'hɔː(r)/ *vt* (*pt/pp* abhorred) verabscheuen. **~rence** /-'hɒrəns/ *n* Abscheu *m*. **~rent** /-'hɒrənt/ *a* abscheulich

abid|e /ə'baɪd/ *vt* (*pt/pp* abided) (*tolerate*) aushalten; ausstehen (*person*) □ *vi* **~e by** sich halten an (+ *acc*). **~ing** *a* bleibend

ability /ə'bɪlətɪ/ *n* Fähigkeit *f*; (*talent*) Begabung *f*

abject /'æbdʒekt/ *a* erbärmlich; (*humble*) demütig

ablaze /ə'bleɪz/ *a* in Flammen; **be ~ in** Flammen stehen

able /'eɪbl/ (*a* **-r, -st**) fähig; **be ~ to do sth** etw tun können. **~-'bodied** *a* körperlich gesund; (*Mil*) tauglich

ably /'eɪblɪ/ *adv* gekonnt

abnormal /æb'nɔːml/ *a* anormal; (*Med*) abnorm. **~ity** /-'mælətɪ/ *n* Abnormität *f*. **~ly** *adv* ungewöhnlich

aboard /ə'bɔːd/ *adv & prep* an Bord (+ *gen*)

abode /ə'bəʊd/ *n* Wohnsitz *m*

abol|ish /ə'bɒlɪʃ/ *vt* abschaffen. **~ition** /æbə'lɪʃn/ *n* Abschaffung *f*

abominable /ə'bɒmɪnəbl/ *a*, **-bly** *adv* abscheulich

abominate /ə'bɒmɪneɪt/ *vt* verabscheuen

aborigines /æbə'rɪdʒəniːz/ *npl* Ureinwohner *pl*

abort /ə'bɔːt/ *vt* abtreiben. **~ion** /-ɔːʃn/ *n* Abtreibung *f*; **have an ~ion** eine Abtreibung vornehmen lassen. **~ive** /-tɪv/ *a* (*attempt*) vergeblich

abound /ə'baʊnd/ *vi* reichlich vorhanden sein; **~ in** reich sein an (+ *dat*)

about /ə'baʊt/ *adv* umher, herum; (*approximately*) ungefähr; **be ~** (*in circulation*) umgehen; (*in existence*) vorhanden sein; **be up and ~** auf den Beinen sein; **be ~ to do sth** im Begriff sein, etw zu tun; **there are a lot ~** es gibt viele; **there was no one ~** es war kein Mensch da; **run/play ~** herumlaufen/-spielen □ *prep* um (+ *acc*) [... herum]; (*concerning*) über (+ *acc*); **what is it ~?** worum geht es? (*book:*) wovon handelt es? **I know nothing ~** it ich weiß nichts davon; **talk/ know ~** reden/wissen von

about: **~-'face** *n*, **~-'turn** *n* Kehrtwendung *f*

above /ə'bʌv/ *adv* oben □ *prep* über (+ *dat/acc*); **~ all** vor allem

above: **~'board** *a* legal. **~-mentioned** *a* oben erwähnt

abrasion /ə'breɪʒn/ *n* Schürfwunde *f*

abrasive /ə'breɪsɪv/ *a* Scheuer-; (*remark*) verletzend □ *n* Scheuermittel *nt*; (*Techn*) Schleifmittel *nt*

abreast /ə'brest/ *adv* nebeneinander; **keep ~ of** Schritt halten mit

abridge /ə'brɪdʒ/ *vt* kürzen

abroad /ə'brɔːd/ *adv* im Ausland; **go ~** ins Ausland fahren

abrupt /ə'brʌpt/ *a*, **-ly** *adv* abrupt; (*sudden*) plötzlich; (*curt*) schroff

abscess /'æbsɪs/ *n* Abszess *m*

abscond /əb'skɒnd/ *vi* entfliehen

absence /'æbsəns/ *n* Abwesenheit *f*

absent¹ /'æbsənt/ *a*, **-ly** *adv* abwesend; **be ~** fehlen

absent² /æb'sent/ *vt* **~ oneself** fernbleiben

absentee /æbsən'tiː/ *n* Abwesende(r) *m/f*

absent-minded /æbsənt'maɪndɪd/ *a*, **-ly** *adv* geistesabwesend; (*forgetful*) zerstreut

absolute /'æbsəluːt/ *a*, **-ly** *adv* absolut

absolution /æbsə'lu:ʃn/ n Absolution f

absolve /əb'zɒlv/ vt lossprechen

absorb /əb'sɔ:b/ vt absorbieren, auf-saugen; ~ed in vertieft in (+ acc). ~ent /-ənt/ a saugfähig

absorption /əb'sɔ:pʃn/ n Absorption f

abstain /əb'steɪn/ vi sich enthalten (from gen); ~ from voting sich der Stimme enthalten

abstemious /əb'sti:mɪəs/ a enthaltsam

abstention /əb'stenʃn/ n (Pol) [Stimm]-enthaltung f

abstinence /'æbstɪnəns/ n Ent-haltsamkeit f

abstract /'æbstrækt/ a abstrakt □ n (sum-mary) Abriss m

absurd /əb'sɜ:d/ a, -ly adv absurd. ~ity n Absurdität f

abundan|ce /ə'bʌndəns/ n Fülle f (of an + dat). ~t a reichlich

abuse¹ /ə'bju:z/ vt missbrauchen; (insult) beschimpfen

abus|e² /ə'bju:s/ n Missbrauch m; (insults) Beschimpfungen pl. ~ive /-ɪv/ ausfallend

abut /ə'bʌt/ vi (pt/pp abutted) angrenzen (on to an + acc)

abysmal /ə'bɪzml/ a (fam) katastrophal

abyss /ə'bɪs/ n Abgrund m

academic /ækə'demɪk/ a, -ally adv aka-demisch □ n Akademiker(in) m(f)

academy /ə'kædəmɪ/ n Akademie f

accede /ək'si:d/ vi ~ to zustimmen (+ dat); besteigen (throne)

accelerat|e /ək'seləreɪt/ vt beschleunigen □ vi die Geschwindigkeit erhöhen. ~ion /-'reɪʃn/ n Beschleunigung f. ~or n (Auto) Gaspedal nt

accent¹ /'æksənt/ n Akzent m

accent² /æk'sent/ vt betonen

accentuate /ək'sentjʊeɪt/ vt betonen

accept /ək'sept/ vt annehmen; (fig) akzep-tieren □ vi zusagen. ~able /-əbl/ a an-nehmbar. ~ance n Annahme f; (of invitation) Zusage f

access /'ækses/ n Zugang m; (road) Zufahrt f. ~ible /ək'sesəbl/ a zugänglich

accession /ək'seʃn/ n (to throne) Thron-besteigung f

accessor|y /ək'sesərɪ/ n (Jur) Mitschul-dige(r) m/f; ~ies pl (fashion) Accessoires pl; (Techn) Zubehör nt

accident /'æksɪdənt/ n Unfall m; (chance) Zufall m; by ~ zufällig; (unintentionally) versehentlich. ~al /-'dentl/ a, -ly adv zufällig; (unintentional) versehentlich

acclaim /ə'kleɪm/ n Beifall m □ vt feiern (as als)

acclimate /'æklɪmeɪt/ vt (Amer) = accli-matize

acclimatize /ə'klaɪmətaɪz/ vt become ~d sich akklimatisieren

accolade /'ækəleɪd/ n Auszeichnung f

accommodat|e /ə'kɒmədeɪt/ vt unter-bringen; (oblige) entgegenkommen (+ dat). ~ing a entgegenkommend. ~ion /-'deɪʃn/ (rooms) Unterkunft f

accompan|iment /ə'kʌmpənɪmənt/ n Begleitung f. ~ist n (Mus) Begleiter(in) m(f)

accompany /ə'kʌmpənɪ/ vt (pt/pp -ied) begleiten

accomplice /ə'kʌmplɪs/ n Komplize/-zin m/f

accomplish /ə'kʌmplɪʃ/ vt erfüllen (task); (achieve) erreichen. ~ed a fähig. ~ment n Fertigkeit f; (achievement) Leis-tung f

accord /ə'kɔ:d/ n (treaty) Abkommen nt; of one ~ einmütig; of one's own ~ aus eigenem Antrieb □ vt gewähren. ~ance n in ~ance with entsprechend (+ dat)

according /ə'kɔ:dɪŋ/ adv ~ to nach (+ dat). ~ly adv entsprechend

accordion /ə'kɔ:dɪən/ n Akkordeon nt

accost /ə'kɒst/ vt ansprechen

account /ə'kaʊnt/ n Konto nt; (bill) Rechnung f; (description) Darstellung f; (report) Bericht m; ~s pl (Comm) Bücher pl; on ~ of wegen (+ gen); on no ~ auf keinen Fall; on this ~ deshalb; on my ~ meinetwegen; of no ~ ohne Bedeutung; take into ~ in Betracht ziehen, berück-sichtigen □ vi ~ for Rechenschaft ablegen für; (explain) erklären

accountant /ə'kaʊntənt/ n Buchhal-ter(in) m(f); (chartered) Wirt-schaftsprüfer m; (for tax) Steuerberater m

accoutrements /ə'ku:trəmənts/ npl Aus-rüstung f

accredited /ə'kredɪtɪd/ a akkreditiert

accrue /ə'kru:/ vi sich ansammeln

accumulat|e /ə'kju:mjʊleɪt/ vt ansam-meln, anhäufen □ vi sich ansammeln, sich anhäufen. ~ion /-'leɪʃn/ n Ansammlung f, Anhäufung f. ~or n (Electr) Akkumu-lator m

accura|cy /'ækʊrəsɪ/ n Genauigkeit f. ~te /-rət/ a, -ly adv genau

accusation /ækju:'zeɪʃn/ n Anklage f

accusative /ə'kju:zətɪv/ a & n ~ [case] (Gram) Akkusativ m

accuse /ə'kju:z/ vt (Jur) anklagen (of gen); ~ s.o. of doing sth jdn beschuldigen, etw getan zu haben. ~d n the ~d der/die An-geklagte

accustom /əˈkʌstəm/ *vt* gewöhnen (**to** an + *dat*); **grow** or **get** ~**ed to** sich gewöhnen an (+ *acc*). ~**ed** *a* gewohnt

ace /eɪs/ *n* (*Cards, Sport*) Ass *nt*

ache /eɪk/ *n* Schmerzen *pl* □ *vi* weh tun, schmerzen

achieve /əˈtʃiːv/ *vt* leisten; (*gain*) erzielen; (*reach*) erreichen. ~**ment** *n* (*feat*) Leistung *f*

acid /ˈæsɪd/ *a* sauer; (*fig*) beißend □ *n* Säure *f*. ~**ity** /əˈsɪdətɪ/ *n* Säure *f*. '~**rain** *n* saurer Regen *m*

acknowledge /əkˈnɒlɪdʒ/ *vt* anerkennen; (*admit*) zugeben; erwidern (*greeting*); ~ **receipt** of den Empfang bestätigen (+ *gen*). ~**ment** *n* Anerkennung *f*; (*of letter*) Empfangsbestätigung *f*

acne /ˈæknɪ/ *n* Akne *f*

acorn /ˈeɪkɔːn/ *n* Eichel *f*

acoustic /əˈkuːstɪk/ *a*, -**ally** *adv* akustisch. ~**s** *npl* Akustik *f*

acquaint /əˈkweɪnt/ *vt* ~ **s.o. with** jdn bekannt machen mit; **be** ~**ed with** kennen; vertraut sein mit (*fact*). ~**ance** *n* Bekanntschaft *f*; (*person*) Bekannte(r) *m/f*; **make s.o.'s** ~**ance** jdn kennen lernen

acquiesce /ækwɪˈes/ *vi* einwilligen (**to** in + *acc*). ~**nce** *n* Einwilligung *f*

acquire /əˈkwaɪə(r)/ *vt* erwerben

acquisit|ion /ækwɪˈzɪʃn/ *n* Erwerb *m*; (*thing*) Erwerbung *f*. ~**ive** /əˈkwɪzətɪv/ *a* habgierig

acquit /əˈkwɪt/ *vt* (*pt/pp* **acquitted**) freisprechen; ~ **oneself well** seiner Aufgabe gerecht werden. ~**tal** *n* Freispruch *m*

acre /ˈeɪkə(r)/ *n* ≈ Morgen *m*

acrid /ˈækrɪd/ *a* scharf

acrimon|ious /ækrɪˈməʊnɪəs/ *a* bitter. ~**y** /ˈækrɪmənɪ/ *n* Bitterkeit *f*

acrobat /ˈækrəbæt/ *n* Akrobat(in) *m(f)*. ~**ic** /-ˈbætrɪk/ *a* akrobatisch

across /əˈkrɒs/ *adv* hinüber/herüber; (*wide*) breit; (*not lengthwise*) quer; (*in crossword*) waagerecht; **come** ~ **sth** auf etw (*acc*) stoßen; **go** ~ hinübergehen; **bring** ~ herüberbringen □ *prep* über (+ *acc*); (*crosswise*) quer über (+ *acc/dat*); (*on the other side of*) auf der anderen Seite (+ *gen*)

act /ækt/ *n* Tat *f*; (*action*) Handlung *f*; (*law*) Gesetz *nt*; (*Theat*) Akt *m*; (*item*) Nummer *f*; **put on an** ~ (*fam*) sich verstellen □ *vi* handeln; (*behave*) sich verhalten; (*Theat*) spielen; (*pretend*) sich verstellen; ~ **as** fungieren als □ *vt* spielen (*role*). ~**ing** *a* (*deputy*) stellvertretend □ *n* (*Theat*) Schauspielerei *f*. ~**ing** **profession** *n* Schauspielerberuf *m*

action /ˈækʃn/ *n* Handlung *f*; (*deed*) Tat *f*; (*Mil*) Einsatz *m*; (*Jur*) Klage *f*; (*effect*) Wirkung *f*; (*Techn*) Mechanismus *m*; **out of** ~ (*machine:*) außer Betrieb; **take** ~ handeln; **killed in** ~ gefallen. ~ '**replay** *n* (*TV*) Wiederholung *f*

activate /ˈæktɪveɪt/ *vt* betätigen; (*Chem, Phys*) aktivieren

activ|e /ˈæktɪv/ *a*, -**ly** *adv* aktiv; **on** ~**e service** im Einsatz. ~**ity** /-ˈtɪvətɪ/ *n* Aktivität *f*

act|or /ˈæktə(r)/ *n* Schauspieler *m*. ~**ress** *n* Schauspielerin *f*

actual /ˈæktʃʊəl/ *a*, -**ly** *adv* eigentlich; (*real*) tatsächlich. ~**ity** /-ˈælətɪ/ *n* Wirklichkeit *f*

acumen /ˈækjʊmən/ *n* Scharfsinn *m*

acupuncture /ˈækjʊ-/ *n* Akupunktur *f*

acute /əˈkjuːt/ *a* scharf; (*angle*) spitz; (*illness*) akut. ~**ly** *adv* sehr

ad /æd/ *n* (*fam*) = **advertisement**

AD *abbr* (**Anno Domini**) n.Chr.

adamant /ˈædəmənt/ *a* **be** ~ **that** darauf bestehen, dass

adapt /əˈdæpt/ *vt* anpassen; bearbeiten (*play*) □ *vi* sich anpassen. ~**ability** /-əˈbɪlətɪ/ *n* Anpassungsfähigkeit *f*. ~**able** /-əbl/ *a* anpassungsfähig

adaptation /ædæpˈteɪʃn/ *n* (*Theat*) Bearbeitung *f*

adapter, adaptor /əˈdæptə(r)/ *n* (*Techn*) Adapter *m*; (*Electr*) (*two-way*) Doppelstecker *m*

add /æd/ *vt* hinzufügen; (*Math*) addieren □ *vi* zusammenzählen, addieren; ~ **to** hinzufügen zu; (*fig: increase*) steigern; (*compound*) verschlimmern. ~ **up** *vt* zusammenzählen (*figures*) □ *vi* zusammenzählen, addieren; ~ **up to** machen; **it doesn't** ~ **up** (*fig*) da stimmt etwas nicht

adder /ˈædə(r)/ *n* Kreuzotter *f*

addict /ˈædɪkt/ *n* Süchtige(r) *m/f*

addict|ed /əˈdɪktɪd/ *a* süchtig; ~**ed to drugs** drogensüchtig. ~**ion** /-ɪkʃn/ *n* Sucht *f*. ~**ive** /-ɪv/ *a* **be** ~**ive** zur Süchtigkeit führen

addition /əˈdɪʃn/ *n* Hinzufügung *f*; (*Math*) Addition *f*; (*thing added*) Ergänzung *f*; **in** ~ zusätzlich. ~**al** *a*, -**ly** *adv* zusätzlich

additive /ˈædɪtɪv/ *n* Zusatz *m*

address /əˈdres/ *n* Adresse *f*, Anschrift *f*; (*speech*) Ansprache *f*; **form of** ~ Anrede *f* □ *vt* adressieren (**to** an + *acc*); (*speak to*) anreden (*person*); sprechen (+ *dat*) (*meeting*). ~**ee** /ædreˈsiː/ *n* Empfänger *m*

adenoids /ˈædənɔɪdz/ *npl* [Rachen]polypen *pl*

adept /ˈædept/ *a* geschickt (**at** in + *dat*)

adequate /'ædɪkwət/ *a*, **-ly** *adv* ausreichend

adhere /əd'hɪə(r)/ *vi* kleben/(*fig*) festhalten (**to** an + *dat.*). **~nce** *n* Festhalten *nt*

adhesive /əd'hi:sɪv/ *a* klebend □ *n* Klebstoff *m*

adjacent /ə'dʒeɪsnt/ *a* angrenzend

adjective /'ædʒɪktɪv/ *n* Adjektiv *nt*

adjoin /ə'dʒɔɪn/ *vt* angrenzen an (+ *acc.*). **~ing** *a* angrenzend

adjourn /ə'dʒɜ:n/ *vt* vertagen (**until** auf + *acc*) □ *vi* sich vertagen. **~ment** *n* Vertagung *f*

adjudicate /ə'dʒu:dɪkeɪt/ *vi* entscheiden; (*in competition*) Preisrichter sein

adjust /ə'dʒʌst/ *vt* einstellen; (*alter*) verstellen □ *vi* sich anpassen (**to** *dat.*). **~able** /-əbl/ *a* verstellbar. **~ment** *n* Einstellung *f*; Anpassung *f*

ad lib /æd'lɪb/ *adv* aus dem Stegreif □ *vi* (*pt/pp* **ad libbed**) (*fam*) improvisieren

administer /əd'mɪnɪstə(r)/ *vt* verwalten; verabreichen (*medicine*)

administrat|ion /ədmɪnɪ'streɪʃn/ *n* Verwaltung *f*; (*Pol*) Regierung *f*. **~or** /əd'mɪnɪstreɪtə(r)/ *n* Verwaltungsbeamte(r) *m* /-beamtin *f*

admirable /'ædmərəbl/ *a* bewundernswert

admiral /'ædmərəl/ *n* Admiral *m*

admiration /ædmə'reɪʃn/ *n* Bewunderung *f*

admire /əd'maɪə(r)/ *vt* bewundern. **~r** *n* Verehrer(in) *m(f)*

admissable /əd'mɪsəbl/ *a* zulässig

admission /əd'mɪʃn/ *n* Eingeständnis *nt*; (*entry*) Eintritt *m*

admit /əd'mɪt/ *vt* (*pt/pp* **admitted**) (*let in*) hereinlassen; (*acknowledge*) zugeben; **~ to sth** etw zugeben. **~tance** *n* Eintritt *m*. **~tedly** *adv* zugegebenermaßen

admoni|sh /əd'mɒnɪʃ/ *vt* ermahnen. **~tion** /ædmə'nɪʃn/ *n* Ermahnung *f*

ado /ə'du:/ *n* **without more ~** ohne weiteres

adolescen|ce /ædə'lesns/ *n* Jugend *f*, Pubertät *f*. **~t** *a* Jugend-; (*boy, girl*) halbwüchsig □ *n* Jugendliche(r) *m/f*

adopt /ə'dɒpt/ *vt* adoptieren; ergreifen (*measure*); (*Pol*) annehmen (*candidate*). **~ion** /-ɒpʃn/ *n* Adoption. *f*. **~ive** /-ɪv/ *a* Adoptiv-

ador|able /ə'dɔ:rəbl/ *a* bezaubernd. **~ation** /ædə'reɪʃn/ *n* Anbetung *f*

adore /ə'dɔ:(r)/ *vt* (*worship*) anbeten; (*fam: like*) lieben

adorn /ə'dɔ:n/ *vt* schmücken. **~ment** *n* Schmuck *m*

adrenalin /ə'drenəlɪn/ *n* Adrenalin *nt*

Adriatic /eɪdrɪ'ætɪk/ *a & n* **~ [Sea]** Adria *f*

adrift /ə'drɪft/ *a* **be ~** treiben; **come ~** sich losreißen

adroit /ə'drɔɪt/ *a*, **-ly** *adv* gewandt, geschickt

adulation /ædjʊ'leɪʃn/ *n* Schwärmerei *f*

adult /'ædʌlt/ *n* Erwachsene(r) *m/f*

adulterate /ə'dʌltəreɪt/ *vt* verfälschen; panschen (*wine*)

adultery /ə'dʌltərɪ/ *n* Ehebruch *m*

advance /əd'vɑ:ns/ *n* Fortschritt *m*; (*Mil*) Vorrücken *nt*; (*payment*) Vorschuss *m*; **in ~** im Voraus □ *vi* vorankommen; (*Mil*) vorrücken; (*make progress*) Fortschritte machen □ *vt* fördern (*cause*); vorbringen (*idea*); vorschießen (*money*). **~ booking** *n* Kartenvorverkauf *m*. **~d** *a* fortgeschritten; (*progressive*) fortschrittlich. **~ment** *n* Förderung *f*; (*promotion*) Beförderung *f*

advantage /əd'vɑ:ntɪdʒ/ *n* Vorteil *m*; **take ~ of** ausnutzen. **~ous** /ædvən'teɪdʒəs/ *a* vorteilhaft

advent /'ædvent/ *n* Ankunft *f*; **A~** (*season*) Advent *m*

adventur|e /əd'ventʃə(r)/ *n* Abenteuer *nt*. **~er** *n* Abenteurer *m*. **~ous** /-rəs/ *a* abenteuerlich; (*person*) abenteuerlustig

adverb /'ædvɜ:b/ *n* Adverb *nt*

adversary /'ædvəsərɪ/ *n* Widersacher *m*

advers|e /'ædvɜ:s/ *a* ungünstig. **~ity** /əd'vɜ:sətɪ/ *n* Not *f*

advert /'ædvɜ:t/ *n* (*fam*) = **advertisement**

advertise /'ædvətaɪz/ *vt* Reklame machen für; (*by small ad*) inserieren □ *vi* Reklame machen; inserieren; **~ for** per Anzeige suchen

advertisement /əd'vɜ:tɪsmənt/ *n* Anzeige *f*; (*publicity*) Reklame *f*; (*small ad*) Inserat *nt*

advertis|er /'ædvətaɪzə(r)/ *n* Inserent *m*. **~ing** *n* Werbung *f* □ *attrib* Werbe-

advice /əd'vaɪs/ *n* Rat *m*. **~ note** *n* Benachrichtigung *f*

advisable /əd'vaɪzəbl/ *a* ratsam

advis|e /əd'vaɪz/ *vt* raten (**s.o.** jdm); (*counsel*) beraten; (*inform*) benachrichtigen; **~e s.o. against sth** jdm von etw abraten □ *vi* raten. **~er** *n* Berater(in) *m(f)*. **~ory** /-ərɪ/ *a* beratend

advocate[1] /'ædvəkət/ *n* [Rechts]anwalt *m*/-anwältin *f*; (*supporter*) Befürworter *m*

advocate[2] /'ædvəkeɪt/ *vt* befürworten

aerial /'eərɪəl/ *a* Luft- □ *n* Antenne *f*

aerobics /eə'rəʊbɪks/ *n* Aerobic *nt*

aero|drome /'eərədrəum/ n Flugplatz m. ~**plane** n Flugzeug nt

aerosol /'eərəsɒl/ n Spraydose f

aesthetic /i:s'θetιk/ a ästhetisch

afar /ə'fɑ:(r)/ adv **from ~** aus der Ferne

affable /'æfəbl/ a, -**bly** adv freundlich

affair /ə'feə(r)/ n Angelegenheit f, Sache f; (scandal) Affäre f; [love-]~ [Liebes]- verhältnis nt

affect /ə'fekt/ vt sich auswirken auf (+ acc); (concern) betreffen; (move) rühren; (pretend) vortäuschen. ~**ation** /æfek- 'teɪʃn/ n Affektiertheit f. ~**ed** a affektiert

affection /ə'fekʃn/ n Liebe f. ~**ate** /-ət/ a, -**ly** adv liebevoll

affiliated /ə'fιlιeιtιd/ a angeschlossen (to dat)

affinity /ə'fιnətι/ n Ähnlichkeit f; (attrac- tion) gegenseitige Anziehung f

affirm /ə'fɜ:m/ vt behaupten; (Jur) eides- stattlich erklären

affirmative /ə'fɜ:mətιv/ a bejahend □ n Bejahung f

affix /ə'fιks/ vt anbringen (to dat); (stick) aufkleben (to auf + acc); setzen (signa- ture) (to unter + acc)

afflict /ə'flιkt/ vt **be ~ed with** behaftet sein mit. ~**ion** /-ιkʃn/ n Leiden nt

affluen|ce /'æfluəns/ n Reichtum m. ~**t** a wohlhabend. ~**t society** n Wohlstandsge- sellschaft f

afford /ə'fɔ:d/ vt (provide) gewähren; **be able to ~ sth** sich (dat) etw leisten können. ~**able** /-əbl/ a erschwinglich

affray /ə'freι/ n Schlägerei f

affront /ə'frʌnt/ n Beleidigung f □ vt be- leidigen

afield /ə'fi:ld/ adv **further ~** weiter weg

afloat /ə'fləut/ a **be ~** ⟨ship:⟩ flott sein; **keep ~** ⟨person:⟩ sich über Wasser halten

afoot /ə'fut/ a im Gange

aforesaid /ə'fɔ:sed/ a (Jur) oben erwähnt

afraid /ə'freιd/ a **be ~** Angst haben (of vor + dat); **I'm ~ not** leider nicht; **I'm ~ so** [ja] leider; **I'm ~ I can't help you** ich kann Ihnen leider nicht helfen

afresh /ə'freʃ/ adv von vorne

Africa /'æfrιkə/ n Afrika nt. ~**n** a afrika- nisch □ n Afrikaner(in) m(f)

after /'ɑ:ftə(r)/ adv danach □ prep nach (+ dat); ~ **that** danach; ~ **all** schließlich; **the day ~ tomorrow** übermorgen; **be ~** aus sein auf (+ acc) □ conj nachdem

after: ~-**effect** n Nachwirkung f. ~**math** /-mɑ:θ/ n Auswirkungen pl. ~**noon** n Nachmittag m; **good ~noon!** guten Tag! ~-**sales service** n Kundendienst m. ~**shave** n Rasierwasser nt. ~**thought** n

nachträglicher Einfall m. ~**wards** adv nachher

again /ə'gen/ adv wieder; (once more) noch einmal; (besides) außerdem; ~ **and ~** im- mer wieder

against /ə'genst/ prep gegen (+ acc)

age /eιdʒ/ n Alter nt; (era) Zeitalter nt; ~**s** (fam) ewig; **under ~** minderjährig; **of ~** volljährig; **two years of ~** zwei Jahre alt □ v (pres p **ageing**) □ vt älter machen □ vi altern; (mature) reifen

aged[1] /eιdʒd/ a ~ **two** zwei Jahre alt

aged[2] /'eιdʒιd/ a betagt □ n **the ~** pl die Alten

ageless /'eιdʒlιs/ a ewig jung

agency /'eιdʒənsι/ n Agentur f; (office) Büro nt; **have the ~ for** die Vertretung haben für

agenda /ə'dʒendə/ n Tagesordnung f; **on the ~** auf dem Programm

agent /'eιdʒənt/ n Agent(in) m(f); (Comm) Vertreter(in) m(f); (substance) Mittel nt

aggravat|e /'ægrəveιt/ vt verschlimmern; (fam: annoy) ärgern. ~**ion** /-'veιʃn/ n (fam) Ärger m

aggregate /'ægrιgət/ a gesamt □ n Ge- samtzahl f; (sum) Gesamtsumme f

aggress|ion /ə'greʃn/ n Aggression f. ~**ive** /-sιv/ a, -**ly** adv aggressiv. ~**iveness** n Aggressivität f. ~**or** n Angreifer(in) m(f)

aggrieved /ə'gri:vd/ a verletzt

aggro /'ægrəu/ n (fam) Ärger m

aghast /ə'gɑ:st/ a entsetzt

agil|e /'ædʒaιl/ a flink, behände; ⟨mind⟩ wendig. ~**ity** /ə'dʒιlətι/ n Flinkheit f, Be- händigkeit f

agitat|e /'ædʒιteιt/ vt bewegen; (shake) schütteln □ vi (fig) ~ **for** agitieren für. ~**ed** a, -**ly** adv erregt. ~**ion** /-'teιʃn/ n Erregung f; (Pol) Agitation f. ~**or** n Agi- tator m

agnostic /æg'nɒstιk/ n Agnostiker m

ago /ə'gəu/ adv vor (+ dat); **a month ~** vor einem Monat; **a long time ~** vor langer Zeit; **how long ~ is it?** wie lange ist es her?

agog /ə'gɒg/ a gespannt

agoniz|e /'ægənaιz/ vi [innerlich] ringen. ~**ing** a qualvoll

agony /'ægənι/ n Qual f; **be in ~** furcht- bare Schmerzen haben

agree /ə'gri:/ vt vereinbaren; (admit) zu- geben; ~ **to do sth** sich bereit erklären, etw zu tun □ vi ⟨people, figures:⟩ über- einstimmen; (reach agreement) sich eini- gen; (get on) gut miteinander auskommen; (consent) einwilligen (to in + acc); **I ~** Meinung bin ich auch; ~ **with s.o.** jdm zustimmen; ⟨food:⟩ jdm bekommen; ~ **with sth** (*approve of*) mit etw einverstanden sein

agreeable /ə'griːəbl/ *a* angenehm; **be ~** einverstanden sein (**to** mit)

agreed /ə'griːd/ *a* vereinbart

agreement /ə'griːmənt/ *n* Übereinstimmung *f*; (*consent*) Einwilligung *f*; (*contract*) Abkommen *nt*; **reach ~** sich einigen

agricultur|al /ægrɪ'kʌltʃərəl/ *a* landwirtschaftlich. **~e** /'ægrɪkʌltʃə(r)/ *n* Landwirtschaft *f*

aground /ə'graʊnd/ *a* gestrandet; **run ~** ⟨ship:⟩ stranden

ahead /ə'hed/ *adv* straight ~ geradeaus; **be ~ of s.o./sth** vor jdm/etw sein; (*fig*) jdm/etw voraus sein; **draw ~** nach vorne ziehen; **go on ~** vorgehen; **get ~** vorankommen; **go ~!** (*fam*) bitte! **look/plan ~** vorausblicken/-planen

aid /eɪd/ *n* Hilfe *f*; (*financial*) Unterstützung *f*; **in ~ of** zugunsten (+ *gen*) □ *vt* helfen (+ *dat*)

aide /eɪd/ *n* Berater *m*

Aids /eɪdz/ *n* Aids *nt*

ail|ing /'eɪlɪŋ/ *a* kränkelnd. **~ment** *n* Leiden *nt*

aim /eɪm/ *n* Ziel *nt*; **take ~** zielen □ *vt* richten (**at** auf + *acc*) □ *vi* zielen (**at** auf + *acc*); **~ to do sth** beabsichtigen, etw zu tun. **~less** *a*, **-ly** *adv* ziellos

air /eə(r)/ *n* Luft *f*; (*tune*) Melodie *f*; (*expression*) Miene *f*; (*appearance*) Anschein *m*; **be on the ~** ⟨programme:⟩ gesendet werden; ⟨person:⟩ senden, auf Sendung sein; **put on ~s** vornehm tun; **by ~** auf dem Luftweg; (*airmail*) mit Luftpost □ *vt* lüften; vorbringen ⟨views⟩

air: **~-bed** *n* Luftmatratze *f*. **~-conditioned** *a* klimatisiert. **~-conditioning** *n* Klimaanlage *f*. **~craft** *n* Flugzeug *nt*. **~fare** *n* Flugpreis *m*. **~field** *n* Flugplatz *m*. **~force** *n* Luftwaffe *f*. **~ freshener** *n* Raumspray *nt*. **~gun** *n* Luftgewehr *nt*. **~ hostess** *n* Stewardess *f*. **~ letter** *n* Aerogramm *nt*. **~line** *n* Fluggesellschaft *f*. **~lock** *n* Luftblase *f*. **~mail** *n* Luftpost *f*. **~man** *n* Flieger *m*. **~plane** *n* (*Amer*) Flugzeug *nt*. **~ pocket** *n* Luftloch *nt*. **~port** *n* Flughafen *m*. **~-raid** *n* Luftangriff *m*. **~-raid shelter** *n* Luftschutzbunker *m*. **~ship** *n* Luftschiff *nt*. **~ ticket** *n* Flugschein *m*. **~tight** *a* luftdicht. **~ traffic** *n* Luftverkehr *m*. **~-traffic controller** *n* Fluglotse *m*. **~worthy** *a* flugtüchtig

airy /'eərɪ/ *a* (**ier,-iest**) luftig; ⟨manner⟩ nonchalant

aisle /aɪl/ *n* Gang *m*

ajar /ə'dʒɑː(r)/ *a* angelehnt

akin /ə'kɪn/ *a* **~ to** verwandt mit; (*similar*) ähnlich (**to** dat)

alabaster /'æləbɑːstə(r)/ *n* Alabaster *m*

alacrity /ə'lækrətɪ/ *n* Bereitfertigkeit *f*

alarm /əlɑːm/ *n* Alarm *m*; (*device*) Alarmanlage *f*; (*clock*) Wecker *m*; (*fear*) Unruhe *f* □ *vt* erschrecken; alarmieren. **~ clock** *n* Wecker *m*

alas /ə'læs/ *int* ach!

album /'ælbəm/ *n* Album *nt*

alcohol /'ælkəhɒl/ *n* Alkohol *m*. **~ic** /-'hɒlɪk/ *a* alkoholisch □ *n* Alkoholiker(in) *m(f)*. **~ism** *n* Alkoholismus *m*

alcove /'ælkəʊv/ *n* Nische *f*

alert /ə'lɜːt/ *a* aufmerksam □ *n* Alarm *m*; **on the ~** auf der Hut □ *vt* alarmieren

algae /'ældʒiː/ *npl* Algen *pl*

algebra /'ældʒɪbrə/ *n* Algebra *f*

Algeria /æl'dʒɪərɪə/ *n* Algerien *nt*

alias /'eɪlɪəs/ *n* Deckname *m* □ *adv* alias

alibi /'ælɪbaɪ/ *n* Alibi *nt*

alien /'eɪlɪən/ *a* fremd □ *n* Ausländer(in) *m(f)*

alienat|e /'eɪlɪəneɪt/ *vt* entfremden. **~ion** /-'neɪʃn/ *n* Entfremdung *f*

alight[1] /ə'laɪt/ *vi* aussteigen (**from** aus); ⟨bird:⟩ sich niederlassen

alight[2] *a* **be ~** brennen; **set ~** anzünden

align /ə'laɪn/ *vt* ausrichten. **~ment** *n* Ausrichtung *f*; **out of ~ment** nicht richtig ausgerichtet

alike /ə'laɪk/ *a & adv* ähnlich; (*same*) gleich; **look ~** sich (*dat*) ähnlich sehen

alimony /'ælɪmənɪ/ *n* Unterhalt *m*

alive /ə'laɪv/ *a* lebendig; **be ~** leben; **be ~ with** wimmeln von

alkali /'ælkəlaɪ/ *n* Base *f*, Alkali *nt*

all /ɔːl/ *a* alle *pl*; (*whole*) ganz; **~ [the] children** alle Kinder; **~ our children** alle unsere Kinder; **~ the others** alle anderen; **~ day** den ganzen Tag; **~ the wine** der ganze Wein; **for ~ that** (*nevertheless*) trotzdem; **in ~ innocence** in aller Unschuld □ *pron* alle *pl*; (*everything*) alles; **~ of you/them** Sie/sie alle; **~ of the town** die ganze Stadt; **not at ~** gar nicht; **in ~** insgesamt; **~ in ~** alles in allem; **most of ~** am meisten; **once and for ~** ein für alle Mal □ *adv* ganz; **~ but** fast; **~ at once** auf einmal; **~ too soon** viel zu früh; **~ the same** (*nevertheless*) trotzdem; **~ the better** umso besser; **be ~ in** (*fam*) völlig erledigt sein; **four ~** (*Sport*) vier zu vier

allay /ə'leɪ/ *vt* zerstreuen

allegation /ælɪ'geɪʃn/ *n* Behauptung *f*

allege /ə'ledʒ/ *vt* behaupten. **~d** *a* **-ly** /-ɪdlɪ/ *adv* angeblich

allegiance /ə'li:dʒəns/ n Treue f

allegor|ical /ælɪ'gɒrɪkl/ a allegorisch. ~y /'æligəri/ n Allegorie f

allerg|ic /ə'lɜːdʒɪk/ a allergisch (to gegen). ~y /'ælədʒi/ n Allergie f

alleviate /ə'li:vɪeɪt/ vt lindern

alley /'æli/ n Gasse f; (for bowling) Bahn f

alliance /ə'laɪəns/ n Verbindung f; (Pol) Bündnis nt

allied /'ælaɪd/ a alliiert; (fig: related) verwandt (to mit)

alligator /'æligeɪtə(r)/ n Alligator m

allocat|e /'æləkeɪt/ vt zuteilen; (share out) verteilen. ~ion /-'keɪʃn/ n Zuteilung f

allot /ə'lɒt/ vt (pt/pp allotted) zuteilen (s.o. jdm). ~ment n ≈ Schrebergarten m

allow /ə'laʊ/ vt erlauben; (give) geben; (grant) gewähren; (reckon) rechnen; (agree, admit) zugeben; ~ for berücksichtigen; ~ s.o. to do sth jdm erlauben, etw zu tun; be ~ed to do sth etw tun dürfen

allowance /ə'laʊəns/ n [finanzielle] Unterstützung f; ~ for petrol Benzingeld nt; make ~s for berücksichtigen

alloy /'ælɔɪ/ n Legierung f

allude /ə'lu:d/ vi anspielen (to auf + acc)

allure /æ'ljʊə(r)/ n Reiz m

allusion /ə'lu:ʒn/ n Anspielung f

ally[1] /'ælaɪ/ n Verbündete(r) m/f; the Allies pl die Alliierten

ally[2] /ə'laɪ/ vt (pt/pp -ied) verbinden; ~ oneself with sich verbünden mit

almighty /ɔːl'maɪtɪ/ a allmächtig; (fam: big) Riesen-. □ n the A ~ der Allmächtige

almond /'ɑːmənd/ n (Bot) Mandel f

almost /'ɔːlməʊst/ adv fast, beinahe

alms /ɑːmz/ npl (liter) Almosen pl

alone /ə'ləʊn/ a & adv allein; leave me ~ lass mich in Ruhe; leave that ~! lass die Finger davon! let ~ ganz zu schweigen von

along /ə'lɒŋ/ prep entlang (+ acc); ~ the river den Fluss entlang □ adv ~ with zusammen mit; all ~ die ganze Zeit; come ~ komm doch; I'll bring it ~ ich bringe es mit; move ~ weitergehen

along'side adv daneben □ prep neben (+ dat)

aloof /ə'lu:f/ a distanziert

aloud /ə'laʊd/ adv laut

alphabet /'ælfəbət/ n Alphabet nt. ~ical /-'betɪkl/ a, -ly adv alphabetisch

alpine /'ælpaɪn/ a alpin; A~ Alpen-

Alps /ælps/ npl Alpen pl

already /ɔːl'redɪ/ adv schon

Alsace /æl'sæs/ n Elsass nt

Alsatian /æl'seɪʃn/ n (dog) [deutscher] Schäferhund m

also /'ɔːlsəʊ/ adv auch

altar /'ɔːltə(r)/ n Altar m

alter /'ɔːltə(r)/ vt ändern □ vi sich verändern. ~ation /-'reɪʃn/ n Änderung f

alternate[1] /'ɔːltəneɪt/ vi [sich] abwechseln □ vt abwechseln

alternate[2] /ɔːl'tɜːnət/ a, -ly adv abwechselnd; (Amer: alternative) andere(r,s); on ~ days jeden zweiten Tag

'alternating current n Wechselstrom m

alternative /ɔːl'tɜːnətɪv/ a andere(r,s) □ n Alternative f. ~ly adv oder aber

although /ɔːl'ðəʊ/ conj obgleich, obwohl

altitude /'æltɪtjuːd/ n Höhe f

altogether /ɔːltə'geðə(r)/ adv insgesamt; (on the whole) alles in allem

altruistic /æltru:'ɪstɪk/ a altruistisch

aluminium /ælju'mɪnɪəm/ n, (Amer) **aluminum** /ə'luːmɪnəm/ n Aluminium nt

always /'ɔːlweɪz/ adv immer

am /æm/ see **be**

a.m. abbr (ante meridiem) vormittags

amalgamate /ə'mælgəmeɪt/ vt vereinigen; (Chem) amalgamieren □ vi sich vereinigen; (Chem) sich amalgamieren

amass /ə'mæs/ vt anhäufen

amateur /'æmətə(r)/ n Amateur m □ attrib Amateur-; (Theat) Laien-. ~ish a laienhaft

amaze /ə'meɪz/ vt erstaunen. ~d a erstaunt. ~ment n Erstaunen nt

amazing /ə'meɪzɪŋ/ a, -ly adv erstaunlich

ambassador /æm'bæsədə(r)/ n Botschafter m

amber /'æmbə(r)/ n Bernstein m □ a (colour) gelb

ambidextrous /æmbɪ'dekstrəs/ a be ~ mit beiden Händen gleich geschickt sein

ambience /'æmbɪəns/ n Atmosphäre f

ambigu|ity /æmbɪ'gjuːətɪ/ n Zweideutigkeit f. ~ous /-'bɪgjʊəs/ a -ly adv zweideutig

ambiti|on /æm'bɪʃn/ n Ehrgeiz m; (aim) Ambition f. ~ous /-ʃəs/ a ehrgeizig

ambivalent /æm'bɪvələnt/ a zwiespältig; be/feel ~ im Zwiespalt sein

amble /'æmbl/ vi schlendern

ambulance /'æmbjʊləns/ n Krankenwagen m. ~ man n Sanitäter m

ambush /'æmbʊʃ/ n Hinterhalt m □ vt aus dem Hinterhalt überfallen

amen /ɑː'men/ int amen

amenable /ə'miːnəbl/ a ~ to zugänglich (+ dat)

amend /ə'mend/ *vt* ändern. **~ment** *n* Änderung *f*. **~s** *npl* **make ~s for sth** etw wieder gutmachen

amenities /ə'mi:nətız/ *npl* Einrichtungen *pl*

America /ə'merıkə/ *n* Amerika *nt*. **~n** *a* amerikanisch □ *n* Amerikaner(in) *m(f)*. **~nism** *n* Amerikanismus *m*

amiable /'eımıəbl/ *a* nett

amicable /'æmıkəbl/ *a*, **-bly** *adv* freundschaftlich; ⟨*agreement*⟩ gütlich

amid[st] /ə'mıd[st]/ *prep* inmitten (+ *gen*)

amiss /ə'mıs/ *a* **be ~** nicht stimmen □ *adv* **not come ~** nicht unangebracht sein; **take sth ~** etw übel nehmen

ammonia /ə'məunıə/ *n* Ammoniak *nt*

ammunition /æmju'nıʃn/ *n* Munition *f*

amnesia /æm'ni:zıə/ *n* Amnesie *f*

amnesty /'æmnəstı/ *n* Amnestie *f*

among[st] /ə'mʌŋ[st]/ *prep* unter (+ *dat/acc*); **~ yourselves** untereinander

amoral /eı'mɒrəl/ *a* amoralisch

amorous /'æmərəs/ *a* zärtlich

amount /ə'maunt/ *n* Menge *f*; ⟨*sum of money*⟩ Betrag *m*; ⟨*total*⟩ Gesamtsumme *f* □ *vi* **~ to** sich belaufen auf (+ *acc*); ⟨*fig*⟩ hinauslaufen auf (+ *acc*)

amp /æmp/ *n* Ampere *nt*

amphibi|an /æm'fıbıən/ *n* Amphibie *f*. **~ous** /-ıəs/ *a* amphibisch

amphitheatre /'æmfı-/ *n* Amphitheater *nt*

ample /'æmpl/ *a* (**-r,-st**), **-ly** *adv* reichlich; ⟨*large*⟩ füllig

amplif|ier /'æmplıfaıə(r)/ *n* Verstärker *m*. **~y** /-faı/ *vt* ⟨*pt/pp* **-ied**⟩ weiter ausführen; verstärken ⟨*sound*⟩

amputat|e /'æmpjuteıt/ *vt* amputieren. **~ion** /-'teıʃn/ *n* Amputation *f*

amuse /ə'mju:z/ *vt* amüsieren, belustigen; ⟨*entertain*⟩ unterhalten. **~ment** *n* Belustigung *f*; Unterhaltung *f*. **~ment arcade** *n* Spielhalle *f*

amusing /ə'mju:zıŋ/ *a* amüsant

an /ən/, *betont* æn/ *see* a

anaem|ia /ə'ni:mıə/ *n* Blutarmut *f*, Anämie *f*. **~ic** *a* blutarm

anaesthesia /ænəs'θi:zıə/ *n* Betäubung *f*

anaesthetic /ænəs'θetık/ *n* Narkosemittel *nt*, Betäubungsmittel *nt*; **under [an] ~** in Narkose; **give s.o. an ~** jdm eine Narkose geben

anaesthet|ist /ə'ni:sθətıst/ *n* Narkosearzt *m*. **~ize** /-taız/ *vt* betäuben

analog[ue] /'ænəlɒg/ *a* Analog-

analogy /ə'nælədʒı/ *n* Analogie *f*

analyse /'ænəlaız/ *vt* analysieren

analysis /ə'næləsıs/ *n* Analyse *f*

analyst /'ænəlıst/ *n* Chemiker(in) *m(f)*; ⟨*Psych*⟩ Analytiker *m*

analytical /ænə'lıtıkl/ *a* analytisch

anarch|ist /'ænəkıst/ *n* Anarchist *m*. **~y** *n* Anarchie *f*

anathema /ə'næθəmə/ *n* Gräuel *m*

anatom|ical /ænə'tɒmıkl/ *a*, **-ly** *adv* anatomisch. **~y** /ə'nætəmı/ *n* Anatomie *f*

ancest|or /'ænsestə(r)/ *n* Vorfahr *m*. **~ry** *n* Abstammung *f*

anchor /'æŋkə(r)/ *n* Anker *m* □ *vi* ankern □ *vt* verankern

anchovy /'æntʃəvı/ *n* Sardelle *f*

ancient /'eınʃənt/ *a* alt

ancillary /æn'sılərı/ *a* Hilfs-

and /ənd/, *betont* ænd/ *conj* und; **~ so on** und so weiter; **six hundred ~ two** sechshundertzwei; **more ~ more** immer mehr; **nice ~ warm** schön warm; **try ~ come** versuche zu kommen

anecdote /'ænıkdəut/ *n* Anekdote *f*

anew /ə'nju:/ *adv* von neuem

angel /'eındʒl/ *n* Engel *m*. **~ic** /æn'dʒelık/ *a* engelhaft

anger /'æŋgə(r)/ *n* Zorn *m* □ *vt* zornig machen

angle¹ /'æŋgl/ *n* Winkel *m*; ⟨*fig*⟩ Standpunkt *m*; **at an ~** schräg

angle² *vi* angeln; **~ for** ⟨*fig*⟩ fischen nach. **~r** *n* Angler *m*

Anglican /'æŋglıkən/ *a* anglikanisch □ *n* Anglikaner(in) *m(f)*

Anglo-Saxon /æŋgləu'sæksn/ *a* angelsächsisch □ *n* Angelsächsisch *nt*

angry /'æŋgrı/ *a* (**-ier,-iest**), **-ily** *adv* zornig; **be ~ with** böse sein auf (+ *acc*)

anguish /'æŋgwıʃ/ *n* Qual *f*

angular /'æŋgjulə(r)/ *a* eckig; ⟨*features*⟩ kantig

animal /'ænıml/ *n* Tier *nt* □ *a* tierisch

animate¹ /'ænımət/ *a* lebendig

animat|e² /'ænımeıt/ *vt* beleben. **~ed** *a* lebhaft. **~ion** /-'meıʃn/ *n* Lebhaftigkeit *f*

animosity /ænı'mɒsətı/ *n* Feindseligkeit *f*

aniseed /'ænısi:d/ *n* Anis *m*

ankle /'æŋkl/ *n* [Fuß]knöchel *m*

annex /ə'neks/ *vt* annektieren

annex[e] /'æneks/ *n* Nebengebäude *nt*; ⟨*extension*⟩ Anbau *m*

annihilat|e /ə'naıəleıt/ *vt* vernichten. **~ion** /-'leıʃn/ *n* Vernichtung *f*

anniversary /ænı'vɜ:sərı/ *n* Jahrestag *m*

annotate /'ænəteıt/ *vt* kommentieren

announce /ə'nauns/ *vt* bekannt geben; ⟨*over loudspeaker*⟩ durchsagen; ⟨*at reception*⟩ ankündigen; ⟨*Radio, TV*⟩ ansagen;

(in newspaper) anzeigen. ~**ment** n Bekanntgabe f; Bekanntmachung f; Durchsage f; Ansage f; Anzeige f. ~**r** n Ansager(in) m(f)

annoy /ə'nɔɪ/ vt ärgern; *(pester)* belästigen; **get** ~**ed** sich ärgern. ~**ance** n Ärger m. ~**ing** a ärgerlich

annual /'ænjʊəl/ a, **-ly** adv jährlich □ n *(Bot)* einjährige Pflanze f; *(book)* Jahresalbum nt

annuity /ə'nju:ətɪ/ n [Leib]rente f

annul /ə'nʌl/ vt *(pt/pp* **annulled)** annullieren

anoint /ə'nɔɪnt/ vt salben

anomaly /ə'nɒməlɪ/ n Anomalie f

anonymous /ə'nɒnɪməs/ a, **-ly** adv anonym

anorak /'ænəræk/ n Anorak m

anorexia /ænə'reksɪə/ n Magersucht f

another /ə'nʌðə(r)/ a & pron ein anderer/ eine andere/ein anderes; *(additional)* noch ein(e); ~ **[one]** noch einer/eine/ eins; ~ **day** an einem anderen Tag; **in** ~ **way** auf andere Weise; ~ **time** ein andermal; **one** ~ einander

answer /'ɑ:nsə(r)/ n Antwort f; *(solution)* Lösung f □ vt antworten (**s.o.** jdm); beantworten *(question, letter)*; ~ **the door/ telephone** an die Tür/ans Telefon gehen □ vi antworten; *(Teleph)* sich melden; ~ **back** eine freche Antwort geben; ~ **for** verantwortlich sein für. ~**able** /-əbl/ a verantwortlich. ~**ing machine** n *(Teleph)* Anrufbeantworter m

ant /ænt/ n Ameise f

antagonis|m /æn'tægənɪzm/ n Antagonismus m. ~**tic** /-'nɪstɪk/ a feindselig

antagonize /æn'tægənaɪz/ vt gegen sich aufbringen

Antarctic /æn't'ɑ:ktɪk/ n Antarktis f

antelope /'æntɪləʊp/ n Antilope f

antenatal /æntɪ'neɪtl/ a ~ **care** Schwangerschaftsfürsorge f

antenna /æn'tenə/ n Fühler m; *(Amer: aerial)* Antenne f

ante-room /'æntɪ-/ n Vorraum m

anthem /'ænθəm/ n Hymne f

anthology /æn'θɒlədʒɪ/ n Anthologie f

anthropology /ænθrə'pɒlədʒɪ/ n Anthropologie f

anti-'aircraft /æntɪ-/ a Flugabwehr-

antibiotic /æntɪbaɪ'ɒtɪk/ n Antibiotikum nt

'antibody n Antikörper m

anticipat|e /æn'tɪsɪpeɪt/ vt vorhersehen; *(forestall)* zuvorkommen (+ dat); *(expect)* erwarten. ~**ion** /-'peɪʃn/ n Erwartung f

anti'climax n Enttäuschung f

anti'clockwise a & adv gegen den Uhrzeigersinn

antics /'æntɪks/ npl Mätzchen pl

anti'cyclone n Hochdruckgebiet nt

antidote /'æntɪdəʊt/ n Gegengift nt

'antifreeze n Frostschutzmittel nt

antipathy /æn'tɪpəθɪ/ n Abneigung f, Antipathie f

antiquarian /æntɪ'kweərɪən/ a antiquarisch. ~ **bookshop** n Antiquariat nt

antiquated /'æntɪkweɪtɪd/ a veraltet

antique /æn'ti:k/ a antik □ n Antiquität f. ~ **dealer** n Antiquitätenhändler m

antiquity /æn'tɪkwətɪ/ n Altertum nt

anti-Semitic /æntɪsɪ'mɪtɪk/ a antisemitisch

anti'septic a antiseptisch □ n Antiseptikum nt

anti'social a asozial; *(fam)* ungesellig

antithesis /æn'tɪθəsɪs/ n Gegensatz m

antlers /'æntləz/ npl Geweih nt

anus /'eɪnəs/ n After m

anvil /'ænvɪl/ n Amboss m

anxiety /æŋ'zaɪətɪ/ n Sorge f

anxious /'æŋkʃəs/ a, **-ly** adv ängstlich; *(worried)* besorgt; **be** ~ **to do sth** etw gerne machen wollen

any /'enɪ/ a irgendein(e); pl irgendwelche; *(every)* jede(r,s); pl alle; *(after negative)* kein(e); pl keine; ~ **colour/number you like** eine beliebige Farbe/Zahl; **have you** ~ **wine/apples?** haben Sie Wein/Äpfel? **for** ~ **reason** aus irgendeinem Grund □ pron [irgend]einer/eine/eins; pl [irgend]welche; *(some)* welche(r,s); pl welche; *(all)* alle pl; *(negative)* keiner/keine/ keins; pl keine; **I don't want** ~ **of it** ich will nichts davon; **there aren't** ~ **es gibt** keine; **I need wine/apples/money— have we** ~? ich brauche Wein/Äpfel/ Geld—haben wir welchen/welche/ welches? □ adv noch; ~**quicker/slower** noch schneller/langsamer; **is it** ~ **better?** geht es etwas besser? **would you like** ~ **more?** möchten Sie noch [etwas]? **I can't eat** ~ **more** ich kann nichts mehr essen; **I can't go** ~ **further** ich kann nicht mehr weiter

'anybody pron [irgend]jemand; *(after negative)* niemand; ~ **can do that** das kann jeder

'anyhow adv jedenfalls; *(nevertheless)* trotzdem; *(badly)* irgendwie

'anyone pron = anybody

'anything pron [irgend]etwas; *(after negative)* nichts; *(everything)* alles

'anyway adv jedenfalls; *(in any case)* sowieso

'anywhere *adv* irgendwo; (*after negative*) nirgendwo; ⟨*be, live*⟩ überall; **I'd go ~** ich würde überallhin gehen

apart /ə'pɑ:t/ *adv* auseinander; **live ~** getrennt leben; **~ from** abgesehen von

apartment /ə'pɑ:tmənt/ *n* Zimmer *nt*; (*Amer: flat*) Wohnung *f*

apathy /'æpəθɪ/ *n* Apathie *f*

ape /eɪp/ *n* [Menschen]affe *m* □ *vt* nachäffen

aperitif /ə'perəti:f/ *n* Aperitif *m*

aperture /'æpətʃə(r)/ *n* Öffnung *f*; (*Phot*) Blende *f*

apex /'eɪpeks/ *n* Spitze *f*; (*fig*) Gipfel *m*

apiece /ə'pi:s/ *adv* pro Person; (*thing*) pro Stück

apologetic /əpɒlə'dʒetɪk/ *a,* **-ally** *adv* entschuldigend; **be ~** sich entschuldigen

apologize /ə'pɒlədʒaɪz/ *vi* sich entschuldigen (**to** bei)

apology /ə'pɒlədʒɪ/ *n* Entschuldigung *f*

apostle /ə'pɒsl/ *n* Apostel *m*

apostrophe /ə'pɒstrəfɪ/ *n* Apostroph *m*

appal /ə'pɔ:l/ *vt* (*pt/pp* **appalled**) entsetzen. **~ling** *a* entsetzlich

apparatus /æpə'reɪtəs/ *n* Apparatur *f*; (*Sport*) Geräte *pl*; (*single piece*) Gerät *nt*

apparel /ə'pærəl/ *n* Kleidung *f*

apparent /ə'pærənt/ *a* offenbar; (*seeming*) scheinbar. **~ly** *adv* offenbar, anscheinend

apparition /æpə'rɪʃn/ *n* Erscheinung *f*

appeal /ə'pi:l/ *n* Appell *m*, Aufruf *m*; (*request*) Bitte *f*; (*attraction*) Reiz *m*; (*Jur*) Berufung *f* □ *vi* appellieren (**to an** + *acc*); (*ask*) bitten (**for** um); (*be attractive*) zusagen (**to** dat); (*Jur*) Berufung einlegen. **~ing** *a* ansprechend

appear /ə'pɪə(r)/ *vi* erscheinen; (*seem*) scheinen; (*Theat*) auftreten. **~ance** *n* Erscheinen *nt*; (*look*) Aussehen *nt*; **to all ~ances** allem Anschein nach

appease /ə'pi:z/ *vt* beschwichtigen

append /ə'pend/ *vt* nachtragen; setzen ⟨*signature*⟩ (**to** unter + *acc*). **~age** /-ɪdʒ/ *n* Anhängsel *nt*

appendicitis /əpendɪ'saɪtɪs/ *n* Blinddarmentzündung *f*

appendix /ə'pendɪks/ *n* (*pl* **-ices** /-ɪsi:z/) (*of book*) Anhang *m* □ (*pl* **-es**) (*Anat*) Blinddarm *m*

appertain /æpə'teɪn/ *vi* **~ to** betreffen

appetite /'æpɪtaɪt/ *n* Appetit *m*

appetizing /'æpɪtaɪzɪŋ/ *a* appetitlich

applaud /ə'plɔ:d/ *vt/i* Beifall klatschen (+ *dat*). **~se** *n* Beifall *m*

apple /'æpl/ *n* Apfel *m*

appliance /ə'plaɪəns/ *n* Gerät *nt*

applicable /'æplɪkəbl/ *a* anwendbar (**to** auf + *acc*); (*on form*) **not ~** nicht zutreffend

applicant /'æplɪkənt/ *n* Bewerber(in) *m(f)*

application /æplɪ'keɪʃn/ *n* Anwendung *f*; (*request*) Antrag *m*; (*for job*) Bewerbung *f*; (*diligence*) Fleiß *m*

applied /ə'plaɪd/ *a* angewandt

apply /ə'plaɪ/ *vt* (*pt/pp* **-ied**) auftragen ⟨*paint*⟩; anwenden ⟨*force, rule*⟩ □ *vi* zutreffen (**to** auf + *acc*); **~ for** beantragen; sich bewerben um (*job*)

appoint /ə'pɔɪnt/ *vt* ernennen; (*fix*) festlegen; **well ~ed** gut ausgestattet. **~ment** *n* Ernennung *f*; (*meeting*) Verabredung *f*; (*at doctor's, hairdresser's*) Termin *m*; (*job*) Posten *m*; **make an ~ment** sich anmelden

apposite /'æpəzɪt/ *a* treffend

appraise /ə'preɪz/ *vt* abschätzen

appreciable /ə'pri:ʃəbl/ *a* merklich; (*considerable*) beträchtlich

appreciat|e /ə'pri:ʃɪeɪt/ *vt* zu schätzen wissen; (*be grateful for*) dankbar sein für; (*enjoy*) schätzen; (*understand*) verstehen □ *vi* (*increase in value*) im Wert steigen. **~ion** /-'eɪʃn/ *n* (*gratitude*) Dankbarkeit *f*; **in ~ion** als Dank (**of** für). **~ive** /-ətɪv/ *a* dankbar

apprehend /æprɪ'hend/ *vt* festnehmen

apprehens|ion /æprɪ'henʃn/ *n* Festnahme *f*; (*fear*) Angst *f*. **~ive** /-sɪv/ *a* ängstlich

apprentice /ə'prentɪs/ *n* Lehrling *m*. **~ship** *n* Lehre *f*

approach /ə'prəʊtʃ/ *n* Näherkommen *nt*; (*of time*) Nahen *nt*; (*access*) Zugang *m*; (*road*) Zufahrt *f* □ *vi* sich nähern; ⟨*time:*⟩ nahen □ *vt* sich nähern (+ *dat*); (*with request*) herantreten an (+ *acc*); (*set about*) sich heranmachen an (+ *acc*). **~able** /-əbl/ *a* zugänglich

approbation /æprə'beɪʃn/ *n* Billigung *f*

appropriate¹ /ə'prəʊprɪət/ *a* angebracht, angemessen

appropriate² /ə'prəʊprɪeɪt/ *vt* sich (*dat*) aneignen

approval /ə'pru:vl/ *n* Billigung *f*; **on ~** zur Ansicht

approv|e /ə'pru:v/ *vt* billigen □ *vi* **~e of** sth/s.o. mit etw/jdm einverstanden sein. **~ing** *a,* **-ly** *adv* anerkennend

approximate¹ /ə'prɒksɪmeɪt/ *vi* **~ to** nahe kommen (+ *dat*)

approximate² /ə'prɒksɪmət/ *a* ungefähr. **~ly** *adv* ungefähr, etwa

approximation /əprɒksɪ'meɪʃn/ *n* Schätzung *f*

apricot /'eɪprɪkɒt/ n Aprikose f

April /'eɪprəl/ n April m; **make an ~ fool of** in den April schicken

apron /'eɪprən/ n Schürze f

apropos /'æprəpəʊ/ adv ~ **[of]** betreffs (+ gen)

apt /æpt/ a, **-ly** adv passend; ⟨pupil⟩ begabt; **be ~ to do sth** dazu neigen, etw zu tun

aptitude /'æptɪtjuːd/ n Begabung f

aqualung /'ækwəlʌŋ/ n Tauchgerät nt

aquarium /ə'kweərɪəm/ n Aquarium nt

Aquarius /ə'kweərɪəs/ n (Astr) Wassermann m

aquatic /ə'kwætɪk/ a Wasser-

Arab /'ærəb/ a arabisch □ n Araber(in) m(f). **~ian** /ə'reɪbɪən/ a arabisch

Arabic /'ærəbɪk/ a arabisch

arable /'ærəbl/ a ~ **land** Ackerland nt

arbitrary /'ɑːbɪtrəri/ a, **-ily** adv willkürlich

arbitrat|e /'ɑːbɪtreɪt/ vi schlichten. **~ion** /-'treɪʃn/ n Schlichtung f

arc /ɑːk/ n Bogen m

arcade /ɑː'keɪd/ n Laubengang m; ⟨shops⟩ Einkaufspassage f

arch /ɑːtʃ/ n Bogen m; ⟨of foot⟩ Gewölbe nt □ vt ~ **its back** ⟨cat:⟩ einen Buckel machen

archaeological /ɑːkɪə'lɒdʒɪkl/ a archäologisch

archaeolog|ist /ɑːkɪ'ɒlədʒɪst/ n Archäologe m/-login f. **~y** n Archäologie f

archaic /ɑː'keɪɪk/ a veraltet

arch'bishop /ɑːtʃ-/ n Erzbischof m

arch-'enemy n Erzfeind m

archer /ɑː'tʃə(r)/ n Bogenschütze m. **~y** n Bogenschießen nt

architect /'ɑːkɪtekt/ n Architekt(in) m(f). **~ural** /ɑːkɪ'tektʃərəl/ a, **-ly** adv architektonisch

architecture /'ɑːkɪtektʃə(r)/ n Architektur f

archives /'ɑːkaɪvz/ npl Archiv nt

archway /'ɑːtʃweɪ/ n Torbogen m

Arctic /'ɑːktɪk/ a arktisch □ n **the ~** die Arktis

ardent /'ɑːdənt/ a, **-ly** adv leidenschaftlich

ardour /'ɑːdə(r)/ n Leidenschaft f

arduous /'ɑːdjʊəs/ a mühsam

are /ɑː(r)/ see **be**

area /'eərɪə/ n ⟨surface⟩ Fläche f; ⟨Geom⟩ Flächeninhalt m; ⟨region⟩ Gegend f; ⟨fig⟩ Gebiet nt. **~ code** n Vorwahlnummer f

arena /ə'riːnə/ n Arena f

aren't /ɑːnt/ = **are not**. See **be**

Argentina /ɑːdʒən'tiːnə/ n Argentinien nt

Argentin|e /'ɑːdʒəntaɪn/, **~ian** /-'tɪnɪən/ a argentinisch

argue /'ɑːgjuː/ vi streiten (**about** über + acc); ⟨two people:⟩ sich streiten; ⟨debate⟩ diskutieren; **don't ~!** keine Widerrede! □ vt ⟨debate⟩ diskutieren; ⟨reason⟩ ~ **that** argumentieren, dass

argument /'ɑːgjʊmənt/ n Streit m, Auseinandersetzung f; ⟨reasoning⟩ Argument nt; **have an ~** sich streiten. **~ative** /-'mentətɪv/ a streitlustig

aria /'ɑːrɪə/ n Arie f

arid /'ærɪd/ a dürr

Aries /'eəriːz/ n (Astr) Widder m

arise /ə'raɪz/ vi (pt **arose**, pp **arisen**) sich ergeben (**from** aus)

aristocracy /ærɪ'stɒkrəsɪ/ n Aristokratie f

aristocrat /'ærɪstəkræt/ n Aristokrat(in) m(f). **~ic** /-'krætɪk/ a aristokratisch

arithmetic /ə'rɪθmətɪk/ n Rechnen nt

ark /ɑːk/ n **Noah's A~** die Arche Noah

arm /ɑːm/ n Arm m; ⟨of chair⟩ Armlehne f; **~s** pl ⟨weapons⟩ Waffen pl; ⟨Heraldry⟩ Wappen nt; **up in ~s** ⟨fam⟩ empört □ vt bewaffnen

armament /'ɑːməmənt/ n Bewaffnung f; **~s** pl Waffen pl

'armchair n Sessel m

armed /ɑːmd/ a bewaffnet; **~ forces** Streitkräfte pl

armistice /'ɑːmɪstɪs/ n Waffenstillstand m

armour /'ɑːmə(r)/ n Rüstung f. **~ed** a Panzer-

'armpit n Achselhöhle f

army /'ɑːmɪ/ n Heer nt; ⟨specific⟩ Armee f; **join the ~** zum Militär gehen

aroma /ə'rəʊmə/ n Aroma nt, Duft m. **~tic** /ærə'mætɪk/ a aromatisch

arose /ə'rəʊz/ see **arise**

around /ə'raʊnd/ adv **[all] ~** rings herum; **he's not ~** er ist nicht da; **look/turn ~** sich umsehen/umdrehen; **travel ~** herumreisen □ prep um (+ acc) ... herum; ⟨approximately⟩ gegen

arouse /ə'raʊz/ vt aufwecken; ⟨excite⟩ erregen

arrange /ə'reɪndʒ/ vt arrangieren; anordnen ⟨furniture, books⟩; ⟨settle⟩ abmachen; **I have ~d to go there** ich habe abgemacht, dass ich dahingehe. **~ment** n Anordnung f; ⟨agreement⟩ Vereinbarung f; ⟨of flowers⟩ Gesteck nt; **make ~ments** Vorkehrungen treffen

arrears /ə'rɪəz/ npl Rückstände pl; **in ~** im Rückstand

arrest /ə'rest/ n Verhaftung f; **under ~** verhaftet □ vt verhaften

arrival /ə'raɪvl/ *n* Ankunft *f*; **new** ~**s** *pl* Neuankömmlinge *pl*

arrive /ə'raɪv/ *vi* ankommen; ~ **at** (*fig*) gelangen zu

arrogan|ce /'ærəgəns/ *n* Arroganz *f*. ~**t** *a*, **-ly** *adv* arrogant

arrow /'ærəʊ/ *n* Pfeil *m*

arse /ɑːs/ *n* (*vulg*) Arsch *m*

arsenic /'ɑːsənɪk/ *n* Arsen *nt*

arson /'ɑːsn/ *n* Brandstiftung *f*. ~**ist** /-sənɪst/ *n* Brandstifter *m*

art /ɑːt/ *n* Kunst *f*; **work of** ~ Kunstwerk *nt*; ~**s and crafts** *pl* Kunstgewerbe *nt*; **A**~**s** *pl* (*Univ*) Geisteswissenschaften *pl*

artery /'ɑːtərɪ/ *n* Schlagader *f*, Arterie *f*

artful /'ɑːtfl/ *a* gerissen

'**art gallery** *n* Kunstgalerie *f*

arthritis /ɑː'θraɪtɪs/ *n* Arthritis *f*

artichoke /'ɑːtɪtʃəʊk/ *n* Artischocke *f*

article /'ɑːtɪkl/ *n* Artikel *m*; (*object*) Gegenstand *m*; ~ **of clothing** Kleidungsstück *nt*

articulate[1] /ɑː'tɪkjʊlət/ *a* deutlich; **be** ~ sich gut ausdrücken können

articulate[2] /ɑː'tɪkjʊleɪt/ *vt* aussprechen. ~**d lorry** *n* Sattelzug *m*

artifice /'ɑːtɪfɪs/ *n* Arglist *f*

artificial /ɑːtɪ'fɪʃl/ *a*, **-ly** *adv* künstlich

artillery /ɑː'tɪlərɪ/ *n* Artillerie *f*

artist /'ɑːtɪst/ *n* Künstler(in) *m(f)*

artiste /ɑː'tiːst/ *n* (*Theat*) Artist(in) *m(f)*

artistic /ɑː'tɪstɪk/ *a*, **-ally** *adv* künstlerisch

artless /'ɑːtlɪs/ *a* unschuldig

as /æz/ *conj* (*because*) da; (*when*) als; (*while*) während □ *prep* als; **as a child/foreigner** als Kind/Ausländer □ *adv* **as well** auch; **as soon as** sobald; **as much as** so viel wie; **as quick as** so schnell wie du; **as you know** wie Sie wissen; **as far as I'm concerned** was mich betrifft

asbestos /æz'bestɒs/ *n* Asbest *m*

ascend /ə'send/ *vi* [auf]steigen □ *vt* besteigen (*throne*)

Ascension /ə'senʃn/ *n* (*Relig*) [Christi] Himmelfahrt *f*

ascent /ə'sent/ *n* Aufstieg *m*

ascertain /æsə'teɪn/ *vt* ermitteln

ascribe /ə'skraɪb/ *vt* zuschreiben (**to** *dat*)

ash[1] /æʃ/ *n* (*tree*) Esche *f*

ash[2] *n* Asche *f*

ashamed /ə'ʃeɪmd/ *a* beschämt; **be** ~ sich schämen (**of** über + *acc*)

ashore /ə'ʃɔː(r)/ *adv* an Land

ash: ~**tray** *n* Aschenbecher *m*. **A**~ '**Wednesday** *n* Aschermittwoch *m*

Asia /'eɪʃə/ *n* Asien *nt*. ~**n** *a* asiatisch □ *n* Asiat(in) *m(f)*. ~**tic** /eɪʃɪ'ætɪk/ *a* asiatisch

aside /ə'saɪd/ *adv* beiseite; ~ **from** (*Amer*) außer (+ *dat*)

ask /ɑːsk/ *vt/i* fragen; stellen (*question*); (*invite*) einladen; ~ **for** bitten um; verlangen (*s.o.*); ~ **after** sich erkundigen nach; ~ **s.o. in** jdn hereinbitten; ~ **s.o. to do sth** jdn bitten, etw zu tun

askance /ə'skɑːns/ *adv* **look** ~ **at** schief ansehen

askew /ə'skjuː/ *a & adv* schief

asleep /ə'sliːp/ *a* **be** ~ schlafen; **fall** ~ einschlafen

asparagus /ə'spærəgəs/ *n* Spargel *m*

aspect /'æspekt/ *n* Aspekt *m*

aspersions /ə'spɜːʃnz/ *npl* **cast** ~ **on** schlecht machen

asphalt /'æsfælt/ *n* Asphalt *m*

asphyxia /æs'fɪksɪə/ *n* Erstickung *f*. ~**te** /æ'sfɪksɪeɪt/ *vt/i* ersticken. ~**tion** /-'eɪʃn/ *n* Erstickung *f*

aspirations /æspə'reɪʃnz/ *npl* Streben *nt*

aspire /ə'spaɪə(r)/ *vi* ~ **to** streben nach

ass /æs/ *n* Esel *m*

assail /ə'seɪl/ *vt* bestürmen. ~**ant** *n* Angreifer(in) *m(f)*

assassin /ə'sæsɪn/ *n* Mörder(in) *m(f)*. ~**ate** *vt* ermorden. ~**ation** /-'neɪʃn/ *n* [politischer] Mord *m*

assault /ə'sɔːlt/ *n* (*Mil*) Angriff *m*; (*Jur*) Körperverletzung *f* □ *vt* [tätlich] angreifen

assemble /ə'sembl/ *vi* sich versammeln □ *vt* versammeln; (*Techn*) montieren

assembly /ə'semblɪ/ *n* Versammlung *f*; (*Sch*) Andacht *f*; (*Techn*) Montage *f*. ~ **line** *n* Fließband *nt*

assent /ə'sent/ *n* Zustimmung *f* □ *vi* zustimmen (**to** *dat*)

assert /ə'sɜːt/ *vt* behaupten; ~ **oneself** sich durchsetzen. ~**ion** /-ɜːʃn/ *n* Behauptung *f*. ~**ive** /-tɪv/ *a* **be** ~**ive** sich durchsetzen können

assess /ə'ses/ *vt* bewerten; (*fig & for tax purposes*) einschätzen: schätzen (*value*). ~**ment** *n* Einschätzung *f*; (*of tax*) Steuerbescheid *m*

asset /'æset/ *n* Vorteil *m*; ~**s** *pl* (*money*) Vermögen *nt*; (*Comm*) Aktiva *pl*

assiduous /ə'sɪdjʊəs/ *a*, **-ly** *adv* fleißig

assign /ə'saɪn/ *vt* zuweisen (**to** *dat*). ~**ment** *n* (*task*) Aufgabe *f*

assimilate /ə'sɪmɪleɪt/ *vt* aufnehmen; (*integrate*) assimilieren

assist /ə'sɪst/ *vt/i* helfen (+ *dat*). ~**ance** *n* Hilfe *f*. ~**ant** *a* Hilfs- □ *n* Assistent(in) *m(f)*; (*in shop*) Verkäufer(in) *m(f)*

associat|e[1] /ə'səʊʃieɪt/ *vt* verbinden; (*Psych*) assoziieren □ *vi* ~ **with** verkehren mit. **~ion** /-'eɪʃn/ *n* Verband *m*. **A~ion 'football** *n* Fußball *m*

associate[2] /ə'səʊʃiət/ *a* assoziiert □ *n* Kollege *m*/-gin *f*

assort|ed /ə'sɔ:tɪd/ *a* gemischt. **~ment** *n* Mischung *f*

assum|e /ə'sju:m/ *vt* annehmen; übernehmen (*office*); **~ing that** angenommen, dass

assumption /ə'sʌmpʃn/ *n* Annahme *f*; **on the ~** in der Annahme (**that** dass)

assurance /ə'ʃʊərəns/ *n* Versicherung *f*; (*confidence*) Selbstsicherheit *f*

assure /ə'ʃʊə(r)/ *vt* versichern (*s.o.* jdm); **I ~ you [of that]** das versichere ich Ihnen. **~d** *a* sicher

asterisk /'æstərɪsk/ *n* Sternchen *nt*

astern /ə'stɜ:n/ *adv* achtern

asthma /'æsmə/ *n* Asthma *nt*. **~tic** /-'mætɪk/ *a* asthmatisch

astonish /ə'stɒnɪʃ/ *vt* erstaunen. **~ing** *a* erstaunlich. **~ment** *n* Erstaunen *nt*

astound /ə'staʊnd/ *vt* in Erstaunen setzen

astray /ə'streɪ/ *adv* **go ~** verloren gehen; (*person:*) sich verlaufen; (*fig*) vom rechten Weg abkommen; **lead ~** verleiten

astride /ə'straɪd/ *adv* rittlings □ *prep* rittlings auf (+ *dat/acc*)

astringent /ə'strɪndʒənt/ *a* adstringierend; (*fig*) beißend

astrolog|er /ə'strɒlədʒə(r)/ *n* Astrologe *m*/-gin *f*. **~y** *n* Astrologie *f*

astronaut /'æstrənɔ:t/ *n* Astronaut(in) *m(f)*

astronom|er /ə'strɒnəmə(r)/ *n* Astronom *m*. **~ical** /æstrə'nɒmɪkl/ *a* astronomisch. **~y** *n* Astronomie *f*

astute /ə'stju:t/ *a* scharfsinnig. **~ness** *n* Scharfsinn *m*

asylum /ə'saɪləm/ *n* Asyl *nt*; **[lunatic] ~** Irrenanstalt *f*

at /ət, *betont* æt/ *prep* **an** (+ *dat/acc*); (*with town*) in; (*price*) zu; (*speed*) mit; **at the station** am Bahnhof; **at the beginning/ end** am Anfang/Ende; **at home** zu Hause; **at John's** bei John; **at work/the hairdresser's** bei der Arbeit/beim Friseur; **at school/the office** in der Schule/im Büro; **at a party/wedding** auf einer Party/Hochzeit; **at one o'clock** um ein Uhr; **at Christmas/Easter** zu Weihnachten/Ostern; **at the age of** im Alter von; **not at all** gar nicht; **at times** manchmal; **two at a time** zwei auf einmal; **good/bad at languages** gut/schlecht in Sprachen

ate /et/ *see* eat

atheist /'eɪθiɪst/ *n* Atheist(in) *m(f)*

athlet|e /'æθli:t/ *n* Athlet(in) *m(f)*. **~ic** /-'letɪk/ *a* sportlich. **~ics** /-'letɪks/ *n* Leichtathletik *f*

Atlantic /ət'læntɪk/ *a & n* **the ~ [Ocean]** der Atlantik

atlas /'ætləs/ *n* Atlas *m*

atmospher|e /'ætməsfɪə(r)/ *n* Atmosphäre *f*. **~ic** /-'ferɪk/ *a* atmosphärisch

atom /'ætəm/ *n* Atom *nt*. **~ bomb** *n* Atombombe *f*

atomic /ə'tɒmɪk/ *a* Atom-

atone /ə'təʊn/ *vi* büßen (**for** für). **~ment** *n* Buße *f*

atrocious /ə'trəʊʃəs/ *a* abscheulich

atrocity /ə'trɒsəti/ *n* Gräueltat *f*

attach /ə'tætʃ/ *vt* befestigen (**to** an + *dat*); beimessen (*importance*) (**to** *dat*); **be ~ed to** (*fig*) hängen an (+ *dat*)

attaché /ə'tæʃeɪ/ *n* Attaché *m*. **~ case** *n* Aktenkoffer *m*

attachment /ə'tætʃmənt/ *n* Bindung *f*; (*tool*) Zubehörteil *nt*; (*additional*) Zusatzgerät *nt*

attack /ə'tæk/ *n* Angriff *m*; (*Med*) Anfall *m* □ *vt/i* angreifen. **~er** *n* Angreifer *m*

attain /ə'teɪn/ *vt* erreichen; (*get*) erlangen. **~able** /-əbl/ *a* erreichbar

attempt /ə'tempt/ *n* Versuch *m* □ *vt* versuchen

attend /ə'tend/ *vt* anwesend sein bei; (*go regularly to*) besuchen; (*take part in*) teilnehmen an (+ *dat*); (*accompany*) begleiten; (*doctor:*) behandeln □ *vi* anwesend sein; (*pay attention*) aufpassen; **~ to** sich kümmern um; (*in shop*) bedienen. **~ance** *n* Anwesenheit *f*; (*number*) Besucherzahl *f*. **~ant** *n* Wärter(in) *m(f)*; (*in car park*) Wächter *m*

attention /ə'tenʃn/ *n* Aufmerksamkeit *f*; **~!** (*Mil*) stillgestanden! **pay ~** aufpassen; **pay ~ to** beachten, achten auf (+ *acc*); **need ~** reparaturbedürftig sein; **for the ~ of** zu Händen von

attentive /ə'tentɪv/ *a*, **-ly** *adv* aufmerksam

attest /ə'test/ *vt/i* **~ [to]** bezeugen

attic /'ætɪk/ *n* Dachboden *m*

attire /ə'taɪə(r)/ *n* Kleidung *f* □ *vt* kleiden

attitude /'ætɪtju:d/ *n* Haltung *f*

attorney /ə'tɜ:nɪ/ *n* (*Amer: lawyer*) Rechtsanwalt *m*; **power of ~** Vollmacht *f*

attract /ə'trækt/ *vt* anziehen; erregen (*attention*); **~ s.o.'s attention** jds Aufmerksamkeit auf sich (*acc*) lenken. **~ion** /-ækʃn/ *n* Anziehungskraft *f*; (*charm*) Reiz *m*; (*thing*) Attraktion *f*. **~ive** /-tɪv/ *a*, **-ly** *adv* attraktiv

attribute[1] /'ætrɪbju:t/ *n* Attribut *nt*

attribut|e² /ə'trɪbjuːt/ *vt* zuschreiben (**to** *dat*). **∼ive** /-tɪv/ *a*, **-ly** *adv* attributiv

attrition /ə'trɪʃn/ *n* war of ∼ Zermürbungskrieg *m*

aubergine /'əʊbəʒiːn/ *n* Aubergine *f*

auburn /'ɔːbən/ *a* kastanienbraun

auction /'ɔːkʃn/ *n* Auktion *f*, Versteigerung *f* □ *vt* versteigern. **∼eer** /-ʃə'nɪə(r)/ *n* Auktionator *m*

audaci|ous /ɔː'deɪʃəs/ *a*, **-ly** *adv* verwegen. **∼ty** /-'dæsətɪ/ *n* Verwegenheit *f*; (*impudence*) Dreistigkeit *f*

audible /'ɔːdəbl/ *a*, **-bly** *adv* hörbar

audience /'ɔːdɪəns/ *n* Publikum *nt*; (*Theat, TV*) Zuschauer *pl*; (*Radio*) Zuhörer *pl*; (*meeting*) Audienz *f*

audio /'ɔːdɪəʊ/: ∼ **typist** *n* Phonotypistin *f*. **∼'visual** *a* audiovisuell

audit /'ɔːdɪt/ *n* Bücherrevision *f* □ *vt* (*Comm*) prüfen

audition /ɔː'dɪʃn/ *n* (*Theat*) Vorsprechen *nt*; (*Mus*) Vorspielen *nt*; (*for singer*) Vorsingen *nt* □ *vi* vorsprechen; vorspielen; vorsingen

auditor /'ɔːdɪtə(r)/ *n* Buchprüfer *m*

auditorium /ɔːdɪ'tɔːrɪəm/ *n* Zuschauerraum *m*

augment /ɔːg'ment/ *vt* vergrößern

augur /'ɔːgə(r)/ *vi* ∼ **well/ill** etwas/ nichts Gutes verheißen

august /ɔː'gʌst/ *a* hoheitsvoll

August /'ɔːgəst/ *n* August *m*

aunt /ɑːnt/ *n* Tante *f*

au pair /əʊ'peə(r)/ *n* ∼ **[girl]** Aupairmädchen *nt*

aura /'ɔːrə/ *n* Fluidum *nt*

auspices /'ɔːspɪsɪz/ *npl* (*protection*) Schirmherrschaft *f*

auspicious /ɔː'spɪʃəs/ *a* günstig; (*occasion*) freudig

auster|e /ɒ'stɪə(r)/ *a* streng; (*simple*) nüchtern. **∼ity** /ɒ'sterətɪ/ *n* Strenge *f*; (*hardship*) Entbehrung *f*

Australia /ɒ'streɪlɪə/ *n* Australien *nt*. ∼**n** *a* australisch □ *n* Australier(in) *m(f)*

Austria /'ɒstrɪə/ *n* Österreich *nt*. ∼**n** *a* österreichisch □ *n* Österreicher(in) *m(f)*

authentic /ɔː'θentɪk/ *a* echt, authentisch. **∼ate** *vt* beglaubigen. **∼ity** /-'tɪsətɪ/ *n* Echtheit *f*

author /'ɔːθə(r)/ *n* Schriftsteller *m*, Autor *m*; (*of document*) Verfasser *m*

authoritarian /ɔːθɒrɪ'teərɪən/ *a* autoritär

authoritative /ɔː'θɒrɪtətɪv/ *a* maßgebend; **be** ∼ Autorität haben

authority /ɔː'θɒrətɪ/ *n* Autorität *f*; (*public*) Behörde *f*; **in** ∼ verantwortlich

authorization /ɔːθəraɪ'zeɪʃn/ *n* Ermächtigung *f*

authorize /'ɔːθəraɪz/ *vt* ermächtigen ⟨*s.o.*⟩; genehmigen ⟨*sth*⟩

autobi'ography /ɔːtə-/ *n* Autobiographie *f*

autocratic /ɔːtə'krætɪk/ *a* autokratisch

autograph /'ɔːtə-/ *n* Autogramm *nt*

automatic /ɔːtə'mætɪk/ *a*, **-ally** *adv* automatisch □ *n* (*car*) Fahrzeug *nt* mit Automatikgetriebe; (*washing machine*) Waschautomat *m*

automation /ɔːtə'meɪʃn/ *n* Automation *f*

automobile /'ɔːtəməbiːl/ *n* Auto *nt*

autonom|ous /ɔː'tɒnəməs/ *a* autonom. **∼y** *n* Autonomie *f*

autopsy /'ɔːtɒpsɪ/ *n* Autopsie *f*

autumn /'ɔːtəm/ *n* Herbst *m*. **∼al** /-'tʌmnl/ *a* herbstlich

auxiliary /ɔːg'zɪlɪərɪ/ *a* Hilfs- □ *n* Helfer(in) *m(f)*, Hilfskraft *f*

avail /ə'veɪl/ *n* **to no** ∼ vergeblich □ *vi* ∼ **oneself of** Gebrauch machen von

available /ə'veɪləbl/ *a* verfügbar; (*obtainable*) erhältlich

avalanche /'ævəlɑːnʃ/ *n* Lawine *f*

avaric|e /'ævərɪs/ *n* Habsucht *f*. **∼ious** /-'rɪʃəs/ *a* habgierig, habsüchtig

avenge /ə'vendʒ/ *vt* rächen

avenue /'ævənjuː/ *n* Allee *f*

average /'ævərɪdʒ/ *a* Durchschnitts-, durchschnittlich □ *n* Durchschnitt *m*; **on** ∼ im Durchschnitt, durchschnittlich □ *vt* durchschnittlich schaffen □ *vi* ∼ **out at** im Durchschnitt ergeben

avers|e /ə'vɜːs/ *a* **not be** ∼**e to sth** etw (*dat*) nicht abgeneigt sein. **∼ion** /-ʒn/ *n* Abneigung *f* (**to** gegen)

avert /ə'vɜːt/ *vt* abwenden

aviary /'eɪvɪərɪ/ *n* Vogelhaus *nt*

aviation /eɪvɪ'eɪʃn/ *n* Luftfahrt *f*

avid /'ævɪd/ *a* gierig (**for** nach); (*keen*) eifrig

avocado /ævə'kɑːdəʊ/ *n* Avocado *f*

avoid /ə'vɔɪd/ *vt* vermeiden; ∼ **s.o.** jdm aus dem Weg gehen. **∼able** /-əbl/ *a* vermeidbar. **∼ance** *n* Vermeidung *f*

await /ə'weɪt/ *vt* warten auf (+ *acc*)

awake /ə'weɪk/ *a* wach; **wide** ∼ hellwach □ *vi* (*pt* **awoke**, *pp* **awoken**) erwachen

awaken /ə'weɪkn/ *vt* wecken □ *vi* erwachen. **∼ing** *n* Erwachen *nt*

award /ə'wɔːd/ *n* Auszeichnung *f*; (*prize*) Preis *m* □ *vt* zuerkennen (**to s.o.** *dat*); verleihen ⟨*prize*⟩

aware /ə'weə(r)/ *a* **become** ∼ gewahr werden (**of** *gen*); **be** ∼ **that** wissen, dass. **∼ness** *n* Bewusstsein *nt*

awash /ə'wɒʃ/ *a* be ~ unter Wasser stehen

away /ə'weɪ/ *adv* weg, fort; (*absent*) abwesend; **be** ~ nicht da sein; **far** ~ weit weg; **four kilometres** ~ vier Kilometer entfernt; **play** ~ (*Sport*) auswärts spielen; **go/stay** ~ weggehen/-bleiben. ~ **game** *n* Auswärtsspiel *nt*

awe /ɔː/ *n* Ehrfurcht *f*

awful /'ɔːfl/ *a*, **-ly** *adv* furchtbar

awhile /ə'waɪl/ *adv* eine Weile

awkward /'ɔːkwəd/ *a* schwierig; (*clumsy*) ungeschickt; (*embarrassing*) peinlich; (*inconvenient*) ungünstig. ~**ly** *adv* ungeschickt; (*embarrassedly*) verlegen

awning /'ɔːnɪŋ/ *n* Markise *f*

awoke(n) /ə'wəʊk(n)/ *see* **awake**

awry /ə'raɪ/ *adv* schief

axe /æks/ *n* Axt *f* □ *vt* (*pres p* **axing**) streichen; (*dismiss*) entlassen

axis /'æksɪs/ *n* (*pl* **axes** /-siːz/) Achse *f*

axle /'æksl/ *n* (*Techn*) Achse *f*

ay[e] /aɪ/ *adv* ja □ *n* Jastimme *f*

B

B /biː/ *n* (*Mus*) H *nt*

BA *abbr of* **Bachelor of Arts**

babble /'bæbl/ *vi* plappern; (*stream:*) plätschern

baboon /bə'buːn/ *n* Pavian *m*

baby /'beɪbɪ/ *n* Baby *nt*; (*Amer, fam*) Schätzchen *nt*

baby: ~ **carriage** *n* (*Amer*) Kinderwagen *m*. ~**ish** *a* kindisch. ~**minder** *n* Tagesmutter *f*. ~**sit** *vi* babysitten. ~**sitter** *n* Babysitter *m*

bachelor /'bætʃələ(r)/ *n* Junggeselle *m*; **B** ~ **of Arts/Science** Bakkalaureus Artium/Scientium

bacillus /bə'sɪləs/ *n* (*pl* **-lli**) Bazillus *m*

back /bæk/ *n* Rücken *m*; (*reverse*) Rückseite *f*; (*of chair*) Rückenlehne *f*; (*Sport*) Verteidiger *m*; **at/**(*Auto*) **in the** ~ hinten; **on the** ~ auf der Rückseite; ~ **to front** verkehrt; **at the** ~ **of beyond** am Ende der Welt □ *a* Hinter- □ *adv* zurück; ~ **here/ there** hier/da hinten; ~ **at home** zu Hause; **go/pay** ~ zurückgehen/-zahlen □ *vt* (*support*) unterstützen; (*with money*) finanzieren; (*Auto*) zurücksetzen; (*Betting*) [Geld] setzen auf (+ *acc*); (*cover the back of*) mit einer Verstärkung versehen □ *vi* (*Auto*) zurücksetzen. ~ **down** *vi* klein beigeben. ~ **in** *vi* rückwärts hineinfahren. ~ **out** *vi* rückwärts hinaus-/

herausfahren; (*fig*) aussteigen (**of** aus). ~ **up** *vt* unterstützen; (*confirm*) bestätigen □ *vi* (*Auto*) zurücksetzen

back: ~**ache** *n* Rückenschmerzen *pl*. ~**biting** *n* gehässiges Gerede *nt*. ~**bone** *n* Rückgrat *nt*. ~**chat** *n* Widerrede *f*. ~**comb** *vt* toupieren. ~**date** *vt* rückdatieren; ~**dated to** rückwirkend von. ~ '**door** *n* Hintertür *f*

backer /'bækə(r)/ *n* Geldgeber *m*

back: ~'**fire** *vi* (*Auto*) fehlzünden; (*fig*) fehlschlagen. ~**ground** *n* Hintergrund *m*; **family** ~**ground** Familienverhältnisse *pl*. ~**hand** *n* (*Sport*) Rückhand *f*. ~'**handed** *a* (*compliment*) zweifelhaft. ~'**hander** *n* (*Sport*) Rückhandschlag *m*; (*fam: bribe*) Schmiergeld *nt*

backing /'bækɪŋ/ *n* (*support*) Unterstützung *f*; (*material*) Verstärkung *f*

back: ~**lash** *n* (*fig*) Gegenschlag *m*. ~**log** *n* Rückstand *m* (**of an** + *dat*). ~'**seat** *n* Rücksitz *m*. ~**side** *n* (*fam*) Hintern *m*. ~**stage** *adv* hinter der Bühne. ~**stroke** *n* Rückenschwimmen *nt*. ~-**up** *n* Unterstützung *f*; (*Amer: traffic jam*) Stau *m*

backward /'bækwəd/ *a* zurückgeblieben; (*country*) rückständig □ *adv* rückwärts. ~**s** rückwärts; ~**s and forwards** hin und her

back: ~**water** *n* (*fig*) unberührtes Fleckchen *nt*. ~ '**yard** *n* Hinterhof *m*; **not in my** ~ **yard** (*fam*) nicht vor meiner Haustür

bacon /'beɪkn/ *n* [Schinken]speck *m*

bacteria /bæk'tɪərɪə/ *npl* Bakterien *pl*

bad /bæd/ *a* (**worse, worst**) schlecht; (*serious*) schwer, schlimm; (*naughty*) unartig; ~ **language** gemeine Ausdrucksweise *f*; **feel** ~ sich schlecht fühlen; (*feel guilty*) ein schlechtes Gewissen haben; **go** ~ schlecht werden

bade /bæd/ *see* **bid²**

badge /bædʒ/ *n* Abzeichen *nt*

badger /'bædʒə(r)/ *n* Dachs *m* □ *vt* plagen

badly /'bædlɪ/ *adv* schlecht; (*seriously*) schwer; ~ **off** schlecht gestellt; ~ **behaved** unerzogen; **want** ~ sich (*dat*) sehnsüchtig wünschen; **need** ~ dringend brauchen

bad-'mannered *a* mit schlechten Manieren

badminton /'bædmɪntən/ *n* Federball *m*

bad-'tempered *a* schlecht gelaunt

baffle /'bæfl/ *vt* verblüffen

bag /bæg/ *n* Tasche *f*; (*of paper*) Tüte *f*; (*pouch*) Beutel *m*; ~**s of** (*fam*) jede Menge □ *vt* (*fam: reserve*) in Beschlag nehmen

baggage /'bægɪdʒ/ *n* [Reise]gepäck *nt*

baggy /'bægɪ/ *a* (*clothes*) ausgebeult

'bagpipes *npl* Dudelsack *m*

bail /beɪl/ n Kaution f; **on ~** gegen Kaution □ vt **~ s.o. out** jdn gegen Kaution freibekommen; (fig) jdm aus der Patsche helfen. **~ out** vt (Naut) ausschöpfen □ vi (Aviat) abspringen

bailiff /'beɪlɪf/ n Gerichtsvollzieher m; (of estate) Gutsverwalter m

bait /beɪt/ n Köder m □ vt mit einem Köder versehen; (fig: torment) reizen

bake /beɪk/ vt/i backen

baker /'beɪkə(r)/ n Bäcker m; **~'s [shop]** Bäckerei f. **~y** n Bäckerei f

baking /'beɪkɪŋ/ n Backen nt. **~-powder** n Backpulver nt. **~-tin** n Backform f

balance /'bæləns/ n (equilibrium) Gleichgewicht nt, Balance f; (scales) Waage f; (Comm) Saldo m; (outstanding sum) Restbetrag m; **[bank] ~** Kontostand m; **in the ~** (fig) in der Schwebe □ vt balancieren; (equalize) ausgleichen; (Comm) abschließen ⟨books⟩ □ vi balancieren; (fig & Comm) sich ausgleichen. **~d** a ausgewogen. **~ sheet** n Bilanz f

balcony /'bælkənɪ/ n Balkon m

bald /bɔːld/ a (-er, -est) kahl; ⟨person⟩ kahlköpfig; **go ~** eine Glatze bekommen

balderdash /'bɔːldədæʃ/ n Unsinn m

bald|ing /'bɔːldɪŋ/ a **be ~ing** eine Glatze bekommen. **~ly** adv unverblümt. **~ness** n Kahlköpfigkeit f

bale /beɪl/ n Ballen m

baleful /'beɪlfl/ a, **-ly** adv böse

balk /bɔːlk/ vt vereiteln □ vi **~ at** zurückschrecken vor (+ dat)

Balkans /'bɔːlknz/ npl Balkan m

ball[1] /bɔːl/ n Ball m; (Billiards, Croquet) Kugel f; (of yarn) Knäuel m & nt; **on the ~** (fam) auf Draht

ball[2] n (dance) Ball m

ballad /'bæləd/ n Ballade f

ballast /'bæləst/ n Ballast m

ball-'bearing n Kugellager nt

ballerina /bælə'riːnə/ n Ballerina f

ballet /'bæleɪ/ n Ballett nt. **~ dancer** n Balletttänzer(in) m(f)

ballistic /bə'lɪstɪk/ a ballistisch. **~s** n Ballistik f

balloon /bə'luːn/ n Luftballon m; (Aviat) Ballon m

ballot /'bælət/ n [geheime] Wahl f; (on issue) [geheime] Abstimmung f. **~-box** n Wahlurne f. **~-paper** n Stimmzettel m

ball: ~-point ['pen] n Kugelschreiber m. **~room** n Ballsaal m

balm /bɑːm/ n Balsam m

balmy /'bɑːmɪ/ a (-ier, -iest) a sanft; (fam: crazy) verrückt

Baltic /'bɔːltɪk/ a & n **the ~ [Sea]** die Ostsee

balustrade /bælə'streɪd/ n Balustrade f

bamboo /bæm'buː/ n Bambus m

bamboozle /bæm'buːzl/ vt (fam) übers Ohr hauen

ban /bæn/ n Verbot nt □ vt (pt/pp **banned**) verbieten

banal /bə'nɑːl/ a banal. **~ity** /-'nælətɪ/ n Banalität f

banana /bə'nɑːnə/ n Banane f

band /bænd/ n Band nt; (stripe) Streifen m; (group) Schar f; (Mus) Kapelle f □ vi **~ together** sich zusammenschließen

bandage /'bændɪdʒ/ n Verband m; (for support) Bandage f □ vt verbinden; bandagieren ⟨limb⟩

b. & b. abbr of **bed and breakfast**

bandit /'bændɪt/ n Bandit m

band: ~stand n Musikpavillon m. **~wagon** n **jump on the ~wagon** (fig) sich einer erfolgreichen Sache anschließen

bandy[1] /'bændɪ/ vt (pt/pp **-ied**) wechseln ⟨words⟩

bandy[2] a (-ier, -iest) **be ~** O-Beine haben. **~-legged** a O-beinig

bang /bæŋ/ n (noise) Knall m; (blow) Schlag m □ adv **go ~** knallen □ int bums! peng! □ vt knallen; (shut noisily) zuknallen; (strike) schlagen auf (+ acc); **~ one's head** sich (dat) den Kopf stoßen (**on** an + acc) □ vi schlagen; ⟨door:⟩ zuknallen

banger /'bæŋə(r)/ n (firework) Knallfrosch m; (fam: sausage) Wurst f; **old ~** (fam: car) Klapperkiste f

bangle /'bæŋgl/ n Armreifen m

banish /'bænɪʃ/ vt verbannen

banisters /'bænɪstəz/ npl [Treppen]geländer nt

banjo /'bændʒəʊ/ n Banjo nt

bank[1] /bæŋk/ n (of river) Ufer nt; (slope) Hang m □ vi (Aviat) in die Kurve gehen

bank[2] n Bank f □ vt einzahlen; **~ with** ein Konto haben bei. **~ on** vt sich verlassen auf (+ acc)

'bank account n Bankkonto nt

banker /'bæŋkə(r)/ n Bankier m

bank: ~ 'holiday n gesetzlicher Feiertag m. **~ing** n Bankwesen nt. **~note** n Banknote f

bankrupt /'bæŋkrʌpt/ a bankrott; **go ~** Bankrott machen □ n Bankrotteur m □ vt Bankrott machen. **~cy** n Bankrott m

banner /'bænə(r)/ n Banner nt; (carried by demonstrators) Transparent nt, Spruchband nt

banns /bænz/ npl (Relig) Aufgebot nt

banquet /'bæŋkwɪt/ n Bankett nt

banter /'bæntə(r)/ n Spöttelei f

bap /bæp/ n weiches Brötchen nt

baptism /'bæptɪzm/ n Taufe f

Baptist /'bæptɪst/ n Baptist(in) m(f)

baptize /bæp'taɪz/ vt taufen

bar /bɑː(r)/ n Stange f; (of cage) [Gitter]stab m; (of gold) Barren m; (of chocolate) Tafel f; (of soap) Stück nt; (long) Riegel m; (café) Bar f; (counter) Theke f; (Mus) Takt m; (fig: obstacle) Hindernis nt; **parallel ∼s** (Sport) Barren m; **be called to the ∼** (Jur) als plädierender Anwalt zugelassen werden; **behind ∼s** (fam) hinter Gittern □ vt (pt/pp **barred**) versperren (way, door); ausschließen (person) □ prep außer; **∼ none** ohne Ausnahme

barbarian /bɑː'beərɪən/ n Barbar m

barbar|ic /bɑː'bærɪk/ a barbarisch. **∼ity** n Barbarei f. **∼ous** /'bɑːbərəs/ a barbarisch

barbecue /'bɑːbɪkjuː/ n Grill m; (party) Grillfest nt □ vt [im Freien] grillen

barbed /bɑːbd/ a **∼ wire** Stacheldraht m

barber /'bɑːbə(r)/ n [Herren]friseur m

barbiturate /bɑː'bɪtjʊrət/ n Barbiturat nt

'bar code n Strichkode m

bare /beə(r)/ a (-r, -st) nackt, bloß; (tree) kahl; (empty) leer; (mere) bloß □ vt entblößen; fletschen (teeth)

bare: **∼back** adv ohne Sattel. **∼faced** a schamlos. **∼foot** adv barfuß. **∼'headed** a mit unbedecktem Kopf

barely /'beəlɪ/ adv kaum

bargain /'bɑːgɪn/ n (agreement) Geschäft nt; (good buy) Gelegenheitskauf m; **into the ∼** noch dazu; **make a ∼** sich einigen □ vi handeln; (haggle) feilschen; **∼ for** (expect) rechnen mit

barge /bɑːdʒ/ n Lastkahn m; (towed) Schleppkahn m □ vi **∼ in** (fam) hereinplatzen

baritone /'bærɪtəʊn/ n Bariton m

bark[1] /bɑːk/ n (of tree) Rinde f

bark[2] n Bellen nt □ vi bellen

barley /'bɑːlɪ/ n Gerste f

bar: **∼maid** n Schankmädchen nt. **∼man** Barmann m

barmy /'bɑːmɪ/ a (fam) verrückt

barn /bɑːn/ n Scheune f

barometer /bə'rɒmɪtə(r)/ n Barometer nt

baron /'bærn/ n Baron m. **∼ess** n Baronin f

baroque /bə'rɒk/ a barock □ n Barock nt

barracks /'bærəks/ npl Kaserne f

barrage /'bærɑːʒ/ n (in river) Wehr nt; (Mil) Sperrfeuer nt; (fig) Hagel m

barrel /'bærl/ n Fass nt; (of gun) Lauf m; (of cannon) Rohr nt. **∼-organ** n Drehorgel f

barren /'bærn/ a unfruchtbar; (landscape) öde

barricade /bærɪ'keɪd/ n Barrikade f □ vt verbarrikadieren

barrier /'bærɪə(r)/ n Barriere f; (across road) Schranke f; (Rail) Sperre f; (fig) Hindernis nt

barring /'bɑːrɪŋ/ prep **∼ accidents** wenn alles gut geht

barrister /'bærɪstə(r)/ n [plädierender] Rechtsanwalt m

barrow /'bærəʊ/ n Karre f, Karren m. **∼ boy** n Straßenhändler m

barter /'bɑːtə(r)/ vt tauschen (for gegen)

base /beɪs/ n Fuß m; (fig) Basis f; (Mil) Stützpunkt m □ a gemein; (metal) unedel □ vt stützen (on auf + acc); **be ∼d on** basieren auf (+ dat)

base: **∼ball** n Baseball m. **∼less** a unbegründet. **∼ment** n Kellergeschoss nt. **∼ment flat** n Kellerwohnung f

bash /bæʃ/ n Schlag m; **have a ∼!** (fam) probier es mal! □ vt hauen; (dent) einbeulen; **∼ed in** verbeult

bashful /'bæʃfl/ a, -ly adv schüchtern

basic /'beɪsɪk/ a Grund-; (fundamental) grundlegend; (essential) wesentlich; (unadorned) einfach; the **∼s** das Wesentliche. **∼ally** adv grundsätzlich

basil /'bæzɪl/ n Basilikum nt

basilica /bə'zɪlɪkə/ n Basilika f

basin /'beɪsn/ n Becken nt; (for washing) Waschbecken nt; (for food) Schüssel f

basis /'beɪsɪs/ n (pl **-ses** /-siːz/) Basis f

bask /bɑːsk/ vi sich sonnen

basket /'bɑːskɪt/ n Korb m. **∼ball** n Basketball m

Basle /bɑːl/ n Basel nt

bass /beɪs/ a Bass-; **∼ voice** Bassstimme f □ n Bass m; (person) Bassist m

bassoon /bə'suːn/ n Fagott nt

bastard /'bɑːstəd/ n (sl) Schuft m

baste[1] /beɪst/ vt (sew) heften

baste[2] vt (Culin) begießen

bastion /'bæstɪən/ n Bastion f

bat[1] /bæt/ n Schläger m; **off one's own ∼** (fam) auf eigene Faust □ vt (pt/pp **batted**) schlagen; **not ∼ an eyelid** (fig) nicht mit der Wimper zucken

bat[2] n (Zool) Fledermaus f

batch /bætʃ/ n (of people) Gruppe f; (of papers) Stoß m; (of goods) Sendung f; (of bread) Schub m

bated /'beɪtɪd/ a **with ∼ breath** mit angehaltenem Atem

bath /bɑːθ/ n (pl **∼s** /bɑːðz/) Bad nt; (tub) Badewanne f; **∼s** pl Badeanstalt f; **have a ∼** baden □ vt/i baden

bathe /beɪð/ n Bad nt □ vt/i baden. ~r n Badende(r) m/f

bathing /'beɪðɪŋ/ n Baden nt. ~cap n Bademütze f. ~costume n Badeanzug m

bath: ~mat n Badematte f. ~robe n (Amer) Bademantel m. ~room n Badezimmer nt. ~towel n Badetuch nt

baton /'bætn/ n (Mus) Taktstock m; (Mil) Stab m

battalion /bə'tælɪən/ n Bataillon nt

batten /'bætn/ n Latte f

batter /'bætə(r)/ n (Culin) flüssiger Teig m □ vt schlagen. ~ed a (car) verbeult; (wife) misshandelt

battery /'bætərɪ/ n Batterie f

battle /'bætl/ n Schlacht f; (fig) Kampf m □ vi (fig) kämpfen (for um)

battle: ~axe n (fam) Drachen m. ~field n Schlachtfeld nt. ~ship n Schlachtschiff nt

batty /'bætɪ/ a (fam) verrückt

Bavaria /bə'veərɪə/ n Bayern nt. ~n a bayrisch □ n Bayer(in) m(f)

bawdy /'bɔːdɪ/ a (-ier, -iest) derb

bawl /bɔːl/ vt/i brüllen

bay[1] /beɪ/ n (Geog) Bucht f; (Archit) Erker m

bay[2] n keep at ~ fern halten

bay[3] n (horse) Braune(r) m

bay[4] n (Bot) [echter] Lorbeer m. ~leaf n Lorbeerblatt nt

bayonet /'beɪənət/ n Bajonett nt

bay 'window n Erkerfenster nt

bazaar /bə'zɑː(r)/ n Basar m

BC abbr (before Christ) v. Chr.

be /biː/ vi (pres am, are, is, pl are; pt was, pl were; pp been) sein; (lie) liegen; (stand) stehen; (cost) kosten; he is a teacher er ist Lehrer; be quiet! sei still! I am cold/hot mir ist kalt/heiß; how are you? wie geht es Ihnen? I am well mir geht es gut; there is/are es gibt; what do you want to be? was willst du werden? I have been to Vienna ich bin in Wien gewesen; has the postman been? war der Briefträger schon da? it's hot, isn't it? es ist heiß, nicht [wahr]? you are coming too, aren't you? du kommst mit, nicht [wahr]? it's yours, is it? das gehört also Ihnen? yes he is/I am ja; (negating previous statement) doch; three and three are six drei und drei macht sechs □ v aux ~ reading/going lesen/gehen; I am coming/staying ich komme/bleibe; what is he doing? was macht er? I am being lazy ich faulenze; I was thinking of you ich dachte an dich; you were going to ... du wolltest ...; I am to stay ich soll bleiben; you are not to ... du darfst nicht ...; you are to do that immediately das musst du sofort machen □ passive werden; be attacked/deceived überfallen/betrogen werden

beach /biːtʃ/ n Strand m. ~wear n Strandkleidung f

beacon /'biːkn/ n Leuchtfeuer nt; (Naut, Aviat) Bake f

bead /biːd/ n Perle f

beak /biːk/ n Schnabel m

beaker /'biːkə(r)/ n Becher m

beam /biːm/ n Balken m; (of light) Strahl m □ vi strahlen. ~ing a [freude]strahlend

bean /biːn/ n Bohne f; spill the ~s (fam) alles ausplaudern

bear[1] /beə(r)/ n Bär m

bear[2] vt/i (pt bore, pp borne) tragen; (endure) ertragen; gebären (child); ~ right sich rechts halten. ~able /-əbl/ a erträglich

beard /bɪəd/ n Bart m. ~ed a bärtig

bearer /'beərə(r)/ n Träger m; (of news, cheque) Überbringer m; (of passport) Inhaber(in) m(f)

bearing /'beərɪŋ/ n Haltung f; (Techn) Lager nt; have a ~ on von Belang sein für; get one's ~s sich orientieren; lose one's ~s die Orientierung verlieren

beast /biːst/ n Tier nt; (fam: person) Biest nt

beastly /'biːstlɪ/ a (-ier, -iest) (fam) scheußlich; (person) gemein

beat /biːt/ n Schlag m; (of policeman) Runde f; (rhythm) Takt m □ vt/i (pt beat, pp beaten) schlagen; (thrash) verprügeln; klopfen (carpet); (hammer) hämmern (on an + acc); ~ a retreat (Mil) sich zurückziehen; ~ it! (fam) hau ab! it ~s me (fam) das begreife ich nicht. ~ up vt zusammenschlagen

beat|en /'biːtn/ a off the ~en track abseits. ~ing n Prügel pl

beautician /bjuː'tɪʃn/ n Kosmetikerin f

beauti|ful /'bjuːtɪfl/ a, -ly adv schön. ~fy /-faɪ/ vt (pt/pp -ied) verschönern

beauty /'bjuːtɪ/ n Schönheit f. ~ parlour n Kosmetiksalon m. ~ spot n Schönheitsfleck m; (place) landschaftlich besonders reizvolles Fleckchen nt

beaver /'biːvə(r)/ n Biber m

became /bɪ'keɪm/ see become

because /bɪ'kɒz/ conj weil □ adv ~ of wegen (+ gen)

beckon /'bekn/ vt/i ~ [to] herbeiwinken

becom|e /bɪ'kʌm/ vt/i (pt became, pp become) werden. ~ing a (clothes) kleidsam

bed /bed/ n Bett nt; (layer) Schicht f; (of flowers) Beet nt; in ~ im Bett; go to ~ ins od zu Bett gehen; ~ and breakfast

Zimmer mit Frühstück. ~**clothes** npl,
~**ding** n Bettzeug nt

bedlam /'bedləm/ n Chaos nt

'**bedpan** n Bettpfanne f

bedraggled /bɪ'drægld/ a nass und
verschmutzt

bed: ~**ridden** a bettlägerig. ~**room** n
Schlafzimmer nt

'**bedside** n at his ~ an seinem Bett. ~
'**lamp** n Nachttischlampe f. ~'**rug** n
Bettvorleger m. ~'**table** n Nachttisch m

bed: ~'**sitter** n, ~'**sitting-room** n
Wohnschlafzimmer nt. ~**spread** n
Tagesdecke f. ~**time** n Schlafenszeit f; at
~**time** vor dem Schlafengehen

bee /biː/ n Biene f

beech /biːtʃ/ n Buche f

beef /biːf/ n Rindfleisch nt. ~**burger** n
Hamburger m

bee: ~**hive** n Bienenstock m. ~**keeper** n
Imker(in) m(f). ~**keeping** n Bienenzucht
f. ~**line** n make a ~**line for** (fam) zusteuern auf (+ acc)

been /biːn/ see **be**

beer /bɪə(r)/ n Bier nt

beet /biːt/ n (Amer: **beetroot**) rote Bete f;
[**sugar**] ~ Zuckerrübe f

beetle /'biːtl/ n Käfer m

'**beetroot** n rote Bete f

before /bɪ'fɔː(r)/ prep vor (+ dat/acc); **the
day** ~ **yesterday** vorgestern; ~ **long** bald
□ adv vorher; (already) schon; **never** ~
noch nie; ~ **that** davor □ conj (time) ehe,
bevor. ~**hand** adv vorher, im Voraus

befriend /bɪ'frend/ vt sich anfreunden
mit

beg /beg/ v (pt/pp **begged**) □ vi betteln □ vt
(entreat) anflehen; (ask) bitten (**for** um)

began /bɪ'gæn/ see **begin**

beggar /'begə(r)/ n Bettler(in) m(f); (fam)
Kerl m

begin /bɪ'gɪn/ vt/i (pt **began**, pp **begun**,
pres p **beginning**) anfangen, beginnen; **to
~ with** anfangs. ~**ner** n Anfänger(in)
m(f). ~**ning** n Anfang m, Beginn m

begonia /bɪ'gəʊnɪə/ n Begonie f

begrudge /bɪ'grʌdʒ/ vt ~ **s.o. sth** jdm etw
missgönnen

beguile /bɪ'gaɪl/ vt betören

begun /bɪ'gʌn/ see **begin**

behalf /bɪ'hɑːf/ n on ~ **of** im Namen von;
on my ~ meinetwegen

behave /bɪ'heɪv/ vi sich verhalten. ~ **oneself** sich benehmen

behaviour /bɪ'heɪvjə(r)/ n Verhalten nt;
good/bad ~ gutes/schlechtes Benehmen
nt; ~ **pattern** Verhaltensweise f

behead /bɪ'hed/ vt enthaupten

beheld /bɪ'held/ see **behold**

behind /bɪ'haɪnd/ prep hinter (+ dat/
acc); **be** ~ **sth** hinter etw (dat) stecken
□ adv hinten; (late) im Rückstand; **a long
way** ~ weit zurück; **in the car** ~ im
Wagen dahinter □ n (fam) Hintern m.
~**hand** adv im Rückstand

behold /bɪ'həʊld/ vt (pt/pp **beheld**) (liter)
sehen

beholden /bɪ'həʊldn/ a verbunden (**to**
dat)

beige /beɪʒ/ a beige

being /'biːɪŋ/ n Dasein nt; **living** ~ Lebe-
wesen nt; **come into** ~ entstehen

belated /bɪ'leɪtɪd/ a, -**ly** adv verspätet

belch /beltʃ/ vi rülpsen □ vt ~ **out** ausstoßen (smoke)

belfry /'belfrɪ/ n Glockenstube f; (tower)
Glockenturm m

Belgian /'beldʒən/ a belgisch □ n Belgi-
er(in) m(f)

Belgium /'beldʒəm/ n Belgien nt

belief /bɪ'liːf/ n Glaube m

believable /bɪ'liːvəbl/ a glaubhaft

believe /bɪ'liːv/ vt/i glauben (**s.o.** jdm; **in**
an + acc). ~**r** n (Relig) Gläubige(r) m/f

belittle /bɪ'lɪtl/ vt herabsetzen

bell /bel/ n Glocke f; (on door) Klingel f

belligerent /bɪ'lɪdʒərənt/ a Krieg
führend; (aggressive) streitlustig

bellow /'beləʊ/ vt/i brüllen

bellows /'beləʊz/ npl Blasebalg m

belly /'belɪ/ n Bauch m

belong /bɪ'lɒŋ/ vi gehören (**to** dat); (be
member) angehören (**to** dat). ~**ings** npl
Sachen pl

beloved /bɪ'lʌvɪd/ a geliebt □ n Geliebte(r)
m/f

below /bɪ'ləʊ/ prep unter (+ dat/acc)
□ adv unten; (Naut) unter Deck

belt /belt/ n Gürtel m; (area) Zone f;
(Techn) [Treib]riemen m □ vi (fam: rush)
rasen □ vt (fam: hit) hauen

bemused /bɪ'mjuːzd/ a verwirrt

bench /bentʃ/ n Bank f; (work-) Werkbank
f; **the B** ~ (Jur) ≈ die Richter pl

bend /bend/ n Biegung f; (in road) Kurve
f; **round the** ~ (fam) verrückt □ v (pt/pp
bent) □ vt biegen; beugen (arm, leg) □ vi
sich bücken; (thing:) sich biegen; (road:)
eine Biegung machen. ~ **down** vi sich
bücken. ~ **over** vi sich vornüberbeugen

beneath /bɪ'niːθ/ prep unter (+ dat/acc);
~ **him** (fig) unter seiner Würde; ~ **contempt** unter aller Würde □ adv darunter

benediction /benɪ'dɪkʃn/ n (Relig) Segen
m

benefactor /'benɪfæktə(r)/ *n* Wohltäter(in) *m(f)*

beneficial /benɪ'fɪʃl/ *a* nützlich

beneficiary /benɪ'fɪʃərɪ/ *n* Begünstigte(r) *m/f*

benefit /'benɪfɪt/ *n* Vorteil *m*; (*allowance*) Unterstützung *f*; (*insurance*) Leistung *f*; **sickness** ~ Krankengeld *nt* □ *v* (*pt/pp* -**fited**, *pres p* -**fiting**) □ *vt* nützen (+ *dat*) □ *vi* profitieren (**from** von)

benevolen|ce /bɪ'nevələns/ *n* Wohlwollen *nt*. ~**t** *a*, -**ly** *adv* wohlwollend

benign /bɪ'naɪn/ *a*, -**ly** *adv* gütig; (*Med*) gutartig

bent /bent/ *see* **bend** □ *a* ⟨*person*⟩ gebeugt; (*distorted*) verbogen; (*fam: dishonest*) korrupt; **be** ~ **on doing sth** darauf erpicht sein, etw zu tun □ *n* Hang *m*, Neigung *f* (**for** zu); **artistic** ~ künstlerische Ader *f*

be|queath /bɪ'kwiːð/ *vt* vermachen (**to** *dat*). ~**quest** /-'kwest/ *n* Vermächtnis *nt*

bereave|d /bɪ'riːvd/ *n* **the** ~**d** *pl* die Hinterbliebenen. ~**ment** *n* Trauerfall *m*; (*state*) Trauer *f*

bereft /bɪ'reft/ *a* ~ **of** beraubt (+ *gen*)

beret /'bereɪ/ *n* Baskenmütze *f*

Berne /bɜːn/ *n* Bern *nt*

berry /'berɪ/ *n* Beere *f*

berserk /bə'sɜːk/ *a* **go** ~ wild werden

berth /bɜːθ/ *n* (*in ship*) [Schlaf]koje *f*; (*ship's anchorage*) Liegeplatz *m*; **give a wide** ~ **to** (*fam*) einen großen Bogen machen um □ *vi* anlegen

beseech /bɪ'siːtʃ/ *vt* (*pt/pp* **beseeched** *or* **besought**) anflehen

beside /bɪ'saɪd/ *prep* neben (+ *dat/acc*); ~ **oneself** außer sich (*dat*)

besides /bɪ'saɪdz/ *prep* außer (+ *dat*) □ *adv* außerdem

besiege /bɪ'siːdʒ/ *vt* belagern

besought /bɪ'sɔːt/ *see* **beseech**

bespoke /bɪ'spəʊk/ *a* ⟨*suit*⟩ maßgeschneidert

best /best/ *a & n* beste(r,s); **the** ~ der/die/das Beste; **at** ~ bestenfalls; **all the** ~! alles Gute! **do one's** ~ sein Bestes tun; **the** ~ **part of a year** fast ein Jahr; **to the** ~ **of my knowledge** so viel ich weiß; **make the** ~ **of it** das Beste daraus machen □ *adv* am besten; **as** ~ **I could** so gut ich konnte. ~ '**man** *n* ≈ Trauzeuge *m*

bestow /bɪ'stəʊ/ *vt* schenken (**on** *dat*)

best'seller *n* Bestseller *m*

bet /bet/ *n* Wette *f* □ *v* (*pt/pp* **bet** *or* **betted**) □ *vt* ~ **s.o. £5** mit jdm um £5 wetten □ *vi* wetten; ~ **on** [Geld] setzen auf (+ *acc*)

betray /bɪ'treɪ/ *vt* verraten. ~**al** *n* Verrat *m*

better /'betə(r)/ *a* besser; **get** ~ sich bessern; (*after illness*) sich erholen □ *adv* besser; ~ **off** besser dran; ~ **not** lieber nicht; **all the** ~ umso besser; **the sooner the** ~ je eher, desto besser; **think** ~ **of sth** sich eines Besseren besinnen; **you'd** ~ **stay** du bleibst am besten hier □ *vt* verbessern; (*do better than*) übertreffen; ~ **oneself** sich verbessern

'**betting shop** *n* Wettbüro *nt*

between /bɪ'twiːn/ *prep* zwischen (+ *dat/acc*); ~ **you and me** unter uns; ~ **us** (*together*) zusammen □ *adv* **[in]** ~ dazwischen

beverage /'bevərɪdʒ/ *n* Getränk *nt*

bevy /'bevɪ/ *n* Schar *f*

beware /bɪ'weə(r)/ *vi* sich in Acht nehmen (**of** vor + *dat*); ~ **of the dog!** Vorsicht, bissiger Hund!

bewilder /bɪ'wɪldə(r)/ *vt* verwirren. ~**ment** *n* Verwirrung *f*

bewitch /bɪ'wɪtʃ/ *vt* verzaubern; (*fig*) bezaubern

beyond /bɪ'jɒnd/ *prep* über (+ *acc*) . . . hinaus; (*further*) weiter als; ~ **reach** außer Reichweite; ~ **doubt** ohne jeden Zweifel; **it's** ~ **me** (*fam*) das geht über meinen Horizont □ *adv* darüber hinaus

bias /'baɪəs/ *n* Voreingenommenheit *f*; (*preference*) Vorliebe *f*; (*Jur*) Befangenheit *f*; **cut on the** ~ schräg geschnitten □ *vt* (*pt/pp* **biased**) (*influence*) beeinflussen. ~**ed** *a* voreingenommen; (*Jur*) befangen

bib /bɪb/ *n* Lätzchen *nt*

Bible /'baɪbl/ *n* Bibel *f*

biblical /'bɪblɪkl/ *a* biblisch

bibliography /bɪblɪ'ɒɡrəfɪ/ *n* Bibliographie *f*

bicarbonate /baɪ'kɑːbəneɪt/ *n* ~ **of soda** doppeltkohlensaures Natron *nt*

bicker /'bɪkə(r)/ *vi* sich zanken

bicycle /'baɪsɪkl/ *n* Fahrrad *nt* □ *vi* mit dem Rad fahren

bid¹ /bɪd/ *n* Gebot *nt*; (*attempt*) Versuch *m* □ *vt/i* (*pt/pp* **bid**, *pres p* **bidding**) bieten (**for** auf + *acc*); (*Cards*) reizen

bid² *vt* (*pt* **bade** *or* **bid**, *pp* **bidden** *or* **bid**, *pres p* **bidding**) (*liter*) heißen; ~ **s.o. welcome** jdn willkommen heißen

bidder /'bɪdə(r)/ *n* Bieter(in) *m(f)*

bide /baɪd/ *vt* ~ **one's time** den richtigen Moment abwarten

biennial /baɪ'enɪəl/ *a* zweijährlich; (*lasting two years*) zweijährig

bier /bɪə(r)/ *n* [Toten]bahre *f*

bifocals /baɪ'fəʊklz/ *npl* **[pair of]** ~ Bifokalbrille *f*

big /bɪɡ/ *a* (**bigger, biggest**) groß □ *adv* **talk** ~ (*fam*) angeben

bigam|ist /'bɪgəmɪst/ n Bigamist m. **~y** n Bigamie f

big-'headed a (fam) eingebildet

bigot /'bɪgət/ n Eiferer m. **~ed** a engstirnig

'bigwig n (fam) hohes Tier nt

bike /baɪk/ n (fam) [Fahr]rad nt

bikini /bɪ'ki:nɪ/ n Bikini m

bilberry /'bɪlbərɪ/ n Heidelbeere f

bile /baɪl/ n Galle f

bilingual /baɪ'lɪŋgwəl/ a zweisprachig

bilious /'bɪljəs/ a (Med) **~ attack** verdorbener Magen m

bill¹ /bɪl/ n Rechnung f; (poster) Plakat nt; (Pol) Gesetzentwurf m; (Amer: note) Banknote f. **~ of exchange** Wechsel m □ vt eine Rechnung schicken (+ dat)

bill² n (break) Schnabel m

billet /'bɪlɪt/ n (Mil) Quartier m □ vt (pt/pp billeted) einquartieren (on bei)

'billfold n (Amer) Brieftasche f

billiards /'bɪljədz/ n Billard nt

billion /'bɪljən/ n (thousand million) Milliarde f; (million million) Billion f

billy-goat /'bɪlɪ-/ n Ziegenbock m

bin /bɪn/ n Mülleimer m; (for bread) Kasten m

bind /baɪnd/ vt (pt/pp bound) binden (to an + acc); (bandage) verbinden; (Jur) verpflichten; (cover the edge of) einfassen. **~ing** a verbindlich □ n Einband m; (braid) Borte f; (on ski) Bindung f

binge /bɪndʒ/ n (fam) go on the **~** eine Sauftour machen

binoculars /bɪ'nɒkjʊləz/ npl **[pair of] ~** Fernglas nt

bio|'chemistry /baɪəʊ-/ n Biochemie f. **~degradable** /-dɪ'greɪdəbl/ a biologisch abbaubar

biograph|er /baɪ'ɒgrəfə(r)/ n Biograph(in) m(f). **~y** n Biographie f

biological /baɪə'lɒdʒɪkl/ a biologisch

biolog|ist /baɪ'ɒlədʒɪst/ n Biologe m. **~y** n Biologie f

birch /bɜ:tʃ/ n Birke f; (whip) Rute f

bird /bɜ:d/ n Vogel m; (fam: girl) Mädchen nt; **kill two ~s with one stone** zwei Fliegen mit einer Klappe schlagen

Biro (P) /'baɪrəʊ/ n Kugelschreiber m

birth /bɜ:θ/ n Geburt f

birth: ~ certificate n Geburtsurkunde f. **~control** n Geburtenregelung f. **~day** n Geburtstag m. **~mark** n Muttermal nt. **~rate** n Geburtenziffer f. **~right** n Geburtsrecht nt

biscuit /'bɪskɪt/ n Keks m

bisect /baɪ'sekt/ vt halbieren

bishop /'bɪʃəp/ n Bischof m; (Chess) Läufer m

bit¹ /bɪt/ n Stückchen nt; (for horse) Gebiss nt; (Techn) Bohreinsatz m; **a ~** ein bisschen; **~ by ~** nach und nach; **a ~ of bread** ein bisschen Brot; **do one's ~** sein Teil tun

bit² see **bite**

bitch /bɪtʃ/ n Hündin f; (sl) Luder nt. **~y** a gehässig

bit|e /baɪt/ n Biss m; (mouthful) Bissen m; **[insect] ~** Stich m □ vt/i (pt bit, pp bitten) beißen; (insect:) stechen; kauen ⟨one's nails⟩. **~ing** a beißend

bitten /'bɪtn/ see **bite**

bitter /'bɪtə(r)/ a, **-ly** adv bitter; **cry ~ly** bitterlich weinen; **~ly cold** bitterkalt □ n bitteres Bier nt. **~ness** n Bitterkeit f

bitty /'bɪtɪ/ a zusammengestoppelt

bizarre /bɪ'zɑ:(r)/ a bizarr

blab /blæb/ vi (pt/pp blabbed) alles ausplaudern

black /blæk/ a (-er, -est) schwarz; **be ~ and blue** grün und blau sein □ n Schwarz nt; (person) Schwarze(r) m/f □ vt schwärzen; boykottieren (goods). **~ out** vt verdunkeln □ vi (lose consciousness) das Bewusstsein verlieren

black: ~berry n Brombeere f. **~bird** n Amsel f. **~board** n (Sch) [Wand]tafel f. **~currant** n schwarze Johannisbeere f

blacken vt/i schwärzen

black: ~ 'eye n blaues Auge nt. **B~ 'Forest** n Schwarzwald m. **~ 'ice** n Glatteis nt. **~leg** n Streikbrecher m. **~list** vt auf die schwarze Liste setzen. **~mail** n Erpressung f □ vt erpressen. **~mailer** n Erpresser(in) m(f). **~market** n schwarzer Markt m. **~out** n Verdunkelung f; **have a ~out** (Med) das Bewusstsein verlieren. **~ 'pudding** n Blutwurst f. **~smith** n [Huf]schmied m

bladder /'blædə(r)/ n (Anat) Blase f

blade /bleɪd/ n Klinge f; (of grass) Halm m

blame /bleɪm/ n Schuld f □ vt die Schuld geben (+ dat); **no one is to ~** keiner ist schuld daran. **~less** a schuldlos

blanch /blɑ:ntʃ/ vi blass werden □ vt (Culin) blanchieren

blancmange /blə'mɒnʒ/ n Pudding m

bland /blænd/ a (-er, -est) mild

blank /blæŋk/ a leer; (look) ausdruckslos □ n Lücke f; (cartridge) Platzpatrone f. **~ 'cheque** n Blankoscheck m

blanket /'blæŋkɪt/ n Decke f; **wet ~** (fam) Spielverderber(in) m(f)

blank 'verse n Blankvers m

blare /bleə(r)/ vt/i schmettern

blasé /'blɑːzeɪ/ a blasiert

blaspheme /blæs'fiːm/ vi lästern

blasphem|ous /'blæsfəməs/ a [gottes]-lästerlich. **~y** n [Gottes]lästerung f

blast /blɑːst/ n (gust) Luftstoß m; (sound) Schmettern nt; (of horn) Tuten nt □ vt sprengen □ int (sl) verdammt. **~ed** a (sl) verdammt

blast: ~furnace n Hochofen m. **~-off** n (of missile) Start m

blatant /'bleɪtənt/ a offensichtlich

blaze /bleɪz/ n Feuer nt □ vi brennen

blazer /'bleɪzə(r)/ n Blazer m

bleach /bliːtʃ/ n Bleichmittel nt □ vt/i bleichen

bleak /bliːk/ a (-er, -est) öde; (fig) trostlos

bleary-eyed /'blɪərɪ-/ a mit trüben/(on waking up) verschlafenen Augen

bleat /bliːt/ vi blöken; (goat:) meckern

bleed /bliːd/ v (pt/pp bled) □ vi bluten □ vt entlüften (radiator)

bleep /bliːp/ n Piepton m □ vi piepsen □ vt mit dem Piepser rufen. **~er** n Piepser m

blemish /'blemɪʃ/ n Makel m

blend /blend/ n Mischung f □ vt mischen □ vi sich vermischen. **~er** n (Culin) Mixer m

bless /bles/ vt segnen. **~ed** /'blesɪd/ a heilig; (sl) verflixt. **~ing** n Segen m

blew /bluː/ see **blow**¹

blight /blaɪt/ n (Bot) Brand m □ vt (spoil) vereiteln

blind /blaɪnd/ a blind; (corner) unübersichtlich; **~ man/woman** Blinde(r) m/f □ n [roller] ~ Rouleau n □ vt blenden

blind: ~ 'alley n Sackgasse f. **~fold** a & adv mit verbundenen Augen □ n Augenbinde f □ vt die Augen verbinden (+ dat). **~ly** adv blindlings. **~ness** n Blindheit f

blink /blɪŋk/ vi blinzeln; (light:) blinken

blinkers /'blɪŋkəz/ npl Scheuklappen pl

bliss /blɪs/ n Glückseligkeit f. **~ful** a glücklich

blister /'blɪstə(r)/ n (Med) Blase f □ vi (paint:) Blasen werfen

blitz /blɪts/ n Luftangriff m; (fam) Großaktion f

blizzard /'blɪzəd/ n Schneesturm m

bloated /'bləʊtɪd/ a aufgedunsen

blob /blɒb/ n Klecks m

bloc /blɒk/ n (Pol) Block m

block /blɒk/ n Block m; (of wood) Klotz m; (of flats) [Wohn]block m □ vt blockieren. **~ up** vt zustopfen

blockade /blɒ'keɪd/ n Blockade f □ vt blockieren

blockage /'blɒkɪdʒ/ n Verstopfung f

block: ~head n (fam) Dummkopf m. **~ 'letters** npl Blockschrift f

bloke /bləʊk/ n (fam) Kerl m

blonde /blɒnd/ a blond □ n Blondine f

blood /blʌd/ n Blut nt

blood: ~count n Blutbild nt. **~-curdling** a markerschütternd. **~ donor** n Blutspender m. **~ group** n Blutgruppe f. **~hound** n Bluthund m. **~-poisoning** n Blutvergiftung f. **~ pressure** n Blutdruck m. **~ relative** n Blutsverwandte(r) m/f. **~shed** n Blutvergießen nt. **~shot** a blutunterlaufen. **~ sports** npl Jagdsport m. **~-stained** a blutbefleckt. **~stream** n Blutbahn f. **~ test** n Blutprobe f. **~thirsty** a blutdürstig. **~ transfusion** n Blutübertragung f. **~-vessel** n Blutgefäß nt

bloody /'blʌdɪ/ a (-ier, -iest) blutig; (sl) verdammt. **~'minded** a (sl) stur

bloom /bluːm/ n Blüte f □ vi blühen

bloom|er /'bluːmə(r)/ n (fam) Schnitzer m. **~ing** a (fam) verdammt

blossom /'blɒsəm/ n Blüte f □ vi blühen. **~ out** vi (fig) aufblühen

blot /blɒt/ n [Tinten]klecks m; (fig) Fleck m □ vt (pt/pp blotted) löschen. **~ out** vt (fig) auslöschen

blotch /blɒtʃ/ n Fleck m. **~y** a fleckig

'blotting-paper n Löschpapier nt

blouse /blaʊz/ n Bluse f

blow¹ /bləʊ/ n Schlag m

blow² v (pt blew, pp blown) □ vt blasen; (fam: squander) verpulvern; **~ one's nose** sich (dat) die Nase putzen □ vi blasen; (fuse:) durchbrennen. **~ away** vt wegblasen □ vi wegfliegen. **~ down** vt umwehen □ vi umfallen. **~ out** vt (extinguish) ausblasen. **~ over** vi umfallen; (fig: die down) vorübergehen. **~ up** vt (inflate) aufblasen; (enlarge) vergrößern; (shatter by explosion) sprengen □ vi explodieren

blow: ~-dry vt föhnen. **~fly** n Schmeißfliege f. **~lamp** n Lötlampe f

blown /bləʊn/ see **blow**²

'blowtorch n (Amer) Lötlampe f

blowy /'bləʊɪ/ a windig

bludgeon /'blʌdʒn/ vt (fig) zwingen

blue /bluː/ a (-r, -st) blau; **feel ~** deprimiert sein □ n Blau nt; **have the ~s** deprimiert sein; **out of the ~** aus heiterem Himmel

blue: ~bell n Sternhyazinthe f. **~berry** n Heidelbeere f. **~bottle** n Schmeißfliege f. **~ film** n Pornofilm m. **~print** n (fig) Entwurf m

bluff /blʌf/ n Bluff m □ vi bluffen

blunder /'blʌndə(r)/ n Schnitzer m □ vi einen Schnitzer machen

blunt /blʌnt/ a stumpf; ⟨person⟩ geradeheraus. **~ly** adv unverblümt, geradeheraus

blur /blɜ:(r)/ n it's all a ~ alles ist verschwommen □ vt (pt/pp **blurred**) verschwommen machen; **~red** verschwommen

blurb /blɜ:b/ n Klappentext m

blurt /blɜ:t/ vt ~ **out** herausplatzen mit

blush /blʌʃ/ n Erröten nt □ vi erröten

bluster /'blʌstə(r)/ n Großtuerei f. **~y** a windig

boar /bɔ:(r)/ n Eber m

board /bɔ:d/ n Brett nt; ⟨for notices⟩ schwarzes Brett nt; ⟨committee⟩ Ausschuss m; ⟨of directors⟩ Vorstand m; on ~ an Bord; **full** ~ Vollpension f; ~ **and lodging** Unterkunft und Verpflegung pl; **go by the** ~ ⟨fam⟩ unter den Tisch fallen □ vt einsteigen in (+ acc); ⟨Naut, Aviat⟩ besteigen □ vi an Bord gehen; ~ **with** in Pension wohnen bei. ~ **up** vt mit Brettern verschlagen

boarder /'bɔ:də(r)/ n Pensionsgast m; ⟨Sch⟩ Internatsschüler(in) m(f)

board: **~-game** n Brettspiel nt. **~ing-house** n Pension f. **~ing-school** n Internat nt

boast /bəust/ vt sich rühmen (+ gen) □ vi prahlen (**about** mit). **~ful** a, **-ly** adv prahlerisch

boat /bəut/ n Boot nt; ⟨ship⟩ Schiff nt. **~er** n ⟨hat⟩ flacher Strohhut m

bob /bɒb/ n Bubikopf m □ vi (pt/pp **bobbed**) ⟨curtsy⟩ knicksen; ~ **up and down** sich auf und ab bewegen

bobbin /'bɒbɪn/ n Spule f

'bob-sleigh n Bob m

bode /bəud/ vi ~ **well/ill** etwas/nichts Gutes verheißen

bodice /'bɒdɪs/ n Mieder nt

bodily /'bɒdɪlɪ/ a körperlich □ adv ⟨forcibly⟩ mit Gewalt

body /'bɒdɪ/ n Körper m; ⟨corpse⟩ Leiche f; ⟨corporation⟩ Körperschaft f; **the main** ~ der Hauptanteil. **~guard** n Leibwächter m. **~work** n ⟨Auto⟩ Karosserie f

bog /bɒg/ n Sumpf m □ vt (pt/pp **bogged**) **get ~ged down** stecken bleiben

boggle /'bɒgl/ vi **the mind ~s** es ist kaum vorstellbar

bogus /'bəugəs/ a falsch

boil¹ /bɔɪl/ n Furunkel m

boil² n **bring/come to the** ~ zum Kochen bringen/kommen □ vt/i kochen; **~ed potatoes** Salzkartoffeln pl. ~ **down to** ⟨fig⟩ hinauslaufen (**to** auf + acc). ~ **over** vi überkochen. ~ **up** vt aufkochen

boiler /'bɔɪlə(r)/ n Heizkessel m. ~ **suit** n Overall m

'boiling point n Siedepunkt m

boisterous /'bɔɪstərəs/ a übermütig

bold /bəuld/ a (-er, -est), **-ly** adv kühn; ⟨Typ⟩ fett. **~ness** n Kühnheit f

bollard /'bɒlɑ:d/ n Poller m

bolster /'bəulstə(r)/ n Nackenrolle f □ vt ~ **up** Mut machen (+ dat)

bolt /bəult/ n Riegel m; ⟨Techn⟩ Bolzen m; **nuts and ~s** Schrauben und Muttern pl □ vt schrauben (**to** an + acc); verriegeln ⟨door⟩; hinunterschlingen ⟨food⟩ □ vi abhauen; ⟨horse:⟩ durchgehen □ adv ~ **upright** kerzengerade

bomb /bɒm/ n Bombe f □ vt bombardieren

bombard /bɒm'bɑ:d/ vt beschießen; ⟨fig⟩ bombardieren

bombastic /bɒm'bæstɪk/ a bombastisch

bomb|er /'bɒmə(r)/ n ⟨Aviat⟩ Bomber m; ⟨person⟩ Bombenleger(in) m(f). **~shell** n **be a ~shell** ⟨fig⟩ wie eine Bombe einschlagen

bond /bɒnd/ n ⟨fig⟩ Band nt; ⟨Comm⟩ Obligation f; **be in** ~ unter Zollverschluss stehen

bondage /'bɒndɪdʒ/ n ⟨fig⟩ Sklaverei f

bone /bəun/ n Knochen m; ⟨of fish⟩ Gräte f □ vt von den Knochen lösen ⟨meat⟩; entgräten ⟨fish⟩. **~-'dry** a knochentrocken

bonfire /'bɒn-/ n Gartenfeuer nt; ⟨celebratory⟩ Freudenfeuer nt

bonnet /'bɒnɪt/ n Haube f

bonus /'bəunəs/ n Prämie f; ⟨gratuity⟩ Gratifikation f; ⟨fig⟩ Plus nt

bony /'bəunɪ/ a (-ier, -iest) knochig; ⟨fish⟩ grätig

boo /bu:/ int buh! □ vt ausbuhen □ vi buhen

boob /bu:b/ n ⟨fam: mistake⟩ Schnitzer m □ vi ⟨fam⟩ einen Schnitzer machen

book /bʊk/ n Buch nt; ⟨of tickets⟩ Heft nt; **keep the ~s** ⟨Comm⟩ die Bücher führen □ vt/i buchen; ⟨reserve⟩ [vor]bestellen; ⟨for offence⟩ aufschreiben. **~able** /-əbl/ a im Vorverkauf erhältlich

book: **~case** n Bücherregal nt. **~-ends** npl Buchstützen pl. **~ing-office** n Fahrkartenschalter m. **~keeping** n Buchführung f. **~let** n Broschüre f. **~maker** n Buchmacher m. **~mark** n Lesezeichen nt. **~seller** n Buchhändler(in) m(f). **~shop** n Buchhandlung f. **~stall** n Bücherstand m. **~worm** n Bücherwurm m

boom /bu:m/ n ⟨Comm⟩ Hochkonjunktur f; ⟨upturn⟩ Aufschwung m □ vi dröhnen; ⟨fig⟩ blühen

boon /bu:n/ n Segen m

boor /bʊə(r)/ n Flegel m. **~ish** a flegelhaft

boost /buːst/ n Auftrieb m □ vt Auftrieb geben (+ dat). ~er n (Med) Nachimpfung f

boot /buːt/ n Stiefel m; (Auto) Kofferraum m

booth /buːð/ n Bude f; (cubicle) Kabine f

booty /ˈbuːtɪ/ n Beute f

booze /buːz/ n (fam) Alkohol m □ vi (fam) saufen

border /ˈbɔːdə(r)/ n Rand m; (frontier) Grenze f; (in garden) Rabatte f □ vi ~ on grenzen an (+ acc). ~line n Grenzlinie f. ~line case n Grenzfall m

bore¹ /bɔː(r)/ see bear²

bore² vt/i (Techn) bohren

bor|e³ n (of gun) Kaliber nt; (person) langweiliger Mensch m; (thing) langweilige Sache f □ vt langweilen; be ~ed sich langweilen. ~edom n Langeweile f. ~ing a langweilig

born /bɔːn/ pp be ~ geboren werden □ a geboren

borne /bɔːn/ see bear²

borough /ˈbʌrə/ n Stadtgemeinde f

borrow /ˈbɒrəʊ/ vt [sich (dat)] borgen od leihen (from von)

bosom /ˈbʊzm/ n Busen m

boss /bɒs/ n (fam) Chef m □ vt herumkommandieren. ~y a herrschsüchtig

botanical /bəˈtænɪkl/ a botanisch

botan|ist /ˈbɒtənɪst/ n Botaniker(in) m(f). ~y n Botanik f

botch /bɒtʃ/ vt verpfuschen

both /bəʊθ/ a & pron beide; ~[of] the children beide Kinder; ~ of them beide [von ihnen] □ adv ~ men and women sowohl Männer als auch Frauen

bother /ˈbɒðə(r)/ n Mühe f; (minor trouble) Ärger m □ int (fam) verflixt! □ vt belästigen; (disturb) stören □ vi sich kümmern (about um); don't ~ nicht nötig

bottle /ˈbɒtl/ n Flasche f □ vt auf Flaschen abfüllen; (preserve) einmachen. ~ up vt (fig) in sich (dat) aufstauen

bottle: ~neck n (fig) Engpass m. ~opener n Flaschenöffner m

bottom /ˈbɒtəm/ a unterste(r,s) □ n (of container) Boden m; (of river) Grund m; (of page, hill) Fuß m; (buttocks) Hintern m; at the ~ unten; get to the ~ of sth (fig) hinter etw (acc) kommen. ~less a bodenlos

bough /baʊ/ n Ast m

bought /bɔːt/ see buy

boulder /ˈbəʊldə(r)/ n Felsblock m

bounce /baʊns/ vi [auf]springen; (cheque:) (fam) nicht gedeckt sein □ vt aufspringen lassen (ball)

bouncer /ˈbaʊnsə(r)/ n (fam) Rausschmeißer m

bouncing /ˈbaʊnsɪŋ/ a ~ baby strammer Säugling m

bound¹ /baʊnd/ n Sprung m □ vi springen

bound² see bind □ a ~ for (ship) mit Kurs auf (+ acc); be ~ to do sth etw bestimmt machen; (obliged) verpflichtet sein, etw zu machen

boundary /ˈbaʊndərɪ/ n Grenze f

'boundless a grenzenlos

bounds /baʊndz/ npl (fig) Grenzen pl; out of ~ verboten

bouquet /bʊˈkeɪ/ n [Blumen]strauß m; (of wine) Bukett nt

bourgeois /ˈbʊəʒwɑː/ a (pej) spießbürgerlich

bout /baʊt/ n (Med) Anfall m; (Sport) Kampf m

bow¹ /bəʊ/ n (weapon & Mus) Bogen m; (knot) Schleife f

bow² /baʊ/ n Verbeugung f □ vi sich verbeugen □ vt neigen (head)

bow³ /baʊ/ n (Naut) Bug m

bowel /ˈbaʊəl/ n Darm m; ~ movement Stuhlgang m. ~s pl Eingeweide pl; (digestion) Verdauung f

bowl¹ /bəʊl/ n Schüssel f; (shallow) Schale f; (of pipe) Kopf m; (of spoon) Schöpfteil m

bowl² n (ball) Kugel f □ vt/i werfen. ~ over vt umwerfen

bow-legged /bəʊˈlegd/ a O-beinig

bowler¹ /ˈbəʊlə(r)/ n (Sport) Werfer m

bowler² n ~ [hat] Melone f

bowling /ˈbəʊlɪŋ/ n Kegeln nt. ~-alley n Kegelbahn f

bowls /bəʊlz/ n Bowlsspiel nt

bow-'tie /bəʊ-/ n Fliege f

box¹ /bɒks/ n Schachtel f; (wooden) Kiste f; (cardboard) Karton m; (Theat) Loge f

box² vt/i (Sport) boxen; ~ s.o.'s ears jdn ohrfeigen

box|er /ˈbɒksə(r)/ n Boxer m. ~ing n Boxen nt. B~ing Day n zweiter Weihnachtstag m

box: ~-office n (Theat) Kasse f. ~-room n Abstellraum m

boy /bɔɪ/ n Junge m

boycott /ˈbɔɪkɒt/ n Boykott m □ vt boykottieren

boy: ~friend n Freund m. ~ish a jungenhaft

bra /brɑː/ n BH m

brace /breɪs/ n Strebe f, Stütze f; (dental) Zahnspange f; ~s npl Hosenträger mpl □ vt ~ oneself sich stemmen (against gegen); (fig) sich gefasst machen (for auf + acc)

bracelet /'breɪslɪt/ n Armband nt

bracing /'breɪsɪŋ/ a stärkend

bracken /'brækn/ n Farnkraut nt

bracket /'brækɪt/ n Konsole f; (group) Gruppe f; **round/square ~s** (Typ) runde/eckige Klammern □ vt einklammern

brag /bræg/ vi (pt/pp **bragged**) prahlen (**about** mit)

braid /breɪd/ n Borte f

braille /breɪl/ n Blindenschrift f

brain /breɪn/ n Gehirn nt; **~s** (fig) Intelligenz f

brain: **~child** n geistiges Produkt nt. **~less** a dumm. **~wash** vt einer Gehirnwäsche unterziehen. **~wave** n Geistesblitz m

brainy /'breɪnɪ/ a (-ier, -iest) klug

braise /breɪz/ vt schmoren

brake /breɪk/ n Bremse f □ vt/i bremsen. **~light** n Bremslicht nt

bramble /'bræmbl/ n Brombeerstrauch m

bran /bræn/ n Kleie f

branch /brɑ:ntʃ/ n Ast m; (fig) Zweig m; (Comm) Zweigstelle f; (shop) Filiale f □ vi sich gabeln. **~ off** vi abzweigen. **~ out** vi **~ out into** sich verlegen auf (+ acc)

brand /brænd/ n Marke f; (on animal) Brandzeichen nt □ vt mit dem Brandeisen zeichnen (animal); (fig) brandmarken

brandish /'brændɪʃ/ vt schwingen

brand-'new a nagelneu

brandy /'brændɪ/ n Weinbrand m

brash /bræʃ/ a nassforsch

brass /brɑ:s/ n Messing nt; (Mus) Blech nt; **get down to ~ tacks** (fam) zur Sache kommen; **top ~** (fam) hohe Tiere pl. **~ band** n Blaskapelle f

brassiere /'bræzɪə(r)/ n Büstenhalter m

brassy /'brɑ:sɪ/ a (-ier, -iest) (fam) ordinär

brat /bræt/ n (pej) Balg nt

bravado /brə'vɑ:dəʊ/ n Forschheit f

brave /breɪv/ a (-r, -st), -ly adv tapfer □ vt die Stirn bieten (+ dat). **~ry** /-ərɪ/ n Tapferkeit f

bravo /brɑ:'vəʊ/ int bravo!

brawl /brɔ:l/ n Schlägerei f □ vi sich schlagen

brawn /brɔ:n/ n (Culin) Sülze f

brawny /'brɔ:nɪ/ a muskulös

bray /breɪ/ vi iahen

brazen /'breɪzn/ a unverschämt

brazier /'breɪzɪə(r)/ n Kohlenbecken nt

Brazil /brə'zɪl/ n Brasilien nt. **~ian** a brasilianisch. **~ nut** n Paranuss f

breach /bri:tʃ/ n Bruch m; (Mil & fig) Bresche f; **~ of contract** Vertragsbruch m □ vt durchbrechen; brechen (contract)

bread /bred/ n Brot nt; **slice of ~ and butter** Butterbrot nt

bread: ~crumbs npl Brotkrümel pl; (Culin) Paniermehl nt. **~line** n **to be on the ~line** gerade genug zum Leben haben

breadth /bredθ/ n Breite f

'bread-winner n Brotverdiener m

break /breɪk/ n Bruch m; (interval) Pause f; (interruption) Unterbrechung f; (fam: chance) Chance f □ v (pt **broke**, pp **broken**) □ vt brechen; (smash) zerbrechen; (damage) kaputtmachen (fam); (interrupt) unterbrechen; **~ one's arm** sich (dat) den Arm brechen □ vi brechen; (day:) anbrechen; (storm:) losbrechen; (thing:) kaputtgehen (fam); (rope, thread:) reißen; (news:) bekannt werden; **his voice is ~ing** er ist im Stimmbruch. **~ away** vi sich losreißen/(fig) sich absetzen (from von). **~ down** vi zusammenbrechen; (Techn) eine Panne haben; (negotiations:) scheitern □ vt aufbrechen (door); aufgliedern (figures). **~ in** vi einbrechen. **~ off** vt/i abbrechen; lösen (engagement). **~ out** vi ausbrechen. **~ up** vt zerbrechen □ vi zerbrechen; (crowd:) sich zerstreuen; (marriage, couple:) auseinander gehen; (Sch) Ferien bekommen

break|able /'breɪkəbl/ a zerbrechlich. **~age** /-ɪdʒ/ n Bruch m. **~down** n (Techn) Panne f; (Med) Zusammenbruch m; (of figures) Aufgliederung f. **~er** n (wave) Brecher m

breakfast /'brekfəst/ n Frühstück nt

break: ~through n Durchbruch m. **~water** n Buhne f

breast /brest/ n Brust f. **~bone** n Brustbein nt. **~feed** vt stillen. **~stroke** n Brustschwimmen nt

breath /breθ/ n Atem m; **out of ~** außer Atem; **under one's ~** vor sich (acc) hin

breathalyse /'breθəlaɪz/ vt ins Röhrchen blasen lassen. **~r (P)** n Röhrchen nt. **~r test** n Alcotest (P) m

breathe /bri:ð/ vt/i atmen. **~ in** vt/i einatmen. **~ out** vt/i ausatmen

breath|er /'bri:ðə(r)/ n Atempause f. **~ing** n Atmen nt

breath /breθ/: **~less** a atemlos. **~taking** a atemberaubend. **~ test** n Alcotest (P) m

bred /bred/ see **breed**

breeches /'brɪtʃɪz/ npl Kniehose f; (for riding) Reithose f

breed /bri:d/ n Rasse f □ v (pt/pp **bred**) □ vt züchten; (give rise to) erzeugen □ vi sich vermehren. **~er** *n* Züchter *m*. **~ing** *n* Zucht *f*; (*fig*) [gute] Lebensart *f*

breez|e /briːz/ *n* Lüftchen *nt*; (*Naut*) Brise *f*. **~y a** [leicht] windig

brevity /'brevətɪ/ *n* Kürze *f*

brew /bruː/ *n* Gebräu *nt* □ *vt* brauen; kochen ⟨*tea*⟩ □ *vi* (*fig*) sich zusammenbrauen. **~er** *n* Brauer *m*. **~ery** *n* Brauerei *f*

bribe /braɪb/ *n* (*money*) Bestechungsgeld *nt* □ *vt* bestechen. **~ry** /-ərɪ/ *n* Bestechung *f*

brick /brɪk/ *n* Ziegelstein *m*, Backstein *m* □ *vt* **~ up** zumauern

'bricklayer *n* Maurer *m*

bridal /'braɪdl/ *a* Braut-

bride /braɪd/ *n* Braut *f*. **~groom** *n* Bräutigam *m*. **~smaid** *n* Brautjungfer *f*

bridge¹ /brɪdʒ/ *n* Brücke *f*; (*of nose*) Nasenrücken *m*; (*of spectacles*) Steg *m* □ *vt* (*fig*) überbrücken

bridge² *n* (*Cards*) Bridge *nt*

bridle /'braɪdl/ *n* Zaum *m*. **~-path** *n* Reitweg *m*

brief¹ /briːf/ *a* (-er, -est) kurz; **be ~** ⟨*person:*⟩ sich kurz fassen

brief² *n* Instruktionen *pl*; (*Jur: case*) Mandat *nt* □ *vt* Instruktionen geben (+ *dat*); (*Jur*) beauftragen. **~case** *n* Aktentasche *f*

brief|ing /'briːfɪŋ/ *n* Informationsgespräch *nt*. **~ly** *adv* kurz. **~ness** *n* Kürze *f*

briefs /briːfs/ *npl* Slip *m*

brigad|e /brɪ'geɪd/ *n* Brigade *f*. **~ier** /-ə'dɪə(r)/ *n* Brigadegeneral *m*

bright /braɪt/ *a* (-er, -est), **-ly** *adv* hell; ⟨*day*⟩ heiter; **~ red** hellrot

bright|en /'braɪtn/ *v* **~en [up]** □ *vt* aufheitern □ *vi* sich aufheitern. **~ness** *n* Helligkeit *f*

brilliance /'brɪljəns/ *n* Glanz *m*; (*of person*) Genialität *f*

brilliant /'brɪljənt/ *a*, **-ly** *adv* glänzend; ⟨*person*⟩ genial

brim /brɪm/ *n* Rand *m*; (*of hat*) Krempe *f* □ *vi* (*pt/pp* brimmed) **~ over** überfließen

brine /braɪn/ *n* Salzwasser *nt*; (*Culin*) [Salz]lake *f*

bring /brɪŋ/ *vt* (*pt/pp* brought) bringen; **~ them with you** bring sie mit; **I can't b~ myself to do it** ich bringe es nicht fertig. **~ about** *vt* verursachen. **~ along** *vt* mitbringen. **~ back** *vt* zurückbringen. **~ down** *vt* herunterbringen; senken ⟨*price*⟩. **~ off** *vt* vollbringen. **~ on** *vt* ⟨*cause*⟩ verursachen. **~ out** *vt* herausbringen. **~ round** *vt* vorbeibringen; ⟨*persuade*⟩ überreden, wieder zum Bewusstsein bringen ⟨*unconscious person*⟩. **~ up** *vt* heraufbringen; (*vomit*) erbrechen; aufziehen ⟨*children*⟩; erwähnen ⟨*question*⟩

brink /brɪŋk/ *n* Rand *m*

brisk /brɪsk/ *a* (-er, -est,) **-ly** *adv* lebhaft; (*quick*) schnell

brist|le /'brɪsl/ *n* Borste *f*. **~ly** *a* borstig

Brit|ain /'brɪtn/ *n* Großbritannien *nt*. **~ish** *a* britisch; **the ~ish** die Briten *pl*. **~on** *n* Brite *m*/Britin *f*

Brittany /'brɪtənɪ/ *n* die Bretagne

brittle /'brɪtl/ *a* brüchig, spröde

broach /brəʊtʃ/ *vt* anzapfen; anschneiden ⟨*subject*⟩

broad /brɔːd/ *a* (-er, -est) breit; ⟨*hint*⟩ deutlich; **in ~ daylight** am helllichten Tag. **~ beans** *npl* dicke Bohnen *pl*

'broadcast *n* Sendung *f* □ *vt/i* (*pt/pp* -cast) senden. **~er** *n* Rundfunk- und Fernsehpersönlichkeit *f*. **~ing** *n* Funk und Fernsehen *pl*

broaden /'brɔːdn/ *vt* verbreitern; (*fig*) erweitern □ *vi* sich verbreitern

broadly /'brɔːdlɪ/ *adv* breit; **~ speaking** allgemein gesagt

broad'minded *a* tolerant

brocade /brə'keɪd/ *n* Brokat *m*

broccoli /'brɒkəlɪ/ *n* *inv* Brokkoli *pl*

brochure /'brəʊʃə(r)/ *n* Broschüre *f*

brogue /brəʊg/ *n* (*shoe*) Wanderschuh *m*; **Irish ~** irischer Akzent *m*

broke /brəʊk/ *see* **break** □ *a* (*fam*) pleite

broken /'brəʊkn/ *see* **break** □ *a* zerbrochen, (*fam*) kaputt; **~ English** gebrochenes Englisch *nt*. **~-hearted** *a* untröstlich

broker /'brəʊkə(r)/ *n* Makler *m*

brolly /'brɒlɪ/ *n* (*fam*) Schirm *m*

bronchitis /brɒŋ'kaɪtɪs/ *n* Bronchitis *f*

bronze /brɒnz/ *n* Bronze *f*

brooch /brəʊtʃ/ *n* Brosche *f*

brood /bruːd/ *n* Brut *f* □ *vi* brüten; (*fig*) grübeln

brook¹ /brʊk/ *n* Bach *m*

brook² *vt* dulden

broom /bruːm/ *n* Besen *m*; (*Bot*) Ginster *m*. **~stick** *n* Besenstiel *m*

broth /brɒθ/ *n* Brühe *f*

brothel /'brɒθl/ *n* Bordell *nt*

brother /'brʌðə(r)/ *n* Bruder *m*

brother: ~-in-law *n* (*pl* **-s-in-law**) Schwager *m*. **~ly** *a* brüderlich

brought /brɔːt/ *see* **bring**

brow /braʊ/ *n* Augenbraue *f*; (*forehead*) Stirn *f*; (*of hill*) [Berg]kuppe *f*

'browbeat *vt* (*pt* -beat, *pp* -beaten) einschüchtern

brown /braun/ *a* (-er, -est) braun; ~ 'paper Packpapier *nt* □ *n* Braun *nt* □ *vt* bräunen □ *vi* braun werden

Brownie /'brauni/ *n* Wichtel *m*

browse /brauz/ *vi* (*read*) schmökern; (*in shop*) sich umsehen

bruise /bru:z/ *n* blauer Fleck *m* □ *vt* beschädigen ⟨*fruit*⟩; ~ one's arm sich ⟨*dat*⟩ den Arm quetschen

brunch /brʌntʃ/ *n* Brunch *m*

brunette /bru:'net/ *n* Brünette *f*

Brunswick /'brʌnzwɪk/ *n* Braunschweig *nt*

brunt /brʌnt/ *n* the ~ of die volle Wucht (+ *gen*)

brush /brʌʃ/ *n* Bürste *f*; (*with handle*) Handfeger *m*; (*for paint, pastry*) Pinsel *m*; (*bushes*) Unterholz *nt*; ⟨*fig: conflict*⟩ Zusammenstoß *m* □ *vt* bürsten putzen ⟨*teeth*⟩; ~ against streifen [gegen]; ~ aside (*fig*) abtun. ~ off *vt* abbürsten; ⟨*reject*⟩ zurückweisen. ~ up *vt/i* (*fig*) ~ up [on] auffrischen

brusque /brusk/ *a*, -ly *adv* brüsk

Brussels /'brʌslz/ *n* Brüssel *nt*. ~ sprouts *npl* Rosenkohl *m*

brutal /'bru:tl/ *a*, -ly *adv* brutal. ~ity /-'tæləti/ *n* Brutalität *f*

brute /bru:t/ *n* Unmensch *m*. ~ force *n* rohe Gewalt *f*

B.Sc. *abbr of* **Bachelor of Science**

bubble /'bʌbl/ *n* [Luft]blase *f* □ *vi* sprudeln

buck[1] /bʌk/ *n* (*deer & Gym*) Bock *m*; (*rabbit*) Rammler *m* □ *vi* ⟨*horse:*⟩ bocken. ~ up *vi* (*fam*) sich aufheitern; (*hurry*) sich beeilen

buck[2] *n* (*Amer, fam*) Dollar *m*

buck[3] *n* pass the ~ die Verantwortung abschieben

bucket /'bʌkɪt/ *n* Eimer *m*

buckle /'bʌkl/ *n* Schnalle *f* □ *vt* zuschnallen □ *vi* sich verbiegen

bud /bʌd/ *n* Knospe *f* □ *vi* (*pt/pp* budded) knospen

Buddhis|m /'bʊdɪzm/ *n* Buddhismus *m*. ~t *a* buddhistisch □ *n* Buddhist(in) *m(f)*

buddy /'bʌdɪ/ *n* (*fam*) Freund *m*

budge /bʌdʒ/ *vt* bewegen □ *vi* sich [von der Stelle] rühren

budgerigar /'bʌdʒərɪgɑ:(r)/ *n* Wellensittich *m*

budget /'bʌdʒɪt/ *n* Budget *nt*; (*Pol*) Haushaltsplan *m*; (*money available*) Etat *m* □ *vi* (*pt/pp* budgeted) ~ for sth etw einkalkulieren

buff /bʌf/ *a* (*colour*) sandfarben □ *n* Sandfarbe *f*; (*Amer, fam*) Fan *m* □ *vt* polieren

buffalo /'bʌfələʊ/ *n* (*inv or pl* -es) Büffel *m*

buffer /'bʌfə(r)/ *n* (*Rail*) Puffer *m*; old ~ (*fam*) alter Knacker *m*; ~ zone Pufferzone *f*

buffet[1] /'bʊfeɪ/ *n* Büfett *nt*; (*on station*) Imbissstube *f*

buffet[2] /'bʌfɪt/ *vt* (*pt/pp* buffeted) hin und her werfen

buffoon /bə'fu:n/ *n* Narr *m*

bug /bʌg/ *n* Wanze *f*; ⟨*fam: virus*⟩ Bazillus *m*; ⟨*fam: device*⟩ Abhörgerät *nt*, (*fam*) Wanze *f* □ *vt* (*pt/pp* bugged) bauen. ~ on *vt* anwanzen ⟨*room*⟩; abhören ⟨*telephone*⟩; (*Amer: annoy*) ärgern

buggy /'bʌgɪ/ *n* [Kinder]sportwagen *m*

bugle /'bju:gl/ *n* Signalhorn *nt*

build /bɪld/ *n* (*of person*) Körperbau *m* □ *vt/i* (*pt/pp* built) bauen. ~ on *vt* anbauen (to an + *acc*). ~ up *vt* aufbauen □ *vi* zunehmen; ⟨*traffic:*⟩ sich stauen

builder /'bɪldə(r)/ *n* Bauunternehmer *m*

building /'bɪldɪŋ/ *n* Gebäude *nt*. ~ site *n* Baustelle *f*. ~ society *n* Bausparkasse *f*

built /bɪlt/ *see* **build**. ~-in *a* eingebaut. ~-in 'cupboard *n* Einbauschrank *m*. ~-up area *n* bebautes Gebiet *nt*; (*Auto*) geschlossene Ortschaft *f*

bulb /bʌlb/ *n* [Blumen]zwiebel *f*; (*Electr*) [Glüh]birne *f*

bulbous /'bʌlbəs/ *a* bauchig

Bulgaria /bʌl'geərɪə/ *n* Bulgarien *nt*

bulg|e /bʌldʒ/ *n* Ausbauchung *f* □ *vi* sich ausbauchen. ~ing *a* prall; ⟨*eyes*⟩ hervorquellend; ~ing with prall gefüllt mit

bulk /bʌlk/ *n* Masse *f*; (*greater part*) Hauptteil *m*; in ~ en gros; (*loose*) lose. ~y *a* sperrig; (*large*) massig

bull /bʊl/ *n* Bulle *m*, Stier *m*

'bulldog *n* Bulldogge *f*

bulldozer /'bʊldəʊzə(r)/ *n* Planierraupe *f*

bullet /'bʊlɪt/ *n* Kugel *f*

bulletin /'bʊlɪtɪn/ *n* Bulletin *nt*

'bullet-proof *a* kugelsicher

'bullfight *n* Stierkampf *m*. ~er *n* Stierkämpfer *m*

'bullfinch *n* Dompfaff *m*

bullion /'bʊlɪən/ *n* gold ~ Barrengold *nt*

bullock /'bʊlək/ *n* Ochse *m*

bull: ~ring *n* Stierkampfarena *f*. ~'s-eye *n* score a ~'s-eye ins Schwarze treffen

bully /'bʊlɪ/ *n* Tyrann *m* □ *vt* tyrannisieren

bum[1] /bʌm/ *n* (*sl*) Hintern *m*

bum[2] *n* (*Amer, fam*) Landstreicher *m*

bumble-bee /'bʌmbl-/ *n* Hummel *f*

bump /bʌmp/ n Bums m; (swelling) Beule f; (in road) holperige Stelle f ▫ vt stoßen; ~ **into** stoßen gegen; (meet) zufällig treffen. ~ **off** vt (fam) um die Ecke bringen

bumper /'bʌmpə(r)/ a Rekord- ▫ n (Auto) Stoßstange f

bumpkin /'bʌmpkɪn/ n country ~ Tölpel m

bumptious /'bʌmpʃəs/ a aufgeblasen

bumpy /'bʌmpɪ/ a holperig

bun /bʌn/ n Milchbrötchen nt; (hair) [Haar]knoten m

bunch /bʌntʃ/ n (of flowers) Strauß m; (of radishes, keys) Bund m; (of people) Gruppe f; ~ **of grapes** [ganze] Weintraube f

bundle /'bʌndl/ n Bündel nt ▫ vt ~ [up] bündeln

bung /bʌŋ/ vt (fam) (throw) schmeißen. ~ **up** vt (fam) verstopfen

bungalow /'bʌŋgələʊ/ n Bungalow m

bungle /'bʌŋgl/ vt verpfuschen

bunion /'bʌnjən/ n (Med) Ballen m

bunk /bʌŋk/ n [Schlaf]koje f. ~**-beds** npl Etagenbett nt

bunker /'bʌŋkə(r)/ n Bunker m

bunkum /'bʌŋkəm/ n Quatsch m

bunny /'bʌnɪ/ n (fam) Kaninchen nt

buoy /bɔɪ/ n Boje f. ~ **up** vt (fig) stärken

buoyan|cy /'bɔɪənsɪ/ n Auftrieb m. ~**t** a be ~t schwimmen; (water:) gut tragen

burden /'bɜːdn/ n Last f ▫ vt belasten. ~**some** /-səm/ a lästig

bureau /'bjʊərəʊ/ n (pl -**x** /-əʊz/ or -**s**) (desk) Sekretär m; (office) Büro nt

bureaucracy /bjʊə'rɒkrəsɪ/ n Bürokratie f

bureaucrat /'bjʊərəkræt/ n Bürokrat m. ~**ic** /-'krætɪk/ a bürokratisch

burger /'bɜːgə(r)/ n Hamburger m

burglar /'bɜːglə(r)/ n Einbrecher m. ~ **alarm** n Alarmanlage f

burglar|ize /'bɜːgləraɪz/ vt (Amer) einbrechen in (+ acc). ~**y** n Einbruch m

burgle /'bɜːgl/ vt einbrechen in (+ acc); **they have been** ~**d** bei ihnen ist eingebrochen worden

Burgundy /'bɜːgəndɪ/ n Burgund nt; **b**~ (wine) Burgunder m

burial /'berɪəl/ n Begräbnis nt

burlesque /bɜː'lesk/ n Burleske f

burly /'bɜːlɪ/ a (-ier, -iest) stämmig

Burm|a /'bɜːmə/ n Birma nt. ~**ese** /-'miːz/ a birmanisch

burn /bɜːn/ n Verbrennung f; (on skin) Brandwunde f; (on material) Brandstelle

f ▫ v (pt/pp **burnt** or **burned**) ▫ vt verbrennen ▫ vi brennen; (food:) anbrennen. ~ **down** vt/i niederbrennen

burnish /'bɜːnɪʃ/ vt polieren

burnt /bɜːnt/ see **burn**

burp /bɜːp/ vi (fam) aufstoßen

burrow /'bʌrəʊ/ n Bau m ▫ vi wühlen

bursar /'bɜːsə(r)/ n Rechnungsführer m. ~**y** n Stipendium nt

burst /bɜːst/ n Bruch m; (surge) Ausbruch m ▫ v (pt/pp **burst**) ▫ vt platzen machen ▫ vi platzen; (bud:) aufgehen; ~ **into tears** in Tränen ausbrechen

bury /'berɪ/ vt (pt/pp -**ied**) begraben; (hide) vergraben

bus /bʌs/ n [Auto]bus m ▫ vt/i (pt/pp **bussed**) mit dem Bus fahren

bush /bʊʃ/ n Strauch m; (land) Busch m. ~**y** a (-ier, -iest) buschig

busily /'bɪzɪlɪ/ adv eifrig

business /'bɪznɪs/ n Angelegenheit f; (Comm) Geschäft nt; **on** ~ geschäftlich; **he has no** ~ er hat kein Recht (**to** zu); **mind one's own** ~ sich um seine eigenen Angelegenheiten kümmern; **that's none of your** ~ das geht Sie nichts an. ~**-like** a geschäftsmäßig. ~**man** n Geschäftsmann m

busker /'bʌskə(r)/ n Straßenmusikant m

'bus-stop n Bushaltestelle f

bust[1] /bʌst/ n Büste f. ~ **size** n Oberweite f

bust[2] a (fam) kaputt; **go** ~ Pleite gehen ▫ v (pt/pp **busted** or **bust**) (fam) ▫ vt kaputtmachen ▫ vt kaputtgehen

bustl|e /'bʌsl/ n Betrieb m, Getriebe nt ▫ vi ~**e about** geschäftig hin und her laufen. ~**ing** a belebt

'bust-up n (fam) Streit m, Krach m

busy /'bɪzɪ/ a (-ier, -iest) beschäftigt; (day) voll; (street) belebt; (with traffic) stark befahren; (Amer Teleph) besetzt; **be** ~ zu tun haben ▫ vt ~ **oneself** sich beschäftigen (**with** mit)

'busybody n Wichtigtuer(in) m(f)

but /bʌt, unbetont bət/ conj aber; (after negative) sondern ▫ prep außer (+ dat); ~ **for** (without) ohne (+ acc); **the last** ~ **one** der/die/das vorletzte; **the next** ~ **one** der/die/das übernächste ▫ adv nur

butcher /'bʊtʃə(r)/ n Fleischer m, Metzger m; ~'**s** [**shop**] Fleischerei f, Metzgerei f ▫ vt [ab]schlachten

butler /'bʌtlə(r)/ n Butler m

butt /bʌt/ n (of gun) [Gewehr]kolben m; (fig: target) Zielscheibe f; (of cigarette) Stummel m; (for water) Regentonne f ▫ vt mit dem Kopf stoßen ▫ vi ~ **in** unterbrechen

butter /'bʌtə(r)/ n Butter f □ vt mit Butter bestreichen. ~ **up** vt (fam) schmeicheln (+ dat)

butter: ~**cup** a Butterblume f, Hahnenfuß m. ~**fly** n Schmetterling m

buttocks /'bʌtəks/ npl Gesäß nt

button /'bʌtn/ n Knopf m □ vt ~ **[up]** zuknöpfen □ vi geknöpft werden. ~**hole** n Knopfloch nt

buttress /'bʌtrɪs/ n Strebepfeiler m; **flying** ~ Strebebogen m

buxom /'bʌksəm/ a drall

buy /baɪ/ n Kauf m □ vt (pt/pp **bought**) kaufen. ~**er** n Käufer(in) m(f)

buzz /bʌz/ n Summen □ vi summen. ~ **off** vi (fam) abhauen

buzzard /'bʌzəd/ n Bussard m

buzzer /'bʌzə(r)/ n Summer m

by /baɪ/ prep (close to) bei (+ dat); (next to) neben (+ dat/acc); (past) an (+ dat) ... vorbei; (to the extent of) um (+ acc); (at the latest) bis; (by means of) durch; **by Mozart/Dickens** von Mozart/Dickens; ~ **oneself** allein; ~ **the sea** am Meer; ~ **car/bus** mit dem Auto/Bus; ~ **sea** mit dem Schiff; ~ **day/night** bei Tag/Nacht; ~ **the hour** pro Stunde; ~ **the metre** meterweise; **six metres ~ four** sechs mal vier Meter; **win ~ a length** mit einer Länge Vorsprung gewinnen; **miss the train ~ a minute** den Zug um eine Minute verpassen □ adv ~ **and** ~ mit der Zeit; ~ **and large** im Großen und Ganzen; **put ~** beiseite legen; **go/pass ~** vorbeigehen

bye /baɪ/ int (fam) tschüs

by: ~**-election** n Nachwahl f. ~**gone** a vergangen. ~**-law** n Verordnung f. ~**pass** n Umgehungsstraße f; (Med) Bypass m □ vt umfahren. ~**-product** n Nebenprodukt nt. ~**-road** n Nebenstraße f. ~**stander** n Zuschauer(in) m(f)

Byzantine /bɪ'zæntaɪn/ a byzantinisch

C

cab /kæb/ n Taxi nt; (of lorry, train) Führerhaus nt

cabaret /'kæbəreɪ/ n Kabarett nt

cabbage /'kæbɪdʒ/ n Kohl m

cabin /'kæbɪn/ n Kabine f; (hut) Hütte f

cabinet /'kæbɪnɪt/ n Schrank m; (TV, Radio) Gehäuse nt; **C~** (Pol) Kabinett nt; **[display]** ~ Vitrine f; ~**-maker** n Möbeltischler m

cable /'keɪbl/ n Kabel nt; (rope) Tau nt. ~ '**railway** n Seilbahn f. ~ '**television** n Kabelfernsehen nt

cache /kæʃ/ n Versteck nt; ~ **of arms** Waffenlager nt

cackle /'kækl/ vi gackern

cactus /'kæktəs/ n (pl **-ti** /-taɪ/ or **-tuses**) Kaktus m

caddie /'kædɪ/ n Caddie m

caddy /'kædɪ/ n **[tea-]**~ Teedose f

cadet /kə'det/ n Kadett m

cadge /kædʒ/ vt/i (fam) schnorren

Caesarean /sɪ'zeərɪən/ a & n ~ **[section]** Kaiserschnitt m

café /'kæfeɪ/ n Café nt

cafeteria /kæfə'tɪərɪə/ n Selbstbedienungsrestaurant nt

caffeine /'kæfiːn/ n Koffein nt

cage /keɪdʒ/ n Käfig m

cagey /'keɪdʒɪ/ a (fam) **be ~** mit der Sprache nicht herauswollen

cajole /kə'dʒəʊl/ vt gut zureden (+ dat)

cake /keɪk/ n Kuchen m; (of soap) Stück nt. ~**d** a verkrustet (with mit)

calamity /kə'læmɪtɪ/ n Katastrophe f

calcium /'kælsɪəm/ n Kalzium nt

calculat|e /'kælkjʊleɪt/ vt berechnen; (estimate) kalkulieren. ~**ing** a (fig) berechnend. ~**ion** /-'leɪʃn/ n Rechnung f, Kalkulation f. ~**or** n Rechner m

calendar /'kælɪndə(r)/ n Kalender m

calf[1] /kɑːf/ n (pl **calves**) Kalb nt

calf[2] n (pl **calves**) (Anat) Wade f

calibre /'kælɪbə(r)/ n Kaliber nt

calico /'kælɪkəʊ/ n Kattun m

call /kɔːl/ n Ruf m; (Teleph) Anruf m; (visit) Besuch m; **be on** ~ ⟨doctor:⟩ Bereitschaftsdienst haben □ vt rufen; (Teleph) anrufen; (wake) wecken; ausrufen ⟨strike⟩; (name) nennen; **be ~ed** heißen □ vi rufen; ~ **[in or round]** vorbeikommen. ~ **back** vt zurückrufen □ vi noch einmal vorbeikommen. ~ **for** vt rufen nach; (demand) verlangen; (fetch) abholen. ~ **off** vt zurückrufen ⟨dog⟩; (cancel) absagen. ~ **on** vt bitten (for um); (appeal to) appellieren an (+ acc); (visit) besuchen. ~ **out** vt rufen; aufrufen ⟨names⟩ □ vi rufen. ~ **up** vt (Mil) einberufen; (Teleph) anrufen

call: ~**box** n Telefonzelle f. ~**er** n Besucher m; (Teleph) Anrufer m. ~**ing** n Berufung f

callous /'kæləs/ a gefühllos

'**call-up** n (Mil) Einberufung f

calm /kɑːm/ a (-er, -est), **-ly** adv ruhig □ n Ruhe f □ vt ~ **[down]** beruhigen □ vi ~ **down** sich beruhigen. ~**ness** n Ruhe f; (of sea) Stille f

calorie /'kælərɪ/ n Kalorie f

calves /kɑ:vz/ npl see calf[1] & [2]

camber /'kæmbə(r)/ n Wölbung f

came /keɪm/ see come

camel /'kæml/ n Kamel nt

camera /'kæmərə/ n Kamera f. ~man n Kameramann m

camouflage /'kæməflɑ:ʒ/ n Tarnung f □ vt tarnen

camp /kæmp/ n Lager nt □ vi campen; (Mil) kampieren

campaign /kæm'peɪn/ n Feldzug m; (Comm, Pol) Kampagne f □ vi kämpfen; (pol) im Wahlkampf arbeiten

camp: ~bed n Feldbett nt. ~er n Camper m; (Auto) Wohnmobil nt. ~ing n Camping nt. ~site n Campingplatz m

campus /'kæmpəs/ n (pl -puses) (Univ) Campus m

can[1] /kæn/ n (for petrol) Kanister m; (tin) Dose f, Büchse f; a ~ of beer eine Dose Bier □ vt in Dosen od Büchsen konservieren

can[2] /kæn, unbetont kən/ v aux (pres can; pt could) können; I cannot/can't go ich kann nicht gehen; he could not go er konnte nicht gehen; if I could go wenn ich gehen könnte

Canad|a /'kænədə/ n Kanada nt. ~ian /kə'neɪdɪən/ a kanadisch □ n Kanadier(in) m(f)

canal /kə'næl/ n Kanal m

Canaries /kə'neərɪz/ npl Kanarische Inseln pl

canary /kə'neərɪ/ n Kanarienvogel m

cancel /'kænsl/ vt/i (pt/pp cancelled) absagen; entwerten ⟨stamp⟩; (annul) rückgängig machen; (Comm) stornieren; abbestellen ⟨newspaper⟩; be ~led ausfallen. ~lation /-ə'leɪʃn/ n Absage f

cancer /'kænsə(r)/ n, & (Astr) C~ Krebs m. ~ous /-rəs/ a krebsig

candelabra /kændə'lɑ:brə/ n Armleuchter m

candid /'kændɪd/ a, -ly adv offen

candidate /'kændɪdət/ n Kandidat(in) m(f)

candied /'kændɪd/ a kandiert

candle /'kændl/ n Kerze f. ~stick n Kerzenständer m, Leuchter m

candour /'kændə(r)/ n Offenheit f

candy /'kændɪ/ n (Amer) Süßigkeiten pl; [piece of] ~ Bonbon m. ~floss /-flɒs/ n Zuckerwatte f

cane /keɪn/ n Rohr nt; (stick) Stock m □ vt mit dem Stock züchtigen

canine /'keɪnaɪn/ a Hunde-. ~ tooth n Eckzahn m

canister /'kænɪstə(r)/ n Blechdose f

cannabis /'kænəbɪs/ n Haschisch nt

canned /kænd/ a Dosen-, Büchsen-; ~ music (fam) Musik f aus der Konserve

cannibal /'kænɪbl/ n Kannibale m. ~ism /-bəlɪzm/ n Kannibalismus m

cannon /'kænən/ n inv Kanone f. ~ball n Kanonenkugel f

cannot /'kænɒt/ see can[2]

canny /'kænɪ/ a schlau

canoe /kə'nu:/ n Paddelboot nt; (Sport) Kanu nt □ vi paddeln; (Sport) Kanu fahren

canon /'kænən/ n Kanon m; (person) Kanonikus m. ~ize /-aɪz/ vt kanonisieren

'can-opener n Dosenöffner m, Büchsenöffner m

canopy /'kænəpɪ/ n Baldachin m

cant /kænt/ n Heuchelei f

can't /kɑ:nt/ = cannot. See can[2]

cantankerous /kæn'tæŋkərəs/ a zänkisch

canteen /kæn'ti:n/ n Kantine f; ~ of cutlery Besteckkasten m

canter /'kæntə(r)/ n Kanter m □ vi kantern

canvas /'kænvəs/ n Segeltuch nt; (Art) Leinwand f; (painting) Gemälde nt

canvass /'kænvəs/ vt/m Stimmen werben

canyon /'kænjən/ n Cañon m

cap /kæp/ n Kappe f, Mütze f; (nurse's) Haube f; (top, lid) Verschluss m □ vt (pt/pp capped) (fig) übertreffen

capability /keɪpə'bɪlətɪ/ n Fähigkeit f

capable /'keɪpəbl/ a, -bly adv fähig; be ~ of doing sth fähig sein, etw zu tun

capacity /kə'pæsətɪ/ n Fassungsvermögen nt; (ability) Fähigkeit f; in my ~ as in meiner Eigenschaft als

cape[1] /keɪp/ n (cloak) Cape nt

cape[2] n (Geog) Kap nt

caper[1] /'keɪpə(r)/ vi herumspringen

caper[2] n (Culin) Kaper f

capital /'kæpɪtl/ a ⟨letter⟩ groß □ n (town) Hauptstadt f; (money) Kapital nt; (letter) Großbuchstabe m

capital|ism /'kæpɪtəlɪzm/ n Kapitalismus m. ~ist /-ɪst/ a kapitalistisch □ n Kapitalist m. ~ize /-aɪz/ vi ~ize on (fig) Kapital schlagen aus. ~ 'letter n Großbuchstabe m. ~ 'punishment n Todesstrafe f

capitulat|e /kə'pɪtjʊleɪt/ vi kapitulieren. ~ion /-'leɪʃn/ n Kapitulation f

capricious /kə'prɪʃəs/ a launisch

Capricorn /'kæprɪkɔ:n/ n (Astr) Steinbock m

capsize /kæp'saɪz/ vi kentern □ vt zum Kentern bringen

capsule /'kæpsjʊl/ n Kapsel f

captain /'kæptɪn/ n Kapitän m; (Mil) Hauptmann m □ vt anführen ⟨team⟩

caption /'kæpʃn/ n Überschrift f; (of illustration) Bildtext m

captivate /'kæptɪveɪt/ vt bezaubern

captiv|e /'kæptɪv/ a hold/take ~e gefangen halten/nehmen □ n Gefangene(r) m/f. ~ity /-'tɪvətɪ/ n Gefangenschaft f

capture /'kæptʃə(r)/ n Gefangennahme f □ vt gefangen nehmen; [ein]fangen ⟨animal⟩; (Mil) einnehmen ⟨town⟩

car /kɑ:(r)/ n Auto nt, Wagen m; by ~ mit dem Auto od Wagen

carafe /kə'ræf/ n Karaffe f

caramel /'kærəmel/ n Karamell m

carat /'kærət/ n Karat nt

caravan /'kærəvæn/ n Wohnwagen m; (procession) Karawane f

carbohydrate /kɑ:bə'haɪdreɪt/ n Kohlenhydrat nt

carbon /'kɑ:bən/ n Kohlenstoff m; (paper) Kohlepapier nt; (copy) Durchschlag m

carbon: ~ copy n Durchschlag m. ~ dioxide n Kohlendioxid nt; (in drink) Kohlensäure f. ~ paper n Kohlepapier nt

carburettor /kɑ:bjʊ'retə(r)/ n Vergaser m

carcass /'kɑ:kəs/ n Kadaver m

card /kɑ:d/ n Karte f

'cardboard n Pappe f, Karton m. ~ 'box n Pappschachtel f; (large) [Papp]karton m

'card-game n Kartenspiel nt

cardiac /'kɑ:dɪæk/ a Herz-

cardigan /'kɑ:dɪgən/ n Strickjacke f

cardinal /'kɑ:dɪnl/ a Kardinal-; ~ number Kardinalzahl f □ n (Relig) Kardinal m

card 'index n Kartei f

care /keə(r)/ n Sorgfalt f; (caution) Vorsicht f; (protection) Obhut f; (looking after) Pflege f; (worry) Sorge f; ~ of (on letter abbr c/o) bei; take ~ vorsichtig sein; take into ~ in Pflege nehmen; take ~ of sich kümmern um □ vi ~ about sich kümmern um; ~ for (like) mögen; (look after) betreuen; I don't ~ das ist mir gleich

career /kə'rɪə(r)/ n Laufbahn f; (profession) Beruf m □ vi rasen

care: ~free a sorglos. ~ful a, -ly adv sorgfältig; (cautious) vorsichtig. ~less a, -ly adv nachlässig. ~lessness n Nachlässigkeit f

caress /kə'res/ n Liebkosung f □ vt liebkosen

'caretaker n Hausmeister m

'car ferry n Autofähre f

cargo /'kɑ:gəʊ/ n (pl -es) Ladung f

Caribbean /kærɪ'bi:ən/ n the ~ die Karibik

caricature /'kærɪkətjʊə(r)/ n Karikatur f □ vt karikieren

caring /'keərɪŋ/ a ⟨parent⟩ liebevoll; ⟨profession, attitude⟩ sozial

carnage /'kɑ:nɪdʒ/ n Gemetzel nt

carnal /'kɑ:nl/ a fleischlich

carnation /kɑ:'neɪʃn/ n Nelke f

carnival /'kɑ:nɪvl/ n Karneval m

carnivorous /kɑ:'nɪvərəs/ a Fleisch fressend

carol /'kærl/ n [Christmas] ~ Weihnachtslied nt

carp[1] /kɑ:p/ n inv Karpfen m

carp[2] vi nörgeln; ~ at herumnörgeln an (+ dat)

'car park n Parkplatz m; (multi-storey) Parkhaus nt; (underground) Tiefgarage f

carpent|er /'kɑ:pɪntə(r)/ n Zimmermann m; (joiner) Tischler m. ~ry n Tischlerei f

carpet /'kɑ:pɪt/ n Teppich m □ vt mit Teppich auslegen

carriage /'kærɪdʒ/ n Kutsche f; (Rail) Wagen m; (of goods) Beförderung f; (cost) Frachtkosten pl; (bearing) Haltung f. ~way n Fahrbahn f

carrier /'kærɪə(r)/ n Träger(in) m(f); (Comm) Spediteur m; ~ [bag] Tragetasche f

carrot /'kærət/ n Möhre f, Karotte f

carry /'kærɪ/ vt/i (pt/pp -ied) tragen; be carried away (fam) hingerissen sein. ~ off vt wegtragen; gewinnen ⟨prize⟩. ~ on vi weitermachen; ~ on at (fam) herumnörgeln an (+ dat); ~ on with (fam) eine Affäre haben mit □ vt führen; (continue) fortführen. ~ out vt hinaus-/heraustragen; (perform) ausführen

'carry-cot n Babytragetasche f

cart /kɑ:t/ n Karren m; put the ~ before the horse das Pferd beim Schwanz aufzäumen □ vt karren; (fam: carry) schleppen

cartilage /'kɑ:tɪlɪdʒ/ n (Anat) Knorpel m

carton /'kɑ:tn/ n [Papp]karton m; (for drink) Tüte f; (of cream, yoghurt) Becher m

cartoon /kɑ:'tu:n/ n Karikatur f; (joke) Witzzeichnung f; (strip) Comic Strips pl; (film) Zeichentrickfilm m; (Art) Karton m. ~ist n Karikaturist m

cartridge /'kɑ:trɪdʒ/ n Patrone f; (for film, typewriter ribbon) Kassette f; (of record player) Tonabnehmer m

carve /kɑ:v/ vt schnitzen; (in stone) hauen; (Culin) aufschneiden

carving /ˈkɑːvɪŋ/ n Schnitzerei f. **~-knife**
n Tranchiermesser nt

'car wash n Autowäsche f; (place) Au-
towaschanlage f

case¹ /keɪs/ n Fall m; **in any ~** auf jeden
Fall; **just in ~** für alle Fälle; **in ~ he
comes** falls er kommt

case² n Kasten m; (crate) Kiste f; (for spectacles) Etui nt; (suitcase) Koffer m; (for
display) Vitrine f

cash /kæʃ/ n Bargeld nt; **pay [in] ~** [in] bar
bezahlen; **~ on delivery** per Nachnahme
□ vt einlösen (cheque). **~ desk** n Kasse f

cashier /kæˈʃɪə(r)/ n Kassierer(in) m(f)

'cash register n Registrierkasse f

casino /kəˈsiːnəʊ/ n Kasino nt

cask /kɑːsk/ n Fass nt

casket /ˈkɑːskɪt/ n Kasten m; (Amer: coffin)
Sarg m

casserole /ˈkæsərəʊl/ n Schmortopf m;
(stew) Eintopf m

cassette /kəˈset/ n Kassette f. **~ recorder**
n Kassettenrecorder m

cast /kɑːst/ n (throw) Wurf m; (mould)
Form f; (model) Abguss m; (Theat) Besetzung f; **[plaster] ~** (Med) Gipsverband
m □ vt (pt/pp cast) (throw) werfen; (shed)
abwerfen; abgeben (vote); gießen (metal);
(Theat) besetzen (role); **~ a glance at**
einen Blick werfen auf (+ acc). **~ off** vi
(Naut) ablegen □ vt (Knitting) abketten. **~
on** vt (Knitting) anschlagen

castanets /kæstəˈnets/ npl Kastagnetten
pl

castaway /ˈkɑːstəweɪ/ n Schiffbrü-
chige(r) m/f

caste /kɑːst/ n Kaste f

cast 'iron n Gusseisen nt

cast-'iron a gusseisern

castle /ˈkɑːsl/ n Schloss nt; (fortified) Burg
f; (Chess) Turm m

'cast-offs npl abgelegte Kleidung f

castor /ˈkɑːstə(r)/ n (wheel) [Lauf]rolle f

'castor sugar n Streuzucker m

castrat|e /kæˈstreɪt/ vt kastrieren. **~ion**
/-eɪʃn/ n Kastration f

casual /ˈkæʒʊəl/ a, **-ly** adv (chance) zufällig; (offhand) lässig; (informal) zwanglos;
(not permanent) Gelegenheits-; **~ wear**
Freizeitbekleidung f

casualty /ˈkæʒʊəltɪ/ n [Todes]opfer nt; (in-
jured person) Verletzte(r) m/f; **~ [depart-
ment]** Unfallstation f

cat /kæt/ n Katze f

catalogue /ˈkætəlɒg/ n Katalog m □ vt kat-
alogisieren

catalyst /ˈkætəlɪst/ n (Chem & fig) Katalysator m

catalytic /kætəˈlɪtɪk/ a **~ converter**
(Auto) Katalysator m

catapult /ˈkætəpʌlt/ n Katapult nt □ vt ka-
tapultieren

cataract /ˈkætərækt/ n (Med) grauer Star
m

catarrh /kəˈtɑː(r)/ n Katarrh m

catastroph|e /kəˈtæstrəfɪ/ n Katastrophe
f. **~ic** /kætəˈstrɒfɪk/ a katastrophal

catch /kætʃ/ n (of fish) Fang m; (fastener)
Verschluss m; (on door) Klinke f; (fam:
snag) Haken m (fam) □ v (pt/pp caught)
□ vt fangen; (be in time for) erreichen;
(travel by) fahren mit; bekommen (illness);
~ a cold sich erkälten; **~ sight of** erblicken; **~ s.o. stealing** jdn beim Stehlen
erwischen; **~ one's finger in the door**
sich (dat) den Finger in der Tür [ein]klem-
men □ vi (burn) anbrennen; (get stuck)
klemmen. **~ on** vi (fam) (understand) kapieren; (become popular) sich durchsetzen.
~ up vt einholen □ vi aufholen; **~ up with**
einholen □ vt (s.o.); nachholen (work)

catching /ˈkætʃɪŋ/ a ansteckend

catch: ~-phrase n, **~word** n Schlagwort
nt

catchy /ˈkætʃɪ/ a (-ier, -iest) einprägsam

catechism /ˈkætɪkɪzm/ n Katechismus m

categor|ical /kætɪˈgɒrɪkl/ a, **-ly** adv kate-
gorisch. **~y** /ˈkætɪgərɪ/ n Kategorie f

cater /ˈkeɪtə(r)/ vi **~ for** beköstigen;
(firm:) das Essen liefern für (party); (fig)
eingestellt sein auf (+ acc). **~ing** n (trade)
Gaststättengewerbe nt

caterpillar /ˈkætəpɪlə(r)/ n Raupe f

cathedral /kəˈθiːdrl/ n Dom m, Kathedrale f

Catholic /ˈkæθəlɪk/ a katholisch □ n Ka-
tholik(in) m(f). **C ~ism** /kəˈθɒlɪsɪzm/ n
Katholizismus m

catkin /ˈkætkɪn/ n (Bot) Kätzchen nt

cattle /ˈkætl/ npl Vieh nt

catty /ˈkætɪ/ a (-ier, -iest) boshaft

caught /kɔːt/ see **catch**

cauldron /ˈkɔːldrən/ n [großer] Kessel m

cauliflower /ˈkɒlɪ-/ n Blumenkohl m

cause /kɔːz/ n Ursache f; (reason) Grund
m; **good ~** gute Sache f □ vt verursachen;
~ s.o. to do sth jdn veranlassen, etw zu
tun

'causeway n [Insel]damm m

caustic /ˈkɔːstɪk/ a ätzend; (fig) beißend

cauterize /ˈkɔːtəraɪz/ vt kauterisieren

caution /ˈkɔːʃn/ n Vorsicht f; (warning)
Verwarnung f □ vt (Jur) verwarnen

cautious /ˈkɔːʃəs/ a, **-ly** adv vorsichtig

cavalry /ˈkævlrɪ/ n Kavallerie f

cave /keɪv/ n Höhle f □ vi **~ in** einstürzen

cavern /'kævən/ n Höhle f

caviare /'kævɪɑ:(r)/ n Kaviar m

caving /'keɪvɪŋ/ n Höhlenforschung f

cavity /'kævətɪ/ n Hohlraum m; (in tooth) Loch nt

cavort /kə'vɔ:t/ vi tollen

cease /si:s/ n without ~ unaufhörlich □ vt/i aufhören. ~-fire n Waffenruhe f. ~less a, -ly adv unaufhörlich

cedar /'si:də(r)/ n Zeder f

cede /si:d/ vt abtreten (to an + acc)

ceiling /'si:lɪŋ/ n [Zimmer]decke f; (fig) oberste Grenze f

celebrat|e /'selɪbreɪt/ vt/i feiern. ~ed a berühmt (for wegen). ~ion /-'breɪʃn/ n Feier f

celebrity /sɪ'lebrətɪ/ n Berühmtheit f

celery /'selərɪ/ n [Stangen]sellerie m & f

celiba|cy /'selɪbəsɪ/ n Zölibat nt. ~te a be ~te im Zölibat leben

cell /sel/ n Zelle f

cellar /'selə(r)/ n Keller m

cellist /'tʃelɪst/ n Cellist(in) m(f)

cello /'tʃeləʊ/ n Cello nt

Celsius /'selsɪəs/ a Celsius

Celt /kelt/ n Kelte m/ Keltin f. ~ic a keltisch

cement /sɪ'ment/ n Zement m; (adhesive) Kitt m □ vt zementieren; (stick) kitten

cemetery /'semətrɪ/ n Friedhof m

censor /'sensə(r)/ n Zensor m □ vt zensieren. ~ship n Zensur f

censure /'senʃə(r)/ n Tadel m □ vt tadeln

census /'sensəs/ n Volkszählung f

cent /sent/ n (coin) Cent m

centenary /sen'ti:nərɪ/ n, (Amer) **centennial** /sen'tenɪəl/ n Hundertjahrfeier f

center /'sentə(r)/ n (Amer) = centre

centi|grade /'sentɪ-/ a Celsius-; 5° ~ 5° Celsius. ~metre m Zentimeter m & nt. ~pede /-pi:d/ n Tausendfüßler m

central /'sentrəl/ a, -ly adv zentral. ~ 'heating n Zentralheizung f. ~ize vt zentralisieren. ~ reser'vation n (Auto) Mittelstreifen m

centre /'sentə(r)/ n Zentrum nt; (middle) Mitte f □ v (pt/pp centred) □ vt zentrieren; ~ on (fig) sich drehen um. ~-'forward n Mittelstürmer m

centrifugal /sentrɪ'fju:gl/ a ~ force Fliehkraft f

century /'sentʃərɪ/ n Jahrhundert nt

ceramic /sɪ'ræmɪk/ a Keramik-. ~s n Keramik f

cereal /'sɪərɪəl/ n Getreide nt; (breakfast food) Frühstücksflocken pl

cerebral /'serɪbrl/ a Gehirn-

ceremon|ial /serɪ'məʊnɪəl/ a, -ly adv zeremoniell, feierlich n Zeremoniell nt. ~i-ous /-ɪəs/ a, -ly adv formell

ceremony /'serɪmənɪ/ n Zeremonie f, Feier f; without ~ ohne weitere Umstände

certain /'sɜ:tn/ a sicher; (not named) gewiss; for ~ mit Bestimmtheit; make ~ (check) sich vergewissern (that dass); (ensure) dafür sorgen (that dass); he is ~ to win er wird ganz bestimmt siegen. ~ly adv bestimmt, sicher; ~ly not! auf keinen Fall! ~ty n Sicherheit f, Gewissheit f; it's a ~ty es ist sicher

certificate /sə'tɪfɪkət/ n Bescheinigung f; (Jur) Urkunde f; (Sch) Zeugnis nt

certify /'sɜ:tɪfaɪ/ vt (pt/pp -ied) bescheinigen; (declare insane) für geisteskrank erklären

cessation /se'seɪʃn/ n Ende nt

cesspool /'ses-/ n Senkgrube f

cf. abbr (compare) vgl.

chafe /tʃeɪf/ vt wund reiben

chaff /tʃɑ:f/ n Spreu f

chaffinch /'tʃæfɪntʃ/ n Buchfink m

chain /tʃeɪn/ n Kette f □ vt ketten (to an + acc). ~ up vt anketten

chain: ~ re'action n Kettenreaktion f. ~-smoker n Kettenraucher m. ~ store n Kettenladen m

chair /tʃeə(r)/ n Stuhl m; (Univ) Lehrstuhl m; (Adm) Vorsitzende(r) m/f □ vt den Vorsitz führen bei. ~-lift n Sessellift m. ~man n Vorsitzende(r) m/f

chalet /'ʃæleɪ/ n Chalet nt

chalice /'tʃælɪs/ n (Relig) Kelch m

chalk /tʃɔ:k/ n Kreide f. ~y a kreidig

challeng|e /'tʃælɪndʒ/ n Herausforderung f; (Mil) Anruf m □ vt herausfordern; (Mil) anrufen; (fig) anfechten (statement). ~er n Herausforderer m. ~ing a herausfordernd; (demanding) anspruchsvoll

chamber /'tʃeɪmbə(r)/ n Kammer f; ~s pl (Jur) [Anwalts]büro nt; C~ of Commerce Handelskammer f

chamber: ~maid n Zimmermädchen nt. ~ music n Kammermusik f. ~-pot n Nachttopf m

chamois¹ /'ʃæmwɑ:/ n inv (animal) Gämse f

chamois² /'ʃæmɪ/ n ~[-leather] Ledertuch nt

champagne /ʃæm'peɪn/ n Champagner m

champion /'tʃæmpɪən/ n (Sport) Meister(in) m(f); (of cause) Verfechter m □ vt sich einsetzen für. ~ship n (Sport) Meisterschaft f

chance /tʃɑːns/ n Zufall m; (prospect) Chancen pl; (likelihood) Aussicht f; (opportinity) Gelegenheit f; **by ~** zufällig; **take a ~** ein Risiko eingehen; **give s.o. a ~** jdm eine Chance geben □ attrib zufällig □ vt ~ **it** es riskieren

chancellor /'tʃɑːnsələ(r)/ n Kanzler m; (Univ) Rektor m; **C~ of the Exchequer** Schatzkanzler m

chancy /'tʃɑːnsɪ/ a riskant

chandelier /ʃændə'lɪə(r)/ n Kronleuchter m

change /tʃeɪndʒ/ n Veränderung f; (alteration) Änderung f; (money) Wechselgeld nt; **for a ~** zur Abwechslung □ vt wechseln; (alter) ändern; (exchange) umtauschen (**for** gegen); (transform) verwandeln; trocken legen ⟨baby⟩; **~ one's clothes** sich umziehen; **~ trains** umsteigen □ vi sich verändern; (~ clothes) sich umziehen; (~ trains) umsteigen; **all ~!** alles aussteigen!

changeable /'tʃeɪndʒəbl/ a wechselhaft

'changing-room n Umkleideraum m

channel /'tʃænl/ n Rinne f; (Radio, TV) Kanal m; (fig) Weg m; **the [English] C~** der Ärmelkanal; **the C~ Islands** die Kanalinseln □ vt (pt/pp **channelled**) leiten; (fig) lenken

chant /tʃɑːnt/ n liturgischer Gesang m □ vt singen; ⟨demonstrators:⟩ skandieren

chao|s /'keɪɒs/ n Chaos nt. **~tic** /-'ɒtɪk/ a chaotisch

chap /tʃæp/ n (fam) Kerl m

chapel /'tʃæpl/ n Kapelle f

chaperon /'ʃæpərəʊn/ n Anstandsdame f □ vt begleiten

chaplain /'tʃæplɪn/ n Geistliche(r) m

chapped /tʃæpt/ a ⟨skin⟩ aufgesprungen

chapter /'tʃæptə(r)/ n Kapitel nt

char[1] /tʃɑː(r)/ n (fam) Putzfrau f

char[2] vt (pt/pp charred) (burn) verkohlen

character /'kærɪktə(r)/ n Charakter m; (in novel, play) Gestalt f; (Typ) Schriftzeichen nt; **out of ~** uncharakteristisch; **quite a ~** (fam) ein Original

characteristic /kærɪktə'rɪstɪk/ a, **-ally** adv charakteristisch (**of** für) □ n Merkmal nt

characterize /'kærɪktəraɪz/ vt charakterisieren

charade /ʃə'rɑːd/ n Scharade f

charcoal /'tʃɑː-/ n Holzkohle f

charge /tʃɑːdʒ/ n (price) Gebühr f; (Electr) Ladung f; (attack) Angriff m; (Jur) Anklage f; **free of ~** kostenlos; **be in ~** verantwortlich sein (**of** für); **take ~** die Aufsicht übernehmen (**of** über + acc) □ vt berechnen (fee); (Electr) laden; (attack) angreifen; (Jur) anklagen (**with** gen); **~ s.o.**

for sth jdm etw berechnen □ vi (attack) angreifen

chariot /'tʃærɪət/ n Wagen m

charisma /kə'rɪzmə/ n Charisma nt. **~tic** /kærɪz'mætɪk/ a charismatisch

charitable /'tʃærɪtəbl/ a wohltätig; (kind) wohlwollend

charity /'tʃærətɪ/ n Nächstenliebe f; (organization) wohltätige Einrichtung f; **for ~** für Wohltätigkeitszwecke; **live on ~** von Almosen leben

charlatan /'ʃɑːlətən/ n Scharlatan m

charm /tʃɑːm/ n Reiz m; (of person) Charme f; (object) Amulett nt □ vt bezaubern. **~ing** a, **-ly** adv reizend; ⟨person, smile⟩ charmant

chart /tʃɑːt/ n Karte f; (table) Tabelle f

charter /'tʃɑːtə(r)/ n ~ **[flight]** Charterflug m □ vt chartern; **~ed accountant** Wirtschaftsprüfer(in) m(f)

charwoman /'tʃɑː-/ n Putzfrau f

chase /tʃeɪs/ n Verfolgungsjagd f □ vt jagen, verfolgen. **~ away** or **off** vt wegjagen

chasm /'kæzm/ n Kluft f

chassis /'ʃæsɪ/ n (pl **chassis** /-sɪz/) Chassis nt

chaste /tʃeɪst/ a keusch

chastise /tʃæ'staɪz/ vt züchtigen

chastity /'tʃæstətɪ/ n Keuschheit f

chat /tʃæt/ n Plauderei f; **have a ~ with** plaudern mit □ vi (pt/pp **chatted**) plaudern. **~ show** n Talkshow f

chatter /'tʃætə(r)/ n Geschwätz nt □ vi schwatzen; ⟨child:⟩ plappern; ⟨teeth:⟩ klappern. **~box** n (fam) Plappermaul n

chatty /'tʃætɪ/ a (-ier, -iest) geschwätzig

chauffeur /'ʃəʊfə(r)/ n Chauffeur m

chauvin|ism /'ʃəʊvɪnɪzm/ n Chauvinismus m. **~ist** n Chauvinist m; **male ~ist** (fam) Chauvi m

cheap /tʃiːp/ a & adv (-er, -est), **-ly** adv billig. **~en** vt entwürdigen; **~en oneself** sich erniedrigen

cheat /tʃiːt/ n Betrüger(in) m(f); (at games) Mogler m □ vt betrügen □ vi (at games) mogeln (fam)

check[1] /tʃek/ a (squared) kariert □ n Karo nt

check[2] n Überprüfung f; (inspection) Kontrolle f; (Chess) Schach nt; (Amer: bill) Rechnung f; (Amer: cheque) Scheck m; (Amer: tick) Haken m; **keep a ~ on** kontrollieren □ vt [über]prüfen; (inspect) kontrollieren; (restrain) hemmen; (stop) aufhalten □ vi [go and] ~ nachsehen. **~ in** vi sich anmelden; (Aviat) einchecken □ vt abfertigen; einchecken. **~ out** vi sich abmelden. ~ **up** *vi* prüfen, kontrollieren; ~ **up on** überprüfen

check|ed /tʃekt/ *a* kariert. ~**ers** *n* (*Amer*) Damespiel *nt*

check: ~**mate** *int* schachmatt! ~**out** *n* Kasse *f*. ~**room** *n* (*Amer*) Garderobe *f*. ~**up** *n* (*Med*) [Kontroll]untersuchung *f*

cheek /tʃiːk/ *n* Backe *f*; (*impudence*) Frechheit *f*. ~**y** *a*, **-ily** *adv* frech

cheep /tʃiːp/ *vi* piepen

cheer /tʃɪə(r)/ *n* Beifallsruf *m*; **three** ~**s** ein dreifaches Hoch (**for** auf + *acc*); ~**s**! prost! (*goodbye*) tschüs! □ *vt* zujubeln (+ *dat*) □ *vi* jubeln. ~ **up** *vt* aufmuntern; aufheitern □ *vi* munterer werden. ~**ful** *a*, **-ly** *adv* fröhlich. ~**fulness** *n* Fröhlichkeit *f*

cheerio /tʃɪərɪ'əʊ/ *int* (*fam*) tschüs!

'**cheerless** *a* trostlos

cheese /tʃiːz/ *n* Käse *m*. ~**cake** *n* Käsekuchen *m*

cheetah /tʃiːtə/ *n* Gepard *m*

chef /ʃef/ *n* Koch *m*

chemical /'kemɪkl/ *a*, **-ly** *adv* chemisch □ *n* Chemikalie *f*

chemist /'kemɪst/ *n* (*pharmacist*) Apotheker(in) *m(f)*; (*scientist*) Chemiker(in) *m(f)*; ~'**s** [**shop**] Drogerie *f*; (*dispensing*) Apotheke *f*. ~**ry** *n* Chemie *f*

cheque /tʃek/ *n* Scheck *m*. ~**book** *n* Scheckbuch *nt*. ~ **card** *n* Scheckkarte *f*

cherish /'tʃerɪʃ/ *vt* lieben; (*fig*) hegen

cherry /'tʃerɪ/ *n* Kirsche *f* □ *attrib* Kirsch-

cherub /'tʃerəb/ *n* Engelchen *nt*

chess /tʃes/ *n* Schach *nt*

chess: ~**board** *n* Schachbrett *nt*. ~**man** *n* Schachfigur *f*

chest /tʃest/ *n* Brust *f*; (*box*) Truhe *f*

chestnut /'tʃesnʌt/ *n* Esskastanie *f*, Marone *f*; (*horse-*) [Ross]kastanie *f*

chest of 'drawers *n* Kommode *f*

chew /tʃuː/ *vt* kauen. ~**ing-gum** *n* Kaugummi *m*

chic /ʃiːk/ *a* schick

chick /tʃɪk/ *n* Küken *nt*

chicken /'tʃɪkɪn/ *n* Huhn *nt* □ *attrib* Hühner- □ *a* (*fam*) feige □ *vi* ~ **out** (*fam*) kneifen. ~**pox** *n* Windpocken *pl*

chicory /'tʃɪkərɪ/ *n* Chicorée *m*; (*in coffee*) Zichorie *f*

chief /tʃiːf/ *a* Haupt- □ *n* Chef *m*; (*of tribe*) Häuptling *m*. ~**ly** *adv* hauptsächlich

chilblain /'tʃɪlbleɪn/ *n* Frostbeule *f*

child /tʃaɪld/ *n* (*pl* ~**ren**) Kind *nt*

child: ~**birth** *n* Geburt *f*. ~**hood** *n* Kindheit *f*. ~**ish** *a* kindisch. ~**less** *a* kinderlos. ~**like** *a* kindlich. ~**minder** *n* Tagesmutter *f*

children /'tʃɪldrən/ *npl see* **child**

Chile /'tʃɪlɪ/ *n* Chile *nt*

chill /tʃɪl/ *n* Kälte *f*; (*illness*) Erkältung *f* □ *vt* kühlen

chilli /'tʃɪlɪ/ *n* (*pl* **-es**) Chili *m*

chilly /'tʃɪlɪ/ *a* kühl; **I felt** ~ mich fröstelte [es]

chime /tʃaɪm/ *vi* läuten; ⟨*clock:*⟩ schlagen

chimney /'tʃɪmnɪ/ *n* Schornstein *m*. ~**pot** *n* Schornsteinaufsatz *m*. ~**sweep** *n* Schornsteinfeger *m*

chimpanzee /tʃɪmpæn'ziː/ *n* Schimpanse *m*

chin /tʃɪn/ *n* Kinn *nt*

china /'tʃaɪnə/ *n* Porzellan *nt*

Chin|a *n* China *nt*. ~**ese** /-'niːz/ *a* chinesisch □ *n* (*Lang*) Chinesisch *nt*; **the** ~**ese** *pl* die Chinesen. ~**ese 'lantern** *n* Lampion *m*

chink[1] /tʃɪŋk/ *n* (*slit*) Ritze *f*

chink[2] *n* Geklirr *nt* □ *vi* klirren; ⟨*coins:*⟩ klimpern

chip /tʃɪp/ *n* (*fragment*) Span *m*; (*in china, paintwork*) angeschlagene Stelle *f*; (*Computing, Gambling*) Chip *m*; ~**s** *pl* (*Culin*) Pommes frites *pl*; (*Amer: crisps*) Chips *pl* □ *vt* (*pt/pp* **chipped**) (*damage*) anschlagen. ~**ped** *a* angeschlagen

chiropod|ist /kɪ'rɒpədɪst/ *n* Fußpfleger(in) *m(f)*. ~**y** *n* Fußpflege *f*

chirp /tʃɜːp/ *vi* zwitschern; (*cricket:*) zirpen. ~**y** *a* (*fam*) munter

chisel /'tʃɪzl/ *n* Meißel *m* □ *vt/i* (*pt/pp* **chiselled**) meißeln

chit /tʃɪt/ *n* Zettel *m*

chival|rous /'ʃɪvlrəs/ *a*, **-ly** *adv* ritterlich. ~**ry** *n* Ritterlichkeit *f*

chives /tʃaɪvz/ *npl* Schnittlauch *m*

chlorine /'klɔːriːn/ *n* Chlor *nt*

chloroform /'klɒrəfɔːm/ *n* Chloroform *nt*

chocolate /'tʃɒkələt/ *n* Schokolade *f*; (*sweet*) Praline *f*

choice /tʃɔɪs/ *n* Wahl *f*; (*variety*) Auswahl *f* □ *a* auserlesen

choir /'kwaɪə(r)/ *n* Chor *m*. ~**boy** *n* Chorknabe *m*

choke /tʃəʊk/ *n* (*Auto*) Choke *m* □ *vt* würgen; (*to death*) erwürgen □ *vi* sich verschlucken; ~ **on** (*fast*) ersticken an (+ *dat*)

cholera /'kɒlərə/ *n* Cholera *f*

cholesterol /kə'lestərɒl/ *n* Cholesterin *nt*

choose /tʃuːz/ *vt/i* (*pt* **chose**, *pp* **chosen**) wählen; (*select*) sich (*dat*) aussuchen; ~ **to do/go** [freiwillig] tun/gehen; **as you** ~ wie Sie wollen

choos[e]y /'tʃuːzɪ/ *a* (*fam*) wählerisch

chop /tʃɒp/ n (*blow*) Hieb m; (*Culin*) Kotelett nt ◻ vt (*pt/pp* **chopped**) hacken. **~ down** vt abhacken; fällen ⟨*tree*⟩. **~ off** vt abhacken

chop|per /'tʃɒpə(r)/ n Beil nt; (*fam*) Hubschrauber m. **~py** a kabbelig

'chopsticks npl Essstäbchen pl

choral /'kɔ:rəl/ a Chor-; **~ society** Gesangverein m

chord /kɔ:d/ n (*Mus*) Akkord m

chore /tʃɔ:(r)/ n lästige Pflicht f; [**household**] **~s** Hausarbeit f

choreography /kɒrɪ'ɒgrəfi/ n Choreographie f

chortle /'tʃɔ:tl/ vi [vor Lachen] glucksen

chorus /'kɔ:rəs/ n Chor m; (*of song*) Refrain m

chose, chosen /tʃəʊz, 'tʃəʊzn/ *see* **choose**

Christ /kraɪst/ n Christus m

christen /'krɪsn/ vt taufen. **~ing** n Taufe f

Christian /'krɪstʃən/ a christlich ◻ n Christ(in) m(f). **~ity** /-stɪ'ænətɪ/ n Christentum nt. **~ name** n Vorname m

Christmas /'krɪsməs/ n Weihnachten nt. **~ card** n Weihnachtskarte f. **~ 'Day** n erster Weihnachtstag m. **~ 'Eve** n Heiligabend m. **~ tree** n Weihnachtsbaum m

chrome /krəʊm/ n, **chromium** /'krəʊmɪəm/ n Chrom nt

chromosome /'krəʊməsəʊm/ n Chromosom nt

chronic /'krɒnɪk/ a chronisch

chronicle /'krɒnɪkl/ n Chronik f

chronological /krɒnə'lɒdʒɪkl/ a, -ly adv chronologisch

chrysalis /'krɪsəlɪs/ n Puppe f

chrysanthemum /krɪ'sænθəməm/ n Chrysantheme f

chubby /'tʃʌbɪ/ a (-ier, -iest) mollig

chuck /tʃʌk/ vt (*fam*) schmeißen. **~ out** vt (*fam*) rausschmeißen

chuckle /'tʃʌkl/ vi in sich (*acc*) hineinlachen

chum /tʃʌm/ n Freund(in) m(f)

chunk /tʃʌŋk/ n Stück nt

church /tʃɜ:tʃ/ n Kirche f. **~yard** n Friedhof m

churlish /'tʃɜ:lɪʃ/ a unhöflich

churn /tʃɜ:n/ n Butterfass nt; (*for milk*) Milchkanne f ◻ vt **~ out** am laufenden Band produzieren

chute /ʃu:t/ n Rutsche f; (*for rubbish*) Müllschlucker m

CID abbr (**Criminal Investigation Department**) Kripo f

cider /'saɪdə(r)/ n Apfelwein m

cigar /sɪ'gɑ:(r)/ n Zigarre f

cigarette /sɪgə'ret/ n Zigarette f

cine-camera /'sɪnɪ-/ n Filmkamera f

cinema /'sɪnɪmə/ n Kino nt

cinnamon /'sɪnəmən/ n Zimt m

cipher /'saɪfə(r)/ n (*code*) Chiffre f; (*numeral*) Ziffer f; (*fig*) Null f

circle /'sɜ:kl/ n Kreis m; (*Theat*) Rang m ◻ vt umkreisen ◻ vi kreisen

circuit /'sɜ:kɪt/ n Runde f; (*racetrack*) Rennbahn f; (*Electr*) Stromkreis m. **~ous** /sə'kju:ɪtəs/ a **~ route** Umweg m

circular /'sɜ:kjʊlə(r)/ a kreisförmig ◻ n Rundschreiben nt. **~ 'saw** n Kreissäge f. **~ 'tour** n Rundfahrt f

circulat|e /'sɜ:kjʊleɪt/ vt in Umlauf setzen ◻ vi zirkulieren. **~ion** /-'leɪʃn/ n Kreislauf m; (*of newspaper*) Auflage f

circumcis|e /'sɜ:kəmsaɪz/ vt beschneiden. **~ion** /-'sɪʒn/ n Beschneidung f

circumference /sə'kʌmfərəns/ n Umfang m

circumspect /'sɜ:kəmspekt/ a, -ly adv umsichtig

circumstance /'sɜ:kəmstəns/ n Umstand m; **~s** pl Umstände pl; (*financial*) Verhältnisse pl

circus /'sɜ:kəs/ n Zirkus m

CIS abbr (**Commonwealth of Independent States**) GUS f

cistern /'sɪstən/ n (*tank*) Wasserbehälter m; (*of WC*) Spülkasten m

cite /saɪt/ vt zitieren

citizen /'sɪtɪzn/ n Bürger(in) m(f). **~ship** n Staatsangehörigkeit f

citrus /'sɪtrəs/ n **~ [fruit]** Zitrusfrucht f

city /'sɪtɪ/ n [Groß]stadt f

civic /'sɪvɪk/ a Bürger-

civil /'sɪvl/ a bürgerlich; ⟨*aviation, defence*⟩ zivil; (*polite*) höflich. **~ engi'neering** n Hoch- und Tiefbau m

civilian /sɪ'vɪljən/ a Zivil-; **in ~ clothes** in Zivil ◻ n Zivilist m

civility /sɪ'vɪlətɪ/ n Höflichkeit f

civiliz|ation /sɪvəlaɪ'zeɪʃn/ n Zivilisation f. **~e** /'sɪvəlaɪz/ vt zivilisieren

civil: ~ 'servant n Beamte(r) m/Beamtin f. **C~ 'Service** n Staatsdienst m

clad /klæd/ a gekleidet (**in** in + *acc*)

claim /kleɪm/ n Anspruch m; (*application*) Antrag m; (*demand*) Forderung f; (*assertion*) Behauptung f ◻ vt beanspruchen; (*apply for*) beantragen; (*demand*) fordern; (*assert*) behaupten; (*collect*) abholen. **~ant** n Antragsteller m

clairvoyant /kleə'vɔɪənt/ n Hellseher(in) m(f)

clam /klæm/ n Klaffmuschel f

clamber /'klæmbə(r)/ vi klettern

clammy /'klæmɪ/ a (-ier, -iest) feucht

clamour /'klæmə(r)/ n Geschrei nt □ vi ∼ for schreien nach

clamp /klæmp/ n Klammer f □ vt [ein]-spannen □ vi (fam) ∼ **down** durchgreifen; ∼ **down on** vorgehen gegen

clan /klæn/ n Clan m

clandestine /klæn'destɪn/ a geheim

clang /klæŋ/ n Schmettern nt. ∼**er** n (fam) Schnitzer m

clank /klæŋk/ vi klirren

clap /klæp/ n **give s.o. a** ∼ jdm Beifall klatschen; ∼ **of thunder** Donnerschlag m □ vt/i (pt/pp **clapped**) Beifall klatschen (+ dat); ∼ **one's hands** [in die Hände] klatschen

claret /'klærət/ n roter Bordeaux m

clari|fication /klærɪfɪ'keɪʃn/ n Klärung f. ∼**fy** /'klærɪfaɪ/ vt/i (pt/pp -ied) klären

clarinet /klærɪ'net/ n Klarinette f

clarity /'klærətɪ/ n Klarheit f

clash /klæʃ/ n Geklirr nt; (fig) Konflikt m □ vi klirren; ⟨colours:⟩ sich beißen; ⟨events:⟩ ungünstig zusammenfallen

clasp /klɑːsp/ n Verschluss m □ vt ergreifen; ⟨hold⟩ halten

class /klɑːs/ n Klasse f; **travel first/second** ∼ erster/zweiter Klasse reisen □ vt einordnen

classic /'klæsɪk/ a klassisch □ n Klassiker m; ∼**s** pl (Univ) Altphilologie f. ∼**al** a klassisch

classi|fication /klæsɪfɪ'keɪʃn/ n Klassifikation f. ∼**fy** /'klæsɪfaɪ/ vt (pt/pp -ied) klassifizieren

'classroom n Klassenzimmer nt

classy /'klɑːsɪ/ a (-ier, -iest) (fam) schick

clatter /'klætə(r)/ n Geklapper nt □ vi klappern

clause /klɔːz/ n Klausel f; (Gram) Satzteil m

claustrophobia /klɔːstrə'fəʊbɪə/ n Klaustrophobie f, (fam) Platzangst m

claw /klɔː/ n Kralle f; ⟨of bird of prey & Techn⟩ Klaue f; ⟨of crab, lobster⟩ Schere f □ vt kratzen

clay /kleɪ/ n Lehm m; (pottery) Ton m

clean /kliːn/ a (-er, -est) sauber □ adv glatt □ vt sauber machen; putzen ⟨shoes, windows⟩; ∼ **one's teeth** sich (dat) die Zähne putzen; **have sth** ∼**ed** etw reinigen lassen. ∼ **up** vt sauber machen

cleaner /'kliːnə(r)/ n Putzfrau f; (substance) Reinigungsmittel nt; [**dry**] ∼'**s** chemische Reinigung f

cleanliness /'klenlɪnɪs/ n Sauberkeit f

cleanse /klenz/ vt reinigen. ∼**r** n Reinigungsmittel nt

clean-shaven a glatt rasiert

cleansing cream /'klenz-/ n Reinigungscreme f

clear /klɪə(r)/ a (-er, -est), **-ly** adv klar; (obvious) eindeutig; (distinct) deutlich; ⟨conscience⟩ rein; ⟨without obstacles⟩ frei; **make sth** ∼ etw klarmachen (**to** dat) □ adv **stand** ∼ zurücktreten; **keep** ∼ **of** aus dem Wege gehen (+ dat) □ vt räumen; abräumen ⟨table⟩; ⟨acquit⟩ freisprechen; ⟨authorize⟩ genehmigen; ⟨jump over⟩ überspringen; ∼ **one's throat** sich räuspern □ vi ⟨fog:⟩ sich auflösen. ∼ **away** vt wegräumen. ∼ **off** vi (fam) abhauen. ∼ **out** vt ausräumen □ vi (fam) abhauen. ∼ **up** vt (tidy) aufräumen; (solve) aufklären □ vi ⟨weather:⟩ sich aufklären

clearance /'klɪərəns/ n Räumung f; (authorization) Genehmigung f; (customs) [Zoll]abfertigung f; (Techn) Spielraum m. ∼ **sale** n Räumungsverkauf m

clear|ing /'klɪərɪŋ/ n Lichtung f. ∼**way** n (Auto) Straße f mit Halteverbot

cleavage /'kliːvɪdʒ/ n Spaltung f; ⟨woman's⟩ Dekolleté nt

clef /klef/ n Notenschlüssel m

cleft /kleft/ n Spalte f

clemen|cy /'klemənsɪ/ n Milde f. ∼**t** a mild

clench /klentʃ/ vt ∼ **one's fist** die Faust ballen; ∼ **one's teeth** die Zähne zusammenbeißen

clergy /'klɜːdʒɪ/ npl Geistlichkeit f. ∼**man** n Geistliche(r) m

cleric /'klerɪk/ n Geistliche(r) m. ∼**al** a Schreib-; (Relig) geistlich

clerk /klɑːk, Amer: /klɜːk/ n Büroangestellte(r) m/f; (Amer: shop assistant) Verkäufer(in) m(f)

clever /'klevə(r)/ a (-er, -est), **-ly** adv klug; (skilful) geschickt

cliché /'kliːʃeɪ/ n Klischee nt

click /klɪk/ vi klicken

client /'klaɪənt/ n Kunde m/ Kundin f; (Jur) Klient(in) m(f)

clientele /kliːɒn'tel/ n Kundschaft f

cliff /klɪf/ n Kliff nt

climat|e /'klaɪmət/ n Klima nt. ∼**ic** /-'mætɪk/ a klimatisch

climax /'klaɪmæks/ n Höhepunkt m

climb /klaɪm/ n Aufstieg m □ vt besteigen ⟨mountain⟩; steigen auf (+ acc) ⟨ladder, tree⟩ □ vi klettern; ⟨rise⟩ steigen; ⟨road:⟩ ansteigen. ∼ **down** vi hinunter-/herunterklettern; ⟨from ladder, tree⟩ heruntersteigen; (fam) nachgeben

climber /'klaɪmə(r)/ n Bergsteiger m; (plant) Kletterpflanze f

clinch /klɪntʃ/ vt perfekt machen ⟨deal⟩ ◻ vi ⟨boxing⟩ clinchen

cling /klɪŋ/ vi ⟨pt/pp clung⟩ sich klammern (to an + acc); ⟨stick⟩ haften (to an + dat). **~film** n Sichtfolie f mit Hafteffekt

clinic /'klɪnɪk/ n Klinik f. **~al** a, **-ly** adv klinisch

clink /klɪŋk/ n Klirren nt; ⟨fam: prison⟩ Knast m ◻ vi klirren

clip¹ /klɪp/ n Klammer f; ⟨jewellery⟩ Klipp m ◻ vt ⟨pt/pp **clipped**⟩ anklammern (to an + acc)

clip² n ⟨extract⟩ Ausschnitt m ◻ vt schneiden; knipsen ⟨ticket⟩. **~board** n Klemmbrett nt. **~pers** npl Schere f. **~ping** n ⟨extract⟩ Ausschnitt m

clique /kliːk/ n Clique f

cloak /kləʊk/ n Umhang m. **~room** n Garderobe f; ⟨toilet⟩ Toilette f

clobber /'klɒbə(r)/ n ⟨fam⟩ Zeug nt ◻ vt ⟨fam: hit, defeat⟩ schlagen

clock /klɒk/ n Uhr f; ⟨fam: speedometer⟩ Tacho m ◻ vi ~ **in/out** stechen

clock: ~ tower n Uhrenturm m. **~wise** a & adv im Uhrzeigersinn. **~work** n Uhrwerk nt; ⟨of toy⟩ Aufziehmechanismus m; **like ~work** ⟨fam⟩ wie am Schnürchen

clod /klɒd/ n Klumpen m

clog /klɒg/ n Holzschuh m ◻ vt/i ⟨pt/pp **clogged**⟩ ~ **[up]** verstopfen

cloister /'klɔɪstə(r)/ n Kreuzgang m

close¹ /kləʊs/ a ⟨-r, -st⟩ nah[e] (to dat); ⟨friend⟩ eng; ⟨weather⟩ schwül; **have a ~ shave** ⟨fam⟩ mit knapper Not davonkommen ◻ adv nahe; ~ **by** nicht weit weg ◻ n ⟨street⟩ Sackgasse f

close² /kləʊz/ n Ende nt; **draw to a ~** sich dem Ende nähern ◻ vt zumachen, schließen; ⟨bring to an end⟩ beenden; sperren ⟨road⟩ ◻ vi sich schließen; ⟨shop:⟩ schließen, zumachen; ⟨end⟩ enden. ~ **down** vt schließen; stilllegen ⟨factory⟩ ◻ vi schließen; ⟨factory:⟩ stillgelegt werden

closed 'shop /kləʊzd-/ n ≈ Gewerkschaftszwang m

closely /'kləʊslɪ/ adv eng, nah[e]; ⟨with attention⟩ genau

close season /'kləʊs-/ n Schonzeit f

closet /'klɒzɪt/ n ⟨Amer⟩ Schrank m

close-up /'kləʊs-/ n Nahaufnahme f

closure /'kləʊʒə(r)/ n Schließung f; ⟨of factory⟩ Stilllegung f; ⟨of road⟩ Sperrung f

clot /klɒt/ n ⟨Blut⟩gerinnsel nt; ⟨fam: idiot⟩ Trottel m ◻ vi ⟨pt/pp **clotted**⟩ ⟨blood:⟩ gerinnen

cloth /klɒθ/ n Tuch nt

clothe /kləʊð/ vt kleiden

clothes /kləʊðz/ npl Kleider pl. **~-brush** n Kleiderbürste f. **~line** n Wäscheleine f

clothing /'kləʊðɪŋ/ n Kleidung f

cloud /klaʊd/ n Wolke f ◻ vi ~ **over** sich bewölken. **~burst** n Wolkenbruch m

cloudy /'klaʊdɪ/ a ⟨-ier, -iest⟩ wolkig, bewölkt; ⟨liquid⟩ trübe

clout /klaʊt/ n ⟨fam⟩ Schlag m; ⟨influence⟩ Einfluss m ◻ vt ⟨fam⟩ hauen

clove /kləʊv/ n [Gewürz]nelke f; ~ **of garlic** Knoblauchzehe f

clover /'kləʊvə(r)/ n Klee m. ~ **leaf** n Kleeblatt nt

clown /klaʊn/ n Clown m ◻ vi ~ **[about]** herumalbern

club /klʌb/ n Klub m; ⟨weapon⟩ Keule f; ⟨Sport⟩ Schläger m; ~**s** pl ⟨Cards⟩ Kreuz nt, Treff nt ◻ v ⟨pt/pp **clubbed**⟩ ◻ vt knüppeln ◻ vi ~ **together** zusammenlegen

cluck /klʌk/ vi glucken

clue /kluː/ n Anhaltspunkt m; ⟨in crossword⟩ Frage f; **I haven't a ~** ⟨fam⟩ ich habe keine Ahnung

clump /klʌmp/ n Gruppe f

clumsiness /'klʌmzɪnɪs/ n Ungeschicklichkeit f

clumsy /'klʌmzɪ/ a ⟨-ier, -iest⟩, **-ily** adv ungeschickt; ⟨unwieldy⟩ unförmig

clung /klʌŋ/ see **cling**

cluster /'klʌstə(r)/ n Gruppe f; ⟨of flowers⟩ Büschel nt ◻ vi sich scharen ⟨round um⟩

clutch /klʌtʃ/ n Griff m; ⟨Auto⟩ Kupplung f; **be in s.o.'s ~es** ⟨fam⟩ in jds Klauen sein ◻ vt festhalten; ⟨grab⟩ ergreifen ◻ vi ~ **at** greifen nach

clutter /'klʌtə(r)/ n Kram m ◻ vt ~ **[up]** vollstopfen

c/o abbr ⟨care of⟩ bei

coach /kəʊtʃ/ n [Reise]bus m; ⟨Rail⟩ Wagen m; ⟨horse-drawn⟩ Kutsche f; ⟨Sport⟩ Trainer m ◻ vt Nachhilfestunden geben (+ dat); ⟨Sport⟩ trainieren

coagulate /kəʊˈægjʊleɪt/ vi gerinnen

coal /kəʊl/ n Kohle f

coalition /kəʊəˈlɪʃn/ n Koalition f

'coal-mine n Kohlenbergwerk nt

coarse /kɔːs/ a ⟨-r, -st⟩, **-ly** adv grob

coast /kəʊst/ n Küste f ◻ vi ⟨freewheel⟩ im Freilauf fahren; ⟨Auto⟩ im Leerlauf fahren. **~al** a Küsten-. **~er** n ⟨mat⟩ Untersatz m

coast: ~guard n Küstenwache f. **~line** n Küste f

coat /kəʊt/ n Mantel m; ⟨of animal⟩ Fell nt; ⟨of paint⟩ Anstrich m; ~ **of arms** Wappen nt ◻ vt überziehen; ⟨with paint⟩ streichen. **~-hanger** n Kleiderbügel m. **~-hook** n Kleiderhaken m

coating /'kəʊtɪŋ/ n Überzug m, Schicht f; (of paint) Anstrich m

coax /kəʊks/ vt gut zureden (+ dat)

cob /kɒb/ n (of corn) [Mais]kolben m

cobble[1] /'kɒbl/ n Kopfstein m; ∼s pl Kopfsteinpflaster nt

cobble[2] vt flicken. ∼r n Schuster m

'cobblestones npl = cobbles

cobweb /'kɒb-/ n Spinnengewebe nt

cocaine /kə'keɪn/ n Kokain nt

cock /kɒk/ n Hahn m; (any male bird) Männchen nt □ vt (animal:) ∼ its ears die Ohren spitzen; ∼ the gun den Hahn spannen. ∼-and-'bull story n (fam) Lügengeschichte f

cockerel /'kɒkərəl/ n [junger] Hahn m

cock-'eyed a (fam) schief; (absurd) verrückt

cockle /'kɒkl/ n Herzmuschel f

cockney /'kɒknɪ/ n (dialect) Cockney nt; (person) Cockney m

cock: ∼pit n (Aviat) Cockpit nt. ∼roach /-rəʊtʃ/ n Küchenschabe f. ∼tail n Cocktail m. ∼-up n (sl) make a ∼-up Mist bauen (of bei)

cocky /'kɒkɪ/ a (-ier, -iest) (fam) eingebildet

cocoa /'kəʊkəʊ/ n Kakao m

coconut /'kəʊkənʌt/ n Kokosnuß f

cocoon /kə'ku:n/ n Kokon m

cod /kɒd/ n inv Kabeljau m

COD abbr (cash on delivery) per Nachnahme

coddle /'kɒdl/ vt verhätscheln

code /kəʊd/ n Kode m; (Computing) Code m; (set of rules) Kodex m. ∼d a verschlüsselt

coedu'cational /kəʊ-/ a gemischt. ∼ school n Koedukationsschule f

coerce /kəʊ'ɜ:s/ vt zwingen. ∼ion /-'ɜ:ʃn/ n Zwang m

coe'xist vi koexistieren. ∼ence n Koexistenz f

coffee /'kɒfɪ/ n Kaffee m

coffee: ∼-grinder n Kaffeemühle f. ∼-pot n Kaffeekanne f. ∼-table n Couchtisch m

coffin /'kɒfɪn/ n Sarg m

cog /kɒg/ n (Techn) Zahn m

cogent /'kəʊdʒənt/ a überzeugend

cog-wheel n Zahnrad nt

cohabit /kəʊ'hæbɪt/ vi (Jur) zusammenleben

coherent /kəʊ'hɪərənt/ a zusammenhängend; (comprehensible) verständlich

coil /kɔɪl/ n Rolle f; (Electr) Spule f; (one ring) Windung f □ vt ∼ [up] zusammenrollen

coin /kɔɪn/ n Münze f □ vt prägen

coincide /kəʊɪn'saɪd/ vi zusammenfallen; (agree) übereinstimmen

coinciden|ce /kəʊ'ɪnsɪdəns/ n Zufall m. ∼tal /-'dentl/ a, -ly adv zufällig

coke /kəʊk/ n Koks m

Coke (P) n (drink) Cola f

colander /'kʌləndə(r)/ n (Culin) Durchschlag m

cold /kəʊld/ a (-er, -est) kalt; **I am** or **feel** ∼ mir ist kalt □ n Kälte f; (Med) Erkältung f

cold: ∼-'blooded a kaltblütig. ∼-'hearted a kaltherzig. ∼ly adv (fig) kalt, kühl. ∼ness n Kälte f

coleslaw /'kəʊlslɔ:/ n Krautsalat m

colic /'kɒlɪk/ n Kolik f

collaborat|e /kə'læbəreɪt/ vi zusammenarbeiten (**with** mit); ∼e **on sth** mitarbeiten bei etw. ∼ion /-'reɪʃn/ n Zusammenarbeit f, Mitarbeit f; (with enemy) Kollaboration f. ∼or n Mitarbeiter(in) m(f); Kollaborateur m

collaps|e /kə'læps/ n Zusammenbruch m; Einsturz m □ vi zusammenbrechen; (roof, building:) einstürzen. ∼ible a zusammenklappbar

collar /'kɒlə(r)/ n Kragen m; (for animal) Halsband nt. ∼-bone n Schlüsselbein nt

colleague /'kɒli:g/ n Kollege m/Kollegin f

collect /kə'lekt/ vt sammeln; (fetch) abholen; einsammeln (tickets); einziehen (taxes) □ vi sich [an]sammeln □ adv call ∼ (Amer) ein R-Gespräch führen. ∼ed /-ɪd/ a gesammelt; (calm) gefasst

collection /kə'lekʃn/ n Sammlung f; (in church) Kollekte f; (of post) Leerung f; (designer's) Kollektion f

collective /kə'lektɪv/ a gemeinsam; (Pol) kollektiv. ∼ 'noun n Kollektivum nt

collector /kə'lektə(r)/ n Sammler(in) m(f)

college /'kɒlɪdʒ/ n College nt

collide /kə'laɪd/ vi zusammenstoßen

colliery /'kɒlɪərɪ/ n Kohlengrube f

collision /kə'lɪʒn/ n Zusammenstoß m

colloquial /kə'ləʊkwɪəl/ a, -ly adv umgangssprachlich. ∼ism n umgangssprachlicher Ausdruck m

Cologne /kə'ləʊn/ n Köln nt

colon /'kəʊlən/ n Doppelpunkt m; (Anat) Dickdarm m

colonel /'kɜ:nl/ n Oberst m

colonial /kə'ləʊnɪəl/ a Kolonial-

colon|ize /'kɒlənaɪz/ vt kolonisieren. ∼y n Kolonie f

colossal /kə'lɒsl/ a riesig

colour /'kʌlə(r)/ n Farbe f; (complexion) Gesichtsfarbe f; (race) Hautfarbe f; ∼s pl (*flag*) Fahne *f*; **off** ~ (*fam*) nicht ganz auf der Höhe □ *vt* färben; ~ **[in]** ausmalen □ *vi* (*blush*) erröten

colour: ~ **bar** *n* Rassenschranke *f*. ~**blind** *a* farbenblind. ~**ed** *a* farbig □ *n* (*person*) Farbige(r) *m/f*. ~**fast** *a* farbecht. ~ **film** *n* Farbfilm *m*. ~**ful** *a* farbenfroh. ~**less** *a* farblos. ~ **photo[graph]** *n* Farbaufnahme *f*. ~ **television** *n* Farbfernsehen *nt*

colt /kəʊlt/ *n* junger Hengst *m*

column /'kɒləm/ *n* Säule *f*; (*of soldiers, figures*) Kolonne *f*; (*Typ*) Spalte *f*; (*Journ*) Kolumne *f*. ~**ist** /-nɪst/ *n* Kolumnist *m*

coma /'kəʊmə/ *n* Koma *nt*

comb /kəʊm/ *n* Kamm *m* □ *vt* kämmen; (*search*) absuchen; ~ **one's hair** sich (*dat*) [die Haare] kämmen

combat /'kɒmbæt/ *n* Kampf *m* □ *vt* (*pt/pp* **combated**) bekämpfen

combination /kɒmbɪ'neɪʃn/ *n* Verbindung *f*; (*for lock*) Kombination *f*

combine[1] /kəm'baɪn/ *vt* verbinden □ *vi* sich verbinden; (*people:*) sich zusammenschließen

combine[2] /'kɒmbaɪn/ *n* (*Comm*) Konzern *m*; ~ **[harvester]** *n* Mähdrescher *m*

combustion /kəm'bʌstʃn/ *n* Verbrennung *f*

come /kʌm/ *vi* (*pt* came, *pp* come) kommen; (*reach*) reichen (**to an** + *acc*); **that** ~**s to £10** das macht £10; ~ **into money** zu Geld kommen; ~ **true** wahr werden; ~ **in two sizes** in zwei Größen erhältlich sein; **the years to** ~ die kommenden Jahre; **how** ~? (*fam*) wie das? ~ **about** *vi* geschehen. ~ **across** *vi* herüberkommen; (*fam*) klar werden □ *vt* stoßen auf (+ *acc*). ~ **apart** *vi* sich auseinander nehmen lassen; (*accidentally*) auseinander gehen. ~ **away** *vi* weggehen; (*thing:*) abgehen. ~ **back** *vi* zurückkommen. ~ **by** *vi* vorbeikommen □ *vt* (*obtain*) bekommen. ~ **in** *vi* hereinkommen. ~ **off** *vi* abgehen; (*take place*) stattfinden; (*succeed*) klappen (*fam*). ~ **out** *vi* herauskommen; (*book:*) erscheinen; (*stain:*) herausgehen. ~ **round** *vi* vorbeikommen; (*after fainting*) [wieder] zu sich kommen; (*change one's mind*) sich umstimmen lassen. ~ **to** *vi* [wieder] zu sich kommen. ~ **up** *vi* heraufkommen; (*plant:*) aufgehen; (*reach*) reichen (**to** bis); ~ **up with** sich (*dat*) einfallen lassen

'**come-back** *n* Comeback *nt*

comedian /kə'miːdɪən/ *n* Komiker *m*

'**come-down** *n* Rückschritt *m*

comedy /'kɒmədɪ/ *n* Komödie *f*

comet /'kɒmɪt/ *n* Komet *m*

come-uppance /kʌm'ʌpəns/ *n* **get one's** ~ (*fam*) sein Fett abkriegen

comfort /'kʌmfət/ *n* Bequemlichkeit *f*; (*consolation*) Trost *m* □ *vt* trösten

comfortable /'kʌmfətəbl/ *a*, **-bly** *adv* bequem

'**comfort station** *n* (*Amer*) öffentliche Toilette *f*

comfy /'kʌmfɪ/ *a* (*fam*) bequem

comic /'kɒmɪk/ *a* komisch □ *n* Komiker *m*; (*periodical*) Comic-Heft *nt*. ~**al** *a*, **-ly** *adv* komisch. ~ **strip** *n* Comic Strips *pl*

coming /'kʌmɪŋ/ *a* kommend □ *n* Kommen *nt*; ~**s and goings** Kommen und Gehen *nt*

comma /'kɒmə/ *n* Komma *nt*

command /kə'mɑːnd/ *n* Befehl *m*; (*Mil*) Kommando *nt*; (*mastery*) Beherrschung *f* □ *vt* befehlen (+ *dat*); kommandieren ⟨*army*⟩

commandeer /kɒmən'dɪə(r)/ *vt* beschlagnahmen

command|er /kə'mɑːndə(r)/ *n* Befehlshaber *m*; (*of unit*) Kommandeur *m*; (*of ship*) Kommandant *m*. ~**ing** *a* ⟨*view*⟩ beherrschend. ~**ing officer** *n* Befehlshaber *m*. ~**ment** *n* Gebot *nt*

commemorat|e /kə'meməreɪt/ *vt* gedenken (+ *gen*). ~**ion** /-'reɪʃn/ *n* Gedenken *nt*. ~**ive** /-ətɪv/ *a* Gedenk-

commence /kə'mens/ *vt/i* anfangen, beginnen. ~**ment** *n* Anfang *m*, Beginn *m*

commend /kə'mend/ *vt* loben; (*recommend*) empfehlen (**to** *dat*). ~**able** /-əbl/ *a* lobenswert. ~**ation** /kɒmen'deɪʃn/ *n* Lob *nt*

commensurate /kə'menʃərət/ *a* angemessen; **be** ~ **with** entsprechen (+ *dat*)

comment /'kɒment/ *n* Bemerkung *f*; **no** ~! kein Kommentar! □ *vi* sich äußern (**on** zu); ~ **on** (*Journ*) kommentieren

commentary /'kɒməntrɪ/ *n* Kommentar *m*; **[running]** ~ (*Radio, TV*) Reportage *f*

commentator /'kɒmənteɪtə(r)/ *n* Kommentator *m*; (*Sport*) Reporter *m*

commerce /'kɒmɜːs/ *n* Handel *m*

commercial /kə'mɜːʃl/ *a*, **-ly** *adv* kommerziell □ *n* (*Radio, TV*) Werbespot *m*. ~**ize** *vt* kommerzialisieren

commiserate /kə'mɪzəreɪt/ *vi* sein Mitleid ausdrücken (**with** *dat*)

commission /kə'mɪʃn/ *n* (*order for work*) Auftrag *m*; (*body of people*) Kommission *f*; (*payment*) Provision *f*; (*Mil*) [Offiziers]patent *nt*; **out of** ~ außer Betrieb □ *vt* beauftragen ⟨*s.o.*⟩; in Auftrag geben ⟨*thing*⟩; (*Mil*) zum Offizier ernennen

commissionaire /kəmɪʃə'neə(r)/ *n* Portier *m*

commissioner /kə'mɪʃənə(r)/ *n* Kommissar *m*; **~ for oaths** Notar *m*

commit /kə'mɪt/ *vt* (*pt/pp* **committed**) begehen; (*entrust*) anvertrauen (**to** *dat*); (*consign*) einweisen (**to in** + *acc*); **~ oneself** sich festlegen; (*involve oneself*) sich engagieren; **~ sth to memory** sich (*dat*) etw einprägen. **~ment** *n* Verpflichtung *f*; (*involvement*) Engagement *nt*. **~ted** *a* engagiert

committee /kə'mɪtɪ/ *n* Ausschuss *m*, Komitee *nt*

commodity /kə'mɒdətɪ/ *n* Ware *f*

common /'kɒmən/ *a* (-er, -est) gemeinsam; (*frequent*) häufig; (*ordinary*) gewöhnlich; (*vulgar*) ordinär □ *n* Gemeindeland *nt*; **have in ~** gemeinsam haben; **House of C~s** Unterhaus *nt*. **~er** *n* Bürgerliche(r) *m/f*

common: **~ 'law** *n* Gewohnheitsrecht *nt*. **~ly** *adv* allgemein. **C~ 'Market** *n* Gemeinsamer Markt *m*. **~place** *a* häufig. **~room** *n* Aufenthaltsraum *m*. **~ 'sense** *n* gesunder Menschenverstand *m*

commotion /kə'məʊʃn/ *n* Tumult *m*

communal /'kɒmjʊnl/ *a* gemeinschaftlich

communicable /kə'mjuːnɪkəbl/ *a* (*disease*) übertragbar

communicate /kə'mjuːnɪkeɪt/ *vt* mitteilen (**to** *dat*); übertragen (disease) □ *vi* sich verständigen; (*be in touch*) in Verbindung stehen

communication /kəmjuːnɪ'keɪʃn/ *n* Verständigung *f*; (*contact*) Verbindung *f*; (*of disease*) Übertragung *f*; (*message*) Mitteilung *f*; **~s** *pl* (*technology*) Nachrichtenwesen *nt*. **~ cord** *n* Notbremse *f*

communicative /kə'mjuːnɪkətɪv/ *a* mitteilsam

Communion /kə'mjuːnɪən/ *n* [Holy] **~** das [heilige] Abendmahl; (*Roman Catholic*) die [heilige] Kommunion

communiqué /kə'mjuːnɪkeɪ/ *n* Kommuniqué *nt*

Communis|m /'kɒmjʊnɪzm/ *n* Kommunismus *m*. **~t** /-ɪst/ *a* kommunistisch □ *n* Kommunist(in) *m(f)*

community /kə'mjuːnətɪ/ *n* Gemeinschaft *f*; **local ~** Gemeinde *f*. **~ centre** *n* Gemeinschaftszentrum *nt*

commute /kə'mjuːt/ *vi* pendeln □ *vt* (*Jur*) umwandeln. **~r** *n* Pendler(in) *m(f)*

compact[1] /kəm'pækt/ *a* kompakt

compact[2] /'kɒmpækt/ *n* Puderdose *f*. **~ disc** *n* CD *f*

companion /kəm'pænjən/ *n* Begleiter(in) *m(f)*. **~ship** *n* Gesellschaft *f*

company /'kʌmpənɪ/ *n* Gesellschaft *f*; (*firm*) Firma *f*; (*Mil*) Kompanie *f*; (*fam:*

guests) Besuch *m*. **~ car** *n* Firmenwagen *m*

comparable /'kɒmpərəbl/ *a* vergleichbar

comparative /kəm'pærətɪv/ *a* vergleichend; (*relative*) relativ □ *n* (*Gram*) Komparativ *m*. **~ly** *adv* verhältnismäßig

compare /kəm'peə(r)/ *vt* vergleichen (**with/to** mit) □ *vi* sich vergleichen lassen

comparison /kəm'pærɪsn/ *n* Vergleich *m*

compartment /kəm'pɑːtmənt/ *n* Fach *nt*; (*Rail*) Abteil *nt*

compass /'kʌmpəs/ *n* Kompass *m*. **~es** *npl* **pair of ~es** Zirkel *m*

compassion /kəm'pæʃn/ *n* Mitleid *nt*. **~ate** /-ʃənət/ *a* mitfühlend

compatible /kəm'pætəbl/ *a* vereinbar; (*drugs*) verträglich; (*Techn*) kompatibel; **be ~** (*people:*) [gut] zueinander passen

compatriot /kəm'pætrɪət/ *n* Landsmann *m* /-männin *f*

compel /kəm'pel/ *vt* (*pt/pp* **compelled**) zwingen

compensat|e /'kɒmpənseɪt/ *vt* entschädigen □ *vi* **~e for** (*fig*) ausgleichen. **~ion** /-'seɪʃn/ *n* Entschädigung *f*; (*fig*) Ausgleich *m*

compère /'kɒmpeə(r)/ *n* Conférencier *m*

compete /kəm'piːt/ *vi* konkurrieren; (*take part*) teilnehmen (**in** an + *dat*)

competen|ce /'kɒmpɪtəns/ *n* Tüchtigkeit *f*; (*ability*) Fähigkeit *f*; (*Jur*) Kompetenz *f*. **~t** *a* tüchtig; fähig; (*Jur*) kompetent

competition /kɒmpə'tɪʃn/ *n* Konkurrenz *f*; (*contest*) Wettbewerb *m*; (*in newspaper*) Preisausschreiben *nt*

competitive /kəm'petətɪv/ *a* (*Comm*) konkurrenzfähig

competitor /kəm'petɪtə(r)/ *n* Teilnehmer *m*; (*Comm*) Konkurrent *m*

compile /kəm'paɪl/ *vt* zusammenstellen; verfassen (*dictionary*)

complacen|cy /kəm'pleɪsənsɪ/ *n* Selbstzufriedenheit *f*. **~t** *a*, **-ly** *adv* selbstzufrieden

complain /kəm'pleɪn/ *vi* klagen (**about/of** über + *acc*); (*formally*) sich beschweren. **~t** *n* Klage *f*; (*formal*) Beschwerde *f*; (*Med*) Leiden *nt*

complement[1] /'kɒmplɪmənt/ *n* Ergänzung *f*; **full ~** volle Anzahl *f*

complement[2] /'kɒmplɪment/ *vt* ergänzen; **~ each other** sich ergänzen. **~ary** /-'mentərɪ/ *a* sich ergänzend; **be ~ary** sich ergänzen

complete /kəm'pliːt/ *a* vollständig; (*finished*) fertig; (*utter*) völlig □ *vt* vervollständigen; (*finish*) abschließen; (*fill in*) ausfüllen. **~ly** *adv* völlig

completion /kəm'pli:ʃn/ n Vervollständigung f; (end) Abschluss m

complex /'kɒmpleks/ a komplex □ n Komplex m

complexion /kəm'plekʃn/ n Teint m; (colour) Gesichtsfarbe f; (fig) Aspekt m

complexity /kəm'pleksəti/ n Komplexität f

compliance /kəm'plaɪəns/ n Einverständnis nt; in ~ with gemäß (+ dat)

complicat|e /'kɒmplɪkeɪt/ vt komplizieren. ~ed a kompliziert. ~ion /-'keɪʃn/ n Komplikation f

complicity /kəm'plɪsəti/ n Mittäterschaft f

compliment /'kɒmplɪmənt/ n Kompliment nt; ~s pl Grüße pl □ vt ein Kompliment machen (+ dat). ~ary /-'mentəri/ a schmeichelhaft; (given free) Frei-

comply /kəm'plaɪ/ vi (pt/pp -ied) ~ with nachkommen (+ dat)

component /kəm'pəʊnənt/ a & n = [part] Bestandteil m, Teil nt

compose /kəm'pəʊz/ vt verfassen; (Mus) komponieren; ~ oneself sich fassen; be ~d of sich zusammensetzen aus. ~d a (calm) gefasst. ~r n Komponist m

composition /kɒmpə'zɪʃn/ n Komposition f; (essay) Aufsatz m

compost /'kɒmpɒst/ n Kompost m

composure /kəm'pəʊʒə(r)/ n Fassung f

compound[1] /kəm'paʊnd/ vt (make worse) verschlimmern

compound[2] /'kɒmpaʊnd/ a zusammengesetzt; (fracture) kompliziert □ n (Chem) Verbindung f; (Gram) Kompositum nt; (enclosure) Einfriedigung f. ~ 'interest n Zinseszins m

comprehen|d /kɒmprɪ'hend/ vt begreifen, verstehen; (include) umfassen. ~sible a, -bly adv verständlich. ~sion /-'henʃn/ n Verständnis nt

comprehensive /kɒmprɪ'hensɪv/ a & n umfassend; ~ [school] Gesamtschule f. ~ insurance n (Auto) Vollkaskoversicherung f

compress[1] /'kɒmpres/ n Kompresse f

compress[2] /kəm'pres/ vt zusammenpressen; ~ed air Druckluft f

comprise /kəm'praɪz/ vt umfassen, bestehen aus

compromise /'kɒmprəmaɪz/ n Kompromiss m □ vt kompromittieren (person) □ vi einen Kompromiss schließen

compuls|ion /kəm'pʌlʃn/ n Zwang m. ~ive /-sɪv/ a zwanghaft; ~ive eating Esszwang m. ~ory /-səri/ a obligatorisch; ~ory subject Pflichtfach nt

compunction /kəm'pʌŋkʃn/ n Gewissensbisse pl

comput|er /kəm'pju:tə(r)/ n Computer m. ~erize vt computerisieren (data); auf Computer umstellen (firm). ~ing n Computertechnik f

comrade /'kɒmreɪd/ n Kamerad m; (Pol) Genosse m/Genossin f. ~ship n Kameradschaft f

con[1] /kɒn/ see pro

con[2] n (fam) Schwindel m □ vt (pt/pp conned) (fam) beschwindeln

concave /'kɒŋkeɪv/ a konkav

conceal /kən'si:l/ vt verstecken; (keep secret) verheimlichen

concede /kən'si:d/ vt zugeben; (give up) aufgeben

conceit /kən'si:t/ n Einbildung f. ~ed a eingebildet

conceivable /kən'si:vəbl/ a denkbar

conceive /kən'si:v/ vt (Biol) empfangen; (fig) sich (dat) ausdenken □ vi schwanger werden. ~ of (fig) sich (dat) vorstellen

concentrat|e /'kɒnsəntreɪt/ vt konzentrieren □ vi sich konzentrieren. ~ion /-'treɪʃn/ n Konzentration f. ~ion camp n Konzentrationslager nt

concept /'kɒnsept/ n Begriff m. ~ion /kən'sepʃn/ n Empfängnis f; (idea) Vorstellung f

concern /kən'sɜ:n/ n Angelegenheit f; (worry) Sorge f; (Comm) Unternehmen nt □ vt (be about, affect) betreffen; (worry) kümmern; be ~ed about besorgt sein um; ~ oneself with sich beschäftigen mit; as far as I am ~ed was mich angeht od betrifft. ~ing prep bezüglich (+ gen)

concert /'kɒnsət/ n Konzert nt; in ~ im Chor. ~ed /kən'sɜ:tɪd/ a gemeinsam

concertina /kɒnsə'ti:nə/ n Konzertina f

'concertmaster n (Amer) Konzertmeister m

concerto /kən'tʃeətəʊ/ n Konzert nt

concession /kən'seʃn/ n Zugeständnis nt; (Comm) Konzession f; (reduction) Ermäßigung f. ~ary a (reduced) ermäßigt

conciliation /kənsɪlɪ'eɪʃn/ n Schlichtung f

concise /kən'saɪs/ a, -ly adv kurz

conclude /kən'klu:d/ vt/i schließen

conclusion /kən'klu:ʒn/ n Schluss m; in ~ abschließend, zum Schluss

conclusive /kən'klu:sɪv/ a schlüssig

concoct /kən'kɒkt/ vt zusammenstellen; (fig) fabrizieren. ~ion /-ɒkʃn/ n Zusammenstellung f; (drink) Gebräu nt

concourse /'kɒŋkɔ:s/ n Halle f

concrete /'kɒŋkri:t/ a konkret □ n Beton m □ vt betonieren

concur /kən'kɜ:(r)/ *vi* (*pt/pp* concurred) übereinstimmen

concurrently /kən'kʌrəntlɪ/ *adv* gleichzeitig

concussion /kən'kʌʃn/ *n* Gehirnerschütterung *f*

condemn /kən'dem/ *vt* verurteilen; (*declare unfit*) für untauglich erklären. ∼ation /kɒndem'neɪʃn/ *n* Verurteilung *f*

condensation /kɒnden'seɪʃn/ *n* Kondensation *f*

condense /kən'dens/ *vt* zusammenfassen; (*Phys*) kondensieren □ *vi* sich kondensieren. ∼d milk *n* Kondensmilch *f*

condescend /kɒndɪ'send/ *vi* sich herablassen (to zu). ∼ing *a*, -ly *adv* herablassend

condiment /'kɒndɪmənt/ *n* Gewürz *nt*

condition /kən'dɪʃn/ *n* Bedingung *f*; (*state*) Zustand *m*; ∼s *pl* Verhältnisse *pl*; on ∼ that unter der Bedingung, dass □ *vt* (*Psych*) konditionieren. ∼al *a* bedingt; be ∼al on abhängen von □ *n* (*Gram*) Konditional *m*. ∼er *n* Haarkur *f*; (*for fabrics*) Weichspüler *m*

condolences /kən'dəʊlənsɪz/ *npl* Beileid *nt*

condom /'kɒndəm/ *n* Kondom *nt*

condominium /kɒndə'mɪnɪəm/ *n* (*Amer*) ≈ Eigentumswohnung *f*

condone /kən'dəʊn/ *vt* hinwegsehen über (+ *acc*)

conducive /kən'dju:sɪv/ *a* förderlich (to dat)

conduct¹ /'kɒndʌkt/ *n* Verhalten *nt*; (*Sch*) Betragen *nt*

conduct² /kən'dʌkt/ *vt* führen; (*Phys*) leiten; (*Mus*) dirigieren. ∼or *n* Dirigent *m*; (*of bus*) Schaffner *m*; (*Phys*) Leiter *m*. ∼ress *n* Schaffnerin *f*

cone /kəʊn/ *n* Kegel *m*; (*Bot*) Zapfen *m*; (*for ice-cream*) [Eis]tüte *f*; (*Auto*) Leitkegel *m*

confectioner /kən'fekʃənə(r)/ *n* Konditor *m*. ∼y *n* Süßwaren *pl*

confederation /kənfedə'reɪʃn/ *n* Bund *m*; (*Pol*) Konföderation *f*

confer /kən'fɜ:(r)/ *v* (*pt/pp* conferred) □ *vt* verleihen (on dat) □ *vi* sich beraten

conference /'kɒnfərəns/ *n* Konferenz *f*

confess /kən'fes/ *vt/i* gestehen; (*Relig*) beichten. ∼ion /-eʃn/ *n* Geständnis *nt*; (*Relig*) Beichte *f*. ∼ional /-eʃənəl/ *n* Beichtstuhl *m*. ∼or *n* Beichtvater *m*

confetti /kən'fetɪ/ *n* Konfetti *nt*

confide /kən'faɪd/ *vt* anvertrauen □ *vi* ∼ in s.o. sich jdm anvertrauen

confidence /'kɒnfɪdəns/ *n* (*trust*) Vertrauen *nt*; (*self-assurance*) Selbstvertrauen *nt*; (*secret*) Geheimnis *nt*; in ∼ im Vertrauen. ∼ trick *n* Schwindel *m*

confident /'kɒnfɪdənt/ *a*, -ly *adv* zuversichtlich; (*self-assured*) selbstsicher

confidential /kɒnfɪ'denʃl/ *a*, -ly *adv* vertraulich

confine /kən'faɪn/ *vt* beschränken (to auf + *acc*); be ∼d to bed das Bett hüten müssen. ∼d *a* (*narrow*) eng. ∼ment *n* Haft *f*

confines /'kɒnfaɪnz/ *npl* Grenzen *pl*

confirm /kən'fɜ:m/ *vt* bestätigen; (*Relig*) konfirmieren; (*Roman Catholic*) firmen. ∼ation /kɒnfə'meɪʃn/ *n* Bestätigung *f*; Konfirmation *f*; Firmung *f*. ∼ed *a* ∼ed bachelor eingefleischter Junggeselle *m*

confiscat|e /'kɒnfɪskeɪt/ *vt* beschlagnahmen. ∼ion /-'keɪʃn/ *n* Beschlagnahme *f*

conflict¹ /'kɒnflɪkt/ *n* Konflikt *m*

conflict² /kən'flɪkt/ *vi* im Widerspruch stehen (with zu). ∼ing *a* widersprüchlich

conform /kən'fɔ:m/ *vi* ⟨*person:*⟩ sich anpassen; ⟨*thing:*⟩ entsprechen (to dat). ∼ist *n* Konformist *m*

confounded /kən'faʊndɪd/ *a* (*fam*) verflixt

confront /kən'frʌnt/ *vt* konfrontieren. ∼ation /kɒnfrən'teɪʃn/ *n* Konfrontation *f*

confus|e /kən'fju:z/ *vt* verwirren; (*mistake for*) verwechseln (with mit). ∼ing *a* verwirrend. ∼ion /-ju:ʒn/ *n* Verwirrung *f*; (*muddle*) Durcheinander *nt*

congeal /kən'dʒi:l/ *vi* fest werden; ⟨*blood:*⟩ gerinnen

congenial /kən'dʒi:nɪəl/ *a* angenehm

congenital /kən'dʒenɪtl/ *a* angeboren

congest|ed /kən'dʒestɪd/ *a* verstopft; (*with people*) überfüllt. ∼ion /-estʃn/ *n* Verstopfung *f*; Überfüllung *f*

congratulat|e /kən'grætjuleɪt/ *vt* gratulieren (+ *dat*) (on zu). ∼ions /-'leɪʃnz/ *npl* Glückwünsche *pl*; ∼ions! [ich] gratuliere!

congregat|e /'kɒngrɪgeɪt/ *vi* sich versammeln. ∼ion /-'geɪʃn/ *n* (*Relig*) Gemeinde *f*

congress /'kɒngres/ *n* Kongress *m*. ∼man *n* Kongressabgeordnete(r) *m*

conical /'kɒnɪkl/ *a* kegelförmig

conifer /'kɒnɪfə(r)/ *n* Nadelbaum *m*

conjecture /kən'dʒektʃə(r)/ *n* Mutmaßung *f* □ *vt/i* mutmaßen

conjugal /'kɒndʒʊgl/ *a* ehelich

conjugat|e /'kɒndʒʊgeɪt/ *vt* konjugieren. ∼ion /-'geɪʃn/ *n* Konjugation *f*

conjunction /kən'dʒʌŋkʃn/ *n* Konjunktion *f*; in ∼ with zusammen mit

conjunctivitis /kənd ʒʌŋktɪ'vaɪtɪs/ n Bindehautentzündung f

conjur|e /'kʌndʒə(r)/ vi zaubern □ vt ~e up heraufbeschwören. ~or n Zauberkünstler m

conk /kɒŋk/ vi ~ out (fam) ⟨machine:⟩ kaputtgehen; ⟨person:⟩ zusammenklappen

conker /'kɒŋkə(r)/ n (fam) Kastanie f

'con-man n (fam) Schwindler m

connect /kə'nekt/ vt verbinden (to mit); (Electr) anschließen (to an + acc) □ vi verbunden sein; ⟨train:⟩ Anschluss haben (with an + acc); be ~ed with zu tun haben mit; (be related to) verwandt sein mit

connection /kə'nek ʃn/ n Verbindung f; (Rail, Electr) Anschluss m; in ~ with in Zusammenhang mit. ~s npl Beziehungen pl

conniv|ance /kə'naɪvəns/ n stillschweigende Duldung f. ~e vi ~e at stillschweigend dulden

connoisseur /kɒnə'sɜ:(r)/ n Kenner m

connotation /kɒnə'teɪ ʃn/ n Assoziation f

conquer /'kɒŋkə(r)/ vt erobern; ⟨fig⟩ besiegen. ~or n Eroberer m

conquest /'kɒŋkwest/ n Eroberung f

conscience /'kɒn ʃəns/ n Gewissen nt

conscientious /kɒn ʃɪ'en ʃəs/ a, -ly adv gewissenhaft. ~ ob'jector n Kriegsdienstverweigerer m

conscious /'kɒn ʃəs/ a, -ly adv bewusst; [fully] ~ bei [vollem] Bewusstsein; be/ become ~ of sth sich (dat) etw (gen) bewusst sein/werden. ~ness n Bewusstsein nt

conscript¹ /'kɒnskrɪpt/ n Einberufene(r) m

conscript² /kən'skrɪpt/ vt einberufen. ~ion /-ɪp ʃn/ n allgemeine Wehrpflicht f.

consecrat|e /'kɒnsɪkreɪt/ vt weihen; einweihen ⟨church⟩. ~ion /-'kreɪ ʃn/ n Weihe f; Einweihung f

consecutive /kən'sekjʊtɪv/ a aufeinanderfolgend. -ly adv fortlaufend

consensus /kən'sensəs/ n Übereinstimmung f

consent /kən'sent/ n Einwilligung f, Zustimmung f □ vi einwilligen (to in + acc), zustimmen (to dat)

consequen|ce /'kɒnsɪkwəns/ n Folge f; (importance) Bedeutung f. ~t a daraus folgend. ~tly adv folglich

conservation /kɒnsə'veɪ ʃn/ n Erhaltung f, Bewahrung f. ~ist n Umweltschützer m

conservative /kən'sɜ:vətɪv/ a konservativ; ⟨estimate⟩ vorsichtig. C~ (Pol) a konservativ □ n Konservative(r) m/f

conservatory /kən'sɜ:vətrɪ/ n Wintergarten m

conserve /kən'sɜ:v/ vt erhalten, bewahren; sparen ⟨energy⟩

consider /kən'sɪdə(r)/ vt erwägen; (think over) sich (dat) überlegen; (take into account) berücksichtigen; (regard as) betrachten als; ~ doing sth erwägen, etw zu tun. ~able /-əbl/ a, -bly adv erheblich

consider|ate /kən'sɪdərət/ a, -ly adv rücksichtsvoll. ~ation /-'reɪ ʃn/ n Erwägung f; (thoughtfulness) Rücksicht f; (payment) Entgelt nt; take into ~ation berücksichtigen. ~ing prep wenn man bedenkt (that dass); ~ing the circumstances unter den Umständen

consign /kən'saɪn/ vt übergeben (to dat). ~ment n Lieferung f

consist /kən'sɪst/ vi ~ of bestehen aus

consisten|cy /kən'sɪstənsɪ/ n Konsequenz f; (density) Konsistenz f. ~t a konsequent; (unchanging) gleichbleibend; be ~t with entsprechen (+ dat). ~tly adv konsequent; (constantly) ständig

consolation /kɒnsə'leɪ ʃn/ n Trost m. ~ prize n Trostpreis m

console /kən'səʊl/ vt trösten

consolidate /kən'sɒlɪdeɪt/ vt konsolidieren

consonant /'kɒnsənənt/ n Konsonant m

consort /'kɒnsɔ:t/ n Gemahl(in) m(f)

conspicuous /kən'spɪkjʊəs/ a auffällig

conspiracy /kən'spɪrəsɪ/ n Verschwörung f

conspire /kən'spaɪə(r)/ vi sich verschwören

constable /'kʌnstəbl/ n Polizist m

constant /'kɒnstənt/ a, -ly adv beständig; (continuous) ständig

constellation /kɒnstə'leɪ ʃn/ n Sternbild nt

consternation /kɒnstə'neɪ ʃn/ n Bestürzung f

constipat|ed /'kɒnstɪpeɪtɪd/ a verstopft. ~ion /-'peɪ ʃn/ n Verstopfung f

constituency /kən'stɪtjʊənsɪ/ n Wahlkreis m

constituent /kən'stɪtjʊənt/ n Bestandteil m; (Pol) Wähler(in) m(f)

constitut|e /'kɒnstɪtju:t/ vt bilden. ~ion /-'tju: ʃn/ n (Pol) Verfassung f; (of person) Konstitution f. ~ional /-'tju: ʃənl/ a Verfassungs- □ n Verdauungsspaziergang m

constrain /kən'streɪn/ vt zwingen. **~t** n Zwang m; (restriction) Beschränkung f; (strained manner) Gezwungenheit f

constrict /kən'strɪkt/ vt einengen

construct /kən'strʌkt/ vt bauen. **~ion** /-ʌkʃn/ n Bau m; (Gram) Konstruktion f; (interpretation) Deutung f; **under ~ion** im Bau. **~ive** /-ɪv/ a konstruktiv

construe /kən'stru:/ vt deuten

consul /'kɒnsl/ n Konsul m. **~ate** /'kɒnsjʊlət/ n Konsulat nt

consult /kən'sʌlt/ vt [um Rat] fragen; konsultieren (doctor); nachschlagen in (+ dat) (book). **~ant** n Berater m; (Med) Chefarzt m. **~ation** /kɒnsl'teɪʃn/ n Beratung f; (Med) Konsultation f

consume /kən'sju:m/ vt verzehren; (use) verbrauchen. **~r** n Verbraucher m. **~r goods** npl Konsumgüter pl

consummat|e /'kɒnsəmeɪt/ vt vollziehen. **~ion** /-'meɪʃn/ n Vollzug m

consumption /kən'sʌmpʃn/ n Konsum m; (use) Verbrauch m

contact /'kɒntækt/ n Kontakt m; (person) Kontaktperson f □ vt sich in Verbindung setzen mit. **~ 'lenses** npl Kontaktlinsen pl

contagious /kən'teɪdʒəs/ a direkt übertragbar

contain /kən'teɪn/ vt enthalten; (control) beherrschen. **~er** n Behälter m; (Comm) Container m

contaminat|e /kən'tæmɪneɪt/ vt verseuchen. **~ion** /-'neɪʃn/ n Verseuchung f

contemplat|e /'kɒntəmpleɪt/ vt betrachten; (meditate) nachdenken über (+ acc); **~e doing sth** daran denken, etw zu tun. **~ion** /-'pleɪʃn/ n Betrachtung f; Nachdenken nt

contemporary /kən'tempərəri/ a zeitgenössisch □ n Zeitgenosse m/ -genossin f

contempt /kən'tempt/ n Verachtung f; **beneath ~** verabscheuungswürdig; **~ of court** Missachtung f des Gerichts. **~ible** /-əbl/ a verachtenswert. **~uous** /-tjʊəs/ a, **-ly** adv verächtlich

contend /kən'tend/ vi kämpfen (with mit) □ vt (assert) behaupten. **~er** n Bewerber(in) m(f); (Sport) Wettkämpfer(in) m(f)

content¹ /'kɒntent/ n & **contents** pl Inhalt m

content² /kən'tent/ a zufrieden □ n **to one's heart's ~** nach Herzenslust □ vt **~ oneself** sich begnügen (with mit). **~ed** a, **-ly** adv zufrieden

contention /kən'tenʃn/ n (assertion) Behauptung f

contentment /kən'tentmənt/ n Zufriedenheit f

contest¹ /'kɒntest/ n Kampf m; (competition) Wettbewerb m

contest² /kən'test/ vt (dispute) bestreiten; (Jur) anfechten; (Pol) kandidieren in (+ dat). **~ant** n Teilnehmer m

context /'kɒntekst/ n Zusammenhang m

continent /'kɒntɪnənt/ n Kontinent m

continental /kɒntɪ'nentl/ a Kontinental-. **~ breakfast** n kleines Frühstück nt. **~ quilt** n Daunendecke f

contingen|cy /kən'tɪndʒənsi/ n Eventualität f. **~t a be ~t upon** abhängen von □ n (Mil) Kontingent nt

continual /kən'tɪnjʊəl/ a, **-ly** adv dauernd

continuation /kəntɪnjʊ'eɪʃn/ n Fortsetzung f

continue /kən'tɪnju:/ vt fortsetzen; **~ doing** or **to do sth** fortfahren, etw zu tun; **to be ~d** Fortsetzung folgt □ vi weitergehen; (doing sth) weitermachen; (speaking) fortfahren; (weather:) anhalten

continuity /kɒntɪ'nju:əti/ n Kontinuität f

continuous /kən'tɪnjʊəs/ a, **-ly** adv anhaltend, ununterbrochen

contort /kən'tɔ:t/ vt verzerren. **~ion** /-ɔ:ʃn/ n Verzerrung f

contour /'kɒntʊə(r)/ n Kontur f; (line) Höhenlinie f

contraband /'kɒntrəbænd/ n Schmuggelware f

contracep|tion /kɒntrə'sepʃn/ n Empfängnisverhütung f. **~tive** /-tɪv/ a empfängnisverhütend □ n Empfängnisverhütungsmittel nt

contract¹ /'kɒntrækt/ n Vertrag m

contract² /kən'trækt/ vi sich zusammenziehen □ vt zusammenziehen; sich (dat) zuziehen (illness). **~ion** /-ækʃn/ n Zusammenziehung f; (abbreviation) Abkürzung f; (in childbirth) Wehe f. **~or** n Unternehmer m

contradict /kɒntrə'dɪkt/ vt widersprechen (+ dat). **~ion** /-ɪkʃn/ n Widerspruch m. **~ory** /-ərɪ/ a widersprüchlich

contra-flow /'kɒntrə-/ n Umleitung f [auf die entgegengesetzte Fahrbahn]

contralto /kən'træltəʊ/ n Alt m; (singer) Altistin f

contraption /kən'træpʃn/ n (fam) Apparat m

contrary¹ /'kɒntrərɪ/ a & adv entgegengesetzt; **~ to** entgegen (+ dat) □ n Gegenteil nt; **on the ~** im Gegenteil

contrary² /kən'treərɪ/ a widerspenstig

contrast¹ /'kɒntrɑ:st/ n Kontrast m

contrast² /kən'trɑ:st/ vt gegenüberstellen (with dat) □ vi einen Kontrast bilden (with zu). **∼ing** *a* gegensätzlich; ⟨*colour*⟩ Kontrast-

contravene| /kɒntrə'viːn/ *vt* verstoßen gegen. **∼tion** /-'venʃn/ *n* Verstoß *m* (of gegen)

contribut|e /kən'trɪbjuːt/ *vt/i* beitragen; beisteuern ⟨*money*⟩; ⟨*donate*⟩ spenden. **∼ion** /kɒntrɪ'bjuːʃn/ *n* Beitrag *m*; ⟨*donation*⟩ Spende *f*. **∼or** *n* Beitragende(r) *m/f*

contrite /kən'traɪt/ *a* reuig

contrivance /kən'traɪvəns/ *n* Vorrichtung *f*

contrive /kən'traɪv/ *vt* verfertigen; **∼ to do sth** es fertig bringen, etw zu tun

control /kən'trəʊl/ *n* Kontrolle *f*; ⟨*mastery*⟩ Beherrschung *f*; ⟨*Techn*⟩ Regler *m*; **∼s** *pl* ⟨*of car, plane*⟩ Steuerung *f*; **get out of ∼** außer Kontrolle geraten □ *vt* ⟨*pt/pp* controlled⟩ kontrollieren; ⟨*restrain*⟩ unter Kontrolle halten; **∼ oneself** sich beherrschen

controvers|ial /kɒntrə'vɜːʃl/ *a* umstritten. **∼y** /'kɒntrəvɜːsɪ/ *n* Kontroverse *f*

conundrum /kə'nʌndrəm/ *n* Rätsel *nt*

conurbation /kɒnɜː'beɪʃn/ *n* Ballungsgebiet *nt*

convalesce /kɒnvə'les/ *vi* sich erholen. **∼nce** *n* Erholung *f*

convalescent /kɒnvə'lesnt/ *a* **be ∼** noch erholungsbedürftig sein. **∼ home** *n* Erholungsheim *nt*

convector /kən'vektə(r)/ *n* **∼ [heater]** Konvektor *m*

convene /kən'viːn/ *vt* einberufen □ *v* sich versammeln

convenience /kən'viːnɪəns/ *n* Bequemlichkeit *f*; **[public]** *~* öffentliche Toilette *f*; **with all modern ∼s** mit allem Komfort

convenient /kən'viːnɪənt/ *a*, **-ly** *adv* günstig; **be ∼ for s.o.** jdm gelegen sein *od* jdm passen; **if it is ∼ [for you]** wenn es Ihnen passt

convent /'kɒnvənt/ *n* [Nonnen]kloster *nt*

convention /kən'venʃn/ *n* ⟨*custom*⟩ Brauch *m*, Sitte *f*; ⟨*agreement*⟩ Konvention *f*; ⟨*assembly*⟩ Tagung *f*. **∼al** *a*, **-ly** *adv* konventionell

converge /kən'vɜːdʒ/ *vi* zusammenlaufen

conversant /kən'vɜːsənt/ *a* **∼ with** vertraut mit

conversation /kɒnvə'seɪʃn/ *n* Gespräch *nt*; ⟨*Sch*⟩ Konversation *f*

converse¹ /kən'vɜːs/ *vi* sich unterhalten

converse² /'kɒnvɜːs/ *n* Gegenteil *nt*. **∼ly** *adv* umgekehrt

conversion /kən'vɜːʃn/ *n* Umbau *m*; ⟨*Relig*⟩ Bekehrung *f*; ⟨*calculation*⟩ Umrechnung *f*

convert¹ /'kɒnvɜːt/ *n* Bekehrte(r) *m/f*, Konvertit *m*

convert² /kən'vɜːt/ *vt* bekehren ⟨*person*⟩; ⟨*change*⟩ umwandeln (**into** in + *acc*); umbauen ⟨*building*⟩; ⟨*calculate*⟩ umrechnen; ⟨*Techn*⟩ umstellen. **∼ible** /-əbl/ *a* verwandelbar □ *n* ⟨*Auto*⟩ Kabriolett *nt*

convex /'kɒnveks/ *a* konvex

convey /kən'veɪ/ *vt* befördern; vermitteln ⟨*idea, message*⟩. **∼ance** *n* Beförderung *f*; ⟨*vehicle*⟩ Beförderungsmittel *nt*. **∼or belt** *n* Förderband *nt*

convict¹ /'kɒnvɪkt/ *n* Sträfling *m*

convict² /kən'vɪkt/ *vt* verurteilen (**of** wegen). **∼ion** /-ɪkʃn/ *n* Verurteilung *f*; ⟨*belief*⟩ Überzeugung *f*; **previous ∼ion** Vorstrafe *f*

convinc|e /kən'vɪns/ *vt* überzeugen. **∼ing** *a*, **-ly** *adv* überzeugend

convivial /kən'vɪvɪəl/ *a* gesellig

convoluted /'kɒnvəluːtɪd/ *a* verschlungen; ⟨*fig*⟩ verwickelt

convoy /'kɒnvɔɪ/ *n* Konvoi *m*

convuls|e /kən'vʌls/ *vt* **be ∼ed** sich krümmen (**with** vor + *dat*). **∼ion** /-ʌlʃn/ *n* Krampf *m*

coo /kuː/ *vi* gurren

cook /kʊk/ *n* Koch *m*/ Köchin *f* □ *vt/i* kochen; **is it ∼ed?** ist es gar? **∼ the books** ⟨*fam*⟩ die Bilanz frisieren. **∼book** *n* ⟨*Amer*⟩ Kochbuch *nt*

cooker /'kʊkə(r)/ *n* [Koch]herd *m*; ⟨*apple*⟩ Kochapfel *m*. **∼y** *n* Kochen *nt*. **∼y book** *n* Kochbuch *nt*

cookie /'kʊkɪ/ *n* ⟨*Amer*⟩ Keks *m*

cool /kuːl/ *a* (**-er, -est**), **-ly** *adv* kühlen □ *n* Kühle *f* □ *vt* kühlen □ *vi* abkühlen. **∼-box** *n* Kühlbox *f*. **∼ness** *n* Kühle *f*

coop /kuːp/ *n* [Hühner]stall *m* □ *vt* **∼ up** einsperren

co-operat|e /kəʊ'ɒpəreɪt/ *vi* zusammenarbeiten. **∼ion** /-'reɪʃn/ *n* Kooperation *f*

co-operative /kəʊ'ɒpərətɪv/ *a* hilfsbereit □ *n* Genossenschaft *f*

co-opt /kəʊ'ɒpt/ *vt* hinzuwählen

co-ordinat|e /kəʊ'ɔːdɪneɪt/ *vt* koordinieren. **∼ion** /-'neɪʃn/ *n* Koordination *f*

cop /kɒp/ *n* ⟨*fam*⟩ Polizist *m*

cope /kəʊp/ *vi* ⟨*fam*⟩ zurechtkommen; **∼ with** fertig werden mit

copious /'kəʊpɪəs/ *a* reichlich

copper¹ /'kɒpə(r)/ *n* Kupfer *nt*; **∼s** *pl* Kleingeld *nt* □ *a* kupfern

copper² *n* ⟨*fam*⟩ Polizist *m*

copper 'beech *n* Blutbuche *f*

coppice /'kɒpɪs/ *n*, **copse** /kɒps/ *n* Gehölz *nt*

copulate /'kɒpjʊleɪt/ vi sich begatten

copy vt /'kɒpɪ/ n Kopie f; (book) Exemplar nt □ vt (pt/pp -ied) kopieren; (imitate) nachahmen; (Sch) abschreiben

copy: ~right n Copyright nt. ~writer n Texter m

coral /'kɒrl/ n Koralle f

cord /kɔːd/ n Schnur f; (fabric) Cordsamt m; ~s pl Cordhose f

cordial /'kɔːdɪəl/ a, -ly adv herzlich □ n Fruchtsirup m

cordon /'kɔːdn/ n Kordon m □ vt ~ off absperren

corduroy /'kɔːdərɔɪ/ n Cordsamt m

core /kɔː(r)/ n Kern m; (of apple, pear) Kerngehäuse nt

cork /kɔːk/ n Kork m; (for bottle) Korken m. ~screw n Korkenzieher m

corn[1] /kɔːn/ n Korn nt; (Amer: maize) Mais m

corn[2] n (Med) Hühnerauge nt

cornea /'kɔːnɪə/ n Hornhaut f

corned beef /kɔːnd'biːf/ n Cornedbeef nt

corner /'kɔːnə(r)/ n Ecke f; (bend) Kurve f; (football) Eckball m □ vt (fig) in die Enge treiben; (Comm) monopolisieren ‹market›. ~stone n Eckstein m

cornet /'kɔːnɪt/ n (Mus) Kornett nt; (for ice-cream) [Eis]tüte f

corn: ~flour n, (Amer) ~starch n Stärkemehl nt

corny /'kɔːnɪ/ a (fam) abgedroschen

coronary /'kɒrənərɪ/ a & n ~ [thrombosis] Koronarthrombose f

coronation /kɒrə'neɪʃn/ n Krönung f

coroner /'kɒrənə(r)/ n Beamte(r) m, der verdächtige Todesfälle untersucht

coronet /'kɒrənet/ n Adelskrone f

corporal[1] /'kɔːpərəl/ n (Mil) Stabsunteroffizier m

corporal[2] a körperlich; ~ punishment körperliche Züchtigung f

corporate /'kɔːpərət/ a gemeinschaftlich

corporation /kɔːpə'reɪʃn/ n Körperschaft f; (of town) Stadtverwaltung f

corps /kɔː(r)/ n (pl corps /kɔːz/) Korps nt

corpse /kɔːps/ n Leiche f

corpulent /'kɔːpjʊlənt/ a korpulent

corpuscle /'kɔːpʌsl/ n Blutkörperchen nt

correct /kə'rekt/ a, -ly adv richtig; (proper) korrekt □ vt verbessern; (Sch, Typ) korrigieren. ~ion /-ekʃn/ n Verbesserung f; (Typ) Korrektur f

correlation /kɒrə'leɪʃn/ n Wechselbeziehung f

correspond /kɒrɪ'spɒnd/ vi entsprechen (to dat); ‹two things:› sich entsprechen;

(write) korrespondieren. ~ence n Briefwechsel m; (Comm) Korrespondenz f. ~ent n Korrespondent(in) m(f). ~ing a, -ly adv entsprechend

corridor /'kɒrɪdɔː(r)/ n Gang m; (Pol, Aviat) Korridor m

corroborate /kə'rɒbəreɪt/ vt bestätigen

corro|de /kə'rəʊd/ vt zerfressen □ vi rosten. ~sion /-'rəʊʒn/ n Korrosion f

corrugated /'kɒrəgeɪtɪd/ a gewellt. ~ iron n Wellblech nt

corrupt /kə'rʌpt/ a korrupt □ vt korrumpieren; (spoil) verderben. ~ion /-ʌpʃn/ n Korruption f

corset /'kɔːsɪt/ n & -s pl Korsett nt

Corsica /'kɔːsɪkə/ n Korsika nt

cortège /kɔː'teɪʒ/ n [funeral] ~ Leichenzug m

cosh /kɒʃ/ n Totschläger m

cosmetic /kɒz'metɪk/ a kosmetisch □ n ~s pl Kosmetika pl

cosmic /'kɒzmɪk/ a kosmisch

cosmonaut /'kɒzmənɔːt/ n Kosmonaut(in) m(f)

cosmopolitan /kɒzmə'pɒlɪtən/ a kosmopolitisch

cosmos /'kɒzmɒs/ n Kosmos m

cosset /'kɒsɪt/ vt verhätscheln

cost /kɒst/ n Kosten pl; ~s pl (Jur) Kosten; at all ~s um jeden Preis; I learnt to my ~ es ist mich teuer zu stehen gekommen □ vt (pt/pp cost) kosten; it ~ me £20 es hat mich £20 gekostet □ vt (pt/pp costed) ~ [out] die Kosten kalkulieren für

costly /'kɒstlɪ/ a (-ier, -iest) teuer

cost: ~ of 'living n Lebenshaltungskosten pl. ~ price n Selbstkostenpreis m

costume /'kɒstjuːm/ n Kostüm nt; (national) Tracht f. ~ jewellery n Modeschmuck m

cosy /'kəʊzɪ/ a (-ier, -iest) gemütlich □ n (tea-, egg-) Wärmer m

cot /kɒt/ n Kinderbett nt; (Amer: camp-bed) Feldbett nt

cottage /'kɒtɪdʒ/ n Häuschen nt. ~ 'cheese n Hüttenkäse m

cotton /'kɒtn/ n Baumwolle f; (thread) Nähgarn nt □ a baumwollen □ vi ~ on (fam) kapieren

cotton 'wool n Watte f

couch /kaʊtʃ/ n Liege f

couchette /kuː'ʃet/ n (Rail) Liegeplatz m

cough /kɒf/ n Husten m □ vi husten. ~ up vt/i husten; (fam: pay) blechen

'cough mixture n Hustensaft m

could /kʊd, unbetont kəd/ see can[2]

council /'kaʊnsl/ n Rat m; (Admin) Stadtverwaltung f; (rural) Gemeindeverwaltung f. ~ house n ≈ Sozialwohnung f

councillor /'kaʊnsələ(r)/ n Stadtverord-
nete(r) m/f

'council tax n Gemeindesteuer f

counsel /'kaʊnsl/ n Rat m; (Jur) Anwalt
m □ vt (pt/pp counselled) beraten. ~lor
n Berater(in) m(f)

count¹ /kaʊnt/ n Graf m

count² n Zählung f; keep ~ zählen □ vt/i
zählen. ~ on vt rechnen auf (+ acc)

countenance /'kaʊntənəns/ n Gesicht nt
□ vt dulden

counter¹ /'kaʊntə(r)/ n (in shop) Ladentisch m; (in bank) Schalter m; (in café)
Theke f; (Games) Spielmarke f

counter² adv ~ to gegen (+ acc) □ a Ge-
gen- □ vt/i kontern

counter'act vt entgegenwirken (+ dat)

'counter-attack n Gegenangriff m

counter-'espionage n Spionageabwehr
f

'counterfeit /-fɪt/ a gefälscht □ n Fälschung f □ vt fälschen

'counterfoil n Kontrollabschnitt m

'counterpart n Gegenstück nt

counter-pro'ductive a be ~ das Gegenteil bewirken

'countersign vt gegenzeichnen

countess /'kaʊntɪs/ n Gräfin f

countless /'kaʊntlɪs/ a unzählig

countrified /'kʌntrɪfaɪd/ a ländlich

country /'kʌntrɪ/ n Land nt; (native land)
Heimat f; (countryside) Landschaft f; in
the ~ auf dem Lande. ~man n [fellow]
~man Landsmann m. ~side n Landschaft f

county /'kaʊntɪ/ n Grafschaft f

coup /kuː/ n (Pol) Staatsstreich m

couple /'kʌpl/ n Paar nt; a ~ of (two) zwei
□ vt verbinden; (Rail) koppeln

coupon /'kuːpɒn/ n Kupon m; (voucher)
Gutschein m; (entry form) Schein m

courage /'kʌrɪdʒ/ n Mut m. ~ous /kə-
'reɪdʒəs/ a, -ly adv mutig

courgettes /kʊə'ʒets/ npl Zucchini pl

courier /'kʊrɪə(r)/ n Bote m; (diplomatic)
Kurier m; (for tourists) Reiseleiter(in)
m(f)

course /kɔːs/ n (Naut, Sch) Kurs m; (Culin)
Gang m; (for golf) Platz m; ~ of treatment (Med) Kur f; of ~ natürlich,
selbstverständlich; in the ~ of im Lauf[e]
(+ gen)

court /kɔːt/ n Hof m; (Sport) Platz m; (Jur)
Gericht nt □ vt werben um; herausfordern
⟨danger⟩

courteous /'kɜːtɪəs/ a, -ly adv höflich

courtesy /'kɜːtəsɪ/ n Höflichkeit f

court: ~ 'martial n (pl ~s martial) Mili-
tärgericht nt. ~ shoes npl Pumps pl.
~yard n Hof m

cousin /'kʌzn/ n Vetter m, Cousin m;
(female) Kusine f

cove /kəʊv/ n kleine Bucht f

cover /'kʌvə(r)/ n Decke f; (of cushion) Bezug m; (of umbrella) Hülle f; (of typewriter)
Haube f; (of book; lid) Deckel m; (of magazine) Umschlag m; (protection) Deckung
f, Schutz m; take ~ Deckung nehmen;
under separate ~ mit getrennter Post
□ vt bedecken; beziehen ⟨cushion⟩; decken
⟨costs, needs⟩; zurücklegen ⟨distance⟩;
(Journ) berichten über (+ acc); (insure)
versichern. ~ up vt zudecken; (fig) vertuschen

coverage /'kʌvərɪdʒ/ n (Journ) Berichter-
stattung f (of über + acc)

cover: ~ charge n Gedeck nt. ~ing n Decke f; (for floor) Belag m. ~-up n Vertu-
schung f

covet /'kʌvɪt/ vt begehren

cow /kaʊ/ n Kuh f

coward /'kaʊəd/ n Feigling m. ~ice /-ɪs/
n Feigheit f. ~ly a feige

'cowboy n Cowboy m; (fam) unsolider
Handwerker m

cower /'kaʊə(r)/ vi sich [ängstlich] ducken

'cowshed n Kuhstall m

cox /kɒks/ n, coxswain /'kɒksn/ n Steuer-
mann m

coy /kɔɪ/ a (-er, -est) gespielt schüchtern

crab /kræb/ n Krabbe f. ~-apple n Holzap-
fel m

crack /kræk/ n Riss m; (in china, glass)
Sprung m; (noise) Knall m; (fam: joke) Witz
m; (fam: attempt) Versuch m □ a (fam)
erstklassig □ vt knacken ⟨nut, code⟩; einen
Sprung machen in (+ acc) ⟨china, glass⟩;
(fam) reißen ⟨joke⟩; (fam) lösen ⟨problem⟩
□ vi ⟨china, glass:⟩ springen; ⟨whip:⟩
knallen. ~ down vi (fam) durchgreifen

cracked /krækt/ a gesprungen; ⟨rib⟩ ange-
brochen; (fam: crazy) verrückt

cracker /'krækə(r)/ n (biscuit) Kräcker m;
(firework) Knallkörper m; [Christmas] ~
Knallbonbon m. ~s a be ~s (fam) einen
Knacks haben

crackle /'krækl/ vi knistern

cradle /'kreɪdl/ n Wiege f

craft¹ /krɑːft/ n inv (boat) [Wasser]-
fahrzeug nt

craft² n Handwerk nt; (technique) Fertigkeit f. ~sman n Handwerker m

crafty /'krɑːftɪ/ a (-ier, -iest), -ily adv
gerissen

crag /kræg/ n Felszacken m. ~gy a felsig;
⟨face⟩ kantig

cram /kræm/ v (pt/pp **crammed**) □ vt hineinstopfen (**into** in + acc); vollstopfen (**with** mit) □ vi (for exams) pauken

cramp /kræmp/ n Krampf m. **~ed** a eng

crampon /'kræmpən/ n Steigeisen nt

cranberry /'krænbəri/ n (Culin) Preiselbeere f

crane /krein/ n Kran m; (bird) Kranich m □ vt ~ one's neck den Hals recken

crank[1] /kræŋk/ n (fam) Exzentriker m

crank[2] n (Techn) Kurbel f. **~shaft** n Kurbelwelle f

cranky /'kræŋki/ a exzentrisch; (Amer: irritable) reizbar

cranny /'kræni/ n Ritze f

crash /kræʃ/ n (noise) Krach m; (Auto) Zusammenstoß m; (Aviat) Absturz m □ vi krachen (into gegen); (cars:) zusammenstoßen; (plane:) abstürzen □ vt einen Unfall haben mit ⟨car⟩

crash: ~ **course** n Schnellkurs m. **~-helmet** n Sturzhelm m. **~-landing** n Bruchlandung f

crate /kreit/ n Kiste f

crater /'kreitə(r)/ n Krater m

cravat /krə'væt/ n Halstuch nt

crav|e /kreiv/ vi ~**e for** sich sehnen nach. **~ing** n Gelüst nt

crawl /krɔːl/ n (Swimming) Kraul nt; **do the** ~ kraulen; **at a** ~ im Kriechtempo □ vi kriechen; ⟨baby:⟩ krabbeln; ~ **with** wimmeln von. **~er lane** n (Auto) Kriechspur f

crayon /'kreiən/ n Wachsstift m; (pencil) Buntstift m

craze /kreiz/ n Mode f

crazy /'kreizi/ a (-ier, -iest) verrückt; **be** ~ **about** verrückt sein nach

creak /kriːk/ n Knarren nt □ vi knarren

cream /kriːm/ n Sahne f; (Cosmetic, Med, Culin) Creme f □ a (colour) cremefarben □ vt (Culin) cremig rühren. ~ 'cheese n ≈ Quark m. **~y** a sahnig; (smooth) cremig

crease /kriːs/ n Falte f; (unwanted) Knitterfalte f □ vt falten; (accidentally) zerknittern □ vi knittern. **~-resistant** a knitterfrei

creat|e /kriː'eit/ vt schaffen. **~ion** /-'eiʃn/ n Schöpfung f. **~ive** /-tiv/ a schöpferisch. **~or** n Schöpfer m

creature /'kriːtʃə(r)/ n Geschöpf nt

crèche /kreʃ/ n Kinderkrippe f

credentials /kri'denʃlz/ npl Beglaubigungsschreiben nt

credibility /kredə'biləti/ n Glaubwürdigkeit f

credible /'kredəbl/ a glaubwürdig

credit /'kredit/ n Kredit m; (honour) Ehre f □ vt glauben; ~ **s.o. with sth** (Comm) jdm etw gutschreiben; (fig) jdm etw zuschreiben. **~able** /-əbl/ a lobenswert

credit: ~ **card** n Kreditkarte f. **~or** n Gläubiger m

creed /kriːd/ n Glaubensbekenntnis nt

creek /kriːk/ n enge Bucht f; (Amer: stream) Bach m

creep /kriːp/ vi (pt/pp **crept**) schleichen □ n (fam) fieser Kerl m; **it gives me the** ~**s** es ist mir unheimlich. **~er** n Kletterpflanze f. **~y** a gruselig

cremat|e /kri'meit/ vt einäschern. **~ion** /-eiʃn/ n Einäscherung f

crematorium /kremə'tɔːriəm/ n Krematorium nt

crêpe /kreip/ n Krepp m. ~ **paper** n Krepppapier nt

crept /krept/ see creep

crescent /'kresənt/ n Halbmond m

cress /kres/ n Kresse f

crest /krest/ n Kamm m; (coat of arms) Wappen nt

Crete /kriːt/ n Kreta nt

crevasse /kri'væs/ n [Gletscher]spalte f

crevice /'krevis/ n Spalte f

crew /kruː/ n Besatzung f; (gang) Bande f. ~ **cut** n Bürstenschnitt m

crib[1] /krib/ n Krippe f

crib[2] vt/i (pt/pp **cribbed**) (fam) abschreiben

crick /krik/ n ~ **in the neck** steifes Genick nt

cricket[1] /'krikit/ n (insect) Grille f

cricket[2] n Kricket nt. **~er** n Kricketspieler m

crime /kraim/ n Verbrechen nt; (rate) Kriminalität f

criminal /'kriminl/ a kriminell, verbrecherisch; (law, court) Straf- □ n Verbrecher m

crimson /'krimzn/ a purpurrot

cringe /krindʒ/ vi sich [ängstlich] ducken

crinkle /'kriŋkl/ vt/i knittern

cripple /'kripl/ n Krüppel m □ vt zum Krüppel machen; (fig) lahm legen. **~d** a verkrüppelt

crisis /'kraisis/ n (pl -ses /-siːz/) Krise f

crisp /krisp/ a (-er, -est) knusprig. **~bread** n Knäckebrot nt. **~s** npl Chips pl

criss-cross /'kris-/ a schräg gekreuzt

criterion /krai'tiəriən/ n (pl -ria /-riə/) Kriterium nt

critic /'kritik/ n Kritiker m. **~al** a kritisch. **~ally** adv kritisch; **~ally ill** schwer krank

criticism /'kritisizm/ n Kritik f

criticize /'kritisaiz/ vt kritisieren

croak /krəʊk/ *vi* krächzen; ⟨*frog:*⟩ quaken

crochet /'krəʊʃeɪ/ *n* Häkelarbeit *f* □ *vt/i* häkeln. ~-**hook** *n* Häkelnadel *f*

crock /krɒk/ *n* (*fam*) **old** ~ (*person*) Wrack *m*; (*car*) Klapperkiste *f*

crockery /'krɒkərɪ/ *n* Geschirr *nt*

crocodile /'krɒkədaɪl/ *n* Krokodil *nt*

crocus /'krəʊkəs/ *n* (*pl* **-es**) Krokus *m*

crony /'krəʊnɪ/ *n* Kumpel *m*

crook /krʊk/ *n* (*stick*) Stab *m*; (*fam: criminal*) Schwindler *m*, Gauner *m*

crooked /'krʊkɪd/ *a* schief; (*bent*) krumm; (*fam: dishonest*) unehrlich

crop /krɒp/ *n* Feldfrucht *f*; (*harvest*) Ernte *f*; (*of bird*) Kropf *m* □ *v* (*pt/pp* **cropped**) □ *vt* stutzen □ *vi* ~ **up** (*fam*) zur Sprache kommen; (*occur*) dazwischenkommen

croquet /'krəʊkeɪ/ *n* Krocket *nt*

croquette /krəʊ'ket/ *n* Krokette *f*

cross /krɒs/ *a*, **-ly** *adv* (*annoyed*) böse (**with** auf + *acc*); **talk at** ~ **purposes** aneinander vorbeireden □ *n* Kreuz *nt*; (*Bot, Zool*) Kreuzung *f*; **on the** ~ schräg □ *vt* kreuzen ⟨*cheque, animals*⟩; überqueren ⟨*road*⟩; ~ **oneself** sich bekreuzigen; ~ **one's arms** die Arme verschränken; ~ **one's legs** die Beine übereinanderschlagen; **keep one's fingers** ~**ed for s.o.** jdm die Daumen drücken; **it** ~**ed my mind** es fiel mir ein □ *vi* (*go across*) hinübergehen/-fahren; ⟨*lines:*⟩ sich kreuzen. ~ **out** *vt* durchstreichen

cross: ~**bar** *n* Querlatte *f*; (*on bicycle*) Stange *f*. ~**-country** *n* (*Sport*) Crosslauf *m*. ~**-ex'amine** *vt* ins Kreuzverhör nehmen. ~**-exami'nation** *n* Kreuzverhör *nt*. ~**-'eyed** *a* schielend; **be** ~**-eyed** schielen. ~**fire** *n* Kreuzfeuer *nt*. ~**ing** *n* Übergang *m*; (*sea journey*) Überfahrt *f*. ~**-'reference** *n* Querverweis *m*. ~**roads** *n* [Straßen]kreuzung *f*. ~**-'section** *n* Querschnitt *m*. ~**-stitch** *n* Kreuzstich *m*. ~**wise** *adv* kreuzweise. ~**word** *n* ~**word [puzzle]** Kreuzworträtsel *nt*

crotchet /'krɒtʃɪt/ *n* Viertelnote *f*

crotchety /'krɒtʃɪtɪ/ *a* griesgrämig

crouch /kraʊtʃ/ *vi* kauern

crow /krəʊ/ *n* Krähe *f*; **as the** ~ **flies** Luftlinie □ *vi* krähen. ~**bar** *n* Brechstange *f*

crowd /kraʊd/ *n* [Menschen]menge *f* □ *vi* sich drängen. ~**ed** /'kraʊdɪd/ *a* [gedrängt] voll

crown /kraʊn/ *n* Krone *f* □ *vt* krönen; überkronen ⟨*tooth*⟩

crucial /'kru:ʃl/ *a* höchst wichtig; (*decisive*) entscheidend (**to** für)

crucifix /'kru:sɪfɪks/ *n* Kruzifix *nt*

cruci|fixion /kru:sɪ'fɪkʃn/ *n* Kreuzigung *f*. ~**y** /'kru:sɪfaɪ/ *vt* (*pt/pp* **-ied**) kreuzigen

crude /'kru:d/ *a* (**-r, -st**) (*raw*) roh

cruel /'kru:əl/ *a* (**crueller, cruellest**), **-ly** *adv* grausam (**to** gegen). ~**ty** *n* Grausamkeit *f*; ~**ty to animals** Tierquälerei *f*

cruis|e /kru:z/ *n* Kreuzfahrt *f* □ *vi* kreuzen; ⟨*car.:*⟩ fahren. ~**er** *n* (*Mil*) Kreuzer *m*; (*motor boat*) Kajütboot *nt*. ~**ing speed** *n* Reisegeschwindigkeit *f*

crumb /krʌm/ *n* Krümel *m*

crumb|le /'krʌmbl/ *vt/i* krümeln; (*collapse*) einstürzen. ~**ly** *a* krümelig

crumple /'krʌmpl/ *vt* zerknittern □ *vi* knittern

crunch /krʌntʃ/ *n* (*fam*) **when it comes to the** ~ wenn es [wirklich] drauf ankommt □ *vt* mampfen □ *vi* knirschen

crusade /kru:'seɪd/ *n* Kreuzzug *m*; (*fig*) Kampagne *f*. ~**r** *n* Kreuzfahrer *m*; (*fig*) Kämpfer *m*

crush /krʌʃ/ *n* (*crowd*) Gedränge *nt* □ *vt* zerquetschen; zerknittern ⟨*clothes*⟩; (*fig: subdue*) niederschlagen

crust /krʌst/ *n* Kruste *f*

crutch /krʌtʃ/ *n* Krücke *f*

crux /krʌks/ *n* (*fig*) springender Punkt *m*

cry /kraɪ/ *n* Ruf *m*; (*shout*) Schrei *m*; **a far** ~ **from** (*fig*) weit entfernt von □ *vi* (*pt/pp* **cried**) (*weep*) weinen; ⟨*baby:*⟩ schreien; (*call*) rufen

crypt /krɪpt/ *n* Krypta *f*. ~**ic** *a* rätselhaft

crystal /'krɪstl/ *n* Kristall *m*; (*glass*) Kristall *nt*. ~**lize** *vi* [sich] kristallisieren

cub /kʌb/ *n* (*Zool*) Junge(s) *nt*; **C**~ **[Scout]** Wölfling *m*

Cuba /'kju:bə/ *n* Kuba *nt*

cubby-hole /'kʌbɪ-/ *n* Fach *nt*

cub|e /kju:b/ *n* Würfel *m*. ~**ic** *a* Kubik-

cubicle /'kju:bɪkl/ *n* Kabine *f*

cuckoo /'kʊku:/ *n* Kuckuck *m*. ~ **clock** *n* Kuckucksuhr *f*

cucumber /'kju:kʌmbə(r)/ *n* Gurke *f*

cuddl|e /'kʌdl/ *vt* herzen □ *vi* ~**e up to** sich kuscheln an (+ *acc*). ~**y** *a* kuschelig. ~**y 'toy** *n* Plüschtier *nt*

cudgel /'kʌdʒl/ *n* Knüppel *m*

cue[1] /kju:/ *n* Stichwort *nt*

cue[2] *n* (*Billiards*) Queue *nt*

cuff /kʌf/ *n* Manschette *f*; (*Amer: turn-up*) [Hosen]aufschlag *m*; (*blow*) Klaps *m*; **off the** ~ (*fam*) aus dem Stegreif □ *vt* einen Klaps geben (+ *dat*). ~**-link** *n* Manschettenknopf *m*

cul-de-sac /'kʌldəsæk/ *n* Sackgasse *f*

culinary /'kʌlɪnərɪ/ *a* kulinarisch

cull /kʌl/ *vt* pflücken ⟨*flowers*⟩; (*kill*) ausmerzen

culminat|e /'kʌlmɪneɪt/ *vi* gipfeln (**in** in + *dat*). **~ion** /-'neɪʃn/ *n* Gipfelpunkt *m*

culottes /kju:'lɒts/ *npl* Hosenrock *m*

culprit /'kʌlprɪt/ *n* Täter *m*

cult /kʌlt/ *n* Kult *m*

cultivate /'kʌltɪveɪt/ *vt* anbauen ⟨*crop*⟩; bebauen ⟨*land*⟩

cultural /'kʌltʃərəl/ *a* kulturell

culture /'kʌltʃə(r)/ *n* Kultur *f*. **~d** *a* kultiviert

cumbersome /'kʌmbəsəm/ *a* hinderlich; (*unwieldy*) unhandlich

cumulative /'kju:mjʊlətɪv/ *a* kumulativ

cunning /'kʌnɪŋ/ *a* listig ⊓ *n* List *f*

cup /kʌp/ *n* Tasse *f*; (*prize*) Pokal *m*

cupboard /'kʌbəd/ *n* Schrank *m*

Cup 'Final *n* Pokalendspiel *nt*

Cupid /'kju:pɪd/ *n* Amor *m*

curable /'kjʊərəbl/ *a* heilbar

curate /'kjʊərət/ *n* Vikar *m*; (*Roman Catholic*) Kaplan *m*

curator /kjʊə'reɪtə(r)/ *n* Kustos *m*

curb /kɜ:b/ *vt* zügeln

curdle /'kɜ:dl/ *vi* gerinnen

cure /kjʊə(r)/ *n* [Heil]mittel *nt* ⊓ *vt* heilen; (*salt*) pökeln; (*smoke*) räuchern; gerben ⟨*skin*⟩

curfew /'kɜ:fju:/ *n* Ausgangssperre *f*

curio /'kjʊərɪəʊ/ *n* Kuriosität *f*

curiosity /kjʊərɪ'ɒsətɪ/ *n* Neugier *f*; (*object*) Kuriosität *f*

curious /'kjʊərɪəs/ *a*, **-ly** *adv* neugierig; (*strange*) merkwürdig, seltsam

curl /kɜ:l/ *n* Locke *f* ⊓ *vt* locken ⊓ *vi* sich locken. **~ up** *vi* sich zusammenrollen

curler /'kɜ:lə(r)/ *n* Lockenwickler *m*

curly /'kɜ:lɪ/ *a* (**-ier, -iest**) lockig

currant /'kʌrənt/ *n* (*dried*) Korinthe *f*

currency /'kʌrənsɪ/ *n* Geläufigkeit *f*; (*money*) Währung *f*; **foreign ~** Devisen *pl*

current /'kʌrənt/ *a* augenblicklich, gegenwärtig; (*in general use*) geläufig, gebräuchlich ⊓ *n* Strömung *f*; (*Electr*) Strom *m*. **~ affairs** *or* **events** *npl* Aktuelle(s) *nt*. **~ly** *adv* zurzeit

curriculum /kə'rɪkjʊləm/ *n* Lehrplan *m*. **~ vitae** /-'vi:taɪ/ *n* Lebenslauf *m*

curry /'kʌrɪ/ *n* Curry *nt* & *m*; (*meal*) Currygericht *nt* ⊓ *vt* (*pt/pp* **-ied**) **~ favour** sich einschmeicheln (**with** bei)

curse /kɜ:s/ *n* Fluch *m* ⊓ *vt* verfluchen ⊓ *vi* fluchen

cursory /'kɜ:sərɪ/ *a* flüchtig

curt /kɜ:t/ *a*, **-ly** *adv* barsch

curtail /kɜ:'teɪl/ *vt* abkürzen

curtain /'kɜ:tn/ *n* Vorhang *m*

curtsy /'kɜ:tsɪ/ *n* Knicks *m* ⊓ *vi* (*pt/pp* **-ied**) knicksen

curve /kɜ:v/ *n* Kurve *f* ⊓ *vi* einen Bogen machen; **~ to the right/left** nach rechts/links biegen. **~d** *a* gebogen

cushion /'kʊʃn/ *n* Kissen *nt* ⊓ *vt* dämpfen; (*protect*) beschützen

cushy /'kʊʃɪ/ *a* (**-ier, -iest**) (*fam*) bequem

custard /'kʌstəd/ *n* Vanillesoße *f*

custodian /kʌ'stəʊdɪən/ *n* Hüter *m*

custody /'kʌstədɪ/ *n* Obhut *f*; (*of child*) Sorgerecht *nt*; (*imprisonment*) Haft *f*

custom /'kʌstəm/ *n* Brauch *m*; (*habit*) Gewohnheit *f*; (*Comm*) Kundschaft *f*. **~ary** *a* üblich; (*habitual*) gewohnt. **~er** *n* Kunde *m*/Kundin *f*

customs /'kʌstəmz/ *npl* Zoll *m*. **~ officer** *n* Zollbeamte(r) *m*

cut /kʌt/ *n* Schnitt *m*; (*Med*) Schnittwunde *f*; (*reduction*) Kürzung *f*; (*in price*) Senkung *f*; **~ [of meat]** [Fleisch]stück *nt* ⊓ *vt/i* (*pt/pp* cut, *pres p* **cutting**) schneiden; (*mow*) mähen; abheben ⟨*cards*⟩; (*reduce*) kürzen; senken ⟨*price*⟩; **~ one's finger** sich in den Finger schneiden; **~ s.o.'s hair** jdm die Haare schneiden; **~ short** abkürzen. **~ back** *vt* zurückschneiden; (*fig*) einschränken, kürzen. **~ down** *vt* fällen; (*fig*) einschränken. **~ off** *vt* abschneiden; (*disconnect*) abstellen; **be ~ off** (*Teleph*) unterbrochen werden. **~ out** *vt* ausschneiden; (*delete*) streichen; **be ~ out for** (*fam*) geeignet sein zu. **~ up** *vt* zerschneiden; (*slice*) aufschneiden

'cut-back *n* Kürzung *f*, Einschränkung *f*

cute /kju:t/ *a* (**-r, -st**) (*fam*) niedlich

cut 'glass *n* Kristall *nt*

cuticle /'kju:tɪkl/ *n* Nagelhaut *f*

cutlery /'kʌtlərɪ/ *n* Besteck *nt*

cutlet /'kʌtlɪt/ *n* Kotelett *nt*

'cut-price *a* verbilligt

cutting /'kʌtɪŋ/ *a* ⟨*remark*⟩ bissig ⊓ *n* (*from newspaper*) Ausschnitt *m*; (*of plant*) Ableger *m*

CV *abbr of* **curriculum vitae**

cyclamen /'sɪkləmən/ *n* Alpenveilchen *nt*

cycl|e /'saɪkl/ *n* Zyklus *m*; (*bicycle*) [Fahr]rad *nt* ⊓ *vi* mit dem Rad fahren. **~ing** *n* Radfahren *nt*. **~ist** *n* Radfahrer(in) *m(f)*

cyclone /'saɪkləʊn/ *n* Wirbelsturm *m*

cylind|er /'sɪlɪndə(r)/ *n* Zylinder *m*. **~rical** /-'lɪndrɪkl/ *a* zylindrisch

cymbals /'sɪmblz/ *npl* (*Mus*) Becken *nt*

cynic /'sɪnɪk/ *n* Zyniker *m*. **~al** *a*, **-ly** *adv* zynisch. **~ism** /-sɪzm/ *n* Zynismus *m*

cypress /'saɪprəs/ n Zypresse f

Cyprus /'saɪprəs/ n Zypern nt

cyst /sɪst/ n Zyste f. ~itis /-'taɪtɪs/ n Blasenentzündung f

Czech /tʃek/ a tschechisch □ n Tscheche m/ Tschechin f

Czechoslovak /tʃekə'sləʊvæk/ a tschechoslowakisch. ~ia /-'vækɪə/ n die Tschechoslowakei. ~ian /-'vækɪən/ a tschechoslowakisch

D

dab /dæb/ n Tupfer m; (of butter) Klecks m; a ~ of ein bisschen □ vt (pt/pp dabbed) abtupfen; betupfen (with mit)

dabble /'dæbl/ vi ~ in sth (fig) sich nebenbei mit etw befassen

dachshund /'dækshʊnd/ n Dackel m

dad[dy] /'dæd[i]/ n (fam) Vati m

daddy-'long-legs n [Kohl]schnake f; (Amer: spider) Weberknecht m

daffodil /'dæfədɪl/ n Osterglocke f, gelbe Narzisse f

daft /dɑːft/ a (-er, -est) dumm

dagger /'dægə(r)/ n Dolch m; (Typ) Kreuz nt; be at ~s drawn (fam) auf Kriegsfuß stehen

dahlia /'deɪlɪə/ n Dahlie f

daily /'deɪlɪ/ a & adv täglich □ n (newspaper) Tageszeitung f; (fam: cleaner) Putzfrau f

dainty /'deɪntɪ/ a (-ier, -iest) zierlich

dairy /'deərɪ/ n Molkerei f; (shop) Milchgeschäft nt. ~ cow n Milchkuh f. ~ products pl Milchprodukte pl

dais /'deɪɪs/ n Podium nt

daisy /'deɪzɪ/ n Gänseblümchen nt

dale /deɪl/ n (liter) Tal nt

dally /'dælɪ/ vi (pt/pp -ied) trödeln

dam /dæm/ n [Stau]damm m □ vt (pt/pp dammed) eindämmen

damage /'dæmɪdʒ/ n Schaden m (to an + dat); ~es pl (Jur) Schadenersatz m □ vt beschädigen; (fig) beeinträchtigen. ~ing a schädlich

damask /'dæməsk/ n Damast m

dame /deɪm/ n (liter) Dame f; (Amer sl) Weib nt

damn /dæm/ a, int & adv (fam) verdammt □ n I don't care or give a ~ (fam) ich schere mich einen Dreck darum □ vt verdammen. ~ation /-'neɪʃn/ n Verdammnis f □ int (fam) verdammt!

damp /dæmp/ a (-er, -est) feucht □ n Feuchtigkeit f □ vt = **dampen**

damp|en vt anfeuchten; (fig) dämpfen. ~ness n Feuchtigkeit f

dance /dɑːns/ n Tanz m; (function) Tanzveranstaltung f □ vt/i tanzen. ~hall n Tanzlokal nt. ~ music n Tanzmusik f

dancer /'dɑːnsə(r)/ n Tänzer(in) m(f)

dandelion /'dændɪlaɪən/ n Löwenzahn m

dandruff /'dændrʌf/ n Schuppen pl

Dane /deɪn/ n Däne m/Dänin f; Great ~ [deutsche] Dogge f

danger /'deɪndʒə(r)/ n Gefahr f; in/out of ~ in/außer Gefahr. ~ous /-rəs/ a, -ly adv gefährlich; ~ously ill schwer erkrankt

dangle /'dæŋgl/ vi baumeln □ vt baumeln lassen

Danish /'deɪnɪʃ/ a dänisch. ~ 'pastry n Hefeteilchen nt, Plunderstück nt

dank /dæŋk/ a (-er, -est) nasskalt

Danube /'dænjuːb/ n Donau f

dare /deə(r)/ n Mutprobe f □ vt/i (challenge) herausfordern (to zu); ~ [to] do sth [es] wagen, etw zu tun; I ~ say! das mag wohl sein! ~devil n Draufgänger m

daring /'deərɪŋ/ a verwegen □ n Verwegenheit f

dark /dɑːk/ a (-er, -est) dunkel; ~ blue/ brown dunkelblau/-braun; ~ horse (fig) stilles Wasser nt; keep sth ~ (fig) etw geheim halten □ n Dunkelheit f; after ~ nach Einbruch der Dunkelheit; in the ~ im Dunkeln; keep in the ~ (fig) im Dunkeln lassen

dark|en /'dɑːkn/ vt verdunkeln □ vi dunkler werden. ~ness n Dunkelheit f

'dark-room n Dunkelkammer f

darling /'dɑːlɪŋ/ a allerliebst □ n Liebling m

darn /dɑːn/ vt stopfen. ~ing-needle n Stopfnadel f

dart /dɑːt/ n Pfeil m; (Sewing) Abnäher m; ~s sg (game) [Wurf]pfeil m □ vi flitzen

dash /dæʃ/ n (Typ) Gedankenstrich m; (in Morse) Strich m; a ~ of milk ein Schuss Milch; make a ~ losstürzen (for auf + acc) □ vi rennen □ vt schleudern. ~ off vi losstürzen □ vt (write quickly) hinwerfen

'dashboard n Armaturenbrett nt

dashing /'dæʃɪŋ/ a schneidig

data /'deɪtə/ npl & sg Daten pl. ~ processing n Datenverarbeitung f

date¹ /deɪt/ n (fruit) Dattel f

date² *n* Datum *nt*; (*fam*) Verabredung *f*; **to ~ bis heute; out of ~** überholt; (*expired*) ungültig; **be up to ~** auf dem Laufenden sein □ *vt/i* datieren; (*Amer, fam: go out with*) ausgehen mit; **~ back to** zurückgehen auf (+ *acc*)

dated /'deɪtɪd/ *a* altmodisch

'date-line *n* Datumsgrenze *f*

dative /'deɪtɪv/ *a & n* (*Gram*) **~ [case]** Dativ *m*

daub /dɔːb/ *vt* beschmieren (**with** mit); schmieren (*paint*)

daughter /'dɔːtə(r)/ *n* Tochter *f*. **~-in-law** *n* (*pl* **~s-in-law**) Schwiegertochter *f*

daunt /dɔːnt/ *vt* entmutigen; **nothing ~ed** unverzagt. **~less** *a* furchtlos

dawdle /'dɔːdl/ *vi* trödeln

dawn /dɔːn/ *n* Morgendämmerung *f*; **at ~** bei Tagesanbruch □ *vi* anbrechen; **it ~ed on me** (*fig*) es ging mir auf

day /deɪ/ *n* Tag *m*; **~ by ~** Tag für Tag; **~ after ~** Tag um Tag; **these ~s** heutzutage; **in those ~s** zu der Zeit; **it's had its ~** (*fam*) es hat ausgedient

day: ~break *n* **at ~break** bei Tagesanbruch *m*. **~dream** *n* Tagtraum *m* □ *vi* [mit offenen Augen] träumen. **~light** *n* Tageslicht *nt*. **~ re'turn** *n* (*ticket*) Tagesrückfahrkarte *f*. **~time** *n* **in the ~time** am Tage

daze /deɪz/ *n* **in a ~** wie benommen. **~d** *a* benommen

dazzle /'dæzl/ *vt* blenden

deacon /'diːkn/ *n* Diakon *m*

dead /ded/ *a* tot; (*flower*) verwelkt; (*numb*) taub; **~ body** Leiche *f*; **be ~ on time** auf die Minute pünktlich kommen; **~ centre** genau in der Mitte □ *adv* **~ tired** todmüde; **~ slow** sehr langsam; **stop ~** stehen bleiben □ *n* **the ~** *pl* die Toten; **in the ~ of night** mitten in der Nacht

deaden /'dedn/ *vt* dämpfen (*sound*); betäuben (*pain*)

dead: ~ 'end *n* Sackgasse *f*. **~ 'heat** *n* totes Rennen *nt*. **~line** *n* [letzter] Termin *m*. **~lock** *n* **reach ~lock** (*fig*) sich festfahren

deadly /'dedlɪ/ *a* (**-ier, -iest**) tödlich; (*fam: dreary*) sterbenslangweilig; **~ sins** *pl* Todsünden *pl*

deaf /def/ *a* (**-er, -est**) taub; **~ and dumb** taubstumm. **~-aid** *n* Hörgerät *nt*

deaf|en /'defn/ *vt* betäuben; (*permanently*) taub machen. **~ening** *a* ohrenbetäubend. **~ness** *n* Taubheit *f*

deal /diːl/ *n* (*transaction*) Geschäft *nt*; **whose ~?** (*Cards*) wer gibt? **a good** *or* **great ~** eine Menge; **get a raw ~** (*fam*) schlecht wegkommen □ *v* (*pt/pp* **dealt**

/delt/) □ *vt* (*Cards*) geben; **~ out** austeilen; **~ s.o. a blow** jdm einen Schlag versetzen □ *vi* **~ in** handeln mit; **~ with** zu tun haben mit; (*handle*) sich befassen mit; (*cope with*) fertig werden mit; (*be about*) handeln von; **that's been dealt with** das ist schon erledigt

deal|er /'diːlə(r)/ *n* Händler *m*; (*Cards*) Kartengeber *m*. **~ings** *npl* **have ~ings with** zu tun haben mit

dean /diːn/ *n* Dekan *m*

dear /dɪə(r)/ *a* (**-er, -est**) lieb; (*expensive*) teuer; (*in letter*) liebe(r,s) (*formal*) sehr geehrte(r,s) □ *n* Liebe(r) *m/f* □ *int* **oh ~!** oje! **~ly** *adv* (*love*) sehr; (*pay*) teuer

dearth /dɜːθ/ *n* Mangel *m* (**of** an + *dat*)

death /deθ/ *n* Tod *m*; **three ~s** drei Todesfälle. **~ certificate** *n* Sterbeurkunde *f*. **~ duty** *n* Erbschaftssteuer *f*

deathly *a* **~ silence** Totenstille *f* □ *adv* **~ pale** totenblass

death: ~ penalty *n* Todesstrafe *f*. **~'s head** *n* Totenkopf *m*. **~-trap** *n* Todesfalle *f*

debar /dɪˈbɑː(r)/ *vt* (*pt/pp* **debarred**) ausschließen

debase /dɪˈbeɪs/ *vt* erniedrigen

debatable /dɪˈbeɪtəbl/ *a* strittig

debate /dɪˈbeɪt/ *n* Debatte *f* □ *vt/i* debattieren

debauchery /dɪˈbɔːtʃərɪ/ *n* Ausschweifung *f*

debility /dɪˈbɪlətɪ/ *n* Entkräftung *f*

debit /'debɪt/ *n* Schuldbetrag *m*; **~ [side]** Soll *nt* □ *vt* (*pt/pp* **debited**) (*Comm*) belasten; abbuchen (*sum*)

debris /'debriː/ *n* Trümmer *pl*

debt /det/ *n* Schuld *f*; **in ~** verschuldet. **~or** *n* Schuldner *m*

début /'deɪbuː/ *n* Debüt *nt*

decade /'dekeɪd/ *n* Jahrzehnt *nt*

decaden|ce /'dekədəns/ *n* Dekadenz *f*. **~t** *a* dekadent

decaffeinated /dɪˈkæfɪneɪtɪd/ *a* koffeinfrei

decant /dɪˈkænt/ *vt* umfüllen. **~er** *n* Karaffe *f*

decapitate /dɪˈkæpɪteɪt/ *vt* köpfen

decay /dɪˈkeɪ/ *n* Verfall *m*; (*rot*) Verwesung *f*; (*of tooth*) Zahnfäule *f* □ *vi* verfallen; (*rot*) verwesen; (*tooth:*) schlecht werden

decease /dɪˈsiːs/ *n* Ableben *nt*. **~d** *a* verstorben □ *n* **the ~d** der/die Verstorbene

deceit /dɪˈsiːt/ *n* Täuschung *f*. **~ful** *a*, **-ly** *adv* unaufrichtig

deceive /dɪˈsiːv/ *vt* täuschen; (*be unfaithful to*) betrügen

December /dɪˈsembə(r)/ *n* Dezember *m*

decency /'di:sənsı/ n Anstand m

decent /'di:sənt/ a, -ly adv anständig

decentralize /di:'sentrəlaız/ vt dezentralisieren

decept|ion /dı'sepʃn/ n Täuschung f; (fraud) Betrug m. ~ive /-tıv/ a, -ly adv täuschend

decibel /'desıbel/ n Dezibel nt

decide /dı'saıd/ vt entscheiden □ vi sich entscheiden (on für)

decided /dı'saıdıd/ a, -ly adv entschieden

deciduous /dı'sıdjuəs/ a ~ tree Laubbaum m

decimal /'desıml/ a Dezimal- □ n Dezimalzahl f. ~ 'point n Komma nt. ~ system n Dezimalsystem nt

decimate /'desımeıt/ vt dezimieren

decipher /dı'saıfə(r)/ vt entziffern

decision /dı'sıʒn/ n Entscheidung f; (firmness) Entschlossenheit f

decisive /dı'saısıv/ a ausschlaggebend; (firm) entschlossen

deck¹ /dek/ vt schmücken

deck² n (Naut) Deck nt; on ~ an Deck; top ~ (of bus) Oberdeck nt; ~ of cards (Amer) [Karten]spiel nt. ~-chair n Liegestuhl m

declaration /deklə'reıʃn/ n Erklärung f

declare /dı'kleə(r)/ vt erklären; angeben (goods); anything to ~? etwas zu verzollen?

declension /dı'klenʃn/ n Deklination f

decline /dı'klaın/ n Rückgang m; (in health) Verfall m □ vt ablehnen; (Gram) deklinieren □ vi ablehnen; (fall) sinken; (decrease) nachlassen

decode /di:'kəud/ vt entschlüsseln

decompos|e /di:kəm'pəuz/ vi sich zersetzen

décor /'deıkɔ:(r)/ n Ausstattung f

decorat|e /'dekəreıt/ vt (adorn) schmücken; verzieren (cake); (paint) streichen; (wallpaper) tapezieren; (award medal to) einen Orden verleihen (+ dat). ~ion /-'reıʃn/ n Verzierung f; (medal) Orden m; ~ions pl Schmuck m. ~ive /-rətıv/ a dekorativ. ~or n painter and ~or Maler und Tapezierer m

decorous /'dekərəs/ a, -ly adv schamhaft

decorum /dı'kɔ:rəm/ n Anstand m

decoy¹ /'di:kɔı/ n Lockvogel m

decoy² /dı'kɔı/ vt locken

decrease¹ /'di:kri:s/ n Verringerung f; (in number) Rückgang m; be on the ~ zurückgehen

decrease² /dı'kri:s/ vt verringern; herabsetzen (price) □ vi sich verringern; (price:) sinken

decree /dı'kri:/ n Erlass m □ vt (pt/pp decreed) verordnen

decrepit /dı'krepıt/ a altersschwach

dedicat|e /'dedıkeıt/ vt widmen; (Relig) weihen. ~ed a hingebungsvoll; (person) aufopfernd. ~ion /-'keıʃn/ n Hingabe f; (in book) Widmung f

deduce /dı'dju:s/ vt folgern (from aus)

deduct /dı'dʌkt/ vt abziehen

deduction /dı'dʌkʃn/ n Abzug m; (conclusion) Folgerung f

deed /di:d/ n Tat f; (Jur) Urkunde f

deem /di:m/ vt halten für

deep /di:p/ a (-er, -est), -ly adv tief; go off the ~ end (fam) auf die Palme gehen □ adv tief

deepen /'di:pn/ vt vertiefen □ vi tiefer werden; (fig) sich vertiefen

deep-'freeze n Gefriertruhe f; (upright) Gefrierschrank m

deer /dıə(r)/ n inv Hirsch m; (roe) Reh nt

deface /dı'feıs/ vt beschädigen

defamat|ion /defə'meıʃn/ n Verleumdung f. ~ory /dı'fæmətərı/ a verleumderisch

default /dı'fɔ:lt/ n (Jur) Nichtzahlung f; (failure to appear) Nichterscheinen nt; win by ~ (Sport) kampflos gewinnen □ vi nicht zahlen; nicht erscheinen

defeat /dı'fi:t/ n Niederlage f; (defeating) Besiegung f; (rejection) Ablehnung f □ vt besiegen; ablehnen; (frustrate) vereiteln

defect¹ /dı'fekt/ vi (Pol) überlaufen

defect² /'di:fekt/ n Fehler m; (Techn) Defekt m. ~ive /dı'fektıv/ a fehlerhaft; (Techn) defekt

defence /dı'fens/ n Verteidigung f. ~less a wehrlos

defend /dı'fend/ vt verteidigen; (justify) rechtfertigen. ~ant n (Jur) Beklagte(r) m/f; (in criminal court) Angeklagte(r) m/f

defensive /dı'fensıv/ a defensiv □ n Defensive f

defer /dı'fɜ:(r)/ vt (pt/pp deferred) (postpone) aufschieben; ~ to s.o. sich jdm fügen

deferen|ce /'defərəns/ n Ehrerbietung f. ~tial /-'renʃl/ a, -ly adv ehrerbietig

defian|ce /dı'faıəns/ n Trotz m; in ~ce of zum Trotz (+ dat). ~t a, -ly adv aufsässig

deficien|cy /dı'fıʃənsı/ n Mangel m. ~t a mangelhaft; he is ~t in ... ihm mangelt es an ... (dat)

deficit /'defısıt/ n Defizit nt

defile /dı'faıl/ vt (fig) schänden

define /dı'faın/ vt bestimmen; definieren (word)

definite /'defınıt/ a, -ly adv bestimmt; (certain) sicher

definition /defɪ'nɪʃn/ n Definition f; (Phot, TV) Schärfe f

definitive /dɪ'fɪnətɪv/ a endgültig; (authoritative) maßgeblich

deflat|e /dɪ'fleɪt/ vt die Luft auslassen aus. ~ion /-eɪʃn/ n (Comm) Deflation f

deflect /dɪ'flekt/ vt ablenken

deform|ed /dɪ'fɔ:md/ a missgebildet. ~ity n Missbildung f

defraud /dɪ'frɔ:d/ vt betrügen (of um)

defray /dɪ'freɪ/ vt bestreiten

defrost /di:'frɒst/ vt entfrosten; abtauen ⟨fridge⟩; auftauen ⟨food⟩

deft /deft/ a (-er, -est), -ly adv geschickt. ~ness n Geschicklichkeit f

defunct /dɪ'fʌŋkt/ a aufgelöst; ⟨law⟩ außer Kraft gesetzt

defuse /di:'fju:z/ vt entschärfen

defy /dɪ'faɪ/ vt (pt/pp -ied) trotzen (+ dat); widerstehen (+ dat) ⟨attempt⟩

degenerate[1] /dɪ'dʒenəreɪt/ vi degenerieren; ~ into ⟨fig⟩ ausarten in (+ acc)

degenerate[2] /dɪ'dʒenərət/ a degeneriert

degrading /dɪ'greɪdɪŋ/ a entwürdigend

degree /dɪ'gri:/ n Grad m; (Univ) akademischer Grad m; **20 ~s** 20 Grad

dehydrate /di:'haɪdreɪt/ vt Wasser entziehen (+ dat). ~d /-ɪd/ a ausgetrocknet

de-ice /di:'aɪs/ vt enteisen

deign /deɪn/ vi ~ to do sth sich herablassen, etw zu tun

deity /'di:ɪtɪ/ n Gottheit f

dejected /dɪ'dʒektɪd/ a, -ly adv niedergeschlagen

delay /dɪ'leɪ/ n Verzögerung f; (of train, aircraft) Verspätung f; **without ~** unverzüglich ◻ vt aufhalten; (postpone) aufschieben; **be ~ed** ⟨person:⟩ aufgehalten werden; ⟨train, aircraft:⟩ Verspätung haben ◻ vi zögern

delegate[1] /'delɪgət/ n Delegierte(r) m/f

delegat|e[2] /'delɪgeɪt/ vt delegieren. ~ion /-'geɪʃn/ n Delegation f

delet|e /dɪ'li:t/ vt streichen. ~ion /-i:ʃn/ n Streichung f

deliberate[1] /dɪ'lɪbərət/ a, -ly adv absichtlich; (slow) bedächtig

deliberat|e[2] /dɪ'lɪbəreɪt/ vt/i überlegen. ~ion /-'reɪʃn/ n Überlegung f; **with ~ion** mit Bedacht

delicacy /'delɪkəsɪ/ n Feinheit f; Zartheit f; (food) Delikatesse f

delicate /'delɪkət/ a fein; ⟨fabric, health⟩ zart; (situation) heikel; (mechanism) empfindlich

delicatessen /delɪkə'tesn/ n Delikatessengeschäft nt

delicious /dɪ'lɪʃəs/ a köstlich

delight /dɪ'laɪt/ n Freude f ◻ vt entzücken ◻ vi ~ in sich erfreuen an (+ dat). ~ed a hocherfreut; **be ~ed** sich sehr freuen. ~ful a reizend

delinquen|cy /dɪ'lɪŋkwənsɪ/ n Kriminalität f. ~t a straffällig ◻ n Straffällige(r) m/f

deli|rious /dɪ'lɪrɪəs/ a **be ~rious** im Delirium sein. ~rium /-rɪəm/ n Delirium nt

deliver /dɪ'lɪvə(r)/ vt liefern; zustellen ⟨post, newspaper⟩; halten ⟨speech⟩; überbringen ⟨message⟩; versetzen ⟨blow⟩; (set free) befreien; ~ **a baby** ein Kind zur Welt bringen. ~ance n Erlösung f. ~y n Lieferung f; (of post) Zustellung f; (Med) Entbindung f; **cash on ~y** per Nachnahme

delta /'deltə/ n Delta nt

delude /dɪ'lu:d/ vt täuschen; ~ **oneself** sich (dat) Illusionen machen

deluge /'delju:dʒ/ n Flut f; (heavy rain) schwerer Guss m ◻ vt überschwemmen

delusion /dɪ'lu:ʒn/ n Täuschung f

de luxe /dɪ'lʌks/ a Luxus-

delve /delv/ vi hineingreifen (into in + acc); ⟨fig⟩ eingehen (into auf + acc)

demand /dɪ'mɑ:nd/ n Forderung f; (Comm) Nachfrage f; **in ~** gefragt; **on ~** auf Verlangen ◻ vt verlangen, fordern (of/from von). ~ing a anspruchsvoll

demarcation /di:mɑ:'keɪʃn/ n Abgrenzung f

demean /dɪ'mi:n/ vt ~ **oneself** sich erniedrigen

demeanour /dɪ'mi:nə(r)/ n Verhalten nt

demented /dɪ'mentɪd/ a verrückt

demise /dɪ'maɪz/ n Tod m

demister /di:'mɪstə(r)/ n (Auto) Defroster m

demo /'deməʊ/ n (pl ~s) (fam) Demonstration f

demobilize /di:'məʊbɪlaɪz/ vt (Mil) entlassen

democracy /dɪ'mɒkrəsɪ/ n Demokratie f

democrat /'deməkræt/ n Demokrat m. ~ic /-'krætɪk/ a, -ally adv demokratisch

demo|lish /dɪ'mɒlɪʃ/ vt abbrechen; (destroy) zerstören. ~lition /-'lɪʃn/ n Abbruch m

demon /'di:mən/ n Dämon m

demonstrat|e /'demənstreɪt/ vt beweisen; vorführen ⟨appliance⟩ ◻ vi (Pol) demonstrieren. ~ion /-'streɪʃn/ n Vorführung f; (Pol) Demonstration f

demonstrative /dɪ'mɒnstrətɪv/ a (Gram) demonstrativ; **be ~** seine Gefühle zeigen

demonstrator /'demənstreɪtə(r)/ n Vorführer m; (Pol) Demonstrant m

demoralize /dɪ'mɒrəlaɪz/ *vt* demoralisieren

demote /dɪ'məʊt/ *vt* degradieren

demure /dɪ'mjʊə(r)/ *a*, **-ly** *adv* sittsam

den /den/ *n* Höhle *f*; (*room*) Bude *f*

denial /dɪ'naɪəl/ *n* Leugnen *nt*; **official ~** Dementi *nt*

denigrate /'denɪgreɪt/ *vt* herabsetzen

denim /'denɪm/ *n* Jeansstoff *m*; **~s** *pl* Jeans *pl*

Denmark /'denmɑ:k/ *n* Dänemark *nt*

denomination /dɪnɒmɪ'neɪʃn/ *n* (*Relig*) Konfession *f*; (*money*) Nennwert *m*

denote /dɪ'nəʊt/ *vt* bezeichnen

denounce /dɪ'naʊns/ *vt* denunzieren; (*condemn*) verurteilen

dens|e /dens/ *a* (**-r, -st**), **-ly** *adv* dicht; (*fam: stupid*) blöd[e]. **~ity** *n* Dichte *f*

dent /dent/ *n* Delle *f*, Beule *f* □ *vt* einbeulen; **~ed** /-ɪd/ verbeult

dental /'dentl/ *a* Zahn-; (*treatment*) zahnärztlich. **~ floss** /flɒs/ *n* Zahnseide *f*. **~ surgeon** *n* Zahnarzt *m*

dentist /'dentɪst/ *n* Zahnarzt *m*/-ärztin *f*. **~ry** *n* Zahnmedizin *f*

denture /'dentʃə(r)/ *n* Zahnprothese *f*; **~s** *pl* künstliches Gebiss *nt*

denude /dɪ'nju:d/ *vt* entblößen

denunciation /dɪnʌnsɪ'eɪʃn/ *n* Denunziation *f*; (*condemnation*) Verurteilung *f*

deny /dɪ'naɪ/ *vt* (*pt/pp* **-ied**) leugnen; (*officially*) dementieren; **~ s.o. sth** jdm etw verweigern

deodorant /di:'əʊdərənt/ *n* Deodorant *nt*

depart /dɪ'pɑ:t/ *vi* abfahren; (*Aviat*) abfliegen; (*go away*) weggehen/-fahren; (*deviate*) abweichen (**from** von)

department /dɪ'pɑ:tmənt/ *n* Abteilung *f*; (*Pol*) Ministerium *nt*. **~ store** *n* Kaufhaus *nt*

departure /dɪ'pɑ:tʃə(r)/ *n* Abfahrt *f*; (*Aviat*) Abflug *m*; (*from rule*) Abweichung *f*; **new ~** Neuerung *f*

depend /dɪ'pend/ *vi* abhängen (**on** von); (*rely*) sich verlassen (**on** auf + *acc*); **it all ~s** das kommt darauf an. **~able** /-əbl/ *a* zuverlässig. **~ant** *n* Abhängige(r) *m/f*. **~ence** *n* Abhängigkeit *f*. **~ent** *a* abhängig (**on** von)

depict /dɪ'pɪkt/ *vt* darstellen

depilatory /dɪ'pɪlətərɪ/ *n* Enthaarungsmittel *nt*

deplete /dɪ'pli:t/ *vt* verringern

deplor|able /dɪ'plɔ:rəbl/ *a* bedauerlich. **~e** *vt* bedauern

deploy /dɪ'plɔɪ/ *vt* (*Mil*) einsetzen □ *vi* sich aufstellen

depopulate /di:'pɒpjʊleɪt/ *vt* entvölkern

deport /dɪ'pɔ:t/ *vt* deportieren, ausweisen. **~ation** /di:pɔ:'teɪʃn/ *n* Ausweisung *f*

deportment /dɪ'pɔ:tmənt/ *n* Haltung *f*

depose /dɪ'pəʊz/ *vt* absetzen

deposit /dɪ'pɒzɪt/ *n* Anzahlung *f*; (*against damage*) Kaution *f*; (*on bottle*) Pfand *nt*; (*sediment*) Bodensatz *m*; (*Geol*) Ablagerung *f* □ *vt* (*pt/pp* **deposited**) legen; (*for safety*) deponieren; (*Geol*) ablagern. **~ account** *n* Sparkonto *nt*

depot /'depəʊ/ *n* Depot *nt*; (*Amer: railway station*) Bahnhof *m*

deprav|e /dɪ'preɪv/ *vt* verderben. **~ed** *a* verkommen. **~ity** /-'prævətɪ/ *n* Verderbtheit *f*

deprecate /'deprəkeɪt/ *vt* missbilligen

depreciat|e /dɪ'pri:ʃɪeɪt/ *vi* an Wert verlieren. **~ion** /-'eɪʃn/ *n* Wertminderung *f*; (*Comm*) Abschreibung *f*

depress /dɪ'pres/ *vt* deprimieren; (*press down*) herunterdrücken. **~ed** *a* deprimiert; **~ed area** Notstandsgebiet *nt*. **~ing** *a* deprimierend. **~ion** /-eʃn/ *n* Vertiefung *f*; (*Med*) Depression *f*; (*Meteorol*) Tief *nt*

deprivation /deprɪ'veɪʃn/ *n* Entbehrung *f*

deprive /dɪ'praɪv/ *vt* entziehen; **~ s.o. of sth** jdm etw entziehen. **~d** *a* benachteiligt

depth /depθ/ *n* Tiefe *f*; **in ~** gründlich; **in the ~s of winter** im tiefsten Winter

deputation /depjʊ'teɪʃn/ *n* Abordnung *f*

deputize /'depjʊtaɪz/ *vi* **~ for** vertreten

deputy /'depjʊtɪ/ *n* Stellvertreter *m* □ *attrib* stellvertretend

derail /dɪ'reɪl/ *vt* **be ~ed** entgleisen. **~ment** *n* Entgleisung *f*

deranged /dɪ'reɪndʒd/ *a* geistesgestört

derelict /'derəlɪkt/ *a* verfallen; (*abandoned*) verlassen

deri|de /dɪ'raɪd/ *vt* verhöhnen. **~sion** /-'rɪʒn/ *n* Hohn *m*

derisive /dɪ'raɪsɪv/ *a*, **-ly** *adv* höhnisch

derisory /dɪ'raɪsərɪ/ *a* höhnisch; (*offer*) lächerlich

derivation /derɪ'veɪʃn/ *n* Ableitung *f*

derivative /dɪ'rɪvətɪv/ *a* abgeleitet □ *n* Ableitung *f*

derive /dɪ'raɪv/ *vt/i* (*obtain*) gewinnen (**from** aus); **be ~d from** (*word:*) hergeleitet sein aus

dermatologist /dɜ:mə'tɒlədʒɪst/ *n* Hautarzt *m* /-ärztin *f*

derogatory /dɪ'rɒgətrɪ/ *a* abfällig

derrick /'derɪk/ *n* Bohrturm *m*

derv /dɜ:v/ *n* Diesel[kraftstoff] *m*

descend /dɪ'send/ vt/i hinunter-/heruntergehen; ⟨vehicle, lift:⟩ hinunter-/herunterfahren; **be ~ed from** abstammen von. **~ant** n Nachkomme m

descent /dɪ'sent/ n Abstieg m; (lineage) Abstammung f

describe /dɪ'skraɪb/ vt beschreiben

descrip|tion /dɪ'skrɪpʃn/ n Beschreibung f; (sort) Art f. **~tive** /-tɪv/ a beschreibend; (vivid) anschaulich

desecrat|e /'desɪkreɪt/ vt entweihen. **~ion** /-'kreɪʃn/ n Entweihung f

desert¹ /'dezət/ n Wüste f □ a Wüsten-; **~ island** verlassene Insel f

desert² /dɪ'zɜ:t/ vt verlassen □ vt desertieren. **~ed** a verlassen. **~er** n (Mil) Deserteur m. **~ion** /-ʃn/ n Fahnenflucht f

deserts /dɪ'zɜ:ts/ npl **get one's ~** seinen verdienten Lohn bekommen

deserv|e /dɪ'zɜ:v/ vt verdienen. **~edly** /-ɪdlɪ/ adv verdientermaßen. **~ing** a verdienstvoll; **~ing cause** guter Zweck m

design /dɪ'zaɪn/ n Entwurf m; (pattern) Muster m; (construction) Konstruktion f; (aim) Absicht f □ vt entwerfen; (construct) konstruieren; **be ~ed for** bestimmt sein für

designat|e /'dezɪgneɪt/ vt bezeichnen; (appoint) ernennen. **~ion** /-'neɪʃn/ n Bezeichnung f

designer /dɪ'zaɪnə(r)/ n Designer m; (Techn) Konstrukteur m; (Theat) Bühnenbildner m

desirable /dɪ'zaɪrəbl/ a wünschenswert; (sexually) begehrenswert

desire /dɪ'zaɪə(r)/ n Wunsch m; (longing) Verlangen nt (for nach); (sexual) Begierde f □ vt [sich (dat)] wünschen; (sexually) begehren

desk /desk/ n Schreibtisch m; (Sch) Pult nt; (Comm) Kasse f; (in hotel) Rezeption f

desolat|e /'desələt/ a trostlos. **~ion** /-'leɪʃn/ n Trostlosigkeit f

despair /dɪ'speə(r)/ n Verzweiflung f; **in ~** verzweifelt □ vi verzweifeln

desperat|e /'despərət/ a, **-ly** adv verzweifelt; (urgent) dringend; **be ~e** ⟨criminal:⟩ zum Äußersten entschlossen sein; **be ~e for** dringend brauchen. **~ion** /-'reɪʃn/ n Verzweiflung f; **in ~ion** aus Verzweiflung

despicable /dɪ'spɪkəbl/ a verachtenswert

despise /dɪ'spaɪz/ vt verachten

despite /dɪ'spaɪt/ prep trotz (+ gen)

despondent /dɪ'spɒndənt/ a niedergeschlagen

despot /'despɒt/ n Despot m

dessert /dɪ'zɜ:t/ n Dessert nt, Nachtisch m. **~ spoon** n Dessertlöffel m

destination /destɪ'neɪʃn/ n [Reise]ziel nt; (of goods) Bestimmungsort m

destine /'destɪn/ vt bestimmen

destiny /'destɪnɪ/ n Schicksal nt

destitute /'destɪtjuːt/ a völlig mittellos

destroy /dɪ'strɔɪ/ vt zerstören; (totally) vernichten. **~er** n (Naut) Zerstörer m

destruc|tion /dɪ'strʌkʃn/ n Zerstörung f; Vernichtung f. **-tive** /-tɪv/ a zerstörerisch; (fig) destruktiv

detach /dɪ'tætʃ/ vt abnehmen; (tear off) abtrennen. **~able** /-əbl/ a abnehmbar. **~ed** a (fig) distanziert; **~ed house** Einzelhaus nt

detachment /dɪ'tætʃmənt/ n Distanz f; (objectivity) Abstand m; (Mil) Sonderkommando nt

detail /'diːteɪl/ n Einzelheit f, Detail nt; **in ~** ausführlich □ vt einzeln aufführen; (Mil) abkommandieren. **~ed** a ausführlich

detain /dɪ'teɪn/ vt aufhalten; ⟨police:⟩ in Haft behalten; (take into custody) in Haft nehmen. **~ee** /diːteɪ'niː/ n Häftling m

detect /dɪ'tekt/ vt entdecken; (perceive) wahrnehmen. **~ion** /-ekʃn/ n Entdeckung f

detective /dɪ'tektɪv/ n Detektiv m. **~ story** n Detektivroman m

detector /dɪ'tektə(r)/ n Suchgerät nt; (for metal) Metalldetektor m

detention /dɪ'tenʃn/ n Haft f; (Sch) Nachsitzen nt

deter /dɪ'tɜ:(r)/ vt (pt/pp deterred) abschrecken; (prevent) abhalten

detergent /dɪ'tɜ:dʒənt/ n Waschmittel nt

deteriorat|e /dɪ'tɪərɪəreɪt/ vi sich verschlechtern. **~ion** /-'reɪʃn/ n Verschlechterung f

determination /dɪtɜːmɪ'neɪʃn/ n Entschlossenheit f

determine /dɪ'tɜ:mɪn/ vt bestimmen; **~ to** (resolve) sich entschließen zu. **~d** a entschlossen

deterrent /dɪ'terənt/ n Abschreckungsmittel nt

detest /dɪ'test/ vt verabscheuen. **~able** /-əbl/ a abscheulich

detonat|e /'detəneɪt/ vt zünden □ vi explodieren. **~or** n Zünder m

detour /'diːtʊə(r)/ n Umweg m; (for traffic) Umleitung f

detract /dɪ'trækt/ vi **~ from** beeinträchtigen

detriment /'detrɪmənt/ n **to the ~** zum Schaden (of gen). **~al** /-'mentl/ a schädlich (to dat)

deuce /djuːs/ n (Tennis) Einstand m

devaluation /diːvæljuˈeɪʃn/ n Abwertung f

de'value vt abwerten ⟨currency⟩

devastat|e /ˈdevəsteɪt/ vt verwüsten. ~ed /-ɪd/ a ⟨fam⟩ erschüttert. ~ing a verheerend. ~ion /-ˈsteɪʃn/ n Verwüstung f

develop /dɪˈveləp/ vt entwickeln; bekommen ⟨illness⟩; erschließen ⟨area⟩ □ vi sich entwickeln (into zu). ~er n [property] ~er Bodenspekulant m

de'veloping country n Entwicklungsland nt

development /dɪˈveləpmənt/ n Entwicklung f

deviant /ˈdiːvɪənt/ a abweichend

deviat|e /ˈdiːvɪeɪt/ vi abweichen. ~ion /-ˈeɪʃn/ n Abweichung f

device /dɪˈvaɪs/ n Gerät nt; ⟨fig⟩ Mittel nt; **leave s.o. to his own ~s** jdn sich ⟨dat⟩ selbst überlassen

devil /ˈdevl/ n Teufel m. ~ish a teuflisch

devious /ˈdiːvɪəs/ a verschlagen; ~ route Umweg m

devise /dɪˈvaɪz/ vt sich ⟨dat⟩ ausdenken

devoid /dɪˈvɔɪd/ a ~ of ohne

devolution /diːvəˈluːʃn/ n Dezentralisierung f; ⟨of power⟩ Übertragung f

devot|e /dɪˈvəʊt/ vt widmen (to dat). ~ed a, -ly adv ergeben; ⟨care⟩ liebevoll; be ~ed to s.o. sehr an jdm hängen. ~ee /devə-ˈtiː/ n Anhänger(in) m(f)

devotion /dɪˈvəʊʃn/ n Hingabe f; ~s pl ⟨Relig⟩ Andacht f

devour /dɪˈvaʊə(r)/ vt verschlingen

devout /dɪˈvaʊt/ a fromm

dew /djuː/ n Tau m

dexterity /dekˈsterətɪ/ n Geschicklichkeit f

diabet|es /daɪəˈbiːtiːz/ n Zuckerkrankheit f. ~ic /-ˈbetɪk/ a zuckerkrank □ n Zuckerkranke(r) m/f, Diabetiker(in) m(f)

diabolical /daɪəˈbɒlɪkl/ a teuflisch

diagnose /daɪəɡˈnəʊz/ vt diagnostizieren

diagnosis /daɪəɡˈnəʊsɪs/ n (pl -oses /-siːz/) Diagnose f

diagonal /daɪˈæɡənl/ a, -ly adv diagonal □ n Diagonale f

diagram /ˈdaɪəɡræm/ n Diagramm nt

dial /ˈdaɪəl/ n ⟨of clock⟩ Zifferblatt nt; ⟨Techn⟩ Skala f; ⟨Teleph⟩ Wählscheibe f □ vt/i (pt/pp dialled) ⟨Teleph⟩ wählen; ~ direct durchwählen

dialect /ˈdaɪəlekt/ n Dialekt m

dialling: ~ code n Vorwahlnummer f. ~ tone n Amtszeichen nt

dialogue /ˈdaɪəlɒɡ/ n Dialog m

'dial tone n ⟨Amer, Teleph⟩ Amtszeichen nt

diameter /daɪˈæmɪtə(r)/ n Durchmesser m

diametrically /daɪəˈmetrɪkəlɪ/ adv ~ opposed genau entgegengesetzt (to dat)

diamond /ˈdaɪəmənd/ n Diamant m; ⟨cut⟩ Brillant m; ⟨shape⟩ Raute f; ~s pl ⟨Cards⟩ Karo nt

diaper /ˈdaɪəpə(r)/ n ⟨Amer⟩ Windel f

diaphragm /ˈdaɪəfræm/ n ⟨Anat⟩ Zwerchfell nt; ⟨Phot⟩ Blende f

diarrhoea /daɪəˈriːə/ n Durchfall m

diary /ˈdaɪərɪ/ n Tagebuch nt; ⟨for appointments⟩ [Termin]kalender m

dice /daɪs/ n inv Würfel m □ vt ⟨Culin⟩ in Würfel schneiden

dicey /ˈdaɪsɪ/ a ⟨fam⟩ riskant

dictat|e /dɪkˈteɪt/ vt/i diktieren. ~ion /-eɪʃn/ n Diktat nt

dictator /dɪkˈteɪtə(r)/ n Diktator m. ~ial /-təˈtɔːrɪəl/ a diktatorisch. ~ship n Diktatur f

diction /ˈdɪkʃn/ n Aussprache f

dictionary /ˈdɪkʃənrɪ/ n Wörterbuch nt

did /dɪd/ see do

didactic /dɪˈdæktɪk/ a didaktisch

diddle /ˈdɪdl/ vt ⟨fam⟩ übers Ohr hauen

didn't /ˈdɪdnt/ = did not

die¹ /daɪ/ n ⟨Techn⟩ Prägestempel m; ⟨metal mould⟩ Gussform f

die² vi ⟨pres p dying⟩ sterben (of an + dat); ⟨plant, animal:⟩ eingehen; ⟨flower:⟩ verwelken; **be dying to do sth** ⟨fam⟩ darauf brennen, etw zu tun; **be dying for sth** ⟨fam⟩ sich nach etw sehnen. ~ down vi nachlassen; ⟨fire:⟩ herunterbrennen. ~ out vi aussterben

diesel /ˈdiːzl/ n Diesel m. ~ engine n Dieselmotor m

diet /ˈdaɪət/ n Kost f; ⟨restricted⟩ Diät f; ⟨for slimming⟩ Schlankheitskur f; be on a ~ Diät leben; eine Schlankheitskur machen □ vi Diät leben; eine Schlankheitskur machen

dietician /daɪəˈtɪʃn/ n Diätassistent(in) m(f)

differ /ˈdɪfə(r)/ vi sich unterscheiden; ⟨disagree⟩ verschiedener Meinung sein

differ|ence /ˈdɪfrəns/ n Unterschied m; ⟨disagreement⟩ Meinungsverschiedenheit f. ~t a andere(r,s); ⟨various⟩ verschiedene; be ~t anders sein (from als)

differential /dɪfəˈrenʃl/ a Differenzial- □ n Unterschied m; ⟨Techn⟩ Differenzial nt

differentiate /dɪfəˈrenʃɪeɪt/ vt/i unterscheiden (between zwischen + dat)

differently /ˈdɪfrəntlɪ/ adv anders

difficult /ˈdɪfɪkəlt/ a schwierig, schwer. ~y n Schwierigkeit f

diffiden|ce /'dɪfɪdəns/ n Zaghaftigkeit f.
~t a zaghaft

diffuse¹ /dɪ'fju:s/ a ausgebreitet; (wordy)
langatmig

diffuse² /dɪ'fju:z/ vt (Phys) streuen

dig /dɪg/ n (poke) Stoß m; (remark) spitze
Bemerkung f; (Archaeol) Ausgrabung f;
~s pl (fam) möbliertes Zimmer nt □ vt/i
(pt/pp dug, pres p digging) graben;
umgraben (garden); ~ s.o. in the ribs jdm
einen Rippenstoß geben. ~ out vt ausgraben. ~ up vt ausgraben; umgraben
(garden); aufreißen (street)

digest¹ /'daɪdʒest/ n Kurzfassung f

digest² /dɪ'dʒest/ vt verdauen. ~ible a
verdaulich. ~ion /-estʃn/ n Verdauung f

digger /'dɪgə(r)/ n (Techn) Bagger m

digit /'dɪdʒɪt/ n Ziffer f; (finger) Finger m;
(toe) Zehe f

digital /'dɪdʒɪtl/ a Digital-; ~ **clock** Di-
gitaluhr f

dignified /'dɪgnɪfaɪd/ a würdevoll

dignitary /'dɪgnɪtəri/ n Würdenträger m

dignity /'dɪgnɪti/ n Würde f

digress /daɪ'gres/ vi abschweifen. ~ion
/-eʃn/ n Abschweifung f

dike /daɪk/ n Deich m; (ditch) Graben m

dilapidated /dɪ'læpɪdeɪtɪd/ a baufällig

dilate /daɪ'leɪt/ vt erweitern □ vi sich
erweitern

dilatory /'dɪlətəri/ a langsam

dilemma /dɪ'lemə/ n Dilemma nt

dilettante /dɪlɪ'tænti/ n Dilettant(in) m(f)

diligen|ce /'dɪlɪdʒəns/ n Fleiß m. ~t a, -ly
adv fleißig

dill /dɪl/ n Dill m

dilly-dally /'dɪlɪdælɪ/ vi (pt/pp -ied)
(fam) trödeln

dilute /daɪ'lu:t/ vt verdünnen

dim /dɪm/ a (dimmer, dimmest), -ly adv
(weak) schwach; (dark) trüb[e]; (indistinct) undeutlich; (fam: stupid) dumm,
(fam) doof □ v (pt/pp dimmed) □ vt
dämpfen □ vi schwächer werden

dime /daɪm/ n (Amer) Zehncentstück nt

dimension /daɪ'menʃn/ n Dimension f;
~s pl Maße pl

diminish /dɪ'mɪnɪʃ/ vt verringern □ vi
sich verringern

diminutive /dɪ'mɪnjʊtɪv/ a winzig □ n
Verkleinerungsform f

dimple /'dɪmpl/ n Grübchen nt

din /dɪn/ n Krach m, Getöse nt

dine /daɪn/ vi speisen. ~r n Speisende(r)
m/f; (Amer: restaurant) Esslokal nt

dinghy /'dɪŋgɪ/ n Dinghi nt; (inflatable)
Schlauchboot nt

dingy /'dɪndʒɪ/ a (-ier, -iest) trübe

dining /'daɪnɪŋ/: ~**car** n Speisewagen m.
~**room** n Esszimmer nt. ~**table** n
Esstisch m

dinner /'dɪnə(r)/ n Abendessen nt; (at midday) Mittagessen nt; (formal) Essen nt. ~
jacket n Smoking m

dinosaur /'daɪnəsɔ:(r)/ n Dinosaurier m

dint /dɪnt/ n **by** ~ **of** durch (+ acc)

diocese /'daɪəsɪs/ n Diözese f

dip /dɪp/ n (in ground) Senke f; (Culin) Dip
m; **go for a** ~ kurz schwimmen gehen □ v
(pt/pp dipped) vt [ein]tauchen; ~ **one's
headlights** (Auto) [die Scheinwerfer] ab-
blenden □ vi sich senken

diphtheria /dɪf'θɪərɪə/ n Diphtherie f

diphthong /'dɪfθɒŋ/ n Diphthong m

diploma /dɪ'pləʊmə/ n Diplom nt

diplomacy /dɪ'pləʊməsɪ/ n Diplomatie f

diplomat /'dɪpləmæt/ n Diplomat m. ~**ic**
/-'mætɪk/ a, -**ally** adv diplomatisch

'dip-stick n (Auto) Ölmessstab m

dire /'daɪə(r)/ a (-r, -st) bitter; (situation,
consequences) furchtbar

direct /dɪ'rekt/ a & adv direkt □ vt (aim)
richten (at auf / (fig) an + acc); (control)
leiten; (order) anweisen; ~ s.o. (show the
way) jdm den Weg sagen; ~ **a film/play**
bei einem Film/Theaterstück Regie
führen. ~ '**current** n Gleichstrom m

direction /dɪ'rekʃn/ n Richtung f; (control) Leitung f; (of play, film) Regie f;
~s pl Anweisungen pl; ~s **for use** Gebrauchsanweisung f

directly /dɪ'rektlɪ/ adv direkt; (at once) sofort □ conj (fam) sobald

director /dɪ'rektə(r)/ n (Comm) Direktor
m; (of play, film) Regisseur m

directory /dɪ'rektərɪ/ n Verzeichnis nt;
(Teleph) Telefonbuch nt

dirt /dɜ:t/ n Schmutz m; (soil) Erde f; ~
cheap (fam) spottbillig

dirty /'dɜ:tɪ/ a (-ier, -iest) schmutzig □ vt
schmutzig machen

dis|a'bility /dɪs-/ n Behinderung f.
~**abled** /dɪ'seɪbld/ a [körper]behindert

disad'van|tage n Nachteil m; **at a** ~**tage**
im Nachteil. ~**taged** a benachteiligt.
~**tageous** a nachteilig

disaf'fected a unzufrieden; (disloyal) illoyal

disa'gree vi nicht übereinstimmen (with
mit); **I** ~ ich bin anderer Meinung; **we** ~
wir sind verschiedener Meinung; **oysters**
~ **with me** Austern bekommen mir nicht

disa'greeable a unangenehm

disa'greement n Meinungsverschie-
denheit f

disap'pear vi verschwinden. ~**ance** n
Verschwinden nt

disap'point *vt* enttäuschen. **~ment** *n* Enttäuschung *f*

disap'proval *n* Missbilligung *f*

disap'prove *vi* dagegen sein; **~ of** missbilligen

dis'arm *vt* entwaffnen □ *vi* (*Mil*) abrüsten. **~ament** *n* Abrüstung *f*. **~ing** *a* entwaffnend

disar'ray *n* Unordnung *f*

disast|er /dı'zɑːstə(r)/ *n* Katastrophe *f*; (*accident*) Unglück *nt*. **~rous** /-rəs/ *a* katastrophal

dis'band *vt* auflösen □ *vi* sich auflösen

disbe'lief *n* Ungläubigkeit *f*; **in ~** ungläubig

disc /dısk/ *n* Scheibe *f*; (*record*) [Schall]platte *f*; (*CD*) CD *f*

discard /dı'skɑːd/ *vt* ablegen; (*throw away*) wegwerfen

discern /dı'sɜːn/ *vt* wahrnehmen. **~ible** *a* wahrnehmbar. **~ing** *a* anspruchsvoll

dis'charge[1] *n* Ausstoßen *nt*; (*Naut, Electr*) Entladung *f*; (*dismissal*) Entlassung *f*; (*Jur*) Freispruch *m*; (*Med*) Ausfluss *m*

dis'charge[2] *vt* ausstoßen; (*Naut, Electr*) entladen; (*dismiss*) entlassen; (*Jur*) freisprechen (*accused*); **~ a duty** sich einer Pflicht entledigen

disciple /dı'saıpl/ *n* Jünger *m*; (*fig*) Schüler *m*

disciplinary /'dısıplınərı/ *a* disziplinarisch

discipline /'dısıplın/ *n* Disziplin *f* □ *vt* Disziplin beibringen (+ *dat*); (*punish*) bestrafen

'disc jockey *n* Diskjockey *m*

dis'claim *vt* abstreiten. **~er** *n* Verzichterklärung *f*

dis'clos|e *vt* enthüllen. **~ure** *n* Enthüllung *f*

disco /'dıskəʊ/ *n* (*fam*) Disko *f*

dis'colour *vt* verfärben □ *vi* sich verfärben

dis'comfort *n* Beschwerden *pl*; (*fig*) Unbehagen *nt*

disconcert /dıskən'sɜːt/ *vt* aus der Fassung bringen

discon'nect *vt* trennen; (*Electr*) ausschalten; (*cut supply*) abstellen

disconsolate /dıs'kɒnsələt/ *a* untröstlich

discon'tent *n* Unzufriedenheit *f*. **~ed** *a* unzufrieden

discon'tinue *vt* einstellen; (*Comm*) nicht mehr herstellen

'discord *n* Zwietracht *f*; (*Mus & fig*) Missklang *m*. **~ant** /dı'skɔːdənt/ *a* **~ant note** Missklang *m*

discothèque /'dıskətek/ *n* Diskothek *f*

'discount[1] *n* Rabatt *m*

dis'count[2] *vt* außer Acht lassen

dis'courage *vt* entmutigen; (*dissuade*) abraten (+ *dat*)

'discourse *n* Rede *f*

dis'courteous *a*, **-ly** *adv* unhöflich

discover /dı'skʌvə(r)/ *vt* entdecken. **~y** *n* Entdeckung *f*

dis'credit *n* Misskredit *m* □ *vt* in Misskredit bringen

discreet /dı'skriːt/ *a*, **-ly** *adv* diskret

discrepancy /dı'skrepənsı/ *n* Diskrepanz *f*

discretion /dı'skreʃn/ *n* Diskretion *f*; (*judgement*) Ermessen *nt*

discriminat|e /dı'skrımıneıt/ *vi* unterscheiden (**between** zwischen + *dat*); **~e against** diskriminieren. **~ing** *a* anspruchsvoll. **~ion** /-'neıʃn/ *n* Diskriminierung *f*; (*quality*) Urteilskraft *f*

discus /'dıskəs/ *n* Diskus *m*

discuss /dı'skʌs/ *vt* besprechen; (*examine critically*) diskutieren. **~ion** /-ʌʃn/ *n* Besprechung *f*; Diskussion *f*

disdain /dıs'deın/ *n* Verachtung *f* □ *vt* verachten. **~ful** *a* verächtlich

disease /dı'ziːz/ *n* Krankheit *f*. **~d** *a* krank

disem'bark *vi* an Land gehen

disen'chant *vt* ernüchtern. **~ment** *n* Ernüchterung *f*

disen'gage *vt* losmachen; **~ the clutch** (*Auto*) auskuppeln

disen'tangle *vt* entwirren

dis'favour *n* Ungnade *f*; (*disapproval*) Missfallen *nt*

dis'figure *vt* entstellen

dis'gorge *vt* ausspeien

dis'grace *n* Schande *f*; **in ~** in Ungnade □ *vt* Schande machen (+ *dat*). **~ful** *a* schändlich

disgruntled /dıs'grʌntld/ *a* verstimmt

disguise /dıs'gaız/ *n* Verkleidung *f*; **in ~** verkleidet □ *vt* verkleiden; verstellen (*voice*); (*conceal*) verhehlen

disgust /dıs'gʌst/ *n* Ekel *m*; **in ~** empört □ *vt* anekeln; (*appal*) empören. **~ing** *a* eklig; (*appalling*) abscheulich

dish /dıʃ/ *n* Schüssel *f*; (*shallow*) Schale *f*; (*small*) Schälchen *nt*; (*food*) Gericht *nt*. **~ out** *vt* austeilen. **~ up** *vt* auftragen

'dishcloth *n* Spültuch *nt*

dis'hearten *vt* entmutigen. **~ing** *a* entmutigend

dishevelled /dı'ʃevld/ *a* zerzaust

dis'honest *a*, **-ly** *adv* unehrlich. **~y** *n* Unehrlichkeit *f*

dis'honour n Schande f □ vt entehren; nicht honorieren ⟨cheque⟩. ～able a, -bly adv unehrenhaft

'dishwasher n Geschirrspülmaschine f

disil'lusion vt ernüchtern. ～ment n Ernüchterung f

disin'fect vt desinfizieren. ～ant n Desinfektionsmittel nt

disin'herit vt enterben

dis'integrate vi zerfallen

dis'interested a unvoreingenommen; ⟨uninterested⟩ uninteressiert

dis'jointed a unzusammenhängend

disk /dɪsk/ n = disc

dis'like n Abneigung f □ vt nicht mögen

dislocate /'dɪsləkeɪt/ vt ausrenken; ～ one's shoulder sich ⟨dat⟩ den Arm auskugeln

dis'lodge vt entfernen

dis'loyal a, -ly adv illoyal. ～ty n Illoyalität f

dismal /'dɪzməl/ a trüb[e]; ⟨person⟩ trübselig; ⟨fam: poor⟩ kläglich

dismantle /dɪs'mæntl/ vt auseinander nehmen; ⟨take down⟩ abbauen

dis'may n Bestürzung f. ～ed a bestürzt

dis'miss vt entlassen; ⟨reject⟩ zurückweisen. ～al n Entlassung f; Zurückweisung f

dis'mount vi absteigen

diso'bedien|ce n Ungehorsam m. ～t a ungehorsam

diso'bey vt/i nicht gehorchen (+ dat); nicht befolgen ⟨rule⟩

dis'order n Unordnung f; ⟨Med⟩ Störung f. ～ly a unordentlich; ～ly conduct ungebührliches Benehmen nt

dis'organized a unorganisiert

dis'orientate vt verwirren; be ～d die Orientierung verloren haben

dis'own vt verleugnen

disparaging /dɪ'spærɪdʒɪŋ/ a, -ly adv abschätzig

disparity /dɪ'spærətɪ/ n Ungleichheit f

dispassionate /dɪs'pæʃənət/ a, -ly adv gelassen; ⟨impartial⟩ unparteiisch

dispatch /dɪ'spætʃ/ n ⟨Comm⟩ Versand m; ⟨Mil⟩ Nachricht f; ⟨report⟩ Bericht m; with ～ prompt □ vt [ab]senden; ⟨deal with⟩ erledigen; ⟨kill⟩ töten. ～-rider n Meldefahrer m

dispel /dɪ'spel/ vt ⟨pt/pp dispelled⟩ vertreiben

dispensable /dɪ'spensəbl/ a entbehrlich

dispensary /dɪ'spensərɪ/ n Apotheke f

dispense /dɪ'spens/ vt austeilen; ～ with verzichten auf (+ acc). ～r n Apotheker(in) m(f); ⟨device⟩ Automat m

dispers|al /dɪ'spɜːsl/ n Zerstreuung f. ～e /dɪ'spɜːs/ vt zerstreuen □ vi sich zerstreuen

dispirited /dɪ'spɪrɪtɪd/ a entmutigt

dis'place vt verschieben; ～d person Vertriebene(r) m/f

display /dɪ'spleɪ/ n Ausstellung f; ⟨Comm⟩ Auslage f; ⟨performance⟩ Vorführung f □ vt zeigen; ausstellen ⟨goods⟩

dis'please vt missfallen (+ dat)

dis'pleasure n Missfallen nt

disposable /dɪ'spəʊzəbl/ a Wegwerf-; ⟨income⟩ verfügbar

disposal /dɪ'spəʊzl/ n Beseitigung f; be at s.o.'s ～ jdm zur Verfügung stehen

dispose /dɪ'spəʊz/ vi ～ of beseitigen; ⟨deal with⟩ erledigen; be well ～d wohlgesinnt sein (to dat)

disposition /dɪspə'zɪʃn/ n Veranlagung f; ⟨nature⟩ Wesensart f

disproportionate /dɪsprə'pɔːʃənət/ a, -ly adv unverhältnismäßig

dis'prove vt widerlegen

dispute /dɪ'spjuːt/ n Disput m; ⟨quarrel⟩ Streit m □ vt bestreiten

disqualifi'cation n Disqualifikation f

dis'qualify vt disqualifizieren; ～ s.o. from driving jdm den Führerschein entziehen

disquieting /dɪs'kwaɪətɪŋ/ a beunruhigend

disre'gard n Nichtbeachtung f □ vt nicht beachten, ignorieren

disre'pair n fall into ～ verfallen

dis'reputable a verrufen

disre'pute n Verruf m

disre'spect n Respektlosigkeit f. ～ful a, -ly adv respektlos

disrupt /dɪs'rʌpt/ vt stören. ～ion /-'ʌpʃn/ n Störung f. ～ive /-ɪv/ a störend

dissatis'faction n Unzufriedenheit f

dis'satisfied a unzufrieden

dissect /dɪ'sekt/ vt zergliedern; ⟨Med⟩ sezieren. ～ion /-ekʃn/ n Zergliederung f; ⟨Med⟩ Sektion f

disseminat|e /dɪ'semɪneɪt/ vt verbreiten. ～ion /-'neɪʃn/ n Verbreitung f

dissent /dɪ'sent/ n Nichtübereinstimmung f □ vi nicht übereinstimmen

dissertation /dɪsə'teɪʃn/ n Dissertation f

dis'service n schlechter Dienst m

dissident /'dɪsɪdənt/ n Dissident m

dis'similar a unähnlich (to dat)

dissociate /dɪ'səʊʃɪeɪt/ vt trennen; ～ oneself sich distanzieren (from von)

dissolute /'dɪsəluːt/ a zügellos; ⟨life⟩ ausschweifend

dissolution /dɪsə'luːʃn/ n Auflösung f

dissolve /dɪ'zɒlv/ vt auflösen □ vi sich auflösen

dissuade /dɪ'sweɪd/ vt abbringen (**from** von)

distance /'dɪstəns/ n Entfernung f; **long/ short ~** lange/kurze Strecke f; **in the/ from a ~** in/aus der Ferne

distant /'dɪstənt/ a fern; ⟨aloof⟩ kühl; ⟨relative⟩ entfernt

dis'taste n Abneigung f. **~ful** a unangenehm

distend /dɪ'stend/ vi sich [auf]blähen

distil /dɪ'stɪl/ vt (pt/pp distilled) brennen; ⟨Chem⟩ destillieren. **~lation** /-'leɪʃn/ n Destillation f. **~lery** /-ərɪ/ n Brennerei f

distinct /dɪ'stɪŋkt/ a deutlich; ⟨different⟩ verschieden. **~ion** /-ɪŋkʃn/ n Unterschied m; ⟨Sch⟩ Auszeichnung f. **~ive** /-tɪv/ a kennzeichnend; ⟨unmistakable⟩ unverwechselbar. **~ly** adv deutlich

distinguish /dɪ'stɪŋgwɪʃ/ vt/i unterscheiden; ⟨make out⟩ erkennen; **~ oneself** sich auszeichnen. **~ed** a angesehen; ⟨appearance⟩ distinguiert

distort /dɪ'stɔːt/ vt verzerren; ⟨fig⟩ verdrehen. **~ion** /-ɔːʃn/ n Verzerrung f; ⟨fig⟩ Verdrehung f

distract /dɪ'strækt/ vt ablenken. **~ed** /-ɪd/ a [völlig] aufgelöst. **~ion** /-ækʃn/ n Ablenkung f; ⟨despair⟩ Verzweiflung f

distraught /dɪ'strɔːt/ a [völlig] aufgelöst

distress /dɪ'stres/ n Kummer m; ⟨pain⟩ Schmerz m; ⟨poverty, danger⟩ Not f □ vt Kummer/Schmerz bereiten (+ dat); ⟨sadden⟩ bekümmern; ⟨shock⟩ erschüttern. **~ing** a schmerzlich; ⟨shocking⟩ erschütternd. **~ signal** n Notsignal nt

distribut|e /dɪ'strɪbjuːt/ vt verteilen; ⟨Comm⟩ vertreiben. **~ion** /-'bjuːʃn/ n Verteilung f; Vertrieb m. **~or** n Verteiler m

district /'dɪstrɪkt/ n Gegend f; ⟨Admin⟩ Bezirk m. **~ nurse** n Gemeindeschwester f

dis'trust n Misstrauen nt □ vt misstrauen (+ dat). **~ful** a misstrauisch

disturb /dɪ'stɜːb/ vt stören; ⟨perturb⟩ beunruhigen; ⟨touch⟩ anrühren. **~ance** n Unruhe f; ⟨interruption⟩ Störung f. **~ed** a beunruhigt; **[mentally] ~ed** geistig gestört. **~ing** a beunruhigend

dis'used a stillgelegt; ⟨empty⟩ leer

ditch /dɪtʃ/ n Graben m □ vt ⟨fam: abandon⟩ fallen lassen ⟨plan⟩; wegschmeißen ⟨thing⟩

dither /'dɪðə(r)/ vi zaudern

ditto /'dɪtəʊ/ n dito; ⟨fam⟩ ebenfalls

divan /dɪ'væn/ n Polsterbett nt

dive /daɪv/ n [Kopf]sprung m; ⟨Aviat⟩ Sturzflug m; ⟨fam: place⟩ Spelunke f □ vi einen Kopfsprung machen; ⟨when in water⟩ tauchen; ⟨Aviat⟩ einen Sturzflug machen; ⟨fam: rush⟩ stürzen

diver /'daɪvə(r)/ n Taucher m; ⟨Sport⟩ [Kunst]springer m

diver|ge /daɪ'vɜːdʒ/ vi auseinander gehen. **~gent** /-ənt/ a abweichend

diverse /daɪ'vɜːs/ a verschieden

diversify /daɪ'vɜːsɪfaɪ/ vt/i (pt/pp -ied) variieren; ⟨Comm⟩ diversifizieren

diversion /daɪ'vɜːʃn/ n Umleitung f; ⟨distraction⟩ Ablenkung f

diversity /daɪ'vɜːsətɪ/ n Vielfalt f

divert /daɪ'vɜːt/ vt umleiten; ablenken ⟨attention⟩; ⟨entertain⟩ unterhalten

divest /daɪ'vest/ vt sich entledigen (**of** + gen); ⟨fig⟩ entkleiden

divide /dɪ'vaɪd/ vt teilen; ⟨separate⟩ trennen; ⟨Math⟩ dividieren (**by** durch) □ vi sich teilen

dividend /'dɪvɪdend/ n Dividende f

divine /dɪ'vaɪn/ a göttlich

diving /'daɪvɪŋ/ n ⟨Sport⟩ Kunstspringen nt. **~-board** n Sprungbrett nt. **~-suit** n Taucheranzug m

divinity /dɪ'vɪnətɪ/ n Göttlichkeit f; ⟨subject⟩ Theologie f

divisible /dɪ'vɪzɪbl/ a teilbar (**by** durch)

division /dɪ'vɪʒn/ n Teilung f; ⟨separation⟩ Trennung f; ⟨Math, Mil⟩ Division f; ⟨Parl⟩ Hammelsprung m; ⟨line⟩ Trennlinie f; ⟨group⟩ Abteilung f

divorce /dɪ'vɔːs/ n Scheidung f □ vt sich scheiden lassen von. **~d** a geschieden; **get ~d** sich scheiden lassen

divorcee /dɪvɔː'siː/ n Geschiedene(r) m/f

divulge /daɪ'vʌldʒ/ vt preisgeben

DIY abbr of **do-it-yourself**

dizziness /'dɪzɪnɪs/ n Schwindel m

dizzy /'dɪzɪ/ a (-ier, -iest) schwindlig; **I feel ~** mir ist schwindlig

do /duː/ n (pl dos or do's) ⟨fam⟩ Veranstaltung f □ v (3 sg pres tense does; pt did; pp done) □ vt/i tun, machen; ⟨be suitable⟩ passen; ⟨be enough⟩ reichen, genügen; ⟨cook⟩ kochen; ⟨clean⟩ putzen; ⟨Sch: study⟩ durchnehmen; ⟨fam: cheat⟩ beschwindeln ⟨out of um⟩; **do without** auskommen ohne; **do away with** abschaffen; **be done** ⟨Culin⟩ gar sein; **well done** gut gemacht! ⟨Culin⟩ gut durchgebraten; **done in** ⟨fam⟩ kaputt, fertig; **done for** ⟨fam⟩ verloren, erledigt; **do the flowers** die Blumen arrangieren; **do the potatoes** die Kartoffeln schälen; **do the washing up** abwaschen, spülen; **do one's hair** sich frisieren; **do well/badly** gut/schlecht abschneiden;

how is he doing? wie geht es ihm? **this won't do** das geht nicht; **are you doing anything today?** haben Sie heute etwas vor? **I could do with a spanner** ich könnte einen Schraubenschlüssel gebrauchen □ *vaux* **do you speak German?** sprechen Sie Deutsch? **yes, I do** ja; *(emphatic)* doch; **no, I don't** nein; **I don't smoke** ich rauche nicht; **don't you/ doesn't he?** nicht [wahr]? **so do I** ich auch; **do come in** kommen Sie doch herein; **how do you do?** guten Tag. **do in** *vt (fam)* um die Ecke bringen. **do up** *vt (fasten)* zumachen; *(renovate)* renovieren; *(wrap)* einpacken

docile /'dəʊsaɪl/ *a* fügsam

dock[1] /dɒk/ *n (Jur)* Anklagebank *f*

dock[2] *n* Dock *nt* □ *vi* anlegen, docken □ *vt* docken. **~er** *n* Hafenarbeiter *m*. **~yard** *n* Werft *f*

doctor /'dɒktə(r)/ *n* Arzt *m*; Ärztin *f*; *(Univ)* Doktor *m* □ *vt* kastrieren; *(spay)* sterilisieren. **~ate** /-ət/ *n* Doktorwürde *f*

doctrine /'dɒktrɪn/ *n* Lehre *f*, Doktrin *f*

document /'dɒkjʊmənt/ *n* Dokument *nt*. **~ary** /-'mentərɪ/ *a* Dokumentar- □ *n* Dokumentarbericht *m*; *(film)* Dokumentarfilm *m*

doddery /'dɒdərɪ/ *a (fam)* tatterig

dodge /dɒdʒ/ *n (fam)* Trick *m*, Kniff *m* □ *vt/i* ausweichen (+ *dat)*; **~ out of the way** zur Seite springen

dodgems /'dɒdʒəmz/ *npl* Autoskooter *pl*

dodgy /'dɒdʒɪ/ *a* (-ier, -iest) *(fam) (awkward)* knifflig; *(dubious)* zweifelhaft

doe /dəʊ/ *n* Ricke *f*; *(rabbit)* [Kaninchen]weibchen *nt*

does /dʌz/ *see* **do**

doesn't /'dʌznt/ = **does not**

dog /dɒg/ *n* Hund *m* □ *vt (pt/pp* dogged) verfolgen

dog: ~-biscuit *n* Hundekuchen *m*. **~-collar** *n* Hundehalsband *nt*; *(Relig, fam)* Kragen *m* eines Geistlichen. **~-eared** *a* **be ~-eared** Eselsohren haben

dogged /'dɒgɪd/ *a*, **-ly** *adv* beharrlich

dogma /'dɒgmə/ *n* Dogma *nt*. **~tic** /-'mætɪk/ *a* dogmatisch

'dogsbody *n (fam)* Mädchen *nt* für alles

doily /'dɔɪlɪ/ *n* Deckchen *nt*

do-it-yourself /'du:ɪtjə'self/ *n* Heimwerken *nt*. **~ shop** *n* Heimwerkerladen *m*

doldrums /'dɒldrəmz/ *npl* **be in the ~** niedergeschlagen sein; *(business:)* daniederliegen

dole /dəʊl/ *n (fam)* Stempelgeld *nt*; **be on the ~** arbeitslos sein □ *vt* **~ out** austeilen

doleful /'dəʊlfl/ *a*, **-ly** *adv* trauervoll

doll /dɒl/ *n* Puppe *f* □ *vt (fam)* **~ oneself up** sich herausputzen

dollar /'dɒlə(r)/ *n* Dollar *m*

dollop /'dɒləp/ *n (fam)* Klecks *m*

dolphin /'dɒlfɪn/ *n* Delphin *m*

domain /də'meɪn/ *n* Gebiet *nt*

dome /dəʊm/ *n* Kuppel *f*

domestic /də'mestɪk/ *a* häuslich; *(Pol)* Innen-; *(Comm)* Binnen-. **~ animal** *n* Haustier *nt*

domesticated /də'mestɪkeɪtɪd/ *a* häuslich; *(animal)* zahm

domestic: ~ flight *n* Inlandflug *m*. **~ 'servant** Hausangestellte(r) *m/f*

dominant /'dɒmɪnənt/ *a* vorherrschend

dominate /'dɒmɪneɪt/ *vt* beherrschen □ *vi* dominieren; **~e over** beherrschen. **~ion** /-'neɪʃn/ *n* Vorherrschaft *f*

domineer /dɒmɪ'nɪə(r)/ *vi* **~ over** tyrannisieren. **~ing** *a* herrschsüchtig

dominion /də'mɪnjən/ *n* Herrschaft *f*

domino /'dɒmɪnəʊ/ *n (pl* -es) Dominostein *m*; **~es** *sg (game)* Domino *nt*

don[1] /dɒn/ *vt (pt/pp* donned) *(liter)* anziehen

don[2] *n* [Universitäts]dozent *m*

donate /dəʊ'neɪt/ *vt* spenden. **~ion** /-eɪʃn/ *n* Spende *f*

done /dʌn/ *see* **do**

donkey /'dɒŋkɪ/ *n* Esel *m*; **~'s years** *(fam)* eine Ewigkeit. **~-work** *n* Routinearbeit *f*

donor /'dəʊnə(r)/ *n* Spender(in) *m(f)*

don't /dəʊnt/ = **do not**

doodle /'du:dl/ *vi* kritzeln

doom /du:m/ *n* Schicksal *nt*; *(ruin)* Verhängnis *nt* □ *vt* **be ~ed to failure** zum Scheitern verurteilt sein

door /dɔ:(r)/ *n* Tür *f*; **out of ~s** im Freien

door: ~man *n* Portier *m*. **~mat** *n* [Fuß]abtreter *m*. **~step** *n* Türschwelle *f*; **on the ~step** vor der Tür. **~way** *n* Türöffnung *f*

dope /dəʊp/ *n (fam)* Drogen *pl*; *(fam: information)* Informationen *pl*; *(fam: idiot)* Trottel *m* □ *vt* betäuben; *(Sport)* dopen

dopey /'dəʊpɪ/ *a (fam)* benommen; *(stupid)* blöd[e]

dormant /'dɔ:mənt/ *a* ruhend

dormer /'dɔ:mə(r)/ *n* **~ [window]** Mansardenfenster *nt*

dormitory /'dɔ:mɪtərɪ/ *n* Schlafsaal *m*

dormouse /'dɔ:-/ *n* Haselmaus *f*

dosage /'dəʊsɪdʒ/ *n* Dosierung *f*

dose /dəʊs/ *n* Dosis *f*

doss /dɒs/ *vi (sl)* pennen. **~er** *n* Penner *m*. **~-house** *n* Penne *f*

dot /dɒt/ *n* Punkt *m*; **on the ~** pünktlich

dote /dəʊt/ vi ~ **on** vernarrt sein in (+ acc)

dotted /'dɒtɪd/ a ~ **line** punktierte Linie f; **be** ~ **with** bestreut sein mit

dotty /'dɒtɪ/ a (-ier, -iest) (fam) verdreht

double /'dʌbl/ a & adv doppelt; ⟨bed, chin⟩ Doppel-; ⟨flower⟩ gefüllt □ n das Doppelte; ⟨person⟩ Doppelgänger m; ~**s** pl (Tennis) Doppel nt; **at the** ~ im Laufschritt □ vt verdoppeln; ⟨fold⟩ falten □ vi sich verdoppeln. ~ **back** vi zurückgehen. ~ **up** vi sich krümmen (**with** vor + dat)

double: ~'**bass** n Kontrabass m. ~'**breasted** a zweireihig. ~'**cross** vt ein Doppelspiel treiben mit. ~'**decker** n Doppeldecker m. ~ '**Dutch** n (fam) Kauderwelsch nt. ~ '**glazing** n Doppelverglasung f. ~ '**room** n Doppelzimmer nt

doubly /'dʌblɪ/ adv doppelt

doubt /daʊt/ n Zweifel m □ vt bezweifeln. ~**ful** a, -**ly** adv zweifelhaft; (disbelieving) skeptisch. ~**less** adv zweifellos

dough /dəʊ/ n [fester] Teig m; (fam: money) Pinke f. ~**nut** n Berliner [Pfannkuchen] m, Krapfen m

douse /daʊs/ vt übergießen; ausgießen ⟨flames⟩

dove /dʌv/ n Taube f. ~**tail** n (Techn) Schwalbenschwanz m

dowdy /'daʊdɪ/ a (-ier, -iest) unschick

down¹ /daʊn/ n ⟨feathers⟩ Daunen pl

down² adv unten; (with movement) nach unten; **go** ~ hinuntergehen; **come** ~ herunterkommen; ~ **there** da unten; **£50** ~ £50 Anzahlung; ~! (to dog) Platz! ~ **with ...!** nieder mit ...! □ prep ~ **the road/stairs** die Straße/Treppe hinunter; ~ **the river** den Fluss abwärts; **be** ~ **the pub** (fam) in der Kneipe sein □ vt (fam) ⟨drink⟩ runterkippen; ~ **tools** die Arbeit niederlegen

down: ~-**and**-'**out** n Penner m. ~**cast** a niedergeschlagen. ~**fall** n Sturz m; (ruin) Ruin m. ~'**grade** vt niedriger einstufen. ~-'**hearted** a entmutigt. ~'**hill** adv bergab. ~ **payment** n Anzahlung f. ~**pour** n Platzregen m. ~**right** a & adv ausgesprochen. ~'**stairs** adv unten; ⟨go⟩ nach unten □ a /'--/ im Erdgeschoss. ~'**stream** adv stromabwärts. ~-to-'**earth** a sachlich. ~**town** adv (Amer) im Stadtzentrum. ~**trodden** a unterdrückt. ~**ward** a nach unten; ⟨slope⟩ abfallend □ adv ~[**s**] abwärts, nach unten

downy /'daʊnɪ/ a (-ier, -iest) flaumig

dowry /'daʊrɪ/ n Mitgift f

doze /dəʊz/ n Nickerchen nt □ vi dösen. ~ **off** vi einnicken

dozen /'dʌzn/ n Dutzend nt

Dr abbr of **doctor**

draft¹ /drɑːft/ n Entwurf m; (Comm) Tratte f; (Amer Mil) Einberufung f □ vt entwerfen; (Amer Mil) einberufen

draft² n (Amer) = **draught**

drag /dræg/ n (fam) Klotz m am Bein; **in** ~ (fam) ⟨man⟩ als Frau gekleidet □ vt (pt/pp **dragged**) schleppen; absuchen ⟨river⟩. ~ **on** vi sich in die Länge ziehen

dragon /'drægən/ n Drache m. ~-**fly** n Libelle f

'**drag show** n Transvestitenshow f

drain /dreɪn/ n Abfluss m; (underground) Kanal m; **the** ~**s** die Kanalisation □ vt entwässern ⟨land⟩; ablassen ⟨liquid⟩; das Wasser ablassen aus ⟨tank⟩; abgießen ⟨vegetables⟩; austrinken ⟨glass⟩ □ vi ~ [**away**] ablaufen; **leave sth to** ~ etw abtropfen lassen

drain|age /'dreɪnɪdʒ/ n Kanalisation f; (of land) Dränage f. ~**ing board** n Abtropfbrett nt. ~-**pipe** n Abflussrohr nt

drake /dreɪk/ n Enterich m

drama /'drɑːmə/ n Drama nt; (quality) Dramatik f

dramatic /drə'mætɪk/ a, -**ally** adv dramatisch

dramat|ist /'dræmətɪst/ n Dramatiker m. ~**ize** vt für die Bühne bearbeiten; (fig) dramatisieren

drank /dræŋk/ see **drink**

drape /dreɪp/ n (Amer) Vorhang m □ vt drapieren

drastic /'dræstɪk/ a, -**ally** adv drastisch

draught /drɑːft/ n [Luft]zug m; ~**s** sg (game) Damespiel nt; **there is a** ~ es zieht

draught: ~ **beer** n Bier nt vom Fass. ~**sman** n technischer Zeichner m

draughty /'drɑːftɪ/ a zugig; **it's** ~ es zieht

draw /drɔː/ n Attraktion f; (Sport) Unentschieden nt; (in lottery) Ziehung f □ v (pt **drew**, pp **drawn**) □ vt ziehen; (attract) anziehen; zeichnen ⟨picture⟩; abheben ⟨money⟩; holen ⟨water⟩; ~ **the curtains** die Vorhänge zuziehen ⟨back⟩ aufziehen; ~ **lots** losen (**for** um) □ vi ⟨tea:⟩ ziehen; (Sport) unentschieden spielen. ~ **back** vt zurückziehen □ vi (recoil) zurückweichen. ~ **in** vt einziehen □ vi einfahren; ⟨days:⟩ kürzer werden. ~ **out** vt herausziehen; abheben ⟨money⟩ □ vi ausfahren; ⟨days:⟩ länger werden. ~ **up** vt aufsetzen ⟨document⟩; heranrücken ⟨chair⟩. ~ **oneself up** sich aufrichten □ vi [an]halten

draw: ~**back** n Nachteil m. ~**bridge** n Zugbrücke f

drawer /drɔː(r)/ n Schublade f

drawing /'drɔːɪŋ/ n Zeichnung f

drawing: ~**-board** n Reißbrett nt. ~**-pin** n Reißzwecke f. ~**-room** n Wohnzimmer nt

drawl /drɔːl/ n schleppende Aussprache f

drawn /drɔːn/ see **draw**

dread /dred/ n Furcht f (**of** vor + dat) □ vt fürchten. ~**ful** a, **-fully** adv fürchterlich

dream /driːm/ n Traum m □ attrib Traum- □ vt/i (pt/pp **dreamt** /dremt/ or **dreamed**) träumen (**about/of** von)

dreary /'drɪərɪ/ a (**-ier, -iest**) trüb[e]; (boring) langweilig

dredge /dredʒ/ vt/i baggern. ~**r** n [Nass]bagger m

dregs /dregz/ npl Bodensatz m

drench /drentʃ/ vt durchnässen

dress /dres/ n Kleid nt; (clothing) Kleidung f □ vt anziehen; (decorate) schmücken; (Culin) anmachen; (Med) verbinden; ~ **oneself, get** ~**ed** sich anziehen □ vi sich anziehen. ~ **up** vi sich schön anziehen; (in disguise) sich verkleiden (**as** als)

dress: ~ **circle** n (Theat) erster Rang m. ~**er** n (furniture) Anrichte f; (Amer: dressing-table) Frisiertisch m

dressing n (Culin) Soße f; (Med) Verband m

dressing: ~ **down** n (fam) Standpauke f. ~**-gown** n Morgenmantel m. ~**-room** n Ankleidezimmer nt; (Theat) [Künstler]-garderobe f. ~**-table** n Frisiertisch m

dress: ~**maker** n Schneiderin f. ~**making** n Damenschneiderei f. ~ **rehearsal** n Generalprobe f

dressy /'dresɪ/ a (**-ier, -iest**) schick

drew /druː/ see **draw**

dribble /'drɪbl/ vi sabbern; (Sport) dribbeln

dried /draɪd/ a getrocknet; ~ **fruit** Dörrobst nt

drier /'draɪə(r)/ n Trockner m

drift /drɪft/ n Abtrift f; (of snow) Schneewehe f; (meaning) Sinn m □ vi treiben; (off course) abtreiben; (snow:) Wehen bilden; (fig) (person:) sich treiben lassen; ~ **apart** (persons:) sich auseinander leben. ~**wood** n Treibholz nt

drill /drɪl/ n Bohrer m; (Mil) Drill m □ vt/i bohren (**for** nach); (Mil) drillen

drily /'draɪlɪ/ adv trocken

drink /drɪŋk/ n Getränk nt; (alcoholic) Drink m; (alcohol) Alkohol m; **have a** ~ etwas trinken □ vt/i (pt **drank**, pp **drunk**) trinken. ~ **up** vt/i austrinken

drink|able /'drɪŋkəbl/ a trinkbar. ~**er** n Trinker m

drinking-water n Trinkwasser nt

drip /drɪp/ n Tropfen nt; (drop) Tropfen m; (Med) Tropf m; (fam: person) Niete f □ vi (pt/pp **dripped**) tropfen. ~'**dry** a bügelfrei. ~**ping** n Schmalz nt

drive /draɪv/ n [Auto]fahrt f; (entrance) Einfahrt f; (energy) Elan m; (Psych) Trieb m; (Pol) Aktion f; (Sport) Treibschlag m; (Techn) Antrieb m □ v (pt **drove**, pp **driven**) □ vt treiben; fahren (car); (Sport: hit) schlagen; (Techn) antreiben; ~ **s.o. mad** (fam) jdn verrückt machen; **what are you driving at?** (fam) worauf willst du hinaus? □ vi fahren. ~ **away** vt vertreiben □ vi abfahren. ~ **in** vi hinein-/hereinfahren. ~ **off** vt vertreiben □ vi abfahren. ~ **on** vi weiterfahren. ~ **up** vi vorfahren

'**drive-in** a ~ **cinema** Autokino nt

drivel /'drɪvl/ n (fam) Quatsch m

driven /'drɪvn/ see **drive**

driver /'draɪvə(r)/ n Fahrer(in) m(f); (of train) Lokführer m

driving /'draɪvɪŋ/ a (rain) peitschend; (force) treibend

driving: ~ **lesson** n Fahrstunde f. ~ **licence** n Führerschein m. ~ **school** n Fahrschule f. ~ **test** Fahrprüfung f; **take one's** ~ **test** den Führerschein machen

drizzle /'drɪzl/ n Nieselregen m □ vi nieseln

drone /drəʊn/ n Drohne f; (sound) Brummen nt

droop /druːp/ vi herabhängen; (flowers:) die Köpfe hängen lassen

drop /drɒp/ n Tropfen m; (fall) Fall m; (in price, temperature) Rückgang m □ v (pt/pp **dropped**) □ vt fallen lassen; abwerfen (bomb); (omit) auslassen; (give up) aufgeben □ vi fallen; (fall lower) sinken; (wind:) nachlassen. ~ **in** vi vorbeikommen. ~ **off** vt absetzen (person) □ vi abfallen; (fall asleep) einschlafen. ~ **out** vi herausfallen; (give up) aufgeben

'**drop-out** n Aussteiger m

droppings /'drɒpɪŋz/ npl Kot m

drought /draʊt/ n Dürre f

drove /drəʊv/ see **drive**

droves /drəʊvz/ npl **in** ~ in Scharen

drown /draʊn/ vi ertrinken □ vt ertränken; übertönen (noise); **be** ~**ed** ertrinken

drowsy /'draʊzɪ/ a schläfrig

drudgery /'drʌdʒərɪ/ n Plackerei f

drug /drʌg/ n Droge f □ vt (pt/pp **drugged**) betäuben

drug: ~**addict** n Drogenabhängige(r) m/f. ~**gist** n (Amer) Apotheker m. ~**store** n (Amer) Drogerie f; (dispensing) Apotheke f

drum /drʌm/ n Trommel f; (for oil) Tonne f □ v (pt/pp **drummed**) □ vi trommeln

◻ *vt* ∼sth into s.o. (*fam*) jdm etw einbläuen. ∼mer *n* Trommler *m*; (*in pop-
group*) Schlagzeuger *m*. ∼stick *n* Trom-
melschlägel *m*; (*Culin*) Keule *f*

drunk /drʌŋk/ *see* **drink** ◻ *a* betrunken;
get ∼ sich betrinken ◻ *n* Betrunkene(r)
m

drunk|ard /'drʌŋkəd/ *n* Trinker *m*. ∼en
a betrunken; ∼en driving Trunkenheit
f am Steuer

dry /draɪ/ *a* (**drier, driest**) trocken ◻ *vt/i*
trocknen; ∼ one's eyes sich *dat* die
Tränen abwischen. ∼ up *vi* austrocknen;
(*fig*) versiegen ◻ *vt* austrocknen; abtrocknen (*dishes*)

dry: ∼'**clean** *vt* chemisch reinigen. ∼-
'**cleaner's** *n* (*shop*) chemische Reinigung
f. ∼ness *n* Trockenheit *f*

dual /'dju:əl/ *a* doppelt

dual: ∼'**carriageway** *n* ≈ Schnellstraße
f. ∼'**purpose** *a* zweifach verwendbar

dub /dʌb/ *vt* (*pt/pp* **dubbed**) synchronisieren (*film*); kopieren (*tape*); (*name*)
nennen

dubious /'dju:bɪəs/ *a* zweifelhaft; **be** ∼
about Zweifel haben über (+ *acc*)

duchess /'dʌtʃɪs/ *n* Herzogin *f*

duck /dʌk/ *n* Ente *f* ◻ *vt* (*in water*) untertauchen; ∼ one's head den Kopf ein-
ziehen ◻ *vi* sich ducken. ∼ling *n* Entchen
nt; (*Culin*) Ente *f*

duct /dʌkt/ *n* Rohr *nt*; (*Anat*) Gang *m*

dud /dʌd/ *a* (*fam*) nutzlos; (*coin*) falsch;
(*cheque*) ungedeckt; (*forged*) gefälscht ◻ *n*
(*fam*) (*banknote*) Blüte *f*; (*Mil: shell*)
Blindgänger *m*

due /dju:/ *a* angemessen; **be** ∼ fällig sein;
(*baby:*) erwartet werden; (*train:*) planmäßig ankommen; ∼ to (*owing to*) wegen
(+ *gen*); **be** ∼ **to** zurückzuführen sein auf
(+ *acc*); **in** ∼ **course** im Laufe der Zeit;
(*write*) zu gegebener Zeit ◻ *adv* ∼ **west**
genau westlich

duel /'dju:əl/ *n* Duell *nt*

dues /dju:z/ *npl* Gebühren *pl*

duet /dju:'et/ *n* Duo *nt*; (*vocal*) Duett *n*

dug /dʌg/ *see* **dig**

duke /dju:k/ *n* Herzog *m*

dull /dʌl/ *a* (**-er, -est**) (*overcast, not bright*)
trüb[e]; (*not shiny*) matt; (*sound*) dumpf;
(*boring*) langweilig; (*stupid*) schwerfällig
◻ *vt* betäuben; abstumpfen (*mind*)

duly /'dju:lɪ/ *adv* ordnungsgemäß

dumb /dʌm/ *a* (**-er, -est**) stumm; (*fam:
stupid*) dumm. ∼**founded** *a* sprachlos

dummy /'dʌmɪ/ *n* (*tailor's*) [Schneider]-
puppe *f*; (*for baby*) Schnuller *m*; (*Comm*)
Attrappe *f*

dump /dʌmp/ *n* Abfallhaufen *m*; (*for refuse*) Müllhalde *f*, Deponie *f*; (*fam: town*)
Kaff *nt*; **be down in the** ∼**s** (*fam*) deprimiert sein ◻ *vt* abladen; (*fam: put down*)
hinwerfen (**on** auf + *acc*)

dumpling /'dʌmplɪŋ/ *n* Kloß *m*, Knödel
m

dunce /dʌns/ *n* Dummkopf *m*

dune /dju:n/ *n* Düne *f*

dung /dʌŋ/ *n* Mist *m*

dungarees /dʌŋgə'ri:z/ *npl* Latzhose *f*

dungeon /'dʌndʒən/ *n* Verlies *nt*

dunk /dʌŋk/ *vt* eintunken

duo /'dju:əʊ/ *n* Paar *nt*; (*Mus*) Duo *nt*

dupe /dju:p/ *n* Betrogene(r) *m/f* ◻ *vt* betrügen

duplicate[1] /'dju:plɪkət/ *a* Zweit- ◻ *n* Doppel *nt*; (*document*) Duplikat *nt*; **in** ∼ in
doppelter Ausfertigung

duplicat|e[2] /'dju:plɪkeɪt/ *vt* kopieren;
(*do twice*) zweimal machen. ∼or *n*
Vervielfältigungsapparat *m*

durable /'djʊərəbl/ *a* haltbar

duration /djʊə'reɪʃn/ *n* Dauer *f*

duress /djʊə'res/ *n* Zwang *m*

during /'djʊərɪŋ/ *prep* während (+ *gen*)

dusk /dʌsk/ *n* [Abend]dämmerung *f*

dust /dʌst/ *n* Staub *m* ◻ *vt* abstauben;
(*sprinkle*) bestäuben (**with** mit) ◻ *vi* Staub
wischen

dust: ∼**bin** *n* Mülltonne *f*. ∼**cart** *n*
Müllwagen *m*. ∼**er** *n* Staubtuch *nt*. ∼-
jacket *n* Schutzumschlag *m*. ∼**man** *n*
Müllmann *m*. ∼**pan** *n* Kehrschaufel *f*

dusty /'dʌstɪ/ *a* (**-ier, -iest**) staubig

Dutch /dʌtʃ/ *a* holländisch; **go** ∼ (*fam*)
getrennte Kasse machen ◻ *n* (*Lang*) Holländisch *nt*; **the** ∼ *pl* die Holländer.
∼**man** *n* Holländer *m*

dutiable /'dju:tɪəbl/ *a* zollpflichtig

dutiful /'dju:tɪfl/ *a*, **-ly** *adv* pflicht-
bewusst; (*obedient*) gehorsam

duty /'dju:tɪ/ *n* Pflicht *f*; (*task*) Aufgabe *f*;
(*tax*) Zoll *m*; **be on** ∼ Dienst haben. ∼-
free *a* zollfrei

duvet /'du:veɪ/ *n* Steppdecke *f*

dwarf /dwɔ:f/ *n* (*pl* **-s** *or* **dwarves**) Zwerg
m

dwell /dwel/ *vi* (*pt/pp* **dwelt**) (*liter*)
wohnen; ∼ **on** (*fig*) verweilen bei. ∼**ing**
n Wohnung *f*

dwindle /'dwɪndl/ *vi* abnehmen, schwind-
en

dye /daɪ/ *n* Farbstoff *m* ◻ *vt* (*pres p* **dyeing**)
färben

dying /'daɪɪŋ/ *see* **die**[2]

dynamic /daɪ'næmɪk/ *a* dynamisch. ∼**s** *n*
Dynamik *f*

dynamite /'daɪnəmaɪt/ *n* Dynamit *nt*
dynamo /'daɪnəməʊ/ *n* Dynamo *m*
dynasty /'dɪnəstɪ/ *n* Dynastie *f*
dysentery /'dɪsəntrɪ/ *n* Ruhr *f*
dyslex|ia /dɪs'leksɪə/ *n* Legasthenie *f*. **~ic** *a* legasthenisch; **be ~ic** Legastheniker sein

E

each /iːtʃ/ *a & pron* jede(r,s); *(per)* je; **~ other** einander; **£1 ~** £1 pro Person/ *(for thing)* pro Stück
eager /'iːgə(r)/ *a*, **-ly** *adv* eifrig; **be ~ to do sth** etw gerne machen wollen. **~ness** *n* Eifer *m*
eagle /'iːgl/ *n* Adler *m*
ear[1] /ɪə(r)/ *n (of corn)* Ähre *f*
ear[2] *n* Ohr *nt*. **~ache** *n* Ohrenschmerzen *pl*. **~drum** *n* Trommelfell *nt*
earl /ɜːl/ *n* Graf *m*
early /'ɜːlɪ/ *a & adv* (**-ier, -iest**) früh; *(reply)* baldig; **be ~** früh dran sein; **~ in the morning** früh am Morgen
'earmark *vt* **~ for** bestimmen für
earn /ɜːn/ *vt* verdienen
earnest /'ɜːnɪst/ *a*, **-ly** *adv* ernsthaft □ *n* **in ~** im Ernst
earnings /'ɜːnɪŋz/ *npl* Verdienst *m*
ear: ~phones *npl* Kopfhörer *pl*. **~-ring** *n* Ohrring *m*; *(clip-on)* Ohrklips *m*. **~shot** *n* **within/out of ~shot** in/außer Hörweite
earth /ɜːθ/ *n* Erde *f*; *(of fox)* Bau *m*; **where/ what on ~?** wo/was in aller Welt? □ *vt (Electr)* erden
earthenware /'ɜːθn-/ *n* Tonwaren *pl*
earthly /'ɜːθlɪ/ *a* irdisch; **be no ~ use** *(fam)* völlig nutzlos sein
'earthquake *n* Erdbeben *nt*
earthy /'ɜːθɪ/ *a* erdig; *(coarse)* derb
earwig /'ɪəwɪg/ *n* Ohrwurm *m*
ease /iːz/ *n* Leichtigkeit *f*; **at ~!** *(Mil)* rührt euch! **be** *or* **feel ill at ~** ein ungutes Gefühl haben □ *vt* erleichtern; lindern *(pain)* □ *vi (pain:)* nachlassen; *(situation:)* sich entspannen
easel /'iːzl/ *n* Staffelei *f*
easily /'iːzɪlɪ/ *adv* leicht, mit Leichtigkeit
east /iːst/ *n* Osten *m*; **to the ~ of** östlich von □ *a* Ost-, ost- □ *adv* nach Osten
Easter /'iːstə(r)/ *n* Ostern *nt* □ *attrib* Oster-. **~ egg** *n* Osterei *nt*
east|erly /'iːstəlɪ/ *a* östlich. **~ern** *a* östlich. **~ward[s]** /-wəd[z]/ *adv* nach Osten

easy /'iːzɪ/ *a* (**-ier, -iest**) leicht; **take it ~** *(fam)* sich schonen; **take it ~!** beruhige dich! **go ~ with** *(fam)* sparsam umgehen mit
easy: ~ chair *n* Sessel *m*. **~'going** *a* gelassen; **too ~going** lässig
eat /iːt/ *vt/i* (*pt* **ate**, *pp* **eaten**) essen; *(animal:)* fressen. **~ up** *vt* aufessen
eat|able /'iːtəbl/ *a* genießbar. **~er** *n* (*apple*) Essapfel *m*
eau-de-Cologne /əʊdəkə'ləʊn/ *n* Kölnischwasser *nt*
eaves /iːvz/ *npl* Dachüberhang *m*. **~drop** *vi* (*pt/pp* **~ dropped**) [heimlich] lauschen; **~drop on** belauschen
ebb /eb/ *n (tide)* Ebbe *f*; **at a low ~** *(fig)* auf einem Tiefstand □ *vi* zurückgehen; *(fig)* verebben
ebony /'ebənɪ/ *n* Ebenholz *nt*
ebullient /ɪ'bʌlɪənt/ *a* überschwänglich
EC *abbr* (**European Community**) EG *f*
eccentric /ɪk'sentrɪk/ *a* exzentrisch □ *n* Exzentriker *m*
ecclesiastical /ɪkliːzɪ'æstɪkl/ *a* kirchlich
echo /'ekəʊ/ *n* (*pl* **-es**) Echo *nt*, Widerhall *m* □ *v* (*pt/pp* **echoed**, *pres p* **echoing**) *vt* zurückwerfen; *(imitate)* nachsagen □ *vi* widerhallen (**with** von)
eclipse /ɪ'klɪps/ *n (Astr)* Finsternis *f* □ *vt (fig)* in den Schatten stellen
ecolog|ical /iːkə'lɒdʒɪkl/ *a* ökologisch. **~y** /iː'kɒlədʒɪ/ *n* Ökologie *f*
economic /iːkə'nɒmɪk/ *a* wirtschaftlich. **~al** *a* sparsam. **~ally** *adv* wirtschaftlich; *(thriftily)* sparsam. **~s** *n* Volkswirtschaft *f*
economist /ɪ'kɒnəmɪst/ *n* Volkswirt *m*; *(Univ)* Wirtschaftswissenschaftler *m*
economize /ɪ'kɒnəmaɪz/ *vi* sparen (**on** an + *dat*)
economy /ɪ'kɒnəmɪ/ *n* Wirtschaft *f*; *(thrift)* Sparsamkeit *f*
ecstasy /'ekstəsɪ/ *n* Ekstase *f*
ecstatic /ɪk'stætɪk/ *a*, **-ally** *adv* ekstatisch
ecu /'eɪkjuː/ *n* Ecu *m*
ecumenical /iːkjuː'menɪkl/ *a* ökumenisch
eczema /'eksɪmə/ *n* Ekzem *nt*
eddy /'edɪ/ *n* Wirbel *m*
edge /edʒ/ *n* Rand *m*; *(of table, lawn)* Kante *f*; *(of knife)* Schneide *f*; **on ~** *(fam)* nervös; **have the ~ on** *(fam)* etwas besser sein als □ *vt* einfassen. **~ forward** *vi* sich nach vorn schieben
edging /'edʒɪŋ/ *n* Einfassung *f*
edgy /'edʒɪ/ *a (fam)* nervös
edible /'edɪbl/ *a* essbar
edict /'iːdɪkt/ *n* Erlass *m*
edifice /'edɪfɪs/ *n* [großes] Gebäude *nt*

edify /'edɪfaɪ/ *vt* ⟨*pt/pp* **-ied**⟩ erbauen. **~ing** *a* erbaulich

edit /'edɪt/ *vt* ⟨*pt/pp* **edited**⟩ redigieren; herausgeben ⟨*anthology, dictionary*⟩; schneiden ⟨*film, tape*⟩

edition /ɪ'dɪʃn/ *n* Ausgabe *f*; (*impression*) Auflage *f*

editor /'edɪtə(r)/ *n* Redakteur *m*; (*of anthology, dictionary*) Herausgeber *m*; (*of newspaper*) Chefredakteur *m*; (*of film*) Cutter(in) *m(f)*

editorial /edɪ'tɔ:rɪəl/ *a* redaktionell, Redaktions- ☐ *n* ⟨*Journ*⟩ Leitartikel *m*

educate /'edjʊkeɪt/ *vt* erziehen; **be ~d at X** auf die X-Schule gehen. **~d** *a* gebildet

education /edjʊ'keɪʃn/ *n* Erziehung *f*; (*culture*) Bildung *f*. **~al** *a* pädagogisch; ⟨*visit*⟩ kulturell

eel /i:l/ *n* Aal *m*

eerie /'ɪərɪ/ *a* (**-ier, -iest**) unheimlich

effect /ɪ'fekt/ *n* Wirkung *f*, Effekt *m*; **in ~** in Wirklichkeit; **take ~** in Kraft treten ☐ *vt* bewirken

effective /ɪ'fektɪv/ *a*, **-ly** *adv* wirksam, effektiv; ⟨*striking*⟩ wirkungsvoll, effektvoll; (*actual*) tatsächlich. **~ness** *n* Wirksamkeit *f*

effeminate /ɪ'femɪnət/ *a* unmännlich

effervescent /efə'vesnt/ *a* sprudelnd

efficiency /ɪ'fɪʃənsɪ/ *n* Tüchtigkeit *f*; (*of machine, organization*) Leistungsfähigkeit *f*

efficient /ɪ'fɪʃənt/ *a* tüchtig; ⟨*machine, organization*⟩ leistungsfähig; ⟨*method*⟩ rationell. **~ly** *adv* gut; ⟨*function*⟩ rationell

effigy /'efɪdʒɪ/ *n* Bildnis *nt*

effort /'efət/ *n* Anstrengung *f*; **make an ~** sich (*dat*) Mühe geben. **~less** *a*, **-ly** *adv* mühelos

effrontery /ɪ'frʌntərɪ/ *n* Unverschämtheit *f*

effusive /ɪ'fju:sɪv/ *a*, **-ly** *adv* überschwänglich

e.g. *abbr* (*exempli gratia*) z.B.

egalitarian /ɪgælɪ'teərɪən/ *a* egalitär

egg[1] /eg/ *vt* **~ on** (*fam*) anstacheln

egg[2] *n* Ei *nt*. **~-cup** *n* Eierbecher *m*. **~shell** *n* Eierschale *f*. **~-timer** *n* Eieruhr *f*

ego /'i:gəʊ/ *n* Ich *nt*. **~centric** /-'sentrɪk/ *a* egozentrisch. **~ism** *n* Egoismus *m*. **~ist** *n* Egoist *m*. **~ism** *n* Ichbezogenheit *f*. **~tist** *n* ichbezogener Mensch *m*

Egypt /'i:dʒɪpt/ *n* Ägypten *nt*. **~ian** /ɪ'dʒɪpʃn/ *a* ägyptisch ☐ *n* Ägypter(in) *m(f)*

eiderdown /'aɪdə-/ *n* (*quilt*) Daunendecke *f*

eigh|t /eɪt/ *a* acht ☐ *n* Acht *f*; (*boat*) Achter *m*. **~'teen** *a* achtzehn. **~'teenth** *a* achtzehnte(r,s)

eighth /eɪtθ/ *a* achte(r,s) ☐ *n* Achtel *nt*

eightieth /'eɪtɪɪθ/ *a* achtzigste(r,s)

eighty /'eɪtɪ/ *a* achtzig

either /'aɪðə(r)/ *a & pron* **~ [of them]** einer von [den] beiden; (*both*) beide; **on ~ side** auf beiden Seiten ☐ *adv* **I don't ~** ich auch nicht ☐ *conj* **~ ... or** entweder ... oder

eject /ɪ'dʒekt/ *vt* hinauswerfen

eke /i:k/ *vt* **~ out** strecken; (*increase*) ergänzen; **~ out a living** sich kümmerlich durchschlagen

elaborate[1] /ɪ'læbərət/ *a*, **-ly** *adv* kunstvoll; ⟨*fig*⟩ kompliziert

elaborate[2] /ɪ'læbəreɪt/ *vi* ausführlicher sein; **~ on** näher ausführen

elapse /ɪ'læps/ *vi* vergehen

elastic /ɪ'læstɪk/ *a* elastisch ☐ *n* Gummiband *nt*. **~ 'band** *n* Gummiband *nt*

elasticity /ɪlæs'tɪsətɪ/ *n* Elastizität *f*

elated /ɪ'leɪtɪd/ *a* überglücklich

elbow /'elbəʊ/ *n* Ellbogen *m*

elder[1] /'eldə(r)/ *n* Holunder *m*

eld|er[2] *a* ältere(r,s) ☐ *n* **the ~er** der/die Ältere. **~erly** *a* alt. **~est** *a* älteste(r,s) ☐ *n* **the ~est** der/die Älteste

elect /ɪ'lekt/ *a* **the president ~** der designierte Präsident ☐ *vt* wählen; **~ to do sth** sich dafür entscheiden, etw zu tun. **~ion** /-ekʃn/ *n* Wahl *f*

elector /ɪ'lektə(r)/ *n* Wähler(in) *m(f)*. **~al** *a* Wahl-; **~al roll** Wählerverzeichnis *nt*. **~ate** /-rət/ *n* Wählerschaft *f*

electric /ɪ'lektrɪk/ *a*, **-ally** *adv* elektrisch

electrical /ɪ'lektrɪkl/ *a* elektrisch; **~ engineering** Elektrotechnik *f*

electric: **~ 'blanket** *n* Heizdecke *f*. **~ 'fire** *n* elektrischer Heizofen *m*

electrician /ɪlek'trɪʃn/ *n* Elektriker *m*

electricity /ɪlek'trɪsətɪ/ *n* Elektrizität *f*; (*supply*) Strom *m*

electrify /ɪ'lektrɪfaɪ/ *vt* ⟨*pt/pp* **-ied**⟩ elektrifizieren. **~ing** *a* ⟨*fig*⟩ elektrisierend

electrocute /ɪ'lektrəkju:t/ *vt* durch einen elektrischen Schlag töten; (*execute*) auf dem elektrischen Stuhl hinrichten

electrode /ɪ'lektrəʊd/ *n* Elektrode *f*

electron /ɪ'lektrɒn/ *n* Elektron *nt*

electronic /ɪlek'trɒnɪk/ *a* elektronisch. **~s** *n* Elektronik *f*

elegance /'elɪgəns/ *n* Eleganz *f*

elegant /'elɪgənt/ *a*, **-ly** *adv* elegant

elegy /'elɪdʒɪ/ *n* Elegie *f*

element /'elɪmənt/ n Element nt. ~ary /-'mentərɪ/ a elementar

elephant /'elɪfənt/ n Elefant m

elevat|e /'elɪveɪt/ vt heben; (fig) erheben. ~ion /-'veɪʃn/ n Erhebung f

elevator /'elɪveɪtə(r)/ n (Amer) Aufzug m, Fahrstuhl m

eleven /ɪ'levn/ a elf □ n Elf f. ~th a elfte(r,s); **at the ~th hour** (fam) in letzter Minute

elf /elf/ n (pl elves) Elfe f

elicit /ɪ'lɪsɪt/ vt herausbekommen

eligible /'elɪdʒəbl/ a berechtigt; ~ young man gute Partie f

eliminate /ɪ'lɪmɪneɪt/ vt ausschalten; (excrete) ausscheiden

élite /eɪ'li:t/ n Elite f

ellip|se /ɪ'lɪps/ n Ellipse f. ~tical a elliptisch

elm /elm/ n Ulme f

elocution /elə'kju:ʃn/ n Sprecherziehung f

elongate /'i:lɒŋgeɪt/ vt verlängern

elope /ɪ'əʊp/ vi durchbrennen (fam)

eloquen|ce /'eləkwəns/ n Beredsamkeit f. ~t a, ~ly adv beredt

else /els/ adv sonst; **who ~?** wer sonst? **nothing ~** sonst nichts; **or ~** oder; (otherwise) sonst; **someone/somewhere ~** jemand/irgendwo anders; **anyone ~** jeder andere; (as question) sonst noch jemand? **anything ~** alles andere; (as question) sonst noch etwas? ~**where** adv woanders

elucidate /ɪ'lu:sɪdeɪt/ vt erläutern

elude /ɪ'lu:d/ vt entkommen (+ dat); (avoid) ausweichen (+ dat)

elusive /ɪ'lu:sɪv/ a be ~ schwer zu fassen sein

emaciated /ɪ'meɪsɪeɪtɪd/ a abgezehrt

emanate /'eməneɪt/ vi ausgehen (from von)

emancipat|ed /ɪ'mænsɪpeɪtɪd/ a emanzipiert. ~ion /-'peɪʃn/ n Emanzipation f; (of slaves) Freilassung f

embalm /ɪm'bɑ:m/ vt einbalsamieren

embankment /ɪm'bæŋkmənt/ n Böschung f; (of railway) Bahndamm m

embargo /em'bɑ:gəʊ/ n (pl -es) Embargo nt

embark /ɪm'bɑ:k/ vi sich einschiffen; ~ **on** anfangen mit. ~**ation** /embɑ:'keɪʃn/ n Einschiffung f

embarrass /ɪm'bærəs/ vt in Verlegenheit bringen. ~**ed** a verlegen. ~**ing** a peinlich. ~**ment** n Verlegenheit f

embassy /'embəsɪ/ n Botschaft f

embedded /ɪm'bedɪd/ a be deeply ~ in tief stecken in (+ dat)

embellish /ɪm'belɪʃ/ vt verzieren; (fig) ausschmücken

embers /'embəz/ npl Glut f

embezzle /ɪm'bezl/ vt unterschlagen. ~**ment** n Unterschlagung f

embitter /ɪm'bɪtə(r)/ vt verbittern

emblem /'embləm/ n Emblem nt

embodiment /ɪm'bɒdɪmənt/ n Verkörperung f

embody /ɪm'bɒdɪ/ vt (pt/pp -ied) verkörpern; (include) enthalten

emboss /ɪm'bɒs/ vt prägen

embrace /ɪm'breɪs/ n Umarmung f □ vt umarmen; (fig) umfassen □ vi sich umarmen

embroider /ɪm'brɔɪdə(r)/ vt besticken; sticken (design); (fig) ausschmücken □ vi sticken. ~**y** n Stickerei f

embroil /ɪm'brɔɪl/ vt become ~**ed in** sth in etw (acc) verwickelt werden

embryo /'embrɪəʊ/ n Embryo m

emerald /'emərəld/ n Smaragd m

emer|ge /ɪ'mɜ:dʒ/ vi auftauchen (from aus); (become known) sich herausstellen; (come into being) entstehen. ~**gence** /-əns/ n Auftauchen nt; Entstehung f

emergency /ɪ'mɜ:dʒənsɪ/ n Notfall m; **in an ~** im Notfall. ~ **exit** n Notausgang m

emery-paper /'emərɪ-/ n Schmirgelpapier nt

emigrant /'emɪgrənt/ n Auswanderer m

emigrat|e /'emɪgreɪt/ vi auswandern. ~**ion** /-'greɪʃn/ n Auswanderung f

eminent /'emɪnənt/ a, -ly adv eminent

emission /ɪ'mɪʃn/ n Ausstrahlung f; (of pollutant) Emission f

emit /ɪ'mɪt/ vt (pt/pp emitted) ausstrahlen (light, heat); ausstoßen (smoke, fumes, cry)

emotion /ɪ'məʊʃn/ n Gefühl nt. ~**al** a emotional; **become ~al** sich erregen

emotive /ɪ'məʊtɪv/ a emotional

empath|ize /'empəθaɪz/ vi ~**ize with** s.o. sich in jdn einfühlen. ~**y** n Einfühlungsvermögen nt

emperor /'empərə(r)/ n Kaiser m

emphasis /'emfəsɪs/ n Betonung f

emphasize /'emfəsaɪz/ vt betonen

emphatic /ɪm'fætɪk/ a, -**ally** adv nachdrücklich

empire /'empaɪə(r)/ n Reich nt

empirical /em'pɪrɪkl/ a empirisch

employ /ɪm'plɔɪ/ vt beschäftigen; (appoint) einstellen; (fig) anwenden. ~**ee** /emplɔɪ'i:/ n Beschäftigte(r) m/f; (in contrast to employer) Arbeitnehmer m. ~**er** n Arbeitgeber m. ~**ment** n Beschäftigung *f*; (*work*) Arbeit *f*. **~ment agency** *n* Stellenvermittlung *f*

empower /ɪm'paʊə(r)/ *vt* ermächtigen

empress /'emprɪs/ *n* Kaiserin *f*

empties /'emptɪz/ *npl* leere Flaschen *pl*

emptiness /'emptɪnɪs/ *n* Leere *f*

empty /'emptɪ/ *a* leer □ *vt* leeren; ausleeren (*container*) □ *vi* sich leeren

emulate /'emjʊleɪt/ *vt* nacheifern (+ *dat*)

emulsion /ɪ'mʌlʃn/ *n* Emulsion *f*

enable /ɪ'neɪbl/ *vt* **~ s.o. to** es jdm möglich machen, zu

enact /ɪ'nækt/ *vt* (*Theat*) aufführen

enamel /ɪ'næml/ *n* Email *nt*; (*on teeth*) Zahnschmelz *m*; (*paint*) Lack *m* □ *vt* (*pt/pp* **enamelled**) emaillieren

enamoured /ɪ'næməd/ *a* **be ~ of** sehr angetan sein von

enchant /ɪn'tʃɑːnt/ *vt* bezaubern. **~ing** *a* bezaubernd. **~ment** *n* Zauber *m*

encircle /ɪn'sɜːkl/ *vt* einkreisen

enclave /'enkleɪv/ *n* Enklave *f*

enclos|e /ɪn'kləʊz/ *vt* einschließen; (*in letter*) beilegen (**with** *dat*). **~ure** /-ʒə(r)/ *n* (*at zoo*) Gehege *nt*; (*in letter*) Anlage *f*

encompass /ɪn'kʌmpəs/ *vt* umfassen

encore /'ɒŋkɔː(r)/ *n* Zugabe *f* □ *int* bravo!

encounter /ɪn'kaʊntə(r)/ *n* Begegnung *f*; (*battle*) Zusammenstoß *m* □ *vt* begegnen (+ *dat*); (*fig*) stoßen auf (+ *acc*)

encourag|e /ɪn'kʌrɪdʒ/ *vt* ermutigen; (*promote*) fördern. **~ement** *n* Ermutigung *f*. **~ing** *a* ermutigend

encroach /ɪn'krəʊtʃ/ *vi* **~ on** eindringen in (+ *acc*) (*land*); beanspruchen (*time*)

encumb|er /ɪn'kʌmbə(r)/ *vt* belasten (**with** mit). **~rance** /-rəns/ *n* Belastung *f*

encyclopaed|ia /ɪnsaɪklə'piːdɪə/ *n* Enzyklopädie *f*, Lexikon *nt*. **~ic** *a* enzyklopädisch

end /end/ *n* Ende *nt*; (*purpose*) Zweck *m*; **in the ~** schließlich; **at the ~ of May** Ende Mai; **on ~** hochkant; **for days on ~** tagelang; **make ~s meet** (*fam*) [gerade] auskommen; **no ~ of** (*fam*) unheimlich viel(e) □ *vt* beenden □ *vi* enden; **~ up in** (*fam: arrive at*) landen in (+ *dat*)

endanger /ɪn'deɪndʒə(r)/ *vt* gefährden

endear|ing /ɪn'dɪərɪŋ/ *a* liebenswert. **~ment** *n* **term of ~ment** Kosewort *nt*

endeavour /ɪn'devə(r)/ *n* Bemühung *f* □ *vi* sich bemühen (**to** zu)

ending /'endɪŋ/ *n* Schluss *m*, Ende *nt*; (*Gram*) Endung *f*

endive /'endaɪv/ *n* Endivie *f*

endless /'endlɪs/ *a*, **-ly** *adv* endlos

endorse /en'dɔːs/ *vt* (*Comm*) indossieren; (*confirm*) bestätigen. **~ment** *n* (*Comm*) Indossament *nt*; (*fig*) Bestätigung *f*; (*on driving licence*) Strafvermerk *m*

endow /ɪn'daʊ/ *vt* stiften; **be ~ed with** (*fig*) haben. **~ment** *n* Stiftung *f*

endur|able /ɪn'djʊərəbl/ *a* erträglich. **~ance** /-rəns/ *n* Durchhaltevermögen *nt*; **beyond ~ance** unerträglich

endur|e /ɪn'djʊə(r)/ *vt* ertragen □ *vi* [lange] bestehen. **~ing** *a* dauernd

enemy /'enəmɪ/ *n* Feind *m* □ *attrib* feindlich

energetic /enə'dʒetɪk/ *a* tatkräftig; **be ~** voller Energie sein

energy /'enədʒɪ/ *n* Energie *f*

enforce /ɪn'fɔːs/ *vt* durchsetzen. **~d** *a* unfreiwillig

engage /ɪn'geɪdʒ/ *vt* einstellen (*staff*); (*Theat*) engagieren; (*Auto*) einlegen (*gear*) □ *vi* sich beteiligen (**in** an + *dat*); (*Techn*) ineinander greifen. **~d** *a* besetzt; (*person*) beschäftigt; (*to be married*) verlobt; **get ~d** sich verloben (**to** mit). **~ment** *n* Verlobung *f*; (*appointment*) Verabredung *f*; (*Mil*) Gefecht *nt*

engaging /ɪn'geɪdʒɪŋ/ *a* einnehmend

engender /ɪn'dʒendə(r)/ *vt* (*fig*) erzeugen

engine /'endʒɪn/ *n* Motor *m*; (*Naut*) Maschine *f*; (*Rail*) Lokomotive *f*; (*of jetplane*) Triebwerk *nt*. **~-driver** *n* Lokomotivführer *m*

engineer /endʒɪ'nɪə(r)/ *n* Ingenieur *m*; (*service, installation*) Techniker *m*; (*Naut*) Maschinist *m*; (*Amer*) Lokomotivführer *m* □ *vt* (*fig*) organisieren. **~ing** *n* [**mechanical**] **~ing** Maschinenbau *m*

England /'ɪŋglənd/ *n* England *nt*

English /'ɪŋglɪʃ/ *a* englisch; **the ~ Channel** der Ärmelkanal □ *n* (*Lang*) Englisch *nt*; **in ~** auf Englisch; **into ~** ins Englische; **the ~** *pl* die Engländer. **~man** *n* Engländer *m*. **~woman** *n* Engländerin *f*

engrav|e /ɪn'greɪv/ *vt* eingravieren. **~ing** *n* Stich *m*

engross /ɪn'grəʊs/ *vt* **be ~ed in** vertieft sein in (+ *acc*)

engulf /ɪn'gʌlf/ *vt* verschlingen

enhance /ɪn'hɑːns/ *vt* verschönern; (*fig*) steigern

enigma /ɪ'nɪgmə/ *n* Rätsel *nt*. **~tic** /en-ɪg'mætɪk/ *a* rätselhaft

enjoy /ɪn'dʒɔɪ/ *vt* genießen; **~ oneself** sich amüsieren; **~ cooking/painting** gern kochen/malen; **I ~ed it** es hat mir gut gefallen; (*food:*) geschmeckt. **~able** /-əbl/ *a* angenehm, nett. **~ment** *n* Vergnügen *nt*

enlarge /ɪn'lɑːdʒ/ vt vergrößern □ vi ~ upon sich näher auslassen über (+ acc). ~ment n Vergrößerung f

enlighten /ɪn'laɪtn/ vt aufklären. ~ment n Aufklärung f

enlist /ɪn'lɪst/ vt (Mil) einziehen; ~ s.o.'s help jdn zur Hilfe heranziehen □ vi (Mil) sich melden

enliven /ɪn'laɪvn/ vt beleben

enmity /'enmɪtɪ/ n Feindschaft f

enormity /ɪ'nɔːmətɪ/ n Ungeheuerlichkeit f

enormous /ɪ'nɔːməs/ a, -ly adv riesig

enough /ɪ'nʌf/ a, adv & n genug; **be** ~ reichen; **funnily** ~ komischerweise; **I've had** ~! (fam) jetzt reicht's mir aber!

enquir|e /ɪn'kwaɪə(r)/ vi sich erkundigen (**about** nach) □ vt sich erkundigen nach. ~y n Erkundigung f; (investigation) Untersuchung f

enrage /ɪn'reɪdʒ/ vt wütend machen

enrich /ɪn'rɪtʃ/ vt bereichern; (improve) anreichern

enrol /ɪn'rəʊl/ v (pt/pp -rolled) □ vt einschreiben □ vi sich einschreiben. ~ment n Einschreibung f

ensemble /ɒn'sɒmbl/ n (clothing & Mus) Ensemble nt

ensign /'ensaɪn/ n Flagge f

enslave /ɪn'sleɪv/ vt versklaven

ensue /ɪn'sjuː/ vi folgen; (result) sich ergeben (**from** aus)

ensure /ɪn'ʃʊə(r)/ vt sicherstellen; ~ that dafür sorgen, dass

entail /ɪn'teɪl/ vt erfordern machen; **what does it** ~? was ist damit verbunden?

entangle /ɪn'tæŋgl/ vt **get** ~d sich verfangen (**in** in + dat); (fig) sich verstricken (**in** in + acc)

enter /'entə(r)/ vt eintreten; (vehicle:) einfahren in (+ acc); einreisen in (+ acc) (country); (register) eintragen; sich anmelden zu (competition) □ vi eintreten; (vehicle:) einfahren; (Theat) auftreten; (register as competitor) sich anmelden; (take part) sich beteiligen (**in** an + dat)

enterpris|e /'entəpraɪz/ n Unternehmen nt; (quality) Unternehmungsgeist m. ~ing a unternehmend

entertain /entə'teɪn/ vt unterhalten; (invite) einladen; (to meal) bewirten (guest); (fig) in Erwägung ziehen □ vi unterhalten; (have guests) Gäste haben. ~er n Unterhalter m. ~ment n Unterhaltung f

enthral /ɪn'θrɔːl/ vt (pt/pp **enthralled**) **be** ~led gefesselt sein (**by** von)

enthuse /ɪn'θjuːz/ vi ~ **over** schwärmen von

enthusias|m /ɪn'θjuːzɪæzm/ n Begeisterung f. ~t n Enthusiast m. ~tic /-'æstɪk/ a, -ally adv begeistert

entice /ɪn'taɪs/ vt locken. ~ment n Anreiz m

entire /ɪn'taɪə(r)/ a ganz. ~ly adv ganz, völlig. ~ty /-rətɪ/ n in its ~ty in seiner Gesamtheit

entitle /ɪn'taɪtl/ vt berechtigen; ~d ... mit dem Titel ...; **be** ~d **to sth** das Recht auf etw (acc) haben. ~ment n Berechtigung f; (claim) Anspruch m (**to** auf + acc)

entity /'entɪtɪ/ n Wesen nt

entomology /entə'mɒlədʒɪ/ n Entomologie f

entourage /'ɒntʊrɑːʒ/ n Gefolge nt

entrails /'entreɪlz/ npl Eingeweide pl

entrance[1] /ɪn'trɑːns/ vt bezaubern

entrance[2] /'entrəns/ n Eintritt m; (Theat) Auftritt m; (way in) Eingang m; (for vehicle) Einfahrt f. ~ **examination** n Aufnahmeprüfung f. ~ **fee** n Eintrittsgebühr f

entrant /'entrənt/ n Teilnehmer(in) m(f)

entreat /ɪn'triːt/ vt anflehen (**for** um)

entrench /ɪn'trentʃ/ vt **be** ~ed **in** verwurzelt sein in (+ dat)

entrust /ɪn'trʌst/ vt ~ **s.o. with sth**, ~ **sth to s.o.** jdm etw anvertrauen

entry /'entrɪ/ n Eintritt m; (into country) Einreise f; (on list) Eintrag m; **no** ~ Zutritt; (Auto) Einfahrt verboten. ~ **form** n Anmeldeformular nt. ~ **visa** n Einreisevisum nt

enumerate /ɪ'njuːməreɪt/ vt aufzählen

enunciate /ɪ'nʌnsɪeɪt/ vt [deutlich] aussprechen; (state) vorbringen

envelop /ɪn'veləp/ vt (pt/pp **enveloped**) einhüllen

envelope /'envələʊp/ n [Brief]umschlag m

enviable /'envɪəbl/ a beneidenswert

envious /'envɪəs/ a, -ly adv neidisch (**of** auf + acc)

environment /ɪn'vaɪərənmənt/ n Umwelt f

environmental /ɪnvaɪərən'mentl/ a Umwelt-. ~ist n Umweltschützer m. ~ly adv ~ly friendly umweltfreundlich

envisage /ɪn'vɪzɪdʒ/ vt sich (dat) vorstellen

envoy /'envɔɪ/ n Gesandte(r) m

envy /'envɪ/ n Neid m □ vt (pt/pp -ied) ~ **s.o. sth** jdn um etw beneiden

enzyme /'enzaɪm/ n Enzym nt

epic /'epɪk/ a episch □ n Epos nt

epidemic /epɪ'demɪk/ n Epidemie f

epilep|sy /'epɪlepsɪ/ n Epilepsie f. ~**tic** /-'leptɪk/ a epileptisch □ n Epileptiker(in) m(f)

epilogue /'epɪlɒg/ n Epilog m

episode /'epɪsəʊd/ n Episode f; (instalment) Folge f

epistle /ɪ'pɪsl/ n (liter) Brief m

epitaph /'epɪtɑːf/ n Epitaph nt

epithet /'epɪθet/ n Beiname m

epitom|e /ɪ'pɪtəmɪ/ n Inbegriff m. ~**ize** vt verkörpern

epoch /'iːpɒk/ n Epoche f. ~-**making** a epochemachend

equal /'iːkwl/ a gleich (**to** dat); **be ~ to a task** einer Aufgabe gewachsen sein □ n Gleichgestellte(r) m/f □ vt (pt/pp **equalled**) gleichen (+ dat); (fig) gleichkommen (+ dat). ~**ity** /ɪ'kwɒlətɪ/ n Gleichheit f

equalize /'iːkwəlaɪz/ vt/i ausgleichen. ~**r** n (Sport) Ausgleich[streffer] m

equally /'iːkwəlɪ/ adv gleich; (divide) gleichmäßig; (just as) genauso

equanimity /ekwə'nɪmətɪ/ n Gleichmut m

equat|e /ɪ'kweɪt/ vt gleichsetzen (**with** mit). ~**ion** /-eɪʒn/ n (Math) Gleichung f

equator /ɪ'kweɪtə(r)/ n Äquator m. ~**ial** /ekwə'tɔːrɪəl/ a Äquator-

equestrian /ɪ'kwestrɪən/ a Reit-

equilibrium /iːkwɪ'lɪbrɪəm/ n Gleichgewicht nt

equinox /'iːkwɪnɒks/ n Tagundnachtgleiche f

equip /ɪ'kwɪp/ vt (pt/pp **equipped**) ausrüsten; (furnish) ausstatten. ~**ment** n Ausrüstung f; Ausstattung f

equitable /'ekwɪtəbl/ a gerecht

equity /'ekwətɪ/ n Gerechtigkeit f

equivalent /ɪ'kwɪvələnt/ a gleichwertig; (corresponding) entsprechend □ n Äquivalent nt; (value) Gegenwert m; (counterpart) Gegenstück nt

equivocal /ɪ'kwɪvəkl/ a zweideutig

era /'ɪərə/ n Ära f, Zeitalter nt

eradicate /ɪ'rædɪkeɪt/ vt ausrotten

erase /ɪ'reɪz/ vt ausradieren; (from tape) löschen; (fig) auslöschen. ~**r** n Radiergummi m

erect /ɪ'rekt/ a aufrecht □ vt errichten. ~**ion** /-ekʃn/ n Errichtung f; (building) Bau m; (Biol) Erektion f

ermine /'ɜːmɪn/ n Hermelin m

ero|de /ɪ'rəʊd/ vt (water:) auswaschen; (acid:) angreifen. ~**sion** /-əʊʒn/ n Erosion f

erotic /ɪ'rɒtɪk/ a erotisch. ~**ism** /-tɪsɪzm/ n Erotik f

err /ɜː(r)/ vi sich irren; (sin) sündigen

errand /'erənd/ n Botengang m

erratic /ɪ'rætɪk/ a unregelmäßig; (person) unberechenbar

erroneous /ɪ'rəʊnɪəs/ a falsch; (belief, assumption) irrig. ~**ly** adv fälschlich; irrigerweise

error /'erə(r)/ n Irrtum m; (mistake) Fehler m; **in ~** irrtümlicherweise

erudit|e /'erudaɪt/ a gelehrt. ~**ion** /-'dɪʃn/ n Gelehrsamkeit f

erupt /ɪ'rʌpt/ vi ausbrechen. ~**ion** /-ʌpʃn/ n Ausbruch m

escalat|e /'eskəleɪt/ vt/i eskalieren. ~**ion** /-'leɪʃn/ n Eskalation f. ~**or** n Rolltreppe f

escapade /'eskəpeɪd/ n Eskapade f

escape /ɪ'skeɪp/ n Flucht f; (from prison) Ausbruch m; **have a narrow ~** gerade noch davonkommen □ vi flüchten; (prisoner:) ausbrechen; entkommen (**from** aus; **from s.o.** jdm); (gas:) entweichen □ vt ~ **notice** unbemerkt bleiben; **the name ~s me** der Name entfällt mir

escapism /ɪ'skeɪpɪzm/ n Flucht f vor der Wirklichkeit, Eskapismus m

escort[1] /'eskɔːt/ n (of person) Begleiter m; (Mil) Eskorte f; **under ~** unter Bewachung

escort[2] /ɪ'skɔːt/ vt begleiten; (Mil) eskortieren

Eskimo /'eskɪməʊ/ n Eskimo m

esoteric /esə'terɪk/ a esoterisch

especial /ɪ'speʃl/ a besondere(r,s). ~**ly** adv besonders

espionage /'espɪənɑːʒ/ n Spionage f

essay /'eseɪ/ n Aufsatz m

essence /'esns/ n Wesen nt; (Chem, Culin) Essenz f; **in ~** im Wesentlichen

essential /ɪ'senʃl/ a wesentlich; (indispensable) unentbehrlich □ n **the ~s** das Wesentliche; (items) das Nötigste. ~**ly** adv im Wesentlichen

establish /ɪ'stæblɪʃ/ vt gründen; (form) bilden; (prove) beweisen. ~**ment** n (firm) Unternehmen nt

estate /ɪ'steɪt/ n Gut nt; (possessions) Besitz m; (after death) Nachlass m; (housing) [Wohn]siedlung f. ~ **agent** n Immobilienmakler m. ~ **car** n Kombi[wagen] m

esteem /ɪ'stiːm/ n Achtung f □ vt hochschätzen

estimate[1] /'estɪmət/ n Schätzung f; (Comm) [Kosten]voranschlag m; **at a rough ~** grob geschätzt

estimat|e[2] /'estɪmeɪt/ vt schätzen. ~**ion** /-'meɪʃn/ n Einschätzung f; (esteem) Achtung f; **in my ~ion** meiner Meinung nach

estuary /'estjʊəri/ n Mündung f

etc. /et'setərə/ abbr (et cetera) und so weiter, usw.

etching /'etʃɪŋ/ n Radierung f

eternal /ɪ'tɜːnl/ a, -ly adv ewig

eternity /ɪ'tɜːnəti/ n Ewigkeit f

ether /'iːθə(r)/ n Äther m

ethic /'eθɪk/ n Ethik f. ∼al a ethisch; (morally correct) moralisch einwandfrei. ∼s n Ethik f

Ethiopia /iːθɪ'əʊpɪə/ n Äthiopien nt

ethnic /'eθnɪk/ a ethnisch

etiquette /'etɪket/ n Etikette f

etymology /etɪ'mɒlədʒɪ/ n Etymologie f

eucalyptus /juːkə'lɪptəs/ n Eukalyptus m

eulogy /'juːlədʒɪ/ n Lobrede f

euphemis|m /'juːfəmɪzm/ n Euphemismus m. ∼tic /-'mɪstɪk/ a, -ally adv verhüllend

euphoria /juː'fɔːrɪə/ n Euphorie f

Euro /'jʊərəʊ/ n Euro m. ∼cheque f Eurocheck m. ∼ passport n Europaß m

Europe /'jʊərəp/ n Europa nt

European /jʊərə'piːən/ a europäisch; ∼ Community Europäische Gemeinschaft f □ n Europäer(in) m(f)

evacuat|e /ɪ'vækjʊeɪt/ vt evakuieren; räumen (building, area). ∼ion /-'eɪʃn/ n Evakuierung f; Räumung f

evade /ɪ'veɪd/ vt sich entziehen (+ dat); hinterziehen (taxes); ∼ the issue ausweichen

evaluate /ɪ'væljʊeɪt/ vt einschätzen

evange|lical /iːvæn'dʒelɪkl/ a evangelisch. ∼list /ɪ'vændʒəlɪst/ n Evangelist m

evaporat|e /ɪ'væpəreɪt/ vi verdunsten; ∼ed milk Kondensmilch f, Dosenmilch f. ∼ion /-'reɪʃn/ n Verdampfung f

evasion /ɪ'veɪʒn/ n Ausweichen nt; ∼ of taxes Steuerhinterziehung f

evasive /ɪ'veɪsɪv/ a, -ly adv ausweichend; be ∼ ausweichen

eve /iːv/ n (liter) Vorabend m

even /'iːvn/ a (level) eben; (same, equal) gleich; (regular) gleichmäßig; (number) gerade; **get ∼ with** (fam) es jdm heimzahlen □ adv sogar, selbst; ∼ **so** trotzdem; **not ∼** nicht einmal □ vt ∼ **the score** ausgleichen. ∼ **up** vt ausgleichen □ vi sich ausgleichen

evening /'iːvnɪŋ/ n Abend m; **this ∼** heute Abend; **in the ∼** abends, am Abend. ∼ **class** n Abendkurs m

evenly /'iːvnlɪ/ adv gleichmäßig

event /ɪ'vent/ n Ereignis nt; (function) Veranstaltung f; (Sport) Wettbewerb m; **in the ∼ of** im Falle (+ gen); **in the ∼** wie es sich ergab. ∼**ful** a ereignisreich

eventual /ɪ'ventjʊəl/ a **his ∼ success** der Erfolg, der ihm schließlich zuteil wurde. ∼**ity** /-'ælətɪ/ n Eventualität f, Fall m. ∼**ly** adv schließlich

ever /'evə(r)/ adv je[mals]; **not ∼** nie; **for ∼** für immer; **hardly ∼** fast nie; ∼ **since** seitdem; ∼ **so** (fam) sehr, furchtbar (fam)

'evergreen n immergrüner Strauch m/ (tree) Baum m

ever'lasting a ewig

every /'evrɪ/ a jede(r,s); ∼ **one** jede(r,s) Einzelne; ∼ **other day** jeden zweiten Tag

every: ∼**body** pron jeder[mann]; alle pl. ∼**day** a alltäglich. ∼ **one** pron jeder [-mann]; alle pl. ∼**thing** pron alles. ∼**where** adv überall

evict /ɪ'vɪkt/ vt [aus der Wohnung] hinausweisen. ∼**ion** /-ɪkʃn/ n Ausweisung f

eviden|ce /'evɪdəns/ n Beweise pl; (Jur) Beweismaterial nt; (testimony) Aussage f; **give ∼ce** aussagen. ∼**t** a, -ly adv offensichtlich

evil /'iːvl/ a böse □ n Böse nt

evocative /ɪ'vɒkətɪv/ a **be ∼ of** heraufbeschwören

evoke /ɪ'vəʊk/ vt heraufbeschwören

evolution /iːvə'luːʃn/ n Evolution f

evolve /ɪ'vɒlv/ vt entwickeln □ vi sich entwickeln

ewe /juː/ n [Mutter]schaf nt

exacerbate /ek'sæsəbeɪt/ vt verschlimmern; verschärfen (situation)

exact /ɪg'zækt/ a, -ly adv genau; **not ∼ly** nicht gerade □ vt erzwingen. ∼**ing** a anspruchsvoll. ∼**itude** /-ɪtjuːd/ n, ∼**ness** n Genauigkeit f

exaggerat|e /ɪg'zædʒəreɪt/ vt/i übertreiben. ∼**ion** /-'reɪʃn/ n Übertreibung f

exalt /ɪg'zɔːlt/ vt erheben; (praise) preisen

exam /ɪg'zæm/ n (fam) Prüfung f

examination /ɪgzæmɪ'neɪʃn/ n Untersuchung f; (Sch) Prüfung f

examine /ɪg'zæmɪn/ vt untersuchen; (Sch) prüfen; (Jur) verhören. ∼**r** n (Sch) Prüfer m

example /ɪg'zɑːmpl/ n Beispiel nt (of für); **for ∼** zum Beispiel; **make an ∼ of** ein Exempel statuieren an (+ dat)

exasperat|e /ɪg'zæspəreɪt/ vt zur Verzweiflung treiben. ∼**ion** /-'reɪʃn/ n Verzweiflung f

excavat|e /'ekskəveɪt/ vt ausschachten; (Archaeol) ausgraben. ∼**ion** /-'veɪʃn/ n Ausgrabung f

exceed /ɪk'siːd/ vt übersteigen. ∼**ingly** adv äußerst

excel /ɪk'sel/ v (pt/pp **excelled**) vi sich
auszeichnen □ vt ~ **oneself** sich selbst
übertreffen

excellen|ce /'eksələns/ n Vorzüglichkeit
f. **E** ~**cy** n (title) Exzellenz f. ~**t** a, -**ly**
adv ausgezeichnet, vorzüglich

except /ɪk'sept/ prep außer (+ dat); ~ **for**
abgesehen von □ vt ausnehmen. ~**ing**
prep außer (+ dat)

exception /ɪk'sepʃn/ n Ausnahme f; **take**
~ **to** Anstoß nehmen an (+ dat). ~**al** a,
-**ly** adv außergewöhnlich

excerpt /'eksɜ:pt/ n Auszug m

excess /ɪk'ses/ n Übermaß nt (**of** an + dat);
(surplus) Überschuss m; ~**es** pl Exzesse
pl; **in** ~ **of** über (+ dat)

excess 'fare /ekses-/ n Nachlösegebühr f

excessive /ɪk'sesɪv/ a, -**ly** adv übermäßig

exchange /ɪks'tʃeɪndʒ/ n Austausch m;
(Teleph) Fernsprechamt nt; (Comm)
[Geld]wechsel m; **[stock]** ~ Börse f; **in** ~
dafür □ vt austauschen (**for** gegen);
tauschen (places, greetings, money). ~
rate n Wechselkurs m

exchequer /ɪks'tʃekə(r)/ n (Pol) Staats-
kasse f

excise[1] /'eksaɪz/ n ~ **duty** Verbrauchs-
steuer f

excise[2] /ek'saɪz/ vt herausschneiden

excitable /ɪk'saɪtəbl/ a [leicht] erregbar

excit|e /ɪk'saɪt/ vt aufregen; (cause) er-
regen. ~**ed** a, -**ly** adv aufgeregt; **get** ~**ed**
sich aufregen. ~**ement** n Aufregung f;
Erregung f. ~**ing** a aufregend; (story)
spannend

exclaim /ɪk'skleɪm/ vt/i ausrufen

exclamation /eksklə'meɪʃn/ n Ausruf m.
~ **mark** n, (Amer) ~ **point** n Ausrufe-
zeichen nt

exclu|de /ɪk'sklu:d/ vt ausschließen.
~**ding** prep ausschließlich (+ gen).
~**sion** /-ʒn/ n Ausschluss m

exclusive /ɪk'sklu:sɪv/ a, -**ly** adv ausch-
ließlich; (select) exklusiv; ~ **of** ausschließlich (+ gen)

excommunicate /ekskə'mju:nɪkeɪt/ vt
exkommunizieren

excrement /'ekskrɪmənt/ n Kot m

excrete /ɪk'skri:t/ vt ausscheiden

excruciating /ɪk'skru:ʃieɪtɪŋ/ a grässlich

excursion /ɪk'skɜ:ʃn/ n Ausflug m

excusable /ɪk'skju:zəbl/ a entschuldbar

excuse[1] /ɪk'skju:s/ n Entschuldigung f;
(pretext) Ausrede f

excuse[2] /ɪk'skju:z/ vt entschuldigen; ~
from freistellen von; ~ **me!** Entschuldigung!

ex-di'rectory a **be** ~ nicht im Telefonbuch stehen

execute /'eksɪkju:t/ vt ausführen; (put to
death) hinrichten

execution /eksɪ'kju:ʃn/ n (see **execute**)
Ausführung f; Hinrichtung f. ~**er** n
Scharfrichter m

executive /ɪg'zekjʊtɪv/ a leitend □ n lei-
tende(r) Angestellte(r) m/f; (Pol) Exekutive f

executor /ɪg'zekjʊtə(r)/ n (Jur)
Testamentsvollstrecker m

exemplary /ɪg'zemplərɪ/ a beispielhaft;
(as a warning) exemplarisch

exemplify /ɪg'zemplɪfaɪ/ vt (pt/pp -**ied**)
veranschaulichen

exempt /ɪg'zempt/ a befreit □ vt befreien
(**from** von). ~**ion** /-empʃn/ n Befreiung f

exercise /'eksəsaɪz/ n Übung f; physical
~ körperliche Bewegung f; **take** ~ sich
bewegen □ vt (use) ausüben; bewegen
⟨horse⟩; spazieren führen ⟨dog⟩ □ vi sich
bewegen. ~ **book** n [Schul]heft nt

exert /ɪg'zɜ:t/ vt ausüben; ~ **oneself** sich
anstrengen. ~**ion** /-ɜ:ʃn/ n Anstrengung
f

exhale /eks'heɪl/ vt/i ausatmen

exhaust /ɪg'zɔ:st/ n (Auto) Auspuff m;
(pipe) Auspuffrohr nt; (fumes) Abgase pl
□ vt erschöpfen. ~**ed** a erschöpft. ~**ing** a
anstrengend. ~**ion** /-ɔ:stʃn/ n Erschöp-
fung f. ~**ive** /-ɪv/ a (fig) erschöpfend

exhibit /ɪg'zɪbɪt/ n Ausstellungsstück nt;
(Jur) Beweisstück nt □ vt ausstellen; (fig)
zeigen

exhibition /eksɪ'bɪʃn/ n Ausstellung f;
(Univ) Stipendium nt. ~**ist** n Exhibi-
tionist(in) m(f)

exhibitor /ɪg'zɪbɪtə(r)/ n Aussteller m

exhilarat|ed /ɪg'zɪləreɪtɪd/ a be-
schwingt. ~**ing** a berauschend. ~**ion**
/-'reɪʃn/ n Hochgefühl nt

exhort /ɪg'zɔ:t/ vt ermahnen

exhume /ɪg'zju:m/ vt exhumieren

exile /'eksaɪl/ n Exil nt; (person) im Exil
Lebende(r) m/f □ vt ins Exil schicken

exist /ɪg'zɪst/ vi bestehen, existieren.
~**ence** /-əns/ n Existenz f; **be in** ~**ence**
existieren

exit /'eksɪt/ n Ausgang m; (Auto) Ausfahrt
f; (Theat) Abgang m □ vi (Theat) abgehen.
~ **visa** n Ausreisevisum nt

exonerate /ɪg'zɒnəreɪt/ vt entlasten

exorbitant /ɪg'zɔ:bɪtənt/ a übermäßig
hoch

exorcize /'eksɔ:saɪz/ vt austreiben

exotic /ɪg'zɒtɪk/ a exotisch

expand /ɪk'spænd/ vt ausdehnen; (explain
better) weiter ausführen □ vi sich ausdehnen; (Comm) expandieren; ~ **on** (fig)
weiter ausführen

expans|e /ɪkˈspæns/ *n* Weite *f*. **∼ion** /-ænʃn/ *n* Ausdehnung *f*; (*Techn, Pol, Comm*) Expansion *f*. **∼ive** /-ɪv/ *a* mitteilsam

expatriate /eksˈpætrɪət/ *n* **be an ∼** im Ausland leben

expect /ɪkˈspekt/ *vt* erwarten; (*suppose*) annehmen; **I ∼ so** wahrscheinlich; **we ∼ to arrive on Monday** wir rechnen damit, dass wir am Montag ankommen

expectan|cy /ɪkˈspektənsɪ/ *n* Erwartung *f*. **∼t** *a*, **-ly** *adv* erwartungsvoll; **∼t mother** werdende Mutter *f*

expectation /ɪkspekˈteɪʃn/ *n* Erwartung *f*; **∼ of life** Lebenserwartung *f*

expedient /ɪkˈspiːdɪənt/ *a* zweckdienlich

expedite /ˈekspɪdaɪt/ *vt* beschleunigen

expedition /ekspɪˈdɪʃn/ *n* Expedition *f*. **∼ary** *a* (*Mil*) Expeditions-

expel /ɪkˈspel/ *vt* (*pt/pp* **expelled**) ausweisen (**from** aus); (*from school*) von der Schule verweisen

expend /ɪkˈspend/ *vt* aufwenden. **∼able** /-əbl/ *a* entbehrlich

expenditure /ɪkˈspendɪtʃə(r)/ *n* Ausgaben *pl*

expense /ɪkˈspens/ *n* Kosten *pl*; **business ∼s** *pl* Spesen *pl*; **at my ∼** auf meine Kosten; **at the ∼ of** (*fig*) auf Kosten (+ *gen*)

expensive /ɪkˈspensɪv/ *a*, **-ly** *adv* teuer

experience /ɪkˈspɪərɪəns/ *n* Erfahrung *f*; (*event*) Erlebnis *nt* □ *vt* erleben. **∼d** *a* erfahren

experiment /ɪkˈsperɪmənt/ *n* Versuch *m*, Experiment *nt* □ /-ment/ *vi* experimentieren. **∼al** /-ˈmentl/ *a* experimentell

expert /ˈekspɜːt/ *a*, **-ly** *adv* fachmännisch □ *n* Fachmann *m*, Experte *m*

expertise /ekspɜːˈtiːz/ *n* Sachkenntnis *f*; (*skill*) Geschick *nt*

expire /ɪkˈspaɪə(r)/ *vi* ablaufen

expiry /ɪkˈspaɪərɪ/ *n* Ablauf *m*. **∼ date** *n* Verfallsdatum *nt*

explain /ɪkˈspleɪn/ *vt* erklären

explana|tion /ekspləˈneɪʃn/ *n* Erklärung *f*. **∼tory** /ɪkˈsplænətərɪ/ *a* erklärend

expletive /ɪkˈspliːtɪv/ *n* Kraftausdruck *m*

explicit /ɪkˈsplɪsɪt/ *a*, **-ly** *adv* deutlich

explode /ɪkˈspləʊd/ *vi* explodieren □ *vt* zur Explosion bringen

exploit[1] /ˈeksplɔɪt/ *n* [Helden]tat *f*

exploit[2] /ɪkˈsplɔɪt/ *vt* ausbeuten. **∼ation** /eksplɔɪˈteɪʃn/ *n* Ausbeutung *f*

explora|tion /ekspləˈreɪʃn/ *n* Erforschung *f*. **∼tory** /ɪkˈsplɒrətərɪ/ *a* Probe-

explore /ɪkˈsplɔː(r)/ *vt* erforschen. **∼r** *n* Forschungsreisende(r) *m*

explos|ion /ɪkˈspləʊʒn/ *n* Explosion *f*. **∼ive** /-sɪv/ *a* explosiv □ *n* Sprengstoff *m*

exponent /ɪkˈspəʊnənt/ *n* Vertreter *m*

export[1] /ˈekspɔːt/ *n* Export *m*, Ausfuhr *f*

export[2] /ɪkˈspɔːt/ *vt* exportieren, ausführen. **∼er** *n* Exporteur *m*

expos|e /ɪkˈspəʊz/ *vt* freilegen; (*to danger*) aussetzen (**to** *dat*); (*reveal*) aufdecken; (*Phot*) belichten. **∼ure** /-ʒə(r)/ *n* Aussetzung *f*; (*Med*) Unterkühlung *f*; (*Phot*) Belichtung *f*; **24 ∼ures** 24 Aufnahmen

expound /ɪkˈspaʊnd/ *vt* erläutern

express /ɪkˈspres/ *a* ausdrücklich; (*purpose*) fest □ *adv* (*send*) per Eilpost □ *n* (*train*) Schnellzug *m* □ *vt* ausdrücken; **∼ oneself** sich ausdrücken. **∼ion** /-ʃn/ *n* Ausdruck *m*. **∼ive** /-ɪv/ *a* ausdrucksvoll. **∼ly** *adv* ausdrücklich

expulsion /ɪkˈspʌlʃn/ *n* Ausweisung *f*; (*Sch*) Verweisung *f* von der Schule

expurgate /ˈekspəgeɪt/ *vt* zensieren

exquisite /ekˈskwɪzɪt/ *a* erlesen

ex-ˈserviceman *n* Veteran *m*

extempore /ɪkˈstempərɪ/ *adv* (*speak*) aus dem Stegreif

extend /ɪkˈstend/ *vt* verlängern; (*stretch out*) ausstrecken; (*enlarge*) vergrößern □ *vi* sich ausdehnen; (*table:*) sich ausziehen lassen

extension /ɪkˈstenʃn/ *n* Verlängerung *f*; (*to house*) Anbau *m*; (*Teleph*) Nebenanschluss *m*; **∼ 7** Apparat 7

extensive /ɪkˈstensɪv/ *a* weit; (*fig*) umfassend. **∼ly** *adv* viel

extent /ɪkˈstent/ *n* Ausdehnung *f*; (*scope*) Ausmaß *nt*, Umfang *m*; **to a certain ∼** in gewissem Maße

extenuating /ɪkˈstenjʊeɪtɪŋ/ *a* mildernd

exterior /ɪkˈstɪərɪə(r)/ *a* äußere(r,s) □ *n* **the ∼** das Äußere

exterminat|e /ɪkˈstɜːmɪneɪt/ *vt* ausrotten. **∼ion** /-ˈneɪʃn/ *n* Ausrottung *f*

external /ɪkˈstɜːnl/ *a* äußere(r,s); **for ∼ use only** (*Med*) nur äußerlich. **∼ly** *adv* äußerlich

extinct /ɪkˈstɪŋkt/ *a* ausgestorben; (*volcano*) erloschen. **∼ion** /-ɪŋkʃn/ *n* Aussterben *nt*

extinguish /ɪkˈstɪŋgwɪʃ/ *vt* löschen. **∼er** *n* Feuerlöscher *m*

extol /ɪkˈstəʊl/ *vt* (*pt/pp* **extolled**) preisen

extort /ɪkˈstɔːt/ *vt* erpressen. **∼ion** /-ɔːʃn/ *n* Erpressung *f*

extortionate /ɪkˈstɔːʃənət/ *a* übermäßig hoch

extra /ˈekstrə/ *a* zusätzlich □ *adv* extra; (*especially*) besonders; **∼ strong** extrastark □ *n* (*Theat*) Statist(in) *m(f)*; **∼s** *pl* Nebenkosten *pl*; (*Auto*) Extras *pl*

extract¹ /'ekstrækt/ n Auszug m; (Culin) Extrakt m

extract² /ɪk'strækt/ vt herausziehen; ziehen ⟨tooth⟩; (fig) erzwingen. ~or [fan] n Entlüfter m

extradit|e /'ekstrədaɪt/ vt (Jur) ausliefern. ~ion /-'dɪʃn/ n (Jur) Auslieferung f

extra'marital a außerehelich

extraordinary /ɪk'strɔːdɪnərɪ/ a, -ily adv außerordentlich; (strange) seltsam

extravagan|ce /ɪk'strævəgəns/ n Verschwendung f; an ~ce ein Luxus m. ~t a verschwenderisch; (exaggerated) extravagant

extrem|e /ɪk'striːm/ a äußerste(r,s); (fig) extrem □ n Extrem nt; in the ~e im höchsten Grade. ~ely adv äußerst. ~ist n Extremist m

extremit|y /ɪk'stremətɪ/ n (distress) Not f; the ~ies pl die Extremitäten pl

extricate /'ekstrɪkeɪt/ vt befreien

extrovert /'ekstrəvɜːt/ n extravertierter Mensch m

exuberant /ɪg'zjuːbərənt/ a überglücklich

exude /ɪg'zjuːd/ vt absondern; (fig) ausstrahlen

exult /ɪg'zʌlt/ vi frohlocken

eye /aɪ/ n Auge nt; (of needle) Öhr nt; (for hook) Öse f; keep an ~ on aufpassen auf (+ acc); see ~ to ~ einer Meinung sein □ vt (pt/pp eyed, pres p ey[e]ing) ansehen

eye: ~ball n Augapfel m. ~brow n Augenbraue f. ~lash n Wimper f. ~let /-lɪt/ n Öse f. ~lid n Augenlid nt. ~shadow n Lidschatten m. ~sight n Sehkraft f. ~sore n (fam) Schandfleck m. ~tooth n Eckzahn m. ~witness n Augenzeuge m

F

fable /'feɪbl/ n Fabel f

fabric /'fæbrɪk/ n Stoff m; (fig) Gefüge nt

fabrication /fæbrɪ'keɪʃn/ n Erfindung f

fabulous /'fæbjʊləs/ a (fam) phantastisch

façade /fə'sɑːd/ n Fassade f

face /feɪs/ n Gesicht nt; (grimace) Grimasse f; (surface) Fläche f; (of clock) Zifferblatt nt; pull ~s Gesichter schneiden; in the ~ of angesichts (+ gen); on the ~ of it allem Anschein nach □ vt/i gegenüberstehen (+ dat); ~ north ⟨house:⟩ nach Norden liegen; ~ me! sieh mich an! ~ the fact that sich damit abfinden, dass; ~ up to s.o. jdm die Stirn bieten

face: ~-flannel n Waschlappen m. ~less a anonym. ~-lift n Gesichtsstraffung f

facet /'fæsɪt/ n Facette f; (fig) Aspekt m

facetious /fə'siːʃəs/ a, -ly adv spöttisch

'face value n Nennwert m

facial /'feɪʃl/ a Gesichts-

facile /'fæsaɪl/ a oberflächlich

facilitate /fə'sɪlɪteɪt/ vt erleichtern

facilit|y /fə'sɪlətɪ/ n Leichtigkeit f; (skill) Gewandtheit f; ~ies pl Einrichtungen pl

facing /'feɪsɪŋ/ n Besatz m

facsimile /fæk'sɪmәlɪ/ n Faksimile nt

fact /fækt/ n Tatsache f; in ~ tatsächlich; (actually) eigentlich

faction /'fækʃn/ n Gruppe f

factor /'fæktə(r)/ n Faktor m

factory /'fæktərɪ/ n Fabrik f

factual /'fæktʃʊəl/ a, -ly adv sachlich

faculty /'fækəltɪ/ n Fähigkeit f; (Univ) Fakultät f

fad /fæd/ n Fimmel m

fade /feɪd/ vi verblassen; ⟨material:⟩ verbleichen; ⟨sound:⟩ abklingen; ⟨flower:⟩ verwelken. ~ in/out vt (Radio, TV) ein-/ausblenden

fag /fæg/ n (chore) Plage f; (fam: cigarette) Zigarette f; (Amer sl) Homosexuelle(r) m

fagged /fægd/ a ~ out (fam) völlig erledigt

Fahrenheit /'færənhaɪt/ a Fahrenheit

fail /feɪl/ n without ~ unbedingt □ vi ⟨attempt:⟩ scheitern; ⟨grow weak⟩ nachlassen; ⟨break down⟩ versagen; (in exam) durchfallen; ~ to do sth etw nicht tun; he ~ed to break the record es gelang ihm nicht, den Rekord zu brechen □ vt nicht bestehen ⟨exam⟩; durchfallen lassen ⟨candidate⟩; (disappoint) enttäuschen; words ~ me ich weiß nicht, was ich sagen soll

failing /'feɪlɪŋ/ n Fehler m □ prep ~ that andernfalls

failure /'feɪljə(r)/ n Misserfolg m; (breakdown) Versagen nt; (person) Versager m

faint /feɪnt/ a (-er, -est), -ly adv schwach; I feel ~ mir ist schwach □ n Ohnmacht f □ vi ohnmächtig werden

faint: ~-'hearted a zaghaft. ~ness n Schwäche f

fair¹ /feə(r)/ n Jahrmarkt m; (Comm) Messe f

fair² a (-er, -est) ⟨hair⟩ blond; ⟨skin⟩ hell; ⟨weather⟩ heiter; (just) gerecht, fair; (quite good) ziemlich gut; (Sch) genügend; a ~ amount ziemlich viel □ adv play ~ fair sein. ~ly adv gerecht; (rather) ziemlich. ~ness n Blondheit f; Helle f; Gerechtigkeit f; (Sport) Fairness f

fairy /'feərɪ/ n Elfe f; **good/wicked ~** gute/böse Fee f. **~ story**, **~tale** n Märchen nt

faith /feɪθ/ n Glaube m; (trust) Vertrauen nt (**in** zu); **in good ~** in gutem Glauben

faithful /'feɪθfl/ a, **-ly** adv treu; (exact) genau; **Yours ~ly** Hochachtungsvoll. **~ness** n Treue f; Genauigkeit f

'faith-healer n Gesundbeter(in) m(f)

fake /feɪk/ a falsch □ n Fälschung f; (person) Schwindler m □ vt fälschen; (pretend) vortäuschen

falcon /'fɔːlkən/ n Falke m

fall /fɔːl/ n Fall m; (heavy) Sturz m; (in prices) Fallen nt; (Amer: autumn) Herbst m; **have a ~** fallen □ vi (pt fell, pp fallen) fallen; (heavily) stürzen; (night:) anbrechen; **~ in love** sich verlieben; **~ back on** zurückgreifen auf (+ acc); **~ for s.o.** (fam) sich in jdn verlieben; **~ for sth** (fam) sich auf etw (acc) hereinfallen. **~ about** vi (with laughter) sich [vor Lachen] kringeln. **~ down** vi umfallen; (thing:) herunterfallen; (building:) einstürzen. **~ in** vi hineinfallen; (collapse) einfallen; (Mil) antreten; **~ in with** sich anschließen (+ dat). **~ off** vi herunterfallen; (diminish) abnehmen. **~ out** vi herausfallen; (hair:) ausfallen; (quarrel) sich überwerfen. **~ over** vi hinfallen. **~ through** vi durchfallen; (plan:) ins Wasser fallen

fallacy /'fæləsɪ/ n Irrtum m

fallible /'fæləbl/ a fehlbar

'fall-out n [radioaktiver] Niederschlag m

fallow /'fæləʊ/ a **lie ~** brachliegen

false /fɔːls/ a falsch; (artificial) künstlich; **~ start** (Sport) Fehlstart m. **~hood** n Unwahrheit f. **~ly** adv falsch. **~ness** n Falschheit f

false 'teeth npl [künstliches] Gebiss nt

falsify /'fɔːlsɪfaɪ/ vt (pt/pp -ied) fälschen; (misrepresent) verfälschen

falter /'fɔːltə(r)/ vi zögern; (stumble) straucheln

fame /feɪm/ n Ruhm m. **~d** a berühmt

familiar /fə'mɪljə(r)/ a vertraut; (known) bekannt; **too ~** familiär. **~ity** /-lɪ'ærətɪ/ n Vertrautheit f. **~ize** vt vertraut machen (**with** mit)

family /'fæməlɪ/ n Familie f

family: ~ al'lowance n Kindergeld nt. **~ 'doctor** n Hausarzt m. **~ 'life** n Familienleben nt. **~ 'planning** n Familienplanung f. **~ 'tree** n Stammbaum m

famine /'fæmɪn/ n Hungersnot f

famished /'fæmɪʃt/ a sehr hungrig

famous /'feɪməs/ a berühmt

fan¹ /fæn/ n Fächer m; (Techn) Ventilator m □ v (pt/pp fanned) □ vt fächeln; **~ one-self** sich fächeln □ vi **~ out** sich fächerförmig ausbreiten

fan² n (admirer) Fan m

fanatic /fə'nætɪk/ n Fanatiker m. **~al** a, **-ly** adv fanatisch. **~ism** /-sɪzm/ n Fanatismus m

'fan belt n Keilriemen m

fanciful /'fænsɪfl/ a phantastisch; (imaginative) phantasiereich

fancy /'fænsɪ/ n Phantasie f; **have a ~ to** Lust haben, zu; **I have taken a real ~ to him** er hat es mir angetan □ a ausgefallen; **~ cakes and biscuits** Feingebäck nt □ vt (believe) meinen; (imagine) sich (dat) einbilden; (fam: want) Lust haben auf (+ acc); **~ that!** stell dir vor! (really) tatsächlich! **~ 'dress** n Kostüm m

fanfare /'fænfeə(r)/ n Fanfare f

fang /fæŋ/ n Fangzahn m; (of snake) Giftzahn m

fan: ~ heater n Heizlüfter m. **~light** n Oberlicht nt

fantas|ize /'fæntəsaɪz/ vi phantasieren. **~tic** /-'tæstɪk/ a phantastisch. **~y** n Phantasie f; (Mus) Fantasie f

far /fɑː(r)/ adv weit; (much) viel; **by ~** bei weitem; **~ away** weit weg; **as ~ as I know** soviel ich weiß; **as ~ as the church** bis zur Kirche □ a **the ~ end** am anderen Ende; **the F~ East** der Ferne Osten

farc|e /fɑːs/ n Farce f. **~ical** a lächerlich

fare /feə(r)/ n Fahrpreis m; (money) Fahrgeld nt; (food) Kost f; **air ~** Flugpreis m. **~-dodger** /-dɒdʒə(r)/ n Schwarzfahrer m

farewell /feə'wel/ int (liter) lebe wohl! □ n Lebewohl nt; **~ dinner** Abschiedsessen nt

far-'fetched a weit hergeholt; **be ~** an den Haaren herbeigezogen sein

farm /fɑːm/ n Bauernhof m □ vi Landwirtschaft betreiben □ vt bewirtschaften (land). **~er** n Landwirt m

farm: ~house n Bauernhaus nt. **~ing** n Landwirtschaft f. **~yard** n Hof m

far: ~-'reaching a weit reichend. **~-'sighted** a (fig) umsichtig; (Amer: long-sighted) weitsichtig

fart /fɑːt/ n (vulg) Furz m □ vi (vulg) furzen

farther /'fɑːðə(r)/ adv weiter; **~ off** weiter entfernt □ a **at the ~ end** am anderen Ende

fascinat|e /'fæsɪneɪt/ vt faszinieren. **~ing** a faszinierend. **~ion** /-'neɪʃn/ n Faszination f

fascis|m /'fæʃɪzm/ n Faschismus m. **~t** n Faschist m □ a faschistisch

fashion /'fæʃn/ *n* Mode *f*; (*manner*) Art *f*
□ *vt* machen; (*mould*) formen. ~**able**
/-əbl/ *a*, -**bly** *adv* modisch; **be** ~**able**
Mode sein

fast[1] /fɑːst/ *a* & *adv* (-**er**, -**est**) schnell;
(*firm*) fest; (*colour*) waschecht; **be** ~
(*clock:*) vorgehen; **be** ~ **asleep** fest schlafen

fast[2] *n* Fasten □ *vi* fasten

'**fastback** *n* (*Auto*) Fließheck *nt*

fasten /'fɑːsn/ *vt* zumachen; (*fix*) befestigen (**to** an + *dat*); ~ **one's seatbelt** sich
anschnallen. ~**er** *n*, ~**ing** *n* Verschluss
m

fastidious /fə'stɪdɪəs/ *a* wählerisch; (*particular*) penibel

fat /fæt/ *a* (**fatter, fattest**) dick; (*meat*) fett
□ *n* Fett *nt*

fatal /'feɪtl/ *a* tödlich; (*error*) verhängnis-
voll. ~**ism** /-təlɪzm/ *n* Fatalismus *m*. ~**ist**
/-təlist/ *n* Fatalist *m*. ~**ity** /fə'tælətɪ/ *n*
Todesopfer *nt*. ~**ly** /-təli/ *adv* tödlich

fate /feɪt/ *n* Schicksal *nt*. ~**ful** *a* verhäng-
nisvoll

'**fat-head** *n* (*fam*) Dummkopf *m*

father /'fɑːðə(r)/ *n* Vater *m*; **F** ~
Christmas der Weihnachtsmann □ *vt*
zeugen

father: ~**hood** *n* Vaterschaft *f*. ~**-in-law**
n (*pl* ~**s-in-law**) Schwiegervater *m*. ~**ly**
a väterlich

fathom /'fæðəm/ *n* (*Naut*) Faden *m* □ *vt*
verstehen; ~ **out** ergründen

fatigue /fə'tiːg/ *n* Ermüdung *f* □ *vt* ermüden

fatten /'fætn/ *vt* mästen (*animal*). ~**ing** *a*
cream is ~**ing** Sahne macht dick

fatty /'fætɪ/ *a* fett; (*foods*) fetthaltig

fatuous /'fætjʊəs/ *a*, -**ly** *adv* albern

faucet /'fɔːsɪt/ *n* (*Amer*) Wasserhahn *m*

fault /fɔːlt/ *n* Fehler *m*; (*Techn*) Defekt *m*;
(*Geol*) Verwerfung *f*; **at** ~ im Unrecht;
find ~ **with** etwas auszusetzen haben an
(+ *dat*); **it's your** ~ du bist schuld □ *vt*
etwas auszusetzen haben an (+ *dat*).
~**less** *a*, -**ly** *adv* fehlerfrei

faulty /'fɔːltɪ/ *a* fehlerhaft

fauna /'fɔːnə/ *n* Fauna *f*

favour /'feɪvə(r)/ *n* Gunst *f*; **I am in** ~ ich
bin dafür; **do s.o. a** ~ jdm einen Gefallen
tun □ *vt* begünstigen; (*prefer*) bevorzugen.
~**able** /-əbl/ *a*, -**bly** *adv* günstig; (*reply*)
positiv

favourit|e /'feɪvərɪt/ *a* Lieblings- □ *n*
Liebling *m*; (*Sport*) Favorit(in) *m(f)*. ~**ism**
n Bevorzugung *f*

fawn[1] /fɔːn/ *a* rehbraun □ *n* Hirschkalb *nt*

fawn[2] *vi* sich einschmeicheln (**on** bei)

fax /fæks/ *n* Fax *nt* □ *vt* faxen (**s.o.** jdm). ~
machine *n* Faxgerät *nt*

fear /fɪə(r)/ *n* Furcht *f*, Angst *f* (**of** vor
+ *dat*); **no** ~! (*fam*) keine Angst! □ *vt/i*
fürchten

fear|ful /'fɪəfl/ *a* besorgt; (*awful*) furcht-
bar. ~**less** *a*, -**ly** *adv* furchtlos. ~**some**
/-səm/ *a* Furcht erregend

feas|ibility /fiːzə'bɪlətɪ/ *n* Durchführbar-
keit *f*. ~**ible** *a* durchführbar; (*possible*)
möglich

feast /fiːst/ *n* Festmahl *nt*; (*Relig*) Fest *nt*
□ *vi* ~ [**on**] schmausen

feat /fiːt/ *n* Leistung *f*

feather /'feðə(r)/ *n* Feder *f*

feature /'fiːtʃə(r)/ *n* Gesichtszug *m*;
(*quality*) Merkmal *nt*; (*Journ*) Feature *nt*
□ *vt* darstellen; (*film:*) in der Hauptrolle
zeigen. ~ **film** *n* Hauptfilm *m*

February /'februərɪ/ *n* Februar *m*

feckless /'feklɪs/ *a* verantwortungslos

fed /fed/ *see* **feed** □ *a* **be** ~ **up** (*fam*) die
Nase voll haben (**with** von)

federal /'fedərəl/ *a* Bundes-

federation /fedə'reɪʃn/ *n* Föderation *f*

fee /fiː/ *n* Gebühr *f*; (*professional*) Honorar
nt

feeble /'fiːbl/ *a* (-**r**, -**st**), -**bly** *adv* schwach

feed /fiːd/ *n* Futter *nt*; (*for baby*) Essen
nt □ *v* (*pt/pp* **fed**) □ *vt* füttern; (*support*)
ernähren; (*into machine*) eingeben;
speisen (*computer*) □ *vi* sich ernähren (**on**
von)

'**feedback** *n* Feedback *nt*

feel /fiːl/ *v* (*pt/pp* **felt**) □ *vt* fühlen; (*experience*) empfinden; (*think*) meinen □ *vi* sich
fühlen; ~ **soft/hard** sich weich/hart anfühlen; **I** ~ **hot/ill** mir ist heiß/schlecht;
I don't ~ **like it** ich habe keine Lust dazu.
~**er** *n* Fühler *m*. ~**ing** *n* Gefühl *nt*; **no
hard** ~**ings** nichts für ungut

feet /fiːt/ *see* **foot**

feign /feɪn/ *vt* vortäuschen

feint /feɪnt/ *n* Finte *f*

feline /'fiːlaɪn/ *a* Katzen-; (*catlike*) katzen-
artig

fell[1] /fel/ *vt* fällen

fell[2] *see* **fall**

fellow /'feləʊ/ *n* (*of society*) Mitglied *nt*;
(*fam: man*) Kerl *m*

fellow: ~-'**countryman** *n* Landsmann *m*.
~ **men** *pl* Mitmenschen *pl*. ~**ship** *n* Kameradschaft *f*; (*group*) Gesellschaft *f*

felony /'felənɪ/ *n* Verbrechen *nt*

felt[1] /felt/ *see* **feel**

felt[2] *n* Filz *m*. ~[**-tipped**] '**pen** *n* Filzstift
m

female /'fi:meɪl/ *a* weiblich □ *nt* Weibchen *nt*; (*pej: woman*) Weib *nt*

femin|ine /'femɪnɪn/ *a* weiblich □ *n* (*Gram*) Femininum *nt*. ~**inity** /-'nɪnɪtɪ/ *n* Weiblichkeit *f*. ~**ist** *a* feministisch □ *n* Feminist(in) *m(f)*

fenc|e /fens/ *n* Zaun *m*; (*fam: person*) Hehler *m* □ *vi* (*Sport*) fechten □ *vt* ~ **e in** einzäunen. ~**er** *n* Fechter *m*. ~**ing** *n* Zaun *m*; (*Sport*) Fechten *nt*

fend /fend/ *vi* ~ **for oneself** sich allein durchschlagen. ~ **off** *vt* abwehren

fender /'fendə(r)/ *n* Kaminvorsetzer *m*; (*Naut*) Fender *m*; (*Amer: wing*) Kotflügel *m*

fennel /'fenl/ *n* Fenchel *m*

ferment[1] /'fɜ:ment/ *n* Erregung *f*

ferment[2] /fə'ment/ *vi* gären □ *vt* gären lassen. ~**ation** /fɜ:men'teɪʃn/ *n* Gärung *f*

fern /fɜ:n/ *n* Farn *m*

feroc|ious /fə'rəʊʃəs/ *a* wild. ~**ity** /-'rɒsətɪ/ *n* Wildheit *f*

ferret /'ferɪt/ *n* Frettchen *nt*

ferry /'ferɪ/ *n* Fähre *f* □ *vt* ~ [**across**] übersetzen

fertil|e /'fɜ:taɪl/ *a* fruchtbar. ~**ity** /fɜ:-'tɪlətɪ/ *n* Fruchtbarkeit *f*

fertilize /'fɜ:təlaɪz/ *vt* befruchten; düngen ⟨*land*⟩. ~**r** *n* Dünger *m*

fervent /'fɜ:vənt/ *a* leidenschaftlich

fervour /'fɜ:və(r)/ *n* Leidenschaft *f*

fester /'festə(r)/ *vi* eitern

festival /'festɪvl/ *n* Fest *nt*; (*Mus, Theat*) Festspiele *pl*

festiv|e /'festɪv/ *a* festlich; ~**e season** Festzeit. *f*. ~**ities** /fe'stɪvətɪz/ *npl* Feierlichkeiten *pl*

festoon /fe'stu:n/ *vt* behängen (**with** mit)

fetch /fetʃ/ *vt* holen; (*collect*) abholen; (*be sold for*) einbringen

fetching /'fetʃɪŋ/ *a* anziehend

fête /feɪt/ *n* Fest *nt* □ *vt* feiern

fetish /'fetɪʃ/ *n* Fetisch *m*

fetter /'fetə(r)/ *vt* fesseln

fettle /'fetl/ *n* **in fine** ~ in bester Form

feud /fju:d/ *n* Fehde *f*

feudal /'fju:dl/ *a* Feudal-

fever /'fi:və(r)/ *n* Fieber *nt*. ~**ish** *a* fiebrig; (*fig*) fieberhaft

few /fju:/ *a* (-**er**, -**est**) wenige; **every** ~ **days** alle paar Tage □ *n* **a** ~ ein paar; **quite a** ~ ziemlich viele

fiancé /fɪ'ɒnseɪ/ *n* Verlobte(r) *m*. **fiancée** *n* Verlobte *f*

fiasco /fɪ'æskəʊ/ *n* Fiasko *nt*

fib /fɪb/ *n* kleine Lüge; **tell a** ~ schwindeln

fibre /'faɪbə(r)/ *n* Faser *f*

fickle /'fɪkl/ *a* unbeständig

fiction /'fɪkʃn/ *n* Erfindung *f*; [**works of**] ~ Erzählungsliteratur *f*. ~**al** *a* [frei] erfunden

fictitious /fɪk'tɪʃəs/ *a* [frei] erfunden

fiddle /'fɪdl/ *n* (*fam*) Geige *f*; (*cheating*) Schwindel *m* □ *vi* herumspielen (**with** mit) □ *vt* (*fam*) frisieren ⟨*accounts*⟩; (*arrange*) arrangieren

fiddly /'fɪdlɪ/ *a* knifflig

fidelity /fɪ'delətɪ/ *n* Treue *f*

fidget /'fɪdʒɪt/ *vi* zappeln. ~**y** *a* zappelig

field /fi:ld/ *n* Feld *nt*; (*meadow*) Wiese *f*; (*subject*) Gebiet *nt*

field: ~ **events** *npl* Sprung- und Wurfdisziplinen *pl*. ~**glasses** *npl* Feldstecher *m*. **F**~ '**Marshal** *n* Feldmarschall *m*. ~**work** *n* Feldforschung *f*

fiend /fi:nd/ *n* Teufel *m*. ~**ish** *a* teuflisch

fierce /fɪəs/ *a* (-**r**, -**st**), -**ly** *adv* wild; (*fig*) heftig. ~**ness** *n* Wildheit *f*; (*fig*) Heftigkeit *f*

fiery /'faɪərɪ/ *a* (-**ier**, -**iest**) feurig

fifteen /fɪf'ti:n/ *a* fünfzehn □ *n* Fünfzehn *f*. ~**th** *a* fünfzehnte(r,s)

fifth /fɪfθ/ *a* fünfte(r,s)

fiftieth /'fɪftɪɪθ/ *a* fünfzigste(r,s)

fifty /'fɪftɪ/ *a* fünfzig

fig /fɪg/ *n* Feige *f*

fight /faɪt/ *n* Kampf *m*; (*brawl*) Schlägerei *f*; (*between children, dogs*) Rauferei *f* □ *v* (*pt/pp* **fought**) □ *vt* kämpfen gegen; (*fig*) bekämpfen □ *vi* kämpfen; (*brawl*) sich schlagen; ⟨*children, dogs:*⟩ sich raufen. ~**er** *n* Kämpfer *m*; (*Aviat*) Jagdflugzeug *nt*. ~**ing** *n* Kampf *m*

figment /'fɪgmənt/ *n* ~ **of the imagination** Hirngespinst *nt*

figurative /'fɪgjərətɪv/ *a*, -**ly** *adv* bildlich, übertragen

figure /'fɪgə(r)/ *n* (*digit*) Ziffer *f*; (*number*) Zahl *f*; (*sum*) Summe *f*; (*carving, sculpture, woman's*) Figur *f*; (*form*) Gestalt *f*; (*illustration*) Abbildung *f*; ~ **of speech** Redefigur *f*; **good at** ~**s** gut im Rechnen □ *vi* (*appear*) erscheinen □ *vt* (*Amer: think*) glauben. ~ **out** *vt* ausrechnen

figure: ~**head** *n* Galionsfigur *f*; (*fig*) Repräsentationsfigur *f*. ~ **skating** *n* Eiskunstlauf *m*

filament /'fɪləmənt/ *n* Faden *m*; (*Electr*) Glühfaden *m*

filch /fɪltʃ/ *vt* (*fam*) klauen

file[1] /faɪl/ *n* Akte *f*; (*for documents*) [Akten]ordner *m* □ *vt* ablegen ⟨*documents*⟩; (*Jur*) einreichen

file[2] *n* (*line*) Reihe *f*; **in single** ~ im Gänsemarsch

file[3] *n* (*Techn*) Feile *f* □ *vt* feilen

filigree /'fɪlɪgri:/ *n* Filigran *nt*

filings /'faɪlɪŋz/ *npl* Feilspäne *pl*

fill /fɪl/ n eat one's ~ sich satt essen □ vt füllen; plombieren ⟨tooth⟩ □ vi sich füllen. ~ **in** vt auffüllen; ausfüllen ⟨form⟩. ~ **out** vt ausfüllen ⟨form⟩. ~ **up** vi sich füllen □ vt vollfüllen; ⟨Auto⟩ volltanken; ausfüllen ⟨form⟩

fillet /'fɪlɪt/ n Filet nt □ vt ⟨pt/pp **filleted**⟩ entgräten

filling /'fɪlɪŋ/ n Füllung f; ⟨of tooth⟩ Plombe f. ~ **station** n Tankstelle f

filly /'fɪlɪ/ n junge Stute f

film /fɪlm/ n Film m; ⟨Culin⟩ [**cling**] ~ Klarsichtfolie f □ vt/i filmen; verfilmen ⟨book⟩. ~ **star** n Filmstar m

filter /'fɪltə(r)/ n Filter m □ vt filtern. ~ **through** vi durchsickern. ~ **tip** n Filter m; ⟨cigarette⟩ Filterzigarette f

filth /fɪlθ/ n Dreck m. ~**y** a (-ier, -iest) dreckig

fin /fɪn/ n Flosse f

final /'faɪnl/ a letzte(r,s); ⟨conclusive⟩ endgültig; ~ **result** Endresultat nt □ n ⟨Sport⟩ Finale nt, Endspiel nt; ~**s** pl ⟨Univ⟩ Abschlussprüfung f

finale /fɪ'nɑːlɪ/ n Finale nt

final|ist /'faɪnlɪst/ n Finalist(in) m(f). ~**ity** /-'nælətɪ/ n Endgültigkeit f

final|ize /'faɪnəlaɪz/ vt endgültig festlegen. ~**ly** adv schließlich

finance /faɪ'næns/ n Finanz f □ vt finanzieren

financial /faɪ'nænʃl/ a, -**ly** adv finanziell

finch /fɪntʃ/ n Fink m

find /faɪnd/ n Fund m □ vt ⟨pt/pp **found**⟩ finden; ⟨establish⟩ feststellen; **go and** ~ holen; **try to** ~ suchen; ~ **guilty** ⟨Jur⟩ schuldig sprechen. ~ **out** vt herausfinden; ⟨learn⟩ erfahren □ vi ⟨enquire⟩ sich erkundigen

findings /'faɪndɪŋz/ npl Ergebnisse pl

fine[1] /faɪn/ n Geldstrafe f □ vt zu einer Geldstrafe verurteilen

fine[2] a (-r, -st,) -**ly** adv fein; ⟨weather⟩ schön; **he's** ~ es geht ihm gut □ adv gut; **cut it** ~ ⟨fam⟩ sich ⟨dat⟩ wenig Zeit lassen. ~ **arts** npl schöne Künste pl

finery /'faɪnərɪ/ n Putz m, Staat m

finesse /fɪ'nes/ n Gewandtheit f

finger /'fɪŋgə(r)/ n Finger m □ vt anfassen

finger: ~**mark** n Fingerabdruck m. ~**nail** n Fingernagel m. ~**print** n Fingerabdruck m. ~**tip** n Fingerspitze f; **have sth at one's** ~**tips** etw im kleinen Finger haben

finicky /'fɪnɪkɪ/ a knifflig; ⟨choosy⟩ wählerisch

finish /'fɪnɪʃ/ n Schluss m; ⟨Sport⟩ Finish nt; ⟨line⟩ Ziel nt; ⟨of product⟩ Ausführung f □ vt beenden; ⟨use up⟩ aufbrauchen; ~

one's drink austrinken; ~ **reading** zu Ende lesen □ vi fertig werden; ⟨performance:⟩ zu Ende sein; ⟨runner:⟩ durchs Ziel gehen

finite /'faɪnaɪt/ a begrenzt

Finland /'fɪnlənd/ n Finnland nt

Finn /fɪn/ n Finne m/ Finnin f. ~**ish** a finnisch

fiord /fjɔːd/ n Fjord m

fir /fɜː(r)/ n Tanne f

fire /'faɪə(r)/ n Feuer nt; ⟨forest, house⟩ Brand m; **be on** ~ brennen; **catch** ~ Feuer fangen; **set** ~ **to** anzünden; ⟨arsonist:⟩ in Brand stecken; **under** ~ unter Beschuss □ vt brennen ⟨pottery⟩; abfeuern ⟨shot⟩; schießen mit ⟨gun⟩; ⟨fam: dismiss⟩ feuern □ vi schießen (**at** auf + acc); ⟨engine:⟩ anspringen

fire: ~**alarm** n Feueralarm m; ⟨apparatus⟩ Feuermelder m. ~**arm** n Schusswaffe f. ~ **brigade** n Feuerwehr f. ~**engine** n Löschfahrzeug nt. ~**escape** n Feuertreppe f. ~ **extinguisher** n Feuerlöscher m. ~**man** n Feuerwehrmann m. ~**place** n Kamin m. ~**side** n **by** or **at the** ~**side** am Kamin. ~ **station** n Feuerwache f. ~**wood** n Brennholz nt. ~**work** n Feuerwerkskörper m; ~**works** pl ⟨display⟩ Feuerwerk nt

'firing squad n Erschießungskommando nt

firm[1] /fɜːm/ n Firma f

firm[2] a (-er, -est), -**ly** adv fest; ⟨resolute⟩ entschlossen; ⟨strict⟩ streng

first /fɜːst/ a & n erste(r,s); **at** ~ zuerst; **who's** ~? wer ist der Erste? **at** ~ **sight** auf den ersten Blick; **for the** ~ **time** zum ersten Mal; **from the** ~ von Anfang an □ adv zuerst; ⟨firstly⟩ erstens

first: ~ '**aid** n erste Hilfe. ~-'**aid kit** n Verbandkasten m. ~-**class** a erstklassig; ⟨Rail⟩ erster Klasse □ /-'-/ adv ⟨travel⟩ erster Klasse. ~ e'**dition** n Erstausgabe f. ~ '**floor** n erster Stock; ⟨Amer: ground floor⟩ Erdgeschoss nt. ~**ly** adv erstens. ~ **name** n Vorname m. ~-**rate** a erstklassig

fish /fɪʃ/ n Fisch m □ vt/i fischen; ⟨with rod⟩ angeln. ~ **out** vt herausfischen

fish: ~**bone** n Gräte f. ~**erman** n Fischer m. ~**farm** n Fischzucht f. ~ '**finger** n Fischstäbchen nt

fishing /'fɪʃɪŋ/ n Fischerei f. ~ **boat** n Fischerboot nt. ~-**rod** n Angel[rute] f

fish: ~**monger** /-mʌŋgə(r)/ n Fischhändler m. ~-**slice** n Fischheber m. ~**y** a Fisch-; ⟨fam: suspicious⟩ verdächtig

fission /'fɪʃn/ n ⟨Phys⟩ Spaltung f

fist /fɪst/ n Faust f

fit[1] /fɪt/ n ⟨attack⟩ Anfall m

fit² *a* (**fitter, fittest**) ⟨*suitable*⟩ geeignet; ⟨*healthy*⟩ gesund; ⟨*Sport*⟩ fit; ~ **to eat** essbar; **keep** ~ sich fit halten; **see** ~ **es für angebracht halten (to** zu**)**

fit³ *n* (*of clothes*) Sitz *m*; **be a good** ~ gut passen □ *v* (*pt/pp* **fitted**) *vi* (*be the right size*) passen □ *vt* anbringen (**to** an + *dat*); ⟨*install*⟩ einbauen; ⟨*clothes:*⟩ passen (+ *dat*); ~ **with** versehen mit. ~ **in** *vi* hineinpassen; ⟨*adapt*⟩ sich einfügen (**with** in + *acc*) □ *vt* ⟨*accommodate*⟩ unterbringen

fit|ful /'fıtfl/ *a*, **-ly** *adv* ⟨*sleep*⟩ unruhig. **~ment** *n* Einrichtungsgegenstand *m*; ⟨*attachment*⟩ Zusatzgerät *nt*. **~ness** *n* Eignung *f*; [**physical**] **~ness** Gesundheit *f*; ⟨*Sport*⟩ Fitness *f*. ~ **ted** *a* eingebaut; ⟨*garment*⟩ tailliert

fitted: ~ **'carpet** *n* Teppichboden *m*. ~ **'cupboard** *n* Einbauschrank *m*. ~ **'kitchen** *n* Einbauküche *f*. ~ **'sheet** *n* Spannlaken *nt*

fitter /'fıtə(r)/ *n* Monteur *m*

fitting /'fıtıŋ/ *a* passend □ *n* (*of clothes*) Anprobe *f*; (*of shoes*) Weite *f*; ⟨*Techn*⟩ Zubehörteil *nt*; **~s** *pl* Zubehör *nt*. ~ **room** *n* Anprobekabine *f*

five /faıv/ *a* fünf □ *n* Fünf *f*. **~r** *n* Fünfpfundschein *m*

fix /fıks/ *n* (*sl: drugs*) Fix *m*; **be in a** ~ (*fam*) in der Klemme sitzen □ *vt* befestigen (**to** an + *dat*); ⟨*arrange*⟩ festlegen; ⟨*repair*⟩ reparieren; ⟨*Phot*⟩ fixieren; ~ **a meal** ⟨*Amer*⟩ Essen machen

fixation /fık'seıʃn/ *n* Fixierung *f*

fixed /'fıkst/ *a* fest

fixture /'fıkstʃə(r)/ *n* ⟨*Sport*⟩ Veranstaltung *f*; **~s and fittings** zu einer Wohnung gehörende Einrichtungen *pl*

fizz /fız/ *vi* sprudeln

fizzle /'fızl/ *vi* ~ **out** verpuffen

fizzy /'fızı/ *a* sprudelnd. ~ **drink** *n* Brauselimonade] *f*

flabbergasted /'flæbəgɑːstıd/ *a* **be** ~ platt sein (*fam*)

flabby /'flæbı/ *a* schlaff

flag¹ /flæg/ *n* Fahne *f*; ⟨*Naut*⟩ Flagge *f* □ *vt* (*pt/pp* **flagged**) ~ **down** anhalten ⟨*taxi*⟩

flag² *vi* (*pt/pp* **flagged**) ermüden

flagon /'flægən/ *n* Krug *m*

'flag-pole *n* Fahnenstange *f*

flagrant /'fleıgrənt/ *a* flagrant

'flagstone *n* [Pflaster]platte *f*

flair /fleə(r)/ *n* Begabung *f*

flake /fleık/ *n* Flocke *f* □ *vi* ~ [**off**] abblättern

flaky /'fleıkı/ *a* blättrig. ~ **pastry** *n* Blätterteig *m*

flamboyant /flæm'bɔıənt/ *a* extravagant

flame /fleım/ *n* Flamme *f*

flammable /'flæməbl/ *a* feuergefährlich

flan /flæn/ *n* [**fruit**] ~ Obsttorte *f*

flank /flæŋk/ *n* Flanke *f* □ *vt* flankieren

flannel /'flænl/ *n* Flanell *m*; ⟨*for washing*⟩ Waschlappen *m*

flannelette /flænə'let/ *n* ⟨*Tex*⟩ Biber *m*

flap /flæp/ *n* Klappe *f*; **in a** ~ (*fam*) aufgeregt □ *v* (*pt/pp* **flapped**) *vi* flattern; (*fam*) sich aufregen □ *vt* ~ **its wings** mit den Flügeln schlagen

flare /fleə(r)/ *n* Leuchtsignal *nt* □ *vi* ~ **up** auflodern; ⟨*fam: get angry*⟩ aufbrausen. **~d** *a* ⟨*garment*⟩ ausgestellt

flash /flæʃ/ *n* Blitz *m*; **in a** ~ (*fam*) im Nu □ *vi* blitzen; ⟨*repeatedly*⟩ blinken; ~ **past** vorbeirasen □ *vt* aufleuchten lassen; ~ **one's headlights** die Lichthupe betätigen

flash: ~back *n* Rückblende *f*. **~bulb** *n* ⟨*Phot*⟩ Blitzbirne *f*. **~er** *n* ⟨*Auto*⟩ Blinker *m*. **~light** *n* ⟨*Phot*⟩ Blitzlicht *nt*; ⟨*Amer: torch*⟩ Taschenlampe *f*. **~y** *a* auffällig

flask /flɑːsk/ *n* Flasche *f*; ⟨*Chem*⟩ Kolben *m*; ⟨*vacuum* ~⟩ Thermosflasche (P) *f*

flat /flæt/ *a* (**flatter, flattest**) flach; ⟨*surface*⟩ eben; ⟨*refusal*⟩ glatt; ⟨*beer*⟩ schal; ⟨*battery*⟩ verbraucht; ⟨*Auto*⟩ leer; ⟨*tyre*⟩ platt; ⟨*Mus*⟩ **A** ~ As *nt*; **B** ~ **B** *nt* □ *n* Wohnung *f*; ⟨*Mus*⟩ Erniedrigungszeichen *nt*; ⟨*fam: puncture*⟩ Reifenpanne *f*

flat: ~ **'feet** *npl* Plattfüße *pl*. **~-fish** *n* Plattfisch *m*. **~ly** *adv* ⟨*refuse*⟩ glatt. ~ **rate** *n* Einheitspreis *m*

flatten /'flætn/ *vt* platt drücken

flatter /'flætə(r)/ *vt* schmeicheln (+ *dat*). **~y** *n* Schmeichelei *f*

flat 'tyre *n* Reifenpanne *f*

flatulence /'flætjʊləns/ *n* Blähungen *pl*

flaunt /flɔːnt/ *vt* prunken mit

flautist /'flɔːtıst/ *n* Flötist(in) *m(f)*

flavour /'fleıvə(r)/ *n* Geschmack *m* □ *vt* abschmecken. **~ing** *n* Aroma *nt*

flaw /flɔː/ *n* Fehler *m*. **~less** *a* tadellos; ⟨*complexion*⟩ makellos

flax /flæks/ *n* Flachs *m*. **~en** *a* flachsblond

flea /fliː/ *n* Floh *m*. ~ **market** *n* Flohmarkt *m*

fleck /flek/ *n* Tupfen *m*

fled /fled/ *see* **flee**

flee /fliː/ *v* (*pt/pp* **fled**) □ *vi* fliehen (**from** vor + *dat*) □ *vt* flüchten aus

fleec|e /fliːs/ *n* Vlies *nt* □ *vt* (*fam*) schröpfen. **~y** *a* flauschig

fleet /fliːt/ *n* Flotte *f*; (*of cars*) Wagenpark *m*

fleeting /'fliːtıŋ/ *a* flüchtig

Flemish /'flemıʃ/ *a* flämisch

flesh /fleʃ/ *n* Fleisch *nt*; **in the** ~ (*fam*) in Person. **~y** *a* fleischig

flew /fluː/ *see* **fly²**

flex¹ /fleks/ *vt* anspannen ⟨*muscle*⟩

flex² *n* (*Electr*) Schnur *f*

flexib|ility /fleksə'bɪlətɪ/ *n* Biegsamkeit *f*; (*fig*) Flexibilität *f*. **~le** *a* biegsam; (*fig*) flexibel

'flexitime /'fleksɪ-/ *n* Gleitzeit *f*

flick /flɪk/ *vt* schnippen. **~ through** *vi* schnell durchblättern

flicker /'flɪkə(r)/ *vi* flackern

flier /'flaɪə(r)/ *n* = **flyer**

flight¹ /flaɪt/ *n* ⟨*fleeing*⟩ Flucht *f*; **take ~** die Flucht ergreifen

flight² *n* ⟨*flying*⟩ Flug *m*; **~ of stairs** Treppe *f*

flight: ~ path *n* Flugschneise *f*. **~ recorder** *n* Flugschreiber *m*

flighty /'flaɪtɪ/ *a* flatterhaft

flimsy /'flɪmzɪ/ *a* (**-ier, -iest**) dünn; ⟨*excuse*⟩ fadenscheinig

flinch /flɪntʃ/ *vi* zurückzucken

fling /flɪŋ/ *n* **have a ~** (*fam*) sich austoben □ *vt* (*pt/pp* **flung**) schleudern

flint /flɪnt/ *n* Feuerstein *m*

flip /flɪp/ *vt/i* schnippen; **~ through** durchblättern

flippant /'flɪpənt/ *a*, **-ly** *adv* leichtfertig

flipper /'flɪpə(r)/ *n* Flosse *f*

flirt /flɜːt/ *n* kokette Frau *f* □ *vi* flirten

flirtat|ion /flɜː'teɪʃn/ *n* Flirt *m*. **~ious** /-ʃəs/ *a* kokett

flit /flɪt/ *vi* (*pt/pp* **flitted**) flattern

float /fləʊt/ *n* Schwimmer *m*; (*in procession*) Festwagen *m*; (*money*) Wechselgeld *nt* □ *vi* ⟨*thing:*⟩ schwimmen; ⟨*person:*⟩ sich treiben lassen; (*in air*) schweben; (*Comm*) floaten

flock /flɒk/ *n* Herde *f*; (*of birds*) Schwarm *m* □ *vi* strömen

flog /flɒg/ *vt* (*pt/pp* **flogged**) auspeitschen; (*fam: sell*) verkloppen

flood /flʌd/ *n* Überschwemmung *f*; (*fig*) Flut *f*; **be in ~** ⟨*river:*⟩ Hochwasser führen □ *vt* überschwemmen □ *vi* ⟨*river:*⟩ über die Ufer treten

'floodlight *n* Flutlicht *nt* □ *vt* (*pt/pp* **floodlit**) anstrahlen

floor /flɔː(r)/ *n* Fußboden *m*; (*storey*) Stock *m* □ *vt* (*baffle*) verblüffen

floor: ~ board *n* Dielenbrett *nt*. **~-cloth** *n* Scheuertuch *nt*. **~-polish** *n* Bohnerwachs *nt*. **~ show** *n* Kabarettvorstellung *f*

flop /flɒp/ *n* (*fam*) (*failure*) Reinfall *m*; (*Theat*) Durchfall *m* □ *vi* (*pt/pp* **flopped**) (*fam*) (*fail*) durchfallen; **~ down** sich plumpsen lassen

floppy /'flɒpɪ/ *a* schlapp. **~ 'disc** *n* Diskette *f*

flora /'flɔːrə/ *n* Flora *f*

floral /'flɔːrl/ *a* Blumen-

florid /'flɒrɪd/ *a* ⟨*complexion*⟩ gerötet; ⟨*style*⟩ blumig

florist /'flɒrɪst/ *n* Blumenhändler(in) *m(f)*

flounce /flaʊns/ *n* Volant *m* □ *vi* **~ out** hinausstolzieren

flounder¹ /'flaʊndə(r)/ *vi* zappeln

flounder² *n* ⟨*fish*⟩ Flunder *f*

flour /'flaʊə(r)/ *n* Mehl *nt*

flourish /'flʌrɪʃ/ *n* große Geste *f*; (*scroll*) Schnörkel *m* □ *vi* gedeihen; (*fig*) blühen □ *vt* schwenken

floury /'flaʊərɪ/ *a* mehlig

flout /flaʊt/ *vt* missachten

flow /fləʊ/ *n* Fluss *m*; (*of traffic, blood*) Strom *m* □ *vi* fließen

flower /'flaʊə(r)/ *n* Blume *f* □ *vi* blühen

flower: ~-bed *n* Blumenbeet *nt*. **~ed** *a* geblümt. **~pot** *n* Blumentopf *m*. **~y** *a* blumig

flown /fləʊn/ *see* **fly²**

flu /fluː/ *n* (*fam*) Grippe *f*

fluctuat|e /'flʌktjʊeɪt/ *vi* schwanken. **~ion** /-'eɪʃn/ *n* Schwankung *f*

fluent /'fluːənt/ *a*, **-ly** *adv* fließend

fluff /flʌf/ *n* Fusseln *pl*; (*down*) Flaum *m*. **~y** *a* (**-ier, -iest**) flauschig

fluid /'fluːɪd/ *a* flüssig; (*fig*) veränderlich □ *n* Flüssigkeit *f*

fluke /fluːk/ *n* [glücklicher] Zufall *m*

flung /flʌŋ/ *see* **fling**

flunk /flʌŋk/ *vt/i* (*Amer, fam*) durchfallen (in + *dat*)

fluorescent /flʊə'resnt/ *a* fluoreszierend; **~ lighting** Neonbeleuchtung *f*

fluoride /'flʊəraɪd/ *n* Fluor *nt*

flurry /'flʌrɪ/ *n* (*snow*) Gestöber *nt*; (*fig*) Aufregung *f*

flush /flʌʃ/ *n* (*blush*) Erröten *nt* □ *vi* rot werden □ *vt* spülen □ *a* in einer Ebene (**with** mit); (*fam: affluent*) gut bei Kasse

flustered /'flʌstəd/ *a* nervös

flute /fluːt/ *n* Flöte *f*

flutter /'flʌtə(r)/ *n* Flattern *nt* □ *vi* flattern

flux /flʌks/ *n* **in a state of ~** im Fluss

fly¹ /flaɪ/ *n* (*pl* **flies**) Fliege *f*

fly² *v* (*pt* **flew**, *pp* **flown**) □ *vi* fliegen; ⟨*flag:*⟩ wehen; (*rush*) sausen □ *vt* fliegen; führen ⟨*flag*⟩

fly³ *n* & **flies** *pl* (*on trousers*) Hosenschlitz *m*

flyer /'flaɪə(r)/ *n* Flieger(in) *m(f)*; (*Amer: leaflet*) Flugblatt *nt*

flying: ~ 'buttress *n* Strebebogen *m*. **~ 'saucer** *n* fliegende Untertasse *f*. **~ 'visit** *n* Stippvisite *f*

fly: ∼**leaf** *n* Vorsatzblatt *nt*. ∼**over** *n* Überführung *f*

foal /fəʊl/ *n* Fohlen *nt*

foam /fəʊm/ *n* Schaum *m*; (*synthetic*) Schaumstoff *m* □ *vi* schäumen. ∼ '**rubber** *n* Schaumgummi *m*

fob /fɒb/ *vt* (*pt/pp* **fobbed**) ∼ **sth off** etw andrehen (**on** s.o. jdm); ∼ **s.o. off** jdn abspeisen (**with** mit)

focal /'fəʊkl/ *n* Brenn-

focus /'fəʊkəs/ *n* Brennpunkt *m*; **in** ∼ scharf eingestellt □ *v* (*pt/pp* **focused** *or* **focussed**) □ *vt* einstellen (**on** auf + *acc*); (*fig*) konzentrieren (**on** auf + *acc*) □ *vi* (*fig*) sich konzentrieren (**on** auf + *acc*)

fodder /'fɒdə(r)/ *n* Futter *nt*

foe /fəʊ/ *n* Feind *m*

foetus /'fi:təs/ *n* (*pl-*tuses) Fötus *m*

fog /fɒg/ *n* Nebel *m*

foggy /'fɒgɪ/ *a* (**foggier, foggiest**) neblig

'**fog-horn** *n* Nebelhorn *nt*

fogy /'fəʊgɪ/ *n* **old** ∼ alter Knacker *m*

foible /'fɔɪbl/ *n* Eigenart *f*

foil[1] /fɔɪl/ *n* Folie *f*; (*Culin*) Alufolie *f*

foil[2] *vt* (*thwart*) vereiteln

foil[3] *n* (*Fencing*) Florett *nt*

foist /fɔɪst/ *vt* andrehen (**on** s.o. jdm)

fold[1] /fəʊld/ *n* (*for sheep*) Pferch *m*

fold[2] *n* Falte *f*; (*in paper*) Kniff *m* □ *vt* falten; ∼ **one's arms** die Arme verschränken □ *vi* sich falten lassen; (*fail*) eingehen. ∼ **up** *vt* zusammenfalten; zusammenklappen (*chair*) □ *vi* sich zusammenfalten/-klappen lassen; (*fam*) (*business:*) eingehen

fold|er /'fəʊldə(r)/ *n* Mappe *f*. ∼**ing** *a* Klapp-

foliage /'fəʊlɪɪdʒ/ *n* Blätter *pl*; (*of tree*) Laub *nt*

folk /fəʊk/ *npl* Leute *pl*

folk: ∼**dance** *n* Volkstanz *m*. ∼**lore** *n* Folklore *f*. ∼**song** *n* Volkslied *nt*

follow /'fɒləʊ/ *vt/i* folgen (+ *dat*); (*pursue*) verfolgen; (*in vehicle*) nachfahren (+ *dat*); ∼ **suit** (*fig*) dasselbe tun. ∼ **up** *vt* nachgehen (+ *dat*)

follow|er /'fɒləʊə(r)/ *n* Anhänger(in) *m(f)*. ∼**ing** *a* folgend □ *n* Folgende(s) *nt*; (*supporters*) Anhängerschaft *f* □ *prep* im Anschluss an (+ *acc*)

folly /'fɒlɪ/ *n* Torheit *f*

fond /fɒnd/ *a* (**-er, -est**), **-ly** *adv* liebevoll; **be** ∼ **of** gern haben; gern essen (*food*)

fondle /'fɒndl/ *vt* liebkosen

fondness /'fɒndnɪs/ *n* Liebe *f* (**for** zu)

font /fɒnt/ *n* Taufstein *m*

food /fu:d/ *n* Essen *nt*; (*for animals*) Futter *nt*; (*groceries*) Lebensmittel *pl*

food: ∼ **mixer** *n* Küchenmaschine *f*. ∼ **poisoning** *n* Lebensmittelvergiftung *f*. ∼ **processor** *n* Küchenmaschine *f*. ∼ **value** *n* Nährwert *m*

fool[1] /fu:l/ *n* (*Culin*) Fruchtcreme *f*

fool[2] *n* Narr *m*; **you are a** ∼ du bist dumm; **make a** ∼ **of oneself** sich lächerlich machen □ *vt* hereinlegen □ *vi* ∼ **around** herumalbern

'**fool|hardy** *a* tollkühn. ∼**ish** *a*, **-ly** *adv* dumm. ∼**ishness** *n* Dummheit *f*. ∼**proof** *a* narrensicher

foot /fʊt/ *n* (*pl* **feet**) Fuß *m*; (*measure*) Fuß *m* (30, 48 cm); (*of bed*) Fußende *nt*; **on** ∼ zu Fuß; **on one's feet** auf den Beinen; **put one's** ∼ **in it** (*fam*) ins Fettnäpfchen treten

foot: ∼**-and-'mouth disease** *n* Maul- und Klauenseuche *f*. ∼**ball** *n* Fußball *m*. ∼**baller** *n* Fußballspieler *m*. ∼**ball pools** *npl* Fußballtoto *nt*. ∼**brake** *n* Fußbremse *f*. ∼**bridge** *n* Fußgängerbrücke *f*. ∼**hills** *npl* Vorgebirge *nt*. ∼**hold** *n* Halt *m*. ∼**ing** *n* Halt *m*; (*fig*) Basis *f*. ∼**lights** *npl* Rampenlicht *nt*. ∼**man** *n* Lakai *m*. ∼**note** *n* Fußnote *f*. ∼**path** *n* Fußweg *m*. ∼**print** *n* Fußabdruck *m*. ∼**step** *n* Schritt *m*; **follow in s.o.'s** ∼**steps** (*fig*) in jds Fußstapfen treten. ∼**stool** *n* Fußbank *f*. ∼**wear** *n* Schuhwerk *nt*

for /fə(r), *betont* fɔ:(r)/ *prep* für (+ *acc*); (*send, long*) nach; (*ask, fight*) um; **what** ∼? wozu? ∼ **supper** zum Abendessen; ∼ **nothing** umsonst; ∼ **all** that trotz allem; ∼ **this reason** aus diesem Grund; ∼ **a month** einen Monat; **I have lived here** ∼ **ten years** ich wohne seit zehn Jahren hier □ *conj* denn

forage /'fɒrɪdʒ/ *n* Futter *nt* □ *vi* ∼ **for** suchen nach

forbade /fə'bæd/ *see* **forbid**

forbear|ance /fɔ:'beərəns/ *n* Nachsicht *f*. ∼**ing** *a* nachsichtig

forbid /fə'bɪd/ *vt* (*pt* **forbade**, *pp* **forbidden**) verbieten (s.o. jdm). ∼**ding** *a* bedrohlich; (*stern*) streng

force /fɔ:s/ *n* Kraft *f*; (*of blow*) Wucht *f*; (*violence*) Gewalt *f*; **in** ∼ gültig; (*in large numbers*) in großer Zahl; **come into** ∼ in Kraft treten; **the** ∼**s** *pl* die Streitkräfte *pl* □ *vt* zwingen; (*break open*) aufbrechen; ∼ **sth on s.o.** jdm etw aufdrängen

forced /fɔ:st/ *a* gezwungen; ∼ **landing** Notlandung *f*

force: ∼**-'feed** *vt* (*pt/pp* **-fed**) zwangsernähren. ∼**ful** *a*, **-ly** *adv* energisch

forceps /'fɔ:seps/ *n inv* Zange *f*

forcibl|e /'fɔːsəbl/ *a* gewaltsam. **~y** *adv* mit Gewalt

ford /fɔːd/ *n* Furt *f* ◻ *vt* durchwaten; ⟨*in vehicle*⟩ durchfahren

fore /fɔː(r)/ *a* vordere(r,s) ◻ *n* **to the ~** im Vordergrund

fore: ~arm *n* Unterarm *m*. **~boding** /-'bəʊdɪŋ/ *n* Vorahnung *f*. **~cast** *n* Voraussage *f*; ⟨*for weather*⟩ Vorhersage *f* ◻ *vt* (*pt/pp* **~cast**) voraussagen, vorhersagen. **~court** *n* Vorhof *m*. **~fathers** *npl* Vorfahren *pl*. **~finger** *n* Zeigefinger *m*. **~front** *n* **be in the ~front** führend sein. **~gone** *a* **be a ~gone conclusion** von vornherein feststehen. **~ground** *n* Vordergrund *m*. **~head** /'fɒrɪd/ *n* Stirn *f*. **~hand** *n* Vorhand *f*

foreign /'fɒrən/ *a* ausländisch; ⟨*country*⟩ fremd; **he is ~** er ist Ausländer. **~ currency** *n* Devisen *pl*. **~er** *n* Ausländer(in) *m(f)*. **~ language** *n* Fremdsprache *f*

Foreign: ~ Office *n* ≈ Außenministerium *nt*. **~ 'Secretary** *n* ≈ Außenminister *m*

fore: ~leg *n* Vorderbein *nt*. **~man** *n* Vorarbeiter *m*. **~most** *a* führend ◻ *adv* **first and ~most** zuallererst. **~name** *n* Vorname *m*

forensic /fə'rensɪk/ *a* **~ medicine** Gerichtsmedizin *f*

'forerunner *n* Vorläufer *m*

fore'see *vt* (*pt* **-saw**, *pp* **-seen**) voraussehen, vorhersehen. **~able** /-əbl/ *a* **in the ~able future** in absehbarer Zeit

'foresight *n* Weitblick *m*

forest /'fɒrɪst/ *n* Wald *m*. **~er** *n* Förster *m*

fore'stall *vt* zuvorkommen (+ *dat*)

forestry /'fɒrɪstrɪ/ *n* Forstwirtschaft *f*

'foretaste *n* Vorgeschmack *m*

fore'tell *vt* (*pt/pp* **-told**) vorhersagen

forever /fə'revə(r)/ *adv* für immer

fore'warn *vt* vorher warnen

foreword /'fɔːwɜːd/ *n* Vorwort *nt*

forfeit /'fɔːfɪt/ *n* ⟨*in game*⟩ Pfand *nt* ◻ *vt* verwirken

forgave /fə'geɪv/ *see* **forgive**

forge[1] /fɔːdʒ/ *vi* **~ ahead** ⟨*fig*⟩ Fortschritte machen

forge[2] *n* Schmiede *f* ◻ *vt* schmieden; ⟨*counterfeit*⟩ fälschen. **~r** *n* Fälscher *m*. **~ry** *n* Fälschung *f*

forget /fə'get/ *vt/i* (*pt* **-got**, *pp* **-gotten**) vergessen; verlernen ⟨*language*, *skill*⟩. **~ful** *a* vergesslich. **~fulness** *n* Vergesslichkeit *f*. **~-me-not** *n* Vergissmeinnicht *nt*

forgive /fə'gɪv/ *vt* (*pt* **-gave**, *pp* **-given**) **~ s.o. for sth** jdm etw vergeben *od* verzeihen. **~ness** *n* Vergebung *f*, Verzeihung *f*

forgo /fɔː'gəʊ/ *vt* (*pt* **-went**, *pp* **-gone**) verzichten auf (+ *acc*)

forgot(ten) /fə'gɒt(n)/ *see* **forget**

fork /fɔːk/ *n* Gabel *f*; ⟨*in road*⟩ Gabelung *f* ◻ *vi* ⟨*road:*⟩ sich gabeln; **~ right** rechts abzweigen. **~ out** *vt* ⟨*fam*⟩ blechen

fork-lift 'truck *n* Gabelstapler *m*

forlorn /fə'lɔːn/ *a* verlassen; ⟨*hope*⟩ schwach

form /fɔːm/ *n* Form *f*; ⟨*document*⟩ Formular *nt*; ⟨*bench*⟩ Bank *f*; ⟨*Sch*⟩ Klasse *f* ◻ *vt* formen; ⟨*create*⟩ bilden ◻ *vi* sich bilden; ⟨*idea:*⟩ Gestalt annehmen

formal /'fɔːml/ *a*, **-ly** *adv* formell, förmlich. **~ity** /-'mælətɪ/ *n* Förmlichkeit *f*; ⟨*requirement*⟩ Formalität *f*

format /'fɔːmæt/ *n* Format *nt*

formation /fɔː'meɪʃn/ *n* Formation *f*

formative /'fɔːmətɪv/ *a* **~ years** Entwicklungsjahre *pl*

former /'fɔːmə(r)/ *a* ehemalig; **the ~** der/die/das Erstere. **~ly** *adv* früher

formidable /'fɔːmɪdəbl/ *a* gewaltig

formula /'fɔːmjʊlə/ *n* (*pl* **-ae** /-liː/ *or* **-s**) Formel *f*

formulate /'fɔːmjʊleɪt/ *vt* formulieren

forsake /fə'seɪk/ *vt* (*pt* **-sook** /-sʊk/, *pp* **-saken**) verlassen

fort /fɔːt/ *n* ⟨*Mil*⟩ Fort *nt*

forte /'fɔːteɪ/ *n* Stärke *f*

forth /fɔːθ/ *adv* **back and ~** hin und her; **and so ~** und so weiter

forth: ~'coming *a* bevorstehend; ⟨*fam: communicative*⟩ mitteilsam. **~right** *a* direkt. **~'with** *adv* umgehend

fortieth /'fɔːtɪɪθ/ *a* vierzigste(r,s)

fortification /fɔːtɪfɪ'keɪʃn/ *n* Befestigung *f*

fortify /'fɔːtɪfaɪ/ *vt* (*pt/pp* **-ied**) befestigen; ⟨*fig*⟩ stärken

fortitude /'fɔːtɪtjuːd/ *n* Standhaftigkeit *f*

fortnight /'fɔːt-/ *n* vierzehn Tage *pl*. **~ly** *a* vierzehntäglich ◻ *adv* alle vierzehn Tage

fortress /'fɔːtrɪs/ *n* Festung *f*

fortuitous /fɔː'tjuːɪtəs/ *a*, **-ly** *adv* zufällig

fortunate /'fɔːtʃʊnət/ *a* glücklich; **be ~** Glück haben. **~ly** *adv* glücklicherweise

fortune /'fɔːtʃuːn/ *n* Glück *nt*; ⟨*money*⟩ Vermögen *nt*. **~-teller** *n* Wahrsagerin *f*

forty /'fɔːtɪ/ *a* vierzig; **have ~ winks** ⟨*fam*⟩ ein Nickerchen machen ◻ *n* Vierzig *f*

forum /'fɔːrəm/ *n* Forum *nt*

forward /'fɔːwəd/ *adv* vorwärts; ⟨*to the front*⟩ nach vorn ◻ *a* Vorwärts-; ⟨*presumptuous*⟩ anmaßend ◻ *n* ⟨*Sport*⟩ Stürmer *m* ◻ *vt* nachsenden ⟨*letter*⟩. **~s** *adv* vorwärts

fossil /'fɒsl/ n Fossil nt. ~ized a versteinert

foster /'fɒstə(r)/ vt fördern; in Pflege nehmen ⟨child⟩. ~-child n Pflegekind nt. ~-mother n Pflegemutter f

fought /fɔ:t/ see fight

foul /faʊl/ a (-er, -est) widerlich; ⟨language⟩ unflätig; ~ play (Jur) Mord m □ n (Sport) Foul nt □ vt verschmutzen; ⟨obstruct⟩ blockieren; (Sport) foulen. ~-smelling a übel riechend

found¹ /faʊnd/ see find

found² vt gründen

foundation /faʊn'deɪʃn/ n (basis) Grundlage f; ⟨charitable⟩ Stiftung f; ~s pl Fundament nt. ~-stone n Grundstein m

founder¹ /'faʊndə(r)/ n Gründer(in) m(f)

founder² vi ⟨ship:⟩ sinken; ⟨fig⟩ scheitern

foundry /'faʊndri/ n Gießerei f

fountain /'faʊntin/ n Brunnen m. ~-pen n Füllfederhalter m

four /fɔ:(r)/ a vier □ n Vier f

four: ~-'poster n Himmelbett nt. ~some /'fɔ:səm/ n in a ~some zu viert. ~'teen a vierzehn □ n Vierzehn f. ~'teenth a vierzehnte(r,s)

fourth /fɔ:θ/ a vierte(r,s)

fowl /faʊl/ n Geflügel nt

fox /fɒks/ n Fuchs m □ vt ⟨puzzle⟩ verblüffen

foyer /'fɔɪeɪ/ n Foyer nt; ⟨in hotel⟩ Empfangshalle f

fraction /'frækʃn/ n Bruchteil m; (Math) Bruch m

fracture /'fræktʃə(r)/ n Bruch m □ vt/i brechen

fragile /'frædʒaɪl/ a zerbrechlich

fragment /'frægmənt/ n Bruchstück nt, Fragment nt. ~ary a bruchstückhaft

fragran|ce /'freɪgrəns/ n Duft m. ~t a duftend

frail /freɪl/ a (-er, -est) gebrechlich

frame /freɪm/ n Rahmen m; ⟨of spectacles⟩ Gestell nt; (Anat) Körperbau m; ~ of mind Gemütsverfassung f □ vt einrahmen; ⟨fig⟩ formulieren; ⟨sl⟩ ein Verbrechen anhängen (+ dat). ~work n Gerüst nt; ⟨fig⟩ Gerippe nt

franc /fræŋk/ n (French, Belgian) Franc m; (Swiss) Franken m

France /frɑ:ns/ n Frankreich nt

franchise /'fræntʃaɪz/ n (Pol) Wahlrecht nt; (Comm) Franchise nt

frank¹ /fræŋk/ vt frankieren

frank² a, -ly adv offen

frankfurter /'fræŋkfɜ:tə(r)/ n Frankfurter f

frantic /'fræntɪk/ a, -ally adv verzweifelt; be ~ außer sich (dat) sein (with vor)

fraternal /frə'tɜ:nl/ a brüderlich

fraud /frɔ:d/ n Betrug m; ⟨person⟩ Betrüger(in) m(f). ~ulent /-jʊlənt/ a betrügerisch

fraught /frɔ:t/ a ~ with danger gefahrvoll

fray¹ /freɪ/ n Kampf m

fray² vi ausfransen

freak /fri:k/ n Missbildung f; ⟨person⟩ Missgeburt f; ⟨phenomenon⟩ Ausnahmeerscheinung f □ a anormal. ~ish a anormal

freckle /'frekl/ n Sommersprosse f. ~d a sommersprossig

free /fri:/ a (freer, freest) frei; ⟨ticket, copy, time⟩ Frei-; ⟨lavish⟩ freigebig; ~ [of charge] kostenlos; set ~ freilassen; ⟨rescue⟩ befreien; you are ~ to ... es steht Ihnen frei, zu ... □ vt (pt/pp freed) freilassen; ⟨rescue⟩ befreien; ⟨disentangle⟩ freibekommen

free: ~dom n Freiheit f. ~hand adv aus freier Hand. ~hold n [freier] Grundbesitz m. ~ 'kick n Freistoß m. ~lance a & adv freiberuflich. ~ly adv frei; ⟨voluntarily⟩ freiwillig; ⟨generously⟩ großzügig. F~mason n Freimaurer m. F~masonry n Freimaurerei f. ~-range a ~-range eggs Landeier pl. ~ 'sample n Gratisprobe f. ~style n Freistil m. ~way n (Amer) Autobahn f. ~-'wheel vi im Freilauf fahren

freez|e /fri:z/ vt (pt froze, pp frozen) einfrieren; stoppen ⟨wages⟩ □ vi gefrieren; it's ~ing es friert

freez|er /'fri:zə(r)/ n Gefriertruhe f; ⟨upright⟩ Gefrierschrank m. ~ing a eiskalt □ n below ~ing unter Null

freight /freɪt/ n Fracht f. ~er n Frachter m. ~ train n (Amer) Güterzug m

French /frentʃ/ a französisch □ n (Lang) Französisch nt; the ~ pl die Franzosen

French: ~ 'beans npl grüne Bohnen pl. ~ 'bread n Stangenbrot nt. ~ 'fries npl Pommes frites pl. ~man n Franzose m. ~ 'window n Terrassentür f. ~woman n Französin f

frenzied /'frenzid/ a rasend

frenzy /'frenzi/ n Raserei f

frequency /'fri:kwənsi/ n Häufigkeit f; (Phys) Frequenz f

frequent¹ /'fri:kwənt/ a, -ly adv häufig

frequent² /fri'kwent/ vt regelmäßig besuchen

fresco /'freskəʊ/ n Fresko nt

fresh /freʃ/ a (-er, -est), -ly adv frisch; ⟨new⟩ neu; (Amer: cheeky) frech

freshen /'freʃn/ *vi* ⟨*wind:*⟩ auffrischen. ~ **up** *vt* auffrischen □ *vi* sich frisch machen

freshness /'freʃnɪs/ *n* Frische *f*

'**freshwater** *a* Süßwasser-

fret /fret/ *vi* (*pt/pp* **fretted**) sich grämen. ~**ful** *a* weinerlich

'**fretsaw** *n* Laubsäge *f*

friar /'fraɪə(r)/ *n* Mönch *m*

friction /'frɪkʃn/ *n* Reibung *f*; ⟨*fig*⟩ Reibereien *pl*

Friday /'fraɪdeɪ/ *n* Freitag *m*

fridge /frɪdʒ/ *n* Kühlschrank *m*

fried /fraɪd/ *see* **fry²** □ *a* gebraten; ~ **egg** Spiegelei *nt*

friend /frend/ *n* Freund(in) *m(f)*. ~**liness** *n* Freundlichkeit *f*. ~**ly** *a* (**-ier, -iest**) freundlich; ~**ly with** befreundet mit. ~**ship** *n* Freundschaft *f*

frieze /friːz/ *n* Fries *m*

fright /fraɪt/ *n* Schreck *m*

frighten /'fraɪtn/ *vt* Angst machen (+ *dat*); ⟨*startle*⟩ erschrecken; **be** ~**ed** Angst haben (**of** vor + *dat*). ~**ing** *a* Angst erregend

frightful /'fraɪtfl/ *a*, **-ly** *adv* schrecklich

frigid /'frɪdʒɪd/ *a* frostig; (*Psych*) frigide. ~**ity** /-'dʒɪdətɪ/ *n* Frostigkeit *f*; Frigidität *f*

frill /frɪl/ *n* Rüsche *f*; ⟨*paper*⟩ Manschette *f*. ~**y** *a* rüschenbesetzt

fringe /frɪndʒ/ *n* Fransen *pl*; ⟨*of hair*⟩ Pony *m*; ⟨*fig: edge*⟩ Rand *m*. ~ **benefits** *npl* zusätzliche Leistungen *pl*

frisk /frɪsk/ *vi* herumspringen □ *vt* ⟨*search*⟩ durchsuchen, ⟨*fam*⟩ filzen

frisky /'frɪskɪ/ *a* (**-ier, -iest**) lebhaft

fritter /'frɪtə(r)/ *vt* ~ **[away]** verplempern ⟨*fam*⟩

frivol|ity /frɪ'vɒlətɪ/ *n* Frivolität *f*. ~**ous** /'frɪvələs/ *a*, **-ly** *adv* frivol, leichtfertig

frizzy /'frɪzɪ/ *a* kraus

fro /frəʊ/ *adv* **to and** ~ hin und her

frock /frɒk/ *n* Kleid *nt*

frog /frɒg/ *n* Frosch *m*. ~**man** *n* Froschmann *m*. ~**spawn** *n* Froschlaich *m*

frolic /'frɒlɪk/ *vi* (*pt/pp* **frolicked**) herumtollen

from /frɒm/ *prep* von (+ *dat*); ⟨*out of*⟩ aus (+ *dat*); ⟨*according to*⟩ nach (+ *dat*); ~ **Monday** ab Montag; ~ **that day** seit dem Tag

front /frʌnt/ *n* Vorderseite *f*; ⟨*fig*⟩ Fassade *f*; ⟨*of garment*⟩ Vorderteil *nt*; ⟨*sea-*⟩ Strandpromenade *f*; (*Mil, Pol, Meteorol*) Front *f*; **in** ~ **of** vor; **in** or **at the** ~ vorne; **to the** ~ nach vorne □ *a* vordere(r,s); ⟨*page, row*⟩ erste(r,s); ⟨*tooth, wheel*⟩ Vorder-

frontal /'frʌntl/ *a* Frontal-

front: ~ '**door** *n* Haustür *f*. ~ '**garden** *n* Vorgarten *m*

frontier /'frʌntɪə(r)/ *n* Grenze *f*

front-wheel 'drive *n* Vorderradantrieb *m*

frost /frɒst/ *n* Frost *m*; ⟨*hoar-*⟩ Raureif *m*; **ten degrees of** ~ zehn Grad Kälte. ~**bite** *n* Erfrierung *f*. ~**bitten** *a* erfroren

frost|ed /'frɒstɪd/ *a* ~**ed glass** Mattglas *nt*. ~**ing** *n* (*Amer Culin*) Zuckerguss *m*. ~**y** *a*, **-ily** *adv* frostig

froth /frɒθ/ *n* Schaum *m* □ *vi* schäumen. ~**y** *a* schaumig

frown /fraʊn/ *n* Stirnrunzeln *nt* □ *vi* die Stirn runzeln; ~ **on** missbilligen

froze /frəʊz/ *see* **freeze**

frozen /'frəʊzn/ *see* **freeze** □ *a* gefroren; (*Culin*) tiefgekühlt; **I'm** ~ ⟨*fam*⟩ mir ist eiskalt. ~ **food** *n* Tiefkühlkost *f*

frugal /'fruːgl/ *a*, **-ly** *adv* sparsam; ⟨*meal*⟩ frugal

fruit /fruːt/ *n* Frucht *f*; ⟨*collectively*⟩ Obst *nt*. ~ **cake** *n* englischer [Tee]kuchen *m*

fruit|erer /'fruːtərə(r)/ *n* Obsthändler *m*. ~**ful** *a* fruchtbar

fruition /fruː'ɪʃn/ *n* **come to** ~ sich verwirklichen

fruit: ~ **juice** *n* Obstsaft *m*. ~**less** *a*, **-ly** *adv* fruchtlos. ~ **machine** *n* Spielautomat *m*. ~ **salad** *n* Obstsalat *m*

fruity /'fruːtɪ/ *a* fruchtig

frumpy /'frʌmpɪ/ *a* unmodisch

frustrat|e /frʌ'streɪt/ *vt* vereiteln; (*psych*) frustrieren. ~**ing** *a* frustrierend. ~**ion** /-eɪʃn/ *n* Frustration *f*

fry¹ /fraɪ/ *n inv* **small** ~ ⟨*fig*⟩ kleine Fische *pl*

fry² *vt/i* (*pt/pp* **fried**) [in der Pfanne] braten. ~**ing-pan** *n* Bratpfanne *f*

fuck /fʌk/ *vt/i* ⟨*vulg*⟩ ficken. ~**ing** *a* ⟨*vulg*⟩ Scheiß-

fuddy-duddy /'fʌdɪdʌdɪ/ *n* ⟨*fam*⟩ verknöcherter Kerl *m*

fudge /fʌdʒ/ *n* weiche Karamellen *pl*

fuel /'fjuːəl/ *n* Brennstoff *m*; ⟨*for car*⟩ Kraftstoff *m*; ⟨*for aircraft*⟩ Treibstoff *m*

fugitive /'fjuːdʒətɪv/ *n* Flüchtling *m*

fugue /fjuːg/ *n* (*Mus*) Fuge *f*

fulfil /fʊl'fɪl/ *vt* (*pt/pp* **-filled**) erfüllen. ~**ment** *n* Erfüllung *f*

full /fʊl/ *a* & *adv* (**-er, -est**) voll; ⟨*detailed*⟩ ausführlich; ⟨*skirt*⟩ weit; ~ **of** voll von (+ *dat*), voller (+ *gen*); **at** ~ **speed** in voller Fahrt □ *n* **in** ~ vollständig

full: ~ '**moon** n Vollmond m. ~-**scale** a ⟨model⟩ in Originalgröße; ⟨rescue, alert⟩ groß angelegt. ~ '**stop** n Punkt m. ~-**time** a ganztägig □ adv ganztags

fully /'fʊlɪ/ adv völlig; ⟨in detail⟩ ausführlich

fulsome /'fʊlsəm/ a übertrieben

fumble /'fʌmbl/ vi herumfummeln (**with** an + dat)

fume /fjuːm/ vi vor Wut schäumen

fumes /fjuːmz/ npl Dämpfe pl; ⟨from car⟩ Abgase pl

fumigate /'fjuːmɪgeɪt/ vt ausräuchern

fun /fʌn/ n Spaß m; **for** ~ aus od zum Spaß; **make** ~ **of** sich lustig machen über (+ acc); **have** ~! viel Spaß!

function /'fʌŋkʃn/ n Funktion f; ⟨event⟩ Veranstaltung f □ vi funktionieren; ⟨serve⟩ dienen (**as** als). ~**al** a zweckmäßig

fund /fʌnd/ n Fonds m; ⟨fig⟩ Vorrat m; ~**s** pl Geldmittel pl □ vt finanzieren

fundamental /fʌndə'mentl/ a grundlegend; ⟨essential⟩ wesentlich

funeral /'fjuːnərl/ n Beerdigung f; ⟨cremation⟩ Feuerbestattung f

funeral: ~ **directors** pl, ⟨Amer⟩ ~ **home** n Bestattungsinstitut nt. ~ **march** n Trauermarsch m. ~ **parlour** n ⟨Amer⟩ Bestattungsinstitut nt. ~ **service** n Trauergottesdienst m

'**funfair** n Jahrmarkt m, Kirmes f

fungus /'fʌngəs/ n (pl -**gi** /-gaɪ/) Pilz m

funicular /fjuː'nɪkjʊlə(r)/ n Seilbahn f

funnel /'fʌnl/ n Trichter m; ⟨on ship, train⟩ Schornstein m

funnily /'fʌnɪlɪ/ adv komisch; ~ **enough** komischerweise

funny /'fʌnɪ/ a (-**ier**, -**iest**) komisch. ~**bone** n ⟨fam⟩ Musikantenknochen m

fur /fɜː(r)/ n Fell nt; ⟨for clothing⟩ Pelz m; ⟨in kettle⟩ Kesselstein m. ~ '**coat** n Pelzmantel m

furious /'fjʊərɪəs/ a, -**ly** adv wütend (**with** auf + acc)

furnace /'fɜːnɪs/ n ⟨Techn⟩ Ofen m

furnish /'fɜːnɪʃ/ vt einrichten; ⟨supply⟩ liefern. ~**ed** a ~**ed room** möbliertes Zimmer nt. ~**ings** npl Einrichtungsgegenstände pl

furniture /'fɜːnɪtʃə(r)/ n Möbel pl

furred /fɜːd/ a ⟨tongue⟩ belegt

furrow /'fʌrəʊ/ n Furche f

furry /'fɜːrɪ/ a ⟨animal⟩ Pelz-; ⟨toy⟩ Plüsch-

further /'fɜːðə(r)/ a weitere(r,s); **at the** ~ **end** am anderen Ende; **until** ~ **notice** bis auf weiteres □ adv weiter; ~ **off** weiter entfernt □ vt befördern

further: ~ **edu'cation** n Weiterbildung f. ~'**more** adv überdies

furthest /'fɜːðɪst/ a am weitesten entfernt □ adv am weitesten

furtive /'fɜːtɪv/ a, -**ly** adv verstohlen

fury /'fjʊərɪ/ n Wut f

fuse[1] /fjuːz/ n ⟨of bomb⟩ Zünder m; ⟨cord⟩ Zündschnur f

fuse[2] n ⟨Electr⟩ Sicherung f □ vt/i verschmelzen; **the lights have** ~**d** die Sicherung [für das Licht] ist durchgebrannt. ~**box** n Sicherungskasten m

fuselage /'fjuːzəlɑːʒ/ n ⟨Aviat⟩ Rumpf m

fusion /'fjuːʒn/ n Verschmelzung f, Fusion f

fuss /fʌs/ n Getue nt; **make a** ~ **of** verwöhnen; ⟨caress⟩ liebkosen □ vi Umstände machen

fussy /'fʌsɪ/ a (-**ier**, -**iest**) wählerisch; ⟨particular⟩ penibel

fusty /'fʌstɪ/ a moderig

futile /'fjuːtaɪl/ a zwecklos. ~**ity** /-'tɪlətɪ/ n Zwecklosigkeit f

future /'fjuːtʃə(r)/ a zukünftig □ n Zukunft f; ⟨Gram⟩ [erstes] Futur nt; ~ **perfect** zweites Futur nt; **in** ~ in Zukunft

futuristic /fjuːtʃə'rɪstɪk/ a futuristisch

fuzz /fʌz/ n **the** ~ ⟨sl⟩ die Bullen pl

fuzzy /'fʌzɪ/ a (-**ier**, -**iest**) ⟨hair⟩ kraus; ⟨blurred⟩ verschwommen

G

gab /gæb/ n ⟨fam⟩ **have the gift of the** ~ gut reden können

gabble /'gæbl/ vi schnell reden

gable /'geɪbl/ n Giebel m

gad /gæd/ vi (pt/pp **gadded**) ~ **about** dauernd ausgehen

gadget /'gædʒɪt/ n [kleines] Gerät nt

Gaelic /'geɪlɪk/ n Gälisch nt

gaffe /gæf/ n Fauxpas m

gag /gæg/ n Knebel m; ⟨joke⟩ Witz m; ⟨Theat⟩ Gag m □ vt (pt/pp **gagged**) knebeln

gaiety /'geɪətɪ/ n Fröhlichkeit f

gaily /'geɪlɪ/ adv fröhlich

gain /geɪn/ n Gewinn m; ⟨increase⟩ Zunahme f □ vt gewinnen; ⟨obtain⟩ erlangen; ~ **weight** zunehmen □ vi ⟨clock:⟩ vorgehen. ~**ful** a ~**ful employment** Erwerbstätigkeit f

gait /geɪt/ n Gang m

gala /'gɑ:lə/ n Fest nt; **swimming ~** Schwimmfest nt □ attrib Gala-

galaxy /'gæləksɪ/ n Galaxie f; **the G~** die Milchstraße

gale /geɪl/ n Sturm m

gall /gɔ:l/ n Galle f; (impudence) Frechheit f

gallant /'gælənt/ a, -ly adv tapfer; (chivalrous) galant. **~ry** n Tapferkeit f

'gall-bladder n Gallenblase f

gallery /'gælərɪ/ n Galerie f

galley /'gælɪ/ n (ship's kitchen) Kombüse f; **~ [proof]** [Druck]fahne f

gallivant /'gælɪvænt/ vi (fam) ausgehen

gallon /'gælən/ n Gallone f (= 4,5 l; Amer = 3,785 l)

gallop /'gæləp/ n Galopp m □ vi galoppieren

gallows /'gæləʊz/ n Galgen m

'gallstone n Gallenstein m

galore /gə'lɔ:(r)/ adv in Hülle und Fülle

galvanize /'gælvənaɪz/ vt galvanisieren

gambit /'gæmbɪt/ n Eröffnungsmanöver nt

gamble /'gæmbl/ n (risk) Risiko nt □ vi [um Geld] spielen; **~ on** (rely) sich verlassen auf (+ acc). **~r** n Spieler(in) m(f)

game /geɪm/ n Spiel nt; (animals, birds) Wild nt; **~s** (Sch) Sport m □ a (brave) tapfer; (willing) bereit (for zu). **~keeper** n Wildhüter m

gammon /'gæmən/ n [geräucherter] Schinken m

gamut /'gæmət/ n Skala f

gander /'gændə(r)/ n Gänserich m

gang /gæŋ/ n Bande f; (of workmen) Kolonne f □ vi **~ up** sich zusammenrotten (on gegen)

gangling /'gæŋglɪŋ/ a schlaksig

gangrene /'gæŋgri:n/ n Wundbrand m

gangster /'gæŋstə(r)/ n Gangster m

gangway /'gæŋweɪ/ n Gang m; (Naut, Aviat) Gangway f

gaol /dʒeɪl/ n Gefängnis nt □ vt ins Gefängnis sperren. **~er** n Gefängniswärter m

gap /gæp/ n Lücke f; (interval) Pause f; (difference) Unterschied m

gap|e /geɪp/ vi gaffen; **~e at** anstarren. **~ing** a klaffend

garage /'gærɑ:ʒ/ n Garage f; (for repairs) Werkstatt f; (for petrol) Tankstelle f

garb /gɑ:b/ n Kleidung f

garbage /'gɑ:bɪdʒ/ n Müll m. **~ can** n (Amer) Mülleimer m

garbled /'gɑ:bld/ a verworren

garden /'gɑ:dn/ n Garten m; **[public] ~s** pl [öffentliche] Anlagen pl □ vi im Garten arbeiten. **~er** n Gärtner(in) m(f). **~ing** n Gartenarbeit f

gargle /'gɑ:gl/ n (liquid) Gurgelwasser nt □ vi gurgeln

gargoyle /'gɑ:gɔɪl/ n Wasserspeier m

garish /'geərɪʃ/ a grell

garland /'gɑ:lənd/ n Girlande f

garlic /'gɑ:lɪk/ n Knoblauch m

garment /'gɑ:mənt/ n Kleidungsstück m

garnet /'gɑ:nɪt/ n Granat m

garnish /'gɑ:nɪʃ/ n Garnierung f □ vt garnieren

garret /'gærɪt/ n Dachstube f

garrison /'gærɪsn/ n Garnison f

garrulous /'gærʊləs/ a geschwätzig

garter /'gɑ:tə(r)/ n Strumpfband nt; (Amer: suspender) Strumpfhalter m

gas /gæs/ n Gas nt; (Amer fam: petrol) Benzin nt □ v (pt/pp **gassed**) □ vt vergasen □ vi (fam) schwatzen. **~ cooker** n Gasherd m. **~ 'fire** n Gasofen m

gash /gæʃ/ n Schnitt m; (wound) klaffende Wunde f □ vt **~ one's arm** sich (dat) den Arm aufschlitzen

gasket /'gæskɪt/ n (Techn) Dichtung f

gas: ~ mask n Gasmaske f. **~-meter** n Gaszähler m

gasoline /'gæsəli:n/ n (Amer) Benzin nt

gasp /gɑ:sp/ vi keuchen; (in surprise) hörbar die Luft einziehen

'gas station n (Amer) Tankstelle f

gastric /'gæstrɪk/ a Magen-. **~ 'flu** n Darmgrippe f. **~ 'ulcer** n Magengeschwür nt

gastronomy /gæ'strɒnəmɪ/ n Gastronomie f

gate /geɪt/ n Tor nt; (to field) Gatter nt; (barrier) Schranke f; (at airport) Flugsteig m

gâteau /'gætəʊ/ n Torte f

gate: ~crasher n ungeladener Gast m. **~way** n Tor nt

gather /'gæðə(r)/ vt sammeln; (pick) pflücken; (conclude) folgern (from aus); (Sewing) kräuseln; **~ speed** schneller werden □ vi sich versammeln; (storm:) sich zusammenziehen. **~ing** n **family ~ing** Familientreffen nt

gaudy /'gɔ:dɪ/ a (-ier, -iest) knallig

gauge /geɪdʒ/ n Stärke f; (Rail) Spurweite f; (device) Messinstrument nt □ vt messen; (estimate) schätzen

gaunt /gɔ:nt/ a hager

gauntlet /'gɔ:ntlɪt/ n **run the ~** Spießruten laufen

gauze /gɔ:z/ n Gaze f

gave /geɪv/ *see* **give**

gawky /'gɔːkɪ/ *a* (**-ier, -iest**) schlaksig

gawp /gɔːp/ *vi* (*fam*) glotzen; ~ **at** anglotzen

gay /geɪ/ *a* (**-er, -est**) fröhlich; (*fam*) homosexuell, (*fam*) schwul

gaze /geɪz/ *n* [langer] Blick *m* □ *vi* sehen; ~ **at** ansehen

gazelle /gə'zel/ *n* Gazelle *f*

GB *abbr of* **Great Britain**

gear /gɪə(r)/ *n* Ausrüstung *f*; (*Techn*) Getriebe *nt*; (*Auto*) Gang *m*; **in ~** mit eingelegtem Gang; **change ~** schalten □ *vt* anpassen (**to** *dat*)

gear: ~**box** *n* (*Auto*) Getriebe *nt*. ~**lever** *n*, (*Amer*) ~**shift** *n* Schalthebel *m*

geese /giːs/ *see* **goose**

geezer /'giːzə(r)/ *n* (*sl*) Typ *m*

gel /dʒel/ *n* Gel *nt*

gelatine /'dʒelətɪn/ *n* Gelatine *f*

gelignite /'dʒelɪgnaɪt/ *n* Gelatinedynamit *nt*

gem /dʒem/ *n* Juwel *nt*

Gemini /'dʒemɪnaɪ/ *n* (*Astr*) Zwillinge *pl*

gender /'dʒendə(r)/ *n* (*Gram*) Geschlecht *nt*

gene /dʒiːn/ *n* Gen *nt*

genealogy /dʒiːnɪ'ælədʒɪ/ *n* Genealogie *f*

general /'dʒenrəl/ *a* allgemein □ *n* General *m*; **in ~** im Allgemeinen. ~ **e'lection** *n* allgemeine Wahlen *pl*

generaliz|ation /dʒenrəlaɪ'zeɪʃn/ *n* Verallgemeinerung *f*. ~**e** /'dʒenrəlaɪz/ *vi* verallgemeinern

generally /'dʒenrəlɪ/ *adv* im Allgemeinen

general prac'titioner *n* praktischer Arzt *m*

generate /'dʒenəreɪt/ *vt* erzeugen

generation /dʒenə'reɪʃn/ *n* Generation *f*

generator /'dʒenəreɪtə(r)/ *n* Generator *m*

generic /dʒɪ'nerɪk/ *a* ~ **term** Oberbegriff *m*

generosity /dʒenə'rɒsɪtɪ/ *n* Großzügigkeit *f*

generous /'dʒenərəs/ *a*, **-ly** *adv* großzügig

genetic /dʒɪ'netɪk/ *a* genetisch. ~ **engineering** *n* Gentechnologie *f*. ~**s** *n* Genetik *f*

Geneva /dʒɪ'niːvə/ *n* Genf *nt*

genial /'dʒiːnɪəl/ *a*, **-ly** *adv* freundlich

genitals /'dʒenɪtlz/ *pl* [äußere] Geschlechtsteile *pl*

genitive /'dʒenɪtɪv/ *a & n* ~ **[case]** Genitiv *m*

genius /'dʒiːnɪəs/ *n* (*pl* **-uses**) Genie *nt*; (*quality*) Genialität *f*

genocide /'dʒenəsaɪd/ *n* Völkermord *m*

genre /'ʒãrə/ *n* Gattung *f*, Genre *nt*

gent /dʒent/ *n* (*fam*) Herr *m*; **the ~s** *sg* die Herrentoilette *f*

genteel /dʒen'tiːl/ *a* vornehm

gentle /'dʒentl/ *a* (**-r, -st**) sanft

gentleman /'dʒentlmən/ *n* Herr *m*; (*well-mannered*) Gentleman *m*

gent|leness /'dʒentlnɪs/ *n* Sanftheit *f*. ~**ly** *adv* sanft

genuine /'dʒenjʊɪn/ *a* echt; (*sincere*) aufrichtig. ~**ly** *adv* (*honestly*) ehrlich

genus /'dʒiːnəs/ *n* (*Biol*) Gattung *f*

geograph|ical /dʒɪə'græfɪkl/ *a*, **-ly** *adv* geographisch. ~**y** /dʒɪ'ɒgrəfɪ/ *n* Geographie *f*, Erdkunde *f*

geological /dʒɪə'lɒdʒɪkl/ *a*, **-ly** *adv* geologisch

geolog|ist /dʒɪ'ɒlədʒɪst/ *n* Geologe *m* /**-gin** *f*. ~**y** *n* Geologie *f*

geometr|ic(al) /dʒɪə'metrɪk(l)/ *a* geometrisch. ~**y** /dʒɪ'ɒmətrɪ/ *n* Geometrie *f*

geranium /dʒə'reɪnɪəm/ *n* Geranie *f*

geriatric /dʒerɪ'ætrɪk/ *a* geriatrisch □ *n* geriatrischer Patient *m*. ~**s** *n* Geriatrie *f*

germ /dʒɜːm/ *n* Keim *m*; ~**s** *pl* (*fam*) Bazillen *pl*

German /'dʒɜːmən/ *a* deutsch □ *n* (*person*) Deutsche(r) *m/f*; (*Lang*) Deutsch *nt*; **in ~** auf Deutsch; **into ~** ins Deutsche

Germanic /dʒə'mænɪk/ *a* germanisch

German: ~ **'measles** *n* Röteln *pl*. ~ **'shepherd [dog]** *n* [deutscher] Schäferhund *m*

Germany /'dʒɜːmənɪ/ *n* Deutschland *nt*

germinate /'dʒɜːmɪneɪt/ *vi* keimen

gesticulate /dʒe'stɪkjʊleɪt/ *vi* gestikulieren

gesture /'dʒestʃə(r)/ *n* Geste *f*

get /get/ *v* (*pt/pp* **got**, *pp Amer also* **gotten**, *pres p* **getting**) □ *vt* bekommen, (*fam*) kriegen; (*procure*) besorgen; (*buy*) kaufen; (*fetch*) holen; (*take*) bringen; (*on telephone*) erreichen; (*fam: understand*) kapieren; machen (*meal*); ~ **s.o. to do sth** jdn dazu bringen, etw zu tun □ *vi* (*become*) werden; ~ **to** kommen zu/nach (*town*); (*reach*) erreichen; ~ **dressed** sich anziehen; ~ **married** heiraten. ~ **at** *vt* herankommen an (+ *acc*); **what are you ~ting at?** worauf willst du hinaus? ~ **away** *vi* (*leave*) wegkommen; (*escape*) entkommen. ~ **back** *vi* zurückkommen □ *vt* (*recover*) zurückbekommen; **one's own back** sich revanchieren. ~ **by** *vi* vorbeikommen; (*manage*) sein Auskommen haben. ~ **down** *vi* heruntersteigen; ~ **down to** sich [heran]machen an (+ *acc*) □ *vt* (*depress*) deprimieren. ~ **in** *vi* einsteigen □ *vt* (*fetch*) hereinholen. ~ **off** *vi* *(dismount)* absteigen; *(from bus)* aussteigen; *(leave)* wegkommen; *(Jur)* freigesprochen werden □ *vt (remove)* abbekommen. ~ **on** *vi (mount)* aufsteigen; *(to bus)* einsteigen; *(be on good terms)* gut auskommen (**with** mit); *(make progress)* Fortschritte machen; **how are you ~ting on?** wie geht's? ~ **out** *vi* herauskommen; *(of car)* aussteigen; ~ **out of** *(avoid doing)* sich drücken um □ *vt* herausholen; herausbekommen ⟨cork, stain⟩. ~ **over** *vi* hinübersteigen □ *vt (fig)* hinwegkommen über *(+ acc)*. ~ **round** *vi* herumkommen; **I never ~round to it** ich komme nie dazu □ *vt* herumkriegen; *(avoid)* umgehen. ~ **through** *vi* durchkommen. ~ **up** *vi* aufstehen

get: ~**away** *n* Flucht *f*. ~**up** *n* Aufmachung *f*

geyser /'giːzə(r)/ *n* Durchlauferhitzer *m*; *(Geol)* Geysir *m*

ghastly /'gɑːstlɪ/ *a* (-ier, -iest) grässlich; *(pale)* blass

gherkin /'gɜːkɪn/ *n* Essiggurke *f*

ghetto /'getəʊ/ *n* Getto *nt*

ghost /gəʊst/ *n* Geist *m*, Gespenst *nt*. ~**ly** *a* geisterhaft

ghoulish /'guːlɪʃ/ *a* makaber

giant /'dʒaɪənt/ *n* Riese *m* □ *a* riesig

gibberish /'dʒɪbərɪʃ/ *n* Kauderwelsch *nt*

gibe /dʒaɪb/ *n* spöttische Bemerkung *f* □ *vi* spotten (**at** über *+ acc*)

giblets /'dʒɪblɪts/ *npl* Geflügelklein *nt*

giddiness /'gɪdɪnɪs/ *n* Schwindel *m*

giddy /'gɪdɪ/ *a* (-ier, -iest) schwindlig; **I feel ~** mir ist schwindlig

gift /gɪft/ *n* Geschenk *nt*; *(to charity)* Gabe *f*; *(talent)* Begabung *f*. ~**ed** /-ɪd/ *a* begabt. ~**-wrap** *vt* als Geschenk einpacken

gig /gɪg/ *n (fam, Mus)* Gig *m*

gigantic /dʒaɪ'gæntɪk/ *a* riesig, riesengroß

giggle /'gɪgl/ *n* Kichern *nt* □ *vi* kichern

gild /gɪld/ *vt* vergolden

gills /gɪlz/ *npl* Kiemen *pl*

gilt /gɪlt/ *a* vergoldet □ *n* Vergoldung *f*. ~**-edged** *a (Comm)* mündelsicher

gimmick /'gɪmɪk/ *n* Trick *m*

gin /dʒɪn/ *n* Gin *m*

ginger /'dʒɪndʒə(r)/ *a* rotblond; ⟨cat⟩ rot □ *n* Ingwer *m*. ~**bread** *n* Pfefferkuchen *m*

gingerly /'dʒɪndʒəlɪ/ *adv* vorsichtig

gipsy /'dʒɪpsɪ/ *n* = **gypsy**

giraffe /dʒɪ'rɑːf/ *n* Giraffe *f*

girder /'gɜːdə(r)/ *n (Techn)* Träger *m*

girdle /'gɜːdl/ *n* Bindegürtel *m*; *(corset)* Hüfthalter *m*

girl /gɜːl/ *n* Mädchen *nt*; *(young woman)* junge Frau *f*. ~**friend** *n* Freundin *f*. ~**ish** *a*, -ly *adv* mädchenhaft

giro /'dʒaɪərəʊ/ *n* Giro *nt*; *(cheque)* Postscheck *m*

girth /gɜːθ/ *n* Umfang *m*; *(for horse)* Bauchgurt *m*

gist /dʒɪst/ *n* **the ~** das Wesentliche

give /gɪv/ *n* Elastizität *f* □ *v* (*pt* gave, *pp* given) □ *vt* geben/*(as present)* schenken (**to** *dat*); *(donate)* spenden; *(lecture)* halten; ⟨one's name⟩ angeben □ *vi* geben; *(yield)* nachgeben. ~ **away** *vt* verschenken; *(betray)* verraten; *(distribute)* verteilen; ~ **away the bride** ≈ Brautführer sein. ~ **back** *vt* zurückgeben. ~ **in** *vt* einreichen □ *vi (yield)* nachgeben. ~ **off** *vt* abgeben. ~ **up** *vt/i* aufgeben; ~ **oneself up** sich stellen. ~ **way** *vi* nachgeben; *(Auto)* die Vorfahrt beachten

given /'gɪvn/ *see* **give** □ *a* ~ **name** Vorname *m*

glacier /'glæsɪə(r)/ *n* Gletscher *m*

glad /glæd/ *a* froh (**of** über *+ acc*). ~**den** /'glædn/ *vt* erfreuen

glade /gleɪd/ *n* Lichtung *f*

gladly /'glædlɪ/ *adv* gern[e]

glamorous /'glæmərəs/ *a* glanzvoll; ⟨film star⟩ glamourös

glamour /'glæmə(r)/ *n* [betörender] Glanz *m*

glance /glɑːns/ *n* [flüchtiger] Blick *m* □ *vi* ~ **at** einen Blick werfen auf *(+ acc)*. ~ **up** *vi* aufblicken

gland /glænd/ *n* Drüse *f*

glandular /'glændjʊlə(r)/ *a* Drüsen-

glare /gleə(r)/ *n* grelles Licht *nt*; *(look)* ärgerlicher Blick *m* □ *vi* ~ **at** böse ansehen

glaring /'gleərɪŋ/ *a* grell; ⟨mistake⟩ krass

glass /glɑːs/ *n* Glas *nt*; *(mirror)* Spiegel *m*; ~**es** *pl (spectacles)* Brille *f*. ~**y** *a* glasig

glaze /gleɪz/ *n* Glasur *f* □ *vt* verglasen; *(Culin, Pottery)* glasieren

glazier /'gleɪzɪə(r)/ *n* Glaser *m*

gleam /gliːm/ *n* Schein *m* □ *vi* glänzen

glean /gliːn/ *vi* Ähren lesen □ *vt (learn)* erfahren

glee /gliː/ *n* Frohlocken *nt*. ~**ful** *a*, -ly *adv* frohlockend

glen /glen/ *n* [enges] Tal *nt*

glib /glɪb/ *a*, -ly *adv (pej)* gewandt

glid|e /glaɪd/ *vi* gleiten; *(through the air)* schweben. ~**er** *n* Segelflugzeug *nt*. ~**ing** *n* Segelfliegen *nt*

glimmer /'glɪmə(r)/ *n* Glimmen *nt* □ *vi* glimmen

glimpse /glɪmps/ *n* **catch a ~ of** flüchtig sehen □ *vt* flüchtig sehen

glint /glɪnt/ n Blitzen nt □ vi blitzen

glisten /'glɪsn/ vi glitzern

glitter /'glɪtə(r)/ vi glitzern

gloat /gləʊt/ vi schadenfroh sein; ~ **over** sich weiden an (+ dat)

global /'gləʊbl/ a, -ly adv global

globe /gləʊb/ n Kugel f; (map) Globus m

gloom /gluːm/ n Düsterkeit f; (fig) Pessimismus m

gloomy /'gluːmɪ/ a (-ier, -iest), -ily adv düster; (fig) perssimistisch

glorif|y /'glɔːrɪfaɪ/ vt (pt/pp -ied) verherrlichen; **a ~ied waitress** eine bessere Kellnerin f

glorious /'glɔːrɪəs/ a herrlich; (deed, hero) glorreich

glory /'glɔːrɪ/ n Ruhm m; (splendour) Pracht f □ vi ~ **in** genießen

gloss /glɒs/ n Glanz m □ a Glanz- □ vi ~ **over** beschönigen

glossary /'glɒsərɪ/ n Glossar nt

glossy /'glɒsɪ/ a (-ier, -iest) glänzend

glove /glʌv/ n Handschuh m. ~ **compartment** n (Auto) Handschuhfach nt

glow /gləʊ/ n Glut f; (of candle) Schein m □ vi glühen; (candle:) scheinen. ~**ing** a glühend; (account) begeistert

'glow-worm n Glühwürmchen nt

glucose /'gluːkəʊs/ n Traubenzucker m, Glukose f

glue /gluː/ n Klebstoff m □ vt (pres p gluing) kleben (to an + acc)

glum /glʌm/ a (glummer, glummest), -ly adv niedergeschlagen

glut /glʌt/ n Überfluss m (of an + dat); ~ **of fruit** Obstschwemme f

glutton /'glʌtn/ n Vielfraß m. ~**ous** /-əs/ a gefräßig. ~**y** n Gefräßigkeit f

gnarled /nɑːld/ a knorrig; (hands) knotig

gnash /næʃ/ vt ~ **one's teeth** mit den Zähnen knirschen

gnat /næt/ n Mücke f

gnaw /nɔː/ vt/i nagen (at an + dat)

gnome /nəʊm/ n Gnom m

go /gəʊ/ n (pl **goes**) Energie f; (attempt) Versuch m; **on the go** auf Trab; **at one go** auf einmal; **it's your go** du bist dran; **make a go of it** Erfolg haben □ vi (pt **went**, pp **gone**) gehen; (in vehicle) fahren; (leave) weggehen; (on journey) abfahren; (time:) vergehen; (vanish) verschwinden; (fail) versagen; (become) werden; (belong) kommen; **go swimming/shopping** schwimmen/einkaufen gehen; **where are you going?** wo gehst du hin? **it's all gone** es ist nichts mehr übrig; **I am not going to** ich werde es nicht tun; **'to go'** (Amer) 'zum Mitnehmen'. **go away** vi weggehen/-fahren. **go back** vi zurückgehen/-fahren.

go by vi vorbeigehen/-fahren; (time:) vergehen. **go down** vi hinuntergehen/-fahren; (sun, ship:) untergehen; (prices:) fallen; (temperature, swelling:) zurückgehen. **go for** vt holen; (fam: attack) losgehen auf (+ acc). **go in** vi hineingehen/-fahren; **go in for** teilnehmen an (+ dat) (competition); (take up) sich verlegen auf (+ acc). **go off** vi weggehen/-fahren; (alarm:) klingeln; (gun, bomb:) losgehen; (go bad) schlecht werden; **go off well** gut verlaufen. **go on** vi weitergehen/-fahren; (continue) weitermachen; (talking) fortfahren; (happen) geschehen; **go on at** (fam) herumnörgeln an (+ dat). **go out** vi ausgehen; (leave) hinausgehen/-fahren. **go over** vi hinübergehen/-fahren □ vt (check) durchgehen. **go round** vi herumgehen/-fahren; (visit) vorbeigehen; (turn) sich drehen; (be enough) reichen. **go through** vi durchgehen/-fahren □ vt (suffer) durchmachen; (check) durchgehen. **go under** vi untergehen; (fail) scheitern. **go up** vi hinaufgehen/-fahren; (lift:) hochfahren; (prices:) steigen. **go without** vt verzichten auf (+ acc) □ vi darauf verzichten

goad /gəʊd/ vt anstacheln (**into** zu); (taunt) reizen

'go-ahead a fortschrittlich; (enterprising) unternehmend □ n (fig) grünes Licht nt

goal /gəʊl/ n Ziel nt; (sport) Tor nt. ~**keeper** n Torwart m. ~**post** n Torpfosten m

goat /gəʊt/ n Ziege f

gobble /'gɒbl/ vt hinunterschlingen

'go-between n Vermittler(in) m(f)

goblet /'gɒblɪt/ n Pokal m; (glass) Kelchglas nt

goblin /'gɒblɪn/ n Kobold m

God, god /gɒd/ n Gott m

god: ~**child** n Patenkind nt. ~**daughter** n Patentochter f. ~**dess** n Göttin f. ~**father** n Pate m. **G**~**forsaken** a gottverlassen. ~**mother** n Patin f. ~**parents** npl Paten pl. ~**send** n Segen m. ~**son** n Patensohn m

goggle /'gɒgl/ vi (fam) ~ **at** anglotzen. ~**s** npl Schutzbrille f

going /'gəʊɪŋ/ a (price, rate) gängig; (concern) gut gehend □ n **it is hard** ~ es ist schwierig; **while the** ~ **is good** solange es noch geht. ~**s-'on** npl [seltsame] Vorgänge pl

gold /gəʊld/ n Gold nt □ a golden

golden /'gəʊldn/ a golden. ~ **'handshake** n hohe Abfindungssumme f. ~ **'wedding** n goldene Hochzeit f

gold: ~**fish** n inv Goldfisch m. ~**mine** n Goldgrube f. ~**plated** a vergoldet. ~**smith** n Goldschmied m

golf /gɒlf/ n Golf nt

golf: ~**club** n Golfklub m; (implement) Golfschläger m. ~**course** n Golfplatz m. ~**er** m Golfspieler(in) m(f)

gondo|la /'gɒndələ/ n Gondel f. ~**lier** /-'lɪə(r)/ n Gondoliere m

gone /gɒn/ see go

gong /gɒŋ/ n Gong m

good /gʊd/ a (better, best) gut; (well-behaved) brav, artig; ~ **at** gut in (+ dat); a ~ **deal** ziemlich viel; **as** ~ **as** so gut wie; (almost) fast; ~ **morning/evening** guten Morgen/Abend; ~ **afternoon** guten Tag; ~ **night** gute Nacht □ n the ~ das Gute; **for** ~ für immer; **do** ~ Gutes tun; **do s.o.** ~ jdm gut tun; **it's no** ~ es ist nutzlos; (hopeless) da ist nichts zu machen; **be up to no** ~ nichts Gutes im Schilde führen

goodbye /gʊd'baɪ/ int auf Wiedersehen; (Teleph, Radio) auf Wiederhören

good: ~**-for-nothing** a nichtsnutzig □ n Taugenichts m. **G~ 'Friday** n Karfreitag m. ~**'looking** a gut aussehend. ~**'natured** a gutmütig

goodness /'gʊdnɪs/ n Güte f; **my** ~! du meine Güte! **thank** ~! Gott sei Dank!

goods /gʊdz/ npl Waren pl. ~ **train** n Güterzug m

good'will n Wohlwollen nt; (Comm) Goodwill m

goody /'gʊdɪ/ n (fam) Gute(r) m/f. ~**goody** n Musterkind nt

gooey /'guːɪ/ a (fam) klebrig

goof /guːf/ vi (fam) einen Schnitzer machen

goose /guːs/ n (pl geese) Gans f

gooseberry /'gʊzbərɪ/ n Stachelbeere f

goose /guːs/: ~**flesh** n, ~**pimples** npl Gänsehaut f

gore¹ /gɔː(r)/ n Blut nt

gore² vt mit den Hörnern aufspießen

gorge /gɔːdʒ/ n (Geog) Schlucht f □ vt ~ **oneself** sich vollessen

gorgeous /'gɔːdʒəs/ a prachtvoll; (fam) herrlich

gorilla /gə'rɪlə/ n Gorilla m

gormless /'gɔːmlɪs/ a (fam) doof

gorse /gɔːs/ n inv Stechginster m

gory /'gɔːrɪ/ a (-ier, -iest) blutig; (story) blutrünstig

gosh /gɒʃ/ int (fam) Mensch!

go-'slow n Bummelstreik m

gospel /'gɒspl/ n Evangelium nt

gossip /'gɒsɪp/ n Klatsch m; (person) Klatschbase f □ vi klatschen. ~**y** a geschwätzig

got /gɒt/ see get; **have** ~ haben; **have** ~ **to** müssen; **have** ~ **to do sth** etw tun müssen

Gothic /'gɒθɪk/ a gotisch

gotten /'gɒtn/ see get

gouge /gaʊdʒ/ vt ~ **out** aushöhlen

goulash /'guːlæʃ/ n Gulasch nt

gourmet /'gʊəmeɪ/ n Feinschmecker m

gout /gaʊt/ n Gicht f

govern /'gʌvn/ vt/i regieren; (determine) bestimmen. ~**ess** n Gouvernante f

government /'gʌvnmənt/ n Regierung f. ~**al** /-'mentl/ a Regierungs-

governor /'gʌvənə(r)/ n Gouverneur m; (on board) Vorstandsmitglied nt; (of prison) Direktor m; (fam: boss) Chef m

gown /gaʊn/ n [elegantes] Kleid nt; (Univ, Jur) Talar m

GP abbr of general practitioner

grab /græb/ vt (pt/pp grabbed) ergreifen; ~ **[hold of]** packen

grace /greɪs/ n Anmut f; (before meal) Tischgebet nt; (Relig) Gnade f; **with good** ~ mit Anstand; **say** ~ [vor dem Essen] beten; **three days'** ~ drei Tage Frist. ~**ful** a, **-ly** adv anmutig

gracious /'greɪʃəs/ a gnädig; (elegant) vornehm

grade /greɪd/ n Stufe f; (Comm) Güteklasse f; (Sch) Note f; (Amer, Sch: class) Klasse f; (Amer) = **gradient** □ vt einstufen; (Comm) sortieren. ~ **crossing** n (Amer) Bahnübergang m

gradient /'greɪdɪənt/ n Steigung f; (downward) Gefälle nt

gradual /'grædʒʊəl/ a, **-ly** adv allmählich

graduate¹ /'grædʒʊət/ n Akademiker(in) m(f)

graduate² /'grædʒʊeɪt/ vi (Univ) sein Examen machen. ~**d** a abgestuft; (container) mit Maßeinteilung

graffiti /grə'fiːtɪ/ npl Graffiti pl

graft /grɑːft/ n (Bot) Pfropfreis nt; (Med) Transplantat nt; (fam: hard work) Plackerei f □ vt (Bot) aufpfropfen; (Med) übertragen

grain /greɪn/ n (sand, salt, rice) Korn nt; (cereals) Getreide nt; (in wood) Maserung f; **against the** ~ (fig) gegen den Strich

gram /græm/ n Gramm nt

grammar /'græmə(r)/ n Grammatik f. ~ **school** n ≈ Gymnasium nt

grammatical /grə'mætɪkl/ a, **-ly** adv grammatisch

granary /'grænərɪ/ n Getreidespeicher m

grand /grænd/ a (-er, -est) großartig

grandad /'grændæd/ n (fam) Opa m

'grandchild n Enkelkind nt

'granddaughter n Enkelin f

grandeur /'grændʒə(r)/ n Pracht f

'grandfather n Großvater m. **∼ clock** n Standuhr f

grandiose /'grændɪəʊs/ a grandios

grand: **∼mother** n Großmutter f. **∼parents** npl Großeltern pl. **∼ pi'ano** n Flügel m. **∼son** n Enkel m. **∼stand** n Tribüne f

granite /'grænɪt/ n Granit m

granny /'grænɪ/ n ⟨fam⟩ Oma f

grant /grɑːnt/ n Subvention f; ⟨Univ⟩ Studienbeihilfe f □ vt gewähren; ⟨admit⟩ zugeben; **take sth for ∼ed** etw als selbstverständlich hinnehmen

granular /'grænjʊlə(r)/ a körnig

granulated /'grænjʊleɪtɪd/ a **∼ sugar** Kristallzucker m

granule /'grænjuːl/ n Körnchen nt

grape /greɪp/ n [Wein]traube f; **bunch of ∼s** [ganze] Weintraube f

grapefruit /'greɪp-/ n invar Grapefruit f, Pampelmuse f

graph /grɑːf/ n Kurvendiagramm nt

graphic /'græfɪk/ a, **-ally** adv grafisch; ⟨vivid⟩ anschaulich. **∼s** n ⟨design⟩ grafische Gestaltung f

'graph paper n Millimeterpapier nt

grapple /'græpl/ vi ringen

grasp /grɑːsp/ n Griff m □ vt ergreifen; ⟨understand⟩ begreifen. **∼ing** a habgierig

grass /grɑːs/ n Gras nt; ⟨lawn⟩ Rasen m; **at the ∼ roots** an der Basis. **∼hopper** n Heuschrecke f. **∼land** n Weideland nt

grassy /'grɑːsɪ/ a grasig

grate¹ /greɪt/ n Feuerrost m; ⟨hearth⟩ Kamin m

grate² vt ⟨Culin⟩ reiben; **∼ one's teeth** mit den Zähnen knirschen

grateful /'greɪtfl/ a, **-ly** adv dankbar (**to** dat)

grater /'greɪtə(r)/ n ⟨Culin⟩ Reibe f

gratify /'grætɪfaɪ/ vt ⟨pt/pp **-ied**⟩ befriedigen. **∼ing** a erfreulich

grating /'greɪtɪŋ/ n Gitter nt

gratis /'grɑːtɪs/ adv gratis

gratitude /'grætɪtjuːd/ n Dankbarkeit f

gratuitous /grə'tjuːɪtəs/ a ⟨uncalled for⟩ überflüssig

gratuity /grə'tjuːətɪ/ n ⟨tip⟩ Trinkgeld nt

grave¹ /greɪv/ a ⟨-r, -st⟩, **-ly** adv ernst; **∼ly ill** schwer krank

grave² n Grab nt. **∼-digger** n Totengräber m

gravel /'grævl/ n Kies m

grave: **∼stone** n Grabstein m. **∼yard** n Friedhof m

gravitate /'grævɪteɪt/ vi gravitieren

gravity /'grævətɪ/ n Ernst m; ⟨force⟩ Schwerkraft f

gravy /'greɪvɪ/ n [Braten]soße f

gray /greɪ/ a ⟨Amer⟩ = **grey**

graze¹ /greɪz/ vi ⟨animal:⟩ weiden

graze² n Schürfwunde f □ vt ⟨car⟩ streifen; ⟨knee⟩ aufschürfen

grease /griːs/ n Fett nt; ⟨lubricant⟩ Schmierfett nt □ vt einfetten; ⟨lubricate⟩ schmieren. **∼-proof 'paper** n Pergamentpapier nt

greasy /'griːsɪ/ a ⟨-ier, -iest⟩ fettig

great /greɪt/ a ⟨-er, -est⟩ groß; ⟨fam: marvellous⟩ großartig

great: **∼'aunt** n Großtante f. **G∼ 'Britain** n Großbritannien nt. **∼'grandchildren** npl Urenkel pl. **∼'grandfather** n Urgroßvater m. **∼'grandmother** n Urgroßmutter f

great|ly /'greɪtlɪ/ adv sehr. **∼ness** n Größe f

great-'uncle n Großonkel m

Greece /griːs/ n Griechenland nt

greed /griːd/ n [Hab]gier f

greedy /'griːdɪ/ a ⟨-ier, -iest⟩, **-ily** adv gierig; **don't be ∼** sei nicht so unbescheiden

Greek /griːk/ a griechisch □ n Grieche m/Griechin f; ⟨Lang⟩ Griechisch nt

green /griːn/ a ⟨-er, -est⟩ grün; ⟨fig⟩ unerfahren □ n Grün nt; ⟨grass⟩ Wiese f; **∼s** pl Kohl m; **the G∼s** pl ⟨Pol⟩ die Grünen pl

greenery /'griːnərɪ/ n Grün nt

'greenfly n Blattlaus f

greengage /'griːngeɪdʒ/ n Reneklode f

green: **∼grocer** n Obst- und Gemüsehändler m. **∼house** n Gewächshaus nt. **∼house effect** n Treibhauseffekt m

Greenland /'griːnlənd/ n Grönland nt

greet /griːt/ vt grüßen; ⟨welcome⟩ begrüßen. **∼ing** n Gruß m; ⟨welcome⟩ Begrüßung f. **∼ings card** n Glückwunschkarte f

gregarious /grɪ'geərɪəs/ a gesellig

grenade /grɪ'neɪd/ n Granate f

grew /gruː/ see **grow**

grey /greɪ/ a ⟨-er, -est⟩ grau □ n Grau nt □ vi grau werden. **∼hound** n Windhund m

grid /grɪd/ n Gitter nt; ⟨on map⟩ Gitternetz nt; ⟨Electr⟩ Überlandleitungsnetz nt

grief /griːf/ n Trauer f; **come to ∼** scheitern

grievance /'griːvəns/ n Beschwerde f

grieve /griːv/ vt betrüben □ vi trauern (**for** um)

grievous /'griːvəs/ a, **-ly** adv schwer

grill /grɪl/ n Gitter nt; ⟨Culin⟩ Grill m; **mixed ∼** Gemischtes nt vom Grill □ vt/i grillen; ⟨interrogate⟩ [streng] verhören

grille /grɪl/ n Gitter nt

grim /grɪm/ a (**grimmer, grimmest**), **-ly** adv ernst; ⟨determination⟩ verbissen

grimace /grɪ'meɪs/ n Grimasse f □ vi Grimassen schneiden

grime /graɪm/ n Schmutz m

grimy /'graɪmɪ/ a (**-ier, -iest**) schmutzig

grin /grɪn/ n Grinsen nt □ vi (pt/pp **grinned**) grinsen

grind /graɪnd/ n (fam: hard work) Plackerei f □ vt (pt/pp **ground**) mahlen; ⟨smooth, sharpen⟩ schleifen; (Amer: mince) durchdrehen; ∼ **one's teeth** mit den Zähnen knirschen

grip /grɪp/ n Griff m; (bag) Reisetasche f □ vt (pt/pp **gripped**) ergreifen; ⟨hold⟩ festhalten; fesseln ⟨interest⟩

gripe /graɪp/ vi (sl: grumble) meckern

gripping /'grɪpɪŋ/ a fesselnd

grisly /'grɪzlɪ/ a (**-ier, -iest**) grausig

gristle /'grɪsl/ n Knorpel m

grit /grɪt/ n [grober] Sand m; (for roads) Streugut nt; ⟨courage⟩ Mut m □ vt (pt/pp **gritted**) streuen ⟨road⟩; ∼ **one's teeth** die Zähne zusammenbeißen

grizzle /'grɪzl/ vi quengeln

groan /grəʊn/ n Stöhnen nt □ vi stöhnen

grocer /'grəʊsə(r)/ n Lebensmittelhändler m; ∼**'s [shop]** Lebensmittelgeschäft nt. ∼**ies** npl Lebensmittel pl

groggy /'grɒgɪ/ a schwach; ⟨unsteady⟩ wackelig [auf den Beinen]

groin /grɔɪn/ n (Anat) Leiste f

groom /gru:m/ n Bräutigam m; (for horse) Pferdepfleger(in) m(f) □ vt striegeln ⟨horse⟩

groove /gru:v/ n Rille f

grope /grəʊp/ vi tasten (for nach)

gross /grəʊs/ a (**-er, -est**) fett; (coarse) derb; ⟨glaring⟩ grob; (Comm) brutto; ⟨salary, weight⟩ Brutto- □ n inv Gros nt. ∼**ly** adv ⟨very⟩ sehr

grotesque /grəʊ'tesk/ a, **-ly** adv grotesk

grotto /'grɒtəʊ/ n (pl **-es**) Grotte f

grotty /'grɒtɪ/ a (fam) mies

ground[1] /graʊnd/ see **grind**

ground[2] n Boden m; (terrain) Gelände nt; (reason) Grund m; (Amer, Electr) Erde f; ∼**s** pl (park) Anlagen pl; (of coffee) Satz m □ vi ⟨ship:⟩ auflaufen □ vt aus dem Verkehr ziehen ⟨aircraft⟩; (Amer, Electr) erden

ground: ∼ **floor** n Erdgeschoss nt. ∼**ing** n Grundlage f. ∼**less** a grundlos. ∼ **'meat** n (Amer) Hackfleisch nt. ∼**sheet** n Bodenplane f. ∼**work** n Vorarbeiten pl

group /gru:p/ n Gruppe f □ vt gruppieren □ vi sich gruppieren

grouse[1] /graʊs/ n inv schottisches Moorschneehuhn nt

grouse[2] vi (fam) meckern

grovel /'grɒvl/ vi (pt/pp **grovelled**) kriechen. ∼**ling** a kriecherisch

grow /grəʊ/ v (pt **grew**, pp **grown**) □ vi wachsen; (become) werden; (increase) zunehmen □ vt anbauen; ∼ **one's hair** sich (dat) die Haare wachsen lassen. ∼ **up** aufwachsen; ⟨town:⟩ entstehen

growl /graʊl/ n Knurren nt □ vi knurren

grown /grəʊn/ see **grow**. ∼**-up** a erwachsen □ n Erwachsene(r) m/f

growth /grəʊθ/ n Wachstum nt; (increase) Zunahme f; (Med) Gewächs nt

grub /grʌb/ n (larva) Made f; (fam: food) Essen nt

grubby /'grʌbɪ/ a (**-ier, -iest**) schmuddelig

grudg|e /grʌdʒ/ n Groll m; **bear s.o. a** ∼**e** einen Groll gegen jdn hegen □ vt ∼**e** s.o. **sth** jdm etw missgönnen. ∼**ing** a, **-ly** adv widerwillig

gruelling /'gru:əlɪŋ/ a strapaziös

gruesome /'gru:səm/ a grausig

gruff /grʌf/ a, **-ly** adv barsch

grumble /'grʌmbl/ vi schimpfen (at mit)

grumpy /'grʌmpɪ/ a (**-ier, -iest**) griesgrämig

grunt /grʌnt/ n Grunzen nt □ vi grunzen

guarant|ee /gærən'ti:/ n Garantie f; ⟨document⟩ Garantieschein m □ vt garantieren; garantieren für ⟨quality, success⟩; **be** ∼**eed** ⟨product:⟩ Garantie haben. ∼**or** n Bürge m

guard /gɑ:d/ n Wache f; ⟨security⟩ Wächter m; (on train) ≈ Zugführer m; (Techn) Schutz m; **be on** ∼ Wache stehen; **on one's** ∼ auf der Hut □ vt bewachen; (protect) schützen □ vi ∼ **against** sich hüten vor (+ dat). ∼**dog** n Wachhund m

guarded /'gɑ:dɪd/ a vorsichtig

guardian /'gɑ:dɪən/ n Vormund m

guerrilla /gə'rɪlə/ n Guerillakämpfer m. ∼ **warfare** n Partisanenkrieg m

guess /ges/ n Vermutung f □ vt erraten □ vi raten; (Amer: believe) glauben. ∼**work** n Vermutung f

guest /gest/ n Gast m. ∼**-house** n Pension f

guffaw /gʌ'fɔ:/ n derbes Lachen nt □ vi derb lachen

guidance /'gaɪdəns/ n Führung f, Leitung f; ⟨advice⟩ Beratung f

guide /gaɪd/ n Führer(in) m(f); ⟨book⟩ Führer m; **[Girl] G**∼ Pfadfinderin f □ vt führen, leiten. ∼**book** n Führer m

guided /'gaɪdɪd/ a ∼ **missile** Fernlenkgeschoss nt; ∼ **tour** Führung f

guide: ∼**-dog** n Blindenhund m. ∼**lines** npl Richtlinien pl

guild /gɪld/ n Gilde f, Zunft f

guile /gaɪl/ n Arglist f

guillotine /'gɪlətiːn/ n Guillotine f; (for paper) Papierschneidemaschine f

guilt /gɪlt/ n Schuld f. **∼ily** adv schuldbewusst

guilty /'gɪltɪ/ a (-ier, -iest) a schuldig (of gen); ⟨look⟩ schuldbewusst; ⟨conscience⟩ schlecht

guinea-pig /'gɪnɪ-/ n Meerschweinchen nt; (person) Versuchskaninchen nt

guise /gaɪz/ n in the ∼ of in Gestalt (+ gen)

guitar /gɪ'tɑː(r)/ n Gitarre f. **∼ist** n Gitarrist(in) m(f)

gulf /gʌlf/ n (Geog) Golf m; (fig) Kluft f

gull /gʌl/ n Möwe f

gullet /'gʌlɪt/ n Speiseröhre f; (throat) Kehle f

gullible /'gʌlɪbl/ a leichtgläubig

gully /'gʌlɪ/ n Schlucht f; (drain) Rinne f

gulp /gʌlp/ n Schluck m □ vi schlucken □ vt ∼ **down** hinunterschlucken

gum[1] /gʌm/ n & -s pl (Anat) Zahnfleisch nt

gum[2] n Gummi[harz] nt; (glue) Klebstoff m; (chewing-gum) Kaugummi m □ vt (pt/pp gummed) kleben (to an + acc). **∼boot** n Gummistiefel m

gummed /gʌmd/ see gum[2] □ a ⟨label⟩ gummiert

gumption /'gʌmpʃn/ n (fam) Grips m

gun /gʌn/ n Schusswaffe f; (pistol) Pistole f; (rifle) Gewehr nt; (cannon) Geschütz nt □ vt (pt/pp gunned) ∼ **down** niederschießen

gun: **∼fire** n Geschützfeuer nt. **∼man** bewaffneter Bandit m

gunner /'gʌnə(r)/ n Artillerist m

gun: **∼powder** n Schießpulver nt. **∼shot** n Schuss m

gurgle /'gɜːgl/ vi gluckern; (of baby) glucksen

gush /gʌʃ/ vi strömen; (enthuse) schwärmen (over von). ∼ **out** vi herausströmen

gusset /'gʌsɪt/ n Zwickel m

gust /gʌst/ n (of wind) Windstoß m; (Naut) Bö f

gusto /'gʌstəʊ/ n with ∼ mit Schwung

gusty /'gʌstɪ/ a böig

gut /gʌt/ n Darm m; ∼s pl Eingeweide pl; (fam: courage) Schneid m □ vt (pt/pp gutted) (Culin) ausnehmen; ∼ted by fire ausgebrannt

gutter /'gʌtə(r)/ n Rinnstein m; (fig) Gosse f; (on roof) Dachrinne f

guttural /'gʌtərl/ a guttural

guy /gaɪ/ n (fam) Kerl m

guzzle /'gʌzl/ vt/i schlingen; (drink) schlürfen

gym /dʒɪm/ n (fam) Turnhalle f; (gymnastics) Turnen nt

gymnasium /dʒɪm'neɪzɪəm/ n Turnhalle f

gymnast /'dʒɪmnæst/ n Turner(in) m(f). **∼ics** /-'næstɪks/ n Turnen nt

gym: ∼ **shoes** pl Turnschuhe pl. **∼-slip** n (Sch) Trägerkleid nt

gynaecolog|ist /gaɪnɪ'kɒlədʒɪst/ n Frauenarzt m /-ärztin f. **∼y** n Gynäkologie f

gypsy /'dʒɪpsɪ/ n Zigeuner(in) m(f)

gyrate /dʒaɪə'reɪt/ vi sich drehen

H

haberdashery /'hæbədæʃərɪ/ n Kurzwaren pl; (Amer) Herrenmoden pl

habit /'hæbɪt/ n Gewohnheit f; (Relig: costume) Ordenstracht f; **be in the** ∼ die Angewohnheit haben (of zu)

habitable /'hæbɪtəbl/ a bewohnbar

habitat /'hæbɪtæt/ n Habitat nt

habitation /hæbɪ'teɪʃn/ n **unfit for human** ∼ für Wohnzwecke ungeeignet

habitual /hə'bɪtjʊəl/ a gewohnt; (inveterate) gewohnheitsmäßig. **∼ly** adv gewohnheitsmäßig; (constantly) ständig

hack[1] /hæk/ n (writer) Schreiberling m; (hired horse) Mietpferd nt

hack[2] vt hacken; ∼ **to pieces** zerhacken

hackneyed /'hæknɪd/ a abgedroschen

'hacksaw n Metallsäge f

had /hæd/ see have

haddock /'hædək/ n inv Schellfisch m

haemorrhage /'hemərɪdʒ/ n Blutung f

haemorrhoids /'hemərɔɪdz/ npl Hämorrhoiden pl

hag /hæg/ n old ∼ alte Hexe f

haggard /'hægəd/ a abgehärmt

haggle /'hægl/ vi feilschen (over um)

hail[1] /heɪl/ vt begrüßen; herbeirufen ⟨taxi⟩ □ vi ∼ **from** kommen aus

hail[2] n Hagel m □ vi hageln. **∼stone** n Hagelkorn nt

hair /heə(r)/ n Haar nt; **wash one's** ∼ sich (dat) die Haare waschen

hair: **∼brush** n Haarbürste f. **∼cut** n Haarschnitt m; **have a** ∼**cut** sich (dat) die Haare schneiden lassen. **∼do** n (fam) Frisur f. **∼dresser** n Friseur m/Friseuse f. **∼drier** n Haartrockner m; (hand-held)

Föhn *m*. **~-grip** *n* [Haar]klemme *f*. **~pin** *n* Haarnadel *f*. **~pin 'bend** *n* Haarnadelkurve *f*. **~-raising** *a* haarsträubend. **~-style** *n* Frisur *f*

hairy /'heəri/ *a* (-ier, -iest) behaart; *(excessively)* haarig; *(fam: frightening)* brenzlig

hake /heik/ *n inv* Seehecht *m*

hale /heil/ *a* **~ and hearty** gesund und munter

half /ha:f/ *n (pl* halves) Hälfte *f*; **cut in ~** halbieren; **one and a ~** eineinhalb, anderthalb; **~ a dozen** ein halbes Dutzend; **~ an hour** eine halbe Stunde □ *a & adv* halb; **~ past two** halb drei; **[at] ~ price** zum halben Preis

half: **~-board** *n* Halbpension *f*. **~-caste** *n* Mischling *m*. **~-'hearted** *a* lustlos. **~-'hourly** *a & adv* halbstündlich. **~-'mast** *n* **at ~mast** auf halbmast. **~-measure** *n* Halbheit *f*. **~-'term** *n* schulfreie Tage nach dem halben Trimester. **~-'timbered** *a* Fachwerk-. **~-'time** *n (Sport)* Halbzeit *f*. **~-'way** *a* the **~-way mark/stage** die Hälfte □ *adv* auf halbem Weg; **get ~way** den halben Weg zurücklegen; *(fig)* bis zur Hälfte kommen. **~-wit** *n* Idiot *m*

halibut /'hælibət/ *n inv* Heilbutt *m*

hall /hɔ:l/ *n* Halle *f*; *(room)* Saal *m*; *(Sch)* Aula *f*; *(entrance)* Flur *m*; *(mansion)* Gutshaus *nt*; **~ of residence** *(Univ)* Studentenheim *nt*

'hallmark *n* [Feingehalts]stempel *m*; *(fig)* Kennzeichen *nt* (**of** für) □ *vt* stempeln

hallo /hə'ləʊ/ *int* [guten] Tag! *(fam)* hallo!

Hallowe'en /hæləʊ'i:n/ *n* der Tag vor Allerheiligen

hallucination /həlu:sɪ'neɪʃn/ *n* Halluzination *f*

halo /'heiləʊ/ *n (pl* -es) Heiligenschein *m*; *(Astr)* Hof *m*

halt /hɔ:lt/ *n* Halt *m*; **come to a ~** stehen bleiben; *(traffic:)* zum Stillstand kommen □ *vi* Halt machen; **~!** halt! **~ing** *a, adv* **-ly** zögernd

halve /ha:v/ *vt* halbieren; *(reduce)* um die Hälfte reduzieren

ham /hæm/ *n* Schinken *m*

hamburger /'hæmbɜ:gə(r)/ *n* Hamburger *m*

hamlet /'hæmlɪt/ *n* Weiler *m*

hammer /'hæmə(r)/ *n* Hammer *m* □ *vt/i* hämmern (**at an** + *acc*)

hammock /'hæmək/ *n* Hängematte *f*

hamper[1] /'hæmpə(r)/ *n* Picknickkorb *m*; [gift] Geschenkkorb *m*

hamper[2] *vt* behindern

hamster /'hæmstə(r)/ *n* Hamster *m*

hand /hænd/ *n* Hand *f*; *(of clock)* Zeiger *m*; *(writing)* Handschrift *f*; *(worker)* Arbeiter(in) *m(f)*; *(Cards)* Blatt *nt*; **all ~s** *(Naut)* alle Mann; **at ~** in der Nähe; **on the one/other ~** einer-/andererseits; **out of ~** außer Kontrolle; *(summarily)* kurzerhand; **in ~** unter Kontrolle; *(available)* verfügbar; **give s.o. a ~** jdm behilflich sein □ *vt* reichen (**to** *dat*). **~ in** *vt* abgeben. **~ out** *vt* austeilen. **~ over** *vt* überreichen

hand: **~bag** *n* Handtasche *f*. **~book** *n* Handbuch *nt*. **~brake** *n* Handbremse *f*. **~cuffs** *npl* Handschellen *pl*. **~ful** *n* Handvoll *f*; **be [quite] a ~ful** *(fam)* nicht leicht zu haben sein

handicap /'hændikæp/ *n* Behinderung *f*; *(Sport & fig)* Handikap *nt*. **~ped** *a* **mentally/physically ~ped** geistig/körperlich behindert

handi|craft /'hændikra:ft/ *n* Basteln *nt*; *(Sch)* Werken *nt*. **~work** *n* Werk *nt*

handkerchief /'hæŋkətʃif/ *n (pl* **~s &** **-chieves)** Taschentuch *nt*

handle /'hændl/ *n* Griff *m*; *(of door)* Klinke *f*; *(of cup)* Henkel *m*; *(of broom)* Stiel *m*; **fly off the ~** *(fam)* aus der Haut fahren □ *vt* handhaben; *(treat)* umgehen mit; *(touch)* anfassen. **~bars** *npl* Lenkstange *f*

hand: **~luggage** *n* Handgepäck *nt*. **~made** *a* handgemacht. **~out** *n* Prospekt *m*; *(money)* Unterstützung *f*. **~rail** *n* Handlauf *m*. **~shake** *n* Händedruck *m*

handsome /'hænsəm/ *a* gut aussehend; *(generous)* großzügig; *(large)* beträchtlich

hand: **~stand** *n* Handstand *m*. **~writing** *n* Handschrift *f*. **~-'written** *a* handgeschrieben

handy /'hændi/ *a* (-ier, -iest) handlich; *(person)* geschickt; **have/keep ~** griffbereit haben/halten. **~man** *n* [home] **~man** *n* Heimwerker *m*

hang /hæŋ/ *vt/i (pt/pp* hung) hängen; **~ wallpaper** tapezieren □ *vt (pt/pp* hanged) hängen *(criminal)*; **~ oneself** sich erhängen □ *n* **get the ~ of it** *(fam)* den Dreh herauskriegen. **~ about** *vi* sich herumdrücken. **~ on** *vi* sich festhalten (**to an** + *dat*); *(fam: wait)* warten. **~ out** *vi* heraushängen; *(fam: live)* wohnen □ *vt* draußen aufhängen *(washing)*. **~ up** *vt/i* aufhängen

hangar /'hæŋə(r)/ *n* Flugzeughalle *f*

hanger /'hæŋə(r)/ *n* [Kleider]bügel *m*

hang: **~-glider** *n* Drachenflieger *m*. **~-gliding** *n* Drachenfliegen *nt*. **~man** *n* Henker *m*. **~over** *n (fam)* Kater *m (fam)*. **~-up** *n (fam)* Komplex *m*

hanker /'hæŋkə(r)/ *vi* **~ after sth** sich *(dat)* etw wünschen

hanky /'hæŋkɪ/ n (fam) Taschentuch nt
hanky-panky /hæŋkɪ'pæŋkɪ/ n (fam) Mauscheleien pl
haphazard /hæp'hæzəd/ a, -ly adv planlos
happen /'hæpn/ vi geschehen, passieren; as it ~s zufälligerweise; I ~ed to be there ich war zufällig da; what has ~ed to him? was ist mit ihm los? (become of) was ist aus ihm geworden? ~ing n Ereignis nt
happi|ly /'hæpɪlɪ/ adv glücklich; (fortunately) glücklicherweise. ~ness n Glück nt
happy /'hæpɪ/ a (-ier, -iest) glücklich. ~-go-'lucky a sorglos
harass /'hærəs/ vt schikanieren. ~ed a abgehetzt. ~ment n Schikane f; (sexual) Belästigung f
harbour /'hɑːbə(r)/ n Hafen m □ vt Unterschlupf gewähren (+ dat); hegen (grudge)
hard /hɑːd/ a (-er, -est) hart; (difficult) schwer; ~ of hearing schwerhörig □ adv hart; (work) schwer; (pull) kräftig; (rain, snow) stark; think ~! denk mal nach! be ~ up (fam) knapp bei Kasse sein; be ~ done by (fam) ungerecht behandelt werden
hard: ~back n gebundene Ausgabe f. ~board n Hartfaserplatte f. ~-boiled a hart gekocht
harden /'hɑːdn/ vi hart werden
hard-'hearted a hartherzig
hard|ly /'hɑːdlɪ/ adv kaum; ~ly ever kaum [jemals]. ~ness n Härte f. ~ship n Not f
hard: ~ 'shoulder n (Auto) Randstreifen m. ~ware n Haushaltswaren pl; (Computing) Hardware f. ~-'wearing a strapazierfähig. ~-'working a fleißig
hardy /'hɑːdɪ/ a (-ier, -iest) abgehärtet; (plant) winterhart
hare /heə(r)/ n Hase m. ~ 'lip n Hasenscharte f
hark /hɑːk/ vi ~! hört! ~ back vi ~ back to (fig) zurückkommen auf (+ acc)
harm /hɑːm/ n Schaden m; out of ~'s way in Sicherheit; it won't do any ~ es kann nichts schaden □ vt ~ s.o. jdm etwas antun. ~ful a schädlich. ~less a harmlos
harmonica /hɑː'mɒnɪkə/ n Mundharmonika f
harmonious /hɑː'məʊnɪəs/ a, -ly adv harmonisch
harmon|ize /'hɑːmənaɪz/ vi (fig) harmonieren. ~y n Harmonie f
harness /'hɑːnɪs/ n Geschirr nt; (of parachute) Gurtwerk nt □ vt anschirren (horse); (use) nutzbar machen

harp /hɑːp/ n Harfe f □ vi ~ on [about] (fam) herumreiten auf (+ dat). ~ist n Harfenist(in) m(f)
harpoon /hɑː'puːn/ n Harpune f
harpsichord /'hɑːpsɪkɔːd/ n Cembalo nt
harrow /'hærəʊ/ n Egge f. ~ing a grauenhaft
harsh /hɑːʃ/ a (-er, -est), -ly adv hart; (voice) rau; (light) grell. ~ness n Härte f; Rauheit f
harvest /'hɑːvɪst/ n Ernte f □ vt ernten
has /hæz/ see have
hash /hæʃ/ n (Culin) Haschee nt; make a ~ of (fam) verpfuschen
hashish /'hæʃɪʃ/ n Haschisch nt
hassle /'hæsl/ n (fam) Ärger m □ vt schikanieren
hassock /'hæsək/ n Kniekissen nt
haste /heɪst/ n Eile f; make ~ sich beeilen
hasten /'heɪsn/ vi sich beeilen (to zu); (go quickly) eilen □ vt beschleunigen
hasty /'heɪstɪ/ a (-ier, -iest), -ily adv hastig; (decision) voreilig
hat /hæt/ n Hut m; (knitted) Mütze f
hatch[1] /hætʃ/ n (for food) Durchreiche f; (Naut) Luke f
hatch[2] vi ~ [out] ausschlüpfen □ vt ausbrüten
'hatchback n (Auto) Modell nt mit Hecktür
hatchet /'hætʃɪt/ n Beil nt
hate /heɪt/ n Hass m □ vt hassen. ~ful a abscheulich
hatred /'heɪtrɪd/ n Hass m
haughty /'hɔːtɪ/ a (-ier, -iest), -ily adv hochmütig
haul /hɔːl/ n (fish) Fang m; (loot) Beute f □ vt/i ziehen (on an + dat). ~age n /-ɪdʒ/ n Transport m. ~ier n /-ɪə(r)/ n Spediteur m
haunt /hɔːnt/ n Lieblingsaufenthalt m □ vt umgehen in (+ dat); this house is ~ed in diesem Haus spukt es
have /hæv/ vt (3 sg pres tense has; pt/pp had) haben; bekommen (baby); holen (doctor); ~ a meal/drink etwas essen/ trinken; ~ lunch zu Mittag essen; ~ a walk spazieren gehen; ~ a dream träumen; ~ a rest sich ausruhen; ~ a swim schwimmen; ~ sth done etw machen lassen; ~ sth made sich (dat) etw machen lassen; ~ to do sth etw tun müssen; ~ it out with zur Rede stellen; so I ~! tatsächlich! he has [got] two houses er hat zwei Häuser; you have got the money, haven't you? du hast das Geld, nicht [wahr]? □ v aux haben; (with verbs of motion & some others) sein; I ~ seen him ich habe ihn gesehen; he has never been

there er ist nie da gewesen. **~ on** vt (be wearing) anhaben; (dupe) anführen

haven /'heɪvn/ n (fig) Zuflucht f

haversack /'hævə-/ n Rucksack m

havoc /'hævək/ n Verwüstung f; **play ~ with** (fig) völlig durcheinander bringen

haw /hɔː/ see **hum**

hawk¹ /hɔːk/ n Falke m

hawk² vt hausieren mit. **~er** n Hausierer m

hawthorn /'hɔː-/ n Hagedorn m

hay /heɪ/ n Heu nt. **~ fever** n Heuschnupfen m. **~stack** n Heuschober m

'haywire a (fam) **go ~** verrückt spielen; ⟨plans:⟩ über den Haufen geworfen werden

hazard /'hæzəd/ n Gefahr f; (risk) Risiko nt □ vt riskieren. **~ous** /-əs/ a gefährlich; (risky) riskant. **~ [warning] lights** npl (Auto) Warnblinkanlage f

haze /'heɪz/ n Dunst m

hazel /'heɪzl/ n Haselbusch m. **~nut** n Haselnuss f

hazy /'heɪzɪ/ a (-ier, -iest) dunstig; (fig) unklar

he /hiː/ pron er

head /hed/ n Kopf m; (chief) Oberhaupt nt; (of firm) Chef(in) m(f); (of school) Schulleiter(in) m(f); (on beer) Schaumkrone f; (of bed) Kopfende nt; **20 ~ of cattle** 20 Stück Vieh; **~ first** kopfüber □ vt anführen; (Sport) köpfen ⟨ball⟩ □ vi **~ for** zusteuern auf (+ acc). **~ache** n Kopfschmerzen pl. **~dress** n Kopfschmuck m

head|er /'hedə(r)/ n Kopfball m; (dive) Kopfsprung m. **~ing** n Überschrift f

head: ~lamp n (Auto) Scheinwerfer m. **~land** n Landspitze f. **~light** n (Auto) Scheinwerfer m. **~line** n Schlagzeile f. **~long** adv kopfüber. **~'master** n Schulleiter m. **~'mistress** n Schulleiterin f. **~on** a & adv frontal. **~phones** npl Kopfhörer m. **~quarters** npl Hauptquartier nt; (Pol) Zentrale f. **~rest** n Kopfstütze f. **~room** n lichte Höhe f. **~scarf** n Kopftuch nt. **~strong** a eigenwillig. **~ 'waiter** n Oberkellner m. **~way** n **make ~way** Fortschritte machen. **~wind** n Gegenwind m. **~word** n Stichwort nt

heady /'hedɪ/ a berauschend

heal /hiːl/ vt/i heilen

health /helθ/ n Gesundheit f

health: ~ farm n Schönheitsfarm f. **~ foods** npl Reformkost f. **~-food shop** n Reformhaus nt. **~ insurance** n Krankenversicherung f

healthy /'helθɪ/ a (-ier, -iest), **-ily** adv gesund

heap /hiːp/ n Haufen m; **~s** (fam) jede Menge □ vt **~ [up]** häufen; **~ed teaspoon** gehäufter Teelöffel

hear /hɪə(r)/ vt/i (pt/pp heard) hören; **~, ~!** hört, hört! **he would not ~ of it** er ließ es nicht zu

hearing /'hɪərɪŋ/ n Gehör nt; (Jur) Verhandlung f. **~-aid** n Hörgerät nt

'hearsay n **from ~** vom Hörensagen

hearse /hɜːs/ n Leichenwagen m

heart /hɑːt/ n Herz nt; (courage) Mut m; **~s** pl (Cards) Herz nt; **by ~** auswendig

heart: ~ache n Kummer m. **~ attack** n Herzanfall m. **~beat** n Herzschlag m. **~break** n Leid nt. **~breaking** a herzzerreißend. **~broken** a untröstlich. **~burn** n Sodbrennen nt. **~en** vt ermutigen. **~felt** a herzlich[st]

hearth /hɑːθ/ n Herd m; (fireplace) Kamin m. **~rug** n Kaminvorleger m

heart|ily /'hɑːtɪlɪ/ adv herzlich; ⟨eat⟩ viel. **~less** a, **-ly** adv herzlos. **~y** a herzlich; ⟨meal⟩ groß; ⟨person⟩ burschikos

heat /hiːt/ n Hitze f; (Sport) Vorlauf m □ vt heiß machen; heizen ⟨room⟩. **~ed** a geheizt; ⟨swimming pool⟩ beheizt; ⟨discussion⟩ hitzig. **~er** n Heizgerät nt; (Auto) Heizanlage f

heath /hiːθ/ n Heide f

heathen /'hiːðn/ a heidnisch □ n Heide m/Heidin f

heather /'heðə(r)/ n Heidekraut nt

heating /'hiːtɪŋ/ n Heizung f

heat: ~stroke n Hitzschlag m. **~wave** n Hitzewelle f

heave /hiːv/ vt/i ziehen; (lift) heben; (fam: throw) schmeißen; **~ a sigh** einen Seufzer ausstoßen

heaven /'hevn/ n Himmel m. **~ly** a himmlisch

heavy /'hevɪ/ a (-ier, -iest), **-ily** adv schwer; ⟨traffic, rain⟩ stark; ⟨sleep⟩ tief. **~weight** n Schwergewicht nt

Hebrew /'hiːbruː/ a hebräisch

heckle /'hekl/ vt [durch Zwischenrufe] unterbrechen. **~r** n Zwischenrufer m

hectic /'hektɪk/ a hektisch

hedge /hedʒ/ n Hecke f □ vi (fig) ausweichen. **~hog** n Igel m

heed /hiːd/ n **pay ~ to** Beachtung schenken (+ dat) □ vt beachten. **~less** a ungeachtet (of gen)

heel¹ /hiːl/ n Ferse f; (of shoe) Absatz m; **down at ~** heruntergekommen; **take to one's ~s** (fam) Fersengeld geben

heel² vi **~ over** (Naut) sich auf die Seite legen

hefty /'heftɪ/ a (-ier, -iest) kräftig; (heavy) schwer

heifer /ˈhefə(r)/ n Färse f

height /haɪt/ n Höhe f; (of person) Größe f. **~en** vt (fig) steigern

heir /eə(r)/ n Erbe m. **~ess** n Erbin f. **~loom** n Erbstück nt

held /held/ see hold²

helicopter /ˈhelɪkɒptə(r)/ n Hubschrauber m

hell /hel/ n Hölle f; go to ~! (sl) geh zum Teufel! □ int verdammt!

hello /həˈləʊ/ int [guten] Tag! (fam) hallo!

helm /helm/ n [Steuer]ruder nt; at the ~ (fig) am Ruder

helmet /ˈhelmɪt/ n Helm m

help /help/ n Hilfe f; (employees) Hilfskräfte pl; there's no ~ das nützt nichts □ vt/i helfen (s.o. jdm); ~ oneself to sth sich (dat) etw nehmen; ~ yourself (at table) greif zu; I could not ~ laughing ich musste lachen; it cannot be ~ed es lässt sich nicht ändern; I can't ~ it ich kann nichts dafür

help|er /ˈhelpə(r)/ n Helfer(in) m(f). **~ful** a, -ly adv hilfsbereit; (advice) nützlich. **~ing** n Portion f. **~less** a, -ly adv hilflos

helter-skelter /heltəˈskeltə(r)/ adv holterdiepolter □ n Rutschbahn f

hem /hem/ n Saum m □ vt (pt/pp hemmed) säumen; ~ in umzingeln

hemisphere /ˈhemɪ-/ n Hemisphäre f

'hem-line n Rocklänge f

hemp /hemp/ n Hanf m

hen /hen/ n Henne f; (any female bird) Weibchen nt

hence /hens/ adv daher; five years ~ in fünf Jahren. **~'forth** adv von nun an

henchman /ˈhentʃmən/ n (pej) Gefolgsmann m

'henpecked a ~ husband Pantoffelheld m

her /hɜ:(r)/ a ihr □ pron (acc) sie; (dat) ihr; I know ~ ich kenne sie; give ~ the money gib ihr das Geld

herald /ˈherəld/ vt verkünden. **~ry** n Wappenkunde f

herb /hɜ:b/ n Kraut nt

herbaceous /hɜ:ˈbeɪʃəs/ a krautartig; ~ border Staudenrabatte f

herd /hɜ:d/ n Herde f □ vt (tend) hüten; (drive) treiben. ~ together vi sich zusammendrängen □ vt zusammentreiben

here /hɪə(r)/ adv hier; (to this place) hierher; in ~ hier drinnen; come/bring ~ herkommen/herbringen. **~'after** adv im Folgenden. **~'by** adv hiermit

heredit|ary /həˈredɪtəri/ a erblich. **~y** n Vererbung f

here|sy /ˈherəsɪ/ n Ketzerei f. **~tic** n Ketzer(in) m(f)

here'with adv (Comm) beiliegend

heritage /ˈherɪtɪdʒ/ n Erbe nt

hermetic /hɜ:ˈmetɪk/ a, -ally adv hermetisch

hermit /ˈhɜ:mɪt/ n Einsiedler m

hernia /ˈhɜ:nɪə/ n Bruch m, Hernie f

hero /ˈhɪərəʊ/ n (pl -es) Held m

heroic /hɪˈrəʊɪk/ a, -ally adv heldenhaft

heroin /ˈherəʊɪn/ n Heroin nt

hero|ine /ˈherəʊɪn/ n Heldin f. **~ism** n Heldentum nt

heron /ˈhern/ n Reiher m

herring /ˈherɪŋ/ n Hering m; red ~ (fam) falsche Spur f. **~bone** n (pattern) Fischgrätenmuster nt

hers /hɜ:z/ poss pron ihre(r), ihrs; a friend of ~ ein Freund von ihr; that is ~ das gehört ihr

her'self pron selbst; (refl) sich; by ~ allein

hesitant /ˈhezɪtənt/ a, -ly adv zögernd

hesitat|e /ˈhezɪteɪt/ vi zögern. **~ion** /-ˈteɪʃn/ n Zögern nt; without ~ion ohne zu zögern

het /het/ a ~ up (fam) aufgeregt

hetero'sexual /hetərəʊ-/ a heterosexuell

hew /hju:/ vt (pt hewed, pp hewed or hewn) hauen

hexagonal /hekˈsægənl/ a sechseckig

heyday /ˈheɪ-/ n Glanzzeit f

hi /haɪ/ int he! (hallo) Tag!

hiatus /haɪˈeɪtəs/ n (pl -tuses) Lücke f

hibernat|e /ˈhaɪbəneɪt/ vi Winterschlaf halten. **~ion** /-ˈneɪʃn/ n Winterschlaf m

hiccup /ˈhɪkʌp/ n Hick m; (fam: hitch) Panne f; have the ~s den Schluckauf haben □ vi hick machen

hid /hɪd/, **hidden** see hide²

hide¹ /haɪd/ n (Comm) Haut f; (leather) Leder nt

hide² vt (pt hid, pp hidden) □ vt verstecken; (keep secret) verheimlichen □ vi sich verstecken. **~-and-'seek** n play ~-and-seek Versteck spielen

hideous /ˈhɪdɪəs/ a, -ly adv hässlich; (horrible) grässlich

'hide-out n Versteck nt

hiding¹ /ˈhaɪdɪŋ/ n (fam) give s.o. a ~ jdn verdreschen

hiding² n go into ~ untertauchen

hierarchy /ˈhaɪərɑ:kɪ/ n Hierarchie f

hieroglyphics /haɪərəˈɡlɪfɪks/ npl Hieroglyphen pl

higgledy-piggledy /hɪɡldɪˈpɪɡldɪ/ adv kunterbunt durcheinander

high /haɪ/ a (-er, -est) hoch; attrib hohe(r,s); (meat) angegangen; (wind) stark;

(on drugs) high; **it's ~ time** es ist höchste Zeit □ *adv* hoch; **~ and low** überall □ *n* Hoch *nt*; *(temperature)* Höchsttemperatur *f*

high: **~brow** *a* intellektuell. **~ chair** *n* Kinderhochstuhl *m*. **~'-handed** *a* selbstherrlich. **~'heeled** *a* hochhackig. **~ jump** *n* Hochsprung *m*

'highlight *n* *(fig)* Höhepunkt *m*; **~s** *pl* *(in hair)* helle Strähnen *pl* □ *vt* *(emphasize)* hervorheben

highly /'haɪlɪ/ *adv* hoch; **speak ~ of** loben; **think ~ of** sehr schätzen. **~'strung** *a* nervös

Highness /'haɪnɪs/ *n* Hoheit *f*

high: **~rise** *a* **~rise flats** *pl* Wohnturm *m*. **~ season** *n* Hochsaison *f*. **~ street** *n* Hauptstraße *f*. **~ tide** *n* Hochwasser *nt*. **~way** *n* **public ~way** öffentliche Straße

hijack /'haɪdʒæk/ *vt* entführen. **~er** *n* Entführer *m*

hike /haɪk/ *n* Wanderung *f* □ *vi* wandern. **~r** *n* Wanderer *m*

hilarious /hɪ'leərɪəs/ *a* sehr komisch

hill /hɪl/ *n* Berg *m*; *(mound)* Hügel *m*; *(slope)* Hang *m*

hill: **~billy** *n* *(Amer)* Hinterwäldler *m*. **~side** *n* Hang *m*. **~y** *a* hügelig

hilt /hɪlt/ *n* Griff *m*; **to the ~** *(fam)* voll und ganz

him /hɪm/ *pron* *(acc)* ihn; *(dat)* ihm; **I know ~** ich kenne ihn; **give ~ the money** gib ihm das Geld. **~'self** *pron* selbst; *(refl)* sich; **by ~self** allein

hind /haɪnd/ *a* Hinter-

hind|er /'hɪndə(r)/ *vt* hindern. **~rance** /-rəns/ *n* Hindernis *nt*

hindsight /'haɪnd-/ *n* **with ~** rückblickend

Hindu /'hɪnduː/ *n* Hindu *m* □ *a* Hindu-. **~ism** *n* Hinduismus *m*

hinge /hɪndʒ/ *n* Scharnier *nt*; *(on door)* Angel *f* □ *vi* **~ on** *(fig)* ankommen auf (+ *acc)*

hint /hɪnt/ *n* Wink *m*, Andeutung *f*; *(advice)* Hinweis *m*; *(trace)* Spur *f* □ *vi* **~ at** anspielen auf (+ *acc)*

hip /hɪp/ *n* Hüfte *f*

hippie /'hɪpɪ/ *n* Hippie *m*

hip 'pocket *n* Gesäßtasche *f*

hippopotamus /hɪpə'pɒtəməs/ *n* *(pl -muses or -mi /-maɪ/)* Nilpferd *nt*

hire /'haɪə(r)/ *vt* mieten *(car)*; leihen *(suit)*; einstellen *(person)*; **~ [out]** vermieten; verleihen □ *n* Mieten *nt*; Leihen *nt*. **~-car** *n* Leihwagen *m*

his /hɪz/ *a* sein □ *poss pron* seine(r), seins; **a friend of ~** ein Freund von ihm; **that is ~** das gehört ihm

hiss /hɪs/ *n* Zischen *nt* □ *vt/i* zischen

historian /hɪ'stɔːrɪən/ *n* Historiker(in) *m(f)*

historic /hɪ'stɒrɪk/ *a* historisch. **~al** *a*, **-ly** *adv* geschichtlich, historisch

history /'hɪstərɪ/ *n* Geschichte *f*

hit /hɪt/ *n* *(blow)* Schlag *m*; *(fam: success)* Erfolg *m*; **direct ~** Volltreffer *m* □ *vt/i* *(pt/pp hit, pres p hitting)* schlagen; *(knock against, collide with, affect)* treffen; **~ the target** das Ziel treffen; **~ on** *(fig)* kommen auf (+ *acc)*; **~ it off** gut auskommen (**with** mit); **~ one's head on sth** sich *(dat)* den Kopf an etw *(dat)* stoßen

hitch /hɪtʃ/ *n* Problem *nt*; **technical ~** Panne *f* □ *vt* festmachen (**to** an + *dat)*; **~ up** hochziehen; **~ a lift** per Anhalter fahren, *(fam)* trampen. **~hiker** *vi* per Anhalter fahren, *(fam)* trampen. **~hiker** *n* Anhalter(in) *m(f)*

hither /'hɪðə(r)/ *adv* hierher; **~ and thither** hin und her. **~'to** *adv* bisher

hive /haɪv/ *n* Bienenstock *m*. **~ off** *vt* *(Comm)* abspalten

hoard /hɔːd/ *n* Hort *m* □ *vt* horten, hamstern

hoarding /'hɔːdɪŋ/ *n* Bauzaun *m*; *(with advertisements)* Reklamewand *f*

hoar-frost /'hɔː-/ *n* Raureif *m*

hoarse /hɔːs/ *a* (-r, -st), **-ly** *adv* heiser. **~ness** *n* Heiserkeit *f*

hoax /həʊks/ *n* übler Scherz *m*; *(false alarm)* blinder Alarm *m*

hob /hɒb/ *n* Kochmulde *f*

hobble /'hɒbl/ *vi* humpeln

hobby /'hɒbɪ/ *n* Hobby *nt*. **~-horse** *n* *(fig)* Lieblingsthema *nt*

hobnailed /'hɒb-/ *a* **~ boots** *pl* genagelte Schuhe *pl*

hock /hɒk/ *n* [weißer] Rheinwein *m*

hockey /'hɒkɪ/ *n* Hockey *nt*

hoe /həʊ/ *n* Hacke *f* □ *vt* *(pres p hoeing)* hacken

hog /hɒg/ *n* [Mast]schwein *nt* □ *vt* *(pt/pp hogged)* *(fam)* mit Beschlag belegen

hoist /hɔɪst/ *n* Lastenaufzug *m* □ *vt* hochziehen; hissen *(flag)*

hold[1] /həʊld/ *n* *(Naut)* Laderaum *m*

hold[2] *n* Halt *m*; *(Sport)* Griff *m*; *(fig: influence)* Einfluss *m*; **get ~ of** fassen; *(fam: contact)* erreichen □ *v* *(pt/pp held)* □ *vt* halten; *(container:)* fassen; *(believe:* meinen; *(possess)* haben; anhalte *(breath)*; **~ one's tongue** den Mun halten □ *vi* *(rope:)* halten; *(weather:)* sic halten; **not ~ with** *(fam)* nicht einver standen sein mit. **~ back** *vt* zurückhalte □ *vi* zögern. **~ on** *vi* *(wait)* warten; *(on telephone)* am Apparat bleiben; **~ on t**

(*keep*) behalten; (*cling to*) sich festhalten an (+ *dat*). ~ **out** *vt* hinhalten □ *vi* (*resist*) aushalten. ~ **up** *vt* hochhalten; (*delay*) aufhalten; (*rob*) überfallen

'hold|all *n* Reisetasche *f*. ~**er** *n* Inhaber(in) *m(f)*; (*container*) Halter *m*. ~**up** *n* Verzögerung *f*; (*attack*) Überfall *m*

hole / həʊl/ *n* Loch *nt*

holiday /'hɒlədeɪ/ *n* Urlaub *m*; (*Sch*) Ferien *pl*; (*public*) Feiertag *m*; (*day off*) freier Tag *m*; **go on** ~ in Urlaub fahren. ~**-maker** *n* Urlauber(in) *m(f)*

holiness /'həʊlɪnɪs/ *n* Heiligkeit *f*

Holland /'hɒlənd/ *n* Holland *nt*

hollow /'hɒləʊ/ *a* hohl; (*promise*) leer □ *n* Vertiefung *f*; (*in ground*) Mulde *f*. ~ **out** *vt* aushöhlen

holly /'hɒlɪ/ *n* Stechpalme *f*

'hollyhock *n* Stockrose *f*

hologram /'hɒləgræm/ *n* Hologramm *nt*

holster /'həʊlstə(r)/ *n* Pistolentasche *f*

holy /'həʊlɪ/ *a* (-ier, -est) heilig. **H~ Ghost** or **Spirit** *n* Heiliger Geist *m*. ~ **water** *n* Weihwasser *nt*. **H~ Week** *n* Karwoche *f*

homage /'hɒmɪdʒ/ *n* Huldigung *f*; **pay** ~ **to** huldigen (+ *dat*)

home /həʊm/ *n* Zuhause *nt*; (*house*) Haus *nt*; (*institution*) Heim *nt*; (*native land*) Heimat *f* □ *adv* **at** ~ zu Hause; **come/go** ~ nach Hause kommen/gehen

home: ~ **ad'dress** *n* Heimatanschrift *f*. ~ **com'puter** *n* Heimcomputer *m*. ~ **game** *n* Heimspiel *m*. ~ **help** *n* Haushaltshilfe *f*. ~**land** *n* Heimatland *nt*. ~**less** *a* obdachlos

homely /'həʊmlɪ/ *a* (-ier, -iest) *a* gemütlich; (*Amer: ugly*) unscheinbar

home: ~-'**made** *a* selbst gemacht. **H~ Office** *n* Innenministerium *nt*. **H~ 'Secretary** *n* Innenminister *m*. ~**sick** *a* **be** ~ **sick** Heimweh haben (**for** nach). ~ **sickness** *n* Heimweh *nt*. ~ '**town** *n* Heimatstadt *f*. ~**work** *n* (*Sch*) Hausaufgaben *pl*

homicide /'hɒmɪsaɪd/ *n* Totschlag *m*; (*murder*) Mord *m*

homoeopath|ic /həʊmɪə'pæθɪk/ *a* homöopathisch. ~**y** /-'ɒpəθɪ/ *n* Homöopathie *f*

homogeneous /hɒmə'dʒiːnɪəs/ *a* homogen

homo'sexual *a* homosexuell □ *n* Homosexuelle(r) *m/f*

honest /'ɒnɪst/ *a*, **-ly** *adv* ehrlich. ~**y** *n* Ehrlichkeit *f*

honey /'hʌnɪ/ *n* Honig *m*; (*fam: darling*) Schatz *m*

honey: ~**comb** *n* Honigwabe *f*. ~**moon** *n* Flitterwochen *pl*; (*journey*) Hochzeitsreise *f*. ~**suckle** *n* Geißblatt *nt*

honk /hɒŋk/ *vi* hupen

honorary /'ɒnərərɪ/ *a* ehrenamtlich; (*member, doctorate*) Ehren-

honour /'ɒnə(r)/ *n* Ehre *f* □ *vt* ehren; honorieren (*cheque*). ~**able** /-əbl/ *a*, **-bly** *adv* ehrenhaft

hood /hʊd/ *n* Kapuze *f*; (*of pram*) [Klapp]verdeck *nt*; (*over cooker*) Abzugshaube *f*; (*Amer, Auto*) Kühlerhaube *f*

hoodlum /'huːdləm/ *n* Rowdy *m*

'hoodwink /hʊd-/ *vt* (*fam*) reinlegen

hoof /huːf/ *n* (*pl* ~**s** or **hooves**) Huf *m*

hook /hʊk/ *n* Haken *m*; **by** ~ **or by crook** mit allen Mitteln □ *vt* festhaken (**to** an + *acc*)

hook|ed /hʊkt/ *a* ~**ed nose** Hakennase *f*; ~**ed on** (*fam*) abhängig von; (*keen on*) besessen von. ~**er** *n* (*Amer, sl*) Nutte *f*

hookey /'hʊkɪ/ *n* **play** ~ (*Amer, fam*) schwänzen

hooligan /'huːlɪgən/ *n* Rowdy *m*. ~**ism** *n* Rowdytum *nt*

hoop /huːp/ *n* Reifen *m*

hooray /hʊ'reɪ/ *int & n* = **hurrah**

hoot /huːt/ *n* Ruf *m*; ~**s of laughter** schallendes Gelächter *nt* □ *vi* (*owl:*) rufen; (*car:*) hupen; (*jeer*) johlen. ~**er** *n* (*of factory*) Sirene *f*; (*Auto*) Hupe *f*

hoover /'huːvə(r)/ *n* **H~** (**P**) Staubsauger *m* □ *vt/i* [staub]saugen

hop[1] /hɒp/ *n*, & ~**s** *pl* Hopfen *m*

hop[2] *n* Hüpfer *m*; **catch s.o. on the** ~ (*fam*) jdm ungelegen kommen □ *vi* (*pt/pp* **hopped**) hüpfen; ~ **it!** (*fam*) hau ab! ~ **in** *vi* (*fam*) einsteigen. ~ **out** *vi* (*fam*) aussteigen

hope /həʊp/ *n* Hoffnung *f*; (*prospect*) Aussicht *f* (**of** auf + *acc*) □ *vt/i* hoffen (**for** auf + *acc*); **I** ~ **so** hoffentlich

hope|ful /'həʊpfl/ *a* hoffnungsvoll; **be** ~**ful that** hoffen, dass. ~**fully** *adv* hoffnungsvoll; (*it is hoped*) hoffentlich. ~**less** *a*, **-ly** *adv* hoffnungslos; (*useless*) nutzlos; (*incompetent*) untauglich

horde /hɔːd/ *n* Horde *f*

horizon /hə'raɪzn/ *n* Horizont *m*; **on the** ~ am Horizont

horizontal /hɒrɪ'zɒntl/ *a*, **-ly** *adv* horizontal. ~ **'bar** *n* Reck *nt*

horn /hɔːn/ *n* Horn *nt*; (*Auto*) Hupe *f*

hornet /'hɔːnɪt/ *n* Hornisse *f*

horny /'hɔːnɪ/ *a* schwielig

horoscope /'hɒrəskəʊp/ *n* Horoskop *nt*

horrible /'hɒrɪbl/ *a*, **-bly** *adv* schrecklich

horrid /'hɒrɪd/ *a* grässlich

horrific /hə'rɪfɪk/ *a* entsetzlich

horrify /'hɒrɪfaɪ/ *vt* (*pt/pp* **-ied**) entsetzen

horror /'hɒrə(r)/ n Entsetzen nt. ~ **film** n Horrorfilm m

hors-d'œuvre /ɔː'dɜːvr/ n Vorspeise f

horse /hɔːs/ n Pferd nt

horse: ~**back** n on ~**back** zu Pferde. ~'**chestnut** n [Ross]kastanie f. ~**man** n Reiter m. ~**play** n Toben nt. ~**power** n Pferdestärke f. ~**racing** n Pferderennen nt. ~**radish** n Meerrettich m. ~**shoe** n Hufeisen nt

horti'cultural /hɔːtɪ-/ a Garten-

'**horticulture** n Gartenbau m

hose /həʊz/ n (pipe) Schlauch m □ vt ~ **down** abspritzen

hosiery /'həʊzərɪ/ n Strumpfwaren pl

hospice /'hɒspɪs/ n Heim nt; (for the terminally ill) Sterbeklinik f

hospitable /hɒ'spɪtəbl/ a, -**bly** adv gastfreundlich

hospital /'hɒspɪtl/ n Krankenhaus nt

hospitality /hɒspɪ'tælətɪ/ n Gastfreundschaft f

host[1] /həʊst/ n a ~ **of** eine Menge von

host[2] n Gastgeber m

host[3] n (Relig) Hostie f

hostage /'hɒstɪdʒ/ n Geisel f

hostel /'hɒstl/ n [Wohn]heim nt

hostess /'həʊstɪs/ n Gastgeberin f

hostile /'hɒstaɪl/ a feindlich; (unfriendly) feindselig

hostilit|y /hɒ'stɪlətɪ/ n Feindschaft f; ~**ies** pl Feindseligkeiten pl

hot /hɒt/ a (**hotter, hottest**) heiß; (meal) warm; (spicy) scharf; **I am** or **feel** ~ mir ist heiß

'**hotbed** n (fig) Brutstätte f

hotchpotch /'hɒtʃpɒtʃ/ n Mischmasch m

hotel /həʊ'tel/ n Hotel nt. ~**ier** n -ɪə(r)/ n Hotelier m

hot: ~**head** n Hitzkopf m. ~'**headed** a hitzköpfig. ~**house** n Treibhaus nt. ~**ly** adv (fig) heiß, heftig. ~**plate** n Tellerwärmer m; (of cooker) Kochplatte f. ~ **tap** n Warmwasserhahn m. ~**tempered** a jähzornig. ~'**water bottle** n Wärmflasche f

hound /haʊnd/ n Jagdhund m □ vt (fig) verfolgen

hour /'aʊə(r)/ n Stunde f. ~**ly** a & adv stündlich; ~**ly pay** or **rate** Stundenlohn m

house[1] /haʊs/ n Haus nt; **at my** ~ bei mir

house[2] /haʊz/ vt unterbringen

house /haʊs/: ~**boat** n Hausboot nt. ~**breaking** n Einbruch m. ~**hold** n Haushalt m. ~**holder** n Hausinhaber(in) m(f). ~**keeper** n Haushälterin f. ~**keeping** n Hauswirtschaft f; (money) Haushaltsgeld

nt. ~**plant** n Zimmerpflanze f. ~**trained** a stubenrein. ~**warming** n **have a** ~**warming party** Einstand feiern. ~**wife** n Hausfrau f. ~**work** n Hausarbeit f

housing /'haʊzɪŋ/ n Wohnungen pl; (Techn) Gehäuse nt. ~ **estate** n Wohnsiedlung f

hovel /'hɒvl/ n elende Hütte f

hover /'hɒvə(r)/ vi schweben; (be undecided) schwanken; (linger) herumstehen. ~**craft** n Luftkissenfahrzeug nt

how /haʊ/ adv wie; ~ **do you do?** guten Tag! ~ **many** wie viele; ~ **much** wie viel; **and** ~! und wie!

how'ever adv (in question) wie; (nevertheless) jedoch, aber; ~ **small** wie klein es auch sein mag

howl /haʊl/ n Heulen nt □ vi heulen; ⟨baby:⟩ brüllen. ~**er** n (fam) Schnitzer m

hub /hʌb/ n Nabe f; (fig) Mittelpunkt m

hubbub /'hʌbʌb/ n Stimmengewirr nt

'**hub-cap** n Radkappe f

huddle /'hʌdl/ vi ~ **together** sich zusammendrängen

hue[1] /hjuː/ n Farbe f

hue[2] n ~ **and cry** Aufruhr m

huff /hʌf/ n **in a** ~ beleidigt

hug /hʌɡ/ n Umarmung f □ vt (pt/pp **hugged**) umarmen

huge /hjuːdʒ/ a, -**ly** adv riesig

hulking /'hʌlkɪŋ/ a (fam) ungeschlacht

hull /hʌl/ n (Naut) Rumpf m

hullo /hə'ləʊ/ int = hallo

hum /hʌm/ n Summen nt; Brummen nt □ vt/i (pt/pp **hummed**) summen; ⟨motor:⟩ brummen; ~ **and haw** nicht mit der Sprache herauswollen

human /'hjuːmən/ a menschlich □ n Mensch m. ~ '**being** n Mensch m

humane /hjuː'meɪn/ a, -**ly** adv human

humanitarian /hjuːmænɪ'teərɪən/ a humanitär

humanit|y /hjuː'mænətɪ/ n Menschheit f; ~**ies** pl (Univ) Geisteswissenschaften pl

humble /'hʌmbl/ a (-**r, -st**), -**bly** adv demütig □ vt demütigen

'**humdrum** a eintönig

humid /'hjuːmɪd/ a feucht. ~**ity** /-'mɪdətɪ/ n Feuchtigkeit f

humiliat|e /hjuː'mɪlɪeɪt/ vt demütigen. ~**ion** /-'eɪʃn/ n Demütigung f

humility /hjuː'mɪlətɪ/ n Demut f

'**humming-bird** n Kolibri m

humorous /'hjuːmərəs/ a, -**ly** adv humorvoll; ⟨story⟩ humoristisch

humour /'hju:mə(r)/ n Humor m; (mood) Laune f; **have a sense of ~** Humor haben □ vt ~ **s.o** jdm seinen Willen lassen

hump /hʌmp/ n Buckel m; (of camel) Höcker m □ vt schleppen

hunch /hʌntʃ/ n (idea) Ahnung f

'hunch|back n Bucklige(r) m/f. **~ed** a ~**ed up** gebeugt

hundred /'hʌndrəd/ a **one/a ~** [ein]hundert □ n Hundert nt; (written figure) Hundert f. **~th** a hundertste(r,s) □ n Hundertstel nt. **~weight** n ≈ Zentner m

hung /hʌŋ/ see hang

Hungarian /hʌŋ'geərɪən/ a ungarisch □ n Ungar(in) m(f)

Hungary /'hʌŋgərɪ/ n Ungar nt

hunger /'hʌŋgə(r)/ n Hunger m. **~-strike** n Hungerstreik m

hungry /'hʌŋgrɪ/ a (-ier, -iest), **-ily** adv hungrig; **be ~** Hunger haben

hunk /hʌŋk/ n [großes] Stück nt

hunt /hʌnt/ n Jagd f; (for criminal) Fahndung f □ vt/i jagen; fahnden nach (criminal); **~ for** suchen. **~er** n Jäger m; (horse) Jagdpferd nt. **~ing** n Jagd f

hurdle /'hɜ:dl/ n (Sport & fig) Hürde f. **~r** n Hürdenläufer(in) m(f)

hurl /hɜ:l/ vt schleudern

hurrah /hu'rɑ:/, **hurray** /hu'reɪ/ int hurra! □ n Hurra nt

hurricane /'hʌrɪkən/ n Orkan m

hurried /'hʌrɪd/ a, **-ly** adv eilig; (superficial) flüchtig

hurry /'hʌrɪ/ n Eile f; **be in a ~** es eilig haben □ vi (pt/pp -ied) sich beeilen; (go quickly) eilen. **~ up** vi sich beeilen □ vt antreiben

hurt /hɜ:t/ n Schmerz m □ vt/i (pt/pp hurt) weh tun (+ dat); (injure) verletzen; (offend) kränken. **~ful** a verletzend

hurtle /'hɜ:tl/ vi **~ along** rasen

husband /'hʌzbənd/ n [Ehe]mann m

hush /hʌʃ/ n Stille f □ vt **~ up** vertuschen. **~ed** a gedämpft. **~-'hush** a (fam) streng geheim

husk /hʌsk/ n Spelze f

husky /'hʌskɪ/ a (-ier, -iest) heiser; (burly) stämmig

hustle /'hʌsl/ vt drängen □ n Gedränge nt; **~ and bustle** geschäftiges Treiben nt

hut /hʌt/ n Hütte f

hutch /hʌtʃ/ n [Kaninchen]stall m

hybrid /'haɪbrɪd/ a hybrid □ n Hybride f

hydrangea /haɪ'dreɪndʒə/ n Hortensie f

hydrant /'haɪdrənt/ n [fire] ~ Hydrant m

hydraulic /haɪ'drɔ:lɪk/ a, **-ally** adv hydraulisch

hydrochloric /haɪdrə'klɔ:rɪk/ a ~ **acid** Salzsäure f

hydroe'lectric /haɪdrəʊ-/ a hydroelektrisch. ~ **power station** n Wasserkraftwerk nt

hydrofoil /'haɪdrə-/ n Tragflügelboot nt

hydrogen /'haɪdrədʒən/ n Wasserstoff m

hyena /haɪ'i:nə/ n Hyäne f

hygien|e /'haɪdʒi:n/ n Hygiene f. **~ic** /haɪ'dʒi:nɪk/ a, **-ally** adv hygienisch

hymn /hɪm/ n Kirchenlied nt. **~-book** n Gesangbuch nt

hyphen /'haɪfn/ n Bindestrich m. **~ate** vt mit Bindestrich schreiben

hypno|sis /hɪp'nəʊsɪs/ n Hypnose f. **~tic** /-'nɒtɪk/ a hypnotisch

hypno|tism /'hɪpnətɪzm/ n Hypnotik f. **~tist** /-tɪst/ n Hypnotiseur m. **~tize** vt hypnotisieren

hypochondriac /haɪpə'kɒndrɪæk/ a hypochondrisch □ n Hypochonder m

hypocrisy /hɪ'pɒkrəsɪ/ n Heuchelei f

hypocrit|e /'hɪpəkrɪt/ n Heuchler(in) m(f). **~ical** /-'krɪtɪkl/ a, **-ly** adv heuchlerisch

hypodermic /haɪpə'dɜ:mɪk/ a & n ~ [syringe] Injektionsspritze f

hypothe|sis /haɪ'pɒθəsɪs/ n Hypothese f. **~tical** /-ə'θetɪkl/ a, **-ly** adv hypothetisch

hyster|ia /hɪ'stɪərɪə/ n Hysterie f. **~ical** /-'sterɪkl/ a, **-ly** adv hysterisch. **~ics** /hɪ'sterɪks/ npl hysterischer Anfall m

I

I /aɪ/ pron ich

ice /aɪs/ n Eis nt □ vt mit Zuckerguss überziehen (cake)

ice: ~ age n Eiszeit f. **~-axe** n Eispickel m. **~berg** /-bɜ:g/ n Eisberg m. **~box** n (Amer) Kühlschrank m. **~-'cream** n [Speise]eis nt. **~-'cream parlour** n Eisdiele f. **~-cube** n Eiswürfel m

Iceland /'aɪslənd/ n Island nt

ice: ~ lolly n Eis nt am Stiel. ~ **rink** n Eisbahn f

icicle /'aɪsɪkl/ n Eiszapfen m

icing /'aɪsɪŋ/ n Zuckerguss m. ~ **sugar** n Puderzucker m

icon /'aɪkɒn/ n Ikone f

icy /'aɪsɪ/ a (-ier, -iest), **-ily** adv eisig; (road) vereist

idea /aɪ'dɪə/ n Idee f; (conception) Vorstellung f; **I have no ~!** ich habe keine Ahnung!

ideal /aɪ'dɪəl/ a ideal. □n Ideal nt. ~**ism** n Idealismus m. ~**ist** n Idealist(in) m(f). ~**istic** /-'lɪstɪk/ a idealistisch. ~**ize** vt idealisieren. ~**ly** adv ideal; (in ideal circumstances) idealerweise

identical /aɪ'dentɪkl/ a identisch; ⟨twins⟩ eineiig

identi|fication /aɪdentɪfɪ'keɪʃn/ n Identifizierung f; (proof of identity) Ausweispapiere pl. ~**fy** /aɪ'dentɪfaɪ/ vt (pt/pp -ied) identifizieren

identity /aɪ'dentətɪ/ n Identität f. ~ **card** n [Personal]ausweis m

ideolog|ical /aɪdɪə'lɒdʒɪkl/ a ideologisch. ~**y** /aɪdɪ'ɒlədʒɪ/ n Ideologie f

idiom /'ɪdɪəm/ n [feste] Redewendung f. ~**atic** /-'mætɪk/ a, -**ally** adv idiomatisch

idiosyncrasy /ɪdɪə'sɪŋkrəsɪ/ n Eigenart f

idiot /'ɪdɪət/ n Idiot m. ~**ic** /-'ɒtɪk/ a idiotisch

idle /'aɪdl/ a (-r, -st), -**ly** adv untätig; (lazy) faul; (empty) leer; ⟨machine⟩ nicht in Betrieb. □ vi faulenzen; ⟨engine:⟩ leer laufen. ~**ness** n Untätigkeit f; Faulheit f

idol /'aɪdl/ n Idol nt. ~**ize** /'aɪdəlaɪz/ vt vergöttern

idyllic /ɪ'dɪlɪk/ a idyllisch

i.e. abbr (id est) d.h.

if /ɪf/ conj wenn; (whether) ob; **as if** als ob

ignite /ɪg'naɪt/ vt entzünden. □ vi sich entzünden

ignition /ɪg'nɪʃn/ n (Auto) Zündung f. ~ **key** n Zündschlüssel m

ignoramus /ɪgnə'reɪməs/ n Ignorant m

ignoran|ce /'ɪgnərəns/ n Unwissenheit f. ~**t** a unwissend; (rude) ungehobelt

ignore /ɪg'nɔ:(r)/ vt ignorieren

ilk /ɪlk/ n (fam) **of that ~** von der Sorte

ill /ɪl/ a krank; (bad) schlecht; **feel ~ at ease** sich unbehaglich fühlen. □ adv schlecht. □ n Schlechte(s) nt; (evil) Übel nt. ~**-advised** a unklug. ~**-bred** a schlecht erzogen

illegal /ɪ'li:gl/ a, -**ly** adv illegal

illegible /ɪ'ledʒəbl/ a, -**bly** adv unleserlich

illegitima|cy /ɪlɪ'dʒɪtɪməsɪ/ n Unehelichkeit f. ~**te** /-mət/ a unehelich; ⟨claim⟩ unberechtigt

illicit /ɪ'lɪsɪt/ a, -**ly** adv illegal

illitera|cy /ɪ'lɪtərəsɪ/ n Analphabetentum nt. ~**te** /-rət/ a **be ~te** nicht lesen und schreiben können. □ n Analphabet(in) m(f)

illness /'ɪlnɪs/ n Krankheit f

illogical /ɪ'lɒdʒɪkl/ a, -**ly** adv unlogisch

ill-treat /ɪl'tri:t/ vt misshandeln. ~**ment** n Misshandlung f

illuminat|e /ɪ'lu:mɪneɪt/ vt beleuchten. ~**ing** a aufschlussreich. ~**ion** /-'neɪʃn/ n Beleuchtung f

illusion /ɪ'lu:ʒn/ n Illusion f; **be under the ~ that** sich (dat) einbilden, dass

illusory /ɪ'lu:sərɪ/ a illusorisch

illustrat|e /'ɪləstreɪt/ vt illustrieren. ~**ion** /-'streɪʃn/ n Illustration f

illustrious /ɪ'lʌstrɪəs/ a berühmt

image /'ɪmɪdʒ/ n Bild nt; (statue) Standbild nt; (figure) Figur f; (exact likeness) Ebenbild nt; [public] ~ Image nt

imagin|able /ɪ'mædʒɪnəbl/ a vorstellbar. ~**ary** /-ərɪ/ a eingebildet

imaginat|ion /ɪmædʒɪ'neɪʃn/ n Phantasie f; (fancy) Einbildung f. ~**ive** /ɪ'mædʒɪnətɪv/ a, -**ly** adv phantasievoll; (full of ideas) einfallsreich

imagine /ɪ'mædʒɪn/ vt sich (dat) vorstellen; (wrongly) sich (dat) einbilden

im'balance n Unausgeglichenheit f

imbecile /'ɪmbəsi:l/ n Schwachsinnige(r) m/f; (pej) Idiot m

imbibe /ɪm'baɪb/ vt trinken; (fig) aufnehmen

imbue /ɪm'bju:/ vt **be ~d with** erfüllt sein von

imitat|e /'ɪmɪteɪt/ vt nachahmen, imitieren. ~**ion** /-'teɪʃn/ n Nachahmung f, Imitation f

immaculate /ɪ'mækjʊlət/ a, -**ly** adv tadellos; (Relig) unbefleckt

imma'terial a (unimportant) unwichtig, unwesentlich

imma'ture a unreif

immediate /ɪ'mi:dɪət/ a sofortig; (nearest) nächste(r,s). ~**ly** adv sofort; ~**ly next to** unmittelbar neben. □ conj sobald

immemorial /ɪmə'mɔ:rɪəl/ a **from time ~** seit Urzeiten

immense /ɪ'mens/ a, -**ly** adv riesig; (fam) enorm; (extreme) äußerst

immers|e /ɪ'mɜ:s/ vt untertauchen; **be ~ed in** (fig) vertieft sein in (+ acc). ~**ion** /-ʃn/ n Untertauchen nt. ~**ion heater** n Heißwasserbereiter m

immigrant /'ɪmɪgrənt/ n Einwanderer m

immigrat|e /'ɪmɪgreɪt/ vi einwandern. ~**ion** /-'greɪʃn/ n Einwanderung f

imminent /'ɪmɪnənt/ a **be ~** unmittelbar bevorstehen

immobil|e /ɪ'məʊbaɪl/ a unbeweglich. ~**ize** /-bəlaɪz/ vt (fig) lähmen; (Med) ruhig stellen

immoderate /ɪ'mɒdərət/ a übermäßig

immodest /ɪ'mɒdɪst/ a unbescheiden

immoral /ɪ'mɒrəl/ a, -**ly** adv unmoralisch. ~**ity** /ɪmə'rælətɪ/ n Unmoral f

immortal /ɪˈmɔːtl/ a unsterblich. ~**ity** /-ˈtælətɪ/ n Unsterblichkeit f. ~**ize** vt verewigen

immovable /ɪˈmuːvəbl/ a unbeweglich; (fig) fest

immune /ɪˈmjuːn/ a immun (**to**/**from** gegen). ~ **system** n Abwehrsystem nt

immunity /ɪˈmjuːnətɪ/ n Immunität f

immunize /ˈɪmjʊnaɪz/ vt immunisieren

imp /ɪmp/ n Kobold m

impact /ˈɪmpækt/ n Aufprall m; (collision) Zusammenprall m; (of bomb) Einschlag m; (fig) Auswirkung f

impair /ɪmˈpeə(r)/ vt beeinträchtigen

impale /ɪmˈpeɪl/ vt aufspießen

impart /ɪmˈpɑːt/ vt übermitteln (**to** dat); vermitteln (knowledge)

im'parti|al a unparteiisch. ~**'ality** n Unparteilichkeit f

im'passable a unpassierbar

impasse /ˈæmpɑːs/ n (fig) Sackgasse f

impassioned /ɪmˈpæʃnd/ a leidenschaftlich

im'passive a, -ly adv unbeweglich

im'patien|ce n Ungeduld f. ~**t** a, -ly adv ungeduldig

impeach /ɪmˈpiːtʃ/ vt anklagen

impeccable /ɪmˈpekəbl/ a, -bly adv tadellos

impede /ɪmˈpiːd/ vt behindern

impediment /ɪmˈpedɪmənt/ n Hindernis nt; (in speech) Sprachfehler m

impel /ɪmˈpel/ vt (pt/pp impelled) treiben; **feel** ~**led** sich genötigt fühlen (**to** zu)

impending /ɪmˈpendɪŋ/ a bevorstehend

impenetrable /ɪmˈpenɪtrəbl/ a undurchdringlich

imperative /ɪmˈperətɪv/ a **be** ~ dringend notwendig sein □ n (Gram) Imperativ m, Befehlsform f

imper'ceptible a nicht wahrnehmbar

im'perfect a unvollkommen; (faulty) fehlerhaft □ n (Gram) Imperfekt nt. ~**ion** /-ˈfekʃn/ n Unvollkommenheit f; (fault) Fehler m

imperial /ɪmˈpɪərɪəl/ a kaiserlich. ~**ism** n Imperialismus m

imperil /ɪmˈperəl/ vt (pt/pp imperilled) gefährden

imperious /ɪmˈpɪərɪəs/ a, -ly adv herrisch

im'personal a unpersönlich

impersonat|e /ɪmˈpɜːsəneɪt/ vt sich ausgeben als; (Theat) nachahmen, imitieren. ~**or** n Imitator m

impertinen|ce /ɪmˈpɜːtɪnəns/ n Frechheit f. ~**t** a frech

imperturbable /ɪmpəˈtɜːbəbl/ a unerschütterlich

impervious /ɪmˈpɜːvɪəs/ a ~ **to** (fig) unempfänglich für

impetuous /ɪmˈpetjʊəs/ a, -ly adv ungestüm

impetus /ˈɪmpɪtəs/ n Schwung m

impish /ˈɪmpɪʃ/ a schelmisch

implacable /ɪmˈplækəbl/ a unerbittlich

im'plant[1] vt einpflanzen

'implant[2] n Implantat nt

implement[1] /ˈɪmplɪmənt/ n Gerät nt

implement[2] /ˈɪmplɪment/ vt ausführen

implicat|e /ˈɪmplɪkeɪt/ vt verwickeln. ~**ion** /-ˈkeɪʃn/ n Verwicklung f; ~**ions** pl Auswirkungen pl; **by** ~**ion** implizit

implicit /ɪmˈplɪsɪt/ a, -ly adv unausgesprochen; (absolute) unbedingt

implore /ɪmˈplɔː(r)/ vt anflehen

imply /ɪmˈplaɪ/ vt (pt/pp -ied) andeuten; **what are you** ~**ing?** was wollen Sie damit sagen?

impo'lite a, -ly adv unhöflich

import[1] /ˈɪmpɔːt/ n Import m, Einfuhr f; (importance) Wichtigkeit f; (meaning) Bedeutung f

import[2] /ɪmˈpɔːt/ vt importieren, einführen

importan|ce /ɪmˈpɔːtns/ n Wichtigkeit f. ~**t** a wichtig

importer /ɪmˈpɔːtə(r)/ n Importeur m

impos|e /ɪmˈpəʊz/ vt auferlegen (**on** dat) □ vi sich aufdrängen (**on** dat). ~**ing** a eindrucksvoll. ~**ition** /ɪmpəˈzɪʃn/ n **be an** ~**ition** eine Zumutung sein

impossi'bility n Unmöglichkeit f

im'possible a, -bly adv unmöglich

impostor /ɪmˈpɒstə(r)/ n Betrüger(in) m(f)

impoten|ce /ˈɪmpətəns/ n Machtlosigkeit f; (Med) Impotenz f. ~**t** a machtlos; (Med) impotent

impound /ɪmˈpaʊnd/ vt beschlagnahmen

impoverished /ɪmˈpɒvərɪʃt/ a verarmt

im'practicable a undurchführbar

im'practical a unpraktisch

impre'cise a ungenau

impregnable /ɪmˈpregnəbl/ a uneinnehmbar

impregnate /ˈɪmpregneɪt/ vt tränken; (Biol) befruchten

im'press vt beeindrucken; ~ **sth [up]on s.o.** jdm etw einprägen

impression /ɪmˈpreʃn/ n Eindruck m; (imitation) Nachahmung f; (imprint) Abdruck m; (edition) Auflage f. ~**ism** n Impressionismus m

impressive /ɪmˈpresɪv/ a eindrucksvoll

'imprint[1] n Abdruck m

im'print[2] vt prägen; (fig) einprägen (**on** dat)

im'prison vt gefangen halten; (put in prison) ins Gefängnis sperren

im'probable a unwahrscheinlich

impromptu /ɪm'prɒmptjuː/ a improvisiert □ adv aus dem Stegreif

im'proper a, -ly adv inkorrekt; (indecent) unanständig

impro'priety n Unkorrektheit f

improve /ɪm'pruːv/ vt verbessern; verschönern (appearance) □ vi sich bessern; ~ **[up]on** übertreffen. ~**ment** /-mənt/ n Verbesserung f; (in health) Besserung f

improvise /'ɪmprəvaɪz/ vt/i improvisieren

im'prudent a unklug

impuden|ce /'ɪmpjʊdəns/ n Frechheit f. ~**t** a, -ly adv frech

impuls|e /'ɪmpʌls/ n Impuls m; **on [an]** ~**e** impulsiv. ~**ive** /-'pʌlsɪv/ a, -ly adv impulsiv

impunity /ɪm'pjuːnətɪ/ n **with** ~ ungestraft

im'pur|e a unrein. ~**ity** n Unreinheit f; ~**ities** pl Verunreinigungen pl

impute /ɪm'pjuːt/ vt zuschreiben (**to** dat)

in /ɪn/ prep in (+ dat/(into) + acc); **sit in the garden** im Garten sitzen; **go in the garden** in den Garten gehen; **in May** im Mai; **in the summer/winter** im Sommer/ Winter; **in 1992** [im Jahre] 1992; **in this heat** bei dieser Hitze; **in the rain/sun** im Regen/in der Sonne; **in the evening** am Abend; **in the sky** am Himmel; **in the world** auf der Welt; **in the street** auf der Straße; **deaf in one ear** auf einem Ohr taub; **in the army** beim Militär; **in English/German** auf Englisch/Deutsch; **in ink/pencil** mit Tinte/Bleistift; **in a soft/loud voice** mit leiser/lauter Stimme; **in doing this, he ...** indem er das tut/tat, ... er □ adv (at home) zu Hause; (indoors) drinnen; **he's not in yet** er ist noch nicht da; **all in** alles inbegriffen; (fam: exhausted) kaputt; **day in, day out** tagaus, tagein; **keep in with** s.o. sich mit jdm gut stellen; **have it in for s.o.** (fam) es auf jdn abgesehen haben; **let oneself in for sth** sich auf etw (acc) einlassen; **send/go in** hineinschicken/-gehen; **come/bring in** hereinkommen/-bringen □ a (fam: in fashion) in □ n **the ins and outs** alle Einzelheiten pl

ina'bility n Unfähigkeit f

inac'cessible a unzugänglich

in'accura|cy n Ungenauigkeit f. ~**te** a, -ly adv ungenau

in'ac|tive a untätig. ~**'tivity** n Untätigkeit f

in'adequate a, -ly adv unzulänglich; **feel** ~ sich der Situation nicht gewachsen fühlen

inad'missable a unzulässig

inadvertently /ɪnəd'vɜːtəntlɪ/ adv versehentlich

inad'visable a nicht ratsam

inane /ɪ'neɪn/ a, -ly adv albern

in'animate a unbelebt

in'applicable a nicht zutreffend

inap'propriate a unangebracht

inar'ticulate a undeutlich; **be** ~ sich nicht gut ausdrücken können

inat'tentive a unaufmerksam

in'audible a, -**bly** adv unhörbar

inaugural /ɪ'nɔːgjʊrl/ a Antritts-

inaugurat|e /ɪ'nɔːgjʊreɪt/ vt [feierlich] in sein Amt einführen. ~**ion** /-'reɪʃn/ n Amtseinführung f

inau'spicious a ungünstig

inborn /'ɪnbɔːn/ a angeboren

inbred /ɪn'bred/ a angeboren

incalculable /ɪn'kælkjʊləbl/ a nicht berechenbar; (fig) unabsehbar

in'capable a unfähig; **be** ~ **of doing sth** nicht fähig sein, etw zu tun

incapacitate /ɪnkə'pæsɪteɪt/ vt unfähig machen

incarcerate /ɪn'kɑːsəreɪt/ vt einkerkern

incarnat|e /ɪn'kɑːnət/ a **the devil** ~**e** der leibhaftige Satan. ~**ion** /-'neɪʃn/ n Inkarnation f

incendiary /ɪn'sendɪərɪ/ a & n ~ **[bomb]** Brandbombe f

incense[1] /'ɪnsens/ n Weihrauch m

incense[2] /ɪn'sens/ vt wütend machen

incentive /ɪn'sentɪv/ n Anreiz m

inception /ɪn'sepʃn/ n Beginn m

incessant /ɪn'sesnt/ a, -ly adv unaufhörlich

incest /'ɪnsest/ n Inzest m, Blutschande f

inch /ɪntʃ/ n Zoll m □ vi ~ **forward** sich ganz langsam vorwärts schieben

inciden|ce /'ɪnsɪdəns/ n Vorkommen nt. ~**t** n Zwischenfall m

incidental /ɪnsɪ'dentl/ a nebensächlich; (remark) beiläufig; (expenses) Neben-. ~**ly** adv übrigens

incinerat|e /ɪn'sɪnəreɪt/ vt verbrennen. ~**or** n Verbrennungsofen m

incipient /ɪn'sɪpɪənt/ a angehend

incision /ɪn'sɪʒn/ n Einschnitt m

incisive /ɪn'saɪsɪv/ a scharfsinnig

incisor /ɪn'saɪzə(r)/ n Schneidezahn m

incite /ɪn'saɪt/ vt aufhetzen. **~ment** n Aufhetzung f

inci'vility n Unhöflichkeit f

in'clement a rau

inclination /ɪnklɪ'neɪʃn/ n Neigung f

incline[1] /ɪn'klaɪn/ vt neigen; **be ~d to do sth** dazu neigen, etw zu tun □ vi sich neigen

incline[2] /'ɪnklaɪn/ n Neigung f

inclu|de /ɪn'kluːd/ vt einschließen; (contain) enthalten; (incorporate) aufnehmen (in in + acc). **~ding** prep einschließlich (+ gen). **~sion** /-uːʒn/ n Aufnahme f

inclusive /ɪn'kluːsɪv/ a Inklusiv-; **~ of** einschließlich (+ gen) □ adv inklusive

incognito /ɪnkɒg'niːtəʊ/ adv inkognito

inco'herent a, **-ly** adv zusammenhanglos; (incomprehensible) unverständlich

income /'ɪnkəm/ n Einkommen nt. **~ tax** n Einkommensteuer f

'incoming a ankommend; ⟨mail, call⟩ eingehend. **~ tide** n steigende Flut f

in'comparable a unvergleichlich

incom'patible a unvereinbar; **be ~** ⟨people:⟩ nicht zueinander passen

in'competen|ce n Unfähigkeit f. **~t** a unfähig

incom'plete a unvollständig

incompre'hensible a unverständlich

incon'ceivable a undenkbar

incon'clusive a nicht schlüssig

incongruous /ɪn'kɒŋgruəs/ a unpassend

inconsequential /ɪnkɒnsɪ'kwenʃl/ a unbedeutend

incon'siderate a rücksichtslos

incon'sistent a, **-ly** adv widersprüchlich; (illogical) inkonsequent; **be ~** nicht übereinstimmen

inconsolable /ɪnkən'səʊləbl/ a untröstlich

incon'spicuous a unauffällig

incontinen|ce /ɪn'kɒntɪnəns/ n Inkontinenz f. **~t** a inkontinent

incon'venien|ce n Unannehmlichkeit f; (drawback) Nachteil m; **put s.o. to ~ce** jdm Umstände machen. **~t** a, **-ly** adv ungünstig; **be ~t for s.o.** jdm nicht passen

incorporate /ɪn'kɔːpəreɪt/ vt aufnehmen; (contain) enthalten

incor'rect a, **-ly** adv inkorrekt

incorrigible /ɪn'kɒrɪdʒəbl/ a unverbesserlich

incorruptible /ɪnkə'rʌptəbl/ a unbestechlich

increase[1] /'ɪnkriːs/ n Zunahme f; (rise) Erhöhung f; **be on the ~** zunehmen

increas|e[2] /ɪn'kriːs/ vt vergrößern; (raise) erhöhen □ vi zunehmen; (rise) sich erhöhen. **~ing** a, **-ly** adv zunehmend

in'credible a, **-bly** adv unglaublich

incredulous /ɪn'kredjʊləs/ a ungläubig

increment /'ɪnkrɪmənt/ n Gehaltszulage f

incriminate /ɪn'krɪmɪneɪt/ vt (Jur) belasten

incubat|e /'ɪŋkjʊbeɪt/ vt ausbrüten. **~ion** /-'beɪʃn/ n Ausbrüten nt. **~ion period** n (Med) Inkubationszeit f. **~or** n (for baby) Brutkasten m

inculcate /'ɪnkʌlkeɪt/ vt einprägen (in dat)

incumbent /ɪn'kʌmbənt/ a **be ~ on s.o.** jds Pflicht sein

incur /ɪn'kɜː(r)/ vt (pt/pp incurred) sich (dat) zuziehen; machen ⟨debts⟩

in'curable a, **-bly** adv unheilbar

incursion /ɪn'kɜːʃn/ n Einfall m

indebted /ɪn'detɪd/ a verpflichtet (to dat)

in'decent a, **-ly** adv unanständig

inde'cision n Unentschlossenheit f

inde'cisive a ergebnislos; ⟨person⟩ unentschlossen

indeed /ɪn'diːd/ adv in der Tat, tatsächlich; **yes ~!** allerdings! **~ I am/do** oh doch! **very much ~** sehr; **thank you very much ~** vielen herzlichen Dank

indefatigable /ɪndɪ'fætɪgəbl/ a unermüdlich

in'definite a unbestimmt. **~ly** adv unbegrenzt; ⟨postpone⟩ auf unbestimmte Zeit

indelible /ɪn'delɪbl/ a, **-bly** adv nicht zu entfernen; (fig) unauslöschlich

indemni|fy /ɪn'demnɪfaɪ/ vt (pt/pp -ied) versichern; (compensate) entschädigen. **~ty** n Versicherung f; Entschädigung f

indent /ɪn'dent/ vt (Typ) einrücken. **~ation** /-'teɪʃn/ n Einrückung f; (notch) Kerbe f

inde'penden|ce n Unabhängigkeit f; (self-reliance) Selbstständigkeit f. **~t** a, **-ly** adv unabhängig; selbstständig

indescribable /ɪndɪ'skraɪbəbl/ a, **-bly** adv unbeschreiblich

indestructible /ɪndɪ'strʌktəbl/ a unzerstörbar

indeterminate /ɪndɪ'tɜːmɪnət/ a unbestimmt

index /'ɪndeks/ n Register nt

index: **~ card** n Karteikarte f. **~ finger** n Zeigefinger m. **~-linked** a ⟨pension⟩ dynamisch

India /'ɪndɪə/ n Indien nt. **~n** a indisch; (American) indianisch □ n Inder(in) m(f); (American) Indianer(in) m(f)

Indian: ~ 'ink *n* Tusche *f*. ~ 'summer *n* Nachsommer *m*

indicat|e /'ɪndɪkeɪt/ *vt* zeigen; (*point at*) zeigen auf (+ *acc*); (*hint*) andeuten; (*register*) anzeigen □ *vi* (*Auto*) blinken. ~ion /-'keɪʃn/ *n* Anzeichen *nt*

indicative /ɪn'dɪkətɪv/ *a* be ~ of schließen lassen auf (+ *acc*) □ *n* (*Gram*) Indikativ *m*

indicator /'ɪndɪkeɪtə(r)/ *n* (*Auto*) Blinker *m*

indict /ɪn'daɪt/ *vt* anklagen. ~ment *n* Anklage *f*

in'differen|ce *n* Gleichgültigkeit *f*. ~t *a*, -ly *adv* gleichgültig; (*not good*) mittelmäßig

indigenous /ɪn'dɪdʒɪnəs/ *a* einheimisch

indi'gest|ible *a* unverdaulich; (*difficult to digest*) schwer verdaulich. ~ion *n* Magenverstimmung *f*

indigna|nt /ɪn'dɪgnənt/ *a*, -ly *adv* entrüstet, empört. ~tion /-'neɪʃn/ *n* Entrüstung *f*, Empörung *f*

in'dignity *n* Demütigung *f*

indi'rect *a*, -ly *adv* indirekt

indi'screet *a* indiskret

indis'cretion *n* Indiskretion *f*

indiscriminate /ɪndɪ'skrɪmɪnət/ *a*, -ly *adv* wahllos

indi'spensable *a* unentbehrlich

indisposed /ɪndɪ'spəʊzd/ *a* indisponiert

indisputable /ɪndɪ'spju:təbl/ *a*, -bly *adv* unbestreitbar

indi'stinct *a*, -ly *adv* undeutlich

indistinguishable /ɪndɪ'stɪŋgwɪʃəbl/ *a* be ~ nicht zu unterscheiden sein; (*not visible*) nicht erkennbar sein

individual /ɪndɪ'vɪdjʊəl/ *a*, -ly *adv* individuell; (*single*) einzeln □ *n* Individuum *nt*. ~ity /-'ælətɪ/ *n* Individualität *f*

indi'visible *a* unteilbar

indoctrinate /ɪn'dɒktrɪneɪt/ *vt* indoktrinieren

indolen|ce /'ɪndələns/ *n* Faulheit *f*. ~t *a* faul

indomitable /ɪn'dɒmɪtəbl/ *a* unbeugsam

indoor /'ɪndɔ:(r)/ *a* Innen-; (*clothes*) Haus-; (*plant*) Zimmer-; (*Sport*) Hallen-. ~s /-'dɔ:z/ *adv* im Haus, drinnen; go ~s ins Haus gehen

induce /ɪn'dju:s/ *vt* dazu bewegen (to zu); (*produce*) herbeiführen. ~ment *n* (*incentive*) Anreiz *m*

indulge /ɪn'dʌldʒ/ *vt* frönen (+ *dat*); verwöhnen (*child*) □ *vi* ~ in frönen (+ *dat*). ~nce /-əns/ *n* Nachgiebigkeit *f*; (*leniency*) Nachsicht *f*. ~nt *a* [zu] nachgiebig; nachsichtig

industrial /ɪn'dʌstrɪəl/ *a* Industrie-; take ~ action streiken. ~ist *n* Industrielle(r) *m*. ~ized *a* industrialisiert

industr|ious /ɪn'dʌstrɪəs/ *a*, -ly *adv* fleißig. ~y /'ɪndəstrɪ/ *n* Industrie *f*; (*zeal*) Fleiß *m*

inebriated /ɪ'ni:brɪeɪtɪd/ *a* betrunken

in'edible *a* nicht essbar

inef'fective *a*, -ly *adv* unwirksam; (*person*) untauglich

ineffectual /ɪnɪ'fektʃʊəl/ *a* unwirksam; (*person*) untauglich

inef'ficient *a* unfähig; (*organization*) nicht leistungsfähig; (*method*) nicht rationell

in'eligible *a* nicht berechtigt

inept /ɪ'nept/ *a* ungeschickt

ine'quality *n* Ungleichheit *f*

inert /ɪ'nɜ:t/ *a* unbeweglich; (*Phys*) träge. ~ia /ɪ'nɜ:ʃə/ *n* Trägheit *f*

inescapable /ɪnɪ'skeɪpəbl/ *a* unvermeidlich

inestimable /ɪn'estɪməbl/ *a* unschätzbar

inevitab|le /ɪn'evɪtəbl/ *a* unvermeidlich. ~ly *adv* zwangsläufig

ine'xact *a* ungenau

inex'cusable *a* unverzeihlich

inexhaustible /ɪnɪg'zɔ:stəbl/ *a* unerschöpflich

inexorable /ɪn'eksərəbl/ *a* unerbittlich

inex'pensive *a*, -ly *adv* preiswert

inex'perience *n* Unerfahrenheit *f*. ~d *a* unerfahren

inexplicable /ɪnɪk'splɪkəbl/ *a* unerklärlich

in'fallible *a* unfehlbar

infam|ous /'ɪnfəməs/ *a* niederträchtig; (*notorious*) berüchtigt. ~y *n* Niederträchtigkeit *f*

infan|cy /'ɪnfənsɪ/ *n* frühe Kindheit *f*; (*fig*) Anfangsstadium *nt*. ~t *n* Kleinkind *nt*. ~tile *a* kindisch

infantry /'ɪnfəntrɪ/ *n* Infanterie *f*

infatuated /ɪn'fætʃʊeɪtɪd/ *a* vernarrt (with in + *acc*)

infect /ɪn'fekt/ *vt* anstecken, infizieren; become ~ed (*wound:*) sich infizieren. ~ion /-'fekʃn/ *n* Infektion *f*. ~ious /-'fekʃəs/ *a* ansteckend

infer /ɪn'fɜ:(r)/ *vt* (*pt/pp* inferred) folgern (from aus); (*imply*) andeuten. ~ence /'ɪnfərəns/ *n* Folgerung *f*

inferior /ɪn'fɪərɪə(r)/ *a* minderwertig; (*in rank*) untergeordnet □ *n* Untergebene(r) *m*/*f*

inferiority /ɪnfɪərɪ'ɒrətɪ/ *n* Minderwertigkeit *f*. ~ complex *n* Minderwertigkeitskomplex *m*

infern|al /ɪnˈfɜ:nl/ *a* höllisch. **~o** *n* flammendes Inferno *nt*

in'fer|tile *a* unfruchtbar. **~'tility** *n* Unfruchtbarkeit *f*

infest /ɪnˈfest/ *vt* be **~ed with** befallen sein von; ⟨*place*⟩ verseucht sein mit

infi'delity *n* Untreue *f*

infighting /ˈɪnfaɪtɪŋ/ *n* (*fig*) interne Machtkämpfe *pl*

infiltrate /ˈɪnfɪltreɪt/ *vt* infiltrieren; (*Pol*) unterwandern

infinite /ˈɪnfɪnət/ *a*, **-ly** *adv* unendlich

infinitesimal /ɪnfɪnɪˈtesɪml/ *a* unendlich klein

infinitive /ɪnˈfɪnɪtɪv/ *n* (*Gram*) Infinitiv *m*

infinity /ɪnˈfɪnətɪ/ *n* Unendlichkeit *f*

infirm /ɪnˈfɜ:m/ *a* gebrechlich. **~ary** *n* Krankenhaus *nt*. **~ity** *n* Gebrechlichkeit *f*

inflame /ɪnˈfleɪm/ *vt* entzünden; **become ~d** sich entzünden. **~d** *a* entzündet

in'flammable *a* feuergefährlich

inflammation /ɪnfləˈmeɪʃn/ *n* Entzündung *f*

inflammatory /ɪnˈflæmətrɪ/ *a* aufrührerisch

inflatable /ɪnˈfleɪtəbl/ *a* aufblasbar

inflat|e /ɪnˈfleɪt/ *vt* aufblasen; (*with pump*) aufpumpen. **~ion** /-eɪʃn/ *n* Inflation *f*. **~ionary** /-eɪʃənərɪ/ *a* inflationär

in'flexible *a* starr; ⟨*person*⟩ unbeugsam

inflexion /ɪnˈflekʃn/ *n* Tonfall *m*; (*Gram*) Flexion *f*

inflict /ɪnˈflɪkt/ *vt* zufügen (**on** *dat*); versetzen (*blow*) (**on** *dat*)

influen|ce /ˈɪnfluəns/ *n* Einfluss *m* □ *vt* beeinflussen. **~tial** /-ˈenʃl/ *a* einflussreich

influenza /ɪnfluˈenzə/ *n* Grippe *f*

influx /ˈɪnflʌks/ *n* Zustrom *m*

inform /ɪnˈfɔ:m/ *vt* benachrichtigen; (*officially*) informieren; **~** s.o. of sth jdm etw mitteilen; **keep s.o. ~ed** jdn auf dem Laufenden halten □ *vi* **~ against** denunzieren

in'for|mal *a*, **-ly** *adv* zwanglos; (*unofficial*) inoffiziell. **~'mality** *n* Zwanglosigkeit *f*

informant /ɪnˈfɔ:mənt/ *n* Gewährsmann *m*

informat|ion /ɪnfəˈmeɪʃn/ *n* Auskunft *f*; **a piece of ~ion** eine Auskunft. **~ive** /ɪnˈfɔ:mətɪv/ *a* aufschlussreich; (*instructive*) lehrreich

informer /ɪnˈfɔ:mə(r)/ *n* Spitzel *m*; (*Pol*) Denunziant *m*

infra-'red /ɪnfrə-/ *a* infrarot

in'frequent *a*, **-ly** *adv* selten

infringe /ɪnˈfrɪndʒ/ *vt*/*i* **[on]** verstoßen gegen. **~ment** *n* Verstoß *m*

infuriat|e /ɪnˈfjʊərɪeɪt/ *vt* wütend machen. **~ing** *a* ärgerlich; **he is ~ing** er kann einen zur Raserei bringen

infusion /ɪnˈfju:ʒn/ *n* Aufguss *m*

ingenious /ɪnˈdʒi:nɪəs/ *a* erfinderisch; ⟨*thing*⟩ raffiniert

ingenuity /ɪndʒɪˈnju:ətɪ/ *n* Geschicklichkeit *f*

ingenuous /ɪnˈdʒenjʊəs/ *a* unschuldig

ingot /ˈɪŋgət/ *n* Barren *m*

ingrained /ɪnˈgreɪnd/ *a* eingefleischt; **be ~** ⟨*dirt:*⟩ tief sitzen

ingratiate /ɪnˈgreɪʃɪeɪt/ *vt* **~ oneself** sich einschmeicheln (**with** bei)

in'gratitude *n* Undankbarkeit *f*

ingredient /ɪnˈgri:dɪənt/ *n* (*Culin*) Zutat *f*

ingrowing /ˈɪngrəʊɪŋ/ *a* ⟨*nail*⟩ eingewachsen

inhabit /ɪnˈhæbɪt/ *vt* bewohnen. **~ant** *n* Einwohner(in) *m(f)*

inhale /ɪnˈheɪl/ *vt*/*i* einatmen; (*Med* & *when smoking*) inhalieren

inherent /ɪnˈhɪərənt/ *a* natürlich

inherit /ɪnˈherɪt/ *vt* erben. **~ance** /-əns/ *n* Erbschaft *f*, Erbe *nt*

inhibit /ɪnˈhɪbɪt/ *vt* hemmen. **~ed** *a* gehemmt. **~ion** /-ˈbɪʃn/ *n* Hemmung *f*

inho'spitable *a* ungastlich

in'human *a* unmenschlich

inimitable /ɪˈnɪmɪtəbl/ *a* unnachahmlich

iniquitous /ɪˈnɪkwɪtəs/ *a* schändlich; (*unjust*) ungerecht

initial /ɪˈnɪʃl/ *a* anfänglich, Anfangs- □ *n* Anfangsbuchstabe *m*; **my ~s** meine Initialen □ *vt* (*pt/pp* **initialled**) abzeichnen; (*Pol*) paraphieren. **~ly** *adv* anfangs, am Anfang

initiat|e /ɪˈnɪʃɪeɪt/ *vt* einführen. **~ion** /-ˈeɪʃn/ *n* Einführung *f*

initiative /ɪˈnɪʃətɪv/ *n* Initiative *f*

inject /ɪnˈdʒekt/ *vt* einspritzen, injizieren. **~ion** /-ekʃn/ *n* Spritze *f*, Injektion *f*

injunction /ɪnˈdʒʌŋkʃn/ *n* gerichtliche Verfügung *f*

injur|e /ˈɪndʒə(r)/ *vt* verletzen. **~y** *n* Verletzung *f*

in'justice *n* Ungerechtigkeit *f*; **do s.o. an ~** jdm unrecht tun

ink /ɪŋk/ *n* Tinte *f*

inkling /ˈɪŋklɪŋ/ *n* Ahnung *f*

inlaid /ɪnˈleɪd/ *a* eingelegt

inland /ˈɪnlənd/ *a* Binnen- □ *adv* landeinwärts. **I ~ Revenue** *n* ≈ Finanzamt *nt*

in-laws /ˈɪnlɔ:z/ *npl* (*fam*) Schwiegereltern *pl*

inlay /'ınleı/ *n* Einlegearbeit *f*

inlet /'ınlet/ *n* schmale Bucht *f*; (*Techn*) Zuleitung *f*

inmate /'ınmeıt/ *n* Insasse *m*

inn /ın/ *n* Gasthaus *nt*

innards /'ınədz/ *npl* (*fam*) Eingeweide *pl*

innate /ı'neıt/ *a* angeboren

inner /'ınə(r)/ *a* innere(r,s). ∼**most** *a* innerste(r,s)

'**innkeeper** *n* Gastwirt *m*

innocen|ce /'ınəsəns/ *n* Unschuld *f*. ∼**t** *a* unschuldig. ∼**tly** *adv* in aller Unschuld

innocuous /ı'nɒkjʊəs/ *a* harmlos

innovat|e /'ınəveıt/ *vi* neu einführen. ∼**ion** /-'veıʃn/ *n* Neuerung *f*. ∼**or** *n* Neuerer *m*

innuendo /ınju:'endəʊ/ *n* (*pl* -**es**) [versteckte] Anspielung *f*

innumerable /ı'nju:mərəbl/ *a* unzählig

inoculat|e /ı'nɒkjʊleıt/ *vt* impfen. ∼**ion** /-'leıʃn/ *n* Impfung *f*

inof'fensive *a* harmlos

in'operable *a* nicht operierbar

in'opportune *a* unpassend

inordinate /ı'nɔ:dınət/ *a*, -**ly** *adv* übermäßig

inor'ganic *a* anorganisch

'**in-patient** *n* [stationär behandelter] Krankenhauspatient *m*

input /'ınpʊt/ *n* Input *m* & *nt*

inquest /'ınkwest/ *n* gerichtliche Untersuchung *f*

inquir|e /ın'kwaıə(r)/ *vi* sich erkundigen (**about** nach); ∼**e into** untersuchen □ *vt* sich erkundigen nach. ∼**y** *n* Erkundigung *f*; (*investigation*) Untersuchung *f*

inquisitive /ın'kwızətıv/ *a*, -**ly** *adv* neugierig

inroad /'ınrəʊd/ *n* Einfall *m*; **make** ∼**s into** sth etw angreifen

in'sane *a* geisteskrank; (*fig*) wahnsinnig

in'sanitary *a* unhygienisch

in'sanity *n* Geisteskrankheit *f*

insatiable /ın'seıʃəbl/ *a* unersättlich

inscri|be /ın'skraıb/ *vt* eingravieren. ∼**ption** /-'skrıpʃn/ *n* Inschrift *f*

inscrutable /ın'skru:təbl/ *a* unergründlich; (*expression*) undurchdringlich

insect /'ınsekt/ *n* Insekt *nt*. ∼**icide** /-'sektısaıd/ *n* Insektenvertilgungsmittel *nt*

inse'cur|e *a* nicht sicher; (*fig*) unsicher. ∼**ity** *n* Unsicherheit *f*

insemination /ınsemı'neıʃn/ *n* Besamung *f*; (*Med*) Befruchtung *f*

in'sensible *a* (*unconscious*) bewusstlos

in'sensitive *a* gefühllos; ∼ **to** unempfindlich gegen

in'separable *a* untrennbar; (*people*) unzertrennlich

insert¹ /'ınsɜ:t/ *n* Einsatz *m*

insert² /ın'sɜ:t/ *vt* einfügen, einsetzen; einstecken 〈key〉; einwerfen 〈coin〉. ∼**ion** /-ɜ:ʃn/ *n* (*insert*) Einsatz *m*; (*in text*) Einfügung *f*

inside /ın'saıd/ *n* Innenseite *f*; (*of house*) Innere(s) *nt* □ *attrib* Innen- □ *adv* innen; (*indoors*) drinnen; **go** ∼ hineingehen; **come** ∼ hereinkommen; ∼ **out** links [herum]; **know sth** ∼ **out** etw in- und auswendig kennen □ *prep* ∼ [**of**] in (+ *dat*/ (*into*) + *acc*)

insidious /ın'sıdıəs/ *a*, -**ly** *adv* heimtückisch

insight /'ınsaıt/ *n* Einblick *m* (**into** in + *acc*); (*understanding*) Einsicht *f*

insignia /ın'sıgnıə/ *npl* Insignien *pl*

insig'nificant *a* unbedeutend

insin'cere *a* unaufrichtig

insinuat|e /ın'sınjʊeıt/ *vt* andeuten. ∼**ion** /-'eıʃn/ *n* Andeutung *f*

insipid /ın'sıpıd/ *a* fade

insist /ın'sıst/ *vi* darauf bestehen; ∼ **on** bestehen auf (+ *dat*) □ *vt* ∼ **that** darauf bestehen, dass. ∼**ence** *n* Bestehen *nt*. ∼**ent** *a*, -**ly** *adv* beharrlich; **be** ∼**ent** darauf bestehen

'**insole** *n* Einlegesohle *f*

insolen|ce /'ınsələns/ *n* Unverschämtheit *f*. ∼**t** *a*, -**ly** *adv* unverschämt

in'soluble *a* unlöslich; (*fig*) unlösbar

in'solvent *a* zahlungsunfähig

insomnia /ın'sɒmnıə/ *n* Schlaflosigkeit *f*

inspect /ın'spekt/ *vt* inspizieren; (*test*) prüfen; kontrollieren 〈ticket〉. ∼**ion** /-ekʃn/ *n* Inspektion *f*. ∼**or** *n* Inspektor *m*; (*of tickets*) Kontrolleur *m*

inspiration /ınspə'reıʃn/ *n* Inspiration *f*

inspire /ın'spaıə(r)/ *vt* inspirieren; ∼ **sth in s.o.** etw jdm etw einflößen

insta'bility *n* Unbeständigkeit *f*; (*of person*) Labilität *f*

install /ın'stɔ:l/ *vt* installieren; [in ein Amt] einführen 〈person〉. ∼**ation** /-stə'leıʃn/ *n* Installation *f*; Amtseinführung *f*

instalment /ın'stɔ:lmənt/ *n* (*Comm*) Rate *f*; (*of serial*) Fortsetzung *f*; (*Radio, TV*) Folge *f*

instance /'ınstəns/ *n* Fall *m*; (*example*) Beispiel *nt*; **in the first** ∼ zunächst; **for** ∼ zum Beispiel

instant /'ınstənt/ *a* sofortig; (*Culin*) Instant- □ *n* Augenblick *m*, Moment *m*. ∼**aneous** /-'teınıəs/ *a* unverzüglich, unmittelbar; **death was** ∼**aneous** der Tod trat sofort ein

instant 'coffee *n* Pulverkaffee *m*

instantly /'ınstəntlı/ *adv* sofort

instead /ın'sted/ *adv* statt dessen; ~ **of** statt (+ *gen*), anstelle von; ~ **of me** an meiner Stelle; ~ **of going** anstatt zu gehen

'instep *n* Spann *m*, Rist *m*

instigat|e /'ınstıgeıt/ *vt* anstiften; einleiten (*proceedings*). ~**ion** /-'geıʃn/ *n* Anstiftung *f*; **at his** ~**ion** auf seine Veranlassung. ~**or** *n* Anstifter(in) *m(f)*

instil /ın'stıl/ *vt* (*pt/pp* **instilled**) einprägen (**into s.o.** *dat*)

instinct /'ınstıŋkt/ *n* Instinkt *m*. ~**ive** /-'stıŋktıv/ *a*, **-ly** *adv* instinktiv

institut|e /'ınstıtju:t/ *n* Institut *nt* □ *vt* einführen; einleiten (*search*). ~**ion** /-'tju:-ʃn/ *n* Institution *f*; (*home*) Anstalt *f*

instruct /ın'strʌkt/ *vt* unterrichten; (*order*) anweisen. ~**ion** /-ʌkʃn/ *n* Unterricht *m*; Anweisung *f*; ~**ions** *pl* **for use** Gebrauchsanweisung *f*. ~**ive** /-ıv/ *a* lehrreich. ~**or** *n* Lehrer(in) *m(f)*; (*Mil*) Ausbilder *m*

instrument /'ınstrəmənt/ *n* Instrument *nt*. ~**al** /-'mentl/ *a* Instrumental-; **be** ~**al in** eine entscheidende Rolle spielen bei

insu'bordi|nate *a* ungehorsam. ~**nation** /-'neıʃn/ *n* Ungehorsam *m*; (*Mil*) Insubordination *f*

in'sufferable *a* unerträglich

insuf'ficient *a*, **-ly** *adv* nicht genügend

insular /'ınsjʊlə(r)/ *a* (*fig*) engstirnig

insulat|e /'ınsjʊleıt/ *vt* isolieren. ~**ing tape** *n* Isolierband *nt*. ~**ion** /-'leıʃn/ *n* Isolierung *f*

insulin /'ınsjʊlın/ *n* Insulin *nt*

insult[1] /'ınsʌlt/ *n* Beleidigung *f*

insult[2] /ın'sʌlt/ *vt* beleidigen

insuperable /ın'su:pərəbl/ *a* unüberwindlich

insur|ance /ın'ʃʊərəns/ *n* Versicherung *f*. ~**e** *vt* versichern

insurrection /ınsə'rekʃn/ *n* Aufstand *m*

intact /ın'tækt/ *a* unbeschädigt; (*complete*) vollständig

'intake *n* Aufnahme *f*

in'tangible *a* nicht greifbar

integral /'ıntıgrl/ *a* wesentlich

integrat|e /'ıntıgreıt/ *vt* integrieren □ *vi* sich integrieren. ~**ion** /-'greıʃn/ *n* Integration *f*

integrity /ın'tegrətı/ *n* Integrität *f*

intellect /'ıntəlekt/ *n* Intellekt *m*. ~**ual** /-'lektjʊəl/ *a* intellektuell

intelligen|ce /ın'telıdʒəns/ *n* Intelligenz *f*; (*Mil*) Nachrichtendienst *m*; (*information*) Meldungen *pl*. ~**t** *a*, **-ly** *adv* intelligent

intelligentsia /ıntelı'dʒentsıə/ *n* Intelligenz *f*

intelligible /ın'telıdʒəbl/ *a* verständlich

intend /ın'tend/ *vt* beabsichtigen; **be** ~**ed for** bestimmt sein für

intense /ın'tens/ *a* intensiv; (*pain*) stark. ~**ly** *adv* äußerst; (*study*) intensiv

intensi|fication /ıntensıfı'keıʃn/ *n* Intensivierung *f*. ~**fy** /-'tensıfaı/ *v* (*pt/pp* **-ied**) □ *vt* intensivieren □ *vi* zunehmen

intensity /ın'tensətı/ *n* Intensität *f*

intensive /ın'tensıv/ *a*, **-ly** *adv* intensiv; **be in** ~ **care** auf der Intensivstation sein

intent /ın'tent/ *a*, **-ly** *adv* aufmerksam; ~ **on** (*absorbed in*) vertieft in (+ *acc*); **be** ~ **on doing sth** fest entschlossen sein, etw zu tun □ *n* Absicht *f*; **to all** ~**s and purposes** im Grunde

intention /ın'tenʃn/ *n* Absicht *f*. ~**al** *a*, **-ly** *adv* absichtlich

inter /ın'tɜ:(r)/ *vt* (*pt/pp* **interred**) bestatten

inter'action *n* Wechselwirkung *f*

intercede /ıntə'si:d/ *vi* Fürsprache einlegen (**on behalf of** für)

intercept /ıntə'sept/ *vt* abfangen

'interchange[1] *n* Austausch *m*; (*Auto*) Autobahnkreuz *nt*

inter'change[2] *vt* austauschen. ~**able** *a* austauschbar

intercom /'ıntəkɒm/ *n* [Gegen]sprechanlage *f*

'intercourse *n* Verkehr *m*; (*sexual*) Geschlechtsverkehr *m*

interest /'ıntrəst/ *n* Interesse *nt*; (*Comm*) Zinsen *pl*; **have an** ~ (*Comm*) beteiligt sein (**in an** + *dat*) □ *vt* interessieren; **be** ~**ed** sich interessieren (**in** für). ~**ing** *a* interessant. ~ **rate** *n* Zinssatz *m*

interfere /ıntə'fıə(r)/ *vi* sich einmischen. ~**nce** /-əns/ *n* Einmischung *f*; (*Radio, TV*) Störung *f*

interim /'ıntərım/ *a* Zwischen-; (*temporary*) vorläufig □ *n* **in the** ~ in der Zwischenzeit

interior /ın'tıərıə(r)/ *a* innere(r,s), Innen- □ *n* Innere(s) *nt*

interject /ıntə'dʒekt/ *vt* einwerfen. ~**ion** /-ekʃn/ *n* Interjektion *f*; (*remark*) Einwurf *m*

inter'lock *vi* ineinander greifen

interloper /'ıntələʊpə(r)/ *n* Eindringling *m*

interlude /'ıntəlu:d/ *n* Pause *f*; (*performance*) Zwischenspiel *nt*

inter'marry *vi* untereinander heiraten; (*different groups:*) Mischehen schließen

intermediary /ıntə'mi:dıərı/ *n* Vermittler(in) *m(f)*

intermediate /ɪntə'miːdɪət/ a Zwischen-
interminable /ɪn'tɜːmɪnəbl/ a endlos [lang]
intermission /ɪntə'mɪʃn/ n Pause f
intermittent /ɪntə'mɪtənt/ a in Abständen auftretend
intern /ɪn'tɜːn/ vt internieren
internal /ɪn'tɜːnl/ a innere(r,s); ⟨matter, dispute⟩ intern. ∼ly adv innerlich; ⟨deal with⟩ intern
inter'national a, -ly adv international □ n Länderspiel nt; ⟨player⟩ Nationalspieler(in) m(f)
internist /ɪn'tɜːnɪst/ n (Amer) Internist m
internment /ɪn'tɜːnmənt/ n Internierung f
'interplay n Wechselspiel nt
interpolate /ɪn'tɜːpəleɪt/ vt einwerfen
interpret /ɪn'tɜːprɪt/ vt interpretieren; auslegen ⟨text⟩; deuten ⟨dream⟩; ⟨translate⟩ dolmetschen □ vi dolmetschen. ∼ation /-'teɪʃn/ n Interpretation f. ∼er n Dolmetscher(in) m(f)
interre'lated a verwandt; ⟨facts⟩ zusammenhängend
interrogat|e /ɪn'terəgeɪt/ vt verhören. ∼ion /-'geɪʃn/ n Verhör nt
interrogative /ɪntə'rɒgətɪv/ a & n ∼ [pronoun] Interrogativpronomen nt
interrupt /ɪntə'rʌpt/ vt/i unterbrechen; don't ∼! red nicht dazwischen! ∼ion /-ʌpʃn/ n Unterbrechung f
intersect /ɪntə'sekt/ vi sich kreuzen; (Geom) sich schneiden. ∼ion /-ekʃn/ n Kreuzung f
interspersed /ɪntə'spɜːst/ a ∼ with durchsetzt mit
inter'twine vi sich ineinander schlingen
interval /'ɪntəvl/ n Abstand m; (Theat) Pause f; (Mus) Intervall nt; at hourly ∼s alle Stunde; bright ∼s pl Aufheiterungen pl
interven|e /ɪntə'viːn/ vi eingreifen; (occur) dazwischenkommen. ∼tion /-'venʃn/ n Eingreifen nt; (Mil, Pol) Intervention f
interview /'ɪntəvjuː/ n (Journ) Interview nt; (for job) Vorstellungsgespräch nt; go for an ∼ sich vorstellen □ vt interviewen; ein Vorstellungsgespräch führen mit. ∼er n Interviewer(in) m(f)
intestine /ɪn'testɪn/ n Darm m
intimacy /'ɪntɪməsɪ/ n Vertrautheit f; (sexual) Intimität f
intimate[1] /'ɪntɪmət/ a, -ly adv vertraut; ⟨friend⟩ eng; ⟨sexually⟩ intim
intimate[2] /'ɪntɪmeɪt/ vt zu verstehen geben; (imply) andeuten

intimidat|e /ɪn'tɪmɪdeɪt/ vt einschüchtern. ∼ion /-'deɪʃn/ n Einschüchterung f
into /'ɪntə, vor einem Vokal 'ɪntʊ/ prep in (+ acc); go ∼ the house ins Haus [hinein]gehen; be ∼ (fam) sich auskennen mit; 7 ∼ 21 21 [geteilt] durch 7
in'tolerable a unerträglich
in'toleran|ce n Intoleranz f. ∼t a intolerant
intonation /ɪntə'neɪʃn/ n Tonfall m
intoxicat|ed /ɪn'tɒksɪkeɪtɪd/ a betrunken; (fig) berauscht. ∼ion /-'keɪʃn/ n Rausch m
intractable /ɪn'træktəbl/ a widerspenstig; ⟨problem⟩ hartnäckig
intransigent /ɪn'trænsɪdʒənt/ a unnachgiebig
in'transitive a, -ly adv intransitiv
intravenous /ɪntrə'viːnəs/ a, -ly adv intravenös
intrepid /ɪn'trepɪd/ a kühn, unerschrocken
intricate /'ɪntrɪkət/ a kompliziert
intrigu|e /ɪn'triːg/ n Intrige f □ vt faszinieren □ vi intrigieren. ∼ing a faszinierend
intrinsic /ɪn'trɪnsɪk/ a ∼ value Eigenwert m
introduce /ɪntrə'djuːs/ vt vorstellen; (bring in, insert) einführen
introduct|ion /ɪntrə'dʌkʃn/ n Einführung f; (to person) Vorstellung f; (to book) Einleitung f. ∼ory /-tərɪ/ a einleitend
introspective /ɪntrə'spektɪv/ a in sich (acc) gerichtet
introvert /'ɪntrəvɜːt/ n introvertierter Mensch m
intru|de /ɪn'truːd/ vi stören. ∼der n Eindringling m. ∼sion /-uːʒn/ n Störung f
intuit|ion /ɪntjuː'ɪʃn/ n Intuition f. ∼ive /-'tjuːɪtɪv/ a, -ly adv intuitiv
inundate /'ɪnəndeɪt/ vt überschwemmen
invade /ɪn'veɪd/ vt einfallen in (+ acc). ∼r n Angreifer m
invalid[1] /'ɪnvəlɪd/ n Kranke(r) m/f
invalid[2] /ɪn'vælɪd/ a ungültig. ∼ate vt ungültig machen
in'valuable a unschätzbar; ⟨person⟩ unersetzlich
in'variab|le a unveränderlich. ∼ly adv immer
invasion /ɪn'veɪʒn/ n Invasion f
invective /ɪn'vektɪv/ n Beschimpfungen pl
invent /ɪn'vent/ vt erfinden. ∼ion /-enʃn/ n Erfindung f. ∼ive /-tɪv/ a erfinderisch. ∼or n Erfinder m

inventory /'ınvəntri/ n Bestandsliste f; **make an ~** ein Inventar aufstellen

inverse /ın'vɜːs/ a, **-ly** adv umgekehrt □ n Gegenteil nt

invert /ın'vɜːt/ vt umkehren. **~ed commas** npl Anführungszeichen pl

invest /ın'vest/ vt investieren, anlegen; **~ in** (fam: buy) sich (dat) zulegen

investigat|e /ın'vestıgeıt/ vt untersuchen. **~ion** /-'geıʃn/ n Untersuchung f

invest|ment /ın'vestmənt/ n Anlage f; **be a good ~ment** (fig) sich bezahlt machen. **~or** n Kapitalanleger m

inveterate /ın'vetərət/ a Gewohnheits-; ⟨liar⟩ unverbesserlich

invidious /ın'vıdıəs/ a unerfreulich; (unfair) ungerecht

invigilate /ın'vıdʒıleıt/ vi (Sch) Aufsicht führen

invigorate /ın'vıgəreıt/ vt beleben

invincible /ın'vınsəbl/ a unbesiegbar

inviolable /ın'vaıələbl/ a unantastbar

in'visible a unsichtbar. **~ mending** n Kunststopfen nt

invitation /ınvı'teıʃn/ n Einladung f

invit|e /ın'vaıt/ vt einladen. **~ing** a einladend

invoice /'ınvɔıs/ n Rechnung f □ vt ~ **s.o.** jdm eine Rechnung schicken

invoke /ın'vəʊk/ vt anrufen

in'voluntary a, **-ily** adv unwillkürlich

involve /ın'vɒlv/ vt beteiligen; (affect) betreffen; (implicate) verwickeln; (entail) mit sich bringen; (mean) bedeuten; **be ~d in** beteiligt sein an (+ dat); (implicated) verwickelt sein in (+ acc); **get ~d with s.o.** sich mit jdm einlassen. **~d** a kompliziert

in'vulnerable a unverwundbar; ⟨position⟩ unangreifbar

inward /'ınwəd/ a innere(r,s). **~ly** adv innerlich. **~s** adv nach innen

iodine /'aıədiːn/ n Jod nt

iota /aı'əʊtə/ n Jota nt, (fam) Funke m

IOU abbr (I owe you) Schuldschein m

Iran /ı'rɑːn/ n der Iran

Iraq /ı'rɑːk/ n der Irak

irascible /ı'ræsəbl/ a aufbrausend

irate /aı'reıt/ a wütend

Ireland /'aıələnd/ n Irland nt

iris /'aıərıs/ n (Anat) Regenbogenhaut f, Iris f; (Bot) Schwertlilie f

Irish /'aıərıʃ/ a irisch □ n **the ~** pl die Iren. **~man** n Ire m. **~woman** n Irin f

irk /ɜːk/ vt ärgern. **~some** /-səm/ a lästig

iron /'aıən/ a Eisen-; (fig) eisern □ n Eisen nt; (appliance) Bügeleisen nt □ vt/i bügeln. **~ out** vt ausbügeln

ironic[al] /aı'rɒnık[l]/ a ironisch

ironing /'aıənıŋ/ n Bügeln nt; (articles) Bügelwäsche f; **do the ~** bügeln. **~-board** n Bügelbrett nt

ironmonger /'-mʌŋgə(r)/ n **~'s [shop]** Haushaltswarengeschäft nt

irony /'aıərənı/ n Ironie f

irradiate /ı'reıdıeıt/ vt bestrahlen

irrational /ı'ræʃənl/ a irrational

irreconcilable /ı'rekənsaıləbl/ a unversöhnlich

irrefutable /ırı'fjuːtəbl/ a unwiderlegbar

irregular /ı'regjʊlə(r)/ a, **-ly** adv unregelmäßig; (against rules) regelwidrig. **~ity** /-'lærətı/ n Unregelmäßigkeit f; Regelwidrigkeit f

irrelevant /ı'reləvənt/ a irrelevant

irreparable /ı'repərəbl/ a unersetzlich; **be ~** nicht wieder gutzumachen sein

irreplaceable /ırı'pleısəbl/ a unersetzlich

irrepressible /ırı'presəbl/ a unverwüstlich; **be ~** ⟨person:⟩ nicht unterzukriegen sein

irresistible /ırı'zıstəbl/ a unwiderstehlich

irresolute /ı'rezəluːt/ a unentschlossen

irrespective /ırı'spektıv/ a **~ of** ungeachtet (+ gen)

irresponsible /ırı'spɒnsəbl/ a, **-bly** adv unverantwortlich; ⟨person⟩ verantwortungslos

irreverent /ı'revərənt/ a, **-ly** adv respektlos

irreversible /ırı'vɜːsəbl/ a unwiderruflich; (Med) irreversibel

irrevocable /ı'revəkəbl/ a, **-bly** adv unwiderruflich

irrigat|e /'ırıgeıt/ vt bewässern. **~ion** /-'geıʃn/ n Bewässerung f

irritability /ırıtə'bılətı/ n Gereiztheit f

irritable /'ırıtəbl/ a reizbar

irritant /'ırıtənt/ n Reizstoff m

irritat|e /'ırıteıt/ vt irritieren; (Med) reizen. **~ion** /-'teıʃn/ n Ärger m; (Med) Reizung f

is /ız/ see **be**

Islam /'ızlɑːm/ n der Islam. **~ic** /-'læmık/ a islamisch

island /'aılənd/ n Insel f. **~er** n Inselbewohner(in) m(f)

isle /aıl/ n Insel f

isolat|e /'aısəleıt/ vt isolieren. **~ed** a (remote) abgelegen; (single) einzeln. **~ion** /-'leıʃn/ n Isoliertheit f; (Med) Isolierung f

Israel /'ızreıl/ n Israel nt. **~i** /ız'reılı/ a israelisch □ n Israeli m/f

issue /'ɪʃuː/ n Frage f; (outcome) Ergebnis nt; (of magazine, stamps) Ausgabe f; (offspring) Nachkommen pl; **what is at ~?** worum geht es? **take ~ with s.o.** jdm widersprechen □ vt ausgeben; ausstellen ⟨passport⟩; erteilen ⟨order⟩; herausgeben ⟨book⟩; **be ~d with** sth etw erhalten □ vi **~ from** herausströmen aus

isthmus /'ɪsməs/ n (pl -muses) Landenge f

it /ɪt/ pron es; (m) er; (f) sie; (as direct object) es; (m) ihn; (f) sie; (as indirect object) ihm; (f) ihr; **it is raining** es regnet; **it's me** ich bin's; **who is it?** wer ist da? **of/from it** davon; **with it** damit; **out of it** daraus

Italian /ɪ'tæljən/ a italienisch □ n Italiener(in) m(f); (Lang) Italienisch nt

italic /ɪ'tælɪk/ a kursiv. **~s** npl Kursivschrift f; **in ~s** kursiv

Italy /'ɪtəlɪ/ n Italien nt

itch /ɪtʃ/ n Juckreiz m; **I have an ~** es juckt mich □ vi jucken; **I'm ~ing** (fam) es juckt mich (to zu). **~y** a be **~y** jucken

item /'aɪtəm/ n Gegenstand m; (Comm) Artikel m; (on agenda) Punkt m; (on invoice) Posten m; (act) Nummer f; **~ [of news]** Nachricht f. **~ize** vt einzeln aufführen; spezifizieren ⟨bill⟩

itinerant /aɪ'tɪnərənt/ a Wander-

itinerary /aɪ'tɪnərərɪ/ n [Reise]route f

its /ɪts/ poss pron sein; (f) ihr

it's = it is, it has

itself /ɪt'self/ pron selbst; (refl) sich; **by ~** von selbst; (alone) allein

ivory /'aɪvərɪ/ n Elfenbein nt □ attrib Elfenbein-

ivy /'aɪvɪ/ n Efeu m

J

jab /dʒæb/ n Stoß m; (fam: injection) Spritze f □ vt (pt/pp jabbed) stoßen

jabber /'dʒæbə(r)/ vi plappern

jack /dʒæk/ n (Auto) Wagenheber m; (Cards) Bube m □ vt **~ up** (Auto) aufbocken

jackdaw /'dʒækdɔː/ n Dohle f

jacket /'dʒækɪt/ n Jacke f; (of book) Schutzumschlag m. **~ po'tato** n in der Schale gebackene Kartoffel f

'jackpot n **hit the ~** das große Los ziehen

jade /dʒeɪd/ n Jade m

jaded /'dʒeɪdɪd/ a abgespannt

jagged /'dʒægɪd/ a zackig

jail /dʒeɪl/ = **gaol**

jalopy /dʒə'lɒpɪ/ n (fam) Klapperkiste f

jam¹ /dʒæm/ n Marmelade f

jam² n Gedränge nt; (Auto) Stau m; (fam: difficulty) Klemme f □ v (pt/pp jammed) □ vt klemmen (**in** in + acc); stören ⟨broadcast⟩ □ vi klemmen

Jamaica /dʒə'meɪkə/ n Jamaika nt

jangle /'dʒæŋgl/ vi klimpern □ vt klimpern mit

janitor /'dʒænɪtə(r)/ n Hausmeister m

January /'dʒænjʊərɪ/ n Januar m

Japan /dʒə'pæn/ n Japan nt. **~ese** /dʒæpə'niːz/ a japanisch □ n Japaner(in) m(f); (Lang) Japanisch nt

jar¹ /dʒɑː(r)/ n Glas nt; (earthenware) Topf m

jar² v (pt/pp jarred) vi stören □ vt erschüttern

jargon /'dʒɑːgən/ n Jargon m

jaundice /'dʒɔːndɪs/ n Gelbsucht f. **~d** a (fig) zynisch

jaunt /dʒɔːnt/ n Ausflug m

jaunty /'dʒɔːntɪ/ a (-ier, -iest) -ily adv keck

javelin /'dʒævlɪn/ n Speer m

jaw /dʒɔː/ n Kiefer m; **~s** pl Rachen m □ vi (fam) quatschen

jay /dʒeɪ/ n Eichelhäher m. **~-walker** n achtloser Fußgänger m

jazz /dʒæz/ n Jazz m. **~y** a knallig

jealous /'dʒeləs/ a, **-ly** adv eifersüchtig (**of** auf + acc). **~y** n Eifersucht f

jeans /dʒiːnz/ npl Jeans pl

jeer /dʒɪə(r)/ n Johlen nt □ vi johlen; **~ at** verhöhnen

jell /dʒel/ vi gelieren

jelly /'dʒelɪ/ n Gelee nt; (dessert) Götterspeise f. **~fish** n Qualle f

jemmy /'dʒemɪ/ n Brecheisen nt

jeopar|dize /'dʒepədaɪz/ vt gefährden. **~dy** /-dɪ/ n **in ~dy** gefährdet

jerk /dʒɜːk/ n Ruck m □ vt stoßen; (pull) reißen □ vi rucken; ⟨limb, muscle:⟩ zucken. **~ily** adv ruckweise. **~y** a ruckartig

jersey /'dʒɜːzɪ/ n Pullover m; (Sport) Trikot nt; (fabric) Jersey m

jest /dʒest/ n Scherz m; **in ~** im Spaß □ vi scherzen

jet¹ /dʒet/ n (Miner) Jett m

jet² n (of water) [Wasser]strahl m; (nozzle) Düse f; (plane) Düsenflugzeug nt

jet: ~-'black a pechschwarz. **~lag** n Jetlag nt. **~-pro'pelled** a mit Düsenantrieb

jettison /'dʒetɪsn/ vt über Bord werfen

jetty /'dʒetɪ/ n Landesteg m; (breakwater) Buhne f

Jew /dʒuː/ n Jude m /Jüdin f

jewel /'dʒuːəl/ n Edelstein m; (fig) Juwel nt. ~ler n Juwelier m; ~ler's [shop] Juweliergeschäft nt. ~lery n Schmuck m

Jew|ess /'dʒuː:ɪs/ n Jüdin f. ~ish a jüdisch

jib /dʒɪb/ vi (pt/pp jibbed) (fig) sich sträuben (at gegen)

jiffy /'dʒɪfɪ/ n (fam) in a ~ in einem Augenblick

jigsaw /'dʒɪgsɔ:/ n ~ [puzzle] Puzzlespiel nt

jilt /dʒɪlt/ vt sitzen lassen

jingle /'dʒɪŋgl/ n (rhyme) Verschen nt □ vi klimpern □ vt klimpern mit

jinx /dʒɪŋks/ n (fam) it's got a ~ on it es ist verhext

jitter|s /'dʒɪtəz/ npl (fam) have the ~s nervös sein. ~y a (fam) nervös

job /dʒɒb/ n Aufgabe f; (post) Stelle f, (fam) Job m; be a ~ (fam) nicht leicht sein; it's a good ~ that es ist [nur] gut, dass. ~ centre n Arbeitsvermittlungsstelle f. ~less a arbeitslos

jockey /'dʒɒkɪ/ n Jockei m

jocular /'dʒɒkjʊlə(r)/ a, -ly adv spaßhaft

jog /'dʒɒg/ n Stoß m; at a ~ im Dauerlauf □ v (pt/pp jogged) □ vt anstoßen; ~ s.o.'s memory jds Gedächtnis nachhelfen □ vi (Sport) joggen. ~ging n Jogging m

john /dʒɒn/ n (Amer, fam) Klo nt

join /dʒɔɪn/ n Nahtstelle f □ vt verbinden (to mit); sich anschließen (+ dat) ⟨person⟩; (become member of) beitreten (+ dat); eintreten in (+ acc) ⟨firm⟩ □ vi ⟨roads:⟩ sich treffen. ~ in vi mitmachen. ~ up vi (Mil) Soldat werden □ vt zusammenfügen

joiner /'dʒɔɪnə(r)/ n Tischler m

joint /dʒɔɪnt/ a, -ly adv gemeinsam □ n Gelenk nt; (in wood, brickwork) Fuge f; (Culin) Braten m; (fam: bar) Lokal nt

joist /dʒɔɪst/ n Dielenbalken m

jok|e /dʒəʊk/ n Scherz m; (funny story) Witz m; (trick) Streich m □ vi scherzen. ~er n Witzbold m; (Cards) Joker m. ~ing n ~ing apart Spaß beiseite. ~ingly adv im Spaß

jollity /'dʒɒlətɪ/ n Lustigkeit f

jolly /'dʒɒlɪ/ a (-ier, -iest) lustig □ adv (fam) sehr

jolt /dʒəʊlt/ n Ruck m □ vt einen Ruck versetzen (+ dat) □ vi holpern

Jordan /'dʒɔ:dn/ n Jordanien nt

jostle /'dʒɒsl/ vt anrempeln □ vi drängeln

jot /dʒɒt/ n Jota nt □ vt (pt/pp jotted) ~ [down] sich (dat) notieren. ~ter n Notizblock m

journal /'dʒɜ:nl/ n Zeitschrift f; (diary) Tagebuch nt. ~ese /-ə'li:z/ n Zeitungsjargon m. ~ism n Journalismus m. ~ist n Journalist(in) m(f)

journey /'dʒɜ:nɪ/ n Reise f

jovial /'dʒəʊvɪəl/ a lustig

joy /dʒɔɪ/ n Freude f. ~ful a, -ly adv freudig, froh. ~ride n (fam) Spritztour f [im gestohlenen Auto]

jubil|ant /'dʒu:bɪlənt/ a überglücklich. ~ation /-'leɪʃn/ n Jubel m

jubilee /'dʒu:bɪli:/ n Jubiläum nt

Judaism /'dʒu:deɪɪzm/ n Judentum nt

judder /'dʒʌdə(r)/ vi rucken

judge /dʒʌdʒ/ n Richter m; (of competition) Preisrichter m □ vt beurteilen; (estimate) [ein]schätzen □ vi urteilen (by nach). ~ment n Beurteilung f; (Jur) Urteil nt; (fig) Urteilsvermögen nt

judic|ial /dʒu:'dɪʃl/ a gerichtlich. ~iary /-'ʃərɪ/ n Richterstand m. ~ious /-'ʃəs/ a klug

judo /'dʒu:dəʊ/ n Judo nt

jug /dʒʌg/ n Kanne f; (small) Kännchen nt; (for water, wine) Krug m

juggernaut /'dʒʌgənɔ:t/ n (fam) Riesenlaster m

juggle /'dʒʌgl/ vi jonglieren. ~r n Jongleur m

juice /dʒu:s/ n Saft m. ~ extractor n Entsafter m

juicy /'dʒu:sɪ/ a (-ier, -iest) saftig; (fam) ⟨story⟩ pikant

juke-box /'dʒu:k-/ n Musikbox f

July /dʒʊ'laɪ/ n Juli m

jumble /'dʒʌmbl/ n Durcheinander nt □ vt ~ [up] durcheinander bringen. ~ sale n [Wohltätigkeits]basar m

jumbo /'dʒʌmbəʊ/ n ~ [jet] Jumbo[jet] m

jump /dʒʌmp/ n Sprung m; (in prices) Anstieg m; (in horse racing) Hindernis nt □ vi springen; (start) zusammenzucken; make s.o. ~ jdn erschrecken; ~ [up] sofort zugreifen bei ⟨offer⟩; ~ to conclusions voreilige Schlüsse ziehen □ vt überspringen; ~ the gun (fig) vorschnell handeln. ~ up vi aufspringen

jumper /'dʒʌmpə(r)/ n Pullover m, Pulli m

jumpy /'dʒʌmpɪ/ a nervös

junction /'dʒʌŋkʃn/ n Kreuzung f; (Rail) Knotenpunkt m

juncture /'dʒʌŋktʃə(r)/ n at this ~ zu diesem Zeitpunkt

June /dʒu:n/ n Juni m

jungle /'dʒʌŋgl/ n Dschungel m

junior /'dʒu:nɪə(r)/ a jünger; (in rank) untergeordnet; (Sport) Junioren- □ n Junior m. ~ school n Grundschule f

juniper /'dʒu:nɪpə(r)/ n Wacholder m

junk /dʒʌŋk/ n Gerümpel nt, Trödel m

junkie /'dʒʌŋkɪ/ n (sl) Fixer m

'junk-shop n Trödelladen m

juris|diction /dʒʊərɪs'dɪkʃn/ n Gerichtsbarkeit f. ~'prudence n Rechtswissenschaft f

juror /'dʒʊərə(r)/ n Geschworene(r) m/f

jury /'dʒʊərɪ/ n the ~ die Geschworenen pl; (for competition) die Jury

just /dʒʌst/ a gerecht ◻ adv gerade; (only) nur; (simply) einfach; (exactly) genau; ~ as tall ebenso groß; ~ listen! hör doch mal! I'm ~ going ich gehe schon; ~ put it down stell es nur hin

justice /'dʒʌstɪs/ n Gerechtigkeit f; do ~ to gerecht werden (+ dat); J~ of the Peace ≈ Friedensrichter m

justifiab|le /'dʒʌstɪfaɪəbl/ a berechtigt. ~ly adv berechtigterweise

justi|fication /dʒʌstɪfɪ'keɪʃn/ n Rechtfertigung f. ~fy /'dʒʌstɪfaɪ/ vt (pt/pp -ied) rechtfertigen

justly /'dʒʌstlɪ/ adv zu Recht

jut /dʒʌt/ vi (pt/pp jutted) ~ out vorstehen

juvenile /'dʒuːvənaɪl/ a jugendlich; (childish) kindisch ◻ n Jugendliche(r) m/f. ~ delinquency n Jugendkriminalität f

juxtapose /dʒʌkstə'pəʊz/ vt nebeneinander stellen

K

kangaroo /kæŋgə'ruː/ n Känguru nt

karate /kə'rɑːtɪ/ n Karate nt

kebab /kɪ'bæb/ n (Culin) Spießchen nt

keel /kiːl/ n Kiel m ◻ vi ~ over umkippen; (Naut) kentern

keen /kiːn/ a (-er, -est) (sharp) scharf; (intense) groß; (eager) eifrig, begeistert; ~ on (fam) erpicht auf (+ acc); ~ on s.o. von jdm sehr angetan; be ~ to do sth etw gerne machen wollen. ~ly adv tief. ~ness n Eifer m, Begeisterung f

keep /kiːp/ n (maintenance) Unterhalt m; (of castle) Bergfried m; for ~s für immer ◻ v (pt/pp kept) ◻ vt behalten; (store) aufbewahren; (not throw away) aufheben; (support) unterhalten; (detain) aufhalten; freihalten (seat); halten (promise, animals); führen, haben (shop); einhalten (law, rules); ~ sth hot etw warm halten; ~ s.o. from doing sth jdn davon abhalten, etw zu tun; ~ s.o. waiting jdn warten lassen; ~ sth to oneself etw nicht weitersagen; where do you ~ the sugar? wo hast du den Zucker? ◻ vi (remain) bleiben; (food:) sich halten; ~ left/right

sich links/rechts halten; ~ doing sth etw dauernd machen; ~ on doing sth etw weitermachen; ~ in with sich gut stellen mit. ~ up vi Schritt halten ◻ vt (continue) weitermachen

keep|er /'kiːpə(r)/ n Wärter(in) m(f). ~ing n Obhut f; be in ~ing with passen zu. ~sake n Andenken nt

keg /keg/ n kleines Fass nt

kennel /'kenl/ n Hundehütte f; ~s pl (boarding) Hundepension f; (for breeding) Zwinger m

Kenya /'kenjə/ n Kenia nt

kept /kept/ see **keep**

kerb /kɜːb/ n Bordstein m

kernel /'kɜːnl/ n Kern m

kerosene /'kerəsiːn/ n (Amer) Petroleum nt

ketchup /'ketʃʌp/ n Ketschup m

kettle /'ketl/ n [Wasser]kessel m; put the ~ on Wasser aufsetzen; a pretty ~ of fish (fam) eine schöne Bescherung f

key /kiː/ n Schlüssel m; (Mus) Tonart f; (of piano, typewriter) Taste f ◻ vt ~ in eintasten

key: ~board n Tastatur f; (Mus) Klaviatur f. ~boarder n Taster(in) m(f). ~hole n Schlüsselloch nt. ~-ring n Schlüsselring m

khaki /'kɑːkɪ/ a khakifarben ◻ n Khaki nt

kick /kɪk/ n [Fuß]tritt m; for ~s (fam) zum Spaß ◻ vt treten; ~ the bucket (fam) abkratzen ◻ vi (animal:) ausschlagen. ~off n (Sport) Anstoß m

kid /kɪd/ n Kitz nt; (fam: child) Kind nt ◻ vt (pt/pp kidded) (fam) ~ s.o. jdm etwas vormachen. ~ gloves npl Glacéhandschuhe pl

kidnap /'kɪdnæp/ vt (pt/pp -napped) entführen. ~per n Entführer m. ~ping n Entführung f

kidney /'kɪdnɪ/ n Niere f. ~ machine n künstliche Niere f

kill /kɪl/ vt töten; (fam) totschlagen (time); ~ two birds with one stone zwei Fliegen mit einer Klappe schlagen. ~er n Mörder(in) m(f). ~ing n Tötung f; (murder) Mord m

'killjoy n Spielverderber m

kiln /kɪln/ n Brennofen m

kilo /'kiːləʊ/ n Kilo nt

kilo /'kɪlə/: ~gram n Kilogramm nt. ~hertz /-hɜːts/ n Kilohertz nt. ~metre n Kilometer m. ~watt n Kilowatt nt

kilt /kɪlt/ n Schottenrock m

kin /kɪn/ n Verwandtschaft f; next of ~ nächster Verwandter m/nächste Verwandte f

kind¹ /kaɪnd/ n Art f; (brand, type) Sorte f; **what ~ of car?** was für ein Auto? **~ of** (fam) irgendwie

kind² a (-er, -est) nett; **~ to animals** gut zu Tieren; **~ regards** herzliche Grüße

kindergarten /'kɪndəgɑːtn/ n Vorschule f

kindle /'kɪndl/ vt anzünden

kind|ly /'kaɪndlɪ/ a (-ier, -iest) nett □ adv netterweise; (if you please) gefälligst. **~ness** n Güte f; (favour) Gefallen m

kindred /'kɪndrɪd/ a **~ spirit** Gleichgesinnte(r) m/f

kinetic /kɪ'netɪk/ a kinetisch

king /kɪŋ/ n König m; (Draughts) Dame f. **~dom** n Königreich nt; (fig & Relig) Reich nt

king: ~fisher n Eisvogel m. **~-sized** a extragroß

kink /kɪŋk/ n Knick m. **~y** a (fam) pervers

kiosk /'kiːɒsk/ n Kiosk m

kip /kɪp/ n **have a ~** (fam) pennen □ vi (pt/pp **kipped**) (fam) pennen

kipper /'kɪpə(r)/ n Räucherhering m

kiss /kɪs/ n Kuss m □ vt/i küssen

kit /kɪt/ n Ausrüstung f; (tools) Werkzeug nt; (construction ~) Bausatz m □ vt (pt/pp **kitted**) **~ out** ausrüsten. **~bag** n See sack m

kitchen /'kɪtʃɪn/ n Küche f □ attrib Küchen-. **~ette** /kɪtʃɪ'net/ n Kochnische f

kitchen: ~ 'garden n Gemüsegarten m. **~ 'sink** n Spülbecken nt

kite /kaɪt/ n Drachen m

kith /kɪθ/ n **with ~ and kin** mit der ganzen Verwandtschaft

kitten /'kɪtn/ n Kätzchen nt

kitty /'kɪtɪ/ n (money) [gemeinsame] Kasse f

kleptomaniac /kleptə'meɪnɪæk/ n Kleptomane m/ -manin f

knack /næk/ n Trick m, Dreh m

knapsack /'næp-/ n Tornister m

knead /niːd/ vt kneten

knee /niː/ n Knie nt. **~cap** n Kniescheibe f

kneel /niːl/ vi (pt/pp **knelt**) knien; **~ [down]** sich [nieder]knien

knelt /nelt/ see **kneel**

knew /njuː/ see **know**

knickers /'nɪkəz/ npl Schlüpfer m

knick-knacks /'nɪknæks/ npl Nippsachen pl

knife /naɪf/ n (pl **knives**) Messer nt □ vt einen Messerstich versetzen (+ dat); (to death) erstechen

knight /naɪt/ n Ritter m; (Chess) Springer m □ vt adeln

knit /nɪt/ vt/i (pt/pp **knitted**) stricken; **~ one, purl one** eine rechts eine links; **~ one's brow** die Stirn runzeln. **~ting** n Stricken nt; (work) Strickzeug nt. **~ting-needle** n Stricknadel f. **~wear** n Strickwaren pl

knives /naɪvz/ npl see **knife**

knob /nɒb/ n Knopf m; (on door) Knauf m; (small lump) Beule f; (small piece) Stückchen nt. **~bly** a knorrig; (bony) knochig

knock /nɒk/ n Klopfen nt; (blow) Schlag m; **there was a ~ at the door** es klopfte □ vt anstoßen; (at door) klopfen an (+ acc); (fam: criticize) heruntermachen; **~ a hole in sth** ein Loch in etw (acc) schlagen; **~ one's head** sich (dat) den Kopf stoßen (on an + dat) □ vi klopfen. **~ about** vt schlagen □ vi (fam) herumkommen. **~ down** vt herunterwerfen; (with fist) niederschlagen; (in car) anfahren; (demolish) abreißen; (fam: reduce) herabsetzen. **~ off** vt herunterwerfen; (fam: steal) klauen; (fam: complete quickly) hinhauen □ vi (fam: cease work) Feierabend machen. **~ out** vt ausschlagen; (make unconscious) bewusstlos schlagen; (Boxing) k.o. schlagen. **~ over** vt umwerfen; (in car) anfahren

knock: ~-down a **~-down prices** Schleuderpreise pl. **~er** n Türklopfer m. **~-kneed** /-'niːd/ a X-beinig. **~-out** n (Boxing) K.o. m

knot /nɒt/ n Knoten m □ vt (pt/pp **knotted**) knoten

knotty /'nɒtɪ/ a (-ier, -iest) verwickelt

know /nəʊ/ vt/i (pt **knew**, pp **known**) wissen; kennen (person); können (language); **get to ~** kennen lernen □ n **in the ~** (fam) im Bild

know: ~-all n (fam) Alleswisser m. **~-how** n (fam) [Sach]kenntnis f. **~ing** a wissend. **~ingly** adv wissend; (intentionally) wissentlich

knowledge /'nɒlɪdʒ/ n Kenntnis f (of von/gen); (general) Wissen nt; (specialized) Kenntnisse pl. **~able** /-əbl/ a **be ~able** viel wissen

known /nəʊn/ see **know** □ a bekannt

knuckle /'nʌkl/ n [Finger]knöchel m; (Culin) Hachse f □ vi **~ under** sich fügen; **~ down** sich dahinter klemmen

kosher /'kəʊʃə(r)/ a koscher

kowtow /kaʊ'taʊ/ vi Kotau machen (**to** vor + dat)

kudos /'kjuːdɒs/ n (fam) Prestige nt

L

lab /læb/ *n* (*fam*) Labor *nt*

label /'leɪbl/ *n* Etikett *nt* ▫ *vt* (*pt/pp* **labelled**) etikettieren

laboratory /ləˈbɒrətrɪ/ *n* Labor *nt*

laborious /ləˈbɔːrɪəs/ *a*, **-ly** *adv* mühsam

labour /'leɪbə(r)/ *n* Arbeit *f*; (*workers*) Arbeitskräfte *pl*; (*Med*) Wehen *pl*; **L~** (*Pol*) die Labourpartei ▫ *attrib* Labour- ▫ *vi* arbeiten ▫ *vt* (*fig*) sich lange auslassen über (+ *acc*). **~er** *n* Arbeiter *m*

'labour-saving *a* arbeitssparend

laburnum /ləˈbɜːnəm/ *n* Goldregen *m*

labyrinth /'læbərɪnθ/ *n* Labyrinth *nt*

lace /leɪs/ *n* Spitze *f*; (*of shoe*) Schnürsenkel *m* ▫ *vt* schnüren; **~d with rum** mit einem Schuss Rum

lacerate /'læsəreɪt/ *vt* zerreißen

lack /læk/ *n* Mangel *m* (**of** an + *dat*) ▫ *vt* **I ~ the time** mir fehlt die Zeit ▫ *vi* **be ~ing** fehlen

lackadaisical /lækəˈdeɪzɪkl/ *a* lustlos

laconic /ləˈkɒnɪk/ *a*, **-ally** *adv* lakonisch

lacquer /'lækə(r)/ *n* Lack *m*; (*for hair*) [Haar]spray *m*

lad /læd/ *n* Junge *m*

ladder /'lædə(r)/ *n* Leiter *f*; (*in fabric*) Laufmasche *f*

laden /'leɪdn/ *a* beladen

ladle /'leɪdl/ *n* [Schöpf]kelle *f* ▫ *vt* schöpfen

lady /'leɪdɪ/ *n* Dame *f*; (*title*) Lady *f*

lady: **~bird** *n*, (*Amer*) **~bug** *n* Marienkäfer *m*. **~like** *a* damenhaft

lag¹ /læg/ *vi* (*pt/pp* **lagged**) **~ behind** zurückbleiben; (*fig*) nachhinken

lag² *vt* (*pt/pp* **lagged**) umwickeln (*pipes*)

lager /'lɑːgə(r)/ *n* Lagerbier *nt*

lagoon /ləˈguːn/ *n* Lagune *f*

laid /leɪd/ *see* **lay³**

lain /leɪn/ *see* **lie²**

lair /leə(r)/ *n* Lager *nt*

laity /'leɪətɪ/ *n* Laienstand *m*

lake /leɪk/ *n* See *m*

lamb /læm/ *n* Lamm *nt*

lame /leɪm/ *a* (**-r**, **-st**) lahm

lament /ləˈment/ *n* Klage *f*; (*song*) Klagelied *nt* ▫ *vt* beklagen ▫ *vi* klagen. **~able** /'læməntəbl/ *a* beklagenswert

laminated /'læmɪneɪtɪd/ *a* laminiert

lamp /læmp/ *n* Lampe *f*; (*in street*) Laterne *f*. **~post** *n* Laternenpfahl *m*. **~shade** *n* Lampenschirm *m*

lance /lɑːns/ *n* Lanze *f* ▫ *vt* (*Med*) aufschneiden. **~-'corporal** *n* Gefreite(r) *m*

land /lænd/ *n* Land *nt*; **plot of ~** Grundstück *nt* ▫ *vt/i* landen; **~ s.o. with sth** (*fam*) jdm etw aufhalsen

landing /'lændɪŋ/ *n* Landung *f*; (*top of stairs*) Treppenflur *m*. **~-stage** *n* Landesteg *m*

land: **~lady** *n* Wirtin *f*. **~-locked** *a* **~-locked country** Binnenstaat *m*. **~lord** *n* Wirt *m*; (*of land*) Grundbesitzer *m*; (*of building*) Hausbesitzer *m*. **~mark** *n* Erkennungszeichen *nt*; (*fig*) Meilenstein *m*. **~owner** *n* Grundbesitzer *m*. **~scape** /-skeɪp/ *n* Landschaft *f*. **~slide** *n* Erdrutsch *m*

lane /leɪn/ *n* kleine Landstraße *f*; (*Auto*) Spur *f*; (*Sport*) Bahn *f*; **'get in ~'** (*Auto*) 'bitte einordnen'

language /'læŋgwɪdʒ/ *n* Sprache *f*; (*speech, style*) Ausdrucksweise *f*. **~ laboratory** *n* Sprachlabor *nt*

languid /'læŋgwɪd/ *a*, **-ly** *adv* träge

languish /'læŋgwɪʃ/ *vi* schmachten

lank /læŋk/ *a* (*hair*) strähnig

lanky /'læŋkɪ/ *a* (**-ier**, **-iest**) schlaksig

lantern /'læntən/ *n* Laterne *f*

lap¹ /læp/ *n* Schoß *m*

lap² *n* (*Sport*) Runde *f*; (*of journey*) Etappe *f* ▫ *vi* (*pt/pp* **lapped**) plätschern (**against** gegen)

lap³ *vt* (*pt/pp* **lapped**) **~ up** aufschlecken

lapel /ləˈpel/ *n* Revers *nt*

lapse /læps/ *n* Fehler *m*; (*moral*) Fehltritt *m*; (*of time*) Zeitspanne *f* ▫ *vi* (*expire*) erlöschen; **~ into** verfallen in (+ *acc*)

larceny /'lɑːsənɪ/ *n* Diebstahl *m*

lard /lɑːd/ *n* [Schweine]schmalz *nt*

larder /'lɑːdə(r)/ *n* Speisekammer *f*

large /lɑːdʒ/ *a* (**-r**, **-st**) & *adv* groß; **by and ~** im Großen und Ganzen; **at ~** auf freiem Fuß; (*in general*) im Allgemeinen. **~ly** *adv* großenteils

lark¹ /lɑːk/ *n* (*bird*) Lerche *f*

lark² *n* (*joke*) Jux *m* ▫ *vi* **~ about** herumalbern

larva /'lɑːvə/ *n* (*pl* **-vae** /-viː/) Larve *f*

laryngitis /lærɪnˈdʒaɪtɪs/ *n* Kehlkopfentzündung *f*

larynx /'lærɪŋks/ *n* Kehlkopf *m*

lascivious /ləˈsɪvɪəs/ *a* lüstern

laser /'leɪzə(r)/ *n* Laser *m*

lash /læʃ/ *n* Peitschenhieb *m*; (*eyelash*) Wimper *f* ▫ *vt* peitschen; (*tie*) festbinden (**to** an + *acc*). **~ out** *vi* um sich schlagen; (*spend*) viel Geld ausgeben (**on** für)

lashings /'læʃɪŋz/ *npl* ~ of (*fam*) eine Riesenmenge von

lass /læs/ *n* Mädchen *nt*

lasso /lə'suː/ *n* Lasso *nt*

last¹ /lɑːst/ *n* (*for shoe*) Leisten *m*

last² *a & n* letzte(r,s); ~ **night** heute *od* gestern Nacht; (*evening*) gestern Abend; **at** ~ endlich; **the** ~ **time** das letzte Mal; **for the** ~ **time** zum letzten Mal; **the** ~ **but one** der/die/das vorletzte; **that's the** ~ **straw** (*fam*) das schlägt dem Fass den Boden aus □ *adv* zuletzt; (*last time*) das letzte Mal; **do sth** ~ **etw** zuletzt *od* als Letztes machen; **he/she went** ~ er/sie ging als Letzter/Letzte □ *vi* dauern; ⟨*weather:*⟩ sich halten; ⟨*relationship:*⟩ halten. ~**ing** *a* dauerhaft. ~**ly** *adv* schließlich, zum Schluss

latch /lætʃ/ *n* [einfache] Klinke *f*; **on the** ~ nicht verschlossen

late /leɪt/ *a & adv* (-r, -st) spät; (*delayed*) verspätet; (*deceased*) verstorben; **the** ~**st news** die neuesten Nachrichten; **stay up** ~ bis spät aufbleiben; **of** ~ in letzter Zeit; **arrive** ~ zu spät ankommen; **I am** ~ ich komme zu spät *od* habe mich verspätet; **the train is** ~ der Zug hat Verspätung. ~**comer** *n* Zuspätkommende(r) *m/f*. ~**ly** *adv* in letzter Zeit. ~**ness** *n* Zuspätkommen *nt*; (*delay*) Verspätung *f*

latent /'leɪtnt/ *a* latent

later /'leɪtə(r)/ *a & adv* später; ~ **on** nachher

lateral /'lætərəl/ *a* seitlich

lathe /leɪð/ *n* Drehbank *f*

lather /'lɑːðə(r)/ *n* [Seifen]schaum *m* □ *vt* einseifen □ *vi* schäumen

Latin /'lætɪn/ *a* lateinisch □ *n* Latein *nt*. ~ **A'merica** *n* Lateinamerika *nt*

latitude /'lætɪtjuːd/ *n* (*Geog*) Breite *f*; (*fig*) Freiheit *f*

latter /'lætə(r)/ *a & n* **the** ~ der/die/das Letztere. ~**ly** *adv* in letzter Zeit

lattice /'lætɪs/ *n* Gitter *nt*

Latvia /'lætvɪə/ *n* Lettland *nt*

laudable /'lɔːdəbl/ *a* lobenswert

laugh /lɑːf/ *n* Lachen *nt*; **with a** ~ lachend □ *vi* lachen (**at/about** über + *acc*); ~ **at s.o.** (*mock*) jdn auslachen. ~**able** /-əbl/ *a* lachhaft, lächerlich. ~**ing-stock** *n* Gegenstand *m* des Spottes

laughter /'lɑːftə(r)/ *n* Gelächter *nt*

launch¹ /lɔːntʃ/ *n* (*boat*) Barkasse *f*

launch² *n* Stapellauf *m*; (*of rocket*) Abschuss *m*; (*of product*) Lancierung *f* □ *vt* vom Stapel lassen ⟨*ship*⟩; zu Wasser lassen ⟨*lifeboat*⟩; abschießen ⟨*rocket*⟩; starten ⟨*attack*⟩; (*Comm*) lancieren ⟨*product*⟩

launder /'lɔːndə(r)/ *vt* waschen. ~**ette** /-'dret/ *n* Münzwäscherei *f*

laundry /'lɔːndrɪ/ *n* Wäscherei *f*; (*clothes*) Wäsche *f*

laurel /'lɒrl/ *n* Lorbeer *m*

lava /'lɑːvə/ *n* Lava *f*

lavatory /'lævətrɪ/ *n* Toilette *f*

lavender /'lævəndə(r)/ *n* Lavendel *m*

lavish /'lævɪʃ/ *a*, **-ly** *adv* großzügig; (*wasteful*) verschwenderisch; **on a** ~ **scale** mit viel Aufwand □ *vt* ~ **sth on s.o.** jdn mit etw überschütten

law /lɔː/ *n* Gesetz *nt*; (*system*) Recht *nt*; **study** ~ Jura studieren; ~ **and order** Recht und Ordnung

law: ~**-abiding** *a* gesetzestreu. ~**court** *n* Gerichtshof *m*. ~**ful** *a* rechtmäßig. ~**less** *a* gesetzlos

lawn /lɔːn/ *n* Rasen *m*. ~**-mower** *n* Rasenmäher *m*

'law suit *n* Prozess *m*

lawyer /'lɔːjə(r)/ *n* Rechtsanwalt *m* /-anwältin *f*

lax /læks/ *a* lax, locker

laxative /'læksətɪv/ *n* Abführmittel *nt*

laxity /'læksətɪ/ *n* Laxheit *f*

lay¹ /leɪ/ *a* Laien-

lay² *see* **lie¹**

lay³ *vt* (*pt/pp* **laid**) legen; decken ⟨*table*⟩; ~ **a trap** eine Falle stellen. ~ **down** *vt* hinlegen; festlegen ⟨*rules, conditions*⟩. ~ **off** *vt* entlassen ⟨*workers*⟩ □ *vi* (*fam: stop*) aufhören. ~ **out** *vt* hinlegen; aufbahren ⟨*corpse*⟩; anlegen ⟨*garden*⟩; (*Typ*) gestalten

lay: ~**about** *n* Faulenzer *m*. ~**-by** *n* Parkbucht *f*; (*on motorway*) Rastplatz *m*

layer /'leɪə(r)/ *n* Schicht *f*

layette /leɪ'et/ *n* Babyausstattung *f*

lay: ~**man** *n* Laie *m*. ~**out** *n* Anordnung *f*; (*design*) Gestaltung *f*; (*Typ*) Layout *nt*. ~ **'preacher** *n* Laienprediger *m*

laze /leɪz/ *vi* ~ **[about]** faulenzen

laziness /'leɪzɪnɪs/ *n* Faulheit *f*

lazy /'leɪzɪ/ *a* (**-ier, -iest**) faul. ~**-bones** *n* Faulenzer *m*

lb /paʊnd/ *abbr* (**pound**) Pfd.

lead¹ /led/ *n* Blei *nt*; (*of pencil*) [Blei]stift]mine *f*

lead² /liːd/ *n* Führung *f*; (*leash*) Leine *f*; (*flex*) Schnur *f*; (*clue*) Hinweis *m*, Spur *f*; (*Theat*) Hauptrolle *f*; (*distance ahead*) Vorsprung *m*; **be in the** ~ in Führung liegen □ *vt/i* (*pt/pp* **led**) führen; leiten ⟨*team*⟩; (*induce*) bringen; (*at cards*) ausspielen; ~ **the way** vorangehen; ~ **up to sth** (*fig*) etw (*dat*) vorangehen. ~ **away** *vt* wegführen

leaded /'ledɪd/ *a* verbleit

leader /'li:də(r)/ n Führer m; (of expedition, group) Leiter(in) m(f); (of orchestra) Konzertmeister m; (in newspaper) Leitartikel m. ~ship n Führung f; Leitung f

leading /'li:dɪŋ/ a führend; ~ **lady** Hauptdarstellerin f; ~ **question** Suggestivfrage f

leaf /li:f/ n (pl **leaves**) Blatt nt; (of table) Ausziehplatte f □ vi ~ **through sth** etw durchblättern. ~ **let** n Merkblatt nt; (advertising) Reklameblatt nt; (political) Flugblatt nt

league /li:g/ n Liga f; **be in** ~ **with** unter einer Decke stecken mit

leak /li:k/ n (hole) undichte Stelle f; (Naut) Leck nt; (of gas) Gasausfluss m □ vi undicht sein; ⟨ship:⟩ leck sein, lecken; ⟨liquid:⟩ auslaufen; ⟨gas:⟩ ausströmen □ vt auslaufen lassen; ~ **sth to s.o.** (fig) jdm etw zuspielen. ~y a undicht; (Naut) leck

lean[1] /li:n/ a (-**er**, -**est**) mager

lean[2] v (pt/pp **leaned** or **leant** /lent/) □ vt lehnen (**against**/**on** an + acc) □ vi ⟨person⟩ sich lehnen (**against**/**on** an + acc); ⟨not be straight⟩ sich neigen; **be** ~**ing against** lehnen an (+ dat); ~ **on s.o.** (depend) bei jdm festen Halt finden. ~ **back** vi sich zurücklehnen. ~ **forward** vi sich vorbeugen. ~ **out** vi sich hinauslehnen. ~ **over** vi sich vorbeugen

leaning /'li:nɪŋ/ a schief □ n Neigung f

leap /li:p/ n Sprung m □ vi (pt/pp **leapt** /lept/ or **leaped**) springen; **he leapt at it** (fam) er griff sofort zu. ~**frog** n Bockspringen nt. ~ **year** n Schaltjahr nt

learn /lɜ:n/ vt/i (pt/pp **learnt** or **learned**) lernen; (hear) erfahren; ~ **to swim** schwimmen lernen

learn|ed /'lɜ:nɪd/ a gelehrt. ~**er** n Anfänger m; ~**er** [**driver**] Fahrschüler(in) m(f). ~**ing** n Gelehrsamkeit f

lease /li:s/ n Pacht f; (contract) Mietvertrag m; (Comm) Pachtvertrag m □ vt pachten; ~ [**out**] verpachten

leash /li:ʃ/ n Leine f

least /li:st/ a geringste(r,s); **have** ~ **time** am wenigsten Zeit haben □ n **the** ~ **das** wenigste; **at** ~ wenigstens, mindestens; **not in the** ~ nicht im Geringsten □ adv am wenigsten

leather /'leðə(r)/ n Leder nt. ~y a ledern; (tough) zäh

leave /li:v/ n Erlaubnis f; (holiday) Urlaub m; **on** ~ auf Urlaub; **take one's** ~ sich verabschieden □ v (pt/pp **left**) □ vt lassen; (go out of, abandon) verlassen; (forget) liegen lassen; (bequeath) vermachen (**to** dat); ~ **it to me!** überlassen Sie es mir! **there is nothing left** es ist nichts mehr übrig □ vi [weg]gehen/-fahren; ⟨train,

bus:⟩ abfahren. ~ **behind** vt zurücklassen; (forget) liegen lassen. ~ **out** vt liegen lassen; (leave outside) draußen lassen; (omit) auslassen

leaves /li:vz/ see **leaf**

Lebanon /'lebənən/ n Libanon m

lecherous /'letʃərəs/ a lüstern

lectern /'lektən/ n [Lese]pult nt

lecture /'lektʃə(r)/ n Vortrag m; (Univ) Vorlesung f; (reproof) Strafpredigt f □ vi einen Vortrag/eine Vorlesung halten (on über + acc) □ vt ~ **s.o.** jdm eine Strafpredigt halten. ~**r** n Vortragende(r) m/f; (Univ) Dozent(in) m(f)

led /led/ see **lead**[2]

ledge /ledʒ/ n Leiste f; (shelf, of window) Sims m; (in rock) Vorsprung m

ledger /'ledʒə(r)/ n Hauptbuch nt

lee /li:/ n (Naut) Lee f

leech /li:tʃ/ n Blutegel m

leek /li:k/ n Stange f Porree; ~s pl Porree m

leer /lɪə(r)/ n anzügliches Grinsen nt □ vi anzüglich grinsen

lee|ward /'li:wəd/ adv nach Lee. ~**way** n (fig) Spielraum m

left[1] /left/ see **leave**

left[2] a linke(r,s) □ adv links; ⟨go⟩ nach links □ n linke Seite f; **on the** ~ links; **from**/**to the** ~ von/nach links; **the** ~ (Pol) die Linke

left: ~-'**handed** a linkshändig. ~-'**luggage** [**office**] n Gepäckaufbewahrung f. ~**overs** npl Reste pl. ~-'**wing** a (Pol) linke(r,s)

leg /leg/ n Bein nt; (Culin) Keule f; (of journey) Etappe f

legacy /'legəsɪ/ n Vermächtnis nt, Erbschaft f

legal /'li:gl/ a, -**ly** adv gesetzlich; (matters) rechtlich; (department, position) Rechts-; **be** ~ [gesetzlich] erlaubt sein; **take** ~ **action** gerichtlich vorgehen

legality /lɪ'gælətɪ/ n Legalität f

legalize /'li:gəlaɪz/ vt legalisieren

legend /'ledʒənd/ n Legende f. ~**ary** a legendär

legible /'ledʒəbl/ a, -**bly** adv leserlich

legion /'li:dʒn/ n Legion f

legislat|e /'ledʒɪsleɪt/ vi Gesetze erlassen. ~**ion** /-'leɪʃn/ n Gesetzgebung f; (laws) Gesetze pl

legislat|ive /'ledʒɪslətɪv/ a gesetzgebend. ~**ure** /-leɪtʃə(r)/ n Legislative f

legitimate /lɪ'dʒɪtɪmət/ a rechtmäßig; (justifiable) berechtigt; (child) ehelich

leisure /'leʒə(r)/ n Freizeit f; **at your** ~ wenn Sie Zeit haben. ~**ly** a gemächlich

lemon /'lemən/ n Zitrone f. **~ade** /-'neɪd/ n Zitronenlimonade f

lend /lend/ vt (pt/pp **lent**) leihen; **~ s.o. sth** jdm etw leihen; **~ a hand** (fam) helfen. **~ing library** n Leihbücherei f

length /leŋθ/ n Länge f; (piece) Stück nt; (of wallpaper) Bahn f; (of time) Dauer f; **at ~** ausführlich; (at last) endlich

length|en /'leŋθən/ vt länger machen □ vi länger werden. **~ways** adv der Länge nach, längs

lengthy /'leŋθɪ/ a (-ier, -iest) langwierig

lenien|ce /'liːnɪəns/ n Nachsicht f. **~t** a, **-ly** adv nachsichtig

lens /lenz/ n Linse f; (Phot) Objektiv nt; (of spectacles) Glas nt

lent /lent/ see **lend**

Lent n Fastenzeit f

lentil /'lentl/ n (Bot) Linse f

Leo /'liːəʊ/ n (Astr) Löwe m

leopard /'lepəd/ n Leopard m

leotard /'liːətɑːd/ n Trikot nt

leper /'lepə(r)/ n Leprakranke(r) m/f; (Bible & fig) Aussätzige(r) m/f

leprosy /'leprəsɪ/ n Lepra f

lesbian /'lezbɪən/ a lesbisch □ n Lesbierin f

lesion /'liːʒn/ n Verletzung f

less /les/ a, adv, n & prep weniger; **~ and ~** immer weniger; **not any the ~** um nichts weniger

lessen /'lesn/ vt verringern □ vi nachlassen; (value:) abnehmen

lesser /'lesə(r)/ a geringere(r,s)

lesson /'lesn/ n Stunde f; (in text-book) Lektion f; (Relig) Lesung f; **teach s.o. a ~** (fig) jdm eine Lehre erteilen

lest /lest/ conj (liter) damit ... nicht

let /let/ vt (pt/pp **let**, pres p **letting**) lassen; (rent) vermieten; **~ alone** (not to mention) geschweige denn; **'to ~'** 'zu vermieten'; **~ us go** gehen wir; **~ me know** sagen Sie mir Bescheid; **~ him do it** lass ihn das machen; **just ~ him!** soll er doch! **~ s.o. sleep/win** jdn schlafen/gewinnen lassen; **~ oneself in for sth** (fam) sich (dat) etw einbrocken. **~ down** vt hinunter-/herunterlassen; (lengthen) länger machen; **~ s.o. down** (fam) jdn im Stich lassen; (disappoint) jdn enttäuschen. **~ in** vt hereinlassen. **~ off** vt abfeuern (gun); hochgehen lassen (firework, bomb); (emit) ausstoßen; (excuse from) befreien von; (not punish) frei ausgehen lassen. **~ out** vt hinaus-/herauslassen; (make larger) auslassen. **~ through** vt durchlassen. **~ up** vi (fam) nachlassen

'let-down n Enttäuschung f, (fam) Reinfall m

lethal /'liːθl/ a tödlich

letharg|ic /lɪ'θɑːdʒɪk/ a lethargisch. **~y** /'leθədʒɪ/ n Lethargie f

letter /'letə(r)/ n Brief m; (of alphabet) Buchstabe m; **by ~** brieflich. **~-box** n Briefkasten m. **~-head** n Briefkopf m. **~ing** n Beschriftung f

lettuce /'letɪs/ n [Kopf]salat m

'let-up n (fam) Nachlassen nt

leukaemia /luː'kiːmɪə/ n Leukämie f

level /'levl/ a eben; (horizontal) waagerecht; (in height) auf gleicher Höhe; (spoonful) gestrichen; **draw ~ with** gleichziehen mit; **one's ~ best** sein Möglichstes □ n Höhe f; (fig) Ebene f, Niveau nt; (stage) Stufe f; **on the ~** (fam) ehrlich □ vt (pt/pp **levelled**) einebnen; (aim) richten (**at** auf + acc)

level: **~ 'crossing** n Bahnübergang m. **~-'headed** a vernünftig

lever /'liːvə(r)/ n Hebel m □ vt **~ up** mit einem Hebel anheben. **~age** /-rɪdʒ/ n Hebelkraft f

levity /'levɪtɪ/ n Heiterkeit f; (frivolity) Leichtfertigkeit f

levy /'levɪ/ vt (pt/pp **levied**) erheben (tax)

lewd /ljuːd/ a (-er, -est) anstößig

liabilit|y /laɪə'bɪlətɪ/ n Haftung f; **~ies** pl Verbindlichkeiten pl

liable /'laɪəbl/ a haftbar; **be ~ to do sth** leicht etw tun können

liaise /lɪ'eɪz/ vi (fam) Verbindungsperson sein

liaison /lɪ'eɪzɒn/ n Verbindung f; (affair) Verhältnis nt

liar /'laɪə(r)/ n Lügner(in) m(f)

libel /'laɪbl/ n Verleumdung f □ vt (pt/pp **libelled**) verleumden. **~lous** a verleumderisch

liberal /'lɪbərl/ a, **-ly** adv tolerant; (generous) großzügig. **L~** a (Pol) liberal □ n Liberale(r) m/f

liberat|e /'lɪbəreɪt/ vt befreien. **~ed** a (woman) emanzipiert. **~ion** /-'reɪʃn/ n Befreiung f. **~or** n Befreier m

liberty /'lɪbətɪ/ n Freiheit f; **take the ~ of doing sth** sich (dat) erlauben, etw zu tun; **take liberties** sich (dat) Freiheiten erlauben

Libra /'liːbrə/ n (Astr) Waage f

librarian /laɪ'breərɪən/ n Bibliothekar(in) m(f)

library /'laɪbrərɪ/ n Bibliothek f

Libya /'lɪbɪə/ n Libyen nt

lice /laɪs/ see **louse**

licence /'laɪsns/ n Genehmigung f; (Comm) Lizenz f; (for TV) ≈ Fernsehgebühr f; (for driving) Führerschein m; (for *alcohol)* Schankkonzession *f*; *(freedom)* Freiheit *f*

license /'laɪsns/ *vt* eine Genehmigung//*(Comm)* Lizenz erteilen (+ *dat*); **be ~d** *(car:)* zugelassen sein; *(restaurant:)* Schankkonzession haben. **~-plate** *n* Nummernschild *nt*

licentious /laɪ'senʃəs/ *a* lasterhaft

lichen /'laɪkən/ *n (Bot)* Flechte *f*

lick /lɪk/ *n* Lecken *nt*; **a ~ of paint** ein bisschen Farbe □ *vt* lecken; *(fam: defeat)* schlagen

lid /lɪd/ *n* Deckel *m*; *(of eye)* Lid *nt*

lie¹ /laɪ/ *n* Lüge *f*; **tell a ~** lügen □ *vi (pt/pp lied, pres p lying)* lügen; **~ to** belügen

lie² *vi (pt lay, pp lain, pres p lying)* liegen; **here ~s . . .** hier ruht . . . **~ down** *vi* sich hinlegen

Liège /lɪ'eɪʒ/ *n* Lüttich *nt*

'lie-in *n* **have a ~** [sich] ausschlafen

lieu /ljuː/ *n* **in ~ of** statt (+ *gen)*

lieutenant /lef'tenənt/ *n* Oberleutnant *m*

life /laɪf/ *n (pl* lives) Leben *nt*; *(biography)* Biographie *f*; **lose one's ~** ums Leben kommen

life: ~belt *n* Rettungsring *m*. **~-boat** *n* Rettungsboot *nt*. **~buoy** *n* Rettungsring *m*. **~-guard** *n* Lebensretter *m*. **~-jacket** *n* Schwimmweste *f*. **~less** *a* leblos. **~like** *a* naturgetreu. **~line** *n* Rettungsleine *f*. **~long** *a* lebenslang. **~ preserver** *n (Amer)* Rettungsring *m*. **~size(d)** *a . . .* in Lebensgröße. **~time** *n* Leben *nt*; **in s.o.'s ~time** zu jds Lebzeiten; **the chance of a ~time** eine einmalige Gelegenheit

lift /lɪft/ *n* Aufzug *m*, Lift *m*; **give s.o. a ~** jdn mitnehmen; **get a ~** mitgenommen werden □ *vt* heben; aufheben *(restrictions)* □ *vi (fog:)* sich lichten. **~ up** *vt* hochheben

'lift-off *n* Abheben *nt*

ligament /'lɪgəmənt/ *n (Anat)* Band *nt*

light¹ /laɪt/ *a (-er, -est) (not dark)* hell; **~ blue** hellblau □ *n* Licht *nt*; *(lamp)* Lampe *f*; **in the ~ of** *(fig)* angesichts (+ *gen)*; **have you [got] a ~?** haben Sie Feuer? □ *vt (pt/pp* lit **or** lighted) anzünden *(fire, cigarette)*; anmachen *(lamp)*; *(illuminate)* beleuchten. **~ up** *vi (face:)* sich erhellen

light² *a (-er, -est) (not heavy)* leicht; **~ sentence** milde Strafe *f* □ *adv* **travel ~** mit wenig Gepäck reisen

'light-bulb *n* Glühbirne *f*

lighten¹ /'laɪtn/ *vt* heller machen □ *vi* heller werden

lighten² *vt* leichter machen *(load)*

lighter /'laɪtə(r)/ *n* Feuerzeug *nt*

light: ~-'headed *a* benommen. **~-'hearted** *a* unbekümmert. **~house** *n* Leuchtturm *m*. **~ing** *n* Beleuchtung *f*.

~ly *adv* leicht; *(casually)* leichthin; **get off ~ly** glimpflich davonkommen

lightning /'laɪtnɪŋ/ *n* Blitz *m*. **~-conductor** *n* Blitzableiter *m*

'lightweight *a* leicht □ *n (Boxing)* Leichtgewicht *nt*

like¹ /laɪk/ *a* ähnlich; *(same)* gleich □ *prep* wie; *(similar to)* ähnlich (+ *dat)*; **~ this** so; **a man ~ that** so ein Mann; **what's he ~?** wie ist er denn? □ *conj (fam: as)* wie; *(Amer: as if)* als ob

like² *vt* mögen; **I should/would ~** ich möchte; **I ~ the car** das Auto gefällt mir; **I ~ chocolate** ich esse gern Schokolade; **~ dancing/singing** gern tanzen/singen; **I ~ that!** *(fam)* das ist doch die Höhe! □ *n* **~s and dislikes** *pl* Vorlieben und Abneigungen *pl*

like|able /'laɪkəbl/ *a* sympathisch. **~lihood** /-lɪhʊd/ *n* Wahrscheinlichkeit *f*. **~ly** *a (-ier, -iest)* & *adv* wahrscheinlich; **not ~ly!** *(fam)* auf gar keinen Fall!

'like-minded *a* gleich gesinnt

liken /'laɪkən/ *vt* vergleichen (**to** mit)

like|ness /'laɪknɪs/ *n* Ähnlichkeit *f*. **~wise** *adv* ebenso

liking /'laɪkɪŋ/ *n* Vorliebe *f*; **is it to your ~?** gefällt es Ihnen?

lilac /'laɪlək/ *n* Flieder *m* □ *a* fliederfarben

lily /'lɪlɪ/ *n*. Lilie *f*. **~ of the valley** *n* Maiglöckchen *nt*

limb /lɪm/ *n* Glied *nt*

limber /'lɪmbə(r)/ *vi* **~ up** Lockerungsübungen machen

lime¹ /laɪm/ *n (fruit)* Limone *f*; *(tree)* Linde *f*

lime² *n* Kalk *m*. **~light** *n* **be in the ~light** im Rampenlicht stehen. **~stone** *n* Kalkstein *m*

limit /'lɪmɪt/ *n* Grenze *f*; *(limitation)* Beschränkung *f*; **that's the ~!** *(fam)* das ist doch die Höhe! □ *vt* beschränken (**to** auf + *acc)*. **~ation** /-ɪ'teɪʃn/ *n* Beschränkung *f*; **~ed** *a* beschränkt; **~ed company** Gesellschaft *f* mit beschränkter Haftung

limousine /'lɪməziːn/ *n* Limousine *f*

limp¹ /lɪmp/ *n* Hinken *nt*; **have a ~** hinken □ *vi* hinken

limp² *a (-er, -est)*, **-ly** *adv* schlaff

limpet /'lɪmpɪt/ *n* **like a ~** *(fig)* wie eine Klette

limpid /'lɪmpɪd/ *a* klar

linctus /'lɪŋktəs/ *n* [cough] **~** Hustensirup *m*

line¹ /laɪn/ *n* Linie *f*; *(length of rope, cord)* Leine *f*; *(Teleph)* Leitung *f*; *(of writing)* Zeile *f*; *(row)* Reihe *f*; *(wrinkle)* Falte *f*; *(of business)* Branche *f*; *(Amer: queue)* Schlange *f*; **in ~ with** gemäß (+ *dat)* □ *vt*

säumen ⟨street⟩. **~ up** vi sich aufstellen
□ vt aufstellen

line² vt füttern ⟨garment⟩; (Techn) auskleiden

lineage /'lɪnɪɪdʒ/ n Herkunft f

linear /'lɪnɪə(r)/ a linear

lined¹ /laɪnd/ a ⟨paper⟩ liniert; ⟨wrinkled⟩ faltig

lined² a ⟨garment⟩ gefüttert

linen /'lɪnɪn/ n Leinen nt; ⟨articles⟩ Wäsche f

liner /'laɪnə(r)/ n Passagierschiff nt

'linesman n (Sport) Linienrichter m

linger /'lɪŋgə(r)/ vi [zurück]bleiben

lingerie /'læʒərɪ/ n Damenunterwäsche f

linguist /'lɪŋgwɪst/ n Sprachkundige(r) m/f

linguistic /lɪŋ'gwɪstɪk/ a, -ally adv sprachlich. **~s** n Linguistik f

lining /'laɪnɪŋ/ n ⟨of garment⟩ Futter nt; (Techn) Auskleidung f

link /lɪŋk/ n ⟨of chain⟩ Glied nt ⟨fig⟩ Verbindung f □ vt verbinden; **~ arms** sich unterhaken

links /lɪŋks/ n or npl Golfplatz m

lino /'laɪnəʊ/ n, **linoleum** /lɪ'nəʊlɪəm/ n Linoleum nt

lint /lɪnt/ n Verbandstoff m

lion /'laɪən/ n Löwe m; **~'s share** ⟨fig⟩ Löwenanteil m. **~ess** n Löwin f

lip /lɪp/ n Lippe f; ⟨edge⟩ Rand m; ⟨of jug⟩ Schnabel m

lip: **~-reading** n Lippenlesen nt. **~-service** n pay **~-service** ein Lippenbekenntnis ablegen (to zu). **~stick** n Lippenstift m

liquefy /'lɪkwɪfaɪ/ vt (pt/pp -ied) verflüssigen □ vi sich verflüssigen

liqueur /lɪ'kjʊə(r)/ n Likör m

liquid /'lɪkwɪd/ n Flüssigkeit f □ a flüssig

liquidat|e /'lɪkwɪdeɪt/ vt liquidieren. **~ion** -'deɪʃn/ n Liquidation f

liquidize /'lɪkwɪdaɪz/ vt [im Mixer] pürieren. **~r** n (Culin) Mixer m

liquor /'lɪkə(r)/ n Alkohol m; ⟨juice⟩ Flüssigkeit f

liquorice /'lɪkərɪs/ n Lakritze f

'liquor store n ⟨Amer⟩ Spirituosengeschäft nt

lisp /lɪsp/ n Lispeln nt □ vt/i lispeln

list¹ /lɪst/ n Liste f □ vt aufführen

list² vi ⟨ship⟩ Schlagseite haben

listen /'lɪsn/ vi zuhören (to dat); **~ to the radio** Radio hören. **~er** n Zuhörer(in) m(f); ⟨Radio⟩ Hörer(in) m(f)

listless /'lɪstlɪs/ a, -ly adv lustlos

lit /lɪt/ see **light¹**

litany /'lɪtənɪ/ n Litanei f

literacy /'lɪtərəsɪ/ n Lese- und Schreibfertigkeit f

literal /'lɪtərl/ a wörtlich. **~ly** adv buchstäblich

literary /'lɪtərərɪ/ a literarisch

literate /'lɪtərət/ a be **~** lesen und schreiben können

literature /'lɪtrətʃə(r)/ n Literatur f; ⟨fam⟩ Informationsmaterial nt

lithe /laɪð/ a geschmeidig

Lithuania /lɪθjʊ'eɪnɪə/ n Litauen nt

litigation /lɪtɪ'geɪʃn/ n Rechtsstreit m

litre /'li:tə(r)/ n Liter m & nt

litter /'lɪtə(r)/ n Abfall m; (Zool) Wurf m □ vt be **~ed with** übersät sein mit. **~-bin** n Abfalleimer m

little /'lɪtl/ a klein; ⟨not much⟩ wenig □ adv & n wenig; **a ~** ein bisschen/wenig; **~ by ~** nach und nach

liturgy /'lɪtədʒɪ/ n Liturgie f

live¹ /laɪv/ a lebendig; ⟨ammunition⟩ scharf; **~ broadcast** Live-Sendung f; **be ~** (Electr) unter Strom stehen □ adv (Radio, TV) live

live² /lɪv/ vi leben; ⟨reside⟩ wohnen; **~ up to** gerecht werden (+ dat). **~ on** vt leben von; ⟨eat⟩ sich ernähren von □ vi weiterleben

liveli|hood /'laɪvlɪhʊd/ n Lebensunterhalt m. **~ness** n Lebendigkeit f

lively /'laɪvlɪ/ a (-ier, -iest) lebhaft, lebendig

liven /'laɪvn/ v **~ up** vt beleben □ vi lebhaft werden

liver /'lɪvə(r)/ n Leber f

lives /laɪvz/ see **life**

livestock /'laɪv-/ n Vieh nt

livid /'lɪvɪd/ a ⟨fam⟩ wütend

living /'lɪvɪŋ/ a lebend □ n **earn one's ~** seinen Lebensunterhalt verdienen; **the ~** pl die Lebenden. **~-room** n Wohnzimmer nt

lizard /'lɪzəd/ n Eidechse f

load /ləʊd/ n Last f; ⟨quantity⟩ Ladung f; (Electr) Belastung f; **~s of** ⟨fam⟩ jede Menge □ vt laden ⟨goods, gun⟩; beladen ⟨vehicle⟩; **~ a camera** einen Film in eine Kamera einlegen. **~ed** a beladen; ⟨fam: rich⟩ steinreich; **~ed question** Fangfrage f

loaf¹ /ləʊf/ n (pl loaves) Brot nt

loaf² vi faulenzen

loan /ləʊn/ n Leihgabe f; ⟨money⟩ Darlehen nt; **on ~** geliehen □ vt leihen (to dat)

loath /ləʊθ/ a be **~ to do sth** etw ungern tun

loath|e /ləʊð/ vt verabscheuen. **~ing** n
Abscheu m. **~some** a abscheulich

loaves /ləʊvz/ see loaf¹

lobby /'lɒbɪ/ n Foyer nt; (ante-room) Vorraum m; (Pol) Lobby f

lobe /ləʊb/ n (of ear) Ohrläppchen nt

lobster /'lɒbstə(r)/ n Hummer m

local /'ləʊkl/ a hiesig; (time, traffic) Orts-;
under ~ anaesthetic unter örtlicher Betäubung; **I'm not ~** ich bin nicht von hier
□ n Hiesige(r) m/f; (fam: public house)
Stammkneipe f. **~ au'thority** n
Kommunalbehörde f. **~ call** n (Teleph)
Ortsgespräch nt

locality /ləʊ'kælətɪ/ n Gegend f

localized /'ləʊkəlaɪzd/ a lokalisiert

locally /'ləʊkəlɪ/ adv am Ort

locat|e /ləʊ'keɪt/ vt ausfindig machen; **be
~ed** sich befinden. **~ion** /-'keɪʃn/ n Lage
f; **filmed on ~ion** als Außenaufnahme
gedreht

lock¹ /lɒk/ n (hair) Strähne f

lock² n (on door) Schloss nt; (on canal)
Schleuse f □ vt abschließen □ vi sich
abschließen lassen. **~ in** vt einschließen.
~ out vt ausschließen. **~ up** vt abschließen; einsperren ⟨person⟩ □ vi zuschließen

locker /'lɒkə(r)/ n Schließfach nt; (Mil)
Spind m; (in hospital) kleiner Schrank m

locket /'lɒkɪt/ n Medaillon nt

lock: ~out n Aussperrung f. **~smith** n
Schlosser m

locomotion /ləʊkə'məʊʃn/ n Fortbe-
wegung f

locomotive /ləʊkə'məʊtɪv/ n Lokomotive
f

locum /'ləʊkəm/ n Vertreter(in) m(f)

locust /'ləʊkəst/ n Heuschrecke f

lodge /lɒdʒ/ n (porter's) Pförtnerhaus nt;
(masonic) Loge f □ vt (submit) einreichen;
(deposit) deponieren □ vi zur Untermiete
wohnen (with bei); (become fixed) stecken
bleiben. **~r** n Untermieter(in) m(f)

lodging /'lɒdʒɪŋ/ n Unterkunft f; **~s** npl
möbliertes Zimmer nt

loft /lɒft/ n Dachboden m

lofty /'lɒftɪ/ a (-ier, -iest) hoch; (haughty)
hochmütig

log /lɒg/ n Baumstamm m; (for fire) [Holz]-
scheit nt; **sleep like a ~** (fam) wie ein
Murmeltier schlafen

logarithm /'lɒgərɪðm/ n Logarithmus m

'log-book n (Naut) Logbuch nt

loggerheads /'lɒgə-/ npl **be at ~** (fam)
sich in den Haaren liegen

logic /'lɒdʒɪk/ n Logik f. **~al** a, **-ly** adv
logisch

logistics /lə'dʒɪstɪks/ npl Logistik f

logo /'ləʊgəʊ/ n Symbol nt, Logo nt

loin /lɔɪn/ n (Culin) Lende f

loiter /'lɔɪtə(r)/ vi herumlungern

loll /lɒl/ vi sich lümmeln

loll|ipop /'lɒlɪpɒp/ n Lutscher m. **~y** n
Lutscher m; (fam: money) Moneten pl

London /'lʌndən/ n London nt □ attrib
Londoner. **~er** n Londoner(in) m(f)

lone /ləʊn/ a einzeln. **~liness** n Einsamkeit f

lonely /'ləʊnlɪ/ a (-ier, -iest) einsam

lone|r /'ləʊnə(r)/ n Einzelgänger m.
~some a einsam

long¹ /lɒŋ/ a (-er /'lɒŋgə(r)/, -est
/'lɒŋgɪst/) lang; (journey) weit; **a ~ time**
lange; **a ~ way** weit; **in the ~ run** auf
lange Sicht; (in the end) letzten Endes
□ adv lange; **all day ~** den ganzen Tag;
not ~ ago vor kurzem; **before ~** bald; **no
~er** nicht mehr; **as or so ~as** solange; **so
~!** (fam) tschüs! **will you be ~?** dauert
es noch lange [bei dir]? **it won't take ~**
es dauert nicht lange

long² vi **~ for** sich sehnen nach

long-'distance a Fern-; (Sport) Langstre-
cken-

longevity /lɒn'dʒevətɪ/ n Langlebigkeit f

'longhand n Langschrift f

longing /'lɒŋɪŋ/ a, **-ly** adv sehnsüchtig □ n
Sehnsucht f

longitude /'lɒŋgɪtjuːd/ n (Geog) Länge f

long: ~ jump n Weitsprung m. **~-life
'milk** n H-Milch f. **~-lived** /-lɪvd/ a lang-
lebig. **~-range** a (Mil, Aviat) Langstre-
cken-; (forecast) langfristig. **~-sighted** a
weitsichtig. **~-sleeved** a langärmelig. **~-
suffering** a langmütig. **~-term** a langfristig. **~ wave** n Langwelle f. **~-winded**
/-'wɪndɪd/ a langatmig

loo /luː/ n (fam) Klo nt

look /lʊk/ n Blick m; (appearance) Aussehen nt; **[good] ~s** pl [gutes] Aussehen
nt; **have a ~ at** sich (dat) ansehen; **go
and have a ~** sieh mal nach □ vi sehen;
(search) nachsehen; (seem) aussehen;
don't ~ sieh nicht hin; **~ here!** hören
Sie mal! **~ at** ansehen; **~ for** suchen; **~
forward to** sich freuen auf (+ acc); **~ in
on** vorbeischauen bei; **~ into** (examine)
nachgehen (+ dat); **~ like** aussehen wie;
~ on to ⟨room:⟩ gehen auf (+ acc). **~ after**
vt betreuen. **~ down** vi hinuntersehen; **~
down on s.o.** (fig) auf jdn herabsehen. **~
out** vi hinaus-/heraussehen; (take care)
aufpassen. **~ out for** Ausschau halten
nach; **~ out!** Vorsicht! **~ round** vi sich
umsehen. **~ up** vi aufblicken; **~ up to s.o.**
(fig) zu jdm aufsehen □ vt nachschlagen
⟨word⟩

'look-out n Wache f; (prospect) Aussicht f; **be on the ~ for** Ausschau halten nach

loom[1] /luːm/ n Webstuhl m

loom[2] vi auftauchen; (fig) sich abzeichnen

loony /ˈluːnɪ/ a (fam) verrückt

loop /luːp/ n Schlinge f; (in road) Schleife f; (on garment) Aufhänger m □ vt schlingen. **~hole** n Hintertürchen nt; (in the law) Lücke f

loose /luːs/ a (-r, -st), **-ly** adv lose; (not tight enough) locker; (inexact) frei; **be at a ~ end** nichts zu tun haben; **set ~** freilassen; **run ~** frei herumlaufen. **~ 'change** n Kleingeld nt. **~ 'chippings** npl Rollsplit m

loosen /ˈluːsn/ vt lockern □ vi sich lockern

loot /luːt/ n Beute f □ vt/i plündern. **~er** n Plünderer m

lop /lɒp/ vt (pt/pp lopped) stutzen. **~ off** vt abhacken

lop'sided a schief

loquacious /ləˈkweɪʃəs/ a redselig

lord /lɔːd/ n Herr m; (title) Lord m; **House of L~s** ≈ Oberhaus nt; **the L~'s Prayer** das Vaterunser; **good L~!** du liebe Zeit!

lore /lɔː(r)/ n Überlieferung f

lorry /ˈlɒrɪ/ n Last[kraft]wagen m

lose /luːz/ v (pt/pp lost) □ vt verlieren; (miss) verpassen □ vi verlieren; (clock:) nachgehen; **get lost** verloren gehen; (person) sich verlaufen. **~r** n Verlierer m

loss /lɒs/ n Verlust m; **be at a ~** nicht mehr weiter wissen; **be at a ~ for words** nicht wissen, was man sagen soll

lost /lɒst/ see lose. **~ 'property office** n Fundbüro nt

lot[1] /lɒt/ n Los nt; (at auction) Posten m; **draw ~s** losen (for um)

lot[2] n **the ~** alle; (everything) alles; **a ~ [of]** viel; (many) viele; **~s of** (fam) eine Menge; **it has changed a ~** es hat sich sehr verändert

lotion /ˈləʊʃn/ n Lotion f

lottery /ˈlɒtərɪ/ n Lotterie f. **~ ticket** n Los nt

loud /laʊd/ a (-er, -est), **-ly** adv laut; (colours) grell □ adv [out] **~** laut. **~ 'hailer** n Megaphon nt. **~'speaker** n Lautsprecher m

lounge /laʊndʒ/ n Wohnzimmer nt; (in hotel) Aufenthaltsraum m. □ vi sich lümmeln. **~ suit** n Straßenanzug m

louse /laʊs/ n (pl lice) Laus f

lousy /ˈlaʊzɪ/ a (-ier, -iest) (fam) lausig

lout /laʊt/ n Flegel m, Lümmel m. **~ish** a flegelhaft

lovable /ˈlʌvəbl/ a liebenswert

love /lʌv/ n Liebe f; (Tennis) null; **in ~** verliebt □ vt lieben; **~ doing sth** etw sehr gerne machen; **I ~ chocolate** ich esse sehr gerne Schokolade. **~-affair** n Liebesverhältnis nt. **~ letter** n Liebesbrief m

lovely /ˈlʌvlɪ/ a (-ier, -iest) schön; **we had a ~ time** es war schön

lover /ˈlʌvə(r)/ n Liebhaber m

love: **~ song** n Liebeslied nt. **~ story** n Liebesgeschichte f

loving /ˈlʌvɪŋ/ a, **-ly** adv liebevoll

low /ləʊ/ a (-er, -est) niedrig; (cloud, note) tief; (voice) leise; (depressed) niedergeschlagen □ adv niedrig; (fly, sing) tief; (speak) leise; **feel ~** deprimiert sein □ n (Meteorol) Tief nt; (fig) Tiefstand m

low: **~brow** a geistig anspruchslos. **~-cut** a (dress) tief ausgeschnitten

lower /ˈləʊə(r)/ a & adv see low □ vt niedriger machen; (let down) herunterlassen; (reduce) senken; **~ oneself** sich herabwürdigen

low: **~-'fat** a fettarm. **~-'grade** a minderwertig. **~lands** /-ləndz/ npl Tiefland nt. **~ 'tide** n Ebbe f

loyal /ˈlɔɪəl/ a, **-ly** adv treu. **~ty** n Treue f

lozenge /ˈlɒzɪndʒ/ n Pastille f

Ltd abbr (Limited) GmbH

lubricant /ˈluːbrɪkənt/ n Schmiermittel nt

lubricat|e /ˈluːbrɪkeɪt/ vt schmieren. **~ion** /-ˈkeɪʃn/ n Schmierung f

lucid /ˈluːsɪd/ a klar. **~ity** /-ˈsɪdətɪ/ n Klarheit f

luck /lʌk/ n Glück nt; **bad ~** Pech nt; **good ~!** viel Glück! **~ily** adv glücklicherweise, zum Glück

lucky /ˈlʌkɪ/ a (-ier, -iest) glücklich; (day, number) Glücks-; **be ~** Glück haben; (thing:) Glück bringen. **~ 'charm** n Amulett nt

lucrative /ˈluːkrətɪv/ a einträglich

ludicrous /ˈluːdɪkrəs/ a lächerlich

lug /lʌg/ vt (pt/pp lugged) (fam) schleppen

luggage /ˈlʌgɪdʒ/ n Gepäck nt

luggage: **~-rack** in Gepäckablage f. **~ trolley** n Kofferkuli m. **~-van** n Gepäckwagen m

lugubrious /luːˈguːbrɪəs/ a traurig

lukewarm /ˈluːk-/ a lauwarm

lull /lʌl/ n Pause f □ vt **~ to sleep** einschläfern

lullaby /ˈlʌləbaɪ/ n Wiegenlied nt

lumbago /lʌmˈbeɪgəʊ/ n Hexenschuss m

lumber /ˈlʌmbə(r)/ n Gerümpel nt; (Amer: timber) Bauholz nt □ vt **~ s.o. with sth** jdm etw aufhalsen. **~jack** n (Amer) Holzfäller m

luminous /ˈluːmɪnəs/ a leuchtend; **be ~** leuchten

lump¹ /lʌmp/ n Klumpen m; (of sugar) Stück nt; (swelling) Beule f; (in breast) Knoten m; (tumour) Geschwulst f; **a ~ in one's throat** (fam) ein Kloß im Hals □ vt **~ together** zusammentun

lump² vt **~ it** (fam) sich damit abfinden

lump: ~ sugar n Würfelzucker m. **~ 'sum** n Pauschalsumme f

lumpy /'lʌmpɪ/ a (-ier, -iest) klumpig

lunacy /'lu:nəsɪ/ n Wahnsinn m

lunar /'lu:nə(r)/ a Mond-

lunatic /'lu:nətɪk/ n Wahnsinnige(r) m/f

lunch /lʌntʃ/ n Mittagessen nt □ vi zu Mittag essen

luncheon /'lʌntʃn/ n Mittagessen nt. **~ meat** n Frühstücksfleisch nt. **~ voucher** n Essensbon m

lunch: ~-hour n Mittagspause f. **~-time** n Mittagszeit f

lung /lʌŋ/ n Lungenflügel m; **~s** pl Lunge f. **~ cancer** n Lungenkrebs m

lunge /lʌndʒ/ vi sich stürzen (**at** auf + acc)

lurch¹ /lɜːtʃ/ n **leave in the ~** (fam) im Stich lassen

lurch² vi schleudern; (person:) torkeln

lure /ljʊə(r)/ n Lockung f; (bait) Köder m □ vt locken

lurid /'lʊərɪd/ a grell; (sensational) reißerisch

lurk /lɜːk/ vi lauern

luscious /'lʌʃəs/ a lecker, köstlich

lush /lʌʃ/ a üppig

lust /lʌst/ n Begierde f □ vi **~ after** gieren nach. **~ful** a lüstern

lustre /'lʌstə(r)/ n Glanz m

lusty /'lʌstɪ/ a (-ier, -iest) kräftig

lute /lu:t/ n Laute f

luxuriant /lʌg'ʒʊərɪənt/ a üppig

luxurious /lʌg'ʒʊərɪəs/ a, **-ly** adv luxuriös

luxury /'lʌkʃərɪ/ n Luxus m □ attrib Luxus-

lying /'laɪɪŋ/ see **lie¹, lie²**

lymph gland /'lɪmf-/ n Lymphdrüse f

lynch /lɪntʃ/ vt lynchen

lynx /lɪŋks/ n Luchs m

lyric /'lɪrɪk/ a lyrisch. **~al** a lyrisch; (fam: enthusiastic) schwärmerisch. **~ poetry** n Lyrik f. **~s** npl [Lied]text m

M

mac /mæk/ n (fam) Regenmantel m

macabre /mə'kɑ:br/ a makaber

macaroni /mækə'rəʊnɪ/ n Makkaroni pl

macaroon /mækə'ru:n/ n Makrone f

mace¹ /meɪs/ n Amtsstab m

mace² n (spice) Muskatblüte f

machinations /mækɪ'neɪʃnz/ pl Machenschaften pl

machine /mə'ʃi:n/ n Maschine f □ vt (sew) mit der Maschine nähen; (Techn) maschinell bearbeiten. **~-gun** n Maschinengewehr nt

machinery /mə'ʃi:nərɪ/ n Maschinerie f

machine tool n Werkzeugmaschine f

machinist /mə'ʃi:nɪst/ n Maschinist m; (on sewing machine) Maschinennäherin f

mackerel /'mækrl/ n inv Makrele f

mackintosh /'mækɪntɒʃ/ n Regenmantel m

mad /mæd/ a (**madder, maddest**) verrückt; (dog) tollwütig; (fam: angry) böse (**at** auf + acc)

madam /'mædəm/ n gnädige Frau f

madden /'mædn/ vt (make angry) wütend machen

made /meɪd/ see **make**; **~ to measure** maßgeschneidert

Madeira cake /mə'dɪərə-/ n Sandkuchen m

mad|ly /'mædlɪ/ adv (fam) wahnsinnig. **~man** n Irre(r) m. **~ness** n Wahnsinn m

madonna /mə'dɒnə/ n Madonna f

magazine /mægə'zi:n/ n Zeitschrift f; (Mil, Phot) Magazin nt

maggot /'mægət/ n Made f. **~y** a madig

Magi /'meɪdʒaɪ/ npl **the ~** die Heiligen Drei Könige

magic /'mædʒɪk/ n Zauber m; (tricks) Zauberkunst f □ a magisch; (word, wand, flute) Zauber-. **~al** a zauberhaft

magician /mə'dʒɪʃn/ n Zauberer m; (entertainer) Zauberkünstler m

magistrate /'mædʒɪstreɪt/ n ≈ Friedensrichter m

magnanim|ity /mægnə'nɪmətɪ/ n Großmut f. **~ous** /-'nænɪməs/ a großmütig

magnesia /mæg'ni:ʃə/ n Magnesia f

magnet /'mægnɪt/ n Magnet m. **~ic** /-'netɪk/ a magnetisch. **~ism** n Magnetismus m. **~ize** vt magnetisieren

magnification /mægnɪfɪ'keɪʃn/ n Vergrößerung f

magnificen|ce /mæg'nɪfɪsəns/ *n* Großartigkeit *f*. **~t** *a*, **-ly** *adv* großartig

magnify /'mægnɪfaɪ/ *vt* (*pt/pp* **-ied**) vergrößern; (*exaggerate*) übertreiben. **~ing glass** *n* Vergrößerungsglas *nt*

magnitude /'mægnɪtjuːd/ *n* Größe *f*; (*importance*) Bedeutung *f*

magpie /'mægpaɪ/ *n* Elster *f*

mahogany /mə'hɒgənɪ/ *n* Mahagoni *nt*

maid /meɪd/ *n* Dienstmädchen *nt*; (*liter: girl*) Maid *f*; **old ~** (*pej*) alte Jungfer *f*

maiden /'meɪdn/ *n* (*liter*) Maid *f* □ *a* (*speech, voyage*) Jungfern-. **~ 'aunt** *n* unverheiratete Tante *f*. **~ name** *n* Mädchenname *m*

mail¹ /meɪl/ *n* Kettenpanzer *m*

mail² *n* Post *f* □ *vt* mit der Post schicken; (*send off*) abschicken

mail: **~bag** *n* Postsack *m*. **~box** *n* (*Amer*) Briefkasten *m*. **~ing list** *n* Postversandliste *f*. **~man** *n* (*Amer*) Briefträger *m*. **~-order firm** *n* Versandhaus *nt*

maim /meɪm/ *vt* verstümmeln

main¹ /meɪn/ *n* (*water, gas, electricity*) Hauptleitung *f*

main² *a* Haupt- □ *n* **in the ~** im Großen und Ganzen

main: **~land** /-lənd/ *n* Festland *nt*. **~ly** *adv* hauptsächlich. **~stay** *n* (*fig*) Stütze *f*. **~ street** *n* Hauptstraße *f*

maintain /meɪn'teɪn/ *vt* aufrechterhalten; (*keep in repair*) instand halten; (*support*) unterhalten; (*claim*) behaupten

maintenance /'meɪntənəns/ *n* Aufrechterhaltung *f*; (*care*) Instandhaltung *f*; (*allowance*) Unterhalt *m*

maisonette /meɪzə'net/ *n* Wohnung *f* [auf zwei Etagen]

maize /meɪz/ *n* Mais *m*

majestic /mə'dʒestɪk/ *a*, **-ally** *adv* majestätisch

majesty /'mædʒəstɪ/ *n* Majestät *f*

major /'meɪdʒə(r)/ *a* größer □ *n* (*Mil*) Major *m*; (*Mus*) Dur *nt* □ *vi* (*Amer*) **~ in** als Hauptfach studieren

Majorca /mə'jɔːkə/ *n* Mallorca *nt*

majority /mə'dʒɒrətɪ/ *n* Mehrheit *f*; **in the ~** in der Mehrzahl

major road *n* Hauptverkehrsstraße *f*

make /meɪk/ *n* (*brand*) Marke *f* □ *v* (*pt/pp* **made**) □ *vt* machen; (*force*) zwingen; (*earn*) verdienen; halten (*speech*); treffen (*decision*); erreichen (*destination*) □ *vi* **~ as if to** Miene machen zu. **~ do** *vi* zurechtkommen (**with** mit). **~ for** *vi* zusteuern auf (+ *acc*). **~ off** *vi* sich davonmachen (**with** mit). **~ out** *vt* (*distinguish*) ausmachen; (*write out*) ausstellen; (*assert*) behaupten. **~ over** *vt* überschreiben (**to** auf + *acc*). **~ up** *vt* (*constitute*) bilden; (*invent*) erfinden; (*apply cosmetics to*) schminken; **~ up one's mind** sich entschließen □ *vi* sich versöhnen; **~ up for sth** etw wieder gutmachen; **~ up for lost time** verlorene Zeit aufholen

'make-believe *n* Phantasie *f*

maker /'meɪkə(r)/ *n* Hersteller *m*

make: **~shift** *a* behelfsmäßig □ *n* Notbehelf *m*. **~-up** *n* Make-up *nt*

making /'meɪkɪŋ/ *n* **have the ~s of** das Zeug haben zu

maladjusted /mælə'dʒʌstɪd/ *a* verhaltensgestört

malaise /mə'leɪz/ *n* (*fig*) Unbehagen *nt*

male /meɪl/ *a* männlich □ *n* Mann *m*; (*animal*) Männchen *nt*. **~ nurse** *n* Krankenpfleger *m*. **~ voice 'choir** *n* Männerchor *m*

malevolen|ce /mə'levələns/ *n* Bosheit *f*. **~t** *a* boshaft

malfunction /mæl'fʌŋkʃn/ *n* technische Störung *f*; (*Med*) Funktionsstörung *f* □ *vi* nicht richtig funktionieren

malice /'mælɪs/ *n* Bosheit *f*; **bear s.o. ~** einen Groll gegen jdn hegen

malicious /mə'lɪʃəs/ *a*, **-ly** *adv* böswillig

malign /mə'laɪn/ *vt* verleumden

malignan|cy /mə'lɪgnənsɪ/ *n* Bösartigkeit *f*. **~t** *a* bösartig

malinger /mə'lɪŋgə(r)/ *vi* simulieren, sich krank stellen. **~er** *n* Simulant *m*

malleable /'mælɪəbl/ *a* formbar

mallet /'mælɪt/ *n* Holzhammer *m*

malnu'trition /mæl-/ *n* Unterernährung *f*

mal'practice *n* Berufsvergehen *nt*

malt /mɔːlt/ *n* Malz *nt*

mal'treat /mæl-/ *vt* misshandeln. **~ment** *n* Misshandlung *f*

mammal /'mæml/ *n* Säugetier *nt*

mammoth /'mæməθ/ *a* riesig □ *n* Mammut *nt*

man /mæn/ *n* (*pl* **men**) Mann *m*; (*mankind*) der Mensch; (*chess*) Figur *f*; (*draughts*) Stein *m* □ *vt* (*pt/pp* **manned**) bemannen (*ship*); bedienen (*pump*); besetzen (*counter*)

manacle /'mænəkl/ *vt* fesseln (**to an** + *acc*); **~d** in Handschellen

manage /'mænɪdʒ/ *vt* leiten; verwalten (*estate*); (*cope with*) fertig werden mit; **~ to do sth** es schaffen, etw zu tun □ *vi* zurechtkommen; **~ on** auskommen mit. **~able** /-əbl/ *a* (*tool*) handlich; (*person*) fügsam. **~ment** /-mənt/ *n* **the ~ment** die Geschäftsleitung *f*

manager /'mænɪdʒə(r)/ *n* Geschäftsführer *m*; (*of bank*) Direktor *m*; (*of estate*)

Verwalter *m*; (*Sport*) [Chef]trainer *m*. **~ess** *n* Geschäftsführerin *f*. **~ial** /-'dʒɪə-rɪəl/ *a* **~ial staff** Führungskräfte *pl*

managing /'mænɪdʒɪŋ/ *a* **~ director** Generaldirektor *m*

mandarin /'mændərɪn/ *n* **~ [orange]** Mandarine *f*

mandat|e /'mændeɪt/ *n* Mandat *nt*. **~ory** /-dətrɪ/ *a* obligatorisch

mane /meɪn/ *n* Mähne *f*

manful /'mænfl/ *a*, **-ly** *adv* mannhaft

manger /'meɪndʒə(r)/ *n* Krippe *f*

mangle[1] /'mæŋgl/ *n* Wringmaschine *f*; (*for smoothing*) Mangel *f*

mangle[2] *vt* (*damage*) verstümmeln

mango /'mæŋgəʊ/ *n* (*pl* **-es**) Mango *f*

mangy /'meɪndʒɪ/ *a* ⟨*dog*⟩ räudig

man: **~'handle** *vt* grob behandeln ⟨*person*⟩. **~hole** *n* Kanalschacht *m*. **~hole cover** *n* Kanaldeckel *m*. **~hood** *n* Mannesalter *nt*; (*quality*) Männlichkeit *f*. **~-hour** *n* Arbeitsstunde *f*. **~hunt** *n* Fahndung *f*

man|ia /'meɪnɪə/ *n* Manie *f*. **~iac** /-ɪæk/ *n* Wahnsinnige(r) *m/f*

manicur|e /'mænɪkjʊə(r)/ *n* Maniküre *f* □ *vt* maniküren. **~ist** *n* Maniküre *f*

manifest /'mænɪfest/ *a*, **-ly** *adv* offensichtlich □ *vt* **~ itself** sich manifestieren

manifesto /mænɪ'festəʊ/ *n* Manifest *nt*

manifold /'mænɪfəʊld/ *a* mannigfaltig

manipulat|e /mə'nɪpjʊleɪt/ *vt* handhaben; (*pej*) manipulieren. **~ion** /-'leɪʃn/ *n* Manipulation *f*

man'kind *n* die Menschheit

manly /'mænlɪ/ *a* männlich

'man-made *a* künstlich. **~ fibre** *n* Kunstfaser *f*

manner /'mænə(r)/ *n* Weise *f*; (*kind, behaviour*) Art *f*; **in this ~** auf diese Weise; **[good/bad] ~s** [gute/schlechte] Manieren *pl*. **~ism** *n* Angewohnheit *f*

mannish /'mænɪʃ/ *a* männlich

manœuvrable /mə'nu:vrəbl/ *a* manövrierfähig

manœuvre /mə'nu:və(r)/ *n* Manöver *nt* □ *vt/i* manövrieren

manor /'mænə(r)/ *n* Gutshof *m*; (*house*) Gutshaus *nt*

man: **~power** *n* Arbeitskräfte *pl*. **~servant** *n* (*pl* **menservants**) Diener *m*

mansion /'mænʃn/ *n* Villa *f*

'manslaughter *n* Totschlag *m*

mantelpiece /'mæntl-/ *n* Kaminsims *m & nt*

manual /'mænjʊəl/ *a* Hand- □ *n* Handbuch *nt*

manufacture /mænjʊ'fæktʃə(r)/ *vt* herstellen □ *n* Herstellung *f*. **~r** *n* Hersteller *m*

manure /mə'njʊə(r)/ *n* Mist *m*

manuscript /'mænjʊskrɪpt/ *n* Manuskript *nt*

many /'menɪ/ *a* viele; **~ a time** oft □ *n* **a good/great ~** sehr viele

map /mæp/ *n* Landkarte *f*; (*of town*) Stadtplan *m* □ *vt* (*pt/pp* **mapped**) **~ out** (*fig*) ausarbeiten

maple /'meɪpl/ *n* Ahorn *m*

mar /mɑ:(r)/ *vt* (*pt/pp* **marred**) verderben

marathon /'mærəθən/ *n* Marathon *m*

marauding /mə'rɔːdɪŋ/ *a* plündernd

marble /'mɑːbl/ *n* Marmor *m*; (*for game*) Murmel *f*

March /mɑːtʃ/ *n* März *m*

march *n* Marsch *m* □ *vi* marschieren □ *vt* marschieren lassen; **~ s.o. off** jdn abführen

mare /meə(r)/ *n* Stute *f*

margarine /mɑːdʒə'riːn/ *n* Margarine *f*

margin /'mɑːdʒɪn/ *n* Rand *m*; (*leeway*) Spielraum *m*; (*Comm*) Spanne *f*. **~al** *a*, **-ly** *adv* geringfügig

marigold /'mærɪgəʊld/ *n* Ringelblume *f*

marijuana /mærɪ'hwɑːnə/ *n* Marihuana *nt*

marina /mə'riːnə/ *n* Jachthafen *m*

marinade /mærɪ'neɪd/ *n* Marinade *f* □ *vt* marinieren

marine /mə'riːn/ *a* Meeres- □ *n* Marine *f*; (*sailor*) Marineinfanterist *m*

marionette /mærɪə'net/ *n* Marionette *f*

marital /'mærɪtl/ *a* ehelich. **~ status** *n* Familienstand *m*

maritime /'mærɪtaɪm/ *a* See-

marjoram /'mɑːdʒərəm/ *n* Majoran *m*

mark[1] /mɑːk/ *n* (*currency*) Mark *f*

mark[2] *n* Fleck *m*; (*sign*) Zeichen *nt*; (*trace*) Spur *f*; (*target*) Ziel *nt*; (*Sch*) Note *f* □ *vt* markieren; (*spoil*) beschädigen; (*characterize*) kennzeichnen; (*Sch*) korrigieren; (*Sport*) decken; **~ time** (*Mil*) auf der Stelle treten; (*fig*) abwarten; **~ my words** das [eine] will ich dir sagen. **~ out** *vt* markieren

marked /mɑːkt/ *a*, **~ly** /-kɪdlɪ/ *adv* deutlich; (*pronounced*) ausgeprägt

marker /'mɑːkə(r)/ *n* Marke *f*; (*of exam*) Korrektor(in) *m(f)*

market /'mɑːkɪt/ *n* Markt *m* □ *vt* vertreiben; (*launch*) auf den Markt bringen. **~ing** *n* Marketing *nt*. **~ re'search** *n* Marktforschung *f*

marking /'mɑːkɪŋ/ *n* Markierung *f*; (*on animal*) Zeichnung *f*

marksman /'mɑːksmən/ n Scharfschütze m

marmalade /'mɑːməleɪd/ n Orangenmarmelade f

marmot /'mɑːmət/ n Murmeltier nt

maroon /mə'ruːn/ a dunkelrot

marooned /mə'ruːnd/ a (fig) von der Außenweit abgeschnitten

marquee /mɑː'kiː/ n Festzelt nt; (Amer: awning) Markise f

marquetry /'mɑːkɪtrɪ/ n Einlegearbeit f

marquis /'mɑːkwɪs/ n Marquis m

marriage /'mærɪdʒ/ n Ehe f; (wedding) Hochzeit f. ~able /-əbl/ a heiratsfähig

married /'mærɪd/ see marry ◻ a verheiratet. ~ life n Eheleben nt

marrow /'mærəʊ/ n (Anat) Mark nt; (vegetable) Kürbis m

marr|y /'mærɪ/ vt/i (pt/pp married) heiraten; (unite) trauen; get ~ied heiraten

marsh /mɑːʃ/ n Sumpf m

marshal /'mɑːʃl/ n Marschall m; (steward) Ordner m ◻ vt (pt/pp marshalled) (Mil) formieren; (fig) ordnen

marshy /'mɑːʃɪ/ a sumpfig

marsupial /mɑː'suːpɪəl/ n Beuteltier nt

martial /'mɑːʃl/ a kriegerisch. ~ 'law n Kriegsrecht nt

martyr /'mɑːtə(r)/ n Märtyrer(in) m(f) ◻ vt zum Märtyrer machen. ~dom /-dəm/ n Martyrium nt

marvel /'mɑːvl/ n Wunder nt ◻ vi (pt/pp marvelled) staunen (at über + acc). ~lous /-vələs/ a, -ly adv wunderbar

Marxis|m /'mɑːksɪzm/ n Marxismus m. ~t a marxistisch ◻ n Marxist(in) m(f)

marzipan /'mɑːzɪpæn/ n Marzipan nt

mascara /mæ'skɑːrə/ n Wimperntusche f

mascot /'mæskət/ n Maskottchen nt

masculin|e /'mæskjʊlɪn/ a männlich ◻ n (Gram) Maskulinum nt. ~ity /-'lɪnətɪ/ n Männlichkeit f

mash /mæʃ/ n (fam, Culin) Kartoffelpüree nt ◻ vt stampfen. ~ed potatoes npl Kartoffelpüree nt

mask /mɑːsk/ n Maske f ◻ vt maskieren

masochis|m /'mæsəkɪzm/ n Masochismus m. ~t /-ɪst/ n Masochist m

mason /'meɪsn/ n Steinmetz m

Mason n Freimaurer m. ~ic /mə'sɒnɪk/ a freimaurerisch

masonry /'meɪsnrɪ/ n Mauerwerk nt

masquerade /mæskə'reɪd/ n (fig) Maskerade f ◻ vi ~ as (pose) sich ausgeben als

mass[1] /mæs/ n (Relig) Messe f

mass[2] n Masse f ◻ vi sich sammeln; (Mil) sich massieren

massacre /'mæsəkə(r)/ n Massaker nt ◻ vt niedermetzeln

massage /'mæsɑːʒ/ n Massage f ◻ vt massieren

masseu|r /mæ'sɜː(r)/ n Masseur m. ~se /-'sɜːz/ n Masseuse f

massive /'mæsɪv/ a massiv; (huge) riesig

mass: ~ 'media npl Massenmedien pl. ~-pro'duce vt in Massenproduktion herstellen. ~pro'duction n Massenproduktion f

mast /mɑːst/ n Mast m

master /'mɑːstə(r)/ n Herr m; (teacher) Lehrer m; (craftsman, artist) Meister m; (of ship) Kapitän m ◻ vt meistern; beherrschen (language)

master: ~-key n Hauptschlüssel m. ~ly a meisterhaft. ~-mind n führender Kopf m ◻ vt der führende Kopf sein von. ~piece n Meisterwerk nt. ~y n (of subject) Beherrschung f

masturbat|e /'mæstəbeɪt/ vi masturbieren. ~ion /-'beɪʃn/ n Masturbation f

mat /mæt/ n Matte f; (on table) Untersatz m

match[1] /mætʃ/ n Wettkampf m; (in ball games) Spiel nt; (Tennis) Match nt; (marriage) Heirat f; be a good ~ (colours:) gut zusammenpassen; be no ~ for s.o. jdm nicht gewachsen sein ◻ vt (equal) gleichkommen (+ dat); (be like) passen zu; (find sth similar) etwas Passendes finden zu ◻ vi zusammenpassen

match[2] n Streichholz nt. ~box n Streichholzschachtel f

matching /'mætʃɪŋ/ a [zusammen]passend

mate[1] /meɪt/ n Kumpel m; (assistant) Gehilfe m; (Naut) Maat m; (Zool) Männchen nt; (female) Weibchen nt ◻ vi sich paaren ◻ vt paaren

mate[2] n (Chess) Matt nt

material /mə'tɪərɪəl/ n Material nt; (fabric) Stoff m; raw ~s Rohstoffe pl ◻ a materiell

material|ism /mə'tɪərɪəlɪzm/ n Materialismus m. ~istic /-'lɪstɪk/ a materialistisch. ~ize /-laɪz/ vi sich verwirklichen

maternal /mə'tɜːnl/ a mütterlich

maternity /mə'tɜːnətɪ/ n Mutterschaft f. ~ clothes npl Umstandskleidung f. ~ ward n Entbindungsstation f

matey /'meɪtɪ/ a (fam) freundlich

mathematic|al /mæθə'mætɪkl/ a, -ly adv mathematisch. ~ian /-mə'tɪʃn/ n Mathematiker(in) m(f)

mathematics /mæθə'mætɪks/ n Mathematik f

maths /mæθs/ n (fam) Mathe f

matinée /'mætɪneɪ/ n (*Theat*) Nachmittagsvorstellung f

matriculat|e /mə'trɪkjʊleɪt/ vi sich immatrikulieren. ~**ion** /-'leɪʃn/ n Immatrikulation f

matrimon|ial /mætrɪ'məʊnɪəl/ a Ehe-. ~**y** /'mætrɪmənɪ/ n Ehe f

matrix /'meɪtrɪks/ n (pl **matrices** /-sɪːz/) n (*Techn: mould*) Matrize f

matron /'meɪtrən/ n (*of hospital*) Oberin f; (*of school*) Hausmutter f. ~**ly** a matronenhaft

matt /mæt/ a matt

matted /'mætɪd/ a verfilzt

matter /'mætə(r)/ n (*affair*) Sache f; (*pus*) Eiter m; (*Phys: substance*) Materie f; **money** ~**s** Geldangelegenheiten pl; **as a** ~ **of fact** eigentlich; **what is the** ~? was ist los? □ vi wichtig sein; ~ **to s.o.** jdm etwas ausmachen; **it doesn't** ~ es macht nichts. ~-**of-fact** a sachlich

matting /'mætɪŋ/ n Matten pl

mattress /'mætrɪs/ n Matratze f

matur|e /mə'tjʊə(r)/ a reif, (*Comm*) fällig □ vi reifen; (*person:*) reifer werden; (*Comm*) fällig werden □ vt reifen lassen. ~**ity** n Reifer f; (*Comm*) Fälligkeit f

maul /mɔːl/ vt übel zurichten

Maundy /'mɔːndɪ/ n ~ **Thursday** Gründonnerstag m

mauve /məʊv/ a lila

mawkish /'mɔːkɪʃ/ a rührselig

maxim /'mæksɪm/ n Maxime f

maximum /'mæksɪməm/ a maximal □ n (pl -**ima**) Maximum nt. ~ **speed** n Höchstgeschwindigkeit f

may /meɪ/ v aux (*nur Präsens*) (*be allowed to*) dürfen; (*be possible*) können; **may I come in?** darf ich reinkommen? **may he succeed** möge es ihm gelingen; **I may as well stay** am besten bleibe ich hier; **it may be true** es könnte wahr sein

May n Mai m

maybe /'meɪbiː/ adv vielleicht

'May Day n der Erste Mai

mayonnaise /meɪə'neɪz/ n Mayonnaise f

mayor /'meə(r)/ n Bürgermeister m. ~**ess** n Bürgermeisterin f; (*wife of mayor*) Frau Bürgermeister f

maze /meɪz/ n Irrgarten m; (*fig*) Labyrinth nt

me /miː/ pron (*acc*) mich; (*dat*) mir; **he knows** ~ er kennt mich; **give** ~ **the money** gib mir das Geld; **it's** ~ (*fam*) ich bin es

meadow /'medəʊ/ n Wiese f

meagre /'miːgə(r)/ a dürftig

meal¹ /miːl/ n Mahlzeit f; (*food*) Essen nt

meal² n (*grain*) Schrot m

mealy-mouthed /miːlɪ'maʊðd/ a heuchlerisch

mean¹ /miːn/ a (-**er**, -**est**) geizig; (*unkind*) gemein; (*poor*) schäbig

mean² a mittlere(r,s) □ n (*average*) Durchschnitt m; **the golden** ~ die goldene Mitte

mean³ vt (*pt/pp* **meant**) heißen; (*signify*) bedeuten; (*intend*) beabsichtigen; **I** ~ **it** das ist mein Ernst; ~ **well** es gut meinen; **be meant for** ⟨*present:*⟩ bestimmt sein für; ⟨*remark:*⟩ gerichtet sein an (+ acc)

meander /mɪ'ændə(r)/ vi sich schlängeln; ⟨*person:*⟩ schlendern

meaning /'miːnɪŋ/ n Bedeutung f. ~**ful** a bedeutungsvoll. ~**less** a bedeutungslos

means /miːnz/ n Möglichkeit f, Mittel nt; ~ **of transport** Verkehrsmittel nt; **by** ~ **of** durch; **by all** ~! aber natürlich! **by no** ~ keineswegs □ npl (*resources*) [Geld]mittel pl. ~ **test** n Bedürftigkeitsnachweis m

meant /ment/ *see* **mean³**

'meantime n **in the** ~ in der Zwischenzeit □ adv inzwischen

'meanwhile adv inzwischen

measles /'miːzlz/ n Masern pl

measly /'miːzlɪ/ a (*fam*) mickerig

measurable /'meʒərəbl/ a messbar

measure /'meʒə(r)/ n Maß nt; (*action*) Maßnahme f □ vt/i messen; ~ **up to** (*fig*) herankommen an (+ acc). ~**d** a gemessen. ~**ment** /-mənt/ n Maß nt

meat /miːt/ n Fleisch nt. ~ **ball** n (*Culin*) Klops m. ~ **loaf** n falscher Hase m

mechan|ic /mɪ'kænɪk/ n Mechaniker m. ~**ical** a, -**ly** adv mechanisch. ~**ical engineering** Maschinenbau m. ~**ics** n Mechanik f □ n pl Mechanismus m

mechan|ism /'mekənɪzm/ n Mechanismus m. ~**ize** vt mechanisieren

medal /'medl/ n Orden m; (*Sport*) Medaille f

medallion /mɪ'dælɪən/ n Medaillon nt

medallist /'medəlɪst/ n Medaillengewinner(in) m(f)

meddle /'medl/ vi sich einmischen (**in** in + acc); (*tinker*) herumhantieren (**with** an + acc)

media /'miːdɪə/ *see* **medium** □ n pl **the** ~ die Medien pl

median /'miːdɪən/ a ~ **strip** (*Amer*) Mittelstreifen m

mediat|e /'miːdɪeɪt/ vi vermitteln. ~**or** n Vermittler(in) m(f)

medical /'medɪkl/ a medizinisch; ⟨*treatment:*⟩ ärztlich □ n ärztliche Untersuchung f. ~ **insurance** n Krankenversicherung f. ~ **student** n Medizinstudent m

medicat|ed /'medɪkeɪtɪd/ *a* medizinisch. **~ion** /-'keɪʃn/ *n* (*drugs*) Medikamente *pl*

medicinal /mɪ'dɪsɪnl/ *a* medizinisch; (*plant*) heilkräftig

medicine /'medsən/ *n* Medizin *f*; (*preparation*) Medikament *nt*

medieval /medɪ'i:vl/ *a* mittelalterlich

mediocr|e /mi:dɪ'əʊkə(r)/ *a* mittelmäßig. **~ity** /-'ɒkrətɪ/ *n* Mittelmäßigkeit *f*

meditat|e /'medɪteɪt/ *vi* nachdenken (**on** über + *acc*); (*Relig*) meditieren. **~ion** /-'teɪʃn/ *n* Meditation *f*

Mediterranean /medɪtə'reɪnɪən/ *n* Mittelmeer *nt* □ *a* Mittelmeer-

medium /'mi:dɪəm/ *a* mittlere(r,s); (*steak*) medium; **of ~ size** von mittlerer Größe □ *n* (*pl* **media**) Medium *nt*; (*means*) Mittel *nt* □ (*pl* **-s**) (*person*) Medium *nt*

medium: **~-sized** *a* mittelgroß. **~ wave** *n* Mittelwelle *f*

medley /'medlɪ/ *n* Gemisch *nt*; (*Mus*) Potpourri *nt*

meek /mi:k/ *a* (**-er, -est**), **-ly** *adv* sanftmütig; (*unprotesting*) widerspruchslos

meet /mi:t/ *v* (*pt/pp* **met**) □ *vt* treffen; (*by chance*) begegnen (+ *dat*); (*at station*) abholen; (*make the acquaintance of*) kennen lernen; stoßen auf (+ *acc*) (*problem*); bezahlen (*bill*); erfüllen (*requirements*) □ *vi* sich treffen; (*for the first time*) sich kennen lernen; **~ with** stoßen auf (+ *acc*) (*problem*); sich treffen mit (*person*) □ *n* Jagdtreffen *nt*

meeting /'mi:tɪŋ/ *n* Treffen *nt*; (*by chance*) Begegnung *f*; (*discussion*) Besprechung *f*; (*of committee*) Sitzung *f*; (*large*) Versammlung *f*

megalomania /megələ'meɪnɪə/ *n* Größenwahnsinn *m*

megaphone /'megəfəʊn/ *n* Megaphon *nt*

melancholy /'melənkəlɪ/ *a* melancholisch □ *n* Melancholie *f*

mellow /'meləʊ/ *a*(**-er, -est**) (*fruit*) ausgereift; (*sound, person*) sanft □ *vi* reifer werden

melodic /mɪ'lɒdɪk/ *a* melodisch

melodious /mɪ'ləʊdɪəs/ *a* melodiös

melodrama /'melə-/ *n* Melodrama *nt*. **~tic** /-drə'mætɪk/ *a*, **-ally** *adv* melodramatisch

melody /'melədɪ/ *n* Melodie *f*

melon /'melən/ *n* Melone *f*

melt /melt/ *vt/i* schmelzen. **~ down** *vt* einschmelzen. **~ing-pot** *n* (*fig*) Schmelztiegel *m*

member /'membə(r)/ *n* Mitglied *nt*; (*of family*) Angehörige(r) *m/f*; **M~ of Parliament** Abgeordnete(r) *m/f*. **~ship** *n* Mitgliedschaft *f*; (*members*) Mitgliederzahl *f*

membrane /'membreɪn/ *n* Membran *f*

memento /mɪ'mentəʊ/ *n* Andenken *nt*

memo /'meməʊ/ *n* Mitteilung *f*

memoirs /'memwɑ:z/ *n pl* Memoiren *pl*

memorable /'memərəbl/ *a* denkwürdig

memorandum /memə'rændəm/ *n* Mitteilung *f*

memorial /mɪ'mɔ:rɪəl/ *n* Denkmal *nt*. **~ service** *n* Gedenkfeier *f*

memorize /'meməraɪz/ *vt* sich (*dat*) einprägen

memory /'memərɪ/ *n* Gedächtnis *nt*; (*thing remembered*) Erinnerung *f*; (*of computer*) Speicher *m*; **from ~** auswendig; **in ~ of** zur Erinnerung an (+ *acc*)

men /men/ *see* **man**

menac|e /'menɪs/ *n* Drohung *f*; (*nuisance*) Plage *f* □ *vt* bedrohen. **~ing** *a*, **~ly** *adv* drohend

mend /mend/ *vt* reparieren; (*patch*) flicken; ausbessern (*clothes*) □ *n* **on the ~** auf dem Weg der Besserung

'menfolk *n pl* Männer *pl*

menial /'mi:nɪəl/ *a* niedrig

meningitis /menɪn'dʒaɪtɪs/ *n* Hirnhautentzündung *f*, Meningitis *f*

menopause /'menə-/ *n* Wechseljahre *pl*

menstruat|e /'menstrʊeɪt/ *vi* menstruieren. **~ion** /-'eɪʃn/ *n* Menstruation *f*

mental /'mentl/ *a*, **-ly** *adv* geistig; (*fam: mad*) verrückt. **~ a'rithmetic** *n* Kopfrechnen *nt*. **~ 'illness** *n* Geisteskrankheit *f*

mentality /men'tælətɪ/ *n* Mentalität *f*

mention /'menʃn/ *n* Erwähnung *f* □ *vt* erwähnen; **don't ~ it** keine Ursache; bitte

menu /'menju:/ *n* Speisekarte *f*

mercantile /'mɜ:kəntaɪl/ *a* Handels-

mercenary /'mɜ:sɪnərɪ/ *a* geldgierig □ *n* Söldner *m*

merchandise /'mɜ:tʃəndaɪz/ *n* Ware *f*

merchant /'mɜ:tʃənt/ *n* Kaufmann *m*; (*dealer*) Händler *m*. **~ 'navy** *n* Handelsmarine *f*

merci|ful /'mɜ:sɪfl/ *a* barmherzig. **~fully** *adv* (*fam*) glücklicherweise. **~less** *a*, **-ly** *adv* erbarmungslos

mercury /'mɜ:kjʊrɪ/ *n* Quecksilber *nt*

mercy /'mɜ:sɪ/ *n* Barmherzigkeit *f*, Gnade *f*; **be at s.o.'s ~** jdm ausgeliefert sein

mere /mɪə(r)/ *a*, **-ly** *adv* bloß

merest /'mɪərɪst/ *a* kleinste(r,s)

merge /mɜ:dʒ/ *vi* zusammenlaufen; (*Comm*) fusionieren □ *vt* (*Comm*) zusammenschließen

merger /'mɜ:dʒə(r)/ *n* Fusion *f*

meridian /məˈrɪdɪən/ n Meridian m

meringue /məˈræŋ/ n Baiser nt

merit /ˈmerɪt/ n Verdienst nt; (advantage) Vorzug m; (worth) Wert m ▫ vt verdienen

mermaid /ˈmɜːmeɪd/ n Meerjungfrau f

merri|ly /ˈmerɪlɪ/ adv fröhlich. ~ment /-mənt/ n Fröhlichkeit f; (laughter) Gelächter nt

merry /ˈmerɪ/ a (-ier, -iest) fröhlich; ~ Christmas! fröhliche Weihnachten!

merry: ~-go-round n Karussell nt. ~-making n Feiern nt

mesh /meʃ/ n Masche f; (size) Maschenweite f; (fig: network) Netz nt

mesmerize /ˈmezməraɪz/ vt hypnotisieren. ~d a (fig) [wie] gebannt

mess /mes/ n Durcheinander nt; (trouble) Schwierigkeiten pl; (something spilt) Bescherung f (fam); (Mil) Messe f; **make a ~ of** (botch) verpfuschen ▫ vt ~ **up** in Unordnung bringen; (botch) verpfuschen ▫ vi ~ **about** herumalbern; (tinker) herumspielen (with mit)

message /ˈmesɪdʒ/ n Nachricht f; **give s.o. a ~** jdm etwas ausrichten

messenger /ˈmesɪndʒə(r)/ n Bote m

Messiah /mɪˈsaɪə/ n Messias m

Messrs /ˈmesəz/ n pl see **Mr**; (on letter) ~ Smith Firma Smith

messy /ˈmesɪ/ a (-ier, -iest) schmutzig; (untidy) unordentlich

met /met/ see **meet**

metabolism /mɪˈtæbəlɪzm/ n Stoffwechsel m

metal /ˈmetl/ n Metall nt ▫ a Metall-. ~lic /mɪˈtælɪk/ a metallisch. ~lurgy /mɪˈtælədʒɪ/ n Metallurgie f

metamorphosis /metəˈmɔːfəsɪs/ n (pl -phoses /-siːz/) Metamorphose f

metaphor /ˈmetəfə(r)/ n Metapher f. ~ical /-ˈfɒrɪkl/ a, -ly adv metaphorisch

meteor /ˈmiːtɪə(r)/ n Meteor m. ~ic /-ˈɒrɪk/ a kometenhaft

meteorological /miːtɪərəˈlɒdʒɪkl/ a Wetter-

meteorolog|ist /miːtɪəˈrɒlədʒɪst/ n Meteorologe m/ -gin f. ~y n Meteorologie f

meter¹ /ˈmiːtə(r)/ n Zähler m

meter² n (Amer) = **metre**

method /ˈmeθəd/ n Methode f; (Culin) Zubereitung f

methodical /mɪˈθɒdɪkl/ a, -ly adv systematisch, methodisch

Methodist /ˈmeθədɪst/ n Methodist(in) m(f)

meths /meθs/ n (fam) Brennspiritus m

methylated /ˈmeθɪleɪtɪd/ a ~ **spirit[s]** Brennspiritus m

meticulous /mɪˈtɪkjʊləs/ a, -ly adv sehr genau

metre /ˈmiːtə(r)/ n Meter m & n; (rhythm) Versmaß nt

metric /ˈmetrɪk/ a metrisch

metropolis /mɪˈtrɒpəlɪs/ n Metropole f

metropolitan /metrəˈpɒlɪtən/ a hauptstädtisch; (international) weltstädtisch

mettle /ˈmetl/ n Mut m

mew /mjuː/ n Miau nt ▫ vi miauen

Mexican /ˈmeksɪkən/ a mexikanisch ▫ n Mexikaner(in) m(f). **'Mexico** n Mexiko nt

miaow /mɪˈaʊ/ n Miau nt ▫ vi miauen

mice /maɪs/ see **mouse**

microbe /ˈmaɪkrəʊb/ n Mikrobe f

micro /ˈmaɪkrəʊ/: ~chip n Mikrochip nt. ~computer n Mikrocomputer m. ~film n Mikrofilm m. ~phone n Mikrofon nt. ~processor n Mikroprozessor m. ~scope /-skəʊp/ n Mikroskop nt. ~scopic /-ˈskɒpɪk/ a mikroskopisch. ~wave n Mikrowelle f. ~wave [oven] n Mikrowellenherd m

mid /mɪd/ a ~ **May** Mitte Mai; **in ~ air** in der Luft

midday /mɪdˈdeɪ/ n Mittag m

middle /ˈmɪdl/ a mittlere(r,s); **the M~ Ages** das Mittelalter; **the ~ class[es]** der Mittelstand; **the M~ East** der Nahe Osten ▫ n Mitte f; **in the ~ of the night** mitten in der Nacht

middle: ~-aged a mittleren Alters. ~-class a bürgerlich. ~man n (Comm) Zwischenhändler m

middling /ˈmɪdlɪŋ/ a mittelmäßig

midge /mɪdʒ/ n [kleine] Mücke f

midget /ˈmɪdʒɪt/ n Liliputaner(in) m(f)

Midlands /ˈmɪdləndz/ npl **the ~** Mittelengland n

'midnight n Mitternacht f

midriff /ˈmɪdrɪf/ n (fam) Taille f

midst /mɪdst/ n **in the ~ of** mitten in (+ dat); **in our ~** unter uns

mid: ~summer n Hochsommer m; (solstice) Sommersonnenwende f. ~way adv auf halbem Wege. ~wife n Hebamme f. ~wifery /-wɪfrɪ/ n Geburtshilfe f. ~winter n Mitte f des Winters

might¹ /maɪt/ v aux I ~ vielleicht; **it ~ be true** es könnte wahr sein; **I ~ as well stay** am besten bleibe ich hier; **he asked if he ~ go** er fragte, ob er gehen dürfte; **you ~ have drowned** du hättest ertrinken können

might² n Macht f

mighty /ˈmaɪtɪ/ a (-ier, -iest) mächtig

migraine /ˈmiːgreɪn/ n Migräne f

migrant /ˈmaɪgrənt/ a Wander- ▫ n (bird) Zugvogel m

migrat|e /maɪˈgreɪt/ *vi* abwandern; ⟨*birds:*⟩ ziehen. **~ion** /-ˈgreɪʃn/ *n* Wanderung *f*; (*of birds*) Zug *m*

mike /maɪk/ *n* (*fam*) Mikrofon *nt*

mild /maɪld/ *a* (**-er, -est**) mild

mildew /ˈmɪldjuː/ *n* Schimmel *m*; (*Bot*) Mehltau *m*

mild|ly /ˈmaɪldlɪ/ *adv* leicht; **to put it ~ly** gelinde gesagt. **~ness** *n* Milde *f*

mile /maɪl/ *n* Meile *f* (= *1,6 km*); **~s too big** (*fam*) viel zu groß

mile|age /-ɪdʒ/ *n* Meilenzahl *f*; (*of car*) Meilenstand *m*. **~stone** *n* Meilenstein *m*

militant /ˈmɪlɪtənt/ *a* militant

military /ˈmɪlɪtrɪ/ *a* militärisch. **~ service** *n* Wehrdienst *m*

militate /ˈmɪlɪteɪt/ *vi* **~ against** sprechen gegen

militia /mɪˈlɪʃə/ *n* Miliz *f*

milk /mɪlk/ *n* Milch *f* □ *vt* melken

milk: ~man *n* Milchmann *m*. **~ shake** *n* Milchmixgetränk *nt*. **~ tooth** *n* Milchzahn *m*

milky /ˈmɪlkɪ/ *a* (**-ier, -iest**) milchig. **M~ Way** *n* (*Astr*) Milchstraße *f*

mill /mɪl/ *n* Mühle *f*; (*factory*) Fabrik *f* □ *vt/i* mahlen; (*Techn*) fräsen. **~ about, ~ around** *vi* umherlaufen

millenium /mɪˈlenɪəm/ *n* Jahrtausend *nt*

miller /ˈmɪlə(r)/ *n* Müller *m*

millet /ˈmɪlɪt/ *n* Hirse *f*

milli|gram /ˈmɪlɪ-/ *n* Milligramm *nt*. **~metre** *n* Millimeter *m* & *nt*

milliner /ˈmɪlɪnə(r)/ *n* Modistin *f*; (*man*) Hutmacher *m*. **~y** *n* Damenhüte *pl*

million /ˈmɪljən/ *n* Million *f*; **a ~ pounds** eine Million Pfund. **~aire** /-ˈneə(r)/ *n* Millionär(in) *m(f)*

'millstone *n* Mühlstein *m*

mime /maɪm/ *n* Pantomime *f* □ *vt* pantomimisch darstellen

mimic /ˈmɪmɪk/ *n* Imitator *m* □ *vt* (*pt/pp* **mimicked**) nachahmen. **~ry** *n* Nachahmung *f*

mimosa /mɪˈməʊzə/ *n* Mimose *f*

mince /mɪns/ *n* Hackfleisch *nt* □ *vt* (*Culin*) durchdrehen; **not ~ one's words** kein Blatt vor den Mund nehmen

mince: ~meat *n* Masse *f* aus Korinthen, Zitronat *usw*; **make ~meat of** (*fig*) vernichtend schlagen. **~'pie** *n* mit 'mincemeat' gefülltes Pastetchen *nt*

mincer /ˈmɪnsə(r)/ *n* Fleischwolf *m*

mind /maɪnd/ *n* Geist *m*; (*sanity*) Verstand *m*; **to my ~** meiner Meinung nach; **give s.o. a piece of one's ~** jdm gehörig die Meinung sagen; **make up one's ~** sich entschließen; **be out of one's ~** nicht bei

Verstand sein; **have sth in ~** etw im Sinn haben; **bear sth in ~** an etw (*acc*) denken; **have a good ~ to** große Lust haben, zu; **I have changed my ~** ich habe es mir anders überlegt □ *vt* aufpassen auf (+ *acc*); **I don't ~ the noise** der Lärm stört mich nicht; **~ the step!** Achtung Stufe! □ *vi* (*care*) sich kümmern (**about** um); **I don't ~** mir macht es nichts aus; **never ~!** macht nichts! **do you ~ if?** haben Sie etwas dagegen, wenn? **~ out** *vi* aufpassen

mind|ful *a* **~ful of** eingedenk (+ *gen*). **~less** *a* geistlos

mine¹ /maɪn/ *poss pron* meine(r), meins; **a friend of ~** ein Freund von mir; **that is ~** das gehört mir

mine² *n* Bergwerk *nt*; (*explosive*) Mine *f* □ *vt* abbauen; (*Mil*) verminen. **~ detector** *n* Minensuchgerät *nt*. **~field** *n* Minenfeld *nt*

miner /ˈmaɪnə(r)/ *n* Bergarbeiter *m*

mineral /ˈmɪnərl/ *n* Mineral *nt*. **~ogy** /-ˈrælədʒɪ/ *n* Mineralogie *f*. **~ water** *n* Mineralwasser *nt*

minesweeper /ˈmaɪn-/ *n* Minenräumboot *nt*

mingle /ˈmɪŋgl/ *vi* **~ with** sich mischen unter (+ *acc*)

miniature /ˈmɪnɪtʃə(r)/ *a* Klein- □ *n* Miniatur *f*

mini|bus /ˈmɪnɪ-/ *n* Kleinbus *m*. **~cab** *n* Taxi *nt*

minim /ˈmɪnɪm/ *n* (*Mus*) halbe Note *f*

minim|al /ˈmɪnɪməl/ *a* minimal. **~ize** *vt* auf ein Minimum reduzieren. **~um** *n* (*pl* **-ima**) Minimum *nt* □ *a* Mindest-

mining /ˈmaɪnɪŋ/ *n* Bergbau *m*

miniskirt /ˈmɪnɪ-/ *n* Minirock *m*

minist|er /ˈmɪnɪstə(r)/ *n* Minister *m*; (*Relig*) Pastor *m*. **~erial** /-ˈstɪərɪəl/ *a* ministeriell

ministry /ˈmɪnɪstrɪ/ *n* (*Pol*) Ministerium *nt*; **the ~** (*Relig*) das geistliche Amt

mink /mɪŋk/ *n* Nerz *m*

minor /ˈmaɪnə(r)/ *a* kleiner; (*less important*) unbedeutend □ *n* Minderjährige(r) *m/f*; (*Mus*) Moll *nt*

minority /maɪˈnɒrətɪ/ *n* Minderheit *f*; (*age*) Minderjährigkeit *f*

minor road *n* Nebenstraße *f*

mint¹ /mɪnt/ *n* Münzstätte *f* □ *a* ⟨*stamp*⟩ postfrisch; **in ~ condition** wie neu □ *vt* prägen

mint² *n* (*herb*) Minze *f*; (*sweet*) Pfefferminzbonbon *m* & *nt*

minuet /mɪnjʊˈet/ *n* Menuett *nt*

minus /ˈmaɪnəs/ *prep* minus, weniger; (*fam: without*) ohne □ *n* **~ [sign]** Minuszeichen *nt*

minute¹ /'mɪnɪt/ n Minute f; **in a ~** (shortly) gleich; **~s** pl (of meeting) Protokoll nt

minute² /maɪ'njuːt/ a winzig; (precise) genau

mirac|le /'mɪrəkl/ n Wunder nt. **~ulous** /-'rækjʊləs/ a wunderbar

mirage /'mɪrɑːʒ/ n Fata Morgana f

mire /'maɪə(r)/ n Morast m

mirror /'mɪrə(r)/ n Spiegel m □ vt widerspiegeln

mirth /mɜːθ/ n Heiterkeit f

misad'venture /mɪs-/ n Missgeschick nt

misanthropist /mɪ'zænθrəpɪst/ n Menschenfeind m

misappre'hension n Missverständnis nt; **be under a ~** sich irren

misbe'hav|e vi sich schlecht benehmen. **~iour** n schlechtes Benehmen nt

mis'calcu|late vt falsch berechnen □ vi sich verrechnen. **~'lation** n Fehlkalkulation f

'miscarriage n Fehlgeburt f; **~ of justice** Justizirrtum m. **mis'carry** vi eine Fehlgeburt haben

miscellaneous /mɪsə'leɪnɪəs/ a vermischt

mischief /'mɪstʃɪf/ n Unfug m; (harm) Schaden m

mischievous /'mɪstʃɪvəs/ a, **-ly** adv schelmisch; (malicious) boshaft

miscon'ception n falsche Vorstellung f

mis'conduct n unkorrektes Verhalten nt; (adultery) Ehebruch m

miscon'strue vt missdeuten

mis'deed n Missetat f

misde'meanour n Missetat f

miser /'maɪzə(r)/ n Geizhals m

miserable /'mɪzrəbl/ a, **-bly** adv unglücklich; (wretched) elend

miserly /'maɪzəlɪ/ adv geizig

misery /'mɪzərɪ/ n Elend nt; (fam: person) Miesepeter m

mis'fire vi fehlzünden; (go wrong) fehlschlagen

'misfit n Außenseiter(in) m(f)

mis'fortune n Unglück nt

mis'givings npl Bedenken pl

mis'guided a töricht

mishap /'mɪshæp/ n Missgeschick nt

misin'form vt falsch unterrichten

misin'terpret vt missdeuten

mis'judge vt falsch beurteilen; (estimate wrongly) falsch einschätzen

mis'lay vt (pt/pp -laid) verlegen

mis'lead vt (pt/pp -led) irreführen. **~ing** a irreführend

mis'manage vt schlecht verwalten. **~ment** n Misswirtschaft f

misnomer /mɪs'nəʊmə(r)/ n Fehlbezeichnung f

'misprint n Druckfehler m

mis'quote vt falsch zitieren

misrepre'sent vt falsch darstellen

miss /mɪs/ n Fehltreffer m □ vt verpassen; (fail to hit or find) verfehlen; (fail to attend) versäumen; (fail to notice) übersehen; (feel the loss of) vermissen □ vi (fail to hit) nicht treffen. **~ out** vt auslassen

Miss n (pl -es) Fräulein nt

misshapen /mɪs'ʃeɪpən/ a missgestaltet

missile /'mɪsaɪl/ n [Wurf]geschoss nt; (Mil) Rakete f

missing /'mɪsɪŋ/ a fehlend (lost) verschwunden; (Mil) vermisst; **be ~** fehlen

mission /'mɪʃn/ n Auftrag m; (Mil) Einsatz m; (Relig) Mission f

missionary /'mɪʃənrɪ/ n Missionar(in) m(f)

mis'spell vt (pt/pp **-spelt** or **-spelled**) falsch schreiben

mist /mɪst/ n Dunst m; (fog) Nebel m; (on window) Beschlag m □ vi **~ up** beschlagen

mistake /mɪ'steɪk/ n Fehler m; **by ~** aus Versehen □ vt (pt **mistook**, pp **mistaken**) missverstehen; **~ for** verwechseln mit

mistaken /mɪ'steɪkən/ a falsch; **be ~** sich irren; **~ identity** Verwechslung f. **~ly** adv irrtümlicherweise

mistletoe /'mɪsltəʊ/ n Mistel f

mistress /'mɪstrɪs/ n Herrin f; (teacher) Lehrerin f; (lover) Geliebte f

mis'trust n Misstrauen nt □ vt misstrauen (+ dat)

misty /'mɪstɪ/ a (**-ier**, **-iest**) dunstig; (foggy) neblig; (fig) unklar

misunder'stand vt (pt/pp **-stood**) missverstehen. **~ing** n Missverständnis nt

misuse¹ /mɪs'juːz/ vt missbrauchen

misuse² /mɪs'juːs/ n Missbrauch m

mite /maɪt/ n (Zool) Milbe f; **little ~** (child) kleines Ding nt

mitigat|e /'mɪtɪgeɪt/ vt mildern. **~ing** a mildernd

mitten /'mɪtn/ n Fausthandschuh m

mix /mɪks/ n Mischung f □ vt mischen □ vi sich mischen; **~ with** (associate with) verkehren mit. **~ up** vt mischen; (muddle) durcheinander bringen; (mistake for) verwechseln (with mit)

mixed /mɪkst/ a gemischt; **be ~ up** durcheinander sein

mixer /'mɪksə(r)/ n Mischmaschine f; (Culin) Küchenmaschine f

mixture /'mıkstʃə(r)/ *n* Mischung *f*; *(medicine)* Mixtur *f*; *(Culin)* Teig *m*

'**mix-up** *n* Durcheinander *nt*; *(confusion)* Verwirrung *f*; *(mistake)* Verwechslung *f*

moan /məʊn/ *n* Stöhnen *nt* □ *vi* stöhnen; *(complain)* jammern

moat /məʊt/ *n* Burggraben *m*

mob /mɒb/ *n* Horde *f*; *(rabble)* Pöbel *m*; *(fam: gang)* Bande *f* □ *vt* (*pt*/*pp* **mobbed**) herfallen über (+ *acc*); belagern *(celebrity)*

mobile /'məʊbaıl/ *a* beweglich □ *n* Mobile *nt*; *(telephone)* Handy *nt*. ∼ '**home** *n* Wohnwagen *m*. ∼ '**phone** *n* Mobiltelefon *nt*, Handy *nt*

mobility /mə'bılətı/ *n* Beweglichkeit *f*

mobi|lization /məʊbılaı'zeıʃn/ *n* Mobilisierung *f*. ∼**lize** /'məʊbılaız/ *vt* mobilisieren

mocha /'mɒkə/ *n* Mokka *m*

mock /mɒk/ *a* Schein- □ *vt* verspotten. ∼**ery** *n* Spott *m*

'**mock-up** *n* Modell *nt*

modal /'məʊdl/ *a* ∼ **auxiliary** Modalverb *nt*

mode /məʊd/ *n* [Art und] Weise *f*; *(fashion)* Mode *f*

model /'mɒdl/ *n* Modell *nt*; *(example)* Vorbild *nt*; **[fashion]** ∼ Mannequin *nt* □ *a* Modell-; *(exemplary)* Muster- □ *v* (*pt*/*pp* **modelled**) □ *vt* formen, modellieren; vorführen *(clothes)* □ *vi* Mannequin sein; *(for artist)* Modell stehen

moderate¹ /'mɒdəreıt/ *vt* mäßigen □ *vi* sich mäßigen

moderate² /'mɒdərət/ *a* mäßig; *(opinion)* gemäßigt □ *n* *(Pol)* Gemäßigte(r) *m*/*f*. ∼**ly** *adv* mäßig; *(fairly)* einigermaßen

moderation /mɒdə'reıʃn/ *n* Mäßigung *f*; **in** ∼ mit Maß[en]

modern /'mɒdn/ *a* modern. ∼**ize** *vt* modernisieren. ∼ '**languages** *npl* neuere Sprachen *pl*

modest /'mɒdıst/ *a* bescheiden; *(decorous)* schamhaft. ∼**y** *n* Bescheidenheit *f*

modicum /'mɒdıkəm/ *n* **a** ∼ **of** ein bisschen

modif|ication /mɒdıfı'keıʃn/ *n* Abänderung *f*. ∼**y** /'mɒdıfaı/ *vt* (*pt*/*pp* **-fied**) abändern

modulate /'mɒdjʊleıt/ *vt*/*i* modulieren

moist /mɔıst/ *a* (**-er, -est**) feucht

moisten /'mɔısn/ *vt* befeuchten

moistur|e /'mɔıstʃə(r)/ *n* Feuchtigkeit *f*. ∼**izer** *n* Feuchtigkeitscreme *f*

molar /'məʊlə(r)/ *n* Backenzahn *m*

molasses /mə'læsız/ *n* *(Amer)* Sirup *m*

mole¹ /məʊl/ *n* Leberfleck *m*

mole² *n* *(Zool)* Maulwurf *m*

mole³ *n* *(breakwater)* Mole *f*

molecule /'mɒlıkjuːl/ *n* Molekül *nt*

'**molehill** *n* Maulwurfshaufen *m*

molest /mə'lest/ *vt* belästigen

mollify /'mɒlıfaı/ *vt* (*pt*/*pp* **-ied**) besänftigen

mollusc /'mɒləsk/ *n* Weichtier *nt*

mollycoddle /'mɒlıkɒdl/ *vt* verzärteln

molten /'məʊltən/ *a* geschmolzen

mom /mɒm/ *n* *(Amer fam)* Mutti *f*

moment /'məʊmənt/ *n* Moment *m*, Augenblick *m*; **at the** ∼ im Augenblick, augenblicklich. ∼**ary** *a* vorübergehend

momentous /mə'mentəs/ *a* bedeutsam

momentum /mə'mentəm/ *n* Schwung *m*

monarch /'mɒnək/ *n* Monarch(in) *m(f)*. ∼**y** *n* Monarchie *f*

monast|ery /'mɒnəstrı/ *n* Kloster *nt*. ∼**ic** /mə'næstık/ *a* Kloster-

Monday /'mʌndeı/ *n* Montag *m*

money /'mʌnı/ *n* Geld *nt*

money: ∼-**box** *n* Sparbüchse *f*. ∼-**lender** *n* Geldverleiher *m*. ∼ **order** *n* Zahlungsanweisung *f*

mongrel /'mʌŋgrəl/ *n* Promenadenmischung *f*

monitor /'mɒnıtə(r)/ *n* *(Techn)* Monitor *m* □ *vt* überwachen *(progress)*; abhören *(broadcast)*

monk /mʌŋk/ *n* Mönch *m*

monkey /'mʌŋkı/ *n* Affe *m*. ∼-**nut** *n* Erdnuss *f*. ∼-**wrench** *n* *(Techn)* Engländer *m*

mono /'mɒnəʊ/ *n* Mono *nt*

monocle /'mɒnəkl/ *n* Monokel *nt*

monogram /'mɒnəgræm/ *n* Monogramm *nt*

monologue /'mɒnəlɒg/ *n* Monolog *m*

monopol|ize /mə'nɒpəlaız/ *vt* monopolisieren. ∼**y** *n* Monopol *nt*

monosyll|abic /mɒnəsı'læbık/ *a* einsilbig. ∼**able** /'mɒnəsıləbl/ *n* einsilbiges Wort *nt*

monotone /'mɒnətəʊn/ *n* **in a** ∼ mit monotoner Stimme

monoton|ous /mə'nɒtənəs/ *a*, -**ly** *adv* eintönig, monoton; *(tedious)* langweilig. ∼**y** *n* Eintönigkeit *f*, Monotonie *f*

monsoon /mɒn'suːn/ *n* Monsun *m*

monster /'mɒnstə(r)/ *n* Ungeheuer *nt*; *(cruel person)* Unmensch *m*

monstrosity /mɒn'strɒsətı/ *n* Monstrosität *f*

monstrous /'mɒnstrəs/ *a* ungeheuer; *(outrageous)* ungeheuerlich

montage /mɒn'tɑːʒ/ *n* Montage *f*

month /mʌnθ/ *n* Monat *m*. ∼**ly** *a* & *adv* monatlich □ *n* *(periodical)* Monatszeitschrift *f*

monument /'mɒnjʊmənt/ *n* Denkmal *nt*. **~al** /-'mentl/ *a* (*fig*) monumental

moo /muː/ *n* Muh *nt* □ *vi* (*pt/pp* mooed) muhen

mooch /muːtʃ/ *vi* **~ about** (*fam*) herumschleichen

mood /muːd/ *n* Laune *f*; **be in a good/bad ~** gute/schlechte Laune haben

moody /'muːdɪ/ *a* (-ier, -iest) launisch

moon /muːn/ *n* Mond *m*; **over the ~** (*fam*) überglücklich

moon: ~light *n* Mondschein *m*. **~lighting** *n* (*fam*) ≈ Schwarzarbeit *f*. **~lit** *a* mondhell

moor[1] /mʊə(r)/ *n* Moor *nt*

moor[2] *vt* (*Naut*) festmachen □ *vi* anlegen. **~ings** *npl* (*chains*) Verankerung *f*; (*place*) Anlegestelle *f*

moose /muːs/ *n* Elch *m*

moot /muːt/ *a* **it's a ~ point** darüber lässt sich streiten □ *vt* aufwerfen ⟨*question*⟩

mop /mɒp/ *n* Mopp *m*; **~ of hair** Wuschelkopf *m* □ *vt* (*pt/pp* mopped) wischen. **~ up** *vt* aufwischen

mope /məʊp/ *vi* Trübsal blasen

moped /'məʊped/ *n* Moped *nt*

moral /'mɒrl/ *a*, **-ly** *adv* moralisch, sittlich; (*virtuous*) tugendhaft □ *n* Moral *f*; **~s** *pl* Moral *f*

morale /məˈrɑːl/ *n* Moral *f*

morality /məˈrælətɪ/ *n* Sittlichkeit *f*

moralize /'mɒrəlaɪz/ *vi* moralisieren

morbid /'mɔːbɪd/ *a* krankhaft; (*gloomy*) trübe

more /mɔː(r)/ *a, adv & n* mehr; (*in addition*) noch; **a few ~** noch ein paar; **any ~** noch etwas; **once ~** noch einmal; **~ or less** mehr oder weniger; **some ~ tea?** noch etwas Tee? **~ interesting** interessanter; **~ [and ~] quickly** [immer] schneller; **no ~, thank you,** nichts mehr, danke; **no ~ bread** kein Brot mehr; **no ~ apples** keine Äpfel mehr

moreover /mɔːˈrəʊvə(r)/ *adv* außerdem

morgue /mɔːg/ *n* Leichenschauhaus *nt*

moribund /'mɒrɪbʌnd/ *a* sterbend

morning /'mɔːnɪŋ/ *n* Morgen *m*; **in the ~** morgens, am Morgen; (*tomorrow*) morgen früh

Morocco /məˈrɒkəʊ/ *n* Marokko *nt*

moron /'mɔːrɒn/ *n* (*fam*) Idiot *m*

morose /məˈrəʊs/ *a*, **-ly** *adv* mürrisch

morphine /'mɔːfiːn/ *n* Morphium *nt*

Morse /mɔːs/ *n* **~ [code]** Morsealphabet *nt*

morsel /'mɔːsl/ *n* (*food*) Happen *m*

mortal /'mɔːtl/ *a* sterblich; (*fatal*) tödlich □ *n* Sterbliche(r) *m/f*. **~ity** /mɔːˈtælətɪ/ *n* Sterblichkeit *f*. **~ly** *adv* tödlich

mortar /'mɔːtə(r)/ *n* Mörtel *m*

mortgage /'mɔːgɪdʒ/ *n* Hypothek *f* □ *vt* hypothekarisch belasten

mortify /'mɔːtɪfaɪ/ *vt* (*pt/pp* -ied) demütigen

mortuary /'mɔːtjʊərɪ/ *n* Leichenhalle *f*; (*public*) Leichenschauhaus *nt*; (*Amer: undertaker's*) Bestattungsinstitut *nt*

mosaic /məʊˈzeɪɪk/ *n* Mosaik *nt*

Moscow /'mɒskəʊ/ *n* Moskau *nt*

Moselle /məʊˈzel/ *n* Mosel *f*; (*wine*) Moselwein *m*

mosque /mɒsk/ *n* Moschee *f*

mosquito /mɒsˈkiːtəʊ/ *n* (*pl* -es) [Stech]mücke *f*, Schnake *f*; (*tropical*) Moskito *m*

moss /mɒs/ *n* Moos *nt*. **~y** *a* moosig

most /məʊst/ *a* der/die/das meiste; (*majority*) die meisten; **for the ~ part** zum größten Teil □ *adv* am meisten; (*very*) höchst; **the ~ interesting day** der interessanteste Tag; **~ unlikely** höchst unwahrscheinlich □ *n* das meiste; **~ of them** die meisten [von ihnen]; **at [the] ~** höchstens; **~ of the time** die meiste Zeit. **~ly** *adv* meist

MOT *n* ≈ TÜV *m*

motel /məʊˈtel/ *n* Motel *nt*

moth /mɒθ/ *n* Nachtfalter *m*; **[clothes-]~** Motte *f*

moth: ~ball *n* Mottenkugel *f*. **~eaten** *a* mottenzerfressen

mother /'mʌðə(r)/ *n* Mutter *f*; **M~'s Day** Muttertag *m* □ *vt* bemuttern

mother: ~hood *n* Mutterschaft *f*. **~-in-law** *n* (*pl* ~s-in-law) Schwiegermutter *f*. **~land** *n* Mutterland *nt*. **~ly** *a* mütterlich. **~-of-pearl** *n* Perlmutter *f*. **~-to-be** *n* werdende Mutter *f*. **~ tongue** *n* Muttersprache *f*

mothproof /'mɒθ-/ *a* mottenfest

motif /məʊˈtiːf/ *n* Motiv *nt*

motion /'məʊʃn/ *n* Bewegung *f*; (*proposal*) Antrag *m* □ *vt/i* **~ [to] s.o.** jdm ein Zeichen geben (**to** zu). **~less** *a*, **-ly** *adv* bewegungslos

motivat|e /'məʊtɪveɪt/ *vt* motivieren. **~ion** /-'veɪʃn/ *n* Motivation *f*

motive /'məʊtɪv/ *n* Motiv *nt*

motley /'mɒtlɪ/ *a* bunt

motor /'məʊtə(r)/ *n* Motor *m*; (*car*) Auto *nt* □ *a* Motor-; (*Anat*) motorisch □ *vi* [mit dem Auto] fahren

Motorail /'məʊtəreɪl/ *n* Autozug *m*

motor: ~ bike *n* (*fam*) Motorrad *nt*. **~ boat** *n* Motorboot *nt*. **~cade** /-keɪd/ *n* (*Amer*) Autokolonne *f*. **~ car** *n* Auto *nt*,

Wagen *m*. ∼ **cycle** *n* Motorrad *nt*. ∼**cyclist** *n* Motorradfahrer *m*. ∼**ing** *n* Autofahren *nt*. ∼**ist** *n* Autofahrer(in) *m(f)*. ∼**ize** *vt* motorisieren. ∼ **vehicle** *n* Kraftfahrzeug *nt*. ∼**way** *n* Autobahn *f*

mottled /'mɒtld/ *a* gesprenkelt

motto /'mɒtəʊ/ *n* (*pl* -**es**) Motto *nt*

mould[1] /məʊld/ *n* (*fungus*) Schimmel *m*

mould[2] *n* Form *f* □ *vt* formen (**into** zu). ∼**ing** *n* (*Archit*) Fries *m*

mouldy /'məʊldɪ/ *a* schimmelig; (*fam: worthless*) schäbig

moult /məʊlt/ *vi* ⟨*bird:*⟩ sich mausern; ⟨*animal:*⟩ sich haaren

mound /maʊnd/ *n* Hügel *m*; (*of stones*) Haufen *m*

mount[1] /maʊnt/ *n* Berg *m*

mount[2] *n* (*animal*) Reittier *nt*; (*of jewel*) Fassung *f*; (*of photo, picture*) Passepartout *nt* □ *vt* (*get on*) steigen auf (+ *acc*); (*on pedestal*) montieren auf (+ *acc*); besteigen ⟨*horse*⟩; fassen ⟨*jewel*⟩; aufzielen ⟨*photo, picture*⟩ □ *vi* aufsteigen; (*increase*) steigen. ∼ **up** *vi* sich häufen; (*add up*) sich anhäufen; (*increase*) steigen

mountain /'maʊntɪn/ *n* Berg *m*

mountaineer /maʊntɪ'nɪə(r)/ *n* Bergsteiger(in) *m(f)*. ∼**ing** *n* Bergsteigen *nt*

mountainous /'maʊntɪnəs/ *a* bergig, gebirgig

mourn /mɔːn/ *vt* betrauern □ *vi* trauern (**for** um). ∼**er** *n* Trauernde(r) *m/f*. ∼**ful** *a*, -**ly** *adv* trauervoll. ∼**ing** *n* Trauer *f*

mouse /maʊs/ *n* (*pl* **mice**) Maus *f*. ∼**trap** *n* Mausefalle *f*

mousse /muːs/ *n* Schaum *m*; (*Culin*) Mousse *f*

moustache /mə'stɑːʃ/ *n* Schnurrbart *m*

mousy /'maʊsɪ/ *a* graubraun; ⟨*person*⟩ farblos

mouth[1] /maʊð/ *vt* ∼ **sth** etw lautlos mit den Lippen sagen

mouth[2] /maʊθ/ *n* Mund *m*; (*of animal*) Maul *nt*; (*of river*) Mündung *f*

mouth- ∼**ful** *n* Mundvoll *m*; (*bite*) Bissen *m*. ∼**organ** *n* Mundharmonika *f*. ∼**piece** *n* Mundstück *nt*; (*fig: person*) Sprachrohr *nt*. ∼**wash** *n* Mundwasser *nt*

movable /'muːvəbl/ *a* beweglich

move /muːv/ *n* Bewegung *f*; (*fig*) Schritt *m*; (*moving house*) Umzug *m*; (*in board-game*) Zug *m*; **on the** ∼ unterwegs; **get a** ∼ **on** (*fam*) sich beeilen □ *vt* bewegen; (*emotionally*) rühren; (*move along*) rücken; (*in board-game*) ziehen; (*take away*) wegnehmen; wegfahren ⟨*car*⟩; (*rearrange*) umstellen; (*transfer*) versetzen ⟨*person*⟩; verlegen ⟨*office*⟩; (*propose*) beantragen; ∼ **house** umziehen □ *vi* sich bewegen; (*move*

house) umziehen; **don't** ∼! stillhalten! (*stop*) stillstehen! ∼ **along** *vt/i* weiterrücken. ∼ **away** *vt/i* wegrücken; (*move house*) wegziehen. ∼ **forward** *vt/i* vorrücken; ⟨*vehicle*⟩ vorwärts fahren. ∼ **in** *vi* einziehen. ∼ **off** *vi* ⟨*vehicle:*⟩ losfahren. ∼ **out** *vi* ausziehen. ∼ **over** *vt/i* [zur Seite] rücken. ∼ **up** *vi* aufrücken

movement /'muːvmənt/ *n* Bewegung *f*; (*Mus*) Satz *m*; (*of clock*) Uhrwerk *nt*

movie /'muːvɪ/ *n* (*Amer*) Film *m*; **go to the** ∼**s** ins Kino gehen

moving /'muːvɪŋ/ *a* beweglich; (*touching*) rührend

mow /məʊ/ *vt* (*pt* **mowed**, *pp* **mown** or **mowed**) mähen. ∼ **down** *vt* (*destroy*) niedermähen

mower /'məʊə(r)/ *n* Rasenmäher *m*

MP *abbr see* **Member of Parliament**

Mr /'mɪstə(r)/ *n* (*pl* **Messrs**) Herr *m*

Mrs /'mɪsɪz/ *n* Frau *f*

Ms /mɪz/ *n* Frau *f*

much /mʌtʃ/ *a, adv & n* viel; **as** ∼ **as** so viel wie; **very** ∼ **loved/interested** sehr geliebt/interessiert

muck /mʌk/ *n* Mist *m*; (*fam: filth*) Dreck *m*. ∼ **about** *vi* herumalbern; (*tinker*) herumspielen (**with** mit). ∼ **in** *vt* (*fam*) mitmachen. ∼ **out** *vt* ausmisten. ∼ **up** *vt* (*fam*) vermasseln; (*make dirty*) schmutzig machen

mucky /'mʌkɪ/ *a* (-**ier**, -**iest**) dreckig

mucus /'mjuːkəs/ *n* Schleim *m*

mud /mʌd/ *n* Schlamm *m*

muddle /'mʌdl/ *n* Durcheinander *nt*; (*confusion*) Verwirrung *f* □ *vt* ∼ [**up**] durcheinander bringen

muddy /'mʌdɪ/ *a* (-**ier**, -**iest**) schlammig; ⟨*shoes*⟩ schmutzig

'mudguard *n* Kotflügel *m*; (*on bicycle*) Schutzblech *nt*

muesli /'muːzlɪ/ *n* Müsli *nt*

muff /mʌf/ *n* Muff *m*

muffle /'mʌfl/ *vt* dämpfen ⟨*sound*⟩; ∼ [**up**] (*for warmth*) einhüllen (**in** in + *acc*)

muffler /'mʌflə(r)/ *n* Schal *m*; (*Amer, Auto*) Auspufftopf *m*

mufti /'mʌftɪ/ *n* **in** ∼ in Zivil

mug[1] /mʌg/ *n* Becher *m*; (*for beer*) Bierkrug *m*; (*fam: face*) Visage *f*; (*fam: simpleton*) Trottel *m*

mug[2] *vt* (*pt/pp* **mugged**) überfallen. ∼**ger** *n* Straßenräuber *m*. ∼**ging** *n* Straßenraub *m*

muggy /'mʌgɪ/ *a* (-**ier**, -**iest**) schwül

mule[1] /mjuːl/ *n* Maultier *nt*

mule[2] *n* (*slipper*) Pantoffel *m*

mull /mʌl/ *vt* ∼ **over** nachdenken über (+ *acc*)

mulled /mʌld/ *a* ∼ **wine** Glühwein *m*

multi /'mʌltɪ/: ~coloured a vielfarbig, bunt. ~lingual /-'lɪŋgwəl/ a mehrsprachig. ~'national a multinational

multiple /'mʌltɪpl/ a vielfach; (with pl) mehrere □ n Vielfache(s) nt

multiplication /mʌltɪplɪ'keɪʃn/ n Multiplikation f

multiply /'mʌltɪplaɪ/ v (pt/pp -ied) □ vt multiplizieren (by mit) □ vi sich vermehren

multi-storey a ~ car park Parkhaus nt

mum¹ /mʌm/ a keep ~ (fam) den Mund halten

mum² n (fam) Mutti f

mumble /'mʌmbl/ vt/i murmeln

mummy¹ /'mʌmɪ/ n (fam) Mutti f

mummy² n (Archaeol) Mumie f

mumps /mʌmps/ n Mumps m

munch /mʌntʃ/ vt/i mampfen

mundane /mʌn'deɪn/ a banal; (worldly) weltlich

municipal /mju:'nɪsɪpl/ a städtisch

munitions /mju:'nɪʃnz/ npl Kriegsmaterial nt

mural /'mjʊərəl/ n Wandgemälde nt

murder /'mɜːdə(r)/ n Mord m □ vt ermorden; (fam: ruin) verhunzen. ~er n Mörder m. ~ess n Mörderin f. ~ous /-rəs/ a mörderisch

murky /'mɜːkɪ/ a (-ier, -iest) düster

murmur /'mɜːmə(r)/ n Murmeln nt □ vt/i murmeln

muscle /'mʌsl/ n Muskel m

muscular /'mʌskjʊlə(r)/ a Muskel-; (strong) muskulös

muse /mju:z/ vi nachsinnen (on über + acc)

museum /mju:'zɪəm/ n Museum nt

mush /mʌʃ/ n Brei m

mushroom /'mʌʃrʊm/ n [essbarer] Pilz m, esp Champignon m □ vi (fig) wie Pilze aus dem Boden schießen

mushy /'mʌʃɪ/ a breiig

music /'mju:zɪk/ n Musik f; (written) Noten pl; set to ~ vertonen

musical /'mju:zɪkl/ a musikalisch □ n Musical nt. ~ box n Spieldose f. ~ instrument Musikinstrument nt

'music-hall n Varieté nt

musician /mju:'zɪʃn/ n Musiker(in) m(f)

'music-stand n Notenständer m

Muslim /'mʊzlɪm/ a mohammedanisch □ n Mohammedaner(in) m(f)

muslin /'mʌzlɪn/ n Musselin m

mussel /'mʌsl/ n [Mies]muschel f

must /mʌst/ v aux (nur Präsens) müssen; (with negative) dürfen □ n a ~ (fam) ein Muss nt

mustard /'mʌstəd/ n Senf m

muster /'mʌstə(r)/ vt versammeln; aufbringen ⟨strength⟩ □ vi sich versammeln

musty /'mʌstɪ/ a (-ier, -iest) muffig

mutation /mju:'teɪʃn/ n Veränderung f; (Biol) Mutation f

mute /mju:t/ a stumm

muted /'mju:tɪd/ a gedämpft

mutilat|e /'mju:tɪleɪt/ vt verstümmeln. ~ion /-'leɪʃn/ n Verstümmelung f

mutin|ous /'mju:tɪnəs/ a meuterisch. ~y n Meuterei f □ vi (pt/pp -ied) meutern

mutter /'mʌtə(r)/ n Murmeln nt □ vt/i murmeln

mutton /'mʌtn/ n Hammelfleisch nt

mutual /'mju:tjʊəl/ a gegenseitig; (fam: common) gemeinsam. ~ly adv gegenseitig

muzzle /'mʌzl/ n (of animal) Schnauze f; (of firearm) Mündung f; (for dog) Maulkorb m □ vt einen Maulkorb anlegen (+ dat)

my /maɪ/ a mein

myopic /maɪ'ɒpɪk/ a kurzsichtig

myself /maɪ'self/ pron selbst; (refl) mich; by ~ allein; I thought to ~ ich habe mir gedacht

mysterious /mɪ'stɪərɪəs/ a, -ly adv geheimnisvoll; (puzzling) mysteriös, rätselhaft

mystery /'mɪstərɪ/ n Geheimnis nt; (puzzle) Rätsel nt; ~ [story] Krimi m

mysti|c[al] /'mɪstɪk[l]/ a mystisch. ~cism /-sɪzm/ n Mystik f

mystification /mɪstɪfɪ'keɪʃn/ n Verwunderung f

mystified /'mɪstɪfaɪd/ a be ~ vor einem Rätsel stehen

mystique /mɪ'sti:k/ n geheimnisvoller Zauber m

myth /mɪθ/ n Mythos m; (fam: untruth) Märchen nt. ~ical a mythisch; (fig) erfunden

mythology /mɪ'θɒlədʒɪ/ n Mythologie f

N

nab /næb/ vt (pt/pp nabbed) (fam) erwischen

nag¹ /næg/ n (horse) Gaul m

nag² vt/i (pp/pp nagged) herumnörgeln (s.o. an jdm). ~ging a (pain) nagend □ n Nörgelei f

nail /neɪl/ n (*Anat, Techn*) Nagel m; **on the ∼** (*fam*) sofort ◻ vt nageln (**to** an + *acc*). **∼ down** vt festnageln; (*close*) zunageln

nail: ∼-brush n Nagelbürste f. **∼-file** n Nagelfeile f. **∼ polish** n Nagellack m. **∼ scissors** npl Nagelschere f. **∼ varnish** n Nagellack m

naïve /naɪˈiːv/ a, **-ly** adv naiv. **∼ty** /-əti/ n Naivität f

naked /ˈneɪkɪd/ a nackt; (*flame*) offen; **with the ∼ eye** mit bloßem Auge. **∼ness** n Nacktheit f

name /neɪm/ n Name m; (*reputation*) Ruf m; **by ∼** dem Namen nach; **by the ∼ of** namens; **call s.o. ∼s** (*fam*) jdn beschimpfen ◻ vt nennen; (*give a name to*) einen Namen geben (+ *dat*); (*announce publicly*) den Namen bekannt geben von. **∼less** a namenlos. **∼ly** adv nämlich

name: ∼-plate n Namensschild nt. **∼sake** n Namensvetter m/Namensschwester f

nanny /ˈnænɪ/ n Kindermädchen nt. **∼-goat** n Ziege f

nap /næp/ n Nickerchen nt; **have a ∼** ein Nickerchen machen ◻ vi **catch s.o. ∼ping** jdn überrumpeln

nape /neɪp/ n **[of the neck]** Nacken m

napkin /ˈnæpkɪn/ n Serviette f; (*for baby*) Windel f

nappy /ˈnæpɪ/ n Windel f

narcotic /nɑːˈkɒtɪk/ a betäubend ◻ n Narkotikum nt; (*drug*) Rauschgift nt

narrat|e /nəˈreɪt/ vt erzählen. **∼ion** /-eɪʃn/ n Erzählung f

narrative /ˈnærətɪv/ a erzählend ◻ n Erzählung f

narrator /nəˈreɪtə(r)/ n Erzähler(in) m(f)

narrow /ˈnærəʊ/ a (**-er, -est**) schmal; (*restricted*) eng; (*margin, majority*) knapp; (*fig*) beschränkt; **have a ∼ escape**, adv **∼ly escape** mit knapper Not davonkommen ◻ vi sich verengen. **∼-minded** a engstirnig

nasal /ˈneɪzl/ a nasal; (*Med & Anat*) Nasen-

nastily /ˈnɑːstɪlɪ/ adv boshaft

nasturtium /nəˈstɜːʃəm/ n Kapuzinerkresse f

nasty /ˈnɑːstɪ/ a (**-ier, -iest**) übel; (*unpleasant*) unangenehm; (*unkind*) boshaft; (*serious*) schlimm; **turn ∼** gemein werden

nation /ˈneɪʃn/ n Nation f; (*people*) Volk nt

national /ˈnæʃənl/ a national; (*newspaper*) überregional; (*campaign*) landesweit ◻ n Staatsbürger(in) m(f)

national: ∼ 'anthem n Nationalhymne f. **N∼ 'Health Service** n staatlicher Gesundheitsdienst m. **N∼ In'surance** n Sozialversicherung f

nationalism /ˈnæʃənəlɪzm/ n Nationalismus m

nationality /næʃəˈnælətɪ/ n Staatsangehörigkeit f

national|ization /næʃənəlaɪˈzeɪʃn/ n Verstaatlichung f. **∼ize** /ˈnæʃənəlaɪz/ vt verstaatlichen. **∼ly** /ˈnæʃənəlɪ/ adv landesweit

'nation-wide a landesweit

native /ˈneɪtɪv/ a einheimisch; (*innate*) angeboren ◻ n Eingeborene(r) m/f; (*local inhabitant*) Einheimische(r) m/f; **a ∼ of Vienna** ein gebürtiger Wiener

native: ∼ 'land n Heimatland nt. **∼ 'language** n Muttersprache f

Nativity /nəˈtɪvətɪ/ n **the ∼** Christi Geburt f. **∼ play** n Krippenspiel nt

natter /ˈnætə(r)/ n **have a ∼** (*fam*) einen Schwatz halten ◻ vi (*fam*) schwatzen

natural /ˈnætʃrəl/ a, **-ly** adv natürlich; **∼[-coloured]** naturfarben

natural: ∼ 'gas n Erdgas nt. **∼ 'history** n Naturkunde f

naturalist /ˈnætʃrəlɪst/ n Naturforscher m

natural|ization /nætʃrəlaɪˈzeɪʃn/ n Einbürgerung f. **∼ize** /ˈnætʃrəlaɪz/ vt einbürgern

nature /ˈneɪtʃə(r)/ n Natur f; (*kind*) Art f; **by ∼** von Natur aus. **∼ reserve** n Naturschutzgebiet nt

naturism /ˈneɪtʃərɪzm/ n Freikörperkultur f

naught /nɔːt/ n = **nought**

naughty /ˈnɔːtɪ/ a (**-ier, -iest**), **-ily** adv unartig; (*slightly indecent*) gewagt

nausea /ˈnɔːzɪə/ n Übelkeit f

nause|ate /ˈnɔːzɪeɪt/ vt anekeln. **∼ating** a ekelhaft. **∼ous** /-ɪəs/ a **I feel ∼ous** mir ist übel

nautical /ˈnɔːtɪkl/ a nautisch. **∼ mile** n Seemeile f

naval /ˈneɪvl/ a Marine-

nave /neɪv/ n Kirchenschiff nt

navel /ˈneɪvl/ n Nabel m

navigable /ˈnævɪgəbl/ a schiffbar

navigat|e /ˈnævɪgeɪt/ vi navigieren ◻ vt befahren (*river*). **∼ion** /-ˈgeɪʃn/ n Navigation f. **∼or** n Navigator m

navvy /ˈnævɪ/ n Straßenarbeiter m

navy /ˈneɪvɪ/ n [Kriegs]marine f ◻ a **∼ [blue]** marineblau

near /nɪə(r)/ a (**-er, -est**) nah[e]; **the ∼est bank** die nächste Bank ◻ adv nahe; **∼ by** nicht weit weg; **∼ at hand** in der Nähe; **draw ∼** sich nähern ◻ prep nahe an (+ *dat*/*acc*); in der Nähe von; **∼ to tears** den Tränen nahe; **go ∼ [to] sth** nahe an etw (*acc*) herangehen ◻ vt sich nähern (+ *dat*)

near: ∼**by** a nahe gelegen, nahe liegend □ adv /-'-/ nicht weit weg. ∼**ly** adv fast, beinahe; **not** ∼**ly** bei weitem nicht. ∼**ness** n Nähe f. ∼ **side** n Beifahrerseite f. ∼**sighted** a (Amer) kurzsichtig

neat /niːt/ a (-er, -est), -ly adv adrett; (tidy) ordentlich; (clever) geschickt; (undiluted) pur. ∼**ness** n Ordentlichkeit f

necessarily /'nesəserəlɪ/ adv notwendigerweise; **not** ∼ nicht unbedingt

necessary /'nesəsərɪ/ a nötig, notwendig

necessit|ate /nɪ'sesɪteɪt/ vt notwendig machen. ∼**y** n Notwendigkeit f; **she works from** ∼**y** sie arbeitet, weil sie es nötig hat

neck /nek/ n Hals m; ∼ **and** ∼ Kopf an Kopf

necklace /'neklɪs/ n Halskette f

neck: ∼**line** n Halsausschnitt m. ∼**tie** n Schlips m

nectar /'nektə(r)/ n Nektar m

née /neɪ/ a ∼ **Brett** geborene Brett

need /niːd/ n Bedürfnis nt; (misfortune) Not f; **be in** ∼ Not leiden; **be in** ∼ **of** brauchen; **in case of** ∼ notfalls; **if** ∼ **be** wenn nötig; **there is a** ∼ **for** es besteht ein Bedarf an (+ dat); **there is no** ∼ **for that** das ist nicht nötig; **there is no** ∼ **for you to go** du brauchst nicht zu gehen □ vt brauchen; **you** ∼ **not go** du brauchst nicht zu gehen; ∼ **I come?** muss ich kommen? **I** ∼ **to know** ich muss es wissen; **it** ∼**s to be done** es muss gemacht werden

needle /'niːdl/ n Nadel f □ vt (annoy) ärgern

needless /'niːdlɪs/ a, -ly adv unnötig; ∼ **to say** selbstverständlich, natürlich

'needlework n Nadelarbeit f

needy /'niːdɪ/ a (-ier, -iest) bedürftig

negation /nɪ'geɪʃn/ n Verneinung f

negative /'negətɪv/ a negativ □ n Verneinung f; (photo) Negativ nt

neglect /nɪ'glekt/ n Vernachlässigung f; **state of** ∼ verwahrloster Zustand m □ vt vernachlässigen; (omit) versäumen (**to** zu). ∼**ed** a verwahrlost. ∼**ful** a nachlässig; **be** ∼**ful of** vernachlässigen

negligen|ce /'neglɪdʒəns/ n Nachlässigkeit f; (Jur) Fahrlässigkeit f. ∼**t** a, -ly adv nachlässig; (Jur) fahrlässig

negligible /'neglɪdʒəbl/ a unbedeutend

negotiable /nɪ'gəʊʃəbl/ a (road) befahrbar; (Comm) unverbindlich; **not** ∼ nicht übertragbar

negotiat|e /nɪ'gəʊʃɪeɪt/ vt aushandeln; (Auto) nehmen (bend) □ vi verhandeln. ∼**ion** /-'eɪʃn/ n Verhandlung f. ∼**or** n Unterhändler(in) m(f)

Negro /'niːgrəʊ/ a Neger- □ n (pl -es) Neger m

neigh /neɪ/ vi wiehern

neighbour /'neɪbə(r)/ n Nachbar(in) m(f). ∼**hood** n Nachbarschaft f; **in the** ∼**hood of** in der Nähe von; (fig) um ... herum. ∼**ing** a Nachbar-. ∼**ly** a [gut]nachbarlich

neither /'naɪðə(r)/ a & pron keine(r, s) [von beiden] □ adv ∼... **nor** weder ... noch □ conj auch nicht

neon /'niːɒn/ n Neon nt. ∼ **light** n Neonlicht nt

nephew /'nevjuː/ n Neffe m

nepotism /'nepətɪzm/ n Vetternwirtschaft f

nerve /nɜːv/ n Nerv m; (fam: courage) Mut m; (fam: impudence) Frechheit f; **lose one's** ∼ den Mut verlieren. ∼**-racking** a nervenaufreibend

nervous /'nɜːvəs/ a, -ly adv (afraid) ängstlich; (highly strung) nervös; (Anat, Med) Nerven-; **be** ∼ Angst haben. ∼ **'breakdown** n Nervenzusammenbruch m. ∼**ness** n Ängstlichkeit f; (Med) Nervosität f

nervy /'nɜːvɪ/ a (-ier, -iest) nervös; (Amer: impudent) frech

nest /nest/ n Nest nt □ vi nisten. ∼**-egg** n Notgroschen m

nestle /'nesl/ vi sich schmiegen (**against** an + acc)

net¹ /net/ n Netz nt; (curtain) Store m □ vt (pt/pp netted) (catch) [mit dem Netz] fangen

net² a netto; (salary, weight) Netto- □ vt (pt/pp netted) netto einnehmen; (yield) einbringen

'netball n ≈ Korbball m

Netherlands /'neðələndz/ npl **the** ∼ die Niederlande pl

netting /'netɪŋ/ n [wire] ∼ Maschendraht m

nettle /'netl/ n Nessel f

'network n Netz nt

neuralgia /njʊə'rældʒə/ n Neuralgie f

neurolog|ist /njʊə'rɒlədʒɪst/ n Neurologe m/ -gin f. ∼**y** n Neurologie f

neur|osis /njʊə'rəʊsɪs/ n (pl -oses /-siːz/) Neurose f. ∼**otic** /-'rɒtɪk/ a neurotisch

neuter /'njuːtə(r)/ a (Gram) sächlich □ n (Gram) Neutrum nt □ vt kastrieren; (spay) sterilisieren

neutral /'njuːtrl/ a neutral □ n **in** ∼ (Auto) im Leerlauf. ∼**ity** /-'trælətɪ/ n Neutralität f. ∼**ize** vt neutralisieren

never /'nevə(r)/ adv nie, niemals; (fam: not) nicht; ∼ **mind** macht nichts; **well I** ∼! ja so was! ∼**ending** a endlos

nevertheless /nevəðə'les/ *adv* dennoch, trotzdem

new /nju:/ *a* (**-er, -est**) neu

new: ~**born** *a* neugeboren. ~**comer** *n* Neuankömmling *m*. ~**fangled** /-'fæŋgld/ *a* (*pej*) neumodisch. ~**laid** *a* frisch gelegt

'**newly** *adv* frisch. ~**weds** *npl* Jung-verheiratete *pl*

new: ~ '**moon** *n* Neumond *m*. ~**ness** *n* Neuheit *f*

news /nju:z/ *n* Nachricht *f*; (*Radio, TV*) Nachrichten *pl*; **piece of** ~ Neuigkeit *f*

news: ~**agent** *n* Zeitungshändler *m*. ~**bulletin** *n* Nachrichtensendung *f*. ~**caster** *n* Nachrichtensprecher(in) *m(f)*. ~**flash** *n* Kurzmeldung *f*. ~**letter** *n* Mit-teilungsblatt *nt*. ~**paper** *n* Zeitung *f*; (*material*) Zeitungspapier *nt*. ~**reader** *n* Nachrichtensprecher(in) *m(f)*

newt /nju:t/ *n* Molch *m*

New: ~ **Year's** '**Day** *n* Neujahr *nt*. ~ **Year's** '**Eve** *n* Silvester *nt*. ~ **Zealand** /'zi:lənd/ *n* Neuseeland *nt*

next /nekst/ *a & n* nächste(r, s); **who's** ~? wer kommt als Nächster dran? **the** ~ **best** das nächstbeste; ~ **door** nebenan; **my** ~ **of kin** mein nächster Verwandter; ~ **to nothing** fast gar nichts; **the week after** ~ übernächste Woche □ *adv* als Nächstes; ~ **to** neben

NHS *abbr see* **National Health Service**

nib /nɪb/ *n* Feder *f*

nibble /'nɪbl/ *vt/i* knabbern (**at** an + *dat*)

nice /naɪs/ *a* (**-r, -st**) nett; (*day, weather*) schön; (*food*) gut; (*distinction*) fein. ~**ly** *adv* nett; (*well*) gut. ~**ties** /'naɪsətɪz/ *npl* Feinheiten *pl*

niche /ni:ʃ/ *n* Nische *f*; (*fig*) Platz *m*

nick /nɪk/ *n* Kerbe *f*; (*fam: prison*) Knast *m*; (*fam: police station*) Revier *nt*; **in the** ~ **of time** (*fam*) gerade noch rechtzeitig; **in good** ~ (*fam*) in gutem Zustand □ *vt* einkerben; (*steal*) klauen; (*fam: arrest*) schnappen

nickel /'nɪkl/ *n* Nickel *nt*; (*Amer*) Fünfcentstück *nt*

'**nickname** *n* Spitzname *m*

nicotine /'nɪkəti:n/ *n* Nikotin *nt*

niece /ni:s/ *n* Nichte *f*

Nigeria /naɪ'dʒɪərɪə/ *n* Nigeria *nt*. ~**n** *a* nigerianisch □ *n* Nigerianer(in) *m(f)*

niggardly /'nɪgədlɪ/ *a* knauserig

niggling /'nɪglɪŋ/ *a* gering; (*petty*) klein-lich; (*pain*) quälend

night /naɪt/ *n* Nacht *f*; (*evening*) Abend *m*; **at** ~ nachts; **Monday** ~ Montag Nacht/Abend

night: ~**cap** *n* Schlafmütze *f*; (*drink*) Schlaftrunk *m*. ~**club** *n* Nachtklub *m*. ~**dress** *n* Nachthemd *nt*. ~**fall** *n* **at** ~**fall** bei Einbruch der Dunkelheit. ~**gown** *n*, (*fam*) ~**ie** /'naɪtɪ/ *n* Nachthemd *nt*

nightingale /'naɪtɪŋgeɪl/ *n* Nachtigall *f*

night: ~**life** *n* Nachtleben *nt*. ~**ly** *a* nächt-lich □ *adv* jede Nacht. ~**mare** *n* Alptraum *m*. ~**shade** *n* (*Bot*) **deadly** ~**shade** Tollkirsche *f*. ~**time** *n* **at** ~**time** bei Nacht. ~**'watchman** *n* Nachtwächter *m*

nil /nɪl/ *n* null

nimble /'nɪmbl/ *a* (**-r, -st**), **-bly** *adv* flink

nine /naɪn/ *a* neun □ *n* Neun *f*. ~'**teen** *a* neunzehn. ~'**teenth** *a* neunzehnte(r, s)

ninetieth /'naɪntɪɪθ/ *a* neunzigste(r, s)

ninety /'naɪntɪ/ *a* neunzig

ninth /naɪnθ/ *a* neunte(r, s)

nip /nɪp/ *n* Kniff *m*; (*bite*) Biss *m* □ *vt* kneifen; (*bite*) beißen; ~ **in the bud** (*fig*) im Keim ersticken □ *vi* (*fam: run*) laufen

nipple /'nɪpl/ *n* Brustwarze *f*; (*Amer: on bottle*) Sauger *m*

nippy /'nɪpɪ/ *a* (**-ier, -iest**) (*fam*) (*cold*) frisch; (*quick*) flink

nitrate /'naɪtreɪt/ *n* Nitrat *nt*

nitrogen /'naɪtrədʒən/ *n* Stickstoff *m*

nitwit /'nɪtwɪt/ *n* (*fam*) Dummkopf *m*

no /nəʊ/ *adv* nein □ *n* (*pl* **noes**) Nein *nt* □ *a* kein(e); (*pl*) keine; **in no time** [sehr] schnell; **no parking/smoking** Parken/Rauchen verboten; **no one = nobody**

nobility /nəʊ'bɪlətɪ/ *n* Adel *m*

noble /'nəʊbl/ *a* (**-r, -st**) edel; (*aristocratic*) adlig. ~**man** *n* Adlige(r) *m*

nobody /'nəʊbədɪ/ *pron* niemand, keiner; **he knows** ~ er kennt niemanden *od* keinen □ *n* **a** ~ ein Niemand *m*

nocturnal /nɒk'tɜ:nl/ *a* nächtlich; (*animal, bird*) Nacht-

nod /nɒd/ *n* Nicken *nt* □ *v* (*pt/pp* **nodded**) □ *vi* nicken □ *vt* ~ **one's head** mit dem Kopf nicken. ~ **off** *vi* einnicken

nodule /'nɒdju:l/ *n* Knötchen *nt*

noise /nɔɪz/ *n* Geräusch *nt*; (*loud*) Lärm *m*. ~**less** *a*, **-ly** *adv* geräuschlos

noisy /'nɔɪzɪ/ *a* (**-ier, -iest**), **-ily** *adv* laut; (*eater*) geräuschvoll

nomad /'nəʊmæd/ *n* Nomade *m*. ~**ic** /-'mædɪk/ *a* nomadisch; (*life, tribe*) Noma-den-

nominal /'nɒmɪnl/ *a*, **-ly** *adv* nominell

nominat|e /'nɒmɪneɪt/ *vt* nominieren, aufstellen; (*appoint*) ernennen. ~**ion** /-'neɪʃn/ *n* Nominierung *f*; Ernennung *f*

nominative /'nɒmɪnətɪv/ *a & n* (*Gram*) ~ [**case**] Nominativ *m*

nonchalant /'nɒnʃələnt/ *a*, **-ly** *adv* non-chalant; (*gesture*) lässig

non-com'missioned /nɒn-/ a ~ **officer** Unteroffizier m

non-com'mittal a unverbindlich; **be ~** sich nicht festlegen

nondescript /'nɒndɪskrɪpt/ a unbestimmbar; (person) unscheinbar

none /nʌn/ pron keine(r)/keins; ~ **of us** keiner von uns; ~ **of it/this** nichts davon □ adv ~ **too** nicht gerade; ~ **too soon** [um] keine Minute zu früh; ~ **the wiser** um nichts klüger; ~ **the less** dennoch

nonentity /nɒ'nentətɪ/ n Null f

non-ex'istent a nicht vorhanden; **be ~** nicht vorhanden sein

non-'fiction n Sachliteratur f

non-'iron a bügelfrei

nonplussed /nɒn'plʌst/ a verblüfft

nonsens|e /'nɒnsəns/ n Unsinn m. ~**ical** /'-sensɪkl/ a unsinnig

non-'smoker n Nichtraucher m; (compartment) Nichtraucherabteil nt

non-'stop adv ununterbrochen; (fly) nonstop; ~ **'flight** Nonstopflug m

non-'swimmer n Nichtschwimmer m

non-'violent a gewaltlos

noodles /'nu:dlz/ npl Bandnudeln pl

nook /nʊk/ n Eckchen nt, Winkel m

noon /nu:n/ n Mittag m; **at ~** um 12 Uhr mittags

noose /nu:s/ n Schlinge f

nor /nɔ:(r)/ adv noch □ conj auch nicht

Nordic /'nɔ:dɪk/ a nordisch

norm /nɔ:m/ n Norm f

normal /'nɔ:ml/ a normal. ~**ity** /-'mælətɪ/ n Normalität f. ~**ly** adv normal; (usually) normalerweise

north /nɔ:θ/ n Norden m; **to the ~ of** nördlich von □ a Nord-, nord- □ adv nach Norden

north: N~ America n Nordamerika nt. ~**-east** a Nordost- □ n Nordosten m

norther|ly /'nɔ:ðəlɪ/ a nördlich. ~**n** a nördlich. **N~n Ireland** n Nordirland nt

north: N~ 'Pole n Nordpol m. **N~ 'Sea** n Nordsee f. ~**ward[s]** /-wəd[z]/ adv nach Norden. ~**-west** a Nordwest- □ n Nordwesten m

Nor|way /'nɔ:weɪ/ n Norwegen nt. ~**wegian** /-'wi:dʒn/ a norwegisch □ n Norweger(in) m(f)

nose /nəʊz/ n Nase f □ vi ~ **about** herumschnüffeln

nose: ~**bleed** n Nasenbluten nt. ~**dive** n (Aviat) Sturzflug m

nostalg|ia /nɒ'stældʒɪə/ n Nostalgie f. ~**ic** a nostalgisch

nostril /'nɒstrəl/ n Nasenloch nt; (of horse) Nüster f

nosy /'nəʊzɪ/ a (-ier, -iest) (fam) neugierig

not /nɒt/ adv nicht; ~ **a** kein(e); **if ~** wenn nicht; ~ **at all** gar nicht; ~ **a bit** kein bisschen; ~ **even** nicht mal; ~ **yet** noch nicht; **he is ~ a German** er ist kein Deutscher

notab|le /'nəʊtəbl/ a bedeutend; (remarkable) bemerkenswert. ~**ly** adv insbesondere

notary /'nəʊtərɪ/ n ~ **'public** ≈ Notar m

notation /nəʊ'teɪʃn/ n Notation f; (Mus) Notenschrift f

notch /nɒtʃ/ n Kerbe f. ~ **up** vt (score) erzielen

note /nəʊt/ n (written comment) Notiz f, Anmerkung f; (short letter) Briefchen nt, Zettel m; (bank ~) Banknote f, Schein m; (Mus) Note f; (sound) Ton m; (on piano) Taste f; **eighth/quarter ~** (Amer) Achtel-/Viertelnote f; **half/whole ~** (Amer) halbe/ganze Note f; **of ~** von Bedeutung; **make a ~ of** notieren □ vt beachten; (notice) bemerken (**that** dass). ~ **down** vt notieren

'notebook n Notizbuch nt

noted /'nəʊtɪd/ a bekannt (**for** für)

note: ~**paper** n Briefpapier nt. ~**worthy** a beachtenswert

nothing /'nʌθɪŋ/ n, pron & adv nichts; **for** ~ umsonst; ~ **but** nichts als; ~ **much** nicht viel; ~ **interesting** nichts Interessantes; **it's ~ to do with you** das geht dich nichts an

notice /'nəʊtɪs/ n (on board) Anschlag m, Bekanntmachung f; (announcement) Anzeige f; (review) Kritik f; (termination of lease, employment) Kündigung f; **[advance] ~** Bescheid m; **give [in one's] ~** kündigen; **give s.o. ~** jdm kündigen; **take no ~ of** keine Notiz nehmen von; **take no ~!** ignoriere es! □ vt bemerken. ~**able** /-əbl/ a, -**bly** adv merklich. ~**-board** n Anschlagbrett nt

noti|fication /nəʊtɪfɪ'keɪʃn/ n Benachrichtigung f. ~**fy** /'nəʊtɪfaɪ/ vt (pt/pp -ied) benachrichtigen

notion /'nəʊʃn/ n Idee f; ~**s** pl (Amer: haberdashery) Kurzwaren pl

notorious /nəʊ'tɔ:rɪəs/ a berüchtigt

notwith'standing prep trotz (+ gen) □ adv trotzdem, dennoch

nought /nɔ:t/ n Null f

noun /naʊn/ n Substantiv nt

nourish /'nʌrɪʃ/ vt nähren. ~**ing** a nahrhaft. ~**ment** n Nahrung f

novel /'nɒvl/ a neu[artig] □ n Roman m. ~**ist** n Romanschriftsteller(in) m(f). ~**ty** n Neuheit f; ~**ties** pl kleine Geschenkartikel pl

November /nəʊ'vembə(r)/ n November m

novice /'nɒvɪs/ n Neuling m; (Relig) Novize m/Novizin f

now /naʊ/ adv & conj jetzt; ~ [that] jetzt; wo; **just** ~ gerade, eben; **right** ~ sofort; ~ **and again** hin und wieder; **now, now!** na, na!

'**nowadays** adv heutzutage

nowhere /'nəʊ-/ adv nirgendwo, nirgends

noxious /'nɒkʃəs/ a schädlich

nozzle /'nɒzl/ n Düse f

nuance /'njuːɑ̃s/ n Nuance f

nuclear /'njuːklɪə(r)/ a Kern-. ~ **de'terrent** n nukleares Abschreckungsmittel nt

nucleus /'njuːklɪəs/ n (pl -lei /-lɪaɪ/) Kern m

nude /njuːd/ a nackt □ n (Art) Akt m; **in the** ~ nackt

nudge /nʌdʒ/ n Stups m □ vt stupsen

nud|ist /'njuːdɪst/ n Nudist m. ~**ity** n Nacktheit f

nugget /'nʌgɪt/ n [Gold]klumpen m

nuisance /'njuːsns/ n Ärgernis nt; (pest) Plage f; **be a** ~ ärgerlich sein; ⟨person:⟩ lästig sein; **what a** ~! wie ärgerlich!

null /nʌl/ a ~ **and void** null und nichtig. ~**ify** /'nʌlɪfaɪ/ vt (pt/pp -ied) für nichtig erklären

numb /nʌm/ a gefühllos, taub; ~ **with cold** taub vor Kälte □ vt betäuben

number /'nʌmbə(r)/ n Nummer f; (amount) Anzahl f; (Math) Zahl f □ vt nummerieren; (include) zählen (**among** zu). ~**plate** n Nummernschild nt

numeral /'njuːmərl/ n Ziffer f

numerate /'njuːmərət/ a **be** ~ rechnen können

numerical /njuː'merɪkl/ a, -ly adv numerisch; **in** ~ **order** zahlenmäßig geordnet

numerous /'njuːmərəs/ a zahlreich

nun /nʌn/ n Nonne f

nuptial /'nʌpʃl/ a Hochzeits-. ~**s** npl (Amer) Hochzeit f

nurse /nɜːs/ n [Kranken]schwester f; (male) Krankenpfleger m; **children's** ~ Kindermädchen nt □ vt pflegen. ~**maid** n Kindermädchen nt

nursery /'nɜːsərɪ/ n Kinderzimmer nt; (Hort) Gärtnerei f; [**day**] ~ Kindertagesstätte f. ~ **rhyme** n Kinderreim m. ~ **school** n Kindergarten m

nursing /'nɜːsɪŋ/ n Krankenpflege f. ~ **home** n Pflegeheim nt

nurture /'nɜːtʃə(r)/ vt nähren; (fig) hegen

nut /nʌt/ n Nuss f; (Techn) [Schrauben]mutter f; (fam: head) Birne f (fam); **be** ~**s** (fam) spinnen (fam). ~**crackers** npl Nussknacker m. ~**meg** n Muskat m

nutrient /'njuːtrɪənt/ n Nährstoff m

nutrit|ion /njuːtrɪʃn/ n Ernährung f. ~**i-ous** /-ʃəs/ a nahrhaft

'**nutshell** n Nussschale f; **in a** ~ (fig) kurz gesagt

nuzzle /'nʌzl/ vt beschnüffeln

nylon /'naɪlɒn/ n Nylon nt; ~**s** pl Nylonstrümpfe pl

nymph /nɪmf/ n Nymphe f

O

O /əʊ/ n (Teleph) null

oaf /əʊf/ n (pl oafs) Trottel m

oak /əʊk/ n Eiche f □ attrib Eichen-

OAP abbr (old-age pensioner) Rentner(in) m(f)

oar /ɔː(r)/ n Ruder nt. ~**sman** n Ruderer m

oasis /əʊ'eɪsɪs/ n (pl oases /-siːz/) Oase f

oath /əʊθ/ n Eid m; (swear-word) Fluch m

oatmeal /'əʊt-/ n Hafermehl nt

oats /əʊts/ npl Hafer m; (Culin) [**rolled**] ~ Haferflocken pl

obedien|ce /ə'biːdɪəns/ n Gehorsam m. ~**t** a, -ly adv gehorsam

obes|e /əʊ'biːs/ a fettleibig. ~**ity** n Fettleibigkeit f

obey /ə'beɪ/ vt/i gehorchen (+ dat); befolgen ⟨instructions, rules⟩

obituary /ə'bɪtjʊərɪ/ n Nachruf m; (notice) Todesanzeige f

object[1] /'ɒbdʒɪkt/ n Gegenstand m; (aim) Zweck m; (intention) Absicht f; (Gram) Objekt nt; **money is no** ~ Geld spielt keine Rolle

object[2] /əb'dʒekt/ vi Einspruch erheben (**to** gegen); (be against) etwas dagegen haben

objection /əb'dʒekʃn/ n Einwand m; **have no** ~ nichts dagegen haben. ~**able** /-əbl/ a anstößig; ⟨person⟩ unangenehm

objectiv|e /əb'dʒektɪv/ a, -ly adv objektiv □ n Ziel nt. ~**ity** /-'tɪvətɪ/ n Objektivität f

objector /əb'dʒektə(r)/ n Gegner m

obligation /ɒblɪ'geɪʃn/ n Pflicht f; **be under an** ~ verpflichtet sein; **without** ~ unverbindlich

obligatory /ə'blɪgətrɪ/ a obligatorisch; **be** ~ Vorschrift sein

oblig|e /ə'blaɪdʒ/ vt verpflichten; (compel) zwingen; (do a small service) einen Gefallen tun (+ dat); **much** ~**ed!** vielen Dank! ~**ing** a entgegenkommend

oblique /ə'bli:k/ a schräg; ⟨angle⟩ schief; ⟨fig⟩ indirekt. **~ stroke** n Schrägstrich m

obliterate /ə'blɪtəreɪt/ vt auslöschen

oblivion /ə'blɪvɪən/ n Vergessenheit f

oblivious /ə'blɪvɪəs/ a **be ~** sich ⟨dat⟩ nicht bewusst sein (of or to gen)

oblong /'ɒblɒŋ/ a rechteckig □ n Rechteck nt

obnoxious /əb'nɒkʃəs/ a widerlich

oboe /'əʊbəʊ/ n Oboe f

obscen|e /əb'si:n/ a obszön; ⟨atrocious⟩ abscheulich. **~ity** /-'senətɪ/ n Obszönität f; Abscheulichkeit f

obscur|e /əb'skjʊə(r)/ a dunkel; ⟨unknown⟩ unbekannt □ vt verdecken; ⟨confuse⟩ verwischen. **~ity** n Dunkelheit f; Unbekanntheit f

obsequious /əb'si:kwɪəs/ a unterwürfig

observa|nce /əb'zɜ:vns/ n ⟨of custom⟩ Einhaltung f. **~nt** a aufmerksam. **~tion** /ɒbzə'veɪʃn/ n Beobachtung f; ⟨remark⟩ Bemerkung f

observatory /əb'zɜ:vətrɪ/ n Sternwarte f; ⟨weather⟩ Wetterwarte f

observe /əb'zɜ:v/ vt beobachten; ⟨say, notice⟩ bemerken; ⟨keep, celebrate⟩ feiern; ⟨obey⟩ einhalten. **~r** n Beobachter m

obsess /əb'ses/ vt **be ~ed by** besessen sein von. **~ion** /-eʃn/ n Besessenheit f; ⟨persistent idea⟩ fixe Idee f. **~ive** /-ɪv/ a, **-ly** adv zwanghaft

obsolete /'ɒbsəli:t/ a veraltet

obstacle /'ɒbstəkl/ n Hindernis nt

obstetrician /ɒbstə'trɪʃn/ n Geburtshelfer m. **obstetrics** /-'stetrɪks/ n Geburtshilfe f

obstina|cy /'ɒbstɪnəsɪ/ n Starrsinn m. **~te** /-nət/ a, **-ly** adv starrsinnig; ⟨refusal⟩ hartnäckig

obstreperous /əb'strepərəs/ a widerspenstig

obstruct /əb'strʌkt/ vt blockieren; ⟨hinder⟩ behindern. **~ion** /-ʌkʃn/ n Blockierung f; Behinderung f; ⟨obstacle⟩ Hindernis nt. **~ive** /-ɪv/ a **be ~ive** Schwierigkeiten bereiten

obtain /əb'teɪn/ vt erhalten, bekommen □ vi gelten. **~able** /-əbl/ a erhältlich

obtrusive /əb'tru:sɪv/ a aufdringlich; ⟨thing⟩ auffällig

obtuse /əb'tju:s/ a ⟨Geom⟩ stumpf; ⟨stupid⟩ begriffsstutzig

obviate /'ɒbvɪeɪt/ vt beseitigen

obvious /'ɒbvɪəs/ a, **-ly** adv offensichtlich, offenbar

occasion /ə'keɪʒn/ n Gelegenheit f; ⟨time⟩ Mal nt; ⟨event⟩ Ereignis nt; ⟨cause⟩ Anlass m, Grund m; **on ~** gelegentlich, hin und wieder; **on the ~ of** anlässlich (+ gen) □ vt veranlassen

occasional /ə'keɪʒənl/ a gelegentlich; **he has the ~ glass of wine** er trinkt gelegentlich ein Glas Wein. **~ly** adv gelegentlich, hin und wieder

occult /ɒ'kʌlt/ a okkult

occupant /'ɒkjʊpənt/ n Bewohner(in) m(f); ⟨of vehicle⟩ Insasse m

occupation /ɒkjʊ'peɪʃn/ n Beschäftigung f; ⟨job⟩ Beruf m; ⟨Mil⟩ Besetzung f; ⟨period⟩ Besatzung f. **~al** a Berufs-. **~al therapy** n Beschäftigungstherapie f

occupier /'ɒkjʊpaɪə(r)/ n Bewohner(in) m(f)

occupy /'ɒkjʊpaɪ/ vt (pt/pp occupied) besetzen ⟨seat, (Mil) country⟩; einnehmen ⟨space⟩; in Anspruch nehmen ⟨time⟩; ⟨live in⟩ bewohnen; ⟨fig⟩ bekleiden ⟨office⟩; ⟨keep busy⟩ beschäftigen; **~ oneself** sich beschäftigen

occur /ə'kɜ:(r)/ vi (pt/pp occurred) geschehen; ⟨exist⟩ vorkommen, auftreten; **it ~red to me that** es fiel mir ein, dass. **occurrence** /ə'kʌrəns/ n Auftreten nt; ⟨event⟩ Ereignis nt

ocean /'əʊʃn/ n Ozean m

o'clock /ə'klɒk/ adv [at] **7 ~** [um] 7 Uhr

octagonal /ɒk'tægənl/ a achteckig

octave /'ɒktɪv/ n ⟨Mus⟩ Oktave f

October /ɒk'təʊbə(r)/ n Oktober m

octopus /'ɒktəpəs/ n (pl -puses) Tintenfisch m

odd /ɒd/ a ⟨-ier, -est⟩ seltsam, merkwürdig; ⟨number⟩ ungerade; ⟨not of set⟩ einzeln; **forty ~** über vierzig; **~ jobs** Gelegenheitsarbeiten pl; **the ~ one out** die Ausnahme; **at ~ moments** zwischendurch; **have the ~ glass of wine** gelegentlich ein Glas Wein trinken

oddity /'ɒdɪtɪ/ n Kuriosität f. **~ly** adv merkwürdig; **~ly enough** merkwürdigerweise. **~ment** n ⟨of fabric⟩ Rest m

odds /ɒdz/ npl ⟨chances⟩ Chancen pl; **at ~ uneinig**; **~ and ends** Kleinkram m; **it makes no ~** es spielt keine Rolle

ode /əʊd/ n Ode f

odious /'əʊdɪəs/ a widerlich, abscheulich

odour /'əʊdə(r)/ n Geruch m. **~less** a geruchlos

oesophagus /i:'sɒfəgəs/ n Speiseröhre f

of /ɒv, unbetont əv/ prep von (+ dat); ⟨made of⟩ aus (+ dat); **the two of us** wir zwei; **a child of three** ein dreijähriges Kind; **the fourth of January** der vierte Januar; **a pound of butter** ein Pfund Butter; **a cup of tea/coffee** eine Tasse Tee/Kaffee; **a bottle of wine** eine Flasche Wein; **half of it** die Hälfte davon; **the whole of the room** das ganze Zimmer

off /ɒf/ *prep* von (+ *dat*); £10 ~ **the price** £10 Nachlass; ~ **the coast** vor der Küste; **get** ~ **the ladder/bus** von der Leiter/aus dem Bus steigen; **take/leave the lid** ~ **the saucepan** den Topf abdecken/nicht zudecken ▯ *adv* weg; ⟨*button, lid, handle*⟩ ab; ⟨*light*⟩ aus; ⟨*brake*⟩ los; ⟨*machine*⟩ abgeschaltet; ⟨*tap*⟩ zu; ⟨*on appliance*⟩ **'off'** 'aus'; **2 kilometres** ~ 2 Kilometer entfernt; **a long way** ~ weit weg; ⟨*time*⟩ noch lange hin; ~ **and on** hin und wieder; **with his hat/coat** ~ ohne Hut/Mantel; **with the light/lid** ~ ohne Licht/Deckel; **20%** ~ 20% Nachlass; **be** ~ ⟨*leave*⟩ [weg]gehen; ⟨*Sport*⟩ starten; ⟨*food:*⟩ schlecht/⟨*all gone*⟩ alle sein; **be better/worse** ~ besser/schlechter dran sein; **be well** ~ gut dran sein; ⟨*financially*⟩ wohlhabend sein; **have a day** ~ einen freien Tag haben; **go/drive** ~ weggehen/-fahren; **turn/take sth** ~ etw abdrehen/-nehmen

offal /'ɒfl/ *n* ⟨*Culin*⟩ Innereien *pl*

offence /ə'fens/ *n* ⟨*illegal act*⟩ Vergehen *nt*; **give/take** ~ Anstoß erregen/nehmen (**at an** + *dat*)

offend /ə'fend/ *vt* beleidigen. ~**er** *n* ⟨*Jur*⟩ Straftäter *m*

offensive /ə'fensɪv/ *a* anstößig; ⟨*Mil, Sport*⟩ offensiv ▯ *n* Offensive *f*

offer /'ɒfə(r)/ *n* Angebot *nt*; **on special** ~ im Sonderangebot ▯ *vt* anbieten (**to** *dat*); leisten ⟨*resistance*⟩; ~ **s.o. sth** jdm etw anbieten; ~ **to do sth** sich anbieten, etw zu tun. ~**ing** *n* Gabe *f*

off'hand *a* brüsk; ⟨*casual*⟩ lässig ▯ *adv* so ohne weiteres

office /'ɒfɪs/ *n* Büro *nt*; ⟨*post*⟩ Amt *nt*; **in** ~ **hours** *pl* Dienststunden *pl*

officer /'ɒfɪsə(r)/ *n* Offizier *m*; ⟨*official*⟩ Beamte(r) *m*/ Beamtin *f*; ⟨*police*⟩ Polizeibeamte(r) *m*/-beamtin *f*

official /ə'fɪʃl/ *a* offiziell, amtlich ▯ *n* Beamte(r) *m*/ Beamtin *f*; ⟨*Sport*⟩ Funktionär *m*. ~**ly** *adv* offiziell

officiate /ə'fɪʃɪeɪt/ *vi* amtieren

officious /ə'fɪʃəs/ *a*, **-ly** *adv* übereifrig

'offing *n* **in the** ~ in Aussicht

'off-licence *n* Wein- und Spirituosenhandlung *f*

off-'load *vt* ausladen

'off-putting *a* ⟨*fam*⟩ abstoßend

off'set *vt* ⟨*pt/pp* **-set**, *pres p* **-setting**⟩ ausgleichen

'offshoot *n* Schössling *m*; ⟨*fig*⟩ Zweig *m*

'offshore *a* offshore-. ~ **rig** *n* Bohrinsel *f*

off'side *a* ⟨*Sport*⟩ abseits

'offspring *n* Nachwuchs *m*

off'stage *adv* hinter den Kulissen

off-'white *a* fast weiß

often /'ɒfn/ *adv* oft; **every so** ~ von Zeit zu Zeit

ogle /'əʊgl/ *vt* beäugeln

ogre /'əʊgə(r)/ *n* Menschenfresser *m*

oh /əʊ/ *int* oh! ach! **oh dear!** o weh!

oil /ɔɪl/ *n* Öl *nt*; ⟨*petroleum*⟩ Erdöl *nt* ▯ *vt* ölen

oil: ~**cloth** *n* Wachstuch *nt*. ~**field** *n* Ölfeld *nt*. ~**painting** *n* Ölgemälde *nt*. ~ **refinery** *n* [Erd]ölraffinerie *f*. ~**skins** *npl* Ölzeug *nt*. ~**slick** *n* Ölteppich *m*. ~**tanker** *n* Öltanker *m*. ~ **well** *n* Ölquelle *f*

oily /'ɔɪlɪ/ *a* (**-ier, -iest**) ölig

ointment /'ɔɪntmənt/ *n* Salbe *f*

OK /əʊ'keɪ/ *a* & *int* ⟨*fam*⟩ in Ordnung; okay ▯ *adv* ⟨*well*⟩ gut ▯ *vt* ⟨*auch* okay⟩ ⟨*pt/pp* **okayed**⟩ genehmigen

old /əʊld/ *a* (**-er, -est**) alt; ⟨*former*⟩ ehemalig

old: ~ **'age** *n* Alter *nt*. ~**age 'pensioner** *n* Rentner(in) *m(f)*. ~ **boy** *n* ehemaliger Schüler. ~**-'fashioned** *a* altmodisch. ~ **girl** ehemalige Schülerin *f*. ~ **'maid** *n* alte Jungfer *f*

olive /'ɒlɪv/ *n* Olive *f*; ⟨*colour*⟩ Oliv *nt* ▯ *a* olivgrün. ~ **branch** *n* Ölzweig *m*; ⟨*fig*⟩ Friedensangebot *nt*. ~ **'oil** *n* Olivenöl *nt*

Olympic /ə'lɪmpɪk/ *a* olympisch ▯ *n* **the** ~**s** die Olympischen Spiele *pl*

omelette /'ɒmlɪt/ *n* Omelett *nt*

omen /'əʊmən/ *n* Omen *nt*

ominous /'ɒmɪnəs/ *a* bedrohlich

omission /ə'mɪʃn/ *n* Auslassung *f*; ⟨*failure to do*⟩ Unterlassung *f*

omit /ə'mɪt/ *vt* ⟨*pt/pp* **omitted**⟩ auslassen; ~ **to do sth** es unterlassen, etw zu tun

omnipotent /ɒm'nɪpətənt/ *a* allmächtig

on /ɒn/ *prep* auf (+ *dat*/⟨*on to*⟩ + *acc*); ⟨*on vertical surface*⟩ an (+ *dat*/⟨*on to*⟩ + *acc*); ⟨*about*⟩ über (+ *acc*); **on Monday** [am] Montag; **on Mondays** montags; **on the first of May** am ersten Mai; **on arriving** als ich ankam; **on one's finger** am Finger; **on the right/left** rechts/links; **on the Rhine/Thames** am Rhein/an der Themse; **on the radio/television** im Radio/Fernsehen; **on the bus/train** im Bus/Zug; **go on the bus/train** mit dem Bus/Zug fahren; **get on the bus/train** in den Bus/Zug einsteigen; **on me** ⟨*with me*⟩ bei mir; **it's on me** ⟨*fam*⟩ das spendiere ich ▯ *adv* ⟨*further on*⟩ weiter; ⟨*switched on*⟩ an; ⟨*brake*⟩ angezogen; ⟨*machine*⟩ angeschaltet; ⟨*on appliance*⟩ **'on'** 'ein'; **with/without his hat/coat on** mit/ohne Hut/Mantel; **with/without the lid on** mit/ohne Deckel; **be on** ⟨*film:*⟩ laufen; ⟨*event:*⟩ stattfinden; **be on at** ⟨*fam*⟩ bedrängen (**zu** to); **it's not on** ⟨*fam*⟩ das geht nicht; **on and on** immer weiter; **on and**

off hin und wieder; **and so on** und so weiter; **later on** später; **drive on** weiterfahren; **stick/sew on** ankleben/-nähen; **from then on** von da an

once /wʌns/ *adv* einmal; *(formerly)* früher; **at ~** sofort; *(at the same time)* gleichzeitig; **~ and for all** ein für alle Mal □ *conj* wenn; *(with past tense)* als. **~-over** *n (fam)* **give s.o./sth the ~-over** sich *(dat)* jdn/etw kurz ansehen

'oncoming *a* **~ traffic** Gegenverkehr *m*

one /wʌn/ *a* ein(e); *(only)* einzig; **not ~** kein(e); **~ day/evening** eines Tages/Abends □ *n* Eins *f* □ *pron* eine(r)/eins; *(impersonal)* man; **which ~** welche(r,s); **~ another** einander; **~ by ~** einzeln; **~ never knows** man kann nie wissen

one: **~-eyed** *a* einäugig. **~-parent 'family** *n* Einelternfamilie *f*. **~'self** *pron* selbst; *(refl)* sich; **by ~self** allein. **~-sided** *a* einseitig. **~-way** *a ⟨street⟩* Einbahn-; *⟨ticket⟩* einfach

onion /'ʌnjən/ *n* Zwiebel *f*

'onlooker *n* Zuschauer(in) *m(f)*

only /'əʊnlɪ/ *a* einzige(r,s); **an ~ child** ein Einzelkind *nt* □ *adv & conj* nur; **~ just** gerade erst; *(barely)* gerade noch

'onset *n* Beginn *m*; *(of winter)* Einsetzen *nt*

onslaught /'ɒnslɔːt/ *n* heftiger Angriff *m*

onus /'əʊnəs/ *n* **the ~ is on me** es liegt an mir **(to** zu)

onward[s] /'ɒnwəd[z]/ *adv* vorwärts; **from then ~** von der Zeit an

ooze /uːz/ *vi* sickern

opal /'əʊpl/ *n* Opal *m*

opaque /əʊ'peɪk/ *a* undurchsichtig

open /'əʊpən/ *a, -ly adv* offen; **be ~** *⟨shop:⟩* geöffnet sein; **in the ~ air** im Freien □ *n* **in the ~** im Freien □ *vt* öffnen, aufmachen; *(start, set up)* eröffnen □ *vi* sich öffnen; *⟨flower:⟩* aufgehen; *⟨shop:⟩* öffnen, aufmachen; *(be started)* eröffnet werden. **~ up** *vt* öffnen, aufmachen; *(fig)* eröffnen □ *vi* sich öffnen; *(fig)* sich eröffnen

open: **~-air 'swimming pool** *n* Freibad *nt*. **~ day** *n* Tag *m* der offenen Tür

opener /'əʊpənə(r)/ *n* Öffner *m*

opening /'əʊpənɪŋ/ *n* Öffnung *f*; *(beginning)* Eröffnung *f*; *(job)* Einstiegsmöglichkeit *f*. **~ hours** *npl* Öffnungszeiten *pl*

open: **~-'minded** *a* aufgeschlossen. **~-plan** *a* **~-plan office** Großraumbüro *nt*. **~ 'sandwich** *n* belegtes Brot *nt*

opera /'ɒpərə/ *n* Oper *f*

operable /'ɒpərəbl/ *a* operierbar

opera: **~-glasses** *npl* Opernglas *nt*. **~ house** *n* Opernhaus *nt*. **~-singer** *n* Opernsänger(in) *m(f)*

operate /'ɒpəreɪt/ *vt* bedienen *⟨machine, lift⟩*; betätigen *⟨lever, brake⟩*; *(fig: run)* betreiben □ *vi ⟨Techn⟩* funktionieren; *(be in action)* in Betrieb sein; *(Mil & fig)* operieren; **~ [on]** *⟨Med⟩* operieren

operatic /ɒpə'rætɪk/ *a* Opern-

operation /ɒpə'reɪʃn/ *n (see operate)* Bedienung *f*; Betätigung *f*; Operation *f*; **in ~** *⟨Techn⟩* in Betrieb; **come into ~** *(fig)* in Kraft treten; **have an ~** *⟨Med⟩* operiert werden. **~al** *a* **be ~al** in Betrieb sein; *⟨law:⟩* in Kraft sein

operative /'ɒpərətɪv/ *a* wirksam

operator /'ɒpəreɪtə(r)/ *n (user)* Bedienungsperson *f*; *(Teleph)* Vermittlung *f*

operetta /ɒpə'retə/ *n* Operette *f*

opinion /ə'pɪnjən/ *n* Meinung *f*; **in my ~** meiner Meinung nach. **~ated** *a* rechthaberisch

opium /'əʊpɪəm/ *n* Opium *nt*

opponent /ə'pəʊnənt/ *n* Gegner(in) *m(f)*

opportun|e /'ɒpətjuːn/ *a* günstig. **~ist** /-'tjuːnɪst/ *a* opportunistisch □ *n* Opportunist *m*

opportunity /ɒpə'tjuːnətɪ/ *n* Gelegenheit *f*

oppos|e /ə'pəʊz/ *vt* Widerstand leisten (+ *dat*); *(argue against)* sprechen gegen; **be ~ed to sth** gegen etw sein; **as ~ed to** im Gegensatz zu. **~ing** *a* gegnerisch; *(opposite)* entgegengesetzt

opposite /'ɒpəzɪt/ *a* entgegengesetzt; *⟨house, side⟩* gegenüberliegend; **~ number** *(fig)* Gegenstück *nt*; **the ~ sex** das andere Geschlecht □ *n* Gegenteil *nt* □ *adv* gegenüber □ *prep* gegenüber (+ *dat*)

opposition /ɒpə'zɪʃn/ *n* Widerstand *m*; *(Pol)* Opposition *f*

oppress /ə'pres/ *vt* unterdrücken. **~ion** /-eʃn/ *n* Unterdrückung *f*. **~ive** /-ɪv/ *a* tyrannisch; *⟨heat⟩* drückend. **~or** *n* Unterdrücker *m*

opt /ɒpt/ *vi* **~ for** sich entscheiden für; **~ out** ausscheiden **(of** aus)

optical /'ɒptɪkl/ *a* optisch; **~ illusion** optische Täuschung *f*

optician /ɒp'tɪʃn/ *n* Optiker *m*

optics /'ɒptɪks/ *n* Optik *f*

optimis|m /'ɒptɪmɪzm/ *n* Optimismus *m*. **~t** /-mɪst/ *n* Optimist *m*. **~tic** /-'mɪstɪk/ *a*, **-ally** *adv* optimistisch

optimum /'ɒptɪməm/ *a* optimal □ *n (pl* **-ima)** Optimum *nt*

option /'ɒpʃn/ *n* Wahl *f*; *(Comm)* Option *f*. **~al** *a* auf Wunsch erhältlich; *⟨subject⟩* wahlfrei; **~al extras** *pl* Extras *pl*

opu|lence /'ɒpjʊləns/ *n* Prunk *m*; *(wealth)* Reichtum *m*. **~lent** *a* prunkvoll; *(wealthy)* sehr reich

or /ɔ:(r)/ *conj* oder; (*after negative*) noch; **or [else]** sonst; **in a year or two** in ein bis zwei Jahren

oracle /'ɒrəkl/ *n* Orakel *nt*

oral /'ɔ:rl/ *a*, **-ly** *adv* mündlich; (*Med*) oral □ *n* (*fam*) Mündliche(s) *nt*

orange /'ɒrɪndʒ/ *n* Apfelsine *f*, Orange *f*; (*colour*) Orange *nt* □ *a* orangefarben. ~**ade** /-'dʒeɪd/ *n* Orangeade *f*

oration /ə'reɪʃn/ *n* Rede *f*

orator /'ɒrətə(r)/ *n* Redner *m*

oratorio /ɒrə'tɔ:rɪəʊ/ *n* Oratorium *nt*

oratory /'ɒrətərɪ/ *n* Redekunst *f*

orbit /'ɔ:bɪt/ *n* Umlaufbahn *f* □ *vt* umkreisen. ~**al** *a* ~**al road** Ringstraße *f*

orchard /'ɔ:tʃəd/ *n* Obstgarten *m*

orches|tra /'ɔ:kɪstrə/ *n* Orchester *nt*. ~**tral** /-'kestrəl/ *a* Orchester-. ~**trate** *vt* orchestrieren

orchid /'ɔ:kɪd/ *n* Orchidee *f*

ordain /ɔ:'deɪn/ *vt* bestimmen; (*Relig*) ordinieren

ordeal /ɔ:'di:l/ *n* (*fig*) Qual *f*

order /'ɔ:də(r)/ *n* Ordnung *f*; (*sequence*) Reihenfolge *f*; (*condition*) Zustand *m*; (*command*) Befehl *m*; (*in restaurant*) Bestellung *f*; (*Comm*) Auftrag *m*; (*Relig, medal*) Orden *m*; **out of ~** (*machine*) außer Betrieb; **in ~ that** damit; **in ~ to help** um zu helfen; **take holy ~s** Geistlicher werden □ *vt* (*put in* ~) ordnen; (*command*) befehlen (+ *dat*); (*Comm, in restaurant*) bestellen; (*prescribe*) verordnen

orderly /'ɔ:dəlɪ/ *a* ordentlich; (*not unruly*) friedlich □ *n* (*Mil, Med*) Sanitäter *m*

ordinary /'ɔ:dɪnərɪ/ *a* gewöhnlich, normal; (*meeting*) ordentlich

ordination /ɔ:dɪ'neɪʃn/ *n* (*Relig*) Ordination *f*

ore /ɔ:(r)/ *n* Erz *nt*

organ /'ɔ:gən/ *n* (*Biol & fig*) Organ *nt*; (*Mus*) Orgel *f*

organic /ɔ:'gænɪk/ *a*, **-ally** *adv* organisch; (*without chemicals*) biodynamisch; (*crop*) biologisch angebaut; (*food*) Bio-; ~**ally grown** biologisch angebaut. ~ **farm** *n* Biohof *m*. ~ **farming** *n* biologischer Anbau *m*

organism /'ɔ:gənɪzm/ *n* Organismus *m*

organist /'ɔ:gənɪst/ *n* Organist *m*

organization /ɔ:gənaɪ'zeɪʃn/ *n* Organisation *f*

organize /'ɔ:gənaɪz/ *vt* organisieren; veranstalten (*event*). ~**r** *n* Organisator *m*; Veranstalter *m*

orgasm /'ɔ:gæzm/ *n* Orgasmus *m*

orgy /'ɔ:dʒɪ/ *n* Orgie *f*

Orient /'ɔ:rɪənt/ *n* Orient *m*. **o~al** /-'entl/ *a* orientalisch; ~**al carpet** Orientteppich *m* □ *n* Orientale *m*/Orientalin *f*

orient|ate /'ɔ:rɪənteɪt/ *vt* ~**ate oneself** sich orientieren. ~**ation** /-'teɪʃn/ *n* Orientierung *f*

orifice /'ɒrɪfɪs/ *n* Öffnung *f*

origin /'ɒrɪdʒɪn/ *n* Ursprung *m*; (*of person, goods*) Herkunft *f*

original /ə'rɪdʒənl/ *a* ursprünglich; (*not copied*) original; (*new*) originell □ *n* Original *nt*. ~**ity** /-'nælətɪ/ *n* Originalität *f*. ~**ly** *adv* ursprünglich

originat|e /ə'rɪdʒɪneɪt/ *vi* entstehen □ *vt* hervorbringen. ~**or** *n* Urheber *m*

ornament /'ɔ:nəmənt/ *n* Ziergegenstand *m*; (*decoration*) Verzierung *f*. ~**al** /-'mentl/ *a* dekorativ. ~**ation** /-'teɪʃn/ *n* Verzierung *f*

ornate /ɔ:'neɪt/ *a* reich verziert

ornithology /ɔ:nɪ'θɒlədʒɪ/ *n* Vogelkunde *f*

orphan /'ɔ:fn/ *n* Waisenkind *nt*, Waise *f* □ *vt* zur Waise machen; ~**ed** verwaist. ~**age** /-ɪdʒ/ *n* Waisenhaus *nt*

orthodox /'ɔ:θədɒks/ *a* orthodox

orthography /ɔ:'θɒgrəfɪ/ *n* Rechtschreibung *f*

orthopaedic /ɔ:θə'pi:dɪk/ *a* orthopädisch

oscillate /'ɒsɪleɪt/ *vi* schwingen

ostensible /ɒ'stensəbl/ *a*, **-bly** *adv* angeblich

ostentat|ion /ɒsten'teɪʃn/ *n* Protzerei *f* (*fam*). ~**ious** /-ʃəs/ *a* protzig (*fam*)

osteopath /'ɒstɪəpæθ/ *n* Osteopath *m*

ostracize /'ɒstrəsaɪz/ *vt* ächten

ostrich /'ɒstrɪtʃ/ *n* Strauß *m*

other /'ʌðə(r)/ *a, pron & n* andere(r,s); **the ~ [one]** der/die/das andere; **the ~ two** die zwei anderen; **two ~s** zwei andere; (*more*) noch zwei; **no ~s** sonst keine; **any ~ questions?** sonst noch Fragen? **every ~ day** jeden zweiten Tag; **the ~ day** neulich; **the ~ evening** neulich abends; **someone/something or ~** irgendjemand/-etwas □ *adv* anders; ~ **than him** außer ihm; **somehow/somewhere or ~** irgendwie/irgendwo

otherwise *adv* sonst; (*differently*) anders

otter /'ɒtə(r)/ *n* Otter *m*

ouch /aʊtʃ/ *int* autsch

ought /ɔ:t/ *v aux* **I/we ~ to stay** ich sollte/wir sollten eigentlich bleiben; **he ~ not to have done it** er hätte es nicht machen sollen; **that ~ to be enough** das sollte eigentlich genügen

ounce /aʊns/ *n* Unze *f* (28, 35 g)

our /'aʊə(r)/ *a* unser

ours /ˈaʊəz/ *poss pron* unsere(r,s); **a friend of** ~ ein Freund von uns; **that is** ~ das gehört uns

ourselves /aʊəˈselvz/ *pron* selbst; (*refl*) uns; **by** ~ allein

oust /aʊst/ *vt* entfernen

out /aʊt/ *adv* (*not at home*) weg; (*outside*) draußen; (*not alight*) aus; (*unconscious*) bewusstlos; **be** ~ (*sun:*) scheinen; (*flower*) blühen; (*workers*) streiken; (*calculation:*) nicht stimmen; (*Sport*) aus sein; (*fig: not feasible*) nicht infrage kommen; ~ **and about** unterwegs; **have it** ~ **with s.o.** (*fam*) jdn zur Rede stellen; **get** ~! (*fam*) raus! ~ **with it!** (*fam*) heraus damit! **to/send** ~ hinausgehen/-schicken; **come/bring** ~ herauskommen/-bringen □ *prep* ~ **of** aus (+ *dat*); **go** ~ **of the door** zur Tür hinausgehen; **be** ~ **of bed/ the room** nicht im Bett/im Zimmer sein; ~ **of breath/danger** außer Atem/Gefahr; ~ **of work** arbeitslos; **nine** ~ **of ten** neun von zehn; **be** ~ **of sugar/bread** keinen Zucker/kein Brot mehr haben □ *prep* aus (+ *dat*); **go** ~ **the door** zur Tür hinausgehen

out'bid *vt* (*pt/pp* -**bid**, *pres p* -**bidding**) überbieten

'outboard *a* ~ **motor** Außenbordmotor *m*

'outbreak *n* Ausbruch *m*

'outbuilding *n* Nebengebäude *nt*

'outburst *n* Ausbruch *m*

'outcast *n* Ausgestoßene(r) *m/f*

'outcome *n* Ergebnis *nt*

'outcry *n* Aufschrei *m* [der Entrüstung]

out'dated *a* überholt

out'do *vt* (*pt* -**did**, *pp* -**done**) übertreffen, übertrumpfen

'outdoor *a* (*life, sports*) im Freien; ~ **shoes** *pl* Straßenschuhe *pl*; ~ **swimming pool** Freibad *nt*

out'doors *adv* draußen; **go** ~ nach draußen gehen

'outer *a* äußere(r,s)

'outfit *n* Ausstattung *f*; (*clothes*) Ensemble *nt*; (*fam: organization*) Betrieb *m*; (*fam*) Laden *m*. ~**ter** *n* **men's** ~**ter's** Herrenbekleidungsgeschäft *nt*

'outgoing *a* ausscheidend; (*mail*) ausgehend; (*sociable*) kontaktfreudig. ~**s** *npl* Ausgaben *pl*

out'grow *vi* (*pt* -**grew**, *pp* -**grown**) herauswachsen aus

'outhouse *n* Nebengebäude *nt*

outing /ˈaʊtɪŋ/ *n* Ausflug *m*

outlandish /aʊtˈlændɪʃ/ *a* ungewöhnlich

'outlaw *n* Geächtete(r) *m/f* □ *vt* ächten

'outlay *n* Auslagen *pl*

'outlet *n* Abzug *m*; (*for water*) Abfluss *m*; (*fig*) Ventil *nt*; (*Comm*) Absatzmöglichkeit *f*

'outline *n* Umriss *m*; (*summary*) kurze Darstellung *f* □ *vt* umreißen

out'live *vt* überleben

'outlook *n* Aussicht *f*; (*future prospect*) Aussichten *pl*; (*attitude*) Einstellung *f*

'outlying *a* entlegen; ~ **areas** *pl* Außengebiete *pl*

out'moded *a* überholt

out'number *vt* zahlenmäßig überlegen sein (+ *dat*)

'out-patient *n* ambulanter Patient *m*; ~**s' department** Ambulanz *f*

'outpost *n* Vorposten *m*

'output *n* Leistung *f*; Produktion *f*

'outrage *n* Gräueltat *f*; (*fig*) Skandal *m*; (*indignation*) Empörung *f* □ *vt* empören. ~**ous** /-ˈreɪdʒəs/ *a* empörend

'outright[1] *a* völlig, total; (*refusal*) glatt

out'right[2] *adv* ganz; (*at once*) sofort; (*frankly*) offen

'outset *n* Anfang *m*; **from the** ~ von Anfang an

'outside[1] *a* äußere(r,s); ~ **wall** Außenwand *f* □ *n* Außenseite *f*; **from the** ~ von außen; **at the** ~ höchstens

out'side[2] *adv* außen; (*out of doors*) draußen; **go** ~ nach draußen gehen □ *prep* außerhalb (+ *gen*); (*in front of*) vor (+ *dat/acc*)

out'sider *n* Außenseiter *m*

'outsize *a* übergroß

'outskirts *npl* Rand *m*

out'spoken *a* offen; **be** ~ kein Blatt vor den Mund nehmen

out'standing *a* hervorragend; (*conspicuous*) bemerkenswert; (*not settled*) unerledigt; (*Comm*) ausstehend

'outstretched *a* ausgestreckt

out'strip *vt* (*pt/pp* -**stripped**) davonlaufen (+ *dat*); (*fig*) übertreffen

out'vote *vt* überstimmen

'outward /-wəd/ *a* äußerlich; ~ **journey** Hinreise *f* □ *adv* nach außen; **be** ~ **bound** (*ship:*) auslaufen. ~**ly** *adv* nach außen hin, äußerlich. ~**s** *adv* nach außen

out'weigh *vt* überwiegen

out'wit *vt* (*pt/pp* -**witted**) überlisten

oval /ˈəʊvl/ *a* oval □ *n* Oval *nt*

ovary /ˈəʊvərɪ/ *n* (*Anat*) Eierstock *m*

ovation /əʊˈveɪʃn/ *n* Ovation *f*

oven /ˈʌvn/ *n* Backofen *m*. ~-**ready** *a* bratfertig

over /ˈəʊvə(r)/ *prep* über (+ *acc/dat*); ~ **dinner** beim Essen; ~ **the weekend**

overall 403 overthrow

übers Wochenende; ∼ **the phone** am Telefon; ∼ **the page** auf der nächsten Seite; **all** ∼ **Germany** in ganz Deutschland; ⟨*travel*⟩ durch ganz Deutschland; **all** ∼ **the place** (*fam*) überall □ *adv* (*remaining*) übrig; (*ended*) zu Ende; ∼ **again** noch einmal; ∼ **and** ∼ immer wieder; ∼ **here/there** hier/da drüben; **all** ∼ (*everywhere*) überall; **it's all** ∼ es ist vorbei; **I ache all** ∼ mir tut alles weh; **go/drive** ∼ hinübergehen/ -fahren; **come/bring** ∼ herüberkommen/-bringen; **turn** ∼ herumdrehen

overall¹ /ˈəʊvərɔːl/ n Kittel m; ∼**s** pl Overall m

overall² /əʊvərˈɔːl/ a gesamt; (*general*) allgemein □ *adv* insgesamt

over'awe vt (*fig*) überwältigen

over'balance vi das Gleichgewicht verlieren

over'bearing a herrisch

'overboard adv (*Naut*) über Bord

'overcast a bedeckt

over'charge vt ∼ **s.o.** jdm zu viel berechnen □ vi zu viel verlangen

'overcoat n Mantel m

over'come vt (pt -came, pp -come) überwinden; **be** ∼ **by** überwältigt werden von

over'crowded a überfüllt

over'do vt (pt -did, pp -done) übertreiben; (*cook too long*) zu lange kochen; ∼ **it** (*fam: do too much*) sich übernehmen

'overdose n Überdosis f

'overdraft n [Konto]überziehung f; **have an** ∼ sein Konto überzogen haben

over'draw vt (pt -drew, pp -drawn) (*Comm*) überziehen

over'due a überfällig

over'estimate vt überschätzen

'overflow¹ n Überschuss m; (*outlet*) Überlauf m

over'flow² vi überlaufen

over'grown a (*garden*) überwachsen

'overhang¹ n Überhang m

over'hang² vt/i (pt/pp -hung) überhängen (über + acc)

'overhaul¹ n Überholung f

over'haul² vt (*Techn*) überholen

over'head¹ adv oben

'overhead² a Ober-; (*ceiling*) Decken-. ∼**s** npl allgemeine Unkosten pl

over'hear vt (pt/pp -heard) mit anhören ⟨*conversation*⟩; **I overheard him saying** it ich hörte zufällig, wie er das sagte

over'heat vi zu heiß werden □ vt zu stark erhitzen

over'joyed a überglücklich

'overland a & adv /--'-/ auf dem Landweg; ∼ **route** Landroute f

over'lap v (pt/pp -lapped) □ vi sich überschneiden □ vt überlappen

over'leaf adv umseitig

over'load vt überladen; (*Electr*) überlasten

'overlook¹ n (*Amer*) Aussichtspunkt m

over'look² vt überblicken; (*fail to see, ignore*) übersehen

overly /ˈəʊvəlɪ/ adv übermäßig

over'night¹ adv über Nacht; **stay** ∼ übernachten

'overnight² a Nacht-; ∼ **stay** Übernachtung f

'overpass n Überführung f

over'pay vt (pt/pp -paid) überbezahlen

over'populated a übervölkert

over'power vt überwältigen. ∼**ing** a überwältigend

over'priced a zu teuer

overpro'duce vt überproduzieren

over'rate vt überschätzen. ∼**d** a überbewertet

over'reach vt ∼ **oneself** sich übernehmen

overre'act vi überreagieren. ∼**ion** n Überreaktion f

over'rid|e vt (pt -rode, pp -ridden) sich hinwegsetzen über (+ acc). ∼**ing** a Haupt-

over'rule vt ablehnen; **we were** ∼**d** wir wurden überstimmt

over'run vt (pt -ran, pp -run, pres p -running) überrennen; überschreiten ⟨*time*⟩; **be** ∼ **with** überlaufen sein von

over'seas¹ adv in Übersee; **go** ∼ nach Übersee gehen

'overseas² a Übersee-

over'see vt (pt -saw, pp -seen) beaufsichtigen

'overseer /-sɪə(r)/ n Aufseher m

over'shadow vt überschatten

over'shoot vt (pt/pp -shot) hinausschießen über (+ acc)

'oversight n Versehen nt

over'sleep vi (pt/pp -slept) [sich] verschlafen

over'step vt (pt/pp -stepped) überschreiten

over'strain vt überanstrengen

overt /əʊˈvɜːt/ a offen

over'tak|e vt/i (pt -took, pp -taken) überholen. ∼**ing** n Überholen nt; **no** ∼**ing** Überholverbot nt

over'tax vt zu hoch besteuern; (*fig*) überfordern

'overthrow¹ n (*Pol*) Sturz m

over'throw² vt (pt -threw, pp -thrown) (*Pol*) stürzen

'overtime *n* Überstunden *pl* □ *adv* **work**
~ Überstunden machen

over'tired *a* übermüdet

'overtone *n* (*fig*) Unterton *m*

overture /'əʊvətjʊə(r)/ *n* (*Mus*) Ouvertüre *f*; ~**s** *pl* (*fig*) Annäherungsversuche
pl

over'turn *vt* umstoßen □ *vi* umkippen

over'weight *a* übergewichtig; **be ~** Übergewicht haben

overwhelm /-'welm/ *vt* überwältigen.
~**ing** *a* überwältigend

over'work *n* Überarbeitung *f* □ *vt* überfordern □ *vi* sich überarbeiten

over'wrought *a* überreizt

ovulation /ɒvjʊ'leɪʃn/ *n* Eisprung *m*

ow|e /əʊ/ *vt* schulden; (*fig*) verdanken
([**to**] s.o. jdm); ~**e s.o. sth** jdm etw schuldig sein; **be ~ing** (*money:*) ausstehen.
'~**ing to** *prep* wegen (+ *gen*)

owl /aʊl/ *n* Eule *f*

own¹ /əʊn/ *a & pron* eigen; **it's my ~** es
gehört mir; **a car of my ~** mein eigenes
Auto; **on one's ~** allein; **hold one's ~**
sich behaupten; **get one's ~ back** (*fam*)
sich revanchieren

own² *vt* besitzen; (*confess*) zugeben; **I don't
~ it** es gehört mir nicht. ~ **up** *vi* es zugeben

owner /'əʊnə(r)/ *n* Eigentümer(in) *m(f)*,
Besitzer(in) *m(f)*; (*of shop*) Inhaber(in)
m(f). ~**ship** *n* Besitz *m*

ox /ɒks/ *n* (*pl* **oxen**) Ochse *m*

oxide /'ɒksaɪd/ *n* Oxid *nt*

oxygen /'ɒksɪdʒən/ *n* Sauerstoff *m*

oyster /'ɔɪstə(r)/ *n* Auster *f*

ozone /'əʊzəʊn/ *n* Ozon *nt*. ~-'**friendly** *a*
≈ ohne FCKW. ~ **layer** *n* Ozonschicht *f*

P

pace /peɪs/ *n* Schritt *m*; (*speed*) Tempo *nt*;
keep ~ with Schritt halten mit □ *vi* ~ **up
and down** auf und ab gehen. ~-**maker** *n*
(*Sport & Med*) Schrittmacher *m*

Pacific /pə'sɪfɪk/ *a & n* **the ~ [Ocean]** der
Pazifik

pacifier /'pæsɪfaɪə(r)/ *n* (*Amer*) Schnuller
m

pacifist /'pæsɪfɪst/ *n* Pazifist *m*

pacify /'pæsɪfaɪ/ *vt* (*pt/pp* **-ied**) beruhigen

pack /pæk/ *n* Packung *f*; (*Mil*) Tornister *m*;
(*of cards*) [Karten]spiel *nt*; (*gang*) Bande *f*;
(*of hounds*) Meute *f*; (*of wolves*) Rudel *nt*; **a
~ of lies** ein Haufen Lügen □ *vt/i* packen;

einpacken ⟨*article*⟩; **be ~ed** (*crowded*) [gedrängt] voll sein; **send s.o. ~ing** (*fam*)
jdn wegschicken. ~ **up** *vt* einpacken □ *vi*
(*fam*) ⟨*machine:*⟩ kaputtgehen; ⟨*person:*⟩
einpacken (*fam*)

package /'pækɪdʒ/ *n* Paket *nt* □ *vt* verpacken. ~ **holiday** *n* Pauschalreise *f*

packed 'lunch *n* Lunchpaket *nt*

packet /'pækɪt/ *n* Päckchen *nt*; **cost a ~**
(*fam*) einen Haufen Geld kosten

packing /'pækɪŋ/ *n* Verpackung *f*

pact /pækt/ *n* Pakt *m*

pad¹ /pæd/ *n* Polster *nt*; (*for writing*)
[Schreib]block *m*; (*fam: home*) Wohnung
f □ *vt* (*pt/pp* **padded**) polstern

pad² *vi* (*pt/pp* **padded**) tappen

padding /'pædɪŋ/ *n* Polsterung *f*; (*in written work*) Füllwerk *nt*

paddle¹ /'pædl/ *n* Paddel *nt* □ *vt* (*row*) paddeln

paddle² *vi* waten

paddock /'pædək/ *n* Koppel *f*

padlock /'pædlɒk/ *n* Vorhängeschloss *nt*
□ *vt* mit einem Vorhängeschloss verschließen

paediatrician /piːdɪə'trɪʃn/ *n* Kinderarzt *m* /-ärztin *f*

pagan /'peɪgən/ *a* heidnisch □ *n* Heide
m /Heidin *f*

page¹ /peɪdʒ/ *n* Seite *f*

page² *n* (*boy*) Page *m* □ *vt* ausrufen ⟨*person*⟩

pageant /'pædʒənt/ *n* Festzug *m*. ~**ry** *n*
Prunk *m*

paid /peɪd/ *see* **pay** □ *a* bezahlt; **put ~ to**
(*fam*) zunichte machen

pail /peɪl/ *n* Eimer *m*

pain /peɪn/ *n* Schmerz *m*; **be in ~**
Schmerzen haben; **take ~s** sich (*dat*)
Mühe geben; ~ **in the neck** (*fam*) Nervensäge *f* □ *vt* (*fig*) schmerzen

pain: ~**ful** *a* schmerzhaft; (*fig*)
schmerzlich. ~-**killer** *n* schmerzstillendes Mittel *nt*. ~**less** *a*, -**ly** *adv*
schmerzlos

painstaking /'peɪnzteɪkɪŋ/ *a* sorgfältig

paint /peɪnt/ *n* Farbe *f* □ *vt/i* streichen;
⟨*artist:*⟩ malen. ~**brush** *n* Pinsel *m*. ~**er**
n Maler *m*; (*decorator*) Anstreicher *m*.
~**ing** *n* Malerei *f*; (*picture*) Gemälde *nt*

pair /peə(r)/ *n* Paar *nt*; ~ **of trousers**
Hose *f*; ~ **of scissors** Schere *f* □ *vt*
paaren □ *vi* ~ **off** Paare bilden

pajamas /pə'dʒɑːməz/ *n pl* (*Amer*)
Schlafanzug *m*

Pakistan /pɑːkɪ'stɑːn/ *n* Pakistan *nt*. ~**i**
a pakistanisch □ *n* Pakistaner(in) *m(f)*

pal /pæl/ *n* Freund(in) *m(f)*

palace /'pælɪs/ *n* Palast *m*

palatable /'pælətəbl/ *a* schmackhaft

palate /'pælət/ *n* Gaumen *m*

palatial /pə'leɪʃl/ *a* palastartig

palaver /pə'lɑːvə(r)/ *n* (*fam: fuss*) Theater *nt* (*fam*)

pale[1] /peɪl/ *n* (*stake*) Pfahl *m*; **beyond the ~** (*fam*) unmöglich

pale[2] *a* (**-r, -st**) blass □ *vi* blass werden. **~ness** *n* Blässe *f*

Palestin|e /'pælɪstaɪn/ *n* Palästina *nt*. **~ian** /pælə'stɪnɪən/ *a* palästinensisch □ *n* Palästinenser(in) *m(f)*

palette /'pælɪt/ *n* Palette *f*

pall /pɔːl/ *n* Sargtuch *nt*; (*fig*) Decke *f* □ *vi* an Reiz verlieren

pall|id /'pælɪd/ *a* bleich. **~or** *n* Blässe *f*

palm /pɑːm/ *n* Handfläche *f*; (*tree, symbol*) Palme *f* □ *vt* **~ sth off on s.o.** jdm etw andrehen. **P~ 'Sunday** *n* Palmsonntag *m*

palpable /'pælpəbl/ *a* tastbar; (*perceptible*) spürbar

palpitat|e /'pælpɪteɪt/ *vi* klopfen. **~ions** /-'teɪʃnz/ *npl* Herzklopfen *nt*

paltry /'pɔːltrɪ/ *a* (**-ier, -iest**) armselig

pamper /'pæmpə(r)/ *vt* verwöhnen

pamphlet /'pæmflɪt/ *n* Broschüre *f*

pan /pæn/ *n* Pfanne *f*; (*saucepan*) Topf *m*; (*of scales*) Schale *f* □ *vt* (*pt/pp* **panned**) (*fam*) verreißen

panacea /pænə'siːə/ *n* Allheilmittel *nt*

panache /pə'næʃ/ *n* Schwung *m*

'pancake *n* Pfannkuchen *m*

pancreas /'pæŋkrɪəs/ *n* Bauchspeicheldrüse *f*

panda /'pændə/ *n* Panda *m*. **~ car** *n* Streifenwagen *m*

pandemonium /pændɪ'məʊnɪəm/ *n* Höllenlärm *m*

pander /'pændə(r)/ *vi* **~ to s.o.** jdm zu sehr nachgeben

pane /peɪn/ *n* [Glas]scheibe *f*

panel /'pænl/ *n* Tafel *f*, Platte *f*; **~ of experts** Expertenrunde *f*; **~ of judges** Jury *f*. **~ling** *n* Täfelung *f*

pang /pæŋ/ *n* **~s of hunger** Hungergefühl *nt*; **~s of conscience** Gewissensbisse *pl*

panic /'pænɪk/ *n* Panik *f* □ *vi* (*pt/pp* **panicked**) in Panik geraten. **~-stricken** *a* von Panik ergriffen

panoram|a /pænə'rɑːmə/ *n* Panorama *nt*. **~ic** /-'ræmɪk/ *a* Panorama-

pansy /'pænzɪ/ *n* Stiefmütterchen *nt*

pant /pænt/ *vi* keuchen; ⟨*dog:*⟩ hecheln

pantechnicon /pæn'teknɪkən/ *n* Möbelwagen *m*

panther /'pænθə(r)/ *n* Panther *m*

panties /'pæntɪz/ *npl* [Damen]slip *m*

pantomime /'pæntəmaɪm/ *n* [zu Weihnachten aufgeführte] Märchenvorstellung *f*

pantry /'pæntrɪ/ *n* Speisekammer *f*

pants /pænts/ *npl* Unterhose *f*; (*woman's*) Schlüpfer *m*; (*trousers*) Hose *f*

'pantyhose *n* (*Amer*) Strumpfhose *f*

papal /'peɪpl/ *a* päpstlich

paper /'peɪpə(r)/ *n* Papier *nt*; (*wall~*) Tapete *f*; (*newspaper*) Zeitung *f*; (*exam ~*) Testbogen *m*; (*exam*) Klausur *f*; (*treatise*) Referat *nt*; **~s** *pl* (*documents*) Unterlagen *pl*; (*for identification*) [Ausweis]papiere *pl*; **on ~** schriftlich □ *vt* tapezieren

paper: ~back *n* Taschenbuch *nt*. **~clip** *n* Büroklammer *f*. **~knife** *n* Brieföffner *m*. **~weight** *n* Briefbeschwerer *m*. **~work** *n* Schreibarbeit *f*

par /pɑː(r)/ *n* (*Golf*) Par *nt*; **on a ~** gleichwertig (**with** *dat*); **feel below ~** sich nicht ganz auf der Höhe fühlen

parable /'pærəbl/ *n* Gleichnis *nt*

parachut|e /'pærəʃuːt/ *n* Fallschirm *m* □ *vi* [mit dem Fallschirm] abspringen. **~ist** *n* Fallschirmspringer *m*

parade /pə'reɪd/ *n* Parade *f*; (*procession*) Festzug *m* □ *vi* marschieren □ *vt* (*show off*) zur Schau stellen

paradise /'pærədaɪs/ *n* Paradies *nt*

paradox /'pærədɒks/ *n* Paradox *nt*. **~ical** *a* /-'dɒksɪkl/ paradox

paraffin /'pærəfɪn/ *n* Paraffin *nt*

paragon /'pærəgən/ *n* **~ of virtue** Ausbund *m* der Tugend

paragraph /'pærəgrɑːf/ *n* Absatz *m*

parallel /'pærəlel/ *a & adv* parallel □ *n* (*Geog*) Breitenkreis *m*; (*fig*) Parallele *f*

paralyse /'pærəlaɪz/ *vt* lähmen; (*fig*) lahm legen

paralysis /pə'ræləsɪs/ *n* (*pl* **-ses** /-siːz/) Lähmung *f*

paramount /'pærəmaʊnt/ *a* überragend; **be ~** vorgehen

paranoid /'pærənɔɪd/ *a* [krankhaft] misstrauisch

parapet /'pærəpɪt/ *n* Brüstung *f*

paraphernalia /pærəfə'neɪlɪə/ *n* Kram *m*

paraphrase /'pærəfreɪz/ *n* Umschreibung *f* □ *vt* umschreiben

paraplegic /pærə'pliːdʒɪk/ *a* querschnittsgelähmt □ *n* Querschnittsgelähmte(r) *m/f*

parasite /'pærəsaɪt/ *n* Parasit *m*, Schmarotzer *m*

parasol /'pærəsɒl/ *n* Sonnenschirm *m*

paratrooper /'pærətruːpə(r)/ *n* Fallschirmjäger *m*

parcel /'pɑːsl/ *n* Paket *nt*

parch /pɑːtʃ/ *vt* austrocknen; **be** ∼**ed** ⟨*person*:⟩ furchtbaren Durst haben

parchment /'pɑːtʃmənt/ *n* Pergament *nt*

pardon /'pɑːdn/ *n* Verzeihung *f*; (*Jur*) Begnadigung *f*; ∼? (*fam*) bitte? **I beg your** ∼ wie bitte? (*sorry*) Verzeihung! □ *vt* verzeihen; (*Jur*) begnadigen

pare /peə(r)/ *vt* (*peel*) schälen

parent /'peərənt/ *n* Elternteil *m*; ∼**s** *pl* Eltern *pl*. ∼**al** /pə'rentl/ *a* elterlich

parenthesis /pə'renθəsɪs/ *n* (*pl* -**ses** /-siːz/) Klammer *f*

parish /'pærɪʃ/ *n* Gemeinde *f*. ∼**ioner** /pə'rɪʃənə(r)/ *n* Gemeindemitglied *nt*

parity /'pærəti/ *n* Gleichheit *f*

park /pɑːk/ *n* Park *m* □ *vt/i* parken

parking /'pɑːkɪŋ/ *n* Parken *nt*; **'no** ∼' 'Parken verboten'. ∼**-lot** *n* (*Amer*) Parkplatz *m*. ∼**-meter** *n* Parkuhr *f*. ∼ **space** *n* Parkplatz *m*

parliament /'pɑːləmənt/ *n* Parlament *nt*. ∼**ary** /-'mentəri/ *a* parlamentarisch

parlour /'pɑːlə(r)/ *n* Wohnzimmer *nt*

parochial /pə'rəʊkɪəl/ *a* Gemeinde-; (*fig*) beschränkt

parody /'pærədi/ *n* Parodie *f* □ *vt* (*pt/pp* -**ied**) parodieren

parole /pə'rəʊl/ *n* **on** ∼ auf Bewährung

paroxysm /'pærəksɪzm/ *n* Anfall *m*

parquet /'pɑːkeɪ/ *n* ∼ **floor** Parkett *nt*

parrot /'pærət/ *n* Papagei *m*

parry /'pæri/ *vt* (*pt/pp* -**ied**) abwehren ⟨*blow*⟩; (*Fencing*) parieren

parsimonious /pɑːsɪ'məʊnɪəs/ *a* geizig

parsley /'pɑːsli/ *n* Petersilie *f*

parsnip /'pɑːsnɪp/ *n* Pastinake *f*

parson /'pɑːsn/ *n* Pfarrer *m*

part /pɑːt/ *n* Teil *m*; (*Techn*) Teil *nt*; (*area*) Gegend *f*; (*Theat*) Rolle *f*; (*Mus*) Part *m*; ∼ **spare** ∼ Ersatzteil *nt*; **for my** ∼ meinerseits; **on the** ∼ **of** vonseiten (+ *gen*); **take s.o.'s** ∼ für jdn Partei ergreifen; **take** ∼ **in** teilnehmen an (+ *dat*) □ *adv* teils □ *vt* trennen; scheiteln ⟨*hair*⟩ □ *vi* ⟨*people*:⟩ sich trennen; ∼ **with** sich trennen von

partake /pɑː'teɪk/ *vt* (*pt* -**took**, *pp* -**taken**) teilnehmen; ∼ **of** (*eat*) zu sich nehmen

part-ex'change *n* **take in** ∼ in Zahlung nehmen

partial /'pɑːʃl/ *a* Teil-; **be** ∼ **to** mögen. ∼**ity** /pɑːʃɪ'æləti/ *n* Voreingenommenheit *f*; (*liking*) Vorliebe *f*. -**ly** *adv* teilweise

particip|ant /pɑː'tɪsɪpənt/ *n* Teilnehmer(in) *m(f)*. ∼**ate** /-peɪt/ *vi* teilnehmen (**in** an + *dat*). ∼**ation** /-'peɪʃn/ *n* Teilnahme *f*

participle /'pɑːtɪsɪpl/ *n* Partizip *nt*; **present/past** ∼ erstes/zweites Partizip

particle /'pɑːtɪkl/ *n* Körnchen *nt*; (*Phys*) Partikel *nt*; (*Gram*) Partikel *f*

particular /pə'tɪkjʊlə(r)/ *a* besondere(r,s); (*precise*) genau; (*fastidious*) penibel; **in** ∼ besonders. ∼**ly** *adv* besonders. ∼**s** *npl* nähere Angaben *pl*

parting /'pɑːtɪŋ/ *n* Abschied *m*; (*in hair*) Scheitel *m* □ *attrib* Abschieds-

partition /pɑː'tɪʃn/ *n* Trennwand *f*; (*Pol*) Teilung *f* □ *vt* teilen. ∼ **off** *vt* abtrennen

partly /'pɑːtli/ *adv* teilweise

partner /'pɑːtnə(r)/ *n* Partner(in) *m(f)*; (*Comm*) Teilhaber *m*. ∼**ship** *n* Partnerschaft *f*; (*Comm*) Teilhaberschaft *f*

partridge /'pɑːtrɪdʒ/ *n* Rebhuhn *nt*

part-'time *a* & *adv* Teilzeit-; **be** *or* **work** ∼ Teilzeitarbeit machen

party /'pɑːti/ *n* Party *f*, Fest *nt*; (*group*) Gruppe *f*; (*Pol, Jur*) Partei *f*; **be** ∼ **to** sich beteiligen an (+ *dat*)

'party line[1] *n* (*Teleph*) Gemeinschaftsanschluss *m*

party 'line[2] *n* (*Pol*) Parteilinie *f*

pass /pɑːs/ *n* Ausweis *m*; (*Geog, Sport*) Pass *m*; (*Sch*) ≈ ausreichend; **get a** ∼ bestehen □ *vt* vorbeigehen/-fahren an (+ *dat*); (*overtake*) überholen; (*hand*) reichen; (*Sport*) abgeben, abspielen; (*approve*) annehmen; (*exceed*) übersteigen; bestehen ⟨*exam*⟩; machen ⟨*remark*⟩; fällen ⟨*judgement*⟩; (*Jur*) verhängen ⟨*sentence*⟩; ∼ **water** Wasser lassen; ∼ **the time** sich (*dat*) die Zeit vertreiben; ∼ **sth off as sth** etw als etw ausgeben; ∼ **one's hand over sth** mit der Hand über etw (*acc*) fahren □ *vi* vorbeigehen/-fahren; (*get by*) vorbeikommen; (*overtake*) überholen; ⟨*time*:⟩ vergehen; (*in exam*) bestehen; **let sth** ∼ (*fig*) etw übergehen; **[I]** ∼! [ich] passe! ∼ **away** *vi* sterben. ∼ **down** *vt* herunterreichen; (*fig*) weitergeben. ∼ **out** *vi* ohnmächtig werden. ∼ **round** *vt* herumreichen. ∼ **up** *vt* heraufreichen; (*fam: miss*) vorübergehen lassen

passable /'pɑːsəbl/ *a* ⟨*road*⟩ befahrbar; (*satisfactory*) passabel

passage /'pæsɪdʒ/ *n* Durchgang *m*; (*corridor*) Gang *m*; (*voyage*) Überfahrt *f*; (*in book*) Passage *f*

passenger /'pæsɪndʒə(r)/ *n* Fahrgast *m*; (*Naut, Aviat*) Passagier *m*; (*in car*) Mitfahrer *m*. ∼ **seat** *n* Beifahrersitz *m*

passer-by /pɑːsə'baɪ/ *n* (*pl* -**s-by**) Passant(in) *m(f)*

'passing place *n* Ausweichstelle *f*

passion /'pæʃn/ *n* Leidenschaft *f*. ∼**ate** /-ət/ *a*, -**ly** *adv* leidenschaftlich

passive /'pæsɪv/ *a* passiv □ *n* Passiv *nt*

Passover /'pɑːsəʊvə(r)/ n Passah nt

pass: ∼**port** n [Reise]pass m. ∼**word** n Kennwort nt; (Mil) Losung f

past /pɑːst/ a vergangene(r,s); (former) ehemalig; **in the** ∼ **few days** in den letzten paar Tagen; **that's all** ∼ das ist jetzt vorbei □ n Vergangenheit f □ prep an (+ dat) ... vorbei; (after) nach; **at ten** ∼ **two** um zehn nach zwei □ adv vorbei; **go/come** ∼ vorbeigehen/-kommen

pasta /'pæstə/ n Nudeln pl

paste /peɪst/ n Brei m; (dough) Teig m; (fish-, meat-) Paste f; (adhesive) Kleister m; (jewellery) Strass m □ vt kleistern

pastel /'pæstl/ n Pastellfarbe f; (crayon) Pastellstift m; (drawing) Pastell nt □ attrib Pastell-

pasteurize /'pɑːstʃəraɪz/ vt pasteurisieren

pastille /'pæstɪl/ n Pastille f

pastime /'pɑːstaɪm/ n Zeitvertreib m

pastoral /'pɑːstərl/ a ländlich; (care) seelsorgerisch

pastr|y /'peɪstrɪ/ n Teig m; **cakes and** ∼**ies** Kuchen und Gebäck

pasture /'pɑːstʃə(r)/ n Weide f

pasty[1] /'pæstɪ/ n Pastete f

pasty[2] /'peɪstɪ/ a blass, (fam) käsig

pat /pæt/ n Klaps m; (of butter) Stückchen nt □ adv **have sth off** ∼ etw aus dem Effeff können □ vt (pt/pp patted) tätscheln; ∼ **s.o. on the back** jdm auf die Schulter klopfen

patch /pætʃ/ n Flicken m; (spot) Fleck m; **not a** ∼ **on** (fam) gar nicht zu vergleichen mit □ vt flicken. ∼ **up** vt [zusammen]flicken; beilegen (quarrel)

patchy /'pætʃɪ/ a ungleichmäßig

pâté /'pæteɪ/ n Pastete f

patent /'peɪtnt/ a, -ly adv offensichtlich □ n Patent nt □ vt patentieren. ∼ **leather** n Lackleder nt

patern|al /pə'tɜːnl/ a väterlich. ∼**ity** n Vaterschaft f

path /pɑːθ/ n (pl ∼s /pɑːðz/) [Fuß]weg m, Pfad m; (orbit, track) Bahn f; (fig) Weg m

pathetic /pə'θetɪk/ a mitleiderregend; (attempt) erbärmlich

patholog|ical /pæθə'lɒdʒɪkl/ a pathologisch. ∼**ist** /pə'θɒlədʒɪst/ n Pathologe m

pathos /'peɪθɒs/ n Rührseligkeit f

patience /'peɪʃns/ n Geduld f; (game) Patience f

patient /'peɪʃnt/ a, -ly adv geduldig □ n Patient(in) m(f)

patio /'pætɪəʊ/ n Terrasse f

patriot /'pætrɪət/ n Patriot(in) m(f). ∼**ic** /-'ɒtɪk/ a patriotisch. ∼**ism** n Patriotismus m

Patrol /pə'trəʊl/ n Patrouille f □ vt/i patrouillieren [in (+ dat)]; (police:) auf Streife gehen/fahren [in (+ dat)]. ∼ **car** n Streifenwagen m

patron /'peɪtrən/ n Gönner m; (of charity) Schirmherr m; (of the arts) Mäzen m; (customer) Kunde m/Kundin f; (Theat) Besucher m. ∼**age** /'pætrənɪdʒ/ n Schirmherrschaft f

patroniz|e /'pætrənaɪz/ vt (fig) herablassend behandeln. ∼**ing** a, -ly adv gönnerhaft

patter[1] /'pætə(r)/ n Getrippel nt; (of rain) Plätschern nt □ vi trippeln; plätschern

patter[2] n (speech) Gerede nt

pattern /'pætn/ n Muster nt

paunch /pɔːntʃ/ n [Schmer]bauch m

pauper /'pɔːpə(r)/ n Arme(r) m/f

pause /pɔːz/ n Pause f □ vi innehalten

pave /peɪv/ vt pflastern; ∼ **the way** den Weg bereiten (for dat). ∼**ment** n Bürgersteig m

pavilion /pə'vɪljən/ n Pavillon m; (Sport) Klubhaus nt

paw /pɔː/ n Pfote f; (of large animal) Pranke f, Tatze f

pawn[1] /pɔːn/ n (Chess) Bauer m; (fig) Schachfigur f

pawn[2] vt verpfänden □ n **in** ∼ verpfändet. ∼ **broker** n Pfandleiher m. ∼**shop** n Pfandhaus nt

pay /peɪ/ n Lohn m; (salary) Gehalt nt; **be in the** ∼ **of** bezahlt werden von □ v (pt/pp paid) □ vt bezahlen; zahlen (money); ∼ **s.o. a visit** jdm einen Besuch abstatten; ∼ **s.o. a compliment** jdm ein Kompliment machen □ vi zahlen; (be profitable) sich bezahlt machen; (fig) sich lohnen; ∼ **for** sth etw bezahlen. ∼ **back** vt zurückzahlen. ∼ **in** vt einzahlen. ∼ **off** vt abzahlen (debt) □ vi (fig) sich auszahlen. ∼ **up** vi zahlen

payable /'peɪəbl/ a zahlbar; **make** ∼ **to** ausstellen auf (+ acc)

payee /peɪ'iː/ n [Zahlungs]empfänger m

payment /'peɪmənt/ n Bezahlung f; (amount) Zahlung f

pay: ∼ **packet** n Lohntüte f. ∼**phone** n Münzfernsprecher m

pea /piː/ n Erbse f

peace /piːs/ n Frieden m; **for my** ∼ **of mind** zu meiner eigenen Beruhigung

peace|able /'piːsəbl/ a friedlich. ∼**ful** a, -ly adv friedlich. ∼**maker** n Friedensstifter m

peach /piːtʃ/ n Pfirsich m

peacock /'piːkɒk/ n Pfau m

peak /piːk/ n Gipfel m; (fig) Höhepunkt m. ∼**ed 'cap** n Schirmmütze f. ∼ **hours** npl

Hauptbelastungszeit *f*; (*for traffic*) Hauptverkehrszeit *f*

peaky /'piːkɪ/ *a* kränklich

peal /piːl/ *n* (*of bells*) Glockengeläut *nt*; ∼s **of laughter** schallendes Gelächter *nt*

'peanut *n* Erdnuss *f*; **for** ∼s (*fam*) für einen Apfel und ein Ei

pear /peə(r)/ *n* Birne *f*

pearl /pɜːl/ *n* Perle *f*

peasant /'peznt/ *n* Bauer *m*

peat /piːt/ *n* Torf *m*

pebble /'pebl/ *n* Kieselstein *m*

peck /pek/ *n* Schnabelhieb *m*; (*kiss*) flüchtiger Kuss *m* □ *vt/i* picken/(*nip*) hacken (**at** nach). ∼**ing order** *n* Hackordnung *f*

peckish /'pekɪʃ/ *a* **be** ∼ (*fam*) Hunger haben

peculiar /pɪ'kjuːlɪə(r)/ *a* eigenartig, seltsam; ∼ **to** eigentümlich (+ *dat*). ∼**ity** /-'ærətɪ/ *n* Eigenart *f*

pedal /'pedl/ *n* Pedal *nt* □ *vt* fahren ⟨*bicycle*⟩ □ *vi* treten. ∼ **bin** *n* Treteimer *m*

pedantic /pɪ'dæntɪk/ *a*, **-ally** *adv* pedantisch

peddle /'pedl/ *vt* handeln mit

pedestal /'pedɪstl/ *n* Sockel *m*

pedestrian /pɪ'destrɪən/ *n* Fußgänger(in) *m(f)* □ *a* (*fig*) prosaisch. ∼ **'crossing** *n* Fußgängerüberweg *m*. ∼ **'precinct** *n* Fußgängerzone *f*

pedicure /'pedɪkjʊə(r)/ *n* Pediküre *f*

pedigree /'pedɪgriː/ *n* Stammbaum *m* □ *attrib* ⟨*animal*⟩ Rasse-

pedlar /'pedlə(r)/ *n* Hausierer *m*

pee /piː/ *vi* (*pt/pp* **peed**) (*fam*) pinkeln

peek /piːk/ *vi* (*fam*) gucken

peel /piːl/ *n* Schale *f* □ *vt* schälen; □ *vi* ⟨*skin:*⟩ sich schälen; ⟨*paint:*⟩ abblättern. ∼**ings** *npl* Schalen *pl*

peep /piːp/ *n* kurzer Blick *m* □ *vi* gucken. ∼**-hole** *n* Guckloch *nt*. **P**∼**ing 'Tom** *n* (*fam*) Spanner *m*

peer[1] /pɪə(r)/ *vi* ∼ **at** forschend ansehen

peer[2] *n* Peer *m*; **his** ∼s *pl* seinesgleichen

peev|ed /piːvd/ *a* (*fam*) ärgerlich. ∼**ish** *a* reizbar

peg /peg/ *n* (*hook*) Haken *m*; (*for tent*) Pflock *m*, Hering *m*; (*for clothes*) [Wäsche]klammer *f*; **off the** ∼ (*fam*) von der Stange □ *vt* (*pt/pp* **pegged**) anpflocken; anklammern ⟨*washing*⟩

pejorative /pɪ'dʒɒrətɪv/ *a*, **-ly** *adv* abwertend

pelican /'pelɪkən/ *n* Pelikan *m*

pellet /'pelɪt/ *n* Kügelchen *nt*

pelt[1] /pelt/ *n* (*skin*) Pelz *m*, Fell *nt*

pelt[2] *vt* bewerfen □ *vi* (*fam: run fast*) rasen; ∼ **[down]** ⟨*rain:*⟩ [hernieder]prasseln

pelvis /'pelvɪs/ *n* (*Anat*) Becken *nt*

pen[1] /pen/ *n* (*for animals*) Hürde *f*

pen[2] *n* Federhalter *m*; (*ball-point*) Kugelschreiber *m*

penal /'piːnl/ *a* Straf-. ∼**ize** *vt* bestrafen; (*fig*) benachteiligen

penalty /'penltɪ/ *n* Strafe *f*; (*fine*) Geldstrafe *f*; (*Sport*) Strafstoß *m*; (*Football*) Elfmeter *m*

penance /'penəns/ *n* Buße *f*

pence /pens/ *see* **penny**

pencil /'pensl/ *n* Bleistift *m* □ *vt* (*pt/pp* **pencilled**) mit Bleistift schreiben. ∼**sharpener** *n* Bleistiftspitzer *m*

pendant /'pendənt/ *n* Anhänger *m*

pending /'pendɪŋ/ *a* unerledigt □ *prep* bis zu

pendulum /'pendjʊləm/ *n* Pendel *nt*

penetrat|e /'penɪtreɪt/ *vt* durchdringen; ∼**e [into]** eindringen in (+ *acc*). ∼**ing** *a* durchdringend. ∼**ion** /-'treɪʃn/ *n* Durchdringen *nt*

'penfriend *n* Brieffreund(in) *m(f)*

penguin /'peŋgwɪn/ *n* Pinguin *m*

penicillin /penɪ'sɪlɪn/ *n* Penizillin *nt*

peninsula /pə'nɪnsʊlə/ *n* Halbinsel *f*

penis /'piːnɪs/ *n* Penis *m*

peniten|ce /'penɪtəns/ *n* Reue *f*. ∼**t** *a* reuig □ *n* Büßer *m*

penitentiary /penɪ'tenʃərɪ/ *n* (*Amer*) Gefängnis *nt*

pen: ∼**knife** *n* Taschenmesser *nt*. ∼**-name** *n* Pseudonym *nt*

pennant /'penənt/ *n* Wimpel *m*

penniless /'penɪlɪs/ *a* mittellos

penny /'penɪ/ *n* (*pl* **pence**; *single coins* **pennies**) Penny *m*; (*Amer*) Centstück *nt*; **spend a** ∼ (*fam*) mal verschwinden; **the** ∼**'s dropped** (*fam*) der Groschen ist gefallen

pension /'penʃn/ *n* Rente *f*; (*of civil servant*) Pension *f*. ∼**er** *n* Rentner(in) *m(f)*; Pensionär(in) *m(f)*

pensive /'pensɪv/ *a* nachdenklich

Pentecost /'pentɪkɒst/ *n* Pfingsten *nt*

pent-up /'pentʌp/ *a* angestaut

penultimate /pe'nʌltɪmət/ *a* vorletzte(r,s)

penury /'penjʊrɪ/ *n* Armut *f*

peony /'pɪənɪ/ *n* Pfingstrose *f*

people /'piːpl/ *npl* Leute *pl*, Menschen *pl*; (*citizens*) Bevölkerung *f*; **the** ∼ das Volk; **English** ∼ die Engländer; ∼ **say** man sagt; **for four** ∼ für vier Personen □ *vt* bevölkern

pep /pep/ *n* (*fam*) Schwung *m*

pepper /'pepə(r)/ n Pfeffer m; (vegetable) Paprika m; a ~ (fruit) eine Paprika[schote] □ vt (Culin) pfeffern

pepper: ~corn n Pfefferkorn nt. ~mint n Pfefferminz nt; (Bot) Pfefferminze f. ~pot n Pfefferstreuer m

per /pɜ:(r)/ prep pro; ~ **cent** Prozent nt

perceive /pə'si:v/ vt wahrnehmen

percentage /pə'sentɪdʒ/ n Prozentsatz m; (part) Teil m

perceptible /pə'septəbl/ a wahrnehmbar

percept|ion /pə'sepʃn/ n Wahrnehmung f. ~**ive** /-tɪv/ a feinsinnig

perch¹ /pɜ:tʃ/ n Stange f □ vi (bird:) sich niederlassen

perch² n inv (fish) Barsch m

percolat|e /'pɜ:kəleɪt/ vi durchsickern. ~**or** n Kaffeemaschine f

percussion /pə'kʌʃn/ n Schlagzeug nt. ~ **instrument** n Schlaginstrument nt

peremptory /pə'remptəri/ a herrisch

perennial /pə'reniəl/ a (problem:) immer wiederkehrend □ n (Bot) mehrjährige Pflanze f

perfect¹ /'pɜ:fɪkt/ a perfekt, vollkommen; (fam: utter) völlig □ n (Gram) Perfekt nt

perfect² /pə'fekt/ vt vervollkommnen. ~**ion** /-ekʃn/ n Vollkommenheit f; **to** ~**ion** perfekt

perfectly /'pɜ:fɪktlɪ/ adv perfekt; (completely) vollkommen, völlig

perforate /'pɜ:fəreɪt/ vt perforieren; (make a hole in) durchlöchern. ~**d** a perforiert

perform /pə'fɔ:m/ vt ausführen; erfüllen (duty:); (Theat) aufführen (play:); spielen (role:) □ vi (Theat) auftreten; (Techn) laufen. ~**ance** n Aufführung f; (at theatre, cinema) Vorstellung f; (Techn) Leistung f. ~**er** n Künstler(in) m(f)

perfume /'pɜ:fju:m/ n Parfüm nt; (smell) Duft m

perfunctory /pə'fʌŋktəri/ a flüchtig

perhaps /pə'hæps/ adv vielleicht

peril /'perəl/ n Gefahr f. ~**ous** /-əs/ a gefährlich

perimeter /pə'rɪmɪtə(r)/ n [äußere] Grenze f; (Geom) Umfang m

period /'pɪərɪəd/ n Periode f; (Sch) Stunde f; (full stop) Punkt m □ attrib (costume) zeitgenössisch; (furniture) antik. ~**ic** /-'ɒdɪk/ a, ~**ally** adv periodisch. ~**ical** /-'ɒdɪkl/ n Zeitschrift f

peripher|al /pə'rɪfərl/ a nebensächlich. ~**y** n Peripherie f

periscope /'perɪskəʊp/ n Periskop nt

perish /'perɪʃ/ vi (rubber:) verrotten; (food:) verderben; (die) ums Leben kommen. ~**ing** a (fam: cold) eiskalt

perjur|e /'pɜ:dʒə(r)/ vt ~**e oneself** einen Meineid leisten. ~**y** n Meineid m

perk¹ /pɜ:k/ n (fam) [Sonder]vergünstigung f

perk² vi ~ **up** munter werden

perky /'pɜ:kɪ/ a munter

perm /pɜ:m/ n Dauerwelle f □ vt ~ **s.o.'s hair** jdm eine Dauerwelle machen

permanent /'pɜ:mənənt/ a ständig; (job, address) fest. ~**ly** adv ständig; (work, live) dauernd, permanent; (employed) fest

permeable /'pɜ:mɪəbl/ a durchlässig

permeate /'pɜ:mɪeɪt/ vt durchdringen

permissible /pə'mɪsəbl/ a erlaubt

permission /pə'mɪʃn/ n Erlaubnis f

permissive /pə'mɪsɪv/ a (society) permissiv

permit¹ /pə'mɪt/ vt (pt/pp -mitted) erlauben (s.o. jdm); ~ **me!** gestatten Sie!

permit² /'pɜ:mɪt/ n Genehmigung f

pernicious /pə'nɪʃəs/ a schädlich; (Med) perniziös

perpendicular /pɜ:pən'dɪkjʊlə(r)/ a senkrecht □ n Senkrechte f

perpetrat|e /'pɜ:pɪtreɪt/ vt begehen. ~**or** n Täter m

perpetual /pə'petjʊəl/ a, ~**ly** adv ständig, dauernd

perpetuate /pə'petjʊeɪt/ vt bewahren; verewigen (error:)

perplex /pə'pleks/ vt verblüffen. ~**ed** a verblüfft. ~**ity** n Verblüffung f

persecut|e /'pɜ:sɪkju:t/ vt verfolgen. ~**ion** /-'kju:ʃn/ n Verfolgung f

perseverance /pɜ:sɪ'vɪərəns/ n Ausdauer f

persever|e /pɜ:sɪ'vɪə(r)/ vi beharrlich weitermachen. ~**ing** a ausdauernd

Persia /'pɜ:ʃə/ n Persien nt

Persian /'pɜ:ʃn/ a persisch; (cat, carpet) Perser-

persist /pə'sɪst/ vi beharrlich weitermachen; (continue) anhalten; (view:) weiter bestehen; ~ **in doing sth** dabei bleiben, etw zu tun. ~**ence** n Beharrlichkeit f. ~**ent** a, ~**ly** adv beharrlich; (continuous) anhaltend

person /'pɜ:sn/ n Person f; **in** ~ persönlich

personal /'pɜ:sənl/ a, ~**ly** adv persönlich. ~ **'hygiene** n Körperpflege f

personality /pɜ:sə'nælətɪ/ n Persönlichkeit f

personify /pə'sɒnɪfaɪ/ *vt* (*pt/pp* -ied) personifizieren, verkörpern

personnel /pɜːsə'nel/ *n* Personal *nt*

perspective /pə'spektɪv/ *n* Perspektive *f*

perspicacious /pɜːspɪ'keɪʃəs/ *a* scharfsichtig

persp|iration /pɜːspɪ'reɪʃn/ *n* Schweiß *m*. ~**ire** /-'spaɪə(r)/ *vi* schwitzen

persua|de /pə'sweɪd/ *vt* überreden; (*convince*) überzeugen. ~**sion** /-eɪʒn/ *n* Überredung *f*; (*powers of* ~*sion*) Überredungskunst *f*; (*belief*) Glaubensrichtung *f*

persuasive /pə'sweɪsɪv/ *a*, -**ly** *adv* beredsam; (*convincing*) überzeugend

pert /pɜːt/ *a*, -**ly** *adv* kess

pertain /pə'teɪn/ *vi* ~ **to** betreffen; (*belong*) gehören zu

pertinent /'pɜːtɪnənt/ *a* relevant (**to** für)

perturb /pə'tɜːb/ *vt* beunruhigen

peruse /pə'ruːz/ *vt* lesen

perva|de /pə'veɪd/ *vt* durchdringen. ~**sive** /-sɪv/ *a* durchdringend

pervers|e /pə'vɜːs/ *a* eigensinnig. ~**ion** /-ɜːʃn/ *n* Perversion *f*

pervert[1] /pə'vɜːt/ *vt* verdrehen; verführen ⟨*person*⟩

pervert[2] /'pɜːvɜːt/ *n* Perverse(r) *m*

perverted /pə'vɜːtɪd/ *a* abartig

pessimis|m /'pesɪmɪzm/ *n* Pessimismus *m*. ~**t** /-mɪst/ *n* Pessimist *m*. ~**tic** /-'mɪstɪk/ *a*, -**ally** *adv* pessimistisch

pest /pest/ *n* Schädling *m*; (*fam: person*) Nervensäge *f*

pester /'pestə(r)/ *vt* belästigen; ~ **s.o. for sth** jdm wegen etw in den Ohren liegen

pesticide /'pestɪsaɪd/ *n* Schädlingsbekämpfungsmittel *nt*

pet /pet/ *n* Haustier *nt*; (*favourite*) Liebling *m* □ *vt* (*pt/pp* petted) liebkosen

petal /'petl/ *n* Blütenblatt *nt*

peter /'piːtə(r)/ *vi* ~ **out** allmählich aufhören; ⟨*stream:*⟩ versickern

petite /pə'tiːt/ *a* klein und zierlich

petition /pə'tɪʃn/ *n* Bittschrift *f* □ *vt* eine Bittschrift richten an (+ *acc*)

pet 'name *n* Kosename *m*

petrif|y /'petrɪfaɪ/ *vt/i* (*pt/pp* -ied) versteinern; ~**ied** (*frightened*) vor Angst wie versteinert

petrol /'petrl/ *n* Benzin *nt*

petroleum /pɪ'trəʊlɪəm/ *n* Petroleum *nt*

petrol: ~**pump** *n* Zapfsäule *f*. ~ **station** *n* Tankstelle *f*. ~ **tank** *n* Benzintank *m*

'pet shop *n* Tierhandlung *f*

petticoat /'petɪkəʊt/ *n* Unterrock *m*

petty /'petɪ/ *a* (-**ier**, -**iest**) kleinlich. ~ **'cash** *n* Portokasse *f*

petulant /'petjʊlənt/ *a* gekränkt

pew /pjuː/ *n* [Kirchen]bank *f*

pewter /'pjuːtə(r)/ *n* Zinn *nt*

phantom /'fæntəm/ *n* Gespenst *nt*

pharmaceutical /fɑːmə'sjuːtɪkl/ *a* pharmazeutisch

pharmac|ist /'fɑːməsɪst/ *n* Apotheker(in) *m(f)*. ~**y** *n* Pharmazie *f*; (*shop*) Apotheke *f*

phase /feɪz/ *n* Phase *f* □ *vt* ~ **in/out** allmählich einführen/abbauen

Ph.D. (*abbr of* **Doctor of Philosophy**) Dr. phil.

pheasant /'feznt/ *n* Fasan *m*

phenomen|al /fɪ'nɒmɪnl/ *a* phänomenal. ~**on** *n* (*pl* -**na**) Phänomen *nt*

phial /'faɪəl/ *n* Fläschchen *nt*

philanderer /fɪ'lændərə(r)/ *n* Verführer *m*

philanthrop|ic /fɪlən'θrɒpɪk/ *a* menschenfreundlich. ~**ist** /fɪ'lænθrəpɪst/ *n* Philanthrop *m*

philately /fɪ'lætəlɪ/ *n* Philatelie *f*, Briefmarkenkunde *f*

philharmonic /fɪlɑː'mɒnɪk/ *n* (*orchestra*) Philharmoniker *pl*

Philippines /'fɪlɪpiːnz/ *npl* Philippinen *pl*

philistine /'fɪlɪstaɪn/ *n* Banause *m*

philosoph|er /fɪ'lɒsəfə(r)/ *n* Philosoph *m*. ~**ical** /fɪlə'sɒfɪkl/ *a*, -**ly** *adv* philosophisch. ~**y** *n* Philosophie *f*

phlegm /flem/ *n* (*Med*) Schleim *m*

phlegmatic /fleg'mætɪk/ *a* phlegmatisch

phobia /'fəʊbɪə/ *n* Phobie *f*

phone /fəʊn/ *n* Telefon *nt*; **be on the** ~ Telefon haben; (*be phoning*) telefonieren □ *vt* anrufen □ *vi* telefonieren. ~ **back** *vt/i* zurückrufen. ~ **book** *n* Telefonbuch *nt*. ~ **box** *n* Telefonzelle *f*. ~ **card** *n* Telefonkarte *f*. ~**in** *n* (*Radio*) Hörersendung *f*. ~ **number** *n* Telefonnummer *f*

phonetic /fə'netɪk/ *a* phonetisch. ~**s** *n* Phonetik *f*

phoney /'fəʊnɪ/ *a* (-**ier**, -**iest**) falsch; (*forged*) gefälscht

phosphorus /'fɒsfərəs/ *n* Phosphor *m*

photo /'fəʊtəʊ/ *n* Foto *nt*, Aufnahme *f*. ~**copier** *n* Fotokopiergerät *nt*. ~**copy** *n* Fotokopie *f* □ *vt* fotokopieren

photogenic /fəʊtəʊ'dʒenɪk/ *a* fotogen

photograph /'fəʊtəgrɑːf/ *n* Fotografie *f*, Aufnahme *f* □ *vt* fotografieren

photograph|er /fə'tɒgrəfə(r)/ *n* Fotograf(in) *m(f)*. ~**ic** /fəʊtə'græfɪk/ *a*, -**ally** *adv* fotografisch. ~**y** *n* Fotografie *f*

phrase /freɪz/ *n* Redensart *f* □ *vt* formulieren. ~**book** *n* Sprachführer *m*

physical /'fızıkl/ *a*, **-ly** *adv* körperlich; ⟨*geography, law*⟩ physikalisch. **∼ edu'ca**-**tion** *n* Turnen *nt*

physician /fı'zıʃn/ *n* Arzt *m*/ Ärztin *f*

physic|ist /'fızısıst/ *n* Physiker(in) *m(f)*. **∼s** *n* Physik *f*

physiology /fızı'ɒlədʒı/ *n* Physiologie *f*

physio'therap|ist /fızıǝʋ-/ *n* Physiotherapeut(in) *m(f)*. **∼y** *n* Physiotherapie *f*

physique /fı'zi:k/ *n* Körperbau *m*

pianist /'pıǝnıst/ *n* Klavierspieler(in) *m(f)*; ⟨*professional*⟩ Pianist(in) *m(f)*

piano /pı'ænǝʋ/ *n* Klavier *nt*

pick[1] /pık/ *n* Spitzhacke *f*

pick[2] *n* Auslese *f*; **take one's ∼** sich ⟨*dat*⟩ aussuchen □ *vt/i* ⟨*pluck*⟩ pflücken; ⟨*select*⟩ wählen, sich ⟨*dat*⟩ aussuchen; **∼ and choose** wählerisch sein; **∼ one's nose** in der Nase bohren; **∼ a quarrel** einen Streit anfangen; **∼ a hole in sth** ein Loch in etw ⟨*acc*⟩ machen; **∼ holes in** ⟨*fam*⟩ kritisieren; **∼ at one's food** im Essen herumstochern. **∼ on** *vt* wählen; ⟨*fam: find fault with*⟩ herumhacken auf (+ *dat*). **∼ up** *vt* in die Hand nehmen; ⟨*off the ground*⟩ aufheben; hochnehmen ⟨*baby*⟩; ⟨*learn*⟩ lernen; ⟨*acquire*⟩ erwerben; ⟨*buy*⟩ kaufen; ⟨*Teleph*⟩ abnehmen ⟨*receiver*⟩; auffangen ⟨*signal*⟩; ⟨*collect*⟩ abholen; aufnehmen ⟨*passengers*⟩; ⟨*police:*⟩ aufgreifen ⟨*criminal*⟩; sich holen ⟨*illness*⟩; ⟨*fam*⟩ aufgabeln ⟨*girl*⟩; **∼ oneself up** aufstehen □ *vi* ⟨*improve*⟩ sich bessern

'pickaxe *n* Spitzhacke *f*

picket /'pıkıt/ *n* Streikposten *m* □ *vt* Streikposten aufstellen vor (+ *dat*). **∼ line** *n* Streikpostenkette *f*

pickle /'pıkl/ *n*, ⟨*Amer: gherkin*⟩ Essiggurke *f*; **∼s** *pl* [Mixed] Pickles *pl* □ *vt* einlegen

pick: ∼pocket *n* Taschendieb *m*. **∼-up** *n* ⟨*truck*⟩ Lieferwagen *m*; ⟨*on record-player*⟩ Tonabnehmer *m*

picnic /'pıknık/ *n* Picknick *nt* □ *vi* ⟨*pt/pp* **-nicked**⟩ picknicken

pictorial /pık'tɔ:rıǝl/ *a* bildlich

picture /'pıktʃǝ(r)/ *n* Bild *nt*; ⟨*film*⟩ Film *m*; **as pretty as a ∼** bildhübsch; **put s.o. in the ∼** ⟨*fig*⟩ jdn ins Bild setzen □ *vt* ⟨*imagine*⟩ sich ⟨*dat*⟩ vorstellen

picturesque /pıktʃǝ'resk/ *a* malerisch

pie /paı/ *n* Pastete *f*; ⟨*fruit ∼*⟩ Kuchen *m*

piece /pi:s/ *n* Stück *nt*; ⟨*of set*⟩ Teil *nt*; ⟨*in game*⟩ Stein *m*; ⟨*Journ*⟩ Artikel *m*; **a ∼ of bread/paper** ein Stück Brot/Papier; **a ∼ of news/advice** eine Nachricht/ein Rat; **take to ∼s** auseinander nehmen □ *vt* **∼ together** zusammensetzen; ⟨*fig*⟩

zusammenstückeln. **∼meal** *adv* stückweise. **∼-work** *n* Akkordarbeit *f*

pier /pıǝ(r)/ *n* Pier *m*; ⟨*pillar*⟩ Pfeiler *m*

pierc|e /pıǝs/ *vt* durchstechen; **∼e a hole in sth** ein Loch in etw ⟨*acc*⟩ stechen. **∼ing** *a* durchdringend

piety /'paıǝtı/ *n* Frömmigkeit *f*

piffle /'pıfl/ *n* ⟨*fam*⟩ Quatsch *m*

pig /pıg/ *n* Schwein *nt*

pigeon /'pıdʒın/ *n* Taube *f*. **∼-hole** *n* Fach *nt*

piggy /'pıgı/ *n* ⟨*fam*⟩ Schweinchen *nt*. **∼back** *n* **give s.o. a ∼back** jdn huckepack tragen. **∼ bank** *n* Sparschwein *nt*

pig'headed *a* ⟨*fam*⟩ starrköpfig

pigment /'pıgmǝnt/ *n* Pigment *nt*. **∼ation** /-men'teıʃn/ *n* Pigmentierung *f*

pig: ∼skin *n* Schweinsleder *nt*. **∼sty** *n* Schweinestall *m*. **∼tail** *n* ⟨*fam*⟩ Zopf *m*

pike /paık/ *n inv* ⟨*fish*⟩ Hecht *m*

pilchard /'pıltʃǝd/ *n* Sardine *f*

pile[1] /paıl/ *n* ⟨*of fabric*⟩ Flor *m*

pile[2] *n* Haufen *m* □ *vt* **∼ sth on to sth** auf etw ⟨*acc*⟩ häufen. **∼ up** *vt* aufhäufen □ *vi* sich häufen

piles /paılz/ *npl* Hämorrhoiden *pl*

'pile-up *n* Massenkarambolage *f*

pilfer /'pılfǝ(r)/ *vt/i* stehlen

pilgrim /'pılgrım/ *n* Pilger(in) *m(f)*. **∼age** /-ıdʒ/ *n* Pilgerfahrt *f*, Wallfahrt *f*

pill /pıl/ *n* Pille *f*

pillage /'pılıdʒ/ *vt* plündern

pillar /'pılǝ(r)/ *n* Säule *f*. **∼-box** *n* Briefkasten *m*

pillion /'pılıǝn/ *n* Sozius[sitz] *m*

pillory /'pılǝrı/ *n* Pranger *m* □ *vt* ⟨*pt/pp* -ied⟩ anprangern

pillow /'pılǝʋ/ *n* Kopfkissen *nt*. **∼case** *n* Kopfkissenbezug *m*

pilot /'paılǝt/ *n* Pilot *m*; ⟨*Naut*⟩ Lotse *m* □ *vt* fliegen ⟨*plane*⟩; lotsen ⟨*ship*⟩. **∼-light** *n* Zündflamme *f*

pimp /pımp/ *n* Zuhälter *m*

pimple /'pımpl/ *n* Pickel *m*

pin /pın/ *n* Stecknadel *f*; ⟨*Techn*⟩ Bolzen *m*, Stift *m*; ⟨*Med*⟩ Nagel *m*; **I have ∼s and needles in my leg** ⟨*fam*⟩ mein Bein ist eingeschlafen □ *vt* ⟨*pt/pp* pinned⟩ anstecken ⟨**to/on** an + *acc*⟩; ⟨*sewing*⟩ stecken; ⟨*hold down*⟩ festhalten; **∼ sth on s.o.** ⟨*fam*⟩ jdm etw anhängen. **∼ up** *vt* hochstecken; ⟨*on wall*⟩ anheften, anschlagen

pinafore /'pınǝfɔ:(r)/ *n* Schürze *f*. **∼ dress** *n* Kleiderrock *m*

pincers /'pınsǝz/ *npl* Kneifzange *f*; ⟨*Zool*⟩ Scheren *pl*

pinch /pıntʃ/ *n* Kniff *m*; ⟨*of salt*⟩ Prise *f*; **at a ∼** ⟨*fam*⟩ zur Not □ *vt* kneifen, zwicken;

(fam: steal) klauen; ~ **one's finger** sich *(dat)* den Finger klemmen □ *vi (shoe:)* drücken

'**pincushion** *n* Nadelkissen *nt*

pine[1] /pain/ *n (tree)* Kiefer *f*

pine[2] *vi* ~ **for** sich sehnen nach; ~ **away** sich verzehren

pineapple /'pain-/ *n* Ananas *f*

ping /piŋ/ *n* Klingeln *nt*

'**ping-pong** *n* Tischtennis *nt*

pink /piŋk/ *a* rosa

pinnacle /'pinəkl/ *n* Gipfel *m*; *(on roof)* Turmspitze *f*

pin: ~**point** *vt* genau festlegen. ~**stripe** *n* Nadelstreifen *m*

pint /paint/ *n* Pint *nt (0,571, Amer: 0,47 l)*

'**pin-up** *n* Pin-up-Girl *nt*

pioneer /paiə'niə(r)/ *n* Pionier *m* □ *vt* bahnbrechende Arbeit leisten für

pious /'paiəs/ *a*, **-ly** *adv* fromm

pip[1] /pip/ *n (seed)* Kern *m*

pip[2] *n (sound)* Tonsignal *nt*

pipe /paip/ *n* Pfeife *f*; *(for water, gas)* Rohr *nt* □ *vt* in Rohren leiten; *(Culin)* spritzen. ~ **down** *vi (fam)* den Mund halten

pipe: ~**dream** *n* Luftschloss *nt*. ~**line** *n* Pipeline *f*; **in the** ~**line** *(fam)* in Vorbereitung

piper /'paipə(r)/ *n* Pfeifer *m*

piping /'paipiŋ/ *a* ~ **hot** kochend heiß

piquant /'pi:kənt/ *a* pikant

pique /pi:k/ *n* **in a fit of** ~ beleidigt

pirate /'paiərət/ *n* Pirat *m*

Pisces /'paisi:z/ *n (Astr)* Fische *pl*

piss /pis/ *vi (sl)* pissen

pistol /'pistl/ *n* Pistole *f*

piston /'pistən/ *n (Techn)* Kolben *m*

pit /pit/ *n* Grube *f*; *(for orchestra)* Orchestergraben *m* □ *vt (pt/pp* **pitted**) *(fig)* messen (**against** mit)

pitch[1] /pitʃ/ *n (steepness)* Schräge *f*; *(of voice)* Stimmlage *f*; *(of sound)* [Ton]höhe *f*; *(Sport)* Feld *nt*; *(of street-trader)* Standplatz *m*; *(fig: degree)* Grad *m* □ *vt* werfen; aufschlagen *(tent)* □ *vi* fallen

pitch[2] *n (tar)* Pech *nt*. ~-'**black** *a* pechschwarz. ~-'**dark** *a* stockdunkel

pitcher /'pitʃə(r)/ *n* Krug *m*

'**pitchfork** *n* Heugabel *f*

piteous /'pitiəs/ *a* erbärmlich

'**pitfall** *n (fig)* Falle *f*

pith /piθ/ *n (Bot)* Mark *nt*; *(of orange)* weiße Haut *f*; *(fig)* Wesentliche(s) *nt*

pithy /'piθi/ *a (-ier, -iest) (fig)* prägnant

piti|ful /'pitifl/ *a* bedauernswert. ~**less** *a* mitleidslos

pittance /'pitns/ *n* Hungerlohn *m*

pity /'piti/ *n* Mitleid *nt*, Erbarmen *nt*; **[what a]** ~**!** *[wie]* schade! **take** ~ **on** sich erbarmen über (+ *acc*) □ *vt* bemitleiden

pivot /'pivət/ *n* Drehzapfen *m*; *(fig)* Angelpunkt *m* □ *vi* sich drehen (**on** um)

pixie /'piksi/ *n* Kobold *m*

pizza /'pi:tsə/ *n* Pizza *f*

placard /'plækɑ:d/ *n* Plakat *nt*

placate /plə'keit/ *vt* beschwichtigen

place /pleis/ *n* Platz *m*; *(spot)* Stelle *f*; *(town, village)* Ort *m*; *(fam: house)* Haus *nt*; **out of** ~ fehl am Platze; **take** ~ stattfinden; **all over the** ~ überall □ *vt* setzen; *(upright)* stellen; *(flat)* legen; *(remember)* unterbringen *(fam)*; ~ **an order** eine Bestellung aufgeben; **be** ~**d** *(in race)* sich platzieren. ~-**mat** *n* Set *nt*

placid /'plæsid/ *a* gelassen

plagiar|ism /'pleidʒərizm/ *n* Plagiat *nt*. ~**ize** *vt* plagiieren

plague /pleig/ *n* Pest *f* □ *vt* plagen

plaice /pleis/ *n inv* Scholle *f*

plain /plein/ *a* (-**er**, -**est**) klar; *(simple)* einfach; *(not pretty)* nicht hübsch; *(not patterned)* einfarbig; *(chocolate)* zartbitter; **in** ~ **clothes** in Zivil □ *adv (simply)* einfach □ *n* Ebene *f*; *(Knitting)* rechte Masche *f*. ~**ly** *adv* klar, deutlich; *(simply)* einfach; *(obviously)* offensichtlich

plaintiff /'pleintif/ *n (Jur)* Kläger(in) *m(f)*

plaintive /'pleintiv/ *a*, **-ly** *adv* klagend

plait /plæt/ *n* Zopf *m* □ *vt* flechten

plan /plæn/ *n* Plan *m* □ *vt (pt/pp* **planned**) planen; *(intend)* vorhaben

plane[1] /plein/ *n (tree)* Platane *f*

plane[2] *n* Flugzeug *nt*; *(Geom & fig)* Ebene *f*

plane[3] *n (Techn)* Hobel *m* □ *vt* hobeln

planet /'plænit/ *n* Planet *m*

plank /plæŋk/ *n* Brett *nt*; *(thick)* Planke *f*

planning /'plæniŋ/ *n* Planung *f*. ~ **permission** *n* Baugenehmigung *f*

plant /plɑ:nt/ *n* Pflanze *f*; *(Techn)* Anlage *f*; *(factory)* Werk *nt* □ *vt* pflanzen; *(place in position)* setzen; ~ **oneself in front of s.o.** sich vor jdn hinstellen. ~**ation** /plæn'teiʃn/ *n* Plantage *f*

plaque /plɑ:k/ *n* [Gedenk]tafel *f*; *(on teeth)* Zahnbelag *m*

plasma /'plæzmə/ *n* Plasma *nt*

plaster /'plɑ:stə(r)/ *n* Verputz *m*; *(sticking* ~*)* Pflaster *nt*; ~ **[of Paris]** Gips *m* □ *vt* verputzen *(wall)*; *(cover)* bedecken mit. ~**ed** *a (sl)* besoffen. ~**er** *n* Gipser *m*

plastic /'plæstik/ *n* Kunststoff *m*, Plastik *nt* □ *a* Kunststoff-, Plastik-; *(malleable)* formbar, plastisch

Plasticine (P) /'plæstisi:n/ *n* Knetmasse *f*

plastic 'surgery *n* plastische Chirurgie *f*

plate /pleɪt/ *n* Teller *m*; (*flat sheet*) Platte *f*; (*with name, number*) Schild *nt*; (*gold and silverware*) vergoldete/versilberte Ware *f*; (*in book*) Tafel *f* □ *vt* (*with gold*) vergolden; (*with silver*) versilbern

plateau /ˈplætəʊ/ *n* (*pl* ～x /-əʊz/) Hochebene *f*

platform /ˈplætfɔːm/ *n* Plattform *f*; (*stage*) Podium *nt*; (*Rail*) Bahnsteig *m*; ～ **5** Gleis 5

platinum /ˈplætɪnəm/ *n* Platin *nt*

platitude /ˈplætɪtjuːd/ *n* Plattitüde *f*

platonic /pləˈtɒnɪk/ *a* platonisch

platoon /pləˈtuːn/ *n* (*Mil*) Zug *m*

platter /ˈplætə(r)/ *n* Platte *f*

plausible /ˈplɔːzəbl/ *a* plausibel

play /pleɪ/ *n* Spiel *nt*; [Theater]stück *nt*; (*Radio*) Hörspiel *nt*; (*TV*) Fernsehspiel *nt*; ～ **on words** Wortspiel *nt* □ *vt/i* spielen; ausspielen ⟨*card*⟩; ～ **safe** sichergehen. ～ **down** *vt* herunterspielen. ～ **up** *vi* (*fam*) Mätzchen machen

play: ～**boy** *n* Playboy *m*. ～**er** *n* Spieler(in) *m(f)*. ～**ful** *a*, **-ly** *adv* verspielt. ～**ground** *n* Spielplatz *m*; (*Sch*) Schulhof *m*. ～**group** *n* Kindergarten *m*

playing: ～**card** *n* Spielkarte *f*. ～**field** *n* Sportplatz *m*

play: ～**mate** *n* Spielkamerad *m*. ～**pen** *n* Laufstall *m*, Laufgitter *nt*. ～**thing** *n* Spielzeug *nt*. ～**wright** /-raɪt/ *n* Dramatiker *m*

plc *abbr* (**public limited company**) ≈ GmbH

plea /pliː/ *n* Bitte *f*; **make a** ～ **for** bitten um

plead /pliːd/ *vt* vorschützen; (*Jur*) vertreten ⟨*case*⟩ □ *vi* flehen (**for** um); ～ **guilty** sich schuldig bekennen; ～ **with s.o.** jdn anflehen

pleasant /ˈplezənt/ *a* angenehm; ⟨*person*⟩ nett. ～**ly** *adv* angenehm; ⟨*say, smile*⟩ freundlich

pleas|e /pliːz/ *adv* bitte □ *vt* gefallen (+ *dat*); ～**e s.o.** jdm eine Freude machen; ～**e oneself** tun, was man will. ～**ed** *a* erfreut; **be** ～**ed with/about sth** sich über etw ⟨*acc*⟩ freuen. ～**ing** *a* erfreulich

pleasurable /ˈpleʒərəbl/ *a* angenehm

pleasure /ˈpleʒə(r)/ *n* Vergnügen *nt*; (*joy*) Freude *f*; **with** ～ gern[e]

pleat /pliːt/ *n* Falte *f* □ *vt* fälteln. ～**ed 'skirt** *n* Faltenrock *m*

plebiscite /ˈplebɪsɪt/ *n* Volksabstimmung *f*

pledge /pledʒ/ *n* Pfand *nt*; (*promise*) Versprechen *nt* □ *vt* verpfänden; versprechen

plentiful /ˈplentɪfl/ *a* reichlich; **be** ～ reichlich vorhanden sein

plenty /ˈplentɪ/ *n* eine Menge; (*enough*) reichlich; ～ **of money/people** viel Geld/viele Leute

pleurisy /ˈplʊərəsɪ/ *n* Rippenfellentzündung *f*

pliable /ˈplaɪəbl/ *a* biegsam

pliers /ˈplaɪəz/ *npl* [Flach]zange *f*

plight /plaɪt/ *n* [Not]lage *f*

plimsolls /ˈplɪmsəlz/ *npl* Turnschuhe *pl*

plinth /plɪnθ/ *n* Sockel *m*

plod /plɒd/ *vi* (*pt/pp* **plodded**) trotten; (*work hard*) sich abmühen

plonk /plɒŋk/ *n* (*fam*) billiger Wein *m*

plot /plɒt/ *n* Komplott *nt*; (*of novel*) Handlung *f*; ～ **of land** Stück *nt* Land □ *vt* einzeichnen □ *vi* ein Komplott schmieden

plough /plaʊ/ *n* Pflug *m* □ *vt/i* pflügen. ～ **back** *vt* (*Comm*) wieder investieren

ploy /plɔɪ/ *n* (*fam*) Trick *m*

pluck /plʌk/ *n* Mut *m* □ *vt* zupfen; rupfen ⟨*bird*⟩; pflücken ⟨*flower*⟩; ～ **up courage** Mut fassen

plucky /ˈplʌkɪ/ *a* (**-ier, -iest**) tapfer, mutig

plug /plʌg/ *n* Stöpsel *m*; (*wood*) Zapfen *m*; (*cotton wool*) Bausch *m*; (*Electr*) Stecker *m*; (*Auto*) Zündkerze *f*; (*fam: advertisement*) Schleichwerbung *f* □ *vt* zustopfen; (*fam: advertise*) Schleichwerbung machen für. ～ **in** *vt* (*Electr*) einstecken

plum /plʌm/ *n* Pflaume *f*

plumage /ˈpluːmɪdʒ/ *n* Gefieder *nt*

plumb /plʌm/ *n* Lot *nt* □ *adv* lotrecht □ *vt* loten. ～ **in** *vt* installieren

plumb|er /ˈplʌmə(r)/ *n* Klempner *m*. ～**ing** *n* Wasserleitungen *pl*

'plumb-line *n* [Blei]lot *nt*

plume /pluːm/ *n* Feder *f*

plummet /ˈplʌmɪt/ *vi* herunterstürzen

plump /plʌmp/ *a* (**-er, -est**) mollig, rundlich □ *vt* ～ **for** wählen

plunder /ˈplʌndə(r)/ *n* Beute *f* □ *vt* plündern

plunge /plʌndʒ/ *n* Sprung *m*; **take the** ～ (*fam*) den Schritt wagen □ *vt/i* tauchen

plu'perfect /pluː-/ *n* Plusquamperfekt *nt*

plural /ˈplʊərl/ *a* pluralisch □ *n* Mehrzahl *f*, Plural *m*

plus /plʌs/ *prep* plus (+ *dat*) □ *a* Plus- □ *n* Pluszeichen *nt*; (*advantage*) Plus *nt*

plush[y] /ˈplʌʃ[ɪ]/ *a* luxuriös

ply /plaɪ/ *vt* (*pt/pp* **plied**) ausüben ⟨*trade*⟩; ～ **s.o. with drink** jdm ein Glas nach dem anderen eingießen. ～**wood** *n* Sperrholz *nt*

p.m. *adv* (*abbr of* **post meridiem**) nachmittags

pneumatic /nju:'mætɪk/ a pneumatisch. ~ 'drill n Presslufthammer m

pneumonia /nju:'məʊnɪə/ n Lungenentzündung f

poach /pəʊtʃ/ vt (Culin) pochieren; (steal) wildern. ~er n Wilddieb m

pocket /'pɒkɪt/ n Tasche f; ~ of resistance Widerstandsnest nt; be out of ~ [an einem Geschäft] verlieren □ vt einstecken. ~-book n Notizbuch nt; (wallet) Brieftasche f. ~-money n Taschengeld nt

pock-marked /'pɒk-/ a pockennarbig

pod /pɒd/ n Hülse f

podgy /'pɒdʒɪ/ a (-ier, -iest) dick

poem /'pəʊɪm/ n Gedicht nt

poet /'pəʊɪt/ n Dichter(in) m(f). ~ic /-'etɪk/ a dichterisch

poetry /'pəʊɪtrɪ/ n Dichtung f

poignant /'pɔɪnjənt/ a ergreifend

point /pɔɪnt/ n Punkt m; (sharp end) Spitze f; (meaning) Sinn m; (purpose) Zweck m; (Electr) Steckdose f; ~s pl (Rail) Weiche f; ~ of view Standpunkt m; good/bad ~s gute/schlechte Seiten; what is the ~? wozu? the ~ is es geht darum; I don't see the ~ das sehe ich nicht ein; up to a ~ bis zu einem gewissen Grade; be on the ~ of doing sth im Begriff sein, etw zu tun □ vt richten (at auf + acc); ausfugen (brickwork) □ vi deuten (at/to auf + acc); (with finger) mit dem Finger zeigen. ~ out vt zeigen auf (+ acc); ~ sth out to s.o. jdn auf etw (acc) hinweisen

point-'blank a aus nächster Entfernung; (fig) rundweg

point|ed /'pɔɪntɪd/ a spitz; (question) gezielt. ~er n (hint) Hinweis m. ~less a zwecklos, sinnlos

poise /pɔɪz/ n Haltung f. ~d a (confident) selbstsicher; ~d to bereit zu

poison /'pɔɪzn/ n Gift nt □ vt vergiften. ~ous a giftig

poke /pəʊk/ n Stoß m □ vt stoßen; schüren (fire); (put) stecken; ~ fun at sich lustig machen über (+ acc)

poker¹ /'pəʊkə(r)/ n Schüreisen nt

poker² n (Cards) Poker nt

poky /'pəʊkɪ/ a (-ier, -iest) eng

Poland /'pəʊlənd/ n Polen nt

polar /'pəʊlə(r)/ a Polar-. ~ 'bear n Eisbär m. ~ize vt polarisieren

Pole /pəʊl/ n Pole m/Polin f

pole¹ n Stange f

pole² n (Geog, Electr) Pol m

'polecat n Iltis m

'pole-star n Polarstern m

'pole-vault n Stabhochsprung m

police /pə'li:s/ npl Polizei f □ vt polizeilich kontrollieren

police: ~man n Polizist m. ~ state n Polizeistaat m. ~ station n Polizeiwache f. ~woman n Polizistin f

policy¹ /'pɒlɪsɪ/ n Politik f

policy² n (insurance) Police f

polio /'pəʊlɪəʊ/ n Kinderlähmung f

Polish /'pəʊlɪʃ/ a polnisch

polish /'pɒlɪʃ/ n (shine) Glanz m; (for shoes) [Schuh]creme f; (for floor) Bohnerwachs m; (for furniture) Politur f; (for silver) Putzmittel nt; (for nails) Lack m; (fig) Schliff m □ vt polieren; bohnern (floor). ~ off vt (fam) verputzen (food); erledigen (task)

polisher /'pɒlɪʃə(r)/ n (machine) Poliermaschine f; (for floor) Bohnermaschine f

polite /pə'laɪt/ a, -ly adv höflich. ~ness n Höflichkeit f

politic /'pɒlɪtɪk/ a ratsam

politic|al /pə'lɪtɪkl/ a, -ly adv politisch. ~ian /pɒlɪ'tɪʃn/ n Politiker(in) m(f)

politics /'pɒlɪtɪks/ n Politik f

polka /'pɒlkə/ n Polka f

poll /pəʊl/ n Abstimmung f; (election) Wahl f; [opinion] ~ [Meinungs]umfrage f; go to the ~s wählen □ vt erhalten (votes)

pollen /'pɒlən/ n Blütenstaub m, Pollen m

polling /'pəʊlɪŋ/ ~-booth n Wahlkabine f. ~-station n Wahllokal nt

'poll tax n Kopfsteuer f

pollutant /pə'lu:tənt/ n Schadstoff m

pollut|e /pə'lu:t/ vt verschmutzen. ~ion /-u:ʃn/ n Verschmutzung f

polo /'pəʊləʊ/ n Polo nt. ~-neck n Rollkragen m. ~ shirt n Polohemd nt

polyester /pɒlɪ'estə(r)/ n Polyester m

polystyrene /pɒlɪ'staɪri:n/ n Polystyrol nt; (for packing) Styropor (P) nt

polytechnic /pɒlɪ'teknɪk/ n ≈ technische Hochschule f

polythene /'pɒlɪθi:n/ n Polyäthylen nt. ~ bag n Plastiktüte f

polyun'saturated a mehrfach ungesättigt

pomegranate /'pɒmɪgrænɪt/ n Granatapfel m

pomp /pɒmp/ n Pomp m

pompon /'pɒmpɒn/ n Pompon m

pompous /'pɒmpəs/ a, -ly adv großspurig

pond /pɒnd/ n Teich m

ponder /'pɒndə(r)/ vi nachdenken

ponderous /'pɒndərəs/ a schwerfällig

pong /pɒŋ/ n (fam) Mief m

pony /'pəʊnɪ/ n Pony nt. ~-tail n Pferdeschwanz m. ~-trekking n Ponyreiten nt

poodle /'pu:dl/ n Pudel m

pool¹ /puːl/ n [Schwimm]becken nt; (pond) Teich m; (of blood) Lache f

pool² n (common fund) [gemeinsame] Kasse f; ~s pl [Fußball]toto nt □ vt zusammenlegen

poor /pʊə(r)/ a (-er, -est) arm; (not good) schlecht; **in** ~ **health** nicht gesund □ npl **the** ~ die Armen. ~**ly** a be ~**ly** krank sein □ adv ärmlich; (badly) schlecht

pop¹ /pɒp/ n Knall m; (drink) Brause f □ v (pt/pp popped) □ vt (fam: put) stecken (**in** in + acc) □ vi knallen; (burst) platzen. ~ **in** vi (fam) reinschauen. ~ **out** vi (fam) kurz rausgehen

pop² n (fam) Popmusik f, Pop m □ attrib Pop-

'popcorn n Puffmais m

pope /pəʊp/ n Papst m

poplar /'pɒplə(r)/ n Pappel f

poppy /'pɒpɪ/ n Mohn m

popular /'pɒpjʊlə(r)/ a beliebt, populär; (belief) volkstümlich. ~**ity** /-'lærətɪ/ n Beliebtheit f, Popularität f

populat|e /'pɒpjʊleɪt/ vt bevölkern. ~**ion** /-'leɪʃn/ n Bevölkerung f

porcelain /'pɔːsəlɪn/ n Porzellan nt

porch /pɔːtʃ/ n Vorbau m; (Amer) Veranda f

porcupine /'pɔːkjʊpaɪn/ n Stachelschwein nt

pore¹ /pɔː(r)/ n Pore f

pore² vi ~ **over** studieren

pork /pɔːk/ n Schweinefleisch nt

porn /pɔːn/ n (fam) Porno m

pornograph|ic /pɔːnə'græfɪk/ a pornographisch. ~**y** /-'nɒgrəfɪ/ n Pornographie f

porous /'pɔːrəs/ a porös

porpoise /'pɔːpəs/ n Tümmler m

porridge /'pɒrɪdʒ/ n Haferbrei m

port¹ /pɔːt/ n Hafen m; (town) Hafenstadt f

port² n (Naut) Backbord nt

port³ n (wine) Portwein m

portable /'pɔːtəbl/ a tragbar

porter /'pɔːtə(r)/ n Portier m; (for luggage) Gepäckträger m

portfolio /pɔːt'fəʊlɪəʊ/ n Mappe f; (Comm) Portefeuille nt

'porthole n Bullauge nt

portion /'pɔːʃn/ n Portion f; (part, share) Teil m

portly /'pɔːtlɪ/ a (-ier, -iest) beleibt

portrait /'pɔːtrɪt/ n Porträt nt

portray /pɔː'treɪ/ vt darstellen. ~**al** n Darstellung f

Portug|al /'pɔːtjʊgl/ n Portugal nt. ~**uese** /-'giːz/ a portugiesisch □ n Portugiese m /-giesin f

pose /pəʊz/ n Pose f □ vt aufwerfen (problem); stellen (question) □ vi posieren; (for painter) Modell stehen; ~ **as** sich ausgeben als

posh /pɒʃ/ a (fam) feudal

position /pə'zɪʃn/ n Platz m; (posture) Haltung f; (job) Stelle f; (situation) Lage f, Situation f; (status) Stellung f □ vt platzieren; ~ **oneself** sich stellen

positive /'pɒzətɪv/ a, -**ly** adv positiv; (definite) eindeutig; (real) ausgesprochen □ n Positiv nt

possess /pə'zes/ vt besitzen. ~**ion** /pə'zeʃn/ n Besitz m; ~**ions** pl Sachen pl

possess|ive /pə'zesɪv/ a Possessiv-; be ~**ive** zu sehr an jdm hängen. ~**or** n Besitzer m

possibility /pɒsə'bɪlətɪ/ n Möglichkeit f

possib|le /'pɒsəbl/ a möglich. ~**ly** adv möglicherweise; **not** ~**ly** unmöglich

post¹ /pəʊst/ n (pole) Pfosten m □ vt anschlagen (notice)

post² n (place of duty) Posten m; (job) Stelle f □ vt postieren; (transfer) versetzen

post³ n (mail) Post f; **by** ~ mit der Post □ vt aufgeben (letter); (send by ~) mit der Post schicken; **keep s.o.** ~**ed** jdn auf dem Laufenden halten

postage /'pəʊstɪdʒ/ n Porto nt. ~ **stamp** n Briefmarke f

postal /'pəʊstl/ a Post-. ~ **order** n ≈ Geldanweisung f

post: ~**box** n Briefkasten m. ~**card** n Postkarte f; (picture) Ansichtskarte f. ~**code** n Postleitzahl f. ~'**date** vt vordatieren

poster /'pəʊstə(r)/ n Plakat nt

posterior /pɒ'stɪərɪə(r)/ a hintere(r,s) □ n (fam) Hintern m

posterity /pɒ'sterətɪ/ n Nachwelt f

posthumous /'pɒstjʊməs/ a, -**ly** adv postum

post: ~**man** n Briefträger m. ~**mark** n Poststempel m

post-mortem /-'mɔːtəm/ n Obduktion f

'post office n Post f

postpone /pəʊst'pəʊn/ vt aufschieben; ~ **until** verschieben auf (+ acc). ~**ment** n Verschiebung f

postscript /'pəʊstskrɪpt/ n Nachschrift f

posture /'pɒstʃə(r)/ n Haltung f

post-'war a Nachkriegs-

posy /'pəʊzɪ/ n Sträußchen nt

pot /pɒt/ n Topf m; (for tea, coffee) Kanne f; ~**s of money** (fam) eine Menge Geld; **go to** ~ (fam) herunterkommen

potassium /pə'tæsɪəm/ *n* Kalium *nt*

potato /pə'teɪtəʊ/ *n* (*pl* -es) Kartoffel *f*

poten|cy /'pəʊtənsɪ/ *n* Stärke *f*. ~**t** *a* stark

potential /pə'tenʃl/ *a*, -**ly** *adv* potenziell □ *n* Potenzial *nt*

pot: ~-**hole** *n* Höhle *f*; (*in road*) Schlagloch *nt*. ~-**holer** *n* Höhlenforscher *m*. ~-**shot** *n* **take a** ~-**shot at** schießen auf (+ *acc*)

potted /'pɒtɪd/ *a* eingemacht; (*shortened*) gekürzt. ~ '**plant** *n* Topfpflanze *f*

potter¹ /'pɒtə(r)/ *vi* ~ [**about**] herumwerkeln

potter² *n* Töpfer(in) *m(f)*. ~**y** *n* Töpferei *f*; (*articles*) Töpferwaren *pl*

potty /'pɒtɪ/ *a* (-**ier**, -**iest**) (*fam*) verrückt □ *n* Töpfchen *nt*

pouch /paʊtʃ/ *n* Beutel *m*

pouffe /puːf/ *n* Sitzkissen *nt*

poultry /'pəʊltrɪ/ *n* Geflügel *nt*

pounce /paʊns/ *vi* zuschlagen; ~ **on** sich stürzen auf (+ *acc*)

pound¹ /paʊnd/ *n* (*money & 0,454 kg*) Pfund *nt*

pound² *vt* hämmern □ *vi* (*heart:*) hämmern; (*run heavily*) stampfen

pour /pɔ:(r)/ *vt* gießen; (*drink*) einschenken □ *vi* strömen; (*with rain*) gießen. ~ **out** *vi* ausströmen □ *vt* ausschütten; einschenken (*drink*)

pout /paʊt/ *vi* einen Schmollmund machen

poverty /'pɒvətɪ/ *n* Armut *f*

powder /'paʊdə(r)/ *n* Pulver *nt*; (*cosmetic*) Puder *m* □ *vt* pudern. ~**y** *a* pulverig

power /'paʊə(r)/ *n* Macht *f*; (*strength*) Kraft *f*; (*Electr*) Strom *m*; (*nuclear*) Energie *f*; (*Math*) Potenz *f*. ~ **cut** *n* Stromsperre *f*. ~**ed** *a* betrieben (**by** mit); ~**ed by electricity** mit Elektroantrieb. ~**ful** *a* mächtig; (*strong*) stark. ~**less** *a* machtlos. ~-**station** *n* Kraftwerk *nt*

practicable /'præktɪkəbl/ *a* durchführbar, praktikabel

practical /'præktɪkl/ *a*, -**ly** *adv* praktisch. ~ '**joke** *n* Streich *m*

practice /'præktɪs/ *n* Praxis *f*; (*custom*) Brauch *m*; (*habit*) Gewohnheit *f*; (*exercise*) Übung *f*; (*Sport*) Training *nt*; **in** ~ (*in reality*) in der Praxis; **out of** ~ außer Übung; **put into** ~ ausführen

practise /'præktɪs/ *vt* üben; (*carry out*) praktizieren; ausüben (*profession*) □ *vi* üben; (*doctor:*) praktizieren. ~**d** *a* geübt

pragmatic /præg'mætɪk/ *a*, ~**ally** *adv* pragmatisch

praise /preɪz/ *n* Lob *nt* □ *vt* loben. ~**worthy** *a* lobenswert

pram /præm/ *n* Kinderwagen *m*

prance /prɑ:ns/ *vi* herumhüpfen; (*horse:*) tänzeln

prank /præŋk/ *n* Streich *m*

prattle /'prætl/ *vi* plappern

prawn /prɔ:n/ *n* Garnele *f*, Krabbe *f*. ~ '**cocktail** *n* Krabbencocktail *m*

pray /preɪ/ *vi* beten. ~**er** /preə(r)/ *n* Gebet *nt*; ~**ers** *pl* (*service*) Andacht *f*

preach /pri:tʃ/ *vt/i* predigen. ~**er** *n* Prediger *m*

preamble /pri:'æmbl/ *n* Einleitung *f*

pre-ar'range /pri:-/ *vt* im Voraus arrangieren

precarious /prɪ'keərɪəs/ *a*, -**ly** *adv* unsicher

precaution /prɪ'kɔ:ʃn/ *n* Vorsichtsmaßnahme *f*; **as a** ~ zur Vorsicht. ~**ary** *a* Vorsichts-

precede /prɪ'si:d/ *vt* vorangehen (+ *dat*)

preceden|ce /'presɪdəns/ *n* Vorrang *m*. ~**t** *n* Präzedenzfall *m*

preceding /prɪ'si:dɪŋ/ *a* vorhergehend

precinct /'pri:sɪŋkt/ *n* Bereich *m*; (*trafficfree*) Fußgängerzone *f*; (*Amer: district*) Bezirk *m*

precious /'preʃəs/ *a* kostbar; (*style*) preziös □ *adv* (*fam*) ~ **little** recht wenig

precipice /'presɪpɪs/ *n* Steilabfall *m*

precipitate¹ /prɪ'sɪpɪtət/ *a* voreilig

precipitat|e² /prɪ'sɪpɪteɪt/ *vt* schleudern; (*fig: accelerate*) beschleunigen. ~**ion** /-'teɪʃn/ *n* (*Meteorol*) Niederschlag *m*

précis /'preɪsɪ/ *n* (*pl* **précis** /-si:z/) Zusammenfassung *f*

precis|e /prɪ'saɪs/ *a*, -**ly** *adv* genau. ~**ion** /-'sɪʒn/ *n* Genauigkeit *f*

preclude /prɪ'klu:d/ *vt* ausschließen

precocious /prɪ'kəʊʃəs/ *a* frühreif

pre|con'ceived /pri:-/ *a* vorgefasst. ~**con'ception** *n* vorgefasste Meinung *f*

precursor /pri:'kɜ:sə(r)/ *n* Vorläufer *m*

predator /'predətə(r)/ *n* Raubtier *nt*

predecessor /'pri:dɪsesə(r)/ *n* Vorgänger(in) *m(f)*

predicament /prɪ'dɪkəmənt/ *n* Zwangslage *f*

predicat|e /'predɪkət/ *n* (*Gram*) Prädikat *nt*. ~**ive** /prɪ'dɪkətɪv/ *a*, -**ly** *adv* prädikativ

predict /prɪ'dɪkt/ *vt* voraussagen. ~**able** /-əbl/ *a* voraussehbar; (*person*) berechenbar. ~**ion** /-'dɪkʃn/ *n* Voraussage *f*

pre'domin|ant /prɪ-/ *a* vorherrschend. ~**antly** *adv* hauptsächlich, überwiegend. ~**ate** *vi* vorherrschen

pre-'eminent /pri:-/ *a* hervorragend

pre-empt /pri:'empt/ *vt* zuvorkommen (+ *dat*)

preen /pri:n/ *vt* putzen; ~ **oneself** (*fig*) selbstgefällig tun

pre|fab /'pri:fæb/ *n* (*fam*) [einfaches] Fertighaus *nt*. ~'**fabricated** *a* vorgefertigt

preface /'prefɪs/ *n* Vorwort *nt*

prefect /'pri:fekt/ *n* Präfekt *m*

prefer /prɪ'fɜ:(r)/ *vt* (*pt/pp* **preferred**) vorziehen; **I ~ to walk** ich gehe lieber zu Fuß; **I ~ wine** ich trinke lieber Wein

prefera|ble /'prefərəbl/ *a* **be ~ble** vorzuziehen sein (**to** *dat*). ~**bly** *adv* vorzugsweise

preferen|ce /'prefərəns/ *n* Vorzug *m*. ~**tial** /-'renʃl/ *a* bevorzugt

prefix /'pri:fɪks/ *n* Vorsilbe *f*

pregnan|cy /'pregnənsɪ/ *n* Schwangerschaft *f*. ~**t** *a* schwanger; ⟨*animal*⟩ trächtig

prehi'storic /pri:-/ *a* prähistorisch

prejudice /'predʒʊdɪs/ *n* Vorurteil *nt*; (*bias*) Voreingenommenheit *f* □ *vt* einnehmen (**against** gegen). ~**d** *a* voreingenommen

preliminary /prɪ'lɪmɪnərɪ/ *a* Vor-

prelude /'prelju:d/ *n* Vorspiel *nt*

pre-'marital *a* vorehelich

premature /'premətjʊə(r)/ *a* vorzeitig; ⟨*birth*⟩ Früh-. ~**ly** *adv* zu früh

pre'meditated /pri:-/ *a* vorsätzlich

premier /'premɪə(r)/ *a* führend □ *n* (*Pol*) Premier[minister] *m*

première /'premɪeə(r)/ *n* Premiere *f*

premises /'premɪsɪz/ *npl* Räumlichkeiten *pl*; **on the ~** im Haus

premiss /'premɪs/ *n* Prämisse *f*

premium /'pri:mɪəm/ *n* Prämie *f*; **be at a ~** hoch im Kurs stehen

premonition /premə'nɪʃn/ *n* Vorahnung *f*

preoccupied /prɪ'ɒkjʊpaɪd/ *a* [in Gedanken] beschäftigt

prep /prep/ *n* (*Sch*) Hausaufgaben *pl*

pre-'packed /pri:-/ *a* abgepackt

preparation /prepə'reɪʃn/ *n* Vorbereitung *f*; (*substance*) Präparat *nt*

preparatory /prɪ'pærətrɪ/ *a* Vor- □ *adv* ~ **to** vor (+ *dat*)

prepare /prɪ'peə(r)/ *vt* vorbereiten; anrichten ⟨*meal*⟩ □ *vi* sich vorbereiten (**for** auf + *acc*); ~**d to** bereit zu

pre'pay /pri:-/ *vt* (*pt/pp* **-paid**) im Voraus bezahlen

preposition /prepə'zɪʃn/ *n* Präposition *f*

prepossessing /pri:pə'zesɪŋ/ *a* ansprechend

preposterous /prɪ'pɒstərəs/ *a* absurd

prerequisite /pri:'rekwɪzɪt/ *n* Voraussetzung *f*

prerogative /prɪ'rɒgətɪv/ *n* Vorrecht *nt*

Presbyterian /prezbɪ'tɪərɪən/ *a* presbyterianisch □ *n* Presbyterianer(in) *m(f)*

prescribe /prɪ'skraɪb/ *vt* vorschreiben; (*Med*) verschreiben

prescription /prɪ'skrɪpʃn/ *n* (*Med*) Rezept *nt*

presence /'prezns/ *n* Anwesenheit *f*, Gegenwart *f*; ~ **of mind** Geistesgegenwart *f*

present¹ /'preznt/ *a* gegenwärtig; **be ~** anwesend sein; (*occur*) vorkommen □ *n* Gegenwart *f*; (*Gram*) Präsens *nt*; **at ~** zurzeit; **for the ~** vorläufig

present² *n* (*gift*) Geschenk *nt*

present³ /prɪ'zent/ *vt* überreichen; (*show*) zeigen; vorlegen ⟨*cheque*⟩; (*introduce*) vorstellen; ~ **s.o. with sth** jdm etw überreichen. ~**able** /-əbl/ *a* **be ~able** sich zeigen lassen können

presentation /prezn'teɪʃn/ *n* Überreichung *f*. ~ **ceremony** *n* Verleihungszeremonie *f*

presently /'prezntlɪ/ *adv* nachher; (*Amer: now*) zurzeit

preservation /prezə'veɪʃn/ *n* Erhaltung *f*

preservative /prɪ'zɜ:vətɪv/ *n* Konservierungsmittel *nt*

preserve /prɪ'zɜ:v/ *vt* erhalten; (*Culin*) konservieren; (*bottle*) einmachen □ *n* (*Hunting & fig*) Revier *nt*; (*jam*) Konfitüre *f*

preside /prɪ'zaɪd/ *vi* den Vorsitz haben (**over** bei)

presidency /'prezɪdənsɪ/ *n* Präsidentschaft *f*

president /'prezɪdənt/ *n* Präsident *m*; (*Amer: chairman*) Vorsitzende(r) *m/f*. ~**ial** /-'denʃl/ *a* Präsidenten-; ⟨*election*⟩ Präsidentschafts-

press /pres/ *n* Presse *f* □ *vt/i* drücken; drücken auf (+ *acc*) ⟨*button*⟩; pressen ⟨*flower*⟩; (*iron*) bügeln; (*urge*) bedrängen; ~ **for** drängen auf (+ *acc*); **be ~ed for time** in Zeitdruck sein. ~ **on** *vi* weitergehen/-fahren; (*fig*) weitermachen

press: ~ **cutting** *n* Zeitungsausschnitt *m*. ~**ing** *a* dringend. ~**-stud** *n* Druckknopf *m*. ~**-up** *n* Liegestütz *m*

pressure /'preʃə(r)/ *n* Druck *m* □ *vt* = **pressurize**. ~**-cooker** *n* Schnellkochtopf *m*. ~ **group** *n* Interessengruppe *f*

pressurize /'preʃəraɪz/ *vt* Druck ausüben auf (+ *acc*). ~**d** *a* Druck-

prestig|e /pre'sti:ʒ/ *n* Prestige *nt*. ~**ious** /-'stɪdʒəs/ *a* Prestige-

presumably /prɪ'zju:məblɪ/ *adv* vermutlich

presume /prɪ'zjuːm/ *vt* vermuten; ∼ **to do sth** sich (*dat*) anmaßen, etw zu tun □ *vi* ∼ **on** ausnutzen

presumpt|ion /prɪ'zʌmpʃn/ *n* Vermutung *f*; (*boldness*) Anmaßung *f*. ∼**uous** /-'zʌmptjuəs/ *a*, **-ly** *adv* anmaßend

presup'pose /priː-/ *vt* voraussetzen

pretence /prɪ'tens/ *n* Verstellung *f*; (*pretext*) Vorwand *m*; **it's all** ∼ das ist alles gespielt

pretend /prɪ'tend/ *vt* (*claim*) vorgeben; ∼ **that** so tun, als ob; ∼ **to be** sich ausgeben als

pretentious /prɪ'tenʃəs/ *a* protzig

pretext /'priːtekst/ *n* Vorwand *m*

pretty /'prɪtɪ/ *a* (**-ier, -iest**), **-ily** *adv* hübsch □ *adv* (*fam: fairly*) ziemlich

pretzel /'pretsl/ *n* Brezel *f*

prevail /prɪ'veɪl/ *vi* siegen; ⟨*custom:*⟩ vorherrschen; ∼ **on s.o. to do sth** jdn dazu bringen, etw zu tun

prevalen|ce /'prevələns/ *n* Häufigkeit *f*. ∼**t** *a* vorherrschend

prevent /prɪ'vent/ *vt* verhindern, verhüten; ∼ **s.o. [from] doing sth** jdn daran hindern, etw zu tun. ∼**able** /-əbl/ *a* vermeidbar. ∼**ion** /-enʃn/ *n* Verhinderung *f*, Verhütung *f*. ∼**ive** /-ɪv/ *a* vorbeugend

preview /'priːvjuː/ *n* Voraufführung *f*

previous /'priːvɪəs/ *a* vorhergehend; ∼ **to** vor (+ *dat*). ∼**ly** *adv* vorher, früher

pre-'war /priː-/ *a* Vorkriegs-

prey /preɪ/ *n* Beute *f*; **bird of** ∼ Raubvogel *m* □ *vi* ∼ **on** Jagd machen auf (+ *acc*); ∼ **on s.o.'s mind** jdm schwer auf der Seele liegen

price /praɪs/ *n* Preis *m* □ *vt* (*Comm*) auszeichnen. ∼**less** *a* unschätzbar; (*fig*) unbezahlbar

prick /prɪk/ *n* Stich *m* □ *vt/i* stechen; ∼ **up one's ears** die Ohren spitzen

prickl|e /'prɪkl/ *n* Stachel *m*; (*thorn*) Dorn *m*. ∼**y** *a* stachelig; ⟨*sensation*⟩ stechend

pride /praɪd/ *n* Stolz *m*; (*arrogance*) Hochmut *m*; (*of lions*) Rudel *nt* □ *vt* ∼ **oneself on** stolz sein auf (+ *acc*)

priest /priːst/ *n* Priester *m*

prig /prɪg/ *n* Tugendbold *m*

prim /prɪm/ *a* (**primmer, primmest**) prüde

primarily /'praɪmərɪlɪ/ *adv* hauptsächlich, in erster Linie

primary /'praɪmərɪ/ *a* Haupt-. ∼ **school** *n* Grundschule *f*

prime¹ /praɪm/ *a* Haupt-; (*first-rate*) erstklassig □ *n* **be in one's** ∼ in den besten Jahren sein

prime² *vt* scharf machen ⟨*bomb*⟩; grundieren ⟨*surface*⟩; (*fig*) instruieren

Prime Minister /praɪ'mɪnɪstə(r)/ *n* Premierminister(in) *m(f)*

primeval /praɪ'miːvl/ *a* Ur-

primitive /'prɪmɪtɪv/ *a* primitiv

primrose /'prɪmrəʊz/ *n* gelbe Schlüsselblume *f*

prince /prɪns/ *n* Prinz *m*

princess /prɪn'ses/ *n* Prinzessin *f*

principal /'prɪnsəpl/ *a* Haupt- □ *n* (*Sch*) Rektor(in) *m(f)*

principality /prɪnsɪ'pælətɪ/ *n* Fürstentum *nt*

principally /'prɪnsəplɪ/ *adv* hauptsächlich

principle /'prɪnsəpl/ *n* Prinzip *nt*, Grundsatz *m*; **in/on** ∼ im/aus Prinzip

print /prɪnt/ *n* Druck *m*; (*Phot*) Abzug *m*; **in** ∼ gedruckt; (*available*) erhältlich; **out of** ∼ vergriffen □ *vt* drucken; (*write in capitals*) in Druckschrift schreiben; (*Computing*) ausdrucken; (*Phot*) abziehen. ∼**ed matter** *n* Drucksache *f*

print|er /'prɪntə(r)/ *n* Drucker *m*. ∼**ing** *n* Druck *m*

'printout *n* (*Computing*) Ausdruck *m*

prior /'praɪə(r)/ *a* frühere(r,s); ∼ **to** vor (+ *dat*)

priority /praɪ'ɒrətɪ/ *n* Priorität *f*, Vorrang *m*; (*matter*) vordringliche Sache *f*

prise /praɪz/ *vt* ∼ **open/up** aufstemmen/ hochstemmen

prism /'prɪzm/ *n* Prisma *nt*

prison /'prɪzn/ *n* Gefängnis *nt*. ∼**er** *n* Gefangene(r) *m/f*

pristine /'prɪstiːn/ *a* tadellos

privacy /'prɪvəsɪ/ *n* Privatsphäre *f*; **have no** ∼ nie für sich sein

private /'praɪvət/ *a*, **-ly** *adv* privat; (*confidential*) vertraulich; (*car, secretary, school*) Privat- □ *n* (*Mil*) [einfacher] Soldat *m*; **in** ∼ privat; (*confidentially*) vertraulich

privation /praɪ'veɪʃn/ *n* Entbehrung *f*

privatize /'praɪvətaɪz/ *vt* privatisieren

privilege /'prɪvəlɪdʒ/ *n* Privileg *nt*. ∼**d** *a* privilegiert

privy /'prɪvɪ/ *a* **be** ∼ **to** wissen

prize /praɪz/ *n* Preis *m* □ *vt* schätzen. ∼**giving** *n* Preisverleihung *f*. ∼**-winner** *n* Preisgewinner(in) *m(f)*

pro /prəʊ/ *n* (*fam*) Profi *m*; **the** ∼**s and cons** das Für und Wider

probability /prɒbə'bɪlətɪ/ *n* Wahrscheinlichkeit *f*

probable /'prɒbəbl/ *a*, **-bly** *adv* wahrscheinlich

probation /prə'beɪʃn/ *n* (*Jur*) Bewährung *f*. ∼**ary** *a* Probe-; ∼**ary period** Probezeit *f*

probe /prəub/ n Sonde f; (fig: investigation) Untersuchung f □ vt/i ~ **[into]** untersuchen

problem /'prɔbləm/ n Problem nt; (Math) Textaufgabe f. ~**atic** /-'mætɪk/ a problematisch

procedure /prə'si:dʒə(r)/ n Verfahren nt

proceed /prə'si:d/ vi gehen; (in vehicle) fahren; (continue) weitergehen/-fahren; (speaking) fortfahren; (act) verfahren □ vt ~ **to do sth** anfangen, etw zu tun

proceedings /prə'si:dɪŋz/ npl Verfahren nt; (Jur) Prozess m

proceeds /'prəusi:dz/ npl Erlös m

process /'prəuses/ n Prozess m; (procedure) Verfahren nt; **in the** ~ dabei □ vt verarbeiten; (Admin) bearbeiten; (Phot) entwickeln

procession /prə'seʃn/ n Umzug m, Prozession f

proclaim /prə'kleɪm/ vt ausrufen

proclamation /prɔklə'meɪʃn/ n Proklamation f

procure /prə'kjʊə(r)/ vt beschaffen

prod /prɔd/ n Stoß m □ vt stoßen; (fig) einen Stoß geben (+ dat)

prodigal /'prɔdɪgl/ a verschwenderisch

prodigious /prə'dɪdʒəs/ a gewaltig

prodigy /'prɔdɪdʒɪ/ n **[infant]** ~ Wunderkind nt

produce¹ /'prɔdju:s/ n landwirtschaftliche Erzeugnisse pl

produce² /prə'dju:s/ vt erzeugen, produzieren; (manufacture) herstellen; (bring out) hervorholen; (cause) hervorrufen; inszenieren; (play); (Radio, TV) redigieren. ~**r** n Erzeuger m, Produzent m; Hersteller m; (Theat) Regisseur m; (Radio, TV) Redakteur(in) m(f)

product /'prɔdʌkt/ n Erzeugnis nt, Produkt nt. ~**ion** /prə'dʌkʃn/ n Produktion f; (Theat) Inszenierung f

productiv|e /prə'dʌktɪv/ a produktiv; (land, talks) fruchtbar. ~**ity** /-'tɪvətɪ/ n Produktivität f

profan|e /prə'feɪn/ a weltlich; (blasphemous) [gottes]lästerlich. ~**ity** /-'fænətɪ/ n (oath) Fluch m

profess /prə'fes/ vt behaupten; bekennen ⟨faith⟩

profession /prə'feʃn/ n Beruf m. ~**al** a, -**ly** adv beruflich; (not amateur) Berufs-; (expert) fachmännisch; (Sport) professionell □ n Fachmann m; (Sport) Profi m

professor /prə'fesə(r)/ n Professor m

proficien|cy /prə'fɪʃnsɪ/ n Können nt. ~**t** a **be** ~**t** in beherrschen

profile /'prəufaɪl/ n Profil nt; (character study) Porträt nt

profit /'prɔfɪt/ n Gewinn m, Profit m □ vi ~ **from** profitieren von. ~**able** /-əbl/ a, -**bly** adv gewinnbringend; (fig) nutzbringend

profound /prə'faund/ a, -**ly** adv tief

profus|e /prə'fju:s/ a, -**ly** adv üppig; (fig) überschwenglich. ~**ion** /-ju:ʒn/ n **in** ~**ion** in großer Fülle

progeny /'prɔdʒənɪ/ n Nachkommenschaft f

program /'prəugræm/ n Programm nt; □ vt (pt/pp **programmed**) programmieren

programme /'prəugræm/ n Programm nt; (Radio, TV) Sendung f. ~**r** n (Computing) Programmierer(in) m(f)

progress¹ /'prəugres/ n Vorankommen nt; (fig) Fortschritt m; **in** ~ im Gange; **make** ~ (fig) Fortschritte machen

progress² /prə'gres/ vi vorankommen; (fig) fortschreiten. ~**ion** /-eʃn/ n Folge f; (development) Entwicklung f

progressive /prə'gresɪv/ a fortschrittlich; ⟨disease⟩ fortschreitend. ~**ly** adv zunehmend

prohibit /prə'hɪbɪt/ vt verbieten (s.o. jdm). ~**ive** /-ɪv/ a unerschwinglich

project¹ /'prɔdʒekt/ n Projekt nt; (Sch) Arbeit f

project² /prə'dʒekt/ vt projizieren ⟨film⟩; (plan) planen □ vi (jut out) vorstehen

projectile /prə'dʒektaɪl/ n Geschoss nt

projector /prə'dʒektə(r)/ n Projektor m

proletariat /prəulɪ'teərɪət/ n Proletariat nt

prolific /prə'lɪfɪk/ a fruchtbar; (fig) produktiv

prologue /'prəulɔg/ n Prolog m

prolong /prə'lɔŋ/ vt verlängern

promenade /prɔmə'nɑ:d/ n Promenade f □ vi spazieren gehen

prominent /'prɔmɪnənt/ a vorstehend; (important) prominent; (conspicuous) auffällig; ⟨place⟩ gut sichtbar

promiscu|ity /prɔmɪ'skju:ətɪ/ n Promiskuität f. ~**ous** /prə'mɪskjʊəs/ a **be** ~**ous** häufig den Partner wechseln

promis|e /'prɔmɪs/ n Versprechen nt □ vt/i versprechen (s.o. jdm); **the P**~**ed Land** das Gelobte Land. ~**ing** a viel versprechend

promot|e /prə'məut/ vt befördern; (advance) fördern; (publicize) Reklame machen für; **be** ~**ed** (Sport) aufsteigen. ~**ion** /-əuʃn/ n Beförderung f; (Sport) Aufstieg m; (Comm) Reklame f

prompt /prɔmpt/ a prompt, unverzüglich; (punctual) pünktlich □ adv pünktlich

□ *vt/i* veranlassen (**to** zu); (*Theat*) soufflieren (+ *dat*). ~**er** *n* Souffleur *m*/Souffleuse *f*. ~**ly** *adv* prompt

prone /prəʊn/ *a* **be** *or* **lie** ~ auf dem Bauch liegen; **be** ~ **to** neigen zu; **be** ~ **to do sth** dazu neigen, etw zu tun

prong /prɒŋ/ *n* Zinke *f*

pronoun /'prəʊnaʊn/ *n* Fürwort *nt*, Pronomen *nt*

pronounce /prə'naʊns/ *vt* aussprechen; (*declare*) erklären. ~**d** *a* ausgeprägt; (*noticeable*) deutlich. ~**ment** *n* Erklärung *f*

pronunciation /prənʌnsɪ'eɪʃn/ *n* Aussprache *f*

proof /pru:f/ *n* Beweis *m*; (*Typ*) Korrekturbogen *m* □ *a* ~ **against water/theft** wasserfest/diebessicher. ~**reader** *n* Korrektor *m*

prop[1] /prɒp/ *n* Stütze *f* □ *vt* (*pt/pp* **propped**) ~ **open** offen halten; ~ **against** (*lean*) lehnen an (+ *acc*). ~ **up** *vt* stützen

prop[2] *n* (*Theat, fam*) Requisit *nt*

propaganda /prɒpə'gændə/ *n* Propaganda *f*

propagate /'prɒpəgeɪt/ *vt* vermehren; (*fig*) verbreiten, propagieren

propel /prə'pel/ *vt* (*pt/pp* **propelled**) [an]treiben. ~**ler** *n* Propeller *m*. ~**ling** 'pencil *n* Drehbleistift *m*

propensity /prə'pensətɪ/ *n* Neigung *f* (**for** zu)

proper /'prɒpə(r)/ *a*, -**ly** *adv* richtig; (*decent*) anständig. ~ 'name, ~ 'noun *n* Eigenname *m*

property /'prɒpətɪ/ *n* Eigentum *nt*; (*quality*) Eigenschaft *f*; (*Theat*) Requisit *nt*; (*land*) [Grund]besitz *m*; (*house*) Haus *nt*. ~ **market** *n* Immobilienmarkt *m*

prophecy /'prɒfəsɪ/ *n* Prophezeiung *f*

prophesy /'prɒfɪsaɪ/ *vt* (*pt/pp* -**ied**) prophezeien

prophet /'prɒfɪt/ *n* Prophet *m*. ~**ic** /prə'fetɪk/ *a* prophetisch

proportion /prə'pɔ:ʃn/ *n* Verhältnis *nt*; (*share*) Teil *m*; ~**s** *pl* Proportionen; (*dimensions*) Maße. ~**al** *a*, -**ly** *adv* proportional

proposal /prə'pəʊzl/ *n* Vorschlag *m*; (*of marriage*) [Heirats]antrag *m*

propose /prə'pəʊz/ *vt* vorschlagen; (*intend*) vorhaben; einbringen (*motion*); ausbringen (*toast*) □ *vi* einen Heiratsantrag machen

proposition /prɒpə'zɪʃn/ *n* Vorschlag *m*

propound /prə'paʊnd/ *vt* darlegen

proprietor /prə'praɪətə(r)/ *n* Inhaber(in) *m*(*f*)

propriety /prə'praɪətɪ/ *n* Korrektheit *f*; (*decorum*) Anstand *m*

propulsion /prə'pʌlʃn/ *n* Antrieb *m*

prosaic /prə'zeɪɪk/ *a* prosaisch

prose /prəʊz/ *n* Prosa *f*

prosecut|e /'prɒsɪkju:t/ *vt* strafrechtlich verfolgen. ~**ion** /-'kju:ʃn/ *n* strafrechtliche Verfolgung *f*; **the** ~**ion** die Anklage. ~**or** *n* [**Public**] **P**~**or** Staatsanwalt *m*

prospect[1] /'prɒspekt/ *n* Aussicht *f*

prospect[2] /prə'spekt/ *vi* suchen (**for** nach)

prospect|ive /prə'spektɪv/ *a* (*future*) zukünftig. ~**or** *n* Prospektor *m*

prospectus /prə'spektəs/ *n* Prospekt *m*

prosper /'prɒspə(r)/ *vi* gedeihen, florieren; (*person*) Erfolg haben. ~**ity** /-'sperətɪ/ *n* Wohlstand *m*

prosperous /'prɒspərəs/ *a* wohlhabend

prostitut|e /'prɒstɪtju:t/ *n* Prostituierte *f*. ~**ion** /-'tju:ʃn/ *n* Prostitution *f*

prostrate /'prɒstreɪt/ *a* ausgestreckt; ~ **with grief** (*fig*) vor Kummer gebrochen

protagonist /prəʊ'tægənɪst/ *n* Kämpfer *m*; (*fig*) Protagonist *m*

protect /prə'tekt/ *vt* schützen (**from** vor + *dat*); beschützen (*person*). ~**ion** /-ekʃn/ *n* Schutz *m*. ~**ive** /-ɪv/ *a* Schutz-; (*fig*) beschützend. ~**or** *n* Beschützer *m*

protégé /'prɒtɪʒeɪ/ *n* Schützling *m*, Protégé *m*

protein /'prəʊti:n/ *n* Eiweiß *nt*

protest[1] /'prəʊtest/ *n* Protest *m*

protest[2] /prə'test/ *vi* protestieren

Protestant /'prɒtɪstənt/ *a* protestantisch, evangelisch □ *n* Protestant(in) *m*(*f*), Evangelische(r) *m*/*f*

protester /prə'testə(r)/ *n* Protestierende(r) *m*/*f*

protocol /'prəʊtəkɒl/ *n* Protokoll *nt*

prototype /'prəʊtə-/ *n* Prototyp *m*

protract /prə'trækt/ *vt* verlängern. ~**or** *n* Winkelmesser *m*

protrude /prə'tru:d/ *vi* [her]vorstehen

proud /praʊd/ *a*, -**ly** *adv* stolz (**of** auf + *acc*)

prove /pru:v/ *vt* beweisen □ *vi* ~ **to be** sich erweisen als

proverb /'prɒvɜ:b/ *n* Sprichwort *nt*. ~**ial** /prə'vɜ:bɪəl/ *a* sprichwörtlich

provide /prə'vaɪd/ *vt* zur Verfügung stellen; spenden (*shade*); ~ **s.o. with sth** jdn mit etw versorgen *od* versehen □ *vi* ~ **for** sorgen für

provided /prə'vaɪdɪd/ *conj* ~ [**that**] vorausgesetzt [dass]

providen|ce /'prɒvɪdəns/ *n* Vorsehung *f*. ~**tial** /-'denʃl/ *a* **be** ~**tial** ein Glück sein

providing /prə'vaɪdɪŋ/ *conj* = **provided**

provinc|e /'prɒvɪns/ *n* Provinz *f*; (*fig*) Bereich *m*. ~**ial** /prə'vɪnʃl/ *a* provinziell

provision /prə'vɪʒn/ n Versorgung f (of mit); ~s pl Lebensmittel pl. ~al a, -ly adv vorläufig

proviso /prə'vaɪzəʊ/ n Vorbehalt m

provocat|ion /prɒvə'keɪʃn/ n Provokation f. ~ive /prə'vɒkətɪv/ a, -ly adv provozierend; (sexually) aufreizend

provoke /prə'vəʊk/ vt provozieren; (cause) hervorrufen

prow /praʊ/ n Bug m

prowess /'praʊɪs/ n Kraft f

prowl /praʊl/ vi herumschleichen □ n be on the ~ herumschleichen

proximity /prɒk'sɪmətɪ/ n Nähe f

proxy /'prɒksɪ/ n Stellvertreter(in) m(f); (power) Vollmacht f

prude /pru:d/ n be a ~ prüde sein

pruden|ce /'pru:dns/ n Umsicht f. ~t a, -ly adv umsichtig; (wise) klug

prudish /'pru:dɪʃ/ a prüde

prune[1] /pru:n/ n Backpflaume f

prune[2] vt beschneiden

pry /praɪ/ vi (pt/pp pried) neugierig sein

psalm /sɑ:m/ n Psalm m

pseudonym /'sju:dənɪm/ n Pseudonym nt

psychiatric /saɪkɪ'ætrɪk/ a psychiatrisch

psychiatr|ist /saɪ'kaɪətrɪst/ n Psychiater(in) m(f). ~y n Psychiatrie f

psychic /'saɪkɪk/ a übersinnlich; I'm not ~ ich kann nicht hellsehen

psycho|analyse /saɪkəʊ-/ vt psychoanalysieren. ~a'nalysis n Psychoanalyse f. ~'analyst Psychoanalytiker(in) m(f)

psychological /saɪkə'lɒdʒɪkl/ a, -ly adv psychologisch; (illness) psychisch

psycholog|ist /saɪ'kɒlədʒɪst/ n Psychologe m/ -login f. ~y n Psychologie f

psychopath /'saɪkəpæθ/ n Psychopath(in) m(f)

P.T.O. abbr (please turn over) b.w.

pub /pʌb/ n (fam) Kneipe f

puberty /'pju:bətɪ/ n Pubertät f

public /'pʌblɪk/ a, -ly adv öffentlich; make ~ publik machen □ the ~ die Öffentlichkeit; in ~ in aller Öffentlichkeit

publican /'pʌblɪkən/ n [Gast]wirt m

publication /pʌblɪ'keɪʃn/ n Veröffentlichung f

public: ~ con'venience n öffentliche Toilette f. ~ 'holiday n gesetzlicher Feiertag m. ~ 'house n [Gast]wirtschaft f

publicity /pʌb'lɪsətɪ/ n Publicity f; (advertising) Reklame f

publicize /'pʌblɪsaɪz/ vt Reklame machen für

public: ~ 'library n öffentliche Bücherei f. ~ 'school n Privatschule f; (Amer)

staatliche Schule f. ~-'spirited a be ~-spirited Gemeinsinn haben. ~ 'transport n öffentliche Verkehrsmittel pl

publish /'pʌblɪʃ/ vt veröffentlichen. ~er n Verleger(in) m(f); (firm) Verlag m. ~ing n Verlagswesen nt

pucker /'pʌkə(r)/ vt kräuseln

pudding /'pʊdɪŋ/ n Pudding m; (course) Nachtisch m

puddle /'pʌdl/ n Pfütze f

puerile /'pjʊəraɪl/ a kindisch

puff /pʌf/ n (of wind) Hauch m; (of smoke) Wölkchen nt; (for powder) Quaste f □ vt blasen, pusten; ~ out ausstoßen □ vi keuchen; ~ at paffen an (+ dat) (pipe). ~ed a (out of breath) aus der Puste. ~ pastry n Blätterteig m

puffy /'pʌfɪ/ a geschwollen

pugnacious /pʌg'neɪʃəs/ a, -ly adv aggressiv

pull /pʊl/ n Zug m; (jerk) Ruck m; (fam: influence) Einfluss m □ vt ziehen; ziehen an (+ dat) (rope); ~ a muscle sich (dat) einen Muskel zerren; ~ oneself together sich zusammennehmen; ~ one's weight tüchtig mitarbeiten; ~ s.o.'s leg (fam) jdn auf den Arm nehmen. ~ down vt herunterziehen; (demolish) abreißen. ~ in vt hereinziehen □ vi (Auto) einscheren. ~ off vt abziehen; (fam) schaffen. ~ out vt herausziehen □ vi (Auto) ausscheren. ~ through vt durchziehen □ vi (recover) durchkommen. ~ up vt heraufziehen; ausziehen (plant); (reprimand) zurechtweisen □ vi (Auto) anhalten

pulley /'pʊlɪ/ n (Techn) Rolle f

pullover /'pʊləʊvə(r)/ n Pullover m

pulp /pʌlp/ n Brei m; (of fruit) [Frucht]-fleisch nt

pulpit /'pʊlpɪt/ n Kanzel f

pulsate /pʌl'seɪt/ vi pulsieren

pulse /pʌls/ n Puls m

pulses /'pʌlsɪz/ npl Hülsenfrüchte pl

pulverize /'pʌlvəraɪz/ vt pulverisieren

pumice /'pʌmɪs/ n Bimsstein m

pummel /'pʌml/ vt (pt/pp pummelled) mit den Fäusten bearbeiten

pump /pʌmp/ n Pumpe f □ vt pumpen; (fam) aushorchen. ~ up vt hochpumpen; (inflate) aufpumpen

pumpkin /'pʌmpkɪn/ n Kürbis m

pun /pʌn/ n Wortspiel nt

punch[1] /pʌntʃ/ n Faustschlag m; (device) Locher m □ vt boxen; lochen (ticket); stanzen (hole)

punch[2] n (drink) Bowle f

punch: ~ line n Pointe f. ~-up n Schlägerei f

punctual /'pʌŋktjuəl/ *a*, **-ly** *adv* pünktlich. ~**ity** /-'ælətɪ/ *n* Pünktlichkeit *f*

punctuat|e /'pʌŋktjuɛɪt/ *vt* mit Satzzeichen versehen. ~**ion** /-'eɪʃn/ *n* Interpunktion *f*. ~**ion mark** *n* Satzzeichen *nt*

puncture /'pʌŋktʃə(r)/ *n* Loch *nt*; (*tyre*) Reifenpanne *f* □ *vt* durchstechen

pundit /'pʌndɪt/ *n* Experte *m*

pungent /'pʌndʒənt/ *a* scharf

punish /'pʌnɪʃ/ *vt* bestrafen. ~**able** /-əbl/ *a* strafbar. ~**ment** *n* Strafe *f*

punitive /'pjuːnɪtɪv/ *a* Straf-

punnet /'pʌnɪt/ *n* Körbchen *nt*

punt /pʌnt/ *n* (*boat*) Stechkahn *m*

punter /'pʌntə(r)/ *n* (*gambler*) Wetter *m*; (*client*) Kunde *m*

puny /'pjuːnɪ/ *a* (**-ier, -iest**) mickerig

pup /pʌp/ *n* = **puppy**

pupil /'pjuːpl/ *n* Schüler(in) *m(f)*; (*of eye*) Pupille *f*

puppet /'pʌpɪt/ *n* Puppe *f*; (*fig*) Marionette *f*

puppy /'pʌpɪ/ *n* junger Hund *m*

purchase /'pɜːtʃəs/ *n* Kauf *m*; (*leverage*) Hebelkraft *f* □ *vt* kaufen. ~**r** *n* Käufer *m*

pure /pjʊə(r)/ *a* (**-r, -st,**) **-ly** *adv* rein

purée /'pjʊəreɪ/ *n* Püree *nt*, Brei *m*

purgatory /'pɜːgətrɪ/ *n* (*Relig*) Fegefeuer *nt*; (*fig*) Hölle *f*

purge /pɜːdʒ/ *n* (*Pol*) Säuberungsaktion *f* □ *vt* reinigen; (*Pol*) säubern

puri|fication /pjʊərɪfɪ'keɪʃn/ *n* Reinigung *f*. ~**fy** /'pjʊərɪfaɪ/ *vt* (*pt/pp* **-ied**) reinigen

puritanical /pjʊərɪ'tænɪkl/ *a* puritanisch

purity /'pjʊərɪtɪ/ *n* Reinheit *f*

purl /pɜːl/ *n* (*Knitting*) linke Masche *f* □ *vt/i* links stricken

purple /'pɜːpl/ *a* [dunkel]lila

purport /pə'pɔːt/ *vt* vorgeben

purpose /'pɜːpəs/ *n* Zweck *m*; (*intention*) Absicht *f*; (*determination*) Entschlossenheit *f*; **on** ~ absichtlich; **to no** ~ unnützerweise. ~**ful** *a*, **-ly** *adv* entschlossen. ~**ly** *adv* absichtlich

purr /pɜː(r)/ *vi* schnurren

purse /pɜːs/ *n* Portemonnaie *nt*; (*Amer: handbag*) Handtasche *f* □ *vt* schürzen (*lips*)

pursue /pə'sjuː/ *vt* verfolgen; (*fig*) nachgehen (+ *dat*). ~**r** /-ə(r)/ *n* Verfolger *m*

pursuit /pə'sjuːt/ *n* Verfolgung *f*; Jagd *f*; (*pastime*) Beschäftigung *f*; **in** ~ hinterher

pus /pʌs/ *n* Eiter *m*

push /pʊʃ/ *n* Stoß *m*, (*fam*) Schubs *m*; **get the** ~ (*fam*) hinausfliegen □ *vt/i* schieben; (*press*) drücken; (*roughly*) stoßen; **be** ~**ed for time** (*fam*) unter Zeitdruck stehen. ~ **off** *vt* hinunterstoßen □ *vi* (*fam: leave*) abhauen. ~ **on** *vi* (*continue*) weitergehen/-fahren; (*with activity*) weitermachen. ~ **up** *vt* hochschieben; hochtreiben (*price*)

push: ~**button** *n* Druckknopf *m*. ~**chair** *n* [Kinder]sportwagen *m*. ~**over** *n* (*fam*) Kinderspiel *nt*. ~**up** *n* (*Amer*) Liegestütz *m*

pushy /'pʊʃɪ/ *a* (*fam*) aufdringlich

puss /pʊs/ *n*, **pussy** /'pʊsɪ/ *n* Mieze *f*

put /pʊt/ *vt* (*pt/pp* **put**, *pres p* **putting**) tun; (*place*) setzen; (*upright*) stellen; (*flat*) legen; (*express*) ausdrücken; (*say*) sagen; (*estimate*) schätzen (**at** *acc*); ~ **aside** *or* **by** beiseite legen; ~ **one's foot down** (*fam*) energisch werden; (*Auto*) Gas geben □ *vi* ~ **to sea** auslaufen □ **a** ~ **stay** = dableiben. ~ **away** *vt* wegräumen. ~ **back** *vt* wieder hinsetzen/-stellen/-legen; zurückstellen (*clock*). ~ **down** *vt* hinsetzen/-stellen/-legen; (*suppress*) niederschlagen; (*kill*) töten; (*write*) niederschreiben; (*attribute*) zuschreiben (**to** *dat*). ~ **forward** *vt* vorbringen; vorstellen (*clock*). ~ **in** *vt* hineinsetzen/-stellen/-legen; (*insert*) einstecken; (*submit*) einreichen □ *vi* ~ **in for** beantragen. ~ **off** *vt* ausmachen (*light*); (*postpone*) verschieben; ~ **s.o. off** jdn abbestellen; (*disconcert*) jdn aus der Fassung bringen; ~ **s.o. off sth** jdm etw verleiden. ~ **on** *vt* anziehen (*clothes, brake*); sich (*dat*) aufsetzen (*hat*); (*Culin*) aufsetzen; anmachen (*light*); aufführen (*play*); annehmen (*accent*); ~ **on weight** zunehmen. ~ **out** *vt* hinaussetzen/-stellen/-legen; ausmachen (*fire, light*); ausstrecken (*hand*); (*disconcert*) aus der Fassung bringen; ~ **s.o./oneself out** jdm/sich Umstände machen. ~ **through** *vt* durchstecken; (*Teleph*) verbinden (**to** mit). ~ **up** *vt* errichten (*building*); aufschlagen (*tent*); aufspannen (*umbrella*); anschlagen (*notice*); erhöhen (*price*); unterbringen (*guest*); ~ **s.o. up to sth** jdn zu etw anstiften (+ *dat*) □ *vi* (**at** *hotel*) absteigen in (+ *dat*); ~ **up with sth** sich (*dat*) etw bieten lassen

putrefy /'pjuːtrɪfaɪ/ *vi* (*pt/pp* **-ied**) verwesen

putrid /'pjuːtrɪd/ *a* faulig

putty /'pʌtɪ/ *n* Kitt *m*

put-up /'pʊtʌp/ *a* **a** ~ **job** ein abgekartetes Spiel *nt*

puzzl|e /'pʌzl/ *n* Rätsel *nt*; (*jigsaw*) Puzzlespiel *nt* □ *vt* **it** ~**es me** es ist mir rätselhaft □ *vi* ~**e over** sich (*dat*) den Kopf zerbrechen über (+ *acc*). ~**ing** *a* rätselhaft

pyjamas /pə'dʒɑːməz/ *npl* Schlafanzug *m*

pylon /'paɪlən/ n Mast m

pyramid /'pɪrəmɪd/ n Pyramide f

python /'paɪθn/ n Pythonschlange f

Q

quack¹ /kwæk/ n Quaken nt □ vi quaken

quack² n (doctor) Quacksalber m

quad /kwɒd/ n (fam: court) Hof m; ~s pl = quadruplets

quadrangle /'kwɒdræŋgl/ n Viereck nt; (court) Hof m

quadruped /'kwɒdrʊped/ n Vierfüßer m

quadruple /'kwɒdrʊpl/ a vierfach □ vt vervierfachen □ vi sich vervierfachen. ~ts /-plɪts/ npl Vierlinge pl

quagmire /'kwɒgmaɪə(r)/ n Sumpf m

quaint /kweɪnt/ a (-er, -est) malerisch; (odd) putzig

quake /kweɪk/ n (fam) Erdbeben nt □ vi beben; (with fear) zittern

Quaker /'kweɪkə(r)/ n Quäker(in) m(f)

qualification /kwɒlɪfɪ'keɪʃn/ n Qualifikation f; (reservation) Einschränkung f. ~ied /-faɪd/ a qualifiziert; (trained) ausgebildet; (limited) bedingt

qualify /'kwɒlɪfaɪ/ v (pt/pp -ied) □ vt qualifizieren; (entitle) berechtigen; (limit) einschränken □ vi sich qualifizieren

quality /'kwɒlətɪ/ n Qualität f; (characteristic) Eigenschaft f

qualm /kwɑ:m/ n Bedenken pl

quandary /'kwɒndərɪ/ n Dilemma nt

quantity /'kwɒntətɪ/ n Quantität f, Menge f; **in** ~ in großen Mengen

quarantine /'kwɒrəntɪ:n/ n Quarantäne f

quarrel /'kwɒrl/ n Streit m □ vi (pt/pp quarrelled) sich streiten. ~some a streitsüchtig

quarry¹ /'kwɒrɪ/ n (prey) Beute f

quarry² n Steinbruch m

quart /kwɔ:t/ n Quart nt

quarter /'kwɔ:tə(r)/ n Viertel nt; (of year) Vierteljahr nt; (Amer) 25-Cent-Stück nt; ~s pl Quartier nt; **at [a]** ~ **to six** um Viertel vor sechs; **from all** ~s aus allen Richtungen □ vt vierteln; (Mil) einquartieren (**on** bei). ~·**final** n Viertelfinale nt

quarterly /'kwɔ:təlɪ/ a & adv vierteljährlich

quartet /kwɔ:'tet/ n Quartett nt

quartz /kwɔ:ts/ n Quarz m. ~ **watch** n Quarzuhr f

quash /kwɒʃ/ vt aufheben; niederschlagen (rebellion)

quaver /'kweɪvə(r)/ n (Mus) Achtelnote f □ vi zittern

quay /ki:/ n Kai m

queasy /'kwi:zɪ/ a **I feel** ~ mir ist übel

queen /kwi:n/ n Königin f; (Cards, Chess) Dame f

queer /kwɪə(r)/ a (-er, -est) eigenartig; (dubious) zweifelhaft; (ill) unwohl; (fam: homosexual) schwul □ n (fam) Schwule(r) m

quell /kwel/ vt unterdrücken

quench /kwentʃ/ vt löschen

query /'kwɪərɪ/ n Frage f; (question mark) Fragezeichen nt □ vt (pt/pp -ied) infrage stellen; reklamieren (bill)

quest /kwest/ n Suche f (**for** nach)

question /'kwestʃn/ n Frage f; (for discussion) Thema nt; **out of the** ~ ausgeschlossen; **without** ~ ohne Frage; **the person in** ~ die fragliche Person □ vt infrage stellen; ~ **s.o.** jdn ausfragen; (police:) jdn verhören. ~**able** /-əbl/ a zweifelhaft. ~ **mark** n Fragezeichen nt

questionnaire /kwestʃə'neə(r)/ n Fragebogen m

queue /kju:/ n Schlange f □ vi ~ **[up]** Schlange stehen, sich anstellen (**for** nach)

quibble /'kwɪbl/ vi Haarspalterei treiben

quick /kwɪk/ a (-er, -est), -**ly** adv schnell; **be** ~! mach schnell! **have a** ~ **meal** schnell etwas essen □ adv schnell □ n **cut to the** ~ (fig) bis ins Mark getroffen. ~**en** vt beschleunigen □ vi sich beschleunigen

quick: ~**sand** n Treibsand m. ~**tempered** a aufbrausend

quid /kwɪd/ n inv (fam) Pfund nt

quiet /'kwaɪət/ a (-er, -est), -**ly** adv still; (calm) ruhig; (soft) leise; **keep** ~ **about** (fam) nichts sagen von □ n Stille f; Ruhe f; **on the** ~ heimlich

quiet|en /'kwaɪətn/ vt beruhigen □ vi ~**en down** ruhig werden. ~**ness** n (see quiet) Stille f; Ruhe f

quill /kwɪl/ n Feder f; (spine) Stachel m

quilt /kwɪlt/ n Steppdecke f. ~**ed** a Stepp-

quince /kwɪns/ n Quitte f

quins /kwɪnz/ npl (fam) = quintuplets

quintet /kwɪn'tet/ n Quintett nt

quintuplets /'kwɪntjʊplɪts/ npl Fünflinge pl

quip /kwɪp/ n Scherz m □ vi (pt/pp quipped) scherzen

quirk /kwɜ:k/ n Eigenart f

quit /kwɪt/ v (pt/pp quitted **or** quit) □ vt verlassen; (give up) aufgeben; ~ **doing sth** aufhören, etw zu tun □ vi gehen; **give**

s.o. notice to ~ jdm die Wohnung kündigen

quite /kwaɪt/ *adv* ganz; (*really*) wirklich; ~ [so]! genau! ~ **a few** ziemlich viele

quits /kwɪts/ *a* quitt

quiver /'kwɪvə(r)/ *vi* zittern

quiz /kwɪz/ *n* Quiz *nt* □ *vt* (*pt/pp* **quizzed**) ausfragen. **~zical** *a*, **-ly** *adv* fragend

quorum /'kwɔːrəm/ *n* **have a ~** beschlussfähig sein

quota /'kwəʊtə/ *n* Anteil *m*; (*Comm*) Kontingent *nt*

quotation /kwəʊ'teɪʃn/ *n* Zitat *nt*; (*price*) Kostenvoranschlag *m*; (*of shares*) Notierung *f*. ~ **marks** *npl* Anführungszeichen *pl*

quote /kwəʊt/ *n* (*fam*) = **quotation**; **in** ~**s** in Anführungszeichen □ *vt/i* zitieren

R

rabbi /'ræbaɪ/ *n* Rabbiner *m*; (*title*) Rabbi *m*

rabbit /'ræbɪt/ *n* Kaninchen *nt*

rabble /'ræbl/ *n* **the ~** der Pöbel

rabid /'ræbɪd/ *a* fanatisch; (*animal*) tollwütig

rabies /'reɪbiːz/ *n* Tollwut *f*

race¹ /reɪs/ *n* Rasse *f*

race² /reɪs/ *n* Rennen *nt*; (*fig*) Wettlauf *m* □ *vi* [am Rennen] teilnehmen; (*athlete, horse:*) laufen; (*fam: rush*) rasen □ *vt* um die Wette laufen mit; an einem Rennen teilnehmen lassen (*horse*)

race: ~**course** *n* Rennbahn *f*. ~**horse** *n* Rennpferd *nt*. ~**-track** *n* Rennbahn *f*

racial /'reɪʃl/ *a*, **-ly** *adv* rassisch; (*discrimination, minority*) Rassen-

racing /'reɪsɪŋ/ *n* Rennsport *m*; (*horse-*) Pferderennen *nt*. ~ **car** *n* Rennwagen *m*. ~ **driver** *n* Rennfahrer *m*

racis|m /'reɪsɪzm/ *n* Rassismus *m*. ~**t** /-ɪst/ *a* rassistisch □ *n* Rassist *m*

rack¹ /ræk/ *n* Ständer *m*; (*for plates*) Gestell *nt* □ *vt* ~ **one's brains** sich (*dat*) den Kopf zerbrechen

rack² *n* **go to ~ and ruin** verfallen; (*fig*) herunterkommen

racket¹ /'rækɪt/ *n* (*Sport*) Schläger *m*

racket² *n* (*din*) Krach *m*; (*swindle*) Schwindelgeschäft *nt*

racy /'reɪsɪ/ *a* (-ier, -iest) schwungvoll; (*risqué*) gewagt

radar /'reɪdɑː(r)/ *n* Radar *nt*

radian|ce /'reɪdɪəns/ *n* Strahlen *nt*. ~**t** *a*, **-ly** *adv* strahlend

radiat|e /'reɪdɪeɪt/ *vt* ausstrahlen □ *vi* (*heat:*) ausgestrahlt werden; (*roads:*) strahlenförmig ausgehen. ~**ion** /-'eɪʃn/ *n* Strahlung *f*

radiator /'reɪdɪeɪtə(r)/ *n* Heizkörper *m*; (*Auto*) Kühler *m*

radical /'rædɪkl/ *a*, **-ly** *adv* radikal □ *n* Radikale(r) *m/f*

radio /'reɪdɪəʊ/ *n* Radio *nt*; **by ~** über Funk □ *vt* funken

radio|'active *a* radioaktiv. ~**ac'tivity** *n* Radioaktivität *f*

radiography /reɪdɪ'ɒɡrəfɪ/ *n* Röntgenographie *f*

'radio ham *n* Hobbyfunker *m*

radio'therapy *n* Strahlenbehandlung *f*

radish /'rædɪʃ/ *n* Radieschen *nt*

radius /'reɪdɪəs/ *n* (*pl* **-dii** /-dɪaɪ/) Radius *m*, Halbmesser *m*

raffle /'ræfl/ *n* Tombola *f* □ *vt* verlosen

raft /rɑːft/ *n* Floß *nt*

rafter /'rɑːftə(r)/ *n* Dachsparren *m*

rag¹ /ræɡ/ *n* Lumpen *m*; (*pej: newspaper*) Käseblatt *nt*; **in ~s** in Lumpen

rag² *vt* (*pt/pp* **ragged**) (*fam*) aufziehen

rage /reɪdʒ/ *n* Wut *f*; **all the ~** (*fam*) der letzte Schrei □ *vi* rasen; (*storm:*) toben

ragged /'ræɡɪd/ *a* zerlumpt; (*edge*) ausgefranst

raid /reɪd/ *n* Überfall *m*; (*Mil*) Angriff *m*; (*police*) Razzia *f* □ *vt* überfallen; (*Mil*) angreifen; (*police*) eine Razzia durchführen in (+ *dat*); (*break in*) eindringen in (+ *acc*). ~**er** *n* Eindringling *m*; (*of bank*) Bankräuber *m*

rail /reɪl/ *n* Schiene *f*; (*pole*) Stange *f*; (*hand~*) Handlauf *m*; (*Naut*) Reling *f*; **by ~** mit der Bahn

railings /'reɪlɪŋz/ *npl* Geländer *nt*

'railroad *n* (*Amer*) = **railway**

'railway *n* [Eisen]bahn *f*. ~**man** *n* Eisenbahner *m*. ~ **station** *n* Bahnhof *m*

rain /reɪn/ *n* Regen *m* □ *vi* regnen

rain: ~**bow** *n* Regenbogen *m*. ~**check** *n* (*Amer*) **take a ~check on** aufschieben. ~**coat** *n* Regenmantel *m*. ~**fall** *n* Niederschlag *m*

rainy /'reɪnɪ/ *a* (-ier, -iest) regnerisch

raise /reɪz/ *n* (*Amer*) Lohnerhöhung *f* □ *vt* erheben; (*upright*) aufrichten; (*make higher*) erhöhen; (*lift*) [hoch]heben; lüften (*hat*); aufziehen (*children, animals*); aufwerfen (*question*); aufbringen (*money*)

raisin /'reɪzn/ *n* Rosine *f*

rake /reɪk/ *n* Harke *f*, Rechen *m* □ *vt* harken, rechen. ~ **up** *vt* zusammenharken; (*fam*) wieder aufrühren

'rake-off n (fam) Prozente pl

rally /'rælɪ/ n Versammlung f; (Auto) Rallye f; (Tennis) Ballwechsel m □ vt sammeln □ vi sich sammeln; (recover strength) sich erholen

ram /ræm/ n Schafbock m; (Astr) Widder m □ vt (pt/pp **rammed**) rammen

rambl|e /'ræmbl/ n Wanderung f □ vi wandern; (in speech) irrereden. **~er** n Wanderer m; (rose) Kletterrose f. **~ing** a weitschweifig; ⟨club⟩ Wander-

ramp /ræmp/ n Rampe f; (Aviat) Gangway f

rampage¹ /'ræmpeɪdʒ/ n be/go on the **~** randalieren

rampage² /ræm'peɪdʒ/ vi randalieren

rampant /'ræmpənt/ a weit verbreitet; (in heraldry) aufgerichtet

rampart /'ræmpɑːt/ n Wall m

ramshackle /'ræmʃækl/ a baufällig

ran /ræn/ see **run**

ranch /rɑːntʃ/ n Ranch f

rancid /'rænsɪd/ a ranzig

rancour /'ræŋkə(r)/ n Groll m

random /'rændəm/ a willkürlich; a **~** sample eine Stichprobe □ n at **~** aufs Geratewohl; ⟨choose⟩ willkürlich

randy /'rændɪ/ a (-ier, -iest) (fam) geil

rang /ræŋ/ see **ring²**

range /reɪndʒ/ n Serie f, Reihe f; (Comm) Auswahl f, Angebot nt (of an + dat); (of mountains) Kette f; (Mus) Umfang m; (distance) Reichweite f; (for shooting) Schießplatz m; (stove) Kohlenherd m; at **~** of auf eine Entfernung von □ vi reichen; **~** from ... to gehen von ... bis. **~r** n Aufseher m

rank¹ /ræŋk/ n (row) Reihe f; (Mil) Rang m; (social position) Stand m; the **~** and file die breite Masse; the **~s** pl die gemeinen Soldaten □ vt/i einstufen; **~** among zählen zu

rank² a (bad) übel; ⟨plants⟩ üppig; (fig) krass

ransack /'rænsæk/ vt durchwühlen; (pillage) plündern

ransom /'rænsəm/ n Lösegeld nt; hold s.o. to **~** Lösegeld für jdn fordern

rant /rænt/ vi rasen

rap /ræp/ n Klopfen nt; (blow) Schlag m □ v (pt/pp **rapped**) □ vt klopfen auf (+ acc) □ vi **~** at/on klopfen an/auf (+ acc)

rape¹ /reɪp/ n (Bot) Raps m

rape² n Vergewaltigung f □ vt vergewaltigen

rapid /'ræpɪd/ a, **-ly** adv schnell. **~ity** /rə'pɪdətɪ/ n Schnelligkeit f

rapids /'ræpɪdz/ npl Stromschnellen pl

rapist /'reɪpɪst/ n Vergewaltiger m

rapport /ræ'pɔː(r)/ n [innerer] Kontakt m

rapt /ræpt/ a, **-ly** adv gespannt; ⟨look⟩ andächtig; **~** in versunken in (+ acc)

raptur|e /'ræptʃə(r)/ n Entzücken nt. **~ous** /-rəs/ a, **-ly** adv begeistert

rare¹ /reə(r)/ a (-r, -st), **-ly** adv selten

rare² a (Culin) englisch gebraten

rarefied /'reərɪfaɪd/ a dünn

rarity /'reərətɪ/ n Seltenheit f

rascal /'rɑːskl/ n Schlingel m

rash¹ /ræʃ/ n (Med) Ausschlag m

rash² a (-er, -est), **-ly** adv voreilig

rasher /'ræʃə(r)/ n Speckscheibe f

rasp /rɑːsp/ n Raspel f

raspberry /'rɑːzbərɪ/ n Himbeere f

rat /ræt/ n Ratte f; (fam: person) Schuft m; **smell a ~** (fam) Lunte riechen

rate /reɪt/ n Rate f; (speed) Tempo nt; (of payment) Satz m; (of exchange) Kurs m; **~s** pl (taxes) ≈ Grundsteuer f; at any **~** auf jeden Fall; at this **~** auf diese Weise □ vt einschätzen; **~** among zählen zu □ vi **~** as gelten als

rather /'rɑːðə(r)/ adv lieber; (fairly) ziemlich; **~!** und ob!

rati|fication /rætɪfɪ'keɪʃn/ n Ratifizierung f. **~fy** /'rætɪfaɪ/ vt (pt/pp **-ied**) ratifizieren

rating /'reɪtɪŋ/ n Einschätzung f; (class) Klasse f; (sailor) [einfacher] Matrose m; **~s** pl (Radio, TV) ≈ Einschaltquote f

ratio /'reɪʃɪəʊ/ n Verhältnis nt

ration /'ræʃn/ n Ration f □ vt rationieren

rational /'ræʃənl/ a, **-ly** adv rational. **~ize** vt/i rationalisieren

'rat race n (fam) Konkurrenzkampf m

rattle /'rætl/ n Rasseln nt; (of china, glass) Klirren nt; (of windows) Klappern nt; (toy) Klapper f □ vi rasseln; klirren; klappern □ vt rasseln mit; (shake) schütteln. **~** off vt herunterrasseln

'rattlesnake n Klapperschlange f

raucous /'rɔːkəs/ a rau

ravage /'rævɪdʒ/ vt verwüsten, verheeren

rave /reɪv/ vi toben; **~** about schwärmen von

raven /'reɪvn/ n Rabe m

ravenous /'rævənəs/ a heißhungrig

ravine /rə'viːn/ n Schlucht f

raving /'reɪvɪŋ/ a **~** mad (fam) total verrückt

ravishing /'rævɪʃɪŋ/ a hinreißend

raw /rɔː/ a (-er, -est) roh; (not processed) Roh-; ⟨skin⟩ wund; ⟨weather⟩ nasskalt; (inexperienced) unerfahren; get a **~** deal (fam) schlecht wegkommen. **~ ma'terials** npl Rohstoffe pl

ray /reɪ/ n Strahl m; ~ **of hope** Hoffnungsschimmer m

raze /reɪz/ vt ~ **to the ground** dem Erdboden gleichmachen

razor /'reɪzə(r)/ n Rasierapparat m. ~ **blade** n Rasierklinge f

re /ri:/ prep betreffs (+ gen)

reach /ri:tʃ/ n Reichweite f; (of river) Strecke f; **within/out of** ~ in/außer Reichweite; **within easy** ~ leicht erreichbar □ vt erreichen; (arrive at) ankommen in (+ dat); (~ as far as) reichen bis zu; kommen zu ⟨decision, conclusion⟩; (pass) reichen □ vi reichen (**to** bis zu); ~ **for** greifen nach; **I can't** ~ ich komme nicht daran

re'act /rɪ-/ vi reagieren (**to** auf + acc)

re'action /rɪ-/ n Reaktion f. ~**ary** a reaktionär

reactor /rɪ'æktə(r)/ n Reaktor m

read /ri:d/ vt/i (pt/pp **read** /red/) lesen; (aloud) vorlesen (**to** dat); (Univ) studieren; ablesen ⟨meter⟩. ~ **out** vt vorlesen

readable /'ri:dəbl/ a lesbar

reader /'ri:də(r)/ n Leser(in) m(f); (book) Lesebuch nt

readi|ly /'redɪlɪ/ adv bereitwillig; (easily) leicht. ~**ness** n Bereitschaft f; **in** ~**ness** bereit

reading /'ri:dɪŋ/ n Lesen nt; (Pol, Relig) Lesung f

rea'djust /ri:-/ vt neu einstellen □ vi sich umstellen (**to** auf + acc)

ready /'redɪ/ a (-ier, -iest) fertig; (willing) bereit; (quick) schnell; **get** ~ sich fertig machen; (prepare to) sich bereitmachen

ready: ~-'**made** a fertig. ~ '**money** n Bargeld nt. ~-**to**-'**wear** a Konfektions-

real /rɪəl/ a wirklich; (genuine) echt; (actual) eigentlich □ adv (Amer, fam) echt. ~ **estate** n Immobilien pl

realis|m /'rɪəlɪzm/ n Realismus m. ~**t** /-lɪst/ n Realist m. ~**tic** /-'lɪstɪk/ a, -**ally** adv realistisch

reality /rɪ'ælətɪ/ n Wirklichkeit f, Realität f

realization /rɪəlaɪ'zeɪʃn/ n Erkenntnis f

realize /'rɪəlaɪz/ vt einsehen; (become aware) gewahr werden; verwirklichen ⟨hopes, plans⟩; (Comm) realisieren; einbringen ⟨price⟩; **I didn't** ~ das wusste ich nicht

really /'rɪəlɪ/ adv wirklich; (actually) eigentlich

realm /relm/ n Reich nt

realtor /'ri:əltə(r)/ n (Amer) Immobilienmakler m

reap /ri:p/ vt ernten

reap'pear /ri:-/ vi wiederkommen

rear[1] /rɪə(r)/ a Hinter-; (Auto) Heck- □ n **the** ~ der hintere Teil; **from the** ~ von hinten

rear[2] vt aufziehen □ vi ~ **[up]** ⟨horse:⟩ sich aufbäumen

'**rear-light** n Rücklicht nt

re'arm /ri:-/ vi wieder aufrüsten

rear'range /ri:-/ vt umstellen

rear-view '**mirror** n (Auto) Rückspiegel m

reason /'ri:zn/ n Grund m; (good sense) Vernunft f; (ability to think) Verstand m; **within** ~ in vernünftigen Grenzen □ vi argumentieren; ~ **with** vernünftig reden mit. ~**able** /-əbl/ a vernünftig; (not expensive) preiswert. ~**ably** /-əblɪ/ adv (fairly) ziemlich

reas'sur|ance /ri:-/ n Beruhigung f; Versicherung f. ~**e** vt beruhigen; ~ **e s.o. of sth** jdm etw ⟨gen⟩ versichern

rebate /'ri:beɪt/ n Rückzahlung f; (discount) Nachlass m

rebel[1] /'rebl/ n Rebell m

rebel[2] /rɪ'bel/ vi (pt/pp **rebelled**) rebellieren. ~**lion** /-ɪən/ n Rebellion f. ~**lious** /-ɪəs/ a rebellisch

re'bound[1] /rɪ-/ vi abprallen

'**rebound**[2] /ri:-/ n Rückprall m

rebuff /rɪ'bʌf/ n Abweisung f □ vt abweisen; eine Abfuhr erteilen (**s.o.** jdm)

re'build /ri:-/ vt (pt/pp -**built**) wieder aufbauen

rebuke /rɪ'bju:k/ n Tadel m □ vt tadeln

rebuttal /rɪ'bʌtl/ n Widerlegung f

re'call /rɪ-/ n Erinnerung f; **beyond** ~ unwiderruflich □ vt zurückrufen; abberufen ⟨diplomat⟩; vorzeitig einberufen ⟨parliament⟩; (remember) sich erinnern an (+ acc)

recant /rɪ'kænt/ vi widerrufen

recap /'ri:kæp/ vt/i (fam) = **recapitulate**

recapitulate /ri:kə'pɪtjʊleɪt/ vt/i zusammenfassen; rekapitulieren

re'capture /ri:-/ vt wieder gefangen nehmen ⟨person⟩; wieder einfangen ⟨animal⟩

reced|e /rɪ'si:d/ vi zurückgehen. ~**ing** a ⟨forehead, chin⟩ fliehend; ~**ing hair** Stirnglatze f

receipt /rɪ'si:t/ n Quittung f; (receiving) Empfang m; ~**s** pl (Comm) Einnahmen pl

receive /rɪ'si:v/ vt erhalten, bekommen; empfangen ⟨guests⟩. ~**r** n (Teleph) Hörer m; (Radio, TV) Empfänger m; (of stolen goods) Hehler m

recent /'ri:sənt/ a kürzlich erfolgte(r,s). ~**ly** adv in letzter Zeit; (the other day) kürzlich, vor kurzem

receptacle /rɪ'septəkl/ n Behälter m

reception /rɪ'sepʃn/ *n* Empfang *m*; ~ **[desk]** (*in hotel*) Rezeption *f*. ~**ist** *n* Empfangsdame *f*

receptive /rɪ'septɪv/ *a* aufnahmefähig; ~ **to** empfänglich für

recess /rɪ'ses/ *n* Nische *f*; (*holiday*) Ferien *pl*; (*Amer, Sch*) Pause *f*

recession /rɪ'seʃn/ *n* Rezession *f*

re'charge /riː-/ *vt* [wieder] aufladen

recipe /'resəpɪ/ *n* Rezept *nt*

recipient /rɪ'sɪpɪənt/ *n* Empfänger *m*

recipro|cal /rɪ'sɪprəkl/ *a* gegenseitig. ~**cate** /-keɪt/ *vt* erwidern

recital /rɪ'saɪtl/ *n* (*of poetry, songs*) Vortrag *m*; (*on piano*) Konzert *nt*

recite /rɪ'saɪt/ *vt* aufsagen; (*before audience*) vortragen; (*list*) aufzählen

reckless /'reklɪs/ *a*, **-ly** *adv* leichtsinnig; (*careless*) rücksichtslos. ~**ness** *n* Leichtsinn *m*; Rücksichtslosigkeit *f*

reckon /'rekən/ *vt* rechnen; (*consider*) glauben □ *vi* ~ **on/with** rechnen mit

re'claim /rɪ-/ *vt* zurückfordern; zurückgewinnen (*land*)

reclin|e /rɪ'klaɪn/ *vi* liegen. ~**ing seat** *n* Liegesitz *m*

recluse /rɪ'kluːs/ *n* Einsiedler(in) *m(f)*

recognition /rekəg'nɪʃn/ *n* Erkennen *nt*; (*acknowledgement*) Anerkennung *f*; **in** ~ als Anerkennung (**of** *gen*); **be beyond** ~ nicht wieder zu erkennen sein

recognize /'rekəgnaɪz/ *vt* erkennen; (*know again*) wieder erkennen; (*acknowledge*) anerkennen

re'coil /rɪ-/ *vi* zurückschnellen; (*in fear*) zurückschrecken

recollect /rekə'lekt/ *vt* sich erinnern an (+ *acc*). ~**ion** /-ekʃn/ *n* Erinnerung *f*

recommend /rekə'mend/ *vt* empfehlen. ~**ation** /-'deɪʃn/ *n* Empfehlung *f*

recompense /'rekəmpens/ *n* Entschädigung *f* □ *vt* entschädigen

recon|cile /'rekənsaɪl/ *vt* versöhnen; ~**cile oneself to** sich abfinden mit. ~**ciliation** /-sɪlɪ'eɪʃn/ *n* Versöhnung *f*

recon'dition /riː-/ *vt* generalüberholen. ~**ed engine** *n* Austauschmotor *m*

reconnaissance /rɪ'kɒnɪsns/ *n* (*Mil*) Aufklärung *f*

reconnoitre /rekə'nɔɪtə(r)/ *vi* (*pres p* -**tring**) auf Erkundung ausgehen

recon'sider /riː-/ *vt* sich (*dat*) noch einmal überlegen

recon'struct /riː-/ *vt* wieder aufbauen; rekonstruieren (*crime*). ~**ion** *n* Wiederaufbau *m*; Rekonstruktion *f*

record¹ /rɪ'kɔːd/ *vt* aufzeichnen; (*register*) registrieren; (*on tape*) aufnehmen

record² /'rekɔːd/ *n* Aufzeichnung *f*; (*Jur*) Protokoll *nt*; (*Mus*) [Schall]platte *f*; (*Sport*) Rekord *m*; ~**s** *pl* Unterlagen *pl*; **keep a** ~ **of** sich (*dat*) notieren; **off the** ~ inoffiziell; **have a [criminal]** ~ vorbestraft sein

recorder /rɪ'kɔːdə(r)/ *n* (*Mus*) Blockflöte *f*

recording /rɪ'kɔːdɪŋ/ *n* Aufzeichnung *f*, Aufnahme *f*

'record-player *n* Plattenspieler *m*

recount /rɪ'kaʊnt/ *vt* erzählen

re-'count¹ /riː-/ *vt* nachzählen

're-count² /riː-/ *n* (*Pol*) Nachzählung *f*

recoup /rɪ'kuːp/ *vt* wieder einbringen; ausgleichen (*losses*)

recourse /rɪ'kɔːs/ *n* **have** ~ **to** Zuflucht nehmen zu

re-'cover /riː-/ *vt* neu beziehen

recover /rɪ'kʌvə(r)/ *vt* zurückbekommen; bergen (*wreck*) □ *vi* sich erholen. ~**y** *n* Wiedererlangung *f*; Bergung *f*; (*of health*) Erholung *f*

recreation /rekrɪ'eɪʃn/ *n* Erholung *f*; (*hobby*) Hobby *nt*. ~**al** *a* Freizeit-; **be** ~**al** erholsam sein

recrimination /rɪkrɪmɪ'neɪʃn/ *n* Gegenbeschuldigung *f*

recruit /rɪ'kruːt/ *n* (*Mil*) Rekrut *m*; **new** ~ (*member*) neues Mitglied *nt*; (*worker*) neuer Mitarbeiter *m* □ *vt* rekrutieren; anwerben (*staff*). ~**ment** *n* Rekrutierung *f*; Anwerbung *f*

rectang|le /'rektæŋgl/ *n* Rechteck *nt*. ~**ular** /-'tæŋgjʊlə(r)/ *a* rechteckig

rectify /'rektɪfaɪ/ *vt* (*pt/pp* -**ied**) berichtigen

rector /'rektə(r)/ *n* Pfarrer *m*; (*Univ*) Rektor *m*. ~**y** *n* Pfarrhaus *nt*

recuperat|e /rɪ'kjuːpəreɪt/ *vi* sich erholen. ~**ion** /-'reɪʃn/ *n* Erholung *f*

recur /rɪ'kɜː(r)/ *vi* (*pt/pp* **recurred**) sich wiederholen; (*illness*) wiederkehren

recurren|ce /rɪ'kʌrəns/ *n* Wiederkehr *f*. ~**t** *a* wiederkehrend

recycle /riː'saɪkl/ *vt* wieder verwerten. ~**d paper** *n* Umweltschutzpapier *nt*

red /red/ *a* (**redder, reddest**) rot □ *n* Rot *nt*. ~**currant** *n* rote Johannisbeere *f*

redd|en /'redn/ *vt* röten □ *vi* rot werden. ~**ish** *a* rötlich

re'decorate /riː-/ *vt* renovieren; (*paint*) neu streichen; (*wallpaper*) neu tapezieren

redeem /rɪ'diːm/ *vt* einlösen; (*Relig*) erlösen

redemption /rɪ'dempʃn/ *n* Erlösung *f*

rede'ploy /riː-/ *vt* an anderer Stelle einsetzen

red: ∼-'haired *a* rothaarig. ∼-'handed *a* catch s.o. ∼-'handed jdn auf frischer Tat ertappen. ∼'herring *n* falsche Spur *f*. ∼-hot *a* glühend heiß. R∼ 'Indian *n* Indianer(in) *m(f)*

redi'rect /ri:-/ *vt* nachsenden ⟨*letter*⟩; umleiten ⟨*traffic*⟩

red: ∼ 'light *n* (*Auto*) rote Ampel *f*. ∼ness *n* Röte *f*

re'do /ri:-/ *vt* (*pt* -did, *pp* -done) noch einmal machen

re'double /ri:-/ *vt* verdoppeln

redress /rɪ'dres/ *n* Entschädigung *f* □ *vt* wieder gutmachen; wiederherstellen ⟨*balance*⟩

red 'tape *n* (*fam*) Bürokratie *f*

reduc|e /rɪ'dju:s/ *vt* verringern, vermindern; (*in size*) verkleinern; ermäßigen ⟨*costs*⟩; herabsetzen ⟨*price, goods*⟩; (*Culin*) einkochen lassen. ∼tion /-'dʌkʃn/ *n* Verringerung *f*; (*in price*) Ermäßigung *f*; (*in size*) Verkleinerung *f*

redundan|cy /rɪ'dʌndənsɪ/ *n* Beschäftigungslosigkeit *f*; (*payment*) Abfindung *f*. ∼t *a* überflüssig; **make** ∼t entlassen; **be made** ∼t beschäftigungslos werden

reed /ri:d/ *n* [Schilf]rohr *nt*; ∼s *pl* Schilf *nt*

reef /ri:f/ *n* Riff *nt*

reek /ri:k/ *vi* riechen (**of** nach)

reel /ri:l/ *n* Rolle *f*, Spule *f* □ *vi* (*stagger*) taumeln □ *vt* ∼ **off** (*fig*) herunterrasseln

refectory /rɪ'fektərɪ/ *n* Refektorium *nt*; (*Univ*) Mensa *f*

refer /rɪ'fɜ:(r)/ *v* (*pt/pp* referred) □ *vt* verweisen (**to** an + *acc*); übergeben, weiterleiten ⟨*matter*⟩ (**to** an + *acc*) □ *vi* ∼ **to** sich beziehen auf (+ *acc*); (*mention*) erwähnen; (*concern*) betreffen; (*consult*) sich wenden an (+ *acc*); nachschlagen in (+ *dat*) ⟨*book*⟩; **are you** ∼**ring to me?** meinen Sie mich?

referee /refə'ri:/ *n* Schiedsrichter *m*; (*Boxing*) Ringrichter *m*; (*for job*) Referenz *f* □ *vt/i* (*pt/pp* refereed) Schiedsrichter/Ringrichter sein (**bei**)

reference /'refərəns/ *n* Erwähnung *f*; (*in book*) Verweis *m*; (*for job*) Referenz *f*; (*Comm*) **'your** ∼' Ihr Zeichen; **with** ∼ **to** in Bezug auf (+ *acc*); (*in letter*) unter Bezugnahme auf (+ *acc*); **make [a]** ∼ **to** erwähnen. ∼ **book** *n* Nachschlagewerk *nt*. ∼ **number** *n* Aktenzeichen *nt*

referendum /refə'rendəm/ *n* Volksabstimmung *f*

re'fill¹ /ri:-/ *vt* nachfüllen

'refill² /ri:-/ *n* (*for pen*) Ersatzmine *f*

refine /rɪ'faɪn/ *vt* raffinieren. ∼**d** *a* fein, vornehm. ∼**ment** *n* Vornehmheit *f*;

(*Techn*) Verfeinerung *f*. ∼**ry** /-ərɪ/ *n* Raffinerie *f*

reflect /rɪ'flekt/ *vt* reflektieren; ⟨*mirror:*⟩ [wider]spiegeln; **be** ∼**ed** in sich spiegeln in (+ *dat*) □ *vi* nachdenken (**on** über + *acc*); ∼ **badly upon** s.o. (*fig*) jdn in ein schlechtes Licht stellen. ∼**ion** /-ekʃn/ *n* Reflexion *f*; (*image*) Spiegelbild *nt*; **on** ∼**ion** nach nochmaliger Überlegung. ∼**ive** /-ɪv/ *a*, **-ly** *adv* nachdenklich. ∼**or** *n* Rückstrahler *m*

reflex /'ri:fleks/ *n* Reflex *m* □ *attrib* Reflex-

reflexive /rɪ'fleksɪv/ *a* reflexiv

reform /rɪ'fɔ:m/ *n* Reform *f* □ *vt* reformieren □ *vi* sich bessern. **R**∼**ation** /refə'meɪʃn/ *n* (*Relig*) Reformation *f*. ∼**er** *n* Reformer *m*; (*Relig*) Reformator *m*

refract /rɪ'frækt/ *vt* (*Phys*) brechen

refrain¹ /rɪ'freɪn/ *n* Refrain *m*

refrain² *vi* ∼ **from doing sth** etw nicht tun

refresh /rɪ'freʃ/ *vt* erfrischen. ∼**ing** *a* erfrischend. ∼**ments** *npl* Erfrischungen *pl*

refrigerat|e /rɪ'frɪdʒəreɪt/ *vt* kühlen. ∼**or** *n* Kühlschrank *m*

re'fuel /ri:-/ *vt/i* (*pt/pp* -fuelled) auftanken

refuge /'refju:dʒ/ *n* Zuflucht *f*; **take** ∼ **in** Zuflucht nehmen in (+ *dat*)

refugee /refju'dʒi:/ *n* Flüchtling *m*

'refund¹ /ri:-/ **get a** ∼ sein Geld zurückbekommen

re'fund² /rɪ-/ *vt* zurückerstatten

refurbish /ri:'fɜ:bɪʃ/ *vt* renovieren

refusal /rɪ'fju:zl/ *n* (*see* refuse¹) Ablehnung *f*; Weigerung *f*

refuse¹ /rɪ'fju:z/ *vt* ablehnen; (*not grant*) verweigern; ∼ **to do sth** sich weigern, etw zu tun □ *vi* ablehnen; sich weigern

refuse² /'refju:s/ *n* Müll *m*, Abfall *m*. ∼ **collection** *n* Müllabfuhr *f*

refute /rɪ'fju:t/ *vt* widerlegen

re'gain /rɪ-/ *vt* wiedergewinnen

regal /'ri:gl/ *a*, **-ly** *adv* königlich

regalia /rɪ'geɪlɪə/ *npl* Insignien *pl*

regard /rɪ'ga:d/ *n* (*heed*) Rücksicht *f*; (*respect*) Achtung *f*; ∼**s** *pl* Grüße *pl*; **with** ∼ **to** in Bezug auf (+ *acc*) □ *vt* ansehen, betrachten (**as** als); **as** ∼**s** in Bezug auf (+ *acc*). ∼**ing** *prep* bezüglich (+ *gen*). ∼**less** *adv* ohne Rücksicht (**of** auf + *acc*)

regatta /rɪ'gætə/ *n* Regatta *f*

regenerate /rɪ'dʒenəreɪt/ *vt* regenerieren □ *vi* sich regenerieren

regime /reɪ'ʒi:m/ *n* Regime *nt*

regiment /'redʒɪmənt/ *n* Regiment *nt*. ∼**al** /-'mentl/ *a* Regiments-. ∼**ation** /-'teɪʃn/ *n* Reglementierung *f*

region /'ri:dʒən/ n Region f; **in the ~ of** (fig) ungefähr. **~al** a, **-ly** adv regional

register /'redʒɪstə(r)/ n Register nt; (Sch) Anwesenheitsliste f □ vt registrieren; (report) anmelden; einschreiben (letter); aufgeben (luggage) □ vi (report) sich anmelden; **it didn't ~** (fig) ich habe es nicht registriert

registrar /redʒɪ'strɑ:(r)/ n Standesbeamte(r) m

registration /redʒɪ'streɪʃn/ n Registrierung f; Anmeldung f. **~ number** n Autonummer f

registry office /'redʒɪstrɪ-/ n Standesamt nt

regret /rɪ'gret/ n Bedauern nt □ vt (pt/pp regretted) bedauern. **~fully** adv mit Bedauern

regrettab|le /rɪ'gretəbl/ a bedauerlich. **~ly** adv bedauerlicherweise

regular /'regjʊlə(r)/ a, **-ly** adv regelmäßig; (usual) üblich; (Mil) Berufs- □ n Berufssoldat m; (in pub) Stammgast m; (in shop) Stammkunde m. **~ity** /-'lærətɪ/ n Regelmäßigkeit f

regulat|e /'regjʊleɪt/ vt regulieren. **~ion** /-'leɪʃn/ n (rule) Vorschrift f

rehabilitat|e /ri:hə'bɪlɪteɪt/ vt rehabilitieren. **~ion** /-'teɪʃn/ n Rehabilitation f

rehears|al /rɪ'hɜ:sl/ n (Theat) Probe f. **~e** vt/i proben

reign /reɪn/ n Herrschaft f □ vi herrschen, regieren

reimburse /ri:ɪm'bɜ:s/ vt **~ s.o. for sth** jdm etw zurückerstatten

rein /reɪn/ n Zügel m

reincarnation /ri:ɪnkɑ:'neɪʃn/ f Reinkarnation f, Wiedergeburt f

reindeer /'reɪndɪə(r)/ n inv Rentier nt

reinforce /ri:ɪn'fɔ:s/ vt verstärken. **~d 'concrete** n Stahlbeton m. **~ment** n Verstärkung f; **send ~ments** Verstärkung schicken

reinstate /ri:ɪn'steɪt/ vt wieder einstellen; (to office) wieder einsetzen

reiterate /ri:'ɪtəreɪt/ vt wiederholen

reject /rɪ'dʒekt/ vt ablehnen. **~ion** /-ekʃn/ n Ablehnung f

rejects /'ri:dʒekts/ npl (Comm) Ausschussware f

rejoic|e /rɪ'dʒɔɪs/ vi (liter) sich freuen. **~ing** n Freude f

re'join /rɪ-/ vt sich wieder anschließen (+ dat); wieder beitreten (+ dat) (club, party); (answer) erwidern

rejuvenate /rɪ'dʒu:vəneɪt/ vt verjüngen

relapse /rɪ'læps/ n Rückfall m □ vi einen Rückfall erleiden

relate /rɪ'leɪt/ vt (tell) erzählen; (connect) verbinden □ vi zusammenhängen (**to** mit). **~d** a verwandt (**to** mit)

relation /rɪ'leɪʃn/ n Beziehung f; (person) Verwandte(r) m/f. **~ship** n Beziehung f; (link) Verbindung f; (blood tie) Verwandtschaft f; (affair) Verhältnis nt

relative /'relətɪv/ n Verwandte(r) m/f □ a relativ; (Gram) Relativ-. **~ly** adv relativ, verhältnismäßig

relax /rɪ'læks/ vt lockern, entspannen □ vi sich lockern, sich entspannen. **~ation** /-'seɪʃn/ n Entspannung f. **~ing** a entspannend

relay[1] /'ri:leɪ/ vt (pt/pp -layed) weitergeben; (Radio, TV) übertragen

relay[2] /'ri:leɪ/ n (Electr) Relais nt; **work in ~s** sich bei der Arbeit ablösen. **~ [race]** n Staffel f

release /rɪ'li:s/ n Freilassung f, Entlassung f; (Techn) Auslöser m □ vt freilassen; (let go of) loslassen; (Techn) auslösen; veröffentlichen (information)

relegate /'relɪgeɪt/ vt verbannen; **be ~d** (Sport) absteigen

relent /rɪ'lent/ vi nachgeben. **~less** a, **-ly** adv erbarmungslos; (unceasing) unaufhörlich

relevan|ce /'reləvəns/ n Relevanz f. **~t** a relevant (**to** für)

reliab|ility /rɪlaɪə'bɪlətɪ/ n Zuverlässigkeit f. **~le** /-'laɪəbl/ a, **-ly** adv zuverlässig

relian|ce /rɪ'laɪəns/ n Abhängigkeit f (**on** von). **~t** a angewiesen (**on** auf + acc)

relic /'relɪk/ n Überbleibsel nt; (Relig) Reliquie f

relief /rɪ'li:f/ n Erleichterung f; (assistance) Hilfe f; (distraction) Abwechslung f; (replacement) Ablösung f; (Art) Relief nt; **in ~** im Relief. **~ map** n Reliefkarte f. **~ train** n Entlastungszug m

relieve /rɪ'li:v/ vt erleichtern; (take over from) ablösen; **~ of** entlasten von

religion /rɪ'lɪdʒən/ n Religion f

religious /rɪ'lɪdʒəs/ a religiös. **~ly** adv (conscientiously) gewissenhaft

relinquish /rɪ'lɪŋkwɪʃ/ vt loslassen; (give up) aufgeben

relish /'relɪʃ/ n Genuss m; (Culin) Würze f □ vt genießen

relo'cate /ri:-/ vt verlegen

reluctan|ce /rɪ'lʌktəns/ n Widerstreben nt. **~t** a widerstrebend; **be ~t** zögern (**to** zu). **~tly** adv ungern, widerstrebend

rely /rɪ'laɪ/ vi (pt/pp -ied) **~ on** sich verlassen auf (+ acc); (be dependent on) angewiesen sein auf (+ acc)

remain /rɪ'meɪn/ vi bleiben; (be left) übrig bleiben. **~der** n Rest m. **~ing** a restlich.

~s *npl* Reste *pl*; [mortal] ~s [sterbliche] Überreste *pl*

remand /rɪ'mɑːnd/ *n* **on** ~ in Untersuchungshaft □ *vt* ~ **in custody** in Untersuchungshaft schicken

remark /rɪ'mɑːk/ *n* Bemerkung *f* □ *vt* bemerken. ~**able** /-əbl/ *a*, **-bly** *adv* bemerkenswert

re'marry /riː-/ *vi* wieder heiraten

remedial /rɪ'miːdɪəl/ *a* Hilfs-; (*Med*) Heil-

remedy /'remədɪ/ *n* [Heil]mittel *nt* (**for** gegen); (*fig*) Abhilfe *f* □ *vt* (*pt/pp* -**ied**) abhelfen (+ *dat*); beheben (*fault*)

rememb|er /rɪ'membə(r)/ *vt* sich erinnern an (+ *acc*); ~**er to do sth** daran denken, etw zu tun; ~**er me to him** grüßen Sie ihn von mir □ *vi* sich erinnern. ~**rance** *n* Erinnerung *f*

remind /rɪ'maɪnd/ *vt* erinnern (**of** an + *acc*). ~**er** *n* Andenken *nt*; (*letter, warning*) Mahnung *f*

reminisce /remɪ'nɪs/ *vi* sich seinen Erinnerungen hingeben. ~**nces** /-ənsɪs/ *npl* Erinnerungen *pl*. ~**nt** *a* **be** ~**nt of** erinnern an (+ *acc*)

remiss /rɪ'mɪs/ *a* nachlässig

remission /rɪ'mɪʃn/ *n* Nachlass *m*; (*of sentence*) [Straf]erlass *m*; (*Med*) Remission *f*

remit /rɪ'mɪt/ *vt* (*pt/pp* **remitted**) überweisen (*money*). ~**tance** *n* Überweisung *f*

remnant /'remnənt/ *n* Rest *m*

remonstrate /'remənstreɪt/ *vi* protestieren; ~ **with s.o.** jdm Vorhaltungen machen

remorse /rɪ'mɔːs/ *n* Reue *f*. ~**ful** *a*, **-ly** *adv* reumütig. ~**less** *a*, **-ly** *adv* unerbittlich

remote /rɪ'məʊt/ *a* fern; (*isolated*) abgelegen; (*slight*) gering. ~ **con'trol** *n* Fernsteuerung *f*; (*for TV*) Fernbedienung *f*. ~-**con'trolled** *a* ferngesteuert; fernbedient

remotely /rɪ'məʊtlɪ/ *adv* entfernt; **not** ~ nicht im Entferntesten

re'movable /riː-/ *a* abnehmbar

removal /rɪ'muːvl/ *n* Entfernung *f*; (*from house*) Umzug *m*. ~ **van** *n* Möbelwagen *m*

remove /rɪ'muːv/ *vt* entfernen; (*take off*) abnehmen; (*take out*) herausnehmen

remunerat|e /rɪ'mjuːnəreɪt/ *vt* bezahlen. ~**ion** /-'reɪʃn/ *n* Bezahlung *f*. ~**ive** /-ətɪv/ *a* einträglich

render /'rendə(r)/ *vt* machen; erweisen (*service*); (*translate*) wiedergeben; (*Mus*) vortragen

renegade /'renɪgeɪd/ *n* Abtrünnige(r) *m/f*

renew /rɪ'njuː/ *vt* erneuern; verlängern (*contract*). ~**al** *n* Erneuerung *f*; Verlängerung *f*

renounce /rɪ'naʊns/ *vt* verzichten auf (+ *acc*); (*Relig*) abschwören (+ *dat*)

renovat|e /'renəveɪt/ *vt* renovieren. ~**ion** /-'veɪʃn/ *n* Renovierung *f*

renown /rɪ'naʊn/ *n* Ruf *m*. ~**ed** *a* berühmt

rent /rent/ *n* Miete *f* □ *vt* mieten; (*hire*) leihen; ~ [**out**] vermieten; verleihen. ~**al** *n* Mietgebühr *f*; Leihgebühr *f*

renunciation /rɪnʌnsɪ'eɪʃn/ *n* Verzicht *m*

re'open /riː-/ *vt/i* wieder aufmachen

re'organize /riː-/ *vt* reorganisieren

rep /rep/ *n* (*fam*) Vertreter *m*

repair /rɪ'peə(r)/ *n* Reparatur *f*; **in good/ bad** ~ in gutem/schlechtem Zustand □ *vt* reparieren

repartee /repɑː'tiː/ *n* **piece of** ~ schlagfertige Antwort *f*

repatriat|e /riː'pætrɪeɪt/ *vt* repatriieren. ~**ion** /-'eɪʃn/ *n* Repatriierung *f*

re'pay /riː-/ *vt* (*pt/pp* -**paid**) zurückzahlen; ~ **s.o. for sth** jdm etw zurückzahlen. ~**ment** *n* Rückzahlung *f*

repeal /rɪ'piːl/ *n* Aufhebung *f* □ *vt* aufheben

repeat /rɪ'piːt/ *n* Wiederholung *f* □ *vt/i* wiederholen; ~ **after me** sprechen Sie mir nach. ~**ed** *a*, **-ly** *adv* wiederholt

repel /rɪ'pel/ *vt* (*pt/pp* **repelled**) abwehren; (*fig*) abstoßen. ~**lent** *a* abstoßend

repent /rɪ'pent/ *vi* Reue zeigen. ~**ance** *n* Reue *f*. ~**ant** *a* reuig

repercussions /riːpə'kʌʃnz/ *npl* Auswirkungen *pl*

repertoire /'repətwɑː(r)/ *n* Repertoire *nt*

repertory /'repətrɪ/ *n* Repertoire *nt*

repetit|ion /repɪ'tɪʃn/ *n* Wiederholung *f*. ~**ive** /rɪ'petɪtɪv/ *a* eintönig

re'place /riː-/ *vt* zurücktun; (*take the place of*) ersetzen; (*exchange*) austauschen, auswechseln. ~**ment** *n* Ersatz *m*. ~**ment part** *n* Ersatzteil *nt*

'replay /riː-/ *n* (*Sport*) Wiederholungsspiel *nt*; [**action**] ~ Wiederholung *f*

replenish /rɪ'plenɪʃ/ *vt* auffüllen (*stocks*); (*refill*) nachfüllen

replete /rɪ'pliːt/ *a* gesättigt

replica /'replɪkə/ *n* Nachbildung *f*

reply /rɪ'plaɪ/ *n* Antwort *f* (**to** auf + *acc*) □ *vt/i* (*pt/pp* **replied**) antworten

report /rɪ'pɔːt/ *n* Bericht *m*; (*Sch*) Zeugnis *nt*; (*rumour*) Gerücht *nt*; (*of gun*) Knall *m* □ *vt* berichten; (*notify*) melden; ~ **s.o. to the police** jdn anzeigen □ *vi* berichten (**on** über + *acc*); (*present oneself*) sich melden (**to** bei). ~**er** *n* Reporter(in) *m(f)*

repose /rɪ'pəʊz/ *n* Ruhe *f*

repos'sess /riː-/ *vt* wieder in Besitz nehmen

reprehensible /reprɪ'hensəbl/ *a* tadelnswert

represent /reprɪ'zent/ *vt* darstellen; (*act for*) vertreten, repräsentieren. ∼**ation** /-'teɪʃn/ *n* Darstellung *f*; **make** ∼**ations to** vorstellig werden bei

representative /reprɪ'zentətɪv/ *a* repräsentativ (**of** für) □ *n* Bevollmächtigte(r) *m*/(*f*); (*Comm*) Vertreter(in) *m*(*f*); (*Amer, Pol*) Abgeordnete(r) *m*/*f*

repress /rɪ'pres/ *vt* unterdrücken. ∼**ion** /-eʃn/ *n* Unterdrückung *f*. ∼**ive** /-ɪv/ *a* repressiv

reprieve /rɪ'priːv/ *n* Begnadigung *f*; (*postponement*) Strafaufschub *m*; (*fig*) Gnadenfrist *f* □ *vt* begnadigen

reprimand /'reprɪmɑːnd/ *n* Tadel *m* □ *vt* tadeln

'reprint[1] /riː-/ *n* Nachdruck *m*

re'print[2] /riː-/ *vt* neu auflegen

reprisal /rɪ'praɪzl/ *n* Vergeltungsmaßnahme *f*

reproach /rɪ'prəʊtʃ/ *n* Vorwurf *m* □ *vt* Vorwürfe *pl* machen (+ *dat*). ∼**ful** *a*, **-ly** *adv* vorwurfsvoll

repro'duc|e /riː-/ *vt* wiedergeben, reproduzieren □ *vi* sich fortpflanzen. ∼**tion** /-'dʌkʃn/ *n* Reproduktion *f*; (*Biol*) Fortpflanzung *f*. ∼**tion furniture** *n* Stilmöbel *pl*. ∼**tive** /-'dʌktɪv/ *a* Fortpflanzungs-

reprove /rɪ'pruːv/ *vt* tadeln

reptile /'reptaɪl/ *n* Reptil *nt*

republic /rɪ'pʌblɪk/ *n* Republik *f*. ∼**an** *a* republikanisch □ *n* Republikaner(in) *m*(*f*)

repudiate /rɪ'pjuːdɪeɪt/ *vt* zurückweisen

repugnan|ce /rɪ'pʌgnəns/ *n* Widerwille *m*. ∼**t** *a* widerlich

repuls|e /rɪ'pʌls/ *vt* abwehren; (*fig*) abweisen. ∼**ion** /-ʌlʃn/ *n* Widerwille *m*. ∼**ive** /-ɪv/ *a* abstoßend, widerlich

reputable /'repjʊtəbl/ *a* (*firm*) von gutem Ruf; (*respectable*) anständig

reputation /repjʊ'teɪʃn/ *n* Ruf *m*

repute /rɪ'pjuːt/ *n* Ruf *m*. ∼**d** /-ɪd/ *a*, **-ly** *adv* angeblich

request *n* /rɪ'kwest/ *n* Bitte *f* □ *vt* bitten. ∼ **stop** *n* Bedarfshaltestelle *f*

require /rɪ'kwaɪə(r)/ *vt* (*need*) brauchen; (*demand*) erfordern; **be** ∼**d to do sth** etw tun müssen. ∼**ment** *n* Bedürfnis *nt*; (*condition*) Erfordernis *nt*

requisite /'rekwɪzɪt/ *a* erforderlich □ *n* **toilet/travel** ∼**s** *pl* Toiletten-/Reiseartikel *pl*

requisition /rekwɪ'zɪʃn/ *n* ∼ **[order]** Anforderung *f* □ *vt* anfordern

re'sale /riː-/ *n* Weiterverkauf *m*

rescind /rɪ'sɪnd/ *vt* aufheben

rescue /'reskjuː/ *n* Rettung *f* □ *vt* retten. ∼**r** *n* Retter *m*

research /rɪ'sɜːtʃ/ *n* Forschung *f* □ *vt* erforschen; (*Journ*) recherchieren □ *vi* ∼ **into** erforschen. ∼**er** *n* Forscher *m*; (*Journ*) Rechercheur *m*

resem|blance /rɪ'zembləns/ *n* Ähnlichkeit *f*. ∼**ble** /-bl/ *vt* ähneln (+ *dat*)

resent /rɪ'zent/ *vt* übel nehmen; einen Groll hegen gegen (*person*). ∼**ful** *a*, **-ly** *adv* verbittert. ∼**ment** *n* Groll *m*

reservation /rezə'veɪʃn/ *n* Reservierung *f*; (*doubt*) Vorbehalt *m*; (*enclosure*) Reservat *nt*

reserve /rɪ'zɜːv/ *n* Reserve *f*; (*for animals*) Reservat *nt*; (*Sport*) Reservespieler(in) *m*(*f*) □ *vt* reservieren; (*client:*) reservieren lassen; (*keep*) aufheben; sich (*dat*) vorbehalten (*right*). ∼**d** *a* reserviert

reservoir /'rezəvwɑː(r)/ *n* Reservoir *nt*

re'shape /riː-/ *vt* umformen

re'shuffle /riː-/ *n* (*Pol*) Umbildung *f* □ *vt* (*Pol*) umbilden

reside /rɪ'zaɪd/ *vi* wohnen

residence /'rezɪdəns/ *n* Wohnsitz *m*; (*official*) Residenz *f*; (*stay*) Aufenthalt *m*. ∼ **permit** *n* Aufenthaltsgenehmigung *f*

resident /'rezɪdənt/ *a* ansässig (**in** in + *dat*); (*housekeeper, nurse*) im Haus wohnend □ *n* Bewohner(in) *m*(*f*); (*of street*) Anwohner *m*. ∼**ial** /-'denʃl/ *a* Wohn-

residue /'rezɪdjuː/ *n* Rest *m*; (*Chem*) Rückstand *m*

resign /rɪ'zaɪn/ *vt* ∼ **oneself to** sich abfinden mit □ *vi* kündigen; (*from public office*) zurücktreten. ∼**ation** /rezɪg-'neɪʃn/ *n* Resignation *f*; (*from job*) Kündigung *f*; Rücktritt *m*. ∼**ed** *a*, **-ly** *adv* resigniert

resilient /rɪ'zɪlɪənt/ *a* federnd; (*fig*) widerstandsfähig

resin /'rezɪn/ *n* Harz *nt*

resist /rɪ'zɪst/ *vt*/*i* sich widersetzen (+ *dat*); (*fig*) widerstehen (+ *dat*). ∼**ance** *n* Widerstand *m*. ∼**ant** *a* widerstandsfähig

resolut|e /'rezəluːt/ *a*, **-ly** *adv* entschlossen. ∼**ion** /-'luːʃn/ *n* Entschlossenheit *f*; (*intention*) Vorsatz *m*; (*Pol*) Resolution *f*

resolve /rɪ'zɒlv/ *n* Entschlossenheit *f*; (*decision*) Beschluss *m* □ *vt* beschließen; (*solve*) lösen. ∼**d** *a* entschlossen (**to** zu)

resonan|ce /'rezənəns/ *n* Resonanz *f*. ∼**t** *a* klangvoll

resort /rɪ'zɔːt/ *n* (*place*) Urlaubsort *m*; **as a last** ∼ wenn alles andere fehlschlägt □ *vi* ∼ **to** (*fig*) greifen zu

resound /rɪ'zaʊnd/ *vi* widerhallen. ∼**ing** *a* widerhallend; (*loud*) laut; (*notable*) groß

resource /rɪ'sɔ:s/ n ∼s pl Ressourcen pl. ∼ful a findig. ∼fulness n Findigkeit f

respect /rɪ'spekt/ n Respekt m, Achtung f (for vor + dat); ⟨aspect⟩ Hinsicht f; with ∼ to in Bezug auf (+ acc) □ vt respektieren, achten

respectability /rɪspektə'bɪlətɪ/ n (see respectable) Ehrbarkeit f; Anständigkeit f

respect|able /rɪ'spektəbl/ a, -bly adv ehrbar; ⟨decent⟩ anständig; ⟨considerable⟩ ansehnlich. ∼ful a, -ly adv respektvoll

respective /rɪ'spektɪv/ a jeweilig. ∼ly adv beziehungsweise

respiration /respə'reɪʃn/ n Atmung f

respite /'respaɪt/ n [Ruhe]pause f; ⟨delay⟩ Aufschub m

resplendent /rɪ'splendənt/ a glänzend

respond /rɪ'spɒnd/ vi antworten; ⟨react⟩ reagieren (to auf + acc); ⟨patient:⟩ ansprechen (to auf + acc)

response /rɪ'spɒns/ n Antwort f; Reaktion f

responsibility /rɪspɒnsɪ'bɪlətɪ/ n Verantwortung f; ⟨duty⟩ Verpflichtung f

responsib|le /rɪ'spɒnsəbl/ a verantwortlich; ⟨trustworthy⟩ verantwortungsvoll. ∼ly adv verantwortungsbewusst

responsive /rɪ'spɒnsɪv/ a be ∼ reagieren

rest[1] /rest/ n Ruhe f; ⟨holiday⟩ Erholung f; ⟨interval & Mus⟩ Pause f; have a ∼ eine Pause machen; ⟨rest⟩ sich ausruhen □ vt ausruhen; ⟨lean⟩ lehnen (on an/auf + acc) □ vi ruhen; ⟨have a rest⟩ sich ausruhen

rest[2] n the ∼ der Rest; ⟨people⟩ die Übrigen pl □ vi it ∼s with you es ist an Ihnen (to zu)

restaurant /'restərɒnt/ n Restaurant nt, Gaststätte f. ∼ car n Speisewagen m

restful /'restfl/ a erholsam

restitution /restɪ'tju:ʃn/ n Entschädigung f; ⟨return⟩ Rückgabe f

restive /'restɪv/ a unruhig

restless /'restlɪs/ a, -ly adv unruhig

restoration /restə'reɪʃn/ n ⟨of building⟩ Restaurierung f

restore /rɪ'stɔ:(r)/ vt wiederherstellen; restaurieren ⟨building⟩; ⟨give back⟩ zurückgeben

restrain /rɪ'streɪn/ vt zurückhalten; ∼ oneself sich beherrschen. ∼ed a zurückhaltend. ∼t n Zurückhaltung f

restrict /rɪ'strɪkt/ vt einschränken; ∼ to beschränken auf (+ acc). ∼ion /-ɪkʃn/ n Einschränkung f; Beschränkung f. ∼ive /-ɪv/ a einschränkend

'rest room n (Amer) Toilette f

result /rɪ'zʌlt/ n Ergebnis nt, Resultat nt; ⟨consequence⟩ Folge f; as a ∼ als Folge (of

gen) □ vi sich ergeben (from aus); ∼ in enden in (+ dat); ⟨lead to⟩ führen zu

resume /rɪ'zju:m/ vt wieder aufnehmen; wieder einnehmen ⟨seat⟩ □ vi wieder beginnen

résumé /'rezuːmeɪ/ n Zusammenfassung f

resumption /rɪ'zʌmpʃn/ n Wiederaufnahme f

resurgence /rɪ'sɜ:dʒəns/ n Wiederaufleben nt

resurrect /rezə'rekt/ vt (fig) wieder beleben. ∼ion /-ekʃn/ n the R∼ion ⟨Relig⟩ die Auferstehung

resuscitat|e /rɪ'sʌsɪteɪt/ vt wieder beleben. ∼ion /-'teɪʃn/ n Wiederbelebung f

retail /'riːteɪl/ n Einzelhandel m □ a Einzelhandels- □ adv im Einzelhandel □ vt im Einzelhandel verkaufen □ vi ∼ at im Einzelhandel kosten. ∼er n Einzelhändler m. ∼ price n Ladenpreis m

retain /rɪ'teɪn/ vt behalten

retaliat|e /rɪ'tælɪeɪt/ vi zurückschlagen. ∼ion /-'eɪʃn/ n Vergeltung f; in ∼ion als Vergeltung

retarded /rɪ'tɑ:dɪd/ a zurückgeblieben

retentive /rɪ'tentɪv/ a ⟨memory⟩ gut

reticen|ce /'retɪsns/ n Zurückhaltung f. ∼t a zurückhaltend

retina /'retɪnə/ n Netzhaut f

retinue /'retɪnjuː/ n Gefolge nt

retire /rɪ'taɪə(r)/ vi in den Ruhestand treten; ⟨withdraw⟩ sich zurückziehen. ∼d a im Ruhestand. ∼ment n Ruhestand m; since my ∼ment seit ich nicht mehr arbeite

retiring /rɪ'taɪərɪŋ/ a zurückhaltend

retort /rɪ'tɔ:t/ n scharfe Erwiderung f; ⟨Chem⟩ Retorte f □ vt scharf erwidern

re'touch /riː-/ vt ⟨Phot⟩ retuschieren

re'trace /riː-/ vt zurückverfolgen; ∼ one's steps denselben Weg zurückgehen

retract /rɪ'trækt/ vt einziehen; zurücknehmen ⟨remark⟩ □ vi widerrufen

re'train /riː-/ vt umschulen □ vi umgeschult werden

retreat /rɪ'triːt/ n Rückzug m; ⟨place⟩ Zufluchtsort m □ vi sich zurückziehen

re'trial /riː-/ n Wiederaufnahmeverfahren nt

retribution /retrɪ'bjuːʃn/ n Vergeltung f

retrieve /rɪ'triːv/ vt zurückholen; ⟨from wreckage⟩ bergen; ⟨Computing⟩ wieder auffinden; ⟨dog:⟩ apportieren

retrograde /'retrəgreɪd/ a rückschrittlich

retrospect /'retrəspekt/ n in ∼ rückblickend. ∼ive /-ɪv/ a, -ly adv rückwirkend; ⟨looking back⟩ rückblickend

return /rɪˈtɜːn/ n Rückkehr f; (giving back) Rückgabe f; (Comm) Ertrag m; (ticket) Rückfahrkarte f; (Aviat) Rückflugschein m; by ~ [of post] postwendend; in ~ dafür; in ~ for für; many happy ~s! herzlichen Glückwunsch zum Geburtstag! □ vt zurückgehen/-fahren; (come back) zurückkommen □ vt zurückgeben; (put back) zurückstellen/-legen; (send back) zurückschicken; (elect) wählen

return: ~ flight n Rückflug m. ~ match n Rückspiel nt. ~ ticket n Rückfahrkarte f; (Aviat) Rückflugschein m

reunion /riːˈjuːnɪən/ n Wiedervereinigung f; (social gathering) Treffen nt

reunite /riːjuːˈnaɪt/ vt wieder vereinigen □ vi sich wieder vereinigen

re'us|able /riː-/ a wieder verwendbar. ~e vt wieder verwenden

rev /rev/ n (Auto, fam) Umdrehung f □ vt/i ~ [up] den Motor auf Touren bringen

reveal /rɪˈviːl/ vt zum Vorschein bringen; (fig) enthüllen. ~ing a (fig) aufschlussreich

revel /ˈrevl/ vi (pt/pp revelled) ~ in sth etw genießen

revelation /revəˈleɪʃn/ n Offenbarung f, Enthüllung f

revelry /ˈrevlrɪ/ n Lustbarkeit f

revenge /rɪˈvendʒ/ n Rache f; (fig & Sport) Revanche f □ vt rächen

revenue /ˈrevənjuː/ n [Staats]einnahmen pl

reverberate /rɪˈvɜːbəreɪt/ vi nachhallen

revere /rɪˈvɪə(r)/ vt verehren. ~nce /ˈrevərəns/ n Ehrfurcht f

Reverend /ˈrevərənd/ a the ~ X Pfarrer X; (Catholic) Hochwürden X

reverent /ˈrevərənt/ a, -ly adv ehrfürchtig

reverie /ˈrevərɪ/ n Träumerei f

revers /rɪˈvɪə/ n (pl revers /-z/) Revers nt

reversal /rɪˈvɜːsl/ n Umkehrung f

reverse /rɪˈvɜːs/ a umgekehrt □ n Gegenteil nt; (back) Rückseite f; (Auto) Rückwärtsgang m □ vt umkehren; (Auto) zurücksetzen; ~ the charges (Teleph) ein R-Gespräch führen □ vi zurücksetzen

revert /rɪˈvɜːt/ vi ~ to zurückfallen an (+ acc); zurückkommen auf (+ acc) (topic)

review /rɪˈvjuː/ n Rückblick m (of auf + acc); (re-examination) Überprüfung f; (Mil) Truppenschau f; (of book, play) Kritik f, Rezension f □ vt zurückblicken auf (+ acc); überprüfen (situation); (Mil) besichtigen; kritisieren, rezensieren (book, play). ~er n Kritiker m, Rezensent m

revile /rɪˈvaɪl/ vt verunglimpfen

revis|e /rɪˈvaɪz/ vt revidieren; (for exam) wiederholen. ~ion /-ˈvɪʒn/ n Revision f; Wiederholung f

revival /rɪˈvaɪvl/ n Wiederbelebung f

revive /rɪˈvaɪv/ vt wieder beleben; (fig) wieder aufleben lassen □ vi wieder aufleben

revoke /rɪˈvəʊk/ vt aufheben; widerrufen (command, decision)

revolt /rɪˈvəʊlt/ n Aufstand m □ vi rebellieren □ vt anwidern. ~ing a widerlich, eklig

revolution /revəˈluːʃn/ n Revolution f; (Auto) Umdrehung f. ~ary a revolutionär. ~ize vt revolutionieren

revolve /rɪˈvɒlv/ vi sich drehen; ~ around kreisen um

revolv|er /rɪˈvɒlvə(r)/ n Revolver m. ~ing a Dreh-

revue /rɪˈvjuː/ n Revue f; (satirical) Kabarett nt

revulsion /rɪˈvʌlʃn/ n Abscheu m

reward /rɪˈwɔːd/ n Belohnung f □ vt belohnen. ~ing a lohnend

re'write /riː-/ vt (pt rewrote, pp rewritten) noch einmal [neu] schreiben; (alter) umschreiben

rhapsody /ˈræpsədɪ/ n Rhapsodie f

rhetoric /ˈretərɪk/ n Rhetorik f. ~al /rɪˈtɒrɪkl/ a rhetorisch

rheuma|tic /ruːˈmætɪk/ a rheumatisch. ~tism /ˈruːmətɪzm/ n Rheumatismus m, Rheuma nt

Rhine /raɪn/ n Rhein m

rhinoceros /raɪˈnɒsərəs/ n Nashorn nt, Rhinozeros nt

rhubarb /ˈruːbɑːb/ n Rhabarber m

rhyme /raɪm/ n Reim m □ vt reimen □ vi sich reimen

rhythm /ˈrɪðm/ n Rhythmus m. ~ic[al] a, -ally adv rhythmisch

rib /rɪb/ n Rippe f □ vt (pt/pp ribbed) (fam) aufziehen (fam)

ribald /ˈrɪbld/ a derb

ribbon /ˈrɪbən/ n Band nt; (for typewriter) Farbband nt; in ~s in Fetzen

rice /raɪs/ n Reis m

rich /rɪtʃ/ a (-er, -est), -ly adv reich; (food) gehaltvoll; (heavy) schwer □ n the ~ pl die Reichen; ~es pl Reichtum m

rickets /ˈrɪkɪts/ n Rachitis f

rickety /ˈrɪkɪtɪ/ a wackelig

ricochet /ˈrɪkəʃeɪ/ vi abprallen

rid /rɪd/ vt (pt/pp rid, pres p ridding) befreien (of von); get ~ of loswerden

riddance /ˈrɪdns/ n good ~! auf Nimmerwiedersehen!

ridden /ˈrɪdn/ see ride

riddle /ˈrɪdl/ n Rätsel nt

riddled /'rɪdld/ a ~ **with** durchlöchert mit

ride /raɪd/ n Ritt m; (in vehicle) Fahrt f; **take s.o. for a ~** (fam) jdn reinlegen □ v (pt **rode**, pp **ridden**) □ vt reiten ⟨horse⟩; fahren mit ⟨bicycle⟩ □ vi reiten; (in vehicle) fahren. ~**r** n Reiter(in) m(f); (on bicycle) Fahrer(in) m(f); (in document) Zusatzklausel f

ridge /rɪdʒ/ n Erhebung f; (on roof) First m; (of mountain) Grat m, Kamm m; (of high pressure) Hochdruckkeil m

ridicule /'rɪdɪkjuːl/ n Spott m □ vt verspotten, spotten über (+ acc)

ridiculous /rɪ'dɪkjʊləs/ a, **-ly** adv lächerlich

riding /'raɪdɪŋ/ n Reiten nt □ attrib Reit-

rife /raɪf/ a **be ~** weit verbreitet sein

riff-raff /'rɪfræf/ n Gesindel nt

rifle /'raɪfl/ n Gewehr nt □ vt plündern; ~ **through** durchwühlen

rift /rɪft/ n Spalt m; (fig) Riss m

rig[1] /rɪg/ n Ölbohrturm m; (at sea) Bohrinsel f □ vt (pt/pp **rigged**) ~ **out** ausrüsten; ~ **up** aufbauen

rig[2] vt (pt/pp **rigged**) manipulieren

right /raɪt/ a richtig; (not left) rechte(r,s); **be ~** ⟨person:⟩ Recht haben; ⟨clock:⟩ richtig gehen; **put ~** wieder in Ordnung bringen; (fig) richtig stellen; **that's ~!** das stimmt! □ adv richtig; (directly) direkt; (completely) ganz; (not left) rechts; ⟨go⟩ nach rechts; ~ **away** sofort □ n Recht nt; (not left) rechte Seite f; **on the ~** rechts; **from/to the ~** von/nach rechts; **be in the ~** Recht haben; **by ~s** eigentlich; **the R~** (Pol) die Rechte. ~ **angle** n rechter Winkel m

righteous /'raɪtʃəs/ a rechtschaffen

rightful /'raɪtfl/ a, **-ly** adv rechtmäßig

right: ~**-'handed** a rechtshändig. ~**-hand 'man** n (fig) rechte Hand f

rightly /'raɪtlɪ/ adv mit Recht

right: ~ **of way** n Durchgangsrecht nt; (path) öffentlicher Fuß weg m; (Auto) Vorfahrt f. ~**-'wing** a (Pol) rechte(r,s)

rigid /'rɪdʒɪd/ a starr; (strict) streng. ~**ity** /-'dʒɪdətɪ/ n Starrheit f; Strenge f

rigmarole /'rɪgmərəʊl/ n Geschwätz nt; (procedure) Prozedur f

rigorous /'rɪgərəs/ a, **-ly** adv streng

rigour /'rɪgə(r)/ n Strenge f

rile /raɪl/ vt (fam) ärgern

rim /rɪm/ n Rand m; (of wheel) Felge f

rind /raɪnd/ n (on fruit) Schale f; (on cheese) Rinde f; (on bacon) Schwarte f

ring[1] /rɪŋ/ n Ring m; (for circus) Manege f; **stand in a ~** im Kreis stehen □ vt umringen; ~ **in red** rot einkreisen

ring[2] n Klingeln nt; **give s.o. a ~** (Teleph) jdn anrufen □ v (pt **rang**, pp **rung**) □ vt läuten; ~ **[up]** (Teleph) anrufen □ vi läuten, klingeln. ~ **back** vt/i (Teleph) zurückrufen. ~ **off** vi (Teleph) auflegen

ring: ~**leader** n Rädelsführer m. ~ **road** n Umgehungsstraße f

rink /rɪŋk/ n Eisbahn f

rinse /rɪns/ n Spülung f; (hair colour) Tönung f □ vt spülen; tönen ⟨hair⟩. ~ **off** vt abspülen

riot /'raɪət/ n Aufruhr m; ~**s** pl Unruhen pl; ~ **of colours** bunte Farbenpracht f; **run ~** randalieren □ vi randalieren. ~**er** n Randalierer m. ~**ous** /-əs/ a aufrührerisch; (boisterous) wild

rip /rɪp/ n Riss m □ vt/i (pt/pp **ripped**) zerreißen; ~ **open** aufreißen. ~ **off** vt (fam) neppen

ripe /raɪp/ a (**-r, -st**) reif

ripen /'raɪpn/ vi reifen □ vt reifen lassen

ripeness /'raɪpnɪs/ n Reife f

'rip-off n (fam) Nepp m

ripple /'rɪpl/ n kleine Welle f □ vt kräuseln □ vi sich kräuseln

rise /raɪz/ n Anstieg m; (fig) Aufstieg m; (increase) Zunahme f; (in wages) Lohnerhöhung f; (in salary) Gehaltserhöhung f; **give ~ to** Anlass geben zu □ vi (pt **rose**, pp **risen**) steigen; ⟨ground:⟩ ansteigen; ⟨sun, dough:⟩ aufgehen; ⟨river:⟩ entspringen; (get up) aufstehen; (fig) aufsteigen (**to** zu); ⟨rebel:⟩ sich erheben; ⟨court:⟩ sich vertagen. ~**r** n **early** ~**r** Frühaufsteher m

rising /'raɪzɪŋ/ a steigend; ⟨sun⟩ aufgehend; **the ~ generation** die heranwachsende Generation □ n (revolt) Aufstand m

risk /rɪsk/ n Risiko nt; **at one's own ~** auf eigene Gefahr □ vt riskieren

risky /'rɪskɪ/ a (**-ier, -iest**) riskant

risqué /'rɪskeɪ/ a gewagt

rissole /'rɪsəʊl/ n Frikadelle f

rite /raɪt/ n Ritus m; **last ~s** Letzte Ölung f

ritual /'rɪtjʊəl/ a rituell □ n Ritual nt

rival /'raɪvl/ a rivalisierend □ n Rivale m/Rivalin f; ~**s** pl (Comm) Konkurrenten pl □ vt (pt/pp **rivalled**) gleichkommen (+ dat); (compete with) rivalisieren mit. ~**ry** n Rivalität f; (Comm) Konkurrenzkampf m

river /'rɪvə(r)/ n Fluss m. ~**-bed** n Flussbett nt

rivet /'rɪvɪt/ n Niete f □ vt [ver]nieten; ~**ed by** (fig) gefesselt von

road /rəʊd/ n Straße f; (fig) Weg m

road: **~-block** n Straßensperre f. **~-hog** n (fam) Straßenschreck m. **~-map** n Straßenkarte f. **~ safety** n Verkehrssicherheit f. **~ sense** n Verkehrssinn m. **~side** n Straßenrand m. **~way** n Fahrbahn f. **~works** npl Straßenarbeiten pl. **~worthy** a verkehrssicher

roam /rəʊm/ vi wandern

roar /rɔː(r)/ n Gebrüll nt; **~s of laughter** schallendes Gelächter nt □ vi brüllen; (with laughter) schallend lachen. **~ing** a (fire) prasselnd; **do a ~ing trade** (fam) ein Bombengeschäft machen

roast /rəʊst/ a gebraten, Brat-; **~ beef/pork** Rinder-/Schweinebraten m □ n Braten m □ vt/i braten; rösten (coffee, chestnuts)

rob /rɒb/ vt (pt/pp **robbed**) berauben (of gen); ausrauben (bank). **~ber** n Räuber m. **~bery** n Raub m

robe /rəʊb/ n Robe f; (Amer: bathrobe) Bademantel m

robin /'rɒbɪn/ n Rotkehlchen nt

robot /'rəʊbɒt/ n Roboter m

robust /rəʊ'bʌst/ a robust

rock¹ /rɒk/ n Fels m; **stick of ~** Zuckerstange f; **on the ~s** (ship) aufgelaufen; (marriage) kaputt; (drink) mit Eis

rock² vt/i schaukeln

rock³ n (Mus) Rock m

rock-'bottom n Tiefpunkt m

rockery /'rɒkəri/ n Steingarten m

rocket /'rɒkɪt/ n Rakete f □ vi in die Höhe schießen

rocking: **~-chair** n Schaukelstuhl m. **~-horse** n Schaukelpferd nt

rocky /'rɒki/ a (-ier, -iest) felsig; (unsteady) wackelig

rod /rɒd/ n Stab m; (stick) Rute f; (for fishing) Angel[rute] f

rode /rəʊd/ see ride

rodent /'rəʊdnt/ n Nagetier nt

roe¹ /rəʊ/ n Rogen m; (soft) Milch f

roe² n (pl roe or roes) **~[-deer]** Reh nt

rogue /rəʊg/ n Gauner m

role /rəʊl/ n Rolle f

roll /rəʊl/ n Rolle f; (bread) Brötchen nt; (list) Liste f; (of drum) Wirbel m □ vi rollen; **be ~ing in money** (fam) Geld wie Heu haben □ vt rollen; walzen (lawn); ausrollen (pastry). **~ over** vi sich auf die andere Seite rollen. **~ up** vt aufrollen; hochkrempeln (sleeves) □ vi (fam) auftauchen

'roll-call n Namensaufruf m; (Mil) Appell m

roller /'rəʊlə(r)/ n Rolle f; (lawn, road) Walze f; (hair) Lockenwickler m. **~ blind**

n Rollo nt. **~-coaster** n Berg-und-Tal-Bahn f. **~-skate** n Rollschuh m

'rolling-pin n Teigrolle f

Roman /'rəʊmən/ a römisch □ n Römer(in) m(f)

romance /rə'mæns/ n Romantik f; (love-affair) Romanze f; (book) Liebesgeschichte f

Romania /rəʊ'meɪnɪə/ n Rumänien nt. **~n** a rumänisch □ n Rumäne m/-in f

romantic /rəʊ'mæntɪk/ a, **-ally** adv romantisch. **~ism** /-tɪsɪzm/ n Romantik f

Rome /rəʊm/ n Rom nt

romp /rɒmp/ n Tollen nt □ vi [herum]tollen. **~ers** npl Strampelhöschen nt

roof /ruːf/ n Dach nt; (of mouth) Gaumen m □ vt □ **~ over** überdachen. **~-rack** n Dachgepäckträger m. **~-top** n Dach nt

rook /rʊk/ n Saatkrähe f; (Chess) Turm m □ vt (fam: swindle) schröpfen

room /ruːm/ n Zimmer nt; (for functions) Saal m; (space) Platz m. **~y** a geräumig

roost /ruːst/ n Hühnerstange f □ vi schlafen

root¹ /ruːt/ n Wurzel f; **take ~** anwachsen □ vi Wurzeln schlagen. **~ out** vt (fig) ausrotten

root² vi **~ about** wühlen; **~ for s.o.** (Amer, fam) für jdn sein

rope /rəʊp/ n Seil nt; **know the ~s** (fam) sich auskennen. **~ in** vt (fam) einspannen

rope-'ladder n Strickleiter f

rosary /'rəʊzəri/ n Rosenkranz m

rose¹ /rəʊz/ n Rose f; (of watering-can) Brause f

rose² see rise

rosemary /'rəʊzməri/ n Rosmarin m

rosette /rəʊ'zet/ n Rosette f

roster /'rɒstə(r)/ n Dienstplan m

rostrum /'rɒstrəm/ n Podest nt, Podium nt

rosy /'rəʊzi/ a (-ier, -iest) rosig

rot /rɒt/ n Fäulnis f; (fam: nonsense) Quatsch m □ vi (pt/pp **rotted**) [ver]faulen

rota /'rəʊtə/ n Dienstplan m

rotary /'rəʊtəri/ a Dreh-; (Techn) Rotations-

rotat|e /rəʊ'teɪt/ vt drehen; im Wechsel anbauen (crops) □ vi sich drehen; (Techn) rotieren. **~ion** /-eɪʃn/ n Drehung f; (of crops) Fruchtfolge f; **in ~ion** im Wechsel

rote /rəʊt/ n **by ~** auswendig

rotten /'rɒtn/ a faul; (fam) mies; (person) fies

rotund /rəʊ'tʌnd/ a rundlich

rough /rʌf/ a (-er, -est) rau; (uneven) uneben; (coarse, not gentle) grob; (brutal) roh; (turbulent) stürmisch; (approximate) ungefähr □ *adv* **sleep** ~ im Freien übernachten; **play** ~ holzen □ *n* **do sth in** ~ etw ins Unreine schreiben □ *vt* ~ **it** primitiv leben. ~ **out** *vt* im Groben entwerfen

roughage /ˈrʌfɪdʒ/ *n* Ballaststoffe *pl*

rough 'draft *n* grober Entwurf *m*

rough|ly /ˈrʌflɪ/ *adv* (*see* **rough**) rau; grob; roh; ungefähr. ~**ness** *n* Rauheit *f*

'rough paper *n* Konzeptpapier *nt*

round /raʊnd/ *a* (-er, -est) rund □ *n* Runde *f*; (*slice*) Scheibe *f*; **do one's** ~**s** seine Runde machen □ *prep* um (+ *acc*); ~ **the clock** rund um die Uhr □ *adv* **all** ~ ringsherum; ~ **and** ~ im Kreis; **ask s.o.** ~ jdn einladen; **turn/look** ~ sich umdrehen/umsehen □ *vt* biegen um (*corner*) □ *vi* ~ **on s.o.** jdn anfahren. ~ **off** *vt* abrunden. ~ **up** *vt* aufrunden; zusammentreiben (*animals*); festnehmen (*criminals*)

roundabout /ˈraʊndəbaʊt/ *a* ~ **route** Umweg *m* □ *n* Karussell *nt*; (*for traffic*) Kreisverkehr *m*

round: ~**'shouldered** *a* mit einem runden Rücken. ~ **'trip** *n* Rundreise *f*

rous|e /raʊz/ *vt* wecken; (*fig*) erregen. ~**ing** *a* mitreißend

route /ruːt/ *n* Route *f*; (*of bus*) Linie *f*

routine /ruːˈtiːn/ *a*, **-ly** *adv* routinemäßig □ *n* Routine *f*; (*Theat*) Nummer *f*

roux /ruː/ *n* Mehlschwitze *f*

rove /rəʊv/ *vi* wandern

row[1] /rəʊ/ *n* (*line*) Reihe *f*; **in a** ~ (*one after the other*) nacheinander

row[2] *vt/i* rudern

row[3] /raʊ/ *n* (*fam*) Krach *m* □ *vi* (*fam*) sich streiten

rowan /ˈrəʊən/ *n* Eberesche *f*

rowdy /ˈraʊdɪ/ *a* (-ier, -iest) laut

rowing boat /ˈrəʊɪŋ-/ *n* Ruderboot *nt*

royal /ˈrɔɪəl/ *a*, **-ly** *adv* königlich

royalt|y /ˈrɔɪəltɪ/ *n* Königtum *nt*; (*persons*) Mitglieder *pl* der königlichen Familie; **-ies** *pl* (*payments*) Tantiemen *pl*

rub /rʌb/ *n* **give sth a** ~ etw reiben/(*polish*) polieren □ *vt* (*pt/pp* **rubbed**) reiben; (*polish*) polieren; **don't** ~ **it in** (*fam*) reib es mir nicht unter die Nase. ~ **off** *vt* abreiben □ *vi* abgehen; ~ **off on** abfärben auf (+ *acc*). ~ **out** *vt* ausradieren

rubber /ˈrʌbə(r)/ *n* Gummi *m*; (*eraser*) Radiergummi *m*. ~ **band** *n* Gummiband *nt*. ~**y** *a* gummiartig

rubbish /ˈrʌbɪʃ/ *n* Abfall *m*, Müll *m*; (*fam: nonsense*) Quatsch *m*; (*fam: junk*) Plunder *m*, Kram *m* □ *vt* (*fam*) schlecht machen. ~ **bin** *n* Mülleimer *m*, Abfalleimer *m*. ~

dump *n* Abfallhaufen *m*; (*official*) Müllhalde *f*

rubble /ˈrʌbl/ *n* Trümmer *pl*, Schutt *m*

ruby /ˈruːbɪ/ *n* Rubin *m*

rucksack /ˈrʌksæk/ *n* Rucksack *m*

rudder /ˈrʌdə(r)/ *n* [Steuer]ruder *nt*

ruddy /ˈrʌdɪ/ *a* (-ier, -iest) rötlich; (*sl*) verdammt

rude /ruːd/ *a* (-r, -st), **-ly** *adv* unhöflich; (*improper*) unanständig. ~**ness** *n* Unhöflichkeit *f*

rudiment /ˈruːdɪmənt/ *n* ~**s** *pl* Anfangsgründe *pl*. ~**ary** /-ˈmentərɪ/ *a* elementar; (*Biol*) rudimentär

rueful /ˈruːfl/ *a*, **-ly** *adv* reumütig

ruffian /ˈrʌfɪən/ *n* Rüpel *m*

ruffle /ˈrʌfl/ *n* Rüsche *f* □ *vt* zerzausen

rug /rʌg/ *n* Vorleger *m*, [kleiner] Teppich *m*; (*blanket*) Decke *f*

rugged /ˈrʌgɪd/ *a* (*coastline*) zerklüftet

ruin /ˈruːɪn/ *n* Ruine *f*; (*fig*) Ruin *m* □ *vt* ruinieren. ~**ous** /-əs/ *a* ruinös

rule /ruːl/ *n* Regel *f*; (*control*) Herrschaft *f*; (*government*) Regierung *f*; (*for measuring*) Lineal *nt*; **as a** ~ in der Regel □ *vt* regieren, herrschen über (+ *acc*); (*fig*) beherrschen; (*decide*) entscheiden; ziehen (*line*) □ *vi* regieren, herrschen. ~ **out** *vt* ausschließen

ruled /ruːld/ *a* (*paper*) liniert

ruler /ˈruːlə(r)/ *n* Herrscher(in) *m(f)*; (*measure*) Lineal *nt*

ruling /ˈruːlɪŋ/ *a* herrschend; (*factor*) entscheidend; (*Pol*) regierend □ *n* Entscheidung *f*

rum /rʌm/ *n* Rum *m*

rumble /ˈrʌmbl/ *n* Grollen *nt* □ *vi* grollen; (*stomach:*) knurren

ruminant /ˈruːmɪnənt/ *n* Wiederkäuer *m*

rummage /ˈrʌmɪdʒ/ *vi* wühlen; ~ **through** durchwühlen

rummy /ˈrʌmɪ/ *n* Rommé *nt*

rumour /ˈruːmə(r)/ *n* Gerücht *nt* □ *vt* **it is** ~**ed that** es geht das Gerücht, dass

rump /rʌmp/ *n* Hinterteil *nt*. ~ **steak** *n* Rumpsteak *nt*

rumpus /ˈrʌmpəs/ *n* (*fam*) Spektakel *m*

run /rʌn/ *n* Lauf *m*; (*journey*) Fahrt *f*; (*series*) Serie *f*, Reihe *f*; (*Theat*) Laufzeit *f*; (*Skiing*) Abfahrt *f*; (*enclosure*) Auslauf *m*; (*Amer: ladder*) Laufmasche *f*; **at a** ~ im Laufschritt; ~ **of bad luck** Pechsträhne *f*; **be on the** ~ flüchtig sein; **have the** ~ **of sth** etw zu seiner freien Verfügung haben; **in the long** ~ auf lange Sicht □ *v* (*pt* **ran**, *pp* **run**, *pres p* **running**) □ *vi* laufen; (*flow*) fließen; (*eyes:*) tränen; (*bus:*) verkehren, fahren; (*butter, ink:*) zerfließen; (*colours:*) [ab]färben; (*in election*) kandidieren; **~ across** s.o./sth auf jdn/ etw stoßen □ vt laufen lassen; einlaufen lassen ⟨bath⟩; ⟨manage⟩ führen, leiten; ⟨drive⟩ fahren; eingehen ⟨risk⟩; ⟨Journ⟩ bringen ⟨article⟩; **~ one's hand over sth** mit der Hand über etw ⟨acc⟩ fahren. **~ away** vi weglaufen. **~ down** vi hinunter-/ herunterlaufen; ⟨clockwork:⟩ ablaufen; ⟨stocks:⟩ sich verringern □ vt ⟨run over⟩ überfahren; ⟨reduce⟩ verringern; ⟨fam: criticize⟩ heruntermachen. **~ in** vi hinein-/ hereinlaufen. **~ off** vi weglaufen □ vt abziehen ⟨copies⟩. **~ out** vi hinaus-/heraus-laufen; ⟨supplies, money:⟩ ausgehen; I've **~ out of sugar** Ich habe keinen Zucker mehr. **~ over** vi hinüber-/herüberlaufen; ⟨overflow⟩ überlaufen □ vt überfahren. **~ through** vi durchlaufen. **~ up** vi hinauf-/ herauflaufen; ⟨towards⟩ hinlaufen □ vt machen ⟨debts⟩; auflaufen lassen ⟨bill⟩; ⟨sew⟩ schnell nähen

'runaway n Ausreißer m

run-'down a ⟨area⟩ verkommen

rung¹ /rʌŋ/ n ⟨of ladder⟩ Sprosse f

rung² see ring²

runner /'rʌnə(r)/ n Läufer m; ⟨Bot⟩ Ausläufer m; ⟨on sledge⟩ Kufe f. **~ bean** n Stangenbohne f. **~-'up** n Zweite(r) m/f

running /'rʌnɪŋ/ a laufend; ⟨water⟩ fließend □ n Laufen nt; ⟨management⟩ Führung f, Leitung f; **be/not be in the ~** eine/keine Chance haben. **~ 'commentary** n fortlaufender Kommentar m

runny /'rʌnɪ/ a flüssig

run: ~-of-the-'mill a gewöhnlich. **~-up** n ⟨Sport⟩ Anlauf m; ⟨to election⟩ Zeit f vor der Wahl. **~way** n Start- und Landebahn f, Piste f

rupture /'rʌptʃə(r)/ n Bruch m □ vt/i brechen; **~ oneself** sich ⟨dat⟩ einen Bruch heben

rural /'rʊərəl/ a ländlich

ruse /ruːz/ n List f

rush¹ /rʌʃ/ n ⟨Bot⟩ Binse f

rush² n Hetze f; **in a ~** in Eile □ vi sich hetzen; ⟨run⟩ rasen; ⟨water:⟩ rauschen □ vt hetzen, drängen; **~ s.o. to hospital** jdn schnellstens ins Krankenhaus bringen. **~-hour** n Hauptverkehrszeit f, Stoßzeit f

rusk /rʌsk/ n Zwieback m

Russia /'rʌʃə/ n Russland nt. **~n** a russisch □ n Russe m/Russin f; ⟨Lang⟩ Russisch nt

rust /rʌst/ n Rost m □ vi rosten

rustic /'rʌstɪk/ a bäuerlich; ⟨furniture⟩ rustikal

rustle /'rʌsl/ vi rascheln □ vt rascheln mit; ⟨Amer⟩ stehlen ⟨cattle⟩. **~ up** vt ⟨fam⟩ improvisieren

'rustproof a rostfrei

rusty /'rʌstɪ/ a (-ier, -iest) rostig

rut /rʌt/ n Furche f; **be in a ~** ⟨fam⟩ aus dem alten Trott nicht herauskommen

ruthless /'ruːθlɪs/ a, **-ly** adv rücksichtslos. **~ness** n Rücksichtslosigkeit f

rye /raɪ/ n Roggen m

S

sabbath /'sæbəθ/ n Sabbat m

sabbatical /sə'bætɪkl/ n ⟨Univ⟩ Forschungsurlaub m

sabot|age /'sæbətɑːʒ/ n Sabotage f □ vt sabotieren. **~eur** /-'tɜː(r)/ n Saboteur m

sachet /'sæʃeɪ/ n Beutel m; ⟨scented⟩ Kissen nt

sack¹ /sæk/ vt ⟨plunder⟩ plündern

sack² n Sack m; **get the ~** ⟨fam⟩ rausgeschmissen werden □ vt ⟨fam⟩ rausschmeißen. **~ing** n Sackleinen nt; ⟨fam: dismissal⟩ Rausschmiss m

sacrament /'sækrəmənt/ n Sakrament nt

sacred /'seɪkrɪd/ a heilig

sacrifice /'sækrɪfaɪs/ n Opfer nt □ vt opfern

sacrilege /'sækrɪlɪdʒ/ n Sakrileg nt

sad /sæd/ a (sadder, saddest) traurig; ⟨loss, death⟩ schmerzlich. **~den** vt traurig machen

saddle /'sædl/ n Sattel m □ vt satteln; **~ s.o. with sth** ⟨fam⟩ jdm etw aufhalsen

sadis|m /'seɪdɪzm/ n Sadismus m. **~t** /-dɪst/ n Sadist m. **~tic** /sə'dɪstɪk/ a, **-ally** adv sadistisch

sad|ly /'sædlɪ/ adv traurig; ⟨unfortunately⟩ leider. **~ness** n Traurigkeit f

safe /seɪf/ a (-r, -st) sicher; ⟨journey⟩ gut; ⟨not dangerous⟩ ungefährlich; **~ and sound** gesund und wohlbehalten □ n Safe m. **~guard** n Schutz m □ vt schützen. **~ly** adv sicher; ⟨arrive⟩ gut

safety /'seɪftɪ/ n Sicherheit f. **~-belt** n Sicherheitsgurt m. **~-pin** n Sicherheitsnadel f. **~-valve** n [Sicherheits]ventil nt

sag /sæg/ vi (pt/pp sagged) durchhängen

saga /'sɑːgə/ n Saga f; ⟨fig⟩ Geschichte f

sage¹ /seɪdʒ/ n ⟨herb⟩ Salbei m

sage² a weise □ n Weise(r) m

Sagittarius /sædʒɪ'teərɪəs/ n ⟨Astr⟩ Schütze m

said /sed/ *see* say

sail /seɪl/ *n* Segel *nt*; (*trip*) Segelfahrt *f* □ *vi* segeln; (*on liner*) fahren; (*leave*) abfahren (*for* nach) □ *vt* segeln mit

'sailboard *n* Surfbrett *nt*. **~ing** *n* Windsurfen *nt*

sailing /'seɪlɪŋ/ *n* Segelsport *m*. **~-boat** *n* Segelboot *nt*. **~-ship** *n* Segelschiff *nt*

sailor /'seɪlə(r)/ *n* Seemann *m*; (*in navy*) Matrose *m*

saint /seɪnt/ *n* Heilige(r) *m/f*. **~ly** *a* heilig

sake /seɪk/ *n* for the **~** of … um … (*gen*) willen; for my/your **~** um meinet-/deinetwillen

salad /'sæləd/ *n* Salat *m*. **~ cream** *n* ≈ Mayonnaise *f*. **~-dressing** *n* Salatsoße *f*

salary /'sæləri/ *n* Gehalt *nt*

sale /seɪl/ *n* Verkauf *m*; (*event*) Basar *m*; (*at reduced prices*) Schlussverkauf *m*; for **~** zu verkaufen

sales|man *n* Verkäufer *m*. **~woman** *n* Verkäuferin *f*

salient /'seɪlɪənt/ *a* wichtigste(r,s)

saliva /sə'laɪvə/ *n* Speichel *m*

sallow /'sæləʊ/ *a* (-er, -est) bleich

salmon /'sæmən/ *n* Lachs *m*. **~-pink** *a* lachsrosa

saloon /sə'luːn/ *n* Salon *m*; (*Auto*) Limousine *f*; (*Amer: bar*) Wirtschaft *f*

salt /sɔːlt/ *n* Salz *nt* □ *a* salzig; (*water, meat*) Salz- □ *vt* salzen; (*cure*) pökeln; streuen (*road*). **~-cellar** *n* Salzfass *nt*. **~ 'water** *n* Salzwasser *nt*. **~y** *a* salzig

salutary /'sæljʊtəri/ *a* heilsam

salute /sə'luːt/ *n* (*Mil*) Gruß *m* □ *vt/i* (*Mil*) grüßen

salvage /'sælvɪdʒ/ *n* (*Naut*) Bergung *f* □ *vt* bergen

salvation /sæl'veɪʃn/ *n* Rettung *f*; (*Relig*) Heil *nt*. **S~** '**Army** *n* Heilsarmee *f*

salvo /'sælvəʊ/ *n* Salve *f*

same /seɪm/ *a & pron* the **~** der/die/das gleiche; (*pl*) die gleichen; (*identical*) der-/die-/dasselbe; (*pl*) dieselben □ *adv* the **~** gleich; all the **~** trotzdem; the **~** to you gleichfalls

sample /'sɑːmpl/ *n* Probe *f*; (*Comm*) Muster *nt* □ *vt* probieren, kosten

sanatorium /sænə'tɔːrɪəm/ *n* Sanatorium *nt*

sanctify /'sæŋktɪfaɪ/ *vt* (*pt/pp* -fied) heiligen

sanctimonious /sæŋktɪ'məʊnɪəs/ *a*, **-ly** *adv* frömmlerisch

sanction /'sæŋkʃn/ *n* Sanktion *f* □ *vt* sanktionieren

sanctity /'sæŋktəti/ *n* Heiligkeit *f*

sanctuary /'sæŋktjʊəri/ *n* (*Relig*) Heiligtum *nt*; (*refuge*) Zuflucht *f*; (*for wildlife*) Tierschutzgebiet *nt*

sand /sænd/ *n* Sand *m* □ *vt* **~ [down]** [ab]schmirgeln

sandal /'sændl/ *n* Sandale *f*

sand: **~bank** *n* Sandbank *f*. **~paper** *n* Sandpapier *nt* □ *vt* [ab]schmirgeln. **~pit** *n* Sandkasten *m*

sandwich /'sænwɪdʒ/ *n* ≈ belegtes Brot *nt*; Sandwich *m* □ *vt* **~ed between** eingeklemmt zwischen

sandy /'sændi/ *a* (-ier, -iest) sandig; (*beach, soil*) Sand-; (*hair*) rotblond

sane /seɪn/ *a* (-r, -st) geistig normal; (*sensible*) vernünftig

sang /sæŋ/ *see* sing

sanitary /'sænɪtəri/ *a* hygienisch; (*system*) sanitär. **~ napkin** *n* (*Amer*), **~ towel** *n* [Damen]binde *f*

sanitation /sænɪ'teɪʃn/ *n* Kanalisation und Abfallbeseitigung *pl*

sanity /'sænɪti/ *n* [gesunder] Verstand *m*

sank /sæŋk/ *see* sink

sap /sæp/ *n* (*Bot*) Saft *m* □ *vt* (*pt/pp* sapped) schwächen

sapphire /'sæfaɪə(r)/ *n* Saphir *m*

sarcas|m /'sɑːkæzm/ *n* Sarkasmus *m*. **~tic** /-'kæstɪk/ *a*, **-ally** *adv* sarkastisch

sardine /sɑː'diːn/ *n* Sardine *f*

Sardinia /sɑː'dɪnɪə/ *n* Sardinien *nt*

sardonic /sɑː'dɒnɪk/ *a*, **-ally** *adv* höhnisch; (*smile*) sardonisch

sash /sæʃ/ *n* Schärpe *f*

sat /sæt/ *see* sit

satanic /sə'tænɪk/ *a* satanisch

satchel /'sætʃl/ *n* Ranzen *m*

satellite /'sætəlaɪt/ *n* Satellit *m*. **~ dish** *n* Satellitenschüssel *f*. **~ television** *n* Satellitenfernsehen *nt*

satin /'sætɪn/ *n* Satin *m*

satire /'sætaɪə(r)/ *n* Satire *f*

satirical /sə'tɪrɪkl/ *a*, **-ly** *adv* satirisch

satir|ist /'sætərɪst/ *n* Satiriker(in) *m(f)*. **~ize** *vt* satirisch darstellen; (*book:*) eine Satire sein auf (+ *acc*)

satisfaction /sætɪs'fækʃn/ *n* Befriedigung *f*; to my **~** zu meiner Zufriedenheit

satisfactory /sætɪs'fæktəri/ *a*, **-ily** *adv* zufrieden stellend

satisf|y /'sætɪsfaɪ/ *vt* (*pt/pp* -fied) befriedigen; zufrieden stellen (*customer*); (*convince*) überzeugen; be **~ied** zufrieden sein. **~ying** *a* befriedigend; (*meal*) sättigend

saturat|e /'sætʃəreɪt/ *vt* durchtränken; (*Chem & fig*) sättigen. **~ed** *a* durchnässt; (*fat*) gesättigt

Saturday /'sætədeɪ/ n Samstag m, Sonnabend m

sauce /sɔːs/ n Soße f; (cheek) Frechheit f. ~pan n Kochtopf m

saucer /'sɔːsə(r)/ n Untertasse f

saucy /'sɔːʃɪ/ a (-ier, -iest) frech

Saudi Arabia /saʊdɪə'reɪbɪə/ n Saudi-Arabien n

sauna /'sɔːnə/ n Sauna f

saunter /'sɔːntə(r)/ vi schlendern

sausage /'sɒsɪdʒ/ n Wurst f

savage /'sævɪdʒ/ a wild; (fierce) scharf; (brutal) brutal □ n Wilde(r) m/f □ vt anfallen. ~ry n Brutalität f

save /seɪv/ n (Sport) Abwehr f □ vt retten (from vor + dat); (keep) aufheben; (not waste) sparen; (collect) sammeln; (avoid) ersparen; (Sport) abwehren (shot); verhindern (goal) □ vi ~ [up] sparen □ prep außer (+ dat), mit Ausnahme (+ gen)

saver /'seɪvə(r)/ n Sparer m

saving /'seɪvɪŋ/ n (see save) Rettung f; Sparen nt; Ersparnis f; ~s pl (money) Ersparnisse pl. ~s account n Sparkonto nt. ~s bank n Sparkasse f

saviour /'seɪvjə(r)/ n Retter m

savour /'seɪvə(r)/ n Geschmack m □ vt auskosten. ~y a herzhaft, würzig; (fig) angenehm

saw[1] /sɔː/ see see[1]

saw[2] n Säge f □ vt/i (pt sawed, pp sawn or sawed) sägen. ~dust n Sägemehl nt

saxophone /'sæksəfəʊn/ n Saxophon nt

say /seɪ/ n Mitspracherecht nt; have one's ~ seine Meinung sagen □ vt/i (pt/pp said) sagen; sprechen (prayer); that is to ~ das heißt; that goes without ~ing das versteht sich von selbst; when all is said and done letzten Endes; I ~! (attracting attention) hallo! ~ing n Redensart f

scab /skæb/ n Schorf m; (pej) Streikbrecher m

scaffold /'skæfəld/ n Schafott nt. ~ing n Gerüst nt

scald /skɔːld/ vt verbrühen

scale[1] /skeɪl/ n (of fish) Schuppe f

scale[2] n Skala f; (Mus) Tonleiter f; (ratio) Maßstab m; on a grand ~ in großem Stil □ vt (climb) erklettern. ~ down vt verkleinern

scales /skeɪlz/ npl (for weighing) Waage f

scalp /skælp/ n Kopfhaut f □ vt skalpieren

scalpel /'skælpl/ n Skalpell nt

scam /skæm/ n (fam) Schwindel m

scamper /'skæmpə(r)/ vi huschen

scan /skæn/ n (Med) Szintigramm nt □ v (pt/pp scanned) □ vt absuchen; (quickly) flüchtig ansehen; (Med) szintigraphisch untersuchen □ vi (poetry:) das richtige Versmaß haben

scandal /'skændl/ n Skandal m; (gossip) Skandalgeschichten pl. ~ize /-dəlaɪz/ vt schockieren. ~ous /-əs/ a skandalös

Scandinavia /skændɪ'neɪvɪə/ n Skandinavien nt. ~n a skandinavisch □ n Skandinavier(in) m(f)

scant /skænt/ a wenig

scanty /'skæntɪ/ a (-ier, -iest), -ily adv spärlich; (clothing) knapp

scapegoat /'skeɪp-/ n Sündenbock m

scar /skɑː(r)/ n Narbe f □ vt (pt/pp scarred) eine Narbe hinterlassen auf (+ dat)

scarc|e /skeəs/ a (-r, -st) knapp; make oneself ~e (fam) sich aus dem Staub machen. ~ely adv kaum. ~ity n Knappheit f

scare /skeə(r)/ n Schreck m; (panic) [allgemeine] Panik f; (bomb ~) Bombendrohung f □ vt Angst machen (+ dat); be ~d Angst haben (of vor + dat)

'scarecrow n Vogelscheuche f

scarf /skɑːf/ n (pl scarves) Schal m; (square) Tuch nt

scarlet /'skɑːlət/ a scharlachrot. ~ 'fever n Scharlach m

scary /'skeərɪ/ a unheimlich

scathing /'skeɪðɪŋ/ a bissig

scatter /'skætə(r)/ vt verstreuen; (disperse) zerstreuen □ vi sich zerstreuen. ~brained a (fam) schusselig. ~ed a verstreut; (showers) vereinzelt

scatty /'skætɪ/ a (-ier, -iest) (fam) verrückt

scavenge /'skævɪndʒ/ vi [im Abfall] Nahrung suchen; (animal:) Aas fressen. ~r n Aasfresser m

scenario /sɪ'nɑːrɪəʊ/ n Szenario nt

scene /siːn/ n Szene f; (sight) Anblick m; (place of event) Schauplatz m; behind the ~s hinter den Kulissen; ~ of the crime Tatort m

scenery /'siːnərɪ/ n Landschaft f; (Theat) Szenerie f

scenic /'siːnɪk/ a landschaftlich schön; (Theat) Bühnen-

scent /sent/ n Duft m; (trail) Fährte f; (perfume) Parfüm nt. ~ed a parfümiert

sceptic|al /'skeptɪkl/ a, -ly adv skeptisch. ~ism /-tɪsɪzm/ n Skepsis f

schedule /'ʃedjuːl/ n Programm nt; (of work) Zeitplan m; (timetable) Fahrplan m; behind ~ im Rückstand; according to ~ planmäßig □ vt planen. ~d flight n Linienflug m

scheme /skiːm/ n Programm nt; (plan) Plan m; (plot) Komplott nt □ vi Ränke schmieden

schizophren|ia /ˌskɪtsə'friːnɪə/ n Schizophrenie f. **~ic** /-'frenɪk/ a schizophren

scholar /'skɒlə(r)/ n Gelehrte(r) m/f. **~ly** a gelehrt. **~ship** n Gelehrtheit f; (grant) Stipendium nt

school /skuːl/ n Schule f; (Univ) Fakultät f □ vt schulen; dressieren (animal)

school: **~boy** n Schüler m. **~girl** n Schülerin f. **~ing** n Schulbildung f. **~master** n Lehrer m. **~mistress** n Lehrerin f. **~teacher** n Lehrer(in) m(f)

sciatica /saɪ'ætɪkə/ n Ischias m

scien|ce /'saɪəns/ n Wissenschaft f. **~tific** /-'tɪfɪk/ a wissenschaftlich. **~tist** n Wissenschaftler m

scintillating /'sɪntɪleɪtɪŋ/ a sprühend

scissors /'sɪzəz/ npl Schere f; **a pair of ~** eine Schere

scoff¹ /skɒf/ vi **~ at** spotten über (+ acc)

scoff² vt (fam) verschlingen

scold /skəʊld/ vt ausschimpfen

scoop /skuːp/ n Schaufel f; (Culin) Portionierer m; (Journ) Exklusivmeldung f □ vt **~ out** aushöhlen; (remove) auslöffeln; **~ up** schaufeln; schöpfen (liquid)

scoot /skuːt/ vi (fam) rasen. **~er** n Roller m

scope /skəʊp/ n Bereich m; (opportunity) Möglichkeiten pl

scorch /skɔːtʃ/ vt versengen. **~ing** a glühend heiß

score /skɔː(r)/ n [Spiel]stand m; (individual) Punktzahl f; (Mus) Partitur f; (Cinema) Filmmusik f; **a ~ [of]** (twenty) zwanzig; **keep [the] ~** zählen; (written) aufschreiben; **on that ~** was das betrifft □ vt erzielen; schießen (goal); (cut) einritzen □ vi Punkte erzielen; (Sport) ein Tor schießen; (keep score) Punkte zählen. **~r** n Punktezähler m; (of goals) Torschütze m

scorn /skɔːn/ n Verachtung f □ vt verachten. **~ful** a, **-ly** adv verächtlich

Scorpio /'skɔːpɪəʊ/ n (Astr) Skorpion m

Scorpion /'skɔːpɪən/ n Skorpion m

Scot /skɒt/ n Schotte m/Schottin f

Scotch /skɒtʃ/ a schottisch □ n (whisky) Scotch m

scotch vt unterbinden

scot-'free a **get off ~** straffrei ausgehen

Scot|land /'skɒtlənd/ n Schottland nt. **~s**, **~tish** a schottisch

scoundrel /'skaʊndrl/ n Schurke m

scour¹ /'skaʊə(r)/ vt (search) absuchen

scour² vt (clean) scheuern

scourge /skɜːdʒ/ n Geißel f

scout /skaʊt/ n (Mil) Kundschafter m □ vi **~ for** Ausschau halten nach

Scout n [Boy] **~** Pfadfinder m

scowl /skaʊl/ n böser Gesichtsausdruck m □ vi ein böses Gesicht machen

scraggy /'skrægɪ/ a (-ier, -iest) (pej) dürr, hager

scram /skræm/ vi (fam) abhauen

scramble /'skræmbl/ n Gerangel nt □ vi klettern; **~ for** sich drängen nach □ vt (Teleph) verschlüsseln. **~d 'egg[s]** n[pl] Rührei nt

scrap¹ /skræp/ n (fam: flight) Rauferei f □ vi sich raufen

scrap² n Stückchen nt; (metal) Schrott m; **~s** pl Reste; **not a ~** kein bisschen □ vt (pt/pp scrapped) aufgeben

'scrap-book n Sammelalbum nt

scrape /skreɪp/ vt schaben; (clean) abkratzen; (damage) [ver]schrammen. **~ through** vi gerade noch durchkommen. **~ together** vt zusammenkriegen

scraper /'skreɪpə(r)/ n Kratzer m

'scrap iron n Alteisen nt

scrappy /'skræpɪ/ a lückenhaft

'scrap-yard n Schrottplatz m

scratch /skrætʃ/ n Kratzer m; **start from ~** von vorne anfangen; **not be up to ~** zu wünschen übrig lassen □ vt/i kratzen; (damage) zerkratzen

scrawl /skrɔːl/ n Gekrakel nt □ vt/i krakeln

scrawny /'skrɔːnɪ/ a (-ier, -iest) (pej) dürr, hager

scream /skriːm/ n Schrei m □ vt/i schreien

screech /skriːtʃ/ n Kreischen nt □ vt/i kreischen

screen /skriːn/ n Schirm m; (Cinema) Leinwand f; (TV) Bildschirm m □ vt schützen; (conceal) verdecken; vorführen (film); (examine) überprüfen; (Med) untersuchen. **~ing** n (Med) Reihenuntersuchung f. **~play** n Drehbuch nt

screw /skruː/ n Schraube f □ vt schrauben. **~ up** vt festschrauben; (crumple) zusammenknüllen; zusammenkneifen (eyes); (sl: bungle) vermasseln; **~ up one's courage** seinen Mut zusammennehmen

'screwdriver n Schraubenzieher m

screwy /'skruːɪ/ a (-ier, -iest) (fam) verrückt

scribble /'skrɪbl/ n Gekritzel nt □ vt/i kritzeln

script /skrɪpt/ n Schrift f; (of speech, play) Text m; (Radio, TV) Skript nt; (of film) Drehbuch nt

Scripture /'skrɪptʃə(r)/ n (Sch) Religion f; **the ~s** pl die Heilige Schrift f

scroll /skrəʊl/ n Schriftrolle f; (decoration) Volute f

scrounge /skraʊndʒ/ *vt/i* schnorren. **~r** *n* Schnorrer *m*

scrub[1] /skrʌb/ *n* (*land*) Buschland *nt*, Gestrüpp *nt*

scrub[2] *vt/i* (*pt/pp* **scrubbed**) schrubben; (*fam: cancel*) absagen; fallen lassen (*plan*)

scruff /skrʌf/ *n* **by the ~ of the neck** beim Genick

scruffy /'skrʌfɪ/ *a* (**-ier, -iest**) vergammelt

scrum /skrʌm/ *n* Gedränge *nt*

scruple /'skruːpl/ *n* Skrupel *m*

scrupulous /'skruːpjʊləs/ *a*, **-ly** *adv* gewissenhaft

scrutin|ize /'skruːtɪnaɪz/ *vt* [genau] ansehen. **~y** *n* (*look*) prüfender Blick *m*

scuff /skʌf/ *vt* abstoßen

scuffle /'skʌfl/ *n* Handgemenge *nt*

scullery /'skʌlərɪ/ *n* Spülküche *f*

sculpt|or /'skʌlptə(r)/ *n* Bildhauer(in) *m(f)*. **~ure** /-tʃə(r)/ *n* Bildhauerei *f*; (*piece of work*) Skulptur *f*, Plastik *f*

scum /skʌm/ *n* Schmutzschicht *f*; (*people*) Abschaum *m*

scurrilous /'skʌrɪləs/ *a* niederträchtig

scurry /'skʌrɪ/ *vi* (*pt/pp* **-ied**) huschen

scuttle[1] /'skʌtl/ *n* Kohleneimer *m*

scuttle[2] *vt* versenken (*ship*)

scuttle[3] *vi* schnell krabbeln

scythe /saɪð/ *n* Sense *f*

sea /siː/ *n* Meer *nt*, See *f*; **at ~** auf See; **by ~** mit dem Schiff. **~board** *n* Küste *f*. **~food** *n* Meeresfrüchte *pl*. **~gull** *n* Möwe *f*

seal[1] /siːl/ *n* (*Zool*) Seehund *m*

seal[2] *n* Siegel *nt*; (*Techn*) Dichtung *f* □ *vt* versiegeln; (*Techn*) abdichten; (*fig*) besiegeln. **~ off** *vt* abriegeln

'sea-level *n* Meeresspiegel *m*

seam /siːm/ *n* Naht *f*; (*of coal*) Flöz *nt*

'seaman *n* Seemann *m*; (*sailor*) Matrose *m*

seamless /'siːmlɪs/ *a* nahtlos

seance /'seɪɑːns/ *n* spiritistische Sitzung *f*

sea: ~plane *n* Wasserflugzeug *nt*. **~port** *n* Seehafen *m*

search /sɜːtʃ/ *n* Suche *f*; (*official*) Durchsuchung *f* □ *vt* durchsuchen; absuchen (*area*) □ *vi* suchen (**for** nach). **~ing** *a* prüfend, forschend

search: ~light *n* [Such]scheinwerfer *m*. **~-party** *n* Suchmannschaft *f*

sea: ~sick *a* seekrank. **~side** *n* **at/to the ~side** am/ans Meer

season /'siːzn/ *n* Jahreszeit *f*; (*social, tourist, sporting*) Saison *f* □ *vt* (*flavour*) würzen. **~able** /-əbl/ *a* der Jahreszeit

gemäß. **~al** *a* Saison-. **~ing** *n* Gewürze *pl*

'season ticket *n* Dauerkarte *f*

seat /siːt/ *n* Sitz *m*; (*place*) Sitzplatz *m*; (*bottom*) Hintern *m*; **take a ~** Platz nehmen □ *vt* setzen; (*have seats for*) Sitzplätze bieten (+ *dat*); **remain ~ed** sitzen bleiben. **~-belt** *n* Sicherheitsgurt *m*; **fasten one's ~-belt** sich anschnallen

sea: ~weed *n* [See]tang *m*. **~worthy** *a* seetüchtig

secateurs /sekə'tɜːz/ *npl* Gartenschere *f*

seclu|de /sɪ'kluːd/ *vt* absondern. **~ded** *a* abgelegen. **~sion** /-ʒn/ *n* Zurückgezogenheit *f*

second[1] /sɪ'kɒnd/ *vt* (*transfer*) [vorübergehend] versetzen

second[2] /'sekənd/ *a* zweite(r,s); **on ~ thoughts** nach weiterer Überlegung □ *n* Sekunde *f*; (*Sport*) Sekundant *m*; **~s** *pl* (*goods*) Waren zweiter Wahl; **the ~** der/die/das Zweite □ *adv* (*in race*) an zweiter Stelle □ *vt* unterstützen (*proposal*)

secondary /'sekəndrɪ/ *a* zweitrangig; (*Phys*) Sekundär-. **~ school** *n* höhere Schule *f*

second: ~-best *a* zweitbeste(r,s). **~ 'class** *adv* (*travel, send*) zweiter Klasse. **~-class** *a* zweitklassig

'second hand *n* (*on clock*) Sekundenzeiger *m*

second-'hand *a* gebraucht □ *adv* aus zweiter Hand

secondly /'sekəndlɪ/ *adv* zweitens

second-'rate *a* zweitklassig

secrecy /'siːkrəsɪ/ *n* Heimlichkeit *f*

secret /'siːkrɪt/ *a* geheim; (*agent, police*) Geheim-; (*drinker, lover*) heimlich □ *n* Geheimnis *nt*; **in ~** heimlich

secretarial /sekrə'teərɪəl/ *a* Sekretärinnen-; (*work, staff*) Sekretariats-

secretary /'sekrətərɪ/ *n* Sekretär(in) *m(f)*

secret|e /sɪ'kriːt/ *vt* absondern. **~ion** /-iːʃn/ *n* Absonderung *f*

secretive /'siːkrətɪv/ *a* geheimtuerisch. **~ness** *n* Heimlichtuerei *f*

secretly /'siːkrɪtlɪ/ *adv* heimlich

sect /sekt/ *n* Sekte *f*

section /'sekʃn/ *n* Teil *m*; (*of text*) Abschnitt *m*; (*of firm*) Abteilung *f*; (*of organization*) Sektion *f*

sector /'sektə(r)/ *n* Sektor *m*

secular /'sekjʊlə(r)/ *a* weltlich

secure /sɪ'kjʊə(r)/ *a*, **-ly** *adv* sicher; (*firm*) fest; (*emotionally*) geborgen □ *vt* sichern; (*fasten*) festmachen; (*obtain*) sich (*dat*) sichern

securit|y /sɪˈkjʊərətɪ/ *n* Sicherheit *f*; (*emotional*) Geborgenheit *f*; ~**ies** *pl* Wertpapiere *pl*; (*Fin*) Effekten *pl*

sedan /sɪˈdæn/ *n* (*Amer*) Limousine *f*

sedate¹ /sɪˈdeɪt/ *a*, **-ly** *adv* gesetzt

sedate² *vt* sedieren

sedation /sɪˈdeɪʃn/ *n* Sedierung *f*; **be under** ~ sediert sein

sedative /ˈsedətɪv/ *a* beruhigend □ *n* Beruhigungsmittel *nt*

sedentary /ˈsedəntərɪ/ *a* sitzend

sediment /ˈsedɪmənt/ *n* [Boden]satz *m*

seduce /sɪˈdjuːs/ *vt* verführen

seduct|ion /sɪˈdʌkʃn/ *n* Verführung *f*. ~**ive** /-tɪv/ *a*, **-ly** *adv* verführerisch

see¹ /siː/ *v* (*pt* **saw**, *pp* **seen**) □ *vt* sehen; (*understand*) einsehen; (*imagine*) sich (*dat*) vorstellen; (*escort*) begleiten; **go and** ~ nachsehen; (*visit*) besuchen; ~ **you later!** bis nachher! ~**ing that** da □ *vi* sehen; (*check*) nachsehen; ~ **about** sich kümmern um. ~ **off** *vt* verabschieden; (*chase away*) vertreiben. ~ **through** *vi* durchsehen □ *vt* (*fig*) ~ **through s.o.** jdn durchschauen

see² *n* (*Relig*) Bistum *nt*

seed /siːd/ *n* Samen *m*; (*of grape*) Kern *m*; (*fig*) Saat *f*; (*Tennis*) gesetzter Spieler *m*; **go to** ~ Samen bilden; (*fig*) herunterkommen. ~**ed** *a* (*Tennis*) gesetzt. ~**ling** *n* Sämling *m*

seedy /ˈsiːdɪ/ *a* (**-ier**, **-iest**) schäbig; ⟨*area*⟩ heruntergekommen

seek /siːk/ *vt* (*pt/pp* **sought**) suchen

seem /siːm/ *vi* scheinen. ~**ingly** *adv* scheinbar

seemly /ˈsiːmlɪ/ *a* schicklich

seen /siːn/ *see* **see**¹

seep /siːp/ *vi* sickern

see-saw /ˈsiːsɔː/ *n* Wippe *f*

seethe /siːð/ *vi* ~ **with anger** vor Wut schäumen

'see-through *a* durchsichtig

segment /ˈsegmənt/ *n* Teil *m*; (*of worm*) Segment *nt*; (*of orange*) Spalte *f*

segregat|e /ˈsegrɪgeɪt/ *vt* trennen. ~**ion** /-ˈgeɪʃn/ *n* Trennung *f*

seize /siːz/ *vt* ergreifen; (*Jur*) beschlagnahmen; ~ **s.o. by the arm** jdn am Arm packen. ~ **up** *vi* (*Techn*) sich festfressen

seizure /ˈsiːʒə(r)/ *n* (*Jur*) Beschlagnahme *f*; (*Med*) Anfall *m*

seldom /ˈseldəm/ *adv* selten

select /sɪˈlekt/ *a* ausgewählt; (*exclusive*) exklusiv □ *vt* auswählen; aufstellen ⟨*team*⟩. ~**ion** /-ekʃn/ *n* Auswahl *f*. ~**ive** /-ɪv/ *a*, **-ly** *adv* selektiv; (*choosy*) wählerisch

self /self/ *n* (*pl* **selves**) Ich *nt*

self: ~**-ad'dressed** *a* adressiert. ~**-ad'hesive** *a* selbstklebend. ~**-as'surance** *n* Selbstsicherheit *f*. ~**-as'sured** *a* selbstsicher. ~**-'catering** *n* Selbstversorgung *f*. ~**-'centred** *a* egozentrisch. ~**-'confidence** *n* Selbstbewusstsein *nt*, Selbstvertrauen *nt*. ~**-'confident** *a* selbstbewusst. ~**-'conscious** *a* befangen. ~**-con'tained** *a* ⟨*flat*⟩ abgeschlossen. ~**-con-'trol** *n* Selbstbeherrschung *f*. ~**-de'fence** *n* Selbstverteidigung *f*; (*Jur*) Notwehr *f*. ~**-de'nial** *n* Selbstverleugnung *f*. ~**-determi'nation** *n* Selbstbestimmung *f*. ~**-em'ployed** selbstständig. ~**-es'teem** *n* Selbstachtung *f*. ~**-'evident** *a* offensichtlich. ~**-'governing** *a* selbst verwaltet. ~**-'help** *n* Selbsthilfe *f*. ~**-in'dulgent** *a* maßlos. ~**-'interest** *n* Eigennutz *m*

self|ish /ˈselfɪʃ/ *a*, **-ly** *adv* egoistisch, selbstsüchtig. ~**less** *a*, **-ly** *adv* selbstlos

self: ~**-'pity** *n* Selbstmitleid *nt*. ~**-'portrait** *n* Selbstporträt *nt*. ~**-pos'sessed** *a* selbstbeherrscht. ~**-preser'vation** *n* Selbsterhaltung *f*. ~**-re'spect** *n* Selbstachtung *f*. ~**-'righteous** *a* selbstgerecht. ~**-'sacrifice** *n* Selbstaufopferung *f*. ~**-'satisfied** *a* selbstgefällig. ~**-'service** *n* Selbstbedienung *f* □ *attrib* Selbstbedienungs-. ~**-suf'ficient** *a* selbstständig. ~**-'willed** *a* eigenwillig

sell /sel/ *v* (*pt/pp* **sold**) □ *vt* verkaufen; **be sold out** ausverkauft sein □ *vi* sich verkaufen. ~ **off** *vt* verkaufen

seller /ˈselə(r)/ *n* Verkäufer *m*

Sellotape (P) /ˈseləʊ-/ *n* ≈ Tesafilm (P) *m*

'sell-out *n* **be a** ~ ausverkauft sein; (*fam: betrayal*) Verrat sein

selves /selvz/ *see* **self**

semblance /ˈsembləns/ *n* Anschein *m*

semen /ˈsiːmən/ *n* (*Anat*) Samen *m*

semester /sɪˈmestə(r)/ *n* (*Amer*) Semester *nt*

semi|breve /ˈsemɪbriːv/ *n* (*Mus*) ganze Note *f*. ~**circle** *n* Halbkreis *m*. ~**'circular** *a* halbkreisförmig. ~**'colon** *n* Semikolon *nt*. ~**-de'tached** *a* & *n* ~**detached [house]** Doppelhaushälfte *f*. ~**-'final** *n* Halbfinale *nt*

seminar /ˈsemɪnɑː(r)/ *n* Seminar *nt*. **-y** /-nərɪ/ *n* Priesterseminar *nt*

'semitone *n* (*Mus*) Halbton *m*

semolina /seməˈliːnə/ *n* Grieß *m*

senat|e /ˈsenət/ *n* Senat *m*. ~**or** *n* Senator *m*

send /send/ *vt/i* (*pt/pp* **sent**) schicken; ~ **one's regards** grüßen lassen; ~ **for** kommen lassen ⟨*person*⟩; sich (*dat*) schicken lassen ⟨*thing*⟩. ~**er** *n* Absender *m*. ~**-off** *n* Verabschiedung *f*

Dispatch

senile 443 settee

senior /'si:nıə(r)/ a älter; (in rank) höher □ n Ältere(r) m/f; (in rank) Vorgesetzte(r) m/f. ∼ 'citizen n Senior(in) m(f)

seniority /si:nı'ɒrətı/ n höheres Alter nt; (in rank) höherer Rang m

sensation /sen'seıʃn/ n Sensation f; (feeling) Gefühl nt. ∼al a, -ly adv sensationell

sense /sens/ n Sinn m; (feeling) Gefühl nt; (common ∼) Verstand m; in a ∼ in gewisser Hinsicht; make ∼ Sinn ergeben □ vt spüren. ∼less a, -ly adv sinnlos; (unconscious) bewusstlos

sensible /'sensəbl/ a, -bly adv vernünftig; (suitable) zweckmäßig

sensitiv|e /'sensətıv/ a, -ly adv empfindlich; (understanding) einfühlsam. ∼ity /-'tıvətı/ n Empfindlichkeit f

sensory /'sensərı/ a Sinnes-

sensual /'sensjʊəl/ a sinnlich. -ity /-'ælətı/ n Sinnlichkeit f

sensuous /'sensjʊəs/ a sinnlich

sent /sent/ see send

sentence /'sentəns/ n Satz m; (Jur) Urteil nt; (punishment) Strafe f □ vt verurteilen

sentiment /'sentımənt/ n Gefühl nt; (opinion) Meinung f; (sentimentality) Sentimentalität f. ∼al a /'mentl/ a sentimental. ∼ality /-'tælətı/ n Sentimentalität f

sentry /'sentrı/ n Wache f

separable /'sepərəbl/ a trennbar

separate¹ /'sepərət/ a, -ly adv getrennt, separat

separat|e² /'sepəreıt/ vt trennen □ vi sich trennen. ∼ion /-'reıʃn/ n Trennung f

September /sep'tembə(r)/ n September m

septic /'septık/ a vereitert; go ∼ vereitern

sequel /'si:kwl/ n Folge f; (fig) Nachspiel nt

sequence /'si:kwəns/ n Reihenfolge f

sequin /'si:kwın/ n Paillette f

serenade /serə'neıd/ n Ständchen nt □ vt ∼ s.o. jdm ein Ständchen bringen

seren|e /sı'ri:n/ a, -ly adv gelassen. ∼ity /-'renətı/ n Gelassenheit f

sergeant /'sɑ:dʒənt/ n (Mil) Feldwebel m; (in police) Polizeimeister m

serial /'sıərıəl/ n Fortsetzungsgeschichte f; (Radio, TV) Serie f. ∼ize vt in Fortsetzungen veröffentlichen/(Radio, TV) senden

series /'sıərı:z/ n inv Serie f

serious /'sıərıəs/ a, -ly adv ernst; (illness, error) schwer. ∼ness n Ernst m

sermon /'sɜ:mən/ n Predigt f

serpent /'sɜ:pənt/ n Schlange f

serrated /se'reıtıd/ a gezackt

serum /'sıərəm/ n Serum nt

servant /'sɜ:vənt/ n Diener(in) m(f)

serve /sɜ:v/ n (Tennis) Aufschlag m □ vt dienen (+ dat); bedienen (customer, guest); servieren (food); (Jur) zustellen (on s.o. jdm); verbüßen (sentence); ∼ its purpose seinen Zweck erfüllen; it ∼s you right! das geschieht dir recht! ∼s two für zwei Personen □ vi dienen; (Tennis) aufschlagen

service /'sɜ:vıs/ n Dienst m; (Relig) Gottesdienst m; (in shop, restaurant) Bedienung f; (transport) Verbindung f; (maintenance) Wartung f; (set of crockery) Service nt; (Tennis) Aufschlag m; ∼s pl Dienstleistungen pl; (on motorway) Tankstelle und Raststätte f; in the ∼s beim Militär; be of ∼ nützlich sein; out of/in ∼ (machine:) außer/ in Betrieb □ vt (Techn) warten. ∼able /-əbl/ a nützlich; (durable) haltbar

service: ∼ area n Tankstelle und Raststätte f. ∼ charge n Bedienungszuschlag m. ∼man n Soldat m. ∼ station n Tankstelle f

serviette /sɜ:vı'et/ n Serviette f

servile /'sɜ:vaıl/ a unterwürfig

session /'seʃn/ n Sitzung f; (Univ) Studienjahr nt

set /set/ n Satz m; (of crockery) Service nt; (of cutlery) Garnitur f; (TV, Radio) Apparat m; (Math) Menge f; (Theat) Bühnenbild nt; (Cinema) Szenenaufbau m; (of people) Kreis m; shampoo and ∼ Waschen und Legen □ a (ready) fertig, bereit; (rigid) fest; (book) vorgeschrieben; be ∼ on doing sth entschlossen sein, etw zu tun; be ∼ in one's ways in seinen Gewohnheiten festgefahren sein □ v (pt/pp set, pres p setting) □ vt setzen; (adjust) einstellen; stellen (task, alarm clock); festsetzen, festlegen (date, limit); aufgeben (homework); zusammenstellen (questions); [ein]fassen (gem); einrichten (bone); legen (hair); decken (table) □ vi (sun:) untergehen; (become hard) fest werden; ∼ about sth sich an etw (acc) machen; ∼ about doing sth sich daranmachen, etw zu tun. ∼ back vt zurücksetzen; (hold up) aufhalten; (fam: cost) kosten. ∼ off vi losgehen; (in vehicle) losfahren □ vt auslösen (alarm); explodieren lassen (bomb). ∼ out vi losgehen; (in vehicle) losfahren; ∼ out to do sth sich vornehmen, etw zu tun □ vt auslegen; (state) darlegen. ∼ up vt aufbauen; (fig) gründen

set 'meal n Menü nt

settee /se'ti:/ n Sofa nt, Couch f

setting /'setɪŋ/ n Rahmen m; (surroundings) Umgebung f; (of sun) Untergang m; (of jewel) Fassung f

settle /'setl/ vt (decide) entscheiden; (agree) regeln; (fix) festsetzen; (calm) beruhigen; (pay) bezahlen □ vi sich niederlassen; (snow, dust:) liegen bleiben; (subside) sich senken; (sediment:) sich absetzen. ~ **down** vi sich beruhigen; (permanently) sesshaft werden. ~ **up** vi abrechnen

settlement /'setlmənt/ n (see settle) Entscheidung f; Regelung f; Bezahlung f; (Jur) Vergleich m; (colony) Siedlung f

settler /'setlə(r)/ n Siedler m

'set-to n (fam) Streit m

'set-up n System nt

seven /'sevn/ a sieben. ~**'teen** a siebzehn. ~**'teenth** a siebzehnte(r,s)

seventh /'sevnθ/ a siebte(r,s)

seventieth /'sevntɪɪθ/ a siebzigste(r,s)

seventy /'sevntɪ/ a siebzig

sever /'sevə(r)/ vt durchtrennen; abbrechen (relations)

several /'sevrl/ a & pron mehrere, einige

sever|e /sɪ'vɪə(r)/ a (-r, -st,) -ly adv streng; (pain) stark; (illness) schwer. ~**ity** /-'verətɪ/ n Strenge f; Schwere f

sew /səʊ/ vt/i (pt sewed, pp sewn or sewed) nähen. ~ **up** vt zunähen

sewage /'suːɪdʒ/ n Abwasser nt

sewer /'suːə(r)/ n Abwasserkanal m

sewing /'səʊɪŋ/ n Nähen nt; (work) Näharbeit f. ~ **machine** n Nähmaschine f

sewn /səʊn/ see sew

sex /seks/ n Geschlecht nt; (sexuality, intercourse) Sex m. ~**ist** a sexistisch. ~ **offender** n Triebverbrecher m

sexual /'seksjʊəl/ a, -ly adv sexuell. ~ **'intercourse** n Geschlechtsverkehr m

sexuality /seksjʊ'ælətɪ/ n Sexualität f

sexy /'seksɪ/ a (-ier, -iest) sexy

shabby /'ʃæbɪ/ a (-ier, -iest), -ily adv schäbig

shack /ʃæk/ n Hütte f

shackles /'ʃæklz/ npl Fesseln pl

shade /ʃeɪd/ n Schatten m; (of colour) [Farb]ton m; (for lamp) [Lampen]schirm m; (Amer: window-blind) Jalousie f □ vt beschatten; (draw lines on) schattieren

shadow /'ʃædəʊ/ n Schatten m □ vt (follow) beschatten. ~**y** a schattenhaft

shady /'ʃeɪdɪ/ a (-ier, -iest) schattig; (fam: disreputable) zwielichtig

shaft /ʃɑːft/ n Schaft m; (Techn) Welle f; (of light) Strahl m; (of lift) Schacht m; ~**s** pl (of cart) Gabeldeichsel f

shaggy /'ʃægɪ/ a (-ier, -iest) zottig

shake /ʃeɪk/ n Schütteln nt □ v (pt shook, pp shaken) □ vt schütteln; (cause to tremble, shock) erschüttern; ~ **hands with s.o.** jdm die Hand geben □ vi wackeln; (tremble) zittern. ~ **off** vt abschütteln

shaky /'ʃeɪkɪ/ a (-ier, -iest) wackelig; (hand, voice) zittrig

shall /ʃæl/ v aux I ~ **go** ich werde gehen; **we ~ see** wir werden sehen; **what ~ I do?** was soll ich machen? **I'll come too, ~ I?** ich komme mit, ja? **thou shalt not kill** (liter) du sollst nicht töten

shallow /'ʃæləʊ/ a (-er, -est) seicht; (dish) flach; (fig) oberflächlich

sham /ʃæm/ a unecht □ n Heuchelei f; (person) Heuchler(in) m(f) □ vt (pt/pp shammed) vortäuschen

shambles /'ʃæmblz/ n Durcheinander nt

shame /ʃeɪm/ n Scham f; (disgrace) Schande f; **be a ~** schade sein; **what a ~!** wie schade! ~**-faced** a betreten

shame|ful /'ʃeɪmfl/ a, -ly adv schändlich. ~**less** a, -ly adv schamlos

shampoo /ʃæm'puː/ n Shampoo nt □ vt schamponieren

shandy /'ʃændɪ/ n Radler m

shan't /ʃɑːnt/ = shall not

shape /ʃeɪp/ n Form f; (figure) Gestalt f; **take ~** Gestalt annehmen □ vt formen (into zu) □ vi ~ **up** sich entwickeln. ~**less** a formlos; (clothing) unförmig

shapely /'ʃeɪplɪ/ a (-ier, -iest) wohlgeformt

share /ʃeə(r)/ n [An]teil m; (Comm) Aktie f □ vt/i teilen. ~**holder** n Aktionär(in) m(f)

shark /ʃɑːk/ n Hai[fisch] m

sharp /ʃɑːp/ a (-er, -est), -ly adv scharf; (pointed) spitz; (severe) heftig; (sudden) steil; (alert) clever; (unscrupulous) gerissen □ adv scharf; (Mus) zu hoch; **at six o'clock ~** Punkt sechs Uhr; **look ~!** beeil dich! □ n (Mus) Kreuz nt. ~**en** vt schärfen; [an]spitzen (pencil)

shatter /'ʃætə(r)/ vt zertrümmern; (fig) zerstören; **be ~ed** (person:) erschüttert sein; (fam: exhausted) kaputt sein □ vi zersplittern

shave /ʃeɪv/ n Rasur f; **have a ~** sich rasieren □ vt rasieren □ vi sich rasieren. ~**r** n Rasierapparat m

shaving /'ʃeɪvɪŋ/ n Rasieren nt. ~**-brush** n Rasierpinsel m

shawl /ʃɔːl/ n Schultertuch nt

she /ʃiː/ pron sie

sheaf /ʃiːf/ n (pl sheaves) Garbe f; (of papers) Bündel nt

shear /ʃɪə(r)/ vt (pt **sheared**, pp **shorn** or **sheared**) scheren

shears /ʃɪəz/ npl [große] Schere f

sheath /ʃiːθ/ n (pl ~s /ʃiːðz/) Scheide f

sheaves /ʃiːvz/ see **sheaf**

shed[1] /ʃed/ n Schuppen m; (for cattle) Stall m

shed[2] vt (pt/pp **shed**, pres p **shedding**) verlieren; vergießen ⟨blood, tears⟩; ~ **light on** Licht bringen in (+ acc)

sheen /ʃiːn/ n Glanz m

sheep /ʃiːp/ n inv Schaf nt. ~-**dog** n Hütehund m

sheepish /ʃiːpɪʃ/ a, -**ly** adv verlegen

'sheepskin n Schaffell nt

sheer /ʃɪə(r)/ a rein; (steep) steil; (transparent) hauchdünn □ adv steil

sheet /ʃiːt/ n Laken nt, Betttuch nt; (of paper) Blatt nt; (of glass, metal) Platte f

sheikh /ʃeɪk/ n Scheich m

shelf /ʃelf/ n (pl **shelves**) Brett nt, Bord nt; (set of shelves) Regal nt

shell /ʃel/ n Schale f; (of snail) Haus nt; (of tortoise) Panzer m; (on beach) Muschel f; (of unfinished building) Rohbau m; (Mil) Granate f □ vt pellen; enthülsen ⟨peas⟩; (Mil) [mit Granaten] beschießen. ~ **out** vi (fam) blechen

'shellfish n inv Schalentiere pl; (Culin) Meeresfrüchte pl

shelter /ʃeltə(r)/ n Schutz m; (air-raid ~) Luftschutzraum m □ vt schützen (**from** vor + dat) □ vi sich unterstellen. ~**ed** a geschützt; ⟨life⟩ behütet

shelve /ʃelv/ vt auf Eis legen; (abandon) aufgeben □ vi ⟨slope:⟩ abfallen

shelves /ʃelvz/ see **shelf**

shelving /ʃelvɪŋ/ n (shelves) Regale pl

shepherd /ʃepəd/ n Schäfer m; (Relig) Hirte m □ vt führen. ~**ess** n Schäferin f. ~**'s pie** n Auflauf m aus mit Kartoffelbrei bedecktem Hackfleisch

sherry /ʃerɪ/ n Sherry m

shield /ʃiːld/ n Schild m; (for eyes) Schirm m; (Techn & fig) Schutz m □ vt schützen (**from** vor + dat)

shift /ʃɪft/ n Verschiebung f; (at work) Schicht f; **make** ~ sich (dat) behelfen (**with** mit) □ vt rücken; (take away) wegnehmen; (rearrange) umstellen; schieben ⟨blame⟩ (**on** to auf + acc) □ vi sich verschieben; (fam: move quickly) rasen

'shift work n Schichtarbeit f

shifty /ʃɪftɪ/ a (-**ier**, -**iest**) (pej) verschlagen

shilly-shally /ʃɪlɪʃælɪ/ vi fackeln (fam)

shimmer /ʃɪmə(r)/ n Schimmer m □ vi schimmern

shin /ʃɪn/ n Schienbein nt

shine /ʃaɪn/ n Glanz m □ v (pt/pp **shone**) □ vi leuchten; (reflect light) glänzen; ⟨sun:⟩ scheinen □ vt ~ **a light on** beleuchten

shingle /ʃɪŋgl/ n (pebbles) Kiesel pl

shingles /ʃɪŋglz/ n (Med) Gürtelrose f

shiny /ʃaɪnɪ/ a (-**ier**, -**iest**) glänzend

ship /ʃɪp/ n Schiff nt □ vt (pt/pp **shipped**) verschiffen

ship: ~**building** n Schiffbau m. ~**ment** n Sendung f. ~**per** n Spediteur m. ~**ping** n Versand m; (traffic) Schifffahrt f. ~**shape** a & adv in Ordnung. ~**wreck** n Schiffbruch m. ~**wrecked** a schiffbrüchig. ~**yard** n Werft f

shirk /ʃɜːk/ vt sich drücken vor (+ dat). ~**er** n Drückeberger m

shirt /ʃɜːt/ n [Ober]hemd nt; (for woman) Hemdbluse f

shit /ʃɪt/ n (vulg) Scheiße f □ vi (pt/pp **shit**) (vulg) scheißen

shiver /ʃɪvə(r)/ n Schauder m □ vi zittern

shoal /ʃəʊl/ n (of fish) Schwarm m

shock /ʃɒk/ n Schock m; (Electr) Schlag m; (impact) Erschütterung f □ vt einen Schock versetzen (+ dat); (scandalize) schockieren. ~**ing** a schockierend; (fam: dreadful) fürchterlich

shod /ʃɒd/ see **shoe**

shoddy /ʃɒdɪ/ a (-**ier**, -**iest**) minderwertig

shoe /ʃuː/ n Schuh m; (of horse) Hufeisen nt □ vt (pt/pp **shod**, pres p **shoeing**) beschlagen ⟨horse⟩

shoe: ~**horn** n Schuhanzieher m. ~-**lace** n Schnürsenkel m. ~**maker** n Schuhmacher m. ~-**string** n on a ~-**string** (fam) mit ganz wenig Geld

shone /ʃɒn/ see **shine**

shoo /ʃuː/ vt scheuchen □ int sch!

shook /ʃʊk/ see **shake**

shoot /ʃuːt/ n (Bot) Trieb m; (hunt) Jagd f □ v (pt/pp **shot**) □ vt schießen; (kill) erschießen; drehen ⟨film⟩ □ vi schießen. ~ **down** vt abschießen. ~ **out** vi (rush) herausschießen. ~ **up** vi (grow) in die Höhe schießen/⟨prices:⟩ schnellen

'shooting-range n Schießstand m

shop /ʃɒp/ n Laden m, Geschäft nt; (workshop) Werkstatt f; **talk** ~ (fam) fachsimpeln □ vi (pt/pp **shopped**, pres p **shopping**) einkaufen; **go** ~**ping** einkaufen gehen

shop: ~ **assistant** n Verkäufer(in) m(f). ~**keeper** n Ladenbesitzer(in) m(f). ~-**lifter** n Ladendieb m. ~-**lifting** n Ladendiebstahl m

shopping /ʃɒpɪŋ/ n Einkaufen nt; (articles) Einkäufe pl; **do the** ~ einkaufen. ~ **bag** n Einkaufstasche f ~ **centre** n

Einkaufszentrum *nt*. ~ **trolley** *n* Einkaufswagen *m*

shop: ~ '**steward** *n* [gewerkschaftlicher] Vertrauensmann *m*. ~-'**window** *n* Schaufenster *nt*

shore /ʃɔː(r)/ *n* Strand *m*; (*of lake*) Ufer *nt*

shorn /ʃɔːn/ *see* **shear**

short /ʃɔːt/ (**er, -est**) kurz; (*person*) klein; (*curt*) schroff; **a ~ time ago** vor kurzem; **be ~ of** ... zu wenig ... haben; **be in ~ supply** knapp sein □ *adv* kurz; (*abruptly*) plötzlich; (*curtly*) kurz angebunden; **in ~** kurzum; ~ **of** (*except*) außer; **go ~** Mangel leiden; **stop ~ of doing sth** davor zurückschrecken, etw zu tun

shortage /'ʃɔːtɪdʒ/ *n* Mangel *m* (**of** an + *dat*); (*scarcity*) Knappheit *f*

short: ~**bread** *n* ≈ Mürbekekse *pl.* ~'**circuit** *n* Kurzschluss *m*. ~**coming** *n* Fehler *m*. ~ '**cut** *n* Abkürzung *f*

shorten /'ʃɔːtn/ *vt* [ab]kürzen; kürzer machen (*garment*)

short: ~**hand** *n* Kurzschrift *f*, Stenographie *f*. ~-'**handed** *a* **be ~-handed** zu wenig Personal haben. ~**hand 'typist** *n* Stenotypistin *f*. ~ **list** *n* engere Auswahl *f*. ~**-lived** /-lɪvd/ *a* kurzlebig

short|ly /'ʃɔːtlɪ/ *adv* in Kürze; ~**ly before/after** kurz vorher/danach. ~**ness** *n* Kürze *f*; (*of person*) Kleinheit *f*

shorts /ʃɔːts/ *npl* kurze Hose *f*, Shorts *pl*

short: ~-'**sighted** *a* kurzsichtig. ~-**sleeved** *a* kurzärmelig. ~-'**staffed** *a* **be ~-staffed** zu wenig Personal haben. ~-'**story** *n* Kurzgeschichte *f*. ~-'**tempered** *a* aufbrausend. ~-**term** *a* kurzfristig. ~ **wave** *n* Kurzwelle *f*

shot /ʃɒt/ *see* **shoot** □ *n* Schuss *m*; (*pellets*) Schrot *m*; (*person*) Schütze *m*; (*Phot*) Aufnahme *f*; (*injection*) Spritze *f*; (*fam: attempt*) Versuch *m*; **like a ~** (*fam*) sofort. ~**gun** *n* Schrotflinte *f*. ~-**putting** *n* (*Sport*) Kugelstoßen *nt*

should /ʃʊd/ *v aux* **you ~ go** du solltest gehen; **I ~ have seen him** ich hätte ihn sehen sollen; **I ~ like** ich möchte; **this ~ be enough** das müsste eigentlich reichen; **if he ~ be there** falls er da sein sollte

shoulder /'ʃəʊldə(r)/ *n* Schulter *f* □ *vt* schultern; (*fig*) auf sich (*acc*) nehmen. ~**blade** *n* Schulterblatt *nt*. ~-**strap** *n* Tragriemen *m*; (*on garment*) Träger *m*

shout /ʃaʊt/ *n* Schrei *m* □ *vt/i* schreien. ~ **down** *vt* niederschreien

shouting /'ʃaʊtɪŋ/ *n* Geschrei *nt*

shove /ʃʌv/ *n* Stoß *m*; (*fam*) Schubs *m* □ *vt* stoßen; (*fam*) schubsen; (*fam: put*) tun □ *vi* drängeln. ~ **off** *vi* (*fam*) abhauen

shovel /'ʃʌvl/ *n* Schaufel *f* □ *vt* (*pt/pp* **shovelled**) schaufeln

show /ʃəʊ/ *n* (*display*) Pracht *f*; (*exhibition*) Ausstellung *f*, Schau *f*; (*performance*) Vorstellung *f*; (*Theat, TV*) Show *f*; **on ~** ausgestellt □ *v* (*pt* **showed**, *pp* **shown**) □ *vt* zeigen; (*put on display*) ausstellen; *verführen* ⟨*film*⟩ □ *vi* sichtbar sein; ⟨*film:*⟩ gezeigt werden. ~ **in** *vt* hereinführen. ~ **off** *vi* (*fam*) angeben □ *vt* vorführen; (*flaunt*) angeben mit. ~ **up** *vi* [deutlich] zu sehen sein; (*fam: arrive*) auftauchen □ *vt* deutlich zeigen; (*fam: embarrass*) blamieren

'**show-down** *n* Entscheidungskampf *m*

shower /'ʃaʊə(r)/ *n* Dusche *f*; (*of rain*) Schauer *m*; **have a ~** duschen □ *vt* ~ **with** überschütten mit □ *vi* duschen. ~**proof** *a* regendicht. ~**y** *a* regnerisch

'**show-jumping** *n* Springreiten *nt*

shown /ʃəʊn/ *see* **show**

show: ~-**off** *n* Angeber(in) *m*(*f*). ~-**piece** *n* Paradestück *nt*. ~**room** *n* Ausstellungsraum *m*

showy /'ʃəʊɪ/ *a* protzig

shrank /ʃræŋk/ *see* **shrink**

shred /ʃred/ *n* Fetzen *m*; (*fig*) Spur *f* □ *vt* (*pt/pp* **shredded**) zerkleinern; (*Culin*) schnitzeln. ~**der** *n* Reißwolf *m*; (*Culin*) Schnitzelwerk *nt*

shrewd /ʃruːd/ *a* (**-er, -est**), **-ly** *adv* klug. ~**ness** *n* Klugheit *f*

shriek /ʃriːk/ *n* Schrei *m* □ *vt/i* schreien

shrift /ʃrɪft/ *n* **give s.o. short ~** jdn kurz abfertigen

shrill /ʃrɪl/ *a*, **-y** *adv* schrill

shrimp /ʃrɪmp/ *n* Garnele *f*, Krabbe *f*

shrine /ʃraɪn/ *n* Heiligtum *nt*

shrink /ʃrɪŋk/ *vi* (*pt* **shrank**, *pp* **shrunk**) schrumpfen; (*garment:*) einlaufen; (*draw back*) zurückschrecken (**from** vor + *dat*)

shrivel /'ʃrɪvl/ *vi* (*pt/pp* **shrivelled**) verschrumpeln

shroud /ʃraʊd/ *n* Leichentuch *nt*; (*fig*) Schleier *m*

Shrove /ʃrəʊv/ *n* ~ '**Tuesday** Fastnachtsdienstag *m*

shrub /ʃrʌb/ *n* Strauch *m*

shrug /ʃrʌg/ *n* Achselzucken *nt* □ *vt/i* (*pt/pp* **shrugged**) ~ [**one's shoulders**] die Achseln zucken

shrunk /ʃrʌŋk/ *see* **shrink**. ~**en** *a* geschrumpft

shudder /'ʃʌdə(r)/ *n* Schauder *m* □ *vi* schaudern; (*tremble*) zittern

shuffle /'ʃʌfl/ *vi* schlurfen □ *vt* mischen ⟨*cards*⟩

shun /ʃʌn/ *vt* (*pt/pp* **shunned**) meiden

shunt /ʃʌnt/ *vt* rangieren

shush /ʃʊʃ/ *int* sch!

shut /ʃʌt/ v (pt/pp **shut**, pres p **shutting**) □ vt zumachen, schließen; **~ one's finger in the door** sich (dat) den Finger in der Tür einklemmen □ vi sich schließen; ⟨shop:⟩ schließen, zumachen. **~ down** vt schließen; stilllegen ⟨factory:⟩ □ vi schließen; ⟨factory:⟩ stillgelegt werden. **~ up** vt abschließen; ⟨lock in⟩ einsperren □ vi (fam) den Mund halten

'shut-down n Stilllegung f

shutter /'ʃʌtə(r)/ n [Fenster]laden m; (Phot) Verschluss m

shuttle /'ʃʌtl/ n (Tex) Schiffchen nt □ vi pendeln

shuttle: **~cock** n Federball m. **~ service** n Pendelverkehr m

shy /ʃaɪ/ a (-er, -est), -ly adv schüchtern; ⟨timid⟩ scheu □ vi (pt/pp **shied**) ⟨horse:⟩ scheuen. **~ness** n Schüchternheit f

Siamese /saɪə'miːz/ a siamesisch

siblings /'sɪblɪŋz/ npl Geschwister pl

Sicily /'sɪsɪlɪ/ n Sizilien nt

sick /sɪk/ a krank; ⟨humour⟩ makaber; **be ~** (vomit) sich übergeben; **be ~ of sth** (fam) etw satt haben; **I feel ~** mir ist schlecht

sicken /'sɪkn/ vt anwidern □ vi **be ~ing for something** krank werden

sickle /'sɪkl/ n Sichel f

sick|ly /'sɪklɪ/ a (-ier, -iest) kränklich. **~ness** n Krankheit f; ⟨vomiting⟩ Erbrechen nt

'sick-room n Krankenzimmer nt

side /saɪd/ n Seite f; **on the ~** (as sideline) nebenbei; **~ by** nebeneinander; (fig) Seite an Seite; **take ~s** Partei ergreifen (**with** für); **to be on the ~** vorsichtshalber □ attrib Seiten- □ vi **~ with** Partei ergreifen für

side: **~board** n Anrichte f. **~burns** npl Koteletten pl. **~effect** n Nebenwirkung f. **~lights** npl Standlicht nt. **~line** n Nebenbeschäftigung f. **~show** n Nebenattraktion f. **~step** vt ausweichen (+ dat). **~track** vt ablenken. **~walk** n (Amer) Bürgersteig m. **~ways** adv seitwärts

siding /'saɪdɪŋ/ n Abstellgleis nt

sidle /'saɪdl/ vi sich heranschleichen (**up to** an + acc)

siege /siːdʒ/ n Belagerung f; ⟨by police⟩ Umstellung f

sieve /sɪv/ n Sieb nt □ vt sieben

sift /sɪft/ vt sieben; (fig) durchsehen

sigh /saɪ/ n Seufzer m □ vi seufzen

sight /saɪt/ n Sicht f; ⟨faculty⟩ Sehvermögen nt; ⟨spectacle⟩ Anblick m; ⟨on gun⟩ Visier nt; **~s** pl Sehenswürdigkeiten pl; **at first ~** auf den ersten Blick; **within/out of ~** in/außer Sicht; **lose ~ of** aus dem Auge verlieren; **know by ~** vom Sehen kennen; **have bad ~** schlechte Augen haben □ vt sichten

'sightseeing n **go ~** die Sehenswürdigkeiten besichtigen

sign /saɪn/ n Zeichen nt; ⟨notice⟩ Schild nt □ vt/i unterschreiben; ⟨author, artist:⟩ signieren. **~ on** vi (as unemployed) sich arbeitslos melden; (Mil) sich verpflichten

signal /'sɪgnl/ n Signal nt □ vt/i (pt/pp signalled) signalisieren; **~ to s.o.** jdm ein Signal geben (**to** zu). **~-box** n Stellwerk nt

signature /'sɪgnətʃə(r)/ n Unterschrift f; ⟨of artist⟩ Signatur f. **~ tune** n Kennmelodie f

signet-ring /'sɪgnɪt-/ n Siegelring m

significan|ce /sɪg'nɪfɪkəns/ n Bedeutung f. **~t** a, -ly adv bedeutungsvoll; (important) bedeutend

signify /'sɪgnɪfaɪ/ vt (pt/pp -ied) bedeuten

signpost /'saɪn-/ n Wegweiser m

silence /'saɪləns/ n Stille f; (of person) Schweigen nt □ vt zum Schweigen bringen. **~r** n (on gun) Schalldämpfer m; (Auto) Auspufftopf m

silent /'saɪlənt/ a, -ly adv still; (without speaking) schweigend; **remain ~** schweigen. **~ film** n Stummfilm m

silhouette /sɪlu'et/ n Silhouette f; ⟨picture⟩ Schattenriss m □ vt **be ~d** sich als Silhouette abheben

silicon /'sɪlɪkən/ n Silizium nt

silk /sɪlk/ n Seide f □ attrib Seiden-. **~worm** n Seidenraupe f

silky /'sɪlkɪ/ a (-ier, -iest) seidig

sill /sɪl/ n Sims m & nt

silly /'sɪlɪ/ a (-ier, -iest) dumm, albern

silo /'saɪləʊ/ n Silo m

silt /sɪlt/ n Schlick m

silver /'sɪlvə(r)/ a silbern; ⟨coin, paper⟩ Silber- □ n Silber nt

silver: **~-plated** a versilbert. **~ware** n Silber nt. **~ wedding** n Silberhochzeit f

similar /'sɪmɪlə(r)/ a, -ly adv ähnlich. **~ity** /-'lærətɪ/ n Ähnlichkeit f

simile /'sɪmɪlɪ/ n Vergleich m

simmer /'sɪmə(r)/ vi leise kochen, ziehen □ vt ziehen lassen

simple /'sɪmpl/ a (-r, -st) einfach; ⟨person⟩ einfältig. **~-minded** a einfältig. **~ton** /'sɪmpltən/ n Einfaltspinsel m

simplicity /sɪm'plɪsətɪ/ n Einfachheit f

simpli|fication /sɪmplɪfɪ'keɪʃn/ n Vereinfachung f. **~fy** /'sɪmplɪfaɪ/ vt (pt/pp -ied) vereinfachen

simply /'sɪmplɪ/ adv einfach

simulat|e /'sɪmjʊleɪt/ vt vortäuschen; (Techn) simulieren. **~ion** /-'leɪʃn/ n Vortäuschung f; Simulation f

simultaneous /sɪml'teɪnɪəs/ a, **-ly** adv gleichzeitig; (interpreting) Simultan-

sin /sɪn/ n Sünde f □ vi (pt/pp **sinned**) sündigen

since /sɪns/ prep seit (+ dat) □ adv seitdem □ conj seit; (because) da

sincere /sɪn'sɪə(r)/ a aufrichtig; (heartfelt) herzlich. **~ly** adv aufrichtig; **Yours ~ly** Mit freundlichen Grüßen

sincerity /sɪn'serətɪ/ n Aufrichtigkeit f

sinew /'sɪnju:/ n Sehne f

sinful /'sɪnfl/ a sündhaft

sing /sɪŋ/ vt/i (pt **sang**, pp **sung**) singen

singe /sɪndʒ/ vt (pres p **singeing**) versengen

singer /'sɪŋə(r)/ n Sänger(in) m(f)

single /'sɪŋgl/ a einzeln; (one only) einzig; (unmarried) ledig; (ticket) einfach; (room, bed) Einzel- □ n (ticket) einfache Fahrkarte f; (record) Single f; **~s** pl (Tennis) Einzel nt □ vt **~ out** auswählen

single: ~-breasted a einreihig. **~-handed** a & adv allein. **~-minded** a zielstrebig. **~ 'parent** n Alleinerziehende(r) m/f

singlet /'sɪŋglɪt/ n Unterhemd nt

singly /'sɪŋglɪ/ adv einzeln

singular /'sɪŋgjʊlə(r)/ a eigenartig; (Gram) im Singular □ n Singular m. **~ly** adv außerordentlich

sinister /'sɪnɪstə(r)/ a finster

sink /sɪŋk/ n Spülbecken nt □ v (pt **sank**, pp **sunk**) □ vi sinken □ vt versenken (ship); senken (shaft). **~ in** vi einsinken; (fam: be understood) kapiert werden

'sink unit n Spüle f

sinner /'sɪnə(r)/ n Sünder(in) m(f)

sinus /'saɪnəs/ n Nebenhöhle f

sip /sɪp/ n Schlückchen nt □ vt (pt/pp **sipped**) in kleinen Schlucken trinken

siphon /'saɪfn/ n (bottle) Siphon m. **~ off** vt mit einem Saugheber ablassen

sir /sɜ:(r)/ n mein Herr; **S~** (title) Sir; **Dear S~s** Sehr geehrte Herren

siren /'saɪrən/ n Sirene f

sissy /'sɪsɪ/ n Waschlappen m

sister /'sɪstə(r)/ n Schwester f; (nurse) Oberschwester f. **~-in-law** n (pl **~s-in-law**) Schwägerin f. **~ly** a schwesterlich

sit /sɪt/ v (pt/pp **sat**, pres p **sitting**) □ vi sitzen; (sit down) sich setzen; (committee:) tagen □ vt setzen; machen (exam). **~ back** vi sich zurücklehnen. **~ down** vi sich setzen. **~ up** vi [aufrecht] sitzen; (rise) sich aufsetzen; (not slouch) gerade sitzen; (stay up) aufbleiben

site /saɪt/ n Gelände nt; (for camping) Platz m; (Archaeol) Stätte f □ vt legen

sitting /'sɪtɪŋ/ n Sitzung f; (for meals) Schub m

situat|e /'sɪtjʊeɪt/ vt legen; **be ~ed** liegen. **~ion** /-'eɪʃn/ n Lage f; (circumstances) Situation f; (job) Stelle f

six /sɪks/ a sechs. **~teen** a sechzehn. **~teenth** a sechzehnte(r,s)

sixth /sɪksθ/ a sechste(r,s)

sixtieth /'sɪkstɪɪθ/ a sechzigste(r,s)

sixty /'sɪkstɪ/ a sechzig

size /saɪz/ n Größe f □ vt **~ up** (fam) taxieren

sizeable /'saɪzəbl/ a ziemlich groß

sizzle /'sɪzl/ vi brutzeln

skate¹ /skeɪt/ n inv (fish) Rochen m

skate² n Schlittschuh m; (roller-) Rollschuh m □ vi Schlittschuh/Rollschuh laufen. **~r** n Eisläufer(in) m(f); Rollschuhläufer(in) m(f)

skating /'skeɪtɪŋ/ n Eislaufen nt. **~-rink** n Eisbahn f

skeleton /'skelɪtn/ n Skelett nt. **~ 'key** n Dietrich m. **~ 'staff** n Minimalbesetzung f

sketch /sketʃ/ n Skizze f; (Theat) Sketch m □ vt skizzieren

sketchy /'sketʃɪ/ a (-ier, -iest), **-ily** adv skizzenhaft

skew /skju:/ n **on the ~** schräg

skewer /'skjʊə(r)/ n [Brat]spieß m

ski /ski:/ n Ski m □ vi (pt/pp **skied**, pres p **skiing**) Ski fahren or laufen

skid /skɪd/ n Schleudern nt □ vi (pt/pp **skidded**) schleudern

skier /'ski:ə(r)/ n Skiläufer(in) m(f)

skiing /'ski:ɪŋ/ n Skilaufen nt

skilful /'skɪlfl/ a, **-ly** adv geschickt

skill /skɪl/ n Geschick nt. **~ed** a geschickt; (trained) ausgebildet

skim /skɪm/ vt (pt/pp **skimmed**) entrahmen (milk). **~ off** vt abschöpfen. **~ through** vt überfliegen

skimp /skɪmp/ vt sparen an (+ dat)

skimpy /'skɪmpɪ/ a (-ier, -iest) knapp

skin /skɪn/ n Haut f; (on fruit) Schale f □ vt (pt/pp **skinned**) häuten; schälen (fruit)

skin: ~-deep a oberflächlich. **~-diving** n Sporttauchen nt

skinflint /'skɪnflɪnt/ n Geizhals m

skinny /'skɪnɪ/ a (-ier, -iest) dünn

skip¹ /skɪp/ n Container m

skip² n Hüpfer m □ v (pt/pp **skipped**) vi hüpfen; (with rope) seilspringen □ vt überspringen

skipper /'skɪpə(r)/ n Kapitän m

'skipping-rope n Sprungseil nt

skirmish /'skɜ:mɪʃ/ n Gefecht nt

skirt /skɜ:t/ n Rock m ▫ vt herumgehen um

skit /skɪt/ n parodistischer Sketch m

skittle /'skɪtl/ n Kegel m

skive /skaɪv/ vi (fam) blaumachen

skulk /skʌlk/ vi lauern

skull /skʌl/ n Schädel m

skunk /skʌŋk/ n Stinktier nt

sky /skaɪ/ n Himmel m. ~light n Dachluke f. ~scraper n Wolkenkratzer m

slab /slæb/ n Platte f; (slice) Scheibe f; (of chocolate) Tafel f

slack /slæk/ a (-er, -est) schlaff, locker; ⟨person⟩ nachlässig; (Comm) flau ▫ vi bummeln

slacken /'slækn/ vi sich lockern; (diminish) nachlassen; ⟨speed:⟩ sich verringern ▫ vt lockern; (diminish) verringern

slacks /slæks/ npl Hose f

slag /slæg/ n Schlacke f

slain /sleɪn/ see slay

slake /sleɪk/ vt löschen

slam /slæm/ v (pt/pp slammed) ▫ vt zuschlagen; (put) knallen (fam); (fam: criticize) verreißen ▫ vi zuschlagen

slander /'slɑ:ndə(r)/ n Verleumdung f ▫ vt verleumden. ~ous /-rəs/ a verleumderisch

slang /slæŋ/ n Slang m. ~y a salopp

slant /slɑ:nt/ n Schräge f; on the ~ schräg ▫ vt abschrägen; (fig) färben ⟨report⟩ ▫ vi sich neigen

slap /slæp/ n Schlag m ▫ vt (pt/pp slapped) schlagen; (put) knallen (fam) ▫ adv direkt

slap: ~dash a (fam) schludrig. ~-up a (fam) toll

slash /slæʃ/ n Schlitz m ▫ vt aufschlitzen; [drastisch] reduzieren ⟨prices⟩

slat /slæt/ n Latte f

slate /sleɪt/ n Schiefer m ▫ vt (fam) heruntermachen; verreißen ⟨performance⟩

slaughter /'slɔ:tə(r)/ n Schlachten nt; (massacre) Gemetzel nt ▫ vt schlachten; abschlachten. ~house n Schlachthaus nt

Slav /slɑ:v/ a slawisch ▫ n Slawe m/ Slawin f

slave /sleɪv/ n Sklave m/ Sklavin f ▫ vi ~ [away] schuften. ~-driver n Leuteschinder m

slav|ery /'sleɪvəri/ n Sklaverei f. ~ish a, -ly adv sklavisch

Slavonic /slə'vɒnɪk/ a slawisch

slay /sleɪ/ vt (pt slew, pp slain) ermorden

sleazy /'sli:zɪ/ a (-ier, -iest) schäbig

sledge /sledʒ/ n Schlitten m. ~hammer n Vorschlaghammer m

sleek /sli:k/ a (-er, -est) seidig; (well-fed) wohlgenährt

sleep /sli:p/ n Schlaf m; go to ~ einschlafen; put to ~ einschläfern ▫ v (pt/pp slept) ▫ vi schlafen ▫ vt (accommodate) Unterkunft bieten für. ~er n Schläfer(in) m(f); (Rail) Schlafwagen m; (on track) Schwelle f

sleeping: ~-bag n Schlafsack m. ~-car n Schlafwagen m. ~-pill n Schlaftablette f

sleep: ~less a schlaflos. ~-walking n Schlafwandeln nt

sleepy /'sli:pɪ/ a (-ier, -iest), -ily adv schläfrig

sleet /sli:t/ n Schneeregen m ▫ vi it is ~ing es gibt Schneeregen

sleeve /sli:v/ n Ärmel m; (for record) Hülle f. ~less a ärmellos

sleigh /sleɪ/ n [Pferde]schlitten m

sleight /slaɪt/ n ~ of hand Taschenspielerei f

slender /'slendə(r)/ a schlank; (fig) gering

slept /slept/ see sleep

sleuth /slu:θ/ n Detektiv m

slew¹ /slu:/ vi schwenken

slew² see slay

slice /slaɪs/ n Scheibe f ▫ vt in Scheiben schneiden; ~d bread Schnittbrot nt

slick /slɪk/ a clever ▫ n (of oil) Ölteppich m

slid|e /slaɪd/ n Rutschbahn f; (for hair) Spange f; (Phot) Dia nt ▫ v (pt/pp slid) ▫ vi rutschen ▫ vt schieben. ~ing a gleitend; ⟨door, seat⟩ Schiebe-

slight /slaɪt/ a (-er, -est), -ly adv leicht; ⟨importance⟩ gering; ⟨acquaintance⟩ flüchtig; ⟨slender⟩ schlank; not in the ~est nicht im Geringsten; ~ly better ein bisschen besser ▫ vt kränken, beleidigen ▫ n Beleidigung f

slim /slɪm/ a (slimmer, slimmest) schlank; ⟨volume⟩ schmal; (fig) gering ▫ vi eine Schlankheitskur machen

slim|e /slaɪm/ n Schleim m. ~y a schleimig

sling /slɪŋ/ n (Med) Schlinge f ▫ vt (pt/pp slung) (fam) schmeißen

slip /slɪp/ n (mistake) Fehler m, (fam) Patzer m; (petticoat) Unterrock m; (for pillow) Bezug m; (paper) Zettel m; give s.o. the ~ (fam) jdm entwischen; ~ of the tongue Versprecher m ▫ v (pt/pp slipped) ▫ vi rutschen; (fall) ausrutschen; (go quickly) schlüpfen; (decline) nachlassen ▫ vt schieben; ~ s.o.'s mind jdm entfallen. ~ away vi sich fortschleichen; ⟨time:⟩ verfliegen. ~ up vi (fam) einen Schnitzer machen

slipped 'disc *n* (*Med*) Bandscheibenvorfall *m*

slipper /'slɪpə(r)/ *n* Hausschuh *m*

slippery /'slɪpərɪ/ *a* glitschig; ⟨*surface*⟩ glatt

slipshod /'slɪpʃɒd/ *a* schludrig

'slip-up *n* (*fam*) Schnitzer *m*

slit /slɪt/ *n* Schlitz *m* □ *vt* (*pt/pp* **slit**) aufschlitzen

slither /'slɪðə(r)/ *vi* rutschen

sliver /'slɪvə(r)/ *n* Splitter *m*

slobber /'slɒbə(r)/ *vi* sabbern

slog /slɒg/ *n* [**hard**] ~ Schinderei *f* □ *v* (*pt/pp* **slogged**) □ *vi* schuften □ *vt* schlagen

slogan /'sləʊgən/ *n* Schlagwort *nt*; (*advertising*) Werbespruch *m*

slop /slɒp/ *v* (*pt/pp* **slopped**) □ *vt* verschütten □ *vi* ~ **over** überschwappen. **~s** *npl* Schmutzwasser *nt*

slop|e /sləʊp/ *n* Hang *m*; (*inclination*) Neigung *f* □ *vi* sich neigen. **~ing** *a* schräg

sloppy /'slɒpɪ/ *a* (**-ier, -iest**) schludrig; (*sentimental*) sentimental

slosh /slɒʃ/ *vi* (*fam*) platschen; ⟨*water:*⟩ schwappen □ *vt* (*fam: hit*) schlagen

slot /slɒt/ *n* Schlitz *m*; (*TV*) Sendezeit *f* □ *v* (*pt/pp* **slotted**) □ *vt* einfügen □ *vi* sich einfügen (**in** in + *acc*)

sloth /sləʊθ/ *n* Trägheit *f*

'slot-machine *n* Münzautomat *m*; (*for gambling*) Spielautomat *m*

slouch /slaʊtʃ/ *vi* sich schlecht halten

slovenly /'slʌvnlɪ/ *a* schlampig

slow /sləʊ/ *a* (**-er, -est**), **-ly** *adv* langsam; **be** ~ ⟨*clock:*⟩ nachgehen; **in** ~ **motion** in Zeitlupe □ *adv* langsam □ *vt* verlangsamen □ *vi* ~ **down**, ~ **up** langsamer werden

slow: **~coach** *n* (*fam*) Trödler *m*. **~ness** *n* Langsamkeit *f*

sludge /slʌdʒ/ *n* Schlamm *m*

slug /slʌg/ *n* Nacktschnecke *f*

sluggish /'slʌgɪʃ/ *a*, **-ly** *adv* träge

sluice /sluːs/ *n* Schleuse *f*

slum /slʌm/ *n* (*house*) Elendsquartier *nt*; **~s** *pl* Elendsviertel *nt*

slumber /'slʌmbə(r)/ *n* Schlummer *m* □ *vi* schlummern

slump /slʌmp/ *n* Sturz *m* □ *vi* fallen; (*crumple*) zusammensacken; ⟨*prices:*⟩ stürzen; ⟨*sales:*⟩ zurückgehen

slung /slʌŋ/ *see* **sling**

slur /slɜː(r)/ *n* (*discredit*) Schande *f* □ *vt* (*pt/pp* **slurred**) undeutlich sprechen

slurp /slɜːp/ *vt/i* schlürfen

slush /slʌʃ/ *n* [Schnee]matsch *m*; (*fig*) Kitsch *m*. ~ **fund** *n* Fonds *m* für Bestechungsgelder

slushy /'slʌʃɪ/ *a* matschig; (*sentimental*) kitschig

slut /slʌt/ *n* Schlampe *f* (*fam*)

sly /slaɪ/ *a* (**-er, -est**), **-ly** *adv* verschlagen □ *n* **on the** ~ heimlich

smack¹ /smæk/ *n* Schlag *m*, Klaps *m* □ *vt* schlagen; ~ **one's lips** mit den Lippen schmatzen □ *adv* (*fam*) direkt

smack² *vi* ~ **of** (*fig*) riechen nach

small /smɔːl/ *a* (**-er, -est**) klein; **in the** ~ **hours** in den frühen Morgenstunden □ *adv* **chop up** ~ klein hacken □ *n* ~ **of the back** Kreuz *nt*

small: ~ **ads** *npl* Kleinanzeigen *pl*. ~ **'change** *n* Kleingeld *nt*. ~**-holding** *n* landwirtschaftlicher Kleinbetrieb *m*. ~**pox** *n* Pocken *pl*. ~ **talk** *n* leichte Konversation *f*

smarmy /'smɑːmɪ/ *a* (**-ier, -iest**) (*fam*) ölig

smart /smɑːt/ *a* (**-er, -est**), **-ly** *adv* schick; (*clever*) schlau, clever; (*brisk*) flott; (*Amer fam: cheeky*) frech □ *vi* brennen

smarten /'smɑːtn/ *vt* ~ **oneself up** mehr auf sein Äußeres achten

smash /smæʃ/ *n* Krach *m*; (*collision*) Zusammenstoß *m*; (*Tennis*) Schmetterball *m* □ *vt* zerschlagen; (*strike*) schlagen; (*Tennis*) schmettern □ *vi* zerschmettern; (*crash*) krachen (**into** gegen). ~**ing** *a* (*fam*) toll

smattering /'smætərɪŋ/ *n* **a** ~ **of German** ein paar Brocken Deutsch

smear /smɪə(r)/ *n* verschmierter Fleck *m*; (*Med*) Abstrich *m*; (*fig*) Verleumdung *f* □ *vt* schmieren; (*coat*) beschmieren (**with** mit); (*fig*) verleumden □ *vi* schmieren

smell /smel/ *n* Geruch *m*; (*sense*) Geruchssinn *m* □ *v* (*pt/pp* **smelt** *or* **smelled**) □ *vt* riechen; (*sniff*) riechen an (+ *dat*) □ *vi* riechen (**of** nach)

smelly /'smelɪ/ *a* (**-ier, -iest**) übel riechend

smelt¹ /smelt/ *see* **smell**

smelt² *vt* schmelzen

smile /smaɪl/ *n* Lächeln *nt* □ *vi* lächeln; ~ **at** anlächeln

smirk /smɜːk/ *vi* feixen

smith /smɪθ/ *n* Schmied *m*

smithereens /smɪðə'riːnz/ *npl* **smash to** ~ in tausend Stücke schlagen

smitten /'smɪtn/ *a* ~ **with** sehr angetan von

smock /smɒk/ *n* Kittel *m*

smog /smɒg/ *n* Smog *m*

smoke /sməʊk/ *n* Rauch *m* □ *vt/i* rauchen; (*Culin*) räuchern. ~**less** *a* rauchfrei; ⟨*fuel*⟩ rauchlos

smoker /'sməʊkə(r)/ n Raucher m; (Rail) Raucherabteil nt

'smoke-screen n [künstliche] Nebelwand f

smoking /'sməʊkɪŋ/ n Rauchen nt; 'no ~' 'Rauchen verboten'

smoky /'sməʊki/ a (-ier, -iest) verraucht; ⟨taste⟩ rauchig

smooth /smu:ð/ a (-er, -est), -ly adv glatt □ vt glätten. ~ **out** vt glatt streichen

smother /'smʌðə(r)/ vt ersticken; (cover) bedecken; (suppress) unterdrücken

smoulder /'sməʊldə(r)/ vi schwelen

smudge /smʌdʒ/ n Fleck m □ vt verwischen □ vi schmieren

smug /smʌg/ a (smugger, smuggest), -ly adv selbstgefällig

smuggl|e /'smʌgl/ vt schmuggeln. ~**er** n Schmuggler m. ~**ing** n Schmuggel m

smut /smʌt/ n Rußflocke f; (mark) Rußfleck m; (fig) Schmutz m

smutty /'smʌti/ a (-ier, -iest) schmutzig

snack /snæk/ n Imbiss m. ~**bar** n Imbissstube f

snag /snæg/ n Schwierigkeit f, (fam) Haken m

snail /sneɪl/ n Schnecke f; at a ~'s pace im Schneckentempo

snake /sneɪk/ n Schlange f

snap /snæp/ n Knacken nt; (photo) Schnappschuss m □ attrib (decision) plötzlich □ v (pt/pp snapped) □ vi [entzwei]brechen; ~ **at** (bite) schnappen nach; (speak sharply) [scharf] anfahren □ vt zerbrechen; (say) fauchen; (Phot) knipsen. ~ **up** vt wegschnappen

snappy /'snæpi/ a (-ier, -iest) bissig; (smart) flott; make it ~! ein bisschen schnell!

'snapshot n Schnappschuss m

snare /sneə(r)/ n Schlinge f

snarl /snɑ:l/ vi [mit gefletschten Zähnen] knurren

snatch /snætʃ/ n (fragment) Fetzen pl; (theft) Raub m; make a ~ at greifen nach □ vt schnappen; (steal) klauen; entführen ⟨child⟩; ~ sth from s.o. jdm etw entreißen

sneak /sni:k/ n (fam) Petze f □ vi schleichen; (fam: tell tales) petzen □ vt (take) mitgehen lassen □ vi ~ **in/out** sich hinein-/hinausschleichen

sneakers /'sni:kəz/ npl (Amer) Turnschuhe pl

sneaking /'sni:kɪŋ/ a heimlich; ⟨suspicion⟩ leise

sneaky /'sni:ki/ a hinterhältig

sneer /snɪə(r)/ vi höhnisch lächeln; (mock) spotten

sneeze /sni:z/ n Niesen nt □ vi niesen

snide /snaɪd/ a (fam) abfällig

sniff /snɪf/ vi schnüffeln □ vt schnüffeln an (+ dat); schnüffeln ⟨glue⟩

snigger /'snɪgə(r)/ vi [boshaft] kichern

snip /snɪp/ n Schnitt m; (fam: bargain) günstiger Kauf m □ vt/i ~ **[at]** schnippeln an (+ dat)

snipe /snaɪp/ vi ~ **at** aus dem Hinterhalt schießen auf (+ acc); (fig) anschießen. ~**r** n Heckenschütze m

snippet /'snɪpɪt/ n Schnipsel m; (of information) Bruchstück nt

snivel /'snɪvl/ vi (pt/pp snivelled) flennen

snob /snɒb/ n Snob m. ~**bery** n Snobismus m. ~**bish** a snobistisch

snoop /snu:p/ vi (fam) schnüffeln

snooty /'snu:ti/ a (fam) hochnäsig

snooze /snu:z/ n Nickerchen nt □ vi dösen

snore /snɔ:(r)/ vi schnarchen

snorkel /'snɔ:kl/ n Schnorchel m

snort /snɔ:t/ vi schnauben

snout /snaʊt/ n Schnauze f

snow /snəʊ/ n Schnee m □ vi schneien; ~**ed under with** (fig) überhäuft mit

snow: ~**ball** n Schneeball m □ vi lawinenartig anwachsen. ~**drift** n Schneewehe f. ~**drop** n Schneeglöckchen nt. ~**fall** n Schneefall m. ~**flake** n Schneeflocke f. ~ **flurry** n Schneegestöber nt. ~**man** n Schneemann m. ~**plough** n Schneepflug m. ~**storm** n Schneesturm m

snub /snʌb/ n Abfuhr f □ vt (pt/pp snubbed) brüskieren

'snub-nosed a stupsnasig

snuff¹ /snʌf/ n Schnupftabak m

snuff² vt ~ **[out]** löschen

snuffle /'snʌfl/ vi schnüffeln

snug /snʌg/ a (snugger, snuggest) behaglich, gemütlich

snuggle /'snʌgl/ vi sich kuscheln (up to + acc)

so /səʊ/ adv so; not so fast nicht so schnell; so am I ich auch; so does he er auch; so I see das sehe ich; that is so das stimmt; so much the better umso besser; so it is tatsächlich; if so wenn ja; so as to um zu; so long! (fam) tschüs! □ pron I hope so hoffentlich; I think so ich glaube schon; I told you so ich hab's dir gleich gesagt; because I say so weil ich es sage; I'm afraid so leider ja; so saying/doing, he/she . . . indem er/sie das sagte/tat, . . .; an hour or so eine Stunde oder so; very much so durchaus □ conj (therefore) also; so that damit; so there! fertig! so what! na und! so you see wie du siehst; so where have you been? wo warst du denn?

soak /səʊk/ *vt* nass machen; *(steep)* einweichen; *(fam: fleece)* schröpfen □ *vi* weichen; *(liquid:)* sickern. ~ **up** *vt* aufsaugen

soaking /'səʊkɪŋ/ *a & adv* ~ **[wet]** patschnass *(fam)*

soap /səʊp/ *n* Seife *f*. ~ **opera** *n* Seifenoper *f*. ~ **powder** *n* Seifenpulver *nt*

soapy /'səʊpɪ/ *a* (-ier, -iest) seifig

soar /sɔː(r)/ *vi* aufsteigen; *(prices:)* in die Höhe schnellen

sob /sɒb/ *n* Schluchzer *m* □ *vi* (pt/pp **sobbed**) schluchzen

sober /'səʊbə(r)/ *a*, **-ly** *adv* nüchtern; *(serious)* ernst; *(colour)* gedeckt. ~ **up** *vi* nüchtern werden

'so-called *a* sogenannt

soccer /'sɒkə(r)/ *n (fam)* Fußball *m*

sociable /'səʊʃəbl/ *a* gesellig

social /'səʊʃl/ *a* gesellschaftlich; *(Admin, Pol, Zool)* sozial

socialis|m /'səʊʃəlɪzm/ *n* Sozialismus *m*. ~**t** /-ɪst/ *a* sozialistisch □ *n* Sozialist *m*

socialize /'səʊʃəlaɪz/ *vi* [gesellschaftlich] verkehren

socially /'səʊʃəlɪ/ *adv* gesellschaftlich; **know** ~ privat kennen

social: ~ **se'curity** *n* Sozialhilfe *f*. ~ **work** *n* Sozialarbeit *f*. ~ **worker** *n* Sozialarbeiter(in) *m(f)*

society /sə'saɪətɪ/ *n* Gesellschaft *f*; *(club)* Verein *m*

sociolog|ist /səʊsɪ'ɒlədʒɪst/ *n* Soziologe *m*. ~**y** *n* Soziologie *f*

sock¹ /sɒk/ *n* Socke *f*; *(knee-length)* Kniestrumpf *m*

sock² *n (fam)* Schlag *m* □ *vt (fam)* hauen

socket /'sɒkɪt/ *n (of eye)* Augenhöhle *f*; *(of joint)* Gelenkpfanne *f*; *(wall plug)* Steckdose *f*; *(for bulb)* Fassung *f*

soda /'səʊdə/ *n* Soda *nt*; *(Amer)* Limonade *f*. ~ **water** *n* Sodawasser *nt*

sodden /'sɒdn/ *a* durchnässt

sodium /'səʊdɪəm/ *n* Natrium *nt*

sofa /'səʊfə/ *n* Sofa *nt*. ~ **bed** *n* Schlafcouch *f*

soft /sɒft/ *a* (-er, -est), **-ly** *adv* weich; *(quiet)* leise; *(gentle)* sanft; *(fam: silly)* dumm; **have a** ~ **spot for s.o.** jdn mögen. ~ **drink** *n* alkoholfreies Getränk *nt*

soften /'sɒfn/ *vt* weich machen; *(fig)* mildern □ *vi* weich werden

soft: ~ **toy** *n* Stofftier *nt*. ~**ware** *n* Software *f*

soggy /'sɒgɪ/ *a* (-ier, -iest) aufgeweicht

soil¹ /sɔɪl/ *n* Erde *f*, Boden *m*

soil² *vt* verschmutzen

solace /'sɒləs/ *n* Trost *m*

solar /'səʊlə(r)/ *a* Sonnen-

sold /səʊld/ *see* **sell**

solder /'səʊldə(r)/ *n* Lötmetall *nt* □ *vt* löten

soldier /'səʊldʒə(r)/ *n* Soldat *m* □ *vi* ~ **on** [unbeirrt] weitermachen

sole¹ /səʊl/ *n* Sohle *f*

sole² *n (fish)* Seezunge *f*

sole³ *a* einzig. ~**ly** *adv* einzig und allein

solemn /'sɒləm/ *a*, **-ly** *adv* feierlich; *(serious)* ernst. ~**ity** /sə'lemnətɪ/ *n* Feierlichkeit *f*; Ernst *m*

solicit /sə'lɪsɪt/ *vt* bitten um □ *vi (prostitute:)* sich an Männer heranmachen

solicitor /sə'lɪsɪtə(r)/ *n* Rechtsanwalt *m* /-anwältin *f*

solicitous /sə'lɪsɪtəs/ *a* besorgt

solid /'sɒlɪd/ *a* fest; *(sturdy)* stabil; *(not hollow, of same substance)* massiv; *(unanimous)* einstimmig; *(complete)* ganz □ *n (Geom)* Körper *m*; ~**s** *pl (food)* feste Nahrung *f*

solidarity /sɒlɪ'dærətɪ/ *n* Solidarität *f*

solidify /sə'lɪdɪfaɪ/ *vi* (pt/pp **-ied**) fest werden

soliloquy /sə'lɪləkwɪ/ *n* Selbstgespräch *nt*

solitary /'sɒlɪtərɪ/ *a* einsam; *(sole)* einzig. ~ con'finement *n* Einzelhaft *f*

solitude /'sɒlɪtjuːd/ *n* Einsamkeit *f*

solo /'səʊləʊ/ *n* Solo *nt* □ *a* Solo-; *(flight)* Allein- □ *adv* solo. ~**ist** *n* Solist(in) *m(f)*

solstice /'sɒlstɪs/ *n* Sonnenwende *f*

soluble /'sɒljʊbl/ *a* löslich; *(solvable)* lösbar

solution /sə'luːʃn/ *n* Lösung *f*

solvable /'sɒlvəbl/ *a* lösbar

solve /sɒlv/ *vt* lösen

solvent /'sɒlvənt/ *a* zahlungsfähig; *(Chem)* lösend □ *n* Lösungsmittel *nt*

sombre /'sɒmbə(r)/ *a* dunkel; *(mood)* düster

some /sʌm/ *a & pron* etwas; *(a little)* ein bisschen; *(with pl noun)* einige; *(a few)* ein paar; *(certain)* manche(r,s); *(one or the other)* [irgend]ein; ~ **day** eines Tages; **I want** ~ ich möchte etwas; *(pl)* welche; **will you have** ~ **wine?** möchten Sie Wein? **I need** ~ **money/books** ich brauche Geld/Bücher; **do** ~ **shopping** einkaufen

some: ~**body** /-bədɪ/ *pron & n* jemand; *(emphatic)* irgendjemand. ~**how** *adv* irgendwie. ~**one** *pron & n* = **somebody**

somersault /'sʌməsɔːlt/ *n* Purzelbaum *m (fam)*; *(Sport)* Salto *m*; **turn a** ~ einen Purzelbaum schlagen/einen Salto springen

'something *pron & adv* etwas; *(emphatic)* irgendetwas; ~ **different** etwas anderes;

~ **like** so etwas wie; **see** ~ **of** s.o. jdn mal sehen

some: ~**time** *adv* irgendwann □ *a* ehemalig. ~**times** *adv* manchmal. ~**what** *adv* ziemlich. ~**where** *adv* irgendwo; ⟨go⟩ irgendwohin

son /sʌn/ *n* Sohn *m*

sonata /sə'nɑ:tə/ *n* Sonate *f*

song /sɒŋ/ *n* Lied *nt*. ~**bird** *n* Singvogel *m*

sonic /'sɒnɪk/ *a* Schall-. ~ '**boom** *n* Überschallknall *m*

'**son-in-law** *n* (*pl* ~**s-in-law**) Schwiegersohn *m*

soon /su:n/ *adv* (-er, -est) bald; ⟨quickly⟩ schnell; **too** ~ zu früh; **as** ~ **as** sobald; **as** ~ **as possible** so bald wie möglich; ~**er or later** früher oder später; **no** ~**er had I arrived than** ... kaum war ich angekommen, da ...; **I would** ~**er stay** ich würde lieber bleiben

soot /sʊt/ *n* Ruß *m*

sooth|e /su:ð/ *vt* beruhigen; lindern ⟨pain⟩. ~**ing** *a*, **-ly** *adv* beruhigend; lindernd

sooty /'sʊtɪ/ *a* rußig

sop /sɒp/ *n* Beschwichtigungsmittel *nt*

sophisticated /sə'fɪstɪkeɪtɪd/ *a* weltgewandt; ⟨complex⟩ hoch entwickelt

soporific /sɒpə'rɪfɪk/ *a* einschläfernd

sopping /'sɒpɪŋ/ *a* & *adv* ~ [**wet**] durchnässt

soppy /'sɒpɪ/ *a* (-ier, -iest) ⟨fam⟩ rührselig

soprano /sə'prɑ:nəʊ/ *n* Sopran *m*; ⟨woman⟩ Sopranistin *f*

sordid /'sɔ:dɪd/ *a* schmutzig

sore /sɔ:(r)/ *a* (-r, -st) wund; ⟨painful⟩ schmerzhaft; **have a** ~ **throat** Halsschmerzen haben □ *n* wunde Stelle *f*. ~**ly** *adv* sehr

sorrow /'sɒrəʊ/ *n* Kummer *m*, Leid *nt*. ~**ful** *a* traurig

sorry /'sɒrɪ/ *a* (-ier, -iest) ⟨sad⟩ traurig; ⟨wretched⟩ erbärmlich; **I am** ~ es tut mir Leid; **she is** *or* **feels** ~ **for him** er tut ihr Leid; **I am** ~ **to say** leider; ~! Entschuldigung!

sort /sɔ:t/ *n* Art *f*; ⟨brand⟩ Sorte *f*; **he's a good** ~ ⟨fam⟩ er ist in Ordnung; **be out of** ~**s** ⟨fam⟩ nicht auf der Höhe sein □ *vt* sortieren. ~ **out** *vt* sortieren; ⟨fig⟩ klären

sought /sɔ:t/ *see* **seek**

soul /səʊl/ *n* Seele *f*. ~**ful** *a* gefühlvoll

sound[1] /saʊnd/ *a* (-er, -est) gesund; ⟨sensible⟩ vernünftig; ⟨secure⟩ solide; ⟨thorough⟩ gehörig □ *adv* **be** ~ **asleep** fest schlafen

sound[2] *vt* ⟨Naut⟩ loten. ~ **out** *vt* ⟨fig⟩ aushorchen

sound[3] *n* ⟨strait⟩ Meerenge *f*

sound[4] *n* Laut *m*; ⟨noise⟩ Geräusch *nt*; ⟨Phys⟩ Schall *m*; ⟨Radio, TV⟩ Ton *m*; ⟨of bells, music⟩ Klang *m*; **I don't like the** ~ **of it** ⟨fam⟩ das hört sich nicht gut an □ *vi* [er]tönen; ⟨seem⟩ sich anhören □ *vt* ⟨pronounce⟩ aussprechen; schlagen ⟨alarm⟩; ⟨Med⟩ abhorchen ⟨chest⟩. ~ **barrier** *n* Schallmauer *f*. ~**less** *a*, **-ly** *adv* lautlos

soundly /'saʊndlɪ/ *adv* solide; ⟨sleep⟩ fest; ⟨defeat⟩ vernichtend

'**soundproof** *a* schalldicht

soup /su:p/ *n* Suppe *f*. ~**ed-up** *a* ⟨fam⟩ ⟨engine⟩ frisiert

soup: ~**-plate** *n* Suppenteller *m*. ~**spoon** *n* Suppenlöffel *m*

sour /'saʊə(r)/ *a* (-er, -est) sauer; ⟨bad-tempered⟩ griesgrämig, verdrießlich

source /sɔ:s/ *n* Quelle *f*

south /saʊθ/ *n* Süden *m*; **to the** ~ **of** südlich von □ *a* Süd-, süd- □ *adv* nach Süden

south: **S**~ '**Africa** *n* Südafrika *nt*. **S**~ **A'merica** *n* Südamerika *nt*. ~-'**east** *n* Südosten *m*

southerly /'sʌðəlɪ/ *a* südlich

southern /'sʌðən/ *a* südlich

South 'Pole *n* Südpol *m*

'**southward**[**s**] /-wəd[z]/ *adv* nach Süden

souvenir /su:və'nɪə(r)/ *n* Andenken *nt*, Souvenir *nt*

sovereign /'sɒvrɪn/ *a* souverän □ *n* Souverän *m*. ~**ty** *n* Souveränität *f*

Soviet /'səʊvɪət/ *a* sowjetisch; ~ **Union** *n* Sowjetunion *f*

sow[1] /saʊ/ *n* Sau *f*

sow[2] /səʊ/ *vt* (*pt* **sowed**, *pp* **sown** *or* **sowed**) säen

soya /'sɔɪə/ *n* ~ **bean** Sojabohne *f*

spa /spɑ:/ *n* Heilbad *nt*

space /speɪs/ *n* Raum *m*; ⟨gap⟩ Platz *m*; ⟨Astr⟩ Weltraum *m*; **leave/clear a** ~ Platz lassen/schaffen □ *vt* ~ [**out**] [in Abständen] verteilen

space: ~**craft** *n* Raumfahrzeug *nt*. ~**ship** *n* Raumschiff *nt*

spacious /'speɪʃəs/ *a* geräumig

spade /speɪd/ *n* Spaten *m*; ⟨for child⟩ Schaufel *f*; ~ *pl* ⟨Cards⟩ Pik *nt*; **call a** ~ **a** ~ das Kind beim rechten Namen nennen. ~**work** *n* Vorarbeit *f*

Spain /speɪn/ *n* Spanien *nt*

span[1] /spæn/ *n* Spanne *f*; ⟨of arch⟩ Spannweite *f* □ *vt* (*pt/pp* **spanned**) überspannen; umspannen ⟨time⟩

span[2] *see* **spick**

Span|iard /'spænjəd/ *n* Spanier(in) *m(f)*. ~**ish** *a* spanisch □ *n* ⟨Lang⟩ Spanisch *nt*; **the** ~**ish** *pl* die Spanier

spank /spæŋk/ *vt* verhauen

spanner /'spænə(r)/ *n* Schraubenschlüssel *m*

spar /spɑː(r)/ *vi* (*pt/pp* **sparred**) (*Sport*) sparren; (*argue*) sich zanken

spare /speə(r)/ *a* (*surplus*) übrig; (*additional*) zusätzlich; (*seat, time*) frei; (*room*) Gäste-; (*bed, cup*) Extra- □ *n* (*part*) Ersatzteil *nt* □ *vt* ersparen; (*not hurt*) verschonen; (*do without*) entbehren; (*afford to give*) erübrigen; **to ~** (*surplus*) übrig. **~ 'wheel** *n* Reserverad *nt*

sparing /'speərɪŋ/ *a*, **-ly** *adv* sparsam

spark /spɑːk/ *n* Funke *m* □ *vt* **~ off** zünden; (*fig*) auslösen. **~ing-plug** *n* (*Auto*) Zündkerze *f*

sparkl|e /'spɑːkl/ *n* Funkeln *nt* □ *vi* funkeln. **~ing** *a* funkelnd; (*wine*) Schaum-

sparrow /'spærəʊ/ *n* Spatz *m*

sparse /spɑːs/ *a* spärlich. **~ly** *adv* spärlich; (*populated*) dünn

Spartan /'spɑːtn/ *a* spartanisch

spasm /'spæzm/ *n* Anfall *m*; (*cramp*) Krampf *m*. **~odic** /-'mɒdɪk/ *a*, **-ally** *adv* sporadisch; (*Med*) krampfartig

spastic /'spæstɪk/ *a* spastisch [gelähmt] □ *n* Spastiker(in) *m(f)*

spat /spæt/ *see* **spit**[2]

spate /speɪt/ *n* Flut *f*; (*series*) Serie *f*; **be in full ~** Hochwasser führen

spatial /'speɪʃl/ *a* räumlich

spatter /'spætə(r)/ *vt* spritzen; **~ with** bespritzen mit

spatula /'spætjʊlə/ *n* Spachtel *m*; (*Med*) Spatel *m*

spawn /spɔːn/ *n* Laich *m* □ *vi* laichen □ *vt* (*fig*) hervorbringen

spay /speɪ/ *vt* sterilisieren

speak /spiːk/ *v* (*pt* **spoke**, *pp* **spoken**) □ *vi* sprechen (**to** mit) **~ing!** (*Teleph*) am Apparat! □ *vt* sprechen; sagen (*truth*). **~ up** *vi* lauter sprechen; **~ up for oneself** seine Meinung äußern

speaker /'spiːkə(r)/ *n* Sprecher(in) *m(f)*; (*in public*) Redner(in) *m(f)*; (*loudspeaker*) Lautsprecher *m*

spear /spɪə(r)/ *n* Speer *m* □ *vt* aufspießen. **~head** *vt* (*fig*) anführen

spec /spek/ *n* **on ~** (*fam*) auf gut Glück

special /'speʃl/ *a* besondere(r,s), speziell. **~ist** *n* Spezialist *m*; (*Med*) Facharzt *m* /-ärztin *f*. **~ity** /-ʃɪ'ælətɪ/ *n* Spezialität *f*

special|ize /'speʃəlaɪz/ *vi* sich spezialisieren (**in** auf + *acc*). **~ly** *adv* speziell; (*particularly*) besonders

species /'spiːʃiːz/ *n* Art *f*

specific /spə'sɪfɪk/ *a* bestimmt; (*precise*) genau; (*Phys*) spezifisch. **~ally** *adv* ausdrücklich

specification /spesɪfɪ'keɪʃn/ *n* & **~s** *pl* genaue Angaben *pl*

specify /'spesɪfaɪ/ *vt* (*pt/pp* **-ied**) [genau] angeben

specimen /spesɪmən/ *n* Exemplar *nt*; (*sample*) Probe *f*; (*of urine*) Urinprobe *f*

speck /spek/ *n* Fleck *m*; (*particle*) Teilchen *nt*

speckled /'spekld/ *a* gesprenkelt

specs /speks/ *npl* (*fam*) Brille *f*

spectacle /'spektəkl/ *n* (*show*) Schauspiel *nt*; (*sight*) Anblick *m*. **~s** *npl* Brille *f*

spectacular /spek'tækjʊlə(r)/ *a* spektakulär

spectator /spek'teɪtə(r)/ *n* Zuschauer(in) *m(f)*

spectre /'spektə(r)/ *n* Gespenst *nt*; (*fig*) Schreckgespenst *nt*

spectrum /'spektrəm/ *n* (*pl* **-tra**) Spektrum *nt*

speculat|e /'spekjʊleɪt/ *vi* spekulieren. **~ion** /-'leɪʃn/ *n* Spekulation *f*. **~or** *n* Spekulant *m*

sped /sped/ *see* **speed**

speech /spiːtʃ/ *n* Sprache *f*; (*address*) Rede *f*. **~less** *a* sprachlos

speed /spiːd/ *n* Geschwindigkeit *f*; (*rapidity*) Schnelligkeit *f*; (*gear*) Gang *m*; **at ~** mit hoher Geschwindigkeit □ *vi* (*pt/pp* **sped**) schnell fahren □ (*pt/pp* **speeded**) (*go too fast*) zu schnell fahren. **~ up** (*pt/pp* **speeded up**) □ *vt* beschleunigen □ *vi* schneller werden; (*vehicle:*) schneller fahren

speed: ~boat *n* Rennboot *nt*. **~ing** *n* Geschwindigkeitsüberschreitung *f*. **~ limit** *n* Geschwindigkeitsbeschränkung *f*

speedometer /spiː'dɒmɪtə(r)/ *n* Tachometer *m*

speedy /'spiːdɪ/ *a* (**-ier, -iest**), **-ily** *adv* schnell

spell[1] /spel/ *n* Weile *f*; (*of weather*) Periode *f*

spell[2] *v* (*pt/pp* **spelled** or **spelt**) □ *vt* schreiben; (*aloud*) buchstabieren; (*fig: mean*) bedeuten □ *vi* richtig schreiben; (*aloud*) buchstabieren. **~ out** *vt* buchstabieren; (*fig*) genau erklären

spell[3] *n* Zauber *m*; (*words*) Zauberspruch *m*. **~bound** *a* wie verzaubert

spelling /'spelɪŋ/ *n* Schreibweise *f*; (*orthography*) Rechtschreibung *f*

spelt /spelt/ *see* **spell**[2]

spend /spend/ *vt/i* (*pt/pp* **spent**) ausgeben; verbringen (*time*)

spent /spent/ *see* **spend**

sperm /spɜːm/ *n* Samen *m*

spew /spjuː/ *vt* speien

spher|e /sfɪə(r)/ n Kugel f; (fig) Sphäre f. ~**ical** /ˈsferɪkl/ a kugelförmig

spice /spaɪs/ n Gewürz nt; (fig) Würze f

spick /spɪk/ a ~ **and span** blitzsauber

spicy /ˈspaɪsɪ/ a würzig, pikant

spider /ˈspaɪdə(r)/ n Spinne f

spik|e /spaɪk/ n Spitze f; (Bot, Zool) Stachel m; (on shoe) Spike m. ~**y** a stachelig

spill /spɪl/ v (pt/pp spilt or spilled) □ vt verschütten; vergießen ⟨blood⟩ □ vi überlaufen

spin /spɪn/ v (pt/pp spun, pres p spinning) □ vt drehen; spinnen ⟨wool⟩; schleudern ⟨washing⟩ □ vi sich drehen. ~ **out** vt in die Länge ziehen

spinach /ˈspɪnɪdʒ/ n Spinat m

spinal /ˈspaɪnl/ a Rückgrat-. ~ '**cord** n Rückenmark nt

spindl|e /ˈspɪndl/ n Spindel f. ~**y** a spindeldürr

spin-'drier n Wäscheschleuder f

spine /spaɪn/ n Rückgrat nt; (of book) [Buch]rücken m; (Bot, Zool) Stachel m. ~**less** a (fig) rückgratlos

spinning /ˈspɪnɪŋ/ n Spinnen nt. ~-**wheel** n Spinnrad nt

'spin-off n Nebenprodukt nt

spinster /ˈspɪnstə(r)/ n ledige Frau f

spiral /ˈspaɪrl/ a spiralig □ n Spirale f □ vi (pt/pp spiralled) sich hochwinden; ⟨smoke:⟩ in einer Spirale aufsteigen. ~ '**staircase** n Wendeltreppe f

spire /ˈspaɪə(r)/ n Turmspitze f

spirit /ˈspɪrɪt/ n Geist m; (courage) Mut m; ~**s** pl (alcohol) Spirituosen pl; **in high** ~**s** in gehobener Stimmung; **in low** ~**s** niedergedrückt. ~ **away** vt verschwinden lassen

spirited /ˈspɪrɪtɪd/ a lebhaft; (courageous) beherzt

spirit: ~-**level** n Wasserwaage f. ~ **stove** n Spirituskocher m

spiritual /ˈspɪrɪtjʊəl/ a geistig; (Relig) geistlich. ~**ism** /-ɪzm/ n Spiritismus m. ~**ist** /-ɪst/ a spiritistisch □ n Spiritist m

spit¹ /spɪt/ n (for roasting) [Brat]spieß m

spit² n Spucke f □ vt/i (pt/pp spat, pres p spitting) spucken; ⟨cat:⟩ fauchen; ⟨fat:⟩ spritzen; **it's** ~**ting with rain** es tröpfelt; **be the** ~**ting image of s.o.** jdm wie aus dem Gesicht geschnitten sein

spite /spaɪt/ n Boshaftigkeit f; **in** ~ **of** trotz (+ gen) □ vt ärgern. ~**ful** a, -**ly** adv gehässig

spittle /ˈspɪtl/ n Spucke f

splash /splæʃ/ n Platschen nt; (fam: drop) Schuss m; ~ **of colour** Farbfleck m □ vt spritzen; ~ **s.o. with sth** jdn mit etw bespritzen □ vi spritzen. ~ **about** vi planschen

spleen /spliːn/ n Milz f

splendid /ˈsplendɪd/ a herrlich, großartig

splendour /ˈsplendə(r)/ n Pracht f

splint /splɪnt/ n (Med) Schiene f

splinter /ˈsplɪntə(r)/ n Splitter m □ vi zersplittern

split /splɪt/ n Spaltung f; (Pol) Bruch m; (tear) Riss m □ v (pt/pp split, pres p splitting) □ vt spalten; (share) teilen; (tear) zerreißen; ~ **one's sides** sich kaputtlachen □ vi sich spalten; (tear) zerreißen; ~ **on s.o.** (fam) jdn verpfeifen. ~ **up** vt aufteilen □ vi ⟨couple:⟩ sich trennen

splutter /ˈsplʌtə(r)/ vi prusten

spoil /spɔɪl/ n ~**s** pl Beute f □ v (pt/pp spoilt or spoiled) □ vt verderben; verwöhnen ⟨person⟩ □ vi verderben. ~**sport** n Spielverderber m

spoke¹ /spəʊk/ n Speiche f

spoke², **spoken** /ˈspəʊkn/ see speak

'spokesman n Sprecher m

sponge /spʌndʒ/ n Schwamm m □ vt abwaschen □ vi ~ **on** schmarotzen bei. ~-**bag** n Waschbeutel m. ~-**cake** n Biskuitkuchen m

spong|er /ˈspʌndʒə(r)/ n Schmarotzer m. ~**y** a schwammig

sponsor /ˈspɒnsə(r)/ n Sponsor m; (godparent) Pate m/Patin f; (for membership) Bürge m □ vt sponsern; bürgen für

spontaneous /spɒnˈteɪnɪəs/ a, -**ly** adv spontan

spoof /spuːf/ n (fam) Parodie f

spooky /ˈspuːkɪ/ a (-ier, -iest) (fam) gespenstisch

spool /spuːl/ n Spule f

spoon /spuːn/ n Löffel m □ vt löffeln. ~-**feed** vt (pt/pp -fed) (fig) alles vorkauen (+ dat). ~**ful** n Löffel m

sporadic /spəˈrædɪk/ a, -**ally** adv sporadisch

sport /spɔːt/ n Sport m; (amusement) Spaß m □ vt [stolz] tragen. ~**ing** a sportlich; **a** ~**ing chance** eine faire Chance

sports: ~**car** n Sportwagen m. ~ **coat** n, ~ **jacket** n Sakko m. ~**man** n Sportler m. ~**woman** n Sportlerin f

sporty /ˈspɔːtɪ/ a (-ier, -iest) sportlich

spot /spɒt/ n Fleck m; (place) Stelle f; (dot) Punkt m; (drop) Tropfen m; (pimple) Pickel m; ~**s** pl (rash) Ausschlag m; **a** ~ **of** (fam) ein bisschen; **on the** ~ auf der Stelle; **be in a tight** ~ (fam) in der Klemme sitzen □ vt (pt/pp spotted) entdecken

spot: ~ '**check** n Stichprobe f. ~**less** a makellos; (fam: very clean) blitzsauber. ~**light** n Scheinwerfer m; (fig) Rampenlicht nt

spotted /'spɒtɪd/ a gepunktet

spotty /'spɒtɪ/ a (-ier, -iest) fleckig; (pimply) pickelig

spouse /spauz/ n Gatte m/Gattin f

spout /spaut/ n Schnabel m, Tülle f □ vi schießen (**from** aus)

sprain /spreɪn/ n Verstauchung f □ vt verstauchen

sprang /spræŋ/ see **spring**[2]

sprat /spræt/ n Sprotte f

sprawl /sprɔ:l/ vi sich ausstrecken; (fall) der Länge nach hinfallen

spray[1] /spreɪ/ n (of flowers) Strauß m

spray[2] n Sprühnebel m; (from sea) Gischt m; (device) Spritze f; (container) Sprühdose f; (preparation) Spray nt □ vt spritzen; (with aerosol) sprühen

spread /spred/ n Verbreitung f; (paste) Aufstrich m; (fam: feast) Festessen nt □ v (pt/pp **spread**) □ vt ausbreiten; streichen ⟨butter, jam⟩; bestreichen ⟨bread, surface⟩; streuen ⟨sand, manure⟩; verbreiten ⟨news, disease⟩; verteilen ⟨payments⟩ □ vi sich ausbreiten. ~ **out** vt ausbreiten; (space out) verteilen □ vi sich verteilen

spree /spri:/ n (fam) **go on a shopping ~** groß einkaufen gehen

sprig /sprɪg/ n Zweig m

sprightly /'spraɪtlɪ/ a (-ier, -iest) rüstig

spring[1] /sprɪŋ/ n Frühling m □ attrib Frühlings-

spring[2] n (jump) Sprung m; (water) Quelle f; (device) Feder f; (elasticity) Elastizität f □ v (pt **sprang**, pp **sprung**) □ vi springen; (arise) entspringen (**from** dat) □ vt ~ **sth on s.o.** jdn mit etw überfallen

spring: ~**board** n Sprungbrett nt. ~'**cleaning** n Frühjahrsputz m. ~**time** n Frühling m

sprinkl|e /'sprɪŋkl/ vt sprengen; (scatter) streuen; bestreuen ⟨surface⟩. ~**er** n Sprinkler m; (Hort) Sprenger m. ~**ing** n dünne Schicht f

sprint /sprɪnt/ n Sprint m □ vi rennen; (Sport) sprinten. ~**er** n Kurzstreckenläufer(in) m(f)

sprout /spraut/ n Trieb m; [**Brussels**] ~**s** pl Rosenkohl m □ vi sprießen

spruce /spru:s/ a gepflegt □ n Fichte f

sprung /sprʌŋ/ see **spring**[2] □ a gefedert

spry /spraɪ/ a (-er, -est) rüstig

spud /spʌd/ n (fam) Kartoffel f

spun /spʌn/ see **spin**

spur /spɜ:(r)/ n Sporn m; (stimulus) Ansporn m; (road) Nebenstraße f; **on the ~**

of the moment ganz spontan □ vt (pt/pp **spurred**) ~ [**on**] (fig) anspornen

spurious /'spjuərɪəs/ a, -**ly** adv falsch

spurn /spɜ:n/ vt verschmähen

spurt /spɜ:t/ n Strahl m; (Sport) Spurt m; **put on a ~** spurten □ vi spritzen

spy /spaɪ/ n Spion(in) m(f) □ vi spionieren; ~ **on s.o.** jdm nachspionieren □ vt (fam: see) sehen. ~ **out** vt auskundschaften

spying /'spaɪɪŋ/ n Spionage f

squabble /'skwɒbl/ n Zank m □ vi sich zanken

squad /skwɒd/ n Gruppe f; (Sport) Mannschaft f

squadron /'skwɒdrən/ n (Mil) Geschwader nt

squalid /'skwɒlɪd/ a, -**ly** adv schmutzig

squall /skwɔ:l/ n Bö f □ vi brüllen

squalor /'skwɒlə(r)/ n Schmutz m

squander /'skwɒndə(r)/ vt vergeuden

square /skweə(r)/ a quadratisch; (metre, mile) Quadrat-; (meal) anständig; **all** ~ (fam) quitt □ n Quadrat nt; (area) Platz m; (on chessboard) Feld nt □ vt (settle) klären; (Math) quadrieren □ vi (agree) übereinstimmen

squash /skwɒʃ/ n Gedränge nt; (drink) Fruchtsaftgetränk nt; (Sport) Squash nt □ vt zerquetschen; (suppress) niederschlagen. ~**y** a weich

squat /skwɒt/ a gedrungen □ n (fam) besetztes Haus nt □ vi (pt/pp **squatted**) hocken; ~ **in a house** ein Haus besetzen. ~**ter** n Hausbesetzer m

squawk /skwɔ:k/ vi krächzen

squeak /skwi:k/ n Quieken nt; (of hinge, brakes) Quietschen nt □ vi quieken; quietschen

squeal /skwi:l/ n Schrei m; (screech) Kreischen nt □ vi schreien; kreischen

squeamish /'skwi:mɪʃ/ a empfindlich

squeeze /skwi:z/ n Druck m; (crush) Gedränge nt □ vt drücken; (to get juice) ausdrücken; (force) zwängen; (fam: extort) herauspressen (**from** aus) □ vi ~ **in/out** sich hinein-/hinauszwängen

squelch /skweltʃ/ vi quatschen

squid /skwɪd/ n Tintenfisch m

squiggle /'skwɪgl/ n Schnörkel m

squint /skwɪnt/ n Schielen nt □ vi schielen

squire /'skwaɪə(r)/ n Gutsherr m

squirm /skwɜ:m/ vi sich winden

squirrel /'skwɪrl/ n Eichhörnchen nt

squirt /skwɜ:t/ n Spritzer m □ vt/i spritzen

St abbr (Saint) St.; (Street) Str.

stab /stæb/ n Stich m; (fam: attempt) Versuch m □ vt (pt/pp **stabbed**) stechen; (to death) erstechen

stability /stə'bɪlətɪ/ n Stabilität f

stabilize /'steɪbɪlaɪz/ vt stabilisieren □ vi sich stabilisieren

stable[1] /'steɪbl/ a (-r, -st) stabil

stable[2] n Stall m; (establishment) Reitstall m

stack /stæk/ n Stapel m; (of chimney) Schornstein m; (fam: large quantity) Haufen m □ vt stapeln

stadium /'steɪdɪəm/ n Stadion nt

staff /stɑːf/ n (stick & Mil) Stab m □ (& pl) (employees) Personal nt; (Sch) Lehrkräfte pl □ vt mit Personal besetzen. **~-room** n (Sch) Lehrerzimmer nt

stag /stæg/ n Hirsch m

stage /steɪdʒ/ n Bühne f; (in journey) Etappe f; (in process) Stadium nt; **by** or **in ~s** in Etappen □ vt aufführen; (arrange) veranstalten

stage: ~ door n Bühneneingang m. **~ fright** n Lampenfieber nt

stagger /'stægə(r)/ vi taumeln □ vt staffeln (holidays); versetzt anordnen (seats); I **was ~ed** es hat mir die Sprache verschlagen. **~ing** a unglaublich

stagnant /'stægnənt/ a stehend; (fig) stagnierend

stagnat|e /stæg'neɪt/ vi (fig) stagnieren. **~ion** /-'neɪʃn/ n Stagnation f

staid /steɪd/ a gesetzt

stain /steɪn/ n Fleck m; (for wood) Beize f □ vt färben; beizen (wood); (fig) beflecken. **~ed glass** farbiges Glas nt. **~less** a fleckenlos; (steel) rostfrei. **~ remover** n Fleckentferner m

stair /steə(r)/ n Stufe f; **~s** pl Treppe f. **~case** n Treppe f

stake /steɪk/ n Pfahl m; (wager) Einsatz m; (Comm) Anteil m; **be at ~** auf dem Spiel stehen □ vt [an einem Pfahl] anbinden; (wager) setzen; **~ a claim to sth** Anspruch auf etw (acc) erheben

stale /steɪl/ a (-r, -st) alt; (air) verbraucht. **~mate** n Patt nt

stalk[1] /stɔːk/ n Stiel m, Stängel m

stalk[2] vt pirschen auf (+ acc) □ vi stolzieren

stall /stɔːl/ n Stand m; **~s** pl (Theat) Parkett nt □ vi (engine:) stehen bleiben; (fig) ausweichen □ vt abwürgen (engine)

stallion /'stæljən/ n Hengst m

stalwart /'stɔːlwət/ a treu □ n treuer Anhänger m

stamina /'stæmɪnə/ n Ausdauer f

stammer /'stæmə(r)/ n Stottern nt □ vt/i stottern

stamp /stæmp/ n Stempel m; (postage ~) [Brief]marke f □ vt stempeln; (impress) prägen; (put postage on) frankieren; **~**

one's feet mit den Füßen stampfen □ vi stampfen. **~ out** vt [aus]stanzen; (fig) ausmerzen

stampede /stæm'piːd/ n wilde Flucht f; (fam) Ansturm m □ vi in Panik fliehen

stance /stɑːns/ n Haltung f

stand /stænd/ n Stand m; (rack) Ständer m; (pedestal) Sockel m; (Sport) Tribüne f; (fig) Einstellung f □ v (pt/pp stood) □ vi stehen; (rise) aufstehen; (be candidate) kandidieren; (stay valid) gültig bleiben; **~ still** stillstehen; **~ firm** (fig) festbleiben; **~ together** zusammenhalten; **~ to lose/gain** gewinnen/verlieren können; **~ to reason** logisch sein; **~ in for** vertreten; **~ for** (mean) bedeuten; **I won't ~ for** that das lasse ich mir nicht bieten □ vt stellen; (withstand) standhalten (+ dat); (endure) ertragen; vertragen (climate); (put up with) aushalten; haben (chance); **~ one's ground** nicht nachgeben; **~ the test of time** sich bewähren; **~ s.o. a beer** jdm ein Bier spendieren; **I can't ~ her** (fam) ich kann sie nicht ausstehen; **~ by** vi daneben stehen; (be ready) sich bereithalten □ vt (support) (fig) stehen zu. **~ by s.o.** (fig) zu jdm stehen. **~ down** vi (retire) zurücktreten. **~ out** vi hervorstehen; (fig) herausragen. **~ up** vi aufstehen; **~ up for** eintreten für; **~ up to sich wehren gegen

standard /'stændəd/ a Normal-; **be ~ practice** allgemein üblich sein □ n Maßstab m; (Techn) Norm f; (level) Niveau nt; (flag) Standarte f; **~s** pl (morals) Prinzipien pl; **~ of living** Lebensstandard m. **~ize** vt standardisieren; (Techn) normen

'standard lamp n Stehlampe f

'stand-in n Ersatz m

standing /'stændɪŋ/ a (erect) stehend; (permanent) ständig □ n Rang m; (duration) Dauer f. **~ 'order** n Dauerauftrag m. **~-room** n Stehplätze pl

stand: ~-offish /stænd'ɒfɪʃ/ a distanziert. **~point** n Standpunkt m. **~still** n Stillstand m; **come to a ~still** zum Stillstand kommen

stank /stæŋk/ see **stink**

staple[1] /'steɪpl/ a Grund- □ n (product) Haupterzeugnis nt

staple[2] n Heftklammer f □ vt heften. **~r** n Heftmaschine f

star /stɑː(r)/ n Stern m; (asterisk) Sternchen nt; (Theat, Sport) Star m □ vi (pt/pp starred) die Hauptrolle spielen

starboard /'stɑːbəd/ n Steuerbord nt

starch /stɑːtʃ/ n Stärke f □ vt stärken. **~y** a stärkehaltig; (fig) steif

stare /steə(r)/ n Starren nt □ vt starren; **~ at** anstarren

'starfish n Seestern m

stark /stɑːk/ a (-er, -est) scharf; ⟨contrast⟩ krass □ adv ~ **naked** splitternackt

starling /'stɑːlɪŋ/ n Star m

'starlit a sternhell

starry /'stɑːrɪ/ a sternklar

start /stɑːt/ n Anfang m, Beginn m; ⟨departure⟩ Aufbruch m; ⟨Sport⟩ Start m; **from the** ~ von Anfang an; **for a** ~ erstens □ vi anfangen, beginnen; ⟨set out⟩ aufbrechen; ⟨engine:⟩ anspringen; ⟨Auto, Sport⟩ starten; ⟨jump⟩ aufschrecken; **to** ~ **with** zuerst □ vt anfangen, beginnen; ⟨cause⟩ verursachen; ⟨found⟩ gründen; starten ⟨car, race⟩; in Umlauf setzen ⟨rumour⟩. ~**er** n ⟨Culin⟩ Vorspeise f; ⟨Auto, Sport⟩ Starter m. ~**ing-point** n Ausgangspunkt m

startle /'stɑːtl/ vt erschrecken

starvation /stɑː'veɪʃn/ n Verhungern nt

starve /stɑːv/ vi hungern; ⟨to death⟩ verhungern □ vt verhungern lassen

stash /stæʃ/ vt ⟨fam⟩ ~ **[away]** beiseite schaffen

state /steɪt/ n Zustand m; ⟨grand style⟩ Prunk m; ⟨Pol⟩ Staat m; ~ **of play** Spielstand m; **be in a** ~ ⟨person:⟩ aufgeregt sein; **lie in** ~ feierlich aufgebahrt sein □ attrib Staats-, staatlich □ vt erklären; ⟨specify⟩ angeben. ~**aided** a staatlich gefördert. ~**less** a staatenlos

stately /'steɪtlɪ/ a (-ier, -iest) stattlich. ~ **'home** n Schloss nt

statement /'steɪtmənt/ n Erklärung f; ⟨Jur⟩ Aussage f; ⟨Banking⟩ Auszug m

'statesman n Staatsmann m

static /'stætɪk/ a statisch; **remain** ~ unverändert bleiben

station /'steɪʃn/ n Bahnhof m; ⟨police⟩ Wache f; ⟨radio⟩ Sender m; ⟨space, weather⟩ Station f; ⟨Mil⟩ Posten m; ⟨status⟩ Rang m □ vt stationieren; ⟨post⟩ postieren. ~**ary** /-ərɪ/ a stehend; **be** ~**ary** stehen

stationer /'steɪʃənə(r)/ n ~**'s [shop]** Schreibwarengeschäft nt. ~**y** n Briefpapier nt; ⟨writing-materials⟩ Schreibwaren pl

'station-wagon n ⟨Amer⟩ Kombi[wagen] n

statistic /stə'tɪstɪk/ n statistische Tatsache f. ~**al** a, -**ly** adv statistisch. ~**s** n & pl Statistik f

statue /'stætjuː/ n Statue f

stature /'stætʃə(r)/ n Statur f; ⟨fig⟩ Format nt

status /'steɪtəs/ n Status m, Rang m. ~ **symbol** n Statussymbol nt

statut|e /'stætjuːt/ n Statut nt. ~**ory** a gesetzlich

staunch /stɔːntʃ/ a (-er, -est), -**ly** adv treu

stave /steɪv/ vt ~ **off** abwenden

stay /steɪ/ n Aufenthalt m □ vi bleiben; ⟨reside⟩ wohnen; ~ **the night** übernachten; ~ **put** dableiben □ vt ~ **the course** durchhalten. ~ **away** vi wegbleiben. ~ **behind** vi zurückbleiben. ~ **in** vi zu Hause bleiben; ⟨Sch⟩ nachsitzen. ~ **up** vi oben bleiben; ⟨upright⟩ stehen bleiben; ⟨on wall⟩ hängen bleiben; ⟨person:⟩ aufbleiben

stead /sted/ n **in his** ~ an seiner Stelle; **stand s.o. in good** ~ jdm zustatten kommen. ~**fast** a, -**ly** adv standhaft

steadily /'stedɪlɪ/ adv fest; ⟨continually⟩ stetig

steady /'stedɪ/ a (-ier, -iest) fest; ⟨not wobbly⟩ stabil; ⟨hand⟩ ruhig; ⟨regular⟩ regelmäßig; ⟨dependable⟩ zuverlässig

steak /steɪk/ n Steak nt

steal /stiːl/ vt/i ⟨pt **stole**, pp **stolen**⟩ stehlen ⟨from dat⟩. ~ **in/out** vi sich hinein-/hinausstehlen

stealth /stelθ/ n Heimlichkeit f; **by** ~ heimlich. ~**y** a heimlich

steam /stiːm/ n Dampf m; **under one's own** ~ ⟨fam⟩ aus eigener Kraft □ vt ⟨Culin⟩ dämpfen, dünsten □ vi dampfen. ~ **up** vi beschlagen

'steam-engine n Dampfmaschine f; ⟨Rail⟩ Dampflokomotive f

steamer /'stiːmə(r)/ n Dampfer m

'steamroller n Dampfwalze f

steamy /'stiːmɪ/ a dampfig

steel /stiːl/ n Stahl m □ vt ~ **oneself** allen Mut zusammennehmen

steep¹ /stiːp/ vt ⟨soak⟩ einweichen

steep² a, -**ly** adv steil; ⟨fam: exorbitant⟩ gesalzen

steeple /'stiːpl/ n Kirchturm m. ~**chase** n Hindernisrennen nt

steer /stɪə(r)/ vt/i steuern; ~ **clear of s.o./sth** jdm/ etw aus dem Weg gehen. ~**ing** n ⟨Auto⟩ Steuerung f. ~**ing-wheel** n Lenkrad nt

stem¹ /stem/ n Stiel m; ⟨of word⟩ Stamm m □ vi ⟨pt/pp **stemmed**⟩ ~ **from** zurückzuführen sein auf ⟨+ acc⟩

stem² vt ⟨pt/pp **stemmed**⟩ eindämmen; stillen ⟨bleeding⟩

stench /stentʃ/ n Gestank m

stencil /'stensl/ n Schablone f; ⟨for typing⟩ Matrize f

step /step/ n Schritt m; ⟨stair⟩ Stufe f; ~**s** pl ⟨ladder⟩ Trittleiter f; **in** ~ im Schritt; ~ **by** ~ Schritt für Schritt; **take** ~**s** ⟨fig⟩ Schritte unternehmen □ vi ⟨pt/pp **stepped**⟩ treten; ~ **in** ⟨fig⟩ eingreifen; ~ **into s.o.'s shoes** an jds Stelle treten; ~ **out of line** aus der Reihe tanzen. ~ **up**

vi hinaufsteigen ◻ *vt* (*increase*) erhöhen, steigern; verstärken (*efforts*)

step: ~**brother** *n* Stiefbruder *m*. ~**child** *n* Stiefkind *nt*. ~**daughter** *n* Stieftochter *f*. ~**father** *n* Stiefvater *m*. ~**ladder** *n* Trittleiter *f*. ~**mother** *n* Stiefmutter *f*

'stepping-stone *n* Trittstein *m*; (*fig*) Sprungbrett *nt*

step: ~**sister** *n* Stiefschwester *f*. ~**son** *n* Stiefsohn *m*

stereo /'sterɪəʊ/ *n* Stereo *nt*; (*equipment*) Stereoanlage *f*; **in** ~ stereo. ~**phonic** /-'fɒnɪk/ *a* stereophon

stereotype /'sterɪətaɪp/ *n* stereotype Figur *f*. ~**d** *a* stereotyp

steril|e /'steraɪl/ *a* steril. ~**ity** /stə'rɪlətɪ/ *n* Sterilität *f*

steriliz|ation /sterəlaɪ'zeɪʃn/ *n* Sterilisation *f*. ~**e** *vt* sterilisieren

sterling /'stɜːlɪŋ/ *a* Sterling-; (*fig*) gediegen ◻ *n* Sterling *m*

stern[1] /stɜːn/ *a* (-er, -est), -ly *adv* streng

stern[2] *n* (*of boat*) Heck *nt*

stew /stjuː/ *n* Eintopf *m*; **in a** ~ (*fam*) aufgeregt ◻ *vt/i* schmoren; ~**ed fruit** Kompott *nt*

steward /'stjuːəd/ *n* Ordner *m*; (*on ship, aicraft*) Steward *m*. ~**ess** *n* Stewardess *f*

stick[1] /stɪk/ *n* Stock *m*; (*of chalk*) Stück *nt*; (*of rhubarb*) Stange *f*; (*Sport*) Schläger *m*

stick[2] *v* (*pt/pp* stuck) ◻ *vt* stecken; (*stab*) stechen; (*glue*) kleben; (*fam: put*) tun; (*fam: endure*) aushalten ◻ *vi* stecken; (*adhere*) kleben, haften (**to an** + *dat*); (*jam*) klemmen; ~ **to sth** (*fig*) bei etw bleiben; ~ **at it** (*fam*) dranbleiben; ~ **at nothing** (*fam*) vor nichts zurückschrecken; ~ **up for** (*fam*) eintreten für; **be stuck** nicht weiterkönnen; (*vehicle:*) festsitzen, festgefahren sein; (*drawer:*) klemmen; **be stuck with sth** (*fam*) etw am Hals haben. ~ **out** *vi* abstehen; (*project*) vorstehen ◻ *vt* (*fam*) hinausstrecken; herausstrecken (*tongue*)

sticker /'stɪkə(r)/ *n* Aufkleber *m*

'sticking plaster *n* Heftpflaster *nt*

stickler /'stɪklə(r)/ *n* **be a** ~ **for** es sehr genau nehmen mit

sticky /'stɪkɪ/ *a* (-ier, -iest) klebrig; (*adhesive*) Klebe-

stiff /stɪf/ *a* (-er, -est), -ly *adv* steif; (*brush*) hart; (*dough*) fest; (*difficult*) schwierig; (*penalty*) schwer; **be bored** ~ (*fam*) sich zu Tode langweilen. ~**en** *vt* steif machen ◻ *vi* steif werden. ~**ness** *n* Steifheit *f*

stifl|e /'staɪfl/ *vt* ersticken; (*fig*) unterdrücken. ~**ing** *a* **be** ~**ing** zum Ersticken sein

stigma /'stɪgmə/ *n* Stigma *nt*

stile /staɪl/ *n* Zauntritt *m*

stiletto /stɪ'letəʊ/ *n* Stilett *nt*; (*heel*) Bleistiftabsatz *m*

still[1] /stɪl/ *n* Destillierapparat *m*

still[2] *a* still; (*drink*) ohne Kohlensäure; **keep** ~ stillhalten; **stand** ~ stillstehen ◻ *n* Stille *f* ◻ *adv* noch; (*emphatic*) immer noch; (*nevertheless*) trotzdem; ~ **not** immer noch nicht

'stillborn *a* tot geboren

still 'life *n* Stillleben *nt*

stilted /'stɪltɪd/ *a* gestelzt, geschraubt

stilts /stɪlts/ *npl* Stelzen *pl*

stimulant /'stɪmjʊlənt/ *n* Anregungsmittel *nt*

stimulat|e /'stɪmjʊleɪt/ *vt* anregen. ~**ion** /-'leɪʃn/ *n* Anregung *f*

stimulus /'stɪmjʊləs/ *n* (*pl* -li /-laɪ/) Reiz *m*

sting /stɪŋ/ *n* Stich *m*; (*from nettle, jellyfish*) Brennen *nt*; (*organ*) Stachel *m* ◻ *v* (*pt/pp* stung) ◻ *vt* stechen ◻ *vi* brennen; (*insect:*) stechen. ~**ing nettle** *n* Brennnessel *f*

stingy /'stɪndʒɪ/ *a* (-ier, -iest) geizig, (*fam*) knauserig

stink /stɪŋk/ *n* Gestank *m* ◻ *vi* (*pt* stank, *pp* stunk) stinken (**of** nach)

stint /stɪnt/ *n* Pensum *nt* ◻ *vi* ~ **on** sparen an (+ *dat*)

stipulat|e /'stɪpjʊleɪt/ *vt* vorschreiben. ~**ion** /-'leɪʃn/ *n* Bedingung *f*

stir /stɜː(r)/ *n* (*commotion*) Aufregung *f* ◻ *v* (*pt/pp* stirred) *vt* rühren ◻ *vi* sich rühren

stirrup /'stɪrəp/ *n* Steigbügel *m*

stitch /stɪtʃ/ *n* Stich *m*; (*Knitting*) Masche *f*; (*pain*) Seitenstechen *nt*; **be in** ~**es** (*fam*) sich kaputtlachen ◻ *vt* nähen

stoat /stəʊt/ *n* Hermelin *nt*

stock /stɒk/ *n* Vorrat *m* (**of** an + *dat*); (*in shop*) [Waren]bestand *m*; (*livestock*) Vieh *nt*; (*lineage*) Abstammung *f*; (*Finance*) Wertpapiere *pl*; (*Culin*) Brühe *f*; (*plant*) Levkoje *f*; **in/out of** ~ vorrätig/nicht vorrätig; **take** ~ (*fig*) Bilanz ziehen ◻ *a* Standard- ◻ *vt* (*shop:*) führen; auffüllen (*shelves*). ~ **up** *vi* sich eindecken (**with** mit)

stock: ~**broker** *n* Börsenmakler *m*. ~ **cube** *n* Brühwürfel *m*. **S**~ **Exchange** *n* Börse *f*

stocking /'stɒkɪŋ/ *n* Strumpf *m*

stockist /'stɒkɪst/ *n* Händler *m*

stock: ~**market** *n* Börse *f*. ~**pile** *vt* horten; anhäufen (*weapons*). ~**'still** *a* bewegungslos. ~**taking** *n* (*Comm*) Inventur *f*

stocky /'stɒkɪ/ *a* (-ier, -iest) untersetzt

stodgy /'stɒdʒɪ/ *a* pappig [und schwer verdaulich]

stoical /'stəʊɪkl/ a, -ly adv stoisch

stoke /stəʊk/ vt heizen

stole[1] /stəʊl/ n Stola f

stole[2], stolen /'stəʊlən/ see steal

stolid /'stɒlɪd/ a, -ly adv stur

stomach /'stʌmək/ n Magen m □ vt vertragen. ~ache n Magenschmerzen pl

stone /stəʊn/ n Stein m; (weight) 6,35kg □ a steinern; ⟨wall, Age⟩ Stein- □ vt mit Steinen bewerfen; entsteinen ⟨fruit⟩. ~-cold a eiskalt. ~'deaf n ⟨fam⟩ stocktaub

stony /'stəʊnɪ/ a steinig

stood /stʊd/ see stand

stool /stu:l/ n Hocker m

stoop /stu:p/ n walk with a ~ gebeugt gehen □ vi sich bücken; ⟨fig⟩ sich erniedrigen

stop /stɒp/ n Halt m; ⟨break⟩ Pause f; ⟨for bus⟩ Haltestelle f; ⟨for train⟩ Station f; ⟨Gram⟩ Punkt m; ⟨on organ⟩ Register nt; come to a ~ stehen bleiben; put a ~ to sth etw unterbinden □ v ⟨pt/pp stopped⟩ □ vt anhalten, stoppen; ⟨switch off⟩ abstellen; ⟨plug, block⟩ zustopfen; ⟨prevent⟩ verhindern; ~ s.o. doing sth jdn daran hindern, etw zu tun; ~ doing sth aufhören, etw zu tun; ~ that! hör auf damit! lass das sein! □ vi anhalten; ⟨cease⟩ aufhören; ⟨clock:⟩ stehen bleiben; ⟨fam: stay⟩ bleiben ⟨with s.o.⟩ □ int halt! stopp!

stop: ~gap n Notlösung f. ~over n Zwischenaufenthalt m; ⟨Aviat⟩ Zwischenlandung f

stoppage /'stɒpɪdʒ/ n Unterbrechung f; ⟨strike⟩ Streik m; ⟨deduction⟩ Abzug m

stopper /'stɒpə(r)/ n Stöpsel m

stop: ~press n letzte Meldungen pl. ~watch n Stoppuhr f

storage /'stɔːrɪdʒ/ n Aufbewahrung f; ⟨in warehouse⟩ Lagerung f; ⟨Computing⟩ Speicherung f

store /stɔː(r)/ n ⟨stock⟩ Vorrat m; ⟨shop⟩ Laden m; ⟨department ~⟩ Kaufhaus nt; ⟨depot⟩ Lager nt; in ~ auf Lager; put in ~ lagern; set great ~ by großen Wert legen auf (+ acc); be in ~ for s.o. ⟨fig⟩ jdm bevorstehen □ vt aufbewahren; ⟨in warehouse⟩ lagern; ⟨Computing⟩ speichern. ~room n Lagerraum m

storey /'stɔːrɪ/ n Stockwerk nt

stork /stɔːk/ n Storch m

storm /stɔːm/ n Sturm m; ⟨with thunder⟩ Gewitter nt □ vt/i stürmen. ~y a stürmisch

story /'stɔːrɪ/ n Geschichte f; ⟨in newspaper⟩ Artikel m; ⟨fam: lie⟩ Märchen nt

stout /staʊt/ a (-er, -est) beleibt; ⟨strong⟩ fest

stove /stəʊv/ n Ofen m; ⟨for cooking⟩ Herd m

stow /stəʊ/ vt verstauen. ~away n blinder Passagier m

straddle /'strædl/ vt rittlings sitzen auf (+ dat); ⟨standing⟩ mit gespreizten Beinen stehen über ⟨dat⟩

straggl|e /'strægl/ vi hinterherhinken. ~er n Nachzügler m. ~y a strähnig

straight /streɪt/ a (-er, -est) gerade; ⟨direct⟩ direkt; ⟨clear⟩ klar; ⟨hair⟩ glatt; ⟨drink⟩ pur; be ~ ⟨tidy⟩ in Ordnung sein □ adv gerade; ⟨directly⟩ direkt, geradewegs; ⟨clearly⟩ klar; ~ away sofort; ~ on or ahead geradeaus; ~ out ⟨fig⟩ geradeheraus; go ~ ⟨fam⟩ ein ehrliches Leben führen; put sth ~ etw in Ordnung bringen; sit/stand up ~ gerade sitzen/stehen

straighten /'streɪtn/ vt gerade machen; ⟨put straight⟩ gerade richten □ vi gerade werden; ~ [up] ⟨person:⟩ sich aufrichten. ~ out vt gerade biegen

straight'forward a offen; ⟨simple⟩ einfach

strain[1] /streɪn/ n Rasse f; ⟨Bot⟩ Sorte f; ⟨of virus⟩ Art f

strain[2] n Belastung f; ~s pl ⟨of music⟩ Klänge pl □ vt belasten; ⟨overexert⟩ überanstrengen; ⟨injure⟩ zerren ⟨muscle⟩; ⟨Culin⟩ durchseihen; abgießen ⟨vegetables⟩ □ vi sich anstrengen. ~ed ⟨relations⟩ gespannt. ~er n Sieb nt

strait /streɪt/ n Meerenge f; in dire ~s in großen Nöten. ~jacket n Zwangsjacke f. ~'laced a puritanisch

strand[1] /strænd/ n ⟨of thread⟩ Faden m; ⟨of beads⟩ Kette f; ⟨of hair⟩ Strähne f

strand[2] vt be ~ed festsitzen

strange /streɪndʒ/ a (-r, -st) fremd; ⟨odd⟩ seltsam, merkwürdig. ~r n Fremde(r) m/f

strangely /'streɪndʒlɪ/ adv seltsam, merkwürdig; ~ enough seltsamerweise

strangle /'stræŋgl/ vt erwürgen; ⟨fig⟩ unterdrücken

strangulation /stræŋgjʊ'leɪʃn/ n Erwürgen nt

strap /stræp/ n Riemen m; ⟨for safety⟩ Gurt m; ⟨to grasp in vehicle⟩ Halteriemen m; ⟨of watch⟩ Armband nt; ⟨shoulder-⟩ Träger m □ vt ⟨pt/pp strapped⟩ schnallen; ~ in or down festschnallen

strapping /'stræpɪŋ/ a stramm

strata /'strɑːtə/ npl see stratum

stratagem /'strætədʒəm/ n Kriegslist f

strategic /strə'tiːdʒɪk/ a, -ally adv strategisch

strategy /'strætədʒɪ/ n Strategie f

stratum /'strɑːtəm/ *n* (*pl* **strata**) Schicht *f*

straw /strɔː/ *n* Stroh *nt*; (*single piece, drinking*) Strohhalm *m*; **that's the last ~** jetzt reicht's aber

strawberry /'strɔːbəri/ *n* Erdbeere *f*

stray /streɪ/ *a* streunend □ *n* streunendes Tier □ *vi* sich verirren; (*deviate*) abweichen

streak /striːk/ *n* Streifen *m*; (*in hair*) Strähne *f*; (*fig: trait*) Zug *m* □ *vi* flitzen. **~y** *a* streifig; (*bacon*) durchwachsen

stream /striːm/ *n* Bach *m*; (*flow*) Strom *m*; (*current*) Strömung *f*; (*Sch*) Parallelzug *m* □ *vi* strömen; **~ in/out** hinaus-/herausströmen

streamer /'striːmə(r)/ *n* Luftschlange *f*; (*flag*) Wimpel *m*

'streamline *vt* (*fig*) rationalisieren. **~d** *a* stromlinienförmig

street /striːt/ *n* Straße *f*. **~car** *n* (*Amer*) Straßenbahn *f*. **~lamp** *n* Straßenlaterne *f*

strength /streŋθ/ *n* Stärke *f*; (*power*) Kraft *f*; **on the ~ of** auf Grund (+ *gen*). **~en** *vt* stärken; (*reinforce*) verstärken

strenuous /'strenjʊəs/ *a* anstrengend

stress /stres/ *n* (*emphasis*) Betonung *f*; (*strain*) Belastung *f*; (*mental*) Stress *m* □ *vt* betonen; (*put a strain on*) belasten. **~ful** *a* stressig (*fam*)

stretch /stretʃ/ *n* (*of road*) Strecke *f*; (*elasticity*) Elastizität *f*; **at a ~** ohne Unterbrechung; **a long ~** eine lange Zeit; **have a ~** sich strecken □ *vt* strecken; (*widen*) dehnen; (*spread*) ausbreiten; fordern (*person*); **~ one's legs** sich (*dat*) die Beine vertreten □ *vt* sich erstrecken; (*become wider*) sich dehnen; (*person:*) sich strecken. **~er** *n* Tragbahre *f*

strew /struː/ *vt* (*pp* **strewn** or **strewed**) streuen

stricken /'strɪkn/ *a* betroffen; **~ with** heimgesucht von

strict /strɪkt/ *a* (**-er, -est**), **-ly** *adv* streng; **~ly speaking** streng genommen

stride /straɪd/ *n* [großer] Schritt *m*; **make great ~s** (*fig*) große Fortschritte machen; **take sth in one's ~** mit etw gut fertig werden □ *vi* (*pt* **strode**, *pp* **stridden**) [mit großen Schritten] gehen

strident /'straɪdnt/ *a*, **-ly** *adv* schrill; (*colour*) grell

strife /straɪf/ *n* Streit *m*

strike /straɪk/ *n* Streik *m*; (*Mil*) Angriff *m*; **be on ~** streiken □ *v* (*pt/pp* **struck**) □ *vt* schlagen; (*knock against, collide with*) treffen; prägen (*coin*); anzünden (*match*); stoßen auf (+ *acc*) (*oil, gold*); abbrechen (*camp*); (*delete*) streichen; (*impress*) beeindrucken; (*occur to*) einfallen (+ *dat*); (*Mil*) angreifen; **~ s.o. a blow** jdm einen Schlag versetzen □ *vi* treffen; (*lightning:*) einschlagen; (*clock:*) schlagen; (*attack*) zuschlagen; (*workers:*) streiken; **~ lucky** Glück haben. **~-breaker** *n* Streikbrecher *m*

striker /'straɪkə(r)/ *n* Streikende(r) *m/f*

striking /'straɪkɪŋ/ *a* auffallend

string /strɪŋ/ *n* Schnur *f*; (*thin*) Bindfaden *m*; (*of musical instrument, racket*) Saite *f*; (*of bow*) Sehne *f*; (*of pearls*) Kette *f*; **the ~s** (*Mus*) die Streicher *pl*; **pull ~s** (*fam*) seine Beziehungen spielen lassen, Fäden ziehen □ *vt* (*pt/pp* **strung**) (*thread*) aufziehen (*beads*). **~ed** *a* (*Mus*) Saiten-; (*played with bow*) Streich-

stringent /'strɪndʒnt/ *a* streng

strip /strɪp/ *n* Streifen *m* □ *v* (*pt/pp* **stripped**) □ *vt* ablösen; ausziehen (*clothes*); abziehen (*bed*); abbeizen (*wood, furniture*); auseinander nehmen (*machine*); (*deprive*) berauben (*of gen*); **~ sth off sth** etw von etw entfernen □ *vi* (*undress*) sich ausziehen. **~ club** *n* Stripteaselokal *nt*

stripe /straɪp/ *n* Streifen *m*. **~d** *a* gestreift

'striplight *n* Neonröhre *f*

stripper /'strɪpə(r)/ *n* Stripperin *f*; (*male*) Stripper *m*

strip-'tease *n* Striptease *m*

strive /straɪv/ *vi* (*pt* **strove**, *pp* **striven**) sich bemühen (**to** zu); **~ for** streben nach

strode /strəʊd/ *see* **stride**

stroke¹ /strəʊk/ *n* Schlag *m*; (*of pen*) Strich *m*; (*Swimming*) Zug *m*; (*style*) Stil *m*; (*Med*) Schlaganfall *m*; **~ of luck** Glücksfall *m*; **put s.o. off his ~** jdn aus dem Konzept bringen

stroke² □ *vt* streicheln

stroll /strəʊl/ *n* Spaziergang *m*, (*fam*) Bummel *m* □ *vi* spazieren, (*fam*) bummeln. **~er** *n* (*Amer: push-chair*) [Kinder]sportwagen *m*

strong /strɒŋ/ *a* (**-er** /-gə(r)/, **-est** /-gɪst/), **-ly** *adv* stark; (*powerful, healthy*) kräftig; (*severe*) streng; (*sturdy*) stabil; (*convincing*) gut

strong: **~-box** *n* Geldkassette *f*. **~hold** *n* Festung *f*; (*fig*) Hochburg *f*. **~-'minded** *a* willensstark. **~-room** *n* Tresorraum *m*

stroppy /'strɒpɪ/ *a* widerspenstig

strove /strəʊv/ *see* **strive**

struck /strʌk/ *see* **strike**

structural /'strʌktʃərl/ *a*, **-ly** *adv* baulich

structure /'strʌktʃə(r)/ *n* Struktur *f*; (*building*) Bau *m*

struggle /'strʌgl/ *n* Kampf *m*; **with a ~** mit Mühe □ *vt* kämpfen; **~ for breath**

nach Atem ringen; ∼ **to do sth** sich abmühen, etw zu tun; ∼ **to one's feet** mühsam aufstehen

strum /strʌm/ v (pt/pp **strummed**) □ vt klimpern auf (+ dat) □ vi klimpern

strung /strʌŋ/ see **string**

strut¹ /strʌt/ n Strebe f

strut² vi (pt/pp **strutted**) stolzieren

stub /stʌb/ n Stummel m; (counterfoil) Abschnitt m □ vt (pt/pp **strubbed**) ∼ **one's toe** sich (dat) den Zeh stoßen (on an + dat). ∼ **out** vt ausdrücken (cigarette)

stubb|le /'stʌbl/ n Stoppeln pl. ∼**ly** a stoppelig

stubborn /'stʌbən/ a, -ly adv starrsinnig; (refusal) hartnäckig

stubby /'stʌbi/ a, (-ier, -iest) kurz und dick

stucco /'stʌkəʊ/ n Stuck m

stuck /stʌk/ see **stick²**. ∼-'**up** a (fam) hochnäsig

stud¹ /stʌd/ n Nagel m; (on clothes) Niete f; (for collar) Kragenknopf m; (for ear) Ohrstecker m

stud² n (of horses) Gestüt nt

student /'stju:dnt/ n Student(in) m(f); (Sch) Schüler(in) m(f). ∼ **nurse** n Lernschwester f

studied /'stʌdid/ a gewollt

studio /'stju:dɪəʊ/ n Studio nt; (for artist) Atelier nt

studious /'stju:dɪəs/ a lerneifrig; (earnest) ernsthaft

stud|y /'stʌdi/ n Studie f; (room) Studierzimmer nt; (investigation) Untersuchung f; ∼**ies** pl Studium nt □ v (pt/pp **studied**) □ vt studieren; (examine) untersuchen □ vi lernen; (at university) studieren

stuff /stʌf/ n Stoff m; (fam: things) Zeug nt □ vt vollstopfen; (with padding, Culin) füllen; ausstopfen (animal); ∼ **sth into sth** etw in etw (acc) [hinein]stopfen. ∼**ing** n Füllung f

stuffy /'stʌfi/ a (-ier, -iest) stickig; (old-fashioned) spießig

stumbl|e /'stʌmbl/ vi stolpern; ∼**e across** zufällig stoßen auf (+ acc). ∼**ing-block** n Hindernis nt

stump /stʌmp/ n Stumpf m □ ∼ **up** vt/i (fam) blechen. ∼**ed** a (fam) überfragt

stun /stʌn/ vt (pt/pp **stunned**) betäuben; ∼**ned by** (fig) wie betäubt von

stung /stʌŋ/ see **sting**

stunk /stʌŋk/ see **stink**

stunning /'stʌnɪŋ/ a (fam) toll

stunt¹ /stʌnt/ n (fam) Kunststück nt

stunt² vt hemmen. ∼**ed** a verkümmert

stupendous /stju:'pendəs/ a, -ly adv enorm

stupid /'stju:pɪd/ a dumm. ∼**ity** /-'pɪdəti/ n Dummheit f. ∼**ly** adv dumm; ∼**ly [enough]** dummerweise

stupour /'stju:pə(r)/ n Benommenheit f

sturdy /'stɜ:di/ a (-ier, -iest) stämmig; (furniture) stabil; (shoes) fest

stutter /'stʌtə(r)/ n Stottern nt □ vt/i stottern

sty¹ /staɪ/ n (pl **sties**) Schweinestall m

sty², **stye** n (pl **styes**) (Med) Gerstenkorn nt

style /staɪl/ n Stil m; (fashion) Mode f; (sort) Art f; (hair∼) Frisur f; **in** ∼ in großem Stil

stylish /'staɪlɪʃ/ a, -ly adv stilvoll

stylist /'staɪlɪst/ n Friseur m/ Friseuse f. ∼**ic** /-'lɪstɪk/ a, -ally adv stilistisch

stylized /'staɪlaɪzd/ a stilisiert

stylus /'staɪləs/ n (on record-player) Nadel f

suave /swɑ:v/ a (pej) gewandt

sub'conscious /sʌb-/ a, -ly adv unterbewusst □ n Unterbewusstsein nt

subcon'tract vt [vertraglich] weitervergeben (**to an** + acc)

'subdivi|de vt unterteilen. ∼**sion** n Unterteilung f

subdue /səb'dju:/ vt unterwerfen; (make quieter) beruhigen. ∼**d** a gedämpft; (person) still

subject¹ /'sʌbdʒɪkt/ a **be** ∼ **to sth** etw (dat) unterworfen sein □ n Staatsbürger(in) m(f); (of ruler) Untertan m; (theme) Thema nt; (of investigation) Gegenstand m; (Sch) Fach nt; (Gram) Subjekt nt

subject² /səb'dʒekt/ vt unterwerfen (**to** dat); (expose) aussetzen (**to** dat)

subjective /səb'dʒektɪv/ a, -ly adv subjektiv

subjugate /'sʌbdʒʊgeɪt/ vt unterjochen

subjunctive /səb'dʒʌŋktɪv/ n Konjunktiv m

sub'let vt (pt/pp -**let**) untervermieten

sublime /sə'blaɪm/ a, -ly adv erhaben

subliminal /sʌ'blɪmɪnl/ a unterschwellig

sub-ma'chine-gun n Maschinenpistole f

subma'rine n Unterseeboot nt

submerge /səb'mɜ:dʒ/ vt untertauchen; **be** ∼**d** unter Wasser stehen □ vi tauchen

submiss|ion /səb'mɪʃn/ n Unterwerfung f. ∼**ive** /-sɪv/ a gehorsam; (pej) unterwürfig

submit /səb'mɪt/ v (pt/pp -**mitted**, pres p -**mitting**) □ vt vorlegen (**to** dat); (hand in) einreichen □ vi sich unterwerfen (**to** dat)

subordinate¹ /sə'bɔ:dɪnət/ a untergeordnet □ n Untergebene(r) m/f

subordinate² /sə'bɔːdɪneɪt/ vt unterordnen (**to** dat)

subscribe /səb'skraɪb/ vi spenden; ~ **to** abonnieren ⟨newspaper⟩; ⟨fig⟩ sich anschließen (+ dat). ~**r** n Spender m; Abonnent m

subscription /səb'skrɪpʃn/ n (to club) [Mitglieds]beitrag m; ⟨to newspaper⟩ Abonnement nt; **by** ~ mit Spenden; ⟨buy⟩ im Abonnement

subsequent /'sʌbsɪkwənt/ a, -ly adv folgend; ⟨later⟩ später

subservient /səb'sɜːvɪənt/ a, -ly adv untergeordnet; ⟨servile⟩ unterwürfig

subside /səb'saɪd/ vi sinken; ⟨ground:⟩ sich senken; ⟨storm:⟩ nachlassen

subsidiary /səb'sɪdɪərɪ/ a untergeordnet □ n Tochtergesellschaft f

subsid|ize /'sʌbsɪdaɪz/ vt subventionieren. ~**y** n Subvention f

subsist /səb'sɪst/ vi leben (**on** von). ~**ence** n Existenz f

substance /'sʌbstəns/ n Substanz f

sub'standard a unzulänglich; ⟨goods⟩ minderwertig

substantial /səb'stænʃl/ a solide; ⟨meal⟩ reichhaltig; ⟨considerable⟩ beträchtlich. ~**ly** adv solide; ⟨essentially⟩ im Wesentlichen

substantiate /səb'stænʃɪeɪt/ vt erhärten

substitut|e /'sʌbstɪtjuːt/ n Ersatz m; ⟨Sport⟩ Ersatzspieler(in) m(f) □ vt ~**e A for B** B durch A ersetzen □ vi ~**e for s.o.** jdn vertreten. ~**ion** /-'tjuːʃn/ n Ersetzung f

subterfuge /'sʌbtəfjuːdʒ/ n List f

subterranean /sʌbtə'reɪnɪən/ a unterirdisch

'subtitle n Untertitel m

subtle /'sʌtl/ a (-r, -st), -tly adv fein; ⟨fig⟩ subtil

subtract /səb'trækt/ vt abziehen, subtrahieren. ~**ion** /-ækʃn/ n Subtraktion f

suburb /'sʌbɜːb/ n Vorort m; **in the** ~**s** am Stadtrand. ~**an** /sə'bɜːbən/ a Vorort-; ⟨pej⟩ spießig. ~**ia** /sə'bɜːbɪə/ n die Vororte pl

subversive /səb'vɜːsɪv/ a subversiv

'subway n Unterführung f; ⟨Amer: railway⟩ U-Bahn f

succeed /sək'siːd/ vi Erfolg haben; ⟨plan:⟩ gelingen; ⟨follow⟩ nachfolgen (+ dat); **I** ~**ed** es ist mir gelungen; **he** ~**ed in escaping** es gelang ihm zu entkommen □ vt folgen (+ dat). ~**ing** a folgend

success /sək'ses/ n Erfolg m. ~**ful** a, -ly adv erfolgreich

succession /sək'seʃn/ n Folge f; ⟨series⟩ Serie f; ⟨to title, office⟩ Nachfolge f; ⟨to throne⟩ Thronfolge f; **in** ~ hintereinander

successive /sək'sesɪv/ a aufeinander folgend. ~**ly** adv hintereinander

successor /sək'sesə(r)/ n Nachfolger(in) m(f)

succinct /sək'sɪŋkt/ a, -ly adv prägnant

succulent /'sʌkjʊlənt/ a saftig

succumb /sə'kʌm/ vi erliegen (**to** dat)

such /sʌtʃ/ a solche(r,s); ~ **a book** ein solches od solch ein Buch; ~ **a thing** so etwas; ~ **a long time** so lange; **there is no** ~ **thing** das gibt es gar nicht; **there is no** ~ **person** eine solche Person gibt es nicht □ pron **as** ~ als solche(r,s); ⟨strictly speaking⟩ an sich; ~ **as** wie [zum Beispiel]; **and** ~ und dergleichen. ~**like** pron ⟨fam⟩ dergleichen

suck /sʌk/ vt/i saugen; lutschen ⟨sweet⟩. ~ **up** vt aufsaugen □ vi ~ **up to s.o.** ⟨fam⟩ sich bei jdm einschmeicheln

sucker /'sʌkə(r)/ n ⟨Bot⟩ Ausläufer m; ⟨fam: person⟩ Dumme(r) m/f

suckle /'sʌkl/ vt säugen

suction /'sʌkʃn/ n Saugwirkung f

sudden /'sʌdn/ a, -ly adv plötzlich; ⟨abrupt⟩ jäh □ n **all of a** ~ auf einmal

sue /suː/ vt (pres p suing) verklagen (**for** auf + acc) □ vi klagen

suede /sweɪd/ n Wildleder nt

suet /'suːɪt/ n [Nieren]talg m

suffer /'sʌfə(r)/ vi leiden (**from an** + dat) □ vt erleiden; ⟨tolerate⟩ dulden. ~**ance** /-əns/ n **on** ~**ance** bloß geduldet. ~**ing** n Leiden nt

suffice /sə'faɪs/ vi genügen

sufficient /sə'fɪʃnt/ a, -ly adv genug, genügend; **be** ~ genügen

suffix /'sʌfɪks/ n Nachsilbe f

suffocat|e /'sʌfəkeɪt/ vt/i ersticken. ~**ion** /-'keɪʃn/ n Ersticken nt

sugar /'ʃʊgə(r)/ n Zucker m □ vt zuckern; ⟨fig⟩ versüßen. ~ **basin**, ~ **bowl** n Zuckerschale f. ~**y** a süß; ⟨fig⟩ süßlich

suggest /sə'dʒest/ vt vorschlagen; ⟨indicate, insinuate⟩ andeuten. ~**ion** /-estʃn/ n Vorschlag m; Andeutung f; ⟨trace⟩ Spur f. ~**ive** /-ɪv/ a, -ly adv anzüglich; **be** ~**ive of** schließen lassen auf (+ acc)

suicidal /suːɪ'saɪdl/ a selbstmörderisch

suicide /'suːɪsaɪd/ n Selbstmord m

suit /suːt/ n Anzug m; ⟨woman's⟩ Kostüm nt; ⟨Cards⟩ Farbe f; ⟨Jur⟩ Prozess m; **follow** ~ ⟨fig⟩ das Gleiche tun □ vt ⟨adapt⟩ anpassen ⟨**to** dat⟩; ⟨be convenient for⟩ passen (+ dat); ⟨go with⟩ passen zu; ⟨clothing:⟩ stehen ⟨s.o. jdm⟩; **be** ~**ed for** geeignet sein für; ~ **yourself!** wie du willst!

suit|able /'suːtəbl/ a geeignet; ⟨convenient⟩ passend; ⟨appropriate⟩ angemessen;

(*for weather, activity*) zweckmäßig. ~**ably** *adv* angemessen; zweckmäßig

'**suitcase** *n* Koffer *m*

suite /swi:t/ *n* Suite *f*; (*of furniture*) Garnitur *f*

sulk /sʌlk/ *vi* schmollen. ~**y** *a* schmollend

sullen /'sʌlən/ *a*, -**ly** *adv* mürrisch

sulphur /'sʌlfə(r)/ *n* Schwefel *f*. ~**ic** /-'fjʊərɪk/ ~**ic acid** Schwefelsäure *f*

sultana /sʌl'tɑːnə/ *n* Sultanine *f*

sultry /'sʌltrɪ/ *a* (-**ier**, -**iest**) (*weather*) schwül

sum /sʌm/ *n* Summe *f*; (*Sch*) Rechenaufgabe *f* □ *vt/i* (*pt/pp* **summed**) ~ **up** zusammenfassen; (*assess*) einschätzen

summar|ize /'sʌməraɪz/ *vt* zusammenfassen. ~**y** *n* Zusammenfassung *f* □ *a*, -**ily** *adv* summarisch; (*dismissal*) fristlos

summer /'sʌmə(r)/ *n* Sommer *m*. ~**house** *n* [Garten]laube *f*. ~**time** *n* Sommer *m*

summery /'sʌmərɪ/ *a* sommerlich

summit /'sʌmɪt/ *n* Gipfel *m*. ~ **conference** *n* Gipfelkonferenz *f*

summon /'sʌmən/ *vt* rufen; holen (*help*); (*Jur*) vorladen. ~ **up** *vt* aufbringen

summons /'sʌmənz/ *n* (*Jur*) Vorladung *f* □ *vt* vorladen

sump /sʌmp/ *n* (*Auto*) Ölwanne *f*

sumptuous /'sʌmptjʊəs/ *a*, -**ly** *adv* prunkvoll; (*meal*) üppig

sun /sʌn/ *n* Sonne *f* □ *vt* (*pt/pp* **sunned**) ~ **oneself** sich sonnen

sun: ~**bathe** *vi* sich sonnen. ~**bed** *n* Sonnenbank *f*. ~**burn** *n* Sonnenbrand *m*

sundae /'sʌndeɪ/ *n* Eisbecher *m*

Sunday /'sʌndeɪ/ *n* Sonntag *m*

'**sundial** *n* Sonnenuhr *f*

sundry /'sʌndrɪ/ *a* verschiedene *pl*; **all and** ~ alle *pl*

'**sunflower** *n* Sonnenblume *f*

sung /sʌŋ/ *see* **sing**

'**sun-glasses** *npl* Sonnenbrille *f*

sunk /sʌŋk/ *see* **sink**

sunken /'sʌŋkn/ *a* gesunken; (*eyes*) eingefallen

sunny /'sʌnɪ/ *a* (-**ier**, -**iest**) sonnig

sun: ~**rise** *n* Sonnenaufgang *m*. ~**roof** *n* (*Auto*) Schiebedach *nt*. ~**set** *n* Sonnenuntergang *m*. ~**shade** *n* Sonnenschirm *m*. ~**shine** *n* Sonnenschein *m*. ~**stroke** *n* Sonnenstich *m*. ~**tan** *n* [Sonnen]bräune *f*. ~**tanned** *a* braun [gebrannt]. ~**tan oil** *n* Sonnenöl *nt*

super /'su:pə(r)/ *a* (*fam*) prima, toll

superb /sʊ'pɜːb/ *a* erstklassig

supercilious /su:pə'sɪlɪəs/ *a* überlegen

superficial /su:pə'fɪʃl/ *a*, -**ly** *adv* oberflächlich

superfluous /sʊ'pɜːflʊəs/ *a* überflüssig

super'human *a* übermenschlich

superintendent /su:pərɪn'tendənt/ *n* (*of police*) Kommissar *m*

superior /su:'pɪərɪə(r)/ *a* überlegen; (*in rank*) höher □ *n* Vorgesetzte(r) *m/f*. ~**ity** /-'ɒrətɪ/ *n* Überlegenheit *f*

superlative /su:'pɜːlətɪv/ *a* unübertrefflich □ *n* Superlativ *m*

'**superman** *n* Übermensch *m*

'**supermarket** *n* Supermarkt *m*

super'natural *a* übernatürlich

'**superpower** *n* Supermacht *f*

supersede /su:pə'si:d/ *vt* ersetzen

super'sonic *a* Überschall-

superstiti|on /su:pə'stɪʃn/ *n* Aberglaube *m*. ~**ous** /-'stɪʃəs/ *a*, -**ly** *adv* abergläubisch

supervis|e /'su:pəvaɪz/ *vt* beaufsichtigen; überwachen (*work*). ~**ion** /-'vɪʒn/ *n* Aufsicht *f*; Überwachung *f*. ~**or** *n* Aufseher(in) *m(f)*

supper /'sʌpə(r)/ *n* Abendessen *nt*

supple /'sʌpl/ *a* geschmeidig

supplement /'sʌplɪmənt/ *n* Ergänzung *f*; (*addition*) Zusatz *m*; (*to fare*) Zuschlag *m*; (*book*) Ergänzungsband *m*; (*to newspaper*) Beilage *f* □ *vt* ergänzen. ~**ary** /-'mentərɪ/ *a* zusätzlich

supplier /sə'plaɪə(r)/ *n* Lieferant *m*

supply /sə'plaɪ/ *n* Vorrat *m*; **supplies** *pl* (*Mil*) Nachschub *m* □ *vt* (*pt/pp* -**ied**) liefern; ~ **s.o. with sth** jdn mit etw versorgen

support /sə'pɔːt/ *n* Stütze *f*; (*fig*) Unterstützung *f* □ *vt* stützen; (*bear weight of*) tragen; (*keep*) ernähren; (*give money to*) unterstützen; (*speak in favour of*) befürworten; (*Sport*) Fan sein von. ~**er** *n* Anhänger(in) *m(f)*; (*Sport*) Fan *m*. ~**ive** /-ɪv/ *a* be ~**ive** [to s.o.] [jdm] eine große Stütze sein

suppose /sə'pəʊz/ *vt* annehmen; (*presume*) vermuten; (*imagine*) sich (*dat*) vorstellen; **be** ~**d to do sth** etw tun sollen; **not be** ~**d to** (*fam*) nicht dürfen; **I** ~ **so** vermutlich. ~**dly** /-ɪdlɪ/ *adv* angeblich

supposition /sʌpə'zɪʃn/ *n* Vermutung *f*

suppository /sʌ'pɒzɪtrɪ/ *n* Zäpfchen *nt*

suppress /sə'pres/ *vt* unterdrücken. ~**ion** /-eʃn/ *n* Unterdrückung *f*

supremacy /su:'preməsɪ/ *n* Vorherrschaft *f*

supreme /su:'pri:m/ *a* höchste(r,s); ⟨*court*⟩ oberste(r,s)

surcharge /'sɜ:tʃɑ:dʒ/ *n* Zuschlag *m*

sure /ʃʊə(r)/ *a* (-r, -st) sicher; **make ~** sich vergewissern (**of** *gen*); (*check*) nachprüfen; **be ~ to do it** sieh zu, dass du es tust □ *adv* (*Amer, fam*) klar; **~ enough** tatsächlich. **~ly** *adv* sicher; (*for emphasis*) doch; (*Amer: gladly*) gern

surety /'ʃʊərəti/ *n* Bürgschaft *f*; **stand ~ for** bürgen für

surf /'sɜ:f/ *n* Brandung *f*

surface /'sɜ:fɪs/ *n* Oberfläche *f* □ *vi* (*emerge*) auftauchen. **~ mail** *n* **by ~ mail** auf dem Land-/Seeweg

'surfboard *n* Surfbrett *nt*

surfeit /'sɜ:fɪt/ *n* Übermaß *nt*;

surfing /'sɜ:fɪŋ/ *n* Surfen *nt*

surge /sɜ:dʒ/ *n* (*of sea*) Branden *nt*; (*fig*) Welle *f* □ *vi* branden; **~ forward** nach vorn drängen

surgeon /'sɜ:dʒən/ *n* Chirurg(in) *m(f)*

surgery /'sɜ:dʒərɪ/ *n* Chirurgie *f*; (*place*) Praxis *f*; (*room*) Sprechzimmer *nt*; (*hours*) Sprechstunde *f*; **have ~** operiert werden

surgical /'sɜ:dʒɪkl/ *a*, **-ly** *adv* chirurgisch

surly /'sɜ:lɪ/ *a* (-ier, -iest) mürrisch

surmise /sə'maɪz/ *vt* mutmaßen

surmount /sə'maʊnt/ *vt* überwinden

surname /'sɜ:neɪm/ *n* Nachname *m*

surpass /sə'pɑ:s/ *vt* übertreffen

surplus /'sɜ:pləs/ *a* überschüssig; **be ~ to requirements** nicht benötigt werden □ *n* Überschuss *m* (**of** an + *dat*)

surpris|e /sə'praɪz/ *n* Überraschung *f* □ *vt* überraschen; **be ~ed** sich wundern (**at** über + *acc*). **~ing** *a*, **-ly** *adv* überraschend

surrender /sə'rendə(r)/ *n* Kapitulation *f* □ *vi* sich ergeben; (*Mil*) kapitulieren □ *vt* aufgeben

surreptitious /sʌrəp'tɪʃəs/ *a*, **-ly** *adv* heimlich, verstohlen

surrogate /'sʌrəgət/ *n* Ersatz *m*. **~ 'mother** *n* Leihmutter *f*

surround /sə'raʊnd/ *vt* umgeben; (*encircle*) umzingeln; **~ed by** umgeben von. **~ing** *a* umliegend. **~ings** *npl* Umgebung *f*

surveillance /sə'veɪləns/ *n* Überwachung *f*; **be under ~** überwacht werden

survey¹ /'sɜ:veɪ/ *n* Überblick *m*; (*poll*) Umfrage *f*; (*investigation*) Untersuchung *f*; (*of land*) Vermessung *f*; (*of house*) Gutachten *nt*

survey² /sə'veɪ/ *vt* betrachten; vermessen ⟨*land*⟩; begutachten ⟨*building*⟩. **~or** *n* Landvermesser *m*; Gutachter *m*

survival /sə'vaɪvl/ *n* Überleben *nt*; (*of tradition*) Fortbestand *m*

surviv|e /sə'vaɪv/ *vt* überleben □ *vi* überleben; ⟨*tradition:*⟩ erhalten bleiben. **~or** *n* Überlebende(r) *m/f*; **be a ~or** (*fam*) nicht unterzukriegen sein

susceptible /sə'septəbl/ *a* empfänglich/ (*Med*) anfällig (**to** für)

suspect¹ /sə'spekt/ *vt* verdächtigen; (*assume*) vermuten; **he ~s nothing** er ahnt nichts

suspect² /'sʌspekt/ *a* verdächtig □ *n* Verdächtige(r) *m/f*

suspend /sə'spend/ *vt* aufhängen; (*stop*) [vorläufig] einstellen; (*from duty*) vorläufig beurlauben. **~er belt** *n* Strumpfbandgürtel *m*. **~ders** *npl* Strumpfbänder *pl*; (*Amer: braces*) Hosenträger *pl*

suspense /sə'spens/ *n* Spannung *f*

suspension /sə'spenʃn/ *n* (*Auto*) Federung *f*. **~ bridge** *n* Hängebrücke *f*

suspici|on /sə'spɪʃn/ *n* Verdacht *m*; (*mistrust*) Misstrauen *nt*; (*trace*) Spur *f*. **~ous** /-ɪʃəs/ *a*, **-ly** *adv* misstrauisch; (*arousing suspicion*) verdächtig

sustain /sə'steɪn/ *vt* tragen; (*fig*) aufrechterhalten; erhalten ⟨*life*⟩; erleiden ⟨*injury*⟩

sustenance /'sʌstɪnəns/ *n* Nahrung *f*

swab /swɒb/ *n* (*Med*) Tupfer *m*; (*specimen*) Abstrich *m*

swagger /'swægə(r)/ *vi* stolzieren

swallow¹ /'swɒləʊ/ *vt/i* schlucken. **~ up** *vt* verschlucken; verschlingen ⟨*resources*⟩

swallow² *n* (*bird*) Schwalbe *f*

swam /swæm/ *see* **swim**

swamp /swɒmp/ *n* Sumpf *m* □ *vt* überschwemmen. **~y** *a* sumpfig

swan /swɒn/ *n* Schwan *m*

swank /swæŋk/ *vi* (*fam*) angeben

swap /swɒp/ *n* (*fam*) Tausch *m* □ *vt/i* (*pt/pp* **swapped**) (*fam*) tauschen (**for** gegen)

swarm /swɔ:m/ *n* Schwarm *m* □ *vi* schwärmen; **be ~ing with** wimmeln von

swarthy /'swɔ:ðɪ/ *a* (-ier, -iest) dunkel

swastika /'swɒstɪkə/ *n* Hakenkreuz *nt*

swat /swɒt/ *vt* (*pt/pp* **swatted**) totschlagen

sway /sweɪ/ *n* (*fig*) Herrschaft *f* □ *vi* schwanken; (*gently*) sich wiegen □ *vt* wiegen; (*influence*) beeinflussen

swear /sweə(r)/ *v* (*pt* **swore**, *pp* **sworn**) □ *vt* schwören (**by** auf + *acc*); (*curse*) fluchen. **~-word** *n* Kraftausdruck *m*

sweat /swet/ *n* Schweiß *m* □ *vi* schwitzen

sweater /'swetə(r)/ *n* Pullover *m*

sweaty /'swetɪ/ *a* verschwitzt

swede /swi:d/ *n* Kohlrübe *f*

Swed|e /swi:d/ *n* Schwede *m* /-din *f*. **~en** *n* Schweden *nt*. **~ish** *a* schwedisch

sweep /swiːp/ n Schornsteinfeger m;
⟨curve⟩ Bogen m; ⟨movement⟩ ausholende
Bewegung f; **make a clean ∼** ⟨fig⟩ gründlich aufräumen ○ v ⟨pt/pp **swept**⟩ ○ vt
fegen, kehren ○ vi ⟨go swiftly⟩ rauschen;
⟨wind:⟩ fegen. **∼ up** vt zusammenfegen/
-kehren

sweeping /'swiːpɪŋ/ a ausholend; ⟨state-
ment⟩ pauschal; ⟨changes⟩ weit reichend

sweet /swiːt/ a (-er, -est) süß; **have a ∼
tooth** gern Süßes mögen ○ n Bonbon m &
nt; ⟨dessert⟩ Nachtisch m. **∼ corn** n [Zu-
cker]mais m

sweeten /'swiːtn/ vt süßen. **∼er** n Süßstoff
m; ⟨fam: bribe⟩ Schmiergeld nt

sweet: ∼heart n Schatz m. **∼shop** n Süß-
warenladen m. **∼ness** n Süße f. **∼ 'pea** n
Wicke f

swell /swel/ n Dünung f ○ v ⟨pt **swelled**, pp
swollen or **swelled**⟩ ○ vi [an]schwellen;
⟨sails:⟩ sich blähen; ⟨wood:⟩ aufquellen
○ vt anschwellen lassen; ⟨increase⟩ vergrößern. **∼ing** n Schwellung f

swelter /'sweltə(r)/ vi schwitzen

swept /swept/ see **sweep**

swerve /swɜːv/ vi einen Bogen machen

swift /swɪft/ a (-er, -est), **-ly** adv schnell

swig /swɪg/ n ⟨fam⟩ Schluck m, Zug m ○ vt
⟨pt/pp **swigged**⟩ ⟨fam⟩ [herunter]kippen

swill /swɪl/ n ⟨for pigs⟩ Schweinefutter nt
○ vt **∼ [out]** [aus]spülen

swim /swɪm/ n **have a ∼** schwimmen ○ vi
⟨pt **swam**, pp **swum**⟩ schwimmen; **my
head is ∼ming** mir dreht sich der Kopf.
∼mer n Schwimmer(in) m(f)

swimming /'swɪmɪŋ/ n Schwimmen nt.
∼-baths npl Schwimmbad nt. **∼-pool** n
Schwimmbecken nt; ⟨private⟩ Swimming-
pool m

'swim-suit n Badeanzug m

swindle /'swɪndl/ n Schwindel m, Betrug
m ○ vt betrügen. **∼r** n Schwindler m

swine /swaɪn/ n Schwein nt

swing /swɪŋ/ n Schwung m; ⟨shift⟩
Schwenk m; ⟨seat⟩ Schaukel f; **in full ∼**
in vollem Gange ○ v ⟨pt/pp **swung**⟩ ○ vi
schwingen; ⟨on swing⟩ schaukeln; ⟨sway⟩
schwanken; ⟨dangle⟩ baumeln; ⟨turn⟩
schwenken ○ vt schwingen; ⟨influence⟩ beeinflussen. **∼'door** n Schwingtür f

swingeing /'swɪndʒɪŋ/ a hart; ⟨fig⟩ drastisch

swipe /swaɪp/ n ⟨fam⟩ Schlag m ○ vt ⟨fam⟩
knallen; ⟨steal⟩ klauen

swirl /swɜːl/ n Wirbel m ○ vt/i wirbeln

swish /swɪʃ/ a ⟨fam⟩ schick ○ vi zischen

Swiss /swɪs/ a Schweizer, schweizerisch
○ n Schweizer(in) m(f); **the ∼** pl die
Schweizer. **∼ 'roll** n Biskuitrolle f

switch /swɪtʃ/ n Schalter m; ⟨change⟩
Wechsel m; ⟨Amer, Rail⟩ Weiche f ○ vt
wechseln; ⟨exchange⟩ tauschen ○ vi wechseln; **∼ to** umstellen auf (+ acc). **∼ off** vt
ausschalten; abschalten ⟨engine⟩. **∼ on** vt
einschalten, anschalten

switch: ∼back n Achterbahn f. **∼board**
n [Telefon]zentrale f

Switzerland /'swɪtsələnd/ n die Schweiz

swivel /'swɪvl/ v ⟨pt/pp **swivelled**⟩ ○ vt
drehen ○ vi sich drehen

swollen /'swəʊlən/ see **swell** ○ a geschwollen. **∼-'headed** a eingebildet

swoop /swuːp/ n Sturzflug m; ⟨by police⟩
Razzia f ○ vi **∼ down** herabstoßen

sword /sɔːd/ n Schwert nt

swore /swɔː(r)/ see **swear**

sworn /swɔːn/ see **swear**

swot /swɒt/ n ⟨fam⟩ Streber m ○ vt ⟨pt/pp
swotted⟩ ⟨fam⟩ büffeln

swum /swʌm/ see **swim**

swung /swʌŋ/ see **swing**

syllable /'sɪləbl/ n Silbe f

syllabus /'sɪləbəs/ n Lehrplan m; ⟨for
exam⟩ Studienplan m

symbol /'sɪmbl/ n Symbol nt ⟨of für⟩. **∼ic**
/-'bɒlɪk/ a, **-ally** adv symbolisch **∼ism**
/-ɪzm/ n Symbolik f. **∼ize** vt symbolisie-
ren

symmetr|ical /sɪ'metrɪkl/ a, **-ly** adv sym-
metrisch. **∼y** /'sɪmətrɪ/ n Symmetrie f

sympathetic /sɪmpə'θetɪk/ a, **-ally** adv
mitfühlend; ⟨likeable⟩ sympathisch

sympathize /'sɪmpəθaɪz/ vi mitfühlen.
∼r n ⟨Pol⟩ Sympathisant m

sympathy /'sɪmpəθɪ/ n Mitgefühl nt; ⟨con-
dolences⟩ Beileid nt

symphony /'sɪmfənɪ/ n Sinfonie f

symptom /'sɪmptəm/ n Symptom nt.
∼atic /-'mætɪk/ a symptomatisch ⟨of für⟩

synagogue /'sɪnəgɒg/ n Synagoge f

synchronize /'sɪŋkrənaɪz/ vt synchronisieren

syndicate /'sɪndɪkət/ n Syndikat nt

syndrome /'sɪndrəʊm/ n Syndrom nt

synonym /'sɪnənɪm/ n Synonym nt. **∼ous**
/-'nɒnɪməs/ a, **-ly** adv synonym

synopsis /sɪ'nɒpsɪs/ n (pl **-opses** /-siːz/
Zusammenfassung f; ⟨of opera, ballet⟩ In-
haltsangabe f

syntax /'sɪntæks/ n Syntax f

synthesis /'sɪnθəsɪs/ n (pl **-ses** /-siːz/
Synthese f

synthetic /sɪn'θetɪk/ a synthetisch ○ n
Kunststoff m

Syria /'sɪrɪə/ n Syrien nt

syringe /sɪ'rɪndʒ/ n Spritze f ○ vt spritzen;
ausspritzen ⟨ears⟩

syrup /'sɪrəp/ n Sirup m

system /'sɪstəm/ n System nt. **~atic** /-'mætɪk/ a, **-ally** adv systematisch

T

tab /tæb/ n (projecting) Zunge f; (with name) Namensschild nt; (loop) Aufhänger m; **keep ~s on** (fam) [genau] beobachten; **pick up the ~** (fam) bezahlen

tabby /'tæbɪ/ n getigerte Katze f

table /'teɪbl/ n Tisch m; (list) Tabelle f; **at [the] ~** bei Tisch □ vt einbringen. **~cloth** n Tischdecke f, Tischtuch nt. **~spoon** n Servierlöffel m

tablet /'tæblɪt/ n Tablette f; (of soap) Stück nt; (slab) Tafel f

'table tennis n Tischtennis nt

tabloid /'tæblɔɪd/ n kleinformatige Zeitung f; (pej) Boulevardzeitung f

taboo /tə'buː/ a tabu □ n Tabu nt

tacit /'tæsɪt/ a, **-ly** adv stillschweigend

taciturn /'tæsɪtɜːn/ a wortkarg

tack /tæk/ n (nail) Stift m; (stitch) Heftstich m; (Naut & fig) Kurs m □ vt festnageln; (sew) heften □ vi (Naut) kreuzen

tackle /'tækl/ n Ausrüstung f □ vt angehen

tacky /'tækɪ/ a klebrig

tact /tækt/ n Takt m, Taktgefühl nt. **~ful** a, **-ly** adv taktvoll

tactic|al /'tæktɪkl/ a, **-ly** adv taktisch. **~s** npl Taktik f

tactless /'tæktlɪs/ a, **-ly** adv taktlos. **~ness** n Taktlosigkeit f

tadpole /'tædpəʊl/ n Kaulquappe f

tag¹ /tæg/ n (label) Schild nt □ vi (pt/pp tagged) **~ along** mitkommen

tag² n (game) Fangen nt

tail /teɪl/ n Schwanz m; **~s** pl (tailcoat) Frack m; **heads or ~s?** Kopf oder Zahl? □ vt (fam: follow) beschatten □ vi **~ off** zurückgehen

tail: ~back n Rückstau m. **~coat** n Frack m. **~-end** n Ende nt. **~ light** n Rücklicht nt

tailor /'teɪlə(r)/ n Schneider m. **~-made** a maßgeschneidert

'tail wind n Rückenwind m

taint /teɪnt/ vt verderben

take /teɪk/ v (pt took, pp taken) □ vt nehmen; (with one) mitnehmen; (take to a place) bringen; (steal) stehlen; (win) gewinnen; (capture) einnehmen; (require) brauchen; (last) dauern; (teach) geben;

machen ⟨exam, subject holiday, photograph⟩; messen ⟨pulse, temperature⟩; **~ s.o. home** jdn nach Hause bringen; **~ sth to the cleaner's** etw in die Reinigung bringen; **~ s.o. prisoner** jdn gefangen nehmen; **be ~n ill** krank werden; **~ sth calmly** etw gelassen aufnehmen □ vi ⟨plant:⟩ angehen; **~ after s.o.** jdm nachschlagen; (in looks) jdm ähnlich sehen; **~ to** (like) mögen; (as a habit) sich (dat) angewöhnen. **~ away** vt wegbringen; (remove) wegnehmen; (subtract) abziehen; '**to ~ away**' 'zum Mitnehmen'. **~ back** vt zurücknehmen; (return) zurückbringen. **~ down** vt herunternehmen; (remove) abnehmen; (write down) aufschreiben. **~ in** vt hineinbringen; (bring indoors) hereinholen; (to one's home) aufnehmen; (understand) begreifen; (deceive) hereinlegen; (make smaller) enger machen. **~ off** vt abnehmen; ablegen ⟨coat⟩; sich (dat) ausziehen ⟨clothes⟩; (deduct) abziehen; (mimic) nachmachen; **~ time off** sich (dat) freinehmen; **~ oneself off** [fort]gehen □ vi (Aviat) starten. **~ on** vt annehmen; (undertake) übernehmen; (engage) einstellen; (as opponent) antreten gegen. **~ out** vt hinausbringen; (for pleasure) ausgehen mit; ausführen ⟨dog⟩; (remove) herausnehmen; (withdraw) abheben ⟨money⟩; (from library) ausleihen; **~ out a subscription to sth** etw abonnieren; **~ it out on s.o.** (fam) seinen Ärger an jdm auslassen. **~ over** vt hinüberbringen; übernehmen ⟨firm, control⟩ □ vi **~ over from s.o.** jdn ablösen. **~ up** vt hinaufbringen; annehmen ⟨offer⟩; ergreifen ⟨profession⟩; sich (dat) zulegen ⟨hobby⟩; in Anspruch nehmen ⟨time⟩; einnehmen ⟨space⟩; aufreißen ⟨floorboards⟩; **~ sth up with s.o.** mit jdm über etw (acc) sprechen □ vi **~ up with s.o.** sich mit jdm einlassen

take: ~-away n Essen zum Mitnehmen; (restaurant) Restaurant nt mit Straßenverkauf. **~-off** n (Aviat) Start m, Abflug m. **~-over** n Übernahme f

takings /'teɪkɪŋz/ npl Einnahmen pl

talcum /'tælkəm/ n **~ [powder]** Körperpuder m

tale /teɪl/ n Geschichte f

talent /'tælənt/ n Talent nt. **~ed** a talentiert

talk /tɔːk/ n Gespräch nt; (lecture) Vortrag m; **make small ~** Konversation machen □ vi reden, sprechen (to/with mit) □ vt reden; **~ s.o. into sth** jdn zu etw überreden. **~ over** vt besprechen

talkative /'tɔːkətɪv/ a gesprächig

'talking-to n Standpauke f

tall /tɔːl/ *a* (-er, -est) groß; ⟨*building, tree*⟩ hoch; **that's a ~ order** das ist ziemlich viel verlangt. **~boy** *n* hohe Kommode *f*. **~ 'story** *n* übertriebene Geschichte *f*

tally /'tælɪ/ *n* **keep a ~ of** Buch führen über (+ *acc*) □ *vi* übereinstimmen

talon /'tælən/ *n* Klaue *f*

tambourine /tæmbə'riːn/ *n* Tamburin *nt*

tame /teɪm/ *a* (-r, -st), **-ly** *adv* zahm; ⟨*dull*⟩ lahm (*fam*) □ *vt* zähmen. **~r** *n* Dompteur *m*

tamper /'tæmpə(r)/ *vi* **~ with** sich (*dat*) zu schaffen machen an (+ *dat*)

tampon /'tæmpɒn/ *n* Tampon *m*

tan /tæn/ *a* gelbbraun □ *n* Gelbbraun *nt*; (*from sun*) Bräune *f* □ *v* (*pt/pp* **tanned**) □ *vt* gerben ⟨*hide*⟩ □ *vi* braun werden

tang /tæŋ/ *n* herber Geschmack *m*; (*smell*) herber Geruch *m*

tangent /'tændʒənt/ *n* Tangente *f*; **go off at a ~** (*fam*) vom Thema abschweifen

tangible /'tændʒɪbl/ *a* greifbar

tangle /'tæŋgl/ *n* Gewirr *nt*; (*in hair*) Verfilzung *f* □ *vt* **~ [up]** verheddern □ *vi* sich verheddern

tango /'tæŋgəʊ/ *n* Tango *m*

tank /tæŋk/ *n* Tank *m*; (*Mil*) Panzer *m*

tankard /'tæŋkəd/ *n* Krug *m*

tanker /'tæŋkə(r)/ *n* Tanker *m*; (*lorry*) Tank[last]wagen *m*

tantaliz|e /'tæntəlaɪz/ *vt* quälen. **~ing** *a* verlockend

tantamount /'tæntəmaʊnt/ *a* **be ~ to** gleichbedeutend sein mit

tantrum /'tæntrəm/ *n* Wutanfall *m*

tap /tæp/ *n* Hahn *m*; (*knock*) Klopfen *nt*; **on ~** zur Verfügung □ *v* (*pt/pp* **tapped**) □ *vt* klopfen an (+ *acc*); anzapfen ⟨*barrel, tree*⟩; erschließen ⟨*resources*⟩; abhören ⟨*telephone*⟩ □ *vi* klopfen. **~-dance** *n* Stepptanz *m* □ *vi* Stepp tanzen, steppen

tape /teɪp/ *n* Band *nt*; (*adhesive*) Klebstreifen *m*; (*for recording*) Tonband *nt* □ *vt* mit Klebstreifen zukleben; (*record*) auf Band aufnehmen

'tape-measure *n* Bandmaß *nt*

taper /'teɪpə(r)/ *n* dünne Wachskerze *f* □ *vi* sich verjüngen

'tape recorder *n* Tonbandgerät *nt*

tapestry /'tæpɪstrɪ/ *n* Gobelinstickerei *f*

'tapeworm *n* Bandwurm *m*

'tap water *n* Leitungswasser *nt*

tar /tɑː(r)/ *n* Teer *m* □ *vt* (*pt/pp* **tarred**) teeren

tardy /'tɑːdɪ/ *a* (-ier, -iest) langsam; (*late*) spät

target /'tɑːgɪt/ *n* Ziel *nt*; (*board*) [Ziel]-scheibe *f*

tariff /'tærɪf/ *n* Tarif *m*; (*duty*) Zoll *m*

tarnish /'tɑːnɪʃ/ *vi* anlaufen

tarpaulin /tɑː'pɔːlɪn/ *n* Plane *f*

tarragon /'tærəgən/ *n* Estragon *m*

tart¹ /tɑːt/ *a* (-er, -est) sauer; (*fig*) scharf

tart² *n* ≈ Obstkuchen *m*; (*individual*) Törtchen *nt*; (*sl: prostitute*) Nutte *f* □ *vt* **~ oneself up** (*fam*) sich auftakeln

tartan /'tɑːtn/ *n* Schottenmuster *nt*; (*cloth*) Schottenstoff *m* □ *attrib* schottisch kariert

tartar /'tɑːtə(r)/ *n* (*on teeth*) Zahnstein *m*

tartar 'sauce /tɑːtə-/ *n* ≈ Remouladensoße *f*

task /tɑːsk/ *n* Aufgabe *f*; **take s.o. to ~** jdm Vorhaltungen machen. **~ force** *n* Sonderkommando *nt*

tassel /'tæsl/ *n* Quaste *f*

taste /teɪst/ *n* Geschmack *m*; (*sample*) Kostprobe *f* □ *vt* kosten, probieren; schmecken ⟨*flavour*⟩ □ *vi* schmecken (**of** nach). **~ful** *a*, **-ly** *adv* (*fig*) geschmackvoll. **~less** *a*, **-ly** *adv* geschmacklos

tasty /'teɪstɪ/ *a* (-ier, -iest) lecker, schmackhaft

tat /tæt/ *see* **tit²**

tatter|ed /'tætəd/ *a* zerlumpt; ⟨*pages*⟩ zerfleddert. **~s** *npl* **in ~s** in Fetzen

tattoo¹ /tə'tuː/ *n* Tätowierung *f* □ *vt* tätowieren

tattoo² *n* (*Mil*) Zapfenstreich *m*

tatty /'tætɪ/ *a* (-ier, -iest) schäbig; ⟨*book*⟩ zerfleddert

taught /tɔːt/ *see* **teach**

taunt /tɔːnt/ *n* höhnische Bemerkung *f* □ *vt* verhöhnen

Taurus /'tɔːrəs/ *n* (*Astr*) Stier *m*

taut /tɔːt/ *a* straff

tavern /'tævən/ *n* (*liter*) Schenke *f*

tawdry /'tɔːdrɪ/ *a* (-ier, -iest) billig und geschmacklos

tawny /'tɔːnɪ/ *a* gelbbraun

tax /tæks/ *n* Steuer *f* □ *vt* besteuern; (*fig*) strapazieren; **~ with** beschuldigen (+ *gen*). **~able** /-əbl/ *a* steuerpflichtig. **~ation** /-'seɪʃn/ *n* Besteuerung *f*. **~-free** *a* steuerfrei

taxi /'tæksɪ/ *n* Taxi *nt* □ *vi* (*pt/pp* **taxied**, *pres p* **taxiing**) ⟨*aircraft:*⟩ rollen. **~ driver** *n* Taxifahrer *m*. **~ rank** *n* Taxistand *m*

'taxpayer *n* Steuerzahler *m*

tea /tiː/ *n* Tee *m*. **~-bag** *n* Teebeutel *m*. **~-break** *n* Teepause *f*

teach /tiːtʃ/ *vt/i* (*pt/pp* **taught**) unterrichten; **~ s.o. sth** jdm etw beibringen. **~er** *n* Lehrer(in) *m(f)*

tea: **~-cloth** *n* (*for drying*) Geschirrtuch *nt*. **~cup** *n* Teetasse *f*

teak /tiːk/ *n* Teakholz *nt*

team /tiːm/ *n* Mannschaft *f*; (*fig*) Team *nt*; (*of animals*) Gespann *nt* □ *vi* ~ **up** sich zusammentun

'team-work *n* Teamarbeit *f*

'teapot *n* Teekanne *f*

tear¹ /teə(r)/ *n* Riss *m* □ *v* (*pt* **tore**, *pp* **torn**) □ *vt* reißen; (*damage*) zerreißen; ~ **open** aufreißen; ~**oneself away** sich losreißen □ *vi* [zer]reißen; (*run*) rasen. ~ **up** *vt* zerreißen

tear² /tɪə(r)/ *n* Träne *f*. ~**ful** *a* weinend. ~**fully** *adv* unter Tränen. ~**gas** *n* Tränengas *nt*

tease /tiːz/ *vt* necken

tea: ~**-set** *n* Teeservice *nt*. ~**shop** *n* Café *nt*. ~**spoon** *n* Teelöffel *m*. ~**-strainer** *n* Teesieb *nt*

teat /tiːt/ *n* Zitze *f*; (*on bottle*) Sauger *m*

'tea-towel *n* Geschirrtuch *nt*

technical /'teknɪkl/ *a* technisch; (*specialized*) fachlich. ~**ity** /-'kælətɪ/ *n* technisches Detail *nt*; (*Jur*) Formfehler *m*. ~**ly** *adv* technisch; (*strictly*) streng genommen. ~ **term** *n* Fachausdruck *m*

technician /tek'nɪʃn/ *n* Techniker *m*

technique /tek'niːk/ *n* Technik *f*

technological /teknə'lɒdʒɪkl/ *a*, **-ly** *adv* technologisch

technology /tek'nɒlədʒɪ/ *n* Technologie *f*

teddy /'tedɪ/ *n* ~ **[bear]** Teddybär *m*

tedious /'tiːdɪəs/ *a* langweilig

tedium /'tiːdɪəm/ *n* Langeweile *f*

teem /tiːm/ *vi* (*rain*) in Strömen gießen; **be** ~**ing with** (*full of*) wimmeln von

teenage /'tiːneɪdʒ/ *a* Teenager-; ~ **boy/girl** Junge *m*/Mädchen *nt* im Teenageralter. ~**r** *n* Teenager *m*

teens /tiːnz/ *npl* **the** ~ die Teenagerjahre *pl*

teeny /'tiːnɪ/ *a* (**-ier, -iest**) winzig

teeter /'tiːtə(r)/ *vi* schwanken

teeth /tiːθ/ *see* **tooth**

teeth|e /tiːð/ *vi* zahnen. ~**ing troubles** *npl* (*fig*) Anfangsschwierigkeiten *pl*

teetotal /tiː'təʊtl/ *a* abstinent. ~**ler** *n* Abstinenzler *m*

telecommunications /telɪkəmjuːnɪ'keɪʃnz/ *npl* Fernmeldewesen *nt*

telegram /'telɪɡræm/ *n* Telegramm *nt*

telegraph /'telɪɡrɑːf/ *n* Telegraf *m*. ~**ic** /-'ɡræfɪk/ *a* telegrafisch. ~ **pole** *n* Telegrafenmast *m*

telepathy /tɪ'lepəθɪ/ *n* Telepathie *f*; **by** ~ telepathisch

telephone /'telɪfəʊn/ *n* Telefon *nt*; **be on the** ~ Telefon haben; (*be telephoning*) telefonieren □ *vt* anrufen □ *vi* telefonieren

telephone: ~ **book** *n* Telefonbuch *nt*. ~ **booth** *n*, ~ **box** *n* Telefonzelle *f*. ~ **directory** *n* Telefonbuch *nt*. ~ **number** *n* Telefonnummer *f*

telephonist /tɪ'lefənɪst/ *n* Telefonist(in) *m(f)*

tele'photo /telɪ-/ *a* ~ **lens** Teleobjektiv *nt*

teleprinter /'telɪ-/ *n* Fernschreiber *m*

telescop|e /'telɪskəʊp/ *n* Teleskop *nt*, Fernrohr *nt*. ~**ic** /-'skɒpɪk/ *a* teleskopisch; (*collapsible*) ausziehbar

televise /'telɪvaɪz/ *vt* im Fernsehen übertragen

television /'telɪvɪʒn/ *n* Fernsehen *nt*; **watch** ~ fernsehen. ~ **set** *n* Fernsehapparat *m*, Fernseher *m*

telex /'teleks/ *n* Telex *nt* □ *vt* telexen

tell /tel/ *vt/i* (*pt/pp* **told**) sagen (**s.o.** jdm); (*relate*) erzählen; (*know*) wissen; (*distinguish*) erkennen; ~ **the time** die Uhr lesen; **time will** ~ das wird man erst sehen; **his age is beginning to** ~ sein Alter macht sich bemerkbar; **don't** ~ **me** sag es mir nicht; **you mustn't** ~ du darfst nichts sagen. ~ **off** *vt* ausschimpfen

teller /'telə(r)/ *n* (*cashier*) Kassierer(in) *m(f)*

telly /'telɪ/ *n* (*fam*) = **television**

temerity /tɪ'merətɪ/ *n* Kühnheit *f*

temp /temp/ *n* (*fam*) Aushilfssekretärin *f*

temper /'tempə(r)/ *n* (*disposition*) Naturell *nt*; (*mood*) Laune *f*; (*anger*) Wut *f*; **lose one's** ~ wütend werden □ *vt* (*fig*) mäßigen

temperament /'tempərəmənt/ *n* Temperament *nt*. ~**al** /-'mentl/ *a* temperamentvoll; (*moody*) launisch

temperance /'tempərəns/ *n* Mäßigung *f*; (*abstinence*) Abstinenz *f*

temperate /'tempərət/ *a* gemäßigt

temperature /'temprətʃə(r)/ *n* Temperatur *f*; **have** *or* **run a** ~ Fieber haben

tempest /'tempɪst/ *n* Sturm *m*. ~**uous** /-'pestjʊəs/ *a* stürmisch

template /'templɪt/ *n* Schablone *f*

temple¹ /'templ/ *n* Tempel *m*

temple² *n* (*Anat*) Schläfe *f*

tempo /'tempəʊ/ *n* Tempo *nt*

temporary /'tempərərɪ/ *a*, **-ily** *adv* vorübergehend; (*measure, building*) provisorisch

tempt /tempt/ *vt* verleiten; (*Relig*) versuchen; herausfordern (*fate*); (*entice*) [ver]locken; **be** ~**ed** versucht sein (**to** zu); **I am** ~**ed by it** es lockt mich. ~**ation** /-'teɪʃn/ *n* Versuchung *f*. ~**ing** *a* verlockend

ten /ten/ *a* zehn

tenable /'tenəbl/ *a* (*fig*) haltbar
tenaci|ous /tɪ'neɪʃəs/ *a*, **-ly** *adv* hartnäckig. **~ty** /-'næsətɪ/ *n* Hartnäckigkeit *f*
tenant /'tenənt/ *n* Mieter(in) *m(f)*; (*Comm*) Pächter(in) *m(f)*
tend¹ /tend/ *vt* (*look after*) sich kümmern um
tend² *vi* **~ to do sth** dazu neigen, etw zu tun
tendency /'tendənsɪ/ *n* Tendenz *f*; (*inclination*) Neigung *f*
tender¹ /'tendə(r)/ *n* □ (*Comm*) Angebot *nt*; **legal ~** gesetzliches Zahlungsmittel *nt* □ *vt* anbieten; einreichen ⟨*resignation*⟩
tender² *a* zart; (*loving*) zärtlich; (*painful*) empfindlich. **~ly** *adv* zärtlich. **~ness** *n* Zartheit *f*; Zärtlichkeit *f*
tendon /'tendən/ *n* Sehne *f*
tenement /'tenəmənt/ *n* Mietshaus *nt*
tenet /'tenɪt/ *n* Grundsatz *m*
tenner /'tenə(r)/ *n* (*fam*) Zehnpfundschein *m*
tennis /'tenɪs/ *n* Tennis *nt*. **~-court** *n* Tennisplatz *m*
tenor /'tenə(r)/ *n* Tenor *m*
tense¹ /tens/ *n* (*Gram*) Zeit *f*
tense² *a* (**-r, -st**) gespannt □ *vt* anspannen ⟨*muscle*⟩
tension /'tenʃn/ *n* Spannung *f*
tent /tent/ *n* Zelt *nt*
tentacle /'tentəkl/ *n* Fangarm *m*
tentative /'tentətɪv/ *a*, **-ly** *adv* vorläufig; (*hesitant*) zaghaft
tenterhooks /'tentəhʊks/ *npl* **be on ~** wie auf glühenden Kohlen sitzen
tenth /tenθ/ *a* zehnte(r,s) □ *n* Zehntel *nt*
tenuous /'tenjʊəs/ *a* (*fig*) schwach
tepid /'tepɪd/ *a* lauwarm
term /tɜ:m/ *n* Zeitraum *m*; (*Sch*) ≈ Halbjahr *nt*; (*Univ*) ≈ Semester *nt*; (*expression*) Ausdruck *m*; **~s** *pl* (*conditions*) Bedingungen *pl*; **~ of office** Amtszeit *f*; **in the short/long ~** kurz-/langfristig; **be on good/bad ~s** gut/nicht gut miteinander auskommen; **come to ~s with** sich abfinden mit
terminal /'tɜ:mɪnl/ *a* End-; (*Med*) unheilbar □ *n* (*Aviat*) Terminal *m*; (*of bus*) Endstation *f*; (*on battery*) Pol *m*; (*Computing*) Terminal *nt*
terminat|e /'tɜ:mɪneɪt/ *vt* beenden; lösen ⟨*contract*⟩; unterbrechen ⟨*pregnancy*⟩ □ *vi* enden. **~ion** /-'neɪʃn/ *n* Beendigung *f*; (*Med*) Schwangerschaftsabbruch *m*
terminology /tɜ:mɪ'nɒlədʒɪ/ *n* Terminologie *f*
terminus /'tɜ:mɪnəs/ *n* (*pl* **-ni** /-naɪ/) Endstation *f*
terrace /'terəs/ *n* Terrasse *f*; (*houses*) Häuserreihe *f*; **the ~s** (*Sport*) die [Steh]ränge *pl*. **~d house** *n* Reihenhaus *nt*
terrain /te'reɪn/ *n* Gelände *nt*
terrible /'terəbl/ *a*, **-bly** *adv* schrecklich
terrier /'terɪə(r)/ *n* Terrier *m*
terrific /tə'rɪfɪk/ *a* (*fam*) (*excellent*) sagenhaft; (*huge*) riesig
terri|fy /'terɪfaɪ/ *vt* (*pt/pp* **-ied**) Angst machen (+ *dat*); **be ~fied** Angst haben. **~fying** *a* Furcht erregend
territorial /terɪ'tɔ:rɪəl/ *a* Territorial-
territory /'terɪtərɪ/ *n* Gebiet *nt*
terror /'terə(r)/ *n* [panische] Angst *f*; (*Pol*) Terror *m*. **~ism** /-ɪzm/ *n* Terrorismus *m*. **~ist** /-ɪst/ *n* Terrorist *m*. **~ize** *vt* terrorisieren
terse /tɜ:s/ *a*, **-ly** *adv* kurz, knapp
test /test/ *n* Test *m*; (*Sch*) Klassenarbeit *f*; **put to the ~** auf die Probe stellen □ *vt* prüfen; (*examine*) untersuchen (**for** auf + *acc*)
testament /'testəmənt/ *n* Testament *nt*; **Old/New T~** Altes/Neues Testament *nt*
testicle /'testɪkl/ *n* Hoden *m*
testify /'testɪfaɪ/ *v* (*pt/pp* **-ied**) □ *vt* beweisen; **~ that** bezeugen, dass □ *vi* aussagen; **~ to** bezeugen
testimonial /testɪ'məʊnɪəl/ *n* Zeugnis *nt*
testimony /'testɪmənɪ/ *n* Aussage *f*
'test-tube *n* Reagenzglas *nt*. **~ 'baby** *n* (*fam*) Retortenbaby *nt*
testy /'testɪ/ *a* gereizt
tetanus /'tetənəs/ *n* Tetanus *m*
tetchy /'tetʃɪ/ *a* gereizt
tether /'teðə(r)/ *n* **be at the end of one's ~** am Ende seiner Kraft sein □ *vt* anbinden
text /tekst/ *n* Text *m*. **~book** *n* Lehrbuch *nt*
textile /'tekstaɪl/ *a* Textil- □ *n* **~s** *pl* Textilien *pl*
texture /'tekstʃə(r)/ *n* Beschaffenheit *f*; (*Tex*) Struktur *f*
Thai /taɪ/ *a* thailändisch. **~land** *n* Thailand *nt*
Thames /temz/ *n* Themse *f*
than /ðən, *betont* ðæn/ *conj* als; **older ~ me** älter als ich
thank /θæŋk/ *vt* danken (+ *dat*); **~ you [very much]** danke [schön]. **~ful** *a*, **-ly** *adv* dankbar. **~less** *a* undankbar
thanks /θæŋks/ *npl* Dank *m*; **~!** (*fam*) danke! **~ to** dank (+ *dat or gen*)
that /ðæt/ *a & pron* (*pl* **those**) der/die/das; (*pl*) die; **~ one** der/die/das da; **I'll take ~** ich nehme den/die/das; **I don't like those** die mag ich nicht; **~ is** das heißt; **is ~ you?** bist du es? **who is ~?** wer ist

da? **with/after** ~ damit/danach; **like** ~ so; **a man like** ~ so ein Mann; ~ **is why** deshalb; ~'**s it!** genau! **all** ~ **I know** alles was ich weiß; **the day** ~ **I saw him** an dem Tag, als ich ihn sah □ *adv* so; ~ **good/ hot** so gut/heiß □ *conj* dass

thatch /θætʃ/ *n* Strohdach *nt*. ~**ed** *a* strohgedeckt

thaw /θɔ:/ *n* Tauwetter *nt* □ *vt/i* auftauen; **it's** ~**ing** es taut

the /ðə, *vor einem Vokal* ði:/ *def art* der/ die/das; (*pl*) die; **play** ~ **piano/violin** Klavier/Geige spielen □ *adv* ~ **more** ~ **better** je mehr, desto besser; **all** ~ **better** umso besser

theatre /'θɪətə(r)/ *n* Theater *nt*; (*Med*) Operationssaal *m*

theatrical /θɪ'ætrɪkl/ *a* Theater-; (*showy*) theatralisch

theft /θeft/ *n* Diebstahl *m*

their /ðeə(r)/ *a* ihr

theirs /ðeəz/ *poss pron* ihre(r), ihrs; **a friend of** ~ ein Freund von ihnen; **those are** ~ die gehören ihnen

them /ðem/ *pron* (*acc*) sie; (*dat*) ihnen; **I know** ~ ich kenne sie; **give** ~ **the money** gib ihnen das Geld

theme /θi:m/ *n* Thema *nt*

them'selves *pron* selbst; (*refl*) sich; **by** ~ allein

then /ðen/ *adv* dann; (*at that time in past*) damals; **by** ~ bis dahin; **since** ~ seitdem; **before** ~ vorher; **from** ~ **on** von da an; **now and** ~ dann und wann; **there and** ~ auf der Stelle □ *a* damalig

theolog|ian /θɪə'ləʊdʒɪən/ *n* Theologe *m*. ~**y** /-'ɒlədʒɪ/ *n* Theologie *f*

theorem /'θɪərəm/ *n* Lehrsatz *m*

theoretical /θɪə'retɪkl/ *a*, -**ly** *adv* theoretisch

theory /'θɪərɪ/ *n* Theorie *f*; **in** ~ theoretisch

therapeutic /θerə'pju:tɪk/ *a* therapeutisch

therap|ist /'θerəpɪst/ *n* Therapeut(in) *m(f)*. ~**y** *n* Therapie *f*

there /ðeə(r)/ *adv* da; (*with movement*) dahin, dorthin; **down/up** ~ da unten/oben; ~ **is/are da ist/sind**; (*in existence*) es gibt; ~ **he/she is** da ist er/sie; **send/take** ~ hinschicken/-bringen □ *int* there, there! nun, nun!

there: ~**abouts** *adv* da [in der Nähe]; **or** ~**abouts** (*roughly*) ungefähr. ~'**after** *adv* danach. ~**by** *adv* dadurch. ~**fore** /-fɔ:(r)/ *adv* deshalb, also

thermal /'θɜ:ml/ *a* Thermal-; ~ '**underwear** *n* Thermowäsche *f*

thermometer /θə'mɒmɪtə(r)/ *n* Thermometer *nt*

Thermos (P) /'θɜ:məs/ *n* ~ **[flask]** Thermosflasche (P) *f*

thermostat /'θɜ:məstæt/ *n* Thermostat *m*

these /ði:z/ *see* this

thesis /'θi:sɪs/ *n* (*pl* -**ses** /-si:z/) Dissertation *f*; (*proposition*) These *f*

they /ðeɪ/ *pron* sie; ~ **say** (*generalizing*) man sagt

thick /θɪk/ *a* (-**er**, -**est**), -**ly** *adv* dick; (*dense*) dicht; (*liquid*) dickflüssig; (*fam: stupid*) dumm □ *adv* dick ~ *n* **in the** ~ **of** mitten in (+ *dat*). ~**en** *vt* dicker machen; eindicken (*sauce*) □ *vi* dicker werden; (*fog:*) dichter werden; (*plot:*) komplizierter werden. ~**ness** *n* Dicke *f*; Dichte *f*; Dickflüssigkeit *f*

thick: ~**set** *a* untersetzt. ~'**skinned** *a* (*fam*) dickfellig

thief /θi:f/ *n* (*pl* **thieves**) Dieb(in) *m(f)*

thieving /'θi:vɪŋ/ *a* diebisch □ *n* Stehlen *nt*

thigh /θaɪ/ *n* Oberschenkel *m*

thimble /'θɪmbl/ *n* Fingerhut *m*

thin /θɪn/ *a* (**thinner**, **thinnest**), -**ly** *adv* dünn □ *adv* dünn □ *v* (*pt/pp* **thinned**) □ *vt* verdünnen (*liquid*) □ *vi* sich lichten. ~ **out** *vt* ausdünnen

thing /θɪŋ/ *n* Ding *nt*; (*subject, affair*) Sache *f*; ~**s** *pl* (*belongings*) Sachen *pl*; **for one** ~ erstens; **the right** ~ das Richtige; **just the** ~! genau das Richtige! **how are** ~**s?** wie geht's? **the latest** ~ (*fam*) der letzte Schrei; **the best** ~ **would be** am besten wäre es

think /θɪŋk/ *vt/i* (*pt/pp* **thought**) denken (**about/of** an + *acc*); (*believe*) meinen; (*consider*) nachdenken; (*regard as*) halten für; **I** ~ **so** ich glaube schon; **what do you** ~? was meinen Sie? **what do you** ~ **of** **it?** was halten Sie davon? ~ **better of it** es sich (*dat*) anders überlegen. ~ **over** *vt* sich (*dat*) überlegen. ~ **up** *vt* sich (*dat*) ausdenken

third /θɜ:d/ *a* dritte(r,s) □ *n* Drittel *nt*. ~**ly** *adv* drittens. ~**rate** *a* drittrangig

thirst /θɜ:st/ *n* Durst *m*. ~**y** *a*, -**ily** *adv* durstig; **be** ~**y** Durst haben

thirteen /θɜ:'ti:n/ *a* dreizehn. ~**th** *a* dreizehnte(r,s)

thirtieth /'θɜ:tɪɪθ/ *a* dreißigste(r,s)

thirty /'θɜ:tɪ/ *a* dreißig

this /ðɪs/ *a* (*pl* **these**) diese(r,s); (*pl*) diese; ~ **one** diese(r,s) da; **I'll take** ~ ich nehme diesen/diese/ dieses; ~ **evening/morning** heute Abend/Morgen; **these days** heutzutage □ *pron* (*pl* **these**) das, dies[es]; (*pl*) die, diese; ~ **and that** dies und das; ~ **or that** dieses oder das da; **like** ~ **so**;

~ **is** Peter das ist Peter; *(Teleph)* hier [spricht] Peter; **who is** ~? wer ist das? *(Amer, Teleph)* wer ist am Apparat?

thistle /'θɪsl/ *n* Distel *f*

thorn /θɔːn/ *n* Dorn *m*. ~**y** *a* dornig

thorough /'θʌrə/ *a* gründlich

thorough: ~**bred** *n* reinrassiges Tier *nt*; *(horse)* Rassepferd *nt*. ~**fare** *n* Durchfahrtsstraße *f*; '**no** ~**fare**' 'keine Durchfahrt'

thorough|ly /'θʌrəlɪ/ *adv* gründlich; *(completely)* völlig; *(extremely)* äußerst. ~**ness** *n* Gründlichkeit *f*

those /ðəʊz/ *see* **that**

though /ðəʊ/ *conj* obgleich, obwohl; **as** ~ als ob □ *adv (fam)* doch

thought /θɔːt/ *see* **think** □ *n* Gedanke *m*; *(thinking)* Denken *nt*. ~**ful** *a*, **-ly** *adv* nachdenklich; *(considerate)* rücksichtsvoll. ~**less** *a*, **-ly** *adv* gedankenlos

thousand /'θaʊznd/ *a* **one**/**a** ~ [ein]tausend □ *n* Tausend *nt*; ~**s of** Tausende von. ~**th** *a* tausendste(r,s) □ *n* Tausendstel *nt*

thrash /θræʃ/ *vt* verprügeln; *(defeat)* [vernichtend] schlagen. ~ **about** *vi* sich herumwerfen; *(fish:)* zappeln. ~ **out** *vt* ausdiskutieren

thread /θred/ *n* Faden *m*; *(of screw)* Gewinde *nt* □ *vt* einfädeln; auffädeln *(beads)*. ~ **one's way through** sich schlängeln durch. ~**bare** *a* fadenscheinig

threat /θret/ *n* Drohung *f*; *(danger)* Bedrohung *f*

threaten /'θretn/ *vt* drohen (+ *dat*); *(with weapon)* bedrohen; ~ **to do sth** drohen, etw zu tun; ~ **s.o. with sth** jdm etw androhen □ *vi* drohen. ~**ing** *a*, **-ly** *adv* drohend; *(ominous)* bedrohlich

three /θriː/ *a* drei. ~**fold** *a* & *adv* dreifach. ~**some** /-səm/ *n* Trio *nt*

thresh /θreʃ/ *vt* dreschen

threshold /'θreʃəʊld/ *n* Schwelle *f*

threw /θruː/ *see* **throw**

thrift /θrɪft/ *n* Sparsamkeit *f*. ~**y** *a* sparsam

thrill /θrɪl/ *n* Erregung *f*; *(fam)* Nervenkitzel *m* □ *vt (excite)* erregen; **be** ~**ed with** sich sehr freuen über (+ *acc*). ~**er** *n* Thriller *m*. ~**ing** *a* aufregend

thrive /θraɪv/ *vi (pt* **thrived** *or* **throve**, *pp* **thrived** *or* **thriven** /'θrɪvn/) gedeihen (**on** bei); *(business:)* florieren

throat /θrəʊt/ *n* Hals *m*; **sore** ~ Halsschmerzen *pl*; **cut s.o.'s** ~ jdm die Kehle durchschneiden

throb /θrɒb/ *n* Pochen *nt* □ *vi (pt/pp* **throbbed**) pochen; *(vibrate)* vibrieren

throes /θrəʊz/ *npl* **in the** ~ **of** *(fig)* mitten in (+ *dat*)

thrombosis /θrɒm'bəʊsɪs/ *n* Thrombose *f*

throne /θrəʊn/ *n* Thron *m*

throng /θrɒŋ/ *n* Menge *f*

throttle /'θrɒtl/ *vt* erdrosseln

through /θruː/ *prep* durch (+ *acc*); *(during)* während (+ *gen*); *(Amer: up to & including)* bis einschließlich □ *adv* durch; **all** ~ die ganze Zeit; ~ **and** ~ durch und durch; **wet** ~ durch und durch nass; **read sth** ~ etw durchlesen; **let**/**walk** ~ durchlassen/-gehen □ *a (train)* durchgehend; **be** ~ *(finished)* fertig sein; *(Teleph)* durch sein

throughout /θruː'aʊt/ *prep* ~ **the country** im ganzen Land; ~ **the night** die Nacht durch □ *adv* ganz; *(time)* die ganze Zeit

throve /θrəʊv/ *see* **thrive**

throw /θrəʊ/ *n* Wurf *m* □ *vt (pt* **threw**, *pp* **thrown**) werfen; schütten *(liquid)*; betätigen *(switch)*; abwerfen *(rider)*; *(fam: disconcert)* aus der Fassung bringen; *(fam)* geben *(party)*; ~ **sth to s.o.** jdm etw zuwerfen; ~ **sth at s.o.** etw nach jdm werfen; *(pelt with)* jdn mit etw bewerfen. ~ **away** *vt* wegwerfen. ~ **out** *vt* hinauswerfen; *(~ away)* wegwerfen; verwerfen *(plan)*. ~ **up** *vt* hochwerfen □ *vi (fam)* sich übergeben

'**throw-away** *a* Wegwerf-

thrush /θrʌʃ/ *n* Drossel *f*

thrust /θrʌst/ *n* Stoß *m*; *(Phys)* Schub *m* □ *vt (pt/pp* **thrust**) stoßen; *(insert)* stecken; ~ **[up]on** aufbürden (**s.o.** jdm)

thud /θʌd/ *n* dumpfer Schlag *m*

thug /θʌg/ *n* Schläger *m*

thumb /θʌm/ *n* Daumen *m*; **rule of** ~ Faustregel *f*; **under s.o.'s** ~ unter jds Fuchtel □ *vt* ~ **a lift** *(fam)* per Anhalter fahren. ~**index** *n* Daumenregister *nt*. ~**tack** *n (Amer)* Reißzwecke *f*

thump /θʌmp/ *n* Schlag *m*; *(noise)* dumpfer Schlag *m* □ *vt* schlagen □ *vi* hämmern (**on** an/auf + *acc*); *(heart:)* pochen

thunder /'θʌndə(r)/ *n* Donner *m* □ *vi* donnern. ~**clap** *n* Donnerschlag *m*. ~**storm** *n* Gewitter *nt*. ~**y** *a* gewittrig

Thursday /'θɜːzdeɪ/ *n* Donnerstag *m*

thus /ðʌs/ *adv* so

thwart /θwɔːt/ *vt* vereiteln; ~ **s.o.** jdm einen Strich durch die Rechnung machen

thyme /taɪm/ *n* Thymian *m*

thyroid /'θaɪrɔɪd/ *n* Schilddrüse *f*

tiara /tɪ'ɑːrə/ *n* Diadem *nt*

tick[1] /tɪk/ *n* **on** ~ *(fam)* auf Pump

tick[2] *n (sound)* Ticken *nt*; *(mark)* Häkchen *nt*; *(fam: instant)* Sekunde *f* □ *vi* ticken

□ *vt* abhaken. **~ off** *vt* abhaken; (*fam*) rüffeln. **~ over** *vi* (*engine:*) im Leerlauf laufen

ticket /'tɪkɪt/ *n* Karte *f*; (*for bus, train*) Fahrschein *m*; (*Aviat*) Flugschein *m*; (*for lottery*) Los *nt*; (*for article deposited*) Schein *m*; (*label*) Schild *nt*; (*for library*) Lesekarte *f*; (*fine*) Strafzettel *m*. **~collector** *n* Fahrkartenkontrolleur *m*. **~office** *n* Fahrkartenschalter *m*; (*for entry*) Kasse *f*

tick|le /'tɪkl/ *n* Kitzeln *nt* □ *vt/i* kitzeln. **~lish** /'tɪklɪʃ/ *a* kitzlig

tidal /'taɪdl/ *a* (*river, harbour*) Tide-. **~ wave** *n* Flutwelle *f*

tiddly-winks /'tɪdlɪwɪŋks/ *n* Flohspiel *nt*

tide /taɪd/ *n* Gezeiten *pl*; (*of events*) Strom *m*; **the ~ is in/out** es ist Flut/Ebbe □ *vt* **~ s.o. over** jdm über die Runden helfen

tidiness /'taɪdɪnɪs/ *n* Ordentlichkeit *f*

tidy /'taɪdɪ/ *a* (**-ier, -iest**), **-ily** *adv* ordentlich □ *vt* **~ [up]** aufräumen; **~ oneself up** sich zurechtmachen

tie /taɪ/ *n* Krawatte *f*; Schlips *m*; (*cord*) Schnur *f*; (*fig: bond*) Band *nt*; (*restriction*) Bindung *f*; (*Sport*) Unentschieden *nt*; (*in competition*) Punktgleichheit *f* □ *v* (*pres p* **tying**) □ *vt* binden; machen (*knot*) □ *vi* (*Sport*) unentschieden spielen; (*have equal scores, votes*) punktgleich sein; **~ in with** passen zu. **~ up** *vt* festbinden; verschnüren (*parcel*); fesseln (*person*); **be ~d up** (*busy*) beschäftigt sein

tier /tɪə(r)/ *n* Stufe *f*; (*of cake*) Etage *f*; (*in stadium*) Rang *m*

tiff /tɪf/ *n* Streit *m*, (*fam*) Krach *m*

tiger /'taɪgə(r)/ *n* Tiger *m*

tight /taɪt/ *a* (**-er, -est**), **-ly** *adv* fest; (*taut*) straff; (*clothes*) eng; (*control*) streng; (*fam: drunk*) blau; **in a ~ corner** (*fam*) in der Klemme □ *adv* fest

tighten /'taɪtn/ *vt* fester ziehen; straffen (*rope*); anziehen (*screw*); verschärfen (*control*) □ *vi* sich spannen

tight: ~-'fisted *a* knauserig. **~rope** *n* Hochseil *nt*

tights /taɪts/ *npl* Strumpfhose *f*

tile /taɪl/ *n* Fliese *f*; (*on wall*) Kachel *f*; (*on roof*) [Dach]ziegel *m* □ *vt* mit Fliesen auslegen; kacheln (*wall*); decken (*roof*)

till[1] /tɪl/ *prep & conj* = **until**

till[2] *n* Kasse *f*

tiller /'tɪlə(r)/ *n* Ruderpinne *f*

tilt /tɪlt/ *n* Neigung *f*; **at full ~** mit voller Wucht □ *vt* kippen; [zur Seite] neigen (*head*) □ *vi* sich neigen

timber /'tɪmbə(r)/ *n* [Nutz]holz *nt*

time /taɪm/ *n* Zeit *f*; (*occasion*) Mal *nt*; (*rhythm*) Takt *m*; **~s** (*Math*) mal; **at any**

~ jederzeit; this ~ dieses Mal, diesmal; **at ~s** manchmal; **~ and again** immer wieder; **two at a ~** zwei auf einmal; **on ~** pünktlich; **in ~** rechtzeitig; (*eventually*) mit der Zeit; **in no ~** im Handumdrehen; **in a year's ~** in einem Jahr; **behind ~** verspätet; **behind the ~s** rückständig; **for the ~ being** vorläufig; **what is the ~?** wie spät ist es? wie viel Uhr ist es? **by the ~ we arrive** bis wir ankommen; **did you have a nice ~?** hat es dir gut gefallen? **have a good ~!** viel Vergnügen! □ *vt* stoppen (*race*); **be well ~d** gut abgepaßt sein

time: ~ bomb *n* Zeitbombe *f*. **~-lag** *n* Zeitdifferenz *f*. **~less** *a* zeitlos. **~ly** *a* rechtzeitig. **~-switch** *n* Zeitschalter *m*. **~-table** *n* Fahrplan *m*; (*Sch*) Stundenplan *m*

timid /'tɪmɪd/ *a*, **-ly** *adv* scheu; (*hesitant*) zaghaft

timing /'taɪmɪŋ/ *n* Wahl *f* des richtigen Zeitpunkts; (*Sport, Techn*) Timing *nt*

tin /tɪn/ *n* Zinn *nt*; (*container*) Dose *f* □ *vt* (*pt/pp* **tinned**) in Dosen *od* Büchsen konservieren. **~ foil** *n* Stanniol *nt*; (*Culin*) Alufolie *f*

tinge /tɪndʒ/ *n* Hauch *m* □ *vt* **~d with** mit einer Spur von

tingle /'tɪŋgl/ *vi* kribbeln

tinker /'tɪŋkə(r)/ *vi* herumbasteln (**with** an + *dat*)

tinkle /'tɪŋkl/ *n* Klingeln *nt* □ *vi* klingeln

tinned /tɪnd/ *a* Dosen-, Büchsen-

'tin opener *n* Dosen-/Büchsenöffner *m*

'tinpot *a* (*pej*) (*firm*) schäbig

tinsel /'tɪnsl/ *n* Lametta *nt*

tint /tɪnt/ *n* Farbton *m* □ *vt* tönen

tiny /'taɪnɪ/ *a* (**-ier, -iest**) winzig

tip[1] /tɪp/ *n* Spitze *f*

tip[2] *n* (*money*) Trinkgeld *nt*; (*advice*) Rat *m*, (*fam*) Tipp *m*; (*for rubbish*) Müllhalde *f* □ *v* (*pt/pp* **tipped**) □ *vt* (*tilt*) kippen; (*reward*) Trinkgeld geben (**s.o.** jdm) □ *vi* kippen. **~ off** *vt* **~ s.o. off** jdm einen Hinweis geben. **~ out** *vt* auskippen. **~ over** *vt/i* umkippen

'tip-off *n* Hinweis *m*

tipped /tɪpt/ *a* Filter-

tipsy /'tɪpsɪ/ *a* (*fam*) beschwipst

tiptoe /'tɪptəʊ/ *n* **on ~** auf Zehenspitzen

tiptop /tɪp'tɒp/ *a* (*fam*) erstklassig

tire /'taɪə(r)/ *vt/i* ermüden. **~d** *a* müde; **be ~d of sth** etw satt haben; **~d out** [völlig] erschöpft. **~less** *a*, **-ly** *adv* unermüdlich. **~some** /-səm/ *a* lästig

tiring /'taɪrɪŋ/ *a* ermüdend

tissue /'tɪʃu/ n Gewebe nt; (handkerchief) Papiertaschentuch nt. **~-paper** n Seidenpapier nt

tit[1] /tɪt/ n (bird) Meise f

tit[2] n **~ for tat** wie du mir, so ich dir

'titbit n Leckerbissen m

titilate /'tɪtɪleɪt/ vt erregen

title /'taɪtl/ n Titel m. **~-role** n Titelrolle f

tittle-tattle /'tɪtltætl/ n Klatsch m

titular /'tɪtjʊlə(r)/ a nominell

to /tu:, unbetont tə/ prep zu (+ dat); (with place, direction) nach; (to cinema, theatre) in (+ acc); (to wedding, party) auf (+ acc); (address, send, fasten) an (+ acc); (per) pro; (up to, until) bis; **to the station** zum Bahnhof; **to Germany/Switzerland** nach Deutschland/ in die Schweiz; **to the toilet/one's room** auf die Toilette/sein Zimmer; **to the office/an exhibition** ins Büro/ in eine Ausstellung; **to university** auf die Universität; **twenty/quarter to eight** zwanzig/Viertel vor acht; **5 to 6 pounds** 5 bis 6 Pfund; **to the end** bis zum Schluss; **to this day** bis heute; **to the best of my knowledge** nach meinem besten Wissen; **give/say sth to s.o.** jdm etw geben/sagen; **go/come to s.o.** zu jdm gehen/ kommen; **I've never been to Berlin** ich war noch nie in Berlin; **there's nothing to it** es ist nichts dabei □ verbal construction **to go** gehen; **to stay** bleiben; **learn to swim** schwimmen lernen; **want to/have to go** gehen wollen/müssen; **be easy/difficult to forget** leicht/schwer zu vergessen sein; **too ill/tired to go** zu krank/müde, um zu gehen; **he did it to annoy me** er tat es, um mich zu ärgern; **you have to** du musst; **I don't want to** ich will nicht; **I'd love to** gern; **I forgot to** ich habe es vergessen; **he wants to be a teacher** er will Lehrer werden; **live to be 90** 90 werden; **he was the last to arrive** er kam als Letzter; **to be honest** ehrlich gesagt □ adv **pull to** anlehnen; **to and fro** hin und her

toad /təʊd/ n Kröte f. **~stool** n Giftpilz m

toast /təʊst/ n Toast m □ vt toasten ⟨bread⟩; (drink a ~ to) trinken auf (+ acc). **~er** n Toaster m

tobacco /tə'bækəʊ/ n Tabak m. **~nist's [shop]** n Tabakladen m

toboggan /tə'bɒgən/ n Schlitten m □ vi Schlitten fahren

today /tə'deɪ/ n & adv heute; **~ week** heute in einer Woche; **~'s paper** die heutige Zeitung

toddler /'tɒdlə(r)/ n Kleinkind nt

to-do /tə'du:/ n (fam) Getue nt, Theater nt

toe /təʊ/ n Zeh m; (of footwear) Spitze f □ vt **~ the line** spuren. **~nail** n Zehennagel m

toffee /'tɒfɪ/ n Karamellbonbon m & nt

together /tə'geðə(r)/ adv zusammen; (at the same time) gleichzeitig

toil /tɔɪl/ n [harte] Arbeit f □ vi schwer arbeiten

toilet /'tɔɪlɪt/ n Toilette f. **~ bag** n Kulturbeutel m. **~ paper** n Toilettenpapier nt

toiletries /'tɔɪlɪtrɪz/ npl Toilettenartikel pl

toilet: **~ roll** n Rolle f Toilettenpapier. **~ water** n Toilettenwasser nt

token /'təʊkən/ n Zeichen nt; (counter) Marke f; (voucher) Gutschein m □ attrib symbolisch

told /təʊld/ see **tell** □ a **all ~** insgesamt

tolerable /'tɒlərəbl/ a, **-bly** adv erträglich; (not bad) leidlich

toleran|ce /'tɒlərəns/ n Toleranz f. **~t** a, **-ly** adv tolerant

tolerate /'tɒləreɪt/ vt dulden, tolerieren; (bear) ertragen

toll[1] /təʊl/ n Gebühr f; (for road) Maut f (Aust); **death ~** Zahl f der Todesopfer; **take a heavy ~** einen hohen Tribut fordern

toll[2] vi läuten

tom /tɒm/ n (cat) Kater m

tomato /tə'mɑːtəʊ/ n (pl -es) Tomate f. **~ purée** n Tomatenmark nt

tomb /tu:m/ n Grabmal nt

tomboy /'tɒm-/ n Wildfang m

'tombstone n Grabstein m

'tom-cat n Kater m

tome /təʊm/ n dicker Band m

tomfoolery /tɒm'fu:lərɪ/ n Blödsinn m

tomorrow /tə'mɒrəʊ/ n & adv morgen; **~ morning** morgen früh; **the day after ~** übermorgen; **see you ~!** bis morgen!

ton /tʌn/ n Tonne f; **~s of** (fam) jede Menge

tone /təʊn/ n Ton m; (colour) Farbton m □ vt **~ down** dämpfen; (fig) mäßigen. **~ up** vt kräftigen; straffen ⟨muscles⟩

tongs /tɒŋz/ npl Zange f

tongue /tʌŋ/ n Zunge f; **~ in cheek** (fam) nicht ernst. **~-twister** n Zungenbrecher m

tonic /'tɒnɪk/ n Tonikum nt; (for hair) Haarwasser nt; (fig) Wohltat f; **~ [water]** Tonic nt

tonight /tə'naɪt/ n & adv heute Nacht; (evening) heute Abend

tonne /tʌn/ n Tonne f

tonsil /'tɒnsl/ n (Anat) Mandel f. **~litis** /-sə'laɪtɪs/ n Mandelentzündung f

too /tu:/ *adv* zu; (*also*) auch; ~ **much/little** zu viel/zu wenig

took /tʊk/ *see* take

tool /tu:l/ *n* Werkzeug *nt*; (*for gardening*) Gerät *nt*

toot /tu:t/ *n* Hupsignal *nt* □ *vi* tuten; (*Auto*) hupen

tooth /tu:θ/ *n* (*pl* teeth) Zahn *m*

tooth: ~**ache** *n* Zahnschmerzen *pl.* ~**brush** *n* Zahnbürste *f.* ~**less** *a* zahnlos. ~**paste** *n* Zahnpasta *f.* ~**pick** *n* Zahnstocher *m*

top¹ /tɒp/ *n* (*toy*) Kreisel *m*

top² *n* oberer Teil *m*; (*apex*) Spitze *f*; (*summit*) Gipfel *m*; (*Sch*) Erste(r) *m/f*; (*top part or half*) Oberteil *nt*; (*head*) Kopfende *nt*; (*of road*) oberes Ende *nt*; (*upper surface*) Oberfläche *f*; (*lid*) Deckel *m*; (*of bottle*) Verschluss *m*; (*garment*) Top *nt*; **at the/on** ~ oben; **on** ~ **of** oben auf (+ *dat/acc*); **on** ~ **of that** (*besides*) obendrein; **from** ~ **to bottom** von oben bis unten □ *a* oberste(r,s); (*highest*) höchste(r,s); (*best*) beste(r,s) □ *vt* (*pt/pp* **topped**) an erster Stelle stehen auf (+ *dat*) ⟨*list*⟩; (*exceed*) übersteigen; (*remove the* ~ *of*) die Spitze abschneiden von. ~ **up** *vt* nachfüllen, auffüllen

top: ~'**hat** *n* Zylinder[hut] *m.* ~**heavy** *a* kopflastig

topic /'tɒpɪk/ *n* Thema *nt.* ~**al** *a* aktuell

top: ~**less** *a & adv* oben ohne. ~**most** *a* oberste(r,s)

topple /'tɒpl/ *vt/i* umstürzen. ~ **off** *vi* stürzen

top-'secret *a* streng geheim

topsy-turvy /tɒpsɪ'tɜːvɪ/ *adv* völlig durcheinander

torch /tɔːtʃ/ *n* Taschenlampe *f*; (*flaming*) Fackel *f*

tore /tɔː(r)/ *see* tear¹

torment¹ /'tɔːment/ *n* Qual *f*

torment² /tɔː'ment/ *vt* quälen

torn /tɔːn/ *see* tear¹ □ *a* zerrissen

tornado /tɔː'neɪdəʊ/ *n* (*pl* -es) Wirbelsturm *m*

torpedo /tɔː'piːdəʊ/ *n* (*pl* -es) Torpedo *m* □ *vt* torpedieren

torrent /'tɒrənt/ *n* reißender Strom *m.* ~**ial** /tə'renʃl/ *a* ⟨*rain*⟩ wolkenbruchartig

torso /'tɔːsəʊ/ *n* Rumpf *m*; (*Art*) Torso *m*

tortoise /'tɔːtəs/ *n* Schildkröte *f.* ~**shell** *n* Schildpatt *nt*

tortuous /'tɔːtjʊəs/ *a* verschlungen; (*fig*) umständlich

torture /'tɔːtʃə(r)/ *n* Folter *f*; (*fig*) Qual *f* □ *vt* foltern; (*fig*) quälen

toss /tɒs/ *vt* werfen; (*into the air*) hochwerfen; (*shake*) schütteln; (*unseat*) abwerfen; mischen ⟨*salad*⟩; wenden ⟨pan cake⟩; ~ **a coin** mit einer Münze losen □ *vi* ~ **and turn** (*in bed*) sich [schlaflos] ir Bett wälzen. ~ **up** *vi* [mit einer Münze losen

tot¹ /tɒt/ *n* kleines Kind *nt*; (*fam: of liquor* Gläschen *nt*

tot² *vt* (*pt/pp* totted) ~ **up** (*fam*) zusam menzählen

total /'təʊtl/ *a* gesamt; (*complete*) völlig total □ *n* Gesamtzahl *f*; (*Sum*) Gesamt summe *f* □ *vt* (*pt/pp* **totalled**) zusam menzählen; (*amount to*) sich belaufen au (+ *acc*)

totalitarian /təʊtælɪ'teərɪən/ *a* totalitär

totally /'təʊtəlɪ/ *adv* völling, total

totter /'tɒtə(r)/ *vi* taumeln; (*rock*) schwanken. ~**y** *a* wackelig

touch /tʌtʃ/ *n* Berührung *f*; (*sense*) Tastsinn *m*; (*Mus*) Anschlag *m*; (*contact*) Kontakt *m*; (*trace*) Spur *f*; (*fig*) Anflug *m*; **get/be in** ~ sich in Verbindung setzen/in Verbindung stehen (**with** mit) □ *vt* berühren; (*get hold of*) anfassen; (*lightly*) tippen auf/an (+ *acc*); (*brush against*) streifen [gegen]; (*reach*) erreichen; (*equal*) herankommen an (+ *acc*); (*fig: move*) rühren; anrühren ⟨*food, subject*⟩; **don't** ~ **that!** fass das nicht an! □ *vi* sich berühren; ~ **on** (*fig*) berühren. ~ **down** *vi* (*Aviat*) landen. ~ **up** *vt* ausbessern

touch|ing /'tʌtʃɪŋ/ *a* rührend. ~**y** *a* empfindlich; ⟨*subject*⟩ heikel

tough /tʌf/ *a* (-**er**, -**est**) zäh; (*severe, harsh*) hart; (*difficult*) schwierig; (*durable*) strapazierfähig

toughen /'tʌfn/ *vt* härten; ~ **up** abhärten

tour /tʊə(r)/ *n* Reise *f*, Tour *f*; (*of building, town*) Besichtigung *f*; (*Theat, Sport*) Tournee *f*; (*of duty*) Dienstzeit *f* □ *vt* fahren durch; besichtigen ⟨*building*⟩ □ *vi* herumreisen

touris|m /'tʊərɪzm/ *n* Tourismus *m*, Fremdenverkehr *m.* ~**t** /-rɪst/ *n* Tourist(in) *m(f)* □ *attrib* Touristen-. ~**t office** *n* Fremdenverkehrsbüro *nt*

tournament /'tʊənəmənt/ *n* Turnier *nt*

'**tour operator** *n* Reiseveranstalter *m*

tousle /'taʊzl/ *vt* zerzausen

tout /taʊt/ *n* Anreißer *m*; (*ticket* ~) Kartenschwarzhändler *m* □ *vi* ~ **for customers** Kunden werben

tow /təʊ/ *n* give s.o./a car a ~ jdn/ein Auto abschleppen; '**on** ~ 'wird geschleppt'; **in** ~ (*fam*) im Schlepptau □ *vt* schleppen; ziehen ⟨*trailer*⟩. ~ **away** *vt* abschleppen

toward[s] /tə'wɔːd(z)/ *prep* zu (+ *dat*); (*with direction*) nach; (*with time*) gegen (+ *acc*); (*with respect to*) gegenüber (+ *dat*)

towel /'taʊəl/ n Handtuch nt. ~**ling** n (Tex) Frottee nt

tower /'taʊə(r)/ n Turm m □ vi ~ **above** überragen. ~ **block** n Hochhaus nt. ~**ing** a hoch aufragend

town /taʊn/ n Stadt f. ~ 'hall n Rathaus nt

tow: ~-**path** n Treidelpfad m. ~-**rope** n Abschleppseil nt

toxic /'tɒksɪk/ a giftig. ~ 'waste n Giftmüll m

toxin /'tɒksɪn/ n Gift nt

toy /tɔɪ/ n Spielzeug nt □ vi ~ **with** spielen mit; stochern in (+ dat) ⟨food⟩. ~**shop** n Spielwarengeschäft nt

trac|e /treɪs/ n Spur f □ vt folgen (+ dat); ⟨find⟩ finden; ⟨draw⟩ zeichnen; ⟨with tracing-paper⟩ durchpausen. ~**ing-paper** n Pauspapier nt

track /træk/ n Spur f; ⟨path⟩ [unbefestigter] Weg m; ⟨Sport⟩ Bahn f; ⟨Rail⟩ Gleis nt; **keep** ~ **of** im Auge behalten □ vt verfolgen. ~ **down** vt aufspüren; ⟨find⟩ finden

'**tracksuit** n Trainingsanzug m

tract[1] /trækt/ n ⟨land⟩ Gebiet nt

tract[2] n ⟨pamphlet⟩ [Flug]schrift f

tractor /'træktə(r)/ n Traktor m

trade /treɪd/ n Handel m; ⟨line of business⟩ Gewerbe nt; ⟨business⟩ Geschäft nt; ⟨craft⟩ Handwerk nt; **by** ~ von Beruf □ vt tauschen; ~ **in** ⟨give in part exchange⟩ in Zahlung geben □ vi handeln (**in** mit)

'**trade mark** n Warenzeichen nt

trader /'treɪdə(r)/ n Händler m

trade: ~ '**union** n Gewerkschaft f. ~ '**unionist** n Gewerkschaftler(in) m(f)

trading /'treɪdɪŋ/ n Handel m. ~ **estate** n Gewerbegebiet nt. ~ **stamp** n Rabattmarke f

tradition /trə'dɪʃn/ n Tradition f. ~**al** a, -**ly** adv traditionell

traffic /'træfɪk/ n Verkehr m; ⟨trading⟩ Handel m □ vi handeln (**in** mit)

traffic: ~ **circle** n (Amer) Kreisverkehr m. ~ **jam** n [Verkehrs]stau m. ~ **lights** npl [Verkehrs]ampel f. ~ **warden** n ≈ Hilfspolizist m; ⟨woman⟩ Politesse f

tragedy /'trædʒədɪ/ n Tragödie f

tragic /'trædʒɪk/ a, -**ally** adv tragisch

trail /treɪl/ n Spur f; ⟨path⟩ Weg m, Pfad m □ vi schleifen; ⟨plant:⟩ sich ranken; ~ [**behind**] zurückbleiben; ⟨Sport⟩ zurückliegen □ vt verfolgen, folgen (+ dat); ⟨drag⟩ schleifen

trailer /'treɪlə(r)/ n (Auto) Anhänger m; (Amer: caravan) Wohnwagen m; ⟨film⟩ Vorschau f

train /treɪn/ n Zug m; ⟨of dress⟩ Schleppe f; ~ **of thought** Gedankengang m □ vt ausbilden; ⟨Sport⟩ trainieren; ⟨aim⟩ richten auf (+ acc); erziehen ⟨child⟩; abrichten ⟨to do tricks⟩ dressieren ⟨animal⟩; ziehen ⟨plant⟩ □ vi eine Ausbildung machen; ⟨Sport⟩ trainieren. ~**ed** a ausgebildet

trainee /treɪ'niː/ n Auszubildende(r) m/f; (Techn) Praktikant(in) m(f)

train|er /'treɪnə(r)/ n ⟨Sport⟩ Trainer m; (in circus) Dompteur m; ~**ers** pl Trainingsschuhe pl. ~**ing** n Ausbildung f; ⟨Sport⟩ Training nt; ⟨of animals⟩ Dressur f

traipse /treɪps/ vi (fam) latschen

trait /treɪt/ n Eigenschaft f

traitor /'treɪtə(r)/ n Verräter m

tram /træm/ n Straßenbahn f. ~-**lines** npl Straßenbahnschienen pl

tramp /træmp/ n Landstreicher m; ⟨hike⟩ Wanderung f □ vi stapfen; ⟨walk⟩ marschieren

trample /'træmpl/ vt/i trampeln (**on** auf + acc)

trampoline /'træmpəliːn/ n Trampolin nt

trance /trɑːns/ n Trance f

tranquil /'træŋkwɪl/ a ruhig. ~**lity** /-'kwɪlətɪ/ n Ruhe f

tranquillizer /'træŋkwɪlaɪzə(r)/ n Beruhigungsmittel nt

transact /træn'zækt/ vt abschließen. ~**ion** /-ækʃn/ n Transaktion f

transcend /træn'send/ vt übersteigen

transcript /'trænskrɪpt/ n Abschrift f; ⟨of official proceedings⟩ Protokoll nt. ~**ion** /-'skrɪpʃn/ n Abschrift f

transept /'trænsept/ n Querschiff nt

transfer[1] /'trænsfɜː(r)/ n (see **transfer**[2]) Übertragung f; Verlegung f; Versetzung f; Überweisung f; ⟨Sport⟩ Transfer m; ⟨design⟩ Abziehbild nt

transfer[2] /træns'fɜː(r)/ v (pt/pp **transferred**) □ vt übertragen; verlegen ⟨firm, prisoners⟩; versetzen ⟨employee⟩; überweisen ⟨money⟩; ⟨Sport⟩ transferieren □ vi [über]wechseln; ⟨when travelling⟩ umsteigen. ~**able** /-əbl/ a übertragbar

transform /træns'fɔːm/ vt verwandeln. ~**ation** /-fə'meɪʃn/ n Verwandlung f. ~**er** n Transformator m

transfusion /træns'fjuːʒn/ n Transfusion f

transient /'trænzɪənt/ a kurzlebig; ⟨life⟩ kurz

transistor /træn'zɪstə(r)/ n Transistor m

transit /'trænsɪt/ n Transit m; ⟨of goods⟩ Transport m; **in** ~ ⟨goods⟩ auf dem Transport

transition /træn'sɪʒn/ n Übergang m. ~al a Übergangs-

transitive /'trænsɪtɪv/ a, -ly adv transitiv

transitory /'trænsɪtərɪ/ a vergänglich; ⟨life⟩ kurz

translat|e /træns'leɪt/ vt übersetzen. ~ion /-'leɪʃn/ n Übersetzung f. ~or n Übersetzer(in) m(f)

translucent /trænz'lu:snt/ a durchscheinend

transmission /trænz'mɪʃn/ n Übertragung f

transmit /trænz'mɪt/ vt (pt/pp transmitted) übertragen. ~ter n Sender m

transparen|cy /træns'pærənsɪ/ n (Phot) Dia nt. ~t a durchsichtig

transpire /træn'spaɪə(r)/ vi sich herausstellen; ⟨fam: happen⟩ passieren

transplant[1] /'trænsplɑ:nt/ n Verpflanzung f, Transplantation f

transplant[2] /træns'plɑ:nt/ vt umpflanzen; (Med) verpflanzen

transport[1] /'trænspɔ:t/ n Transport m

transport[2] /træn'spɔ:t/ vt transportieren. ~ation /-'teɪʃn/ n Transport m

transpose /træns'pəʊz/ vt umstellen

transvestite /træns'vestaɪt/ n Transvestit m

trap /træp/ n Falle f; ⟨fam: mouth⟩ Klappe f; pony and ~ Einspänner m ▫ vt (pt/pp trapped) [mit einer Falle] fangen; ⟨jam⟩ einklemmen; be ~ped festsitzen; ⟨shut in⟩ eingeschlossen sein; ⟨cut off⟩ abgeschnitten sein. ~door n Falltür f

trapeze /trə'pi:z/ n Trapez nt

trash /træʃ/ n Schund m; ⟨rubbish⟩ Abfall m; ⟨nonsense⟩ Quatsch m. ~can n (Amer) Mülleimer m. ~y a Schund-

trauma /'trɔ:mə/ n Trauma nt. ~tic /-'mætɪk/ a traumatisch

travel /'trævl/ n Reisen nt ▫ v (pt/pp travelled) ▫ vi reisen; ⟨go in vehicle⟩ fahren; ⟨light, sound:⟩ sich fortpflanzen; (Techn) sich bewegen ▫ vt bereisen; fahren ⟨distance⟩. ~ agency n Reisebüro nt. ~ agent n Reisebürokaufmann m

traveller /'trævələ(r)/ n Reisende(r) m/f; (Comm) Vertreter m; ~s pl (gipsies) fahrendes Volk. ~'s cheque n Reisescheck m

trawler /'trɔ:lə(r)/ n Fischdampfer m

tray /treɪ/ n Tablett nt; ⟨for oven⟩ [Back]blech nt; ⟨for documents⟩ Ablagekorb m

treacher|ous /'tretʃərəs/ a treulos; ⟨dangerous⟩ tückisch. ~y n Verrat m

treacle /'tri:kl/ n Sirup m

tread /tred/ n Schritt m; ⟨step⟩ Stufe f; ⟨of tyre⟩ Profil nt ▫ v (pt trod, pp trodden)

▫ vi ⟨walk⟩ gehen; ~ on/in treten auf/ in (+ acc) ▫ vt treten

treason /'tri:zn/ n Verrat m

treasure /'treʒə(r)/ n Schatz m ▫ vt in Ehren halten. ~r n Kassenwart m

treasury /'treʒərɪ/ n Schatzkammer f; the T~ das Finanzministerium

treat /tri:t/ n [besonderes] Vergnügen nt; give s.o. a ~ jdm etwas Besonderes bieten ▫ vt behandeln; ~ s.o. to sth jdm etw spendieren

treatise /'tri:tɪz/ n Abhandlung f

treatment /'tri:tmənt/ n Behandlung f

treaty /'tri:tɪ/ n Vertrag m

treble /'trebl/ a dreifach; ~ the amount dreimal so viel ▫ n (Mus) Diskant m; ⟨voice⟩ Sopran m ▫ vt verdreifachen ▫ vi sich verdreifachen. ~ clef n Violinschlüssel m

tree /tri:/ n Baum m

trek /trek/ n Marsch m ▫ vi (pt/pp trekked) latschen

trellis /'trelɪs/ n Gitter nt

tremble /'trembl/ vi zittern

tremendous /trɪ'mendəs/ a, -ly adv gewaltig; ⟨fam: excellent⟩ großartig

tremor /'tremə(r)/ n Zittern nt; [earth] ~ Beben nt

trench /trentʃ/ n Graben m; (Mil) Schützengraben m

trend /trend/ n Tendenz f; ⟨fashion⟩ Trend m. ~y a (-ier, -iest) ⟨fam⟩ modisch

trepidation /trepɪ'deɪʃn/ n Beklommenheit f

trespass /'trespəs/ vi ~ on unerlaubt betreten. ~er n Unbefugte(r) m/f

trial /'traɪəl/ n (Jur) [Gerichts]verfahren nt, Prozess m; ⟨test⟩ Probe f; ⟨ordeal⟩ Prüfung f; be on ~ auf Probe sein; (Jur) angeklagt sein ⟨for wegen⟩; by ~ and error durch Probieren

triang|le /'traɪæŋgl/ n Dreieck nt; (Mus) Triangel m. ~ular /-'æŋgjʊlə(r)/ a dreieckig

tribe /traɪb/ n Stamm m

tribulation /trɪbjʊ'leɪʃn/ n Kummer m

tribunal /traɪ'bju:nl/ n Schiedsgericht nt

tributary /'trɪbjʊtərɪ/ n Nebenfluss m

tribute /'trɪbju:t/ n Tribut m; pay ~ Tribut zollen ⟨to dat⟩

trice /traɪs/ n in a ~ im Nu

trick /trɪk/ n Trick m; ⟨joke⟩ Streich m; (Cards) Stich m; ⟨feat of skill⟩ Kunststück nt; that should do the ~ ⟨fam⟩ damit dürfte es klappen ▫ vt täuschen, ⟨fam⟩ hereinlegen

trickle /'trɪkl/ vi rinnen

trick|ster /'trɪkstə(r)/ n Schwindler m. **~y** a (-ier, -iest) a schwierig

tricycle /'traɪsɪkl/ n Dreirad nt

tried /traɪd/ see **try**

trifl|e /'traɪfl/ n Kleinigkeit f; (Culin) Trifle nt. **~ing** a unbedeutend

trigger /'trɪgə(r)/ n Abzug m; (fig) Auslöser m □ vt **~ [off]** auslösen

trigonometry /trɪgə'nɒmɪtrɪ/ n Trigonometrie f

trim /trɪm/ a (trimmer, trimmest) gepflegt □ n (cut) Nachschneiden nt; (decoration) Verzierung f; (condition) Zustand m □ vt schneiden; (decorate) besetzen; (Naut) trimmen. **~ming** n Besatz m; **~mings** pl (accessories) Zubehör nt; (decorations) Verzierungen pl; **with all the ~mings** mit allem Drum und Dran

Trinity /'trɪnətɪ/ n the [Holy] **~** die [Heilige] Dreieinigkeit f

trinket /'trɪŋkɪt/ n Schmuckgegenstand m

trio /'triːəʊ/ n Trio nt

trip /trɪp/ n Reise f; (excursion) Ausflug m □ v (pt/pp tripped) □ vt **~ s.o. up** jdm ein Bein stellen □ vi stolpern (**on/over** über + acc)

tripe /traɪp/ n Kaldaunen pl; (nonsense) Quatsch m

triple /'trɪpl/ a dreifach □ vt verdreifachen □ vi sich verdreifachen

triplets /'trɪplɪts/ npl Drillinge pl

triplicate /'trɪplɪkət/ n **in ~** in dreifacher Ausfertigung

tripod /'traɪpɒd/ n Stativ nt

tripper /'trɪpə(r)/ n Ausflügler m

trite /traɪt/ a banal

triumph /'traɪʌmf/ n Triumph m □ vi triumphieren (**over** über + acc). **~ant** /-'ʌmfnt/ a, **-ly** adv triumphierend

trivial /'trɪvɪəl/ a belanglos. **~ity** /-'ælətɪ/ n Belanglosigkeit f

trod, trodden /trɒd, 'trɒdn/ see **tread**

trolley /'trɒlɪ/ n (for serving food) Servierwagen m; (for shopping) Einkaufswagen m; (for luggage) Kofferkuli m; (Amer: tram) Straßenbahn f. **~ bus** n O-Bus m

trombone /trɒm'bəʊn/ n Posaune f

troop /truːp/ n Schar f; **~s** pl Truppen pl □ vi **~ in/out** hinein-/hinausströmen

trophy /'trəʊfɪ/ n Trophäe f; (in competition) ≈ Pokal m

tropic /'trɒpɪk/ n Wendekreis m; **~s** pl Tropen pl. **~al** a tropisch; (fruit) Süd-

trot /trɒt/ n Trab m □ vi (pt/pp trotted) traben

trouble /'trʌbl/ n Ärger m; (difficulties) Schwierigkeiten pl; (inconvenience) Mühe f; (conflict) Unruhe f; (Med) Beschwerden pl; (Techn) Probleme pl; **get into ~** Ärger bekommen; **take ~** sich (dat) Mühe geben □ vt (disturb) stören; (worry) beunruhigen □ vi sich bemühen. **~-maker** n Unruhestifter m. **~some** /-səm/ a schwierig; (flies, cough) lästig

trough /trɒf/ n Trog m

trounce /traʊns/ vt vernichtend schlagen; (thrash) verprügeln

troupe /truːp/ n Truppe f

trousers /'traʊzəz/ npl Hose f

trousseau /'truːsəʊ/ n Aussteuer f

trout /traʊt/ n inv Forelle f

trowel /'traʊəl/ n Kelle f; (for gardening) Pflanzkelle f

truant /'truːənt/ n **play ~** die Schule schwänzen

truce /truːs/ n Waffenstillstand m

truck /trʌk/ n Last[kraft]wagen m; (Rail) Güterwagen m

truculent /'trʌkjʊlənt/ a aufsässig

trudge /trʌdʒ/ n [mühseliger] Marsch m □ vi latschen

true /truː/ a (-r, -st) wahr; (loyal) treu; (genuine) echt; **come ~** in Erfüllung gehen; **is that ~?** stimmt das?

truism /'truːɪzm/ n Binsenwahrheit f

truly /'truːlɪ/ adv wirklich; (faithfully) treu; **Yours ~** Hochachtungsvoll

trump /trʌmp/ n (Cards) Trumpf m □ vt übertrumpfen. **~ up** vt (fam) erfinden

trumpet /'trʌmpɪt/ n Trompete f. **~er** n Trompeter m

truncheon /'trʌntʃn/ n Schlagstock m

trundle /'trʌndl/ vt/i rollen

trunk /trʌŋk/ n [Baum]stamm m; (body) Rumpf m; (of elephant) Rüssel m; (for travelling) [Übersee]koffer m; (for storage) Truhe f; (Amer: of car) Kofferraum m; **~s** pl Badehose f

truss /trʌs/ n (Med) Bruchband nt

trust /trʌst/ n Vertrauen nt; (group of companies) Trust m; (organization) Treuhandgesellschaft f; (charitable) Stiftung f □ vt trauen (+ dat), vertrauen (+ dat); (hope) hoffen □ vi vertrauen (**in/to** auf + acc)

trustee /trʌs'tiː/ n Treuhänder m

trust|ful /'trʌstfl/ a, **-ly** adv vertrauensvoll. **~ing** a vertrauensvoll. **~worthy** a vertrauenswürdig

truth /truːθ/ n (pl **-s** /truːðz/) Wahrheit f. **~ful** a, **-ly** adv ehrlich

try /traɪ/ n Versuch m □ v (pt/pp tried) □ vt versuchen; (sample, taste) probieren; (be a strain on) anstrengen; (Jur) vor Gericht stellen; verhandeln (case) □ vi versuchen; (make an effort) sich bemühen. **~ on** vt anprobieren; aufprobieren (hat). **~ out** vt ausprobieren

trying /'traɪɪŋ/ *a* schwierig

T-shirt /'tiː-/ *n* T-Shirt *nt*

tub /tʌb/ *n* Kübel *m*; (*carton*) Becher *m*; (*bath*) Wanne *f*

tuba /'tjuːbə/ *n* (*Mus*) Tuba *f*

tubby /'tʌbɪ/ *a* (**-ier, -iest**) rundlich

tube /tjuːb/ *n* Röhre *f*; (*pipe*) Rohr *nt*; (*flexible*) Schlauch *m*; (*of toothpaste*) Tube *f*; (*Rail, fam*) U-Bahn *f*

tuber /'tjuːbə(r)/ *n* Knolle *f*

tuberculosis /tjuːbɜːkjʊ'ləʊsɪs/ *n* Tuberkulose *f*

tubing /'tjuːbɪŋ/ *n* Schlauch *m*

tubular /'tjuːbjʊlə(r)/ *a* röhrenförmig

tuck /tʌk/ *n* Saum *m*; (*decorative*) Biese *f* ◻ *vt* (*put*) stecken. **~ in** *vt* hineinstecken; **~ s.o.** in jdn zudecken ◻ *vi* (*fam: eat*) zulangen. **~ up** *vt* hochkrempeln ⟨sleeves⟩; (*in bed*) zudecken

Tuesday /'tjuːzdeɪ/ *n* Dienstag *m*

tuft /tʌft/ *n* Büschel *nt*

tug /tʌg/ *n* Ruck *m*; (*Naut*) Schleppdampfer *m* ◻ *v* (*pt/pp* **tugged**) ◻ *vt* ziehen ◻ *vi* zerren (**at** an + *dat*). **~ of war** *n* Tauziehen *nt*

tuition /tjuː'ɪʃn/ *n* Unterricht *m*

tulip /'tjuːlɪp/ *n* Tulpe *f*

tumble /'tʌmbl/ *n* Sturz *m* ◻ *vi* fallen; **~ to sth** (*fam*) etw kapieren. **~down** *a* verfallen. **~-drier** *n* Wäschetrockner *m*

tumbler /'tʌmblə(r)/ *n* Glas *nt*

tummy /'tʌmɪ/ *n* (*fam*) Magen *m*; (*abdomen*) Bauch *m*

tumour /'tjuːmə(r)/ *n* Geschwulst *f*, Tumor *m*

tumult /'tjuːmʌlt/ *n* Tumult *m*. **~uous** /-'mʌltjʊəs/ *a* stürmisch

tuna /'tjuːnə/ *n* Thunfisch *m*

tune /tjuːn/ *n* Melodie *f*; **out of ~** ⟨instrument⟩ verstimmt; **to the ~ of** (*fam*) in Höhe von ◻ *vt* stimmen; (*Techn*) einstellen. **~ in** *vt* einstellen ◻ *vi* **~ in to a station** einen Sender einstellen. **~ up** *vi* (*Mus*) stimmen

tuneful /'tjuːnfl/ *a* melodisch

tunic /'tjuːnɪk/ *n* (*Mil*) Uniformjacke *f*; (*Sch*) Trägerkleid *nt*

Tunisia /tjuː'nɪzɪə/ *n* Tunesien *nt*

tunnel /'tʌnl/ *n* Tunnel *m* ◻ *vi* (*pt/pp* **tunnelled**) einen Tunnel graben

turban /'tɜːbən/ *n* Turban *m*

turbine /'tɜːbaɪn/ *n* Turbine *f*

turbot /'tɜːbət/ *n* Steinbutt *m*

turbulen|ce /'tɜːbjʊləns/ *n* Turbulenz *f*. **~t** *a* stürmisch

tureen /tjʊə'riːn/ *n* Terrine *f*

turf /tɜːf/ *n* Rasen *m*; (*segment*) Rasenstück *nt*. **~ out** *vt* (*fam*) rausschmeißen

'turf accountant *n* Buchmacher *m*

Turk /tɜːk/ *n* Türke *m*/Türkin *f*

turkey /'tɜːkɪ/ *n* Pute *f*, Truthahn *m*

Turk|ey *n* die Türkei. **~ish** *a* türkisch

turmoil /'tɜːmɔɪl/ *n* Aufruhr *m*; (*confusion*) Durcheinander *nt*

turn /tɜːn/ *n* (*rotation*) Drehung *f*; (*in road*) Kurve *f*; (*change of direction*) Wende *f*; (*short walk*) Runde *f*; (*Theat*) Nummer *f*; (*fam: attack*) Anfall *m*; **do s.o. a good ~** jdm einen guten Dienst erweisen; **take ~s** sich abwechseln; **in ~** der Reihe nach; **out of ~** außer der Reihe; **it's your ~** du bist an der Reihe ◻ *vt* drehen; (**~** *over*) wenden; (*reverse*) umdrehen; (*Techn*) drechseln ⟨wood⟩; **~ the page** umblättern; **~ the corner** um die Ecke biegen ◻ *vi* sich drehen; (**~** *round*) sich umdrehen; ⟨car:⟩ wenden; ⟨leaves:⟩ sich färben; ⟨weather:⟩ umschlagen; (*become*) werden; **~ right/left** nach rechts/links abbiegen; **~ to s.o.** sich an jdn wenden; **have ~ed against s.o.** gegen jdn sein. **~ away** *vt* abweisen ◻ *vi* sich abwenden. **~ down** *vt* herunterschlagen ⟨collar⟩; herunterdrehen ⟨heat, gas⟩; leiser stellen ⟨sound⟩; (*reject*) ablehnen; abweisen ⟨person⟩. **~ in** *vt* einschlagen ⟨edges⟩ ◻ *vi* ⟨car:⟩ einbiegen; (*fam: go to bed*) ins Bett gehen. **~ off** *vt* zudrehen ⟨tap⟩; ausschalten ⟨light, radio⟩; abstellen ⟨water, gas, engine, machine⟩ ◻ *vi* abbiegen. **~ on** *vt* aufdrehen ⟨tap⟩; einschalten ⟨light, radio⟩; anstellen ⟨water, gas, engine, machine⟩. **~ out** *vt* (*expel*) vertreiben, (*fam*) hinauswerfen; ausschalten ⟨light⟩; abdrehen ⟨gas⟩; (*produce*) produzieren; (*empty*) ausleeren; [gründlich] aufräumen ⟨room, cupboard⟩ ◻ *vi* (*go out*) hinausgehen; (*transpire*) sich herausstellen; **~ out well/badly** gut/ schlecht gehen. **~ over** *vt* umdrehen ◻ *vi* sich umdrehen. **~ up** *vt* hochschlagen ⟨collar⟩; aufdrehen ⟨heat, gas⟩; lauter stellen ⟨sound, radio⟩ ◻ *vi* auftauchen

turning /'tɜːnɪŋ/ *n* Abzweigung *f*. **~ point** *n* Wendepunkt *m*

turnip /'tɜːnɪp/ *n* weiße Rübe *f*

turn|: **~-out** *n* (*of people*) Teilnahme *f*, Beteiligung *f*; (*of goods*) Produktion *f*. **~over** *n* (*Comm*) Umsatz *m*; (*of staff*) Personalwechsel *m*. **~pike** *n* (*Amer*) gebührenpflichtige Autobahn *f*. **~stile** *n* Drehkreuz *nt*. **~table** *n* Drehscheibe *f*; (*on record-player*) Plattenteller *m*. **~-up** *n* [Hosen]aufschlag *m*

turpentine /'tɜːpəntaɪn/ *n* Terpentin *nt*

turquoise /'tɜːkwɔɪz/ *a* türkis[farben] ◻ *n* (*gem*) Türkis *m*

turret /'tʌrɪt/ *n* Türmchen *nt*

turtle /'tɜːtl/ *n* Seeschildkröte *f*

tusk /tʌsk/ *n* Stoßzahn *m*

tussle /'tʌsl/ n Balgerei f; (fig) Streit m
□ vi sich balgen

tutor /'tju:tə(r)/ n [Privat]lehrer m

tuxedo /tʌk'si:dəʊ/ n (Amer) Smoking m

TV /ti:'vi:/ abbr of television

twaddle /'twɒdl/ n Geschwätz nt

twang /twæŋ/ n (in voice) Näseln n □ vt
zupfen

tweed /twi:d/ n Tweed m

tweezers /'twi:zəz/ npl Pinzette f

twelfth /twelfθ/ a zwölfter(r,s)

twelve /twelv/ a zwölf

twentieth /'twentiɪθ/ a zwanzigste(r,s)

twenty /'twenti/ a zwanzig

twerp /twɜ:p/ n (fam) Trottel m

twice /twaɪs/ adv zweimal

twiddle /'twɪdl/ vt drehen an (+ dat)

twig[1] /twɪg/ n Zweig m

twig[2] vt/i (pt/pp twigged) (fam) kapieren

twilight /'twaɪ-/ n Dämmerlicht nt

twin /twɪn/ n Zwilling m □ attrib Zwil-
lings-. ～ **beds** npl zwei Einzelbetten pl

twine /twaɪn/ n Bindfaden m □ vi sich
winden; ⟨plant:⟩ sich ranken

twinge /twɪndʒ/ n Stechen nt; ～ **of conscience** Gewissensbisse pl

twinkle /'twɪŋkl/ n Funkeln nt □ vi funkeln

twin 'town n Partnerstadt f

twirl /twɜ:l/ vt/i herumwirbeln

twist /twɪst/ n Drehung f; ⟨curve⟩ Kurve
f; ⟨unexpected occurrence⟩ überraschende
Wendung f □ vt drehen; ⟨distort⟩ verdrehen; ⟨fam: swindle⟩ beschummeln; ～
one's ankle sich (dat) den Knöchel verrenken □ vi sich drehen; ⟨road:⟩ sich
winden. ～**er** n (fam) Schwindler m

twit /twɪt/ n (fam) Trottel m

twitch /twɪtʃ/ n Zucken nt □ vi zucken

twitter /'twɪtə(r)/ n Zwitschern nt □ vi
zwitschern

two /tu:/ a zwei

two: ～**-faced** a falsch. ～**-piece** a zweitei-
lig. ～**some** /-səm/ n Paar nt. ～**-way** a ～**-
way traffic** Gegenverkehr m

tycoon /taɪ'ku:n/ n Magnat m

tying /'taɪɪŋ/ see tie

type /taɪp/ n Art f, Sorte f; ⟨person⟩ Typ
m; ⟨printing⟩ Type f □ vt mit der Maschine
schreiben, (fam) tippen; ～**d letter** ma-
schinegeschriebener Brief □ vi Maschine
schreiben, (fam) tippen. ～**writer** n
Schreibmaschine f. ～**written** a
maschinegeschrieben

typhoid /'taɪfɔɪd/ n Typhus m

typical /'tɪpɪkl/ a, -ly adv typisch (of für)

typify /'tɪpɪfaɪ/ vt (pt/pp -ied) typisch sein
für

typing /'taɪpɪŋ/ n Maschineschreiben nt.
～ **paper** n Schreibmaschinenpapier nt

typist /'taɪpɪst/ n Schreibkraft f

typography /taɪ'pɒgrəfɪ/ n Typographie
f

tyrannical /tɪ'rænɪkl/ a tyrannisch

tyranny /'tɪrənɪ/ n Tyrannei f

tyrant /'taɪrənt/ n Tyrann m

tyre /'taɪə(r)/ n Reifen m

U

ubiquitous /ju:'bɪkwɪtəs/ a allgegenwär-
tig; be ～ überall zu finden sein

udder /'ʌdə(r)/ n Euter nt

ugl|iness /'ʌglɪnɪs/ n Hässlichkeit f. ～**y**
a (-ier, -iest) hässlich; ⟨nasty⟩ übel

UK abbr see United Kingdom

ulcer /'ʌlsə(r)/ n Geschwür nt

ulterior /ʌl'tɪərɪə(r)/ a ～ **motive** Hintergedanke m

ultimate /'ʌltɪmət/ a letzte(r,s); ⟨final⟩
endgültig; ⟨fundamental⟩ grundlegend,
eigentlich. ～**ly** adv schließlich

ultimatum /ʌltɪ'meɪtəm/ n Ultimatum nt

ultrasound /'ʌltrə-/ n (Med) Ultraschall
m

ultra'violet a ultraviolett

umbilical /ʌm'bɪlɪkl/ a ～ **cord** Nabel-
schnur f

umbrella /ʌm'brelə/ n [Regen]schirm m

umpire /'ʌmpaɪə(r)/ n Schiedsrichter m
□ vt/i Schiedsrichter sein (bei)

umpteen /ʌmp'ti:n/ a (fam) zig. ～**th** a
(fam) zigste(r,s); **for the ～th time** zum
zigsten Mal

un'able /ʌn-/ a be ～ **to do sth** etw nicht
tun können

una'bridged a ungekürzt

unac'companied a ohne Begleitung;
⟨luggage⟩ unbegleitet

unac'countab|le a unerklärlich. ～**y** adv
unerklärlicherweise

unac'customed a ungewohnt; **be ～ to
sth** etw nicht gewohnt sein

una'dulterated a unverfälscht, rein;
⟨utter⟩ völlig

un'aided a ohne fremde Hilfe

unal'loyed /ʌnə'lɔɪd/ a (fig) ungetrübt

unanimity /ju:nə'nɪmətɪ/ n Einstimmig-
keit f

unanimous /ju:'nænɪməs/ a, -ly adv einmütig; ⟨vote, decision⟩ einstimmig

un'armed *a* unbewaffnet; ~ **combat** Kampf *m* ohne Waffen

unas'suming *a* bescheiden

unat'tached *a* nicht befestigt; ⟨*person*⟩ ungebunden

unat'tended *a* unbeaufsichtigt

un'authorized *a* unbefugt

una'voidable *a* unvermeidlich

una'ware *a* be ~ **of** sth sich (*dat*) etw (*gen*) nicht bewusst sein. ~s /-eəz/ *adv* catch s.o. ~s jdn überraschen

un'balanced *a* unausgewogen; (*mentally*) unausgeglichen

un'bearable *a*, -bly *adv* unerträglich

unbeat|able /ʌn'biːtəbl/ *a* unschlagbar. ~en *a* ungeschlagen; ⟨*record*⟩ ungebrochen

unbeknown /ʌnbɪ'nəʊn/ *a* (*fam*) ~ **to me** ohne mein Wissen

unbe'lievable *a* unglaublich

un'bend *vi* (*pt/pp* -bent) (*relax*) aus sich herausgehen

un'biased *a* unvoreingenommen

un'block *vt* frei machen

un'bolt *vt* aufriegeln

un'breakable *a* unzerbrechlich

unbridled /ʌn'braɪdld/ *a* ungezügelt

un'burden *vt* ~ **oneself** (*fig*) sich aussprechen

un'button *vt* aufknöpfen

uncalled-for /ʌn'kɔːldfɔː(r)/ *a* unangebracht

un'canny *a* unheimlich

un'ceasing *a* unaufhörlich

uncere'monious *a*, -ly *adv* formlos; (*abrupt*) brüsk

un'certain *a* (*doubtful*) ungewiss; ⟨*origins*⟩ unbestimmt; **be** ~ nicht sicher sein; **in no** ~ **terms** ganz eindeutig. ~ty *n* Ungewissheit *f*

un'changed *a* unverändert

un'charitable *a* lieblos

uncle /'ʌŋkl/ *n* Onkel *m*

un'comfortable *a*, -bly *adv* unbequem; **feel** ~ (*fig*) sich nicht wohl fühlen

un'common *a* ungewöhnlich

un'compromising *a* kompromisslos

uncon'ditional *a*, ~ly *adv* bedingungslos

un'conscious *a* bewusstlos; (*unintended*) unbewusst; **be** ~ **of** sth sich (*dat*) etw (*gen*) nicht bewusst sein. ~ly *adv* unbewusst

uncon'ventional *a* unkonventionell

unco'operative *a* nicht hilfsbereit

un'cork *vt* entkorken

uncouth /ʌn'kuːθ/ *a* ungehobelt

un'cover *vt* aufdecken

unctuous /'ʌŋktjʊəs/ *a*, -ly *adv* salbungsvoll

unde'cided *a* unentschlossen; (*not settled*) nicht entschieden

undeniable /ʌndɪ'naɪəbl/ *a*, -bly *adv* unbestreitbar

under /'ʌndə(r)/ *prep* unter (+ *dat/acc*); ~ **it** darunter; ~ **there** da drunter; ~ **repair** in Reparatur; ~ **construction** im Bau; ~ **age** minderjährig; ~ **way** unterwegs; (*fig*) im Gange ◻ *adv* darunter

'undercarriage *n* (*Aviat*) Fahrwerk *nt*, Fahrgestell *nt*

'underclothes *npl* Unterwäsche *f*

under'cover *a* geheim

'undercurrent *n* Unterströmung *f*; (*fig*) Unterton *m*

under'cut *vt* (*pt/pp* -cut) (*Comm*) unterbieten

'underdog *n* Unterlegene(r) *m*

under'done *a* nicht gar; (*rare*) nicht durchgebraten

under'estimate *vt* unterschätzen

under'fed *a* unterernährt

under'foot *adv* am Boden; **trample** ~ zertrampeln

under'go *vt* (*pt* -went, *pp* -gone) durchmachen; sich unterziehen (+ *dat*) ⟨*operation, treatment*⟩; ~ **repairs** repariert werden

under'graduate *n* Student(in) *m(f)*

under'ground¹ *adv* unter der Erde; ⟨*mining*⟩ unter Tage

'underground² *a* unterirdisch; (*secret*) Untergrund- ◻ *n* (*railway*) U-Bahn *f*. ~ **car park** *n* Tiefgarage *f*

'undergrowth *n* Unterholz *nt*

'underhand *a* hinterhältig

'underlay *n* Unterlage *f*

under'lie *vt* (*pt* -lay, *pp* -lain, *pres p* -lying) (*fig*) zugrunde liegen (+ *dat*)

under'line *vt* unterstreichen

underling /'ʌndəlɪŋ/ *n* (*pej*) Untergebene(r) *m/f*

under'lying *a* (*fig*) eigentlich

under'mine *vt* (*fig*) unterminieren, untergraben

underneath /ʌndə'niːθ/ *prep* unter (+ *dat/acc*); ~ **it** darunter ◻ *adv* darunter

'underpants *npl* Unterhose *f*

'underpass *n* Unterführung *f*

under'privileged *a* unterprivilegiert

under'rate *vt* unterschätzen

'underseal *n* (*Auto*) Unterbodenschutz *m*

'undershirt *n* (*Amer*) Unterhemd *nt*

understaffed /-'staːft/ *a* unterbesetzt

under'stand *vt/i* (*pt/pp* -stood) verstehen; **I ~ that** ... (*have heard*) ich habe gehört, dass ... **~able** /-əbl/ *a* verständlich. **~ably** /-əblɪ/ *adv* verständlicherweise

under'standing *a* verständnisvoll □ *n* Verständnis *int*; (*agreement*) Vereinbarung *f*; **reach an ~** sich verständigen; **on the ~ that** unter der Voraussetzung, dass

'understatement *n* Untertreibung *f*

'understudy *n* (*Theat*) Ersatzspieler(in) *m(f)*

under'take *vt* (*pt* -took, *pp* -taken) unternehmen; **~ to do sth** sich verpflichten, etw zu tun

'undertaker *n* Leichenbestatter *m*; [firm of] **~s** Bestattungsinstitut *n*

under'taking *n* Unternehmen *nt*; (*promise*) Versprechen *nt*

'undertone *n* (*fig*) Unterton *m*; **in an ~** mit gedämpfter Stimme

under'value *vt* unterbewerten

'underwater[1] *a* Unterwasser-

under'water[2] *adv* unter Wasser

'underwear *n* Unterwäsche *f*

under'weight *a* untergewichtig; **be ~** Untergewicht haben

'underworld *n* Unterwelt *f*

'underwriter *n* Versicherer *m*

unde'sirable *a* unerwünscht

undies /'ʌndɪz/ *npl* (*fam*) [Damen]unterwäsche *f*

un'dignified *a* würdelos

un'do *vt* (*pt* -did, *pp* -done) aufmachen; (*fig*) ungeschehen machen; (*ruin*) zunichte machen

un'done *a* offen; (*not accomplished*) unerledigt

un'doubted *a* unzweifelhaft. **~ly** *adv* zweifellos

un'dress *vt* ausziehen; **get ~ed** sich ausziehen □ *vi* sich ausziehen

un'due *a* übermäßig

undulating /'ʌndjʊleɪtɪŋ/ *a* Wellen-; (*country*) wellig

un'duly *adv* übermäßig

un'dying *a* ewig

un'earth *vt* ausgraben; (*fig*) zutage bringen. **~ly** *a* unheimlich; **at an ~ly hour** (*fam*) in aller Herrgottsfrühe

un'eas|e *n* Unbehagen *nt*. **~y** *a* unbehaglich; **I feel ~y** mir ist unbehaglich zumute

un'eatable *a* ungenießbar

uneco'nomic *a*, **-ally** *adv* unwirtschaftlich

uneco'nomical *a* verschwenderisch

unem'ployed *a* arbeitslos □ *npl* **the ~** die Arbeitslosen

unem'ployment *n* Arbeitslosigkeit *f*. **~ benefit** *n* Arbeitslosenunterstützung *f*

un'ending *a* endlos

un'equal *a* unterschiedlich; (*struggle*) ungleich; **be ~ to a task** einer Aufgabe nicht gewachsen sein. **~ly** *adv* ungleichmäßig

unequivocal /ʌnɪ'kwɪvəkl/ *a*, **-ly** *adv* eindeutig

unerring /ʌn'ɜ:rɪŋ/ *a* unfehlbar

un'ethical *a* unmoralisch; **be ~** gegen das Berufsethos verstoßen

un'even *a* uneben; (*unequal*) ungleich; (*not regular*) ungleichmäßig; (*number*) ungerade. **~ly** *adv* ungleichmäßig

unex'pected *a*, **-ly** *adv* unerwartet

un'failing *a* nie versagend

un'fair *a*, **-ly** *adv* ungerecht, unfair. **~ness** *n* Ungerechtigkeit *f*

un'faithful *a* untreu

unfa'miliar *a* ungewohnt; (*unknown*) unbekannt

un'fasten *vt* aufmachen; (*detach*) losmachen

un'favourable *a* ungünstig

un'feeling *a* gefühllos

un'finished *a* unvollendet; (*business*) unerledigt

un'fit *a* ungeeignet; (*incompetent*) unfähig; (*Sport*) nicht fit; **~ for work** arbeitsunfähig

unflinching /ʌn'flɪntʃɪŋ/ *a* unerschrocken

un'fold *vt* auseinander falten, entfalten; (*spread out*) ausbreiten □ *vi* sich entfalten

unfore'seen *a* unvorhergesehen

unforgettable /ʌnfə'getəbl/ *a* unvergesslich

unforgivable /ʌnfə'gɪvəbl/ *a* unverzeihlich

un'fortunate *a* unglücklich; (*unfavourable*) ungünstig; (*regrettable*) bedauerlich; **be ~** (*person:*) Pech haben. **~ly** *adv* leider

un'founded *a* unbegründet

unfurl /ʌn'fɜ:l/ *vt* entrollen □ *vi* sich entrollen

un'furnished *a* unmöbliert

ungainly /ʌn'geɪnlɪ/ *a* unbeholfen

ungodly /ʌn'gɒdlɪ/ *a* gottlos; **at an ~ hour** (*fam*) in aller Herrgottsfrühe

un'grateful *a*, **-ly** *adv* undankbar

un'happi|ly *adv* unglücklich; (*unfortunately*) leider. **~ness** *n* Kummer *m*

un'happy *a* unglücklich; (*not content*) unzufrieden

un'harmed *a* unverletzt

un'healthy *a* ungesund

un'hook vt vom Haken nehmen; aufhaken ⟨dress⟩

un'hurt a unverletzt

unhy'gienic a unhygienisch

unicorn /'ju:nɪkɔ:n/ n Einhorn nt

unification /ju:nɪfɪ'keɪʃn/ n Einigung f

uniform /'ju:nɪfɔ:m/ a, -ly adv einheitlich ◻ n Uniform f

unify /'ju:nɪfaɪ/ vt (pt/pp -ied) einigen

uni'lateral /ju:nɪ-/ a, -ly adv einseitig

uni'maginable a unvorstellbar

unim'portant a unwichtig

unin'habited a unbewohnt

unin'tentional a, -ly adv unabsichtlich

union /'ju:nɪən/ n Vereinigung f; (Pol) Union f; (trade ~) Gewerkschaft f. ~ist n (Pol) Unionist m

unique /ju:'ni:k/ a einzigartig. ~ly adv einmalig

unison /'ju:nɪsn/ n in ~ einstimmig

unit /'ju:nɪt/ n Einheit f; (Math) Einer m; (of furniture) Teil nt, Element nt

unite /ju:'naɪt/ vt vereinigen ◻ vi sich vereinigen

united /ju:'naɪtɪd/ a einig. U~ 'Kingdom n Vereinigtes Königreich nt. U~ 'Nations n Vereinte Nationen pl. U~ States [of America] n Vereinigte Staaten pl [von Amerika]

unity /'ju:nətɪ/ n Einheit f; (harmony) Einigkeit f

universal /ju:nɪ'vɜ:sl/ a, -ly adv allgemein

universe /'ju:nɪvɜ:s/ n [Welt]all nt, Universum nt

university /ju:nɪ'vɜ:sətɪ/ n Universität f ◻ attrib Universitäts-

un'just a, -ly adv ungerecht

unkempt /ʌn'kempt/ a ungepflegt

un'kind a, -ly adv unfreundlich; (harsh) hässlich. ~ness n Unfreundlichkeit f; Hässlichkeit f

un'known a unbekannt

un'lawful a, -ly adv gesetzwidrig

unleaded /ʌn'ledɪd/ a bleifrei

un'leash vt (fig) entfesseln

unless /ən'les/ conj wenn ... nicht; ~ I am mistaken wenn ich mich nicht irre

un'like a nicht ähnlich, unähnlich; (not the same) ungleich ◻ prep im Gegensatz zu (+ dat)

un'likely a unwahrscheinlich

un'limited a unbegrenzt

un'load vt entladen; ausladen ⟨luggage⟩

un'lock vt aufschließen

un'lucky a unglücklich; ⟨day, number⟩ Unglücks-; be ~ Pech haben; ⟨thing:⟩ Unglück bringen

un'manned a unbemannt

un'married a unverheiratet. ~ 'mother n ledige Mutter f

un'mask vt (fig) entlarven

unmistakable /ʌnmɪ'steɪkəbl/ a, -bly adv unverkennbar

un'mitigated a vollkommen

un'natural a, -ly adv unnatürlich; (not normal) nicht normal

un'necessary a, -ily adv unnötig

un'noticed a unbemerkt

unob'tainable a nicht erhältlich

unob'trusive a, -ly adv unaufdringlich; ⟨thing⟩ unauffällig

unof'ficial a, -ly adv inoffiziell

un'pack vt/i auspacken

un'paid a unbezahlt

un'palatable a ungenießbar

un'paralleled a beispiellos

un'pick vt auftrennen

un'pleasant a, -ly adv unangenehm. ~ness n ⟨bad feeling⟩ Ärger m

un'plug vt (pt/pp -plugged) den Stecker herausziehen von

un'popular a unbeliebt

un'precedented a beispiellos

unpre'dictable a unberechenbar

unpre'meditated a nicht vorsätzlich

unpre'pared a nicht vorbereitet

unprepos'sessing a wenig attraktiv

unpre'tentious a bescheiden

un'principled a skrupellos

unpro'fessional a be ~ gegen das Berufsethos verstoßen; (Sport) unsportlich sein

un'profitable a unrentabel

un'qualified a unqualifiziert; (fig: absolute) uneingeschränkt

un'questionable a unbezweifelbar; ⟨right⟩ unbestreitbar

unravel /ʌn'rævl/ vt (pt/pp -ravelled) entwirren; (Knitting) aufziehen

un'real a unwirklich

un'reasonable a unvernünftig; be ~ zu viel verlangen

unre'lated a unzusammenhängend; be ~ nicht verwandt sein; ⟨events:⟩ nicht miteinander zusammenhängen

unre'liable a unzuverlässig

unrequited /ʌnrɪ'kwaɪtɪd/ a unerwidert

unreservedly /ʌnrɪ'zɜ:vɪdlɪ/ adv uneingeschränkt; (frankly) offen

un'rest n Unruhen pl

un'rivalled a unübertroffen

un'roll vt aufrollen ◻ vi sich aufrollen

unruly /ʌn'ru:lɪ/ a ungebärdig

un'safe *a* nicht sicher
un'said *a* ungesagt
un'salted *a* ungesalzen
unsatis'factory *a* unbefriedigend
un'savoury *a* unangenehm; (*fig*) unerfreulich
unscathed /ʌnˈskeɪðd/ *a* unversehrt
un'screw *vt* abschrauben
un'scrupulous *a* skrupellos
un'seemly *a* unschicklich
un'selfish *a* selbstlos
un'settled *a* ungeklärt; (*weather*) unbeständig; (*bill*) unbezahlt
unshakeable /ʌnˈʃeɪkəbl/ *a* unerschütterlich
unshaven /ʌnˈʃeɪvn/ *a* unrasiert
unsightly /ʌnˈsaɪtlɪ/ *a* unansehnlich
un'skilled *a* ungelernt; (*work*) unqualifiziert
un'sociable *a* ungesellig
unso'phisticated *a* einfach
un'sound *a* krank, nicht gesund; (*building*) nicht sicher; (*advice*) unzuverlässig; (*reasoning*) nicht stichhaltig; **of ∼ mind** unzurechnungsfähig
unspeakable /ʌnˈspiːkəbl/ *a* unbeschreiblich
un'stable *a* nicht stabil; (*mentally*) labil
un'steady *a*, **-ily** *adv* unsicher; (*wobbly*) wackelig
un'stuck *a* **come ∼** sich lösen; (*fam: fail*) scheitern
unsuc'cessful *a*, **-ly** *adv* erfolglos; **be ∼** keinen Erfolg haben
un'suitable *a* ungeeignet; (*inappropriate*) unpassend; (*for weather, activity*) unzweckmäßig
unsu'specting *a* ahnungslos
un'sweetened *a* ungesüßt
unthinkable /ʌnˈθɪŋkəbl/ *a* unvorstellbar
un'tidiness *n* Unordentlichkeit *f*
un'tidy *a*, **-ily** *adv* unordentlich
un'tie *vt* aufbinden; losbinden (*person, boat, horse*)
until /ənˈtɪl/ *prep* bis (+ *acc*); **not ∼** erst; **∼ the evening** bis zum Abend; **∼ his arrival** bis zu seiner Ankunft □ *conj* bis; **not ∼** erst wenn; (*in past*) erst als
untimely /ʌnˈtaɪmlɪ/ *a* ungelegen; (*premature*) vorzeitig
un'tiring *a* unermüdlich
un'told *a* unermesslich
unto'ward *a* ungünstig; (*unseemly*) ungehörig; **if nothing ∼ happens** wenn nichts dazwischenkommt
un'true *a* unwahr; **that's ∼** das ist nicht wahr

unused[1] /ʌnˈjuːzd/ *a* unbenutzt; (*not utilized*) ungenutzt
unused[2] /ʌnˈjuːst/ *a* **be ∼ to sth** etw nicht gewohnt sein
un'usual *a*, **-ly** *adv* ungewöhnlich
un'veil *vt* enthüllen
un'versed *a* nicht bewandert (**in** in + *dat*)
un'wanted *a* unerwünscht
un'warranted *a* ungerechtfertigt
un'welcome *a* unwillkommen
un'well *a* **be** *or* **feel ∼** sich nicht wohl fühlen
unwieldy /ʌnˈwiːldɪ/ *a* sperrig
un'willing *a*, **-ly** *adv* widerwillig; **be ∼ to do sth** etw nicht tun wollen
un'wind *v* (*pt/pp* **unwound**) □ *vt* abwickeln □ *vi* sich abwickeln; (*fam: relax*) sich entspannen
un'wise *a*, **-ly** *adv* unklug
unwitting /ʌnˈwɪtɪŋ/ *a*, **-ly** *adv* unwissentlich
un'worthy *a* unwürdig
un'wrap *vt* (*pt/pp* **-wrapped**) auswickeln; auspacken (*present*)
un'written *a* ungeschrieben
up /ʌp/ *adv* oben; (*with movement*) nach oben; (*not in bed*) auf; (*collar*) hochgeklappt; (*road*) aufgerissen; (*price*) gestiegen; (*curtains*) aufgehängt; (*shelves*) angebracht; (*notice*) angeschlagen; (*tent*) aufgebaut; (*building*) gebaut; **be up for sale** zu verkaufen sein; **up there** da oben; **up to** (*as far as*) bis; **time's up** die Zeit ist um; **what's up?** (*fam*) was ist los? **what's he up to?** (*fam*) was hat er vor? **I don't feel up to it** ich fühle mich dem nicht gewachsen; **be one up on s.o.** (*fam*) jdm etwas voraushaben; **go up** hinaufgehen; **come up heraufkommen** □ *prep* **be up on sth** [oben] auf etw (*dat*) sein; **up the mountain** oben am Berg; (*movement*) den Berg hinauf; **be up the tree** oben im Baum sein; **up the road** die Straße entlang; **up the river** stromaufwärts; **go up the stairs** die Treppe hinaufgehen; **be up the pub** (*fam*) in der Kneipe sein
'upbringing *n* Erziehung *f*
up'date *vt* auf den neuesten Stand bringen
up'grade *vt* aufstufen
upheaval /ʌpˈhiːvl/ *n* Unruhe *f*; (*Pol*) Umbruch *m*
up'hill *a* (*fig*) mühsam □ *adv* bergauf
up'hold *vt* (*pt/pp* **upheld**) unterstützen; bestätigen (*verdict*)
upholster /ʌpˈhəʊlstə(r)/ *vt* polstern. **∼er** *n* Polsterer *m*. **∼y** *n* Polsterung *f*
'upkeep *n* Unterhalt *m*
up-'market *a* anspruchsvoll
upon /əˈpɒn/ *prep* auf (+ *dat*/*acc*)

upper /'ʌpə(r)/ *a* obere(r,s); ⟨*deck, jaw, lip*⟩ Ober-; **have the ∼ hand** die Oberhand haben □ *n* (*of shoe*) Obermaterial *nt*

upper: ∼ **circle** *n* zweiter Rang *m*. ∼ **class** *n* Oberschicht *f*. ∼**most** *a* oberste(r,s)

'upright *a* aufrecht □ *n* Pfosten *m*

'uprising *n* Aufstand *m*

'uproar *n* Aufruhr *m*

up'root *vt* entwurzeln

up'set[1] *vt* (*pt/pp* upset, *pres p* upsetting) umstoßen; ⟨*spill*⟩ verschütten; durcheinander bringen ⟨*plan*⟩; ⟨*distress*⟩ erschüttern; ⟨*food:*⟩ nicht bekommen (+ *dat*); **get ∼ about sth** sich über etw (*acc*) aufregen; **be very ∼** sehr bestürzt sein

'upset[2] *n* Aufregung *f*; **have a stomach ∼** einen verdorbenen Magen haben

'upshot *n* Ergebnis *nt*

upside 'down *adv* verkehrt herum; **turn ∼** umdrehen

up'stairs[1] *adv* oben; ⟨*go*⟩ nach oben

'upstairs[2] *a* im Obergeschoss

'upstart *n* Emporkömmling *m*

'up'stream *adv* stromaufwärts

'upsurge *n* Zunahme *f*

'uptake *n* **slow on the ∼** schwer von Begriff; **be quick on the ∼** schnell begreifen

up'tight *a* nervös

'upturn *n* Aufschwung *m*

upward /'ʌpwəd/ *a* nach oben; ⟨*movement*⟩ Aufwärts-; ∼ **slope** Steigung *f* □ *adv* ∼[s] aufwärts, nach oben

uranium /jʊ'reɪnɪəm/ *n* Uran *nt*

urban /'ɜːbən/ *a* städtisch

urbane /ɜː'beɪn/ *a* weltmännisch

urge /ɜːdʒ/ *n* Trieb *m*, Drang *m* □ *vt* drängen; ∼ **on** antreiben

urgen|cy /'ɜːdʒənsɪ/ *n* Dringlichkeit *f*. ∼**t** *a*, **-ly** *adv* dringend

urinate /'jʊərɪneɪt/ *vi* urinieren

urine /'jʊərɪn/ *n* Urin *m*, Harn *m*

urn /ɜːn/ *n* Urne *f*; (*for tea*) Teemaschine *f*

us /ʌs/ *pron* uns; **it's us** wir sind es

US[A] *abbr* USA *pl*

usable /'juːzəbl/ *a* brauchbar

usage /'juːzɪdʒ/ *n* Brauch *m*; (*of word*) [Sprach]gebrauch *m*

use[1] /juːs/ *n* (*see* use[2]) Benutzung *f*; Verwendung *f*; Gebrauch *m*; **be of ∼** nützlich sein; **be of no ∼** nichts nützen; **make ∼ of** Gebrauch machen von; (*exploit*) ausnutzen; **it is no ∼** es hat keinen Zweck; **what's the ∼?** wozu?

use[2] /juːz/ *vt* benutzen ⟨*implement, room, lift*⟩; verwenden ⟨*ingredient, method, book, money*⟩; gebrauchen ⟨*words, force, brains*⟩; ∼ **[up]** aufbrauchen

used[1] /juːzd/ *a* benutzt; ⟨*car*⟩ Gebraucht-

used[2] /juːst/ *pt* **be ∼ to sth** an etw (*acc*) gewöhnt sein; **get ∼ to** sich gewöhnen an (+ *acc*); **he ∼ to say** er hat immer gesagt; **he ∼ to live here** er hat früher hier gewohnt

useful /'juːsfl/ *a* nützlich. ∼**ness** *n* Nützlichkeit *f*

useless /'juːslɪs/ *a* nutzlos; (*not usable*) unbrauchbar; (*pointless*) zwecklos

user /'juːzə(r)/ *n* Benutzer(in) *m(f)*. ∼-'friendly *a* benutzerfreundlich

usher /'ʌʃə(r)/ *n* Platzanweiser *m*; (*in court*) Gerichtsdiener *m* □ *vt* ∼ **in** hineinführen

usherette /ʌʃə'ret/ *n* Platzanweiserin *f*

USSR *abbr* UdSSR *f*

usual /'juːʒʊəl/ *a* üblich. ∼**ly** *adv* gewöhnlich

usurp /juː'zɜːp/ *vt* sich (*dat*) widerrechtlich aneignen

utensil /juː'tensl/ *n* Gerät *nt*

uterus /'juːtərəs/ *n* Gebärmutter *f*

utilitarian /juːtɪlɪ'teərɪən/ *a* zweckmäßig

utility /juː'tɪlətɪ/ *a* Gebrauchs- □ *n* Nutzen *m*. ∼ **room** *n* ≈ Waschküche *f*

utiliz|ation /juːtɪlaɪ'zeɪʃn/ *n* Nutzung *f*. ∼**e** /'juːtɪlaɪz/ *vt* nutzen

utmost /'ʌtməʊst/ *a* äußerste(r,s), größte(r,s) □ *n* **do one's ∼** sein Möglichstes tun

utter[1] /'ʌtə(r)/ *a*, **-ly** *adv* völlig

utter[2] *vt* von sich geben ⟨*sigh, sound*⟩; sagen ⟨*word*⟩. ∼**ance** /-əns/ *n* Äußerung *f*

U-turn /'juː-/ *n* (*fig*) Kehrtwendung *f*; '**no ∼s**' (*Auto*) 'Wenden verboten'

V

vacan|cy /'veɪkənsɪ/ *n* (*job*) freie Stelle *f*; (*room*) freies Zimmer *nt*; '**no ∼cies**' 'belegt'. ∼**t** *a* frei; ⟨*look*⟩ [gedanken]leer

vacate /və'keɪt/ *vt* räumen

vacation /və'keɪʃn/ *n* (*Univ & Amer*) Ferien *pl*

vaccinat|e /'væksɪneɪt/ *vt* impfen. ∼**ion** /-'neɪʃn/ *n* Impfung *f*

vaccine /'væksiːn/ *n* Impfstoff *m*

vacuum /'vækjʊəm/ *n* Vakuum *nt*, luftleerer Raum *m* □ *vt* saugen. ∼ **cleaner** *n* Staubsauger *m*. ∼ **flask** *n* Thermosflasche (P) *f*. ∼-**packed** *a* vakuumverpackt

vagaries /'veɪgərɪz/ *npl* Launen *pl*

vagina /vəˈdʒaɪnə/ n (Anat) Scheide f

vagrant /ˈveɪgrənt/ n Landstreicher m

vague /veɪg/ a (-r,-st), -ly adv vage; ⟨outline⟩ verschwommen

vain /veɪn/ a (-er,-est) eitel; ⟨hope, attempt⟩ vergeblich; in ~ vergeblich. ~ly adv vergeblich

vale /veɪl/ n (liter) Tal nt

valet /ˈvæleɪ/ n Kammerdiener m

valiant /ˈvæliənt/ a, -ly adv tapfer

valid /ˈvælɪd/ a gültig; ⟨claim⟩ berechtigt; ⟨argument⟩ stichhaltig; ⟨reason⟩ triftig. ~ate vt ⟨confirm⟩ bestätigen. ~ity /vəˈlɪdəti/ n Gültigkeit f

valley /ˈvæli/ n Tal nt

valour /ˈvælə(r)/ n Tapferkeit f

valuable /ˈvæljʊəbl/ a wertvoll. ~s npl Wertsachen pl

valuation /væljʊˈeɪʃn/ n Schätzung f

value /ˈvælju:/ n Wert m; ⟨usefulness⟩ Nutzen m ▢ vt schätzen. ~ 'added tax n Mehrwertsteuer f

valve /vælv/ n Ventil nt; (Anat) Klappe f; (Electr) Röhre f

vampire /ˈvæmpaɪə(r)/ n Vampir m

van /væn/ n Lieferwagen m

vandal /ˈvændl/ n Rowdy n. ~ism /-ɪzm/ n mutwillige Zerstörung f. ~ize vt demolieren

vanilla /vəˈnɪlə/ n Vanille f

vanish /ˈvænɪʃ/ vi verschwinden

vanity /ˈvænəti/ n Eitelkeit f. ~ bag n Kosmetiktäschchen nt

vantage-point /ˈvɑːntɪdʒ-/ n Aussichtspunkt m

vapour /ˈveɪpə(r)/ n Dampf m

variable /ˈveərɪəbl/ a unbeständig; (Math) variabel; ⟨adjustable⟩ regulierbar

variance /ˈveərɪəns/ n be at ~ nicht übereinstimmen

variant /ˈveərɪənt/ n Variante f

variation /veərɪˈeɪʃn/ n Variation f; ⟨difference⟩ Unterschied m

varicose /ˈværɪkəʊs/ a ~ veins Krampfadern pl

varied /ˈveərɪd/ a vielseitig; ⟨diet:⟩ abwechslungsreich

variety /vəˈraɪəti/ n Abwechslung f; ⟨quantity⟩ Vielfalt f; (Comm) Auswahl f; ⟨type⟩ Art f; (Bot) Abart f; (Theat) Varieté nt

various /ˈveərɪəs/ a verschieden. ~ly adv unterschiedlich

varnish /ˈvɑːnɪʃ/ n Lack m ▢ vt lackieren

vary /ˈveərɪ/ v (pt/pp -ied) ▢ vi sich ändern; ⟨be different⟩ verschieden sein ▢ vt [ver]ändern; ⟨add variety to⟩

abwechslungsreicher gestalten. ~ing a wechselnd; ⟨different⟩ unterschiedlich

vase /vɑːz/ n Vase f

vast /vɑːst/ a riesig; ⟨expanse⟩ weit. ~ly adv gewaltig

vat /væt/ n Bottich m

VAT /viːeɪˈtiː:, væt/ abbr (value added tax) Mehrwertsteuer f, MwSt.

vault¹ /vɔːlt/ n ⟨roof⟩ Gewölbe nt; (in bank) Tresor m; ⟨tomb⟩ Gruft f

vault² n Sprung m ▢ vt/i ~ [over] springen über (+ acc)

VDU abbr (visual display unit) Bildschirmgerät nt

veal /viːl/ n Kalbfleisch nt ▢ attrib Kalbs-

veer /vɪə(r)/ vi sich drehen; (Naut) abdrehen; (Auto) ausscheren

vegetable /ˈvedʒtəbl/ n Gemüse nt; ~s pl Gemüse nt ▢ attrib Gemüse-; ⟨oil, fat⟩ Pflanzen-

vegetarian /vedʒɪˈteərɪən/ a vegetarisch ▢ n Vegetarier(in) m(f)

vegetat|e /ˈvedʒɪteɪt/ vi dahinvegetieren. ~ion /-ˈteɪʃn/ n Vegetation f

vehemen|ce /ˈviːəmən s/ n Heftigkeit f. ~t a, -ly adv heftig

vehicle /ˈviːɪkl/ n Fahrzeug nt; ⟨fig: medium⟩ Mittel nt

veil /veɪl/ n Schleier m ▢ vt verschleiern

vein /veɪn/ n Ader f; ⟨mood⟩ Stimmung f; ⟨manner⟩ Art f; ~s and arteries Venen und Arterien. ~ed a geädert

Velcro (P) /ˈvelkrəʊ/ n ~ fastening Klettverschluss m

velocity /vɪˈlɒsəti/ n Geschwindigkeit f

velvet /ˈvelvɪt/ n Samt m. ~y a samtig

vending-machine /ˈvendɪŋ-/ n [Verkaufs]automat m

vendor /ˈvendə(r)/ n Verkäufer(in) m(f)

veneer /vəˈnɪə(r)/ n Furnier nt; ⟨fig⟩ Tünche f. ~ed a furniert

venerable /ˈvenərəbl/ a ehrwürdig

venereal /vɪˈnɪərɪəl/ a ~ disease Geschlechtskrankheit f

Venetian /vəˈniːʃn/ a venezianisch. v~ blind n Jalousie f

vengeance /ˈvendʒəns/ n Rache f; with a ~ (fam) gewaltig

Venice /ˈvenɪs/ n Venedig nt

venison /ˈvenɪsn/ n (Culin) Wild nt

venom /ˈvenəm/ n Gift nt; ⟨fig⟩ Hass m. ~ous /-əs/ a giftig

vent¹ /vent/ n Öffnung f; ⟨fig⟩ Ventil nt; give ~ to Luft machen (+ dat) ▢ vt Luft machen (+ dat)

vent² n (in jacket) Schlitz m

ventilat|e /'ventɪleɪt/ *vt* belüften. **~ion** /-'leɪʃn/ *n* Belüftung *f*; (*installation*) Lüftung *f*. **~or** *n* Lüftungsvorrichtung *f*; (*Med*) Beatmungsgerät *nt*

ventriloquist /ven'trɪləkwɪst/ *n* Bauchredner *m*

venture /'ventʃə(r)/ *n* Unternehmung *f* □ *vt* wagen □ *vi* sich wagen

venue /'venju:/ *n* Treffpunkt *m*; (*for event*) Veranstaltungsort *m*

veranda /və'rændə/ *n* Veranda *f*

verb /vɜ:b/ *n* Verb *nt*. **~al** *a*, **-ly** *adv* mündlich; (*Gram*) verbal

verbatim /vɜ:'beɪtɪm/ *a* & *adv* [wort]wörtlich

verbose /vɜ:'bəʊs/ *a* weitschweifig

verdict /'vɜ:dɪkt/ *n* Urteil *nt*

verge /vɜ:dʒ/ *n* Rand *m*; **be on the ~ of doing sth** im Begriff sein, etw zu tun □ *vi* **~ on** (*fig*) grenzen an (+ *acc*)

verger /'vɜ:dʒə(r)/ *n* Küster *m*

verify /'verɪfaɪ/ *vt* (*pt/pp* **-ied**) überprüfen; (*confirm*) bestätigen

vermin /'vɜ:mɪn/ *n* Ungeziefer *nt*

vermouth /'vɜ:məθ/ *n* Wermut *m*

vernacular /və'nækjʊlə(r)/ *n* Landessprache *f*

versatil|e /'vɜ:sətaɪl/ *a* vielseitig. **~ity** /-'tɪlətɪ/ *n* Vielseitigkeit *f*

verse /vɜ:s/ *n* Strophe *f*; (*of Bible*) Vers *m*; (*poetry*) Lyrik *f*

version /'vɜ:ʃn/ *n* Version *f*; (*translation*) Übersetzung *f*; (*model*) Modell *nt*

versus /'vɜ:səs/ *prep* gegen (+ *acc*)

vertebra /'vɜ:tɪbrə/ *n* (*pl* **-brae** /-bri:/) (*Anat*) Wirbel *m*

vertical /'vɜ:tɪkl/ *a*, **-ly** *adv* senkrecht □ *n* Senkrechte *f*

vertigo /'vɜ:tɪgəʊ/ *n* (*Med*) Schwindel *m*

verve /vɜ:v/ *n* Schwung *m*

very /'verɪ/ *adv* sehr; **~ much** *adv* sehr; (*quantity*) sehr viel; **~ little** sehr wenig; **~ probably** höchstwahrscheinlich; **at the ~ most** allerhöchstens □ *a* (*mere*) bloß; **the ~ first** der/die/das allererste; **the ~ thing** genau das Richtige; **at the ~ end/beginning** ganz am Ende/Anfang; **only a ~ little** nur ein ganz kleines bisschen

vessel /'vesl/ *n* Schiff *nt*; (*receptacle* & *Anat*) Gefäß *nt*

vest /vest/ *n* [Unter]hemd *nt*; (*Amer: waistcoat*) Weste *f* □ *vt* **~ sth in s.o.** jdm etw verleihen; **have a ~ed interest in sth** ein persönliches Interesse an etw (*dat*) haben

vestige /'vestɪdʒ/ *n* Spur *f*

vestment /'vestmənt/ *n* (*Relig*) Gewand *nt*

vestry /'vestrɪ/ *n* Sakristei *f*

vet /vet/ *n* Tierarzt *m* /-ärztin *f* □ *vt* (*pt/pp* **vetted**) überprüfen

veteran /'vetərən/ *n* Veteran *m*. **~ car** *n* Oldtimer *m*

veterinary /'vetərɪnərɪ/ *a* tierärztlich. **~ surgeon** *n* Tierarzt *m* /-ärztin *f*

veto /'vi:təʊ/ *n* (*pl* **-es**) Veto *nt* □ *vt* sein Veto einlegen gegen

vex /veks/ *vt* ärgern. **~ation** /-'seɪʃn/ *n* Ärger *m*. **~ed** *a* verärgert; **~ed question** viel diskutierte Frage *f*

VHF *abbr* (**very high frequency**) UKW

via /'vaɪə/ *prep* über (+ *acc*)

viable /'vaɪəbl/ *a* lebensfähig; (*fig*) realisierbar; (*firm*) rentabel

viaduct /'vaɪədʌkt/ *n* Viadukt *nt*

vibrant /'vaɪbrənt/ *a* (*fig*) lebhaft

vibrat|e /vaɪ'breɪt/ *vi* vibrieren. **~ion** /-'breɪʃn/ *n* Vibrieren *nt*

vicar /'vɪkə(r)/ *n* Pfarrer *m*. **~age** /-rɪdʒ/ *n* Pfarrhaus *nt*

vicarious /vɪ'keərɪəs/ *a* nachempfunden

vice¹ /vaɪs/ *n* Laster *nt*

vice² *n* (*Techn*) Schraubstock *m*

vice 'chairman *n* stellvertretender Vorsitzender *m*

vice 'president *n* Vizepräsident *m*

vice versa /vaɪsɪ'vɜ:sə/ *adv* umgekehrt

vicinity /vɪ'sɪnətɪ/ *n* Umgebung *f*; **in the ~ of** in der Nähe von

vicious /'vɪʃəs/ *a*, **-ly** *adv* boshaft; (*animal*) bösartig. **~ 'circle** *n* Teufelskreis *m*

victim /'vɪktɪm/ *n* Opfer *nt*. **~ize** *vt* schikanieren

victor /'vɪktə(r)/ *n* Sieger *m*

victor|ious /vɪk'tɔ:rɪəs/ *a* siegreich. **~y** /'vɪktərɪ/ *n* Sieg *m*

video /'vɪdɪəʊ/ *n* Video *nt*; (*recorder*) Videorecorder *m* □ *attrib* Video- □ *vt* [auf Videoband] aufnehmen

video: **~ cas'sette** *n* Videokassette *f*. **~ game** *n* Videospiel *nt*. **~ 'nasty** *n* Horrorvideo *nt*. **~ recorder** *n* Videorecorder *m*

vie /vaɪ/ *vi* (*pres p* **vying**) wetteifern

Vienn|a /vɪ'enə/ *n* Wien *nt*. **~ese** /vɪə'ni:z/ *a* Wiener

view /vju:/ *n* Sicht *f*; (*scene*) Aussicht *f*, Blick *m*; (*picture, opinion*) Ansicht *f*; **in my ~** meiner Ansicht nach; **in ~ of** angesichts (+ *gen*); **keep/have sth in ~** etw im Auge behalten/haben; **be on ~** besichtigt werden können □ *vt* sich (*dat*) ansehen; besichtigen (*house*); (*consider*) betrachten □ *vi* (*TV*) fernsehen. **~er** *n* (*TV*) Zuschauer(in) *m(f)*; (*Phot*) Diabetrachter *m*

view: **~finder** *n* (*Phot*) Sucher *m*. **~point** *n* Standpunkt *m*

vigil /'vɪdʒɪl/ n Wache f

vigilan|ce /'vɪdʒɪləns/ n Wachsamkeit f. ~t a, -ly adv wachsam

vigorous /'vɪgərəs/ a, -ly adv kräftig; (fig) heftig

vigour /'vɪgə(r)/ n Kraft f; (fig) Heftigkeit f

vile /vaɪl/ a abscheulich

villa /'vɪlə/ n (for holidays) Ferienhaus nt

village /'vɪlɪdʒ/ n Dorf nt. ~r n Dorfbewohner(in) m(f)

villain /'vɪlən/ n Schurke m; (in story) Bösewicht m

vim /vɪm/ n (fam) Schwung m

vindicat|e /'vɪndɪkeɪt/ vt rechtfertigen. ~ion /-'keɪʃn/ n Rechtfertigung f

vindictive /vɪn'dɪktɪv/ a nachtragend

vine /vaɪn/ n Weinrebe f

vinegar /'vɪnɪgə(r)/ n Essig m

vineyard /'vɪnjɑːd/ n Weinberg m

vintage /'vɪntɪdʒ/ a erlesen □ n (year) Jahrgang m. ~ 'car n Oldtimer m

viola /vɪ'əʊlə/ n (Mus) Bratsche f

violat|e /'vaɪəleɪt/ vt verletzen; (break) brechen; (disturb) stören; (defile) schänden. ~ion /-'leɪʃn/ n Verletzung f; Schändung f

violen|ce /'vaɪələns/ n Gewalt f; (fig) Heftigkeit f. ~t a gewalttätig; (fig) heftig. ~tly adv brutal; (fig) heftig

violet /'vaɪələt/ a violett □ n (flower) Veilchen nt

violin /vaɪə'lɪn/ n Geige f, Violine f. ~ist n Geiger(in) m(f)

VIP abbr (very important person) Prominente(r) m/f

viper /'vaɪpə(r)/ n Kreuzotter f; (fig) Schlange f

virgin /'vɜːdʒɪn/ a unberührt □ n Jungfrau f. ~ity /-'dʒɪnətɪ/ n Unschuld f

Virgo /'vɜːgəʊ/ n (Astr) Jungfrau f

viril|e /'vɪraɪl/ a männlich. ~ity /-'rɪlətɪ/ n Männlichkeit f

virtual /'vɜːtjʊəl/ a a ~ ... praktisch ein ... ~ly adv praktisch

virtu|e /'vɜːtjuː/ n Tugend f; (advantage) Vorteil m; by or in ~e of auf Grund (+ gen)

virtuoso /vɜːtjʊ'əʊzəʊ/ n (pl -si /-zɪː/) Virtuose m

virtuous /'vɜːtjʊəs/ a tugendhaft

virulent /'vɪrʊlənt/ a bösartig; (poison) stark; (fig) scharf

virus /'vaɪərəs/ n Virus nt

visa /'viːzə/ n Visum nt

vis-à-vis /viːzɑː'viː/ adv & prep gegenüber (+ dat)

viscous /'vɪskəs/ a dickflüssig

visibility /vɪzə'bɪlətɪ/ n Sichtbarkeit f; (Meteorol) Sichtweite f

visible /'vɪzəbl/ a, -bly adv sichtbar

vision /'vɪʒn/ n Vision f; (sight) Sehkraft f; (foresight) Weitblick m

visit /'vɪzɪt/ n Besuch m □ vt besuchen; besichtigen (town, building). ~ing hours npl Besuchszeiten pl. ~or n Besucher(in) m(f); (in hotel) Gast m; have ~ors Besuch haben

visor /'vaɪzə(r)/ n Schirm m; (on helmet) Visier nt; (Auto) [Sonnen]blende f

vista /'vɪstə/ n Aussicht f

visual /'vɪzjʊəl/ a, -ly adv visuell; ~ly handicapped sehbehindert. ~ aids npl Anschauungsmaterial nt. ~ dis'play unit n Bildschirmgerät nt

visualize /'vɪzjʊəlaɪz/ vt sich (dat) vorstellen

vital /'vaɪtl/ a unbedingt notwendig; (essential to life) lebenswichtig. ~ity /vaɪ'tælətɪ/ n Vitalität f. ~ly /'vaɪtəlɪ/ adv äußerst

vitamin /'vɪtəmɪn/ n Vitamin nt

vitreous /'vɪtrɪəs/ a glasartig; (enamel) Glas-

vivaci|ous /vɪ'veɪʃəs/ a, -ly adv lebhaft. ~ty /-'væsətɪ/ n Lebhaftigkeit f

vivid /'vɪvɪd/ a, -ly adv lebhaft; (description) lebendig

vixen /'vɪksn/ n Füchsin f

vocabulary /və'kæbjʊlərɪ/ n Wortschatz m; (list) Vokabelverzeichnis nt; learn ~ Vokabeln lernen

vocal /'vəʊkl/ a, -ly adv stimmlich; (vociferous) lautstark. ~ cords npl Stimmbänder pl

vocalist /'vəʊkəlɪst/ n Sänger(in) m(f)

vocation /və'keɪʃn/ n Berufung f. ~al a Berufs-

vociferous /və'sɪfərəs/ a lautstark

vodka /'vɒdkə/ n Wodka m

vogue /vəʊg/ n Mode f; in ~ in Mode

voice /vɔɪs/ n Stimme f □ vt zum Ausdruck bringen

void /vɔɪd/ a leer; (not valid) ungültig; ~ of ohne □ n Leere f

volatile /'vɒlətaɪl/ a flüchtig; (person) sprunghaft

volcanic /vɒl'kænɪk/ a vulkanisch

volcano /vɒl'keɪnəʊ/ n Vulkan m

volition /və'lɪʃn/ n of one's own ~ aus eigenem Willen

volley /'vɒlɪ/ n (of gunfire) Salve f; (Tennis) Volley m

volt /vəʊlt/ n Volt nt. ~age /-ɪdʒ/ n (Electr) Spannung f

voluble /'vɒljʊbl/ a, **-bly** adv redselig; ⟨protest⟩ wortreich

volume /'vɒljuːm/ n ⟨book⟩ Band m; ⟨Geom⟩ Rauminhalt m; ⟨amount⟩ Ausmaß nt; ⟨Radio, TV⟩ Lautstärke f. ~ **control** n Lautstärkeregler m

voluntary /'vɒləntərɪ/ a, **-ily** adv freiwillig

volunteer /vɒlən'tɪə(r)/ n Freiwillige(r) m/f □ vt anbieten; geben ⟨information⟩ □ vi sich freiwillig melden

voluptuous /və'lʌptjʊəs/ a sinnlich

vomit /'vɒmɪt/ n Erbrochene(s) nt □ vt erbrechen □ vi sich übergeben

voracious /və'reɪʃəs/ a gefräßig; ⟨appetite⟩ unbändig

vot|e /vəʊt/ n Stimme f; ⟨ballot⟩ Abstimmung f; ⟨right⟩ Wahlrecht nt; **take a** ~**e on** abstimmen über (+ acc) □ vi abstimmen; ⟨in election⟩ wählen □ vt ~**e s.o. president** jdn zum Präsidenten wählen. ~**er** n Wähler(in) m(f)

vouch /vaʊtʃ/ vi ~ **for** sich verbürgen für. ~**er** n Gutschein m

vow /vaʊ/ n Gelöbnis nt; ⟨Relig⟩ Gelübde nt □ vt geloben

vowel /'vaʊəl/ n Vokal m

voyage /'vɔɪɪdz/ n Seereise f; ⟨in space⟩ Reise f, Flug m

vulgar /'vʌlgə(r)/ a vulgär, ordinär. ~**ity** /-'gærətɪ/ n Vulgarität f

vulnerable /'vʌlnərəbl/ a verwundbar

vulture /'vʌltʃə(r)/ n Geier m

vying /'vaɪɪŋ/ see **vie**

W

wad /wɒd/ n Bausch m; ⟨bundle⟩ Bündel nt. ~**ding** n Wattierung f

waddle /'wɒdl/ vi watscheln

wade /weɪd/ vi waten; ~ **through** ⟨fam⟩ sich durchackern durch ⟨book⟩

wafer /'weɪfə(r)/ n Waffel f; ⟨Relig⟩ Hostie f

waffle[1] /'wɒfl/ vi ⟨fam⟩ schwafeln

waffle[2] n ⟨Culin⟩ Waffel f

waft /wɒft/ vt/i wehen

wag /wæg/ v ⟨pt/pp **wagged**⟩ □ vt wedeln mit; ~ **one's finger at s.o.** jdm mit dem Finger drohen □ vi wedeln

wage[1] /weɪdʒ/ vt führen

wage[2] n, & ~**s** pl Lohn m. ~ **packet** n Lohntüte f

wager /'weɪdʒə(r)/ n Wette f

waggle /'wægl/ vt wackeln mit □ vi wackeln

wagon /'wægən/ n Wagen m; ⟨Rail⟩ Waggon m

wail /weɪl/ n [klagender] Schrei m □ vi heulen; ⟨lament⟩ klagen

waist /weɪst/ n Taille f. ~**coat** /'weɪskəʊt/ n Weste f. ~**line** n Taille f

wait /weɪt/ n Wartezeit f; **lie in** ~ **for** auflauern (+ dat) □ vi warten ⟨**for** auf + acc⟩; ⟨at table⟩ servieren; ~ **on** bedienen □ vt ~ **one's turn** warten, bis man an der Reihe ist

waiter /'weɪtə(r)/ n Kellner m; ~! Herr Ober!

waiting: ~**-list** n Warteliste f. ~**-room** n Warteraum m; ⟨doctor's⟩ Wartezimmer nt

waitress /'weɪtrɪs/ n Kellnerin f

waive /weɪv/ vt verzichten auf (+ acc)

wake[1] /weɪk/ n Totenwache f □ v ⟨pt **woke**, pp **woken**⟩ ~ [**up**] □ vt [auf]wecken □ vi aufwachen

wake[2] n ⟨Naut⟩ Kielwasser nt; **in the** ~ **of** im Gefolge (+ gen)

waken /'weɪkn/ vt [auf]wecken □ vi aufwachen

Wales /weɪlz/ n Wales nt

walk /wɔːk/ n Spaziergang m; ⟨gait⟩ Gang m; ⟨path⟩ Weg m; **go for a** ~ spazieren gehen □ vi gehen; ⟨not ride⟩ laufen, zu Fuß gehen; ⟨ramble⟩ wandern; **learn to** ~ laufen lernen □ vt ausführen ⟨dog⟩. ~ **out** vi hinausgehen; ⟨workers:⟩ in den Streik treten; ~ **out on s.o.** jdn verlassen

walker /'wɔːkə(r)/ n Spaziergänger(in) m(f); ⟨rambler⟩ Wanderer m/Wanderin f

walking /'wɔːkɪŋ/ n Gehen nt; ⟨rambling⟩ Wandern nt. ~**-stick** n Spazierstock m

walk: ~**-out** n Streik m. ~**-over** n ⟨fig⟩ leichter Sieg m

wall /wɔːl/ n Wand f; ⟨external⟩ Mauer f; **go to the** ~ ⟨fam⟩ eingehen; **drive s.o. up the** ~ ⟨fam⟩ jdn auf die Palme bringen □ vt ~ **up** zumauern

wallet /'wɒlɪt/ n Brieftasche f

'wallflower n Goldlack m

wallop /'wɒləp/ n ⟨fam⟩ Schlag m □ vt ⟨pt/pp **walloped**⟩ ⟨fam⟩ schlagen

wallow /'wɒləʊ/ vi sich wälzen; ⟨fig⟩ schwelgen

'wallpaper n Tapete f □ vt tapezieren

walnut /'wɔːlnʌt/ n Walnuss f

waltz /wɔːlts/ n Walzer m □ vi Walzer tanzen; **come** ~**ing up** ⟨fam⟩ angetanzt kommen

wan /wɒn/ a bleich

wand /wɒnd/ n Zauberstab m

wander /'wɒndə(r)/ vi umherwandern, (fam) bummeln; (fig: digress) abschweifen. ∼ **about** vi umherwandern. ∼**lust** n Fernweh nt

wane /weɪn/ n **be on the** ∼ schwinden; ⟨moon:⟩ abnehmen □ vi schwinden; abnehmen

wangle /'wæŋgl/ vt (fam) organisieren

want /wɒnt/ n Mangel m (**of** an + dat); (hardship) Not f; (desire) Bedürfnis nt □ vt wollen; (need) brauchen; ∼ **[to have] sth** etw haben wollen; ∼ **to do sth** etw tun wollen; **we** ∼ **to stay** wir wollen bleiben; **I** ∼ **you to go** ich will, dass du gehst; **it** ∼**s painting** es müsste gestrichen werden; **you** ∼ **to learn to swim** du solltest schwimmen lernen □ vi **he doesn't** ∼ **for anything** ihm fehlt es an nichts. ∼**ed** a gesucht. ∼**ing** a **be** ∼**ing** fehlen; **he is** ∼**ing in** ihm fehlt es an (+ dat)

wanton /'wɒntən/ a, -ly adv mutwillig

war /wɔ:(r)/ n Krieg m; **be at** ∼ sich im Krieg befinden

ward /wɔ:d/ n [Kranken]saal m; (unit) Station f; (of town) Wahlbezirk m; (child) Mündel nt □ vt ∼ **off** abwehren

warden /'wɔ:dn/ n Heimleiter(in) m(f); (of youth hostel) Herbergsvater m; (supervisor) Aufseher(in) m(f)

warder /'wɔ:də(r)/ n Wärter(in) m(f)

wardrobe /'wɔ:drəʊb/ n Kleiderschrank m; (clothes) Garderobe f

warehouse /'weəhaʊs/ n Lager nt; (building) Lagerhaus nt

wares /weəz/ npl Waren pl

war: ∼**fare** n Krieg m. ∼**head** n Sprengkopf m. ∼**like** a kriegerisch

warm /wɔ:m/ a (-er, -est), -ly adv warm; ⟨welcome⟩ herzlich; **I am** ∼ mir ist warm □ vt wärmen. ∼ **up** vt aufwärmen □ vi warm werden; (Sport) sich aufwärmen. ∼**-hearted** a warmherzig

warmth /wɔ:mθ/ n Wärme f

warn /wɔ:n/ vt warnen (**of** vor + dat). ∼**ing** n Warnung f; (advance notice) Vorwarnung f; (caution) Verwarnung f

warp /wɔ:p/ vt verbiegen □ vi sich verziehen

'**war-path** n **on the** ∼ auf dem Kriegspfad

warrant /'wɒrənt/ n (for arrest) Haftbefehl m; (for search) Durchsuchungsbefehl m □ vt (justify) rechtfertigen; (guarantee) garantieren

warranty /'wɒrənti/ n Garantie f

warrior /'wɒrɪə(r)/ n Krieger m

'**warship** n Kriegsschiff nt

wart /wɔ:t/ n Warze f

'**wartime** n Kriegszeit f

wary /'weəri/ a (-ier, -iest), -ily adv vorsichtig; (suspicious) misstrauisch

was /wɒz/ see **be**

wash /wɒʃ/ n Wäsche f; (Naut) Wellen pl; **have a** ∼ sich waschen □ vt waschen; spülen ⟨dishes⟩; aufwischen ⟨floor⟩; (flow over) bespülen; ∼ **one's hands** sich (dat) die Hände waschen □ vi sich waschen; ⟨fabric:⟩ sich waschen lassen. ∼ **out** vt auswaschen; ausspülen ⟨mouth⟩. ∼ **up** vt abwaschen, spülen □ vi abwaschen; (Amer) sich waschen

washable /'wɒʃəbl/ a waschbar

wash: ∼**basin** n Waschbecken nt. ∼**cloth** n (Amer) Waschlappen m

washed 'out a (faded) verwaschen; (tired) abgespannt

washer /'wɒʃə(r)/ n (Techn) Dichtungsring m; (machine) Waschmaschine f

washing /'wɒʃɪŋ/ n Wäsche f. ∼**machine** n Waschmaschine f. ∼**powder** n Waschpulver nt. ∼'**up** n Abwasch m; **do the** ∼**up** abwaschen, spülen. ∼'**up liquid** n Spülmittel nt

wash: ∼**out** n Pleite f; (person) Niete f. ∼**room** n Waschraum m

wasp /wɒsp/ n Wespe f

wastage /'weɪstɪdʒ/ n Schwund m

waste /weɪst/ n Verschwendung f; (rubbish) Abfall m; ∼**s** pl Öde f; ∼ **of time** Zeitverschwendung f □ a ⟨product⟩ Abfall-; **lay** ∼ verwüsten □ vt verschwenden □ vi ∼ **away** immer mehr abmagern

waste: ∼**di'sposal unit** n Müllzerkleinerer m. ∼**ful** a verschwenderisch. ∼**land** n Ödland nt. ∼ '**paper** n Altpapier nt. ∼-'**paper basket** n Papierkorb m

watch /wɒtʃ/ n Wache f; (timepiece) [Armband]uhr f; **be on the** ∼ aufpassen □ vt beobachten; sich (dat) ansehen ⟨film, match⟩; (be careful of, look after) achten auf (+ acc); ∼ **television** fernsehen □ vi zusehen. ∼ **out** vi Ausschau halten (**for** nach); (be careful) aufpassen

watch: ∼**dog** n Wachhund m. ∼**ful** a, -ly adv wachsam. ∼**maker** n Uhrmacher m. ∼**man** n Wachmann m. ∼**strap** n Uhrarmband nt. ∼**tower** n Wachturm m. ∼**word** n Parole f

water /'wɔ:tə(r)/ n Wasser nt; ∼**s** pl Gewässer pl □ vt gießen ⟨garden, plant⟩; (dilute) verdünnen; (give drink to) tränken □ vi ⟨eyes:⟩ tränen; **my mouth was** ∼**ing** mir lief das Wasser im Munde zusammen. ∼ **down** vt verwässern

water: ∼**colour** n Wasserfarbe f; (painting) Aquarell nt. ∼**cress** n Brunnenkresse f. ∼**fall** n Wasserfall m

'**watering-can** *n* Gießkanne *f*

water: ∼-lily *n* Seerose *f*. ∼**logged** *a* be ∼**logged** ⟨ground:⟩ unter Wasser stehen. ∼-**main** *n* Hauptwasserleitung *f*. ∼**mark** *n* Wasserzeichen *nt*. ∼ **polo** *n* Wasserball *m*. ∼-**power** *n* Wasserkraft *f*. ∼**proof** *a* wasserdicht. ∼**shed** *n* Wasserscheide *f*; ⟨fig⟩ Wendepunkt *m*. ∼-**skiing** *n* Wasserskilaufen *nt*. ∼**tight** *a* wasserdicht. ∼**way** *n* Wasserstraße *f*

watery /'wɔːtərɪ/ *a* wässrig

watt /wɒt/ *n* Watt *nt*

wave /weɪv/ *n* Welle *f*; (gesture) Handbewegung *f*; (as greeting) Winken *nt* □ *vt* winken mit; (brandish) schwingen; (threateningly) drohen mit; wellen ⟨hair⟩; ∼ **one's hand** winken □ *vi* winken (to dat); ⟨flag:⟩ wehen. ∼**length** *n* Wellenlänge *f*

waver /'weɪvə(r)/ *vi* schwanken

wavy /'weɪvɪ/ *a* wellig

wax[1] /wæks/ *vi* ⟨moon:⟩ zunehmen; (fig: become) werden

wax[2] *n* Wachs *nt*; (in ear) Schmalz *nt* □ *vt* wachsen. ∼**works** *n* Wachsfigurenkabinett *nt*

way /weɪ/ *n* Weg *m*; (direction) Richtung *f*; (respect) Hinsicht *f*; (manner) Art *f*; (method) Art und Weise *f*; ∼**s** *pl* Gewohnheiten *pl*; **in the** ∼ im Weg; **on the** ∼ auf dem Weg (to nach/zu); (under way) unterwegs; **a little/long** ∼ ein kleines/ ganzes Stück; **a long** ∼ **off** weit weg; **this** ∼ hierher; (like this) so; **which** ∼ in welche Richtung; (how) wie; **by the** ∼ übrigens; **in some** ∼**s** in gewisser Hinsicht; **either** ∼ so oder so; **in this** ∼ auf diese Weise; **in a** ∼ in gewisser Weise; **in a bad** ∼ ⟨person⟩ in schlechter Verfassung; **lead the** ∼ vorausgehen; **make** ∼ Platz machen (for dat); '**give** ∼' (Auto) 'Vorfahrt beachten'; **go out of one's** ∼ (fig) sich (dat) besondere Mühe geben (to zu); **get one's [own]** ∼ seinen Willen durchsetzen □ *adv* weit; ∼ **behind** weit zurück. ∼ '**in** *n* Eingang *m*

way'lay *vt* (pt/pp -laid) überfallen; (fam: intercept) abfangen

way 'out *n* Ausgang *m*; (fig) Ausweg *m*

way-'out *a* (fam) verrückt

wayward /'weɪwəd/ *a* eigenwillig

WC *abbr* WC *nt*

we /wiː/ *pron* wir

weak /wiːk/ *a* (-er, -est), -**ly** *adv* schwach; ⟨liquid⟩ dünn. ∼**en** *vt* schwächen □ *vi* schwächer werden. ∼**ling** *n* Schwächling *m*. ∼**ness** *n* Schwäche *f*

wealth /welθ/ *n* Reichtum *m*; (fig) Fülle *f* (**of** an + dat). ∼**y** *a* (-ier, -iest) reich

wean /wiːn/ *vt* entwöhnen

weapon /'wepən/ *n* Waffe *f*

wear /weə(r)/ *n* (clothing) Kleidung *f*; ∼ **and tear** Abnutzung *f*, Verschleiß *m* □ *v* (pt wore, pp worn) □ *vt* tragen; (damage) abnutzen; ∼ **a hole in sth** etw durchwetzen; **what shall I** ∼? was soll ich anziehen? □ *vi* sich abnutzen; (last) halten. ∼ **off** *vi* abgehen; ⟨effect:⟩ nachlassen. ∼ **out** *vt* abnutzen; (exhaust) erschöpfen □ *vi* sich abnutzen

wearable /'weərəbl/ *a* tragbar

weary /'wɪərɪ/ *a* (-ier, -iest), -**ily** *adv* müde □ *v* (pt/pp wearied) □ *vt* ermüden □ *vi* ∼ **of sth** etw (gen) überdrüssig werden

weasel /'wiːzl/ *n* Wiesel *nt*

weather /'weðə(r)/ *n* Wetter *nt*; **in this** ∼ bei diesem Wetter; **under the** ∼ (fam) nicht ganz auf dem Posten □ *vt* abwettern ⟨storm⟩; (fig) überstehen

weather: ∼-**beaten** *a* verwittert; wettergegerbt ⟨face⟩. ∼**cock** *n* Wetterhahn *m*. ∼ **forecast** *n* Wettervorhersage *f*. ∼-**vane** *n* Wetterfahne *f*

weave[1] /wiːv/ *vi* (pt/pp weaved) sich schlängeln (**through** durch)

weave[2] *n* (Tex) Bindung *f* □ *vt* (pt wove, pp woven) weben; (plait) flechten; (fig) einflechten (**in** in + acc). ∼**r** *n* Weber *m*

web /web/ *n* Netz *nt*. ∼**bed feet** *npl* Schwimmfüße *pl*

wed /wed/ *vt/i* (pt/pp wedded) heiraten. ∼**ding** *n* Hochzeit *f*; (ceremony) Trauung *f*

wedding: ∼ **day** *n* Hochzeitstag *m*. ∼ **dress** *n* Hochzeitskleid *nt*. ∼-**ring** *n* Ehering *m*, Trauring *m*

wedge /wedʒ/ *n* Keil *m*; (of cheese) [keilförmiges] Stück *nt* □ *vt* festklemmen

wedlock /'wedlɒk/ *n* (liter) Ehe *f*; **in/out of** ∼ ehelich/unehelich

Wednesday /'wenzdeɪ/ *n* Mittwoch *m*

wee /wiː/ *a* (fam) klein □ *vi* Pipi machen

weed /wiːd/ *n* & ∼**s** *pl* Unkraut *nt* □ *vt/i* jäten. ∼ **out** *vt* (fig) aussieben

'**weed-killer** *n* Unkrautvertilgungsmittel *nt*

weedy /'wiːdɪ/ *a* (fam) spillerig

week /wiːk/ *n* Woche *f*. ∼**day** *n* Wochentag *m*. ∼**end** *n* Wochenende *nt*

weekly /'wiːklɪ/ *a* & *adv* wöchentlich □ *n* Wochenzeitschrift *f*

weep /wiːp/ *vi* (pt/pp wept) weinen. ∼**ing** '**willow** *n* Trauerweide *f*

weigh /weɪ/ *vt/i* wiegen; ∼ **anchor** den Anker lichten. ∼ **down** *vt* (fig) niederdrücken. ∼ **up** *vt* (fig) abwägen

weight /weɪt/ *n* Gewicht *nt*; **put on/lose** ∼ zunehmen/abnehmen. ∼**ing** *n* (allowance) Zulage *f*

weight: ~**lessness** *n* Schwerelosigkeit *f*. ~**-lifting** *n* Gewichtheben *nt*

weighty /'weɪtɪ/ *a* (-**ier**, -**iest**) schwer; (*important*) gewichtig

weir /wɪə(r)/ *n* Wehr *nt*

weird /wɪəd/ *a* (-**er**, -**est**) unheimlich; (*bizarre*) bizarr

welcome /'welkəm/ *a* willkommen; **you're** ~! nichts zu danken! **you're** ~ **to have it** das können Sie gerne haben ◻ *n* Willkommen *nt* ◻ *vt* begrüßen

weld /weld/ *vt* schweißen. ~**er** *n* Schweißer *m*

welfare /'welfeə(r)/ *n* Wohl *nt*; (*Admin*) Fürsorge *f*. **W~ State** *n* Wohlfahrtsstaat *m*

well[1] /wel/ *n* Brunnen *m*; (*oil* ~) Quelle *f*; (*of staircase*) Treppenhaus *nt*

well[2] *adv* (**better**, **best**) gut; **as** ~ auch; **as** ~ **as** (*in addition*) sowohl ... als auch; ~ **done!** gut gemacht! ◻ *a* gesund; **he is not** ~ es geht ihm nicht gut; **get** ~ **soon!** gute Besserung! ◻ *int* nun, na

well: ~**-behaved** *a* artig. ~**-being** *n* Wohl *nt*. ~**-bred** *a* wohlerzogen. ~**-heeled** *a* (*fam*) gut betucht

wellingtons /'welɪŋtənz/ *npl* Gummistiefel *pl*

well: ~**-known** *a* bekannt. ~**-meaning** *a* wohlmeinend. ~**-meant** *a* gut gemeint. ~**-off** *a* wohlhabend; **be** ~**-off** gut dran sein. ~**-read** *a* belesen. ~**-to-do** *a* wohlhabend

Welsh /welʃ/ *a* walisisch ◻ *n* (*Lang*) Walisisch *nt*; **the** ~ *pl* die Waliser. ~ **man** *n* Waliser *m*. ~ **rabbit** *n* überbackenes Käsebrot *nt*

went /went/ *see* go

wept /wept/ *see* weep

were /wɜ:(r)/ *see* be

west /west/ *n* Westen *m*; **to the** ~ **of** westlich von ◻ *a* West-, west- ◻ *adv* nach Westen; **go** ~ (*fam*) flöten gehen. ~**erly** *a* westlich. ~**ern** *a* westlich ◻ *n* Western *m*

West: ~ **'Germany** *n* Westdeutschland *nt*. ~ **'Indian** *a* westindisch ◻ *n* Westinder(in) *m(f)*. ~ **'Indies** /-'ɪndɪz/ *npl* Westindische Inseln *pl*

'westward[s] /-wəd[z]/ *adv* nach Westen

wet /wet/ *a* (**wetter**, **wettest**) nass; (*fam: person*) weichlich, lasch; '~ **paint**' 'frisch gestrichen' ◻ *vt* (*pt/pp* **wet** or **wetted**) nass machen. ~ **'blanket** *n* Spaßverderber *m*

whack /wæk/ *n* (*fam*) Schlag *m* ◻ *vt* (*fam*) schlagen. ~**ed** *a* (*fam*) kaputt

whale /weɪl/ *n* Wal *m*; **have a** ~ **of a time** (*fam*) sich toll amüsieren

wharf /wɔ:f/ *n* Kai *m*

what /wɒt/ *pron* & *int* was; ~ **for?** wozu? ~ **is it like?** wie ist es? ~ **is your name?** wie ist Ihr Name? ~ **is the weather like?** wie ist das Wetter? ~**'s he talking about?** wovon redet er? ◻ *a* welche(r,s); ~ **kind of a** was für ein(e); **at** ~ **time?** um wie viel Uhr?

what'ever *a* [egal] welche(r,s) ◻ *pron* was ... auch; ~ **is it?** was ist das bloß? ~ **he does** was er auch tut; ~ **happens** was auch geschieht; **nothing** ~ überhaupt nichts

whatso'ever *pron* & *a* ≈ **whatever**

wheat /wi:t/ *n* Weizen *m*

wheedle /'wi:dl/ *vt* gut zureden (+ *dat*); ~ **sth out of s.o.** jdm etw ablocken

wheel /wi:l/ *n* Rad *nt*; (*pottery*) Töpferscheibe *f*; (*steering* ~) Lenkrad *nt*; **at the** ~ am Steuer ◻ *vt* (*push*) schieben ◻ *vi* kehrtmachen; (*circle*) kreisen

wheel: ~**barrow** *n* Schubkarre *f*. ~**chair** *n* Rollstuhl *m*. ~**-clamp** *n* Parkkralle *f*

wheeze /wi:z/ *vi* keuchen

when /wen/ *adv* wann; **the day** ~ der Tag, an dem ◻ *conj* wenn; (*in the past*) als; (*although*) wo ... doch; ~ **swimming**/ **reading** beim Schwimmen/Lesen

whence /wens/ *adv* (*liter*) woher

when'ever *conj* & *adv* [immer] wenn; (*at whatever time*) wann immer; ~ **did it happen?** wann ist das bloß passiert?

where /weə(r)/ *adv* & *conj* wo; ~ **[to]** wohin; ~ **[from]** woher

whereabouts[1] /weərə'baʊts/ *adv* wo

'whereabouts[2] *n* Verbleib *m*; (*of person*) Aufenthaltsort *m*

where'as *conj* während; (*in contrast*) wohingegen

where'by *adv* wodurch

whereu'pon *adv* worauf[hin]

wher'ever *conj* & *adv* wo immer; (*to whatever place*) wohin immer; (*from whatever place*) woher immer; (*everywhere*) überall wo; ~ **is he?** wo ist er bloß? ~ **possible** wenn irgend möglich

whet /wet/ *vt* (*pt/pp* **whetted**) wetzen; anregen (*appetite*)

whether /'weðə(r)/ *conj* ob

which /wɪtʃ/ *a* & *pron* welche(r,s); ~ **one** welche(r,s) ◻ *rel pron* der/die/das, (*pl*) die; (*after clause*) was; **after** ~ wonach; **on** ~ worauf

which'ever *a* & *pron* [egal] welche(r,s); ~ **it** is was es auch ist

whiff /wɪf/ *n* Hauch *m*

while /waɪl/ *n* Weile *f*; **a long** ~ lange; **be worth** ~ sich lohnen; **its worth my** ~ es lohnt sich für mich ◻ *conj* während; (*as* *long as*) solange; (*although*) obgleich □ *vt* ~ **away** sich (*dat*) vertreiben

whilst /waɪlst/ *conj* während

whim /wɪm/ *n* Laune *f*

whimper /'wɪmpə(r)/ *vi* wimmern; ⟨*dog:*⟩ winseln

whimsical /'wɪmzɪkl/ *a* skurril

whine /waɪn/ *n* Winseln *nt* □ *vi* winseln

whip /wɪp/ *n* Peitsche *f*; (*Pol*) Einpeitscher *m* □ *vt* (*pt/pp* **whipped**) peitschen; (*Culin*) schlagen; (*snatch*) reißen; (*fam: steal*) klauen. ~ **up** *vt* (*incite*) anheizen; (*fam*) schnell hinzaubern ⟨*meal*⟩. **~ped** 'cream *n* Schlagsahne *f*

whirl /wɜːl/ *n* Wirbel *m*; **I am in a** ~ mir schwirrt der Kopf □ *vt/i* wirbeln. **~pool** *n* Strudel *m*. **~wind** *n* Wirbelwind *m*

whirr /wɜː(r)/ *vi* surren

whisk /wɪsk/ *n* (*Culin*) Schneebesen *m* □ *vt* (*Culin*) schlagen. ~ **away** *vt* wegreißen

whisker /'wɪskə(r)/ *n* Schnurrhaar *nt*; **~s** *pl* (*on man's cheek*) Backenbart *m*

whisky /'wɪskɪ/ *n* Whisky *m*

whisper /'wɪspə(r)/ *n* Flüstern *nt*; (*rumour*) Gerücht *nt*; **in a** ~ im Flüsterton □ *vt/i* flüstern

whistle /'wɪsl/ *n* Pfiff *m*; (*instrument*) Pfeife *f* □ *vt/i* pfeifen

white /waɪt/ *a* (**-r, -st**) weiß □ *n* Weiß *nt*; (*of egg*) Eiweiß *nt*; (*person*) Weiße(r) *m/f*

white: ~ '**coffee** *n* Kaffee *m* mit Milch. ~ '**collar worker** *n* Angestellte(r) *m*. ~ '**lie** *n* Notlüge *f*

whiten /'waɪtn/ *vt* weiß machen □ *vi* weiß werden

whiteness /'waɪtnɪs/ *n* Weiß *nt*

'**whitewash** *n* Tünche *f*; (*fig*) Schönfärberei *f* □ *vt* tünchen

Whitsun /'wɪtsn/ *n* Pfingsten *nt*

whittle /'wɪtl/ *vt* ~ **down** reduzieren; kürzen ⟨*list*⟩

whiz[z] /wɪz/ *vi* (*pt/pp* **whizzed**) zischen. **~-kid** *n* (*fam*) Senkrechtstarter *m*

who /huː/ *pron* wer; (*acc*) wen; (*dat*) wem □ *rel pron* der/die/das, (*pl*) die

who'ever *pron* wer [immer]; ~ **he is** wer er auch ist; ~ **is it?** wer ist das bloß?

whole /həʊl/ *a* ganz; ⟨*truth*⟩ voll □ *n* Ganze(s) *nt*; **as a** ~ als Ganzes; **on the** ~ im Großen und Ganzen; **the** ~ **lot** alle; (*everything*) alles; **the** ~ **of Germany** ganz Deutschland; **the** ~ **time** die ganze Zeit

whole: **~food** *n* Vollwertkost *f*. ~ '**hearted** *a* rückhaltlos. **~meal** *a* Vollkorn-

'**wholesale** *a* Großhandels- □ *adv* en gros; (*fig*) in Bausch und Bogen. **~r** *n* Großhändler *m*

wholesome /'həʊlsəm/ *a* gesund

wholly /'həʊlɪ/ *adv* völlig

whom /huːm/ *pron* wen; **to** ~ wem □ *rel pron* den/die/das, (*pl*) die; (*dat*) dem/der/ dem, (*pl*) denen

whooping cough /'huːpɪŋ-/ *n* Keuchhusten *m*

whopping /'wɒpɪŋ/ *a* (*fam*) Riesen-

whore /hɔː(r)/ *n* Hure *f*

whose /huːz/ *pron* wessen; ~ **is that?** wem gehört das? □ *rel pron* dessen/ deren/dessen, (*pl*) deren

why /waɪ/ *adv* warum; (*for what purpose*) wozu; **that's** ~ darum □ *int* na

wick /wɪk/ *n* Docht *m*

wicked /'wɪkɪd/ *a* böse; (*mischievous*) frech, boshaft

wicker /'wɪkə(r)/ *n* Korbgeflecht *nt* □ *attrib* Korb-

wide /waɪd/ *a* (**-r, -st**) weit; (*broad*) breit; (*fig*) groß; **be** ~ (*far from target*) danebengehen □ *adv* weit; (*off target*) daneben; ~ **awake** hellwach; **far and** ~ weit und breit. **~ly** *adv* weit; ⟨*known, accepted*⟩ weithin; ⟨*differ*⟩ stark

widen /'waɪdn/ *vt* verbreitern; (*fig*) erweitern □ *vi* sich verbreitern

'**widespread** *a* weit verbreitet

widow /'wɪdəʊ/ *n* Witwe *f*. **~ed** *a* verwitwet. **~er** *n* Witwer *m*

width /wɪdθ/ *n* Weite *f*; (*breadth*) Breite *f*

wield /wiːld/ *vt* schwingen; ausüben ⟨*power*⟩

wife /waɪf/ *n* (*pl* **wives**) [Ehe]frau *f*

wig /wɪg/ *n* Perücke *f*

wiggle /'wɪgl/ *vi* wackeln □ *vt* wackeln mit

wild /waɪld/ *a* (**-r, -est**), **-ly** *adv* wild; ⟨*animal*⟩ wild lebend; ⟨*flower*⟩ wild wachsend; (*furious*) wütend; **be** ~ **about** (*keen on*) wild sein auf (+ *acc*) □ *adv* wild; **run** ~ frei herumlaufen □ *n* **in the** ~ wild; **the** ~**s** *pl* die Wildnis *f*

'**wildcat strike** *n* wilder Streik *m*

wilderness /'wɪldənɪs/ *n* Wildnis *f*; (*desert*) Wüste *f*

wild: ~'**goose chase** *n* aussichtslose Suche *f*. **~life** *n* Tierwelt *f*

will[1] /wɪl/ *v aux* wollen; (*forming future tense*) werden; **he** ~ **arrive tomorrow** er wird morgen kommen; ~ **you go?** gehst du? **you** ~ **be back soon, won't you?** du kommst doch bald wieder, nicht? **he** ~ **be there, won't he?** er wird doch da sein? **she** ~ **be there by now** sie wird jetzt schon da sein; ~ **you be quiet!** willst du wohl ruhig sein! ~ **you have some wine?**

möchten Sie Wein? **the engine won't start** der Motor will nicht anspringen

will² n Wille m; (*document*) Testament nt

willing /'wɪlɪŋ/ a willig; (*eager*) bereitwillig; **be ~** bereit sein. **~ly** adv bereitwillig; (*gladly*) gern. **~ness** n Bereitwilligkeit f

willow /'wɪləʊ/ n Weide f

'will-power n Willenskraft f

willy-'nilly adv wohl oder übel

wilt /wɪlt/ vi welk werden, welken

wily /'waɪlɪ/ a (**-ier, -iest**) listig

wimp /wɪmp/ n Schwächling m

win /wɪn/ n Sieg m; **have a ~** gewinnen □ v (pt/pp **won**; pres p **winning**) □ vi gewinnen; bekommen (*scholarship*) □ vi gewinnen; (*in battle*) siegen. **~ over** vt auf seine Seite bringen

wince /wɪns/ vi zusammenzucken

winch /wɪntʃ/ n Winde f □ vt **~ up** hochwinden

wind¹ /wɪnd/ n Wind m; (*breath*) Atem m; (*fam: flatulence*) Blähungen pl; **have the ~ up** (*fam*) Angst haben □ vt **~ s.o.** jdm den Atem nehmen

wind² /waɪnd/ v (pt/pp **wound**) □ vt (*wrap*) wickeln; (*move by turning*) kurbeln; aufziehen (*clock*) □ vi (*road:*) sich winden. **~ up** vt aufziehen (*clock*); schließen (*proceedings*)

wind /wɪnd/: **~fall** n unerwarteter Glücksfall m; **~falls** pl (*fruit*) Fallobst nt. **~ instrument** n Blasinstrument nt. **~mill** n Windmühle f

window /'wɪndəʊ/ n Fenster nt; (*of shop*) Schaufenster nt

window: **~-box** n Blumenkasten m. **~-cleaner** n Fensterputzer m. **~-dresser** n Schaufensterdekorateur(in) m(f). **~-dressing** n Schaufensterdekoration f; (*fig*) Schönfärberei f. **~-pane** n Fensterscheibe f. **~-shopping** n Schaufensterbummel m. **~-sill** n Fensterbrett nt

'windpipe n Luftröhre f

'windscreen n, (*Amer*) **'windshield** n Windschutzscheibe f. **~ washer** n Scheibenwaschanlage f. **~-wiper** n Scheibenwischer m

wind: **~ surfing** n Windsurfen nt. **~swept** a windgepeitscht; (*person*) zersaust

windy /'wɪndɪ/ a (**-ier, -iest**) windig; **be ~** (*fam*) Angst haben

wine /waɪn/ n Wein m

wine: **~-bar** n Weinstube f. **~glass** n Weinglas nt. **~-list** n Weinkarte f

winery /'waɪnərɪ/ n (*Amer*) Weingut nt

'wine-tasting n Weinprobe f

wing /wɪŋ/ n Flügel m; (*Auto*) Kotflügel m; **~s** pl (*Theat*) Kulissen pl

wink /wɪŋk/ n Zwinkern nt; **not sleep a ~** kein Auge zutun □ vi zwinkern; (*light:*) blinken

winner /'wɪnə(r)/ n Gewinner(in) m(f); (*Sport*) Sieger(in) m(f)

winning /'wɪnɪŋ/ a siegreich; (*smile*) gewinnend. **~-post** n Zielpfosten m. **~s** npl Gewinn m

wint|er /'wɪntə(r)/ n Winter m. **~ry** a winterlich

wipe /waɪp/ n **give sth a ~** etw abwischen □ vt abwischen; aufwischen (*floor*); (*dry*) abtrocknen. **~ off** vt abwischen; (*erase*) auslöschen. **~ out** vt (*cancel*) löschen; (*destroy*) ausrotten. **~ up** vt aufwischen; abtrocknen (*dishes*)

wire /'waɪə(r)/ n Draht m. **~-haired** a rauhaarig

wireless /'waɪəlɪs/ n Radio nt

wire 'netting n Maschendraht m

wiring /'waɪərɪŋ/ n [elektrische] Leitungen pl

wiry /'waɪərɪ/ a (**-ier, -iest**) drahtig

wisdom /'wɪzdəm/ n Weisheit f; (*prudence*) Klugheit f. **~ tooth** n Weisheitszahn m

wise /waɪz/ a (**-r, -st**), **-ly** adv weise; (*prudent*) klug

wish /wɪʃ/ n Wunsch m □ vt wünschen; **~ s.o. well** jdm alles Gute wünschen; **I ~ you could stay** ich wünschte, du könntest hier bleiben □ vi sich (dat) etwas wünschen. **~ful** a **~ful thinking** Wunschdenken nt

wishy-washy /'wɪʃɪwɒʃɪ/ a labberig; (*colour*) verwaschen; (*person*) lasch

wisp /wɪsp/ n Büschel nt; (*of hair*) Strähne f; (*of smoke*) Fahne f

wisteria /wɪs'tɪərɪə/ n Glyzinie f

wistful /'wɪstfl/ a, **-ly** adv wehmütig

wit /wɪt/ n Geist m, Witz m; (*intelligence*) Verstand m; (*person*) geistreicher Mensch m; **be at one's ~s' end** sich (dat) keinen Rat mehr wissen; **scared out of one's ~s** zu Tode erschrocken

witch /wɪtʃ/ n Hexe f. **~craft** n Hexerei f. **~-hunt** n Hexenjagd f

with /wɪð/ prep mit (+ dat); **~ fear/cold** vor Angst/Kälte; **~ it** damit; **I'm going ~ you** ich gehe mit; **take it ~ you** nimm es mit; **I haven't got it ~ me** ich habe es nicht bei mir; **I'm not ~ you** (*fam*) ich komme nicht mit

with'draw v (pt **-drew**, pp **-drawn**) □ vt zurückziehen; abheben (*money*) □ vi sich zurückziehen. **~al** n Zurückziehen nt; (*of money*) Abhebung f; (*from drugs*) Entzug m. **~al symptoms** npl Entzugserscheinungen pl

with'drawn *see* **withdraw** □ *a* ⟨*person*⟩ verschlossen

wither /'wɪðə(r)/ *vi* [ver]welken

with'hold *vt* (*pt/pp* **-held**) vorenthalten (from s.o. jdm)

with'in *prep* innerhalb (+ *gen*); ~ **the law** im Rahmen des Gesetzes □ *adv* innen

with'out *prep* ohne (+ *acc*); ~ **my notic- ing it** ohne dass ich es merkte

with'stand *vt* (*pt/pp* **-stood**) standhalten (+ *dat*)

witness /'wɪtnɪs/ *n* Zeuge *m*/ Zeugin *f*; (*evidence*) Zeugnis *nt* □ *vt* Zeuge/Zeugin sein (+ *gen*); bestätigen ⟨*signature*⟩. ~ **box** *n*, (*Amer*) ~**stand** *n* Zeugenstand *m*

witticism /'wɪtɪsɪzm/ *n* geistreicher Aus- spruch *m*

wittingly /'wɪtɪŋlɪ/ *adv* wissentlich

witty /'wɪtɪ/ *a* (**-ier, -iest**) witzig, geist- reich

wives /waɪvz/ *see* **wife**

wizard /'wɪzəd/ *n* Zauberer *m*. ~**ry** *n* Zau- berei *f*

wizened /'wɪznd/ *a* verhutzelt

wobb|le /'wɒbl/ *vi* wackeln. ~**ly** *a* wa- ckelig

woe /wəʊ/ *n* (*liter*) Jammer *m*; ~ **is me!** wehe mir!

woke, woken /wəʊk, 'wəʊkn/ *see* **wake**[1]

wolf /wʊlf/ *n* (*pl* **wolves** /wʊlvz/) Wolf *m* □ *vt* ~ **[down]** hinunterschlingen

woman /'wʊmən/ *n* (*pl* **women**) Frau *f*. ~**izer** *n* Schürzenjäger *m*. ~**ly** *a* fraulich

womb /wuːm/ *n* Gebärmutter *f*

women /'wɪmɪn/ *npl see* **woman**; **W~'s Libber** /'lɪbə(r)/ *n* Frauenrechtlerin *f*. **W~'s Liberation** *n* Frauenbewegung *f*

won /wʌn/ *see* **win**

wonder /'wʌndə(r)/ *n* Wunder *nt*; (*sur- prise*) Staunen *nt* □ *vt/i* sich fragen; (*be surprised*) sich wundern; **I** ~ da frage ich mich; **I** ~ **whether she is ill** ob sie wohl krank ist? ~**ful** *a*, **-ly** *adv* wunderbar

won't /wəʊnt/ = **will not**

woo /wuː/ *vt* (*liter*) werben um; (*fig*) umwerben

wood /wʊd/ *n* Holz *nt*; (*forest*) Wald *m*; **touch** ~! unberufen!

wood: ~**cut** *n* Holzschnitt *m*. ~**ed** /-ɪd/ *a* bewaldet. ~**en** *a* Holz-; (*fig*) hölzern. ~**pecker** *n* Specht *m*. ~**wind** *n* Holzblä- ser *pl*. ~**work** *n* (*wooden parts*) Holzteile *pl*; (*craft*) Tischlerei *f*. ~**worm** *n* Holz- wurm *m*. ~**y** *a* holzig

wool /wʊl/ *n* Wolle *f* □ *attrib* Woll-. ~**len** *a* wollen. ~**lens** *npl* Wollsachen *pl*

woolly /'wʊlɪ/ *a* (**-ier, -iest**) wollig; (*fig*) unklar

word /wɜːd/ *n* Wort *nt*; (*news*) Nachricht *f*; **by** ~ **of mouth** mündlich; **have a** ~ **with** sprechen mit; **have** ~**s** einen Wortwechsel haben. ~**ing** *n* Wortlaut *m*. ~ **processor** *n* Textverarbeitungssystem *nt*

wore /wɔː(r)/ *see* **wear**

work /wɜːk/ *n* Arbeit *f*; (*Art, Literature*) Werk *nt*; ~**s** *pl* (*factory, mechanism*) Werk *nt*; **at** ~ bei der Arbeit; **out of** ~ arbeitslos □ *vi* arbeiten; ⟨*machine, system*⟩ funktio- nieren; (*have effect*) wirken; (*study*) ler- nen; **it won't** ~ (*fig*) es klappt nicht □ *vt* arbeiten lassen; bedienen ⟨*machine*⟩; betä- tigen ⟨*lever*⟩; ~ **one's way through sth** sich durch etw hindurcharbeiten. ~ **off** *vt* abarbeiten. ~ **out** *vt* ausrechnen; (*solve*) lösen □ *vi* gut gehen, (*fam*) klappen. ~ **up** *vt* aufbauen; sich ⟨*dat*⟩ holen ⟨*appetite*⟩; **get** ~**ed up** sich aufregen

workable /'wɜːkəbl/ *a* (*feasible*) durch- führbar

workaholic /wɜːkə'hɒlɪk/ *n* arbeits- wütiger Mensch *m*

worker /'wɜːkə(r)/ *n* Arbeiter(in) *m(f)*

working /'wɜːkɪŋ/ *a* berufstätig; (*day, clothes*) Arbeits-; **be in** ~ **order** funktio- nieren. ~ **class** *n* Arbeiterklasse *f*. ~ **class** *a* Arbeiter-; **be** ~**-class** zur Arbei- terklasse gehören

work: ~**man** *n* Arbeiter *m*; (*craftsman*) Handwerker *m*. ~**manship** *n* Arbeit *f*. ~**out** *n* [Fitness]training *nt*. ~**shop** *n* Werk- statt *f*

world /wɜːld/ *n* Welt *f*; **in the** ~ auf der Welt; **a** ~ **of difference** ein himmelweiter Unterschied; **think the** ~ **of s.o.** große Stücke auf jdn halten. ~**ly** *a* weltlich; ⟨*person*⟩ weltlich gesinnt. ~**-wide** *a & adv* /-'-/ weltweit

worm /wɜːm/ *n* Wurm *m* □ *vi* ~ **one's way into s.o.'s confidence** sich in jds Ver- trauen einschleichen. ~**-eaten** *a* wurm- stichig

worn /wɔːn/ *see* **wear** □ *a* abgetragen. ~**out** *a* abgetragen; ⟨*carpet*⟩ abgenutzt; ⟨*per- son*⟩ erschöpft

worried /'wʌrɪd/ *a* besorgt

worry /'wʌrɪ/ *n* Sorge *f* □ *v* (*pt/pp* **wor- ried**) □ *vt* beunruhigen, Sorgen machen (+ *dat*); (*bother*) stören □ *vi* sich beun- ruhigen, sich (*dat*) Sorgen machen. ~**ing** *a* beunruhigend

worse /wɜːs/ *a & adv* schlechter; (*more serious*) schlimmer □ *n* Schlechtere(s) *nt*; Schlimmere(s) *nt*

worsen /'wɜːsn/ *vt* verschlechtern □ *vi* sich verschlechtern

worship /'wɜːʃɪp/ *n* Anbetung *f*; (*service*) Gottesdienst *m*; **Your/His W** ~ Euer/

Seine Ehren □ *v* (*pt/pp* **-shipped**) □ *vt* anbeten □ *vi* am Gottesdienst teilnehmen

worst /wɜːst/ *a* schlechteste(r,s); (*most serious*) schlimmste(r,s) □ *adv* am schlechtesten; am schlimmsten □ *n* the ~ das Schlimmste; **get the ~ of it** den Kürzeren ziehen

worsted /'wʊstɪd/ *n* Kammgarn *m*

worth /wɜːθ/ *n* Wert *m*; **£10's ~ of petrol** Benzin für £10 □ *a* **be ~ £5** £5 wert sein; **be ~ it** (*fig*) sich lohnen. **~less** *a* wertlos. **~while** *a* lohnend

worthy /'wɜːðɪ/ *a* würdig

would /wʊd/ *v aux* **I ~ do it** ich würde es tun, ich täte es; **~ you go?** würdest du gehen? **he said he ~n't** er sagte, er würde es nicht tun; **what ~ you like?** was möchten Sie?

wound[1] /wuːnd/ *n* Wunde *f* □ *vt* verwunden

wound[2] /waʊnd/ *see* **wind**[2]

wove, woven /wəʊv, 'wəʊvn/ *see* **weave**[2]

wrangle /'ræŋgl/ *n* Streit *m* □ *vi* sich streiten

wrap /ræp/ *n* Umhang *m* □ *vt* (*pt/pp* **wrapped**) ~ **[up]** wickeln; einpacken (*present*) □ *vi* ~ **up warmly** sich warm einpacken; **be ~ped up in** (*fig*) aufgehen in (+ *dat*). **~per** *n* Hülle *f*. **~ping** *n* Verpackung *f*. **~ping paper** *n* Einwickelpapier *nt*

wrath /rɒθ/ *n* Zorn *m*

wreak /riːk/ *vt* ~ **havoc** Verwüstungen anrichten

wreath /riːθ/ *n* (*pl* ~**s** /-ðz/) Kranz *m*

wreck /rek/ *n* Wrack *nt* □ *vt* zerstören; zunichte machen (*plans*); zerrütten (*marriage*). **~age** /-ɪdʒ/ *n* Wrackteile *pl*; (*fig*) Trümmer *pl*

wren /ren/ *n* Zaunkönig *m*

wrench /rentʃ/ *n* Ruck *m*; (*tool*) Schraubenschlüssel *m*; **be a ~** (*fig*) weh tun □ *vt* reißen; ~ **sth from s.o.** jdm etw entreißen

wrest /rest/ *vt* entwinden (**from s.o.** jdm)

wrestl|e /'resl/ *vi* ringen. **~er** *n* Ringer *m*. **~ing** *n* Ringen *nt*

wretch /retʃ/ *n* Kreatur *f*. **~ed** /-ɪd/ *a* elend; (*very bad*) erbärmlich

wriggle /'rɪgl/ *n* Zappeln *nt* □ *vi* zappeln; (*move forward*) sich schlängeln; ~ **out of sth** (*fam*) sich vor etw (*dat*) drücken

wring /rɪŋ/ *vt* (*pt/pp* **wrung**) wringen; (~ *out*) auswringen; umdrehen (*neck*); ringen (*hands*); **be ~ing wet** tropfnass sein

wrinkle /'rɪŋkl/ *n* Falte *f*; (*on skin*) Runzel *f* □ *vt* kräuseln □ *vi* sich kräuseln, sich falten. **~d** *a* runzlig

wrist /rɪst/ *n* Handgelenk *nt*. **~-watch** *n* Armbanduhr *f*

writ /rɪt/ *n* (*Jur*) Verfügung *f*

write /raɪt/ *vt/i* (*pt* **wrote**, *pp* **written**, *pres p* **writing**) schreiben. ~ **down** *vt* aufschreiben. ~ **off** *vt* abschreiben; zu Schrott fahren (*car*)

'write-off *n* ≈ Totalschaden *m*

writer /'raɪtə(r)/ *n* Schreiber(in) *m(f)*; (*author*) Schriftsteller(in) *m(f)*

'write-up *n* Bericht *m*; (*review*) Kritik *f*

writhe /raɪð/ *vi* sich winden

writing /'raɪtɪŋ/ *n* Schreiben *nt*; (*handwriting*) Schrift *f*; **in ~** schriftlich. **~-paper** *n* Schreibpapier *nt*

written /'rɪtn/ *see* **write**

wrong /rɒŋ/ *a*, **-ly** *adv* falsch; (*morally*) unrecht; (*not just*) ungerecht; **be ~** nicht stimmen; (*person:*) Unrecht haben; **what's ~?** was ist los? □ *adv* falsch; **go ~** (*person:*) etwas falsch machen; (*machine:*) kaputtgehen; (*plan:*) schief gehen □ *n* Unrecht *nt* □ *vt* Unrecht tun (+ *dat*). **~ful** *a* ungerechtfertigt. **~fully** *adv* (*accuse*) zu Unrecht

wrote /rəʊt/ *see* **write**

wrought 'iron /rɔːt-/ *n* Schmiedeeisen *nt* □ *attrib* schmiedeeisern

wrung /rʌŋ/ *see* **wring**

wry /raɪ/ *a* (**-er, -est**) ironisch; (*humour*) trocken

X

xerox (P) /'zɪərɒks/ *vt* fotokopieren

Xmas /'krɪsməs, 'eksməs/ *n* (*fam*) Weihnachten *nt*

X-ray /'eks-/ *n* (*picture*) Röntgenaufnahme *f*; ~**s** *pl* Röntgenstrahlen *pl*; **have an ~** geröntgt werden □ *vt* röntgen; durchleuchten (*luggage*)

Y

yacht /jɒt/ *n* Jacht *f*; (*for racing*) Segelboot *nt*. **~ing** *n* Segeln *nt*

yank /jæŋk/ *vt* (*fam*) reißen

Yank *n* (*fam*) Amerikaner(in) *m(f)*, (*fam*) Ami *m*

yap /jæp/ *vi* (*pt/pp* **yapped**) (*dog:*) kläffen

yard[1] /jɑːd/ *n* Hof *m*; (*for storage*) Lager *nt*

yard² /jɑːd/ n Yard nt (= 0,91 m). ~**stick** n (fig) Maßstab m

yarn /jɑːn/ n Garn nt; (fam: tale) Geschichte f

yawn /jɔːn/ n Gähnen nt □ vi gähnen. ~**ing** a gähnend

year /jɪə(r)/ n Jahr nt; (of wine) Jahrgang m; **for** ~**s** jahrelang. ~**book** n Jahrbuch nt. ~**ly** a & adv jährlich

yearn /jɜːn/ vi sich sehnen (**for** nach). ~**ing** n Sehnsucht f

yeast /jiːst/ n Hefe f

yell /jel/ n Schrei m □ vi schreien

yellow /'jeləʊ/ a gelb □ n Gelb nt. ~**ish** a gelblich

yelp /jelp/ vi jaulen

yen /jen/ n Wunsch m (**for** nach)

yes /jes/ adv ja; (contradicting) doch □ n Ja nt

yesterday /'jestədeɪ/ n & adv gestern; ~**'s paper** die gestrige Zeitung; **the day before** ~ vorgestern

yet /jet/ adv noch; (in question) schon; (nevertheless) doch; **as** ~ bisher; **not** ~ noch nicht; **the best** ~ das bisher beste □ conj doch

yew /juː/ n Eibe f

Yiddish /'jɪdɪʃ/ n Jiddisch nt

yield /jiːld/ n Ertrag m □ vt bringen; abwerfen (profit) □ vi nachgeben; (Amer, Auto) die Vorfahrt beachten

yodel /'jəʊdl/ vi (pt/pp yodelled) jodeln

yoga /'jəʊgə/ n Yoga m

yoghurt /'jɒgət/ n Joghurt m

yoke /jəʊk/ n Joch nt; (of garment) Passe f

yokel /'jəʊkl/ n Bauerntölpel m

yolk /jəʊk/ n Dotter m, Eigelb nt

yonder /'jɒndə(r)/ adv (liter) dort drüben

you /juː/ pron du; (acc) dich; (dat) dir; (pl) ihr; (acc, dat) euch; (formal) (nom & acc, sg & pl) Sie; (dat, sg & pl) Ihnen; (one) man; (acc) einen; (dat) einem; **all of** ~ ihr/Sie alle; **I know** ~ ich kenne dich/euch/Sie; **I'll give** ~ **the money** ich gebe dir/euch/Ihnen das Geld; **it does** ~ **good** es tut einem gut; **it's bad for** ~ es ist ungesund

young /jʌŋ/ a (-**er** /-gə(r)/, -**est** /-gɪst/) jung □ npl (animals) Junge pl; **the** ~ die

Jugend f. ~**ster** n Jugendliche(r) m/f; (child) Kleine(r) m/f

your /jɔː(r)/ a dein; (pl) euer; (formal) Ihr

yours /jɔːz/ poss pron deine(r), deins; (pl) eure(r), euers; (formal, sg & pl) Ihre(r), Ihr[e]s; **a friend of** ~ ein Freund von dir/Ihnen/euch; **that is** ~ das gehört dir/Ihnen/euch

your'self pron (pl -**selves**) selbst; (refl) dich; (dat) dir; (pl) euch; (formal) sich; **by** ~ allein

youth /juːθ/ n (pl youths /-ðːz/) Jugend f; (boy) Jugendliche(r) m. ~**ful** a jugendlich. ~ **hostel** n Jugendherberge f

Yugoslav /'juːgəslɑːv/ a jugoslawisch. ~**ia** /-'slɑːvɪə/ n Jugoslawien nt

Z

zany /'zeɪnɪ/ a (-**ier**, -**iest**) närrisch, verrückt

zeal /ziːl/ n Eifer m

zealous /'zeləs/ a, -**ly** adv eifrig

zebra /'zebrə/ n Zebra nt. ~ '**crossing** n Zebrastreifen m

zenith /'zenɪθ/ n Zenit m; (fig) Gipfel m

zero /'zɪərəʊ/ n Null f

zest /zest/ n Begeisterung f

zigzag /'zɪgzæg/ n Zickzack m □ vi (pt/pp -zagged) im Zickzack laufen/ (in vehicle) fahren

zinc /zɪŋk/ n Zink nt

zip /zɪp/ n **[fastener]** Reißverschluss m □ vt ~ **[up]** den Reißverschluss zuziehen an (+ dat)

'Zip code n (Amer) Postleitzahl f

zipper /'zɪpə(r)/ n Reißverschluss m

zither /'zɪðə(r)/ n Zither f

zodiac /'zəʊdɪæk/ n Tierkreis m

zombie /'zɒmbɪ/ n (fam) **like a** ~ ganz benommen

zone /zəʊn/ n Zone f

zoo /zuː/ n Zoo m

zoological /zəʊə'lɒdʒɪkl/ a zoologisch

zoolog|ist /zəʊ'ɒlədʒɪst/ n Zoologe m /-gin f. ~**y** Zoologie f

zoom /zuːm/ vi sausen. ~ **lens** n Zoomobjektiv nt

Phonetic symbols used for German words

a	Hand	hant	ŋ	lang	laŋ
aː	Bahn	baːn	o	Moral	moˈraːl
ɐ	Ober	ˈoːbɐ	oː	Boot	boːt
ɐ̯	Uhr	uːɐ̯	o̜	Foyer	fo̜aˈjeː
ã	Conférencier	kõferãˈsi̯eː	õ	Konkurs	kõˈkʊrs
ãː	Abonnement	abɔnəˈmãː	õː	Ballon	baˈlõː
ai̯	weit	vai̯t	ɔ	Post	pɔst
au̯	Haut	hau̯t	ø	Ökonom	økoˈnoːm
b	Ball	bal	øː	Öl	øːl
ç	ich	ɪç	œ	göttlich	ˈɡœtlɪç
d	dann	dan	ɔy	heute	ˈhɔytə
dʒ	Gin	dʒɪn	p	Pakt	pakt
e	Metall	meˈtal	r	Rast	rast
eː	Beet	beːt	s	Hast	hast
ɛ	mästen	ˈmɛstən	ʃ	Schal	ʃaːl
ɛː	wählen	ˈvɛːlən	t	Tal	taːl
ɛ̃	Cousin	kuˈzɛ̃ː	ts	Zahl	tsaːl
ə	Nase	ˈnaːzə	tʃ	Couch	kau̯tʃ
f	Faß	fas	u	kulant	kuˈlant
ɡ	Gast	ɡast	uː	Hut	huːt
h	haben	ˈhaːbən	u̯	aktuell	akˈtu̯ɛl
i	Rivale	riˈvaːlə	ʊ	Pult	pʊlt
iː	viel	fiːl	v	was	vas
i̯	Aktion	akˈtsi̯oːn	x	Bach	bax
ɪ	Birke	ˈbɪrkə	y	Physik	fyˈziːk
j	ja	jaː	yː	Rübe	ˈryːbə
k	kalt	kalt	ỹ	Nuance	ˈnỹãːsə
l	Last	last	ʏ	Fülle	ˈfʏlə
m	Mast	mast	z	Nase	ˈnaːzə
n	Naht	naːt	ʒ	Regime	reˈʒiːm

ʔ	Glottal stop, e.g. Koordination /koʔɔrdinaˈtsi̯oːn/.
ː	Length sign after a vowel, e.g. Chrom /kroːm/.
ˈ	Stress mark before stressed syllable, e.g. Balkon /balˈkõː/.

Die für das Englische verwendeten Zeichen der Lautschrift

ɑː	barn	bɑːn	l	lot	lɒt
ɑ̃	nuance	ˈnjuːɑ̃s	m	mat	mæt
æ	fat	fæt	n	not	nɒt
æ̃	lingerie	ˈlæ̃ʒərɪ	ŋ	sing	sɪŋ
aɪ	fine	faɪn	ɒ	got	gɒt
aʊ	now	naʊ	ɔː	paw	pɔː
b	bat	bæt	ɔɪ	boil	bɔɪl
d	dog	dɒg	p	pet	pet
dʒ	jam	dʒæm	r	rat	ræt
e	met	met	s	sip	sɪp
eɪ	fate	feɪt	ʃ	ship	ʃɪp
eə	fairy	ˈfeərɪ	t	tip	tɪp
əʊ	goat	gəʊt	tʃ	chin	tʃɪn
ə	ago	əˈgəʊ	θ	thin	θɪn
ɜː	fur	fɜː(r)	ð	the	ðə
f	fat	fæt	uː	boot	buːt
g	good	gʊd	ʊ	book	bʊk
h	hat	hæt	ʊə	tourism	ˈtʊərɪzm
ɪ	bit, happy	bɪt, ˈhæpɪ	ʌ	dug	dʌg
ɪə	near	nɪə(r)	v	van	væn
iː	meet	miːt	w	win	wɪn
j	yet	jet	z	zip	zɪp
k	kit	kɪt	ʒ	vision	ˈvɪʒn

ː bezeichnet Länge des vorhergehenden Vokals, z. B. boot [buːt].

ˈ Betonung, steht unmittelbar vor einer betonten Silbe, z. B. ago [əˈgəʊ].

(r) Ein „r" in runden Klammern wird nur gesprochen, wenn im Textzusammenhang ein Vokal unmittelbar folgt, z. B. fire /ˈfaɪə(r); fire at /ˈfaɪər æt/.

Guide to German pronunciation

Consonants are pronounced as in English with the following exceptions:

b	as	p	
d	as	t	} *at the end of a word or syllable*
g	as	k	

ch	as in Scottish lo<u>ch</u> *after a, o, u, au*	
	like an exaggerated h as in <u>h</u>uge	
		after i, e, ä, ö, ü, eu, ei
-chs	as	x	(as in bo<u>x</u>)
-ig	as	-ich /ɪç/	*when a suffix*
j	as	y	(as in <u>y</u>es)

ps	}	the p is pronounced
pn		

qu	as	k+v	
s	as	z	(as in <u>z</u>ero) *at the beginning of a word*
	as	s	(as in bu<u>s</u>) *at the end of a word or syllable, before a consonant, or when doubled*
sch	as	sh	
sp	as	shp	*at the beginning of a word*
st	as	sht	
v	as	f	(as in <u>f</u>or)
	as	v	(as in <u>v</u>ery) *within a word*
w	as	v	(as in <u>v</u>ery)
z	as	ts	

Vowels are approximately as follows:

a	short	as	u	(as in b<u>u</u>t)
	long	as	a	(as in c<u>a</u>r)
e	short	as	e	(as in p<u>e</u>n)
	long	as	a	(as in p<u>a</u>per)
i	short	as	i	(as in b<u>i</u>t)
	long	as	ee	(as in qu<u>ee</u>n)
o	short	as	o	(as in h<u>o</u>t)
	long	as	o	(as in p<u>o</u>pe)
u	short	as	oo	(as in f<u>oo</u>t)
	long	as	oo	(as in b<u>oo</u>t)

Vowels are always short before a double consonant, and long when followed by an h or when double

ie	is pronounced ee	(as in k<u>ee</u>p)

Diphthongs

au		as	ow	(as in h<u>ow</u>)
ei				
ai		as	y	(as in m<u>y</u>)
eu				
äu		as	oy	(as in b<u>oy</u>)

German irregular verbs

1st, 2nd and 3rd person present are given after the infinitive, and past subjunctive after the past indicative, where there is a change of vowel or any other irregularity.

Compound verbs are only given if they do not take the same forms as the corresponding simple verb, e.g. *befehlen*, or if there is no corresponding simple verb, e.g. *bewegen*.

An asterisk (*) indicates a verb which is also conjugated regularly.

Infinitive Infinitiv	Past Tense Präteritum	Past Participle 2. Partizip
abwägen	wog (wöge) ab	abgewogen
ausbedingen	bedang (bedänge) aus	ausbedungen
*backen (du bäckst, er bäckt)	buk (büke)	gebacken
befehlen (du befiehlst, er befiehlt)	befahl (beföhle, befähle)	befohlen
beginnen	begann (begänne)	begonnen
beißen (du/er beißt)	biss (bisse)	gebissen
bergen (du birgst, er birgt)	barg (bärge)	geborgen
bersten (du/er birst)	barst (bärste)	geborsten
bewegen[2]	bewog (bewöge)	bewogen
biegen	bog (böge)	gebogen
bieten	bot (böte)	geboten
binden	band (bände)	gebunden
bitten	bat (bäte)	gebeten
blasen (du/er bläst)	blies	geblasen
bleiben	blieb	geblieben
*bleichen	blich	geblichen
braten (du brätst, er brät)	briet	gebraten
brechen (du brichst, er bricht)	brach (bräche)	gebrochen
brennen	brannte (brennte)	gebrannt
bringen	brachte (brächte)	gebracht
denken	dachte (dächte)	gedacht
dreschen (du drischst, er drischt)	drosch (drösche)	gedroschen

Infinitive Infinitiv	Past Tense Präteritum	Past Participle 2. Partizip
dringen	drang (dränge)	gedrungen
dürfen (ich/er darf, du darfst)	durfte (dürfte)	gedurft
empfehlen (du empfiehlst, er empfiehlt)	empfahl (empföhle)	empfohlen
erlöschen (du erlischst, er erlischt)	erlosch (erlösche)	erloschen
*erschallen	erscholl (erschölle)	erschollen
*erschrecken (du erschrickst, er erschrickt)	erschrak (erschräke)	erschrocken
erwägen	erwog (erwöge)	erwogen
essen (du/er isst)	aß (äße)	gegessen
fahren (du fährst, er fährt)	fuhr (führe)	gefahren
fallen (du fällst, er fällt)	fiel	gefallen
fangen (du fängst, er fängt)	fing	gefangen
fechten (du fichtst, er ficht)	focht (föchte)	gefochten
finden	fand (fände)	gefunden
flechten (du flichtst, er flicht)	flocht (flöchte)	geflochten
fliegen	flog (flöge)	geflogen
fliehen	floh (flöhe)	geflohen
fließen (du/er fließt)	floss (flösse)	geflossen
fressen (du/er frisst)	fraß (fräße)	gefressen
frieren	fror (fröre)	gefroren
*gären	gor (göre)	gegoren
gebären (du gebierst, sie gebiert)	gebar (gebäre)	geboren
geben (du gibst, er gibt)	gab (gäbe)	gegeben
gedeihen	gedieh	gediehen
gehen	ging	gegangen
gelingen	gelang (gelänge)	gelungen
gelten (du giltst, er gilt)	galt (gölte, gälte)	gegolten
genesen (du/er genest)	genas (genäse)	genesen
genießen (du/er genießt)	genoss (genösse)	genossen
geschehen (es geschieht)	geschah (geschähe)	geschehen
gewinnen	gewann (gewönne, gewänne)	gewonnen
gießen (du/er gießt)	goss (gösse)	gegossen
gleichen	glich	geglichen

Infinitive Infinitiv	Past Tense Präteritum	Past Participle 2. Partizip
gleiten	glitt	geglitten
glimmen	glomm (glömme)	geglommen
graben (du gräbst, er gräbt)	grub (grübe)	gegraben
greifen	griff	gegriffen
haben (du hast, er hat)	hatte (hätte)	gehabt
halten (du hältst, er hält)	hielt	gehalten
hängen[2]	hing	gehangen
hauen	haute	gehauen
heben	hob (höbe)	gehoben
heißen (du/er heißt)	hieß	geheißen
helfen (du hilfst, er hilft)	half (hülfe)	geholfen
kennen	kannte (kennte)	gekannt
klingen	klang (klänge)	geklungen
kneifen	kniff	gekniffen
kommen	kam (käme)	gekommen
können (ich/er kann, du kannst)	konnte (könnte)	gekonnt
kriechen	kroch (kröche)	gekrochen
laden (du lädst, er lädt)	lud (lüde)	geladen
lassen (du/er lässt)	ließ	gelassen
laufen (du läufst, er läuft)	lief	gelaufen
leiden	litt	gelitten
leihen	lieh	geliehen
lesen (du/er liest)	las (läse)	gelesen
liegen	lag (läge)	gelegen
lügen	log (löge)	gelogen
mahlen	mahlte	gemahlen
meiden	mied	gemieden
melken	molk (mölke)	gemolken
messen (du/er misst)	maß (mäße)	gemessen
misslingen	misslang (misslänge)	misslungen
mögen (ich/er mag, du magst)	mochte (möchte)	gemocht
müssen (ich/er muss, du musst)	musste (müsste)	gemusst
nehmen (du nimmst, er nimmt)	nahm (nähme)	genommen
nennen	nannte (nennte)	genannt
pfeifen	pfiff	gepfiffen
preisen (du/er preist)	pries	gepriesen
quellen (du quillst, er quillt)	quoll (quölle)	gequollen

Infinitive Infinitiv	Past Tense Präteritum	Past Participle 2. Partizip
raten (du rätst, er rät)	riet	geraten
reiben	rieb	gerieben
reißen (du/er reißt)	riss	gerissen
reiten	ritt	geritten
rennen	rannte (rennte)	gerannt
riechen	roch (röche)	gerochen
ringen	rang (ränge)	gerungen
rinnen	rann (ränne)	geronnen
rufen	rief	gerufen
*salzen (du/er salzt)	salzte	gesalzen
saufen (du säufst, er säuft)	soff (söffe)	gesoffen
*saugen	sog (söge)	gesogen
schaffen[1]	schuf (schüfe)	geschaffen
scheiden	schied	geschieden
scheinen	schien	geschienen
scheißen (du/er scheißt)	schiss	geschissen
schelten (du schiltst, er schilt)	schalt (schölte)	gescholten
scheren[1]	schor (schöre)	geschoren
schieben	schob (schöbe)	geschoben
schießen (du/er schießt)	schoss (schösse)	geschossen
schinden	schindete	geschunden
schlafen (du schläfst, er schläft)	schlief	geschlafen
schlagen (du schlägst, er schlägt)	schlug (schlüge)	geschlagen
schleichen	schlich	geschlichen
schleifen[2]	schliff	geschliffen
schließen (du/er schließt)	schloss (schlösse)	geschlossen
schlingen	schlang (schlänge)	geschlungen
schmeißen (du/er schmeißt)	schmiss (schmisse)	geschmissen
schmelzen (du/er schmilzt)	schmolz (schmölze)	geschmolzen
schneiden	schnitt	geschnitten
*schrecken (du schrickst, er schrickt)	schrak (schräke)	geschreckt
schreiben	schrieb	geschrieben
schreien	schrie	geschrie[e]n
schreiten	schritt	geschritten
schweigen	schwieg	geschwiegen
schwellen (du schwillst, er schwillt)	schwoll (schwölle)	geschwollen

Infinitive Infinitiv	Past Tense Präteritum	Past Participle 2. Partizip
schwimmen	schwamm (schwömme)	geschwommen
schwinden	schwand (schwände)	geschwunden
schwingen	schwang (schwänge)	geschwungen
schwören	schwor (schwüre)	geschworen
sehen (du siehst, er sieht)	sah (sähe)	gesehen
sein (ich bin, du bist, er ist, wir sind, ihr seid, sie sind)	war (wäre)	gewesen
senden[1]	sandte (sendete)	gesandt
sieden	sott (sötte)	gesotten
singen	sang (sänge)	gesungen
sinken	sank (sänke)	gesunken
sinnen	sann (sänne)	gesonnen
sitzen (du/er sitzt)	saß (säße)	gesessen
sollen (ich/er soll, du sollst)	sollte	gesollt
*spalten	spaltete	gespalten
speien	spie	gespie[e]n
spinnen	spann (spönne, spänne)	gesponnen
sprechen (du sprichst, er spricht)	sprach (spräche)	gesprochen
sprießen (du/er sprießt)	spross (sprösse)	gesprossen
springen	sprang (spränge)	gesprungen
stechen (du stichst, er sticht)	stach (stäche)	gestochen
stehen	stand (stünde, stände)	gestanden
stehlen (du stiehlst, er stiehlt)	stahl (stähle)	gestohlen
steigen	stieg	gestiegen
sterben (du stirbst, er stirbt)	starb (stürbe)	gestorben
stinken	stank (stänke)	gestunken
stoßen (du/er stößt)	stieß	gestoßen
streichen	strich	gestrichen
streiten	stritt	gestritten
tragen (du trägst, er trägt)	trug (trüge)	getragen
treffen (du triffst, er trifft)	traf (träfe)	getroffen
treiben	trieb	getrieben
treten (du trittst, er tritt)	trat (träte)	getreten
*triefen	troff (tröffe)	getroffen

Infinitive Infinitiv	Past Tense Präteritum	Past Participle 2. Partizip
trinken	trank (tränke)	getrunken
trügen	trog (tröge)	getrogen
tun (du tust, er tut)	tat (täte)	getan
verderben (du verdirbst, er verdirbt)	verdarb (verdürbe)	verdorben
vergessen (du/er vergisst)	vergaß (vergäße)	vergessen
verlieren	verlor (verlöre)	verloren
verschleißen (du/er verschleißt)	verschliss	verschlissen
verzeihen	verzieh	verziehen
wachsen[1] (du/er wächst)	wuchs (wüchse)	gewachsen
waschen (du wäschst, er wäscht)	wusch (wüsche)	gewaschen
weichen[2]	wich	gewichen
weisen (du/er weist)	wies	gewiesen
*wenden[2]	wandte (wendete)	gewandt
werben (du wirbst, er wirbt)	warb (würbe)	geworben
werden (du wirst, er wird)	wurde (würde)	geworden
werfen (du wirfst, er wirft)	warf (würfe)	geworfen
wiegen[1]	wog (wöge)	gewogen
winden	wand (wände)	gewunden
wissen (ich/er weiß, du weißt)	wusste (wüsste)	gewusst
wollen (ich/er will, du willst)	wollte	gewollt
wringen	wrang (wränge)	gewrungen
ziehen	zog (zöge)	gezogen
zwingen	zwang (zwänge)	gezwungen